Newsmakers®

ISSN 0899-0417

Newsmakers®

The People Behind Today's Headlines

Terrie M. Rooney
Editor

1998
Cumulation

Includes Indexes from
1985 through 1998

GALE

DETROIT · LONDON

STAFF

Terrie M. Rooney, *Editor*

Luann Brennan, Leah Burton, and Andrea Henderson, *Contributing Editors*

Laura Hightower, *Associate Editor*

Geri Speace, *Senior Sketchwriter*

Neil E. Walker, *Managing Editor, General Biography/Genealogy*

Susan M. Trosky, *Permissions Manager*
Margaret Chamberlain, *Permissions Specialist*
Keasha Jack-Lyles, *Permissions Assistant*

Deborah Milliken, *Production Assistant*
Gary Leach, *Macintosh Artist*

Randy Bassett, *Image Database Supervisor*
Robert Duncan and Mike Logusz, *Imaging Specialists*
Pamela A. Reed, *Imaging Coordinator*

Victoria B. Cariappa, *Research Manager*
Barbara McNeil, *Research Specialist*
Phyllis Spinelli, *Editorial Assistant*

Cover Photos: Pam Grier (Pacha/Corbis)
and John Glenn (AP/Wide World Photos)

ISBN 0-7876-1230-8 (this volume)
ISBN 0-7876-1226-X (complete 1998 set)
ISSN 0899-0417

Printed in the United States of America

Contents

Obituaries

Introduction

Newsmakers provides informative profiles of the world's most interesting people in a crisp, concise, contemporary format. Make *Newsmakers* the first place you look for biographical information on the people making today's headlines.

Important Features

- **Attractive, modern page design** pleases the eye while making it easy to locate the information you need.

- **Coverage of all the newsmakers** you want to know about—people in business, education, technology, law, politics, religion, entertainment, labor, sports, medicine, and other fields.

- **Clearly labeled data sections** allow quick access to vital personal statistics, career information, major awards, and mailing addresses.

- **Informative sidelights essays** include the kind of in-depth analysis you're looking for.

- **Sources for additional information** provide lists of books, magazines, newspapers, and internet sites where you can find out even more about *Newsmakers* listees.

- **Enlightening photographs** are specially selected to further enhance your knowledge of the subject.

- **Separate obituaries section** provides you with concise profiles of recently deceased newsmakers.

- **Publication schedule and price** fit your budget. *Newsmakers* is published in three paperback issues per year, each containing approximately 50 entries, and a hardcover cumulation, containing approximately 200 entries (those from the preceding three paperback issues *plus* an additional 50 entries), *all at a price you can afford!*

- And much, much more!

Indexes Provide Easy Access

Familiar and indispensable: The *Newsmakers* indexes! You can easily locate entries in a variety of ways through our four versatile, comprehensive indexes. The Nationality, Occupation, and Subject Indexes list names from the current year's *Newsmakers* issues. These are cumulated in the annual hardbound volume to include all names from the entire *Contemporary Newsmakers* and *Newsmakers* series. The Newsmakers Index is cumulated in all issues as well as the hardbound annuals to provide concise coverage of the entire series.

- **Nationality Index**—Names of newsmakers are arranged alphabetically under their respective nationalities.

- **Occupation Index**—Names are listed alphabetically under broad occupational categories.

- **Subject Index**—Includes key subjects, topical issues, company names, products, organizations, etc., that are discussed in *Newsmakers*. Under each subject heading are listed names of newsmakers associated with that topic. So the unique Subject Index provides access to the information in *Newsmakers* even when readers are unable to connect a name with a particular topic. This index also invites browsing, allowing *Newsmakers* users to discover topics they may wish to explore further.

- **Cumulative Newsmaker Index**—Listee names, along with birth and death dates, when available, are arranged alphabetically followed by the year and issue number in which their entries appear.

Available in Electronic Formats

Diskette/Magnetic Tape. *Newsmakers* is available for licensing on magnetic tape or diskette in a fielded format. The database is available for internal data processing and nonpublishing purposes only. For more information, call 1-800-877-GALE.

Online. *Newsmakers* is available online as part of the Gale Biographies (GALBIO) database accessible through LEXIS-NEXIS, P.O. Box 933, Dayton, OH 454012-0933; phone: (513) 865-6800; toll-free: 1-800-543-6862.

Suggestions Are Appreciated

The editors welcome your comments and suggestions. In fact, many popular *Newsmakers* features were implemented as a result of readers' suggestions. We will continue to shape the series to best meet the needs of the greatest number of users. Send comments or suggestions to:

The Editor
Newsmakers
Gale Research
27500 Drake Rd.
Farmington Hills, MI 48331-3535

Or, call toll-free at 1-800-877-GALE

Bella Abzug

AP/Wide World Photos

Lawyer, politician, and activist

Born Bella Savitzky, July 24, 1920, in New York, NY; died of complications following heart surgery, March 31, 1998, in New York, NY; daughter of Emmanuel (a butcher) and Esther Savitzky; married Maurice Martin Abzug (a stockbroker and novelist), June 4, 1944; children: Eve Gail, Isobel Jo. *Education:* Hunter College, B.A., 1942; Columbia University, LL.B., 1947. *Politics:* Democrat. *Religion:* Jewish.

Career

Admitted to the New York Bar, 1947; employed as a New York City-based attorney specializing in labor law and civil rights cases, 1947-70; U.S. House of Representatives, member from New York, 1971-77; co-founder, National Women's Political Caucus and the Women's Environment and Development Organization.

Member: American Civil Liberties Union, American Jewish Congress, National Organization for Women, National Urban League, New York State Bar, Women USA, Women's Environment and Development Organization, Women's Political Caucus.

Sidelights

A longtime activist for the rights of workers, racial minorities, and women, Bella Abzug became a nationally known figure when she was elected to the U.S. Congress in 1970. Her flamboyant personal style, wisecracking public statements, relentless advocacy of liberal issues, and mastery of parliamentary procedure enabled her to instantly become a force in Congress. "It has been some time since the U.S. Congress has seen the likes—male or female—of Bella Abzug.... Her partisans know her as a raucously passionate crusader for minority rights, Women's Lib and the anti-war movement, a truculent and courageous woman. To the less friendly, she comes on as a sumo liberal, a lady wrestler, Joan of Arc resurrected as an elemental *yenta*," wrote a reporter for *Time* in 1971.

Bella Abzug was born Bella Savitzky in New York City in 1920. Her Russian-Jewish immigrant parents also had another daughter, Bella's older sister, and ran the Live and Let Live Meat Market on Manhattan's Ninth Avenue. Growing up in the Bronx, Abzug attended local public schools and began her political activist career as a teenager by handing out leaflets at subway stops advocating a Jewish homeland and raising alarm about increasing anti-Semitism in Europe. When Abzug was 13 years old her father died. Showing the feminist spirit for which she would become famous as an adult, the young Abzug went to synagogue every day for a year to say Kaddish for her father, even though Jewish law restricted the saying of Kaddish to males.

Graduating from Walton High School in 1938, Abzug entered Hunter College, an all-women's institution operated by the City University of New York. At Hunter, Abzug was elected class president and addressed an assembly gathered to greet First Lady Eleanor Roosevelt. Abzug was also active in Zionist organizations while a student. Ironically, during her days as a politician, Abzug, who was the first Jewish woman elected to Congress, was sometimes criticized for letting her "doveish" views on foreign policy lead her to only tepid support of Israel. According to *Newsweek*, Abzug responded to this criticism with the quip—"I'm an Egyptian maybe?"

Abzug's childhood ambition was to be a lawyer. After receiving her bachelor's degree from Hunter, she worked briefly in the wartime shipbuilding industry, then applied to law schools. Harvard was her first choice but she discovered that it did not accept female students. Instead, she enrolled at Columbia University's law school, becoming one of just a handful of women there. In 1944, Bella married (Maurice) Martin Abzug, an aspiring writer. The couple eventually had two daughters, Eve Gail and Isobel Jo.

Receiving her law degree and passing the bar exam in 1947, Abzug began to practice law, specializing in labor disputes and civil rights cases that brought in little or no money. To support the family, her husband put his writing career on a back burner and became a stockbroker (although he did eventually have two novels published). Abzug was never reluctant to credit her husband's emotional and financial support for her career. "From the beginning, he did everything and anything to make possible what I was doing. If I had to work 18 hours a day as a young labor lawyer, he would keep me company reading a book or typing in the room next to my office.... When I practiced law he said I was the greatest lawyer that ever was. When I became a member of Congress he said I was the greatest member of Congress and later he said I was the greatest stateswoman. He never felt competitive—only proud," Abzug wrote in *Ms.* magazine in 1990.

Among the groups Abzug represented during her 23 years as a practicing attorney were fur industry workers, restaurant employees, longshoremen, and the United Auto Workers. While pregnant with her first child, she went to Mississippi to be chief counsel in the case of Willie McGee, a black man convicted of rape and sentenced to execution. Though her efforts won McGee two stays of execution, he was put to death in 1951. In the later 1950s Abzug represented clients accused of "subversive activities" by anti-Communist politicians. In the 1960s, Abzug helped found Women Strike for Peace, and led protests against American military involvement in Vietnam. She gathered support for the campaigns of left-wing "peace" candidates, including Senator Eugene McCarthy's presidential bid in 1968.

Abzug's passionate activism led to her dissatisfaction with liberal politicians whom she felt were not assertive enough in espousing their beliefs. Also, she felt it was very important for more women to be elected to office. In 1970, at the age of 50, Abzug began her career as a politician when she announced her candidacy for the Democratic nomination for Congress from New York's nineteenth district. A fishhook shaped area of Manhattan stretching from the Upper West Side through Chelsea and Greenwich Village to the Lower East Side, the nineteenth district had been represented since 1957 by Leonard Farbstein, a mild-mannered, constituent services oriented Democrat who rarely made news. Farbstein had defeated a number of strong challengers over the years and he enjoyed the backing of Democratic party regulars. Abzug was a "reform" Democrat. Commenting on her uphill battle, Abzug told *Newsweek*—"I'm a woman. I'm strong. I have something to say. And I like the big fight."

Since Abzug's liberal views differed little from those of Farbstein, the race was characterized as a battle of style rather than substance. "She just wants my job," Farbstein told Grace Lichtenstein of the *New York Times*. Adopting the slogan "A Woman's Place is in the House ... the House of Representatives!," Abzug ran an aggressive campaign throughout the multiethnic nineteenth district, sometimes speaking in Yiddish, in which she was fluent, and delivering short, memorized speeches in Spanish. In the June 1970 primary, the underdog Abzug defeated Farbstein by a comfortable margin. "I think quite a few people voted for me because I'm a woman and they thought they'd like to see a compassionate woman in Congress, to find some morality in what seems like a hopeless morass in society," Abzug told Margaret Crimmins of the *Washington Post* in July 1970. Republicans made up a small percentage of nineteenth district voters, and in the November general election Abzug was handily victorious over GOP candidate Barry Farber, a radio talk show host.

Calling herself a "freshwoman Congresswoman" the outspoken Abzug quickly made her presence known in the House. "I think [Abzug] has turned off some of the members by coming on too strong," an unnamed Democratic member of Congress told Richard L. Madden of the *New York Times* in 1971. "She'll call me and start shouting about this or that outrage, and I'll have to say, 'Bella! Don't make me hold the phone a foot away from my ear. I'm on your side!' But I think it's good for the House to have her here. God knows, the place needs shaking up." Abzug desired a seat on the powerful Armed Services Committee but was given typical new member assignments on the Public Works and Government Operations Committees.

To avoid being mistaken for a secretary, Abzug had made it a habit to wear a hat in the courtroom during her years as a lawyer. She continued to wear a hat on the floor of the House, in violation of Congressional protocol. Hats became her much joked about trademark. "When I was a young lawyer, I would go to people's offices and they would always say, 'Sit here. We'll wait for the lawyer.' Working women wore hats. It was the only way they would take you seriously. After a while, I started liking them. When I got to Congress, they made a big thing of it. So I was watching—did they want me to wear it or not? They didn't want me to wear it, so I did," Abzug told Seth Faison of the New York Times in 1995.

In 1972, New York's congressional districts were redrawn and reduced in number. Abzug's fishhook shaped nineteenth district was broken up and distributed into four other districts. In order to retain a seat in Congress, Abzug ran against another incumbent member of Congress, William Fitts Ryan, in the Democratic primary in the newly configured twentieth district. About one quarter of Abzug's old district was included in the new twentieth district, a narrow belt running along the West Side of Manhattan and into the Bronx. A small extension in the southern part of the district took in Abzug's Greenwich Village home. Ryan was one of the most liberal members of the House, and the Abzug-Ryan battle created bitter internecine warfare among left-wing Democrats. Almost half of Abzug's old district had been joined with the seventeenth Congressional district represented by John Murphy, a conservative Democrat from Staten Island, and many of her fellow "reform" Democrats criticized Abzug for not changing her address by a few blocks and running against Murphy. Abzug defended her decision to run against Ryan by explaining that she stood no chance of defeating Murphy since her liberal views would not garner many votes on politically moderate Staten Island and that, while Ryan may have an impeccably liberal voting record, a voting record alone was not enough. The times called for more aggressive tactics. Also, she pointed out that Congress needed more women, not just male supporters of women's rights. "I'm an activist and Bill isn't. It's as simple as that. Why should there just be 11

women in Congress? Why should I be told either to retire or go into a race I can't win?" Abzug told Tom Buckley of the New York Times. Abzug lost the Democratic primary to Ryan by a margin of two to one.

Rumors had circulated throughout the campaign that Ryan was in poor health. These rumors were confirmed when Ryan died of throat cancer in September 1972, two months before the general election. Primary runner-up Abzug was selected by the Democratic Party to take his place on the ticket. However, many of Ryan's followers refused to throw their support to Abzug and mounted a campaign by Ryan's widow under the Liberal Party banner. Despite this split of left-wing votes, Abzug emerged victorious.

> "I'm a woman. I'm strong. I have something to say. And I like the big fight."

During her tenure as a member of the U.S. Congress, Abzug demanded withdrawal of American forces from Vietnam, led the way in drafting legislation to prevent discrimination against women by lending institutions, helped obtain federal grants to clean up New York Harbor and to stop erosion on Long Island beaches, advocated increased funding for social programs and mass transit, and supported efforts towards statehood for New York City.

Like many ambitious members of the House of Representatives, Abzug began looking towards the more prestigious and powerful Senate. In 1976, instead of running for re-election to the House, she entered the Democratic primary for a seat in Congress' upper house, facing opponents Ramsey Clark, a former U.S. attorney general, and Daniel Patrick Moynihan, a college professor who had served as a domestic issues advisor to President Nixon. "I ran because I felt it was essential for me to be a Senator. It was important for me to try to be a Senator. It was important that women get elected to the Senate," Abzug told Carey Winfrey of the New York Times in 1977. Abzug did well among African-American, Hispanic, and liberal white voters but ended up a very close second to the moderate Moynihan who went on to defeat Republican incumbent James Buckley in the general election.

In 1977, Abzug ran for mayor of New York City, joining a crowded field of Democratic candidates that included incumbent mayor Abraham Beame, secretary of state and future governor Mario Cuomo, and Congressman Edward Koch. New York City was plagued with seemingly insurmountable fiscal and social problems at this time. A power blackout in the summer of 1977 brought the city to a halt, provoked widespread looting, and symbolized the chaotic situation into which the nation's largest metropolis had descended. Abzug felt the city needed firmer leadership and that she could provide it. "You just cannot accept the fact that a place like New York will not pull out of it. It therefore requires somebody who has the energy and the creativity ... and the leadership to keep it going, find the ways, put it together, give it something," Abzug explained to Winfrey during the 1977 campaign. Though Abzug came out on top in Manhattan, she did not fare as well in the outer boroughs and ended up in fourth place, behind Koch, Cuomo, and Beame. Koch went on the become mayor. In a 1978 interview with Patricia Burstein of *People,* Abzug dismissed the newly installed Mayor Koch as "a bore."

In early 1978, Abzug made an effort to return to Washington by running in a special election for Koch's vacated seat in the eighteenth Congressional district on Manhattan's posh East Side, often referred to as the "Bluestocking" district because of its proliferation of longtime wealthy families. Abzug was denied the Democratic nomination when she narrowly lost a Democratic Party Committee election to Carter Burden, a former New York City councilman. She successfully contested the vote count in court and was named the Democratic candidate. Abzug's ultra-liberal opinions and blunt style did not go over as well on the patrician East Side as they did on the more freewheeling West Side and she was defeated by Republican S. William Green in the February election.

Three defeats in a row did not sour Abzug on the idea of elected office. "I'm a politician—I run for office! That's my profession! ... I get up feeling frustrated about not being able to make a more direct contribution," Abzug told Leslie Bennetts of the *New York Times* in December 1978. However, Abzug did not run for office again. Many believe that the deteriorating health of her husband, who died of a heart ailment in 1986, and large post-campaign debts influenced her decision to stay out of the electoral fray.

After leaving elective politics, Abzug devoted most of her attention to women's rights. In the early 1980s, she worked for passage of the Equal Rights Amendment (ERA) to the United States Constitution. Unable to gather sufficient support in state legislatures within a proscribed time limit, the ERA failed in its bid for ratification in 1982. Extending her concerns beyond the status of American women, Abzug made efforts to mobilize women on an international level. She was a special advisor to the Secretary General of the United Nations Conference on Environment and Development and co-founded the Women's Environment and Development Organization (WEDO) which works to give women around the world greater access to political power. "Women are the very core of the environment, which is the sine qua non of existence. Women's knowledge, skills, experience and instincts have not been taken into consideration.... I believe that the political empowerment of women may well provide the missing part of the equation that is needed to restore the health of our planet," Abzug wrote in the *UNESCO Courier* in 1992.

Heart disease and a bout with breast cancer did not quell Abzug's activism and passion. "When we're sick, most of us would go to bed, but [Abzug] just goes to another meeting," Mim Kelber, a longtime associate of Abzug's, told Seth Faison of the *New York Times.* Despite difficulties with walking that sometimes forced her to use a wheelchair, Abzug continued to attend conferences around the world, usually playing a major role in the proceedings. She presided over the World Women's Congress for a Healthy Planet in 1991 and addressed the United Nations World Conference on Women held in Beijing in 1995. While talking with people from other nations, Abzug discovered how far her reputation has traveled. She told the *New Yorker* that at one meeting "this young woman came in and said, 'Hi, I'm the Bella Abzug of Mongolia.'"

In March of 1998, Abzug's health failed and she was hospitalized. She died the last day of the month following an operation on her heart. "[Abzug] was an original," opined Edward Koch, former New York Mayor, as quoted in the *Chicago Tribune.* He continued, "The women of the world, not just the country, owe her a great debt. She stood up for them as nobody else. She was their champion." U.S. Health and Human Services Secretary Donna Shalala also had praise for Abzug, commenting in the *Los Angeles Times* that "[Abzug] was bigger than life, a true pioneer in the struggle for women's equality." "She was one of the most exciting, enlightened legislators that ever served in the Congress," judged Representative Charles Rangel of Manhattan in the *New York Times.* Gloria Steinem, as noted in the *Chicago Tribune,* declared: "There's just no one else with her vision and her compassion and combination of head and heart. She was larger than life and full of life, and president of the United States is the least she should have been."

Selected writings

Bella! Ms. Abzug Goes to Washington, Saturday Review Press, 1972.

Sources

Chicago Tribune, April 1, 1998.
Harper's, November 1983, pp. 69-72.
Los Angeles Times, April 1, 1998.
Ms., April 1974, pp. 64-65; July/August 1990, pp. 94-96; January/February 1996, p. 63.
Nation, November 28, 1981, pp. 576-578.
Newsweek, October 5, 1970, pp. 28-29.
New Yorker, September 4, 1995, p. 32.

New York Times, June 9, 1970, p. 30; October 11, 1971, pp. 37, 40; March 22, 1972, p. 35; April 12, 1972, p. 47; April 29, 1972, p. 29; June 12, 1972, p. 37; July 2, 1972, sec. 7, pp. 5-7; September 15, 1976, pp. 1, 28; August 15, 1977, p. 27; August 21, 1977, sect. 6, p. 15; December 1, 1978, p. B6; July 26, 1985, p. B3; March 12, 1995, p. 6; September 12, 1995, p. 3; April 1, 1998.
People, November 13, 1978, pp. 46-47.
Time, August 16, 1971, pp. 14-16.
Times (London), April 2, 1998.
UNESCO Courier, March 1992, pp. 36-37.
Washington Post, July 5, 1970, p. G1-2.

—*Mary Kalfatovic*

Sherman Alexie

Author

Born Sherman Joseph Alexie, Jr, October 7, 1966, in Spokane, WA; son of Sherman Joseph (a truck driver and logger) and Lillian Agnes (a quilter; maiden name, Cox) Alexie; married; wife's name, Diane. *Education:* Attended Gonzaga University, 1985-87; Washington State University, B.A., 1991.

Addresses: *Home*—P.O. Box 376, Wellpinit, WA.

Career

Writer. First published in *Hanging Loose* magazine, 1990. Writer and producer of film *Smoke Signals,* 1998.

Awards: Washington State Arts Commission, poetry fellow, 1991; National Endowment for the Arts poetry fellowship, 1992; winner, Slipstream's fifth annual chapbook contest, 1992, for *I Would Steal Horses;* American Book Award, 1996, for *Reservation Blues;* Granta's Best of Young American Novelists award, 1996; Sundance Film Festival, Audience Award and Filmmakers Trophy, 1998, for *Smoke Signals;* PEN/ Hemingway fiction citation for *The Lone Ranger and Tonto Fistfight in Heaven.*

Sidelights

Author Sherman Alexie, using poetry and prose saturated with imagery, drama, and humor, has shed light on what it means to be an Indian in contemporary American society. His works have helped his fellow Indians to understand themselves better by honing in on typical problems rampant on reserva-

tions, including poverty, alcoholism, and racism. However, Alexie's characters are not the cliched stone-faced people who accept their lot in defeat; rather, he exposes the rich sense of humor that Indians commonly use to deal with their problems. His works are also useful in helping non-Indians recognize the issues that Indians face and dispelling old mistaken notions of who Indians are, although his writings are disdainful of whites who claim to sympathize with Indians for their own selfish reasons. Alexie's mission to break down Indian stereotypes jumped from the page to the screen in 1998 with the release of his film, *Smoke Signals,* based on a collection of stories titled *The Lone Ranger and Tonto Fistfight in Heaven.* Also directed and produced by Indians, *Smoke Signals* brought Alexie's frequently recurring characters to life. As the author noted to Jeffrey Ressner in *Time,* "I love the way movies have more power than books. They continue the oral tradition, the way we all sit around the fire and listen to stories."

Alexie was born October 7, 1966, in Spokane, Washington, to Sherman Joseph and Lillian Agnes (Cox) Alexie. Upon his birth, he had fluid pressure on the brain and underwent brain surgery at six months. As a result, Alexie was a weak and sickly child until about age seven. Though his father was a Coeur d'Alene Indian, Alexie's mother was Spokane, and thus he grew up in Wellpinit, Washington, on the Spokane Indian Reservation, where his mother would sell her handmade quilts at the Wellpinit Trading Post. His father was a truck driver and logger, but also an alcoholic who was away from home much of the time. As a youngster, Alexie loved to read, and would pore over everything he could find, including auto repair manuals, basketball biographies, and corny westerns. When he began the eighth grade, Alexie decided to venture off of the reservation in order to attend Reardan High School some 32 miles away. Though he was the only Indian at the mostly white school, a year later, his twin sisters joined him. He originally aspired to become a doctor, but a series of fainting spells during high school anatomy courses prompted him to reconsider. He was a top student nevertheless, and was admitted to Gonzaga University, a Jesuit school in Spokane, in 1985.

> *"According to TV and the movies, Indians don't exist past 1950. So I hope my books show that the dispossession of Indians is still occurring."*

However, the academic pressure and the stress of being different weighed on him. Though he never drank while on the reservation, he fell into the trap of alcohol abuse during college. He was also disillusioned with much of the education. "The teachers are mostly terrible, the books are old and useless, and they teach you the same lies that every high school in the country teaches," Alexie complained to Rita Kempley in the *Washington Post,* reprinted in the *Arizona Republic.* "Iconoclastic thought can get you a C-plus on an essay test. Outright agreement will get you an A-minus. So, I hated it, but I knew I needed the degree. I played the game, got drunk, and I graduated summa cum laude." He told Kempley that he drank for five years, from age 18 to 23, but "they were like dog years. I tried to put about 35 years of drinking into that period."

In 1987, Alexie transferred to Washington State University, where his high school sweetheart was enrolled, and began writing fiction and poetry. There, a creative writing instructor, Alex Kuo, encouraged him to try to get published. When the magazine *Hanging Loose* published a number of his works in 1990, Alexie found the motivation to quit drinking and devote himself to a writing career. As the author told Liane Hansen on Na-

tional Public Radio's *Weekend Edition,* "I was sort of into that suffering artists routine. You know, you had to drink ... you had to cause yourself more pain in order to write, but you know, that's a lie. You know, you don't need substances of any variety to be an artist." Alexie's works would soon become appreciated by many. He graduated from Washington State in 1991, and also that year, the university granted him a poetry fellowship. The next year, he was granted a National Endowment for the Arts fellowship and also won a chapbook (a poetry collection) contest from Slipstream for *I Would Steal Horses,* which they published. In addition to this debut, Alexie went on to create more books of poetry, including *First Indian on the Moon,* 1993, *Old Shirts & New Skins,* 1993, *Water Flowing Home,* 1994, and *Seven Mourning Songs for the Cedar Flute I Have Yet to Learn to Play,* 1994. The poems in these books mainly focus on the fight to maintain self-respect in the face of obstacles such as racism, alcohol and drugs, and a sense of powerlessness.

In 1992 Alexie published *The Business of Fancydancing,* his first major release. This collection of short stories and poetry was spawned from the first writing workshop that he attended at Washington State, and centers on "Crazy Horse Dreams," a saying for goals—whether reachable or improbable—that either materialize or fail without any apparent reason. The book introduced an assortment of characters, many of whom have reappeared in subsequent works. They generally deal with the same themes as his poetry, serving to convey the despair, poverty, and alcoholism that often envelops Indian society on reservations. However, his work does not fail to interject the vein of humor that is so important in Indian culture. *The Business of Fancydancing* received positive reviews, with James R. Kincaid in *New York Times Book Review* calling Alexie "one of the major lyric voices of our time." Writing in the *Kenyon Review,* Leslie Ullman commented on the work, "Alexie's collection ... weaves a curiously soft-blended tapestry of humor, humility, pride and metaphysical provocation out of the hard realities that make up its material: the tin-shack lives, the alcohol dreams, the bad luck and burlesque disasters, and the self-destructive courage of his characters."

After *The Business of Fancydancing,* Alexie was courted by agents and editors. His next short story collection, *The Lone Range and Tonto Fistfight in Heaven,* 1993, reprises many of the characters from his earlier collection and focuses on themes of survival and forgiveness. Big Mom, a spiritual and maternal figure, is known for her outstanding fry bread, a staple of Indian meals. Thomas Builds-the-Fire, an autobiographical character, spins the best tales. The book was noted for its smooth and detailed narratives about life on a reservation, from the poverty and desperation to the strong bonds of community and the comfort of time-worn traditions. This insider's look can be appreciated by Indians as well as non-Indians who can read it in order to better understand the Indian experience. Another of the book's important elements was, again, the incisive humor pervading the daily lives of those on the reservation. Refuting the stereotype of stoicism, Alexie's characters joke with ease and irony about the Bureau of Indian Affairs, racist police officers, government food, and even cancer. The book received a PEN/Hemingway fiction citation.

Alexie published his first novel in 1995, titled *Reservation Blues,* which won the American Book Award in 1996. In the story, protagonist Thomas Builds-the-Fire, along with his friends Victor Joseph and Junior Polatkin, all thirty-something, get a hold of legendary bluesman Robert Johnson's magical guitar, which provides Victor with amazing talent. The pals decide to form a rock band, the Coyote Springs, and their adventures result in a cacophony of cultures as Indian and Anglo worlds collide. Frederick Busch, writing in the *New York Times,* felt the book was funny and stirring, but commented, "Though there is wonderful humor and profound sorrow in this novel, and brilliant renditions of each, there is not enough structure to carry the dreams and tales that Mr. Alexie needs to portray and that we need to read. His talent may be for the short form." However, Busch added, "But the talent is real, and it is very large, and I will gratefully read whatever he writes, in whatever form."

In 1996, Alexie came out with another novel, *Indian Killer,* about a trio of Indians living in Seattle. The novel traces their personal lives, and the action is driven by the fact that an Indian has been stalking and killing white men in the area, and vigilantes are retaliating by murdering homeless Indians. Richard E. Nicholls in the *New York Times* claimed, "It's difficult not to make "Indian Killer" sound unrelievedly grim. It is leavened, however, by flashes of sardonic wit, the humor that Indians use to assuage pain.... It's also difficult not to make the novel seem more angry than reflective. But Sherman Alexie is too good a writer, too devoted to the complexities of the story, to settle for a diatribe. His vigorous prose, his haunted, surprising characters and his meditative exploration of the sources of human identity transform into a resonant tragedy what might have been a melodrama in less assured hands." In addition to addressing racial tensions, *Indian Killer* also exposes the inherent problems of whites who try to co-opt Indian culture and by doing so, display their ignorance and hypocrisy.

After *Indian Killer,* Alexie went to work on a screenplay incorporating much of the material in *The Lone Range and Tonto Fistfight in Heaven.* Released in 1998, *Smoke Signals* was written, directed, and produced by Indians, and also starred Indians. It was financed by a multimedia company in Seattle and helped along by Robert Redford's Sundance Institute, which sponsors a program to aid Indian filmmakers. The story revolved around two friends, Thomas and Victor, who embark on a road trip from their reservation in Idaho down to Arizona to retrieve the ashes of Victor's father. The father left the family when Victor was much younger, so the tale also involves the young man's feelings about his now-deceased father as he begins his journey. Thomas, as the cheery, geeky motormouth tagalong provides a perfect comic foil to the troubled Victor, but he also has private issues with which to contend as well. The film pokes fun of Indian stereotypes such as the serious warrior face and mystical visions while also maintaining a sense of humor about the white culture that Indians also experience, like John Wayne movies or "breakfast anytime" at Denny's. "Sure we have different specific cultural customs," Alexie told Jeffrey Ressner in *Time,* "but we also read Stephen King and watch *ER* like everyone else."

Smoke Signals was praised, winning both the Audience Award and Filmmakers Trophy at the Sundance Film Festival after its release, and Alexie was hailed as possibly the Spike Lee of the Indian world. "I want to write books and make films that will change the world's perception of Indians," he told John Clark in the *Los Angeles Times.* "And a tiny goal, a more specific goal, I want it so that Indian actors never have to put on a loincloth again." Alexie had other offers to produce *Smoke Signals,* but waited until he found one that would work with an Indian director. One producer even wanted to work on the project, but only if he could make the characters white. As he told Kempley, he has rejected numerous offers from what he calls the "evil White bastards" in Hollywood. When asked what the proposals involved, Alexie replied, "I can't talk about it. The evil White bastards are litigious."

Alexie, who is married (his wife, Diane, is a member of the Hidatsa tribe of North Dakota), has continued to live on the Spokane reservation. He is a large man, six feet, two inches tall, with long dark hair and glasses. He prefers not to use the term "Native American," and has expressed happiness that he has been able to write for reservation Indians, even though most of the other Spokane Indians have expressed dissatisfaction with Alexie and his work. The author, however, chalks it up to jealousy and the fact that he's "airing dirty laundry" about his tribe, as he told della Cava. Alexie even mused to Erik Himmelsbach in the *Los Angeles Times* that one tribal leader resented that he was a "ball hog" on the basketball team, or perhaps his tribal members did not agree with his decision to pursue his education at a white high school.

Nevertheless, Alexie is much in demand by other tribes, and is often asked to appear at events and commencements. He has also given hundreds of readings from his works over the years and teaches writing workshops on numerous reservations. He plans to continue to work to erase stereotypes and share Indian strengths and traditions while revealing the continuing oppression that Indians continue to face. Some future plans include directing a scrip based on *Indian Killer* and continuing to write novels and poetry. As Alexie remarked to Marco R. della Cava in *USA Today*, "According to TV and the movies, Indians don't exist past 1950. So I hope my books show that the dispossession of Indians is still occurring. They might not be giving up smallpox blankets anymore, but they're dumping nuclear waste on our reservations, which isn't much different."

Selected writings

I Would Steal Horses (poems), Slipstream, 1992.
The Business of Fancydancing: Stories and Poems, Hanging Loose Press, 1992.
First Indian on the Moon (poems), Hanging Loose Press, 1993.
The Lone Ranger and Tonto Fistfight in Heaven (short stories), Atlantic Monthly Press, 1993.
Old Shirts & New Skins (poems), UCLA American Indian Studies Center, 1993.
Water Flowing Home (poems), Limberlost Press, 1994.
Seven Mourning Songs for the Cedar Flute I Have Yet to Learn to Play (poems), Whitman College Press, 1994.

Reservation Blues (novel), Grove/Atlantic, 1994.
Indian Killer, Atlantic Monthly Press, 1996.
The Summer of Black Widows, Hanging Loose Press, 1996.
Smoke Signals (screenplay), Hyperion, 1998.

Sources

On-line

"Sherman (Jospeh, Jr.) Alexie," Contemporary Authors, Gale Literary Databases web site, http://www.galenet.com (July 7, 1998).
"Sherman Alexie," Contemporary Literary Criticism, Gale Literary Databases web site, http://www.galenet.com (July 7, 1998).
"Sherman Alexie," DISCovering Biography, Gale Literary Databases web site, http://www.galenet.com (August 13, 1998).

Books

Notable Native Americans, Gale Research, 1995.

Periodicals

American Indian Quarterly, January 1, 1996, p. 123.
Arizona Republic, July 10, 1998, p. D1.
Kenyon Review, Summer, 1993, p. 182.
Los Angeles Times, December 17, 1996; June 28, 1998.
Newsday, December 23 1993, p. 48; November 3, 1996, p. C39; June 26, 1998, p. B11.
New York Times, July 16, 1995; November 24, 1996.
New York Times Book Review, May 3, 1992, p. 28.
Star Tribune (Minneapolis, MN), July 8, 1998, p. 9E.
Time, June 29, 1998, p. 69.
USA Today, June 15, 1995.

Other

Weekend Edition (radio transcript), National Public Radio, September 26, 1993.

—Geri Speace

Debbie Allen

Director, actress, dancer, choreographer, and producer

Born January 16, 1950, in Houston, TX; daughter of Vivian Ayers (an artist) and a dentist; married Win Wilford (divorced); married Norm Nixon; children: (with Nixon) Vivian, Norman Jr. *Education:* Howard University, B.A., 1972.

Addresses: *Office*—c/o Lisa Kasteler, Wolf Kasteler, 1033 Gayley Avenue, Suite 208, Los Angeles, CA 90024-3417.

Career

Actress and dancer in Broadway musicals, including *Purlie* (1972), *West Side Story* (revival, 1980), *Guys and Dolls, Raisin, Ain't Misbehavin'*, and *Sweet Charity* (revival, 1986); choreographer for Broadway musical *Carrie* (1988), for television series *Fame* (1982-87), and for Academy Awards shows (1991-94); director of television series *A Different World* (1988-92), episodes of *Family Ties* and *Fame*, pilot and first episode of *Fresh Prince of Bel Air* (1990), and made-for-television movie *Stompin' at the Savoy* (1992); released musical album, *Special Look* (1989); director and choreographer for Disney television musicals *Polly* (1989) and *Polly II* (1990); actress in films including *The Fish That Saved Pittsburgh* (1979), *Fame* (1980), and *Jo Jo Dancer, Your Life Is Calling* (1986); actress in television sitcom *In the House* (1995-96); director of film *Out of Sync* (1995); co-producer of film *Amistad* (1997). University of California, Los Angeles, School of Theatre, Film and Television, member of executive committee of dean's advisory board, 1993.

Awards: Drama Desk Award, 1980, for *West Side Story*; Antoinette Perry Award, 1986, for *Sweet Charity*; two Emmy Awards for choreography, for *Fame*.

Sidelights

Dubbed "Miss Versatile" by her high school class, accomplished actress, dancer, director, producer, choreographer, and singer Debbie Allen has lived up to that nickname. Determined and never afraid to tackle new challenges, Allen has accomplished more than most in the entertainment industry: acting, dancing, singing, writing, producing, directing and choreographing on stage, screen, and television. In doing so she continually has broken new grounds for African American entertainers. "I've never put any limitations on myself," Allen once told *Ebony* magazine. "I liken myself to an octopus, having hands on so many things." Feisty and blunt speaking, Allen is supremely self-confident. "I'm good, I'm fast and I come in on budget," she told Pamela Johnson of *Essence,* explaining why she is so often sought as a director and producer.

From her beginnings as a dancer in Broadway musicals and films, Allen has taken her career in unexpected directions. Her behind the camera work in television and movies has made her one of Hollywood's top female executives, earning more than a million dollars a year. In 1997 Allen realized a career long dream when her tireless efforts at reclaiming a forgotten piece of American history resulted in the release of the acclaimed movie *Amistad*. Allen co-produced the film, which was directed by Stephen Spielberg.

Allen was born and raised in Houston, Texas. Her father was a dentist and her mother was an artist. They divorced when she was four old years. Her mother, Vivian Ayres, had primary responsibility for raising Debbie, her sister and two brothers, though Debbie always remained close to her father. Allen told Allison Adato of *Life* that her mother was "responsible for all of our creative development. She was a writer; the first plays we did were hers." Her father, she said, loved history. "My father would rather quote history than, almost, the Bible." Much later in life, Allen would name her production company Red Bird, a nickname her father gave her when she grew her hair into a huge Afro and it turned reddish.

From an early age, Allen was interested in dancing, taking up to ten ballet classes a week. She immediately displayed a determination to succeed and benefited from the rigors of strict training. "The discipline from dance training has been invaluable in helping me succeed," she told *Ebony*. "I learned to focus on the work, even when my toes hurt all the time."

The accomplishments of her older sister Phylicia provided additional motivation. One year, Phylicia was the drum majorette in Houston's Thanksgiving Day parade. "I wanted to be Phylicia," Allen told Adato. "She won the twirling competition one year, I won it the next. She went to Howard University, then I found myself there. When I got to New York, she was already doing plays."

At Howard University in Washington, D.C., Allen majored in classics, studied Greek and dance, and graduated cum laude in 1972. Afterward, she moved to New York to live with her sister. At first, they lived at the YWCA, and Allen recalled dividing up a can of tuna fish for dinner. Her sister, Phylicia Rashad, began an acting career that would culminate in the high-profile role of Bill Cosby's wife on *The Cosby Show*.

In 1972 Allen landed a role in a Broadway production of *Purlie* and soon became a regular performer in Broadway musicals. In 1980 she won a Drama Desk award for a revival of *West Side Story*. For six years, she was married to record executive Win Wilford, but they had no children. Allen made her film debut in the 1979 comedy *The Fish That Saved Pittsburgh*, playing a basketball cheerleader. On the set she met Norm Nixon, a star guard for the Los Angeles Lakers. They became friends but did not become romantically involved until years later. They married in 1984 and started a family.

In 1980 Allen appeared in the hit movie musical *Fame*, playing Lydia Grant, a stern taskmaster of a dance teacher. For six seasons starting in 1982, she played the same role in the television spin-off series. It was during the run of *Fame* on television that Allen began to branch out into managerial roles. She won two Emmys for her choreography in the series and also directed eleven episodes.

In 1986 Allen won an Antoinette Perry Award for acting and dancing in the Broadway musical *Sweet Charity*. That year, Bill Cosby asked her to direct the first season of his *Cosby Show* spin-off *A Different World*. Allen initially turned him down because she was hard at work choreographing a musical version of Stephen King's *Carrie*. But after the show flopped on Broadway, Allen took up Cosby's offer for the second season and stayed with *A Different World* for four seasons, until 1992. The series had been slammed by critics after its debut, but Allen incorporated more realistic stories about life at a black college as well as a few dazzling dance numbers. While directing *A Different World*, Allen also was raising her daughter Vivian and son Norman Jr., who were frequently with her on the set. Allen often rushed home after shooting for dinner with the family.

In 1989 Allen showed off all her talents in *The Debbie Allen Special* on ABC, which she co-wrote, directed, produced, choreographed, and starred. That same year, she recorded an album, but singing proved to be the other entertainment venture in which she failed to make a splash. Also in 1989, she directed her sister in a remake of the Disney classic *Pollyanna* with a predominately black cast.

In 1992 Allen directed *Stompin' at the Savoy*, a made-for-television movie about four young black women who share a room in Harlem in 1939 and escape from their struggles by doing the jitterbug at the Savoy ballroom. David Hiltbrand of *People* called it a "standard gals with dreams melodrama," noting Allen gave it "a fatalistic twist." That same year, Allen choreographed the glitzy Academy Awards telecast, and the dance numbers were so dazzling that the Oscars used her talents for several more years.

While making her mark as a director and choreographer, Allen never forsook her acting career. In 1995 she landed a starring role in the NBC sitcom, *In the House,* playing a recently divorced, downwardly mobile tenant who rents a house from an injured football star, played by rapper LL Cool J. That same year, Allen directed her first feature film, *Out of Sync,* in which LL Cool J starred as a disc jockey who gets in trouble with bookies. The movie got mixed reviews and little box office attention.

"The discipline from dance training has been invaluable in helping me succeed. I learned to focus on the work, even when my toes hurt all the time."

Much more attention would be given to the next movie project in which Allen was involved. One of her most persistent quests was rewarded in 1997 with the release of *Amistad.* For 19 years Allen had tried to bring the story about a shipboard slave rebellion to the screen, but she was repeatedly rejected by countless studios. "They didn't think it was commercially viable, they weren't moved, didn't think it warranted the attention," Allen told Adato. "It was tough for me to hear all of that."

Around 1978 she had bought a book to read on a long plane ride. The book was about 53 Africans from Sierra Leone who revolted on a Spanish ship in 1839, were captured by the U.S. Navy and brought to trial in the United States, where they eventually were acquitted by the Supreme Court and returned home as free men. "It's really the first civil rights case," Allen told Adato. But it was forgotten history. "It's this little blemish left out to protect the images of men who wanted to be looked at a certain way. They obliterated it."

In 1984 Allen found two volumes of essays and articles by African American writers, historians, and philosophers, which delved deeply into the Amistad incident. Allen told *People:* "It was just incredible to me that I had never been taught that story. I felt robbed."

Rejections only stoked Allen's determination to bring the project to fruition. "What kept me going was Belief," Allen said in an interview for the *Amistad* web page. "I believed in the power and the truth of this story. I believed that the enormous tapestry upon which it occurred related to all our ancestors the Africans, the abolitionists, the pro slavers, the Spanish, the Cubans, the British. It tells us all a lot about our history."

After seeing *Schlinder's List,* Allen went to Spielberg's Dream Works Pictures to pitch her longtime pet project. "*Schindler's List* made me want to get to Steven," Allen told Adato. "Black people and Jewish people have a lot in common. He was also compelled by the story."

Spielberg said: "I was inspired by her passion for the story. She had a remarkable ability to make me see it through her eyes." With Spielberg signed on, Allen traveled widely to find actors for the film. She consulted historians to ensure accuracy of dialect and customs. The film used the real language of the Mendes of West Africa. "I guided the research, picked out cultural advisors and went to Africa," she told Adato. She oversaw wardrobes, taught the actors gospel hymns, and did whatever chores were needed to give the film its remarkable authenticity. On the set of *Amistad,* Allen literally went undercover to help teenage actress Anna Paquin, who played a Spanish queen; Allen hid under Paquin's huge hoop skirt and fed her some of the Spanish lines she had to recite.

The project hit a legal bump when author Barbara Chase Riboud filed a lawsuit claiming parts of the script was stolen from her 1989 historical novel, *Echo of Lions.* Allen claimed the film was based solely on the 1953 historical novel *Black Mutiny* by William Owen, the book Allen had read in 1978 and had bought the rights to in 1984. Chase Riboud dropped the suit in February 1998, two months after the film was released.

To continue publicizing the forgotten piece of history she had unearthed, Allen created an Amistad Research Center at the Dream Works studio in Los Angeles. Another was founded at Tulane University. The original ship, *La Amistad,* toured the United States. "This is the hardest I have ever worked on a single project," Allen said.

And it seemed to be her proudest accomplishment. Allen said to *Life:* "This movie will raise questions about history and the way it's written and taught. People will be wondering, well, what else is missing? What else don't we know?" She told *Jet:* "This story is about all of us! ... What is so unnerving is that this story could be so quieted, so lost, so ignored." But thanks to Allen, the historic event is now familiar to the millions who have seen the film *Amistad*.

Sources

Ebony, November 1989, p. 54; March 1991, p. 24.
Entertainment Weekly, October 13, 1995, p. 85.
Essence, June 1990, p. 64.
Jet, October 28, 1981, p. 65; December 16, 1991, p. 55; April 24, 1995, p. 56; December 22, 1997, p. 58.
Life, December 1997, p. 44.
People, November 14, 1988, p. 105; September 15, 1997, p. 55; December 22, 1997, p. 22.

—Michael Betzold

Joan Allen

Actress

Born August 20, 1956, in Rochelle, IL; married Peter Friedman (a stage actor); children: Sadie. *Education:* Attended Eastern Illinois University and Northern Illinois University.

Addresses: *Office*—International Creative Management, c/o Bill Mann, 40 West 57th St., New York, NY 10019-4001; and International Creative Management, 8942 Wilshire Blvd., Beverly Hills, CA 90211.

Career

Theatrical appearances include *And a Nightingale Sang*, New York, 1984; *The Marriage of Bette and Boo*, New York, 1986; *Burn This!*, Los Angeles and New York, 1988; *The Heidi Chronicles*, New York, 1988-89; and *Earthly Possessions*, Chicago, 1991. Films include *Compromising Positions*, 1985; *Peggy Sue Got Married*, 1986; *Manhunter*, 1986; *Tucker: The Man and His Dream*, 1988; *In Country*, 1989; *Ethan Frome*, 1993; *Searching for Bobby Fischer*, 1993; *Josh and S.A.M.*, 1993; *Nixon*, 1995; *Mad Love*, 1995; *The Crucible*, 1996; *Face/Off*, 1997; *The Ice Storm*, 1997; and *Pleasantville*, 1998. Television appearances include *Evergreen*, 1985; *All My Sons*, 1986; *American Playhouse*, 1987; *The Room Upstairs*, 1987; and *Without Warning: The James Brady Story*, 1991; also appeared in an episode of *Frasier*, 1993.

Awards: Clarence Derwent Award, Drama Desk award, and Outer Critics Circle award, all 1983, all for *And a Nightingale Sang*; Antoinette Perry Award, 1988, for *Burn This!*

Reuters/Fred Prouser/Archive Photos

Sidelights

Joan Allen plays the dutiful wife, the quiet mother, the unsung woman behind the man. Artfully, she fades into the scenery as the role requires. She is considered cool, detached, prim. She has clear blue eyes and pristine beauty, but in an era of fiery, sexy, flamboyant roles for actresses, Allen gets the unembellished parts and makes the best of them. Two consecutive Academy Award nominations—for playing Pat Nixon in *Nixon* and Elizabeth Proctor in *The Crucible*—attest to that.

One of Allen's triumphs was playing dutiful wife to Kevin Kline's philandering husband in the family drama *The Ice Storm*. Her frosty, commanding performance garned much praise from critics. Allen has a way of wringing emotion out of the driest characters. *The Ice Storm* director Ang Lee was amazed after he put her through thirteen takes of a tense scene with Kline. "Most actors, they're like boxers," Lee once commented. "They become nasty before big scenes. You can't even talk with them because they're honing all day. Not Joan. She showed no trace of preparation. I gave her a cue, and she was right there, shaking with emotion." Afterwards, "she walked away calm. I don't know where that power comes from." Few people do, for Allen keeps an extremely low profile. In addition, her roles are not the kind that garner cover stories in entertainment magazines.

Allen was born in 1956, in Rochelle, Illinois. After attending two Illinois universities, she gravitated to the Chicago stage scene. She was a founding member of Chicago's Steppenwolf Theatre Company, and performed in more than twenty plays there before moving to New York in 1983, where she worked steadily throughout the 1980s. Her New York debut in 1983 in *And a Nightingale Sang* brought her three prestigious drama awards. She won an Antoinette Perry Award playing opposite John Malkovich in *Burn This!* In 1988, she played the lead role in the Pulitzer Prize-winning play *The Heidi Chronicles*.

Allen's subtle displays of emotion were even more suited to the big screen than to theater. Her film debut came in *Compromising Positions* in 1985, and she landed a role in Francis Ford Coppola's *Peggy Sue Got Married*. "I didn't do films until my late 20s," Allen told *Entertainment Weekly*. "I was so entrenched in theater, I didn't know how to act in front of a camera. I tend to feel I'm the one not up to speed."

In Coppola's 1988 film *Tucker: The Man and His Dream,* about the failed automobile tycoon, Allen played the magnate's spouse. Peter Travers of *People* observed: "The family drama plays like *Father Knows Best* and wastes the talents of Joan Allen in the one-note role of Tucker's dutiful wife." Already, Allen seemed destined to play only spouses and mothers. She was a Vietnam War widow in the 1989 film *In Country*. Ralph Novak, writing in *People*, noted Allen "brings off a tough role as a woman who feels vaguely guilty because she isn't obsessed with Vietnam and a man she knew so little, so long ago."

While her film career gave her steady work, Allen also appeared in several television roles. She was praised by *People* contributor David Hiltbrand for her "fine acting" as the wife of the wounded presidential press secretary in the 1991 made-for-television movie *Without Warning: The James Brady Story*.

Hollywood had her in a well-worn groove. In *Searching for Bobby Fischer,* the 1993 film about a chess whiz kid, "Allen has little to do as the boy's passive mom," judged Novak in *People*. Bruce Williamson, writing in

Playboy, noted that "Joan Allen fumes as the sickly wife" in *Ethan Frome,* a film based on Edith Wharton's story about lust in icy New England. Allen's parade of traditional wife roles had her perfectly poised to win the part of the former First Lady in Oliver Stone's *Nixon*. She cultivated a "constricted" body language to play "Plastic Pat" Nixon, and endlessly watched the one extensive TV interview she could find with the reclusive presidential spouse. Critics loved her performance, and it earned her an Oscar nomination. John Simon of the *National Review* declared: "[B]est of all is the Pat Nixon of Joan Allen, a fine and restrained actress who manages to look the part to boot."

Allen played the prim Elizabeth Proctor in Arthur Miller's screen adaptation of his play *The Crucible,* directed by Nicholas Hynter. The *New Republic*'s Stanley Kauffmann observed that Allen "has always been a rather cool actress, so the part fits her." She earned an Academy Award nomination for best supporting actress for the second consecutive year, but once again didn't win the Oscar. Her experience as Hollywood's favorite movie wife earned her a part in *Face/Off* without an audition. Playing opposite Nicholas Cage and John Travolta, Allen earned her highest salary ever, but it was still not seven figures.

Allen grew tired of playing the tortured spouse. Director Gary Rose persuaded her into playing yet "one more married mom" for his comedy *Pleasantville*, released in 1998, but she turned down Whoopi Goldberg's request to play a wife in an HBO adaptation of the August Strindberg play *The Father*. While searching for roles that might stretch her abilities a little more, Allen spends time off from acting with her husband, actor Peter Friedman, and young daughter Sadie.

Sources

Entertainment Weekly, December 22, 1995, p. 43; October 10, 1997, p. 34.
Nation, May 1, 1989, p. 605.
National Review, February 12, 1996, p. 57.
New Republic, December 16, 1996, p. 30.
People, August 22, 1988, p. 15; September 25, 1989, p. 16; June 17, 1991, p. 11; August 16, 1993, p. 17.
Playboy, December 1992, p. 20.

—*Michael Betzold*

Joan Baez

Library of Congress

Singer, musician, and activist

Born Joan Chandos Baez, January 9, 1941, in Staten Island, NY; daughter of Albert Vinicio (a physicist) and Joan (a drama teacher; maiden name, Bridge) Baez; married David Victor Harris (an activist), March 1968 (divorced, 1973); children: Gabriel Earl. *Education:* Attended Boston University.

Addresses: *Home*—Woodside, CA. *Office*—Diamonds & Rust Productions, P.O. Box 1026, Menlo Park, CA 94026. *Manager*—Mark Spector and Julia Hepfer, The Mark Spector Co., 44 Post Rd. West, Westport, CT 06880. *Publicist*—Tracy Bufferd, Kathryn Schenker Associates, 1776 Broadway, 14th Floor, New York, NY 10019.

Career

Singer, guitarist, recording artist, activist, author. Learned to play guitar, age 14; sang in high school choir, Palo Alto, CA; first public performance singing folk ballads and playing guitar with others at Club 47 coffeehouse, Cambridge, MA, 1958-60; regular performer in coffeehouses near Harvard Square, Cambridge and Boston, MA, 1958-60; appeared at The Gate of Horn folk club, Chicago, IL, 1958; played at Newport (RI) Folk Festival, summer, 1959, 1960; recorded on Vanguard Records, 1960-72, A & M, 1973-76, Portrait Records, 1977-80, CBS International, 1980; Gold Castle Records, 1986-89, Virgin Records, 1990-93, Grapevine Label Records (UK), 1995—, and Guardian Records, 1995—; toured the U.S., 1961—, Europe, 1965—, Japan, 1966, 1982, Latin America, 1981, Australia, 1985, and Israel, 1988; extensive television appearances and speaking tours for anti-militarism, U.S. and Canada, 1967-68. Founder, Institute for the Study of Nonviolence, Palo Alto, CA (now the Resource Center for Nonviolence, Santa Cruz, CA), 1965; founded Humanitas International, 1979, president, 1979-92. Starred with David V. Harris and sung title song for film *Carry It On,* New Film Production Company, 1970; also appeared in *Renaldo and Clara,* produced by Bob Dylan; documentary film *There But for Fortune: Joan Baez in Latin America,* 1982; and German television documentary *Music Alone Is Not Enough.*

Awards: Award from Chicago business executives for peace activism, 1971; Thomas Menton Award for commitment to peace, 1975; public service award for work on behalf of abused children, 1977; Bay Area Music award for top female vocalist in the San Francisco Bay area, 1978, 1979; Earl Warren Civil Liberties Award, American Civil Liberties Union, 1979; Jefferson Award for public service, 1980; Americans for Democratic Action award, 1982; Lennon Peace Tribute Award, 1982; SANE Education Fund Peace Award, 1983; named Chevalier, Legion d'honneur, government of France, 1983; award for best live album, Academy Charles Cros (France), 1983; Leadership Award, ACLU of Southern California, 1989; Death Penalty Focus of California Award for work against death penalty, 1992; Award of Achievement, Gleitsman Foundation, 1994.

Sidelights

Singer, songwriter, and activist Joan Baez, the queen of folk music, is one of the icons of the 1960s whose career has continued throughout the subsequent decades. The pacifist soprano with the pure voice came to epitomize the "hippie" look and attitude with her long hair and involvement in activist causes. Although she later shed her flower child image, cutting her hair short and swinging her focus from activism to her music, she never lost her verve for social responsibility. She is known for songs such as "The Night They Drove Old Dixie Down," "Diamonds and Rust," "Blue Sky," and her version of "We Shall Overcome."

Throughout her 40 years of music-making, Baez has inspired numerous singer/songwriters, such as Sarah McLachlan and Jewel, as she has cranked out her own albums at a dedicated rate. Though she always claimed a loyal fan base, Baez in the late 1990s saw a resurgence of her popularity, thanks to artists such as Tracy Chapman, The Indigo Girls, and others who ushered in a new wave of earthy tunes. In late 1997, she released another album, *Gone from Danger*, which addressed issues that had always concerned her—homelessness, single motherhood, war, and sexual abuse—even though she only wrote one song for the release. "I don't want to write anymore," Baez told Kevin C. Johnson in the *St. Louis Post-Dispatch*. "If they [her songwriters] can do that well, I'd rather stay home and feed the goats and watch the chickens lay eggs." Perhaps only partially serious, Baez embarked on a 1998 tour and kept busy writing poetry.

Baez was born on January 9, 1941, in Staten Island, New York, the second of three daughters of Albert Vinicio and Joan (Bridge) Baez. Her father was a Mexican American physicist who turned down the more lucrative path of government defense work for a career in academia. Her mother, born in Scotland, was a drama teacher. The Baez family moved often, as her father took positions at various universities, including overseas in Paris and Baghdad. Baez spent most of her junior high years in southern California, where she faced discrimination from children of Mexican heritage, since she spoke no Spanish, and whites, due to her dark skin and hair. Raised as a Quaker, Baez stayed true to the pacifist teachings throughout her life.

Baez's "debut" as a musician was at age 14 playing "Honey Love" with a ukulele in a school talent show. She also sang with the school choir. Shortly after she graduated from high school in Palo Alto, California, her father got a job at Massachusetts Institute of Technology (MIT) and moved the family to the Boston area.

There she blossomed in the burgeoning coffeeshop folk scene around Harvard Square. Baez enrolled at Boston University, but after attending an amateur night at a coffee house with her father, she decided to pursue music. Though she was never formally trained, Baez became a favorite in the folk scene, appearing at places like Club 47 and Tulla's Coffee Grinder. In 1959, she played at the Gate of Horn in Chicago, where folk singer Bob Gibson noticed her and invited her to perform at the Newport Folk Festival in Rhode Island. This breakthrough gig led to friendships with other major folk acts of the day, including the Seeger family and Odetta, as well as recording offers. But she returned to Boston's coffeehouse folk scene.

The following summer, Baez again appeared at the Newport Folk Festival, and rejected an offer from Columbia Records and signed with Vanguard, a small folk label. Her first album, *Joan Baez*, was released that same year. She became a sensation. With her pure, three-octave soprano voice, her long hair and natural good looks, and her unpretentious presence, she came to earn the nickname "Madonna" because she represented the "Earth Mother" for the 1960s generation. On her first national tour, she displayed her strong convictions which would continue to endear her to the younger, socially active generation. After discovering that blacks were not allowed to attend her concerts at white colleges in the South, she subsequently only performed at black colleges. She also refused to pay income tax, citing that as a Quaker, it violated her pacifist religion, since the government used part of the money for the military. And in 1963, she performed at the Washington rally where Martin Luther King, Jr. gave his "I Have a Dream" speech.

Baez became involved in a number of causes during the Vietnam era, including founding the Institute for the Study of Nonviolence (later renamed the Resource Center for Nonviolence) in Palo Alto, California. Because of her anti-military views, the Daughters of the American Revolution (DAR) refused to let her perform at Constitution Hall in Washington, D.C. in 1967. After widespread publicity, Secretary of the Interior, Morris Udall, let her stage the concert at the Washington Monument, drawing a crowd of 30,000. Later, she was arrested twice and jailed on civil disobedience charges during protests. In March of 1968, she married David Victor Harris, who was jailed for resisting the draft in the summer of 1969. Baez was pregnant with their son, Gabriel, at the time of her husband's arrest. Around the same time, she sang at the Woodstock Festival. Harris remained in prison for 20 months, which constituted a large part of their short marriage. He was released in 1971, and together they wrote *Coming Out,* but they separated in 1972 and were divorced in 1973.

In the early 1970s, Baez offended some former leftist allies, including attorney William Kunstler and actress Jane Fonda, when she denounced Communist re-education centers in Vietnam for reported human rights violations. She stood up, however, against abuse at the hands of all governments and continued her work throughout the decade, singing in bomb shelters in Hanoi during Vietnam and Laotian refugee camps in Thailand. She also became involved with Amnesty International and spoke out in favor of nuclear disarmament. In 1975, she released one of her most important albums, *Diamonds and Rust,* and took time for a good old-fashioned rock concert tour with fellow folkie Bob Dylan. Baez, in fact, is credited with folk legend Bob Dylan's rise to fame. After meeting at Gerde's Folk City in Manhattan's Greenwich Village in 1961, the pair became romantically involved. She performed and popularized his songs and took him on tour with her to boost his fame, but he cheated on her, and they later broke up.

Baez doggedly pursued justice, founding Humanitas International, a human rights organization, in 1979. She served as its president until its demise in 1992. In the late 1970s, she also toured the former Soviet Union, meeting with prominent Russian dissidents Elena Bonner and Andrei Sakharov. In 1981, she visited Latin America to probe human rights abuse cases there. By the mid-1980s, she headlined the Live Aid concert in Philadelphia and in 1986 performed on the "Conspiracy of Hope" tour organized by Amnesty International. Later in the decade, she would visit with the Dalai Lama and Polish Solidarity leader Lech Walesa. She published her autobiography, *And a Voice to Sing With,* in 1987. In 1988, she visited Israel to plead for peace with Palestine and held a concert in Tel Aviv.

Unfortunately, Baez's commitment to human rights had interfered with her life as a performer. Late in the 1980s, with a new manager, Mark Spector, she orchestrated a return to her roots. In 1988 she released *Recently,* her first studio album in eight years, and one of the tracks, "Asimbonanga," was nominated for a Grammy Award. After touring with the contemporary folk duo, the Indigo Girls in 1990, PBS produced the documentary, *Joan Baez in Concert.* Then she released *Play Me Backwards* in October of 1992, collaborating on the songwriting with Nashville-based Kenny Greenberg and Wally Wilson. For that album, she released her first-ever music video at age 51. In 1993, Vanguard released a three-CD boxed set titled *Rare,*

Live & Classic, featuring 60 songs recorded between 1958 and 1989. Bruce Pilato for the Gannett News Service remarked, "There simply is no other woman—with the possible exception of Joni Mitchell—who has made such an outstanding contribution to acoustic vocal music." *Rolling Stone* magazine gave *Rare, Live & Classic* a five-star review.

> *Bruce Pilato for the Gannett News Service remarked, "There simply is no other woman—with the possible exception of Joni Mitchell—who has made such an outstanding contribution to acoustic vocal music."*

Revving up her musical career required Baez to concentrate more on herself and her voice. She went through counseling, took yoga, listened to self-help tapes, and more diligently practiced guitar and voice. Her voice coach told her that "the voice is a muscle and if you don't exercise it every day it starts to calcify," she explained to Jeremy Lovell of the Reuters news service. "That scared me to death. I didn't realize I needed to work on it." Though Baez shut down Humanitas International in 1992, she did not lose sight of her mission. She visited war-torn Bosnia-Herzegovina in April of the following year to perform at refugee camps in Sarajevo and Zagreb. That same year, she was the first major artist to give a concert on Alcatraz Island, a former prison off the shore of San Francisco. The concert proceeds went to benefit her sister Mimi Farina's organization, Bread & Roses. In 1996, she returned to the island to perform with Dar Williams and the Indigo Girls. A supporter of gay rights, she joined Janis Ian in 1995 for "Fight the Right," a concert to benefit the National Gay & Lesbian Task Force. Also in 1995, Baez released the live album *Ring Them Bells,* recorded at New York City's Bottom Line during concerts she gave with fellow performers Mary Chapin Carpenter, the Indigo Girls, Tish Hinojosa, Ireland's Mary Black, her sister Mimi Farina, Dar Williams, and others.

In 1997, Baez came out with *Gone from Danger,* her first album of new material in five years. Baez only composed one of the songs on *Gone from Danger,* leaving the task to a cadre of younger writers, including Dar Williams, Richard Shindell, Mark Addison, Sinead

Lohan, and others. Tammy Paolino for the Gannett News Service called the collection "a beautiful, reflective, and coherent album." Ian Phillips in the *Independent* lauded, "Baez's voice has always had a soothing, vibrant quality to it, but with age, it has also grown in complexity and sophistication." Baez commented to Johnson about the songwriting, "They're powerful, well-crafted, beautiful songs," and explained, "For me, in the early days, the political areas were cut and dried and clear. The songs were quite blunt. These songs are better crafted. They (her current writers) put a lot of time into these songs." However, Baez noted that it was difficult for her to get airplay for the new effort.

Though Baez expressed reluctance to write any more of her own songs, she does enjoy writing poetry. She hopes that the work, which she posts on her web site, may eventually be published in book form. Baez also continues to tour, embarking on a set of dates in the United States and Europe in 1998. On the personal side, she also enjoys tending to her goats and chickens at her home in Woodside, California. She also keeps track of her son, Gabriel, who tours playing the African drums, much to his mother's satisfaction. Though Baez remarked to Rogers in the *Columbian* in 1998 that she has changed somewhat over the years, becoming less stern and more able to loosen up and have fun, she reminded him, "My principles really haven't budged much.... The foundations are rooted in nonviolence, and that hasn't changed." However, she added, "The major difference is in the last nine years I've dropped everything to pursue a musical career. I'd never done that before, and I think it shows."

Selected writings

Daybreak, Dial, 1968.
(With David V. Harris) *Coming Out*, Pocket Books, 1971.
And a Voice to Sing With (autobiography), Summit Books, 1987.
(With Albert V. Baez) *A Year in Baghdad*, illustrated by Joan Baez, J. Daniel, 1988.
(With John H. Yoder and others) *What Would You Do?: A Serious Answer to a Standard Question*, Herald Press, 1992.

Selected recordings

Folksingers round Harvard Square, Veritas Recordings, 1959.
Joan Baez, Vanguard, 1960.
Joan Baez, Volume II, Vanguard, 1961.
Joan Baez in Concert, Vanguard, 1962.
Joan Baez in Concert, Part II, Vanguard, 1963.

Joan Baez/5, Vanguard, 1964.
Farewell, Angelina, Vanguard, 1965.
Noel, Vanguard, 1966.
Portrait, Vanguard, 1966.
Joan, Vanguard, 1967.
Baptism: A Journey Through Our Time, Vanguard, 1968.
Any Day Now (songs by Bob Dylan), Vanguard, 1968.
(With Mimi and Richard Farina) *Memories*, Vanguard, 1969.
One Day at a Time, Vanguard, 1969.
David's Album, Vanguard, 1969.
Joan Baez—The First Ten Years, Vanguard, 1970.
(With others) *Woodstock* (soundtrack), Cotillion, 1970.
Carry It On (soundtrack), Vanguard, 1971.
Celebration at Big Sur (soundtrack), Twentieth Century-Fox, 1971.
Celebration, Ode, 1971.
Live in Milan June 21, 1971, 1971.
Blessed Are..., Vanguard, 1971.
Golden Hour, Pye, 1972.
The Joan Baez Ballad Book, Vanguard, 1972.
Big Sur Folk Festival (One Hand Clapping), Columbia, 1972.
Come from the Shadows, A & M Records, 1972.
Hits/Greatest and Others, Vanguard, 1973.
Where Are You Now My Son, A & M, 1973.
Gracias a la Vida, A & M Records, 1974.
Contemporary Ballad Book, Vanguard, 1974.
Live in Japan, Vanguard, 1975.
Diamonds and Rust, A & M Records, 1975.
From Every Stage, A & M Records, 1976.
Gulf Winds, A & M Records, 1976.
Love Song Album, Vanguard, 1976.
Blowin' Away, Portrait, 1977.
Sacco and Vanzetti, 1977.
Best of Joan C. Baez, A & M Records, 1977.
House of the Rising Sun, Musidisc, 1978.
Country Music, Vanguard, 1979.
Honest Lullaby, Portrait, 1979.
Joan Baez Twenty-four Juglio 1970, Portrait, 1979.
Joan Baez in Italy, Portrait, 1979.
Joan Baez Live in Japan, Portrait, 1979.
Joan Baez—European Tour, CBS International, 1980.
Live in Concert, Portrait, 1980.
Spotlight on Joan Baez, Portrait, 1980.
Very Early Joan, Vanguard, 1982.
Live Europe '83, 1984.
Recently, Gold Castle Records, 1987.
Joan Baez in Concert, Vanguard, 1988.
Diamonds and Rust in the Bullring, Gold Castle Records, 1989.
Speaking of Dreams, Gold Castle Records, 1989.
Brothers in Arms, Gold Castle Records, 1991.
Play Me Backwards, Virgin Records, 1992.

Rare, Live and Classic, Vanguard, 1993.
Ring Them Bells, Guardian Records, 1995.
Gone from Danger, 1997.
Baez Sings Dylan, Vanguard, 1998.

Sources

On-line

Joan Baez web site, http://www.baez.woz.org (April 3, 1998).
"Joan Baez," Gale Literary Databases, http://www.galenet.com (May 6, 1998).

Books

Contemporary Heroes and Heroines, Book II, Gale Research, 1992.
Contemporary Musicians, Volume 1, Gale Research, 1989.
Dictionary of Hispanic Biography, Gale Research, 1996.

Encyclopedia of World Biography, second edition, Gale Research, 1997.
Meier, Matt S., Conchita Franco Serri, and Richard A. Garcia, *Notable Latino Americans: A Biographical Dictionary,* Greenwood Press, 1997.

Periodicals

Atlanta Journal and Constitution, August 1, 1995, p. C6.
Columbian, February 8, 1998, p. D8.
Gannett News Service, January 21, 1994; April 10, 1998.
Independent, June 29, 1996, p. 12; November 21, 1997, p. 21.
Newsday, April 4, 1993, p. 10.
Reuters news service, April 15, 1996.
Rolling Stone, November 13, 1997, p. 52.
St. Louis Post-Dispatch, April 15, 1998, p. E1.
USA Today, April 24, 1995.

—Geri Speace

Robert D. Ballard

Scientist and explorer

Born Robert Duane Ballard, June 30, 1942, in Wichita, KS; son of Chester Patrick (an aerospace executive) and Harriet Nell (May) Ballard; married Marjorie Constance Jacobsen (a medical receptionist), July 1, 1966; children: Todd Alan and Douglas Matthew. *Education:* University of California at Santa Barbara, B.S. in chemistry and geology, 1965; Ph.D, 1974; attended University of Hawaii Institute of Geophysics, 1965-66, and University of Southern California, 1966-67; University of Rhode Island, Ph.D. in marine geology and geophysics, 1974.

Addresses: *Home*—Hatchville, MA. *Office*—Woods Hole Oceanographic Institution, Woods Hole, MA 02543.

Career

North American Aviation, Ocean Systems Operations, Long Beach, CA, in deep submersible engineering, 1961 and 1966-67; Woods Hole Oceanographic Institution, Woods Hole, MA, research associate in ocean engineering, 1970-74, assistant scientist in geology and geophysics, 1974-76, associate scientist, 1976-78; associate scientist in ocean engineering, 1978-79; Stanford University, Stanford, CA, visiting scholar in geology, 1979-80; Woods Hole Oceanographic Institution, associate scientist in ocean engineering, 1980-83, senior scientist, 1983—. Consulting professor at Stanford University, 1980-81; director of Ocean Exploration and Mining Consultants, Inc. (OEMC), 1982—; consultant to Research Systems Corporation Industries, Inc. (RSC), 1970-71, and Benthos, Inc., 1982-83; founder, JASON Foundation for Educa-

AP/Wide World Photos

tion; president, Institute for Exploration, Mystic, CT. Author of books and contributor of articles to journals and magazines. *Military service*—U.S. Army intelligence unit, 1965-67, became second lieutenant; U.S. Navy, naval oceanographic liaison officer, 1967-70; became lieutenant junior grade.

Awards: Science award, Underwater Society of America, 1976, for exploration and research conducted in the Cayman Trough; Compass Distinguished Achievement Award, Marine Technology Society, 1977, for leadership in the area of deep submergence exploration; Newcomb Cleveland Prize, American Association for the Advancement of Science, 1981, for best scientific paper in a journal of science; Cutty Sark Science Award, *Science Digest,* 1982, for exploration conducted in Mid-Ocean Ridge, including the discovery of underwater hot springs and their unique animal communities; Secretary of the Navy Research Chair in Oceanography, 1985; Washburn Award, Boston Museum of Science, 1986; Hubbard Medal, National Geographic Society, 1996.

Sidelights

Robert D. Ballard has made some of the most important underwater discoveries in the late twentieth century in regards to science and exploration. Not only did he help advance the concept of plate tectonics and make important discoveries about ocean life, he also managed to find some of the most famous shipwrecks in history, including the German battleship *Bismarck*, the *U.S.S. Yorktown* from World War II, and the luxury liner *Titanic*. Thanks to advances in technology, including night-vision cameras and fiber optics, scientists like Ballard can help bring information about the ships back up to the surface. "There's more history preserved in the deep sea than in all the museums of the world combined," Ballard suggested to Paul Karon in the *Los Angeles Times*. Despite all of his accomplishments in geology, oceanography, and archaeology, Ballard still gets most excited about his capability to scout new territories. "I think of myself as an explorer—that was always my career goal," he told Karon. "If I could go to Mars tomorrow, I'm gone."

Robert Duane Ballard was born June 30, 1942, in Wichita, Kansas, to Chester Patrick (an aerospace executive) and Harriet Nell (May) Ballard. However, Ballard and his three siblings were raised in southern California, where he developed a passion for the sea. The fair-haired teenager would spend much of his time at the beach near his home in San Diego, becoming an avid swimmer, surfer, fisherman, and scuba diver. Ballard's father was a flight engineer at a testing ground in the Mojave Desert, but was later appointed the U.S. Navy's representative to the famous Scripps Institute of Oceanography. When he was still in high school, Ballard wrote a letter to the Scripps Institute that asked, "I love the ocean—what can I do?" he recalled to Bayard Webster in the *New York Times*. Subsequently, the school invited him to attend a summer program.

Ballard went on to earn a bachelor of science degree in chemistry and geology in 1965 from the University of California at Santa Barbara, but he never lost interest in the sea. After graduating, he pursued post-graduate work at the University of Hawaii Institute of Geophysics in 1965-66, where he made money as the keeper of two trained porpoises at Sea Life Park. He went back to the University of Southern California in 1966-67, and meanwhile, in 1965, he signed up to the U.S. Army in the intelligence unit, where he eventually became second lieutenant. In 1967, he joined the U.S. Navy as a naval oceanographic liaison officer, making lieutenant junior grade. For this stint, he was sent to Woods Hole Oceanographic Institution, a private, not-for-profit research organization on Cape Cod, Massachusetts. After his naval assignment was complete, he decided to stay on the East Coast and work at Woods Hole, continuing his research in marine geology and ocean engineering.

Joining Woods Hole as a research associate in ocean engineering in 1970, Ballard also pursued his doctorate degree at the University of Rhode Island. He began studying plate tectonics, which was a vanguard theory at the time, and earned his Ph.D. in 1974 with a dissertation on the subject. Plate tectonics suggests that the Earth's land masses are divided into sections, or plates, that move independently of the planet's mantle. This movement causes shifting of the land, which results in earthquakes at the boundaries (fault lines) and can also cause the shape of the land masses to change over time. Also in 1974, Ballard was promoted to assistant scientist in geology and geophysics at Woods Hole. Meanwhile, he was becoming interested in the research submarine *Alvin*, which was equipped with a remote arm for retrieving samples from the floor of the ocean. He was also intrigued by the idea of studying the Mid-Atlantic Ridge, a portion of a global underseas mountain range called the Mid-Ocean Ridge. When he suggested that the three-person *Alvin* be sent down, other scientists doubted the value of using a submarine for the project. "There were quite a few people ... who felt that submarines were expensive toys that geologists played with, and that no real good science would come out of them," Ballard remarked to James Lardner in the *Washington Post*.

Nevertheless, by 1974, Ballard was named head of Project FAMOUS (French-American Mid-Ocean Underseas Study) and proved the naysayers wrong. The expedition began in the summer of 1974 with a fleet of four ships and three research submarines. During the project, Ballard designed a survey sled called *Angus* that carried a camera and could be controlled acoustically. It was sent down before *Alvin*'s dives in order to take pictures so that the scientists could determine where they wanted to go. Ballard was on board the *Alvin* during most of its 17 dives to the ocean floor and thus was able to witness the rift formed at the juncture of the plates that form the eastern and western sides of the Atlantic seabed. In addition to the geological importance of the mission, Ballard and his team came back with data that could help predict earthquakes, and they also found beds of natural resources such as petroleum and minerals.

Following that endeavor, Ballard in 1975 and 1976, along with many of the Project FAMOUS team, went to the Cayman Trough, a depression in the ocean floor just south of Cuba. There they found that they had correctly predicted that there had recently been volcanic activity under the sea, and they picked up rock samples from the mantle of the Earth's crust. In 1976, Ballard was named an associate scientist at Woods

Hole, and would later be promoted to associate scientist in ocean engineering in 1978 and senior scientist in 1983. In 1979, he embarked on what would yield one of his most exciting discoveries. Off the coast of Ecuador on the Galapagos Rift, where plates were moving more quickly and strange variances in water temperature were recorded, he discovered that hydrothermal vents were erupting from cracks in the Earth's crust and that marine life—crabs, clams, and tube worms—could survive there by chemosynthesis. The journey and the underwater footage was used in a 1980 National Geographic special called *Dive to the Edge of Creation.*

The amazing creatures and their means of survival led biologists to hypothesize that life may have begun by this chemical method, but in shallow water. On another trip later that year near Baja California, Ballard took along some biologists and found even more proof. Tall geysers that he dubbed "black smokers" were found to sustain surrounding marine life, never before seen, that fed on the chemical-rich dark smoke gushing out of the 10- to 20-foot spews that threatened to melt the submarine's port holes. Marine biologists, up to that point, had assumed that no creature could survive so deep in the sea, where sunlight never penetrates. Though he is not a biologist and cannot authoritatively comment on whether life may have started by chemical methods, Ballard does believe that the smoky chimneys may be responsible for much of the world's mineral deposits.

In the early 1980s Ballard went to work on developing technology for unmanned sea exploration. Sending teams of scientists is expensive and often fruitless, so Ballard decided that robotic means could lower costs and increase productivity for such projects. With funding from the U.S. Navy and the National Science Foundation, Ballard formed the Deep Submergence Laboratory at Woods Hole in 1981. He thus designed the *Argo-Jason* system, an automated submarine loaded with robotic equipment that could function as the scientists' eyes and ears underwater. *Argo,* about the size of a car, has three video cameras that can see in almost total darkness, and its smaller assistant, *Jason,* has a robotic lens and arms and can be sent out to retrieve items from the ocean. With it, Ballard told Webster in the *New York Times,* "We hope to get even clearer pictures of the sea floor and what goes on down there."

Some of Ballard's colleagues were dubious that his system would allow for unmanned exploration, but he did not waver. For its maiden run, Ballard sent *Argo-Jason* down to search for the British luxury liner *Ti-*

tanic, which had hit an iceberg and sunk during its first voyage on the night of April 14-15, 1912, killing more than 1,500 of the 2,200 passengers. Ballard had long been intrigued by the legendary ship and its story, and eventually convinced the U.S. Navy to furnish a research ship, *Knorr,* and maps of the area where the ship was thought to have gone down. He assembled a group of French sonar researchers who set out for the North Atlantic in the summer of 1985. In late August, Ballard and his crew arrived on the *Knorr,* sending down the cameras and waiting for a sign. "The bottom was just going by and going by," Ballard told Karon in the *Los Angeles Times.* "And it's a boring bottom."

Less than a week later, on September 1, 1985, the *Argo* sent up an image of one of the *Titanic's* boilers as Ballard watched on a television monitor. He immediately knew it was the right ship, because he had studied it in detail. "It was a fluke," Ballard noted in *U.S. News and World Report.* "Any fishing boat could have done it." In a week and one day, the *Argo* videotape camera and the still camera on the *Angus* captured over 20,000 images of the shipwreck, including the damaged area and hundreds of artifacts such as bottles, china, a silver tray, and the barren lifeboat cranes. Ballard was strongly moved by the scenes and opposed anyone who wanted to profit from it, stating that instead, it should be declared an international memorial. The next summer, July of 1986, Ballard went down in the *Alvin* along with *Jason Jr.,* a remote "eyeball" that went inside the ship, and saw even more personal items, including a man's shoe and a porcelain doll's head. In 1997 a blockbuster film would be released based on the events of that tragic night, but fictionalized to provide an old-fashioned love story as well. Ballard remarked in *Newsday,* "The movie is excellent. It's a great Romeo and Juliet love story. I saw the ship I never saw, in all of its beauty and elegance."

After this notable discovery, Ballard also found the German battleship *Bismarck* in the Atlantic Ocean and in 1997 announced that he had found eight sailing ships, some dating back before the days of Jesus Christ, 2,500 feet below the surface off the coast of Tunisia in the Mediterranean. By then, Ballard was president of the Institute for Exploration based out of Mystic, Connecticut, and a senior scientist emeritus at Woods Hole. The finding of the Roman ships was especially important because it established that underwater archaeology could be performed in the deep seas of up to 20,000 feet. Previously, archaeologists limited their research to shipwrecks in coastal waters of less than 200 feet because they thought ancient mariners did not venture into deeper waters. In May of 1998, Ballard made another major discovery when he photographed the aircraft carrier *U.S.S. Yorktown*, sunk in the Pacific Ocean by Japanese forces on June 7, 1942, during World War II's Battle of Midway. It was located in almost 17,000 feet of water, one mile deeper than the *Titanic*, about 1,200 miles northwest of Honolulu, Hawaii. The National Geographic Society helped sponsor the work.

Ballard has raised eyebrows among some fellow scientists due to what they consider his enthusiasm to seek publicity. He has appeared in television programs, given lectures, and written for *National Geographic Magazine* in addition to writing in professional journals. He also established the Jason Foundation for Education and the Jason Project, which aims to increase students' interest in science. Like cosmologist Carl Sagan and underwater explorer Jacques Cousteau, Ballard has done much to bring science into the homes of laypeople, an accomplishment that he considers his public duty. "[Sagan and Cousteau] have probably sometimes lost some of the regard of their fellow scientists," Ballard admitted to Webster in the *New York Times*. "But look at the good they've done by making science exciting and making people aware of it! And don't forget that my science is paid for by some poor coal miner whose taxes go to support me while I'm having fun, so I feel it's responsible to go to him and the public and tell them what I'm doing."

Ballard in 1966 married Marjorie Constance Jacobsen, a medical receptionist. They have two sons, Todd Alan and Douglas Matthew, and live in Hatchville, Massachusetts. Ballard has won a number of awards, including the Science award from the Underwater Society of America in 1976 for exploration and research conducted in the Cayman Trough; the Compass Distinguished Achievement Award from the Marine Technology Society in 1977 for leadership in the area of deep submergence exploration; and the Newcomb Cleveland Prize from the American Association for the Advancement of Science in 1981 for the best scientific paper in a journal of science. He also received the Cutty Sark Science Award from *Science Digest*, 1982, for exploration conducted in Mid-Ocean Ridge, including the discovery of underwater hot springs and their unique animal communities. In 1985 he won a grant for $800,000 along with the Secretary of the Navy Research Chair in Oceanography, and in 1986, he was given the Washburn Award from the Boston Museum of Science. He was awarded the prestigious Hubbard Medal from the National Geographic Society in 1996. Ballard has written or cowritten 15 books and has published numerous articles in journals and magazines, including *National Geographic*.

Selected writings

(With K. O. Emery) *Research Submersibles in Ocean Technology*, Marine Technology Society, 1970.

(With James G. Moore) *Photographic Atlas of the Mid-Atlantic Ridge Rift Valley*, Springer-Verlag, 1977.

Exploring Our Living Planet, National Geographic Society, 1983.

(With Rick Archbold) *The Discovery of the Titanic*, Warner Books, 1987.

Exploring the Titanic, Scholastic, 1988.

(With Rick Archbold) *The Discovery of the Bismarck*, Warner Books, 1990.

(With Rick Archbold) *The Lost Wreck of the Isis*, Scholastic/Madison Press, 1990.

Exploring the Bismarck, Scholastic, 1991.

(With Rick Archbold) *The Lost Ships of Guadacanal*, Warner Books, 1993.

Explorer: A Pop-Up Book, Andrews and McMeel, 1992.

(With Nan Froman) *Finding the Titanic*, Scholastic, 1993.

(With Malcolm McConnell) *Explorations: My Quest for Adventure and Discovery Under the Sea*, Hyperion, 1995.

(With Spencer Dunmore) *Exploring the Lusitania: Probing the Mysteries of the Sinking that Changed History*, Warner Books, 1995.

(With Rick Archbold) *Lost Liners*, Hyperion, 1997.

(With Rick Archbold) *Ghost Liners*, Little, Brown, 1998.

Sources

On-line

"Biography: Dr. Robert Ballard," National Geographic web site, http://www.nationageographic.com (July 12, 1998).

Books

Contemporary Authors, volume 112, Gale Research, 1985.

Contemporary Heroes and Heroines, Book II, Gale Research, 1985.

Periodicals

Atlanta Journal and Constitution, May 20, 1998, p. A3; June 5, 1998, p. B4.

Dallas Morning News, July 31, 1997, p. 1A.

Los Angeles Times, January 6, 1997, p. D3.

Newsday, February 5, 1998, p. A8.

New York Times, December 28, 1982. p. C1; September 10, 1985, pp. A1, C3.

Star Tribune (Minneapolis, MN), July 31, 1997, p. 1A.
U.S. News & World Report, September 23, 1985, p. 9.
Washington Post, August 31, 1982, p. B1.

Other

Good Morning America (transcript), ABC-TV, June 5, 1998.

—Geri Speace

Jeffrey Banks

Fashion designer

Full name, Jeffrey Laurence Banks; born November 3, 1953, in Washington, DC. *Education:* Attended Pratt Institute, Brooklyn, NY, 1971–73; Parsons School of Design, New York, NY, B.A., 1975.

Addresses: *Home*—New York, NY. *Office*—Jeffrey Banks Ltd., 15 East 26th Street, Suite 1811, New York, NY 10010.

Career

Ralph Lauren/Polo, design assistant to the president, 1971–73; Calvin Klein/Calvin Klein Ltd., design assistant to the president, 1973–76; Nik-Nik Clothing & Sportswear, clothes designer, 1976–78; Alixandre, designer of furs for men and boys, beginning c. 1977; Jeffrey Banks Ltd. (a design business), founder, 1978, president and chief designer, 1978—; Merona Sports (a sportswear company), head designer, 1980s; Jeffrey Banks International, founder, c. 1988; licensing agreement with Neema Clothing Ltd., beginning 1995; has designed clothes for Concorde International, B. Glanzrock, L'Aiglon, Lakeland, and Oxford Industries.

Awards: Special Coty Award for Men's Furs, Coty Fashion Critics Award, 1977; Excellence in Men's Wear Design, Harvey's Bristol Cream Tribute to Black Designers, 1978–80; Special Coty Award for Menswear, 1982; Cutty Sark Award, outstanding U.S. designer, 1987.

Member: Designers Collective, Fashion Institute of Technology (member of board of directors).

Sidelights

Known for his ability to merge practical comfort, whimsy, and casual sophistication, clothing designer Jeffrey Banks made his reputation in the fashion industry by putting a modern twist on classical elegance. "While he retains the classicist's concern for quality, elegance and simplicity, he cannot help but infuse his clothes with color, exuberance—a wholly American sensibility," stated a publicity release from his design firm, Jeffrey Banks Ltd.

Banks' designs have reflected his own enchantment with the glamour of movie stars in Hollywood's golden era. "A self-avowed romanticist," continued the publicity release, "Banks often draws upon the 'silver screen' Hollywood of the 1920s and 30s for his icons; but whatever the inspiration, his clothes always maintain a crisp, contemporary edge." Banks' interest in timeless elegance is also shown by his private collection of well over 300 black-and-white photographs by famous photographers that showcase fashions worn by famous film stars, writers, and fashion designers in the 1930s, 1940s, and 1950s.

Successful at both the creative and business ends of the design world, Banks established his own firm in

1978 at the age of 25. Weathering the storms of a challenging business and a continually changing fashion style, he has survived and thrived. He later formed a second firm to deal with demands for his designs. According to Lloyd Gite in a 1997 issue of *Black Enterprise,* millions of people around the globe were wearing designs by Jeffrey Banks at that time. "From Bloomingdale's in New York to fine shops in Japan, his name appears on everything from shirts and suits to neckwear and small leather goods, even sunshades and prescription eyewear," claimed Gite.

Jeffrey Laurence Banks knew from an early age while growing up in Washington, D.C., that he was going to be a fashion designer. "I was only 10 years old when I designed an Easter suit for my mother," he told *Black Enterprise.* "The dress was raw silk and it had a banana-colored, wool jersey coat that buttoned to one side. I picked out the fabric, went to the dressmaker with my mother and even picked out the accessories. She loved it and wore it with lots of pride." As a child Banks was also fascinated by fashion photography, especially Richard Avedon's spreads in *Vogue* magazine.

As a design student at Pratt Institute in Brooklyn, New York, Banks proved his ability to rise in the professional ranks. While still a student there he worked as a design assistant to Ralph Lauren, one of the biggest names in the fashion industry. Next he honed his skill as an assistant to the president of another fashion giant, Calvin Klein, while completing his degree at the prestigious Parsons School of Design in New York City.

Armed with his design ideas and a relentless work ethic, Banks quickly moved up the ranks. Among his first jobs was a position as a clerk at an elegant haberdashery in Washington, D.C. Later, he worked for three years as a designer for Nik-Nik Clothing & Sportswear during the late 1970s, and in 1977 won a special Coty Award for a men's fur collection that he designed for Alixandre. Still only 23 years old at the time, Banks was the youngest person ever to win this coveted honor—the "Oscar of the fashion industry," according to *Ebony.*

Banks cashed in on his increasing visibility in fashion by creating his own design firm in 1978, with himself as president and chief designer. He continued building on his reputation as a designer of furs for both men and boys. According to André Leon-Talley in *Ebony,* by 1980 Banks was creating furs for males "so smart and tailored that some women want to wear them." At this time he was also designing outerwear for L'Aiglon, and men's clothes for B. Glanzrock. Perhaps he made his biggest mark as a designer with his line of so-called "spectator sportswear" for men, women, and children for Merona Sports that were cited as both practical and offbeat. According to Teri Agins in the *Wall Street Journal,* Banks' clothing for Merona Sports was "a hot-selling line of boldly colored knit weekend clothes that became as trendy in the early 1980s as jogging suits once were." Banks himself became known during this period for his own impeccable yet breezy tailoring that "earned him a niche on the 'Best Dressed List,'" noted a publicity release from Jeffrey Banks Ltd. By age 26 he already had 130 pairs of shoes, according to *Ebony.*

Despite receiving frequent praise for his design vision and creativity at such a young age, Banks has never harbored any illusions about what it takes to be successful in the clothes business. He has also lamented the downfall of many young designers who fail to grasp the financial aspects of their trade. "Fashion is not art," he said in *Black Enterprise.* "It comes very close, but at the end of the day it's commerce. The more you know about business, the better designer you'll be. Many young designers don't realize that they can't go to a bank or the investment community without a business plan. They just think that everyone will look at their sketches and see their talent shining through."

Banks himself struggled on the business end during the mid 1980s, but then received financial help from Japanese businessman Tomio Taki. In 1988 Taki, who already owned a successful design company in New York City, agreed to invest in a new business with Banks that would give Taki a one third share in the company. Banks claimed at the time that Taki's infusion of money would "free me up to design after spending the last three years so enmeshed in the business side of my company," according to the *Wall Street Journal.* Various ups and downs were also experienced by Banks during the 1990s. He was beset by legal difficulties in 1994 when he was sued by the artist Gloria Fox Lynn, who said that he had produced shirts using her copyrighted paintings without her permission. In 1995 Banks bounced back by signing a licensing agreement with Neema Clothing Ltd., granting them permission to manufacture and market clothing that had the Banks label on it. By 1996, Banks was heading two companies—Jeffrey Banks Ltd. and Jeffrey Banks International—with combined annual sales of almost $20 million a year. After nearly a quarter century of active designing, Banks continues to be a force in the fashion world.

Sources

Periodicals

Architectural Digest, September 1989, pp. 78–84.
Black Enterprise, June 1997, p. 277.
Daily News Record, December 19, 1997.
Ebony, November 1980, p. 172.
Forbes, December 3, 1983, p. 153.
Inc., November 1990, p. 68.
Wall Street Journal, August 30, 1988, p. 27.

Other

Additional information for this profile was obtained from publicity materials of Jeffrey Banks Ltd.

—*Ed Decker*

James L. Barksdale

CEO of Netscape Communications Corp.

Born in 1943, in Jackson, MS; married; wife's name, Sally; children: Susan, Betsy, David. *Education:* Graduated from University of Mississippi, 1965.

Addresses: *Office*—Netscape Communications Corp., 501 East Middlefield Rd., Mountain View, CA 94043.

Career

IBM Corp., held several positions, 1965-73; Cook Industries, Inc., vice president, 1973-79; Federal Express Corp., senior vice president for information systems, 1979-83; executive vice president and chief operating officer, 1983-91; McCaw Cellular Communications, Inc., president and chief operating officer, 1991-94; AT&T Wireless Services, chief executive officer, September 1994-January 1995; Netscape Communications Corp., president and chief executive officer, 1995–.

Sidelights

At Netscape Communications Corp., president and chief executive officer James L. Barksdale is aiming for an entrepreneurial hat-trick as he tries for the third time in his career to successfully navigate a company through a period of monumental growth. First, there was Federal Express Corp.; during Barksdale's tenure as its chief operating officer in the 1980s, the company's sales jumped sevenfold to $7.7 billion a year. Next, Barksdale helped build McCaw Cellular Communications into the largest company in one of the world's fastest-growing industries, the cellular industry. Then came Netscape, the fastest-growing software company ever. When Netscape became a publicly owned company in August 1995, its stock was initially priced at $28 a share, quickly raced to $75, then fell to $58.25—all in its first day of trading on the stock market. At $58.25 per share, the company's market value was $2.21 billion—and Barksdale's 4.2 million shares were worth more than $200 million. After that head-turning arrival, Netscape settled in for a fight that promised fireworks in years ahead—a market-share battle with $100-billion software giant Microsoft Corp.

Barksdale is described as a courtly Southern gentleman, unpretentious and modest, charismatic and funny, a great communicator and leader whose laid-back style belies a relentless competitive drive. "He's like everyone's dad," McCaw vice president of corporate communications Bob Ratliffe told M. Sharon Baker of *Puget Sound Business Journal.* "He's warm-hearted and friendly, driven and occasionally intense." Tom Martin, public relations director for Federal Express, told Baker that Barksdale can talk with employees in the break room and make them feel at ease. "He combines brilliance with the common touch," Martin said. "It's not an artificial veneer, it's the genuine article." Mary Meeker, technology analyst at Morgan Stanley, told *Forbes* that Barksdale is "one of the most phenomenal managers I've ever encountered. He's a great motivator and shrewd businessman and understands technology." L. John Doerr, a Silicon Valley venture capitalist and member of the Netscape board of directors, offered this evidence of Barksdale's impact to Steve Lohr of the *New York Times:* "Fedex drivers would see him on the street, come over and give him a high-five. He's inspired great loyalty wherever he has been. He is one of the great business leaders of America."

Barksdale was born and reared in Jackson, Mississippi, and attended the University of Mississippi, where a single 'B' marred his 'A' average. After graduating in 1965, he went to work selling computers for IBM Corp. in Memphis, Tennessee. Thirty years later, he took the helm at Netscape. "Barksdale is an unlikely software executive," Lohr wrote in the *New York Times.* "At 54, he is twice the age of many of his employees.... He is laconic of speech, fond of homespun one-liners populated by snakes, dogs, chickens and country porches.... His is not a personal style familiar to the software business, a hyperkinetic industry where people typically try to win arguments by simply talking faster than anyone else." Barksdale's "homespun one-liners"— which have been dubbed "Barksdalisms" at both McCaw and Netscape—include "You're such a good salesman you could talk a hungry dog off a meat truck" and "If you can't run with the big dogs, don't get off the porch." Barksdale's take-no-prisoners approach to business is evidenced by his urging the federal government to crack down on alleged monopolistic practices by Microsoft. The Netscape campaign is reminiscent of a "Nixon-era dirty tricks team," Microsoft's chief technology officer, Nathan Myhrvold, told Lohr. "Don't believe this notion that Barksdale is some gracious Southern gentleman. That's nonsense."

Netscape's claim to fame and market share is Netscape Navigator, point-and-click software that allows computer users to easily move around the World Wide Web portion of the Internet. It was born at the University of Illinois in Urbana-Champaign in 1993, the cyber-child of a small team of student programmers led by Marc Andreessen. Working for $6.85 an hour, Andreessen and his fellow techies developed the Mosaic Internet browser. After graduating 18 months later, Andreessen moved to Silicon Valley, the high-tech entrepreneurial enclave in northern California. There, he connected with James H. Clark, who was leaving Silicon Graphics Inc., a company he founded, to explore other business ventures. The pair moved ahead with a new and improved version of Mosaic, to be called Netscape Navigator. In January 1995, they named Barksdale

president and CEO of their high-flying fledgling company. His job was to bring order to the creative chaos at the fast growing software firm, prepare for an impending public stock offering, and "convert Clark's entrepreneurial vision and Andreessen's technological genius into a viable, well-run business," as Charles McCoy put it in the *Raleigh News & Observer.* Richard Shaffer of the research firm Technologic Partners told Lohr that "Barksdale is the guy who adds adult credibility to what would otherwise be a band of techies."

Barksdale's track record suggested he could handle the job. After holding several posts at computer giant IBM, he joined Federal Express as head of its systems group in 1979 and worked his way up to the company's number two position, at the right hand of Fedex's legendary founder and CEO Fred Smith. Barksdale was credited with creating Federal Express's computerized tracking and delivery system, which revolutionized the parcel delivery industry and spurred the company's staggering growth. At McCaw Cellular, he gained additional experience with computer networks and developed an appreciation of the way they can create growth, new markets, and new business opportunities. "Jim Barksdale's great strength is in understanding the uses of technology," Smith reported to Lohr of the *New York Times.* "He's not a technologist, but a manager who is technologically literate." That, Barksdale says, gives Netscape an advantage in the competitive software business. "I've probably implemented more software in businesses than any CEO of any software company in the world," Barksdale was quoted in *Asian Business.* "Certainly more than [Microsoft founder] Bill Gates. So I know what's in the mind of the buyer."

Barksdale left Federal Express—where he was earning $500,000 a year and held $4 million in the company's stock—to become the president and chief operating officer of McCaw Cellular Communications in 1991. "Both [McCaw and Fedex] are young, aggressive companies trying to build something out of nothing," he told Baker of the *Puget Sound Business Journal.* "There's a willingness to learn; there are no wheels already invented. Both are dealing with the same problems: managing growth and dealing with a service business." His greatest accomplishment at McCaw, where his earnings grew to $1 million a year in cash compensation, was engineering the firm's $12 billion merger with AT&T in 1994. Barksdale had told AT&T he'd stay on board through the merger and a short transition period, but he preferred to run an independent company. True to his word, he stepped down after a few months heading the newly formed AT&T Wireless Services and took the Netscape job.

"If you go around Netscape, you'll observe a passion to be successful," he said in *Asian Business*. "And one of the best things we have going for us is we have good competitors. It keeps us as sharp as we can be, and pushing as hard as we can.... I personally enjoy this better than the other jobs I've done, because it is so competitive. I think that's what keeps the blood going and the heart racing and your mind thinking."

In the year or so following Netscape's super-charged public offering, the company's market value plummeted 69 percent. Microsoft was stealing away a growing share of the browser market; Netscape's share shrank from 87 percent of the market to 62 percent between April 1996 and November 1997. Analysts predicted the losses to Microsoft would continue. Business publications openly questioned whether Netscape could continue to compete, even whether it would ultimately survive. In a high-profile gesture which undoubtedly engendered loyalty within the company, Barksdale announced that he would work for a salary of $1 in 1997, compared with $100,000 he earned the previous year. (He had received a multi-million dollar stock option package when he joined the company.) Eventually, Netscape's fortunes began to turn around. By the third-quarter of 1997, the company announced that both revenues and profits had risen 50 percent. "Barksdale, by all accounts, deserves much of the credit for Netscape's resilience to date," Lohr wrote in the *New York Times*. "He has brought strategic direction and management discipline to the young company, according to industry executives and analysts, and he has proved to be a skillful salesman who can persuade button-down corporate America to buy from an Internet pioneer."

When Microsoft leapt into the Internet business it began packaging its browser, called Internet Explorer, into Windows, the Microsoft computer operating system used in most personal computers. Barksdale charged that this strategy gives Microsoft an unfair competitive advantage, that it can, in effect, force people to use its browser. "If Windows ... can be whatever they say it is, look out," Barksdale was quoted in the *Buffalo News*. "With the Internet, everything is hooked together, and the start of the hook is the operating system." Such allegations triggered Congress and the U.S. Justice Department to investigate whether Microsoft is, indeed, building a monopoly on Internet software. Microsoft denies any impropriety. In the end, Lohr wrote, the federal probe might slow Microsoft's move into the Internet arena, but it won't stop it. It's got the entrepreneurial savvy, marketing budget, and the quality. Numerous product reviews, in fact, have judged Microsoft's Internet Explorer superior to Netscape Navigator. To retain a sizable market share, Netscape will certainly have to continue putting up a fight.

Barksdale says further erosion of his company's slice of the browser pie would not be a critical problem, because Netscape's future growth will occur in the broader Internet software market. "The browser was our technique for getting known," he said in an interview with Eric Nee of *Upside,* a software publication. "It was never the core of our business strategy. The first step was to get known. The second step was to get into the corporate software business.... [It's] a $10 billion industry, far bigger than the browser business.... People now know our name. So when companies are bidding on intranet software ... we're always invited to the party, because we're seen as a viable vendor."

Sources

Asian Business, January 1997, p. 30.
Buffalo News, November 19, 1997, p. C1.
Communications Week, September 30, 1996, p. 92.
Forbes, October 7, 1996, p. 72.
Informationweek, January 21, 1995, p. 20.
Journal of Commerce and Commercial, January 23, 1984.
New York Times, November 10, 1997.
PC Week, January 16, 1995, p. 97; October 13, 1997, p. 88.
Puget Sound Business Journal, December 17, 1993.
Raleigh News & Observer, January 12, 1995, p. C8; August 11, 1995, p. C8; August 15, 1995, p. D1.
Upside, November 1996, p. 86.
U.S. News & World Report, May 12, 1997, p. 57.

—*Dave Wilkins*

Kathleen Battle

UPI/Corbis Images

Opera singer

Born August 13, 1948, in Portsmouth, OH; daughter of Grady (a steelworker) and Ollie Layne (a volunteer) Battle. *Education:* University of Cincinnati Conservatory of Music, M.Mus. *Religion:* African Methodist Episcopal.

Addresses: *Office*—c/o Columbia Artist Management, 165 West 57th St., New York, NY 10019.

Career

Taught upper elementary classes in Cleveland, OH, late 1960s; made professional debut with the Cincinnati Symphony in Brahms's *German Requiem,* 1972; made European debut at Italy's Spoleto Festival, 1972; debut with the Metropolitan Opera of New York as a shepherd in Richard Wagner's *Tannhaeuser,* 1977; repertoire includes Sophie, *Der Rosenkavalier;* Despina, *Cosi fan Tutte;* Susanna, *Le Marriage de Figaro;* has appeared with opera companies or orchestras in San Francisco, Chicago, Boston, London, and Vienna; released from her contract with the Metropolitan Opera of New York, 1994.

Awards: Grammy Awards, 1987 and 1988, for classical recordings.

Sidelights

In the world of opera, huge names—and equally outsized egos—reign supreme, and American-born lyric soprano Kathleen Battle is among its royalty. Diminutive in stature but strong in stage presence and personality, Battle's exceptional talent in interpreting some of opera's most delightfully feminine roles has made her one of the century's best-known classical-music celebrities. For some years, Battle was the star of Metropolitan Opera of New York productions, but was released from her contract with them in 1994 in a well-publicized fracas; ostensibly, management deemed her "difficult," but music-lovers noted that diva-like behavior is far from unusual in opera circles. Battle remains one of classical music's best-selling recorded artists of the modern era.

Battle was born in August of 1948, in Portsmouth, Ohio, a predominantly African American Ohio River town on that state's border with Kentucky. She was the last of seven children of Grady and Ollie Battle. Her father was a steelworker, while her mother was active in church and community organizations. In fact, most of the Battles were active in their local African Methodist Episcopal church; even her father sang in a gospel quartet. His daughter began to sing in church at an early age, and from the start her choir directors and music teachers singled out her voice as exceptional. Yet a career in the performing arts seemed out of the question for Battle: as an African American teenager, she saw few role models for her inside the realm of serious music. Moreover, music was but one of her gifts—she was a National Merit Scholar in mathematics—but in the end heeded her mentor's advice and majored in music studies in college.

At the University of Cincinnati Conservatory of Music, Battle earned a master's degree in music education. "I would never have done anything as impractical as be a performance major," she once said, according to a profile on her by Annalyn Swan in *Vanity Fair*. By the early 1970s Battle was teaching music at an elementary school in a rough Cincinnati neighborhood and still singing in public only with her church choir.

> *"I had never come across a more complete talent than hers."*
> *—conductor James Levine, in*
> New York.

The director of the Conservatory was aware of Battle's promise as a singer, however, and helped her return to the school on a scholarship. Opportunity struck in the form of a labor dispute at the Cincinnati Symphony in early 1972. When its conductor, Thomas Schippers, announced a call for open auditions in the Cincinnati area—with the entire orchestra on the picket lines, his days were long and uneventful—Battle arrived and sang for him. Schippers immediately offered her solo slot with the Symphony when it appeared at the prestigious Spoleto Festival in Italy that summer. In a blue dress she sewed herself, she went onstage with a bit of red wine to ward off stage fright and sang Brahms's *German Requiem*.

After Battle's professional debut at Spoleto, she began to sing regularly with the Cincinnati Symphony, and in 1973, at its annual May Festival, she met guest conductor James Levine. A fellow Ohioan, Levine was an up-and-coming name in American classical-music circles, and was enchanted by Battle's vocal abilities. Echoing the impression Battle imparted to others during these early years, Levine said, "I had never come across a more complete talent than hers," he told Phoebe Hoban in *New York*. Levine would become her unofficial vocal coach and professional mentor for much of her career; by 1976 he had been hired as the music director of the Metropolitan Opera of New York, where Battle auditioned for him and won a beginner's role in a Richard Wagner opera slated for the following season.

Battle's debut on the stage of the Met came in 1977 while wearing the rather unglamorous robes of a boy shepherd in *Tannhaeuser*. Yet within a few years, she was one of the Met's biggest stars. Battle's repertoire as a singer revolved around *soubrette* ("servant") roles—parts integral to the comic operas and best sung by a youthful, light-on-the-feet soprano. These were charming characters such as Sophie in *Der Rosenkavalier*, Susanna in *Le Marriage de Figaro*, Rosina in *The Barber of Seville*, Zerbinetta in *Ariadne auf Naxos*, or Despina in *Cosi Fan Tutte*. Generally, the soubrette part did not deliver an opera's most dramatic entrances and arias, but Battle excelled in them and soon became a favorite with audiences. Her very name began to sell out shows, both at the Met and in guest performances around the country. "Thanks to her supple, dulcet soprano and winning stage personality," wrote Michael Walsh of *Time*, Battle "has risen to worldwide fame in secondary roles that ordinarily do not make stars."

Levine remained a close professional associate of Battle's, and was even known to blow kisses to her onstage when he was conducting the orchestra. Critics were dazzled by her performances, and the published accounts that deemed her talents sublime, and called her character interpretations some of the best the Met had ever seen, only served to increase adoration of Battle. She wore spectacular gowns that enhanced her figure and coloring, and her performances often drew ardent responses from opera fans—a group not known for its public restraint. The recordings she made for Sony and Deutsche Grammophon attained astonishing sales records and won her Grammys. In the studio she was able to explore other styles of music outside of opera, and often collaborated with other famous names in American classics, such as Jessye Norman and Itzhak Perlman. In a review of her 1992 effort with Wynton Marsalis, *Baroque Duets*, *Time* critic Christopher Porterfield wrote that "it is hard not to be dazzled and delighted by the pyrotechnics they provide in these predominantly bright, florid selections."

Yet by the mid-1980s, with just over a decade of professional experience behind her, Battle began to gain a reputation as a troublesome colleague behind the scenes. There were reports of imperiousness to underlings on the production crew, and outright viciousness toward her fellow performers. In a profession filled with large egos and lordly behavior, Battle nevertheless managed to frustrate her associates at the Met by arriving late for rehearsals, and allegedly instructing people not to look at her. That behavior extended to her touring appearances as well—for which she reportedly received $40,000 a night—when she was dissatisfied with hotel accommodations or food.

In one notorious incident she canceled her appearance with the esteemed Vienna Philharmonic only hours beforehand. Audiences felt cheated on some occasions when she sung at half-voice and they couldn't hear some notes. Even her professional relationship with Levine fell into decline.

Nevertheless, Battle remained a favorite with opera fans worldwide. In New York City in 1988, thousands showed up to hear her sing in Central Park with Luciano Pavarotti in *L'Elisir d'Amore,* and opera insiders explain that singers have naturally fragile personalities, which might be attributed to the very delicacy of their voices. "Because they can't touch their instrument, they can't see it, that makes for sensitive and fragile people," Elma Kanefeld, a New York City psychotherapist who specializes in performance-related anxieties, told Walsh in the *Time* article. "I think they play out this vulnerability in other areas of life. Instead of their voices being vulnerable, *they* feel vulnerable."

By the 1990s, Battle was one of the best-known names in opera, but she also was exploring other musical realms far removed from the soubrette. In 1991, Carnegie Hall commissioned a work especially for her in celebration of their centennial anniversary; Nobel Prize laureate Toni Morrison wrote six prose poems and composer Andre Previn set them to music. Leighton Kerner, reviewing the performance for the *Village Voice,* described Battle's singing as a welcome departure: "No longer for her were those seizures of cooing, glutinous coyness that spoiled her opera performances a few years ago." Another recital that same year was recorded and released by Deutsche Grammophon as *Kathleen Battle: At Carnegie Hall;* a *Stereo Review* critique of the record noted her selections—including Mozart and Strauss—were "all performed charmingly," and the audience response "ranges here from enthusiasm to near-hysteria."

Some have suggested that Battle's skin color may have played some part in the worsening relations with colleagues inside the extremely Eurocentric world of opera. Dr. Alvin Poussaint, an authority on race matters, surmised that Battle may have always felt—and indeed been—an outsider, he told Swan in *Vanity Fair.* "When you're a token, sometimes people do not respond to you in normal ways," Poussaint explained. "They may overreact to the point that, to the performer, their reactions seem patronizing or condescending." Adding to the unsavory drama were reports that Battle's opera associates flagrantly derided her with racial epithets—behind her back, of course. Toni Morrison called Battle "tough and resilient as a violin string," the novelist told *New York's* Hoban. "She would never have reached the pinnacle she's reached without being very determined and very demanding." Morrison also noted that the typical African American opera diva had been, before Battle came along, "a spiritual, modest religious woman. People like Marian Anderson didn't rock the boat. Kathy rocks the boat."

Battle apparently rocked the Met's boat one time too many. In early 1993, general manager Joseph Volpe replaced Battle with her understudy after she kept walking out of rehearsals for *Der Rosenkavalier* in disputes with its conductor. A year later, Volpe summarily released her from her contract just a week before she was scheduled to appear in *The Daughter of the Regiment,* and announced that her future appearances with the Met were also canceled. Battle—notoriously interview-shy—released a brief statement that offered the subsequent explanation: "To my knowledge, we were working out all of the artistic problems in the rehearsals, and I don't know the reason behind this unexpected dismissal," *Time* reported. "All I can say is, I am saddened by this decision."

Some music-lovers theorized that Battle's career in opera as an ingenue was on the wane. The soubrette roles require youthfulness, and Battle was nearing fifty. She had refused to expand her live repertoire to other roles more suitable for her age, for fear they might damage her voice—a warranted danger. "She's been typecast as the perpetual ingenue, and she has to sound as sweet, as radiant, as glistening as she did at the beginning of her career," *Boston Globe* opera critic Richard Dyer told Swan in *Vanity Fair.* "And that's impossible, of course."

Battle still enjoys a thriving career in the studio. In 1995 she released *So Many Stars,* a collection of songs performed with musicians such as Grover Washington Jr. and Cyrus Chestnut. Serving as its co-producer as well, Battle and the record's stellar cast explored jazz and Brazilian musical styles, and opened the 1995 Jazz at Lincoln Center series that September in a concert of their work. The following year, Battle performed selections from a few opera roles she had never performed on stage in *French Opera Arias.* Sacred music by Bach and Mozart, among other composers, was the theme for her 1997 Sony release, *Grace.*

Selected discography

Ariadne auf Naxos, Deutsche Grammophon, 1989.
A Carnegie Hall Christmas Concert, Sony, 1992.
Kathleen Battle: At Carnegie Hall, Deutsche Grammophon, 1992.

(With Wynton Marsalis) *Baroque Duets,* Sony, 1992.
New Year's Eve Concert 1992, Sony, 1993.
Verdi: Don Carlo, Sony, 1993.
French Opera Arias, Deutsche Grammophon, 1996.
Grace, Sony, 1997.
Angel's Glory, Sony, 1997.

Sources

Online

http://www.sony.com

Periodicals

New York, July 12, 1993.
Opera News, April 15, 1989, p. 27; July 1997, pp. 38-39.
Ovation, February 1989, p. 44; March 1989, pp. 52-53.
Stereo Review, December 1992; December 1996.
Time, June 8, 1992, p. 93; February 21, 1994, pp. 60-62.
Vanity Fair, May 1994, p. 80.
Village Voice, January 21, 1992.

—*Carol Brennan*

Sister Wendy Beckett

Nun, author, and art critic

Born in 1930, in South Africa; daughter of a physician. *Education:* Oxford University, degree in English, 1954.

Addresses: *Home*—Norfolk, England.

Career

Entered Sisters of Notre Dame convent, 1946; began teaching in South Africa, 1954, becoming a Reverend Mother; began pursuing life of solitude, 1970; began writing for British journals, mid-1980s; published first book, *Contemporary Women Artists,* 1988; wrote *The Story of Painting,* Dorling Kindersley, 1994, which was made into a television series; appeared in *Sister Wendy's Odyssey,* BBC, 1994; *Sister Wendy's Grand Tour,* BBC, 1994; *Sister Wendy's Story of Painting,* PBS, 1997 (first produced by and aired on BBC).

Sidelights

No one would have suspected that a hermit-like nun from rural England would emerge to become a popular television personality known for her insightful commentary on art. Yet the toothy, bespectacled, habit-wearing Sister Wendy Beckett, known as the Art Nun, is one of the most popular British Broadcasting Company (BBC) show hosts of all time. *Sister Wendy's Odyssey* and *Sister Wendy's Grand Tour* at times received a 25 percent audience share in Britain, rivaling Kenneth Clark's hit *Civilisation* in the late 1960s. Though her fame is relegated to public television in the United States, she is well-known across Europe: a Saturday morning children's show parodies her, impressionists mimic her slight South African accent and her speech impediment (her R's come out as W's), and she even has her own publicist. Marshall Sella in the *New York Times* observed, "She is both a Consecrated Virgin and a pop star."

Beckett was born in South Africa, but moved to Britain when she was young. Although she knew that she wanted to become a nun, her father, a doctor, encouraged her to go to college in case she changed her mind. Beckett, however, entered the Sisters of Notre Dame at age 16. "I've never experienced doubt, " she told Sella in the *New York Times.* "I was given ... an abiding and constant sense of what God is." She took the name Sister Michael, but reverted back to Wendy after the Vatican Council suggested that nuns drop their baptismal names.

In 1950 Beckett went to Oxford University to study literature. There she lived in a hostel for nuns and never once spoke with another student. She graduated in 1954 with top honors and was awarded a Congratulatory First, a commendation usually given annually by each department. She also attended a teacher's college in Liverpool before returning to South Africa to teach for the next 15 years, where she would eventually take the title Reverend Mother. When her health became fragile, she asked the Vatican if she could pursue a life of solitude.

Beckett moved back to England, where she lived in a leaky, run-down, poorly insulated trailer with no bath facility on the grounds of a Carmelite monastery in rural Quidenham, Norfolk. (In 1994, after she became a celebrity, she upgraded to a newer—though not much warmer—trailer with a small bath.) During much of the 1970s, permitted to work only two hours a day, she translated from the Latin the sermons of the medieval English prelate John, Abbot of Ford. The work was published from 1977 to 1984. Then in 1980, she decided to study art, and began examining works on postcards and in books. Eager to contribute financially to the Carmelite order, Beckett around the mid-1980s began to write for British journals before finishing her first book, *Contemporary Women Artists.*

Beckett surprised herself with her choice of subject matter, since she later compared contemporary art to a newspaper: it makes a point, but after seeing it, it can be discarded. She told Alan Riding in the *New York Times,* "I like art that you can go on and on looking at. The more you look, the more it gives you." She admitted that her decision to write about contemporary art had something to do with her fellow nuns: "I was living with Philistines, my sisters, who scoffed at people like Picasso," she remarked to Riding. Later, however, she would write more books on contemporary art (including a great deal of abstract works in *The Gaze of Love*) in addition to art from past ages, as well as prayer books.

Her life changed completely at an art exhibit in Norfolk when a camera crew, who had come to film Australian author and feminist Germaine Greer, overheard her comments to a friend and asked if they could film her. Randall Wright, a BBC producer, spotted the piece when it aired, and knew she had potential. The idea for *Sister Wendy's Odyssey* seemed almost fictional: a semi-cloistered nun, who devours art reproductions on cards and in books, travels the world to see the originals and give her reactions. This series was followed by *Sister Wendy's Grand Tour* and the 10-part *Sister Wendy's Story of Paintings,* for which she logged 30,000 miles in over 12 countries.

Though Beckett's programs are not flashy, featuring the nun standing in front of artworks and matter-of-factly relating her thoughts directly into the camera, they are not stagnant, either. Beckett's down-to-earth

explanations are spiced up by her storytelling prowess and quirky insights. "A Greek vase painted in 500 B.C. isn't a dusty old depiction of Achilles slaying Penthesilea; it's an emotional drama, splashy as a miniseries," quipped Sella in the *New York Times.* Sella also noted that Beckett does not shy away from moralizing, as when she states, "Guercino shows us the sad inadequacy of lust," or chastising, "You have a cold heart, Degas!" She really sent people tittering, though, with her comments on fluffy pubic hair in a Stanley Spencer nude. However, Beckett sees no reason to dodge issues of the body, since much of art deals with the human form. She unswervingly lectures about love, sex, and romance in relation to art works. "There's too much puritanical fear of pleasure," she told Sella.

A complex person, Beckett remains true to her vows of poverty, giving her BBC earnings to the Carmelite order, and continues to practice self-denial—in general. She wakes at 3 a.m. to pray and have a little coffee, attends Mass at 8 a.m., and spends seven hours a day praying. She never puts in more than two hours of work, writing books or responding to letters. She eats frugal meals of milk, crackers or bread, some salad and maybe cheese. When Beckett is traveling, though, she indulges in lunch at hot spots such as London's 33, and will not turn away a good glass of wine, explaining to *Financial Post* writer Lucy Kellaway, "God made the grape."

Beckett also catches reporters off guard with her love of military history ("I love the chaos of a battle," Beckett revealed to Kellaway), detective stories, snooker, and horse racing. However, she heard her first Beatles song, "Yesterday," in 1997 when producer David Willcock sang it for her, and she has not been to a movie theater since shortly after World War II. She does, however, watch *Star Trek* on television when she stays in hotels, and approves of the show's morals. The Vatican seems to affirm her actions; the Pope has praised her for conveying a positive image of the Catholic Church.

Beckett, like all in the entertainment industry, has her naysayers. Typically, the elite of the art establishment dislike the simplicity of her commentaries. Producer Randall Wright mused in the *New York Times,* "Personally, I'm delighted that she annoys the art world." However, Beckett's intent is, innocently enough, to open up the world of art to the average person. "This is what I want, everyone realizing they can look at a picture and have their own views."

Selected writings

(Translator) John, Abbot of Ford, *Sermons on the Final Verses of the Song of Songs,* Cistercian Publications, 1977-84.

Contemporary Women Artists, Phaidon, 1988, Universe, 1988.

Peggy Glanville-Hicks, Angus & Robertson, 1992.

The Gaze of Love: Meditations on Art and Spiritual Transformation, Harper, San Francisco, 1993.

The Mystical Now: Art and the Sacred, Universe, 1993.

Sister Wendy's Odyssey: A Journey of Artistic Discovery, BBC Books, 1993.

The Story of Painting, Dorling Kindersley, 1994.

A Child's Book of Prayer in Art, Dorling Kindersley, 1995.

Meditations on Love, Dorling Kindersley, 1995.

Meditations on Peace, Dorling Kindersley, 1995.

Meditations on Silence, Dorling Kindersley, 1995.

Meditations on Joy, Dorling Kindersley, 1995.

The Mystery of Love: Saints in Art through the Centuries, Harper, San Francisco, 1996.

Pains of Glass: The Story of the Passion from King's College Chapel, Lutterworth, Parkwest, 1996.

Sister Wendy's Grand Tour: Discovering Europe's Great Art, Stewart, Tabori & Chang, 1996.

The Duke and the Peasant: Life in the Middle Ages: The Calendar Pictures in the Duc de Berry's Traes Riches Heures, Prestel, 1997.

Max Beckmann and the Self, Prestel, 1997.

Sister Wendy's Book of Saints, DK, 1998.

Sister Wendy's Book of Meditations, DK, 1998.

Sources

America, November 4, 1995, p. 34; September 20, 1997, p. 28.

Booklist, November 1, 1994, p. 468.

Catholic Reporter, December 23, 1994, p. 10.

Financial Post, August 3, 1997, p. 19.

Library Journal, February 15, 1997, p. 130.

New York Times, January 26, 1997; September 1, 1997.

—*Geri Speace*

Susan V. Berresford

President of the Ford Foundation

Born Susan Vail Berresford, January 8, 1943, in New York, NY; daughter of Richard Case and Katherine Vail (Marsters) Berresford Hurd; married David F. Stein (divorced); children: Jeremy Vail Stein. *Education:* Attended Vassar College, 1961-63; Radcliffe University, B.A. in American history, 1965.

Addresses: *Office*—Ford Foundation, 320 E. 43ʳᵈ St., New York, NY 10017-4816.

Career

United Nations Volunteer Services, 1962; secretary, 1964; Neighborhood Youth Corps, New York City, 1965-67; Manpower Career Development Agency, program specialist, 1967, human resources administration specialist, 1968; freelance consultant and writer, 1968-70; Ford Foundation, New York City, project assistant in the national affairs division, 1970-72; program officer, National Affairs division, 1972-80; officer in charge of women's programs, 1980-81; vice president, U.S. and International Affairs programs, 1981-89, vice president, Program Division, in charge of worldwide programming, beginning 1989-95, executive vice president and chief operating officer (COO), 1995-96, elected the first female president of Ford Foundation, 1996.

Sidelights

Susan V. Berresford is the president of the Ford Foundation, the second-largest philanthropic organization in the United States. The foundation gives grants and loans to people and institutions involved in activities that promote democratic values, fight poverty and injustice, increase international cooperation, and advance human achievement. Berresford began working with the program in 1970 and worked her way up to become its first female president in 1996, overseeing an organization that boasts about $9 billion in assets. She quickly saw the need to reorganize the foundation into three main focus areas in order to better serve its grant recipients and stick to its mission. Berresford also worked to update the group's staid image from silent and shadowy to communicative and outreaching, stepping up the advertising and working more closely with the media, public policy people, and officials. Though some pegged her influence as a whole new approach for the institution, Berresford in the *New York Times* remarked that the changes were "evolutionary, not a sharp turn in one direction or another."

Susan Vail Berresford was born on January 8, 1943, to Richard Case and Katherine Vail (Marsters) Berresford Hurd. Not much is known about her childhood, since she has not divulged information about that subject readily. Berresford attended Vassar College from 1961 to 1963, then moved to Radcliffe University, where she graduated cum laude in 1965 with a bachelor of arts in American history. Her history of involvement with social causes goes back to her early college years. In 1962, during her summer vacation, Berresford worked with the United Nations Volunteer Services in New York City, and in the summer of 1964, she served as a secretary to Theodore H. White. She decided early on that she wanted to get involved in the fight against poverty.

After graduating from Radcliffe, Berresford worked as a program officer with the Neighborhood Youth Corps in New York City from 1965 to 1967, then took a job as a program specialist for Manpower Career Development Agency, also in New York. There, she was involved with education, training, and work programs. The next year, she was promoted to program specialist. In 1968 she began working as a freelance consultant and writer in Europe and the United States. Upon her return, she joined the Ford Foundation in 1970 as a project assistant in the division of National Affairs. In 1980 Berresford was promoted to officer in charge of women's programs for the Ford Foundation.

In 1981, Berresford was promoted to vice president for the U.S. and International Affairs programs, a position she held until 1989, when she took over as vice president of the program division in charge of worldwide programming. That job entailed managing efforts aimed at reducing poverty, championing human rights, and promoting education and cultural programs, among others. Berresford, in 1995, took over as executive vice president and chief operating officer (COO) of the foundation. Effective April 3, 1996, she was elected the first female president of the organization, replacing Franklin I. Thomas, who was the first African American to head the agency. The board of directors conducted no outside search, maintaining that Berresford was clearly their top choice for the position.

The Ford Foundation is a private, nonprofit charitable agency formed in 1936 that funds people and institutions involved in promoting its stated goals. According to its mission statement, these are to "strengthen democratic values, reduce poverty and injustice, promote international cooperation, and advance human achievement." In 1936, automobile mogul Henry Ford and his son, Edsel, set up the Ford Foundation with the general purpose of enhancing the welfare of the people. It was a local philanthropy in Michigan until 1950, when it was made a national and international organization. At that time, Ford Motor Company stock from the two men's estates composed virtually all of its assets. From 1956 to 1974, the foundation gradually shed its Ford stock and diversified its investments. Henry Ford II quit the board in 1976, so now all that remains of the connection to Ford is the foundation's name and legacy.

Meanwhile, the ideology of the group was changing as well. In the 1960s, the Ford Foundation mainly functioned as a springboard for liberal ideas, then relied on the government to follow through, which they often did. Some of Ford's plans that were enacted this way include the War on Poverty, public television, and Head Start, the program to give a boost to disadvantaged children. Ford was also instrumental in exporting knowledge of advances in agriculture, which was effective in helping other countries raise their own food sources. The group has also had its dark moments, such as its role in decentralizing the New York school system, a move many criticized as severely detrimental. Issues like this and other controversies irked conservatives, and Berresford now rejects the notion that the group only supports liberal programs, although she still supports civil rights litigation and social causes.

As head of the Ford Foundation, Berresford instituted a number of changes. Some critics were initially skeptical of promoting an "insider" to president. As Karen W. Arenson stated in the New York Times, "To critics who viewed Ford … as a sleeping giant in need of shaking up, wedded to many of the same projects it supported 15 years ago, the appointment did not seem a prescription for change." However, Berresford actively sought new ideas, reeling in department heads from international offices as well as some outsiders to spur action. She began to emphasize communications, establishing it as a new department in order to beef up public relations and advertising. This was a huge shift in style for the organization, as it previously operated as more of a silent benefactor behind the curtain of smaller programs and nonprofits that it funded. In addition, perhaps one of Berresford's most important contributions was the reorganization of grant-giving around three focus areas.

Berresford outlined three general areas for grant recipients: Asset Building and Community Development, Peace and Social Justice, and Education, Media, Arts, and Culture (EMAC). Asset Building and Community Development focuses on fighting poverty by helping people and communities build assets and give them future options, which includes bank-like programs to assist low-income individuals and areas. Peace and Social Justice promotes democracy and freedom, and helps fund organizations that work for civil rights and fair laws. EMAC funds the arts and cultural institutions and promotes awareness of various cultures in hopes of building strong international relationships.

As of mid-1997, the Ford Foundation had assets of about $9 billion, making it larger in terms of finances than 99 percent of all American businesses, and the second-largest foundation in the country, having been surpassed by the Lilly Endowment in the mid-1990s. Ford has given away $8 billion during its lifetime to about 9,000 institutions and 100,000 individuals around the globe. It dispenses about $400 million annually and employs roughly 400 people in its New York office and about 200 in 16 offices overseas. As the president of such a giant organization, Berresford is in the position to make a difference in the nation's welfare, especially in light of many recent governmental cuts in social spending. Conservatives, especially, believe that the burden of social problems should be relegated more and more to private and nonprofit groups, which places Ford in a high-profile position even without her new dedication to making the group more visible.

Berresford has seemed to welcome the Ford Foundation's larger role in this shift of social responsibility. Though the Ford Foundation had developed a reputation of repeatedly giving funds to certain established groups, Berresford made it a goal to reach out into new territory, instituting an innovative test plan that matches funds to those saved by low-income individuals to buy a house, pay for tuition, or open a business, among other programs. On April 24, 1997, it was announced that the foundation would be granting $50 million to support what Berresford called "promising approaches to long-term problems," Peter McCoy reported in *Business Week*. Ford was dedicating $20 million to "create or expand institutions that lend and invest in low-income communities in the U.S. and overseas," $15 million to "seed and strengthen foundations in such fields as economic development, women's rights, and the arts," and $15 million to "revitalize college-level research and teaching on understudied places, languages, and cultures," as cited in *Business Week*. In addition, Berresford out-

lined a goal to increase the amount of grants given outside the borders of the United States from 40 up to 50 percent, and pledged to hire more African American, Asian American, and Latin American staff.

Berresford married David F. Stein and has one son, Jeremy Vail Stein, but the union ended in divorce. She is known as an elegant but unpretentious woman who is intelligent, detail-oriented, and willing to listen. Committed to her cause, Berresford puts in long hours and wants to use her leadership to make more people aware of the mission of the Ford Foundation and others like it. "Philanthropy is less well understood than it should be," she remarked in *Working Woman*. "This is a real opportunity to engage more people in the question of what philanthropies ought to be doing."

Sources

On-line

"The Ford Foundation," Ford Foundation web site, http://www.fordfound.org (June 1, 1998).

Periodicals

Business Week, May 12, 1997, 39.
Business Wire, September 14, 1997.
Chronicle of Higher Education, August 15, 1997, A29.
Hoover's Company Capsules, March 26, 1998.
Jet, January 23, 1995, p. 7.
New York Times, February 14, 1996, p. A14.
Working Woman, April 1996, p. 11.

—*Geri Speace*

Jeff Bezos

Courtesy of AMAZON.COM Inc.

CEO of Amazon.com

Born Jeffrey P. Bezos c. 1964 in Albuquerque, New Mexico; married; wife's name, MacKenzie (a writer). *Education:* Princeton University, B.S. in electrical engineering and computer science, 1986.

Addresses: *Office*—Amazon.com, Inc., 1516 2nd Ave., Seattle, WA 98101.

Career

FITEL fiber optics, manager of administration and development, became associate director of technology and development, 1986-88; Banker's Trust Co., New York City, assistant vice president for global fiduciary services, became vice president of global fiduciary services, 1988-90; D. E. Shaw & Co., New York City, vice president, became senior vice president, 1990-94; Amazon.com online bookseller, founder and CEO, 1994—.

Sidelights

Entrepreneur Jeff Bezos helped revolutionize the way people buy books and proved that the World Wide Web was a valid arena for sales when he started up a "virtual" bookstore online in 1994. Bezos, intrigued by the potential of the Web, struck upon the idea of selling books online because of the large number of titles in print and the inability of traditional stores to carry more than a few hundred in any given location. He realized that he could offer shoppers over a million choices, at their fingertips, around the clock. The enterprise Amazon.com (pronounced "Amazon dot com" and located at the address http://www.amazon.com) was named after the world's largest river. From a spartan affair launched in a garage, the company ballooned. At the end of 1997 it boasted sales of over $147 million, a growth of over 841 percent from the previous year, and stock rose from $18 a share at its initial offering in May of 1997 to almost $100 a year later. Though it still had not turned a profit into 1998, Bezos was not worried, expecting the first five years to be a process of getting the giant infant business firmly established. As of 1998, users had access to three million titles, and Bezos by then had added music to the mix as well, an idea he had initially dismissed.

Bezos was born in New Mexico around 1964 and spent summers herding cattle and repairing wind mills for his grandfather's farm in Cotulla, Texas. He graduated summa cum laude and Phi Beta Kappa from Princeton University in 1986 with a bachelor's degree in electrical engineering and computer science. From 1986 to 1988, he worked at FITEL fiber optics, first as a manager of administration and development, then as an associate director of technology and development. He then took a job developing systems for managing investment funds at Banker's Trust in New York City. He held the position of assistant vice president and then vice president there from 1988 to 1990. After that, he was hired as vice president at D. E. Shaw & Co. in New York as a computer specialist working in hedge funds, and worked his way up to senior vice president of the firm by age 30. However, he had always been brewing ideas for his own enterprises.

Bezos in early 1994 read that the Web was growing at a rate of over 2,000 percent each year. He decided that online commerce would be lucrative and compiled a list of 20 products that he thought might do well in the arena, including books, music, magazines, and computer hardware and software. He eventually narrowed it to books and music. Bezos initially settled on books because of the vast number of titles available: there were only about 300,000 albums in print, compared to almost 1.5 million English language books. Bezos claimed in *Reuters Business Report*, "That makes books totally unusual in this respect, no other product category has this many products." In addition, Bezos figured that music would be a tough field to crack since six major companies dominate the recording industry, whereas book distribution is more scattered. In 1996, Barnes & Noble, the largest bookseller, held only 12 percent of the market.

Bezos knew he had hit upon a good idea. He started packing and told the movers that he would phone them as soon as he knew where he was going—he had figured he would head to Boulder, Colorado; Portland, Oregon; or Seattle, Washington. He finally settled on the Seattle area due to its base of technically skilled workers and the fact that a major book warehouse, Ingram, was close by in Roseburg, Oregon. His wife, MacKenzie, an aspiring novelist, drove across the country as he hammered out a business plan on his laptop, contacting investors via his cell phone on the way (he later said he raised several million dollars for his start-up). Bezos and four employees in 1994 opened shop in the garage of their rented suburban home, writing the software for the fledgling company even before their furniture had arrived. He discarded the name "Cadabra" for the enterprise because it sounded too much like "cadaver" and instead chose Amazon. The first book was sold in July of 1995.

Bezos soon moved his staff to a 400-square foot office and hoped that his enterprise would thrive. Six weeks later, Bezos and crew upgraded to a 2,000-square-foot space, and in six months, they were in a 17,000-square-foot building. Later, they outgrew their space again. Employee growth saw over a 300 percent increase from 1996 to 1997, with 614 on the payroll. By December of 1996 the web site was getting about 2,200 visitors per day; by the end of 1997, it was up to about 50,000. Annual sales shot from about $511,000 in 1995 to $15.7

in 1996, and by the end of 1997 had reached over $147 million. Amazon.com stock went public in 1997, selling for $18 a share, and by mid-1998, it was up to about $100 a share. The company had yet to turn a profit, but Bezos claimed that heavy investment in advertising and technology costs were to blame. With over 100,000 other sites worldwide combined only pulling in about $324 million in 1995, it could not be overlooked that Bezos had found a way to successfully sell products online.

One of the obvious ways that Bezos built a bookstore without books and without stores is by offering a wider selection of titles than an actual store, which can only house perhaps a few hundred titles. Starting with over a million books, Amazon.com in 1998 was listing three million, ordering the titles directly from the warehouses. It also added value by including information about the books it was selling, offering book excerpts and reviews to read, printing interviews with authors, and showing lists of titles by an author or about a subject. Another focus of Amazon.com was to instill fun in the process of online book buying. "One of the things you find out pretty quickly in bookselling," Bezos told Ann Treneman in the *Independent*, "is that people don't just buy books because they need them. They buy them because shopping for them is fun. Many will spend two hours in an afternoon in a bookstore. I do that!" Bezos added that sinceAmazon.com cannot offer its patrons the relaxed atmosphere of plush sofas and steaming cappuccinos, it has had to develop creative ways to intrigue and satisfy customers. It does this by developing a personalized culture, allowing customers to post their own reviews and offering story writing contests.

Amazon also began offering discounts of 10 to 30 percent on many titles. Some or all of the savings incurred, however, are sometimes lost when customers pay for postage and handling charges ($3.95 per book). This is one drawback to any online shopping services, in addition to the risk factor of credit card transactions over the Web. Amazon.com allows customers to phone in their credit card numbers if they are concerned, but Bezos noted in the *Wall Street Journal* that only about five percent do so. Amazon also encrypts all credit information, and offers to pay the minimum $50 charge to a credit card company if numbers are stolen.

Amazon.com continues to expand by urging people and businesses with their own web sites to join forces with them, either by including an advertisement linking to Amazon.com, or by developing a kind of franchise store on their own site. For example, a site devoted to rock climbing could include a list of Amazon.com titles on the subject. For this help, the web site owner receives a cut of the profits of anything sold through the link or their site. The extensive use of computers to track orders allows Amazon to track customer preferences and suggest other titles a user may enjoy, and has led to a giant database full of potential marketing information for other businesses. Bezos expressed reluctance at releasing the data, however, fearing the wrath of customers' ill will.

Once Barnes & Noble caught wind of Amazon.com's success, they joined the land of online commerce as well, providing stiff competition. Amazon.com rose to the challenge and has managed to stay afloat. When Barnes & Noble opened shop online with over a million titles and began offering hardcovers at a 30 percent discount, Amazon.com raised theirs to 40 percent and doubled its offerings to 2.5 million. Bezos, however, eventually had to drop the motto "the Earth's largest bookseller" after Barnes & Noble took legal issue with it (Barnes & Noble now claims to be the "world's largest bookseller online"). However, Amazon.com is proud of the fact that 58 percent of its business are return shoppers, as opposed to 40 percent at Barnes & Noble. Though other bookstores have entered the Web, Bezos plans to maintain a large presence by holding on to a strong brand name and customer loyalty.

Bezos owns 41 percent of Amazon.com, worth close to $1 billion in May of 1998, with his family's interest boosting it to a controlling share of 51 percent. "We were optimistic when we wrote our business plan for Amazon.com but we didn't expect to have as many customers and as much success as we've had," Bezos told Ann Treneman in the *Independent.* "Anybody who had predicted what has happened would have been committed to an institution immediately! It is rather fun to think that two years ago I would put all the packages in the back of my Chevy Blazer and drive them to the post office myself. Now the post office brings 18-wheel trucks and big 40 ft. containers and parks them at the warehouse to be filled up over one day." Amazon.com in 1997 was shipping to over 160 countries, with over a quarter of sales outside of the United States, including many military bases.

As for the future of online retail, Bezos told Christine Bushey in an MSNBC interview that vendors will be offering people more of a browsing experience rather than just going online to find a specific item. "One of the things that we're focused on is moving beyond E-commerce into what we're calling E-merchandising," Bezos explained. He added, "One of the huge things you'll see us be focused on is doing that in a way that's individualized for each and every customer. So we won't be focused just on making a great store that is entertaining for sort of the average customer. But a great store that's perfect for you and a different one that's perfect for me and each of our customers. You can only do that online."

Sources

On-line

"About Amazon.com," Amazon.com web site, http://www.amazon.com (July 7, 1998).

"Amazon.com, Inc.," Hoover's Online web site, http://www.hoovers.com (July 7, 1998).

"One-on-One Interview, CEO, Amazon.com (AMZN)," October 16, 1997, MSNBC web site, http://www.msnbc.com (July 8, 1998).

Periodicals

Advertising Age, July 14, 1997, p. S2.

Business Week, September 23, 1996, p. 106.

Communications Week, September 2, 1996, p. S13.

Economist, May 10, 1997; June 21, 1997.

Fortune, December 9, 1996, p. 169.

Independent, September 10, 1997, p. 2; May 12, 1998, p. 4.

Nation's Business, March 1, 1997, p. 34.

New York Times, May 18, 1997, section 3, p. 1.

Reuters Business Report, May 15, 1997; October 31, 1996.

Star Tribune (Minneapolis, MN), December 23, 1997, p. 11E.

Time, April 14, 1997, p. 71.

USA Today, May 8, 1997, p. D7.

Wall Street Journal, May 16, 1996, p. A1; March 25, 1997, p. B7.

—Geri Speace

Cathleen Black

Publishing executive

Born April 26, 1944, in Chicago, IL; daughter of James Hamilton (a food company executive) and Margaret (Harrington) Black; married Thomas Harvey (an attorney); children: one son; one daughter. *Education:* Trinity College, B.A., 1966.

Addresses: *Office*—959 Eighth Ave., New York, NY 10019.

Career

Curtis Publishing, telephone ad salesperson, 1966; *Holiday* magazine, ad salesperson, 1966-70; *New York* magazine, ad salesperson, 1970-72; *Ms.* magazine, advertising director, 1972-75, associate publisher, 1975-77; *New York* magazine, associate publisher, 1977-79, publisher, 1979- 83; *USA Today,* president, 1983, publisher, 1984-91; Newspaper Association of America, 1991- 96; Hearst Magazines, publisher, 1996—. Board of directors, Hearst Corp., IBM, Coca-Cola Co.

Awards: *Adweek* magaine woman of the year, 1985.

Sidelights

Cathleen Black is the first female president of Hearst Magazines, the longstanding media conglomerate known for some of America's favorite titles. The world's biggest publisher of monthly magazines, Hearst is a private, family-owned business long known for its "old boy network." Black broke through this barrier, one in a long series throughout her career, to be placed in charge of 16 high-profile periodicals, including *Cosmopolitan, Esquire, Harper's Bazaar,* *Popular Mechanics,* and *Redbook.* She has made a steady climb in publishing, first selling advertising at magazines such as *Holiday* and *New York,* then taking a risk as the advertising director of the fledgling feminist publication *Ms.* in 1972. After being promoted to associate publisher there, she was called back to *New York* as an associate publisher, and within two years, was named publisher—the first woman to hold that position at a weekly consumer magazine. In 1984, the trailblazing *USA Today* summoned her to run its operations, and in 1991, she set her own salary as CEO of the National Newspaper Association of America, an important lobbying group in Washington, DC. Black took over at Hearst Magazines in 1996, when chief executive officer (CEO) Frank A Bennack, Jr. announced her appointment as publisher.

Black was born on April 26, 1944, in Chicago, Illinois, to James Hamilton Black, a food company executive, and Margaret (Harrington) Black. She has one brother and one sister. Growing up in an environment where current events were openly discussed, Black was around newspapers from a very young age. The major cultural center of Chicago, meanwhile, exposed Black to the world of arts and entertainment. At age 14, Black's life was altered when her father lost his eyesight. Undaunted by his handicap, he changed careers in order to keep working, becoming an investor. "We both have a strong determination to succeed," Black remarked to Paul Farhi in the *Washington Post.* "We both have outgoing, forceful personalities. I owe him a lot."

Black graduated from Aquinas Dominican High School, then received her bachelor of arts degree from Trinity College in northeast Washington state in 1966. Soon after graduating, she headed for New York City and landed a job selling ads over the phone for Curtis Publishing. Later that year, she began selling ads at *Holiday* magazine, and in 1969, switched to *Travel & Leisure.* There, she ran into sexual discrimination. Larger ad accounts were generally given to men, which she knew was unfair, because her sales figures were impressive. She complained to her boss, who gave her a raise, but it still did not match the salary of her male colleagues. In 1970, Black left *Travel & Leisure* in 1970 to join the advertising department at *New York* magazine, staying only two years until an exciting offer prompted her to move once again.

In 1972, Black took over as advertising manager at *Ms.,* a new feminist magazine at a time when society was still wary of changes in gender roles, such as women in the workforce. "We were watching tens of thousands of women joining the work force," Black recalled to Phyllis Furman in *Crain's New York Business.* The shift in societal attitudes toward women's roles made it difficult to sell ads. "This was a time when feminism was still very new and misunderstood," Black recalled to Lindsy Van Gelder in *Ms.* "We would travel around the country selling ads, and people would literally be hanging out windows to see what the freaks and weirdos looked like." Women as well as men were threatened; men were baffled by women going to work and the changing mores of female behavior, while some women who were already working were concerned about other women competing for their positions. Black managed to convince her clients that the new economic power of women made it worth their while to buy advertising. They did, and she was promoted to associate publisher in 1975.

After overcoming obstacles to make *Ms.* a success, *New York* magazine called Black to be their advertising director. They needed someone who could bail them out of a rut. Australian-born media mogul Rupert Murdoch had just purchased the periodical, scaring advertisers away in droves. He had an unsavory reputation, deserved or not, of printing articles ripe with sex and violence, and rumor had it that *New York* would follow suit. Black went back in 1977 under the condition that if she increased business, she would be named publisher within a year and a half. She overcame the image, sold the ads, helped *New York* turn a profit, and in 1979 became the first female publisher of a weekly consumer magazine.

Black's record caught the attention of Allen H. Neuharth, CEO of Gannett Newspapers. In 1983, he asked her to take the job of president at the innovative *USA Today.* It was the first to be a truly national newspaper, and it adopted a then-unique look; it ran short, easy-to-read stories with a broad interest, used bright colors on the section heads and full-color photos, and boasted more graphically interesting layouts. The following year, 1984, Black became publisher, and later joined its board of directors. She was in charge for eight years, boosting circulation to 1.8 million by 1991, making it the second-largest paper in the country after the *Wall Street Journal.* Her efforts helped get it off the ground and established a new era in newspapers. "To have taken [*USA Today*] from the infant stage to a mature product is something I take great pride in," Black commented to Paul Farhi in the *Washington Post.* "Every cynic wouldn't have given us a prayer to make it to our first birthday."

Though *USA Today* did not actually turn a profit under Black, it did go into the black a year after she left. Her involvement in the project was significant on a greater scale as well. The publication revolutionized the world of newspapers, leading other publishers across the nation to alter the look of their papers in order to compete on newsstands with the jazzy newcomer. Initially, a bevy of journalists and critics were skeptical of the brightly colored pages and brief stories written in simple language, derisively calling it "McPaper" and predicting that it would never work. Readers, however—especially business travelers—enjoyed the product, and its circulation soared. Even the *New York Times,* long known affectionately as the "Gray Lady" due to its bland design, added color late in 1997. In addition, *USA Today* established an identity for Gannett, making it a leading presence in journalism. "It has been a very important investment for this company," Black remarked to Farhi in the *Washington Post.* "*USA Today* put Gannett into the big leagues."

In May of 1991, Black resigned from Gannett to become the president and CEO of the American Newspaper Publishers Association. At the time, newspapers were experiencing steady declines in circulation, thus causing ad sales to drop off, sending profits into decline. The group hired her to turn around their ailing industry, agreeing to match her $600,000 annual salary that she earned at Gannett. This caused waves with some, since her predecessor had earned less than half that amount. In taking the job, Black became one of the highest-paid lobbyists in Washington, D.C., with a salary reaching $885,000 by 1995. The group wanted someone, though, with a high profile, and she fit the bill.

Functioning mainly as a spokesperson and lobbyist, Black increased spending on lobbying efforts from $40,000 in 1988 to $2.78 million, tackling topics such as First Amendment rights, telecommunications, taxes, and environmental issues. She also merged six separate trade groups into one under the new name of the Newspaper Association of America, thus uniting a previously scattered assembly under one umbrella. Some smaller papers were upset that Black seemed to concentrate her energy on representing the larger daily papers, and others complained that she raised dues too high. However, others applauded Black's improvements in the group's restructuring. One person impressed with her accomplishments was Hearst president and CEO Frank Bennack, Jr., who had recruited her for the position in the first place. He asked her to join the media conglomerate as president of Hearst Magazines.

In 1995, Black took over as the first woman president of Hearst Magazines. In this position, she became responsible for the world's largest publisher of monthly magazines, with 16 titles in the United States and 95 international editions sold in more than 100 countries. The Hearst Corporation magazines division includes *Cosmopolitan, Esquire, Harper's Bazaar, Marie Claire, Motor Boating & Sailing, Popular Mechanics, Redbook, Sports Afield,* and *Town & Country.* Some of the titles under their control have been published for over one hundred years. Again, she faced immediate challenges. A recent increase in ad rates, combined with lagging circulation, had turned away some of its top advertisers. Kraft, for one, pulled $30 million of its food ads and $20 million of its tobacco ads.

Though Black publicly defended the company's decision, Jeff Gremillion in *Mediaweek* reported that at least one agency said that Hearst had negotiated a lower rate with them behind-the-scenes. Black originally denied giving discounts, but in 1997 Constance L. Hays in the *New York Times* wrote, "Black argues that discounting ad pages is a way of life for every magazine publisher." Black told Hays, "We are doing nothing different than anybody else. Conde Nast always says itdoesn't discount, but then it rolls in a semi truck full of merchandising and value-added programs and events." Though total number of pages were down in

1996 from 1995, Black maintained that the magazines were financially healthy in 1997 and were on pace to reap their highest profits ever. Hayes wrote that ad revenue for some titles, including *Cosmopolitan* and *Marie Claire,* had increased at an astonishing rate, but did note that some magazines were not performing as well.

Despite the problems, Black made the important contribution of establishing Hearst as a brand name. Some had accused the publishing giant of becoming a stuffy behemoth—a reputation that can mean imminent doom in the constantly-changing, trendy world of magazines. Black updated the image and launched a number of new titles, including *Bob Vila's American Home, Mr. Food's Easy Cooking,* and *Healthy Living.* Though some titles, such as *Esquire,* continued to struggle, Hearst was managing to rake in over $1 billion a year in revenues. Black's rise to president of this media mammoth was an important step for women as well as for publishing. *Newsday* even trumpeted her appointment with the headline, "New Gender at Men's Club," pointing to Hearst's reputation as an "old boys' club," a place where women were simply shut out of opportunities to advance.

Black is married to attorney Thomas Harvey, and they have a son and daughter. The family lives in New York City. Known to have a charming and positive personality, Black is a hands-off boss who trusts editors to do their part. In addition to the board of directors at IBM and the Coca-Cola Company, Black is a member of the corporate board of directors at Hearst, a position that does not hold as much power as CEO Frank Bennack, who sits on the board that runs the Hearst family trust. "Her power is limited by not being part of the family," remarked Steven Cohen, editor of *Media Industry Newsletter,* in the *New York Times.* However, if Black has her way, she might just tear down another wall. According to the *New York Times,* Black mused to the *New York Post,* "I'd love to run the company."

Sources

On-line

"Before Hours," November 12, 1997, CNNfn web site, http://www.cnnfn.com. (June 17, 1998).
"Hearst Magazines," Hearst Corporation web site, http://www.hearstcorp.com (
"Hearst Corporation." Hoover's Online web site, http://www.hoovers.com (June 17, 1998).

Books

Encyclopedia of Twentieth-Century Journalists, Garland
Publishing, 1986.

Periodicals

Advertising Age, September 16, 1996, p. 26; April 28,
1997, p. 3.
Crain's New York Business, March 25, 1996.
Editor & Publisher, December 2, 1995, p. 15.
Folio: The Magazine for Magazine Management, September 15, 1996, p. 44.
Inside Media, December 13, 1995, p. 27.
Mediaweek, October 14, 1996, p. 32; April 28, 1997, p. 6.
Ms., January 1988, p. 71.
Newsday, December 7, 1995, p. B2.
New York Times, June 2, 1997, p. C1.
Washington Post, 13 May 1991, p. 1.

—Geri Speace

Ruben Blades

Actor, singer, and composer

Born July 16, 1948, in Panama City, Panama; son of Ruben Dario (a musician and police officer) and Anoland Benita (a singer, piano player, and radio actress) Blades; married Lisa A. Lebenzon, December 13, 1986. *Education:* University of Panama, degree in political science and law, 1974; Harvard University, master's degree in international law, 1985.

Addresses: *Office*—4 Expressway Plaza, Roslyn Heights, NY 11577.

Career

Banco Nacional de Panama, attorney, 1972-74; professional singer and actor, 1974—; Fania Records, mailroom clerk, then legal adviser, 1975-78; Papa Egoro (political party), founder, 1992, party candidate for president of Panama, 1994. Film appearances include *The Last Fight, Crossover Dreams, Critical Condition, The Milagro Beanfield War, Fatal Beauty, Predator II, The Super, Homeboy, Disorganized Crime, The Lemon Sisters, Mo' Better Blues, The Two Jakes, Life with Mikey, A Million to Juan, Color of Night;* television appearances include *Dead Man Out, One Man's War, The Josephine Baker Story, Crazy from the Heart, The Heart of the Deal, Miracle on I-880;* film scores include *Crossover Dreams, Beat Street, Oliver & Company, Caminos Verdes, Q&A.*

Awards: Two Grammy Awards, National Academy of Recording Arts and Sciences; numerous gold records presented by record companies; National CableACE Award, best actor, for *Dead Man Out.*

Member: Papa Egoro (founder), American Society of Composers, Authors and Publishers, Screen Actors Guild, National Academy of Recording Arts and Sciences, American Federation of Television and Radio Artists, Colegio Nacional de Abogados, Harvard Law School Association.

Sidelights

The seeds of Ruben Blades' musical, theatrical, and political destiny were planted early. His Cuban-born mother was a bolero singer, a pianist, and an actress on radio soap operas in their Panamanian homeland. His father, of West Indian descent, played bongos and was so talented at basketball that he was recruited to play on the national secret police team—and, in the process, became a detective on Panamanian General Omar Torrijos' police force. The Blades were forced to leave the country for Miami in 1973, when then-Colonel Manuel Noriega accused Detective Blades, who was a narcotics investigator, of participating in a CIA plot to assassinate Torrijos. The unique circumstances of his upbringing gave young Ruben, the second of Anoland and Ruben Blades' five children, a strong Afro-Cuban musical heritage and a heightened sense of social injustice. His most profound influence, however, was his paternal grandmother, Emma Bosques Laurenza, a Rosicrucian, vegetarian, yogi, painter, poet, and feminist who taught Ruben to read, introduced him to modern art, and took him to

American musicals. Blades told *Time* magazine writer Jay Cocks that his grandmother was a "wonderfully crazy woman who practiced levitation and instilled in me the silly notion that justice is important and that we can all serve and be part of the solution."

Musically, Blades was raised on the doo-wop and early rock 'n' roll of Bill Haley and the Comets, the Platters, and other bands he heard on the radio in his Panama City barrio. As a result of his exposure to American music, Blades sang in English before he ever sang in his native Spanish. As a teenager, he performed with his brother Luis' band, the Saints, covering Frank Sinatra standards and American pop staples, including the Beatles' "And I Love Her" and the Monkees' "Last Train to Clarksville." His love of American music and admiration of the nation's heroic, liberty-loving image evaporated, however, when Americans refused to honor the regulation requiring the Panamanian flag to be flown alongside the Stars and Stripes at Balboa High School in the Panama Canal Zone. The result was a riot in which American troops killed 21 Panamanians and wounded almost 500. Blades reacted with shock and disgust. "Until then, the North Americans were always the good guys. We knew that from the movies, didn't we?" he told Pete Hamill during an interview for *New York* magazine. "They were the guys we'd seen kicking the Nazis, beating the bad guys. All of a sudden, you had them on the other side and they were shooting at you." Blades stopped singing in English, immersed himself in Latin American music, and began reading more about history and politics.

In the late 1960s, Blades performed with a series of Latin bands and began studying law at the University of Panama. While still a student, he traveled to New York and recorded an album, *De Panama a Nueva York*, with Pete Rodriguez and his combo. Nearly all the lyrics on the record were from Blades. After a few months in New York, Blades returned to Panama to complete his law degree. Following graduation, he served as an attorney for the Bank of Panama and worked to rehabilitate prisoners. Blades' muse was persistent, however, and he returned to New York in 1974 to pursue a career in music. He landed a job in the mailroom of Fania Records, America's leading producer of salsa music, and soon was singing with the Ray Barretto band. In 1976 Blades began performing with trombonist Willie Colon, a collaboration which created three groundbreaking albums, including *Siembra*, which became the largest-selling salsa LP in history.

Over the next few years Blades revolutionized salsa music, experimenting with guitar and vibraphone, swapping the requisite horn section for synthesizers, and adding Caribbean and Latin rhythms and strains of jazz and '50s rock to the traditional Afro-Cuban beat. He also crafted lyrics which poignantly told human stories and explored social injustice. "In Latin America we do not have a strong movie industry, and a lot of people don't have the habit of reading," Blades told Eric Levin in *People*. "So I am reverting to the original popular way of communicating, which is song. I tell stories I see are not being presented. I feel if it's interesting to me as a human being, it will be interesting to other human beings." In story songs often compared to the work of Bob Dylan, Bruce Springsteen and Randy Newman, Blades sings about a priest gunned down while giving communion, a desperate, unemployed man who tries to rob a bank with his son's squirt gun, a secret policeman assigned to make political arrests, and a teen-aged girl contemplating abortion. In 1980 Blades released a song called "Tiburon" which depicted global superpowers intervening in the Caribbean as prowling, sleepless sharks. The song was banned by Miami's top Latin radio station, which aired a commentary calling Blades a Communist. It also spurred at least one death threat, after which the singer wore a bulletproof vest when he performed in Miami. In *New York*, Pete Hamill wrote: "Blades does not write jingles for teenagers or moony ballads of self-pity and abandonment; his songs are about people, one at a time, and their universal problems; they're about exile, too, and brutality and the loss of political innocence; they're about the struggle to be decent." Blades routinely prints both Spanish and English versions of his lyrics on his album jackets; he also included his home phone number until his increasingly itinerant schedule made it difficult to answer fans' calls.

After parting ways with Willie Colon, Blades released his debut solo album, *Maestra Vida*, on the Fania label in 1982. He then made his major-label debut on Elektra Records with 1984's *Buscandro America*, which *People* magazine called "as uplifting as it is ambitious." Next came *Escenas* and *Agua de Luna*, an eight-song cycle based on early short stories of Colombian Nobel laureate Gabriel Garcia Marquez. Reviewer Eric Levin, writing in *People*, lauded the album's "dashing energy and intelligence.... Thanks to [Blades'] bright voice and precise diction, every darting syllable tingles." Levin continued: "Considering how beguilingly these words snake by in Spanish, you admire even more Blades's rare ability to combine sense and sensuousness in music." On the follow-up album *Nothing But the Truth*, which was Blades' first English-language album, he collaborated with Elvis Costello, Lou Reed and other artists. The album made several music critics' Top Ten lists for 1988, but it failed commercially.

As Blades evolved musically in the 1980s, he also had his eyes on another prize: Political office, possibly the presidency, in his native Panama. In 1985 he put his music career on hold to earn a master's degree in international law from Harvard University—a move calculated to bolster his resume for a future political campaign. He also regularly wrote columns on art and politics for Panamanian newspapers. Blades' determination to enter politics in his homeland was heightened when the United States invaded Panama in 1989 to remove Dictator Manuel Noriega from office. Blades called the invasion, which left nearly 5,000 dead and produced thousands of refugees, a "flagrant transgression of international law." After an 18-year absence from his homeland, he returned briefly in 1992 to establish Papa Egoro (it means "Mother Earth" in one of Panama's indigenous languages), a political party built on a platform calling for participatory democracy, Panamanian self-determination, and an end to political corruption. Two years later, Blades became the party's presidential nominee. "There's a lot of anger, resentment, and despair," he told Guy Garcia during a 1994 interview for *Harper's Bazaar*. "After Noriega, everyone's hopes were so high. But we've all been taken for a ride. The politicians are lying most of the time; there's so much corruption.... The dimension of change we are trying to create is mind-boggling. We are trying to change the attitudes of a whole country, and it's exciting as hell." It was not to be, however, as Blades finished third in a field of seven candidates.

Blades' film career, meanwhile, has prospered. The Emmy Award-nominated actor has worked with a laundry list of top actors and directors, including Spike Lee, Robert Redford, Jack Nicholson, Diane Keaton, Richard Pryor and Whoopi Goldberg. Blades first gained notice for his work onscreen in the 1985 independent film *Crossover Dreams*. In the film he portrayed a "Nuyorican" musician struggling for mainstream success—even when it requires him to turn away from his heritage. "Blades proves himself a natural," Eric Levin wrote in *People*. "His innocence and charm are as well outlined as his callousness; he makes clear the cruel tug-of-war between ethnic identity and the hunger for outside validation." From there, Blades went on to appear in Lee's *Mo' Better Blues,* Nicholson's film *The Two Jakes,* and Redford's charmer *The Milagro Beanfield War*—a film in which the actor "exudes sly star power," Richard Corliss wrote in *Time*. Blades also won critical acclaim—and a cable industry ACE Award—for his portrayal of a death-row prisoner in the powerful HBO movie *Dead Man Out*. Richard Rush, who directed Blades in the 1994 erotic thriller

The Color of Night, has said that the same qualities serve Blades both as a politician and an actor. "He's extremely intuitive and bright," Rush told *Harper's Bazaar.* "He totally immerses himself in the moment. He becomes the character. And that's why it works in every take—because he won't lie. It has to do with the truth."

Selected discography

(With Pete Rodriguez) *De Panama a Nueva York,* c. 1969.
(With the Willie Colon Combo) *Metiendo Mano* (includes "Pablo Pueblo"), Fania Records, 1976.
(With the Willie Colon Combo) *Siembra* (includes "Pedro Navaja"), Fania Records, 1977.
Cacniones del Solar de los Aburridos, Fania Records, 1982.

Solo albums

Maestra Vida, Fania Records, 1982.
Buscandro America (includes "El Padre Antonio y el Monanguillo Andres," "Desapariciones," "GDBD," "Decisiones," and "Todos Vuelven"), Elektra, 1984.
Escenas (includes "Silencios," "La Sorpresa," "Tierra Dura," "Cuentes del Alma," and "Muevete"), Elektra, 1985.
Agua de Luna, Elektra, 1987.
Nothing But the Truth (collaboration with other artists, including Elvis Costello and Lou Reed), Elektra, 1988.

Sources

Books

International Motion Picture Almanac, Quigley Publishing Co., 1996.

Periodicals

Harper's Bazaar, March 1994, p. 326.
Hispanic, September 1993, p. 22.
Los Angeles Magazine, September 1995, p. 145.
National Catholic Reporter, May 6, 1994, p. 8.
New Republic, November 1, 1993, p. 10.
New York, August 19, 1985.
People, May 7, 1984, p. 26; August 13, 1984, p. 75; September 30, 1985, p. 10; March 30, 1987, p. 26; May 9, 1994.
Playboy, December 1985, p. 30.
Time, July 2, 1984, p. 82; March 28, 1988, p. 74; January 29, 1990, p. 70; October 14, 1991, p. 17.

—Dave Wilkins

Judy Blume

Author

Born February 12, 1936, in Elizabeth, NJ; daughter of Rudolph (a dentist) and Esther (a homemaker; maiden name, Rosenfeld) Sussman; married John M. Blume (an attorney), August 15, 1959 (divorced, 1975); married Thomas Kitchens (a physicist), 1976 (divorced, 1979); married George Cooper (a law professor and writer), June 6, 1987; children: (from first marriage) Randy Lee (daughter), Lawrence Andrew; stepchildren: Amanda. *Education:* New York University, B.S. in education, 1961.

Addresses: *Home*—New York, NY. *Agent*—William Morris Agency, 1325 Avenue of the Americas, New York, NY 10022.

Career

Author of books for children and adults. Founder of Kids Fund, 1981. Board member, Society of Children's Book Writers, Authors Guild, National Coalition Against Censorship, and Planned Parenthood Advocates.

Awards: For *Are You There God? It's Me, Margaret:* New York Times best books for children list, 1970, Nene Award, 1975, Young Hoosier Book Award, 1976, and North Dakota Children's Choice Award, 1979; for *Tales of a Fourth Grade Nothing:* Charlie May Swann Children's Book Award, 1972, Young Readers Choice Award, Pacific Northwest Library Association, and Sequoyah Children's Book Award of Oklahoma, both 1975, Massachusetts Children's Book Award, Georgia Children's Book Award, and South Carolina Children's Book Award, all 1977, Rhode Island Library Association Award, 1978, North Dakota Children's Choice Award, and West Australian Young Readers' Book Award, both 1980, United States Army in Europe Kinderbuch Award, and Great Stone Face Award, New Hampshire Library Council, both 1981; For *Blubber:* Arizona Young Readers Award, and Young Readers Choice Award, Pacific Northwest Library Association, both 1977, and North Dakota Childrens' Choice Award, 1983; Golden Archer Award, 1974; for *Otherwise Known as Sheila the Great:* South Carolina Children's Book Award, 1978; for *Superfudge:* Texas Bluebonnet List, 1980, Michigan Young Reader's Award, and International Reading Association Children's Choice Award, both 1981, First Buckeye Children's Book Award, Nene Award, Sue Hefley Book Award, Louisiana Association of School Libraries, United States Army in Europe Kinderbuch Award, West Australian Readers' Book Award, North Dakota Children's Choice Award, Colorado Children's Book Award, Georgia Children's Book Award, Tennessee Children's Choice Book Award, and Utah Children's Book Award, all 1982, Northern Territory Young Readers' Book Award, Young Readers Choice Award, Pacific Northwest Library Association, Garden State Children's Book Award, Iowa Children's Choice Award, Arizona Young Readers' Award, California Young Readers' Medal, and Young Hoosier Book

Award, all 1983; Today's Woman Award, 1981; Eleanor Roosevelt Humanitarian Award, Favorite Author—Children's Choice Award, Milner Award, and Jeremiah Ludington Memorial Award, all 1983; for *Tiger Eyes:* Dorothy Canfield Fisher Children's Book Award, Buckeye Children's Book Award, and California Young Readers' Medal, all 1983; Carl Sandburg Freedom to Read Award, Chicago Public Library,1984; Civil Liberties Award, Atlanta American Civil Liberties Union, and John Rock Award, Center for Population Options, Los Angeles, both 1986; South Australian Youth Medal Award for Best Author, South Australian Association for Media Education, 1988; Margaret A. Edwards Award for Lifetime Achievement, for outstanding literature for teens with a special citation for *Forever,* American Library Association, 1996.

Sidelights

Many a young reader has been given a hand through the tough adolescent years with the help of author Judy Blume, known for her realistic portrayals of pre-teen and teenage characters and the issues they face growing up in modern, middle-class America. With books like *Are You There God? It's Me, Margaret, Tales of a Fourth Grade Nothing, Blubber,* and more, Blume opened up a dialogue for kids struggling to figure out life's mysteries. Her straightforward treatment of puberty, friendships, family relationships, and even sex earned her the devotion of millions of readers who found that they were not alone in their confusion, while at the same time provoking legions of parents to protest her work, sometimes banning them from local libraries. Her controversial, humorous, and touching works have remained favorites since the 1970s, selling more than 65 million copies and prompting fans to send tons of mail to Blume asking for advice or complimenting her for the guidance she provided. As her career progressed, Blume branched out into writing adult fiction as well, publishing the racy *Wifey* in 1978, *Smart Women* in 1984, and *Summer Sisters* in 1998.

Blume was born on February 12, 1936, in Elizabeth, New Jersey, to Rudolph and Esther (Rosenfeld) Sussman. Her father, a dentist, was an outgoing, fun-loving man who nurtured her vivid imagination and love of game-playing. Her mother was more introspective and quiet, and loved to read. Blume and her older brother, David, grew up in a home brimming with books as well as a radio tuned to their favorite shows. She took after her father's vibrant personality and started dance classes at age three. In third grade, Blume was separated from her father for two years when she, her mother, and brother moved to Miami Beach, Florida, to help improve her brother's health. She

would later use her experiences during this period to form ideas for many of the incidents in her books. An all-A student, Blume attended the girls-only Battin High School, where she was active in the chorus and on the student newspaper.

Blume graduated with honors and went to college at Boston University for a year but suffered from mononucleosis and was forced to quit. She then transferred to New York University and graduated in 1961 with her bachelor of science in early childhood education. During her sophomore year, she met John Blume, a lawyer, and they were married about a year later, on August 15, 1959. Upon graduation she was already expecting their first child. Her daughter, Randy Lee, was born in 1961, and the following year she had a son, Lawrence Andrew. She found life as a homemaker not completely satisfying, so she began writing books by the time her kids were in nursery school. While she was taking a writing course at New York University, she began composing chapters of what would become her first book, *Iggie's House.* Soon, she was selling some short stories, but receiving even more rejection notices. She was ecstatic when Reilly & Lee finally bought her picture book *The One in the Middle is the Green Kangaroo.*

In 1969, Blume took note of a new publishing company, Bradbury Press, looking for children's fiction. They met with her, and after looking over her book *Iggie's House,* asked for a rewrite. A month later, they accepted the manuscript. Many of the reviews for *Iggie's House* criticized its simplification of racial issues, and later Blume herself admitted that her first two books were not very good. Though she was hurt by the negative reaction, she had already finished her next work, *Are You There God? It's Me, Margaret,* published in 1970. This would establish her as a perceptive chronicler of modern pre-teen angst, filling a literary void and helping innumerable young women through their "awkward years." The story is told in a realistic, first-person narrative by a sixth-grade girl, Margaret Simon, suffering from self-doubt as she tries to cope with the physical and emotional changes of puberty. Worrying about breast development, menstruation, and boys take up much of her emotional energy, and she also has an array of concerns about religion. To help her sort things out, she has conversations with God instead of her parents, illuminating Blume's conviction that parents and children need to communicate more.

Are You There God? It's Me, Margaret initially garnered mixed reviews, but it was a smash success among young readers who felt that Blume expertly related to the issues important to them. The *New York Times* named it one of the outstanding children's books of 1970, and it went on to win a few regional awards as well. It eventually became one of the top five all-time childrens' best-sellers in paperback, selling six million copies by the mid-1990s. Despite the fact that the book was trumpeted for its realism, many parents felt the subject matter was too explicit and wrote scathing letters to the author and publisher. Some tried to ban the book. The attempt at censoring this book and subsequent works of hers led Blume to get involved with the National Coalition Against Censorship. As she remarked to Peter Gorner in the *Chicago Tribune*, "I wasn't aware at the time that I was writing anything controversial. I just know what these books would have meant to me when I was a kid."

For Blume's next novel, 1971's *Then Again, Maybe I Won't*, she told the tale from the perspective of a 12-year-old boy, Tony Miglione. This time, Blume covered issues like erections and wet dreams, as well as the changes in Tony's family as they move up the socioeconomic scale. Not one of her best sellers, *Then Again, Maybe I Won't* was again a target of censors for its treatment of emerging sexuality, even though that was a minor aspect of the story. After that, Blume released *Freckle Juice*, a cute, humorous book for younger readers. Then, when her own children were seeing the divorce rate rise in their own neighborhood, Blume penned *It's Not the End of the World*, relating the feelings and action of two sisters and a brother going through the pain of their parents' breakup.

In 1972, Blume had another major hit with *Tales of a Fourth Grade Nothing*, revolving around sibling rivalry between Peter Hatcher and his two-year-old brother, Fudge. Blume again used her own experiences raising children in order to pinpoint common problems and recreate believable conversations. The enduring tale became the third-best-selling children's book of all time, with over 6.3 million paperbacks sold by the mid-1990s. It won a slew of regional and overseas awards. The same year, 1972, Blume also released *Otherwise Known as Sheila the Great*, which the author based on many of her own childhood fears, including thunderstorms, dogs, and swimming. The mix of humor and pathos highlighted human fragility and promoted the ability to accept one's self and others. Blume's next book, *Deenie*, 1973, continues this theme. It involves a beautiful young woman who discovers she has scoliosis. For background, Blume researched children with the affliction, and her accurate portrayal of the brace-wearing Deenie prompted many children with scoliosis to write to her. It also tackled masturbation, which again upset many parents. Blume considers *Blubber*, published in 1974, to be one of her most important books. It is about a fifth-grade girl whose weight problem earns the ridicule of the other students, and again stems from a real-life experience that Blume's daughter had when a similar incident happened to one of her classmates. Blume drew fire for her use of profanity in the dialogue, but she explained that she was using language as kids really use it at that age.

> *"I don't think the basic characters or things I write about have changed over 20 years. It's always families, friendships and schools. And I think that except for the fact children have had more limited experiences that adults their feelings aren't any different."*

The novel *Forever*, published in 1975, created perhaps her biggest wave of controversy for its frank treatment of adolescent sex. The publisher was even unsure if it was truly fit for young readers and thus labeled it as an adult book without asking Blume. According to Blume, the book was undoubtedly meant for young readers. It was dedicated to her teenage daughter, who had asked her to write a story about teens having sex, but without the heavy-handed moralizing. The graphic intercourse scene was shocking for many parents, but the book was generally well-received critically. Over two decades later, in 1996, the American Library Association gave Blume a lifetime achievement award with a specific citation for *Forever*. Blume's next effort, *Starring Sally J. Freedman as Herself*, is largely autobiographical, based on the author's recollections of herself as a child growing up in the 1940s. It reveals her fears, such as those of the Holocaust and of death in general, and tells of the time that her family spent apart when her father was working in New Jersey while she and her brother were in Florida with their mother. Though the reviews were mixed, Blume has said it is one of her favorite books that she has written.

In 1980, Blume returned to the characters she had constructed in *Tales of a Fourth Grade Nothing*, the brothers who were going through sibling rivalry. In the sequel, *Superfudge* (1980), Blume adds a baby sister,

Tootsie, to the mix to complicate the boys' lives. Reviewers and readers were pleased with this wry, solidly told story, and it was showered with a variety of regional children's book awards. It became her best-selling hardcover. The following year, Blume turned her attention back to more mature topics with *Tiger Eyes*, the runner-up to *Superfudge* in Blume's hardcover sales. *Tiger Eyes*, about a family coping with the murder of the father during a robbery, addresses adult conflicts as well as teen issues such as dating and drugs. Set mainly in the town of Los Alamos, New Mexico, the story also explores death and the threat of nuclear bombs. Her other works for young readers include *The Pain and the Great One*, 1984, *Just as Long as We're Together*, 1987, *Fudge-A-Mania*, 1990, and *Here's to You, Rachel Robinson*, 1993. She also published in 1986 *Letters to Judy: What Your Kids Wish They Could Tell You*, a collection of some of the mail she has received that illuminates the need for children to be able to talk to someone. The proceeds from the book have gone toward her Kids Fund project, an effort she founded in 1981 that donates money to nonprofit groups that help young people.

Blume began writing specifically for adults in 1978 with the release of *Wifey*, about a bored woman in a stale marriage who seeks freedom in sexual encounters with a number of men. She carried over her candid style from her books for young readers, and the risque *Wifey* outsold most of her children's titles. In 1984 Blume's second adult novel, *Smart Women*, focuses on a divorced, professional woman of 40 who falls in love with one of her ex-husband's friends. Her next adult novel was not released until 1998, when she came out with *Summer Sisters*, a story about two girls who vacation together each year on Martha's Vineyard. The novel traces their lives from age 12 to age 30; one is a clean-cut "girl next door," the other a sultry bad girl. Reviews, as usual, were mixed, with some critics faulting it for lacking depth, while others enjoyed the breezy tale that Carolyn Mackler in *Ms.* called "vintage Judy Blume, yet with a very nineties flair."

Blume was divorced from her first husband in 1975 and married Thomas Kitchens, a physicist, the following year. They divorced in 1979. In 1987 she married George Cooper, a law professor and writer. Blume has a daughter, Randy Lee, and son, Lawrence Andrew, from her first marriage and one stepdaughter, Amanda. Blume serves on the board of the Society of Children's Book Writers, the Authors Guild, Planned Parenthood Advocates, and the National Coalition Against Censorship, for which she is a spokesperson. Though many of her better-known books are a couple decades old or more, they have enjoyed longstanding popularity. "I don't think the basic characters or things I write about have changed over 20 years," Blume commented to Andrew Graham-Dixon in the *Independent*. "It's always families, friendships and schools. And I think that except for the fact children have had more limited experiences that adults their feelings aren't any different." When Brangien Davis from the Amazon.com online bookseller asked Blume what she considered was her contribution to literature, she replied, "I'm happy that so many children like to read. And if they like to read in part because of what I gave them to read, that's great. To touch lives, I guess, is the best thing that anybody can ask for."

Selected writings

The One in the Middle is the Green Kangaroo, Reilly & Lee, 1969.
Iggie's House, Bradbury, 1970.
Are You There God? It's Me, Margaret, Bradbury, 1970.
Then Again, Maybe I Won't, Bradbury, 1971.
Freckle Juice, Four Winds, 1971.
Tales of a Fourth Grade Nothing, Dutton, 1972.
It's Not the End of the World, Bradbury, 1972.
Otherwise Known as Sheila the Great, Dutton, 1972.
Deenie, Bradbury, 1973.
Blubber, Bradbury, 1974.
Forever, Bradbury, 1975.
Starring Sally J. Freedman as Herself, Bradbury, 1977.
Wifey (adult novel), Putnam, 1977.
Superfudge, Dutton, 1980.
The Judy Blume Diary: The Place to Put Your Own Feelings, Dell, 1981.
Tiger Eyes, Bradbury, 1981.
The Pain and the Great One, Bradbury, 1984.
Smart Women (adult novel), Putnam, 1984.
Just as Long as We're Together, Orchard, 1987.
The Judy Blume Memory Book, Dell, 1988.
Fudge-A-Mania, Dutton, 1990.
Here's to You, Rachel Robinson, Orchard, 1993.
Summer Sisters (adult novel), Delacorte, 1998.

Sources

On-line

"In Full Blume" (interview), Amazon.com web site, http://www.amazon.com (September 2, 1998).
Judy Blume Official Web Site, http://www.judyblume.com (September 2, 1998).
"Judy Blume," *Contemporary Authors*, Gale Literary Databases web site, http://www.galenet.com (July 7, 1998).

"Judy Blume," *Dictionary of Literary Biography*, Gale Literary Databases web site, http://www .galenet.com (July 7, 1998).

Books

Authors & Artists for Young Adults, Volume 3, Gale Research, 1990.

Periodicals

Booklist, March 15, 1998, p. 1179.
Chicago Tribune, September 24, 1978; March 15, 1985.
Dallas Morning News, July 26, 1998, p. 9J.
Gannett News Service, March 4, 1996.
Independent, October 15, 1996, p. 10.
Library Journal, April 15 1998, p. 111.
Ms., July/August 1998, p. 89.
People, June 15, 1998, p. 49.
Rocky Mountain News, May 31, 1998, p. 2E.
St. Louis Post-Dispatch, January 27, 1998, p. D3.
USA Today, June 4, 1998, p. 9D.

Helena Bonham Carter

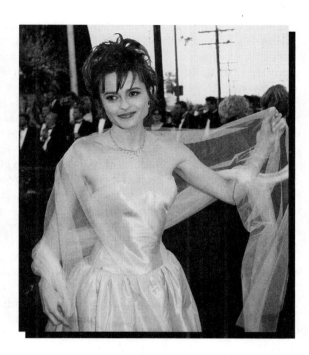

AP/Wide World Photos

Actress

Born May 23, 1966, in London, England; daughter of Raymond (a merchant banker) and Elena (a psychotherapist; maiden name, Propper de Callejon) Bonham Carter.

Addresses: *Home*—London, England. *Office*—c/o Fulton Entertainment, 335 N. Maple Dr., Suite 350, Beverly Hills, CA 90210-3856. *Agent*—c/o United Talent Agency, 9560 Wilshire Blvd., Suite 500, Beverly Hills, CA 90212; Conway Van Gelder, 18-21 Jermyn St., London SW1Y 6HP, England.

Career

Actress. Stage appearances include *The Woman in White*, Greenwich Theatre, London, 1988; and *Trelawny of the "Wells,"* Comedy Theatre, London, 1992. Television appearances include episodes of *Miami Vice*, NBC, 1987, and *Absolutely Fabulous*, Comedy Central, 1994; specials *Arms and the Man*, BBC, 1988; and *Classic Mel: The Making of Mel Gibson's Hamlet*, HBO, 1991; and movies *A Pattern of Roses*, Channel Four, 1982; *The Vision*, BBC, 1987; *A Hazard of Hearts*, CBS, 1987; *Fatal Deception: Mrs. Lee Harvey Oswald*, NBC, 1993; and *Dancing Queen*, 1993. Film appearances include *Lady Jane*, 1986; *A Room with a View*, 1986; *Maurice*, 1987; *La Maschera*, 1987; *Francesco*, 1988; *Getting It Right*, 1989; *Hamlet*, 1990; *Where Angels Fear to Tread*, 1991; *Howards End*, 1992; *Mary Shelley's Frankenstein*, 1994; *Mighty Aphrodite*, 1995; *Margaret's Museum*, 1995; *Twelfth Night: Or What You Will*, 1996; *Portraits chinois*, 1996; *The Wings of the Dove*, 1997; *Keep the Aspidistra Flying*, 1997; *The Theory of Flight*, 1998; and *The Revengers' Comedies*, 1998.

Awards: Genie Award for best performance by an actress in a leading role, 1995, for *Margaret's Museum*; Boston Society of Film Critics Award, Broadcast Film Critics Association Award, Los Angeles Film Critics Association Award, National Board of Review Award, and Society of Texas Film Critics Award, all for best actress, all 1997, for *Wings of the Dove*.

Sidelights

British actress Helena Bonham Carter built her career on playing the quintessential English lady, done up in corsets and hatpins; she is known as the queen of the period piece, acting in adaptations of works by Henry James, E. M. Forster, Mary Shelley, and William Shakespeare. With her delicate features and true-to-life aristocratic blood, Bonham Carter seems made for such parts, and she does not apologize for her tendency to keep taking them. "They're all dynamic women. Fully fleshed. Fully dimensional," she explained to Eleanor Ringel in the *Atlanta Journal and Constitution*. "And it's difficult to find contemporary heroines who are the protagonists and aren't just an ornament. These are the best parts around. So when they come my way, I can't turn them down." Nevertheless, Bonham Carter has proven that she can also do quite well as a modern woman when the role is right.

Bonham Carter was born on May 23, 1966, in London, England, with a notable pedigree. Hergreat-grandfather Lord Herbert Henry Asquith was Britain's liberal prime minister from 1908 to 1916, and her grandmother (Asquith's only daughter by his first wife) was the prominent politician Lady Violet Bonham Carter, a member of the House of Lords. Her great-uncle is screenwriter Anthony Asquith (*The Importance of Being Earnest*). Bonham Carter's father, Raymond, is a merchant banker, and her mother, Elena (Propper de Callejon) Bonham Carter, is a Spanish-French psychotherapist whose father was the Spanish ambassador to the United States, Canada, and Norway. When Helena was five, her mother had a nervous breakdown. Subsequently, her mother recovered and decided to study psychotherapy. Her mother established her own practice, but meanwhile, Bonham Carter's father developed a brain tumor. After the operation he had a massive stroke which left him confined to a wheelchair and partially blind, though his mind remained sharp.

With her father still in the intensive care unit, Bonham Carter decided that she had better learn to fend for herself. At age 13, she dialed up an agent out of the phone book and by age 16 was appearing in television commercials. Her first role was in a stereo advertisement playing Juliet from Shakespeare's classic tale *Romeo and Juliet*, perhaps a sign of things to come. Her next role was as an Edwardian ghost. At 18, all set to take college entrance exams for Cambridge and Oxford, she landed the lead in director Trevor Nunn's *Lady Jane* after he saw a picture of her taken from a magazine. The 1986 film was about Jane Grey, the sixteenth-century queen of England who ruled just nine days. Bonham Carter initially refused the offer, determined to continue her academic career, but Nunn persuaded her to audition.

In her next film, Bonham Carter snagged the lead role of Lucy Honeychurch in the Merchant-Ivory adaptation of E. M. Forster's *A Room with a View*. A sleeper hit internationally, *A Room with a View* was nominated for eight Academy Awards, but Bonham Carter's performance was not always praised. After this running start, the actress was typecast as the corset-wearing archetypical British heroine. In the subsequent years, she made some smaller films, including another Forster tale, *Maurice*, in 1987, and took the lead in *La Maschera* (*The Mask*), an Italian work, in 1988. She also worked in television and theater, appearing in episodes of *Miami Vice* and on stage in *The Woman in White* and others.

By 1989, Bonham Carter was back in the mainstream of cinema with *Getting It Right,* playing Lady Minerva Munday. Her talent this time around drew acclaim, although the film itself was not universally liked. After that, she starred opposite Mickey Rourke in *Francesco,* a docudrama about the life of St. Francis of Assisi. Then in 1990, Bonham Carter played Ophelia in the film version of *Hamlet,* starring Mel Gibson, winning further accolades. The next two years saw her again in Forster adaptations, 1991's *Where Angels Fear to Tread* and 1992's *Howards End.* Though she was esteemed in both, she was overlooked for formal awards.

After that run of period pieces, Bonham Carter played a stripper in the BBC television production *Dancing Queen* in 1993, baring "the whole and utter object. The whole doo-dah. The full monte," she remarked to Jasper Rees in the *Independent on Sunday.* Then in 1994, she played Elizabeth in *Mary Shelley's Frankenstein,* costarring with Kenneth Branagh, who also directed. Though the film was not well-received, it would have a profound effect on both of them. Rumors that they were having an affair circulated, and though they denied them, it became more and more obvious that the two were seeing each other. Bonham Carter was thus credited forbreaking up Branagh's fairy tale marriage to actress Emma Thompson.

In 1995, Bonham Carter shattered her typecasting to play the bratty Manhattan wife of Woody Allen's character in *Mighty Aphrodite.* As she told Rees, "I made a vow to myself. Don't sound like Mia Farrow, and by the end I was saying, Oh my God, I'm beginning to sound like Mia Farrow," comparing herself to Allen's former partner and frequent costar. The same year, she won a Genie Award (a Canadian Oscar) for best performance by an actress in a leading role for *Margaret's Museum,* about a coal miner's daughter in Nova Scotia. The next year, 1996, Bonham Carter took parts in the French film *Portrait chinois* and in Shakespeare's *Twelfth Night,* again directed by Nunn.

Bonham Carter's real breakthrough part, though, came in 1997 when she portrayed Kate Croy in the adaptation of Henry James's *The Wings of the Dove.* She was finally nominated for an Academy Award for her depiction of a young woman who returns to the privileged life that her mother abandoned, then schemes to defy her rich aunt and marry her working-class journalist boyfriend. Though she did not win the Oscar, she did receive best actress honors for her performance from the Boston Society of Film Critics Award, the Broadcast Film Critics Association Award, the Los Angeles Film Critics Association Award, the National Board of Review Award, and the Society of Texas Film Critics Award.

Bonham Carter finally, at about age 30, bought her own place not too far from her parents' place in the Golders Green area of London. She began fixing it up, hoping to move out "sometime before the millennium," she told Marshall Fine in the Gannett News Service. She continues to date Branagh, working with him on the drama *The Theory of Flight*, in which she plays a woman afflicted with Lou Gehrig's disease. They are also reportedly scouting for a project to do together. Despite her steady rise, doubts about her ability continue to plague Bonham Carter. "It would be different if I believed I deserved all the praise, but then I never do," she commented to James Fallon in the *St. Louis Post-Dispatch*. "I'm my own worst critic."

Sources

On-line

"Helena Bonham Carter," Internet Movie Database, http://www.imdb.com (July 30, 1998).

Books

Contemporary Theatre, Film and Television, volume 14, Gale Research, 1996.

Periodicals

Atlanta Journal and Constitution, November 9, 1997, p. K5.
Gannett News Service, November 14, 1997.
Independent, January 10, 1998, p. 4.
Independent on Sunday, July 20, 1997, p. 14.
Newsday, November 23, 1997, p. D4.
New York Times, March 2, 1986.
Premiere, November 1994, p. 105.
St. Louis Post-Dispatch, November 16, 1997, p. D4; March 15, 1998, p. C3.
Time, November 10, 1997, p. 101.
USA Today, November 21, 1997, p. 4D.

—Geri Speace

David Bowie

AP/Wide World Photos

Rock singer, songwriter, and actor

Born David Robert Jones, January 8, 1947, in London, England; son of Hayward (a publicist) and Margaret Mary (a movie theater usher; maiden name, Burns) Jones; married Angela Barnet, 1970 (divorced, 1980); married Iman (a model), 1992; children: (first marriage) Joey (formerly known as Zowie).

Addresses: *Record company*—Virgin, 338 North Foothills Road, Beverly Hills, CA 90210. *Internet*—David Bowie—The Official Web Site: www.davidbowie.com/2.0

Career

Performed with various London area bands including the Kon-Rads, King Bees, Mannish Boys, and the Lower Third; embarked on a solo career in 1966; signed with Mercury and released *The Man Who Sold the World*, 1971; signed with RCA and released *Hunky Dory*, 1972; released *The Rise and Fall of Ziggy Stardust and the Spiders from Mars*, 1972; released *Aladdin Sane*, 1973; released *Pin Ups*, 1973; released *Diamond Dogs*, 1974; released *David Live*, 1974; released *Young Americans*, 1975; released *Station to Station*, 1976; released *Changesonebowie*, 1976; released *Low*, 1977; released *Heroes*, 1977; released *Stage*, 1978; released *Lodger*, 1979; released *Scary Monsters*, 1980; released *Changestwobowie*, 1982; signed to EMI and released *Let's Dance*, 1983; released *Tonight*, 1984; released *Never Let Me Down*, 1987; released *Sound + Vision* box set on Rykodisc, 1989; formed Tin Machine and signed to Virgin; released *Tin Machine*, 1989; signed to Victory and released *Tin Machine II*, 1991; released *Oy Vey Baby*, 1992; disbanded Tin Machine, re-signed to Virgin and

released *Black Tie White Noise*, 1993; released *Outside*, 1995; released *Earthling*, 1997. Film appearances included *The Man Who Fell to Earth*, 1976; *Just a Gigolo*, ca. 1977; *The Hunger*, 1982; *Merry Christmas Mr. Lawrence*, 1982; *Basquiat*, 1996. Stage appearances included *The Elephant Man*, 1980.

Sidelights

David Bowie has been called a cultural chameleon throughout his long and colorful career. From music and film to art and the internet, Bowie has challenged the perceptions of fans and critics alike with his many malleable personas which seemed to mirror the cutting edge trends of the day. In 1996, Bowie became the first artist of his stature to release a single, "Telling Lies," exclusively via the internet.

Born and raised in Brixton, a poor section of London, Bowie claims to have mapped out his destiny at an early age. After having heard a single by Little Richard, the nine-year-old Bowie decided he wanted to be one of Little Richard's saxophone players. A short time later, he got his first saxophone and began working as a butcher's delivery boy in order to pay it off. Upon learning that jazz player Ronnie Ross lived in the neighborhood, Bowie persuaded Ross to give him some lessons. After ten or so lessons, Bowie quit going to see Ross because he felt that he was ready to become a rock star.

Bowie immersed himself in music because of the lack of communication between his parents and himself. He told Hanif Kureishi of *Interview* that "I could never, ever talk to my father. I really loved him, but we couldn't talk about anything together. There was this really British thing that being even remotely emotional was absolutely verboten." Putting it down to the "classic case of British reserve," Bowie consoled himself by withdrawing to his room where he was alone with his books and music and thoughts.

Nicholas Roeg summed up the Bowie mystique in Time *as "David's a real living Renaissance figure. That's what makes him spectacular. He goes away and re-emerges bigger than before."*

While a teenager, Bowie plied his trade with numerous London area bands including the Kon-Rads, King Bees, Mannish Boys, and the Lower Third. During this time he flirted with a number of the musical styles and genres popular in Britain in the early- to mid-1960s, most notably folk and mod. Bowie also studied commercial art, worked briefly at an advertising agency, painted, and acted in some small stage roles.

The worldwide success of the made-for-television American pop band The Monkees forced Bowie to change his name in the late 1960s. The Monkees' lead singer was named Davey Jones and Bowie did not want to be confused with him, so he adopted the surname Bowie. Bowie started to release his first singles about the same time. The singles were mostly unmemorable and easily forgettable until 1969. In that year, Bowie released his first classic signature song "Space Oddity," which eventually peaked at number five on the British pop singles chart. Two years later, his album, *The Man Who Sold the World*, was released. It has been claimed that the birth of the glam rock movement occurred when this album was released. Also that year, Bowie went on his first promotional tour of America and in the summer, his wife Angela Barnet gave birth to a son, Zowie, now known as Joey.

The year 1972 was a rather eventful one for Bowie. He went on another promotional tour of America, although this time it was to cement relations with his new label RCA. *Hunky Dory,* was culled from tracks on the demo that got Bowie his new recording contract. It contained the singles "Life on Mars" and "Changes". The follow-up to *Hunky Dory* established Bowie as a star. *The Rise and Fall of Ziggy Stardust and the Spiders from Mars* gave Bowie not only the abbreviated title track but it also gave him his first and perhaps most beloved personas—Ziggy Stardust. On his chameleon-like character changes, Bowie told Kureishi of *Interview* that "I know now for a fact that so much of my ambition and drive came from wanting to escape from myself and from feelings of inadequacy and vulnerability and not feeling I was loved by anybody, particularly. I would drive those feelings out by throwing myself not only into work, but eventually into characters." The tour to support the album was a rock spectacle full of theatrics and innovations.

During this time, Bowie produced Lou Reed's *Transformer* album and Mott the Hoople's *All the Young Dudes*. He also discussed his bisexuality in an interview with the British music magazine *Melody Maker*. The resulting controversy lingered on for years. Later Bowie told Kurt Loder in *Rolling Stone:* "The biggest mistake I ever made ... was telling that ... writer that I was bisexual. Christ, I was so *young* then. I was *experimenting*."

Aladdin Sane was released in the spring of 1973, while the world was still enchanted by Ziggy Stardust. In June of that year, Bowie gave up the Ziggy Stardust persona which started a trend that would continue throughout his career. The shock of this announcement was heightened by the fact that it was made on the last date of the Ziggy Stardust tour and not even members of Bowie's band had known about it ahead of time.

Bowie then went to France and started to work on his next album *Pin Ups*, which was released in the fall of 1973. It was in homage to the artists who had influenced him when he was starting out in the music industry. Six months later saw the release of *Diamond Dogs*, which was a reaction to the disco music that was slowly starting to inundate society. The success of Bowie's biggest American tour to date was chronicled on *David Live*, a recording of the Philadelphia concert.

Bowie's fascination with America manifested itself on his 1975 release *Young Americans.* It gave Bowie his first American number one single, "Fame," which was a collaboration with John Lennon that barely made the album. Shortly after the release of the album, Bowie moved to Los Angles and began his film career with a role in the 1976 movie *The Man Who Fell to Earth.* Also that year, Bowie released *Station to Station* and RCA released his first greatest hits album *Changesonebowie.*

Not long after this, Bowie moved to Berlin and began collaborations with avante garde experimentalists Brian Eno and Robert Fripp. According to Bowie's official web site, the vibe of the Berlin recording sessions with Fripp and Eno featured "surrealism and experimentation [as] the themes of the day. The incorporation of cut and paste techniques into unique instrumentation birthed what are now heralded as luminary ambient soundscapes." *Low,* which was released in 1977, perplexed both RCA and Bowie's fans although the single "Sound & Vision" made it to number two on the British pop charts. During this time, Bowie also produced and collaborated on *The Idiot* by his friend Iggy Pop.

Stage was released in the fall of 1978 and featured material culled from Bowie's Berlin period and material from his most recent American concert tour. He then relocated to Switzerland before setting off on expeditions to the continents of Asia and Africa. His next album *Lodger* was recorded in France and released in the spring of 1979. In September of the following year, Bowie made his debut on a Broadway stage in the role of the Elephant Man. He received numerous positive reviews for his performance. Around the same time as his Broadway debut, Bowie divorced his wife, Angela Barnet.

Bowie chose to drop out of the music scene for awhile, in order to concentrate on acting. His first film role during his self-imposed sabbatical was in *The Hunger,* which was released in 1982. This was followed very closely by *Merry Christmas Mr. Lawrence.* RCA released his second greatest hits package *Changestwobowie* in that year as well.

With the 1983 signing of Bowie to EMI came the release of yet another of his signature albums *Let's Dance.* Jay Cocks of *Time* called it a "record of shrewd and unsentimental dynamism." It introduced the former Thin White Duke and Ziggy Stardust to a whole new generation of fans through videos on MTV. *Let's Dance* included the hit singles "Let's Dance," "Modern Love," and "China Girl," which was a collaboration between Bowie and Pop from their time spent in Berlin. His next album, *Tonite,* was released in 1984. Three years later saw the release of *Never Let Me Down.*

In 1988, Bowie announced the formation of his new band Tin Machine. This was notable for two reasons. It was the first time Bowie would be part of a group as opposed to a solo singer with a backing band. Also, as Bowie was quick to point out, this was to be a collaborative effort, not a Bowie side project. Virgin released Tin Machine's self titled debut album in 1989. Tin Machine signed to Victory and released *Tin Machine II* in 1991. The following year, the live album *Oy Vey Baby* was released. In 1992, Tin Machine was put on indefinite hold as Bowie decided to revive his solo career.

Bowie toured the world in support of the Rykodisc box set *Sound + Vision.* This tour served as the long awaited and much anticipated greatest hits tour. On April 24, 1992, not far from his home in Switzerland, Bowie wed his second wife, the Somalian model, Iman. The following year brought the Virgin release *Black Tie White Noise,* which was also informally called the wedding album in honor of his nuptials from the previous year. It marked the first solo Bowie record since 1987. Two years later, Bowie was once again collaborating with Eno, this time on *Outside.*

In 1995, Bowie toured the United States with the group Nine Inch Nails, and featured his songs from *Outside.* In 1996, he was inducted into the Rock and Roll Hall of Fame, starred in the film *Basquiat,* and released the Internet-only single "Telling Lies." One of the challenges Bowie faced in 1997 was the marketing and selling of the "Bowie Bonds." The sale of the bonds enabled him to obtain royalty money up front as opposed to waiting for it. The bonds were backed by the future royalties from his albums which were released prior to 1990. He also released *Earthling* in 1997.

Bowie has developed a solid reputation in the art world as an artist and writer. According to the Virgin Records website, during 1996 and 1997 Bowie had art exhibitions in Switzerland, Italy, and England. He also sold art exclusively through his "Bowieart" website, and his interview with the late pop artist Roy Lichtenstein was published in the January 1998 issue of *Interview.* In May of 1997, Bowie and three colleagues founded *21 Publishing* in Great Britain. According to the "Bowieart" website, "21 aims to address the cultural issues of the 21st century and will create a platform for new words, new images and new ideas."

Nicholas Roeg, who directed Bowie in *The Man Who Fell to Earth,* summed up the Bowie mystique to Cocks of *Time* as "David's a real living Renaissance figure. That's what makes him spectacular. He goes away and re-emerges bigger than before. He doesn't have a fashion, he's just constantly expanding. It's the world that has to stop occasionally and say 'My God, he's still going on.'"

Selected discography

David Bowie: Man of Words/Man of Music (includes "Space Oddity"), Mercury, 1969, later reissued as *Space Oddity*, RCA, 1984.
The Man Who Sold the World, Mercury, 1971.
Hunky Dory (includes "Changes" and "Life on Mars), RCA, 1972.
The Rise and Fall of Ziggy Stardust and the Spiders from Mars (includes "Ziggy Stardust"), RCA, 1972.
Aladdin Sane, RCA, 1973.
Pin Ups, RCA, 1973.
Diamond Dogs, RCA, 1974.
David Live, RCA, 1974.
Young Americans (includes "Fame"), RCA, 1975.
Changesonebowie, RCA, 1976.
Station to Station, RCA, 1976.
Low (includes "Sound & Vision"), RCA, 1977.
Heroes, RCA, 1977.
Stage, RCA, 1978.
Lodger, RCA, 1979.
Scary Monsters, RCA, 1980.
Changestwobowie, RCA, 1982.
Let's Dance (includes "Let's Dance," "Modern Love," and "China Girl"), EMI, 1983.
Tonight, EMI, 1984.
Never Let Me Down, EMI, 1987.
Sound + Vision, Rykodisc, 1989.
Tin Machine, Virgin, 1989.
Tin Machine II, Victory, 1991.
Oy Vey Baby, Victory, 1992.
Black Tie White Noise, Virgin, 1993.
Outside, Virgin, 1995.
Earthling, Virgin, 1997.

Sources

On-line

"Bowieart," http://www.bowieart.com (March 9, 1998).
"David Bowie," *Celeb site,* http://www.celebsite.com/people/davidbowie/ (March 9, 1998).
"David Bowie," http://www.davidbowie.com/2.0/history/biography (February 13, 1998).
"David Bowie," http://www.virginrecords.com/artists (February 13, 1998).

Books

Buckley, David, *David Bowie,* Omnibus, 1996.
Thompson, Dave, and Dave Thomson, *David Bowie: Moonage Daydream,* Plexus Pub, 1994.
Tremlett, George, *David Bowie: Living on the Brink,* Carroll & Graf, 1997.

Periodicals

Amusement Business, October 30, 1995, p. 8.
Billboard, August 2, 1997, p. 6.
CFO, April 1997, p. 20.
Entertainment Weekly, April 4, 1997, p. 26; November 14, 1997, p. 89.
Fortune, April 28, 1997, p. 50.
Interview, May 1993, pp. 92-97; February 1997, pp. 46-50.
People, May 18, 1992, p. 72.
Rolling Stone, May 12, 1983; October 25, 1984; April 23, 1987.
Time, July 18, 1983, pp. 54-60; February 17, 1997, p. 70.

—Mary Alice Adams

Scotty Bowman

Courtesy of John Giamundo/B. Bennett

Professional hockey coach

Born William Scott Bowman, September 18, 1933, in Montreal, Quebec, Canada; son of John and Jane Thomson (Scott) Bowman; married Suella Belle Chitty (a nurse), August 16, 1969; children: Alicia Jean, Stanley Glen, David Scott, Nancy Elizabeth and Robert Gordon (twins). *Education:* Attended Sir George Williams Business School, 1954.

Addresses: *Office*—c/o Detroit Red Wings, Joe Louis Arena, 600 Civic Center Dr., Detroit, MI 48226-4408.

Career

Junior Canadiens Hockey Club assistant coach, 1956-58; Club de Hockey Canadien (Montreal Canadiens Hockey Club), Montreal, scout executive, 1958-66, head coach, 1971-79; St. Louis Blues Hockey Club, head coach 1966-71, general manager, 1970-71; Buffalo Sabres Hockey Club, head coach, general manager, and director of hockey operations, 1979-86; Hockey Night in Canada television program, hockey analyst, 1987-90; Pittsburgh Penguins Hockey Club, director of player personnel, 1990-91, interim head coach, 1991-92, head coach, 1992-93; Detroit Red Wings Hockey Club, director of player personnel and head coach, 1993—.

Awards: Stanley Cup as head coach of Montreal Canadiens, 1973, 1976, 1977, 1978, 1979, as head coach of Pittsburgh Penguins, 1992, as head coach of Detroit Red Wings, 1997, 1998; Jack Adams award, 1977, 1996; Victor Award for NHL coach of the year, 1993, 1996, for Stanley Cup Championship, 1997; *Sporting News* NHL executive of the year, 1979-80; inducted into Hockey Hall of Fame, 1991.

Sidelights

Hockey coach Scotty Bowman holds the record for most number of games won in the history of the National Hockey League (NHL) and backs it up with eight Stanley Cup rings, tying for most coaching victories with the legendary Toe Blake. Starting out with junior leagues, he worked his way into a scouting position with the Montreal Canadiens and eventually began coaching a new expansion team, the St. Louis Blues, 1967. He returned to coach the Canadiens in 1971 and landed five Stanley Cups in his eight years there. After a stormy few seasons with the Buffalo Sabres from 1979 to 1986, Bowman retired for a few years before taking to the bench again in 1990 with the Pittsburgh Penguins, leading them to a cup in 1992. When the Detroit Red Wings summoned his skills the following year, he had the opportunity to call his own shots and took the job as a personal challenge, since the team had not won a championship since 1955. He stuck with it, and in 1997 and 1998, landed back-to-back Stanley Cups in Detroit. Known to be abrasive yet fair, Bowman commands respect from players and knows how to manage them to extract their best performance. "The players have to know what you stand for," Bowman stated in the *Sporting News*. "Times have changed immensely, but I don't think our standards and demands change.... You have to lay down what you expect from the start and not make any 90-degree turns."

Bowman was born William Scott Bowman on September 18, 1933, in Montreal, Quebec, Canada, to Scottish immigrants from Dundee. His father, John, pounded sheet metal for 31 years for the railroad, teaching him the value of hard work. His mother, Jane, instilled a sense of competitiveness. Bowman was the second-oldest of four children and grew up in Verdun, a blue-collar suburb of Montreal. When he was young, Bowman skated down his street to the city ice rinks and learned to play hockey. The slight, fast player had promise; by age 17, he was a forward for the prestigious Junior Canadiens hockey team and had caught the attention of the pro league. A terrible ordeal, however, would shatter his future as a player.

In a Junior A playoff game in the early 1950s with the Three Rivers Reds at the Montreal Forum, Bowman broke away alone and scored a goal with defenseman Jean-Guy Talbot on his heels. Facing defeat, Talbot swung his stick twice at Bowman in the heat of frustration. Back in those days, players did not wear helmets. The stick caught Bowman first on the shoulder, then the head, sending him down. When he lifted his hand up to his head, a piece of his skull came off. "It was like being scalped," Bowman told E. M. Swift in *Sports Illustrated*. Talbot received a temporary suspension, but went on to play 17 years in the NHL. Bowman had a metal plate inserted in his head and veered into coaching. Later, the incident long behind him, Bowman chose Talbot to play for him when he was coaching the St. Louis Blues, and the two worked together for three years. Bowman never held a grudge.

Bowman began coaching 12- and 13-year-old youth hockey, then graduated to 14- and 15-year-olds. He also attended college briefly at Sir George Williams Business School in 1954. At age 22, Bowman was coaching 20-year-olds at the Junior B level, earning $250 a year for his efforts while also working at a paint company. In 1956, at age 23, the coach and general manager of the Junior Canadiens, Sam Pollock, asked Bowman to be his assistant. The team that year moved to Ottawa and Bowman went along. In 1958, they landed the top honors in junior hockey, the Memorial Cup, and Bowman subsequently moved up to coaching a Junior A team in Peterborough, Ontario. After three seasons with the team, he joined the Montreal Canadiens as their head talent scout for eastern Canada.

Bowman would work as a scout until 1966, but meanwhile, began to miss coaching and went back to the Junior Canadiens during the 1963-64 season. There he

met Toe Blake, coach of the Montreal Canadiens, the only other NHL coach to win eight Stanley Cups. "[Blake] knew how each of his players did against everyone else. Certain guys do well against one team but not another. He was a good strategist and a good matchup man and wasn't afraid to sit guys out to change his ammunition." In 1966, Bowman was hired as assistant coach for the expansion team the St. Louis Blues starting in their first season, 1967-68, overseeing the defense. By the end of the year, coach Lynn Patrick stepped back and let Bowman take over, leading the team to a third-place finish in the Western Division. In 1969 and 1970, the Blues took the Western Division title and went on to the Stanley Cup finals.

In addition to coaching, Bowman took over as general manager of the Blues in 1970, but saw his team slip to second place in the division in 1971, losing in the first round of the Stanley Cup playoffs to the Minnesota North Stars. After that loss, the son of the owner of the Blues dismissed a couple of players, and Bowman resigned as well. The move was not wise on the part of the Blues, who have not yet seen a Stanley Cup win. Pollack, meanwhile, had become the general manager of the Canadiens and hired Bowman in 1971 to coach the team in the same arena where he had lost part of his skull about two decades prior. Bowman was taking over a legacy rich with Stanley Cup wins. "That creates pressure," Bowman told Dave Anderson in the *New York Times*. "But it's also a plus. That pressure works to your advantage. You know the whole city is watching you. You know the tradition of the club. And all that makes you work harder to accomplish what you know everyone expects you to accomplish."

Of course, it was perhaps easy for Bowman to make those comments in retrospect, after he had led the team to five victories in his eight years as head coach. The Montreal Canadiens under Bowman took the Stanley Cup in 1973, 1976, 1977, 1978, and 1979. There, he developed his reputation as a tough leader, but one who did not play favorites. Aloof and somewhat shy, Bowman did not pal around with his team, and he did not care about hurting someone's feelings by making them sit out a game, placing the desire to win above all else. Players did not like him, but they gave him respect. Bowman did not condescend to them or berate them, preferring to treat them as professionals; he was known to ignore violations of curfew and rules, instead focusing on performance.

When Montreal overlooked Bowman for a general manager job, he left in 1979 to join the Buffalo Sabres as their GM and head coach. He had a rocky road with this team. Used to being gruff and demanding, his style often did not set well with this set of younger, less experienced players. He left the bench after his first season with the team, but then waffled on his choice of coaches. After promoting assistant coach Roger Neilson to head coach in 1980-81, Bowman later ended up taking over instead. He then hired Jimmy Roberts, but stepped back in as coach late in the 1981-82 season. Bowman retired from coaching in the mid-1980s and hired Jim Schoenfeld, but ended up back on the bench. Bowman in the mid-1980s set a record for the most regular-season victories of any coach in NHL history, but the Sabres were still scraping along. In late 1986 the team fired him.

Bowman spent three years as an analyst for the popular Hockey Night in Canada television program on CBC from 1987 to 1990, but as usual, missed the thrill of coaching. He signed on to the Pittsburgh Penguins as director of player personnel in 1990 and the next year, the team, with star Mario Lemieux, won a Stanley Cup under coach Bob Johnson. Johnson was diagnosed with brain cancer during the summer, and Bowman was subsequently appointed head coach. He changed his style slightly in order to get the same results as Johnson had. "I knew I had to be different. If you're critical of a player today, especially openly, it's perceived as being negative.... You have to stroke them more." At the end of the 1992 season, the Penguins shot through 11 straight playoff wins to take home the Stanley Cup—Bowman's fifth championship as head coach.

Bowman stayed with Pittsburgh another season and was then beckoned to Detroit, where the Red Wings had not handled Lord Stanley's coveted cup since 1955. One of the original six NHL teams, Detroit had a long history with the sport, but not a proud record since the heyday of the revered Gordie Howe. While with the Wings, Bowman set a record for coaching the most games in NHL history when he stood behind the bench at Dallas's Reunion Arena on December 29, 1995, for number 1,607. By 1997, he had surpassed the 2,000-game mark. In 1995, fans were revved up when he took the Wings all the way to the final round of the playoffs, but spirits fell when the New Jersey Devils wiped out the Wings in four straight games. In 1996, they lost to the Colorado Avalanche in six games in the conference finals, but that year, they did set a record for most wins in a single season, surpassing the record set by the Montreal Canadiens under Bowman's leadership back in the 1970s.

The team was back with a vengeance in 1997 after honing the talents of their famous Russian Five defensive crew, building up the skill of left wingers Darren McCarty and Martin Lapointe, and acquiring key trades, such as Brendan Shanahan. Finally, under the leadership of Bowman and longtime captain Steve Yzerman, who had been on the team 14 years, the Wings swept the Philadelphia Flyers in the first four games of the 1997 Stanley Cup playoffs. In a rare display of glee, Bowman, smiling broadly, laced up his skates and joined the players on the ice for his turn at carrying the trophy. An estimated one million fans flocked to downtown Detroit to honor the Wings in a victory parade the following week.

Speculation swirled as to whether Bowman would be back the next season for a stab at tying Toe Blake's record for most Stanley Cup wins by a coach. He admitted to Larry Wigge in the *Sporting News*, "I've always had a warm spot in my heart for the Stanley Cup. So, when my wife and I had our first son, we named him Stanley." The lure of number eight perhaps did draw him back, as did his dedication to the team. At the start of the 1997-98 season, the Wings were still reeling from the loss of its top defenseman, Vladimir Konstantinov, who, along with the team trainer Sergei Mnatsakanov, was seriously injured and paralyzed in a limousine accident shortly after the 1997 victory. It was also suffering the absence of star player Sergei Federov, who sat out most of the season in a salary dispute, and prize-winning goaltender Mike Vernon, who was traded to the San Jose Sharks. However, Bowman maintained control. "He's got an entire team that believes in him and trusts him and we don't have a single guy that ever sulks or questions any of his moves," assistant captain Shanahan remarked to Jim Smith in *Newsday*. "So regardless of what our game plan is, he's got 20 guys going out and not questioning it." They were smart to follow instructions, because Bowman once again led the Red Wings to the Stanley Cup victory in 1998, eliminating Washington Capitals in just four games.

Bowman met a nurse, Suella Belle Chitty, in St. Louis in 1967, and they were married on August 16, 1969. They have five children: Alicia Jean, Stanley Glen, David Scott, and a set of twins, Nancy Elizabeth and Robert Gordon. The family has kept their home in Buffalo since Bowman's coaching stint there, despite his subsequent career moves; he and his wife commute to see each other between Buffalo and Bowman's rented townhome in the Detroit suburb of Bloomfield Hills. Their son David was born with hydrocephalus, an overabundance of fluid in the skull, which causes mental degeneration. Bowman is an aficionado of classic cars, driving a 1950 Chrysler Town & Country with real wood sides. Only 698 were made, and only 65 are in existence. Bowman knows these figures and many more; his amazing ability to recall statistics and numbers won him the nickname "Rain Man," after the Tom Cruise-Dustin Hoffman film, from some of his players. Bowman also collects toy trains from as far back as the 1930s, but has not had the opportunity to set them up for many years due to his hectic schedule. Due to extensive health problems that began to plague him during the 1997-98 season, it is unclear whether Bowman will return to the game, but his legacy will surely stand.

Sources

Detroit News, September 7, 1997.

Gannett News Service, May 1, 1997.

Knight-Ridder/Tribune News Service, December 28, 1995; April 16, 1996; April 22, 1997.

Newsday, June 16, 1998, p. A83.

New York Times, May 21, 1979; November 22, 1984.

Rocky Mountain News, May 19, 1997, p. 4N.

Sports Illustrated, May 10, 1993, p. 58; June 16, 1997, p. 28; June 18, 1997, p. 82; June 29, 1998, p. 64.

Sporting News, December 12, 1994, p. 12; February 10, 1997, p. 43; August 4, 1997, p. 40.

St. Louis Post-Dispatch, February 22, 1997, p. 6.

—Geri Speace

Ellen Bravo

Courtesy of Ellen Bravo

Co-Director, 9to5: National Association of Working Women

Born March 25, 1944, in Cleveland, OH; daughter of James and Dorothy Bravo; married Larry Miller; children: Nat, Craig. *Education:* Cornell University, B.A., 1966; Cambridge University, M.A., 1968; McGill University, postgraduate studies, 1970.

Addresses: *Office*—9to5: National Association of Working Women, 231 West Wisconsin Ave., Suite 900, Milwaukee, WI 53203-2308.

Career

St. Mary's College, St. Mary's City, MD, instructor in women's studies, early 1970s; San Diego University, San Diego, CA, instructor in women's studies, early 1970s; worked in an office in Milwaukee, WI, early 1980s; 9to5: National Association of Working Women, founder of Milwaukee chapter, 1982, co-director of national organization, 1993—; University of Wisconsin at Milwaukee, instructor, late 1980s; member of Commission on the Skills of the U.S. Workforce; appointed to federal commission to study impact of 1993 Family and Medical Leave Act.

Awards: Stateswoman of the Year, Wisconsin's Women's Network, 1989; Gloria Steinem Women of Vision Award, *Ms.* Foundation for Women, 1997.

Sidelights

In 1993 Ellen Bravo became co-director of 9to5: National Association of Working Women, an influential organization that works to insure equal pay, healthy and harassment-free workplaces, and more balanced personal and professional lives for millions of American women. Bravo, herself a working mother, founded the Milwaukee chapter of 9to5 in 1982, but had a long career as an activist, women's-studies instructor, and advocate for fairness in the workplace already behind her. In her books, newspaper columns, public-speaking engagements, and other work on behalf of 9to5, Bravo has emphasized the fact that most women need to work, usually for financial reasons, and that balancing the demands of work and family life can be extremely stressful. Her organization aims to educate employers, via public-awareness and political lobbying, of the need to adapt to this reality.

Bravo was born in 1944 in Cleveland, Ohio, one of three children whose mother worked so that the family could save money toward the children's college tuition. When Bravo's father found himself out of a job after an accident, her mother became the breadwinner of the family for a while. At the time, Bravo was a student at Shaker Heights High School, in an era when help-wanted ads were divided by gender, and was shocked to learn just how little her mother was paid in comparison to her father.

A few years later, she struggled herself with the inner conflict over whether to settle down with a husband and family, as many women of her day did, or to pursue academic and professional goals. "I remember sitting on the steps of a building at college, agonizing over how to choose between marriage and children on the one hand and a career on the other," Bravo wrote in her second book, *The Job/Family Challenge: A 9to5 Guide.* One of her professors happened upon her that day in 1963, and she related her dilemma to him. He told her he knew of at least three women who had successfully accomplished both, and so "I decided I'd try to be one of the exceptions," Bravo wrote.

Bravo studied classical languages at Cornell University, from which she earned a literature degree in 1966, and then went to England for further study at Cambridge University on a Fulbright scholarship. She later arrived at McGill University in Montreal, and completed all requirements for a Ph.D. except for her dissertation. Yet during the course of her college career, Bravo became active in the civil-rights movement and anti-war activism, both of which sharpened her zeal to eradicate institutionalized discrimination. In the early 1970s, she became a teacher of women's studies, first at a college in Maryland and later at San Diego University. Later in the decade, she married and began a family. She continued to work, and counted herself lucky to have a supportive partner. "Our children were in day care since infancy, and, because it was good care combined with good parenting, they've thrived," Bravo wrote in *The Job/Family Challenge.*

Yet it was as a working mother in the early 1980s that Bravo began to see just how difficult the lives of most working women really were. Some were the sole supporters in single-parent households; others were forced to take unpaid time off when their children became sick; but most problematic was the attitude of management and the business community in general. She became aware of 9to5: National Association of Working Women, which was founded in Boston in 1973 by Karen Nussbaum and Ellen Cassedy. The organization grew out of an impromptu meeting of ten women who had participated in a seminar on employment-related issues. The group 9to5 culled many of its 15,000-plus members from the secretarial and office professions, since that sector employed the majority of working women in America, and promoted a "Bill of Rights for Working Women" as the backbone of its activities: "That means the right to ... fair pay, family-friendly policies, [and] workplaces free from all forms of discrimination and harassment," according to its publicity materials.

Bravo founded the Milwaukee chapter of 9to5 in 1982, and within a few years had become one of Wisconsin's primary activists for women's workplace rights. In 1984, she was appointed as an observer to Wisconsin's Comparable Worth Task Force, which investigated gender disparities in earnings, and two years later was named to the state's Minimum Wage Advisory Council. She also became a well-known public speaker, training-seminar leader, and media pundit on workplace rights, sexual harassment, and family/career balancing issues. By the early 1990s, Bravo had moved to the national stage. Her efforts in pushing Wisconsin state legislators to enact a family-leave bill—a law that required companies to provide workers with certain rights regarding maternity and paternity leave, retaining their same jobs upon their return, and providing health-care benefits for unpaid leaves of absence—led to Bravo's appointment to the Federal Commission on Leave in 1993. She became part of a task force that studied the impact of that year's hotly contested legislative reform, the Family and Medical Leave Act (FMLA), which enforced similar benefits on a national level, covering about half the American workforce.

The year 1993 also marked another noteworthy professional achievement for Bravo—she became co-director of the 9to5's national organization, coinciding with founder and executive director Karen Nussbaum's presidential appointment to lead the Women's Bureau of the U.S. Department of Labor. Since then, Bravo has worked to bring 9to5's "Bill of Rights for Working Women" to the bargaining table at several levels. She appears often on television news programs such as *Good Morning America*, the *Today* show, and CNN's *Crossfire*. She is a regular contributor to *USA Today* and *Parenting* magazine, and has written two books. The first was authored with 9to5 founder Ellen Cassedy and published in 1992, *The 9to5 Guide to Combating Sexual Harassment.*

Bravo's next book, *The Job/Family Challenge: A 9to5 Guide,* was published in 1995. In this volume, she explains the focus behind her work, 9to5's aims, and the need for legislation such as the FMLA. Only eight percent of American families have a stay-at-home mom, Bravo pointed out, and the sometimes over-ballyhooed trend of women abandoning the workforce in order to stay at home with their children hardly reflected any return to a bygone era—"one could also argue that it's the result of the family having so little value in the workplace," Bravo noted. Furthermore, many of those women "jumping ship" were part of households that allowed them the freedom to do so, which is not the case for the majority of Americans, who either head single-parent households or need two incomes to make ends meet. "The workforce is changing, and the work*place* hasn't kept pace," Bravo declared in *The Job/Family Challenge.* For this she cast blame on the statistic that it is mostly men who comprise the highest management positions inside corporate America, many of whom have very little experience with the challenges that most Americans face daily. "In selecting upper-level managers, American corporations reward those who can meet, move, or travel at a moment's notice. Long hours on the job are a prerequisite for advancement," Bravo wrote in *The Job/Family Challenge,* and pointed out that most men who are able to climb this ladder enjoy a support system of a household managed by a wife who does not work outside the home.

Bravo was selected as a participant at the 1995 United Nations Fourth World Conference on Women in Beijing, China. Her activism on behalf of "pink-collar" workers continues, even though many of 9to5's early goals—flexible schedules, job-sharing, work-at-home options, and on-site childcare, were becoming more available as the decade progressed. "We need a new vision of success," Bravo wrote in the conclusion of *The Job/Family Challenge,* "where you don't have to sacrifice your family in order to contribute or to advance. Imagine the results if people running companies—or countries, for that matter—resembled more closely the people they serve. Chances are we wouldn't have a $700 billion deficit or 38 million people without health insurance."

Selected writings

(With Ellen Cassedy) *The 9to5 Guide to Combating Sexual Harassment,* John Wiley & Sons, 1992.
The Job/Family Challenge: A 9to5 Guide, John Wiley & Sons, 1995.

Sources

Books

Bravo, Ellen, *The Job/Family Challenge: A 9to5 Guide,* John Wiley & Sons, 1995.

Periodicals

Training and Development, October 1995, p. 64.

Additional information for this profile was obtained from publicity materials provided by 9to5: National Association of Working Women, 1998.

—*Carol Brennan*

Gwendolyn Brooks

Poet and novelist

Born June 7, 1917, in Topeka, KS; daughter of David Anderson and Keziah Corinne (Wims) Brooks; married Henry Lowington Blakely II, September 17, 1939; children: Henry Lowington III, Nora. *Education:* Graduate of Wilson Junior College, 1936.

Addresses: *Home*—5530 South Shore Drive, Apt. 2A, Chicago, IL 60637.

Career

National Association for the Advancement of Colored People (NAACP) Youth Council, Chicago, IL, publicity director, 1937-38; instructor in poetry at numerous colleges and universities, including Columbia College, Elmhurst College, Northeastern Illinois State College (now Northwestern Illinois University), and University of Wisconsin-Madison, 1969; City College of the City University of New York, Distinguished Professor of the Arts, 1971; currently professor at Chicago State University. Member, Illinois Arts Council.

Awards: Named one of ten women of the year, *Mademoiselle* magazine, 1945; National Institute of Arts and Letters grant in literature, 1946; American Academy of Arts and Letters Award for creative writing, 1946; Guggenheim fellowships, 1946 and 1947; Eunice Tietjens Memorial Prize, *Poetry* magazine, 1949; Pulitzer Prize in poetry, 1950, for *Annie Allen*; Robert F. Ferguson Memorial Award, Friends of Literature, 1964, for *Selected Poems*; Thormod Monsen Literature Award, 1964; Anisfield-Wolf Award, 1968, for *In the Mecca*; named Poet Laureate of Illinois, 1968; National Book Award nomination, for *In the Mecca*; Black Acad-

emy of Arts and Letters Award, 1971, for outstanding achievement in letters; Shelley Memorial Award, 1976; Poetry Consultant to the Library of Congress, 1985-86; inducted into National Women's Hall of Fame, 1988; *Essence* Award, 1988; Frost Medal, Poetry Society of America, 1989; Lifetime Achievement Award, National Endowment for the Arts, 1989; Society for Literature Award, University of Thessoloniki (Athens, Greece), 1990; Kuumba Liberation Award; Aiken-Taylor award, 1992; Jefferson Lecturer award, 1994; National Book Foundation medal for Lifetime Achievement, 1994; Gwendolyn Brooks Elementary School named in her honor, Aurora, Illinois, 1995; approximately fifty honorary degrees from universities and colleges, including Columbia College, 1964, Lake Forest College, 1965, and Brown University, 1974.

Member: National Institute of Arts and Letters, American Academy of Arts and Letters, Society of Midland Authors (Chicago), Cliff Dwellers Club, Tavern Club (honorary member), Caxton Club (honorary member).

Sidelights

One of the major modern poets and the first African American writer to win a Pulitzer Prize, Gwendolyn Brooks has worked at her craft for well over fifty years. While she devoted the first half of her career to producing verse characterized by traditional forms and language, she has spent the second half boldly experimenting with free verse and the urban black vernacular. Her thematic focus, however, has remained much the same—the lives of ordinary African Americans and their struggle against the devastating effects of poverty and racism. As George E. Kent noted in *Black World*, "Brooks shares with Langston Hughes the achievement of being most responsive to turbulent changes in the Black Community's vision of itself and to the changing forms of its vibrations during decades of rapid change. The depth of her responsiveness and her range of poetic resources make her one of the most distinguished poets to appear in America during the 20th Century."

Although she was born in Topeka, Kansas, in 1917, Gwendolyn Elizabeth Brooks grew up in Chicago, Illinois, and has always considered it her hometown. Her mother, Keziah Wims Brooks, was a schoolteacher, while her father, David Anderson Brooks, was a janitor who had been forced to abandon his dream of becoming a doctor because he didn't have enough money to finish school. The family also included a son, Raymond, who was sixteen months younger than his sister.

The Brooks household was a happy one, and Gwendolyn thrived on a steady diet of love and encouragement from her parents, who read stories and sang songs to their two children. The outside world, however, was somewhat less supportive. According to Kent, as a youngster Gwendolyn "was spurned by members of her own race because she lacked social or athletic abilities, a light skin, and good grade hair." Hurt by such rejection, the little girl took comfort in the solitary pursuits of reading and writing. She composed her first poem at the age of seven and by the age of eleven was regularly entering her thoughts in a notebook. "I felt that I had to write," she later explained in an *Ebony* article. "Even if I had never been published, I knew that I would go on writing, enjoying it and experiencing the challenge." When her parents discovered her aptitude for writing, they excused her from many household chores and set up a desk at which she could work.

Brooks published her first poem at the age of only thirteen in an issue of *American Child* magazine; over the next few years, she frequently contributed to the *Chicago Defender*, one of the nation's most distinguished African American newspapers. During high school, she devoted much of her time to studying poetry and writing and even struck up a correspondence with promi-

nent African American poets Langston Hughes and James Weldon Johnson, whose readings she had attended in Chicago. Brooks asked each of them to critique some of her work, and while both were complimentary and offered helpful suggestions, Hughes was especially enthusiastic and influential. (He and Brooks later became good friends.) His words of encouragement meant a great deal to the young woman and helped ease any doubts she had that black urban life could inspire worthwhile poetry.

By the age of sixteen, Brooks had compiled a substantial portfolio, including about seventy-five published poems. After completing high school in 1935, she attended Wilson Junior College and graduated with a degree in English in 1936. Brooks then worked briefly as a cleaning woman and secretary to a "spiritual advisor" who sold potions and charms to residents of the Mecca, a Chicago tenement building. In 1937, she became the publicity director of the local National Association for the Advancement of Colored People (NAACP) Youth Council.

Around 1941, Brooks began taking part in poetry workshops at Chicago's South Side Community Art Center. They were taught by Inez Cunningham Stark, a wealthy writer and scholar from the city's famous "Gold Coast" who had an interest in cultivating the talents of aspiring black poets. She introduced her pupils—more than a few of whom went on to successful writing careers—to a wide variety of verse, with a particular emphasis on contemporary works, and guided them to an understanding of the principles of poetry. Furthermore, she allowed them to develop their own poetic voices, even if those voices were at odds with what she herself appreciated. "This class of [Stark's] was very alive," Brooks later recalled in her autobiography, *Report from Part One*. "We were encouraged to tear each other to pieces.... It helped me to have somebody tell me what he thought was wrong with my work, and then bounce the analysis back and forth." Brooks blossomed under this form of instruction and produced poems that soon began to garner a fair amount of attention in and around Chicago.

In 1943, Brooks won a poetry award from the Midwestern Writers' Conference. Not long afterward, she pulled together a group of her poems and submitted them to Harper & Row for publication. Editors there liked what they saw, and in 1945 the collection appeared under the title *A Street in Bronzeville*. In its pages, Brooks chronicles the everyday lives, aspirations, and disappointments of ordinary black Americans living in Bronzeville, a Chicago neighborhood that serves as the setting for many of her poems. The first part of *A Street in Bronzeville* provides a realistic depiction of the area and its residents; the second section explores the unfair treatment of African Americans in the U.S. Armed Forces during World War II. In these poems, Brooks introduced thematic issues that would feature prominently in her works during the next two decades—family life, war, the quest for contentment and honor, and the hardships caused by racism and poverty.

A Street in Bronzeville was met with widespread critical acclaim, and Brooks was lauded as a major new voice in contemporary poetry for her technical expertise, innovative use of imagery and idiom, and fresh perspective on the lives of African Americans. Shortly after its publication, she was awarded a Guggenheim fellowship, and *Mademoiselle* magazine named her one of its "Ten Women of the Year."

Brooks's second collection of poetry, *Annie Allen* (1949), garnered even more praise and attention, including the first Pulitzer Prize ever given to an African American writer. Similar in structure to a prose narrative, the poems in *Annie Allen* tell the story of an African American woman's journey from childhood to adulthood in an environment marked by poverty and discrimination. Critics generally praised Brooks for her subtle humor and irony, her skillful handling of conventional stanzaic forms, and her invention of the sonnet-ballad, a verse structure that integrates colloquial speech and formal diction.

Brooks followed up this award-winning effort with an autobiographical novel, *Maud Martha* (1953), which examines racism, sexism, and classism through the eyes of an African American woman just before, during, and after World War II. Often overlooked, it is, according to several critics, nearly as lyrical and as affecting as any of Brooks's poems. Her next major collection of poetry, *The Bean Eaters* (1960), deals with the integration of the school system in Little Rock, Arkansas, the lynchings of black men across the South, and the well-meaning but misguided efforts of white liberals to help African Americans. Written during the early years of the civil rights movement, it reflects Brooks's growing interest in social issues. Her poetic style also underwent a transformation of sorts around this time as she began to rely less on traditional forms in favor of experimenting with free verse.

In 1967, Brooks attended the Second Black Writers' Conference at Fisk University. Witnessing the energy, confidence, and combative spirit of many of the young authors she met there (including LeRoi Jones, now known as Imamu Amiri Baraka; Larry Neal; Ron

Milner; and Don L. Lee, now known as Haki R. Madhubuti) proved to be a life-changing experience. Brooks left the gathering with a new political consciousness and artistic direction shaped by the tenets of black cultural nationalism. As she later explained in the book *Black Women Writers at Work,* the new generation of black activists and artists she became acquainted with at Fisk "seemed proud and so committed to their own people.... The poets among them felt that black poets should write as blacks, about blacks, and address themselves to blacks." As for herself, Brooks noted in her autobiography, "I—who have 'gone the gamut' from an almost angry rejection of my dark skin by some of my brainwashed brothers and sisters to a surprised queenhood in the new Black sun—am qualified to enter at least the kindergarten of new consciousness now.... I have hopes for myself."

> *"What I'm fighting for now in my work, [is] for an* expression *relevant to all manner of blacks, poems I could take into a tavern, into the street, into the halls of a housing project.... I want to* clarify *my language. I want these poems to be free. I want them to be direct without sacrificing the kinds of music, the picturemaking I've always been interested in."*

With the collection entitled *In the Mecca* (1968), which most critics regard as a transitional work, Brooks abandoned the traditional poetic forms of her earlier pieces in favor of free verse and increased her use of vernacular to make her poetry more accessible to black readers. Summarizing the differences between her old and new style, the poet herself wrote in *Say That the River Turns: The Impact of Gwendolyn Brooks,* "The forties and fifties were years of high poet-incense; the language-flowers were thickly sweet. Those flowers whined and begged white folks to pick them, to find them lovable. Then—the sixties: Independent fire!" In an effort to support black publishers, Brooks also made another major change at this point in her career, leaving her longtime publisher Harper & Row for Broadside Press, a small, Detroit-based company operated by African American poet Dudley Randall.

Poverty, unfulfilled dreams, and violence figure prominently as themes of *In the Mecca,* which are based on Brooks's experiences working in the Chicago tenement building known as the Mecca. The title poem, for example, traces a mother's search for her missing daughter, whom she later discovers has been murdered by a fellow resident. Other pieces in the collection are dedicated to slain black activists Medgar Evers and Malcolm X as well as to the Blackstone Rangers, a Chicago street gang.

In *Riot* (1969) and *Family Pictures* (1970), Brooks examined the social upheavals of the late 1960s with objectivity and compassion. Writing in *A Life Distilled: Gwendolyn Brooks, Her Poetry and Fiction,* Norris B. Clark noted that with these works, the poet's "emphasis shifted from a private, internal, and exclusive assessment of the identity crises of twentieth-century persons to a communal, external, and inclusive assessment of the black communal experience." As Brooks herself explained in *Black Women Writers at Work,* "What I'm fighting for now in my work, [is] for an *expression* relevant to all manner of blacks, poems I could take into a tavern, into the street, into the halls of a housing project. I don't want to say that these poems have to be simple, but I want to *clarify* my language. I want these poems to be free. I want them to be direct without sacrificing the kinds of music, the picturemaking I've always been interested in."

Revolution, black power, and black nationalism continued to dominate Brooks's verse during the early 1970s. By the end of the decade, however, the energy and optimism that had characterized *Riot* and *Family Pictures* were replaced with disenchantment as a result of the discord that had developed between the civil rights and black power movements. In *Beckonings* (1975) and *To Disembark* (1981), a more radical Brooks urged blacks to break free from the repression of white American society and advocated violence and anarchy as acceptable means of doing so.

Critics have occasionally debated the literary quality of Brooks's post-1967 poetry. Some have faulted her for sacrificing formal complexity and subtlety for political polemic. Others, however, have noted that she displays the same technical skill as always and the same compassion and understanding that marked her earlier works. And nearly all agree that no matter what the content or form of her poems, Brooks has always remained devoted to what Lerone Bennett described in *Say That the River Turns* as "the sounds, sights and flavors of the Black community." As D.H. Melhem observed in the book *Gwendolyn Brooks: Poetry and the Heroic Voice,* she "enriches both black and white cultures by revealing essential life, its universal identities, and the challenge it poses to a society beset with corruption and decay."

In addition to her own writing, Brooks has actively encouraged other poets through teaching, lecturing, sponsoring poetry competitions, giving poetry readings, and visiting schools, prisons, and other institutions. As poet laureate of Illinois since 1968, she established and continues to support the Poet Laureate Awards competition for young writers in her state in an effort to promote poetry among schoolchildren. In recognition of her many accomplishments, Brooks has received over seventy honorary degrees, a lifetime achievement award from the National Endowment for the Arts, the National Book Foundation Award for Distinguished Contribution to American Letters, and induction into the National Women's Hall of Fame. She served as Consultant in Poetry to the Library of Congress from 1985-86, and in 1994, the National Endowment for the Humanities named her its Jefferson Lecturer, the government's highest honor for achievement in the humanities.

Brooks rejects the notion of retirement, declaring that she sees no reason to stop doing what she loves. "I think there are things for all of us to do as long as we're here and we're healthy," she remarked in *Ebony.* Besides, she went on to point out, "I've always thought of myself as a reporter. When people ask why I don't stop writing, I say, 'Look at what's happening in this world. Every day there's something exciting or disturbing to write about.' With all that's going on, how could I stop?"

Selected writings

A Street in Bronzeville (poetry), Harper (New York City), 1945.

Annie Allen (poetry), Harper, 1949, reprinted, Greenwood Press, 1972.

Maud Martha (novel), Harper, 1953.

Bronzeville Boys and Girls (juvenile), Harper, 1956.

The Bean Eaters (poetry), Harper, 1960.

Selected Poems (poetry), Harper, 1963.

In the Mecca (poetry), Harper, 1968.

Riot (poetry), Broadside Press (Highland Park, MI), 1969.

Family Pictures (poetry), Broadside Press, 1970.

(Editor) *A Broadside Treasury* (poetry), Broadside Press, 1971.

(Editor) *Jump Bad: A New Chicago Anthology,* Broadside Press, 1971.

Aloneness (poetry), Broadside Press, 1971.

Report from Part One: An Autobiography, Broadside Press, 1972.

Aurora (poetry), Broadside Press, 1972.

The Tiger Who Wore White Gloves: Or You Are What You Are (juvenile), Third World Press, 1974, reissued, 1987.

Beckonings (poetry), Broadside Press, 1975.

To Disembark (poetry), Third World Press (Chicago, IL), 1981.

Young Poet's Primer (writing manual), Brooks Press, 1981.

Black Love (poetry), Brooks Press, 1982.

Very Young Poets (writing manual), Brooks Press, 1983.

The Near-Johannesburg Boy, and Other Poems (poetry), David Co., 1987.

Gottschalk and the Grande Tarantelle (poetry), David Co., 1988.

Winnie (poetry), Third World Press, 1988.

Children Coming Home (poetry), David Co., 1991.

Sources

Books

Bigsby, C.W.E., *The Second Black Renaissance: Essays in Black Literature,* Greenwood Press, 1980.

Brooks, Gwendolyn, *Report from Part One: An Autobiography,* Broadside Press, 1972.

Brown, Patricia L., Don L. Lee, and Francis Ward, editors, *To Gwen with Love: An Anthology Dedicated to Gwendolyn Brooks,* Johnson Publishing, 1971.

Evans, Mari, editor, *Black Women Writers (1950-1980): A Critical Evaluation,* Anchor Press/Doubleday, 1984.

Kent, George E., *Gwendolyn Brooks: A Life,* University Press of Kentucky, 1988.

Madhubuti, Haki R., editor, *Say That the River Turns: The Impact of Gwendolyn Brooks,* Third World Press, 1987.

Melhem, D.H., *Gwendolyn Brooks: Poetry and the Heroic Voice,* University Press of Kentucky, 1987.

Mootry, Maria K., and Gary Smith, editors, *A Life Distilled: Gwendolyn Brooks, Her Poetry and Fiction,* University of Illinois Press, 1987.

Shaw, Harry F., *Gwendolyn Brooks,* Twayne, 1980.

Tate, Claudia, editor, *Black Women Writers at Work,* Continuum, 1983.

Periodicals

Black World, September, 1971.

CLA Journal, September, 1972, pp. 23-31.

Ebony, June, 1987.

Jet, February 21, 1994.

—Deborah Gillan Straub

Kobe Bryant

AP/Wide World Photos

Basketball player

Born August 23, 1978, in Philadelphia, PA; son of Joe (a basketball player and coach) and Pam (a homemaker) Bryant. *Education:* Graduated from Lower Merion High School, Ardmore, PA.

Addresses: *Home*—Pacific Palisades, CA. *Office*—Los Angeles Lakers, 401 South Prairie, Inglewood, CA 90301-2824.

Career

As a high school basketball star, was the all-time leading scorer in Southeastern Pennsylvania history; youngest player to enter the National Basketball Association (NBA), 1996; drafted by Charlotte Hornets, then traded to Los Angeles Lakers, 1996; youngest player to start an NBA game, 1997; won Nestle Crunch Slam Dunk, 1997, during the All-Star Weekend in Cleveland, OH; youngest player to be chosen for the NBA All-Star Game, 1998.

Awards: Gatorade Circle of Champions High School Player of the Year, 1996; Naismith Player of the Year, 1996; *USA Today* and *Parade* magazine National High School Player of the Year, 1996; named to the McDonald's All-America Team, 1996.

Sidelights

There is a popular rallying cry for youth of the day to "be like Mike," meaning Michael Jordan, the undisputable superstar of 1990s basketball—but the new kid on the court, Kobe Bryant, has taken that catch phrase to heart. Magazines have extolled Bryant as the next Jordan, as headlines like "Air Apparent" (*Newsweek*) and "Boy Wonder" (*People Weekly*) began to appear after the high school senior became the youngest player to enter the NBA. His stats may not have reached the stratosphere, but with such a short time in the pros, fans should have plenty to look forward to from this exciting talent.

Bryant was born on August 23, 1978, in Philadelphia, Pennsylvania, into an atmosphere of basketball. His father, Joe "Jellybean" Bryant, spent eight seasons in the NBA, mostly with the Philadelphia 76ers. Bryant's parents set up a pint-size court behind their home when Kobe was just three so that the boy could mimic his dad. His mother, Pam, was a homemaker, and the family also included Bryant's two sisters, Shaya and Sharia. When Kobe was five, the family moved to Italy so the elder Bryant could play pro basketball there. Bryant's father told the *Sporting News* that the experience helped to shape his son: "Living in Italy was the key. [Our kids learned] maturity and responsibility." Though Kobe did not know how to speak Italian, he worked with his sisters after school to swap the words they had learned, and he became rather fluent within a few months. He also learned how to steer a gondola and played soccer with schoolmates, while his dad taught him technical basketball skills as well as American street-court tricks.

The family returned to the United States when Bryant was 13 and settled into a comfortable lifestyle. His father ended up coaching at LaSalle University while his mother got the family caught up on American culture by showing tapes of the *Cosby* show and Janet Jackson videos, as well as giving her kids the autobiography of Jackie Robinson to read. Bryant described his upbringing in the *New York Times Magazine* as "a Beaver Cleaver life." Nevertheless, Bryant had a bit of difficulty adjusting. His school, Lower Merion, was 90 percent white, and the other black students did not take him seriously as a basketball player. "They acted as if, if you weren't from the 'hood, you had no game," his mother, Pam, recalled in the *New York Times Magazine*. Of course, he proved them wrong.

> "My parents raised me to be an individual. The key to success at anything, I think, is avoiding peer pressure."

As a high school star, Bryant was a starter all four years, leading Lower Merion High School to the Class AAAA State Title with a record of 31-3 in 1996. He broke the record for most points scored in the history of Southeastern Pennsylvania with 2,883, a healthy margin above Hall of Fame legend Wilt Chamberlain's 2,359 and former St. Joseph's player Carlin Wiley's 2,441. He was *USA Today* and *Parade* magazine's National High School Player of the Year, Naismith Player of the Year, Gatorade Circle of Champions High School Player of the Year, and named to the McDonald's All-America Team, all in 1996. Not too busy for a social life, Bryant also made headlines for a non-basketball event: he took the lovely teen pop singer/actress Brandy to his prom, while remaining adamant that the two are just friends.

With such a stellar display of talent as a teen, the big question was which college would snap up Bryant. Every major university offered him a scholarship. The well-rounded student was not only an athletic hero, he held a B average with an SAT score of 1,080 and still spoke Italian fluently. When the time came, the Lower Merion school newspaper, *The Merionite*, shared space in the gym with hometown papers, ESPN and other national media, the R&B singing group Boyz II

Men, and fellow Philadelphia residents to hear Bryant's decision. He confirmed what was hinted at previously as he announced to the crowd, "I've decided to skip college and take my talent to the NBA," as *Sports Illustrated* reported.

Many derided the young player and his family for making the jump, and there was speculation that his talent would not hold up in the big league. The press dubbed Bryant and his father "Main Line brats," after the name of their suburban area, and accused them of developing the wily plan to get him traded to a high-profile team. He later signed with a major agency, William Morris, and has indicated that he would be interested in pursuing film and music careers. However, he explained in *Newsweek*, "My parents taught me that there would be criticisms out there all the time by many people, but you just got to do what you think is right."

Plenty of people agreed. "He's got star written all over him," remarked NBA Hall of Fame center Bob Lanier to the Knight-Ridder/Tribune Service. "He's got razzle-dazzle, personality, and he's flamboyant." Laker Jerry West affirmed in the Knight-Ridder/Tribune Service, "Guys he has played against will tell you his talent is not 17 years old. He was the most skilled player we've ever worked out, the kind of skill you don't see very often." Lakers Coach Del Harris, also in the Knight-Ridder/Tribune Service, lauded, "There's nothing about him that hasn't impressed me." Though Bryant is indeed the youngest player ever to be drafted in the NBA, some pointed out that Lakers superstar Earvin "Magic" Johnson was only 20 when he was signed, a fact that almost certainly was not overlooked when the team decided to bring the young Bryant on board.

The Los Angeles Lakers had their sights on the prodigy but were late in the draft, so they struck a deal with the Charlotte Hornets. The Hornets selected him 13th overall in the first round of the 1996 draft pick, then traded him to the Lakers for center Vlade Divac. "It was a dream to find out I was going to be playing for the Los Angeles Lakers," exclaimed Bryant to the Knight-Ridder/Tribune Service. "And now it's like another dream on top of a dream to find out I'm going to be playing with Shaq[uille O'Neal]."

Bryant signed a three-year, $3.5 million deal with the Lakers and promptly purchased a six-bedroom, six-bathroom mansion for himself and his family in the Pacific Palisades. The home features a Jacuzzi in the master bedroom, Italian-marble floors, and an ocean view, plus the perk of having Tom Cruise and Arnold Schwarzenegger for neighbors. Bryant also splurged on a new Toyota and BMW, but his mom commented in the *New York Times Magazine* that fame did not change her son. He surely will have no problem affording it all: *Los Angeles Times* writer Mark Heisler revealed in 1998 that Bryant's lucrative endorsement deals with Adidas, Sprite, and Spalding, in addition to his basketball salary, would probably net him about $5 million a year.

Though he lacked college playing experience, Bryant did well, if not outstanding, on the court, scoring in the double digits 25 times during his first season in the NBA. Displaying his skills further, he won the Nestle Crunch Slam Dunk at the All-Star Weekend in 1996 and led the scoring with a record 31 points at the Schick Rookie Classic. The next season, Bryant made the record books again when he became the youngest player to start for an NBA team. In the meantime, he attended summer school at UCLA, picking up 12 credits, perhaps to the dismay of many who criticized his decision to go pro immediately after high school.

In just his second season in the pros, the 19-year-old Bryant was tapped to possibly fill the shoes of superstar Michael Jordan. Indeed, Bryant's sneaker, the Adidas KB8, was the runner-up top seller in the malls during the 1997-98 holiday shopping season, finishing only under the Air Jordan and doing better than the Grant Hill, Penny Hardaway, Allen Iverson, and Shaquille O'Neal styles, according to Mark Heisler in the *Los Angeles Times*. Adidas creative director Peter Moore told Heisler, "Kobe has a magical appeal to young people. I think they sort of see the kid in him." Certainly Bryant has the kind of appeal firms like to attach to their products. In the world of "bad boy" sports mentality, he flaunts no earrings or tattoos, wears a natural afro hair style, does not drink alcohol, and according to *Newsweek*, "He is unfailingly polite, signing autographs and answering questions, and dutiful in his civic and charity obligations."

Bryant does not only captivate the young and style-conscious. "He amazes me," claimed Lakers captain Nick Van Exel in the *Sporting News*. "I see him every day, and he still amazes me." Bryant's spectacular plays have earned him the title "the most exciting player in the NBA" according to *Sporting News* writer Bill Plaschke. Yet, Plaschke warned in his article, "Remember, this is a story about the most exciting player in the NBA. This is not a story about the greatest. Not yet anyway." Plaschke went on to note that although Bryant is averaging 16.2 points a game at the time of the article, he was shooting 39 percent.

Plaschke also described one of Bryant's most embarrassing—and unfortunately most memorable—moments: an airball during the playoffs in 1997. At the end of Game 5 of the playoffs in Utah, he threw the ball from 14 feet, ending the game in overtime in a tie and thus closing the door on the Lakers' season. Bryant told Plaschke that viewing the highlight reel would have been worse if he had not taken the shot. Then, in the first game against Utah in the 1997-98 season, Bryant blocked Byron Russell's three-point try and zipped across the court to score the game-winning dunk. To add to the redemption, Bryant was picked as the youngest player to make the NBA All-Star game in 1998. The Lakers' Jerry West told Mark Heisler in the *Los Angeles Times*, "We do not stuff ballots, period. These votes came from other people that obviously like to watch him play."

Perhaps one of the most astounding facets of this wunderkind is his ability to maintain the balance in his life. While he admittedly seeks celebrity, he does not abuse it. Though Bryant's first season with the Lakers had some rough moments, coach Del Harris commented to Heisler in the *Los Angeles Times*, "He's very tough-minded. He never was disrespectful. He didn't complain publicly and he easily could have because he had a great fan base." He stays close with his family; his oldest sister, Sharia, graduated from Temple University in 1998 with a degree in international business and planned to work for her brother. "He's such a sweetheart. Such a gentleman," Bryant's mother, Pam, insisted in the *New York Times Magazine*. "My parents raised me to be an individual," Bryant told Plaschke in the *Sporting News*. "The key to success at anything, I think, is avoiding peer pressure."

The 6-foot, 7-inch, 210-pound Bryant further revealed his down-to-earth nature in a *Sports Illustrated for Kids* interview. What did he perceive the biggest difference to be in playing for the NBA as opposed to high school? "Traveling.... It's exhausting." Asked about which sports stars he admires, Bryant asserted that his favorite non-NBA player was Emmitt Smith of the Dallas Cowboys, and legendary baseball star Hank Aaron, who played for the Atlanta Braves. He also remarked in the interview that his favorite foods were macaroni and cheese, sweet potatoes, and apple pie, and that his favorite cartoon character was the Road Runner, "because he can't be caught."

Sources

On-line

"Official NBA website biography," www.nba.com/playerfile/bio/kobe_bryant.html

Periodicals

Knight-Ridder/Tribune, June 27, 1996; July 13, 1996; August 1, 1996.

Los Angeles Times, March 10, 1997, p. E1; February 6, 1998.

Los Angeles Times Magazine, May 1997, p. 64.

Newsweek, March 16, 1998, p. 58.

New York Times Magazine, January 19, 1997, p. 23.

Sporting News, December 8, 1997, p. 66.

Sports Illustrated, May 6, 1996, p. 50; June 24, 1996, p. 19.

Sports Illustrated for Kids, October 1997, p. 28.

—Geri Speace

Charles Busch

Playwright and actor

Born Charles Louis Busch, August 23, 1954, in New York, NY; son of Benjiman (a merchant) and Gertrude (a homemaker; maiden name, Young) Busch; partner of Eric Myers (a film publicist). *Education:* Northwestern University, B.A. in drama, 1976.

Addresses: *Home*—New York City. *Office*—c/o attorney Marc Glick, Glick and Weintraub, 1501 Broadway, Suite 2401, New York, NY 10036-5503; Theatre-in-Limbo, 123 West 3rd St., Suite C, New York, NY 10012. *Agent*—Jeffrey Melnick, Harry Gold Agency, 3500 West Olive, Suite 1400, Burbank, CA 91505.

Career

Playwright; actor in stage plays. Worked variously as an office temp, apartment cleaner, portrait artist, encyclopedia salesperson, jeans salesperson, memorabilia shop manager, ice cream server, sports handicapper, and artists' model, 1976-84. Cofounder, actor, and writer for Theatre-in-Limbo, New York City. Stage appearances in his own works include *Sister Act*, 1976; *Alone with a Cast of Thousands*, 1978; *Vampire Lesbians of Sodom*, 1985; *Sleeping Beauty or Coma*, 1985; *Psycho Beach Party*, 1987; *The Lady in Question*, 1989; *Red Scare on Sunset*, 1991; *The Charles Busch Review*, 1993; *You Should Be So Lucky*, 1994, *Swingtime Canteen*, 1995; and *Queen Amarantha*, 1997. Stage appearances in plays by others include *The Maids* by Jean Genet, 1993, and *Little Me* by Neil Simon. Film appearances include *Light Years* (voice only; animated), 1988, and *Addams Family Values*, 1993. Other stage work: associate director of *Ankles Aweigh*, 1988-89. Contributor to periodicals, including *Advocate, Interview, New York,* and *New York Times Book Review.*

AP/Wide World Photos

Awards: Charlie Local and National Comedy Award, Association of Comedy Artists, 1985, for special contribution to the art of comedy; Manhattan Academy of Cabaret Award, 1985 and 1993.

Sidelights

New York playwright Charles Busch could probably be described as the anti-Andrew Lloyd Webber. His campy productions, with their outrageous drag costuming, hilariously raunchy lines, and over-the-top acting, do not have the mainstream appeal to hold up in slick Broadway venues like Webbers' *Cats* or other long-running features. He has, however, blended classic film nostalgia with gay sensibilities, tossed in some overly dramatic glamour, and added a healthy dose of kitsch to come up with rollicking off-Broadway plays that provide a quirky, slightly surreal presence in American theater. His first big hit, *Vampire Lesbians of Sodom,* set a new standard in comedy for the stage and established him as the reigning drag queen of off-Broadway.

Charles Louis Busch was born on August 23, 1954, and grew up with his two sisters, Meg and Betsy, in a middle-class Jewish family in the New York City suburb of Hartsdale in Westchester County. His father, a would-be opera singer who owned a record store, took

Busch to the Metropolitan Opera House when he was eight to see Joan Sutherland, thus whetting his appetite for the arts. His mother, Gertrude, died when he was just seven, so he closed himself off by immersing himself in film. One web site proclaimed that by the age of ten, Busch had viewed every single Metro-Goldwyn-Mayer (MGM) and Warner Brothers movie of the 1930s and 1940s. His family was tolerant of his odd fantasy life, however, and did not seem to care that he idolized zesty actresses like Bette Davis. "I was the androgynous child," he remarked to *Chicago Tribune* contributor Lisa Anderson. "You wonder why so many gay people love Bette Davis? ... Bette Davis is battling the man's world as much as any little gay child does."

> *"By the time I was in college I had already come to the conclusion that I was perhaps too unconventional to be successful in a commercial acting career.... I tried to turn my liabilities into assets and transformed myself from an unsuccessful juvenile into a glamorous leading lady."*

Luckily, Busch's aunt, Lillian Blum, a former teacher, brought him to live with her in Manhattan. "She was Auntie Mame meets the Miracle Worker," Busch later recalled to Alex Witchel in the *New York Times*. "It was a rebirth for me." His aunt concurred, commenting to Witchel, "[H]e was so shy it was almost pathological.... Before he moved in with me, I would pick him up in Hartsdale on a Friday afternoon, and he would be like a zombie. But the minute we crossed the river to New York he was absolutely a new boy."

Witchel reported that Busch's aunt demanded that he read the *New York Times*'s front page on a daily basis to broaden his interests and curb his cinematic addiction. "I didn't do drugs," Busch commented to Witchel, "I did Warner Brothers movies." Blum proved to be a source of inspiration in Busch's formative years. She and his other aunt, Belle Grohs, would later provide financial backing for his plays. Busch enrolled at New York's High School of Music and Art, and after graduating in 1972, attended Northwestern University in Evanston, Illinois, where he received a bachelor's degree in drama in 1976.

Busch's college years were both frustrating and fruitful. He was skipped over for stage parts at Northwestern because he was "[t]oo thin, too light," he explained to Witchel, "which is the euphemism for gay." Busch's disappointments with mainstream theater caused him to pen his own scripts. He discovered that he could find strength in his androgynous appearance and his identification with old screen stars. As he told *Contemporary Authors*, "By the time I was in college I had already come to the conclusion that I was perhaps too unconventional to be successful in a commercial acting career.... I tried to turn my liabilities into assets and transformed myself from an unsuccessful juvenile into a glamorous leading lady."

Busch's first foray into playwrighting was an unproduced script called *Out Takes of a B-Movie*, which enjoyed a brief run of five readings at Northwestern's Joseph T Public Theatre. His first produced endeavor was *Sister Act*. This outrageous play about twin Siamese showgirls, Hester and Esther, was produced at the university in 1976. Busch quipped to Anderson of the *Chicago Tribune*, "It made a big sensation at Northwestern. They'd never seen anything like it." The production was a revelation for Busch as well, as he commented to Patrick Pacheco in the *New York Times*: "I never defined myself theatrically until I put on the lashes and heels."

After graduation, Busch returned to New York City and wrote *Alone with a Cast of Thousands*, a one-person show which featured him as various characters, although he did not perform in drag (wearing women's clothes). With the help of the show's director, Kenneth Elliot, a fellow Northwesterner, he toured throughout the United States from 1978 to 1984. In between bookings, Busch did an assortment of jobs, working as an office temp, apartment cleaner, betting oddsmaker, ice cream scooper, sketch artist, telephone salesperson for encyclopedias, and jeans salesperson. He told Witchel that he never wanted a full-time job, because he was concerned that he would lose ambition for his creative aspirations.

When the show's bookings became extremely slim, Busch seriously considered giving up the stage. As a swan song, he put together a drag skit to be produced at the Limbo Lounge, a gay bar in the East Village area of Manhattan. Audiences loved it, and it evolved into *Vampire Lesbians of Sodom*. He and his cohorts began calling themselves Theatre-in-Limbo and went on to provide more of these spoofs at the bar, including *Theodora, She-Bitch of Byzantium*—a take-off of the epic sagas of legendary film director Cecil B. DeMille—and *Times Square Angel*. Busch explained his inspiration for these plays in *Contemporary Authors*: "Wouldn't it be fun to be Barbara Stanwyck in a Capra Christmas film? Wouldn't it be fun to be Joan Crawford in an anti-Nazi espionage film? While I reveled in the romantic melodrama of those stories, I also satirized the conventions of those films and their heightened acting style." Busch noted to Pacheco, however, in the *New York Times,* "I may spoof the movies, but I don't spoof the message. I really believe in them."

After obtaining backing from family and friends, Busch took *Vampire Lesbians* to the Provincetown Playhouse in Manhattan's Greenwich Village around 1985, where he starred in the two lead roles in drag. The story revolves around a pair of female nemeses, reincarnated as various melodramatic personalities throughout the centuries, from ancient Sodom to contemporary Las Vegas. The lavish and laughable costumes accented the fast-paced, witty dialogue and the homages to screenplays and fashions of a past age. Critics raved, and Busch was lauded as a comic hero. D. J. R. Bruckner in the *New York Times* observed that "the audience laughs at the first line and goes right on laughing at every line to the end, and even at some of the silences. That's no mean achievement." *Vampire Lesbians* became the longest-running non-musical in the history of off-Broadway.

Busch continued his reign with 1987's *Psycho Beach Party,* a send-up of 1960s surfer flicks. As usual, he added his own twist to the formula, starring as Chicklet, a deranged beach bunny who completely shaves off other people's hair and exhibits multiple personalities. Daniel Mendelsohn in *American Theatre* called it "*Gidget* meets *The Three Faces of Eve*—meets *Mommie Dearest*" and described Busch's repertoire in general as akin to "fiendish theatrical cross-fertilizations dreamt up by some star-struck high school chemistry whiz."

Busch was especially proud of his next production, *The Lady in Question,* a 1988 throwback to World War II dramas about the Nazi threat. The plot involves an American celebrity actress, an evil Nazi doctor, a cigar-chomping grandmother, a Lolita type, and an ex-vaudeville performer who, in one memorable line, points out to Hitler that he is missing a testicle. Mendelsohn recounted Busch's anecdote about a fan who "recognized every hairstyle in *Lady in Question* and what movie I stole it from. And, he was right!"

Busch followed this success with *Red Scare on Sunset* in 1991, a McCarthy-era farce set in Hollywood with the players facing the anti-Communist sentiment running amok during the 1950s. Radio personality Pat Pilford is a main accuser, and she proves to her friend, screen legend Mary Dale, that all of her associates are Communists. In *Red Scare,* a much more subtle play than his earlier works, Busch gave more attention to the conceit of actors than to politics. Some politically-correct minded critics were concerned that the play contained a message that made the left wing look bad. Busch denied the accusation, reasoning to Mendelsohn, "I'm not a political satirist at all. It's not my sense of humor." Perhaps just a touch of Busch's own views can be spied in the scripts, though: the Communist-peppered *Red Scare,* along with the Nazi-laden *Lady in Question,* can both be read with the fact in mind that gays were heavily discriminated against during those ultra-oppressive times as well as Jews and suspected Communists.

In 1993, Busch wrote a novel titled *Whores of Lost Atlantis,* which he told *Contemporary Authors* is "a highly autobiographical novel about how I became a drag performer." The main character, Julian, is indeed a strong facsimile of Busch, as he attempts to convince an East Village hot spot to run his play and enlists a motley and eccentric group of friends to assist him. To accomplish the task, he must battle an evil performance artist named Kiko and her friend, Thirteen, a washed-up, menacing drag queen. *New York Times Book Review* critic Robert Plunket remarked, "Busch describes his characters' antics in a comic tone that is so right and so entertaining it becomes ... [an] important virtue." A review in *Publishers Weekly* noted that the book betrayed his lack of experience in novel-writing, but pointed out, "Busch is a natural storyteller and he spins a highly amusing—and at times highly erotic—tale."

Also in 1993, Busch finally got his chance to act in a play that he himself did not write when he agreed to act in director David Esbjornson's version of the Jean Genet play *The Maids.* The play was written in 1954 for a three-man cast—specifically, Jean Genet's fellow prison inmates—to portray a rich woman, Madame, and her two female servants, Solange (played by Busch) and Claire. Though Busch, as usual, acted a female part, the play is certainly not a comedy. "I was desperate to do a dramatic role," Busch commented to Jerry Tallmer in *Back Stage.* "Even in my own plays there are moments of melodrama when the spoof gets serious, and those are my favorite parts." Irene Backalenic praised *The Maids* in *Back Stage,* remarking that all three actors "are perfectly attuned to the mood. Their polished performances provide humor and pathos and shock in equal doses."

In 1994, Busch made the unexpected and perhaps ironic move of writing himself a male lead part to play in *You Should Be So Lucky*, though it is a homosexual role. The fairy-tale plot involves Busch as a shy electrologist who ends up at a charity function at the Rainbow Room, thanks to the help of an elderly man whom he has assisted. There he meets a publicist who becomes his true love, hinting at Busch's real-life long-term relationship with film publicist Eric Myers. The older character dies and bequeaths the electrologist $10 million. Busch quipped to Witchel in the *New York Times* that although he finally plays a man, the character happens to be a gentile, while in fact Busch is really Jewish—a cross-dress of a different color.

Busch teamed up with Linda Thorsen Bond and William Repicci to knock out his first musical, 1995's *Swingtime Canteen*, a subdued World War II-era nostalgia trip. Stefan Kanfer in the *New Leader* observed that Busch acts "with scarcely a hint of his usual overstated camp" and noted that the show features "31 surefire hits from the War years." Remarkably, the cast even included the veteran singing sensation Maxene Andrews as herself, until she passed away during a break from the show.

In 1997, Busch kept up his pace with *The Green Heart*, a novel that he wrote to become a play. Kenneth Elliot, who has directed most of Busch's works, also handled this black comedy, which again featured music. The plot revolves around a quirky horticulturist widow and a destitute schemer. The role of head housekeeper, meant to be played in drag, was actually portrayed by a woman. William Stevenson in *Back Stage* mentioned that some of *The Green Heart*'s songs could use stronger melodies, but lauded the excellent acting and remarked, "Everyone involved deserve[s] praise for launching this high-spirited new musical in high style." Also in 1997, Busch debuted *Queen Amarantha*, which David A. Rosenberg in *Back Stage* dubbed a mix of "Alexander Dumas and the Brothers Grimm."

Though critics have noticed that Busch's plays have considerably mellowed over the years, they still bear his unmistakable trademark: that certain combination of camp, black comedy, and gay culture, as well as the mark of a true film buff. He told Witchel in the *New York Times*, "The lesson I've learned is to be totally true to your origins and just go with it." All signs indicate that he will indeed keep going. As Busch commented in *Contemporary Dramatists*, "Ultimately, I remain hopelessly stagestruck and I write in order to act. It's not enough for an audience to read my stories. I am compelled to get up there and tell it to them myself."

Selected writings; plays, except as noted

Sister Act, produced at Northwestern University, Evanston, IL, 1976.

Hollywood Confidential (one-person show), produced in New York City at One Sheridan Square Theatre, 1978.

Alone with a Cast of Thousands (one-person show), produced in Washington, DC, at the Source Theatre, 1980.

Theodora, She-Bitch of Byzantium, produced in New York City at the Limbo Lounge, 1984.

Vampire Lesbians of Sodom (produced in New York City at the Limbo Lounge, 1984, then in New York City at the Provincetown Playhouse, 1985-90, later in Los Angeles at the Coronet Theatre, 1990), published with *Sleeping Beauty or Coma*, Samuel French, 1985.

Times Square Angel (produced in New York City at the Provincetown Playhouse, 1985-86), Samuel French, 1985.

Pardon My Inquisition, or Kiss the Blood off My Castanets, produced in New York City at the Limbo Lounge, 1986.

Psycho Beach Party (produced in New York City at the Players Theatre, 1987-88), Samuel French, 1989.

Adaptor, *Ankles Aweigh* (musical by Guy Bolton and Eddie Davis), produced at Godspeed Opera House, East Haddam, CT, 1988-89.

The Lady in Question (two-act; produced in New York City at the WPA Theatre, 1988, then in New York City at the Orpheum Theatre, 1989), Samuel French, 1989.

Four Plays by Charles Busch (contains *Vampire Lesbians of Sodom; Sleeping Beauty or Coma; Psycho Beach Party;* and *The Lady in Question*), Fireside Theatre Book Club, 1990.

Red Scare on Sunset (produced in New York City at WPA Theatre, 1991), Samuel French, 1991.

Three Plays by Charles Busch (contains *Theodora, She-Bitch of Byzantium; Times Square Angel;* and *Pardon My Inquisition, or Kiss the Blood off My Castanets*), Fireside Theatre Book Club, 1992.

Charles Busch Revue, produced in New York City at the Ballroom Theatre, 1993.

Whores of Lost Atlantis (novel), Hyperion, 1993.

You Should Be So Lucky: A New Comedy, Fireside Theatre (Garden City, NY), 1994.

(With Linda Thorsen Bond and William Repicci) *Swingtime Canteen,* produced in New York City at the Blue Angel Supper Club, 1995.

Queen Amarantha, produced in New York City at the WPA Theatre, 1997.

The Green Heart (novel written to become a musical adaptation), produced in New York City at the Variety Arts Theatre, 1997.

Sources

On-line

"Charles Busch as *Mrs. Ellen*," http://www. troubleonthecorner.com/docs/Busch.htm (April 9, 1998).

Books

Contemporary Authors, Volume 145, Gale Research, 1995.
Contemporary Dramatists, St. James Press, 1993.

Gay & Lesbian Biography, St. James Press, 1997.
Gay & Lesbian Literature 2, St. James Press, 1998.

Periodicals

America, May 10, 1997, p. 22.
American Theatre, December 1993, p. 44.
Back Stage, September 24, 1993, p. 7; October 8, 1993, p. 44; November 11, 1994, p. 40; April 1, 1997, p. 39; October 31, 1997, p. 38.
Chicago Tribune, November 10, 1993.
New Leader, October 9, 1995, p. 22.
New York Times, June 20, 1985; July 23, 1989; October 19, 1994, p. C1.
New York Times Book Review, November 21, 1993.
Publishers Weekly, September 27, 1993, p. 42.
Variety, October 27, 1997, p. 56.

—Geri Speace

Herman Cain

Courtesy of Herman Cain

Businessman

Born December 13, 1945, in Memphis, TN; son of Luther (a janitor, chauffeur, and barber) and Lenora (a domestic; maiden name, Davis) Cain; married; wife's name, Gloria; children: Melanie, Vincent. *Education:* Morehouse College, B.S. in mathematics, 1967; Purdue University, M.A. in computer science, 1971. *Politics:* Republican.

Addresses: *Office*—National Restaurant Association, 1200 17th St. NW, Washington, DC 20036; Godfather's Pizza Inc., 9140 West Dodge Rd., Omaha, NE 68114.

Career

Worked for Department of the Navy and the Coca-Cola Co., 1970s; Pillsbury Co., Minneapolis, MN, 1977-82, became vice president of corporate systems and services; Burger King Corp., Philadelphia, PA, regional vice president, 1982-86; Godfather's Pizza Inc., Omaha, NE, president, 1986-88, president/CEO, 1988-96, chairman, 1996—; National Restaurant Association, president, 1994-95, CEO, 1996—. Author, *Leadership Is Common Sense*, 1996.

Awards: Named one of Top 25 Black Executives, *Black Enterprise*, 1988; Entrepreneur of the Year, 1990; Operator of the Year/Gold Plate Award, International Foodservice Manufacturers Association, 1991; Horatio Alger Award, 1996; numerous honorary doctorates, humanitarian awards, and other recognitions.

Sidelights

As president and CEO of the National Restaurant Association (NRA), Herman Cain leads one of the top 20 political action committees in Washington, D.C. An active Republican who supported Bob Dole's presidential attempt in 1996, Cain is outspoken when it comes to political issues affecting his group's interests. He also has been open about his personal political ambitions, although he tucked them away for a while to lead the NRA. He hoped to increase its membership and act as a major lobbying force against government initiatives that he felt were threatening free enterprise.

Cain was born in Memphis, Tennessee, on December 13, 1945, to Luther Cain, Jr. and Lenora Davis Cain. When Cain was very young, the family moved to Atlanta, Georgia. Luther Cain displayed the ambition that his son would later embrace, working three jobs at one time. He was a part-time chauffeur for the CEO of the Coca-Cola company, a janitor at a bakery in the evenings, and a barber. His mother was a domestic. "I never heard my father complain about somebody owing him anything," Cain commented to Wallace Terry in *Parade* magazine. "All I ever saw was how hard my father worked to get what he wanted out of life." He also told Terry that his mother instilled in him a strong sense of spirituality.

Cain grew up dreaming of a well-paying job, something in the range of $20,000. He got a math degree from Morehouse College and went to work for the Department of the Navy making a scant $7,729 a year. Five years later, he had reached his goal of earning $20,000 and set his sights on new aspirations. He got a job at Coca-Cola and later jumped to the Pillsbury Company in 1977, where he stayed for several years. He worked his way up to vice president of systems and services, becoming the youngest vice president in the history of the firm, then left for Pillsbury's Burger King subsidiary.

At Burger King, instead of settling into a comfortable office with all the accouterments of a vice president, Cain started in the management training program in 1982, cleaning toilets and grilling burgers at a store in Minneapolis. Burger King quickly promoted him to vice president and general manager in Philadelphia. Ironically, Cain and his friends had once been refused service when they tried to buy a hamburger at a restaurant in 1952. Impressed with his accomplishments at Burger King, Cain moved to the floundering Godfather's Pizza in 1986, where he took over as president, becoming president and CEO in 1988 after prompting a turnaround. Godfather's went from $8 million in the red in 1985 to profits of $4 million in 1988. By 1995, Godfather's was the nation's fifth-largest pizza chain.

Throughout his service in the food industry, Cain was acknowledged as a top manager, thus leading to his election as the first African American to head the National Restaurant Association (NRA), a position he assumed in 1994. As the 73rd president in the organization's history, Cain was in the position to represent 25,000 companies with over 150,000 restaurants employing almost 10 million people—over nine percent of the workforce—throughout the United States. He immediately stepped up to powerful political challenges, feverishly seeking to shut down President Bill Clinton's health care plan, which called for employers to cover 80 percent of costs of health care coverage for employees working over 30 hours per week. Citing the financial burden on restaurants in a face-to-face conversation on the NBC television show *Nightline,* he straightforwardly told Clinton, "Mr. President, with all due respect, your calculation on what the impact would do, quite honestly, is incorrect." The president's initiative was later tabled.

Taking this hard-line conservative economic approach has earned Cain the nickname "The Hermanator." He is known to give evangelical-style speeches using phrases such as "raising Cain," "bite back," and

"Cainniption fit," according to Patricia B. Dailey in *Restaurants & Institutions.* As NRA president, he immediately lobbied against the costs of welfare, Medicare, and Social Security, claiming they interfered with the free market. "Our ability to pursue happiness in a free-enterprise system is deteriorating," he noted at a conference reported in *Nation's Restaurant News.*

Cain's term as president of the NRA ended in 1995, but he continued to remain active in Washington, serving on Jack Kemp's tax reform commission along with 13 other important business leaders. He later resumed leadership of the NRA on a full-time basis, becoming president and CEO of the group on December 2, 1996. He added the title of chief executive—never before granted to the group's leader—to ensure that the association would have a more corporate image and to allow him to more effectively institute policy. Gearing up for the job, Cain laid out some of his goals for the NRA: to lobby in Washington, D.C., specifically in order to reconstruct the tax structure; to educate members; and to expand membership. The position called for much travel, which he readily accepted. Godfather's co-owner and president Ron Gartlan took over Cain's CEO duties at the Omaha office.

Cain also had been pushing for quite some time to polish up the restaurant industry's image, telling young African Americans to stop looking at the food business as a dead-end job. "It is a $320 billion gold mine of opportunity," Cain told conference attendees in Oklahoma, Dailey reported. "There is no other industry where you can start out as a dishwasher and end up owning the company." An NRA survey in 1994 showed that 60 percent of restaurant owners and managers began as workers, such as bussers, servers, or prep cooks.

Though Cain and Kemp's goals for a flat tax have not been realized, it has not dissuaded Cain from pursuing a career in politics. Indeed, the tax committee service and the NRA position has primed him for networking around Washington, and he told Jeffrey P. Berlind in a *Restaurant Business* article that he planned to run for an office "soon." In the meantime, however, he has been committed to running the NRA, hoping to increase its contributions from $1 million to $2 million. Active in many facets of the business world, Cain has served on a number of boards, including the Federal Reserve Bank of Kansas City, Creighton University of Omaha, Nabisco, SuperValue, UtiliCorp United, and Whirlpool. He has an array of honorary doctorates and recognition from a variety of organizations, including the Horatio Alger Society, which honors those who reach great accomplishments by hard work, honesty, and religious principles. An avid singer, he was once featured with the Omaha Symphony Orchestra, and it is possible that his bass-tenor voice will become a familiar sound as it rings out to announce his candidacy in an American political race someday.

Selected writings

Leadership Is Common Sense, Van Nostrand Reinhold, 1996.

Sources

American Visions, April-May 1995, p. 41.

Nation's Restaurant News, June 6, 1994, p. 48; October 10, 1994, p. 56; January 1995, p. 38; February 1996, p. 44; April 8, 1996, p. 22; November 18, 1996, p. 1; February 24, 1997, p. 1; March 24, 1997, p. 41.

Parade, October 13, 1996, p. 4.

Restaurant Business, November 1, 1996, p. 227; December 10, 1996, p. 27; June 1, 1997, p. 6.

Restaurant Hospitality, May 1994, p. 36.

Restaurants & Institutions, June 1, 1997, p. 57.

—*Geri Speace*

Ben Nighthorse Campbell

United States Senator

AP/Wide World Photos

Born April 13, 1933, in Auburn, CA; son of Albert (a hospital orderly) and Mary (a nurse; maiden name, Vierra) Campbell; two early marriages; married Linda Aline Price (a teacher), July 23, 1966; children: Colin, Shanan. *Education:* Attended San Jose City College, San Jose, CA; San Jose State University, B.A., 1957; attended Meiji University, Tokyo, Japan, 1960-64. *Politics:* Republican. *Religion:* Protestant.

Addresses: *Office*—380 Russell Senate Office Building, United States Senate, Washington, DC 20510-0605; and 1129 Pennsylvania St., Denver, CO 80203.

Career

Worked as teacher, c. 1953-70; trained as judoist, participated in Pan American Games, 1963, and Olympics, 1964; raised horses, c. 1972-81; Nighthorse Jewelry Designs, founder and owner, c. 1980—; Colorado State Legislature, representative, 1982-86; elected member of U.S. House of Representatives, 1987-93; elected member of U.S. Senate, 1993—, member of various Senate committees, including Appropriations, Energy and Natural Resources, Veteran's Affairs, Indian Affairs, Agriculture, Nutrition, and Forestry, and served as chair, subcommittee on Parks, Historic Preservation, and Recreation; switched party affiliation from Democrat to Republican, 1995. *Military service:* U.S. Air Force, 1951-53; served in Korea.

Awards: Syngman Rhee Unit Citation, 1953; gold medal, Pan-American Games, 1963; voted one of the "Ten Best Legislators" for Colorado, *Denver Post-News Center 4* poll, 1986; three-time U.S. Judo Champion; over 200 jewelry design awards; numerous horse-show awards.

Member: Northern Cheyenne Indian Tribe Council of 44 Chiefs, U.S. Judo Association (senior technical advisor), Durango Chamber of Commerce, American Quarter Horse Association, American Indian Education Association, Colorado Pilots Association.

Sidelights

As the first Native American to serve in the United States Senate since the 1930s, Ben Nighthorse Campbell is noted for a free-spirited manner characterized by his appearance as well as his avocations. Known for his pony tail, bolo ties, and motorcycle, Campbell does not exactly blend in on Capitol Hill. In 1995, after thirteen years as a Democrat, Campbell switched his affiliation to the Republican Party. In 1996, a Banana Republic ad played on his image as a maverick, as Campbell stated in the print ad, "I'm part of the establishment, but I'm not a conformist."

Campbell was born on April 13, 1933, in Auburn, California. His father, Albert, was part Cheyenne, part Pueblo, and part Apache Indian, and his mother, Mary, was a Portugese immigrant. They lived in the Sacramento Valley of California, and also had a daughter, Alberta, born in 1930. Albert Campbell had served in the Army in World War I, and during that time he had begun drinking; by the 1930s, he was often so incapacitated by his alcoholism that he could not hold down a steady job. In addition, Mary Campbell suffered from tuberculosis, but she managed to find jobs for both of them at the sanatorium where she was receiving treatment, in the town of Weimar. In 1939, however, she found herself unable to take care of the family, so she placed her children in an orphanage in Sacramento.

Later the family fortunes improved, and she brought Ben and Alberta to live in their new home, a cabin in Weimar from which she operated a grocery store. But his experience of abandonment left psychological scars on young Ben, and not surprisingly, he grew up to be a troublemaker. Though he excelled in art classes, his record at Placer High School was otherwise distinguished only by disciplinary problems, both inside and outside the classroom. His had not been an easy childhood, and he was becoming a rough, young man. Although he became involved in crimes such as car theft, he also worked at various jobs including logging and fruit-picking.

As Campbell approached the end of high school, two positive things happened in his life. While working as a fruit-picker, Campbell's Japanese co-workers sparked his interest in judo, and he took up the sport. Secondly, in 1950, his junior year of high school, he enlisted in the U.S. Air Force. (Only later did he earn his general equivalency diploma.) During his service in the Korean War, he studied judo, and at the end of his service in 1953, he moved to San Jose, California. There Campbell took classes at San Jose City College and later San Jose State University, where he earned his B.A. in physical education and fine arts in 1957.

His interest in judo continued, and as a student, Campbell became captain of San Jose State's team. After his graduation, he worked as an elementary teacher for a time, but in 1960 he went to Japan to study judo at Tokyo's Meiji University. He was a determined student, and became so obsessed with defeating one particular opponent that he kept his photo on his wall and would often shout at the picture, "I will beat you!" Eventually, he did beat him. Along the way, he became a sixth-degree black belt, and by 1963 was a participant in the Pan American Games in Sao Paolo, Brazil, where he earned a gold medal. A year later, Campbell became a member of the U.S. judo team at the Olympics in Tokyo, the first time the Games had included that sport. Campbell did not win a medal, however; a

torn ligament caused him to collapse during a match, and his German opponent won. Nonetheless, Campbell became known as one of the world's foremost judoists.

Back in the United States, Campbell continued teaching—he had supported himself in Japan by giving English lessons, and by playing small film roles—and underwent further judo training. He became involved in several judo associations, established several programs for high school students and others, and trained several judoists who became members of the 1972 U.S. Olympic team. He also found time to work as a volunteer mounted police officer and a prison counselor. His judo career ended in 1972, and Campbell began a new career at the age of 39, breeding, raising, and training championship horses. This led to his move to Colorado, when in 1978 he became director of a training center in the town of Ignacio. Campbell served in that role until 1981, during which time he had discovered another lucrative business that would eventually supplant the horse enterprise: jewelry-making.

Even in high school, Campbell had shown a talent for making jewelry, and now he applied elements of Native American and Japanese art to making items which became noted for their highly original designs. Out of this enterprise grew his company, Nighthorse Jewelry Design, which he continued to operate in the 1990s—making him without a doubt the only jewelry-maker with a seat in the U.S. Senate.

His jewelry business itself had an odd connection to the political career which would make Campbell famous. Always more inclined to be a participant than a spectator, Campbell became a pilot so that he could expedite delivery of his jewelry pieces to other states, and one day while his plane was grounded due to bad weather, he decided to attend a meeting of the local Democratic Party. The leaders were looking for someone to run for a legislative seat in the 1982 elections, and they picked the charismatic Ben Nighthorse Campbell (who had adopted the middle name in 1980 in honor of ancestors). So now Campbell, the sometime judoist, horseman, and jewelry-maker, added "politician" to his resumé.

In his 1982 race against Republican Don Whalen for the Colorado State Legislature, Campbell established a pattern for later campaigns, positioning himself as the rough-and-tumble "man of the people" as opposed to Whalen, whom he depicted as a stuffy ultraconservative. Thus the 1982 Campbell-Whalen race gained the nickname "buckskins vs. Brooks Brothers," and when Campbell ran against Republican incumbent Mike Strang for the U.S. House of Representatives seat in 1986, he made much of the fact that Strang had attended an Ivy League school. As for Campbell's record as a legislator, it was not particularly distinguished, and he won his races by narrow margins. But people liked the charismatic Campbell, which may explain why a 1986 poll conducted by the *Denver Post* and a local television station named Campbell one of the state's ten best legislative leaders.

> *"I'm still the only Member of Congress who goes to work on a motorcycle, hates neckties, and is never accused of using the Senate barber shop."*

In Washington, D.C., as the Representative of the Third District of Colorado, Campbell served on the Interior, Agriculture, and Insular Affairs committees. As the only Native American in the entire U.S. Congress— and the only one in the House of Representatives for the preceding two generations—he became the de facto leading representative of all Native Americans in the United States. He sponsored a number of successful pieces of legislation, including the Colorado Ute Indian Water Rights Settlement Act; the creation of the Museum of the American Indian as part of the Smithsonian Institution in Washington; and the renaming of the battlefield where his great-grandfather, Ruben Black Horse, had fought alongside Sitting Bull against General George Armstrong Custer and his troops, to the Little Bighorn National Battlefield Monument.

Political allies had suggested that Campbell run for the Senate in 1990, but he declined; yet when the state's other seat became vacant in 1992, he decided to run. The ensuing campaign against Republican challenger Terry Considine proved to be a bitter one, and Campbell, who started out in the lead, dropped back in the race. It was then that Campbell, if he had not already, proved he was no ordinary Senatorial candidate; after all, few candidates have ever had Northern Cheyenne supporters taking part in "sweats," a religious ceremony among Native Americans, to help them win divine favor. Under the guidance of a medicine man, Campbell also underwent ritual painting of places on his body and carried a sacred eagle feather. Whether through spiritual intercession or more vigorous campaigning, Campbell won the Senate election with just 55 percent of the vote.

The media in 1992 and 1993 tended to portray the new Senator as part of the multiracial, gender-balanced "Clinton Revolution" that ousted President George Bush and other Republicans from Washington, but the reality was rather more complex. Though a Democrat, Campbell showed himself to be a conservative on fiscal issues, as well as many social ones. On the one hand, he championed Native American causes; on the other, he favored the passing of a constitutional amendment that would ban the burning of the American flag. In 1992, dressed in full regalia, he served as co-grand marshall of the Tournament of Roses Parade. In 1993, he again represented Native Americans as he participated in the inaugural parade of President Clinton.

Yet, contrasts abounded. Campbell supported legislation protecting Colorado's wilderness, but he also introduced a bill that would facilitate the development of certain natural gas reserves in his home state. He was in favor of the right to abortion, a definitely liberal stance, but he also belonged to the politically conservative National Rifle Association (NRA). No doubt the conflicts became a concern to Campbell in the mid-1990s, and he threw himself into the relatively apolitical cause of increasing public awareness of Fetal Alcohol Syndrome.

In early 1995, Campbell decided to switch political parties. *Congressional Quarterly Weekly Report* quoted him as stating, "I can no longer continue to support the Democratic agenda nor the administration's goals.... My personal beliefs and that of the Democratic party are far apart." Campbell was joined by Senator Richard Shelby of Alabama and Congressman Nathan Deal of Georgia in moving from the Democratic to the Republican Party.

The response was swift and decisive. On one side of the aisle, his new fellow Republicans welcomed the Senator from Colorado, who as it turned out was part of a wave of defections that spread to several members of the Senate and House. In *Newsweek*, Joe Klein cited Campbell's action as a sign of what was to come, Democratic defeat in 1996. Among many of his old party members and their supporters, Campbell became a source of anger; a *New Republic* article noted that Senator Bob Kerrey of Nebraska wrote a letter to Campbell asking that he return $250,000 worth of Democratic money used in his campaign.

In 1996, Campbell was again involved in controversy. Banana Republic, a popular clothing store owned by The Gap, had featured Campbell in its advertising, for which he was paid $2,000. Campbell donated the money to a Native American school in Montana, Dull Knife Memorial College. But Jonathan Turley, a George Washington University law professor and leader of the Environmental Law Advocacy Center at his school, led a boycott of Banana Republic and threatened demonstrations because Campbell had voted against several environmental measures. Banana Republic quickly responded to the threats by pulling the Campbell spots—which were, ironically, part of a series celebrating freedom of expression.

An article in *Advertising Age* noted that Banana Republic had chosen Campbell as its symbol of a free spirit because of his "image as a renegade." He had made himself known not only for challenging the dress code, but for actions that embarrassed his conservative colleagues, such as his attendance at a fund-raiser for the legal defense of a Hell's Angels motorcycle gang member. True to his unflappable image, Campbell did not let the Banana Republic incident, or the larger furor surrounding his change of party affiliation, affect him. In an April 21, 1997, interview with *Insight on the News*, Campbell noted he did not regret his switch to the Republican party, and criticized President Clinton for attempts to "coerce" votes from Native Americans.

When Campbell spoke at the 1996 Republican National Convention in San Diego, he noted that he was one of the few people who had attended both Democratic and Republican conventions. He made light of his well-known personal characteristics, noting "I'm still the only Member of Congress who goes to work on a motorcycle, hates neckties, and is never accused of using the Senate barber shop." On a more serious note, he listed the reasons for his change of party affiliation, citing his adopted party's stance in favor of a balanced budget and property rights, and against crime. But higher than these, he stressed a quality that knows no party affiliation, an essential characteristic of being an American: freedom.

Selected writings

Judo Drill Training, Zenbei Publishing Co., 1974.
"Reflections on the Columbus Quincentenary (1492-1992)," [Washington, D.C.], 1992.

Sources

On-line

"Ben Nighthorse Campbell," *Republican National Convention,* http://rnc.org/convention96 (November 26, 1997).
"Biography: Ben Nighthorse Campbell," *Powersource,* http://www.powersource.com (October 24, 1997).
"People, places & things in the news," *The Standard Times,* (March 4, 1996),
http://www.s-t.com (November 26, 1997).
"Senator Ben Nighthorse Campbell," *U.S. Senate,* http://www.senate.gov (November 26, 1997).

Books

Allen, Paula Gunn, and Patricia Clark Smith, *As Long As the Rivers Flow: Nine Stories of Native Americans,* Scholastic Press, 1996.
Henry, Christopher E., *Ben Nighthorse Campbell: Cheyenne Chief and Campbell, An American Warrior,* Orion Books, 1993.

Periodicals

Advertising Age, April 15, 1996, p. 25.
American Spectator, November 1993, p. 16.
Congressional Quarterly Weekly Report, January 16, 1993, p. 20; March 4, 1995, p. 664, pp. 702-705; March 11, 1995, p. 764; October 14, 1995, p. 3113.
Insight on the News, May 15, 1995, p. 16; April 21, 1997.
Life, June 1994, p. 108.
National Journal, March 18, 1995, p. 694.
New Republic, March 27, 1995, p. 9.
News for You, March 22, 1995, p. 2.
Newsweek, March 20, 1995, p. 31.
San Francisco Business Times, April 12, 1996, p. 2.

—*Judson Knight*

Neve Campbell

Actress and dancer

Born Neve Adrianne Campbell, October 3, 1973, in Guelph, Ontario, Canada; daughter of Gerry Campbell (a high school drama and media teacher) and Marnie Neve (a psychologist and manager of Neve's fan club); married Jeff Colt (an actor and songwriter), April 3, 1995 (divorced, November 1997). *Education:* Attended the National Ballet School of Canada, 1982-87.

Addresses: *Office*—c/o Fox Broadcasting Company, P.O. Box 900, Beverly Hills, CA 90213. *Fan Club*—Performance Unlimited, 101-1184 Denman St., Box 138, Vancouver, BC, Canada V6G 2M9.

Career

Film appearances include *Web of Deceit,* 1993; *Northern Passage (Baree),* 1994; *The Dark,* 1994; *The Forget-Me-Not Murders,* 1994; *The Canterville Ghost,* 1995; *Love Child,* 1995; *The Craft,* 1996; *Scream,* 1996; *Scream 2,* 1997; *Wild Things,* 1998; *54,* 1998; producer and actress in *Hairshirt,* 1998. Television appearances include *Catwalk,* 1992; *Party of Five,* 1994—; *Mad TV; Saturday Night Live.* Appeared as a dancer in the Toronto production of *Phantom of the Opera,* 1989-91.

Sidelights

Neve Campbell's successful career in television and feature films was established through a combination of talent, rigorous training, and hard work. In her pre-teen years she was already performing with Canada's prestigious National Ballet, where she had been enrolled since age nine. During her five years with the company, she was thoroughly trained in six different types of dance. At 14, accumulated injuries and what she once referred to as "a nervous breakdown" forced her to abandon her dance career, and she resumed attendance at an alternative high school in Toronto, Canada.

Always a serious and gifted student, Campbell turned to drama but dropped out of school at age 16 when she landed a role with the Toronto production of *Phantom of the Opera.* With this popular production she gave 800 performances during the two-year period from 1989-91. Her ex-husband, actor and songwriter Jeff Colt, was a bartender at the theater where *Phantom of the Opera* was appearing. They married in England in 1995, while Campbell was filming *The Canterville Ghost,* a remake of the 1944 comedy.

In 1994 Campbell got her big break on television, when she won out over 300 other actresses for the role of Julia Salinger in *Party of Five.* "I read to them for two minutes," she recalled to Bernard Weinraub of *Cosmopolitan.* "Within two weeks, I was offered the role."

The Emmy Award-winning hour-long family drama series on the Fox network is about five San Francisco children who keep the family together after their parents are killed in an automobile accident. Although the show initially received poor ratings, it eventually won a following of ten million viewers weekly. Weinraub referred to Campbell as the show's "bright light" who plays "a smart and serious everygirl whose problems—including pregnancy—are far more realistic than those of the pencil-thin bubble-heads on shows like *Beverly Hills 90210.*"

Campbell's character, the headstrong teenager Julia, quickly became the most noticeable of the cast and developed a large and loyal following. However, she once admitted that success does have its pitfalls: "It's okay when people come up on the street and say, 'I love your show,' but in a public bathroom? That is something else. Fans have knocked on the stall to get an autograph. Some people have no tact at all."

Campbell also came to the attention of feature film makers, and won a role as the terrorized Sidney Prescott in horror director Wes Craven's *Scream,* which was chosen best movie of the year in 1996 at the MTV film awards. Also in 1996, Campbell played another insecure teenager in *The Craft,* a black comedy about four misfit girls with supernatural powers. Tom Soter of *Video Magazine* called the film a "well-constructed but predictable horror tale, a parable of how a good girl can be led astray."

Scream was the surprise success of 1996, and the sequel, 1997's *Scream 2,* also starred Campbell as Sidney Prescott. The sequel has a movie-within-a-movie based on Campbell's role in the original film. Yet, in a discussion with *Interview's* Steven Goldman, Campbell confessed that she does not even watch horror films. When asked to identify her greatest fear, she responded, "Death of happiness."

Next, Campbell played teenage drug addict Suzie Toller in the 1998 erotic thriller *Wild Things,* her fourth major role in a feature film. The movie's website described the picture as "an irreverent tale of revenge, lust and murder played out in the murky swamps of the Florida Everglades." The role was strongly psycho-sexual, calling for her to play a boozy ex-convict who participates in sexual threesomes. The young actress chose the challenging role in order to avoid being typecast.

Once firmly established in both television and feature films, Campbell formed her own production company, The Blue Sphere Alliance, in Los Angeles, in partnership with her older brother Christian, and Matthew Lillard, who co-starred with Campbell in *Scream.* The company's first production, *Hairshirt* (1998) starred Campbell, her brother Christian, and Katie Wright.

After southern California became her home and business base, Campbell quickly adopted a more relaxed lifestyle. Her intensity was directed toward her work, and yoga and meditation gave her calmness and creative energy release. Her excellent muscle tone and trim weight are maintained with regular exercise and a low-fat diet. She enjoys swimming, horseback riding, and roller blading. When *Interview's* Goldman asked what she loved most about acting, Campbell replied: "Touching people's souls."

Sources

On-line

"Neve Heaven," www.geocities.com/Hollywood/Lot/8595 (March 19, 1998).
"*Wild Things,*" www.spe.sony.com/movies/wildthings/intro.html (March 19, 1998).

Books

McNeil, Alex, *Total Television,* 4th edition, Penguin Books, 1996, pp. 150, 643-44.

Periodicals

Cosmopolitan, January 1997, p. 80.
Interview, January 1997, p. 60.
People, May 27, 1996, p. 79; March 3, 1997, p. 78.
Rolling Stone, October 6, 1994, p. 93; September 18, 1997, pp. 56-60, 116.
Video Magazine, December 1996, p. 96.

—*Ralph Westbrook*

Ben Carson

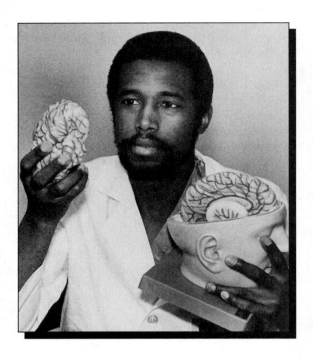

Neurosurgeon

Born Benjamin S. Carson, September 18, 1951, in Detroit, MI; son of Robert Solomon and Sonya (a domestic worker; maiden name, Copeland) Carson; married Lacena Rustin, July 6, 1975; children: Murray, Benjamin Jr., Rhoeyce. *Education:* Yale University, B.A., 1973; University of Michigan, M.D., 1977. *Religion:* Seventh-Day Adventist.

Addresses: *Office*—Johns Hopkins Hospital, 600 North Wolfe St., Baltimore, MD 21205-2110.

Career

Johns Hopkins Hospital, intern, 1977-78, neurosurgery resident, 1978-82, chief resident, 1982-83; Sir Charles Gairdner Hospital, Perth, Australia, senior registrar, 1983-84; Johns Hopkins Hospital, director of pediatric neurosurgery, 1985—.

Awards: Cum Laude Award, American Radiological Society, 1982; American Black Achievement Award, *Ebony* magazine, 1988; Paul Harris Fellow, Rotary International, 1988; honorary DSc., Gettysburg College, 1988; Candle Award, Morehouse College, Atlanta, 1989; honorary DSc., North Carolina AT&T, Andrews University, Sojourner-Douglas College, all in 1989, Shippenburg University, 1990.

Member: American Association of Neurological Surgeons, Congress of Neurological Surgeons, Pediatric Oncology Group, National Medical Association, Children's Cancer Foundation (Baltimore; Medical Advisory Board), Maryland Red Cross (honorary medical chairman).

Sidelights

In 1987, neurosurgeon Ben Carson successfully performed an operation to separate Siamese twins who were born joined at the head. It was a milestone in neurosurgery, but was far from the only noteworthy achievement of Carson's career. He also performed groundbreaking surgery on a twin suffering from an abnormal expansion of the head. Carson was able to relieve the swelling and remove the surplus fluid—all while the unborn twin remained in its mother's uterus. This too was a first, and in other instances Carson has performed operations which have greatly expanded scientific knowledge of the brain and its functions. His "can-do" spirit, combined with his medical expertise, has made him the surgeon of choice for parents with children suffering rare neurological conditions.

If Carson seemed destined for any position when he was a child growing up on the streets of Detroit, he appeared most qualified for the role of putting someone else in the hospital—or even the morgue. In his profile on the American Academy of Achievement website, it was noted that Carson "had a temper so violent that he would attack other children, even his mother, at the slightest provocation." No doubt some of his anger stemmed from the conditions of his childhood. Carson's father left his mother, Sonya, when he was only eight; his mother, who had only a third-grade education, was faced with the daunting task of raising her sons Ben and Curtis by herself. She worked as a maid, sometimes holding two or even three jobs to support her family. The family was poor, and Carson often endured the cruel taunts of his classmates.

A further source of frustration in Carson's life was his poor performance as a student. During a two-year period when his family lived in Boston, he fell behind in his studies. By the time he returned to elementary school in Detroit, he was, according to his profile on the American Academy of Achievement website, "considered the 'dummy' of the class." It was a position for which he "had no competition," he related in his book *Gifted Hands.*

After Carson brought home a report card of failing grades, his mother quickly limited her sons' television viewing and required them to read two books a week. The boys then had to give written reports to their mother on what they read. While other children were outside playing, Sonya Carson forced her boys to stay inside and read, an act for which her friends criticized her, saying that her sons would grow up to hate her. Carson later realized that because of her own limited education, his mother often could not read her sons' reports, and was moved by her efforts to motivate them to a better life.

Before long, Carson moved from the bottom of the class to the top. However, there was resentment from his classmates at the predominantly white school. After awarding Carson a certificate of achievement at the end of his freshman year, a teacher berated his white classmates for letting an African-American student outshine them academically. In his high school years and later, Carson faced racism in a number of situations, but as he said in his 1996 interview with the American Academy of Achievement, "It's something that I haven't invested a great deal of energy in. My mother used to say, 'If you walk into an auditorium full of racist, bigoted people ... you don't have a problem, they have a problem.'"

Despite his academic improvement, Carson still had a violent temper. In his interview with the American Academy of Achievement, he recalled trying to hit his mother over the head with a hammer because of a disagreement over what clothes he should wear. In a dispute with a classmate over a locker, he cut a three-inch gash in the other boy's head. However, at the age of

14, Carson reached a turning point after he nearly stabbed a friend to death because the boy had changed the radio station.

Terrified by his own capacity for violence, he ran home and locked himself in the bathroom with the Bible. "I started praying," he said in his American Academy of Achievement interview, "and asking God to help me find a way to deal with this temper." Reading from the Book of Proverbs, he found numerous verses about anger, but the one that stood out to him was "Better a patient man than a warrior, a man who controls his temper than one who takes a city." After that, he realized he could control his anger, rather than it controlling him.

> *"After several months, I realized that I had a special reason to thank God for leading us to Australia. In my one year there I got so much surgical experience that my skills were honed tremendously, and I felt remarkably capable and comfortable working on the brain."*

With his outstanding academic record, Carson was in demand among the nation's highest-ranking colleges and universities. He graduated at the top of his high school class and enrolled at Yale University. He had long been interested in psychology and, as he related in *Gifted Hands,* decided to become a doctor when he was eight-years-old and heard his pastor talk about the activities of medical missionaries. College would prove difficult, not just academically but financially, and in his book Carson credits God and a number of supportive people for helping him graduate successfully with his B.A. in 1973. He then enrolled in the School of Medicine at the University of Michigan.

Carson decided to become a neurosurgeon rather than a psychologist, and this would not be the only important decision at this juncture of his life. In 1975 he married Lacena Rustin whom he had met at Yale, and they eventually had three children. Carson earned his medical degree in 1977, and the young couple moved to Maryland, where he became a resident at Johns

Hopkins University. By 1982 he was the chief resident in neurosurgery in Johns Hopkins. In his 1996 interview on the American Academy of Achievement website, Carson noted that being a young, African American made things different in the work setting. He recalled that in his early days as a surgeon, nurses would often mistake him for a hospital orderly, and speak to him as such. "I wouldn't get angry," he remembered. "I would simply say, 'Well, that's nice, but I'm Dr. Carson.'" He continued, "I recognize[d] that the reason they said that was not necessarily because they were racist, but because from their perspective … the only black man they had ever seen on that ward with scrubs on was an orderly, so why should they think anything different?"

In 1983, Carson received an important invitation. Sir Charles Gairdner Hospital in Perth, Australia, needed a neurosurgeon, and they invited Carson to take the position. Initially resistant to the idea, as he related in *Gifted Hands,* the choice to go to Australia became one of the most significant of his career. The Carsons were deeply engaged in their life in Australia, and Lacena Rustin Carson, a classically-trained musician, was the first violinist in the Nedlands Symphony. For Ben Carson, his experience in Australia was invaluable, because it was a country without enough doctors with his training. He gained several years' worth of experience in a short time. "After several months," he wrote in *Gifted Hands,* "I realized that I had a special reason to thank God for leading us to Australia. In my one year there I got so much surgical experience that my skills were honed tremendously, and I felt remarkably capable and comfortable working on the brain."

Carson drew upon his previous experiences after he returned to Johns Hopkins in 1984. Shortly thereafter in 1985, and only in his early 30s, Carson became director of pediatric neurosurgery at Johns Hopkins Hospital. He faced several challenging cases, the first being four-year-old Maranda Francisco. Since the age of 18 months, the little girl had been having seizures, and by the time her parents brought her to Johns Hopkins, she was having more than 100 of them a day. In consultation with another doctor, Carson decided to take a radical step: a hemispherectomy, the removal of half the patient's brain. It was a risky procedure, as he told the girl's parents, but if they did nothing, Maranda would probably die. In *Gifted Hands* he described the painstaking surgery, which took more than eight hours and at the end of which the tearful Franciscos learned that their daughter would recover. Carson went on to perform numerous successful hemispherectomies, and only lost one patient; but that loss, of an 11-month-old, was devastating.

Carson described numerous other important operations in his book, *Gifted Hands,* but one which attracted international attention was the case of the Binder Siamese twins, Patrick and Benjamin. The Binders were born to German parents on February 2, 1987, and they were not merely twins: they were joined at the head. Ultimately the parents contacted Carson, who performed the 22-hour surgery on September 5 with a team of some 70 people. Although the twins would turn out to have some brain damage, both would survive the separation, making Carson's the first successful such operation. Part of its success owed to Carson's application of a technique he had seen used in cardiac surgery: by drastically cooling down the patients' bodies, he was able to stop the flow of blood. This ensured the patients' survival during the delicate period when he and the other surgeons were separating their blood vessels.

This type of surgery was in its developmental stages in the 1980s and early 1990s. When Carson and a surgical team of more than two dozen doctors performed a similar operation on the Makwaeba twins in South Africa in 1994, they were unsuccessful, and the twins died. Perhaps more representative of Carson's cases is the one chronicled in the July 1995 issue of *US News and World Report,* entitled "Matthew's Miracle." Matthew Anderson was five-years-old when his parents learned that their son had a brain tumor. According to the article, right before the little boy was to begin radiation treatments, a friend recommended the autobiography of a brain surgeon "who thrived on cases that other doctors deemed hopeless." After the Andersons read *Gifted Hands,* they decided that they wanted Carson to operate on their son. Carson performed two surgeries, one in 1993, and one in 1995. Ultimately, Matthew Anderson recovered.

According to the *US News and World Report* article, Carson performs 500 operations a year, three times as many as most neurosurgeons, a fact for which he credits his "very, very efficient staff." He works with the music of Bach, Schubert, and other composers playing, "to keep me calm," he told the magazine. In 1994, *US News and World Report* rated Johns Hopkins Hospital the finest specialty institution in the country, ranking it above such highly respected hospitals as Mayo Clinic and Massachusetts General.

Because Carson's career has represented a triumph over circumstances, he has become a well-known inspirational writer and speaker. He is not short on advice for young people. In his 1996 American Academy of Achievement interview, he commented, "We don't need to be talking about Madonna, and Michael Jordan, and Michael Jackson. I don't have anything against these people, I really don't. But the fact of the matter is, that's not uplifting anybody. That's not creating the kind of society we want to create." He has noted that the most important thing is to bring value to the world through improving the lives of one's fellow human beings. Carson has done this through perseverance and example.

Selected writings

(With Cecil Murphey) *Gifted Hands,* Zondervan , 1990.
(With Murphey) *Think Big: Unleashing Your Potential for Excellence,* Zondervan, 1992.
(With Murphey and Nathan Aaseng) *Ben Carson,* Zondervan, 1992.

Sources

On-line

"Dr. Benjamin S. Carson," *American Academy of Achievement,* http://www.achievement.org (February 27, 1998).
"Skull Basher to Brain Healer," *Connection Magazine,* http://www.connectionmagazine.org (February 27, 1998).

Books

Carson, Ben, with Cecil Murphey, *Gifted Hands,* Zondervan, 1990.

Periodicals

Black Enterprise, October 1993, p. 147.
Christianity Today, May 27, 1991, pp. 24-26.
People, fall 1991 (special issue), pp. 96-99.
Readers Digest, April 1990, pp. 71-75.
US News and World Report, July 24, 1995, pp. 46-49.

—*Judson Knight*

Tom Clancy

Author

Born Thomas L. Clancy, Jr., in 1947 in Baltimore, MD; son of a postal carrier and a store credit employee; married Wanda Thomas (an eye surgeon and insurance agency manager) in August, 1969 (divorced, 1998); children: Michelle, Christine, Tom, Kathleen. *Education:* Loyola College, Baltimore, MD, degree in English, 1969.

Addresses: *Home*—P.O. Box 800, Huntingtown, MD 20639-0800. *Publisher*—G. P. Putnam's Sons, 200 Madison Ave., New York, NY 10016.

Career

Writer. Insurance agent, Baltimore, MD, and Hartford, CT, until 1973; O.F. Bowen Agency (insurance company), Owings, MD, agent, beginning 1973, owner, 1980. *Military service*—U.S. Army Reserve Officers' Training Corps.

Sidelights

Tom Clancy, the "King of the Techno-Thriller," according to Patrick Anderson in the *New York Times*, has forged a lucrative career as one of the pre-eminent authors of gripping novels mired in detailed accounts of military technology and espionage. His hero, Jack Ryan, combines a rugged all-American heroism with a sophisticated knowledge of high-tech equipment and top military secrets, as well as other intellectual prowess. To many in the know, Clancy's works reflect a remarkable accuracy, although experts generally concede that technology is not usually as dependable as he purports. Nevertheless, Clancy has a devoted legion of fans willing to overlook some of the minor points in order to become enveloped in his captivating global adventures. He has been a mainstay on the best-seller lists since his debut, *The Hunt for Red October,* in 1984. Clancy's 1998 release, *Rainbow Six,* continued to deliver his trademark blend of "splendid technical detail and expert pacing and crosscutting," according to Harry Levins of the *St. Louis Post-Dispatch.* Before his quick ascent to fame, the author was not a top military intelligence officer as fans might have thought; natch, he was never in the service at all. Instead, Clancy was actually a mild-mannered insurance salesman who had always harbored a love of technology and military history and the secret ambition to be a writer.

Thomas L. Clancy, Jr., was born in Baltimore, Maryland, in 1947, the son of a postal carrier and a credit-department employee. He was educated in Catholic schools and grew up with a love of technology and the military. He loved gadgets of all kinds and was often engrossed in books on military history. When he was a student at Loyola College in Baltimore, he joined the Army Reserve Officers' Training Corps (ROTC) but was not allowed to serve in Vietnam because he was so extremely nearsighted. His childhood dreams were sidetracked. "I thought I would have made a good tank commander," Clancy told Evan Thomas in *Newsweek*. "I had read all the books on Rommel." Clancy also had aspired to become a rich and famous writer, but shortly after graduating with his English degree from Loyola, ended up getting married. He wed a nursing student who became an eye surgeon, Wanda Thomas, in August of 1969 and settled into the world of insurance sales, inarguably a more sedate profession than a military officer or big-name writer.

After working as an insurance agent for some years in Baltimore and Hartford, Connecticut, Clancy and his wife in 1973 joined the O.F. Bowen Agency, a small insurance firm that her grandfather founded in 1939 in Owings, Maryland, about 20 miles south of Annapolis. The couple had two daughters, Michelle and Christine, and after about eight years, had a boy, Tommy, and another girl, Katie. The Clancys were financially comfortable and enjoyed the normal things like cookouts with their friends. However, though he loved his wife and children, Clancy could not help feeling trapped, weighed down with the typical middle-class bills and responsibilities. He stuck with insurance, though, and the business grew to service about a thousand clients with fire, casualty, and automobile policies. In August of 1980, Clancy and his wife bought out the office.

Meanwhile, Clancy's dreams of writing continued to brew. In the mid-1970s he had heard about the crew of the Soviet frigate *Storozhevov* who unsuccessfully attempted to defect to Sweden, and it caught his imagination. Clancy, meanwhile, was intrigued by tales of military goings-on that he heard from his customers, many of them connected to the nearby naval base. By 1979, Clancy was finishing up his insurance work early in order to concentrate on his novels. His wife was skeptical of his efforts, but Clancy knew he needed to write. By 1982, he had developed a character, Jack Ryan, a manly hero of Irish-American descent who dropped out of Wall Street to teach at Annapolis. The ex-Marine also worked part-time for the CIA. Clancy worked on three stories about Ryan concurrently; one of them was about a Russian submarine commander who wanted to defect to the West. A complicated game ensues between the Americans who try to help him and the Soviets, who want the crew and their state-of-the-art sub safely returned. To make his book realistic, Clancy began researching military facts and details and even enlisted the help of a former submariner, Ralph Chatam, who gave him insight about life in an underwater vessel.

Clancy finished the work, *The Hunt for Red October*, and heard that the Naval Institute Press, known for publishing scholarly and strategic works, wanted to expand it into novels. He had previously written a brief article about the MX missile for *Proceedings*, the magazine of the U.S. Naval Institute, but had no other literary credentials. It did not matter; the editors loved his manuscript, and after some minor tweaks, published the book in 1984. Initially, some naval officers were shocked at the level of detail and were even concerned that someone had breached security. However, Clancy had amassed all of his information from public documents, military books, talks with Chatam, and a widely available war game called Harpoon. He had never even been on a submarine. Without the backing of publicity from a large publisher, the book began gaining an audience by recommendations and a couple of good reviews. The novel then received a push from two high-profile men not usually noted for being literary critics: President Ronald Reagan, who proclaimed *The Hunt for Red October* "the perfect yarn," according to Edwin McDowell in the *New York Times,* and Secretary of Defense Caspar Weinberger, who also gave his stamp of approval. The book won glowing reviews and sold more than 300,000 copies in hardback and two million in paperback during the first two years after its release. The rights were sold to make a motion picture starring Sean Connery, which was also a hit.

Based on this success, Clancy landed a three-book contract worth $3 million with G.P. Putnam'sSons. His second work, *Red Storm Rising,* published in 1986, was even bigger. In this work, heavily based on the war game Harpoon, the United States and the Soviet Union clash in World War III without breaking out the nuclear weapons. Instead, after Muslim terrorists attack a Siberian oil refinery, the Soviets plan to take over the oil-rich Middle East and try to prevent NATO forces from interfering. Clancy breaks out an arsenal of high-tech air, land, and sea weapons in describing the showdown, including spy satellites, Stealth planes, and advanced tanks. Some reviewers expressed disbelief that such a conflict could take place without chemical or nuclear weapons, but fans obviously were not concerned, nor were they rattled by many critics' accusations that Clancy's characterizations were skimpy. *Red Storm Rising* topped the charts again, selling over a million hardcover copies by the end of the year, and became required reading for students at the Naval War College.

Thanks to *The Hunt for Red October* and *Red Storm Rising,* Clancy soon became the darling of the Pentagon. He was allowed to drive an M-1 tank and fire two rounds; he spent a week at sea on a navy frigate carrying surface-to-air missiles; and he was allowed to speak with a Soviet defector. In June of 1986 while touring a British ship in Baltimore harbor, he met Prince Andrew, who was serving as a helicopter pilot for the British navy. "The military has adopted me," Clancy remarked to Evan Thomas in *Newsweek.* Thomas followed up by adding, "It is not hard to understand why. In Clancy's novels, America's warriors are always brave and true, the weapons always work and the 'good guys' always win."

Clancy's third novel, *Patriot Games,* involved a terrorist plot against the British royal family by a fictional splinter group of the Irish Republican Army. Jack Ryan again was the hero, saving the Prince and Princess of Wales from certain doom only to invoke the wrath of the Irish terrorists. Though *Patriot Games* was criticized, like his other works, for its poor character development and its simplistic moralizing, readers enjoyed the formula thriller and pushed it on to the best-seller lists. It was made into a film starring Harrison Ford and Anne Archer. After *Patriot Games,* Clancy's next book, *The Cardinal of the Kremlin,* returned to the tensions between the Soviet Union and the United States. It featured prominently the Star Wars system, a controversial laser-satellite defense system that was developed during the Reagan era.

Clancy received a $4 million advance for his fifth book, *Clear and Present Danger,* 1989, which continued to trace the adventures of Jack Ryan, this time in cahoots with the CIA in order to combat South American drug runners. It also was adapted for screen, and again, saw Harrison Ford and Anne Archer as the leads, along with Willem Dafoe. Clancy followed this with *The Sum of All Fears,* 1991, a post-Cold War terrorist tale in which a nuclear bomb is set off at the Super Bowl. In *Without Remorse,* 1994, character John Clark, a former Navy SEAL and Ryan's darker alter ego, is sent to Vietnam to free POWs, and the same year, *Debt of Honor* addressed military downsizing and the threat of Japanese competition. *Executive Orders,* 1996, was a sequel to *Debt of Honor,* featuring Jack Ryan as the U.S. president trying to reinstate the country's power.

Clancy's next hardcover, *Rainbow Six,* released in 1998, was inspired by Clancy's CD-ROM game of the same name. It reprised John Clark as the head of a top-secret international anti-terrorism team. Though some critics still complained about the wooden characterization, many noted that all of the typical Clancy elements were in place for a suspenseful and satisfyingride. *Entertainment Weekly* writer Dana Kennedy commented that Clancy "writes action scenes beautifully, and he weaves them into a sprawl-

ing, Bondesque plot.... It may be decoder-ring literature, but within the genre, there's no doubt that Clancy is king." The novel, as usual, shot to the top of the best-seller lists.

In addition to writing books, Clancy was a pioneer in melding literature and computer games. After a first attempt, called SSN, failed due to what he saw as poor marketing efforts, he established a company called Red Storm Entertainment and first released the game Politika in 1997. "Fundamentally, what we are trying to do is create a new art form," Clancy remarked to Ian Grayson in the *Independent.* "It's a different way to tell stories. Instead of just telling them to people as you do if you're a playwright or an author, we present the reader with stories in which he can participate." The novel was written to accompany the interactive game, not the other way around. He also created the games ruthless.com and Dominant Species, although Clancy admitted in a *Publishers Weekly* interview that he does not even play the games himself: "They're more fun to design than they are to play," he quipped. Clancy has also penned a number of nonfiction titles about military matters, such as *Submarine: A Guided Tour Inside a Nuclear Warship,* 1993; *Armed Cav: A Guided Tour of an Armored Cavalry Regiment,* 1994, and *Into the Storm: A Study in Command,* 1997.

After finding fortune with his talent, Clancy and his wife bought a five-bedroom, $200,000 home in Maryland about a mile from their old place. They later upgraded to a $2 million, 24-room stone mansion on a 400-acre site on Chesapeake bay. Clancy's wife even bought him an M-1A1 tank to decorate the front lawn. He also bought the Baltimore Orioles baseball team and planned to go in on a purchase of the Minnesota Vikings football team in early 1998. However, he had to back away from the deal when his finances were thrown into turmoil during a separation from his wife. Wanda Clancy moved out of the house in November of 1997 and was seeking rights to potential future earnings from the use of Clancy's name in future projects, such as books, television shows, computer games, and videos. Meanwhile, Clancy was eager to get through the divorce, because he expressed desire to marry Alexandra Llewellyn, a wealthy television reporter and a cousin of General Colin Powell, who introduced them in 1996 when Clancy was separated from his wife.

The bespectacled Clancy is known to espouse right-wing politics, not surprising given the content of his books. He is afraid to fly and shies away from roller coasters, but he was a risk-taker when it came to shucking the insurance business to become a writer. Going from having nothing in print except the one small article on missiles, he has since become number 27 on the *Forbes* list of the top 40 earners in the entertainment world with a worth of about $190 million. He urges others to follow their true goals as well, commenting to Curt Brown in the Minneapolis *Star Tribune*: "If you're afraid to go for your dream, then about the time you retire, you'll have the condo down in Florida, and you'll be there in the elephant graveyard waiting to die and you'll think ... 'What if when I was 30, I had gone and sailed around the world or bought that airplane I always wanted to buy?'"

Selected writings

Novels

The Hunt for Red October, Naval Institute Press, 1984.
Red Storm Rising, Putnam, 1986.
Patriot Games, Putnam, 1987.
The Cardinal of the Kremlin, Putnam, 1988.
Clear and Present Danger, Putnam, 1989.
The Sum of All Fears, Putnam, 1989.
Submarine, Berkeley, 1993.
Without Remorse, Putnam, 1994.
Debt of Honor, Putnam, 1994.
Executive Orders, Putnam, 1996.
Rainbow Six, Putnam, 1998.

Nonfiction

Submarine: A Guided Tour Inside a Nuclear Warship, Putnam, 1993.
Armed Cav: A Guided Tour of an Armored Cavalry Regimen, Putnam, 1994.
Fighter Wing: A Guided Tour of an Air Force Combat Wing, Berkley, 1995.
Marine: A Guided Tour of a Marine Expeditionary Unit, Berkley, 1996.
Into the Storm: A Study in Command, 1997.
Reality Check: What's Going On Out There?, Putnam, 1997.

Sources

On-line

"Tom Clancy," *Contemporary Authors,* Gale Literary Databases web site, http://www.galenet.com (July 7, 1998).
"Tom Clancy," Penguin Putnam Inc. web site, http://www.penguinputnam.com (August 19, 1998).
Red Storm web site, http://www.redstorm.com (August 19, 1998).

Books

Authors & Artists for Young Adults, volume 9, Gale Research, 1992.

Periodicals

Arizona Republic, May 16, 1998, p. A18.
Dallas Morning News, August 9, 1998, p. 8J.
Entertainment Weekly, August 14, 1998, p. 73.
Independent, December 9, 1997, p. N6.
Los Angeles Times, June 30, 1998, p. E2.
Newsweek, August 8, 1988, p. 60.
New York Times, July 17, 1986, p. C21; July 27, 1986, sec. 7, p. 7; August 12 1986, p. C13; August 2, 1987, sec. 7, p. 11; August 13, 1989, sec. 7, p. 9.
New York Times Magazine, May 1, 1988, p. 54.
People, June 15, 1998, p. 151; August 17, 1998, p. 37.
Publishers Weekly, July 13, 1998, p. 43; July 27, 1998, p. 55.
St. Louis Post-Dispatch, September 12, 1994, p. 3E; June 17, 1998, p. E6; August 9, 1998, p. D5.
Star Tribune (Minneapolis, MN), February 4, 1998, p. 1A; February 6, 1998, p. 1A.
USA Today, August 3, 1998, p. 1D.
U.S. News & World Report, September 15, 1986, p. 66.
Washington Post, January 29, 1985, p. C1.

—*Geri Speace*

William S. Cohen

Secretary of Defense

Born August 28, 1940, in Bangor, ME; son of Ruben (an owner of a family bakery) and Clara (Hartley) Cohen; married Diane Dunn (a landscape and portrait painter), January 6, 1962 (marriage ended); married Janet Langhart (the president of Langhart Communications), 1996; children: (first marriage) Kevin, Christopher. *Education:* Bowdoin College, B.A. (Latin), 1962; Boston University Law School, LL.B. (cum laude), 1965; St. Joseph's College, Windham, ME, LL.D., 1974; University of Maine, LL.D., 1975. *Politics:* Republican. *Religion:* Unitarian-Universalist.

Addresses: *Home*—Bangor, ME. *Office*—Office of the Secretary of Defense, The Pentagon, Washington, DC 20301.

Career

Admitted to the bar, State of Maine, 1965; Paine, Cohen, Lynch, Weatherbee, & Kobritz, Inc. (law firm), Bangor, ME, became partner, 1965-72; Husson College, Bangor, instructor, 1968; University of Maine, Orono, instructor, 1968-72; Penobscot County, ME, assistant county attorney, 1968-70; member of Bangor City Council, Bangor, ME, 1969-72; mayor of Bangor, ME, 1971-72; U.S. House of Representatives, congress member for 2nd Congressional District, State of Maine, 1973-79; U.S. Senate, senator for State of Maine, 1979-97; secretary of defense with the Clinton administration, 1997—. Member, Senate Armed Services Committee and Governmental Affairs Committee, 1979-97, Select Committee on Intelligence, 1983-91 and 1995-97, Vice Chair, 1987-91; member of board of directors, Council on Foreign Relations, 1989-98, chair

of Middle East Study Group, 1996. Member of board of overseers, Bowdoin College, 1973-85; trustee, Unity College.

Awards: James Bowdoin scholar, 1961-62; alumni fund scholar, 1962; *Time* magazine selected Cohen as one of America's 200 future leaders, 1974; U.S. Junior Chamber of Commerce citation, one of the Ten Outstanding Young Men in America, 1975; Boston University Law School, "Young Lawyer's Chair," 1975; Alumni Award for Distinguished Public Service, Boston University, 1976; Vanguard Award, Non-Commissioned Officers Association, 1980; named to New England Hall of Fame basketball team, 1982; L. Mendel Rivers Award, Non-Commissioned Officers Association, 1983; Silver Anniversary Award, National Collegiate Athletic Association (NCAA), 1987; selected for Balfour Silver Anniversary All-American Team, National Association of Basketball coaches, United States, 1987; U.S. Special Operations Command Medal, 1996.

Member: American Trial Lawyers Association, Maine Trial Lawyers Association.

Sidelights

Former Senator William S. Cohen of Maine, nominated for the position of 20th Secretary of Defense in January of 1997, has after 24 years in national governmental service a reputation as a "maverick," a person who places ideals and morality above party loyalties. "Cohen won the label in 1974, when, as a 33-year-old freshman Congressman, he was the first Republican on the House Judiciary Committee to oppose Richard Nixon on the question of providing 'edited' transcripts of Oval Office plotting in the Watergate cover-up," explained *Nation* contributor Doug Ireland, "and was one of seven Republicans who voted for Nixon's impeachment." President Clinton nominated Cohen for the position because of his reputation as a moderate-to-liberal Republican and because of his extensive record of service on the Senate Armed Services Committee.

Cohen was born in Bangor, Maine, to an ethnically and religiously mixed set of parents. His father was a Russian-Jewish immigrant, while his mother was of Irish Protestant extraction. At his father's wish he was raised Jewish, attending Hebrew school and preparing for the Bar Mitzvah examination. When he was told that he would have to undergo a conversion ceremony, however, he decided not to follow through with the ceremony. Instead, he followed his mother's example in refusing to convert to Judaism and became a Christian.

By the time Cohen entered Bowdoin College in 1958 he had developed a reputation as an athlete, excelling in basketball. He had been co-captain of Bangor High School's basketball team and had earned Maine All State honors during his senior year. He originally majored in Latin, with the idea of becoming a teacher after graduation. After receiving his bachelor's degree, however, Cohen entered Boston University's Law School in 1962 to study for his law degree. He passed the Maine state bar exams in 1965 and the same year entered the Bangor law firm of Paine, Cohen, Lynch, Weatherbee, & Kobritz, Inc., eventually becoming a partner. In 1972 he took advantage of Maine's Representative William Dodd Hathaway's decision to run for a Senate seat to launch his own campaign for national office. He was elected by the Second Congressional District to the House of Representatives that year.

As a freshman representative, Cohen was assigned to a position on the House Judiciary Committee—a position regarded by many of his colleagues as a political dead-end, because he could not use it to benefit his constituents directly. However, "Fate played its ultimate trick on me," Cohen related in his memoir *Roll Call: One Year in the United States Senate*, "and turned my assignment to the Judiciary Committee into a ren-

dezvous with history." Only a few months later, Congress instructed the Judiciary Committee to investigate whether or not there were grounds to impeach President Richard M. Nixon. When a vote to inform the president that he had failed to answer the committee's subpoena for tapes and documents came before the committee in May of 1974, Cohen sided with the Democrats in favor of the motion instead of with his fellow Republicans. He later sided with the Democrats again to vote in favor of impeachment.

Although Cohen's cross-party voting record on these important issues angered some of the Republican constituents who had elected him, the Representative was able to use his new reputation to seek higher office. "In 1978," Ireland reported, "he won the first of three Senate terms by knocking off moderate Democratic incumbent William Hathaway with a demogogically nationalist campaign in which Cohen 'mov[ed] briskly to his right,' as the Associated Press noted that year, attacking Hathaway and the Carter Administration on the Panama Canal treaties, strategic arms negotiations with the Soviet Union and neutron weapons." During his succeeding terms Cohen cemented his reputation as a conservative on defense issues, helping to create and sponsor the G.I. Bill of 1984 and the Goldwater-Nichols Defense Reorganization Act of 1986. He also worked for the Council on Foreign Relations, including a stint as the chair of the Middle East Study Group in 1996. Cohen became a published author during his terms as Senator, completing a volume of memoirs, several collections of poetry, some nonfiction works, and a couple of novels, including one—*The Double Man*—co-written with then-fellow Senator Gary Hart.

In 1996 Cohen announced his retirement from the U.S. Senate. In part, Ireland suggested, this was because of "his recent marriage to longtime girlfriend Janet Langhart, a former Marshall Field runway model and TV weather announcer who went on to a lucrative career as a talk-show host and now works for Black Entertainment Television." On December 5, 1996, however, President Clinton announced Cohen's nomination as Secretary of Defense. On January 22, 1997, Cohen was confirmed by the Senate, and he was sworn into office on January 24th.

As Secretary of Defense, Cohen has faced many problems concerning the nature of military life and making military training fair for both male and female recruits. During his first year in office, he had to confront the issue of sexual harassment in the military. Following the conviction of an Army drill sergeant of using his position of authority to demand sexual favors from female recruits, Cohen appointed a panel to investigate the military's policy of mingling male and female recruits during training. In December of 1997, the panel recommended segregating the genders for at least the first twelve weeks of training. Cohen also faced criticism for his support of General Joseph Ralston as successor to Joint Chiefs of Staff chair John Shalikashvilli. Ralston confessed to having an adulterous affair with a civilian woman while he was separated from his wife.

At the same time, Cohen has led the military toward more aggressive prosecution of sex offenders in the armed services. "Three Army sergeants were given prison terms for raping female recruits," wrote Johnathan S. Landay in the *Christian Science Monitor,* "and their commander, Major General John Longhouser, resigned ... after admitting to having an adulterous affair years ago." Landay adds that both an Army general and a Navy admiral "were stripped of their commands during investigations for alleged adultery and sexual harassment respectively." At the same time, the Army's chief noncommissioned officer and the Air Force's first female B-52 pilot both left the armed services to avoid prosecution for sex-related offenses.

As Secretary of Defense, Cohen faces the challenge of preparing the United States' armed services for work in "a world where the only constant is change," noted Linda D. Kozaryn quoting Cohen in a report for the *American Forces Press Service,* "where threats to American interests can erupt anywhere at any time ... where rogue states and freelance terrorists can spread fear and death with a truck full of fertilizer, a vial of volatile liquid or a homemade nuclear device. It is a world that demands American leadership and a strong, capable and ready American military force." Future plans, Kozaryn reported, "include continuing to reduce Russia's remaining 20,000 nuclear weapons, continuing the Partnership for Peace program, enlarging [the North Atlantic Treaty Organization (NATO)] and stabilizing Bosnia."

Selected writings

Of Sons and Seasons (poetry), Simon & Schuster (New York City), 1978, reprinted, Hamilton Press (Lanham, MD), 1987.

Roll Call: One Year in the United States Senate, Simon & Schuster, 1981.

(With Kenneth Lasson) *Getting the Most out of Washington,* Facts on File (New York City), 1982.

Europe and the Middle East: Strains of Key Elements on America's Vital Interests; Report of William S. Cohen to the Committee on Armed Services, United States Senate, April 23, 1982, United States Government Printing Office (Washington, DC), 1982.

(With Gary Hart) *The Double Man,* Morrow (New York City), 1985.

A Baker's Nickel: Poetry, Morrow, 1986.

(With others) *U.S. Strategic Airlift Choices,* Institute for Foreign Policy Analysis (Cambridge, MA), 1986.

(With George J. Mitchell) *Men of Zeal: A Candid Inside Story of the Iran-Contra Hearings,* Viking (New York City), 1988.

One-Eyed Kings: A Novel, Nan A. Talese/Doubleday (New York City), 1991.

(With Thomas B. Allen) *Murder in the Senate,* Nan A. Talese (New York City), 1993.

Easy Prey: The Fleecing of America's Senior Citizens— And How to Stop It, Boomer Books/Marlowe (Washington, DC), 1997.

Sources

On-line

"Biography of William S. Cohen," http:// www.defenselink.mil/bios/secdef_bio.html (December 16, 1997).

"Biography: William S. Cohen," *American Forces Press Service,* http://www.dtic.dla.mil/afps/news/9701238.html (November, 1997).

"Senator William S. Cohen (R-Me)," http:// www.bates.edu/~jwallace/reps/billcohen.html (November, 1997).

"Armed Forces Welcomes Cohen," *American Forces Press Service,* http://www.dtic.dla.mil/sfps/news/9702184.html (November, 1997).

Periodicals

Christian Science Monitor, June 6, 1997, p. 3.

Nation, January 6, 1997, pp. 17-20.

New York Times, April 12, 1978.

New York Times Book Review, March 1, 1981; May 5, 1985.

Time, November 20, 1978; May 6, 1985.

Washington Post, December 22, 1987.

—Kenneth R. Shepherd

Sean "Puffy" Combs

Producer, executive, and singer

Born November 9, 1969 (some sources say 1970 or 1971) in Harlem, New York, NY; son of Melvin and Janice (a teacher and model) Combs; children: (with ex-girlfriend, Misa Hylton) Justin. *Education:* Attended Howard University; studied business administration.

Addresses: *Office*—Bad Boy Entertainment, 8-10 W. 19th St., New York, NY 10011.

Career

Record producer, songwriter, video director, rap singer. Uptown Records, intern, 1990, vice president, A&R department, 1991-93; head of Bad Boy Records division, 1993; president of Bad Boy Records as division of Arista Records, 1993—.

Awards: ASCAP songwriter of the year, 1996.

Sidelights

Sean Combs, also known as "Puffy" or "Puff Daddy," has established himself as a bridge between the music being made on the street and the high-quality studios of the major labels. With an ear for talent and an unstoppable enthusiasm for music, especially rap and hip-hop, Combs worked diligently to bring new acts to the mainstream. Barely out of his teens, he made his name as a top-quality producer for multiplatinum artists like Mary J. Blige and Jodeci, and went on to discover names like Craig Mack and Notorious B.I.G. He signs acts to his own label, Bad Boy Records, first a division of Uptown, now an arm of Arista Records. Snugly at the top of his game in the music business, Combs lost his best friend, rapper Notorious B.I.G., on March 9, 1997. However, he bounced back with what seems like enough energy for three people, continuing to head his business and produce while embarking on projects like restaurants, clothing, and charities. On top of it all, he recorded his own chart-topping album in 1997, *No Way Out.*

Sean Combs was born on November 9, 1969; however, some sources state that he was born in 1970 or 1971. His mother, Janice, was a teacher and model. When Combs was about three years old, his mother gave birth to another son. Shortly after that, Combs's father died, and Combs was led to believe he was killed in a car accident. However, he became suspicious, and when he was around 14 years old, he went to the library and learned that his father had been a hustler who was shot in the head on Central Park West. Combs told Mikal Gilmore in *Rolling Stone,* "All the stories I heard about him, he was a good man and all that, he was just hustling. He was running numbers or selling some drugs or whatever. He wasn't known as a gangsta."

Combs grew up for a while in Harlem during the late 1970s and early 1980s, when rap music and hip-hop culture were beginning to bloom with songs like "Rapper's Delight" by the Sugar Hill Gang in 1979 and "The Message" by Grandmaster Flash in 1982. This style used two or more turntables to mix together new rhythms from old songs, while a singer chanted, or "rapped" overtop of the music. Artists such as L.L. Cool J, Run-DMC, KRS-One, and the Beastie Boys were gaining popularity, and Combs would sneak out as young as 12 years old to go experience the music. However, when he was 12, Combs and his family moved to Mount Vernon, New York, where he went to Mount St. Michael's Academy, an all-boys school, and reportedly was a good student. As the story goes, he got his nickname "Puffy" because as a school football player on the slim side, he used to puff out his chest to make himself look heavier.

Growing up, Combs was an indefatigable entrepreneur. When he found out he could only have one paper route, he signed up some friends and then ran their routes as well as his own to make extra cash. As a teen, he worked double-shifts at an amusement park to rake in a bigger paycheck. When he began attending Howard University in the late 1980s, he naturally studied business administration. Though he was dedicated to his studies, he was also eager to break out of academia and put his knowledge to practical use. He began selling term papers and concert tickets, and became known for promoting hip-hop parties around campus. He was in college for a couple of years before leaving to begin his career.

At age 19, Combs landed an internship at Uptown Records under Andre Harrell, who had been a rapper with the group Dr. Jekyll and Mr. Hyde. Harrell took Combs under his wing and eventually promoted him to head of the A&R (artists and repertoire) department. However, a tragic incident occurred during an event Combs promoted while he was in that capacity. In 1991 he helped organize a celebrity basketball game between rap stars at the City College of New York that left nine people dead following a stampede. Combs tried in vain to revive one of the victims and remained depressed for months following the event. Though many others were implicated as well as being at fault, Combs's grief was compounded when he was blamed for not providing enough security, and for not insuring the event, as required by the college.

Though Combs's future looked bleak at Uptown, he returned to his position after a few months. He had made a name for himself there previously as the producer of multiplatinum hits for R&B artists Mary J. Blige and Jodeci, and he still considered Harrell his mentor. After Combs's return, Harrell allowed him to start up his own label under the Uptown umbrella, Bad Boy Records. As vice president and head of this new division, Combs became more confident and outspoken. "I have to believe at the end of the day: I'm going to be the greatest," Combs told Gilmore in *Rolling Stone*. He later added, "Sometimes people say I'm cocky and arrogant, but that comes with it." Unfortunately for him, Harrell considered him a bit too cocky, claiming that he had tantrums and could not work with the company executives. He fired Combs in 1993. Combs initially accused Harrell of being jealous of his success, but later painted the falling out as a conflict between Combs's creative aspirations versus Harrell's need to address corporate issues. Harrell later went on to head Motown Records, and the two patched up their differences.

Two weeks after leaving Uptown, Combs signed a contract with Arista Records to form Bad Boy Entertainment. As president of the firm, he makes about $700,000 a year, operates a $2 million studio called Daddy's House, and has a credit account of $50 million and $6 million for cash advances, according to Gilmore in *Rolling Stone*. He also has the first option to buy out the business in 2001. Combs soon proved his worth when he signed Craig Mack and Notorious B.I.G., two unknowns who would go on to become huge names in rap. Combs discovered the homeless and destitute Mack rapping one night at a Manhattan club, and B.I.G. was peddling drugs as well as homemade tapes made in a basement studio in the Bedford-Stuyvesant area of New York when Combs got a hold of his sound. This was what gave Bad Boy the edge; Combs had a direct line to what was new on the streets, and knew how to connect with this fresh talent. "I don't just listen to the music with my head, it has to give me a rush," he told Anita M. Samuels in the *New York Times*. Also, because Bad Boy had connections to a major label, Combs was able to attract and keep those acts that he felt had promise.

Combs kept his hand in the business of his artists, helping mold their images, directing some of their videos, and even occasionally dancing or singing in a video himself. Working 18 to 20 hours a day, by his own estimates, he scored 15 consecutive gold or platinum hits, and he wrote or cowrote five top records in 1995, including "Be Happy," by Blige; "Can't You See," and "Think of You," by Total; "One More Chance," by Notorious B.I.G.; and "You Used to Love Me," by Faith Evans. In 1996 he was named ASCAP's songwriter of the year.

Combs gained a best friend while working with Notorious B.I.G., also known as Biggie Smalls, whose

1994 album *Ready to Die* sold more than a million copies. The title was sadly prophetic. Combs lost more than a top artist when B.I.G. was shot to death while sitting in his Suburban sport utility vehicle outside a party on March 9, 1997. Combs had been extremely close to Biggie, spending much of his free time with the beefy but soft-spoken former crack dealer. Apparently the target of a planned attack, B.I.G. was supposedly at odds with Death Row Records star Tupac Shakur, who was killed a few months after B.I.G., in September of 1997. Many speculated that the killings had something to do with the rivalry between the two stars' labels or styles of rap. Bad Boy Records, out of New York, was known as East Coast rap, and Death Row, in California, was West Coast. Combs, though, has insisted that the bad blood was all hype and that neither company has anything against each other. Neither murder was solved as the year faded and 1998 progressed.

After the murder, Combs vowed to donate to charity part of the profits from B.I.G.'s posthumously released album *Life After Death.* Combs then began rewriting some of the lyrics for his own debut album, *No Way Out,* issued in July of 1997. It sold more than half a million copies during its first week in stores and by early 1998 had passed the five million mark. The album boasted three hit singles, including "I'll Be Missing You," a tribute to Biggie. Its melody was based on the song "Every Breath You Take" by Sting. Combs has been heavily criticized for his prolific use of "samples," or excerpts taken from old songs—often easily recognizable top 40 or classic rock hits—and used as a basis for a new one. Fans do not seem to mind, however, because he creates catchy tunes based on time-proven favorites. Jeannine Amber in the *Source* noted, "He's floated rhymes over Diana Ross, over Sting, over infectious pop beats, disco beat; jacked entire hooks. Of course he gets us to dance. We danced the first time we heard it."

Combs himself is aware of his method. "I'm not afraid of using samples," he remarked to Amber. "That's how I started producing. I never played no instruments. I never programmed no drum machines. So if I was at a party and heard a record that I loved, I would figure out a way to bring that record to life. Make it like it was some brand new shit." Combs defends his style, as well, insisting that it produces irresistible beats that make for good dance music. The number of hits underscore his point, although, as with most underground music that becomes popular, he has been taken to task for making rap too mainstream. Amber in the *Source,* however, stated, "As much as he is derided for being too commercial, the man's singlehandedly

changed the face of urban music.... You kind of *have* to give it up to him."

In addition to his wild success as a record executive and rap artist, Combs, who lives in Southampton on Long Island, New York, opened a soul food restaurant in Manhattan in 1997 called Justin's Place. It was named after the son he had with former girlfriend Misa Hylton, with whom he remains friendly. In addition to the eatery, Combs started a clothing label in 1997 called Sean John, and also helped start up a charity arm of Bad Boy Records run by Sister Souljah to help disadvantaged youths. He also hopes to get involved in the film industry, perhaps acting and producing, and plans to write a book. Combs's image has spawned a generation of imitators, young men who like the casual yet elegant air that he exudes, exemplified by a *Rolling Stone* cover photo in which he wore a baseball cap, fur coat, Versace underwear, and a gold medallion. Alisa Valdez in the *Boston Globe* called it "a sort of sporty, Harlem-goes-Beverly Hills look."

Combs focuses on his goal of becoming a "mogul entrepreneur" and noted to Gilmore in *Rolling Stone* that he was "more hurt than mad" that the media kept pursuing the story of Tupac's murder instead of his own contributions to African American culture. He insisted that his accomplishments have been ignored in favor of people concentrating on the tragedies in his life, and that he does not want to become known as the guy mixed up in warring factions of the rap world, but as an ace producer who makes hit records and helps improve communities. He told Gilmore, "I'm the guy that every record I produced went platinum. I'm the guy that makes you dance. I'm the guy that just wants to make good music. That's the only guy I am. And I'm the guy that wants to make history for my race and wants to be a leader of my race."

Sources

Books

Contemporary Musicians, volume 16, Gale Research, 1996.

Periodicals

Business Wire, February 19, 1998.
Dallas Morning News, July 27, 1997, p. 6C.
Entertainment Weekly, December 26, 1997, p. 30.
Essence, November 1, 1997, p. 111.
Gannett News Service, July 19, 1996.
Los Angeles Times, May 25, 1997, p. 8; July 22, 1997.
New York Amsterdam News, August 19, 1995.

New York Times, November 6, 1994, section 13, p. 4; July 20, 1997, section 2, p. 28.

Rolling Stone, August 7, 1997, p. 52.

Source, September 1997, p. 190.

St. Louis Post-Dispatch, November 20, 1997, p. G7.

Star Tribune (Minneapolis, MN), May 26, 1997, p. 9E.

USA Today, July 22, 1997, p. 1D.

—Geri Speace

Merce Cunningham

Choreographer

Born Mercier Philip Cunningham, April 19, 1919, in Centralia, WA; father, a lawyer. *Education:* Attended George Washington University; attended the Cornish School of Fine and Applied Arts (now Cornish College of the Arts); attended Bennington School of Arts, Bennington College; studied modern dance under Bonnie Bird in Seattle, WA.

Addresses: *Office*—Merce Cunningham Studio, Bethune St., New York, NY 10014.

Career

Lester Horton Dance Theatre, dancer, 1938, and Martha Graham Company, soloist, 1940-45; School of American Ballet, New York City, modern dance instructor, 1947-51. Martha Graham Company, choreographer, 1943-45; Merce Cunningham Dance Company, founder, 1952, choreographer and instructor, 1952—. Works choreographed include *Seeds of Brightness* (with Jean Erdman), 1942; *Credo in US* (with Erdman), 1942; *Renaissance Testimonials*, 1942; *Ad Lib* (with Erdman), 1942; *Totem Ancestor*, 1942; *In the Name of the Holocaust*, 1943; *Shimmers*, 1943; *The Wind Remains*, 1943; *Triple-Paced*, 1944; *Root of an Unfocus*, 1944; *Tossed as It Is Untroubled*, 1944; *The Unavailable Memory Of*, 1944; *Spontaneous Earth*, 1944; *Four Walls*, 1944; *Idyllic Song*, 1944; *Mysterious Adventure*, 1945; *Experiences*, 1945; *The Encounter*, 1946; *Invocation to Vahakn*, 1946; *Fast Blues*, 1946; *The Princess Zoodilda and her Entourage*, 1946; *The Seasons*, 1947; *The Open Road*, 1947; *Dromemon*, 1947; *Dream*, 1948; *A Diversion*, 1948; *Orestes*, 1948; *The Monkey Dances*, 1948; *Effusions avant l'heure* (later called *Games* and *Trio*), 1949; *Amores*, 1949;

Duet, 1949; *Two Step*, 1949; *Pool of Darkness*, 1950; *Before Dawn*, 1950; *Waltz*, 1950; *Rag-Time Parade*, 1950; *Sixteen Dances for Soloist and Company of Three*, 1951; *Variation*, 1951; *Boy Who Wanted to Be a Bird*, 1951; *Suite of Six Short Dances*, 1952; *Excerpts from Symphonie pur un homme seul* (also known as *Collage*), 1952; *Les Noces*, 1952; *Suite by Chance*, 1953; *Solo Suite in Space and Time*, 1953; *Demonstration Piece*, 1953; *Epilogue*, 1953; *Banjo*, 1953; *Dime a Dance*, 1953; *Septet*, 1953; *Untitled Solo*, 1953; *Fragments*, 1953; *Minutiae*, 1954; *Springweather and People*, 1955; *Galaxy*, 1956; *Lavish Escapade*, 1956; *Suite for Five in Space and Time*, 1956; *Nocturnes*, 1956; *Labyrinthian Dances*, 1957; *Changeling*, 1957; *Picnic Polka*, 1957; *Collage III*, 1958; *Antic Meet*, 1958; *Summerspace*, 1958; *Night Wandering*, 1958; *From the Poems of White Stone*, 1959; *Gambit for Dancers and Orchestra*, 1959; *Rune*, 1959; *Theatre Piece*, 1960; *Crises*, 1960; *Hands Birds*, 1960; *Waka*, 1960; *Music Walk with Dancers*, 1960; *Aeon*, 1961; *Field Dances*, 1963; *Story*, 1963; *Open Session*, 1964; *Paired*, 1964; *Winterbranch*, 1964; *Cross Currents*, 1964; *Variations V*, 1965; *How to Pass, Kick, Fall and Run*, 1965; *Place*, 1966; *Scramble*, 1967; *Rain Forest*, 1968; *Walkaround Time*, 1968; *Canfield*, 1969; *Tread*, 1970; *Second Hand*, 1970; *Signals*, 1970; *Objects*, 1970; *Loops*, 1970; *Landrover*, 1972; *TV Rerun*, 1972; *Borst Park*, 1972; *Un jour ou deux*, 1973; *Exercise Piece*, 1975; *Changing Steps*, 1975; *Rebus*, 1975; *Solo*,

1975; *Sounddance*, 1975; *Blue Studio: Five Segments*, 1975; *Torse*, 1976; *Squaregame*, 1976; *Travelogue*, 1977; *Inlets*, 1977; *Exercise Piece I*, 1978; *Exercise Piece II*, 1978; *Exchange*, 1978; *Tango*, 1978; *Roadrunners*, 1979; *Exercise Piece III*, 1980; *Duets*, 1980; *Fielding Sixes*, 1980; *10's with Shoes*, 1981; *Gallopade*, 1981; *Trails*, 1982; *Quartet*, 1982; *Inlets 2*, 1983; *Roaratorio*, 1983; *Pictures*, 1984; *Doubles*, 1984; *Phrases*, 1984; *Deli Commedia*, 1985; *Native Green*, 1985; *Arcade*, 1985; *Grange Eve*, 1986; *Points in Space*, 1986; *Fabrications*, 1987; *Shards*, 1987; *Carousel*, 1987; *Eleven*, 1988; *Five Stone*, 1988; *Five Stone Wind*, 1988; *Cargo X*, 1989; *Field and Figures*, 1989; *August Pace*, 1989; *Inventions*, 1989; *Polarity*, 1990; *Neighbors*, 1991; *Trackers*, 1991; *Beach Birds*, 1991; *Beach Birds for Camera*, 1992; *Loosestrife*, 1991; *Change of Address*, 1992; *Touchbase*, 1992; *Enter*, 1992; *Doubletoss*, 1993; *CRWDSPCR*, 1993; *Breakers*, 1994; *Ocean*, 1994; *Ground Level Overlay*, 1995; *Windows*, 1995; *Tune In / Spin Out*, 1996; *Rondo*, 1996.

Awards: Guggenheim fellowships, John Simon Guggenheim Memorial Foundation, 1954 and 1959; *Dance Magazine* Award, 1960; Medal from the Society for the Advancement of Dancing in Sweden, 1964; Gold Medal for Choreographic Invention, Fourth International Festival of Dance, 1964; honorary D.L.L., University of Illinois, 1972; New York State Award, New York State Council on the Arts, 1975; Samuel H. Scripps Award for Lifetime Contribution to Dance, American Dance Festival, 1982; Commander of the Order of Arts and Letters, French Ministry of Culture, 1982; Award of Honor for Arts and Culture, Mayor of New York, 1983; made honorary member of the American Academy and Institute of Arts and Letters, 1984; MacArthur Fellowship, John D. and Catherine T. MacArthur Foundation, 1985; Kennedy Center Honors, Kennedy Center, Washington, DC, 1985; Laurence Olivier Award, best new dance production, Society of West End Theatre, 1985, for *Pictures*; Bessie Award for Sustained Achievement (with John Cage), Dance Theatre Workshop Annual New York Dance and Performance Awards, 1986; Algur H. Meadows Award for Excellence in the Arts, Southern Methodist University, 1987; Dance/USA National Honor, 1988; named Chevalier de la Legion D'Honneur by President Francois Mitterand of France, 1989; Porselli Prize, Cremona, Italy, 1990; National Medal of Arts from President George Bush, 1990; Digital Dance Premier Award, Digital Equipment Company, 1990; Award of Merit, Association of Performing Arts, 1990; Wexner Prize (with Cage), Wexner Center for the Arts, Ohio State University, 1993; inducted into the Hall of Fame, National Museum of Dance, 1993; Medal of Honor, Universidad Complutense of Madrid, 1993; Bessie Award for Outstanding Creative Achievement, 1993, for *Enter*; Dance and Performance Award, best performance by a visiting artist, Dance and Performance Awards, London, England, 1993; International Society of Performing Arts Administrators (ISPAA)/Tiffany Award for Outstanding Contribution to Dance, ISPAA, 1993; Grand Prix Video Danse/Carina Ari Award (with Elliot Caplan), Carina Ari Foundation, 1994; April 16, 1994 named "Merce Cunningham Day" by New York City Mayor Rudolph Giuliani, in honor of Cunningham's 75th birthday; honorary D.F.A., Wesleyan University, 1995; Golden Lion of Venice Biennale, Teatro La Fenice, 1995; Grand Prix Video Danse/Carina Ari Award (with Caplan), 1995; Nellie Cornish Arts Achievement Award, Cornish College of the Arts, 1996; Medal of Distinction, Barnard College, 1997; Grand Prix, Societe des Auteurs et Compositeurs Dramatiques, Teatro La Fenice, 1997.

Sidelights

A trailblazing figure in the modern dance community who has influenced generations of dancers and choreographers, Merce Cunningham is renowned world-wide for his distinctive, often controversial concepts and his experimental choreography. Departing from the romantic style of modern dance pioneer Martha Graham, of whose company he was once a member, Cunningham began in the 1940s to develop his modernist dance style, which utilizes free-flowing organization and movement that is not based upon a particular story or theme, as are most ballet and modern dance works. Cunningham began his collaboration with composer John Cage in the 1940s, and until Cage's death in 1992 the two produced a vast array of works—utilizing Cage's unique brand of music and sound compositions—in which music, dance, and set are presented as occupying the same space and time, but are kept as separate elements and are not linked as they would be in a conventional dance production. Cunningham has remained committed to finding innovative ways of creating and organizing his works, including the use of a computer to discover and direct the movements of the dancers in his company.

In May of 1997, Cunningham was honored by his peers for his contributions to dance at the Brooklyn Academy of Music in New York City; the event was attended by a number of notable figures in the dance world, including famed Russian-born ballet maestro Mikhail Baryshnikov, who told *Harper's Bazaar* contributor Joan Acocella that when he defected to the United States in 1974, leaving the traditional, strict ballet community in the Soviet Union, he was amazed by Cunningham's choreography. Baryshnikov remarked: "It was like discovering modern painting. The way Cunningham dancers cover space, that kind of organized chaos—it was very much like neo-Expressionist painting."

Cunningham was born Mercier Philip Cunningham on April 19, 1919, in Centralia, Washington, a small lumbering and coal-mining town where he grew up and developed an interest in the theatre and dance, an interest that was neither encouraged nor discouraged by his father, who was a lawyer. He began studying piano and dance as a teenager, learning from a local teacher and former vaudeville performer who instructed him in the arts of folk, tap, and ballroom dancing. Upon graduation from Centralia High School, Cunningham enrolled at George Washington University in Washington, DC, but only attended for one year before returning to Washington state and enrolling at the Cornish School of Fine and Applied Arts (now Cornish College of the Arts) in Seattle. While a student at Cornish, Cunningham began performing in amateur and vaudeville productions as well as in a few night clubs in Oregon and California; after honing his performance skills in this manner, he joined the Lester Horton Dance Theatre, a repertory company in California, for the summer of 1938. In 1939 Cunningham attended the Bennington School of Arts at Bennington College in Vermont, and it was there that he was seen by Martha Graham, who asked him to come to New York City and become a member of her dance company.

Cunningham's talents as a dancer quickly led him to become one of Graham's most favored students and earned him roles as a soloist and partner in the company's productions shortly after he joined the group in 1940; he continued to perform with Graham's company until 1945. As a dancer, Cunningham earned a solid reputation for his mastery of the demanding technical and physical aspects of modern dance, and was widely considered a gifted performer. In a review of one of Cunningham's early performances in the New York *Herald Tribune,* critic Edwin Denby asserted that Cunningham danced with "imagination and subtlety" and noted the dancer's "improvisatory naturalness of emphasis which keeps his gestures from ever looking stylized or formalized."

Cunningham began to experiment with choreography in the early 1940s, creating such works as *Shimmers* and *The Wind Remains,* both in 1943, and *Root of an Unfocus, Tossed as It Is Untroubled,* and *Four Walls,* all in 1944. Graham supported the choreographic efforts of her dancers and often presented their works in production; Cunningham took advantage of the oppor-

tunity presented to him by Graham and performed his own work, *Mysterious Adventure,* in 1945. This early work was marked by Cunningham's use of the technique of stopping motion so that the dancer remains immobile on stage, something that had never before been done in dance performance; it was the first of many innovations to American modern dance created by the young choreographer.

> "Movement remains endlessly fascinating to me. Within the scale of the human being there are endless possibilities. And that's really what interests me, to find something that I don't know about and find a way to use it."

Cunningham left the Martha Graham company in 1945, and for a short time thereafter he worked as an independent dancer. Soon, however, he formed his own company and returned to the work of choreography. From the outset of his career as a choreographer, Cunningham was a pioneer, delving into previously unexplored kinds of movement and music with each and every new work he composed. Many critics and fans in the dance community were at first puzzled by his unconventional productions, but some were immediately appreciative of his talent. The lack of a narrative to lend continuity and cohesiveness to the set, music, and dance movements was difficult for audiences to understand, and some critics, like the New York *Herald Tribune*'s Walter Terry responded negatively. In a review of Cunningham's *Sixteen Dances for Soloist and Company of Three,* Terry concluded that the kind of experimentation displayed in the production, which was intended to present assorted types of human conduct, was "carrying [Cunningham] farther and farther away from the theater and closer and closer to a sort of self-indulgent self-expressionism."

Such disapproval did not discourage Cunningham from continuing to seek out original means of composing and presenting his works, and in creating his 1952 production, *Suite by Chance,* Cunningham first tested a method known as "choreography by chance," which meant simply that Cunningham would compose various movements for individual body parts—the bending of an elbow, the turning of a head—and place the movements on slips of paper, which were shuffled and then chosen randomly according to the toss of a coin or simply by chance, but never by design. The coin tosses would determine which movements Cunningham would include in his compositions, and then the choreographer would put them together. In the mid-1960s Cunningham began to try the system called "indeterminacy," which involved the use of dance, film clips, music, and electronic sounds—hums, whistles, beeps, and the like—in a blend of movement and sound created by the dancers as they improvised movement. This system was employed in Cunningham's *Variations V,* a 1965 production that continually varied in length, due to its impromptu construction. In the 1990s Cunningham found a new tool to assist him in choreographing his productions: the computer. Using the computer, he is capable of breaking down a single movement into tiny segments, discovering in the process new body positions that he then incorporates into his choreography. In an interview with *Los Angeles Times* contributor Jordan Levin, Cunningham observed: "Movement remains endlessly fascinating to me. Within the scale of the human being there are endless possibilities. And that's really what interests me, to find something that I don't know about and find a way to use it."

Cunningham's experiments with different types of music and sounds have had less to do with the way in which the audio would complement or blend with the movement and more to do with how the sounds themselves are perceived and for what length of time they are sustained. In the 1950s, Cunningham and his colleague, composer John Cage, began using a variety of audio effects in their dance productions, including a piano that was altered so that it would produce an array of noises, and a series of mechanical-sounding, electronically produced sounds recorded on tape and sometimes played at extremely high decibel levels. The loudness of the music was often responded to negatively by critics, who expressed sentiments similar to the *New York Times*'s Allen Hughes, who remarked: "The attention the public can give to looking, is only what it has left after attending to the crashing assaults on its eardrums."

On May 19, 1997, Cunningham was honored by his friends and colleagues at the Brooklyn Academy of Music in New York City. The event, sponsored by the Cunningham Dance Foundation and hosted by Garrison Keillor, was attended by such dignitaries of the dance world as modern dance innovator and famed choreographer Twyla Tharp, who, according to the *New York Times*'s Anna Kisselgoff, "thanked Cunningham for being Cunningham." Other well-known figures

from the dance community expressed their appreciation for Cunningham's contributions to modern dance, including dancer Trisha Brown, who performed a solo dance entitled "For Merce," and famed dancer and film star Mikhail Baryshnikov, who performed the solo—originally performed by Cunningham himself—from Cunningham's 1968 work, *Walkaround Time.* By Kisselgoff's account of Baryshnikov's performance, the distinguished dancer "jogged in place behind a plastic box ... while taking off layers of sweaters and tights, stripping down to briefs and getting dressed again." Other performers honored Cunningham with their movements and their words, and as Kisselgoff expressed in the conclusion of her article, the evening ended as "Cunningham stepped onstage to move with spiritual and gleeful grace, his hands swiping at the air while his feet traveled in the other direction."

Despite his reputation for excellence and the praise that his works have received from both critics and audiences, Cunningham continues to be questioned about why his works are they way they are—why his dancers do not move with the music, why the movements seem so disjointed and unconnected. For Cunningham, dance is not intended to tell a story or communicate an idea; instead he views dance as something to watch and experience with one's eyes. In addition to his concept of dance as a purely visual art, he embodies with his works the idea of allowing each moment to stand on its own, without being concerned with how it relates to the moment that precedes or follows it. This is why his dancers often stand still or assume a series of bizarre, sometimes awkward-looking positions that appear to be unrelated to one another; to Cunningham there is no need to connect the movements, because each is a visual experience in and of itself that can be appreciated in isolation. The way in which he views dance is, it appears, the way in which Cunningham views the world at large; in the *Los Angeles Times* interview with Jordan Levin, Cunningham explained: "What people don't catch—some do, I don't doubt—is that everything is fragmented in a way. Maybe that's why they can't see it in another form, I don't know, but the society is so fragmented, everything about how we have to work is so fragmented." Cunningham's works continue to elicit rave reviews from audiences and critics who are mesmerized by his imaginative, unique choreography, impeccably performed by highly skilled, well-conditioned dancers. In a tribute to Cunningham in *Dance Ink*, which appears on the Cunningham Dance Foundation's website, Nancy Dalva declared: "There is no greater choreographer, no braver or more truthful performer. There is no one more innovative; his dances encompass a technique and a philosophy yet are full of the everyday." Dalva continued her praise of Cunningham and his works, commenting about his dances: "[Cunningham's dances] are commanding and rigorous, and submit themselves readily to explication and analysis. Recollected in tranquillity, they absorb all thought, all conjecture—a strange and wonderful power common to all profound works of imagination.... One might even come to think, after a long time of looking and thinking, that these dances offer a proposition about the nature of life, and how to go through it." At the conclusion of her review of a 1994 performance of Cunningham's *Ocean, Dance Magazine* contributor Luisa Moffett revealed: "As Cunningham came out to bow to the wildly cheering audience, walking with his crippled gait, so small at the center of that large circle, I was overwhelmed with admiration for this seventy-five-year-old master who can't stop being amazed by the world, or amazing it."

Sources

On-line

Cunningham Dance Foundation, http://www.merce.org (November 1997).
Dance Ink, http://www.merce.org; ink@webcom.com (November 1997).

Periodicals

Dance Magazine, October 1994, p. 82.
Harper's Bazaar, March 1, 1994, pp. 159-60.
Herald Tribune (New York), January 10, 1945; January 28, 1951.
Los Angeles Times, January 12, 1997.
New York Times, August 25, 1963; May 21, 1997.

—*Lynn M. Spampinato*

Angela Davis

AP/Wide World Photos

Activist, educator, and author

Born Angela Yvonne Davis, January 26, 1944, in Birmingham, AL; daughter of B. Frank (a teacher and businessman) and Sallye E. (a teacher) Davis. *Education:* Attended the Sorbonne, University of Paris, 1963-64; Brandeis University, B.A. (magna cum laude), 1965; graduate study at University of Frankfurt (Germany), 1965-67; University of California, San Diego, M.A., 1968, doctoral study, 1968-69.

Addresses: *Office*—History of Consciousness, University of California at Santa Cruz, 218 Oakes College, Santa Cruz, CA 95064.

Career

University of California, Los Angeles, assistant professor of philosophy, 1969-70; activist and author of books on civil rights, women's issues, and global policy, 1970—; Claremont Black Studies Center, instructor, 1975; San Francisco State University, professor, 1979-91; University of California at Santa Cruz, professor, 1992—. Communist Party candidate for vice president of the United States, 1980 and 1984. Member, Communist Party of the U.S.A. (member of Central Committee), National Alliance Against Racist and Political Oppression (founder and co-chairperson), National Political Congress of Black Women (national board member), National Black Women's Health Project (national board member), Phi Beta Kappa.

Sidelights

Angela Davis became a household name in 1970 as an outlaw and a radical freedom fighter, but throughout the decades, her reputation has evolved to that of a dedicated activist, respected educator, and popular public speaker. An avowed Communist who was embroiled in a battle for academic freedom early in her teaching career, she was also an outspoken activist for civil rights, especially concerning prison reforms and the oppression of the poor. Davis was suddenly thrust into the spotlight in 1970 when she was accused of supplying guns to a young man trying to free an inmate in a bloody courtroom escape attempt. She ended up on the FBI's Ten Most Wanted list and spent about a year and a half in jail awaiting trial. Worldwide, supporters rallied to "Free Angela," and she came to symbolize political repression. Acquitted of all charges, Davis published her autobiography at age 30 and later resumed her teaching career. Throughout her life, she has remained an unyielding force in the pursuit of justice and equality, involving herself not only in civil rights, but also in world peace and health care. She has also remained an active Communist who twice ran for the office of vice president, and is a popular lecturer who travels around the globe giving speeches. In 1998, Davis published a work showcasing her theories about women blues artists and their political effects in *Blues Legacies and Black Feminism: Gertrude "Ma" Rainey, Bessie Smith, and Billie Holiday.*

Davis was born January 26, 1944, in Birmingham, Alabama, to B. Frank and Sallye E. Davis, the oldest of four children. (One of her brothers, Benjamin Davis, played professional football with the Cleveland Browns.) Both of her college-educated parents went into teaching, but her father soon went into business for himself as a gas station owner. The family moved to an all-white neighborhood when Davis was a girl, where she took piano and dance lessons (albeit against her will), joined the Girl Scouts, and lived rather comfortably financially. She also faced discrimination, however. Blacks were segregated in schools, stores, churches, and restaurants, sometimes with signs posted reading "white only" or "colored only," and other times with unspoken barriers. After a number of other black families began living in the Davis' neighborhood, white supremacists bombed so many of the houses that the neighborhood was dubbed "Dynamite Hill." Davis and her mother began attending civil rights demonstrations. Police harassed her and her friends for attempting to organize interracial study groups.

Davis often spent her summers in Manhattan, where her mother was pursuing a master's degree. There she experienced a different set of rules. She rode in the front of the bus behind the driver, instead of in the back, as in Alabama. She saw first-run films at glamorous theaters; whereas in Birmingham, blacks were relegated to watching old Tarzan movies at beat-up auditoriums, while only whites were allowed in the one nice cinema. A *New York Times* review of her autobiography reprinted a line that described her confusion about her separate lives: "'If only we lived in New York....' I constantly thought.... In New York we could buy a hot dog anywhere." Viewing this injustice firsthand sowed the seeds of her radicalism. She knew even as a teenager that she wanted to somehow help blacks and the poor.

Due to her academic superiority at Parker High School, Davis earned a scholarship for her junior year of high school to attend Elizabeth Irwin High, a private school in Manhattan's Greenwich Village. It was sponsored by the American Friends Service Committee, a program to foster Southern blacks' integration into the northern white educational system. She also had the opportunity to enter Fisk University on an early-admissions basis, but she took the opportunity to escape the South and went to New York, where she lived in Brooklyn with progressive white Episcopalian minister and civil rights activist William Howard Melish, who won the 1956 Stockholm Peace Prize. Though she found the new school to be more of a challenge than her school in Birmingham, she took summer classes

and repeated the more difficult courses in order to catch up. In New York, she learned more about socialism and communism, becoming interested in the idea of overthrowing the elite power structure.

After graduating from high school in 1961, Davis was awarded a scholarship to Brandeis University in Waltham, Massachusetts, where she was one of only a few African Americans on campus. She began studying French literature, spent her junior year at the prestigious Sorbonne in Paris, France, and met students from Algeria and other African nations who had been raised under French colonialism. Their tales of discrimination heightened her dedication to social change. Also while in Europe, she heard about a church bombing by white racists in her hometown in September of 1963 that killed four young black girls, three of whom she knew.

Returning to Brandeis, Davis studied philosophy privately with Marxist philosopher Herbert Marcuse, later to become her graduate advisor. After graduating magna cum laude in 1965, she again went overseas to study at the University of Frankfurt in Germany. She read philosophers Immanuel Kant and Georg Wilhelm Friedrich Hegel for two years, but was drawn back to the United States because she wanted to get involved with the civil rights movement. In 1967, she went back to America and enrolled at the University of California, San Diego, where she finished her master's degree in 1968 and began doctoral studies. She also joined activist groups, including the Student Nonviolent Coordinating Committee (SNCC) and the Black Panthers, but eventually decided to solely align herself with the Che-Lumumba Club, a black unit of the Communist Party in Los Angeles. She became an official member of the party on June 22, 1968. With the Che-Lumumba Club, she helped organize demonstrations and protests to draw attention to the oppression of minorities.

In the spring of 1969, Davis was hired to teach four courses at the University of California at Los Angeles: Dialectical Materialism, Kant, Existentialism, and Recurring Philosophical Themes in Black Literature. In July, the press got hold of information that revealed Davis was an active Communist Party member, and UCLA's board of regents, which included then-governor Ronald Reagan, dismissed her. Their position was based on the theories of Sidney Hook, who asserted that a Communist, due to his or her loyalty to the party, was not capable of critical thought and independent judgment. The regents used this argument to deem Davis incompetent as an educator, but the incident provoked obvious comparisons to the Red Scare tactics of anti-Communist Senator Joseph McCarthy in the 1950s. Most faculty and students— and even the university's president—opposed the board's action, claiming it infringed on academic freedom. Davis went to court and won her job back, but when her contract expired on June 19, 1970, the regents did not re-hire her, despite her overwhelming popularity and the administration's affirmation that her courses were excellent and unbiased. The board cited their reasons: her outside activism surrounding the Soledad Brothers, and her failure to complete her dissertation.

Davis had indeed become known for her involvement with three unrelated inmates at California's Soledad Prison who became known as the Soledad Brothers. Their struggle and Davis' support for them formed the basis for one of the most publicized trials in American history. The three men were known to be Marxist agitators for prison reform, and were thus often brutalized by guards. On January 13, 1970, a prison yard fight ensued among inmates, and a white guard shot and killed three black men. Half an hour later, a white guard was killed inside, and the activists—John W. Cluchette, Fleeta Drumgo, George Lester Jackson— were indicted for murder. Over the following months, Davis began corresponding with Jackson and they fell in love. Davis worked diligently to bring public attention to the prisoners' cause.

On August 7, 1970, Jackson's trial was set to begin in the Marin County Civic Center in California, when his teenage brother, Jonathan, entered the courtroom, slipped arms to his brother and other convicts there, and tried to take hostages. Gunfire erupted, killing Jonathan Jackson, the judge, and two of the other prisoners, although Bettina Aptheker in *The Morning Breaks* asserted that Jonathan Jackson never fired any bullets. She maintained that the prosecutor who had been taken hostage had fired one convict's gun until it was empty, and that guards opened fire on the prisoners as well. A *New York Times* article also noted that the question of how the shooting began was never answered. The weapons, however, that the convicts possessed were registered in Davis's name, and she fled to New York. She was put on the FBI's Ten Most Wanted List and apprehended in New York City two months later. After spending time in jail in New York, she was extradited to California and imprisoned for 16 months. Prosecutors accused Davis of masterminding the plot and furnishing the guns due to her love for George Jackson, but she maintained her innocence, claiming that she was being railroaded for her political activism.

International support for Davis was overwhelming. Demonstrators of all nationalities displayed "Free Angela" signs, stickers, and buttons, and the slogan came to represent the plight of all those mistreated within the legal system. After spending almost a year and a half in jail, Davis's trial began in February of 1972. In June of 1972, after deliberating for 13 hours, a jury of 11 whites and one Mexican American acquitted Davis of all three charges of murder, kidnapping, and conspiracy. Following the trial, Davis embarked on a speaking tour and appeared in the Soviet Union, where she was warmly received. She published *Angela Davis: An Autobiography* in 1974, which Elinor Langer in a *New York Times* review called "an act of political communication" rather than one of self-discovery. Langer continued, "It is sometimes the voice of Every Prisoner, a little familiar. But it is also a strong, idiosyncratic account of her childhood, youth and growth, and her choice of the Communist party as the agency through which to act."

> *"History is important, but it also can stifle young people's ability to think in new ways and to present ideas that may sound implausible now but that really may help us to develop radical strategies for moving into the next century."*

After a hiatus from teaching, Davis was hired amid much controversy at the Claremont Black Studies Center in Claremont, California, part of the Claremont cluster of six colleges. Everett R. Holles in the *New York Times* reported, "Angered alumni and wealthy benefactors who had talked of canceling their bequest to the richly endowed schools have received letters explaining that although Miss Davis' $3,000 contract with the Claremont Black Studies Center was 'unauthorized and regrettable,' it was legally binding." The article explained that the director of the Black Studies Center, James Garrett, was accused of hiring Davis without discussing it with school officials, and later was dismissed. The center, forced to let her teach lest they be sued for breach of contract, tried to limit her presence on campus by scheduling her classes on Friday evenings and Saturdays. They held her classes in different clandestine locations each week, contacting students via telephone 45 minutes before each session to inform them where to go. Her lectures focused on teaching the history and political-economic situations of black women.

After that difficult position, Davis found an academic home for over a decade at San Francisco State University, where she taught from 1979 to 1991. Meanwhile, she remained active in the Communist party, giving lectures around the world and even running for vice president on the party's ticket in 1980 and 1984. In 1981, she wrote one of her major works, *Women, Race & Class,* which documents the historical development of feminism and asserts that black women are triply oppressed due to race, class, and sex. She brings up examples of racism in the feminist movement beginning in the nineteenth century. Ann Jones in the *New York Times Book Review* stated, "Against this intricate background of the separate and unequal histories of black and white women, Miss Davis sets in perspective some contemporary women's issues: rape, reproductive freedom, housework and child care."

In 1992, Davis took a position as a tenured professor at the University of California at Santa Cruz teaching the history of consciousness. She continued to be popular on the lecture circuit as well, espousing the same hard-line views of the necessity of social change as always. In a 1981 interview with Sid Cassese in *Essence,* excerpted in *Contemporary Literary Criticism,* she noted that blacks were seen more often in the media in a variety of places that were previously closed to them, but that they represented a minority of blacks: though middle-class blacks were becoming a more apparent presence, more blacks were entering poverty as well. In *Essence* in 1995 she remarked, "The struggle is much more difficult now because racism is more entrenched and complicated." She went on to say that the battle for equality must extend beyond color to culture, gender, class, and sexual orientation. And in *Essence* in 1996, she continued to try to find avenues for change, discussing issues from the Million Man March to Snoop Doggy Dogg with Katherine Cleaver, wife of Black Panther leader Eldridge Cleaver. She also acknowledged a different climate for young people, relating that she studied philosophy in college not as a career path, but to find a way to make a difference in the civil rights struggle. "Today the economic situation is a lot worse," Davis conceded in *Essence.* "Even the most politically conscious students are forced to think about how they're going to market themselves in order to get a job."

Into the 1990s, Davis worked for women's rights, nuclear disarmament, and affordable health care. She was active in the Prisoners' Rights Movement, founded the National Alliance Against Racist and Political Repression, and served as a national board member for the National Political Congress of Black Women and the National Black Women's Health Project. In 1998, she published another book, *Blues Legacies and Black Feminism: Gertrude "Ma" Rainey, Bessie Smith, and Billie Holiday,* in which she uses Marxist ideology to assert that female blues singers of the 1920s and '30s helped give rise to a black working-class consciousness. She had been studying the subject since the 1980s and had taught courses on the topic as well.

Davis into her 50s remained physically fit by riding bikes, hiking, running, and working out. No longer sporting the trademark large Afro hairstyle that she wore during her younger years, Davis grew her hair out in long natural braids. In the 1996 *Essence* conversation with Cleaver, Davis suggested that the old guard of the civil rights movement should encourage younger visionaries to assume confidence and take on leadership. "There's ... a tendency to raise past leaders to the status of icons so that political commitment becomes judged in relation to how much an individual measures up to Malcolm X, Marcus Garvey or some other historical figure," she noted in *Essence.* "History is important, but it also can stifle young people's ability to think in new ways and to present ideas that may sound implausible now but that really may help us to develop radical strategies for moving into the next century."

Selected writings

(With Ruchell Magee, the Soledad Brothers, and others) *If They Come in the Morning: Voices of Resistance,* Third Press, 1971.
Angela Davis: An Autobiography, Random House, 1974.
Women, Race & Class, Random House, 1981.
Violence Against Women and the Ongoing Challenge to Racism, Kitchen Table, 1985.
Women, Culture & Politics, Random House, 1989.
Blues Legacies and Black Feminism: Gertrude "Ma" Rainey, Bessie Smith, and Billie Holiday, Pantheon, 1998.

Sources

Books

Aptheker, Bettina, *The Morning Breaks: The Trial of Angela Davis,* International Publishers, 1975.
Contemporary Authors, New Revision Series, Volume 10, Gale Research, 1983.
Contemporary Black Biography, Volume 5, Gale Research, 1994.

Contemporary Literary Criticism, Volume 77, Gale Research, 1993.
Encyclopedia of World Biography, second edition, Gale Research, 1998.
Historic World Leaders, Gale Research, 1994.

Periodicals

Ebony, August 1996, p. 108.
Essence, January 1995, p. 80; May 1996, p. 82.
New York Times, June 5, 1970; October 29, 1972; June 4, 1972; June 5, 1972; October 27, 1974; November 16, 1975; November 20, 1979; January 10, 1982; March 8, 1998.

—Geri Speace

Terrell Davis

Football player

Born October 28, 1972, in San Diego, CA; son of John and Kateree Davis. *Education:* Attended Long Beach State University, 1990-92, and University of Georgia, 1992-95.

Addresses: *Office*—c/o Denver Broncos Administrative Offices, 13655 Broncos Parkway, Englewood, CO 80112.

Career

Drafted and signed by Denver Broncos, 1995; single-season records for rushing attempts, rushing yards, and total yards: 35 passes caught, 1996; second in American Football Conference (AFC) total touchdowns (15), 1996; signed a five-year, seven-figure contract before the season start of his second year in professional football, 1996; AFC rushing leader with 1750 yards, 1997.

Awards: Denver Broncos, offensive MVP, 1995; named Rookie of the Year, *Football Digest;* voted All-Rookie teams—*Pro Football Weekly* and *Football News;* AFC Player of the Week for Week 8, 1996; *Sporting News* NFL All-Pro team, 1996; twice AFC Offensive Player of the Month, September 1996 and September 1997; Miller Lite NFL Player of the Week; Pro Bowl 1996 and 1997; Broncos Offensive MVP for the season, 1997; All Pro Bowl, 1998; MVP, Super Bowl XXXII, 1998.

Sidelights

In January of 1998, running back Terrell Davis emerged as the hero of Super Bowl XXXII, gaining 157 yards (rushing) and winning the award for most valuable player (MVP). He completed the 1997 football season (and post season) with a record-breaking 2,331 yards rushing, and went on to represent the American Football Conference (AFC) in the 1998 All Pro Game. Davis, a sixth-round draft pick in the National Football League (NFL), was an unlikely hero; having suffered from painful migraine headaches since childhood, he developed a serious headache during the Super Bowl. He continued to play and scored the winning touchdown in spite of the pain.

Terrell Davis was born on October 28, 1972, to John and Kateree Davis. The youngest sibling, he and his five older brothers were raised in San Diego, California. The boys were still very young when their father became ill with lupus, an immune deficiency disease. John Davis died when his youngest son was only 12, leaving Kateree Davis to raise the family by herself. Terrell was deeply affected by the tragedy and has maintained a very close relationship with his mother ever since. Years later, in 1994, Davis grieved deeply again, over the senseless shooting death of his cousin and close friend.

As a boy growing up, Davis loved to play Pop Warner football. He distinguished himself as an awesome opponent, so that the other players gave him the nickname "Boss Hog." So reluctant was Davis to give up his status and reputation with the Pop Warner league that he continued with the pee-wee clubs into his freshman year at Morse High School, dehydrating himself with plastic bags to keep from exceeding the weight limit.

When he transferred to Lincoln High School (former Heisman trophy winner Marcus Allen's alma mater) Davis joined the football team as a nose guard in his junior year. In his senior year he played several different positions, including nose guard and fullback. He also threw discus (he broke the high school record) and ran track. Although he lettered in track, his running abilities went largely untapped on the gridiron because, at nearly 200 pounds, he was an excellent blocker.

After graduating from high school in 1990, Davis attended Long Beach State University where he played under the late George Allen for two years. Long Beach eliminated their football program after Allen's untimely death, and Davis transferred to the University of Georgia, where he played for three seasons. At Georgia the coaches used a passing offense, so Davis had little opportunity to shine, although he showed promise, especially in his junior year when he rushed for 824 yards.

His college career took a nose dive when he suffered a severe hamstring injury during pre-season practice before his senior year. He ended up on the sick list, and he aggravated the injury when he tried playing football before it had completely healed. He reinjured the hamstring so badly that he was out of commission for most of his senior year, ending the season with less than 450 yards rushing, a mediocre statistic.

Davis was less than sought after by the National Football League (NFL) in the draft in 1995. He was eventually picked up by the Denver Broncos in the sixth round of the draft. As the 196th player drafted, Davis was an unlikely pick to be a star running back. He assumed that if he ever played at all it would be as "camp meat," a slang term for low-round draft picks who never make the players roster but end up as human scrimmage obstacles for the regular players during practice.

However, Davis fared much better than anticipated, impressing the coaches during pre-season with his power and speed. By the start of the regular season in 1996, he had graduated from fourth string to first string. Along with his ability to "rush" down the field and avoid being blocked, Davis possesses a keen intelligence which has served to his advantage as a football player. Observers have noted that although he's not very fast, his quick mind, dexterity, and accuracy make him a player that any coach can count on to run a game plan and follow the plays.

Despite another torn hamstring near the end of his rookie season, Davis made his presence felt during that first year in the NFL. He rushed for an amazing 1,117 yards, which landed him an NFL record as the lowest drafted player to rush the field for over 1,000 yards in a single season. By the end of the season he ranked fifth in rushing in the AFC conference and sixteenth in the league.

"We spent all this money on scouting, and he makes us look like jackasses, " noted Billy Devaney of Chargers' player personnel in a quote by Paul Attner of *Sporting News,* "You see a different guy right now than you saw in college.... And what is incredible is that he did it right away; he didn't need time to develop." Davis himself was impressed with his first season performance, and he was not alone. The Broncos rewrote his contract after that first year, and raised his salary from the rookie minimum of $131,700 to $6.8 million for five years.

Yet Davis never bought a new wardrobe, or even a new car after signing the seven-figure contract. He remained content to share an apartment with his brother as they always did in the past, and he saved most of his earnings. He rejected the affluence, as he lamented ironically to Attner, "Why is it when you have money, everyone wants to give you something free, but when you are poor, no one wants to buy anything for you?" His needs are modest; he likes to go four-wheeling in the snow, spend time on-line on his computer, watch "sitcoms" on television, and play video games.

In 1996 Davis "hit the ground running" both literally and figuratively. He rushed for 1,538 yards that season, to lead the AFC, and he finished second in the NFL. Tom TJ Jacques of *Urban Spectrum* called Davis "the consummate athlete.... He is powerful and explosive, but is shifty like a halfback."

In September of 1997 Davis was named AFC Offensive Player of the Month for the second time in his brief career. That season his career rushing topped 3,000 yards in 34 games, surpassing the great John Elway and setting a new Broncos record. Davis missed the end of that season with a separated right shoulder, but he led the conference in rushing yards, and he was back again for the end-of-year play-offs (the "wild card" game) against the Jacksonville Jaguars.

The Broncos were successful in the play-off games, winning the AFC championship and the right to compete for the world championship in Super Bowl XXXII.

Super Bowl XXXII was hosted in San Diego, Davis' home town. He traveled under an assumed name, but he made a stop at Lincoln High School in San Diego, where his identity was anything but a secret. He attended a ceremony at the school whereby they retired his old football number from high school. "It was a warm feeling to see that happen.... [It] was kind of cool," Davis admitted to Austin Murphy of *Sports Illustrated.*

On January 23, 1998, during Super Bowl XXXII, Davis rushed for 157 yards and three touchdowns, a Super Bowl record. The Broncos won the championship, and Davis won the MVP award, but the big news was a migraine headache that nearly eliminated Davis from the game. Even the debilitating headache played a part in the Broncos success—Davis, who was seeing double from the pain, managed to decoy the opposition when Elway faked a hand-off to him. The opposing defenders charged for Davis, and that left Elway with a clear shot at the goal line. Davis took medication for the headache before he became incapacitated, successfully playing out the second half of the Super Bowl, and scoring the winning touchdown.

After the game, endorsement offers were plentiful, but not just for sporting goods and cereal. Davis and his headache medicine became a lucrative commodity. *Sporting News* dubbed Davis' discomfort, "One of the most famous migraines of all time." The medication he'd taken for the Super Bowl was newly released, and the manufacturers were eager to sign Davis to endorse the product. But the contract deal took an unusual twist; it included a stipulation for the pharmaceutical distributor to donate money to migraine research and education every time Davis scored a touchdown.

Davis was only seven years old when he first developed migraines, with accompanying blurred vision, nausea, and extreme sensitivity to light. The headaches came most often while he was a teenager, plaguing his high-school days and causing him a great deal of pain and discomfort.

By the time he played ball in college at the University of Georgia, he found a prescription nasal spray that successfully reduced the frequency and intensity of the attacks, although nothing completely cured the problem. He has also tried vitamin B-6 and magne-sium supplements, dietary restrictions, orthodontia, chiropractic treatment, and breathing straight oxygen. Despite the excruciating bouts of pain, Davis maintained that by far the biggest challenge of his life was coming into the NFL in the sixth round of the college draft.

The 1997 football season was a long one for Davis; after the play-offs and the Super Bowl, he went to the All Pro Bowl, the final game. Davis, who personally answers his own fan mail, has managed to keep a cool head amid the accolades and hoopla. Friends describe Davis as popular, personable, and friendly. He attests that his mother was the greatest influence in his life.

Next to football, his favorite sport is bowling, but he admits that his favorite recreation is sleeping. He was fined once by Broncos head coach Mike Shanahan for sleeping during a club meeting, but there were no hard feelings. According to Attner of *Sporting News,* Shanahan said, "He's such a class act, you feel for him so much as a person."

Sources

On-line

"Broncos RB Terrell Davis Named AFC Player of Month for September," http://www.denverbroncos.com/DENVERBRONCOS/newsroom/releases/971002-00.html, October 1, 1997.
"Broncos RB Terrell Davis Named AFC Offensive Player of Week for Week 8," http://www.denverbroncos.com/DENVERBRONCOS/newsroom/releases/961023-03.html, October 23, 1996.
Davis, Terrell, "Broncos Diary," *Denver Post On-line,* http://www.denverpost.com/broncos/super116.html, January 22, 1998.
Jacques, Tom TJ, "Doctor Terrell Davis Has the Perfect Prescription," *Urban Spectrum,* http://www.orci.com/us1/terdavis.html/.
"Terrell Davis, Career Highlights," http://www.nfl.com/players/highlights/1538.html.

Periodicals

People, December 26, 1996, pp. 96-100.
Sporting News, January 30, 1998; February 5, 1998.
Sports Illustrated, October 28, 1996, p. 54; February 2, 1998, p. 8.
U.S. News & World Report, February 9, 1998, p. 68.

—*Gloria Cooksey*

Oscar De La Hoya

AP/Wide World Photos

Boxer

Born February 4, 1973, in East Los Angeles, CA; son of Joel (a former professional boxer and warehouse clerk) and Cecilia (a seamstress and singer) De La Hoya.

Addresses: *Home*—Whittier, CA, and Big Bear, CA. *Office*—Oscar De La Hoya Enterprises, 2401 South Atlantic Blvd., Monterey Park, CA 91754-6807.

Career

Began organized recreational boxing at age six; amateur boxing record was 223-5, with 153 victories by knockout, and culminated in a gold-medal performance at the 1992 Summer Olympic Games in Barcelona, Spain; professional boxing record of 27-0, with 22 knockouts.

Awards: U.S. National Junior Champion, 1988; 125-pound champion, Golden Gloves competition, 1989; Gold Medalist, U.S. Olympic Cup, 1990; Gold Medalist, Goodwill Games, 1990; Gold Medalist, U.S. National Championships, 1990; Gold Medalist, USA vs. Olympic Festival, 1991; Gold Medalist, USA vs. Boxing National Champions, 1991; Gold Medalist, USA vs. Bulgaria, 1992; Gold Medalist, USA vs. Hungary, 1992; Gold Medalist, World Challenge, 1992; Gold Medalist, Olympic Games, 1992; junior lightweight champion and later lightweight champion, World Boxing Organization, 1994; champion, International Boxing Federation, 1995; super-lightweight champion, World Boxing Council, 1996; welterweight champion, World Boxing Council, 1997.

Sidelights

Known as the "Golden Boy" of boxing since his upset victory in the 1992 Olympic championships, the World Boxing Council (WBC) welterweight title-holder Oscar De La Hoya is widely considered the best boxer, "pound-for-pound," active in the sport. De La Hoya's Olympic Gold Medal performance in Barcelona, Spain, capped an amateur career of 223 victories and five defeats that included championships in such competitions as the Golden Gloves, Junior Olympics, Goodwill Games, and U.S. National Championships between 1988 and 1992.

As a professional, De La Hoya has won World Boxing Organization, International Boxing Federation, and WBC titles and carries a 27-0 record, with 22 victories by knockout. His athletic accomplishments, combined with his youth, physical attractiveness, and polite manners, have made De La Hoya a media and fan favorite, and have earned him wealth enough to place third on the *Forbes* magazine list of the world's highest paid athletes. In naming De La Hoya 1997's "Fighter of the Year" the editors of *KO* proclaimed that he is "well on his way to becoming the biggest star boxing has produced in decades."

De La Hoya was born in East Los Angeles, California, in 1973, the son of Joel and Cecilia De La Hoya, who had immigrated to the United States from Mexico. His participation in organized boxing began at an early age and constituted a continuation of a family legacy that included his grandfather and father before him. De La Hoya told Bill Davidson in *Los Angeles Magazine,* "My first boxing match came when I was six. On Sundays, Dad would take me to the Pico Rivera Sports Arena, where there was kind of a boys' club. He got me a little pair of boxing gloves and taught me jabs and feints. One day, there was a boxing tournament for kids ... and Dad entered me in it. They put me in the ring with another kid, and I won."

In a 1997 interview with Alex Tresniowski of *People* De La Hoya revealed, "Boxing is in my blood.... From the day I put on the gloves, it's what I wanted to do." By the time the fighter was 11-years-old, he was winning competitions and working with professional trainers, including Al Stankie and Robert Alcazar. At age 15 De La Hoya won the National Junior Boxing Championship and the following year became the Golden Gloves title-holder in the 125-pound division.

In the summer of 1990 De La Hoya competed in the Goodwill Games in Seattle, Washington, but his gold-medal victory proved bittersweet when he learned that his mother was terminally ill and that the gravity of her condition had been kept a secret from him until the competition was over. His mother succumbed to cancer in October of that year, expressing her hope that her son would win an Olympic Gold Medal. Fulfilling his mother's dream became the focus of De La Hoya's training, and in 1992 in the Barcelona Olympics, he achieved his goal—and became the only U.S. boxer to win a medal in the competition—with a victory against Marco Rudolph, a German fighter who had defeated him the previous year at the world championships in Sydney, Australia.

Commenting on the Olympic competition, which included bouts against Adilson Silva, Dimitrov Tontchev, and Hong Sung Sik, Davidson called De La Hoya's first-round defeat of the Cuban fighter Julio Gonzalez "probably the biggest boxing upset of the '92 Olympics.... [De La Hoya] confounded Gonzalez with footwork, jabs and uppercuts." Following his gold-medal bout, which ended in a knockout in the third round, De La Hoya hoisted both the American and Mexican flags and later returned home to place his gold medal on his mother's grave.

Under Alcazar's direction and backed by the management team of Robert Mittleman and Steve Nelson, De La Hoya turned professional after the Olympics. His first professional fight came November 23, 1992, a first-round knockout of Lamar Williams in Inglewood, California, and in December 1992, he won another first-round victory versus Cliff Hicks. Through early 1993 De La Hoya gained professional experience in bouts against Paris Alexander, Curtis Strong, Jeff Mayweather, and Mike Grable, whom De La Hoya knocked down—but not out— seven times in their eight-round contest. Still, Grable won the distinction of becoming the first fighter to go the distance against De La Hoya in a professional match.

The remainder of the year saw additional knock-out victories against Frank Avelar, Troy Dorsey, Renaldo Carter, Angelo Nunez, and Narcisco Valenzuela, and in December of that year De La Hoya severed his relationship with Mittleman and Nelson. Acting as his own manager, De La Hoya captured his first professional title in Los Angeles on March 5, 1994, with the tenth-round technical knockout of the Danish fighter Jimmi Bredahl for the junior lightweight championship of the World Boxing Organization (WBO). His second-round defeat of Jorge Paez in Las Vegas in July 1994 secured the WBO lightweight title.

Over the next several months De La Hoya faced such competitors as Carl Griffith, John Avila, and John-John Molina (the first fighter ever to last 12 rounds against De La Hoya), in preparation for his May 6, 1995, championship fight against Rafael Ruelas for the International Boxing Federation (IBF) title. After gaining the title in his match with Ruelas, De La Hoya defeated Genaro Hernandez and "Jesse" James Leija in his remaining bouts in 1995.

The following February he knocked out Darryl Tyson in the second round of their Las Vegas contest, the final fight before his June challenge of WBC junior welterweight champion Julio Cesar Chavez, a seasoned Mexican fighter who had 97 professional victories. De La Hoya opened a cut about Chavez's eye in the first round of the contest held at Caesars Palace in Las Vegas, and when the fight was stopped in round four of the bout, many observers were stunned, particularly the large contingent of Mexican-American fans who had long supported Chavez.

De La Hoya defeated another favorite of the Mexican fans, the previously-undefeated Miguel Angel Gonzales, and retained his junior welterweight title in January 1997, the beginning of a busy and highly successful year for De La Hoya. Moving up to the 147-pound weight class, he gained the WBC welterweight title in April with a decision victory against the reigning champion Pernell Whitaker in Las Vegas, and followed that victory with a second-round knockout of David Kamau in June. He retained his welterweight title through additional challenges by Hector "Macho" Camacho and Wilfredo Rivera to conclude 1997. De La Hoya's title defense versus French contender Patrick Charpentier was scheduled for February 28, 1998, but was postponed due to a training injury sustained by the champion.

Describing De La Hoya's strengths in the ring, Mark Kriegel in *Esquire* noted his "cobra quickness, an unnaturally strong lead hand ... and the advantage of superior reach and leverage." Vic Ziegel, in *Playboy*, remarked that "De La Hoya is good and he knows it. He's as fast as anyone out there. He's the thinking man's fighter. Right-handed only when he's in the ring, he has a potent left hand. He also has height and reach and know how to use both."

Davidson reported in *Los Angeles Magazine* that De La Hoya's training regimen at his Big Bear Lake facility in the San Bernardino Mountains includes "two hours of boxing with sparring partners in the afternoon—the gym deliberately heated to 95 degrees to simulate the warmth from the lights and the crowd in an actual arena."

According to Dimitri Ehrlich in *Interview,* De La Hoya "fights classically, with clean, controlled fury and a shockingly powerful jab, whose sting derives from his beginnings as a southpaw." When Ehrlich asked what talent in boxing means to him, De La Hoya responded, "It means being able to accomplish what no other boxer could ever accomplish and to win fights easily. It's about being able to overcome any challenge. And not get hit."

As the editors of *KO* magazine noted, De La Hoya "fights with passion every time out. It's hard to be the best in your field if you don't love what you're doing." Promoter Don Elbaum, quoted in the same magazine, commented, "I'm becoming a big believer in De La Hoya. He's a helluva fighter, he's a great kid, and I'm convinced he's as good as everyone thinks he is."

In addition to the continued presence of Roberto Alcazar, De La Hoya has employed several trainers throughout his professional career, including Carlo Ortiz, a former lightweight champion, who was hired in November 1993. Following Ortiz, Mexican trainer Jesus Rivero combined study of Shakespeare with ring conditioning in order to develop De La Hoya's mind as well as his body but saw De La Hoya through only

seven fights before being replaced by Emanual Steward, the highly regarded Kronk Boxing Team taskmaster. At the time Steward praised De La Hoya as possibly "the most natural fighter I've ever trained." On November 13, 1997, Steward was replaced by Hall of Fame trainer Gil Clancy.

De La Hoya's accomplishments in the ring, his rags-to-riches story, and his dazzling good looks have combined to make him a marketable figure, and advertisers have been quick to seize on his appeal. According to Davidson in *Los Angeles Magazine,* "De La Hoya is a Madison Avenue dream." He has won several lucrative endorsement contracts with such companies as John Henry Menswear, Budweiser, Edge, Mennen, B.U.M. Equipment clothing, and Champion athletic shoes.

However, De La Hoya makes a point to share his success and his fortune with the Latino community in which he was raised. Chief among his community service efforts is the Oscar De La Hoya Foundation, a nonprofit organization dedicated to sponsoring Olympic hopefuls and to providing educational scholarships. And, in 1997 De La Hoya spent $500,000 to purchase the Resurrection Gym, a converted church where he trained as a youngster; now considered one of the leading role models in the Hispanic community, he plans to spend an estimated $250,000 for renovations to the facility, which has been renamed the Oscar De La Hoya Youth Boxing Center.

> "Boxing is in my blood.... From the day I put on the gloves, it's what I wanted to do."

Despite these efforts, De La Hoya has been frustrated by a growing number of detractors among Latino boxing enthusiasts, who express displeasure with his commercial success and his move to a more exclusive neighborhood. According to De La Hoya in the *Esquire* interview with Kriegel, "If I was scarred, if my nose was all busted up, they'd love me.... But I'm not going to apologize to the Mexican fans for not getting hit. I'm not going to apologize for being better than my opponents."

At 25, De La Hoya is unmarried but has many female fans. He is an avid golfer and has long expressed a desire to pursue architecture after retiring from the ring. He told Jose Torres of the *Daily Breeze,* "I have felt violent inside the ring.... Outside the ring, I want no trouble with anybody. I want peace and tranquility. I want to be happy and enjoy life."

Sources

On-line

Oscar De La Hoya Homepage, www.//oscardelahoya .com (February 26, 1998).

Books

Who's Who among Hispanic Americans, third edition, Gale Research, 1994.

Periodicals

Daily Breeze, March 30, 1997.
Esquire, November 1996, p. 78.
Harper's Bazaar, June 1996, p. 136.
Interview, June 1997, p. 84.
KO, April 1998.
Los Angeles Magazine, March 1994, p. 74.
Los Angeles Times, October 12, 1996.
People, January 20, 1997, p. 93.
Playboy, July 1996, p. 114.
Sports Illustrated, December 20, 1993, p. 13; December 8, 1997, p. 24.

—*Laurie DiMauro*

Brian Dickinson

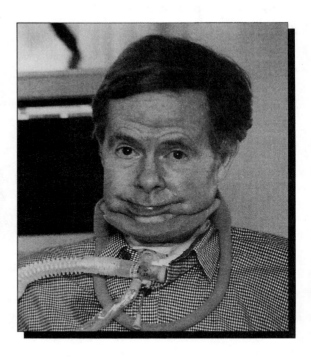

AP/Wide World Photos

Journalist

Born Brian Ward Dickinson, September 28, 1937, in Chicago, IL; son of Leon (a college professor) and Margaret (a secretary and editor) Dickinson; married Barbara Jaros (a magazine editor), December 29, 1961; children: Andrew, Matthew, Jonathan. *Education:* Harvard University, B.A., 1959; Brown University, M.A., 1976.

Addresses: *Office—Providence Journal-Bulletin,* 75 Fountain St., Providence, RI 02902.

Career

New York Times, New York City, news assistant, 1959-61; *New York Times* Washington Bureau, 1963; *Providence Journal-Bulletin,* reporter, political writer, chief editorial writer, editorial page editor, editorial columnist, 1964—; nationally syndicated columnist, 1988—. *Military service:* U.S. Army, 1961-63.

Awards: American Political Science Association fellow, 1969; John McCloy fellow, American Council of Germany, 1976; Best Feature Series citation, New England, UPI, 1986; American Society of Newspaper Editors Award for Distinguished Commentary, 1993; American Society of Newspaper Editors Award for Distinguished Writing, 1995; Poynter Institute for Media Studies, Best Newspaper Writing, Commentary, 1995.

Member: International American Press Association, (board of directors, 1984—), National Conference of Editorial Writers (president, 1987).

Sidelights

Each week Brian Dickinson sends his newspaper column to his editor at the *Providence Journal-Bulletin,* in Providence, Rhode Island. According to his editor, the columns rarely need editing. That may not seem noteworthy for a journalist who has been on the job since the 1960s, but in this case, it is remarkable. Brian Dickinson is a man imprisoned in his own body. He cannot move, talk or walk, and without a ventilator, he cannot breathe. He is battling amyotrophic lateral sclerosis (ALS), commonly known as Lou Gehrig's disease. However, he can still challenge himself and his readers. For the past three years, he has used an eye-activated computer, blinking each letter of each word, to write his newspaper column.

According to Florence George Graves on the *American Journalism Review* website, ALS is named after the New York Yankees star who died of the disease in 1941. It "strikes about 5,000 Americans a year, gradually destroying all of their voluntary muscles, leaving them paralyzed." She added, "Doctors don't know what causes it or how to cure it. Most victims die within two to five years." The disorder usually occurs after age 40 and affects more men than women.

In his December 3, 1997 *Providence Journal-Bulletin* column, Dickinson described ALS : "The disease that has chosen my nervous systems—mine!—to cripple and ravage quaintly bore the name of a long-ago baseball hero.... As a disease, this one is a champ. Invisibly, and by mechanisms not yet understood, its agents choke off the motor neurons, the cells in the brain and spinal column that are the vital electrical triggers governing almost all bodily movement. The patient, denied the capacity to move, succumbs."

Dickinson is aware that ALS is regarded as a fatal disease, but chooses not to dwell on it. He can still think, see, hear and write. And even though it takes him 10-12 hours to finish a column when it used to take him 3 hours, he concentrates on his writing. In fact, he was nominated for a Pulitzer Prize in the Journalism for Commentary category in 1995. He is also working on his memoirs, recounting his battle with ALS.

> *"In some ways I as a kid was pretty wimpy," Dickinson blinks, "BUT when ALS came along, I saw it as a chance to show that I did have some grit."*

The son of Leon and Margaret Dickinson, this diligent columnist was born in Chicago, Illinois, on September 28, 1937. At the time of his birth, his father was a graduate student who would later become a professor with a specialty in 19th-century American literature. His mother was a secretary who later edited a wildlife journal. She died in 1969 from Hodgkin's disease. When Dickinson was nine years old, his father accepted a teaching position at the University of Missouri. The family, which now included sisters Toby and Catherine, moved to Columbia.

Six years later, his father was offered a Fulbright fellowship to teach at the University of Groningen in Holland. The family enjoyed the opportunity to travel around Europe, and the 15-year-old Dickinson soaked in the history of the region and even learned some Dutch. When he returned to high school in Missouri, he was the student manager of the basketball team and the editor of the school yearbook. He attended Harvard University, graduating in 1959, and landed a job writing for the *Week in Review* section of the *New York Times*.

In 1960, Dickinson went on a blind date and met his future wife, Barbara Jaros. She had recently graduated from Smith College in Massachusetts and was working at *Mademoiselle* magazine as an assistant beauty editor. Although she thought her future husband was handsome, she shared with Geoff Williams of *Biography*, "what I liked the most is that he had a sense of humor, that he had an enthusiasm for life—and that has never changed."

The couple married 14 months later in Washington, D.C. By this time, Dickinson had been drafted into the U.S. Army and was working at the Pentagon as an editor for the *Pentagon News*. As he recalled to Williams, "It wasn't a bad duty at all, seeing the President and Mrs. Kennedy at the airport every so often as they welcomed some foreign bigwig."

Dickinson and his wife remained in Washington while he attended law school and worked at the Washington Bureau of the *New York Times*. He was working the day President Kennedy was assassinated and noted, "That drama turned me toward journalism irreversibly."

In 1964, Dickinson began working for the *Providence Journal-Bulletin*. He and his wife had three sons, Andrew, and twins Matthew and Jonathan. The family had a good life, and they enjoyed leisure time, outdoor activities and vacations. Dickinson enjoyed the rewards of his job. He traveled the world, won writing awards, earned his master's degree, and helped plan an annual Public Affairs conference sponsored by his newspaper and his alma mater (Brown University). As noted by Williams, one day on their sailboat, Dickinson told his wife, "This is as good as it gets."

In the spring of 1992, Dickinson began to notice a strange tingling sensation in his right leg. At first, it didn't seem like much, but it eventually got worse. He began falling down and his right arm wouldn't move correctly. Finally deciding it could be a serious problem, he went to the doctor.

According to Williams, neither of the Dickinsons will ever forget December 2, 1992. That was the day the doctor told Dickinson: "You have Lou Gehrig's disease, and there's not a damn thing you can do about it." Although Barbara Dickinson didn't really know much about the disease, Brian Dickinson did, and recalled that "the skin crawled on my bare arms and legs, and my vision grayed out."

The doctor was blunt about the future; there was nothing they could do. But, of course, neither of the Dickinsons accepted that. Instead, they vowed to fight against the disease. Dickinson shared with Williams (through his computer) that as a kid, he was likely to run from a fight. "In some ways I as a kid was pretty wimpy," he blinked, "BUT when ALS came along,I saw it as a chance to show that I did have some grit."

Since that devastating day in 1992, Dickinson's condition has worsened. He spends his time in bed or in his wheelchair. He cannot speak; he replies to conversation with a smile or blink. His head is supported by a metal brace. He is fed through a feeding tube. Each day one of his three sons comes to the house to lift him from the bed to the wheelchair, as his nurses are not allowed to because of insurance restrictions.

Dickinson shared some of his professional struggles in an column that appeared in the *Detroit Free Press.* After being diagnosed with ALS and losing his ability to type, he used "'voice recognition' technology" to write his column. Late in 1993, his speech began to slur and he "could no longer speak words that the machine (or my family) understood.

His wife then heard about a computer which could be operated with the wiggle of a finger, but by early 1995, he had lost the ability to move any of his fingers. Dickinson elaborated, "For the first time since falling ill, I grew deeply depressed about my chances to keep writing. Every door seemed shut.... Had I reached the end of the road?"

In the *Detroit Free Press* column, Dickinson continued, "It was then that we got wind of a revolutionary computer, named Eyegaze, that a user could operate solely by tiny movements of one eye." He added, "We had nothing to lose and decided to try it."

In August 1995, Dickinson had an in-home demonstration and found that he could make it work. As Williams noted in *Biography,* the *Providence Journal-Bulletin* paid the $20,000 for the Eyegaze system (they have also continued to pay Dickinson's full-time salary and health benefits), and Dickinson was back to writing. As he explained to Graves on the *American Journalism Review* website, "I could not overstate enough how important it has been that I could continue to write through all this. The writing has given me focus, purpose, a precious sense of involvement, of being connected to the greater world."

Although Dickinson is successfully working, he does acknowledge that he has much more support than most ALS victims. Most of all, he has his family. In 1995, when he nearly died after a bout with pneumo-

nia, the family's insurance company wanted to place him in a nursing home. His wife and sons said no. "We all wanted Brian here," his wife emphasized to Williams. Dickinson later elaborated on this issue in his December 3, 1997, column for the *Journal-Bulletin.* The column was aimed at those who have the difficult decision of choosing in-home or nursing home care for a loved one. He chronicled his reasons for choosing in-home care for most chronically ill people, noting that: there is more comfort and quiet in the home environment, there are generally less germs in the home, and that the patient can usually be given more personal care in the home.

According to Williams of *Biography,* "Letter by letter, Dickinson aims his right eye at the alphabet on the monitor" of his 'Eyegaze' system, and "blink by blink, he forms words that form paragraphs that form essays that appear on the *Journal-Bulletin's* editorial page." The Eyegaze also keeps him connected to his family and friends, as they ask questions and he slowly blinks the answers.

Even with ALS, he tries to lead as normal a life as possible. That also includes having a difference of opinion with his wife. As a friend explained to Williams, "They argue via the computer. She'll yell at him and he'll swear at her. Of course, Barbara has to be patient enough to stand there and wait until he finishes typing [his epithet] out."

Dickinson's struggle with ALS and his chronicles on the course of his own disease have amazed his local readers over the years. But on December 12, 1997, a national audience got the chance to see him and learn of his struggle. On that night, the television program *20/20* featured a 13-minute segment on Dickinson. Host Hugh Downs opened the show by stating, "Now a story about one of the most amazing men we've ever met." ABC reporter Dr. Tim Johnson told viewers that, in Dickinson's case, ALS "has already passed the point where 95 percent of all victims choose to stop breathing. But Brian Dickinson has chosen to keep on breathing, and to keep on writing."

Surrounded by his wife, sons, and Boswell, the family terrier, Dickinson smiled in approval as the feature detailed his life and his work. It included a dinner held the previous May at which Dickinson was honored by the Rhode Island ALS Association. Also included was a thank you from a chef in Providence, Louise Wilcox. She, too, has ALS, and she told the television audience that she had thought of taking her own life. "But," she said, "Brian, through his articles, really helped me out of that."

Dickinson's sister Toby shared with Williams that before the ALS, her brother would question whether he was doing the right thing or pursuing the right goals. He later told her, "It's such an irony, that when you lose something, when you lose all your ability to really live, you suddenly don't worry about these questions any more." From this, it can probably be said that he truly believes what he wrote in one of his columns: "Seize the moment. Make it your own.... Seize the moment—while you can."

Graves of the *American Journalism Review* website contemplated, "What keeps Brian Dickinson going when so many others might be calling [assisted suicide activist] Jack Kevorkian?" Dickinson's wife responded, "The same quality that has made Brian a good journalist.... I think he just wants to see how all of this is going to turn out. He's got to follow the story."

Sources

On-line

"Writing for His Life," *AJR NewsLink* (March 24-30, 1998), http://www.newslink.org/ajrgraves.html (March 31, 1998).

"How to Live," *Brown Alumni Magazine,* http://www.brown.edu/Administration/Brown_Alumni_Monthly/3-96/features/dickinson.html (March 31, 1998).

Eyegaze Gazette, http://www.lctinc.com/doc/newsmay.htm (March 31, 1998).

"Best Newspaper Writing 1995—Lessons from the Winners," *The Poynter Institute for Media Studies,* http://www.poynter.org/pub/bnw/rwe_bnw95c.htm (March 31, 1998).

Periodicals

Biography, January 1998.

Detroit Free Press, March 1, 1998, p. 3, section E.

Providence Journal-Bulletin, December 3, 1997; December 12, 1997.

Other

Barbara Dickinson, telephone interview by Rose Blue, March 2, 1998.

20/20 (prime time news show), December 12, 1997.

—Rose Blue and Corrine Naden

David Duchovny

AP/Wide World Photos

Actor

Born August 7, 1960, in New York, NY; son of Amram Duchovny (a writer; changed surname to Ducovny) and Meg (a teacher and school administrator) Duchovny; married Tea Leoni (an actress), 1997. *Education:* Princeton University, B.A. in English literature; Yale University, master's degree in English; doctoral studies.

Addresses: *Home*—Los Angeles, CA. *Agent*—William Morris Agency, Inc., 151 El Camino Dr., Beverly Hills, CA 90212.

Career

Actor in television and film, 1988—. Television series appearances include *The Red Shoe Diaries*, Showtime, 1992, as Jake; *The X-Files*, Fox, 1993—, as Fox Mulder; and in *Twin Peaks* as Dennis Denise. Television movie appearances include *Baby Snatcher*, CBS, 1992, and *The Red Shoe Diaries*, Showtime, 1992. Film appearances include *Working Girl*, Twentieth Century-Fox, 1988; *New Year's Day*, International Rainbow Pictures, 1989; *Bad Influence*, Columbia, 1990; *Julia Has Two Lovers*, South Gate Entertainment, 1991; *The Rapture*, Fine Line Features, 1991; *Don't Tell Mom the Babysitter's Dead*, Warner Bros., 1991; *Venice/Venice*, International Rainbow Pictures, 1992; *Ruby*, Triumph Releasing, 1992; *Chaplin*, TriStar, 1992; *Beethoven*, Universal, 1992; *Kalifornia*, Gramercy Pictures, 1993; *Playing God*, Buena Vista, 1997, and *The X-Files: Fight the Future*, Twentieth Century-Fox, 1998.

Sidelights

David Duchovny was well on his way to making his mother proud of him. A Princeton graduate with a master's degree from Yale, he was working on his doctoral dissertation for his Ph.D. in English when acting caught his fancy. He never finished his Ph.D., but he did find fame and fortune playing FBI investigator Fox Mulder in the science-fiction television drama series *The X-Files*. When he signed on, he thought it would just be another small step in his budding career. But the show blossomed, making him a celebrity, not to mention one of television's sexiest men, according to *Cosmopolitan* and his dedicated fans. There is a twist: Mulder does not play the cliched swaggering, macho G-man who rounds up bad guys, but rather an inquisitive, compassionate truth-seeker who desperately wishes to understand paranormal activity such as aliens, ghosts, and magic. According to his co-star, Gillian Anderson, who plays Dana Scully, the character of Mulder is not the only thing that makes Duchovny so popular. "There's a sensitivity to David that's very appealing to women," she remarked in *Cosmopolitan*.

Duchovny was born on August 7, 1960, in New York City, the second of three children. He has an older brother, Danny, and a younger sister, Lori. His father, Amram Ducovny (he modified his last name), was an author and publicist for the American Jewish Committee, and his mother, Meg, was a Scottish-born teacher and school administrator. When Duchovny was 11, his parents divorced, and he went to live with his mother. He mentioned in *Cosmopolitan* that he was brainy but introverted as a youngster, and has said that his parents' breakup caused him to become an over-achiever. His application to the prestigious Collegiate School in Manhattan was initially rejected and the spot given to John F. Kennedy, Jr., but Duchovny was admitted on a scholarship. There he "discovered what preppy really was," as he told *Entertainment Weekly*. His classmates called him "Hayseed," because he lived so far from uptown, in a less-than-desirable neighborhood on Eleventh Street near Second Avenue. While in New York, he got his first job, a bicycle delivery person for a meat shop. He also worked as a lifeguard on Fire Island during the summers.

Duchovny's mother had high hopes for her son's academic career, a dream he would almost see to fruition. After earning board scores of 690 in both math and English and graduating as valedictorian of his class, he was accepted to Harvard, Princeton, Yale, and Brown Universities. He went to Princeton University on a partial scholarship, earning a bachelor of arts in literature. He also played on the basketball team there. After graduation, he spent a year trying to write a novel about a young man's self-discoveries, admitting to *Cosmopolitan*'s Nina Malkin, "It wasn't at all autobiographical." That project fizzled out, and he won a fellowship to Yale, where he obtained his master's degree in English literature and sailed on to doctoral studies. While writing his thesis (titled *Magic and Technology in Contemporary American Fiction and Poetry*, perhaps an omen of his future *X-Files* fame), he began associating with drama folks and tried his hand at writing plays. He never finished his Ph.D. thesis. "My mom was disappointed," Duchovny told Benjamin Svetkey in *Entertainment Weekly*. "I think she'll always be disappointed.... But I was never fully convinced that I was meant to be an academic."

Duchovny began commuting back to New York City to study acting and to take roles in some off-Broadway productions. At age 27, he got his first mainstream gig, in a Lowenbrau beer commercial. After a tiny part ("Tess's Birthday Party Friend") in the Melanie Griffith comedy *Working Girl*, Duchovny was granted a large role as Billy in *New Year's Day*, a low-budget art film. His agent persuaded him to move to the West Coast just in case the part generated a stir; his career did not take off immediately, but he did switch agents. During the late 1980s and early 1990s, he ended up in a rash of quirky parts. He was a sexual adventurer who became a born-again cultist in *The Rapture* (for Fine Line Features; his first major-studio role) and a jealous office employee in *Don't Tell Mom the Babysitter's*

Dead, both in 1991. He went on to play a mean yuppie who experiences a large share of dog slobber in 1992's canine caper flick Beethoven; a cameraman in *Chaplin*, also in 1992; and a hostage in the 1993 Brad Pitt vehicle *Kalifornia*. Meanwhile, he made appearances as a cross-dressing FBI agent in *Twin Peaks*, and was cast as Jake, the narrator for Showtime's sexy nighttime show *Red Shoe Diaries*. "I'm the conduit through which America views the soft underbelly of women's erotic desires," he commented of his character to Svetkey in *Entertainment Weekly*.

Duchovny made his name, though, as the nerdy-yet-sexy Fox Mulder on the television series *The X-Files*. At his audition in 1993, he figured it would bomb after one season: "Two FBI agents investigating the paranormal? sounds like, 'Oh, God! Nothing could be worse,'" he related to Svetkey. A sleeper hit for its first couple of seasons, the show was in danger of being canceled when in 1995 it beat out *NYPD Blue* and *ER* for the Golden Globe award for best drama. Soon after, *The X-Files* blasted off, keeping faithful viewers glued to the set every Sunday night. Coffee mugs, T-shirts, comic books, and other commercialization followed as the devoted audience, now known as "X-philes," grew. In the fall of 1997, older episodes were syndicated for daily broadcasts.

One of the main elements of *The X-Files'* popularity is the chemistry between Duchovny and his co-star, Gillian Anderson, who plays agent Dana Scully. Nina Malkin in *Cosmopolitan* wrote, "Their bond is the most intimate thing on television. Consummate professionals, they rarely so much as touch, but the space between them is all spark, sexier than any grope-and-tumble cliche Aaron Spelling could ever produce." Unlike most dramas, which eventually pair off characters in romantic situations, Scully and Mulder have remained platonic, despite some teaser episodes that hint at it, but never come through.

Another big draw is the gender role-reversal that has earned Duchovny his reputation as a sensitive guy. Throughout the series, Mulder has been unconventionally cast with a more feminine personality; he is the one to believe in UFOs, paranormal happenings, and the spiritual arena. Scully, on the other hand, has a medical degree and a logic to rival Spock's (from the classic *Star Trek* series), and thus tries to provide down-to-earth explanations for the spooky situations that the agents find themselves investigating. Their characters did start to swap ideologies in the 1998 season, with Mulder convinced that his previously-held conspiracy theories were bunk, and Scully gaining more of a spiritual outlook. However, Anderson is generally portrayed as a straightforward, business-only partner to Mulder, whereas he obviously has romantic feelings for her and is not afraid to display deep emotion; his tears flowed in an episode in which Scully was on her deathbed.

Perhaps that is one of the biggest reasons, in addition to his boyish yet imperfect good looks, why, Duchovny is widely seen as a sex symbol. Also, though his character normally wears a suit, glances of his well-defined body are another of the show's major appeals, especially for his legion of female fans. There are numerous web sites dedicated to Duchovny, including "Are You Truly Obsessed with David?," "David Duchovny Drool Brigade," "David Duchovny Worship Page," and "David Duchovny Page of Lust." Baring all but what a teeny bikini covers in one show apparently inspired the "David Duchovny Red Speedo Poems Page." "Oh, that was completely gratuitous," he admitted to James Grant in *Cosmopolitan*. Female fans, however, should not plan to get lucky anytime soon: Duchovny married actress Tea Leoni after a three-and-half month courtship in May of 1997. Previously, he was in a long-term relationship with actress Perrey Reeves (who once played a female vampire on *The X-Files*), and Duchovny continues to deny rumors that there are off-screen romantic hijinks with Anderson, who was divorced in 1996.

Duchovny signed a five-year contract with *The X-Files* in 1996, for which he reportedly makes $100,000 an episode. He also supposedly made $4 million for the film, The X-Files: Fight the Future, released in June of 1998. After his marriage, Duchovny insisted that the television show, which had been filmed around Vancouver, Canada, had to be relocated to Los Angeles, California, so that he could spend more time with his wife. His busy schedule shooting the *X-Files* series ten months a year precludes him from most other work, which irritates him, as he would like to work on more films.

Duchovny is a vegetarian and practices yoga, and he told *TV Guide* that he enjoys watching *The Larry Sanders Show, King of the Hill, Seinfeld,* and *Dr. Katz, Professional Therapist,* in addition to the Animal Channel. He has hinted that he may not stick with the *X-Files* after his contract is up, surely to the dismay of the show's fans. But much like the characters on the X-files, Duchovny can offer surprises. As he commented to Svetkey in *Entertainment Weekly,* "I feel I've got 10 more years of playing the guy [Fox Mulder]. When I'm 45, I'll start thinking about what else I want to do."

Sources

Books

Contemporary Theatre, Film and Television, Volume 14, Gale Research, 1996.

Periodicals

Biography, June 1998.
Cosmopolitan, October 1995, p. 144; March 1997, p. 204.
Entertainment Weekly, December 2, 1994, p. 32; September 29, 1995, p. 20.
TV Guide, October 16, 1997.
US, March 1998.
Vanity Fair, June 1998.

—Geri Speace

Karen Duffy

Actress, model, and television personality

Born May 23, 1962, in New York, NY; daughter of Phil (a developer) and Carol (a homemaker) Duffy; married John Lambrose (an investment banker), February 28, 1997. *Education:* University of Colorado, B.S. (recreational therapy).

Addresses: *Office*—c/o *Cosmopolitan*, The Hearst Corporation, 224 West 57th St., New York, NY 10019.

Career

Worked as a model, appearing in print and television advertisements, c. 1989-91. Appeared on television as a veejay on MTV, 1991-95; appeared as a correspondent in the television series *TV Nation*, 1994. Actress in films, including *McBain*, 1991; *29th Street*, 1991; *Malcolm X*, 1992; *Who's the Man?*, 1993; *Last Action Hero*, 1993; *Blank Check*, 1994; *Reality Bites*, 1994; *Dumb & Dumber*, 1994; *Memory Run*, 1996; *Nothing Sacred*, 1997; and *Meet Wally Sparks*, 1997. Appeared as spokesperson for Revlon, 1995—. Columnist for *Cosmopolitan* magazine, 1996—. Has worked as a writer for television. Worked as a recreational therapist in a nursing home.

Sidelights

Known for her striking beauty, dynamic personality, and irreverent sense of humor, Karen "Duff" Duffy has, through her battle with the incurable disease sarcoidosis that has ravaged her central nervous system, become a source of inspiration to many and an example of personal courage. Duffy first gained fame as the popular prime-time MTV veejay "Duff"

in the early 1990s, and was beginning a promising career in acting and modeling when she became ill in 1995. Despite her health challenges, Duffy has continued to work as an actress, spokesperson, and writer, and has expressed confidence in her chances for a healthy, fulfilling future. In an article for *Cosmopolitan*, Duffy declared: "I'm feeling great, and I'm very optimistic. I'm playing the hand I've been dealt the best I can."

Karen Duffy was born on May 23, 1962, in New York City, the second child of Phil Duffy, a developer, and Carol Duffy, a homemaker; Karen has an older brother, Jim, and two younger sisters, Kate and Laura. Duffy displayed her relaxed, no-nonsense personality at an early age, according to her mother, who reported in an article by *People* contributor Maria Speidel, "I love the name Karen. But in third grade she just started calling herself Duff." Duffy attended the University of Colorado, where she earned a degree in recreational therapy, and then returned to New York, where she worked as a recreational therapist at a nursing home. Duffy told *People*'s Speidel that in her work as a therapist she found that "working with others [makes you] stronger and richer," and she continued to utilize her skills as a therapist on a volunteer basis long after she found fame as a television personality, model, and actress. It was during the same time that she was working at the New York nursing home that Duffy was discovered in a Greenwich Village bar by a photographer who suggested that she try her hand at a career in modeling. She quickly achieved success as a print model, appeared in television commercials, and landed small film roles.

Despite the fact that she knew little to nothing about contemporary rock and roll music, preferring to listen to the music of generations-old singers like Frank Sinatra, Sammy Davis, Jr., Tom Jones, Al Green, and Englebert Humperdinck, Duffy decided to audition for a job as an MTV veejay in 1991. MTV hired her after viewing her home-made audition tape, which consisted of Duffy displaying her natural wit, charm, and unaffected beauty. MTV's vice president of production, Joel Stillerman, told *People*'s Speidel that it wasn't important for Duffy to be knowledgeable about rock and roll. "She's obviously beautiful, obviously smart, obviously funny," Stillerman explained. "And she pretty much says party."

Duffy became a popular on-air personality while working at MTV from 1991 to 1994, and quickly emerged as one of the most recognizable celebrities in Hollywood. She was named one of *Esquire*'s "Women We Love" in 1992 and was included among *People* magazine's "50 Most Beautiful People in the World" in 1993, which was also the year she signed, along with star athletes Christian Laettner and Doug Flutie, to promote the Starter company's line of athletic and outdoor apparel. She signed with the Walt Disney company in 1993 as well, accepting their offer of roles in four films, and subsequently appeared in such films as *Blank Check* and *Dumb and Dumber*, both of which were released in 1994.

In 1994 Duffy's career was given another boost when she left MTV and became a correspondent for the satirical television news program *TV Nation*, which was the brainchild of filmmaker Michael Moore. Her personal life was filled with excitement as well, as she dated a number of prominent men in the entertainment industry, including country music singer Dwight Yoakam, whom she dated for two years. Duffy's social and professional calendar was filled with new opportunities, including film roles and a job as Revlon's spokesperson, and she looked forward to a successful career.

Then, in the fall of 1995, Duffy suffered an extreme setback. She attended the Emmy Awards ceremony and gala with actor George Clooney and celebrated when *TV Nation* was awarded the Emmy for best informa-

tional program. However, the next morning, Duffy awoke in her Los Angeles hotel suite with an intense headache. She described the pain in an article for *Cosmopolitan*: "It was like a red-hot poker trying to poke its way out of the top of my skull." At first she thought that she was suffering from a hangover, but soon realized that the pain in her head was not due to overindulging in alcohol and contacted her doctor in New York City. After arriving in New York, Duffy went directly from the airport to her doctor's office, and, because her doctor feared that she was suffering from a brain aneurysm, she was sent without delay to the hospital for a battery of tests. The tests results shocked Duffy, who had felt confident that because she was in peak physical condition she could not be seriously ill. Duffy explained the results of the tests in her *Cosmopolitan* article: "The doctors had found a lesion, or growth, reaching from the base of my brain to partway down my spinal cord.... It's in an extremely delicate area of the brain, where all my wires connect. There was no possibility of removing it with surgery, and even a biopsy to remove a tissue sample would be dangerous; I could lose motor skills during the operation."

> "She's obviously beautiful, obviously smart, obviously funny," Stillerman explained in People. "And she pretty much says party."

Although initially she was diagnosed with multiple sclerosis, a degenerative neurological disease, Duffy underwent months of agonizing tests to determine exactly what had caused the lesion to grow on her brain and spinal cord. While she endured the testing, Duffy's physical condition rapidly grew worse and worse. She lost feeling in her left hand and arm, and then she began to lose feeling in her other extremities. Duffy related her experience during late 1995 in her *Cosmopolitan* article: "Periodically, I would have flare-ups where the pain was so bad I would cry, and even a tear would hurt if it rolled down my neck.... The doctors were baffled. I was in and out of the hospital for tests, and in November, they put me on steroids to reduce the size of the lesion in my brain." At this time, Duffy explained, she was embarrassed by her condition, and although she was grateful for the support of her parents and three siblings, who took turns caring for her and accompanying her to various doctors' offices and hospitals, she reported that accepting their help was "difficult."

Predictably, Duffy had periods of despondency and feelings of hopelessness as she underwent the testing and awaited her diagnosis, but she also revealed that she had periods during which she felt confident that she would ultimately overcome her condition and be well again. It was during one of the latter periods that a friend introduced her to actor Richard Gere, with whom Duffy spent what she called in *Cosmopolitan* "a memorable evening, to say the least." In order to hide the fact that she had lost the use of her hands, Duffy fashioned a sling from a scarf, pretending that she had sprained her arm. All went well until Gere accidently brushed Duffy's leg with his own under the dinner table, and as Duffy recounted in *Cosmopolitan:* "I've got hyper reflexes—a side effect of the condition. I kicked the dining table and knocked over the candles and set the centerpiece on fire." Gere quickly extinguished the burning centerpiece, but Duffy was left to explain that she was battling an as yet undiagnosed illness and had not told anyone because she had not wanted the sympathy of her dinner companions. Following her admission, Duffy reported, her friends, including Gere, "were all really cool."

Duffy endured the painful tests and treatments with her characteristic sense of humor and positive attitude. She reported in *People* magazine that although she was often treated as an outpatient, she sometimes had to stay at New York Hospital for a week at a time. In the *People* article she recalled: "I was doing everything I could to brighten it up. I had a picture of Dr. Kevorkian [the Michigan-based doctor known for helping terminally-ill patients to commit suicide] over my bed just to shake up the doctors." Duffy continued to work during this period, but the illness and treatment brought about dramatic changes in her appearance that were often extremely difficult to conceal. In April, 1996, Duffy was filmed for the entertainment news program *Entertainment Tonight* as part of her assignment as Revlon spokesperson. The segment was to depict Duffy and two other Revlon spokespeople, models Daisy Fuentes and Claudia Schiffer, preparing for the Academy Awards presentation. Duffy was bloated because of the steroids she had to take to reduce the size of her lesion, and her hair was falling out because of the chemotherapy that was also being used to shrink the lesion. She recounted the experience in the *People* article: "While they were filming, a big swatch of my hair fell out, and the manicurist screamed. I tried to pretend everything was okay, but there were tears in my eyes."

In June, 1996, Duffy was finally diagnosed with sarcoidosis of the central nervous system, an extremely rare immune response of unknown origin. In a *People* article, Dr. Nicholas Schiff, a neurologist who treated Duffy in 1996, reported that there are only "'tens of cases' like hers, with an isolated brain-stem lesion." Very little is known about the condition, except that there is no known cure; however, the condition can go into remission. Duffy began treatment in April, 1996, with steroids, chemotherapy, and morphine (for pain management), a combination which has proven effective for her in controlling the disease's progress. Although the disease and treatment ravaged her appearance, Duffy continued to work and kept her condition a secret, except from Revlon, for whom she was serving as spokesperson and starring in commercials for the company's fragrance Charlie. Other than her employer, only close friends and family knew of her condition, and Duffy expressed appreciation in *Cosmopolitan* for her friends' ability to be "compassionate without being smarmy."

On February 28, 1997, Duffy married John Lambrose, an investment banker with whom she had been acquainted since 1992, but with whom she began a romantic relationship in September, 1996. Although she was hesitant to enter into a serious romantic commitment while she was still battling her illness, Duffy reported in *People* that Lambrose's faith in her future and in their future together encouraged her to believe as well. She quoted her husband in *People* as saying "'So I fell in love with somebody who has a lump in their head. Big deal.'" Duffy publicly disclosed her condition to Oprah Winfrey on the talk show hostess's television program in March, 1997, and has since been very candid about her experience with sarcoidosis.

After disclosing her disease to the public, many media sources reported that Duffy's health appeared to be improving, and, indeed Duffy continued to land lucrative jobs, including a stint as Revlon's spokesperson for their Almay products and a role in a Woody Allen film. In an interview with *US* contributor Brantley Bardin, Duffy was asked about her professional activities following her announcement that she suffered from sarcoidosis, and she quipped, laughing: "Everyone keeps saying, 'Oh, you're doing so much better. Why is that?' They all think it's my treatments and falling in love, and I'm like, 'No, I just couldn't die and have my entire *oeuvre* be *Dumb and Dumber* and *Blank Check*.' I've got *so* much more bad acting in me." Evidently, sarcoidosis has failed to dampen Duffy's passion for living or her take-charge attitude toward life. In the 1992 *People* article by Speidel, Duffy was quoted as saying "My whole view is that no matter what you're doing, you've got to bloom where you're planted." Similarly, Duffy concluded her 1997 *People* article by asserting: "You have to play the hand you're dealt—and squeeze every ounce of fun out of every minute."

Sources

On-line

Internet Movie Database, http://www.imdb.com (November 1997).

Periodicals

Cosmopolitan, April 1997, p. 206.
Daily News Record, June 23, 1993, p. 119.
Entertainment Weekly, September 4, 1992, p. 61; March 21, 1997, p. 371.
Esquire, August 1992, p. 78.
New York, February 3, 1992, p. 16.
People, March 15, 1993, p. 111; May 3, 1993, p. 112; June 30, 1997, p. 42.
Time, July 26, 1993, p. 77.
US, November 1997, pp. 123, 131.

—*Lynn M. Spampinato*

Bob Dylan

Rock singer, songwriter, musician, and poet

Original name, Robert Allen Zimmerman; name legally changed, August 9, 1962; born May 24, 1941, in Duluth, MN; son of Abraham (in furniture and appliance sales) and Beatty (Stone) Zimmerman; married Sara Lowndes, November 22, 1965 (divorced, 1977); children: Jesse, Maria, Jakob, Samuel, Anna. *Education:* Attended University of Minnesota, 1959-60.

Addresses: *Office*—c/o 264 Cooper Station, New York, NY 10003.

Career

Songwriter, composer of more than five hundred songs since early 1960s, including "Blowin' in the Wind," "The Times They Are A-Changin'," "A Hard Rain's A-Gonna Fall," "It Ain't Me, Babe," "Mr. Tambourine Man," "Desolation Row," "Like a Rolling Stone," "Lay Lady Lay," "Forever Young," "Tangled Up in Blue," and "Idiot Wind"; singer and musician (guitarist, pianist, autoharpist, and harmonica player); has recorded with rock groups, including the Band, 1975, The Traveling Wilburys (with Jeff Lynne, Tom Petty, George Harrison, and Roy Orbison), 1988 and 1990, and The Grateful Dead, 1989; has appeared in concert and performed with rock bands, including Tom Petty and the Heartbreakers and the Grateful Dead in the mid 1980s; solo singer and musician in concerts since early 1960s, including appearances at the Newport Folk Festival in 1962 and 1965, appearances at the Woodstock Festivals in 1969 and 1994, an appearance at the Live Aid benefit concert in 1985; and appearances in numerous American cities on tour, including a national tour in 1995-96; international appearances include concerts in Europe, Australia, Japan, and a special performance for Pope John Paul II at a Roman Catholic Youth rally in Bologna, Italy, on September 27, 1997. Has performed on television programs, including *Hard to Handle,* 1986; *Columbia Records Celebrates the Music of Bob Dylan,* 1992; *One Irish Rover,* 1992; *The Bob Dylan 30th Anniversary Celebration,* 1993; and *MTV Unplugged,* 1995. Has appeared in films, including *Don't Look Back,* 1965; *Eat the Document,* 1966; *Johnny Cash: The Man, His World, His Music,* 1970; *Pat Garrett and Billy the Kid* (also director), 1972; *Concert for Bangladesh,* 1972; *Rolling Thunder,* 1977; *Renaldo and Clara,* 1978; *The Last Waltz,* 1978; *Hearts of Fire,* 1987; *A Vision Shared: A Tribute to Woody Guthrie and Leadbelly,* 1988; *Imagine: John Lennon,* 1988.

Awards: Tom Paine Award, Emergency Civil Liberties Committee, 1963; honorary Mus. D., Princeton University, 1970; Grammy Awards, National Academy of Recording Arts and Sciences, best rock vocal performance, 1979, for "Gotta Serve Somebody"; *Rolling Stone* Music Award, artist of the year (tied with Bruce Springsteen), 1975, album of the year, 1975, for *The Basement Tapes* and *Blood on the Tracks*; inducted into the Rock and Roll Hall of Fame, 1988; Commander

Dans L'Ordre des Arts et Lettres from the French Minister of Culture, 1990; Lifetime Achievement Award, National Academy of Recording Arts and Sciences, 1991; Grammy Award, 1993, for *World Gone Wrong;* arts award, Dorothy and Lillian Gish Prize Trust, 1997; Lifetime Achievement Award, John F. Kennedy Center honors, 1997.

Sidelights

Singer and songwriter Bob Dylan is recognized worldwide for the impact he has had on rock music since his career began in the early 1960s, and has managed to maintain his popularity among fans and critics alike over the ensuing decades. Although known primarily for his sometimes caustic, always candid lyrics that reveal the defiant stance on authority, politics, and social norms that was prevalent among the generation of Americans who came of age in the 1960s, Dylan has fans from a variety of age groups, all of whom identify with the raw human emotion expressed in his lyrics, especially feelings of alienation, anger, anxiety, and desperation. Dylan's own humanity was brought to the public's attention in May, 1997, when the legendary artist canceled a planned European tour and was hospitalized to undergo treatment for a sometimes fatal fungal infection known as histoplasmosis, which caused the sac surrounding his heart to swell, resulting in a serious health condition called pericarditis. Despite his health challenges early in 1997, Dylan performed in the United States in August, released *Time Out of Mind* to rave reviews in September, and received an arts award from the Dorothy and Lillian Gish Prize Trust in October. As further evidence of Dylan's broad appeal and the magnitude of his contributions to music, he performed in Bologna, Italy, in September, 1997, after receiving a special invitation from Pope John Paul II, and in December, 1997, he became the first rock star to receive the prestigious Kennedy Center honors. Despite the tributes and testimonials he has received throughout his career, Dylan remains nonchalant about his celebrity status and his impact upon society. In an October, 1997, interview with *Newsweek*'s David Gates, Dylan, commenting on his history of changing religious philosophy, remarked: "I don't think I'm tangible to myself. I mean, I think one thing today and I think another thing tomorrow. I change during the course of a day. I wake and I'm one person, and when I go to sleep I know for certain I'm somebody else. I don't know who I am most of the time. It doesn't even matter to me."

Dylan was born Robert Allen Zimmerman on May 24, 1941, in Duluth, Minnesota to Abraham Zimmerman, a furniture and appliance salesman, and Beatty Stone Zimmerman. In 1947 the Zimmerman family moved to the small town of Hibbing, Minnesota, where Dylan spent his unremarkable childhood and youth. He wrote his first poems at the age of ten, and as a teenager Dylan taught himself to play the piano, harmonica, and guitar. Dylan's musical tastes as a teenager included an appreciation for the talents of a variety of country music and rock and roll performers, such as Elvis Presley, Hank Williams, Little Richard, and Jerry Lee Lewis. Dylan played in many bands during his high school years, including the Golden Chords and Elston Gunn and His Rock Boppers, before enrolling at the University of Minnesota in 1959.

It was while he was a student at the University of Minnesota in Minneapolis that Robert Zimmerman began performing as a folk singer and musician under the name Bob Dylan at such popular Minneapolis night clubs as Ten O'Clock Scholar cafe and St. Paul's Purple Onion Pizza Parlor. Dylan soon became more involved with his musical career than with his studies and dropped out of school in 1960; he immediately moved to New York City. The young performer's interest in New York City was based upon his desire to become involved in the folk music scene that was then emerging in the city's Greenwich Village and upon his wish to meet his idol, folk singer Woody Guthrie, who was hospitalized in New Jersey with a rare disease of the nervous system. Dylan promptly became a popular performer in Greenwich Village coffee houses and night clubs, and also managed to become a regular performer for Guthrie, whom he visited often and for whom he sang his renditions of Guthrie's folk songs. The young Dylan quickly gained the respect and admiration of his peers in the folk music scene with his ability to play songs he had heard only once perfectly and with his ability to compose his own melodies and lyrics at an astonishing pace. Dylan became well known outside of the folk music scene in New York City in 1961, when *New York Times* critic Robert Shelton witnessed one of his performances at a club called Gerde's Folk City and declared that Dylan was "bursting at the seams with talent."

Dylan was twenty years old when he released his first album, entitled *Bob Dylan,* in 1962. The songs on the album were primarily his versions of blues and folk songs by such artists as Jesse Fuller, Bukka White, and Blind Lemon Jefferson, but the album included two original Dylan compositions, "Song to Woody," which was a tribute to Guthrie, and "Talkin' New York." The album achieved limited success, and Dylan followed it in 1963 with *The Freewheelin' Bob Dylan,* which contained more original songs that shared a common theme of protest and predictions of radical social and political change. Two of the songs from Dylan's second album, "Blowin' In the Wind" and "A Hard Rain's Gonna Fall," became enduring anthems of the 1960s, largely because they definitively illustrate the thoughts and feelings of the young members of the counterculture. As confirmation of Dylan's success, the renowned folk group Peter, Paul, and Mary recorded a cover version of "Blowin' In the Wind" that rose to the number two spot on the pop music charts.

By 1964, the year in which Dylan released his third album, *The Times They Are A-Changin'*, he had been thrust into the role of media spokesperson for the counterculture protest movement in the 1960s which sought to abolish the social and political norms of the time and establish a new society. *The Times They Are A-Changin'* included songs similar in theme to those on Dylan's second album, particularly the title song, "The Times They Are A-Changin'," which achieved a status similar to that of "Blowin' In the Wind" and "A Hard Rain's A-Gonna Fall" as a protest song. This third album also contained the protest song "The Lonesome Death of Hattie Carroll," but at the same time the album was released Dylan was making it clear with his public statements that he was growing increasingly pessimistic about the ability of the counterculture to affect change, and that he was uncomfortable with his role as the movement's mouthpiece. Indeed, in the final song on *The Times They Are A-Changin'*, Dylan included a line that articulated his feelings about his current role, asserting that he'd "bid farewell and not give a damn."

Another Side of Bob Dylan, Dylan's follow-up album to *The Times They Are A-Changin'*, contained, instead of his trademark protest songs, extremely personal folk ballads and love songs, and further evidenced his disillusionment with the counterculture movement; the final song on the album, "It Ain't Me, Babe," was an obvious departure from the folk music scene and its community of counterculturalists. The album also contained the song "Ballad in Plain D," which was an angry, uncharitable account of Dylan's breakup with his longtime girlfriend Suze Rotolo. Dylan was introduced to more folk music fans through his next romantic involvement with legendary folk singer Joan Baez, who sang some of Dylan's unreleased songs in concert; however, Dylan was ready to move beyond folk music, and after some tension-filled months, his relationship with Baez dissolved. In 1965 Dylan enraged his folk music following by performing on an electric guitar at the Newport Folk Festival—fans there booed Dylan and his band off the stage—and by releasing *Bringing It All Back Home,* an album on which Dylan returned to his earlier musical influences of rock and roll and rhythm and blues, accompanying half of the album's songs on an electric guitar. The songs on *Bringing It All Back Home* remained critical of society, but none contained any of the direct references to racism, war, or political activism that had marked his earlier works and that had captivated his followers. In one of the album's most insistent and angry songs, "Subterranean Homesick Blues," which contains the famous line "you don't need a weatherman to know which way the wind blows," Dylan suggests that truly creative individuals are forced to become outsiders by society, which rejects individuality and vision and seeks to instill subjective cultural standards. The acoustic song "Mr. Tambourine Man" from *Bringing It All Back Home* was soon recorded in an electrified form by the popular 1960s band the Byrds and reached the top of the pop music charts; by that time a new brand of music known as "folk rock" had become widely favored among young Americans.

Dylan continued to record songs that fused his folk and rock influences, using mystical, ominous lyrics filled with imagery and allusions, and in 1965 he released *Highway 61 Revisited*. This album featured songs with themes of alienation and loss of identity, including the well-known "Like a Rolling Stone," which was comprised of over six minutes of angry, harsh sentiments, and which quickly rose to the number two spot on the *Billboard* singles chart. That same year Dylan married Sara Lowndes, who was a friend of his manager's wife. In 1966 Dylan released *Blonde on Blonde*, which most critics consider among his best albums because it polished the edgy, harsh rock sounds of *Highway 61 Revisited* and introduced music unlike anything that had come before it. Although he was wildly successful, Dylan was suffering from the strains of fame. In the 1971 biography *Bob Dylan*, Dylan commented to Anthony Scaduto about his feelings during that period of his life: "The pressures were unbelievable. They were just something you can't imagine unless you go through them yourself. Man, they hurt so much." Similarly, in a 1997 interview with *Newsweek*'s David Gates, Dylan asserted "I'm not the songs. It's like somebody expecting [William] Shakespeare to be Hamlet, or [Wolfgang von] Goethe to be Faust. If you're not prepared for fame, there's really no way you can imagine what a crippling thing it can be." On July 29, 1966, at the peak of his popularity, Dylan's neck was broken in a near-fatal motorcycle crash, and his public speculated as to whether he was alive or dead.

The accident left Dylan with time to recuperate and rest at his Woodstock, New York, home with Sara and their newborn son Jesse. During this time of solitude, Dylan began reflecting upon his religious beliefs and personal priorities, and wrote songs that reflected his new-found sense of inner peace and satisfaction; many of these songs were recorded in 1967 with the Band and later released on the 1975 album *The Basement Tapes,* while others were released on Dylan's first album following the motorcycle accident, 1968's *John Wesley Harding.* A primarily slow-paced, acoustical album, *John Wesley Harding* was followed in 1969 by *Nashville Skyline,* an album comprised of straightforward country music that contained the hit single "Lay, Lady, Lay," and in 1970 by *Self Portrait* and *New Morning,* both of which were comprised of subdued, simple songs that proclaimed Dylan's personal happiness. These three albums were greeted with derision by his public and Dylan was criticized harshly by his fans for what they perceived as his failure to comment in his music upon the harsh realities of the time, namely the Vietnam War and the struggle for racial equality and civil rights for African Americans.

During the early 1970s Dylan's musical output was minimal, but in 1971 he published *Tarantula,* a collection of prose, poems, letters, and other works written between 1965 and 1966; the volume was faulted by critics as lacking cohesiveness. In 1973 Dylan appeared in and composed the score for the film *Pat Garrett and Billy the Kid;* although the experience was largely negative—the film's director, filmmaker Sam Peckinpah of *The Wild Bunch* fame, proved difficult to work with and Dylan's role as Alias, Billy the Kid's sidekick, was viewed as a poor acting effort—the soundtrack included the single "Knockin' On Heaven's Door," which made it into the top twenty on the music charts and later became one of the Dylan songs most often recorded by other artists. Dylan's first album to reach the number one spot on music charts was his 1974 effort, *Planet Waves,* which he recorded with the Band. Although it was not a critical success, the album led to a flood of interest in Dylan's 1974 tour of the United States and audience demand for tickets far exceeded available seating for his concerts. In 1974, following the tour, Dylan released *Before the Flood,* a two-album set of music recorded live during the tour; the album rose to number three on music charts.

While Dylan's musical career was on an upswing, his personal life was in a shambles as he became involved in a bitter separation with Sara—the divorce became final in 1977—that included a fierce custody battle over their children. Dylan's 1975 album *Blood On the Tracks* features songs reflecting the sorrow, passion, and bit-

terness of his personal life at the time; "If You See Her, Say Hello" directly refers to the breakup of his marriage. Most critics hailed *Blood On the Tracks* as Dylan's best album since the 1960s, praising the artist's use of visual imagery to blur distinctions between reality and illusion to challenge everyday ideas about the world. The album's searing songs about love and loss, including "Tangled Up in Blue," "Shelter from the Storm," and "Idiot Wind," were well-received by Dylan's fans and the album soon reached number one on the charts. Dylan's 1976 album, *Desire,* which contained a mournful tune entitled "Sara," also reached number one on the charts, and along with *Blood On the Tracks,* achieved widespread success in both the United States and Europe; this period marked another high point in Dylan's career.

> *"He invented a new way a pop singer could sound, broke through the limitations of what a recording artist could achieve, and changed the face of rock and roll forever,"* Bruce Springteen commented at Dylan's 1988 induction into the Rock and Roll Hall of Fame.

Although Dylan's 1978 album *Street Legal* was unpopular with his fans, who feared that the performer's personal crises had interfered with his musical abilities, it did not prepare the fans for what was soon to follow. In 1978, while touring to support *Street Legal,* Dylan experienced a religious vision that he later asserted made him question his moral values and saved him from self-destructive behavior. Pronouncing his belief in fundamentalist Christianity, Dylan began to communicate in his music a concern with religious salvation and the end of the world; many fans expressed displeasure with Dylan's blatant attempts to persuade his listeners to adopt his religious philosophy, but others viewed the lyrics as similar to Dylan's earlier songs about social change and prophecy. Among Dylan's albums during his Christian period, only the 1979 album *Slow Train Coming* was a commercial success, largely due to the popularity of the Grammy Award-winning single "Gotta Serve Somebody." The other albums Dylan released during this period, 1980's *Saved* and 1981's *Shot of Love,* were generally considered commercially and critically unsuccessful.

In 1983 Dylan released *Infidels,* an album on which he departed from his overtly religious themes and returned to his more complex, emotionally subtle lyrics in songs such as "Jokerman" and "Don't Fall Apart on Me Tonight." Dylan produced his 1985 album, *Empire Burlesque,* which displayed a wide range of musical sounds, from gospel to acoustic ballad. In the mid-1980s Dylan remained prominent in the public eye by performing with various other music stars, including 1980s superstar Michael Jackson, on the 1985 single "We Are the World" and at the Live Aid benefit concert, both which were designed to raise money for famine relief in Ethiopia. Also in 1985, Dylan released *Biograph,* a five-album set that contained previously released material and "bootleg" recordings (unreleased recordings) and which also included Dylan's brief commentaries; the set was highly popular and proved a top seller. The year 1988 marked the beginning of Dylan's collaboration with the Traveling Wilburys, which was a group made up of Dylan and veteran music stars George Harrison, Jeff Lynne, Roy Orbison, and Tom Petty, on two albums, 1988's *Traveling Wilburys* and *Traveling Wilburys Volume 3*— no second volume was ever recorded—which was released in 1990. Dylan's releases during the late 1980s and the first half of the 1990s, including *Knocked Out Loaded, Oh Mercy, Under the Red Sky, Good As I Been to You,* and *World Gone Wrong,* although satisfying his fans with songs reminiscent of his earlier work, did not break any new ground musically. In 1988 Dylan was inducted into the Rock and Roll Hall of Fame, and was honored by noted rock star Bruce Springsteen, who commented during the induction ceremony that "Bob [Dylan] freed the mind the way Elvis [Presley] freed the body. He showed us that just because the music was innately physical did not mean that it was anti-intellectual.... He invented a new way a pop singer could sound, broke through the limitations of what a recording artist could achieve, and changed the face of rock and roll forever."

The year 1997 proved to be a pivotal year for Dylan, both professionally and personally. In May, 1997, Dylan was stricken with a sometimes fatal fungal infection called histoplasmosis, which caused the sac surrounding his heart to swell, resulting in a condition known as pericarditis. The news of his subsequent hospitalization was important news among music fans, who, when faced with the very real possibility of Dylan's death, recognized that if Dylan were to die the world would lose an influential contemporary

cultural figure. Dylan, however, was too ill to reflect on the significance of his own mortality. He told *Newsweek*'s David Gates, "Mostly I was in a lot of pain. Pain that was intolerable. That's the only way I can put it." Nevertheless, Dylan recovered, and although he needed to take a variety of medications, he began performing again in August, 1997. In September, 1997, Dylan performed for Pope John Paul II—reportedly at the Pope's request—at a eucharistic conference in Bologna, Italy, and in October, 1997, he received an arts award—given to artists who make an "outstanding contribution to the beauty of the world and to mankind's enjoyment and understanding of life"— from the Dorothy and Lillian Gish Prize Trust. In December, 1997, Dylan became the first rock star ever to receive Kennedy Center honors.

In addition to the struggle with illness and the professional accolades that marked Dylan's experience during 1997, the artist's album *Time Out of Mind,* which was released in September, 1997, was greeted with rave reviews from critics who hailed it as Dylan's victory over the effects of mortality, which became particularly significant in light of the legendary performer's recent health crisis. Unlike the reviews of the Dylan albums of the late 1980s and early 1990s, which maintained that the performer was simply rehashing previously covered ground musically, reviews of *Time Out of Mind* declared that Dylan had again managed to reinvent himself and provide his fans with a fresh sound at a relatively advanced age by rock and roll's standards. *Time*'s Christopher John Farley applauded the album, pronouncing: "Dylan has found purpose in his inner battle to reignite his imagination. Turning the quest for inspiration itself into relevant rock—that is alchemic magic." *Newsweek* contributor Karen Schoemer, in a cover story on Dylan's influence on contemporary musicians—including Dylan's son, Jakob, who is a member of the popular alternative band the Wallflowers and who was named one of *People*'s "Sexiest Men Alive" in 1997—, maintained: "*Time Out of Mind* is rewarding precisely because it's so outside the present. In an era defined by novelty hits and slick video edits, it's a reminder that music can mean something more: it can be personal, uncompromised and deeply felt." Similarly, *USA Today*'s Edna Gundersen declared: "The music's spontaneity, rough edges and earthy feel deliver an honest sound that's nearly extinct in current pop." Despite all of the hype that surrounded him in 1997, Dylan remained unruffled. In a September 1997 article by Edna Gundersen in *USA Today,* Dylan asserted that he was "very appreciative" of the honors he had received, maintaining that "in some sense it really does matter," he told *Newsweek*'s David Gates in an October 1997 interview that he often comes close to ending his career, remarking: "Some days I get up and it just makes me sick that I'm doing what I'm doing. Because basically—I mean, you're one cut above a pimp. That's what everybody who's a performer is. I have this voice in my head saying, 'Just be done with it'."

Selected discography

Bob Dylan, Columbia, 1962.
The Freewheelin' Bob Dylan, Columbia, 1963.
The Times They Are A-Changin', Columbia, 1964.
Another Side of Bob Dylan, Columbia, 1964.
Bringing It All Back Home, Columbia, 1965.
Highway 61 Revisited, Columbia, 1965.
Blonde on Blonde, Columbia, 1966.
Bob Dylan's Greatest Hits I, Columbia, 1967.
John Wesley Harding, Columbia, 1968.
Nashville Skyline, Columbia, 1969.
New Morning, Columbia, 1970.
Self Portrait, Columbia, 1970.
Bob Dylan's Greatest Hits, Volume II, Columbia, 1971.
Dylan, Columbia, 1973.
Pat Garrett and Billy the Kid, Columbia, 1973.
Planet Waves, Asylum, 1974.
Before the Flood, Asylum, 1974.
(With the Band) *The Basement Tapes*, Columbia, 1975.
Blood on the Tracks, Columbia, 1975.
Desire, Columbia, 1976.
Hard Rain, Columbia, 1976.
Street Legal, Columbia, 1978.
Bob Dylan at Budokan, Columbia, 1978.
Bob Dylan: Masterpieces, Columbia, 1978.
Slow Train Coming, Columbia, 1979.
Saved, Columbia, 1980.
Shot of Love, Columbia, 1981.
Infidels, Columbia, 1983.
Real Live, Columbia, 1984.
Empire Burlesque, Columbia, 1985.
Biograph, Columbia, 1985.
Knocked Out Loaded, Columbia, 1986.
(With the Traveling Wilburys: Tom Petty, Roy Orbison, George Harrison, and Jeff Lynne) *Traveling Wilburys*, Warner Bros., 1988.
Down in the Groove, Columbia, 1988.
(With the Grateful Dead) *Dylan and the Dead*, Columbia, 1989.
Oh, Mercy, Columbia, 1989.
Traveling Wilburys, Volume 3, Warner Bros., 1990.
Under the Red Sky, Columbia, 1990.
Bootleg Series I-III, Columbia, 1991.
Good As I Been to You, Columbia, 1992.
World Gone Wrong, Columbia, 1993.
Bob Dylan 30th Anniversary Concert, Columbia, 1993.
MTV Unplugged, Columbia, 1995.
Bob Dylan's Greatest Hits, Volume III, Columbia, 1995.
Time Out of Mind, Columbia, 1997.

Selected writings

Tarantula (prose), Macmillan, 1971.
Poem to Joanie, Aloes Press, 1972.
Words (poem), J. Cape, 1973.
Writings and Drawings (songs, poems, drawings, and writings), Knopf, 1973; expanded edition published as *Lyrics: 1962-1985*, 1985.
Renaldo and Clara (screenplay), Circuit Films, 1978.

Sources

On-line

http://www.celebsite.com (October 1997).
USA Today, http://www.usatoday.com/life/dcovmon.htm (September 29, 1997); http://www.usatoday.com/life/music/lmds040.htm (September 29, 1997).

Books

Scaduto, Anthony, *Bob Dylan*, Grosset & Dunlap, 1971.
Shelton, Robert, *No Direction Home: The Life and Music of Bob Dylan*, Beech Tree Books/William Morrow, 1986.
Spitz, Bob, *Dylan: A Biography*, McGraw-Hill, 1989.

Periodicals

Newsweek, October 6, 1997, pp. 62-71.
New York Times, September 29, 1961.
Time, September 29, 1997, p. 87.

—Lynn M. Spampinato

Bernie Ebbers

President and CEO of LDDS WorldCom, Inc.

Full name, Bernard J. Ebbers; born in 1943, in Edmonton, Alberta, Canada; married; children: several. *Education:* Mississippi College, B.A., 1967. *Religion:* Southern Baptist.

Addresses: *Office*—LDDS WorldCom, Inc., 515 East Amite, Jackson, MS 39201.

Career

Delivered milk door-to-door; high school physical education teacher, 1967; managed garment warehouse, c. 1970; motel-restaurant (became a chain of nine hotels), owner and operator, beginning 1974; LDDS (a telecommunications company; renamed LDDS WorldCom, Inc., 1995), owner, 1983—, president, 1985—; Resurgens Communications Group and Metromedia Communications Corp., owner, beginning 1993; WilTel Network services, owner, beginning 1995; MFS Communications and its subsidiary UUNET (an Internet provider), owner, beginning 1996; Brooks Fiber Properties, owner, beginning 1997; CompuServe, co-owner, beginning 1997.

Sidelights

When Bernie Ebbers's LDDS WorldCom, Inc., came a-courting MCI in the largest telecommunications takeover bid in history, many people asked "What is WorldCom?" Perhaps they should have asked "Who is Bernie Ebbers?" Although on the surface the answer seems simple; in fact, Bernie Ebbers is an enigma. An apparently casual and open sort of

person, he has refused to discuss his family with the media. He presented the world with a simple, unassuming appearance while masterminding some of the swiftest and largest takeovers in history.

Born in Edmonton, Alberta, Canada, Ebbers got a job delivering milk door-to-door as soon as he completed high-school. This proved a great incentive for leaving Edmonton and traveling south to Clinton, Mississippi, to attend Mississippi College, a small Southern Baptist school, on a basketball scholarship. He has often been quoted as saying "delivering milk day to day in 30-below-zero weather isn't a real interesting thing to do with the rest of your life." Instead, he found that the school not only provided him with a degree in physical education, but also with a firm grounding in his spiritual development. In a 1996 alumni magazine article Ebbers wrote, "I came to have a fuller understanding of what my purpose was in life, what a personal relationship with Jesus Christ really meant and how I would try to live my life from that point on."

Ebbers presents the appearance of a "good old country boy" with his faded jeans, cowboy boots, and turquoise jewelry. He claimed in *Time*, "Our personality is to be very loose. We aren't stuffed shirt people." He is considered a brash, free-wheeling, western Canadian, shoot-from-the-hip sort of entrepreneur whose casual exterior camouflages a driving ambition. According to John Sidgmore, WorldCom's vice-chair, in *Time*: "Don't fall for that 'Aw shucks' stuff.... [Ebbers]'s extremely street smart. Most of all, he has a vision for the company. He is extremely aggressive and simply wants to build the biggest company in the industry."

Ebbers's rags to riches story was based on shrewd analysis of the breakup of the telephone company in the early 1980s. His purchase of LDDS (Long Distance Discount Services) gave him access to the new and lucrative long distance services. From there, he was able to consolidate his position in the industry and began buying up smaller firms. Through the remainder of the 1980s he put together more than forty mergers and acquisitions to establish LDDS as a leader in the telecommunications industry.

In 1995, Ebbers renamed the company LDDS WorldCom, Inc. This name change reflects the international vision that the company undertook in the 1990s. He has aggressively pursued deals that would offer subscribers to WorldCom a complete array of telecommunications services. In 1996 he purchased MFS Communications for $12 billion which gave him the rights to UUNET, the world's largest Internet provider. In October 1997, he became part of a three-way deal with America On-line to purchase CompuServe for $1.2 billion. These acquisitions were all part of Ebbers's strategy to create a 'one stop' telecommunications service for his subscribers. This from a man who, although he runs a major telecommunications firm, doesn't have a cellular phone, or a pager, and won't use e-mail.

Not everyone is happy with Ebbers's style and takeovers. Allegiance Telecom, founded by Royce Holland, former president and chief executive officer of MFS Communications, alleged in a lawsuit against WorldCom and Ebbers that WorldCom was unfairly preventing former employees from continuing their careers outside the company and not meeting its financial commitments. Similar lawsuits, filed by several other former MFS Communications officials claim that WorldCom denied them their stock options or sued them for taking new jobs. These types of legal difficulties often arise in the wake of takeovers. However, impartial industry analysts expressed concern over Ebbers's tendency to downsize his new properties, and cut what he considered fat. David Goodtree, a telecommunications analyst with Foresster Research in Cambridge, Massachusetts, told *MSNBC*, "WorldCom has a history of swallowing companies and squeezing the creativity out of them ... MFS has great assets, but they wiped out any sense of leadership." While Ebbers disagreed with the assessment, as would shareholders who saw WorldCom stock skyrocket in five years, there is indication that Ebbers's blustery manner often threatened to obscure his message.

In October 1997, Ebbers demolished a British Telecommunications (BT) takeover bid of $18 billion for MCI by offering MCI $30 billion instead. When confronted with the fact that his bid had shattered BT's plan to make MCI the focus of its global strategy, Ebbers responded in *Time*, "We can realize far greater savings and synergies than BT can." In most mergers of this kind, the offer of stock would send stockholders and investors fleeing, but due to the strength and growth of WorldCom stock over the past few years, the deal became both lucrative and positive. Even as he was bidding for MCI, Ebbers unveiled his buyout plans for Brooks Fiber Properties, a company that provides local phone service to business customers in more than thirty U.S. cities. These multiple mergers and acquisitions are part of Ebbers overall plan. He "sees the industry at a historic turning point," Sidgmore said to *Time*. "That's why WorldCom is moving so quickly. We've made big bets and moved faster than anybody else."

By the time he is done creating the all-service telecommunications company that he envisions, Ebbers may find that he needs to broaden his vision. Once, when he was asked if had any new deals up his sleeve, he answered "Are we alive?" Ebbers's ability to recognize the need to serve subscribers in data and Internet traffic, on local, long distance, and international levels, on a massive scale, meant survival for his company. In order to assure this, he combined the right people and the right deals to corner the market on all aspects of the industry that he transformed. Ebbers's WorldCom developed the size and scale to challenge anyone in the telecommunications industry.

Sources

On-line

"The Man behind the Mega-deal," *MSNBC*, http://207.68.146.11/News/114259.asp (November 14, 1997).

"Press Releases," *WorldCom Homepage*, http://www.wcom.com/ (November 17, 1997).

"With Telecoms, It's More Than Money," *MSNBC*, http://207.68.146.11/News/117350.asp (November 17, 1997).

Periodicals

Electronic News, October 6, 1997, p. 1; October 10, 1997, p. 1.

Internet Week, October 6, 1997, p. 175.

Mississippi College Alumni Magazine, 1996.

Time, October 13, 1997, p. 61; October 27, 1997, p. 100.

U.S.A. Today, August 28, 1996, p. 4B; November 11, 1997, p. 3B.

—Paula M. Kalamaras and Paul T. Kraly

Roger Ebert

Film critic and author

Born Roger Joseph Ebert, June 18, 1942, in Urbana, IL; son of Walter H. and Annabel E. (Stumm) Ebert; married Chaz Hammelsmith, 1992. *Education:* University of Illinois, B.S., 1964; attended University of Cape Town, 1965, and University of Chicago, 1966-67.

Addresses: *Home*—Chicago, IL. *Office*—*Chicago Sun-Times,* 401 North Wabash, Chicago, IL 60611-3532.

Career

News Gazette, Champaign-Urbana, IL, staff reporter, 1958-66; film critic for *US* magazine, 1978-79, WMAQ-TV, Chicago, IL, 1980-83, WLS-TV, Chicago, 1984—, *Chicago Sun-Times,* 1967—, *New York Post,* 1986-88, *New York Daily News,* 1988-92, CompuServe, 1991—, Microsoft *Cinemania,* 1994—, and *Yahoo Internet Life;* author of interviews and film reviews for Universal Press Syndicate, 1986—. Co-host of *Sneak Previews,* WTTW and PBS, 1976-82, *At the Movies* (also called *Siskel & Ebert at the Movies*), syndicated by Tribune Entertainment, 1982-86, and *Siskel and Ebert,* syndicated by Buena Vista Television, 1986—; *NBC News,* film critic, 1980-83; *Movie News,* ABC Radio, commentator, 1982-85; *Critics at Large,* WBBM- Radio, Chicago, contributor. President of Ebert Co., Ltd., 1981—. Chicago City College, instructor of English, 1967-68; University of Chicago, lecturer of film criticism, c. 1970—; Columbia College, Chicago, lecturer, 1973-74, 1977-80; Kluge fellow, University of Virginia, 1995-96. Member of juries at Venice, Chicago, and U.S. film festivals; has also covered Cannes, Teheran, Moscow, and New York film festivals; consultant to National En-

dowment for the Humanities and National Endowment for the Arts. Author of books and screenplays. Member, American Newspaper Guild, Writers Guild of America (West), National Society of Film Critics, Arts Club of Chicago, Cliff Dwellers Club of Chicago, Academy of London, University of Illinois Alumni Association (member of board of directors, 1975-77), Phi Delta Theta, and Sigma Delta Chi. Author and contributor to popular magazines and newspapers, including *American Film, Esquire, Film Comment,* and *Rolling Stone.*

Awards: Overseas Press Club Award, 1963; award from Chicago Headline Club, 1963; Rotary fellow, 1965; Stick o' Type Award, Chicago Newspaper Guild, 1973; Pulitzer Prize for distinguished criticism, Columbia University, 1975, for reviews and essays in *Chicago Sun-Times;* Chicago Emmy Award, 1979; inducted into Chicago Journalism Hall of Fame, 1997.

Sidelights

Possessor of one of the most famous fingers in the entertainment world, Roger Ebert has established a simple yet effective film rating system by pointing his thumb either up or down, depending on his general opinion of the effort. Ebert and his cohort, *Chi-*

cago Tribune critic Gene Siskel, have been teaming up since the mid-1970s to provide television audience with their summaries of a flick's pros and cons, and to give a "yes" or "no" vote establishing their overall opinion. Ebert, however, is not just an everyday film buff. After becoming the first (and so far, only) film critic to win the prestigious Pulitzer Prize for distinguished criticism in 1975 for his reviews in the *Chicago Sun-Times*, Chicago's WTTW-TV asked him to cohost a movie reviewing television show with cross-town competitor Siskel. In 1978, PBS signed the quarrelsome critics for the syndicated series *Sneak Previews*. Since then, Ebert has become a hot commodity for publishers and software makers eager to tap into his one-man warehouse of film knowledge. He estimated once in 1995 that he had seen about 5,000 films, and he has written a number of titles on the subject, including the annual *Roger Ebert's Video Companion* and 1997's *Questions for the Movie Answer Man*, and his work can be found online and on the Microsoft CD-ROM *Cinemania*.

Ebert was born on June 18, 1942, in Urbana, Illinois, to Walter H. and Annabel E. (Stumm) Ebert. As a youngster, he enjoyed watching movies at the Princess Theater in his home town, where his first foray into film was *A Day at the Races* featuring the Marx Brothers comedy team. Ebert served as a sports reporter for a local paper, the *News Gazette*, beginning in 1958 at age 15, and went on to attend the University of Illinois. There he became editor of the *Daily Illini*, the student newspaper. While still in college, he began contributing to the *Chicago Sun-Times*. Ebert graduated in 1964 with his journalism degree and attended the University of Cape Town in South Africa in 1965 on a Rotary fellowship. The next year, he began doctoral work at the University of Chicago. He left academia in 1967, however, to take a position as a feature writer with the *Chicago Sun-Times*.

When Ebert started writing movie reviews a little later at around age 25, he did not have any knowledge of the behind-the-scenes view of filmmaking. This changed when he took on a screenwriting project for producer Russ Meyer, known for his campy B-flicks featuring busty women. Ebert wrote the screen adaptation of the novel *Beyond the Valley of the Dolls* by Jacqueline Susann, for which he was paid $15,000. The sequel to *Valley of the Dolls, Beyond the Valley of the Dolls* concerns a group of young women who pursue rock stardom in Los Angeles. Panned by fellow critics, the film would remain a blemish on Ebert's otherwise admirable career. He prefers to keep quiet on the issue, but in 1979 he teamed up with Meyer for yet another forgettable screenplay, *Beneath the Valley of the Ultra Vixens*.

Despite the *Beyond the Valley of the Dolls* fiasco, Ebert in the early- to mid-1970s was becoming recognized for his high-quality reviews of other people's work for the *Chicago Sun-Times*. In 1975, he became the first—and so far, only—film critic to win a Pulitzer Prize for distinguished criticism. Undoubtedly, this must have stuck in the craw of cross-town movie maven Gene Siskel, a Yale philosophy graduate who was busy with picks and pans for the *Chicago Tribune*. The two critics had been fierce rivals in print when WTTW, the pubic broadcasting channel in Chicago, approached them to cohost an onscreen review program. "The answer," Ebert related in *Time*, "was at the tip of my tongue: no." He later claimed that he just did not want to give attention to the competition. Siskel was similarly underwhelmed with the idea, not convinced he that wanted to join forces with "the most hated guy in my life," as he noted in *Time*. Somehow the duo was coerced into getting on stage together.

In a pair of cozy armchairs, Siskel and Ebert began their trademark barbs at the films as well as each other in the show *Opening Soon at a Theater Near You*, which was later renamed *Sneak Previews*. The show's basic format has not changed since its inception. One of the men introduces a clip from an upcoming movie, offers a plot summary, and gives a quick review, then the pair engages in an ad-libbed dialogue about the film's strengths and weaknesses while sometimes tossing in seemingly good-natured insults at each other. Their final word for each review has become their trademark. A "thumbs up" or "thumbs down" signals to potential movie-goers whether the film is overall worth seeing or not. No one knows for sure how much impact their approval or disapproval has on the success of any given film, but reviews for years have been proud to announce "TWO THUMBS UP!" in screaming type whenever the men both express their satisfaction, which is actually not that rare. Richard Zoglin in *Time* noted, "[T]hey agree much more often than they disagree. Their tastes are generally similar.... Both rail regularly against teen sex comedies, violent horror films and car chases. Good movies are almost always those that have 'characters you can identify with.'" Viewers seem to enjoy their unpretentious approach to the medium. Though Ebert is slightly more of a populist and Siskel seems to be a bit more highbrow, they are just as likely to applaud a Hollywood blockbuster as they are a foreign documentary.

Audiences, however, tune in not only to get the Midwesterners' opinions of the pictures, but also to get a laugh at their wisecracks, volleyed back and forth like a tennis ball. Siskel's balding head and Ebert's bulging belly are usually the focus of many jabs, but they also make personal attacks on each other's intelligence when they disagree about the quality of a film. Barbara Kleban Mills in *People Weekly* compared them to comedians Abbott and Costello, and reprinted a few of their gems: "Gene to Roger (who's overweight): *Has your application for a zip code come through yet?* Roger to Gene (who's balding): *The only things the astronauts saw from outer space were Three Mile Island and your forehead.* Gene to Roger: *Yeah? When they passed over your house, you were sunbathing in the garden and they thought they'd discovered a second moon.*"

Though the critics have a general idea of what they will say when the camera rolls, they do not rehearse, nor do they recite lines word-for-word. Ebert told Mills in *People Weekly*, "We're not actors saying the same lines over and over." They will, however, reshoot a scene if one of them trips over his tongue, but they usually do not repeat the sequence exactly as before, and sometimes will launch into a much different version of their speech. Although they have been accused of beefing up their onscreen arguments, they insist the battles are real, and apparently rage offscreen as well: Zoglin in *Time* reported that they have even been known to fight on airplanes.

Just because they argue, however, does not mean they are mortal enemies. Ebert told Steve Lowery of the *Long Beach Press-Telegram*, carried by the Knight-Ridder/Tribune News Service, that he and Siskel "I think, do like each other and we respect each other.... Now, we don't always get along very well. We have our good days and bad days, but we don't hate each other." Their dynamic interactions have led to invitations to talk shows, including *Late Night with David Letterman*, where they delight the host and audience with their bickering, and the iconic duo has spawned parodies in comedy films and television programs. There have also been other attempts to replicate the show's success, including *At the Movies* with Rex Reed and Bill Harris, and the second generation of *Sneak Previews*, with Jeffrey Lyons and Michael Medved. No one, so far, has matched the spark of Siskel and Ebert.

Sneak Previews was an instant success in Chicago, and in 1978 PBS syndicated it nationwide. It soon became the highest-rated series in the history of public broadcasting. In 1982, Siskel and Ebert signed with Tribune Entertainment, which produced the show commercially as *At the Movies*, and after another four years, they moved to Buena Vista Television, which renamed the show simply *Siskel & Ebert*. Each critic reportedly earns $1 million annually for their onscreen antics;

they are seen by about three and a half million viewers weekly on about 200 stations. Ebert pads his income with his reviews for the *Sun-Times*, which are posted on the paper's web site and are fully searchable, and has also been a regular critic for *US* magazine (1978-79), the *New York Post* (1986-88), and the *New York Daily News* (1988-92). Since 1991, his work has been featured on the Internet service CompuServe, and his writing can also be found in *Yahoo Internet Life*, an online magazine.

> *Ebert is not just an everyday film buff. He was the first (and so far, only) film critic to win the prestigious Pulitzer Prize for distinguished criticism in 1975 for his reviews in the* Chicago Sun-Times.

Ebert has also enjoyed a prolific book publishing career. In 1985, he began churning out an annual encyclopedia of over a thousand film reviews titled *Roger Ebert's Movie Home Companion*, which was renamed *Roger Ebert's Video Companion* in 1994. It also includes some celebrity interviews and essays. He published a full book about stars, featuring biographies and interviews, as *A Kiss Is Still a Kiss*, released in 1984. Focusing attention on those behind the camera, in 1991 he and Siskel put out *The Future of the Movies: Interviews with Martin Scorsese, Steven Spielberg, and George Lucas*. A yearly presence at the noted Cannes Film Festival in France, Ebert published an account of the event in 1987 as *Two Weeks in the Midday Sun: A Cannes Notebook*, which he also illustrated. He ventured into fiction in 1993 with *Behind the Phantom's Mask*, a murder mystery serial spoofing Hollywood that was first published in newspapers, and put out a witty guide to film cliches with 1994's *Ebert's Little Movie Glossary*. In addition, his movie reviews are featured on Microsoft's multimedia CD-ROM *Cinemania*. In 1996 he came out with *Roger Ebert's Book of Film: From Tolstoy to Tarantino, the Finest Writing from a Century of Film*, a collection of what others have had to say about the experience of the movies, from memoirs and biographies to articles and novel excerpts (but no criticism). Stanley Kauffmann in the *New Republic* voted it "a prize package," and it was given a grade of "A" by *Entertainment Weekly* and *Publishers Weekly*, the later of which also deemed that it offers "a wealth of lore and legend."

Ebert has been a jury member at the Sundance, Montreal, Chicago, Hawaii, and Venice film festivals, in addition to Cannes. He has taught courses in Chicago colleges since the 1960s. He spent a year at the Chicago City College teaching English from 1967 to 1968, and around 1970 began lecturing on film at the University of Chicago, where he has remained since. He also did a couple of stints at Chicago's Columbia College, during the academic years 1973-74 and 1977-80, and was named a Kluge fellow at the University of Virginia for 1995-96. Ebert enjoys drawing, painting, collecting art, reading, walking, computers, traveling, cosmology, and Darwinianism. He married trial attorney Chaz Hammelsmith in 1992, and the couple live in Chicago. In 1995 Frank Bruni for the Knight-Ridder/Tribune News Service asked Ebert, "In heaven, what movie do they show over and over again and what snack is free of both calories and charge?" Ebert replied, "*Citizen Kane*, and vanilla Haagen-Dazs ice cream."

Selected writings

An Illini Century, University of Illinois Press, 1967.

Beyond the Valley of the Dolls (screenplay), Twentieth Century-Fox, 1970.

Beyond Narrative: The Future of the Feature Film, 1978.

(With Russ Meyer) *Beneath the Valley of the Ultra Vixens* (screenplay), RM Films, 1979.

A Kiss Is Still a Kiss (biographies of film stars), Andrews and McMeel, 1984.

Roger Ebert's Movie Home Companion (film reviews), Andrews and McMeel, annual editions, 1985-93, renamed *Roger Ebert's Video Companion*, 1994—.

(With Daniel Curley) *The Perfect London Walk*, photographs by Jack Lane, Andrews, McMeel, & Parker, 1986.

Two Weeks in the Midday Sun: A Cannes Notebook, Andrews and McMeel, 1987.

(With Gene Siskel) *The Future of the Movies: Interviews with Martin Scorsese, Steven Spielberg, and George Lucas*, Andrews and McMeel, 1991.

Behind the Phantom's Mask: A Serial (novel), illustrations by Victor Juhasz, Andrews and McMeel, 1993.

Ebert's Little Movie Glossary: A Compendium of Movie Cliches, Stereotypes, Obligatory Scenes, Hackneyed Formulas, Shopworn Conventions, and Outdated Archetypes, Andrews McMeel, 1994.

Roger Ebert's Book of Film: From Tolstoy to Tarantino, the Finest Writing from a Century of Film, W. W. Norton, 1997.

Questions for the Movie Answer Man, Andrews McMeel, 1997.

Sources

On-line

"Roger's Biography," Siskel & Ebert web site, http://www.siskel-ebert.com (May 26, 1998).

"Roger's Biography," http://www.tvplex.com/BuenaVista/SiskelAndEbert (May 26, 1998).

Books

Contemporary Authors, New Revision Series, Volume 45, Gale Research, 1995.

Periodicals

Entertainment Weekly, February 21, 1997, p. 120.

Knight-Ridder/Tribune News Service, March 10, 1995; July 3, 1995; August 3, 1995.

New Republic, November 18, 1996, p. 26.

People Weekly, August 20, 1984, p. 61.

Publishers Weekly, October 14, 1996, p. 71.

Time, May 25, 1987, p. 64.

—*Geri Speace*

Mia Farrow

Actress

Born Maria de Lourdes Villiers Farrow, February 9, 1945, in Los Angeles, CA; daughter of John Villiers Farrow (a writer and film director) and Maureen Paula O'Sullivan (an actress); married Frank Sinatra (a singer and actor), July 19, 1966 (divorced, 1968); married Andre Previn (a composer and orchestra conductor), September 10, 1970 (divorced, February, 1979); children: (with Previn) Matthew Phineas and Sascha Villiers Previn (twin boys), Fletcher Previn; (with Woody Allen) Satchel O'Sullivan (named changed to Seamus); (adopted) Lark Song Previn, Summer Song ("Daisy") Previn, Soon-Yi Farrow Previn, Moses Amadeus ("Misha") Farrow, Dylan O'Sullivan Farrow (name changed to Eliza), Tam Farrow, Thaddeus W. Farrow, Isaiah Justus Farrow, Kaeli-Shea Farrow, Gabriel Wilk Farrow, Frankie-Minh Farrow.

Addresses: *Home*—Connecticut. *Agent*—William Morris Agency, 151 El Camino Dr., Beverly Hills, CA 90212.

Career

Actress. Stage appearances include *The Importance of Being Earnest*, Madison Avenue Playhouse (New York City), 1966; *Jeanne d'Arc*, London, 1971; *Mary Rose*, Shaw Theatre (London), 1972; *The House of Bernarda Alba*, Greenwich Theatre (London), 1973; *The Three Sisters*, Greenwich Theatre, 1973; *The Marrying of Ann Leete*, Royal Shakespeare Company (RSC), Aldwych Theatre (London), 1975; *The Zykovs*, RSC, Aldwych Theatre, 1976; *Ivanov*, RSC, Aldwych Theatre, 1976; *Romantic Comedy*, Ethel Barrymore Theatre (New York City), 1979; lead role, *Peter Pan*; and summer theater productions in Warren, OH, 1963. Television appearances include series *Peyton Place*, ABC, 1964-66; and television movies *Goodbye Raggedy Ann*, CBS, 1971; *Murder in Peyton Place* (flashback scenes), NBC, 1977. Television specials include *Johnny Belinda*, ABC, 1967; and "Peter Pan," *Hallmark Hall of Fame*, NBC, 1976. Film appearances include *John Paul Jones*, 1959; *The Age of Curiosity* (short film), 1963; *Guns at Batasi*, 1964; *Rosemary's Baby*, 1968; *Secret Ceremony*, 1968; *A Dandy in Aspic*, 1968; *John and Mary*, 1969; *See No Evil*, 1971; *Docteur Popaul*, 1972; *The Public Eye*, 1972; *The Great Gatsby*, 1974; *The Haunting of Julia*, 1976; *A Wedding*, 1978; *Death on the Nile*, 1978; *Avalanche*, 1978; *Hurricane*, 1979; *High Heels*, 1981; *A Midsummer Night's Sex Comedy*, 1982; *Zelig*, 1983; *Broadway Danny Rose*, 1984; *Supergirl*, 1984; *The Purple Rose of Cairo*, 1985; *Hannah and Her Sisters*, 1986; *Radio Days*, 1986; *September*, 1987; *Another Woman*, 1988; *Crimes and Misdemeanors*, 1989; *New York Stories* ("Oedipus Wrecks" segment), 1989; *Alice*, 1991; *Shadows and Fog*, 1992; *Husbands and Wives*, 1992; *Widow's Peak*, 1994; *Miami Rhapsody*, 1995. Also voice in animated films *The Last Unicorn*, 1982; *Sarah*, 1982; *Stories to Remember—Beauty & the Beast*; and *Stories to Remember—Pegasus*. Author of autobiography *What Falls Away*, Doubleday, 1997.

Awards: Golden Globe Award for most promising newcomer, 1965; French Academy Award for best actress, David Di Donatello Award, Rio de Janeiro Film Festival Award, and San Sebastian Film Festival Award, all 1969, for *Rosemary's Baby*.

Sidelights

Actress Mia Farrow has played a wide range of characters in almost four decades in entertainment, ranging from an innocent, confused teen to a tough Brooklyn mobster moll. She can be just as versatile off screen as well. This mother of over a dozen children is also a successful screen star who has weathered her share of troubles. She began her life in a posh Beverly Hills setting, the daughter of a famous movie star and director and survived polio at age nine. She rose to stardom in the 1960s playing a doe-eyed, waif-like teen in the prime time TV soap opera, *Peyton Place*, then captured audiences as the bride of Satan and mother of the Antichrist in the spooky *Rosemary's Baby*. Her marriage to Frank Sinatra, who died in 1998, was marred by *paparazzi* and plagued with difficulty, partly as a result of his Las Vegas lifestyle and her commitment to her career. She continued making films in the 1970s and worked in London theaters during her marriage to conductor/composer Andre Previn.

In the 1980s, she began a professionally rewarding but personally stormy relationship with director Woody Allen. The court case that followed their breakup sent the nation reeling with his accusations that she was an unfit mother and her charges that he molested one of her young daughters. After the eruption had settled, Allen ended up marrying one of Farrow's older adopted daughters, Soon-Yi Previn. Though Farrow has continued making films, she prefers a private existence in Connecticut where she raises her younger children, goes grocery shopping, and watches television. In 1997 she published her memoir, *What Falls Away*, outlining her highs and lows and giving an in-depth look at the custody battle that Allen waged. "You can acknowledge terrible things, then you move on," Farrow told Merle Ginsberg in *McCall's*. "You hope you've planted enough positive things in your life, enough good people, and that becomes all that matters."

Farrow was born on February 9, 1945, in Los Angeles, California. She was the eldest daughter of John Farrow, a writer and film director, and Maureen O'Sullivan, a glamorous actress. Her father was born in Australia, and her mother hailed from Ireland. The couple had seven children in all: Michael, Patrick, John, Maria ("Mia"), Prudence ("Prudy"), Stephanie ("Steffie"), and Theresa Magdalena ("Tisa"). Farrow was raised Roman Catholic in this extremely close-knit family, enjoying the company of her siblings and other children in their Beverly Hills neighborhood. She also used to play with the merchandise at the Beverly Pet Store, bringing home an array of creatures. At one time Farrow owned a duck, five guinea pigs, a garter snake, two turtles, a toad, and 87 hamsters in addition to the family dog and cat. She sometimes took one of the hamsters to school with her in a pocket.

Farrow suffered a painful bout with polio at age nine, which afflicted many in the 1950s. She stayed in the hospital and had to endure being put in an "iron lung." After pulling through, she went home to find that most of her belongings had been burned so as not to spread the contagion, and she was not allowed contact with other children for months except visits through the window with a friend next door. This experience molded a large part of her being, as she related in her autobiography, *What Falls Away*: "I discovered that whatever your losses, you can still for the most part choose your attitude.... I learned that you can't truly own anything, that true ownership comes only in the moment of giving. And I learned a little about friendship and how it can light the darkest abyss."

In 1958 Farrow's father relocated the family to Spain temporarily to shoot the film *John Paul Jones*. She began attending parochial school and continued at a convent school in Surrey, England, when her father moved to England to edit the film. In 1959, her older brother, Mike, to whom she felt closest, died in a plane crash in California while the rest of the family was in England. Farrow stayed at the boarding school for a couple more years, traveling throughout Europe and the Middle East with other students and nuns and considered joining the convent. When the family returned to California, their finances were not doing so well, and they sold their roomy Beverly Hills home for a smaller house in a less prestigious area. Farrow graduated from the Marymount School, a Catholic college preparatory high school in Los Angeles, where she won awards for her dramatic skills and decided against becoming a nun.

Farrow returned to England in 1962 to prepare for A-level exams, hoping to pursue higher education and perhaps become a pediatrician in developing nations. By Christmas, she was back in the United States visiting her mother, who was in New York starring in the Broadway comedy *Never Too Late*. Farrow and her mother moved into an Upper West Side apartment in early 1963, when she began noticing a relationship developing between her mother and the play's director, George Abbott. When Farrow's father tried to reach his wife one night in January of 1963, Farrow did not tell him of her whereabouts and later in the night let the phone ring without answering. The next day, she learned her father had died of a heart attack during the night with his hand on the telephone.

Farrow was drawn to acting despite her father's admonition that he had "never met a happy actress," as she noted in her book. She had her professional stage debut on July 2, 1963, in the role of Cecily in *The Importance of Being Earnest.* After rave reviews, she was asked to do a screen test for a new television pilot, *Peyton Place,* a nighttime soap opera based on the novel about small-town scandals. At the table with her in the coffee shop as she agonized over whether to sign the contract were her mother and surrealist artist Salvador Dali, whom she had befriended during her time in New York. After signing the papers, Farrow spent the summer of 1963 performing with a stock company in Warren, Ohio.

Farrow had a deal to shoot the *Peyton Place* pilot and five films for Twentieth Century-Fox, so she briefly returned to California. Dubious of the pilot's possibilities, she went back to New York and told Dali that she was anxious to find work. He told her, "If you want dramatic change, put your shoes on the opposite feet," as she recalled in her memoir. Farrow heeded his advice, and immediately got a phone call asking her to fly to Paris, where she got a part in the Fox film *Guns at Batasi* starring Richard Attenborough. Much to her dismay, ABC bought *Peyton Place,* and she had to go back to California. The 19-year old began earning $50,000 a year as Allison MacKenzie, a frail, naive blond teenager. Farrow began acting opposite heartthrob Ryan O'Neal in 1964, but her character was written out of the script in 1966.

Around 1965, before she turned 20, Farrow became involved with crooner Frank Sinatra, who was almost 30 years her senior. He was her first lover and became her first husband when they married in Las Vegas, Nevada, on July 19, 1966. While they were dating, she cropped her waist-length mane to less than an inch in length, stunning *Peyton Place* producers and creating a media frenzy. Sinatra loved the new look, and she kept it short for many years. However, the press coverage was hard on the newlyweds, and the singer did not approve of Farrow's career. When she was offered the starring role in *Rosemary's Baby,* directed by Roman Polanski, he wanted her to turn it down and shoot *The Detective* with him. She figured *Rosemary's Baby*

would be done filming by the start of *The Detective,* so she agreed to take both projects.

Filming took longer than expected for *Rosemary's Baby,* and Farrow decided to continue the project rather than quit the film to begin on *The Detective.* Sinatra served her with divorce papers on the set in November of 1967. After this, in early 1968, Farrow and her sister, Prudence, spent some time in India studying transcendental meditation with the Maharishi Mahesh Yogi and the Beatles, who were followers. (Farrow maintained in *What Falls Away* that the Beatles penned the song "Dear Prudence" about her sister.) Farrow's split with Sinatra was finalized in Mexico in August of 1968 when she was 21 years old. She received no alimony and remained fond of Sinatra throughout her life, paying her respects at his funeral in May of 1998. After their divorce, she traveled extensively in the United States, Europe, and Mexico.

> *"You can acknowledge terrible things, then you move on. You hope you've planted enough positive things in your life, enough good people, and that becomes all that matters."*

Though Farrow's marriage had failed, *Rosemary's Baby,* released in 1968, propelled her to stardom and critical acclaim. The adaptation of Ira Levin's book about the mother of the Antichrist has remained a favorite of audiences for decades. Many were shocked that Farrow was not nominated for an Academy Award for her performance, but she was honored with several international prizes in 1969, including a French Academy Award for best actress, David Di Donatello Award, Rio de Janeiro Film Festival Award, and San Sebastian Film Festival Award. After that big break, she donned a long dark wig to play Elizabeth Taylor's daughter in *Secret Ceremony,* a psychological thriller that did not measure up to *Rosemary's Baby.* Then in 1969, she costarred with Dustin Hoffman in *John and Mary,* a tale of two singles who have intercourse before they know each others' names. The film got mixed reviews.

During filming for *John and Mary,* Farrow began a relationship over the telephone with composer and conductor Andre Previn, who was married. In October of 1969, after spending a short time with him in Ireland, she told him she was pregnant. She had twins, Matthew Phineas and Sascha Villiers, on February 29, 1970. Previn divorced his wife, Dory, who was reluctant to grant the breakup, and married Farrow on September 10, 1970, in London, England. Farrow and Previn were together most of the decade and adopted more children together. Their first was a Vietnamese war orphan in 1973 whom they named Lark Song. The next year, they had another biological child, Fletcher. Six months after his birth, she was admitted to the hospital with a ruptured appendix, which was misdiagnosed almost causing her death.

In 1973, Farrow filmed *The Great Gatsby*, released in 1974, and also made a return to the stage. Living in London with Previn and the children, she appeared in a number of plays, including *The Marrying of Ann Leete, The Zykovs,* and *Ivanov* with the Royal Shakespeare Company. In 1974, she adopted another Vietnamese child, Summer Song, nicknamed Daisy. Despite extreme health problems, the child was nursed to health by Farrow. By 1976, Farrow and Previn added an orphaned Korean girl, about age five (no one was exactly sure) to the household, Soon-Yi. Because Farrow and Previn already had two adopted children, they had used up the allotted number of visas for adoptions, but managed to get the law changed in order to bring Soon-Yi home.

In 1978, Farrow and Previn were having problems, and they divorced in 1979, although they continued to maintain a friendship. Farrow and her children went back to New York and moved into the same Upper West Side apartment that she had shared with her mother. Also that year, Farrow starred with Tony Perkins in *Romantic Comedy*, while her mother, O'Sullivan, was onstage two blocks away in *Morning's at Seven*. They became the first mother and daughter to concurrently headline on Broadway. Meanwhile, in January of 1980, Farrow adopted a Korean boy with cerebral palsy, whom she named Moses Amadeus (also called Misha, her deceased brother Mike's nickname).

Farrow's life would begin a new phase in 1980. In April of that year, she began dating filmmaker Woody Allen, and the two had a professionally productive relationship for a dozen years. Farrow appeared in or starred in many of Allen's critically-acclaimed and usually popular comedies throughout this period, including *A Midsummer Night's Sex Comedy*, 1982; *Zelig*, 1983; *The Purple Rose of Cairo*, 1985; *Hannah and Her Sisters* (which was shot in Farrow's New York City apartment), 1986; *Radio Days*, 1986; the "Oedipus Wrecks" segment of *New York Stories*, 1989; *Crimes and Misdemeanors*, 1989;

Alice, 1991; *Shadows and Fog*, 1992; and *Husbands and Wives*, 1992. Farrow and Allen also entered a romantic relationship, despite their many differences. As Allen remarked in a *New York Times* biography, "She doesn't like the city and I adore it.... She doesn't like sports at all and I love sports. She loves to eat in, early—5:30, 6—and I love to eat out, late. She likes simple, unpretentious restaurants; I like fancy places. She can't sleep with an air-conditioner on; I can only sleep with an air-conditioner on."

Though they never married, Farrow and Allen had a child together, named Satchel O'Sullivan, after the baseball player, Satchel Paige, and Farrow's mother (the boy later changed his name to Seamus). Farrow also continued adopting many more children through the decade, including Dylan O'Sullivan, who later changed her name to Eliza. The couple, however, maintained separated residences for the duration of their time together. Farrow kept her rent-controlled Upper West Side apartment and a country home in Connecticut that she calls "Frog Hollow." Allen did not give up his place across Central Park on the Upper East Side. She was dismayed at his reluctance to get involved with her family; he even referred to the kids in a *New York Times* article as "her little orphan children."

Though Farrow suspected for some time that Allen was sexually molesting their cute toddler, Dylan, she continued seeing him. She also accused him in *What Falls Away* of scaring her with his rages. However, the final blow was her discovery in 1992 of nude and explicit photographs of her 21-year-old daughter Soon-Yi in his apartment. Farrow asserted in *What Falls Away* that the two had been having sexual relations since the girl's senior year in high school; Soon-Yi in *Time* claimed they began seeing each other when she was about 20. Messy litigation ensued, with Allen trying to gain custody of Moses, Dylan, and Satchel. All of the details were made public, causing a public outcry. Farrow was made out to be an unstable scatterbrain unfit to raise her many children, and Allen was painted as an incestuous lecher. In the end, Allen was denied visitation of Dylan and Satchel, and Moses, at 15, was allowed to decide for himself. Allen was ordered to pay all court costs for bringing a "frivolous petition," as reported in the legal documents in *What Falls Away*.

Farrow went on to make more films, including *Widow's Peak* in 1994 and *Miami Rhapsody* in 1995. She also appeared on the cover of *People* in 1994 to celebrate that magazine's twentieth anniversary; she had been the cover model on its very first issue in 1974. Allen continued seeing Soon-Yi, and married her on December 23, 1997, in Venice, Italy. The following month, the Mr. Showbiz web site reported that Allen, 62 at the time, said having children with his 27-year-old bride was "a reasonable option." Farrow moved her family out of the New York apartment in 1994 and took up permanent residence at Frog Hollow, her eight-bedroom home in Connecticut. She adopted more children, including Tam, Thaddeus, Isaiah, Kaeli-Shea, Frankie-Minh (named after her first husband, Frank Sinatra), and Gabriel. She wrote a memoir in 1997 titled *What Falls Away*, giving details of her life and reprinting the court's decision of the custody case and appeared on various talk shows to discuss Allen and her book. She told Ginsberg in *McCall's* that she is happy with her children and animals in the country. "I really don't miss New York City," she remarked. "And I don't miss the company of adult friends. I should miss it more.... Is it wrong to prefer tucking my children in at night to going out to a concert or having dinner? Weighed against what I've got here, nothing else seems as important."

Selected writings

What Falls Away, Doubleday, 1997.

Sources

On-line

"Woody Wants Kids with Soon-Yi," Mr. Showbiz web site, January 16, 1998, http://www.mrshowbiz.com (May 18, 1998).

Books

Contemporary Theatre, Film, and Television, Volume 7, Gale Research, 1989.
What Falls Away, Doubleday, 1997.

Periodicals

Biography, January 1998, p. 14.
Interview, April 1994, p. 78.
McCall's, April 1997, p. 48.
New Statesman, March 7, 1997, p. 45.
Newsweek, January 4, 1965, p. 31.
New York Times, February 24, 1991.
People Weekly, September 7, 1992, p. 55; June 21, 1993, p. 85; March 7, 1994, p. 3.
Time, August 31, 1992, pp. 54, 61.

—*Geri Speace*

Farrah Fawcett

Actress

Born Mary Farrah Leni Fawcett, February 2, 1947, in Corpus Christi, TX; daughter of James William (founder of a pipeline construction company and custodial service) and Pauline (Evans) Fawcett; married Lee Majors (an actor), July 28, 1973 (divorced, 1982); children: (with actor Ryan O'Neal) Redmond O'Neal. *Education:* Attended the University of Texas at Austin.

Addresses: *Agent*—c/o William Morris Agency, 151 El Camino Dr., Beverly Hills, CA 90212.

Career

Model, actress. Stage appearances include *Butterflies Are Free*, Burt Reynolds Dinner Theatre, Jupiter, FL; and *Extremities*, West Side Arts Theatre, 1983. Television appearances include series *Harry O*, ABC, 1974-76; *Charlie's Angels*, ABC, 1976-77; and *Good Sports*, 1991; movies *Three's a Crowd*, 1969; *The Feminist and the Fuzz*, 1970; *The Great American Beauty Contest*, 1973; *The Girl Who Came Gift-Wrapped*, 1974; *Murder on Flight 502*, 1975; *Murder in Texas*, 1981; *The Red-Light Sting*, 1984; *The Burning Bed*, 1984; *Nazi Hunter: The Beate Klarsfeld Story*, 1986; *Between Two Women*, 1986; *Poor Little Rich Girl: The Barbara Hutton Story*, 1987; *Margaret Bourke-White*, 1989; *Small Sacrifices*, 1989; *Criminal Behavior*, 1992; *The Substitute Wife*, 1994; *A Good Day to Die*, 1995; and *Dalva*, 1996; and episodes of *I Dream of Jeannie; The Dating Game; The Flying Nun; The Partridge Family; Owen Marshall, Counselor at Law; Days of Our Lives; McCloud; Apple's Way; The Six-Million Dollar Man; Marcus Welby, M.D.;* and *The Larry Sanders Show*. Film appearances include *Love Is a Funny Thing*, 1969; *Myra Breckenridge*, 1970; *Logan's Run*, 1976; *Somebody Killed Her Husband*, 1978; *Sunburn*, 1979; *Strictly Business*, 1979; *The Helper*, 1979; *Saturn 3*, 1980; *Cannonball Run*, 1981; *Extremities*, 1986; *See You in the Morning*, 1989; *Man of the House*, 1995; *The Apostle*, 1997; and *The Brave Little Toaster Goes to Mars* (animation voiceover), 1998. Video appearance in *All of Me*, 1996.

Sidelights

Actress Farrah Fawcett rose to superstardom in the 1970s with a campy hit television series, *Charlie's Angels*, about a trio of sexy female private investigators. Fawcett's ubiquitous poster that revealed many of her finer assets, including a shining set of pearly whites and bushy feathered blonde hair, set the standard for coiffures of the era. The vivacious, petite Fawcett tried to spread her wings after just one season with the *Angels* and land parts in more substantive roles, but suffered setbacks when her attempts were considered less than heavenly. She finally found her stride appearing in made-for-television movies during the 1980s, making an important breakthrough in 1984's domestic abuse drama *The Burning Bed*. After that, her reputation was boosted again with a starring role in the gripping *Extremities*, 1986, about a rape victim who seeks revenge. After spending about a decade in the television movie genre, Fawcett appeared in 1997's *The Apostle,* Robert Duvall's acclaimed pet project about a Southern preacher. Shortly thereafter, she unfortunately made headlines when she had to go to court to testify against her ex-boyfriend for her own domestic abuse case. Meanwhile, Fawcett shocked many—albeitpleasantly for male fans—when she appeared in a naughty 1996 Playboy video called *All of Me,* which fully reveals her still-athletic figure as she creates art in the nude. Though this and some of her other actions in the late 1990s raised eyebrows, *Newsday* reported that Fawcett told columnist Liz Smith, "I am getting such great offers.... Working with Duvall was my best break ever!"

Mary Farrah Leni Fawcett was born on February 2, 1947, in Corpus Christi, Texas. Her father, James William Fawcett, was an oil pipefitter who also founded a pipeline construction company and later, a custodial service. Her mother, Pauline (Evans) Fawcett, came up with the name Farrah because it sounded good with her surname, Fawcett. As a baby, Fawcett was born with a tumor in her digestive tract and underwent surgery when she was less than a month old. Growing up, she attended Catholic school and remembered being an obedient child. After finishing the sixth grade at St. Patrick's Church in Corpus Christi, Fawcett began public school at W. B. Ray High School, where she was generally a quiet student.

After high school, Fawcett enrolled at the University of Texas in Austin, planning to study microbiology. She later changed her major to art. A pretty, well-dressed student, she began modeling for a local clothing store that ran ads in the college newspaper, and she also sat for artists. After she was voted one of the ten most beautiful women on campus, her picture caught the eye of David Mirisch, a Hollywood publicist, who encouraged her to leave school and pursue a career in entertainment. Though she was eager to go, her parents were not so sure, urging her to finish her education first. By the end of her junior year in college, though, they let her test the waters in Hollywood. Fawcett immediately hired an agent and soon met actor Lee Majors, who helped her along. She managed to sign a contract with Screen Gems, who cast her in guest roles on television series such as *I Dream of Jeannie, The Dating Game, The Flying Nun,* and *The Partridge Family* in 1969 and 1970. "I didn't come to Los Angeles expecting to be anything," Fawcett once said, according to *People.* "I was led. Events happened, fell into place. I really gave no thought to my career."

Fawcett continued to win roles on television and in movies in addition to maintaining a lucrative career on the side as a model. She appeared in top magazines such as *Cosmopolitan* and *Vogue* and made a decent income from commercials for Noxema shaving cream, Ultra-Brite toothpaste, and Wella Balsam shampoo. Her film debut came in 1969 with the French film *Love Is a Funny Thing.* Following that, in 1970 she played Mary Ann in *Myra Breckenridge,* starring Raquel Welch and Rex Reed. This story of a man who undergoes a sex change operation is based on a novel by Gore Vidal. Subsequently, Fawcett landed parts in the made-for-television movies *Three's a Crowd,* 1969; *The Feminist and the Fuzz,* 1970; *The Great American Beauty Contest,* 1973; *The Girl Who Came Gift-Wrapped,* 1974; and *Murder on Flight 502,* 1975. Meanwhile, Fawcett in 1974 was cast on the television cop drama *Harry O* as the title character's girlfriend and secured a small role in the series *Apple's Way* the same year. She landed her next role playing Holly in the science-fiction dystopian thriller *Logan's Run* in 1976. She also married Lee Majors on July 28, 1973 (and changed her name to Farrah Fawcett-Majors) and began appearing with him on his hit show, *The Six-Million Dollar Man.*

Many of the television movies that Fawcett made were produced by Leonard Goldberg, who had headed production at Screen Gems, and Aaron Spelling. In 1976, the two men devised an idea for a television series about three attractive female private eyes working for a mysterious, wealthy man who is never seen on camera, giving his instructions for their assignments over the telephone and via his assistant, John Bosley (David Doyle). They sold their idea, called *Charlie's Angels,* to ABC and cast Fawcett as one of the agents. She played the athletic Jill Munroe, known for her sense of humor and card sharp skills. Kate Jackson was cast as the bright Sabrina Duncan, while Jaclyn Smith provided street smarts as Kelly Garrett. *Charlie's Angels* was undoubtedly erotic, and many men surely liked to see the three beautiful women strutting around disguised as prostitutes or go-go dancers, or tied up by dangerous criminals. However, *Charlie's Angels* was also considered somewhat feminist at the time, breaking new ground as a prime-time action-adventure program that featured the women in all kinds of daring situations. Women viewers appreciated that the angels displayed courage, quick thinking, and resourcefulness, as well as adeptness with guns and brute force, in addition to their stylish sensuality.

The program soared in the ratings and spawned a huge following, with Fawcett standing out as the most admired of the three stars. Her likeness spawned a cottage industry of merchandise, from lunch boxes,

T-shirts, and dolls to wigs, pillows, and a plumbing device (the Farrah faucet). One of the defining pieces of 1970s popular culture is, of course, the famous Farrah Fawcett poster. The picture showed her wearing a wet one-piece swimsuit and a sparkling, toothy smile, seated with one knee up, fingering her signature dishwater-blonde feathered hair. An estimated six million such posters were eventually sold by Pro-Arts, Inc., out of Medina, Ohio. Women and girls nationwide copied the curled-back, slightly messy hairdo, and teenage boys everywhere tacked the photo to their bedroom walls. Her career at its peak, Fawcett only starred in *Charlie's Angels* for one season, 1976-77, before leaving to search for new projects that would broaden her scope as an actress. Cheryl Ladd took her place in the series. Fawcett and her husband, Majors, then started up a production company and made a television movie called *Just a Little Inconvenience* in 1977, but she did not appear in it. A contract with Faberge led to a line of her own personal care products in 1978, for which she reportedly stood to make millions of dollars.

In 1978, Fawcett tried her dramatic skills with the film *Somebody Killed Her Husband,* a poor attempt which many took to calling "Somebody Killed Her Career." Over the next couple of years, she made three more forgettable movies, *Sunburn, The Helper,* and *Saturn 3.* In 1981 she had a role in the comedy *Cannonball Run,* starring Burt Reynolds, and also that year starred in the made-for-television movie *Murder in Texas.* This spurred a long-lasting run for her in the television movie genre, which generally features plots based on true stories. In the 1984 television movie, *The Burning Bed,* Fawcett fully transformed her image from pampered pinup into tragic, sympathetic real-person heroine as she portrayed a battered wife who is driven to murder her husband. Before this, producers were reluctant to give the bubbly beauty a chance at serious roles, but the highly-rated tale of domestic abuse proved that Fawcett had a wider range, and even earned her an Emmy nomination.

In 1986, Fawcett reiterated her abilities as a talented actress in the drama *Extremities,* a role she also played off Broadway in 1983 at the West Side Arts Theatre. In it, she is a woman who is attacked by a rapist in her own house. She manages to lock him up, but then has to face the decision of what to do next. Fawcett told Stephen Farber of the *New York Times* that it was "the most grueling, the most intense, the most physically demanding and emotionally exhausting" role of her career. Following these projects, Fawcett found a real niche in television movies, going on to star in the

miniseries *Poor Little Rich Girl: The Barbara Hutton Story* in 1987 and *Margaret Bourke-White,* a biography of the famous photographer, in 1989. The 1990s saw her in a bevy of television movies as well, including *The Substitute Wife,* 1994, *A Good Day to Die,* 1995, and *Dalva* in 1996. She also starred in the humorous film *Man of the House,* 1995, and played a "dream date" in 1996's *The Lovemaster.*

Fawcett grabbed attention in 1995 when she posed partially nude in the Christmas edition of *Playboy,* and again in 1996 when she released a Playboy video titled *All of Me,* originally aired as a pay-per-view special. The project featured Fawcett sculpting and painting in the nude, even using her body as a brush, and *Playboy* followed it up by printing a 14-page layout of photos from the session in its June, 1997 issue. At 50 years old, Fawcett's figure reportedly still rivaled that of a 25-year-old. According to Diane White in the *Star Tribune,* Fawcett called the body painting experience a "renaissance" and remarked, "I no longer feel ... restrictions emotionally, artistically, creatively or in my everyday life. I don't feel those borders anymore." Perhaps this new freedom helped Fawcett excel in the 1997 film *The Apostle,* written and directed by Robert Duvall, who also starred in it. The story involves Sonny Dewey, a Pentecostal preacher from Texas who, though he has had affairs of his own, discovers that his wife (Fawcett) is carrying on with a younger minister. The enraged Dewey strikes the young man with a bat, putting him in a coma, and then flees town, becomes born again, and starts up a new church in bayou country. The project was highly lauded and re-established Fawcett as an accomplished dramatic actress.

Fawcett was divorced from Lee Majors in 1982 and began a long-term relationship with actor Ryan O'Neal. They had a son, Redmond O'Neal, and the couple was long known as one of Hollywood's most stable couples, despite the fact that they were not married. After over fifteen years together, they split up in February of 1997 and Fawcett later began seeing producer James Orr. When she declined a marriage proposal in January of 1998, Orr assaulted Fawcett at his Bel-Air mansion, leading to obvious physical injuries on her face, neck, and head. Though she never filed charges, Fawcett was subpoenaed to testify in court, since prosecutors in California are allowed to pursue cases of suspected domestic abuse charges even if the victims refuse. Orr was convicted of one count of misdemeanor battery, but planned to appeal. Meanwhile, Fawcett began seeing tennis pro Martin Barba, many years her junior, but called it off once she found out that he pleaded guilty to sexual battery in 1993.

Fawcett shrugged off a surge of bad press that emerged in the late 1990s, including rumors that she stole $72,000 worth of clothes from a fellow actress (no charges were filed and Fawcett later dismissed the affair as a case of extortion) and a barrage of accusations that she was abusing drugs. This last charge stemmed from an appearance on *The Late Show with David Letterman* on June 6, 1997, in which she seemed confused and detached, though she later explained her actions as failed attempts at humor. She has noted that she would like to continue making films, although she is considering moving away from Hollywood in order to regain some sense of privacy.

Sources

On-line

"Farrah Fawcett," CelebSite web site, http://www.celebsite.com (July 12, 1998).

"Farrah Fawcett," Internet Movie Database web site, http://us.imdb.com (July 7, 1998).

"Farrah at Bat," August 13, 1998, Mr. Showbiz web site, http://www.mrshowbiz.com/news (August 17, 1998).

"Farrah's Latest Breakup," July 31, 1998, Mr. Showbiz web site, http://www.mrshowbiz.com/news (August 12, 1998).

"Fawcett Tearfully Testifies," August 12, 1998, Mr. Showbiz web site, http://www.mrshowbiz.com/news (August 12, 1998).

Books

Contemporary Theatre, Film, and Television, volume 4, Gale Research, 1987.

Periodicals

Atlanta Journal and Constitution, January 30, 1998.

Entertainment Weekly, August 15, 1997; December 19, 1997.

Newsday, March 16, 1998, p. A13.

New York Times, August 17, 1986.

People, May 4, 1989; June 30, 1997; February 23, 1998.

Reuters, March 13, 1998.

Star Tribune (Minneapolis, MN), June 29, 1997, p. 10E.

USA Today, May 23, 1994; December 18, 1997.

—*Geri Speace*

Geraldine Ferraro

Attorney and politician

Born August 26, 1935, in Newburgh, NY; daughter of Dominick and Antonetta L. (Corrieri) Ferraro; married John Zaccaro, 1960; children: Donna, John, Jr., and Laura. *Education:* Attended Hunter College; Marymount Manhattan College, B.A., 1956; Fordham University, J.D., 1960; attended New York University Law School, 1978.

Addresses: *Office*—218 Lafayette, New York, NY 10012-4021.

Career

New York Public Schools, Queens, NY, teacher, 1956-60; lawyer in private practice, New York City, 1961-74; assistant district attorney, Queens County, NY, 1974-78, chief of Special Victims Bureau and Confidential Unit, 1977-78; member of U.S. Congress, ninth district, New York, 1978-84; chairman, Democratic platform committee, 1984; nominated to run for U.S. vice president on Democratic ticket, 1984; Harvard Institute of Politics, Cambridge, MA, fellow, 1988; Democratic candidate for U.S. Senate, 1992; Keck, Mahin, Cate & Koether, New York, managing partner, 1993-94; representative to UN Human Rights Commission, 1993; ambassador to UN Human Rights Commission, 1994, 1995; vice chair of U.S. Delegation at the Fourth World Conference on Women, Beijing, China, 1995. Guest moderator, *Crossfire*, CNN, 1996-97. Author of articles and books. Board of directors, New York Easter Seal Society. Member, Queens County Bar Association, Queens County Women's Bar Association (past president), National Democratic Institute for International Affairs (board of directors),

Council of Foreign Relations, International Institute for Women's Political Leadership (past president), Fordham Law School Board of Visitors, National Italian American Foundation, Planned Parenthood Federation of America (board of advocates), National Breast Cancer Research Fund (board of advisors), Pension Rights Center.

Sidelights

Geraldine Ferraro served three terms as a Democratic congresswoman from Queens, New York, before Walter Mondale named her to be his vice presidential running mate in 1984. A trailblazer for women's issues while in office, Ferraro thus became the first female vice presidential nominee for a major party in the history of the United States. Though they lost the election, Ferraro emerged as a inspirational symbol for equal rights for women and as a role model for those hoping to enter the overwhelmingly male field of politics. After her defeat, Ferraro endured a rocky period when her family went through some legal troubles. She actively campaigned for female Democrats in 1990, and tried to return to politics herself in 1992, running in the primary for a U.S. Senate seat. When that fell through, she published a book in 1993 and acted as a host on the CNN cable network program *Crossfire* in 1996 and 1997. By early 1998, she was ready for another challenge, as she began fundraising for another try at the senate.

Ferraro was born on August 26, 1935, in Newburgh, New York, about 70 miles north of New York City on the Hudson River. She was the youngest of three children born to Dominick and Antonetta L. (Corrieri) Ferraro. One son, Gerard, had died in an automobile accident two years before Geraldine was born. Ferraro's parents were Italian Americans who were financially secure thanks to her father's nightclub business. In 1944, however, her father was arrested for allegedly running a numbers operation. The day he was scheduled to appear in court, he had a heart attack and died. Left to support her two children, Ferraro's mother moved the family to New York City, where they lived in the Bronx, then Queens. She earned a living by sewing beads on to wedding dresses and evening gowns.

> *In Congress, Ferraro cosponsored the Economic Equity Act, which opposed economic discrimination against women working both inside and outside of the home. With this, she hoped to institute reforms for women that were lost when the Equal Rights Amendment was defeated.*

Though Ferraro's mother was not well-off to begin with, she further sacrificed so that her daughter could enroll at the prestigious Catholic all-female Marymount School in Tarrytown, New York. Ferraro was an excellent student. She was allowed to skip from sixth to eighth grade, and thus graduated from high school at age 16. She won a full scholarship to Marymount Manhattan College, where she was the editor of the student newspaper. Concurrently, she took teaching courses at Hunter College so that she could immediately begin a career in education. After getting a bachelor of arts at Marymount in 1956, Ferraro taught English in Queens for the New York City public schools while attending law school at Fordham University at night. In 1960, she received her law degree and then passed the bar exam. Later, she married fourth-gen-

eration Italian American John Zaccaro, although she kept her maiden name. The couple had three children, Donna, John, Jr., and Laura.

Though raising her children from 1961 to 1974 kept most of Ferraro's time occupied, she also helped out her husband's real estate business with her legal knowledge. Meanwhile, she became active with the Democratic party, at one point helping her cousin, Nicholas Ferraro, win a campaign for a New York state senate seat. In 1974, when her youngest child was a second-grader, her cousin helped her secure the job of assistant district attorney for Queens County. She worked there until 1978, setting up and running the Special Victims Bureau and the Confidential Unit. In this capacity, she focused on trying cases involving sex crimes, crimes against the elderly, family violence, and child abuse. Though many of the cases were stomach-churning, Ferraro built a reputation as a capable prosecutor. Simultaneously, she served on the Advisory Council for the Housing Court of the City of New York and as president of the Queens County Women's Bar Association.

In 1978, Ferraro decided to pursue a seat in the U.S. Congress from New York's ninth district (Queens). With plenty of financial backing, the once-conservative crime fighter won the Democratic nomination. Competing now as a staunch liberal in a blue-collar, right-wing area against a Republican, Ferraro stressed her background as a prosecutor, her commitment to law and order, and her pledge to improve neighborhoods. Her campaign slogan, "Finally, a Tough Democrat," won over the voters, who elected her with a 54 percent majority. In Congress, Ferraro mainly followed the liberal party line and feminist ideals, but also represented her more conservative constituency. For example, she supported social programs, including government funding for abortions, despite her Roman Catholic background. She also cosponsored the Economic Equity Act, which opposed economic discrimination against women working both inside and outside of the home. With this, she hoped to institute reforms for women that were lost when the Equal Rights Amendment was defeated, but the bill was shot down. Standing slightly to the right, however, she also tended to favor more military spending than most liberals, and opposed school busing.

Ferraro's record impressed the voters, who reelected her again in 1980 and 1982. She also caught the attention of Speaker of the House Tip O'Neill, who began sending her some prime assignments. Coming from a district with two airports, she served on the House Committee on Public Works and Transportation, advocating noise control and air safety. She also sat on the Select Committee on Aging, working to prevent crimes against the elderly, expand health coverage, and provide senior citizen centers. In 1982, she was named to the respected Budget Committee, which sets priorities for spending. She also served as a delegate to the Democratic party's 1982 mid-term convention and was a key member of the Hunt Commission, which developed delegate selection rules for the 1984 convention. In 1983, she traveled to Central America and the Middle East , attempting to beef up her foreign policy expertise. In 1984, she became chair of the Democratic Platform Committee.

In 1984, Ferraro made history when, 64 years to the day that women won the right to vote, she was named the first woman candidate for the vice presidency from a major party. Walter Mondale, the Democratic nominee for president, chose her as his running mate for the 1984 election against incumbent Ronald Reagan and his vice president, George Bush. Democrats were hoping Ferraro would allow them to use the "gender gap" in politics to gain more votes. Traditionally, more women than men showed up at the polls, and they usually favored Democrats. A female candidate would help solidify this support. In addition, Ferraro appealed to blue-collar, working-class voters who had been defecting to the Republican party in greater numbers.

Unfortunately for the Democrats, having a woman on the ticket did not make that much of a difference. Over half of the women voted Republican. The election instead was split on racial and economic lines, with 91 percent of blacks voting Democratic as opposed to 34 percent of whites. Reagan and Bush won reelection in 1984 with a total of 59 percent of the popular vote and 525 out of 538 electoral votes, taking every state except Minnesota (Mondale's home state) and the District of Columbia. Ferraro came under scrutiny for her husband's tax returns, which were filed separately from hers. She made the records public, which revealed no wrongdoing, although she had just a few days prior sent the IRS a check for $53,000 in back taxes. Questions also arose regarding her family's contributions to her 1978 campaign fund, and many were concerned that her family's annual income of almost $4 million belied her image of being "for the people." In addition, she and her husband were chided because he (apparently unknowingly) rented part of a building to a man trafficking in child pornography, and her husband was also accused of having ties to the Mafia. Perhaps the most damaging issue for the Democrats, however, was Mondale's admission during the campaign that he planned to raise taxes. In addition, most

analysts figure that Democrats were out of the running before they began in the heavily Republican era of the 1980s. *Working Woman* quoted Ferraro herself as saying, "Nobody could have beaten President Reagan."

Ferraro subsequently wrote a book about her experiences as a vice presidential nominee titled *Ferraro: My Story,* published in 1985. That same year, her husband pleaded guilty to fraud—he had given misinformation on a bank loan application—and an undercover sting operation caught her son, John, Jr., selling a small amount of cocaine. After his conviction, John, Jr. returned to law school and later, in 1988, Ferraro spent time in academia as a fellow at the Harvard Institute of Politics. Though she wanted to return to the political arena, she let the furor over her family problems die down and stayed out of the 1986 senate elections. Meanwhile, she continued campaigning for other women in New York, lending her support until 1991, when she announced that she was running for the senate.

In 1992, Ferraro embarked on a bid to become the Democratic party's candidate for U.S. Senate. Hoping to unseat right-wing incumbent Alfonse D'Amato, it seemed she had an edge in the race with three others. New York State Attorney Robert Abrams, however, inched past her in the polls, winning by a margin of one percentage point: 37 to 36 percent. After her defeat, Ferraro wrote another book in 1993, *Geraldine Ferraro: Changing History: Women, Power, and Politics,* and returned to practicing law as a managing partner in the New York firm of Keck, Mahin, Cate & Koether from 1993 to 1994. Though she was not in office, she maintained a political presence. In 1993, President Bill Clinton named her U.S. representative to the United Nations Human Rights Commission, then in 1994 and 1995 named her ambassador to the commission. She also served as vice chair of the U.S. Delegation at the Fourth World Conference on Women in Beijing, China, in September of 1995. In 1996, she began appearing every other week as a guest moderator on the nightly high-rated CNN cable network program *Crossfire,* which features political debates. Referencing liberal roots, her sign-off line at the end of the show was, "From the left."

On January 5, 1998, Ferraro announced that she would run again for the U.S. Senate from New York, noting that her debates with conservatives on *Crossfire* had been wonderful training for a potential senator. Some disagreed with her view that entertaining nightly debates were adequate preparation to hold office, and others wondered why she, at age 62, would even want to go through another grueling round: by early May, she was already agreeing again to let the media scrutinize her and her husband's tax records. One reason she gave was to more capably represent women's issues: despite her high-profile bid for the vice presidency, which remains symbolic of women's advances in society, offices at all levels are still overwhelmingly held by men.

An ugly race was predicted if Ferraro made it through the primary. Even though she had raised the least amount of money of all the candidates vying for the Democratic nomination—only $1.35 million as of April, 1998—some predicted that her name recognition surely counted for quite a bit. Other critics noted that she had not held office since the early 1980s, but Ferraro countered by playing up her law experience and involvement with the United Nations Human Rights Commission. *Newsday* quoted her as saying, "The fact that I have not been in elected office doesn't mean I've been dead for the last 12 years." Along with her pursuit of a Senate seat, Ferraro said she is writing a book about her family's struggle and the role that education has played in the lives of women in her family.

Selected writings

Ferraro: My Story, Bantam Books, 1985.

Geraldine Ferraro: Changing History: Women, Power, and Politics, Moyer Bell, 1993.

Sources

Books

Encyclopedia of World Biography, Second Edition, Gale Research, 1997.

Periodicals

Gannett News Service, January 5, 1998; January 15, 1998.
Knight-Ridder/Tribune News Service, February 7, 1996; January 5, 1998; January 9, 1998.
Newsday, September 13, 1992, p. 4; January 6, 1998, pp. A4, A5; April 7, 1998, p. A28; May 2, 1998.
New York Times, October 20, 1991; March 22, 1992.
Washington Monthly, April 1993, p. 21.
Washington Times, February 1, 1998, p. 45.
Working Woman, November-December 1996.

Additional information for this profile was obtained from a transcript of *Good Morning America*, ABC-TV, January 6, 1998.

—*Geri Speace*

David Filo and Jerry Yang

Co-founders of Yahoo!

Filo born in Wisconsin, in 1966; son of Jerry (an architect) and Carol (an accountant) Filo. *Education:* Tulane University, bachelor's degree, computer engineering, 1988; doctoral studies at Stanford University.

Yang born Chih-Yuan Yang, in Taiwan, in 1968; son of Lily Yang (an English and drama teacher). *Education:* Stanford University, bachelor's and master's degrees in electrical engineering, 1990, also doctoral studies.

Addresses: *Office*—Yahoo! Inc., 3400 Central Expressway, Suite 201, Santa Clara, CA 95051.

Career

Stanford University, both taught in Kyoto, Japan, early 1990s; began cataloging web sites, 1993-94; established "Jerry's Guide to the World Wide Web" (later called "Jerry and David's Guide to the World Wide Web" and then "Yahoo!"), 1994; Yahoo! created as a company, April, 1995; Yahoo! begins accepting advertisements, August, 1995; Yahoo! begins selling stock publicly, April 12, 1996; Yahoo! begins offering Internet service through MCI, 1998.

Sidelights

It sounds like a modern-day fairy tale, only it is indeed real and becoming more common as the Information Age continues: a couple of computer geeks get an idea for how to make things easier to use, they begin fashioning some software, and almost overnight, their cobbled-together product becomes legitimate, making them multimillionaires. This happened to David Filo and Jerry Yang, a couple of web surfers who wanted to be able to find their favorite sites more readily. In the dark ages of the Internet way back in the early 1990s, the World Wide Web was an anarchic mass of data, uncategorized and only accessible via a lengthy address, or URL (universal resource locator; the line that begins with http://). The Stanford doctoral students started a system of organizing these addresses by subject matter, and the online catalog eventually evolved into Yahoo! What began as a project for a couple of pals goofing off when their faculty advisor was out of town has become one of the easiest and most efficient ways to retrieve information in today's online arena, as well as one of the hottest stocks on the market. In an increasingly competitive arena, Yang and Filo have continued to nurture Yahoo! to become what most say is the most popular search engine available, and one of the few to become profitable, making the duo millionaires before they were 30 while literally changing the way the world views the Internet.

David Filo was born in Wisconsin in 1966 to Jerry, an architect, and Carol, an accountant, but he was raised in Moss Bluff, Louisiana. Moss Bluff was an "alternative community" in which the Filos lived semi-communally with six other families, sharing gardening duties and a kitchen. Filo attended Tulane University in New Orleans, Louisiana, receiving a bachelor's degree in computer engineering. He continued his education at Stanford University in Palo Alto, California, where he met Jerry Yang. The two went to Kyoto, Japan, together in a teaching program through Stanford during the early 1990s, where they became friends. Filo shared an office with Yang at Stanford during the 1993-94 academic year.

Yang was born Chih-Yuan Yang in Taiwan in 1968, and was raised by his mother, Lily, an English and drama teacher, after his father died when he was only two. He immigrated to the United States at age ten with his mother, grandmother, and younger brother Ken, settling in the Berryessa suburb of San Jose. Yang spoke Mandarin Chinese and hardly any English, but honed his skills and became a straight-A student. He was admitted to Stanford University, where he obtained his bachelor's and master's degrees in electrical engineering in 1990. There, he met Filo, taught with him in Kyoto, and then shared the office where they would spawn their creation.

Doctoral students Filo and Yang in 1993-94 were involved with a project on the computer-aided design of computer chip circuitry. Their office was in a trailer containing a couple of computers, an array of golf clubs, and a sleeping bag. "I was terribly bored," Filo related in the San Jose *Metro* online. With their faculty adviser on sabbatical in Italy, the pair began fooling around with the World Wide Web, a computer network of sites, or "pages," that can be linked together, or "hyperlinked," featuring text and graphics. The web can be used for uncountable tasks, from accessing photographs of celebrities to finding out more about a company to consulting academic papers. Early on, though, many of the sites were put there by creative graduate students like Yang, who posted a "home page" (a main site giving general information about a person or a company) with his picture, some golf scores, his name as it appears in Chinese, and hyperlinks to sumo wrestling sites.

One of the problems with this maze of pages on the web was the lack of organization. Akin to entering a library without the aid of a card catalog or other system to direct patrons to the correct shelf, it was difficult, if not impossible, to locate information on the web without a URL, or domain name. This is the address that begins with "http://" and usually contains the letters "www." for World Wide Web, followed by a word that somewhat describes the topic of the site, such as a person's or company's name, followed by a three-letter code indicating whether the site is a nonprofit site (.org), a company or personal site (.com), an educational institution (.edu), or a governmental branch (.gov). Filo and Yang, after becoming frustrated when they could not locate a page they found interesting,

simply began collecting these confusing codes for their favorite sites so that they could access them again. Others were doing this as well, with some companies publishing books listing numerous sites and describing the content. The web, however, was changing and growing too quickly. Books could not adequately catalog the universe of information, and often sites would "move" to a different server (main computer) or change names, rendering the books outdated before they rolled off the presses.

Filo and Yang came up with the idea to provide a kind of road map for online users. They designed some crude software that organized web pages into topics and that could be used immediately to "link" to those pages. In early 1994, "Jerry's Guide to the World Wide Web" was born, and the name was later revised to "Jerry and David's Guide to the World Wide Web." The two provided the service free to all Stanford users. As their list grew, they began subdividing the topics to provide more structure. Later that summer, the system was dubbed Yahoo!, or Yet Another Hierarchical Officious Oracle.

Although Yahoo! wasn't the first search engine to exist, its categorization was vanguard, and it was the only one to offer whimsy. David Matsukawa in *Transpacific* explained, "Yahoo! had an attitude. It was start-up culture, not corporate. It talked to the folks making the pages. And it talked to the folks venturing out on the waves for the very first time. It said, `Hey, the Internet is a fun place.'" They built it, and people came. By November of 1994, 170,000 people a day were using the site. By 1998, Yahoo! was counting about 26 million unique visitors out of a staggering one billion "hits," per month, which averages out to more than 850,000 a day. America Online (AOL), the giant Internet access service, offered a buy-out, and deals poured in from Microsoft and Prodigy as well. Filo and Yang, working 20 hours a day for the sheer enjoyment of it, turned them all down.

However, Stanford was irked that Yahoo! was tying up their network with all the traffic. "They told us we were crashing their system and that we'd have to move the thing off campus," Yang stated in the San Jose *Metro*. He and Filo began considering starting up a business from this hobby that was becoming overwhelming. "It was a really gradual thing, but we'd find ourselves spending more and more time on it," explained Yang in the *Metro*. "It was getting to be a burden." Not to mention, they were not making any money off of their labor of love. A friend at Harvard, Tim Brady, devised a business plan for Yahoo! for a class project, which allowed the pair to really visualize the potential. Around March or April of 1995, the partners packed up, dropped out, and moved on. They accepted a $1 million investment offer from Mike Mortiz at Sequoia Capital, a fund that had financed other Silicon Valley winners such as Apple and Oracle. Filo and Yang rented an office suite, ordered business cards defining themselves as Chief Yahoos, and hired a staff made up of graduate school friends and interns.

By the summer of 1995, Yahoo! was rapidly establishing itself in the online world. Netscape Navigator, the software most people were using to run the web on their computers, added a "Directory" button on their interface which linked users to Yahoo! About that time, in August of 1995, Yahoo! began selling advertising space on their pages. Initially frowned upon as "sell-outs" by web purists, who had worked to ban all commercial activity on the new technology, the practice quickly became accepted. Also that month, Yahoo! teamed up with Reuters news service, based in London, so that users could access news wire stories online with a click of a button. Since then, they have added other user-friendly elements, such as links to weather, stock quotes, phone listings, interactive maps, and loads of other information that web users now take for granted. In addition, their graphics were bright and slick, and they later hired an expert to assist with logical categorization.

Despite the ballooning success, Filo and Yang suffered some setbacks. A *San Francisco Chronicle* columnist kept a long-standing pessimistic view of the fledgling operation, even printing a litany of anonymous reader's comments that gushed over the legion of Yahoo! competitors, touting the superiority of the many other services. Then, in late 1995, Netscape ditched its Yahoo! link for that of a competing search engine, for which it was paid handsomely. Pundits predicted the offbeat little company would drown in the sea of other search directories, many of whom had corporate backing. Though the Netscape back-out resulted in a temporary drop in the amount of traffic on Yahoo!, the numbers rose again. Yang and Filo also approached Netscape with the idea of offering their users a variety of search engines to choose from when they are surfing, instead of limiting them to only one that is willing to pay big bucks for the spot. Netscape agreed, deciding to charge each company a set amount to be included on its directory list.

Yahoo! also scored points when it developed a "personalized" page called My Yahoo!, which allows users to customize the Yahoo! page with all of the links that interest them the most. A popular culture aficio-

nado, for example, could design a page with links to movie and music data and reviews, celebrity sites, online magazines, and more, while a business executive may want to pull up business periodicals and other relevant news sources, stock quotes, and competitors' home pages. Early in 1996, they started offering a directory tailored to children ages eight through 14 called "Yahooligans!" They later added a "get local" option, which included sites containing information specific to certain cities in the United States.

> *Yahoo!, claimed Yang in the San Jose* Metro, *"conveys the sense of fun involved in all this, the sense of adventure. That is what really distinguishes our site. It is a place for adventures. A place to discover things."*

Although the World Wide Web was booming in the mid-1990s, investors were still trying to figure out how to turn a profit. When Yahoo! first offered its stock publicly on April 12, 1996, the value at the end of the day was $848 million. However, by the end of the year, stock was down 44 percent. *Fortune* magazine in December of 1996 reported that "Internet advertising doesn't seem to work. The search companies are generating paltry revenues and losing money." By late 1997, however, the outlook had drastically changed for the better. In September, another *Fortune* writer remarked that Yahoo!'s "stock price has continued to defy gravity," and a *Computerworld* article two months later noted, "Yahoo is still the only search engine company posting profits several quarters in a row now and its revenue this year has more than doubled compared with last year's." As far along as March of 1998, the only other search engine boasting a profit was Lycos.

Yahoo! was making money not only by charging advertisers for space on its pages, they were also getting a cut from any online sales. For instance, if a customer orders a volume from Amazon online booksellers, Yahoo! would get a flat fee and a commission from that sale. Because of this new avenue for profits, Yahoo! decided to cancel a pending deal with Visa, which would limit its ability to work with other merchants. Other partnerships have been established, however.

In 1998, Yahoo! joined forces with MCI to become an Internet provider as well as a search provider. The strong brand name was expected to be a boon in wooing users. Yahoo! also that year teamed up with *National Geographic Traveler* magazine in order to offer information about cities of the world, and expanded its television listings by partnering with Gist.

Meanwhile, Yahoo!'s main men, Yang and Filo, had remained pretty much the same. At the start of their mammoth operation, the two paid themselves around $40,000 a year and lived in modest apartments. Yang continued dressing in preppy chinos and button-down shirts, even to business conferences. Though Yang eventually bought a nice home in Los Altos, California, and a new Isuzu Rodeo, he told *Forbes*, "It's nice to know that your family is provided for, but the money isn't that important." He is still very close with his family, spending every Sunday with his brother and mother at her house for dinner. Filo, meanwhile, was driving a beat-up, junk-filled Datsun to the company's headquarters in Santa Clara where his office resembled a dorm-room nightmare, littered with empty cans, Rollerblades, and assorted CDs. Throughout the company's rise, Yang functioned as the public relations man, happy to grant interviews and appear on television, while Filo was reluctant to be in the spotlight, spending most of his time behind the scenes and often sleeping on a blanket in his office. The two have also been known to donate money to help disadvantaged people learn about computers.

As long as people are using the web, it seems there will be a need for the creative, continuously expanding search service of Yahoo! Although there are other engines, Yahoo! has staked its place, perhaps because of its co-founders passion for their work, which shows through in the product, and also because it is easy for even web novices to use. Yahoo!, claimed Yang in the San Jose *Metro*, "conveys the sense of fun involved in all this, the sense of adventure. That is what really distinguishes our site. It is a place for adventures. A place to discover things."

Sources

On-line

"A Couple of Yahoos," San Jose *Metro*, April 11, 1996, http://www.metroactive.com (April 20, 1998).

Periodicals

Advertising Age, January 19, 1998, p. 36.
Computerworld, November 17, 1997, p. 138.
Entrepreneur, September 1997, p. 106.
Forbes, December 1, 1997, p. S51; March 9, 1998, p. 48.
Fortune, December 9, 1996, p. 174; September 8, 1997, p. 154.
PC Magazine, January 6, 1998, p. 114; April 7, 1998, p. 40.
PC Week, May 27, 1996, p. A2.
People Weekly, December 4, 1995, p. 123.
Rolling Stone, November 30, 1995, p. 15.
Time, April 20, 1998, p. 50.
Transpacific, March-April 1996, p. 64.

—*Geri Speace*

Calista Flockhart

Actress

Born November 11, 1964, in Freeport, IL; daughter of Ronald (a businessman) and Kay (a teacher) Flockhart. *Education:* Rutgers University, New Jersey, drama degree, 1987.

Addresses: *Agent*—The Gersh Agency, P.O. Box 5617, Beverly Hills, CA 90210. *Office*—Ally McBeal, Ren Mar Studios, 846 Cahuenga Blvd., Bldg. A, 2nd Floor, Hollywood, CA 90038.

Career

Actress. Stage appearances include *Death Takes a Holiday, The Loop; Wrong Turn at Lungfish, Sophistry and Sons, All for One, The Glass Menagerie, Beside Herself,* and *The Three Sisters.* Television appearances include various spots on daytime dramas; *Darrow,* 1991; "The Secret Life of Mary-Margaret: Portrait of a Bulimic" episode on *Lifestories: Families in Crisis,* HBO, 1992; title role, *Ally McBeal,* Fox, 1997—; guest appearance, *The Practice,* 1997. Film appearances include *Quiz Show,* 1994; *Getting In,* 1994; *Naked in New York,* 1994; *Drunks,* 1995; *The Birdcage,* 1996; *Milk and Money,* 1997; and *Telling Lies in America,* 1997.

Awards: Theater World Award and Clarence Derwent Award, both 1994, for *The Glass Menagerie;* Golden Globe for best actress in a comedy series, 1998, for *Ally McBeal.*

Sidelights

When little-known actress Calista Flockhart took the lead role in the Fox series *Ally McBeal,* it is

unlikely that she expected to become a gauge for measuring women's roles in the 1990s. "If that happens, it's out of my control," stated Flockhart in the *Atlanta Journal and Constitution.* "[McBeal's] a character who is just simply that, independent of any kind of role model or some sort of symbolic woman of the '90s who embraces womanhood. God forbid!" However, during its first season in 1997-1998, *Ally McBeal* quickly became one of the most hotly discussed programs on the air. Centering on a young female lawyer who freely exposes her insecurities as well as a good deal of leg, Flockhart's character is either elevated as a fresh, realistic, modern version of the career woman, or struck down as a whiny, weak, female caricature obsessed with men, marriage, and babies. Whether McBeal is the new Mary Tyler Moore or a feminist's nightmare, the real-life Flockhart takes the argument in stride as her career, not the overnight success that it seems, glides along in full gear.

Flockhart was born on November 11, 1964, in Freeport, Illinois, to Ronald and Kay Flockhart; she also has an older brother, Gary. Her mother was a teacher and her father rose through the ranks at Kraft Foods, causing the family to move around quite a bit. Besides Illinois, Flockhart also lived in small towns in Iowa, Minnesota, New York, and New Jersey while she was growing up, finally settling for a time in Medford, New Jersey. As a child, Flockhart told Steven D. Stark in the *New Republic,* she used to put on plays all the time. "I'd give my friends bit parts," Flockhart recalled, "but I was the lead, the director, the set designer." She added, "I was in control. I'm sure the other kids were like, 'She's difficult; she's a diva already.'" Perhaps her name had some effect: Calista (also her great-grandmother's name) means "most beautiful" in Greek. In 1983, she graduated from Medford's Shawnee High School, where she was a cheerleader and a student council member.

After graduation, Flockhart attended the nearby Rutgers University in New Jersey, where she enrolled in the fine arts program and studied drama under acting coach William Esper. There, she got her feet wet on the stage in university and community theater productions, graduating in 1987. After that, she spent about seven years on and off Broadway, acting in *Death Takes a Holiday* at the Williamstown Theater Festival; appearing in plays such as *Wrong Turn at Lungfish, The Loop,* and *Sophistry and Sons* off-Broadway; and portraying the disabled Laura in *The Glass Menagerie* on Broadway. Part-time, she supplemented her income teaching aerobics and taking parts in daytime soap operas. In 1991, she finally got a major television role, in the biographical movie *Darrow,* starring Kevin Spacey as attorney Clarence Darrow of the Scopes trial regarding teaching evolution in schools. The next year she landed a lead part in "The Secret Life of Mary-Margaret: Portrait of a Bulimic," an episode of the HBO series *Lifestories: Families in Crisis.*

Flockhart by this time was getting some attention and had hired an agent and manager. She continued her stage work, winning the lead part in *Beside Herself* for the Circle Repertory Company and playing Irina in Anton Chekhov's *The Three Sisters* at Chicago's Goodman Theater. Her career had its low moments, too, however. At one point, in 1993, she worked for eight weeks in an obscure production that paid a total of just $400. During this time, she survived on cans of ravioli donated by her brother Gary. Soon after, she landed her role in the Tennessee Williams classic *The Glass Menagerie,* for which she earned both a Theater World Award and Clarence Derwent Award in 1994. Also that year, she was cast in the acclaimed *Quiz Show,* director Robert Redford's film about corrupt 1950s television game shows. A large supporting role in the Showtime film *Drunks* followed, then in 1996, she played the fiancee of Robin Williams's son in *The Birdcage.* In 1997, she appeared as the love interest in *Telling Lies in America.*

As her Broadway career was starting to gain speed, Flockhart caught the attention of writer-producer David E. Kelley back in Hollywood. He had already auditioned hundreds of prospects for the lead role in his new television series *Ally McBeal,* without finding a good fit. Negotiations with Bridget Fonda, his ideal choice, did not pan out. Flockhart's friends urged her to try out, despite her reluctance to return to television. After just one meeting, Kelley gave her the job. "I didn't feel particularly great about my audition," Flockhart revealed to Benjamin Svetkey in *Entertainment Weekly.* "Afterward, one of the producers was walking me across the street and he asked, 'Why are you so bummed out?' I told him, and he said, 'Well, cheer up, you got the part." Rumors have flowed, saying that Flockhart's resemblance to Kelley's wife, Michelle Pfeiffer, had something to do with his decision. Flockhart responded in *TV Guide,* as a *People* article pointed out, "I find it hugely flattering although I don't necessarily see it. I feel like I have to apologize to her." She should not worry about living up to the comparison, especially after being named one of *People*'s 50 Most Beautiful People in the World in 1998.

In addition, Flockhart experienced amazing success in just her first season on *Ally McBeal.* She won a Golden Globe Award for best actress in a comedy in 1998, and the show took the Golden Globe for best comedy series. *Ally McBeal* concerns an attorney in her twenties and her cohorts at a Boston firm, including her boss—an old enemy from law school—and an ex-boyfriend, Billy (in fact, her childhood sweetheart) as a coworker. A large part of the plot centers on her desire for Billy, who is married but still attracted to Ally. She struggles with her emotional side while trying to maintain a tough veneer on the job. Despite its awards, the program has gotten its share of critical backlash as well, perhaps only fueling its popularity. Some paint Ally McBeal as a believable, imperfect heroine; one with the usual female conflicts between work and love. Others decry the show's use of female stereotypes, calling out for the portrayal of a more confident lead character.

Ally McBeal is bubbly and strong, but has a vulnerable side. She gets frustrated with sexual harassment, but secretly lusts after her old boyfriend as she works side-by-side with him. An independent working woman, she nevertheless longs for marriage and children, haunted by an computer-enhanced image of a baby dancing to and "ooga-chuka" beat behind the song "I Can't Fight This Feeling" as she acknowledges her proverbial biological clock. Humorous voice-overs convey her innermost thoughts, and her expressive face often reveals more than words. Super-short miniskirts—one of the most hotly contested, and probably least realistic, aspects of the show—barely cover her rail-thin thighs as she struts into the courtroom. Flockhart, however, defends McBeal, telling Greg Braxton in the *Los Angeles Times*, "Ally is complicated, a woman who is struggling to get through the day and do the right thing. She's flawed. It's exciting to have a character that breaks the idea that women have to be perfect."

Flockhart keeps her personal life very private. She found it funny when tabloid stories painted her as a love-'em-and-leave-'em cold-hearted career woman, and though she has denied having any romantic connections, her CelebSite biographical information claims that she is linked with producer Jeffrey Kramer. One constant companion for sure is her dog, Webster; he even accompanies her to filming on the set of *Ally McBeal*. When not working on the series, Flockhart returns to her apartment in New York City. Though she wants to continue performing on stage between seasons, has other films in the works, and hopes to eventually direct, Flockhart is enjoying the wave of *Ally McBeal*'s success as it lasts. "I love that the show is controversial, that it's thought-provoking," she told Svetkey in *Entertainment Weekly*. "I love that people either love it or hate it. It's more interesting."

Sources

On-line

"Calista Flockhart," CelebSite web site, http://www.celebsite.com (July 12, 1998).
"Calista Flockhart," Internet Movie Database web site, http://www.imdb.com (July 7, 1998).

Periodicals

Atlanta Journal and Constitution, February 2, 1998, p. B1.
Biography, May 1998, p. 82.
Business Wire, May 5, 1998.
Cosmopolitan, January 1998, p. 128.
Daily Telegraph, June 13, 1998, p. 9.
Dallas Morning News, January 14, 1998, p. 31A.
Entertainment Weekly, January 30, 1998, p. 20.
Independent, June 15, 1998, p. 13.
Los Angeles Times, September 21, 1997, p. 16.
New Republic, December 29, 1997, p. 13.
Newsday, February 9, 1998, p. B6.
People, May 11, 1998, p. 175.

—*Geri Speace*

Dario Fo

Jerry Bauer

Playwright and actor

Born March 24, 1926, in San Giano (some sources say Lago Maggiore), Italy; son of Felice (a railroad stationmaster and part-time actor) and Pina (Rota) Fo; married Franca Rame (a playwright and actress), June, 1954; children: three. *Education:* Attended Academia di Belle Arti, Milan.

Addresses: *Agent*—Maria Nadotti, 349 East 51st St., New York, NY 10022.

Career

Playwright, director, actor, and theatrical company leader. Author of more than forty plays, including *No se paga! No se paga!* (*We Won't Pay! We Won't Pay!*), 1974; *Morte accidentale di un anarchico* (*Accidental Death of an Anarchist*), 1976; (with wife, Franca Rame) *Tutta casa, letto e chiesa* (*Female Parts: One Woman Plays*), 1981; *The Tale of a Tiger*, 1984; *One Was Nude and One Wore Tails*, 1985; *The Open Couple and an Ordinary Day*, 1990; *The Pope and the Witch*, 1993. Many of Fo's plays have been translated and performed in more than thirty countries, beginning in 1953; performer in plays in Italy, Europe, and the United States, and director of classes and workshops for actors, beginning in the 1970s. Worked as a member of small theatrical group, headed by Franco Parenti, performing semi-improvised sketches for radio before local audiences, 1950; wrote and performed comic monologues for his own radio program, *Poer nana* ("Poor Dwarf"), broadcast by the Italian national radio network RAI, 1951; formed revue company, *I Dritti* ("The Stand Ups"), with Giustino Durano and Parenti, 1953; screenwriter in Rome, Italy, 1956-58; formed improvisational troupe *Compagnia Fo-Rame,* with wife, Franca Rame, 1958; named artistic director of Italian state television network's weekly musical revue, *Chi l'ha visto?* ("Who's Seen It?"), and writer and performer of sketches for variety show *Canzonissima* ("Really Big Song"), 1959; formed theatre cooperative Nuova Scena, with Rame, 1968, and La Comune, 1970.

Awards: Recipient of Sonning Award, Denmark, 1981; Obie Award, 1987; awarded honorary doctorate, University of Westminster, 1996; Nobel Prize in Literature, 1997.

Sidelights

Although he has been hailed by critics worldwide for his acting abilities and especially for his artful, satirical works that convey his leftist ideology, Italian playwright Dario Fo was an unexpected winner of the 1997 Nobel Prize in Literature.

Fo, who according to the press release from the Swedish Academy, "emulates the jesters of the Middle Ages in scourging authority and upholding the dignity of the downtrodden," was by his own admission "amazed" to learn that he had won the prestigious award, according to an article by *Chicago Tribune* contributor Tom Hundley. The Nobel committee's choice was indeed unpopular among many segments of the world population, especially with the Italian government and with the Roman Catholic Church, which have both been favorite targets of Fo's in such works as *A Madhouse for the Sane* and *Mistero buffo*. According to an article by the *New York Times*'s Celestine Bohlen, "the Vatican newspaper *L'Osservatore Romano* said it was flabbergasted by [Fo's] selection. 'Giving the prize to someone who is also the author of questionable works is beyond all imagination,' the paper said."

Fo was born on March 24, 1926, in San Giano, a small fishing village in northern Italy where his father, Felice, was a railroad stationmaster and part-time actor. His father and the local storytellers provided the young Fo with his first lessons in the art of dramatic presentation, and he emulated their animated gestures and vocalizations in his own acting performances. He attended the Academia di Belle Arti (Academy of Fine Arts) in Milan, but left without earning a degree, instead opting to write plays and perform with several improvisational theatre groups.

Fo's first success as a playwright came with his 1953 work, *Il dito nell'occhio* (*A Finger in the Eye*), which was a social satire that presented Marxist concepts with a circus-like backdrop. Fo became an outspoken opponent of the Italian government with his 1954 play, *I sani de legare* (*A Madhouse for the Sane*), which charged several government officials with being fascist sympathizers; the government ordered Fo to cut some of the original material from his script and mandated the presence of state inspectors at each performance to ensure that Italian libel laws were not being broken. Between 1956 and 1958 Fo worked as a screenwriter in Rome, but he returned to the stage and began to produce, along with his wife, actress and playwright Franca Rame, a less conspicuously political variety of satirical plays. Of the works produced during this period of his career, Fo's best is considered by many to be 1959's *Gli arcangeli non giocano a flipper* (*Archangels Don't Play Pinball*), which was the first of his plays to be staged outside of Italy.

In 1968 Fo and Rame, with the support of the Italian communist party, formed Nuova Scena, a nonprofit theatre organization whose works were aimed at the working class audience; the couple's decision to form the group was prompted by their rejection of the theatrical establishment. Nuova Scena productions were marked by an intensely radical tone and dealt with political issues of the time. In one such work, 1968's *Grande pantomima con bandiere e pupazzi piccoli e medi* (*Grand Pantomime with Flags and Small and Medium-Sized Puppets*), Fo took a satirical look at Italy's politi-

cal history following World War II, depicting the way in which he believed the communist party had given in to the temptation of capitalism; the Italian communist party withdrew its support of Nuova Scena following the production of *Grand Pantomime*, and Fo and Rame formed Il Colletive Teatrale La Comune, known as La Comune, in 1970.

Fo was highly popular during the 1960s, perhaps due to the prevailing feelings of social and political upheaval that marked that decade and provided him with exposure to a much broader audience than any with which he had previously been acquainted. *Mistero buffo* (*The Comic Mystery*), considered by many to be Fo's foremost work for the stage as well as his most controversial, was first produced in 1969.

Although the actual script is improvised and thus changes with each performance, the narrative always involves a depiction of events based upon the gospels of the Bible's New Testament presented in a disparaging manner that accuses the Catholic church, landowners, and the government of persecuting the masses. Fo took the idea for this play from the Middle Ages, when traveling performers known as *giullari* would enact medieval mystery plays in the streets.

In Fo's production, a single actor—Fo himself—performs the series of sketches on an empty stage, introducing each segment with a short prologue and linking them together, portraying as many as a dozen characters at one time. The parables from the gospels portrayed in *Mistero buffo* include the resurrection of Lazarus, with pickpockets who steal from those who witness the miracle, the story of a crippled man who avoids Jesus' healing power because he makes a good living as a beggar, and a scornful depiction of the corrupt activities of Pope Boniface VIII.

Mistero buffo was broadcast on television in 1977, and, according to an *Atlantic Monthly* article by Charles C. Mann, the Vatican proclaimed the work to be "the most blasphemous" program ever televised; Fo was, as Mann reported, delighted with the church officials' response. Despite the church's disapproval, or perhaps because of it, *Mistero buffo* was a popular success throughout Europe; when it was performed in London in 1983, the revenue brought in by the play was enough to save the theatre in which it was produced from financial ruin.

Fo and Rame were eventually given permission to enter the United States in 1986, after having been denied visas in both 1980 and 1984 because of reports that they had helped to raise funds to support an Italian terrorist organization; the couple denied taking part in any such activities. *Mistero buffo* opened in New York City in the spring of 1986, and was hailed by the *New York Times*'s Ron Jenkins as "a brilliant one-man version of biblical legends and church history" whose humor "echo[es] the rhythms of revolt."

In response to the premature death of anarchist railway worker Giuseppi Pinelli in 1969, Fo composed the absurdist play *Morte accidentale di un anarchico (Accidental Death of an Anarchist)*, which was the only one of his plays produced during his La Comune period to become an enduring favorite and a popular success. Pinelli's death was, Fo believed, the result of a plot by right-wing extremist members of the Italian military and secret service to undermine the credibility of the Italian Communist party by executing a string of bombings and making it appear that they were the work of leftist terrorists.

Pinelli was charged with the 1969 bombing of the Agricultural Bank of Milan, one of the most devastating of the bombings that killed numerous innocent bystanders. At some point during the time in which the railway worker was held for interrogation by police in Milan, he fell—later it was argued that he was pushed—from a window on the fourth floor of police headquarters.

In *Accidental Death of an Anarchist*, his play based on the events surrounding Pinelli's death, Fo uses a character known as the maniac to reveal the attempts by the police to cover up the truth. In an article in *American Theatre*, Fo observed: "When I injected absurdity into the situation, the lies became apparent. The maniac plays the role of the judge, taking the logic of the authorities to their absurd extremes." In this way, Fo was able to demonstrate that Pinelli was murdered, and could not have died accidentally as the police maintained.

Los Angeles Times contributor John Lahr reported that around the time *Accidental Death of an Anarchist* was first staged Fo was assaulted and imprisoned and Rame was kidnapped and brutalized as punishment for their part in exposing the police cover-up. *Accidental Death of an Anarchist* was enormously popular in Italy, and attracted large audiences during the four years following its first production.

In a review of the play in *New Society,* John Lahr proclaimed it "loud, vulgar, kinetic, scurrilous, smart, [and] sensational.... Everything theatre should be." Although the play was also popular in London, where it ran successfully for two and a half years, it failed to win over audiences in the United States in 1984, when it opened and closed within a matter of months.

Most commentators assert that Fo's plays are not as popular with American audiences as they are with European audiences because they are loosely translated into English or performed in Italian, and because they are based upon historical, political, and social events that even if they are known to Americans are not as significant to them as they are to Europeans.

New York Times contributor Mel Gussow contended that "dealing with topical Italian materials in colloquial Italian language ... presents problems for adapters and directors." Specifically, critics faulted as distracting the use of an onstage translator during an American performance of *Mistero buffo*, and characterized a production based upon the English translation of *Accidental Death of an Anarchist* as considerably less effective than the original Italian production. The *New York Times*'s Frank Rich declared that the insertion of puns based on contemporary American occurrences into the script of *Accidental Death* by adapter Richard Nelson served to "wreck the play's farcical structure and jolt both audience and cast out of its intended grip."

> The Swedish Academy declared that Fo's plays "simultaneously amuse, engage and provide perspectives.... His is an oeuvre of impressive artistic vitality and range."

During the 1980s Fo collaborated extensively with Rame, and the couple produced several plays with distinctly feminist themes. Their most successful of these plays was *Tutta casa, letto e chiesa*, which is comprised of eight monologues that focus on women's position in a male-dominated society. The work, which includes a varying number and combination of the eight monologues in each production, was performed in England and the United States under several different titles, including *Woman Plays, Female Parts*, and *Orgasmo Adulto Escapes from the Zoo.*

According to the *Washington Post*'s David Richards, who reviewed an American production of the play, although the play is admirably candid, because it depicts a brand of sexism practiced more commonly in

Italy, the play "may have lost some of its punch crossing the Atlantic," noting that to American audiences "the women in *Orgasmo* seem to be fighting battles that have long been conceded on these shores."

Another of Fo and Rame's woman-centered plays, 1974's *No se paga! No se paga! (We Won't Pay! We Won't Pay!)*, concerns a group of homemakers who organize a boycott of their local supermarket to protest its outrageous prices; this play was a moderate success in the United States when it was produced Off-Broadway in 1980 and enjoyed a fairly lengthy run.

Fo has continued to produce works that provoke anger and controversy. His 1992 play, *The Pope and the Witch,* which has as its subject a news conference during which the Pope, as described by *New York Times* contributor Celestine Bohlen, "confuses a children's gathering in St. Peter's Square with an abortion rights rally," incited fury among Catholics worldwide. His 1997 play, *Devil with Boobs,* is, according to Bohlen, "a comedy set in the Renaissance featuring a zealous judge and a woman possessed by the devil."

Fo has also continued to appear in productions of his works, and his acting style has been compared to that of the members of the comedy troupe Monty Python, but most often Fo as an actor is "compared to the comedian Lenny Bruce for his activism, scatological humor, sarcasm and barely submerged bitterness," as *New York Times* contributor Rick Lyman related. Nevertheless, Lyman continued, a comparison between Bruce and Fo "ignores a chameleonlike aspect to [Fo's] performances that recalls [comedian] Sid Caesar. In a style reminiscent of Mr. Caesar's double-talk routines, Mr. Fo uses a gibberish called 'grammelot,' often accompanied by a 'translator.' The language is a jumble of syllables that evokes, without actually simulating, Italian, French and American technological jargon."

Because his works have invited such tremendous controversy throughout the world, and because although some of his plays have been successful outside of Italy he is by far more popular and well-known to Italians than to the rest of the world, it was a shock to many when it was announced that Fo would receive the 1997 Nobel Prize for Literature.

The announcement, according to the *New York Times*'s Bohlen, was greeted with "the guarded amazement of Italy's literary establishment and the outright dismay of the Vatican." In its press release, published on the Nobel Prize Internet Archive, the Swedish Academy declared that Fo's plays "simultaneously amuse, engage and provide perspectives.... His is an oeuvre of impressive artistic vitality and range."

Despite the furor surrounding his selection as a Nobel laureate, Fo has maintained his characteristic irreverence; as related in an unsigned article in the *Chicago Tribune* covering his news conference to discuss his prize, Fo remarked on the controversy surrounding his selection: "God is a jester because he bitterly disappointed a lot of people, including the Vatican newspaper. I feel almost guilty, but it was a great joke on them."

Fo's plans as a Nobel laureate have included using his status to promote the fight for civil rights in such countries as China, Algeria, Turkey, and Argentina, and donating portions of his $1 million prize to the movement to ban the use of land mines and to aid the legal defense of three men—Fo has steadfastly proclaimed their innocence—prosecuted for the 1971 murder of the police officer who was in charge of interrogating Giuseppe Pinelli, the railway worker whose death was the inspiration for Fo's *Accidental Death of an Anarchist*. At the time he announced his intentions for his prize money, Fo had already outlined a sequel to *Accidental Death* based upon one of the accused men's struggle to prove his innocence.

Sources

On-line

Nobel Prize Internet Archive, http://www.almaz.com (October 9, 1997).

Swedish Academy Press Release, *The Permanent Secretary,* Nobel Prize Internet Archive, http://www.almaz.com (October 9, 1997).

Periodicals

American Theatre, June 1986.
Atlantic Monthly, September 1985.
Chicago Tribune, October 9, 1997; October 10, 1997; October 11, 1997; November 6, 1997.
Los Angeles Times, January 16, 1983; January 21, 1983.
New Society, March 13, 1980, pp. 559-60.
New York Times, December 18, 1980; April 17, 1983; August 5, 1983; August 14, 1983; August 27, 1983; February 15, 1984; October 31, 1984; November 16, 1984; May 29, 1986; May 30, 1986; May 9, 1987; November 27, 1987; October 10, 1997.
Washington Post, August 27, 1983; November 17, 1984; January 17, 1985; June 12, 1986.

—*Lynn M. Spampinato*

Aretha Franklin

AP/Wide World Photos

Singer and songwriter

Born March 25, 1942, in Memphis, TN; daughter of Clarence La Vaughan (a Baptist minister) and Barbara (a gospel singer; maiden name, Siggers) Franklin; married Ted White (a businessman and music manager), 1961 (divorced, 1969); married Glynn Turman (an actor), April 12, 1978 (divorced, 1984); children: Clarence, Edward, Teddy Richards, Kecalf Cunningham.

Addresses: *Home*—Detroit, MI. *Record company*—Arista Records, 6 West 57th St., New York, NY 11019; 9975 Santa Monica Blvd., Beverly Hills, CA 90212.

Career

Performed with father's touring revue, recorded on Chess label, 1950s; signed with Columbia Records and released debut album *The Great Aretha Franklin*, 1960; signed with Atlantic Records and released *I Never Loved a Man (the Way I Love You)*, 1967; performed at funeral of Rev. Martin Luther King, Jr., 1968; performed at Democratic National Convention, 1968; performed at inauguration of President Jimmy Carter, 1977; appeared in television specials *Aretha*, 1986, *Aretha Franklin: The Queen of Soul, 1988*, and *Duets, 1993*; performed at inauguration of President Bill Clinton, 1993; signed contract with Villard publisher for autobiography, 1995; contributor to the songs of *West Side Story*, 1996; appeared in films *The Blues Brothers*, 1980, and *Blues Brothers 2000*, Universal, 1998.

Awards: American Black Achievement Award, Ebony magazine, 1984; American Music Awards, 1976, 1977, 1983, 1984, 1986; Grammy Award for best female rhythm and blues vocal performance, 1967-74 (every year), 1981, 1985, 1987; Grammy Award for best rhythm and blues recording, 1967; Grammy Award for best gospel, soul performance, 1972; Grammy Award for best rhythm and blues duo vocal (with George Michael), 1987; Grammy Award for best female gospel, soul performance, 1988; Grammy Legend Award, 1991; Grammy Award, lifetime achievement award, 1994; R&B Foundation, lifetime achievement award, 1987; *Rolling Stone* Magazine Music Award, best artist—other, 1985, best singer (with Marla McKee), 1985; first woman inducted into the Rock and Roll Hall of Fame, 1987.

Sidelights

Often when the word "legendary" is used to describe someone of outstanding achievement, the heyday is long gone, and that person is known for resting on past laurels. Not so for the "Queen of Soul," singer Aretha Franklin. The winner of 17 Grammy Awards and numerous other honors began her prodigious career as the embodiment of 1960s soul music and continued to top the charts into the 1990s. Later in that decade, she branched out into producing films and videos and announced that she would release her autobiography—a long-awaited moment for many fans.

Aretha Franklin was born on March 25, 1942 in Memphis, Tennessee, but moved to Detroit, Michigan, at age two with her famed minister father and gospel singer mother. She was the fourth of five children: the older siblings were Vaughan, Erma, and Cecil (who managed Aretha's career for many years), and the younger was Carolyn. Her mother, Barbara Franklin, died when she was ten, so Clarence La Vaughan Franklin (known as C. L.) encouraged his daughter's talents. "Most of what I learned vocally came from him," Franklin commented in *Jet*. Reverend Franklin also stood by her when she later decided to sing popular music instead of gospel.

Guests at the Franklin house included celebrities like Mahalia Jackson, Clara Ward, Dinah Washington, B. B. King, Lou Rawls, and Sam Cooke. James Cleveland helped the Franklin girls form a gospel group that appeared in local churches for a few months. Aretha sang her first solo at age 12 in her father's church, New Bethel Baptist in Detroit, and by age 14 was on the road with her father's touring revival. This experience exposed her to drinking and other adult activities, however, and by age 15 she had her first child and gave birth again two years later. During this time, she recorded her first solo performance on Chess Records, a powerful set of hymns with a vocal quality that belied her age.

At age 18, Franklin set out for New York City to forge a name as a blues singer just like her idol, Dinah Washington. John Hammond at Columbia Records, who had also signed legendary blueswomen Billie Holiday and Bessie Smith, was bowled over by Franklin's voice and signed her to a five-year contract. She released her first album for Columbia in the fall of 1960, *The Great Aretha Franklin*. Although some of the singles made it on the charts, no overwhelming success resulted from these tracks, probably due to the poor choice of material on the part of the label. She never characterized herself as a jazz singer but dabbled in it at the company's request, and then was miscast in orchestra-laden pop songs with a nightclub feel. Hammond admitted later that Columbia had not adequately showcased her immense talents.

Franklin's manager-husband, Ted White, urged her to seek another company when her Columbia contract expired, and Atlantic drew her away in 1967. Producer Jerry Wexler, responsible for her first sides for the label, took her to the Florence Alabama Music Emporium (FAME) in Muscle Shoals, Alabama, where Franklin was thrust into a capable group of musicians. There her vocal and piano abilities shined through and she was able to personally take charge of the arrangements.

Unfortunately, Franklin only finished one song, "I Never Loved a Man (the Way I Love You)," before an altercation between a musician and White caused Franklin and her husband to dash out and disappear for a few weeks. Shortly thereafter, Wexler released the song to radio stations, who begged for more. Finally Franklin returned to New York and finished "Do Right Woman, Do Right Man," and later in 1967 released her first album for Atlantic, *I Never Loved a Man (the Way I Love You)*. The late 1960s saw Franklin's career skyrocket with one hit single after another, including the million-selling "Baby I Love You," 1967, "Chain of Fools," 1967, "(Sweet Baby) Since You've Been Gone," 1968, "Think," 1968, "I Say a Little Prayer," 1968. Also in 1967, she recorded two of her trademark tunes, "(You Make Me Feel Like a) Natural Woman" and "Respect."

Franklin's rousing, thumping version of Otis Redding's "Respect" was released at an eventful moment in time, with civil rights, feminism, and sexual liberation all emerging into the forefront of American culture. Her fervent performance epitomized these movements and the record served as a theme song for social change. Franklin again represented an era, sadly, when she sang "Precious Lord" at the funeral of civil rights leader Reverend Dr. Martin Luther King, Jr., in 1968. King had been a close friend of Franklin's father. Franklin also sang the National Anthem at the Democratic Party's 1968 convention in Chicago, where riots ensued.

In 1969, Franklin divorced Ted White and later began a romance with her road manager, Ken Cunningham. With him, she had her fourth child, Kecalf, whose name combines Cunningham's first name and Franklin's initials. Their six-year relationship ended in 1977. While in Los Angeles for a benefit for underprivileged children, Franklin met actor Glynn Turman and the two were married on April 12, 1978 in her father's New Bethel Baptist Church in Detroit.

From the late 1960s to the mid-1970s, Franklin's career was nonstop. She won Grammy Awards every year from 1969 to 1975, and reinvented herself by covering pop songs by the Band, the Beatles, Jimi Hendrix, Elton John, Paul Simon, and others. Tragically, on June 11, 1979, Franklin's father, C. L., was shot in his home by a burglar and slipped into a coma from which he never awoke. Franklin returned to Detroit in 1982 and was with him when he died on July 24, 1984. Compounding this, her marriage to Turman ended in divorce in 1984. She told Laura B. Randolph in *Ebony*, "I think just growing apart ... and miscommunicating" led to the demise of the relationship, and mentioned that they remain friends.

Franklin's career had experienced a bit of a slowdown in the late 1970s, but the 1980 blockbuster film, the *Blues Brothers*, with its upbeat soundtrack, helped revive 1960s soul music and her popularity. She had an acting part in the film as well as a scene showcasing her singing "Respect." The year 1980 also saw her break from Atlantic Records to sign with Arista.

> *"I'm a very versatile vocalist. That's what I think a singer should be. Whatever it is, I can sing it."*

Arista Records in 1985 released the album *Who's Zoomin' Who?*, featuring the hit single "Freeway of Love." The slick production values were criticized by some, but Franklin saw her sales go up with this hit. Honors started pouring in around this time as well. Michigan legislators acclaimed her voice as one of the state's greatest natural resources in 1986 for her remarkable accomplishment of 24 gold records over 20 years. Senator Carl Levin presented her with a plaque in 1989 for her outstanding musical career and her involvement in the effort to stop drunk drivers.

Franklin throughout the years has been active in holding concerts for charity causes. She attends her father's former parish, New Bethel Baptist Church, and often sings solo. In 1996, she organized a "Christmas Extravaganza at New Bethel," where film crews from the cable network, Showtime, and the British Broadcasting Corporation (BBC) were on hand to record the event.

In 1987, Franklin became the first woman inducted into the Rock and Roll Hall of Fame in Cleveland, Ohio, and the Grammy Awards continued to roll in, including a special Grammy Award for lifetime achievement in 1994. She was featured in a star-studded documentary tribute on public television, and later, in 1998, was again featured in a one-hour profile in "Aretha Franklin: Legends" as part of the *6 Days of Soul* broadcast on the cable network VH-1. She sang at the inauguration of President Bill Clinton in 1993 and at the wedding of Vice President Al Gore's eldest daughter, Karenna, in 1997.

Despite all of her awesome accomplishments, Franklin has harbored a fear of flying for many years. She declared to Waldron in *Jet* that she may be close to overcoming it, telling him that she has tried listening to anti-anxiety tapes and attending classes. She remarked, "I'm not going to jet off tomorrow, but I am expecting to soon. All things in time." She mentioned to Kenneth "Babyface" Edmonds in *Interview* in 1994 that she travels by custom bus, which has "cooking facilities, movies, fax, phones, and a fun driver." She commented, however, to Christopher John Farley in *Time* in 1998 that nothing had worked to conquer the phobia, so she still enjoys the bus. "You can pull over, go to Red Lobster," in the bus, she explained. "You can't pull over at 35,000 feet."

Franklin never let her flying phobia or anything else get in the way of her continuing success, though. Toward the mid- to late-1990s, she began branching out into several directions, giving no indication of settling down and letting her past describe her. In 1995, it was announced that she signed a $1.2 million deal with Villard Books to write her autobiography with David Ritz, and she promised it would be juicy. "My tongue will be smoking when I get through," she jokingly told Clarence Waldron in *Jet*, adding that some things will remain private. She told Brian McCollum in the *Detroit Free Press* that it is "time to correct any inaccuracies." Also in the works were plans for a cooking video; she collected recipes from family and friends for the effort.

Also in the 1990s, Franklin started up her own film production company, Crown Productions, and in 1997, *Jet* reported that she optioned Jesse Jackson's autobiography, *A Time to Speak: The Autobiography of the Rev. Jesse Jackson*, for a television movie for which she will serve as executive producer and coproducer. *Jet* also noted that she made plans for a documentary on her late father as well as a full-length feature on herself. Franklin was accepted to the prestigious Juilliard School in New York City in 1997 to study classical piano, and in 1998 she reprised her popular role as a restaurant owner from the 1980 *Blues Brothers* movie in the comedy *Blues Brothers 2000*. For the film, she recorded yet another version of her theme song, "Respect," which she insists she never tires of performing.

Franklin continued to record music, signing a three-album contract with Arista in 1996 for an estimated $10 million, reported J.R. Reynolds in *Billboard*. In 1998, she released *A Rose Is Still a Rose*, her first full-length album in seven years. All-star producers Kenneth

"Babyface" Edmonds and Sean "Puffy" Combs were on board, as well as Lauryn Hill, who worked with the hip-hop group the Fugees. When Christopher John Farley in *Time* remarked that some fans may be surprised to hear Franklin doing hip-hop songs on the release, she answered, "I'm a very versatile vocalist. That's what I think a singer should be. Whatever it is, I can sing it."

Selected discography

On Atlantic

I Never Loved a Man (the Way I Love You), 1967.
Aretha Arrives, 1967.
Lady Soul, 1968.
Aretha Now, 1968.
Aretha in Paris, 1968.
Soul '69, 1969.
Aretha's Gold, 1969.
This Girl's in Love with You, 1970.
Spirit in the Dark, 1970.
Aretha Live at Fillmore West, 1971.
Aretha's Greatest Hits, 1971.
Young, Gifted, and Black, 1972.
Amazing Grace, 1972.
Hey Now Hey (The Other Side of the Sky), 1973.
Let Me in Your Life, 1974.
With Everything I Feel in Me, 1975.
You, 1975.
Ten Years of Gold, 1977.
Sweet Passion, 1977.
Almighty Fire, 1978.
La Diva, 1979.
Aretha's Jazz, 1984.
The Best of Aretha Franklin, 1984.
Aretha Franklin—30 Greatest Hits, 1986.
Queen of Soul: The Atlantic Recordings, 1992.
The Very Best of Aretha Franklin, Volumes 1 and 2, Rhino/ Atlantic, 1994.
Love Songs, Rhino/Atlantic, 1997.

On Arista

Aretha, 1980.
Jump to It, 1982.
Get It Right, 1984.
Who's Zoomin' Who? (includes "Freeway of Love"), 1985.
Aretha, 1987.
Love All the Hurt Away, 1987.
One Lord, One Faith, One Baptism, 1988.
Through the Storm, 1989.
What You See Is What You Sweat, 1991.
Jazz to Soul, 1992.
Greatest Hits: 1980-1994, 1994.
A Rose Is Still a Rose, 1998.

On Columbia

The Great Aretha Franklin, 1960.
The Electrifying Aretha Franklin, 1960.
The Tender, the Moving, the Swinging Aretha Franklin, 1962.
Laughing on the Outside, 1963.
Unforgettable: A Tribute to Dinah Washington, 1964.
Running Out of Fools, 1964.
Yeah! Aretha Franklin in Person, 1965.
Soul Sister, 1965.
Aretha Franklin's Greatest Hits, 1967.
Take a Look, 1967.
Take It Like You Give It, 1967.
Aretha Franklin's Greatest Hits, Volume 1 and 2, 1967.
Queen of Soul, 1968.
Once in a Lifetime, 1969.
Soft and Beautiful, 1969.
Two Sides of Love, 1970.
Sweet Bitter Love, 1970.
In The Beginning/The World of Aretha Franklin, 1960-1972, 1972.
The Great Aretha Franklin—The First 12 Sides, 1973.
Today I Sing the Blues, 1973.
Aretha Sings the Blues, 1980.
Aretha Franklin—Legendary Queen of Soul, 1981.
Aretha After Hours, 1987.

Other

Songs of Faith, Chess, 1956.
With Curtis Mayfield, *Sparkle* (soundtrack), 1976.
"Think," *The Blues Brothers* (soundtrack), 1979.
With Rev. C. L. Franklin, *Never Grow Old*, Chess, 1984.
"Jumpin' Jack Flash," *Jumpin' Jack Flash* (soundtrack), 1986.
With George Michael, "I Knew You Were Waiting (for Me)," Columbia, 1987.
"If I Lose," *White Men Can't Jump* (soundtrack), EMI, 1992.
All Men Are Brothers: A Tribute to Curtis Mayfield, 1994.
"It Hurts Like Hell," *Waiting to Exhale* (soundtrack), Arista, 1995.

Sources

On-line

http://www.wallofsound.com
http://www.globalserve.net/~ebutler/

Books

Contemporary Musicians, Volume 17, Gale Research, 1997.
Notable Black American Women, Gale Research, 1992.

Periodicals

Billboard, October 26, 1996, p. 26.
Detroit Free Press, December 6, 1996; November 5, 1997; February 17, 1998.
Ebony, April 1995, p. 28; January 1998, p. 52.
Interview, March 1994, p. 20; December 1997, p. 110.
Jet, August 21, 1995, p. 33; October 7, 1996, p. 20; June 16, 1997, pp. 32, 56.
Time, March 2, 1998, p. 78.

—Geri Speace

Jean-Paul Gaultier

Clothing designer

Born April 24, 1952, in Arcueil, Paris, France; son of Paul Rene (an accountant) and Solange (a secretary) Gaultier; companion of Francis Menuge (died, 1990), beginning c. 1975.

Addresses: *Office*—Jean-Paul Gaultier S.A., 30 rue du Faubourg-Saint-Antoine, 75012 Paris, France.

Career

Apprenticed with design house of Pierre Cardin for several years beginning in 1970; affiliated with House of Jean Patou, mid-1970s; first collection shown in Paris, 1976; successful launch of Jean-Paul Gaultier S.A. after financing from Japanese company Kashiyama, 1978; launched Junior Gaultier, 1988; designed costumes for the film *The Cook, the Thief, His Wife, and Her Lover,* 1989, for singer Madonna's world tour, 1990, and for the films *La Cite des Enfants Perdus,* 1995, and *The Fifth Element,* 1997; launched women's fragrance line, 1993, and men's fragrance line, 1995.

Awards: France's Designer of the Year award, 1987.

Sidelights

French designer Jean-Paul Gaultier has been called a maverick, the "high priest of provocation," and for years was considered fashion's *enfant terrible.* For his theatrically outrageous women's line, he borrowed from sources as diverse as 1930s films, political events, African tribal designs, and London street gear. Featuring corsets and semi-bondage latex gear, sarongs,

fresh mixes of fabric and pattern, and a general iconoclasm throughout, Gaultier's designs have been termed unwearable or overpriced, but many of them nevertheless became part of mainstream fashion. The designer is responsible for rubber dresses, the cone-shaped bra, the Cyrillic lettering fad, needlepoint-patterned sweaters, cowl necks that turn into hoods, and was also the first to use sweatshirt jersey material for dresses.

He shocked many in the 1980s when he showed undergarments as outerwear. "Gaultier ... sees himself as the agent provocateur of the Paris couture," Deborah Drier asserted in a 1987 essay in *Art in America.* "Taking his inspiration from the street and from pop fashion, he is audacious, often lurid, sometimes even grotesque." Rock star David Bowie was an early fan of Gaultier's designs, and later Madonna would make the designer a household name when she asked him to outfit her for her 1990 Blond Ambition tour.

Gaultier was born in a suburb of Paris in April of 1952, the son of an accountant. Since his mother also worked, Gaultier often spent time with his grandmother, who lived in Paris proper. She was a faith healer and tarot reader who would sometimes walk about in unusual ensembles; she also became a tremendous influence on Gaultier during his youth. From an early age Gaultier was interested in costume, design, and fashion, and used to dress his stuffed animals in elaborate get-ups. While his grandmother was telling fortunes, he would sit and do before-and-after sketches on her clients. As a teenager, he began drawing costumes, then put his entire "collection" on paper, "which he then lavishly praised in short reviews that he wrote for his own amusement," according to *People*.

This sense of the absurd did portend a career in academia, as Gaultier's parents hoped for him. Instead, he obtained an apprenticeship at the design house of Pierre Cardin on his eighteenth birthday in 1970. He remained there for several years, leaving for a time to apprentice at famous Paris couturier Jean Patou, and then decided to launch his own house in earnest in 1976. To do so, he obtained a loan from his father that was ostensibly to purchase an apartment; Gaultier used the money instead to hold a show of his designs which only sixteen people attended.

Two years later, Gaultier secured the backing of a Japanese company, Kashiyama, and launched a more well received collection. His early designs had a retro feel to them, partly based on the hit movie *Grease*, which was set in the 1950s, as well as the "Bond Girl" look cultivated by 1960s James Bond films.

Within a few years Gaultier's line of women's clothing was launched in earnest. Though his label was still relatively unknown to American buyers, in 1982 Gaultier and his Paris atelier/apartment were selected by *New York Times Magazine* interior design editors for an illustrated piece about its minimalist aesthetic. At the time, he had pinball machines in the foyer and only a bed and a large-screen television in his bedchamber.

By 1984 *Vogue* was singling out his clothes as "inventive, well-tailored," and noted that a ticket to one of his collection's circus-inspired premiers was a much-sought-after commodity among Parisian fashion cognoscenti. Yet fashion editors were not always so flattering when writing about Gaultier's somewhat bizarre designs. This spiraled into a war of words that occurred over several years, with Gaultier dismissing the press and their opinions in interviews, and at one point banning several fashion journalists from his shows for a few seasons. He even penned his own comic-book style biography, *A nous deux la mode*, when he tired of interviewers' standard questions. An excerpt from his school days reads, "One could put up with the teacher if only she were better dressed."

In 1985 Gaultier opened a Paris boutique with a unique ambiance—there were video screens built into the floor, for example—that reflected the spirit of his clothes. He became a well-known presence to American fashion mavens when department stores began carrying his line in mini-Gaultier boutiques; there were several more stores in Europe as well. In Paris, he grew into a cult icon of sorts, recognizable to many by his trademark bleached-blond crew cut. His shows continued to attract the spectacle-seeking, and his line of women's wear grew more accepted by both the fashion press and the general public, though some other designers dismissed his work as too "street" for high fashion.

Gaultier's mid-eighties designs were famous for their armor-like construction; this was also the period when he first showed odd, cone-shaped bras worn over a garment, or integrated a spiral wedge of velvet into the front of the dress itself. Other body-accentuating items—a molded leather jumpsuit, for instance, or clothing constructed from latex—seemed to fit in perfectly with the eighties zeitgeist and the new mixed feelings about sexuality. "Gaultier is creating armor for the knighthood of eros," wrote Drier in the 1987 *Art in America* essay. "In psychoanalytic terms such clothing as ... Gaultier's might seem to incarnate denial of the present, rather desperate state of affairs," Drier reflected, "or a nostalgic throwback to a time when acting out one's sexual fantasies didn't carry a potential death sentence."

Gaultier was awarded France's Designer of the Year award that same year, in 1987, for his consistently fresh approach to couture. While ladylike suits and elaborate ball gowns were mainstays of eighties high fashion, Gaultier worked around new and sometimes odd themes for each season. "Concierge" dressing was one example; another was Gaultier's "idea of White Russians escaping to Paris [after the 1917 Bolshevik Revolution] with their jewelry and formal clothes and then taking jobs as taxi drivers and manicurists," explained *Vogue*'s Georgina Howell.

True to his avant-garde ideas, Gaultier moved into Pigalle, the seedy area of Paris, long before it became fashionable in the mid-1990s. He also shopped in Miami for 1950s American kitsch objects prior to the city's 1990s boost in popularity. When his menswear line was launched, Gaultier merged the two shows into one and put men and women on the runway together, which was considered a radical move at the time. "In a world of recycled fashion ideas, Jean Paul's originality is a big commodity," wrote Howell. In the late 1980s, Gaultier began using high-tech fabrics developed by athletic-wear firms. He was invited to costume the characters in the futuristic sci-fi thriller *The Fifth Element*, released in 1997. That same year he looked to 1930s Mexico for inspiration and designed a collection based on the unique style of painter Frida Kahlo.

"Vulgarity always makes itself obvious," Gaultier told *Vogue*'s Javier Arroyuelo. "You can't hide it under clothes, because it's in your mind." The designer, who admits his favorite shopping emporiums are flea markets around the globe, possesses an eye for the unusual that has suited him well over the years, and many of his far-fetched designs eventually filtered down to teenage mall fashion. "The object used to be to dress a certain social set and to dress the poor to look as though they were rich," Gaultier told Howell in 1991.

Fashion, by then, was no longer so restricting. Neither were Gaultier's still-infamous shows. He was known for holding cattle call auditions for models in an effort to recruit the extraordinary or the extraordi-narily odd. Always a maverick, the designer has asserted, according to *Vogue*, that the best article of clothing for anyone is "their own blue jeans."

Selected writings

A nous deux la mode (biography).

Selected discography

(With Tony Mansfield) *How to Do That*, 1989.

Sources

Art in America, September 1987, pp. 47-49.
New York Times Magazine, December 26, 1982, pp. 30-33; April 10, 1994, sec. 6, p. 62.
People, May 6, 1985; December 10, 1990, p. 123; October 12, 1992.
Vogue, June 1984, p. 194; July 1986; August 1988; January 1989; March 1991, pp. 392.

—*Carol Brennan*

Margaret Joan Geller

Astrophysicist

Born December 8, 1947, in Ithaca, NY; daughter of Seymour (a chemist) and Sarah (Levine) Geller. *Education:* University of California—Berkeley, A.B., 1970; Princeton University, M.A., 1972, Ph.D., 1975.

Addresses: *Office*—Harvard/Smithsonian Center for Astrophysics, 60 Garden St., Cambridge, MA 02138-1516.

Career

Center for Astrophysics, Cambridge, MA, research fellow, 1974-78; Harvard College Observatory, Cambridge, research fellow, 1978-80; Institute of Astronomy, Cambridge, England, senior visiting fellow, 1978-82; Harvard University, assistant professor, 1980-83, professor of astronomy, 1988—; Smithsonian Astrophysical Observatory, Cambridge, astrophysicist, 1983—; University of Pennsylvania, Goodspeed-Richards lecturer, 1992; Royal Astronomical Society of Canada, Hogg lecturer, 1993; Harvard University, orator, 1995; Cornell University, Bethe lecturer, 1996. Contributor to numerous scientific and professional journals; *Science* magazine, board of reviewing editors.

Awards: National Science Foundation fellow, 1970-73; Newcomb-Cleveland prize, 1989-90; MacArthur Foundation fellow, 1990-95; received D.S.H.C. from Connecticut College, 1995, and from Gustavus Adolphus College, 1996; Klopsteg award, American Association of Physics Teachers, 1996; Library Lion, New York Public Library, 1997.

Member: International Astronomy Union, National Academy of Sciences, American Academy of Arts and Sciences, American Physical Society (fellow), American Astronomical Society (councillor), Association of Universities for Research in Astronomy (director-at-large).

Sidelights

Astrophysicist Margaret Joan Geller has devoted much of her career to a project that, to the lay mind, sounds nearly impossible in scope: the mapping of the universe. Since the mid-1980s, the Harvard professor and her colleagues at one of the preeminent centers for astronomy in the United States have won praise for their efforts and inspired other scientists into entering this entirely new field of research in astrophysics.

Geller's work involves scanning the skies with a telescope and feeding the collected data into computers that then display maps of the positions of galaxies in the universe. The often surprising published results have sometimes made Geller an interview subject in the mainstream media; she has also collaborated with a filmmaker on projects that explain patterns in the cosmos.

Geller was born in 1947 in Ithaca, New York. Her father was a physical chemist who occasionally took his young daughter to his workplace in the hopes of encouraging her to follow a scientific career. Geller, however, dreamed of a career on the stage. The Gellers allowed their above-average child to stay at home and work under their supervision; she read prodigiously from the library and went in to her school infrequently, usually only to take her exams. Nevertheless, the time she spent at her father's office, the renowned Bell Labs of New Jersey, did make somewhat of an impression. For college, Geller was an undergraduate at the prestigious University of California at Berkeley.

The decision was a well-timed one. During the mid-1960s, Berkeley was not just a hotbed of radical politics, but also an encouraging and positive place for undergraduates like Geller. Her first major was math, but she soon switched to physics. "I didn't know what kinds of questions to ask in mathematics," Geller recalled in an interview with Gary Taubes of *Discover*. "In physics, I could see there were things that were known and things that weren't."

After receiving her undergraduate degree, Geller enrolled in a Ph.D. program at Princeton University—a dramatically different academic atmosphere than Berkeley. The Ivy League enclave had only recently begun admitting women, and she was uncomfortable. "Students would ask me what I was doing in physics at Princeton when men couldn't get jobs in physics," Geller recalled in the *Discover* interview.

Unhappy, she considered leaving Princeton, but her father pointed out that she had "never failed at anything, and if I left I'd feel that I failed and that would haunt me my whole life," Geller told Taubes in *Discover*. Instead, she was urged to "get the degree and *then* quit."

She took the advice. Geller received her M.A. from Princeton in 1972 and her Ph.D. three years later, becoming only the second woman to receive a Ph.D. in physics from the university at the time. In choosing where to focus her studies, she had considered solid-state physics. But one prescient advisor had told her to choose a field that would be exciting a decade or so after she completed graduate school, and thus Geller chose astrophysics and the undiscovered frontiers of space.

She spent time as a research fellow at the Center for Astrophysics (CfA) in Cambridge, Massachusetts. and did another stint as a research fellow at the prestigious Harvard College Observatory from 1978 to 1980. In 1979, she traveled abroad after winning a visiting fellowship at the Institute of Astronomy in Cambridge, England. It was a good experience for her, and a period in which, after some reflective thought about her career and the status of astrophysics research, Geller found her calling.

As she recalled in *Discover*, "I realized almost nothing was known about anything outside our galaxy." She decided that she wanted to explore the actual physical structure of the universe and how it might be mapped.

Geller teamed with scientific colleagues—in particular John Huchra at the Smithsonian Astrophysical Observatory, where she has worked as an astrophysicist since 1983—to carry out this idea. Much of their research would involve redshifts, which Taubes of *Discover* explained as "measures of how much the wavelengths of light from distant objects stretch toward the red end of the spectrum the farther away those objects happen to be." In other words, a redshift shows how fast a galaxy moves away from the Milky Way, which is our galaxy.

Geller and Huchra began publishing three-dimensional maps of the universe in 1986, and their first maps printed out in two-dimensional form surprised both them and the astrophysics community. This first map of around a thousand galaxies was astounding in its pattern: there appeared to be a stickman figure in the middle—in other words, "the distribution of galaxies looked like a child's drawing of a somewhat bowlegged person," wrote Taubes. The figure came to be called the Stickman.

Prior to the Stickman, the scientific community generally believed that the distribution of galaxies in the universe was random; Geller's Stickman showed that galaxies clustered together in well-organized and large voids of space were common. This finding had important implications for the study of the origins and history of the universe: scientists knew already that at the beginning of time the cosmos was smooth, but the patterns found in Geller's maps offered a whole new set of questions concerning the origins of structure in the universe.

The Stickman made Geller famous; she even appeared on the *Today* show to explain it as "news that the universe was a considerably more perplexing place than previously imagined," wrote Taubes in *Discover*. Geller received further media attention with her and Huchra's 1989 discovery of the "Great Wall," a huge array of galaxies that spans 500 million light years.

Not surprisingly, these attempts to "map" the universe have created an entirely new research area in astrophysics, and Geller is just one of about a hundred astronomers around the world now working in the field.

In late 1998, she and fellow CfA scientist Dan Fabricant will launch their next massive project, a mapping project that will look deep into the universe and locate about 50,000 galaxies, covering a distance of five billion light years and looking back one-third of the age of the universe.

The woman who once considered a career on the stage still professes a love of the arts, and Geller has found satisfaction collaborating with filmmaker Boyd Estus on video projects showcasing her galaxy maps. This union of science and art came about partly as a result of her 1990 MacArthur Fellowship, a distinguished (and generous) five-year grant bestowed to those making outstanding contributions in their field.

Geller has taught at Harvard since 1980, and has been a professor of astronomy there since 1988, but has yet to be awarded University tenure. "I've had periods where I find it very difficult to work because of this," she confessed to Taubes in the *Discover* interview. "Then I think, 'The hell with it, I've shown I can do it. Why don't I go do something else?'"

Sources

On-line

http://www.physics.sfsu.edu/grad/gmarcy/cswa/history/geller.html (February 11, 1998).

Periodicals

Discover, August 1997, pp. 52-59.
Science, November 17, 1989, p. 885.
Time, November 27, 1989, pp. 57-58.

Other

Additional information supplied by Margaret Joan Geller, March 1998.

—*Carol Brennan*

John Glenn

Pilot, astronaut, and senator

Born John Herschel Glenn, Jr., July 18, 1921, in Cambridge, OH; son of John Herschel (a plumbing and heating business owner) and Clara Sproat (an elementary school teacher) Glenn; married Anna Margaret Castor, April 6, 1943; children: David, Carolyn. *Education:* Attended Muskingum College, New Concord, OH; 1939-41, Muskingum College, B.S. in engineering, early 1960s; graduated from Test Pilot School, Naval Air Test Center, Patuxent River, MD, c. 1956; attended University of Maryland, 1956-59.

Addresses: *Office*—503 Hart Senate Office Bldg., Washington, DC 20510.

Career

Entered Naval Aviation Cadet Program, 1942; Marine Corps, 1943-65; flew 59 combat missions during World War II; member of Marine Fighter Squadron 218 on Guam; flight instructor, Corpus Christi, TX, 1948-50; as member of Marine Fighter Squadrons 311 and 27, flew 63 missions in Korea, 1953; assigned to Fighter Design Branch, Navy Bureau of Aeronautics (now Bureau of Naval Weapons), Washington, D.C., 1956-59; set transcontinental speed record, 1957; NASA Space Task Group, Langley, VA, Project Mercury Astronaut, 1959-62; became first American to orbit the earth, 1962; group moved to NASA Manned Spacecraft Center, Houston, TX, 1962-64; promoted to colonel, 1964; retired from Marine Corp and became business executive, 1965; elected to U.S. Senate, 1974, re-elected, 1980, 1986, 1992; selected to be sent into space as oldest person ever to undertake space flight, 1998.

Awards: Six Distinguished Flying Cross honors; Air Medal with 18 clusters for service during World War II and Korea; Asiatic-Pacific Campaign Medal; American Campaign Medal; World War II Victory Medal; China Service Medal; National Defense Service Medal; Korean Service Medal; United Nations Service Medal; Korean Presidential Unit Citation; Navy's Astronaut Wings; Marine Corps' Astronaut Medal; NASA Distinguished Service Medal; Congressional Space Medal of Honor.

Sidelights

For almost 25 years, the world was used to calling him "Senator John Glenn of Ohio." Before his distinguished political career, however, Glenn was a U.S. Marine. He became a World War II and Korean War hero before joining The National Aeronautics and Space Administration (NASA) as the oldest of the original Mercury Seven astronauts. At age 40, he became the first American to orbit the Earth and was showered with praise upon returning from his scenic but almost-fatal trip into space. Though his transformation from all-American hero to politician was not as swift as expected, he finally won a U.S. Senate seat in 1974 and ended up becoming Ohio's first four-term senator elected by its citizens. On the verge of a possible fifth term, however, Glenn decided he would not run. Early in 1998, he surprised many when he announced that was donning a spacesuit once again, this time as NASA's oldest astronaut ever. After a series of medical tests proving the 76-year-old was in prime condition, he was ready to ride. The liftoff was scheduled for October 8, 1998. "I'm very proud to have been part of the beginning of the space program and I'm proud to be back," Glenn commented, as reported in the Knight-Ridder/Tribune News Service.

Glenn was born on July 18, 1921, in Cambridge, Ohio, and grew up in nearby New Concord, a town of just over 1,000 at the time, but one with an uncanny number of businesses for so small an area. His father, John Herschel Glenn, Sr., owned a plumbing and heating business, and his mother, Clara Sproat Glenn, was an elementary school teacher. The Glenns also had an adopted daughter, Jean, reportedly a difficult child and not often mentioned in biographies of Glenn. As a child, Glenn, nicknamed "Bud," loved planes, collecting numerous models, and attending air shows. His family were devout Presbyterians and instilled a strong religious spirit in Glenn. New Concord was a "dry" town, meaning it had outlawed the sale of alcoholic beverages. In this atmosphere of simple pleasures and adherence to faith and the free market, Glenn matured into a noble citizen with old-fashioned American values.

Glenn met his wife, Anna Margaret Castor, whom everyone called "Annie," when he was three years old and she was four. They were inseparable, playing together as children and starting to go steady in the eighth grade. Growing up, the freckle-faced, redheaded Glenn and the pretty, brown-eyed Castor went roller skating and ice skating, flew kites, went on hay rides and to ice cream socials, and held cookouts. Glenn and Castor attended New Concord High School together, where she would ride with him in his 1929 roadster convertible. Sometimes a daredevil driver, Glenn never pulled any stunts with his girlfriend in the car. Despite Castor's 85 percent stutter, which was not treated until 1978, she was a cheerful and outgoing woman with a wry sense of humor. They married on April 6, 1943, and had two children, Dave and Carolyn (called Lyn), and two grandchildren.

Glenn entered high school in 1935 and emerged as a class leader: honor student, junior class president, lead actor in the senior play, and letterman in football, basketball, and tennis, even though his athletic prowess was not top-notch. After graduation, Glenn and Castor both enrolled at nearby Muskingum College in 1939. Glenn played football, but was too small to ex-

cel. Glenn and Castor often hung out after class at the ice cream shop, playing the jukebox. World events, however, would draw Glenn away from his idyllic Midwestern life. In 1939, Nazi Germany began its invasions of other European countries, and Glenn believed American involvement was impending. He volunteered for civilian pilot training at the New Philadelphia airport.

Glenn's parents were disappointed that he would not take over his father's plumbing business, and were devastated that he was undertaking such a dangerous pursuit, convinced that he would eventually end up in combat. "We were sick when he took up aviation," his father recalled in Frank Van Riper's Glenn: The Astronaut Who Would be President. Glenn, however, was thrilled with being in the air. He received his pilot's license on July 1, 1941, just five months and six days before Japan attacked Pearl Harbor and plunged the nation into the midst of World War II. Glenn abandoned academics to enter the Naval Aviation Cadet Program in Corpus Christi, Texas. After a year, Glenn rose to the challenging words of a Marine Corps recruiter and joined that branch of the service. He was eventually sent to Hawaii and was highly decorated with Distinguished Flying Cross medals and Air Medals for his 59 missions in the South Pacific.

In 1945 Glenn decided to become a career Marine. He and his family were sent to Guam in 1947, where they lived in a Quonset hut on base for a few months. From 1948 to 1950, he was a flight instructor back in Corpus Christi. In 1953, Glenn entered combat again during the Korean War with Marine Fighter Squadron 311 as a bomber pilot. Although he had a close call and was almost killed in that capacity, he asked to be put on the front lines. His first day in the F86 Sabrejet, he downed an enemy MiG, and shot down two more within a total of nine days' combat, earning the nickname the "MiG Mad Marine." The war ended a few days later, on July 27, 1953, and Glenn returned to the United States to enroll in the Test Pilot School at the Naval Air Test Center in Patuxent River, Maryland.

By 1956, Glenn was assigned to the fighter design branch at the Navy Bureau of Aeronautics (now called the Bureau of Naval Weapons) in Washington, D.C. While working as a test pilot there for three years, Glenn set the transcontinental speed record across North America on July 16, 1957. He was the first pilot to make a coast-to-coast flight at a speed higher than Mach 1, the speed of sound. His plane was refueled in mid-air on the three-hour, 23-minute trip from

Los Angeles to New York. Also during his time as a test pilot, Glenn volunteered for tests on the Navy's human centrifuge machine in Johnsville, Pennsylvania, in 1958. These tests simulated the kind of gravity pull that would occur if a human were ever sent into space. Then in March of 1959, Glenn began assisting with overseeing the development of the Mercury space capsule.

Glenn was chosen, in April of 1959, as one of the first team of Americans preparing to be sent into space. The "Mercury Seven" were called astronauts, to distinguish them from cosmonauts, the name given to Russian space pilots. Glenn and the others began training at Langley Air Force Base in Newport News, Virginia, and were later transferred to the Cape Canaveral Space Center on the east coast of Florida. All seven wanted to be the first man in space, but Glenn, a high achiever and confident of his position, was stunned when Alan Shepard was chosen as the first pilot, with Virgil I. ("Gus") Grissom and himself as back-ups. The project was made high priority when a Russian cosmonaut, Yuri Gagarin, became the first person in space on April 12, 1961, orbiting the Earth in one hour and 48 minutes. Shepard made it up on May 5, 1961, but did not orbit, spending only 15 minutes in the Mercury-Redstone rocket. That May, President John F. Kennedy stressed the importance of the United States putting a man on the moon by the end of the decade. Space flight continued, with Shepard flying again on July 21 with Grissom as pilot. Glenn was again the back-up.

In August of 1961, the Russians sent Gherman Titov into orbit on Vostok 2. He made 17 complete passes around the globe. The United States quickly announced that Glenn had been chosen to be the first American in orbit. The flight was originally scheduled for December 20, 1961, but weather conditions forced a delay until January 27, 1962. Technical problems put off the endeavor again. Finally, on February 20, 1962, at 9:45 a.m., John Glenn was sent into space from Cape Canaveral in the *Friendship* capsule attached to a Mercury-Atlas rocket. Traveling 17,500 miles per hour at 100 miles above the planet, Glenn's first words were, "Oh, that view is tremendous!" As he headed east, he was treated to a shimmering sight as he spotted the city of Perth, Australia, where residents had turned on all of the lights at midnight just for his pleasure. Suddenly, however, a serious problem arose. The automatic controls had given out, and Glenn had to manually maneuver back down after only three orbits. On re-entering the atmosphere, his capsule's heat shields were burning up and whizzing off. He was almost burned alive, but managed to get out of the

capsule just in time. His family, hounded by the media and waiting anxiously for his safe return, were relieved. Glenn was given a hero's welcome on return, and Muskingum College, which had been disputing his bachelor of science over a residency requirement, finally granted him his engineering degree. Years later, author Tom Wolfe's popular book *The Right Stuff* would recount personal histories of the Mercury astronauts in addition to vanguard pilot Chuck Yeager.

> *"I'm very proud to have been part of the beginning of the space program and I'm proud to be back."*

After Glenn's remarkable journey, he was eager to start a political career. He became friends with President Kennedy and wanted to run for the U.S. Senate in 1964, but a bad fall in the bathtub caused inner ear problems and thwarted him. He retired from the Marine Corps in 1965 and took a job as an executive at Royal Crown International. He ran again in 1970, but was defeated in the primary by Howard Metzenbaum. In 1974, Glenn pulled through, winning his party's candidacy away from Metzenbaum and becoming elected as a Democratic U.S. senator from his home state of Ohio. In 1980, he was re-elected by the largest margin in that state's history, and began a third term in 1986. In 1992, he became the first popularly elected Ohio senator to win the seat in four consecutive elections. He put a bid in for the Democratic presidential nomination in 1984, but was overlooked for Walter Mondale, who lost the race to incumbent Ronald Reagan.

As a four-term senator, Glenn was a liberal Democrat who supported education and health care programs. He served on the Governmental Affairs Committee, the Senate Armed Services Committee, the Select Committee on Intelligence, and the Special Committee on Aging. As a former military man, he could be known to be slightly "hawkish," but overall took a moderate stance on such affairs and actively sought to limit nuclear weapons. In addition, he sought to make government more accountable by implementing the Government Management Reform Act of 1994, which required all federal agencies to appoint a chief financial officer and to produce annual reports and financial statements. He also helped enact the Cash Management Improvement Act of 1990, the Federal

Financial Management Improvement Act of 1996, and the Single Audit Act of 1996. Interested in the environment, Glenn also endorsed the creation of the National Institute for the Environment (NIE) and served as co-chair of the Great Lakes Task Force, which aimed to improve that region. He also set up a web site to keep constituents informed of his activities. From 1976 to 1994, Glenn was accompanied in the Senate by his old foe, Metzenbaum, who became a good friend after winning the state's other seat.

Glenn announced in early 1998 that he would not seek a fifth term. One reason was because of his age—he would be into his 80s if he served the full six years—but he had another issue as well: he had persuaded NASA to send him back up in space. The active, healthy, 76-year-old would be 77 by the time the mission would blast off for a ten-day run in October of 1998, and the oldest person to enter space since astronaut Story Musgrave, who was 61 when he went up in 1996. The media pounced on the story, with articles playing up the romantic notion of the legendary astronaut returning to his first love while serving once again as a guinea pig—this time helping NASA study the effects of aging. In February, Glenn was again spinning in the centrifuge to prepare himself.

Some critics, however, suspected that Glenn was a willing pawn in a NASA publicity stunt to revive enthusiasm for the program and to counteract the lingering horror of the 1986 *Challenger* disaster, in which a shuttle blew up on takeoff and killed four, including the first civilian astronaut, school teacher Christa McAuliffe. "[E]ven Glenn's supporters admit the research isn't critical," Matt Bai remarked in *Newsweek.* "The significance of his mission lies, as always, in the symbolism that surrounds him." Others believed that it was a ploy by Glenn himself. "It's about John keeping his name in the paper," claimed former Apollo astronaut Edgar Mitchell in a Knight-Ridder/Tribune News Service piece. "He wants to keep life interesting for himself," Mitchell noted, while adding that he did not have a problem with that. Still others pointed out

that Glenn's journey could have a positive benefit in the way our society views seniors. NASA administrator Daniel Goldin commented in a Knight-Ridder/Tribune News Service article, "Children will look at their grandparents differently. It shows that senior citizens have the right stuff."

Sources

On-line

"John Glenn Returns to Space," January 30, 1998, CNN Interactive web site, http://cnn.com (May 21, 1998).
"Senator John Glenn web site," http://www.senate.gov/~glenn (May 21, 1998).

Books

Contemporary Heroes and Heroines, Book I, Gale Research, 1990.
Explorers and Discoverers of the World, first edition, Gale Research, 1993.
Van Riper, Frank, *Glenn: The Astronaut Who Would be President,* Empire Books, 1983.

Periodicals

Associated Press, February 19, 1998.
Coal & Synfuels Technology, March 1, 1993, p. 8.
Defense Daily, February 21, 1997, p. 270.
Detroit Free Press, January 16, 1998.
Detroit News, January 13, 1998; January 16, 1998.
Houston Chronicle, February 19, 1998.
Knight-Ridder/Tribune News Service, August 25, 1996; February 21, 1997; January 15, 1998; January 16, 1998; January 20, 1998; February 19, 1998.
Newsweek, January 26, 1998, p. 32.
Time, January 26, 1998, pp. 25, 58.
U.S. News & World Report, January 26, 1998, p. 12.

—*Geri Speace*

Danny Glover

Actor

Born July 22, 1947, in San Francisco, CA; son of James (a postal worker) and Carrie (a postal worker; maiden name, Hunley) Glover; married Asake Bomani (a jazz singer and art gallery manager), 1975; children: daughter, Mandisa. *Education:* San Francisco State College, degree in economics; studied acting at the Black Actors' Workshop of the American Conservatory Theatre, beginning 1975.

Addresses: *Home*—San Francisco, CA. *Office*—c/o Warner Brothers, 4000 Warner Blvd. Burbank, CA 91522.

Career

Began acting, late 1960s, with San Francisco State College's Black Students Union. Worked as an evaluator of social programs for City of Berkeley, CA; researcher, mayor's office, San Francisco, CA, 1971-75; lecturer. Stage appearances include *Blood Knot,* Roundabout Theatre, 1980; *Master Harold ... and the Boys,* Lyceum Theatre, 1982; and *Macbeth,* Actors Theatre, Los Angeles, CA. Television appearances include movies *The Face of Rage,* 1983; *Mandela,* 1987; *A Raisin in the Sun,* 1989; and *Deadly Voyage,* 1996 (also executive producer); miniseries *Chiefs,* 1983; *Lonesome Dove,* 1989; and *Queen,* 1993; and episodes of *Storybook Classics, Lou Grant, Gimme a Break,* and *Hill Street Blues.* Film appearances include *Escape from Alcatraz,* 1979; *Places in the Heart,* 1984; *The Color Purple,* 1985; *Lethal Weapon,* 1987; *Lethal Weapon 2,* 1989; *To Sleep with Anger,* 1990 (also executive producer); *Grand Canyon,* 1991; *A Rage in Harlem,* 1991; *Lethal Weapon 3,* 1993; *Bopha!,* 1993; *Lethal Weapon 4,* 1998.

Awards: *Theatre World* Award, 1982, for *Master Harold ... and the Boys;* Image Award, National Association for the Advancement of Colored People (NAACP), 1988, for *Mandela;* MTV Movie Award (with Mel Gibson), 1993, for *Lethal Weapon 3;* inducted into Black Filmmakers Hall of Fame.

Sidelights

African American actor Danny Glover has not lost hold of his social conscience as he has made his mark in Hollywood. From his activist roots in San Francisco as a college student, he has kept his perspective as an actor while choosing roles in plays, television shows, and top films. He got his start in the late 1960s acting as a student, appearing in works by Amiri Baraka. Then he gave up the footlights to work as an administrator for social programs. By the mid-1970s, he had caught the acting bug again, and gave up his steady job to drive a taxi and go to auditions. His first big stage role was in South African writer Athol Fugard's *Master Harold ... and the Boys,* for which he won acclaim and garnered Hollywood's interest. Though his role in 1985's *The Color Purple* caused controversy amid criticism that it perpetuated stereotypes of African American males, Glover thoughtfully entered the debate with a cool head and remained focused on his goal of bringing multidimensional African American roles to life. The fun thriller *Lethal Weapon* with Mel Gibson fully elevated Glover to star status. It broke from the traditional typecasting of African American characters and has spawned a number of sequels. Glover's relaxed charm onscreen has made him an admired actor in a range of characters, from sympathetic to evil.

Glover was born July 22, 1947, in San Francisco, California, the oldest of five children—three boys and two girls. His parents, James and Carrie (Hunley) Glover, both worked for the postal service, and were active in their union and the NAACP. Glover was raised in the famed Haight-Ashbury district of San Francisco, known for being the birthplace of hippies and flower children during the 1960s, but spent his summers on his grandparents' farm in Georgia. Though he enjoyed singing with his church choir, Glover did not aspire to show business, but rather, wanted to be an economist. School was frightening at times because Glover was mildly dyslexic, but he worked through it. After graduating from high school, where he played tight end on the football team, he went on to San Francisco State College (now San Francisco State University). There, he worked to set up an African American studies department, taking part in a successful student strike when the school planned to get rid of the ethnic studies curriculum. Along the way he became interested in perhaps working in developing countries.

His social awareness stirred, Glover got involved with community politics, joining groups like the African Liberation Support Committee and the Black Panthers, and helping to tutor inner-city youth. Around the same time, he began acting as an outgrowth of his activism, appearing in the late 1960s in plays by noted poet and author Amiri Baraka. "At the time it was a new outlook for Black theater," Glover recalled to Aldore Collier in *Ebony*. "I did activist roles in many of the plays. I felt I was making a statement in the plays." Glover performed with the Black Students' Union in college and even took drama courses. He dabbled in some community theater as well, and joined an improvisational theater group, but did not seriously considering acting as a livelihood. Instead, he kept on his original track and received his degree in economics.

After graduating, Glover remained active in social issues by holding administrative jobs for the cities of San Francisco and Berkeley, evaluating housing and education programs. In 1971, he was granted a fellowship to get involved with the planning commission on zoning for the city of Berkeley, and in the mid-1970s

he was an evaluator for reading programs at the youth and adult levels. By the mid-1970s Glover drifted back into acting. "I kind of felt my way into it," he told Lisa Belkin in the *New York Times.* "There are so many talented cats around, so much of it was luck." By 1977 he was working steadily with the Black Actors' Workshop of the American Conservatory Theatre, driving a taxi to pay the bills. "Thank God for Yellow Cab," Glover remarked to Cynthia Gorney of the *Washington Post.* "When I found out I could drive a cab and make $100 a day, I was in seventh heaven. I could do whatever I wanted to do."

Glover remembered getting up at 4 a.m. to work until late morning, then flying down to Los Angeles for auditions. Glover began acting in productions such as *The Island* and *Suicide in B Flat* in San Francisco; *Macbeth, Sizwe Banzi is Dead,* and *Nevis Mountain Dew* in Los Angeles, and *Jukebox* in Oakland, California. He had his film debut in a small part in 1979's *Escape from Alcatraz.* In 1980 he appeared off-Broadway at the Roundabout Theatre in South African writer Athol Fugard's *Blood Knot,* turning down a part in the successful cop series *Hill Street Blues* in order to take it. Of the play, Glover told Gene Siskel in the *Chicago Tribune,* "I found in this beautiful piece of political poetry a more human way of saying the same things I had performed as part of the more strident, agitprop theatre in college. Here was a real play with characters and not just positions.... His humanity and justice became what I wanted." In 1982, Fugard's first play to premiere outside of South Africa, *Master Harold ... and the Boys,* was staged at the Yale Repertory Theatre in New Haven, Connecticut, and the playwright offered Glover one of the lead parts. The production later moved to New York, marking Glover's Broadway debut.

For his performance in *Master Harold ... and the Boys,* Glover won critical accolades and a *Theatre World* award in 1982 as one of the most promising new actors of the year. While the play was still in New Haven, director Robert Benton noticed Glover and asked him to take the role of Moze in the 1984 film *Places in the Heart.* Though the part was originally meant for an older actor, Benton was so impressed with Glover that he had the script rewritten. In the film, Sally Field stars as a white widow in danger of losing her Texas farm during the Great Depression. She takes in Glover, a transient farm hand, who helps save the property. *Places in the Heart* was nominated for an Academy Award for best picture, and Glover was widely acclaimed for his performance. His next film, 1985's crime drama/romance *Witness,* was also up for a best picture Oscar. In it, Glover played a former police officer who commits a murder. That year he also appeared in *Silverado* as an African American cowboy-hero.

In 1986, Glover was thrust into a controversy after he appeared in Steven Spielberg's screen version of Alice Walker's 1983 Pulitzer Prize-winning novel, *The Color Purple*. The story takes place in Georgia in 1909 and concerns a vulnerable young woman, Celie (Whoopi Goldberg) whose cruel husband, known for most of the tale simply as "Mister," abuses her and separates her from her beloved sister. As Celie is exploited for housework and child-rearing, Mister carries on an affair with a blues singer, Shug Avery. Though the film was nominated for 11 Academy Awards, critical reaction was mixed, with some carrying the opinion that Spielberg made a feel-good picture out of a dark, dramatic tale. Also, a heated debate ensued about African American stereotypes, with Glover's character at the center. A *People* writer noted that Spielberg was accused of creating "a portrait of the black man as a sadistic, sexually abusive ogre," but Glover disagreed, stating in the article, "Mister was an adequate representation of one particular story. He's a product of his past and his present and I think we showed that he has some capabilities for changing. It was a complex, multidimensional role." However, he did not denounce those who felt otherwise. "It's important for the NAACP and other organizations to question the film," he remarked in *People*. "It makes us actors more conscious of what we're doing. And that's all positive."

Following *The Color Purple*, Glover teamed up with Mel Gibson in 1987's classic action-suspense romp, *Lethal Weapon*. One of the biggest hits of the year, the movie established a new "buddy picture" formula, with Glover playing Roger Murtaugh, a homicide detective and stable family man, opposite Mel Gibson as Martin Riggs, a loose cannon with little regard for danger to the point of being suicidal. This reversed the racial stereotypes previously rampant in Hollywood and introduced a duo with a winning chemistry. Glover's straight man persona was a perfect foil to the comic and energetic antics of Gibson. Though Glover had made big films before, *Lethal Weapon* firmly established him as a star. Two years later, *Lethal Weapon 2* proved that sequels do not have to be stale rehashes, winning positive reaction and big box-office sales.

In 1990 Glover was the star as well as executive producer of *To Sleep with Anger*, directed by the noted Charles Burnett. Though it fared poorly at the box office, some critics consider it one of Glover's finest performances. In it, he plays Harry Mention, a slick, superstitious con man from the Deep South who visits some old friends in Los Angeles. Emotions run deep as he stirs up trouble in the family, and it is suggested that Harry may even be the devil himself. After that, Glover in 1991 was praised for his portrayal of Simon, the diligent and moral tow-truck driver in the well-received *Grand Canyon*. After that, *Lethal Weapon 3* came out in 1993, landing him an MTV Movie Award, along with costar Gibson, and beating the box-office sales for either of the first two. Glover also played in *Bopha!*, 1993; *Angels in the Outfield*, 1994; *Operation Dumbo Drop*, 1995; and *Gone Fishin'*, 1997.

Meanwhile, Glover was active in television as well. After a stint in the ABC movie *Face of Rage*, he portrayed the still-imprisoned Nelson Mandela, who would later become president of South Africa, in the 1986 PBS movie *Mandela*. For this role, he won an Image Award from the National Association for the Advancement of Colored People (NAACP) in 1988. He also had roles in the miniseries *Chiefs*, 1983, and in 1989 appeared in the noted *Lonesome Dove*, in which he played an African American cowboy, and *Queen*, written by Alex Haley of *Roots* fame. Also, in the 1989 HBO movie *Dead Man Out*, he played a psychiatrist trying to treat a mentally ill murderer so that the government can institute the death penalty for him. He also hosted a number of episodes of the children's show *Storybook Classics* in the late 1980s and early 1990s, and has appeared in episodes of *Lou Grant*, *Gimme a Break*, *Hill Street Blues*, and *B.J. and the Bear*.

Five years after the third *Lethal Weapon* was released, Glover and Gibson were paired for yet another sequel, *Lethal Weapon 4*. Initial reaction to the idea was dubious. Critics doubted that the storyline could be freshened up, and pointed to the actors' advancing age as an unbelievable element in the plot. An *Entertainment Weekly* writer remarked, "[Gibson and Glover are] still very attractive men, to be sure, but it's distracting to worry about their coronary health while they're being battered and shot at in the course of a day's work. Shouldn't they just cash out and discuss pension plans?" Audiences apparently did not concur, as *Lethal Weapon 4* surpassed opening-weekend revenues of the first three, reaping $34 million upon release.

Glover met his wife, jazz singer Asake Bomani, when they were both students at San Francisco State. She later became an art gallery manager. The couple has a daughter, Mandisa, and they live in a three-story Victorian home in San Francisco that they renovated during the 1980s. It is located just blocks from where Glover grew up. They also own a small cottage an hour from the city on a chardonnay vineyard. The six-foot, four-inch distinguished-looking actor counts his parents and grandparents as his major role models, and he sees himself as being an important role model for African Americans because of his high-profile status. He has been inducted into Black Filmmakers Hall of Fame, and in March of 1998, he was named celebrity spokesperson for United Nations development projects. Glover takes into account his image with every Hollywood project he undertakes. "I have to be careful about the parts I take," he commented to Belkin in the *New York Times*. "Given how this industry has dealt with people like me, the parts I take have to be political choices." Glover added, "[Kids are] watching me. That's a responsibility."

Sources

On-line

"Danny Glover," Internet Movie Database web site, http://www.imdb.com (July 7, 1998).

Books

Contemporary Black Biography, Volume 1, Gale Research, 1992.
Contemporary Theatre, Film and Television, Volume 12, Gale Research, 1994.

Periodicals

Chicago Tribune, March 8, 1987.
Dallas Morning News, November 27, 1997, p. 9C.
Ebony, March 1986, p. 82.
Entertainment Weekly, June 12, 1992, pp. 22, 26; July 17, 1998, p. 56; July 24, 1998, p. 54.
In Style, July 1, 1998, p. 180.
New York Times, January 26, 1986, section 2, p. 21.
People, March 10, 1986, p. 102.
Washington Post, December 18, 1985, p. D1.

—*Geri Speace*

Jean-Luc Godard

Filmmaker

Born December 3, 1930, in Paris, France; son of Paul (a doctor) and Odile (Monad) Godard; married Anna Karina, 1961 (divorced); married Anne Wiazemsky, 1967. *Education:* Received degree in ethnology from the Sorbonne, c. early 1950s.

Addresses: *Office*—26 Ave. Pierre 1er de Serbie, 75116 Paris, France; and 15 rue du Nord, 1180 Roulle, Switzerland.

Career

Filmmaker, screenwriter, actor, and critic.

Awards: Golden Lion, Venice Film Festival, 1983, for *Prenom Carmen* (also known as *First Name: Carmen*).

Sidelights

Jean-Luc Godard may be one of cinema's greatest names, but his films remain consistently abstruse and unseen by mainstream audiences. This is a situation the French-Swiss screenwriter, director, and occasional performer most likely prefers. "Godard's work exhibits his egg-headedness to the point where it has got people scared," opined Ian Cameron in *The Films of Jean-Luc Godard* as far back as 1967. Later critics cited the years prior to this as Godard's most masterful period, when he and other young French directors broke new ground in what came to be known as cinema's New Wave movement, hallmarked by fresh conceptualization and technical tricks that challenged viewers' perceptions. Though a true Hollywood out-

Archive Photos

sider vociferously critical of directors like Steven Spielberg, Godard has always paid homage to American film's golden era by including fleeting references to its bygone works—a poster on the wall, or a bit of dialogue—in his own films. In turn, Godard has influenced a new generation of filmmakers. Elements of his style—the arch dialogue, the quirky camera work—can be seen in the films of Quentin Tarantino, Gregg Araki, and John Woo, among others.

Godard was born in Paris in 1930, but grew up in Switzerland. He attended school there in Nyon, and as a young man returned to Paris for his university education. He studied ethnology at the Sorbonne, the University of Paris, but also experienced the heady intellectual and freewheeling spirit of the Latin Quarter, the Parisian neighborhood that is home to the Sorbonne and its students. His primary interests were in theater and the written word, but "little by little the cinema began to interest me more than the rest," Godard told Jean Collet in *Jean-Luc Godard*. He began frequenting the Cine-Club du Quartier Latin, where he became friends with Francois Truffaut, Eric Rohmer, and Jacques Rivette. Like Godard, the other three would also achieve fame as the most influential of France's postwar filmmakers. The group skipped their classes for visits to the Cinematheque Francaise,

France's museum of film with its steady program of classic works. "We systematically saw everything there was to see," Godard told Collet.

With Rohmer and Rivette, Godard co-founded *La Gazette du Cinema* in 1950, which published their criticism of mainstream French films and their directors. It survived only five issues. Godard had yet to make his own film. "I had ideas, but they were absolutely ridiculous," he commented to Collet, and instead acted in the short works his friends were making in order to observe and learn. In 1954 Godard made his first foray into directing with *Operation Beton*, a short film centered around the construction of a dam ("beton" means concrete); Godard had worked as a laborer on the very project in order to save the money to make the film.

With his next short, 1955's *Une Femme Coquette*, comes evidence of Godard's interest in experimentation—the hand-held camera, jump-cutting from one scene to another, and other quirks which would later become hallmarks of his style are manifest here. By 1956 Godard was writing regularly for France's respected journal of film criticism, *Le Cahiers du Cinema*, and becoming well-known for his polemics on mainstream filmmakers. He directed a project from after a script by Rohmer, *Tous les Garcons s'appellent Patrick* (title means "All Boys Are Called Patrick"), in 1957; the following year's short *Charlotte et son Jules* was both written and directed by Godard. He also appeared briefly, but its real star was a young French actor with a swagger, Jean-Paul Belmondo.

The year 1959 marks the formal birth of France's Nouvelle Vague (New Wave) cinema, when Godard, Truffaut, Rohmer and the others obtained the means to make the quirky, unconventional films they desired. Perhaps Godard's most famous film, and considered his first full-length feature, was made that same year and realized New Wave's concepts memorably. *A Bout de souffle* (also known as *Breathless*) premiered in March of 1960 and was an immediate sensation. It pioneered the use of hand-held cameras, filming at actual, recognizable locations, and most radically, was shot with the barest of script. *Breathless* made stars of Belmondo and his co-star, American actress Jean Seberg, who each appear as entirely vacuous characters, seemingly roused only by images from pop culture.

In *Breathless*'s famous opening shot, Seberg's character, an American student living in Paris, is walking down the Champs-Elysees selling the *New York Herald Tribune*. She encounters her intermittent boyfriend, Belmondo's handsome thug who has just arrived in Paris to hide out from the authorities after a shootout in the countryside with police. Though there is talk of the two fleeing to Italy, and a hint that she may be pregnant, she realizes that Belmondo is wanted for killing a cop, and in the end she turns him in. When Godard began the film, it was almost a freeform experiment, as he said in a 1962 interview in *Le Cahiers du Cinema*. "I had written the first scene, and for the rest I had a pile of notes for each scene. I said to myself, this is terrible. I stopped everything. Then I thought: in a single day, if one knows how to go about it, one should be able to complete a dozen takes. Only instead of planning ahead, I shall invent at the last minute."

Godard's next film, 1960's *Le Petit Soldat* ("The Little Soldier") was banned by the French government. At the time, France had been fighting a nationalist uprising in its North African colony of Algeria for several years, and *Le Petit Soldat* is set amidst this political backdrop. It chronicles the dilemma plaguing a right-wing terrorist assigned to kill a journalist sympathetic to the Arab cause; instead he falls in love with an operative for the other side, the Algerian liberation movement. "The burning political issue in France at that moment, the Algerian war, *Le Petit Soldat* addressed with an implicative urgency summed up in the image of a hesitant assassin walking behind his victim with a large pointed pistol along a crowded street without attracting anybody's notice—a startling image of the daily unbelievability of political violence," wrote Gilberto Perez in the *Nation* of the film and its message.

In 1961 Godard married the female lead of *Le Petit Soldat*, Anna Karina. She went on to play several leading roles in his subsequent works: she was the exotic dancer who wants a child from her unwilling boyfriend in 1961's *Une Femme est une Femme* ("A Woman Is a Woman"). In 1962's *Vivre sa Vie* ("My Life to Live") she was a record-shop clerk who drifts into prostitution for extra money with predictably disastrous consequences. In these and subsequent films of the decade, Godard perfected the signature elements of his work. The theme of alienation is prevalent in his films: Godard's protagonist is nearly always an outsider of some sort or at odds with "normal" (i.e., bourgeois) society. The techniques Godard and his camera operators developed were similarly revolutionary: in some cases, the camera would follow a character walking down a street for minutes on end—virtually unheard-of experimentalism at the time. Godard also had no qualms about confounding viewers with nearly inaudible dialogue.

Une Femme mariee ("A Married Woman"), released in 1964, typified the absence-of-plot style that Godard came to favor. It chronicles a twenty-four hour period in the life of a bored French fashion editor, and serves as a commentary on the seductive power of advertising imagery. The alienation of bourgeois society was a theme continued in *Pierrot le Fou*, a 1965 release that starred Belmondo as a man who escapes his tedious life with his criminal-minded mistress, played by Karina. *Alphaville*, released the same year, was Godard's foray into science fiction. The film's hero is Lemmy Caution, played by American actor Eddie Constantine. Caution is posing as a journalist for a paper comically titled "Figaro-Pravda"—in the 1960s, the leading papers of France and the Soviet Union, respectively. He arrives in bleak Alphaville in a Ford Galaxy to track down the scientist in charge of Alpha-60, the computer that controls Alphaville and robs its citizens of individuality. Called at times Godard's only optimistic film, in the end Caution falls in love with the scientist's daughter and the pair flee.

> *"After 40 years, Godard can still astonish and amuse in the cinematic shorthand he virtually created,"* wrote **Time's** *Richard Corliss.*

Increasing evidence of Godard's left-leaning politics came with the 1967 film *La Chinoise*, but his real politicization occurred with the 1968 student riots in France, a week of street and labor unrest that galvanized the entire country and brought it to a virtual standstill. The following year, Godard released *Un Film comme les autres*, parts of which—interviews with workers at a car factory, for instance—were shot during the days of protest. At this point Godard began to make short films in 16mm he called *cine-tracts*, which crystallized his radical political views and offered up a heavy dose of propaganda; they are almost like commercials for a revolution. He also became involved with the militant Dziga Vertov group, who would finance many of his works of this era.

Another famous Godard work from these days was 1970's *One Plus One*, described by some critics as one of his dullest cinematic experiments. To make it, he traveled to England immediately after the May 1968 demonstrations, and in the middle of nearly three months of filming a movie that basically showed the behind-the-scenes genesis of the Rolling Stones song "Sympathy for the Devil," band member Brian Jones was arrested, and production was held up by both fire and rain. "The result was Godard's most disjointed film to date," noted *The Oxford Companion to Film*. Godard also journeyed to the Czechoslovak capital of Prague to shoot *Pravda* ("truth" in Russian), which depicted the nation in the year since invading Russian tanks had arrived to quell a democratic uprising.

Godard was involved in a serious car accident in 1971, and for a time ceased to make standard-format films. He was still a political rebel, however. In the 1972 short *Letter to Jane*, he lets loose a 45-minute invective against American actor and activist Jane Fonda, then known for her similarly leftist politics. In the film, Godard discusses a photograph of her published in a French newspaper. "The narration calls attention to her facial expression which, Godard claims, differs from that of a North Vietnamese soldier in the background because she is the product of a jaded, capitalist society," according to *The Oxford Companion to Film*. Rather than full-length feature films, much of what Godard produced over the next few years were video collaborations with his partner Anne-Marie Mieville. These include *Numero deux*, filmed in a television studio and ostensibly intent on examining relationships within a traditional family, but what instead occurs is that Godard "makes explicit the relationship between home video and pornography—the fetishization of the primal scene," wrote Amy Taubin in the *Village Voice*.

By 1980 Godard returned to longer films with *Sauve qui peut (la vie)* (titled *Every Man for Himself* for its American debut). Over the next few years he made several acclaimed works, including *Prenom Carmen* (also known as *First Name: Carmen*) and *Je Vous Salue, Marie* ("Hail Mary"). This latter work was a retelling of the story of the Virgin Mary and the immaculate conception that received a great deal of publicity from Roman Catholic groups objecting to its nudity and sexual content. In 1987, Godard released his modern-day urban version of the Shakespearean family drama, *King Lear*. In the film, Burgess Meredith plays the doomed monarch, and Molly Ringwald his daughter Cordelia; Woody Allen also shows up. *Time's* Richard Corliss called it "Godard's most infuriating, entertaining pastiche in two decades."

Godard contributed a segment to *Aria*, a 1988 film conceived as a series of vignettes based on well-known opera works. The following year he released parts one and two of an ongoing video-essay project, *Histoire(s) du Cinema*. Typically Godard, the quintessential anti-film, *Histoire(s)* blends bits and pieces from hundreds of films into a critique on the art form itself and a look at its relation to society. Katherine Dieckmann, writing in *Art in America*, called it "an expansive, densely layered, elegiac treatise on the fate of cinema." The title, which can mean either "history" or "story" in French, also serves to point out how filmgoers are beguiled by the false (the story) rather than the real (actual history), "and Godard struggles to expose how cinema's capacity to seduce and lull implicates it in certain atrocities of this century," Dieckmann wrote. In *Histoire(s)*, she noted, "gritty newsreel footage of war mingles with an image of the 20th Century Fox logo and its sweeping klieg lights, with the none-too-covert message that these forms of spectacle aren't completely separate."

Two Godard films were released in 1990: *Nouvelle vague* ("New Wave"), a pastoral work filmed in the Swiss countryside, and *Allemagne annee 90 neuf zero* (also known as *Germany Year 90 Nine Zero*). Here Godard offers a sequel of sorts to Alphaville, set in a newly reunited Germany. Critics had once compared the bleak urban future-world of the 1965 film to the real East Berlin; in the later work, Lemmy Caution tours the actual Berlin. In 1992, New York's Museum of Modern Art feted Godard with a retrospective of his work; not surprisingly, he did not attend his scheduled appearance, ostensibly because he was in the midst of finishing his next work, *Helas pour moi*. The 1993 film starred Gerard Depardieu in the tale of the Greek deity Zeus and his transformation into human shape. *JLG/JLG*, released in 1995, shows Godard alone in a series of interviews. Some of it takes place in Switzerland, where the filmmaker has a home in Roulle with a large video studio and editing facilities.

Godard's 1963 film, *Le Mepris* ("Contempt"), was re-released in 1997. In this work, French actor Brigitte Bardot plays a woman married to a screenwriter, a man hired to adapt the Greek literary saga *The Odyssey*. Famed German moviemaker Fritz Lang plays the actual director of the fake film. Bardot hates her husband, a weak-willed type caught between Lang, who wants to remain faithful to the original story, and a crass American producer played by Jack Palance who wants nudity and mermaids. Godard's actual film had been partly bankrolled by a well-known Hollywood executive whom he hated, and Palance's character is an evident mockery of the real-life producer. The film was done in only 149 shots.

The year 1997 also marked the release of another work to American filmgoers, *For Ever Mozart*. Shot in 1995 in Sarajevo, Godard again makes another film-within-a-film about a movie crew attempting to get their job done while battling the moral bankruptcy they feel all around, an after-effect of the former Yugoslavia's years-long civil war. "After 40 years, Godard can still astonish and amuse in the cinematic shorthand he virtually created," wrote *Time*'s Corliss in reviewing *For Ever Mozart*. The critic lauded Godard's "encyclopedic wit, the glamour of his imagery, the doggedness of a man who won't give up on modernism. His crabby films are, in truth, breathlessly romantic—because he keeps searching for first principles in the pettiest human affairs. Godard gazes at the intimate and finds the infinite."

Selected filmography

Operation Beton (short), 1954.
Une Femme Coquette (short), 1955.
Tous les Garcons s'appellent Patrick ("All Boys Are Called Patrick"), 1957
Charlotte et son Jules (short), 1958.
Une Histoire d'Eau (short), 1958.
A Bout de souffle ("Breathless"), 1960.
Le Petit Soldat, 1960.
Une Femme est une Femme ("A Woman Is a Woman"), 1961.
Les Sept Peches capitaux ("The Seven Capital Sins"; director of "La Paresse" [Laziness] segment), 1961.
Vivre sa Vie ("My Life to Live"), 1962.
Le Mepris ("Contempt"), 1963.
Les Carabiniers, 1963.
Bande a part ("Band of Outsiders"), 1964.
Les Plus belles escroqueries du monde, 1964.
Une Femme mariee ("A Married Woman"), 1964.
Reportage sur Orly (short), 1964.
Alphaville, 1965.
Pierrot le Fou, 1965.
L'Espion ("The Defector"), 1966.
Made in U.S.A., 1966.
Masculine-Feminine, 1966.
Deux ou trois choses que je sais d'elle ("Two or Three Things I Know about Her"), 1966.
Loin du Vietnam ("Far from Vietnam"), 1967.
La Chinoise, 1967.
Le Week-End, 1967.
Le Gai Savoir, 1968.
Un Film comme les autres, 1969.
British Sounds, 1969.
Pravda, 1969.
Lotte in Italia ("Struggle in Italy"), 1969.
Le Vent d'est ("Wind from the East"), 1969.
Jusqu'a la victoire ("'Til Victory"), 1970.
One Plus One, 1970.
Vladimir et Rosa, 1970.

1 A.M./One American Movie, 1971.
Letter to Jane, 1972.
Tout va bien, 1972.
Comment ca va, 1975.
Ici et ailleurs, 1975.
Numero Deux ("Number Two"), 1975.
Sauve qui peut (la vie) (released in England under title
     Slow Motion; in the United States as *Every Man for*
     Himself), 1980.
Passion, 1982.
Prenom Carmen ("First Name: Carmen"), 1983.
Detective, 1985.
Je Vous Salue, Marie ("Hail Mary"), 1985.
Grandeur et decadence d'un petit commerce de cinema,
     1986.
King Lear, 1987.
Soigne ta droite, 1987.
Aria ("Armide" segment), 1988.
Histoire(s) du Cinema, 1989 (ongoing).
Nouvelle vague ("New Wave"), 1990.
Allemagne annee 90 neuf zero ("Germany Year 90 Nine
     Zero"), 1991.
Contre l'oubli, 1992.
Helas pour moi, 1993.
JLG/JLG, 1995.
For Ever Mozart, 1995.

Selected writings

Godard on Godard, Viking Press, 1972.

Sources

Books

Bawden, Liz-Anne, editor, *The Oxford Companion to*
     Film, Oxford University Press, 1976.
Collet, Jean, *Jean-Luc Godard,* Crown, 1970.
The Films of Jean-Luc Godard, Studio Vista, 1967.
Kreidl, John, *Jean-Luc Godard,* Twayne, 1980.

Periodicals

Art in America, October 1993, pp. 65-67.
ARTnews, February 1993, pp. 57-58.
Le Cahiers du Cinema, 1962.
Film Comment, March 1996, pp. 26-30, pp. 31-41.
Nation, February 18, 1991, pp. 209-212.
Time, February 1, 1988; August 4, 1997.
Village Voice, November 24, 1992, p. 45; July 1, 1997, p.
     89.

—*Carol Brennan*

Gong Li

Actress

Born December 31, 1965, in Shenyang, Liaoning, China; daughter of two university professors; married Ooi Hoe-Seong (a businessman), February 15, 1996. *Education:* Central Drama Academy, Beijing, China, graduated, 1989.

Addresses: *Office*—c/o Miramax Films, 375 Greenwich St., New York, NY 10013.

Career

Central Drama Academy, Beijing, China, teacher; actress in films including *Red Sorghum,* 1987; *Codename Cougar,* 1989; *The Empress Dowager,* 1989; *The Terra-Cotta Warrior,* 1989; *Ju Dou,* 1990; *The Banquet,* 1991; *Back to Shanghai,* 1991; *Raise the Red Lantern,* 1991; *The Story of Qiu Ju,* 1992; *Mary from Beijing,* 1992; *Flirting Scholar,* 1993; *The Painter,* 1993; *Farewell My Concubine,* 1993; *8 Guardians of Buddhism,* 1994; *The Great Conqueror's Concubine,* 1994; *To Live,* 1994; *Shanghai Triad,* 1995; *Temptress Moon,* 1996; *Chinese Box,* 1997; *The Assassin,* 1998.

Awards: Venice Film Festival, Volpi Cup, 1992, for *The Story of Qiu Ju;* New York Film Critics Circle Award, best supporting actress, 1993, for *Farewell My Concubine;* Cannes Film Festival, best actress award, 1994, for *To Live;* French Government, Officer des Arts et Lettres award for contributions to the cinema, 1998.

Sidelights

In America, Chinese actress Gong Li has not become a household name, but in her own country, the most populous in the world, she stands out among 1.2 billion citizens as one of their most revered public figures. As the lead actress in controversial films, some of which have been banned in her native land for their criticisms of Chinese society, Gong Li has exposed cultural injustices and come to personify the fight against oppression. Scarlet Cheng noted in *Premiere,* "To millions of Chinese filmgoers, Gong represents the modern spirit, a beautiful female warrior fighting history, sexism, and bureaucracy for a chance to live in freedom." Her films *Ju Dou, Raise the Red Lantern,* and *Farewell My Concubine* have all been nominated for Academy Awards for best foreign language films; *Farewell My Concubine* shared the top prize, Palm d'Or, at the Cannes Film Festival; and *To Live* won the Cannes Grand Jury Prize. An ongoing romance with the director of many of her films also brought a wave of publicity to the rising star, who, after an inauspicious debut, went on to radiate in a quick succession of his works, which are known for their stylized appearance and moving drama.

Gong Li was born on December 31, 1965, in Shenyang, in the province of Liaoning in northeastern China, shortly before the onset of the Cultural Revolution (1966-76), a period of harsh oppression of intellectuals. Her mother and father were economics professors who were later forced to work in a factory. The couple had four children before Gong Li, and her mother even had her tubes tied, but became pregnant a number of years later. When she was young, Gong Li's brothers and sisters were separated from the family and sent to work in the fields, a practice called "re-education" by Chinese leaders. Luckily, Gong Li was too young and escaped such a fate. Instead, she went through school and considered becoming a kindergarten teacher before a high school teacher suggested she consider attending Beijing's Central Drama Academy. In 1985, she passed an extensive series of auditions and tests, ignoring her parents' warnings that she was not pretty enough.

Gong Li met prominent Chinese director Zhang Yimou while she was a 22-year-old student at the academy and he was about 15 years older. He cast her in the drama *Red Sorghum* in 1988, and they fell in love. Zhang ended up leaving his wife and child for a romance with the young actress. Together, they would create such impressive cinematic works that Chinese fans hounded them incessantly, requiring them to move to new homes frequently to escape the attention. The fame was also due, however, to an element of notoriety. Their affair was followed closely and frowned upon by many in the conservative culture, as Zhang Yimou was not actually granted a divorce until a few years later.

However, Gong Li's introduction as the female lead in *Red Sorghum,* about a woman who is sold into marriage and resists, was initially overlooked, despite the film's box-office success in China and its Golden Bear Award for best film at the Berlin Film Festival in 1988. Howard Feinstein, writing in the *New York Times*, remarked, "In Chinese, hua ping, actually a flower vase, is a pejorative term for a beautiful but empty actress. Some Chinese-speaking moviegoers reportedly applied the words to Gong Li after her debut in ... *Red Sorghum*." She swept away any skepticism after her next two films with Zhang Yimou, 1990's *Ju Dou* and 1991's *Raise the Red Lantern*. Meanwhile, she also worked on more commercial vehicles, including *The Empress Dowager* with prominent veteran director Lihan Xiang, who told Gong Li, "You will become an international star," according to Kevin Thomas in the *Los Angeles Times*.

Gong Li's moving performances, however, did not immediately lift her to star status in China, mainly because filmgoers were cautious to praise her in light of the government's disapproval. *Ju Dou,* about a woman who initiates an affair with her husband's nephew and urges him to kill her abusive spouse, was banned, ostensibly for its immoral content. Critics,

though, believed that the Chinese government was more upset with the symbolism; the old husband represented the government, while the wife stood for a political uprising. Later, the film was nominated for China's version of the Oscar, but the film officials were later punished by having to write essays critical of themselves. Then, *Raise the Red Lantern*, 1991, concerned a woman whose family makes her marry a wealthy man who already has three wives. The women compete with one another for the man's favors and thus control within the home. This, too, was banned in China, but enthusiastically received in the West.

Zhang Yimou and Gong Li's next project, *The Story of Qiu Ju*, won acceptance by the Chinese authorities who then released the two previously banned movies. Though the story is critical of Chinese bureaucracy, the government appreciated that it portrayed peasants in a positive light. In The *Story of Qiu Ju*, Gong Li plays the headstrong pregnant wife of a farmer who is unjustly injured by the village leader. To prepare for the role, the actress lived in a rural area for two months to study the mannerisms and language of the residents. Unlike some of her other roles, where she played elegant, upscale characters, this part called for her to bundle up in layers of padding and trudge around looking frumpy and humble. However, she later told Cheng in *Interview* that Qiu Ju (pronounced cho-ju) was her favorite role because the character is "able to fight for what she wants because she lives in a modern society." For her performance, Gong Li won the Volpi Cup for best actress at the Venice Film Festival in 1992.

In her next notable film, Gong Li, this time with director Chen Kaige, again offended the Communist leaders with *Farewell My Concubine*, which shared the 1993 Palm d'Or at Cannes for best film (along with Australian director Jane Campion's *The Piano*) and landed her a New York Film Critics Circle Award for best supporting actress. In the film, Gong Li portrays a prostitute who marries an opera singer, and the story is intertwined with Chinese history throughout the twentieth century, from the Japanese invasion in the 1930s to the Communist victory in 1949 and eventually the Cultural Revolution and its results. After that, Gong Li teamed again with Zhang Yimou for the 1994 epic picture *To Live*, a melodrama that follows a family over the course of three decades. In this story as well, the country's history is reflected through the characters, and once more provoked the authorities, who banned it. In the *New York Times*, Carolyn James commented, "Gong Li is, as always, a powerful heroine," and the film took the Grand Jury Prize in 1994 at Cannes.

In 1995, Gong Li and Zhang Yimou made *Shanghai Triad*, a 1930s gangster film in which Gong Li plays a crime king's mistress. Plastered with loud makeup and sequins, her chorus-girl role is "a desperate, larger-than-life character, at once a wicked witch and a queen," remarked Adina Hoffman in the *Jerusalem Post*. After that, in 1996 Gong Li made *Temptress Moon*, about a woman in love with two men. It was nominated for an award at Cannes. Surprisingly, the admired actress freely admits that she only reads her scripts one time before showing up for the shoot, noting that it prevents her from giving a diluted and wooden delivery. Stirring up interest in Hollywood, Gong Li told John Powers in *Vogue*, "The one thing that would get me to work in the West is a good director and a good script. But I will never work outside and stay outside. I'll always come back to China." She began taking English lessons in 1995, but about the same time, turned down an offer to star in *Heat* with Al Pacino (one of her favorite American actors) and Robert DeNiro because she was not allowed to read the script beforehand.

In 1997 Gong Li finally released her first English-language film, *Chinese Box*, a love story that takes place just before Hong Kong reverts back to Chinese rule in 1997, after being British for 156 years. Starring opposite Jeremy Irons, Gong Li had a language coach help her with her lines. However, she still did not have to travel to the United States, since the movie was set in and shot in Hong Kong—a good break for her, since she remained fluent only in Mandarin and had to speak her English lines phonetically (media interviews all along had been held through translators). After that, she was cast in another Chen Kaige film, *The Assassin*, in which she plays an emperor's courtesan in ancient times. She told Cheng in *The World & I* that she would be interested in doing more Western films if the parts were good. "They have some fine actors and actresses, good budgets, but the roles they create for Asians are just too superficial, too unnatural. It's clear they don't understand Chinese character at all. That kind of thing isn't at all interesting to me."

Gong Li left Zhang Yimou in 1995, reportedly because he refused to marry her. On February 15, 1996, she married a wealthy executive at the British American Tobacco Company, Ooi Hoe-Song, whom she met at a car race. The couple rents a five-bedroom home in the hills in Hong Kong, and they also live part-time in Beijing and Singapore. Ooi Hoe-Song has a young daughter from a previous marriage. In addition to her films, Gong Li appears often in Chinese advertisements and is her nation's representative for L'Oreal cosmetics. The athletically built actress never watches her diet, but does 150 sit-ups each day. Known for being "temperamental" and "demanding," according to Howard Feinstein in *GQ*, Gong Li told Evelyn Chi'en in *A. Magazine*, "Since I was little, I was strong-willed and independent." When Scarlet Cheng in *Interview* asked how she found her self-confidence, Gong Li replied, "I live my way, that's it. Every human has frustrations and unhappinesses, but hopefully they pass."

Sources

Online

"Li Gong," Internet Movie Database web site, http://us.imdb.com (August 12, 1998).

Periodicals

A. Magazine, June 30, 1994; January 31, 1996.
Entertainment Weekly, January 27, 1995, p. 14.
Esquire, December 1994, p. 38.
GQ, October 1995, p. 124.
Independent on Sunday, March 3, 1997, p. 14.
Interview, May 1997, p. 54.
Jerusalem Post, May 31, 1996.
Los Angeles Times, January 30, 1996, p. F1.
Newsday, November 13, 1994, p. 14.
New York Times, February 25, 1991, p. C11; March 20, 1992, p. C18; April 11, 1993, sec.2, p. 22; October 8, 1993, p. C22; September 30, 1994, p. C30.
People, April 27, 1998, p. 135.
Premiere, March 1996, p. 74.
Reuters, February 23, 1996.
USA Today, February 8, 1994, p. 10.
Vogue, January 1996, p. 66.
World & I, January 1, 1998, p. 83.

—*Geri Speace*

Pam Grier

Actress

Born Pamala Suzette Grier, May 26, 1949, in Winston-Salem, NC; daughter of Clarence Ransom (a U.S. Air Force maintenance mechanic) and Gwendolyn S. (a registered nurse; maiden name, Samuels) Grier. *Education:* Attended Metropolitan State College, Denver, CO.

Addresses: *Agent*—The Irv Schecter Company, 9300 Wilshire Blvd., Beverly Hills, CA 90212. *Office*—Actress, 9000 Sunset Blvd., #1200, Los Angeles, CA 90069.

Career

Worked as a switchboard operator at a talent agency and American International Pictures, c. 1969. Actress. Film appearances include *The Big Bird Cage*, 1969; *Beyond the Valley of the Dolls*, 1969; *The Big Doll House*, 1971; *Cool Breeze*, 1972; *Hit Man*, 1972; *Twilight People*, 1972; *Women in Cages*, 1972; *Black Mama, White Mama*, 1973; *Scream, Blacula, Scream*, 1973; *Coffy*, 1973; *Foxy Brown*, 1974; *The Arena*, 1975; *Bucktown*, 1975; *Friday Foster*, 1975; *Sheba, Baby*, 1975; *Drum*, 1976; *Twilight People*, 1977; *Greased Lightning*, 1977; *Fort Apache: The Bronx*, 1981; *Something Wicked This Way Comes*, 1983; *Tough Enough*, 1983; *Stand Alone*, 1985; *On the Edge*, 1986; *The Vindicator*, 1986; *The Allnighter*, 1987; *Tough Enough*, 1987; *Above the Law*, 1987; *Class of 1999*, 1989; *The Package*, 1989; *Bill and Ted's Bogus Journey*, 1991; *Posse*, 1994; *Serial Killer*, 1995; *Mars Attacks*, 1996; *Escape from L.A.*, 1996; *Original Gangstas*, 1996; *Fakin' Da Funk*, 1997; *Jackie Brown*, 1997, *Strip Search*, 1997, and *Woo*, 1997. Television appearances include *Roots: The Next Generations*, 1979; *Miami Vice*, 1985; *Crime Story*, 1986; *The Cosby Show*, 1987; *Love Boat,* *Badge of the Assassin, The Elizabeth Morgan Story, Knots Landing, Frank's Place,* and *Monsters.* Stage appearances include *Fool for Love, Frankie and Johnny at the Clair de Lune,* and *The Piano Lesson.*

Awards: NAACP Image Award for best actress, 1986, for *Fool for Love;* National Black Theatre Festival Achievement Award and African American Film Society Achievement Award, both 1993.

Sidelights

In an industry that tends to phase out women as they get older or relegate them to watered-down roles, Pam Grier is one of the standout actresses that has never lost her sass and sex appeal, even as she approaches her fourth decade in films. Although she has worked steadily in films since her debut in 1969, her starring role in director Quentin Tarantino's *Jackie Brown* once again thrust her into the spotlight as the sharp, tough heroine with a heart. Grier made a name for herself in the 1970s as the queen of the blaxploitation genre of films, which showcased her as a beautiful and aggressive fighter for justice in urban communities. She introduced a new kind of female lead to Hollywood and thus holds a crucial place in the history of film.

Grier was born May 26, 1949, in Winston-Salem, North Carolina, the second of three children to Clarence Ransom and Gwendolyn (Samuels) Grier. Her father's job as an Air Force maintenance mechanic kept the family on the move. He was transferred to Swindon, England, and Grier spent much of her childhood in Europe until age 14, when the family returned to the United States. She claimed in a 1976 *Ebony* interview that she did not plan on becoming an actress: "I never thought of television, of fans, movie stars, signing autographs. It never crossed my mind."

The family ended up in Denver, Colorado, where Grier found it hard to get along with her peers and described the city as "rough" to Jamaica Kincaid in *Ms.* She spoke with a trace of an English accent, wore used clothing from Goodwill thrift stores, and enjoyed afternoon tea. Despite her rocky introduction to the area, she excelled in track at Smiley Junior High, and after some years, returned to the state to set up home at a ranch outside Denver. Grier told Deborah Gregory in *Essence*, "I go stir-crazy if I'm not near fresh air, the desert and mountains." She eventually applied to the Metropolitan State College in Denver and dreamed of having a career in the medical field. It was around this time that she did a stint as a Denver Broncos cheerleader and toyed with the idea of acting.

After a year of college, Grier entered the Colorado State Miss Universe beauty pageant to see if she could take home some prize money to help pay for more tuition. Black beauty contest winners were rare at the time, and she knew her chances were slim; still, she exuded confidence and came in second place. At a second contest in Colorado Springs, agent David Baumgarten—manager of the popular comedians Rowan & Martin of the television show *Laugh In*—took note. He asked her to attend acting classes and operate the office switchboard at his Agency of the Performing Arts. At first she declined his offer, not wanting to leave college, but her mother urged her on, telling her she could always return to school if things did not work out. In 1968, she moved to Los Angeles with her cousin, football player and actor Roosevelt (Rosey) Grier.

Unfortunately, the acting jobs did not pour in, so Grier took a job as a switchboard operator at the low-budget studio, American International Pictures (AIP), where she earned $25 more per week than she had at the Agency of the Performing Arts. Although she did not know how to work their larger switchboard, she went in to work early to figure it out. She also listened to calls in order to decipher the business world of making movies. Eventually, she called the B-picture king Roger Corman and asked to be cast in *The Big Bird Cage*.

He gave her a small part. During filming in the Philippines, she contracted a terrible tropical disease; her temperature reached 105 degrees. She explained to a writer for *Entertainment Weekly*, "I was in bed for four weeks. I lost my hair, I couldn't see, I couldn't walk. I was dying. The doctor actually kind of froze me to kill the cell that was in my brain, and I started getting better."

After that inglorious introduction to films, Grier went on to other minor parts in low-budget flicks, such as *Beyond the Valley of the Dolls* (1969) and *Twilight People* (1972), before capturing the lead in *Black Mama, White Mama,* a prison escape story based loosely on *The Defiant Ones,* starring Tony Curtis and Sidney Poitier. This Corman melodrama brought her some attention and spurred her on to the lead role in her first big production, *Coffy* (1972). Christopher John Farley in *Time* recalls the message that the film's poster blared: "THE BADDEST ONE-CHICK HIT-SQUAD THAT EVER HIT TOWN!" Criticized for their glorification of violence among African Americans as well as praised for their portrayals of smart, strong, and self-sufficient black characters, blaxploitation films like *Shaft* and *Superfly* were all the rage in the early 1970s. With women's rights issues making gains, audiences were ready for a female action lead as well.

In *Coffy,* Grier plays a nurse with a vendetta against the drug dealers who bring down her sister. The film is memorable for the character's particularly nasty form of punishment for the bad guys: emasculation by shotgun blast. Another one of Grier's memorable vehicles, the title of which would later be used as an homage for her big comeback film, was *Foxy Brown.* In this grass-roots justice picture, her neighborhood crime-fighting league castrates one of the main villains, and she delivers the unattached body part to the man's girlfriend in a jar. To protect herself from the woman and her guards, she whips her pistol out of the back of her Afro hairstyle after the deed in order to make a getaway.

Grier's celebrity in the 1970s led to her appearance in numerous films, including *Scream, Blacula, Scream* and the plantation melodrama *Drum.* Though the movies were mostly low-budget, Grier was an unusual spectacle in Hollywood: the bankable female lead. Her combination of tough-yet-sultry attitude led to a cover story in the feminist periodical *Ms.* as well as a photo shoot for *Playboy.* Grier's characters were especially tricky for feminist critics because, despite the objections of her image as a pinup girl, she filled a void; independent, self-confident women in Hollywood films were almost nonexistent for many decades. Jamaica Kincaid in *Ms.* derided Grier's films for being "mostly simplistic, sensational, violent, and technically faulty," but rejoiced that they represented "the only films to show us a woman who triumphs!"

Grier personally was unhappy with the sensational editing of the films as well. She complained to *Ms.* that AIP took *Coffy* and "cut it up—taking out the most important parts, like tender scenes between me and my sister. So all you see is *bang, bang, bang,* shoot 'em up tits and ass." Her characters wore revealing outfits and huge fake eyelashes, and the stories usually included her romantic involvement with a man, which also did not do much to set a new standard for complex female leads in film. However, it did sweeten up the scripts to make them more palatable for male viewers who may have been uneasy with such a strong-willed, karate-kicking, gun slinging, revenge-seeking woman, not to mention the violence toward male genitalia.

In 1977, Grier veered into conventional drama with *Greased Lightning,* costarring as the wife of actor-comedian Richard Pryor's character, who played a race-car driver. The two became romantically linked in real life as well, and he encouraged her to try new kinds of films. She began to decline work—against the advice of some who warned that her career would suffer—and though the parts tapered off, the blaxploitation genre was faltering anyway. She explained to *Los Angeles Times* writer Dennis Hunt, "I played those parts because they had women in positions of power. It was a good positive image for black women. But the films became redundant, and I don't like being redundant."

For a time, Grier pursued other interests, such as dance training, singing, and piano, and made appearances on the television shows *Roots: The Next Generations* and *Love Boat.* She was, however, out of the public eye for the most part. She was encouraged to return to acting by her friend, singer Minnie Riperton, who died of cancer. Grier went back into the business and landed a part as a drug-addled prostitute/murderer in 1981's *Fort Apache: The Bronx.* Grier immersed herself in the part, losing weight and letting her looks wither to the point where her friends were concerned. She researched the character's attitude and moves by prowling the streets. The effort did not go unnoticed; her performance was widely praised.

However, her success only led to some small parts for most of the 1980s. She appeared in the Disney screen adaptation of Ray Bradbury's fantasy-horror novel *Something Wicked This Way Comes* in 1983, for which she was cast as the Dust Witch, a beautiful belly dancer. Grier commented to Farber in *Moviegoer* that Bradbury was one of her favorite science fiction authors. Unfortunately in 1988, Grier was diagnosed with cancer and was not sure she wanted to live at times. She remarked in *Entertainment Weekly,* "My doctor gave me 18 months to live. My whole life changed." She was in treatment for two years and managed to pull out of it.

> *"All I wanted to show when I played Foxy Brown was that here was someone who was independent, who could take care of herself ... and that's a lot about me."*

Throughout the 1980s and for much of the 1990s, Grier did not snag any leading film roles, but she did have minor spots in films like *Above the Law* (1988), in which she plays Steven Seagal's partner; *Class of 1999* (1989); *The Package* (1989); *Bill and Ted's Bogus Journey,* (1991); *Posse* (1994); and *Mars Attacks,* (1996); as well as appearances on such television shows as *Miami Vice* in 1985 and *The Cosby Show* in 1987. Grier did, however, shine in her stage role in the acclaimed Sam Shepard play *Fool for Love,* which brought her an NAACP Image Award for best actress in 1986. She also purposely gained 80 pounds to act in the play *Frankie and Johnny at the Clair de Lune* in 1990. She told Michael Keaton in *Interview,* "That was hard because people have such a prejudice against overweight women. I have never been so ostracized and criticized as I was at that time."

Grier's fame still existed well into the 1990s in the realm of cult-film buffs who remembered her 1970s blaxploitation efforts, especially with the growth in popularity of 1970s pop culture nostalgia. One of her biggest fans of this type was writer/director Quentin Tarantino, who rose to success first with the gory crime film *Reservoir Dogs* in 1992 but more prominently with 1994's wildly popular and unconventional *Pulp Fiction.* Tarantino penned an adaptation of crime writer Elmore Leonard's novel *Rum Punch* specifically with Grier in mind to play the lead. He even renamed the character Jackie Brown (she was called Jackie Burke in the print version) as an homage to Grier's film *Foxy Brown,* and titled the film *Jackie Brown* as well.

Though the film was not as warmly received as director Tarantino's previous success, *Pulp Fiction,* it was generally popular and a big step for Grier's career. In *Jackie Brown*, Grier plays a middle-aged flight attendant making some extra cash running money to Mexico for a small-time gun dealer, played by Samuel L. Jackson. When the Feds catch up to them, Jackie, with the help of an understanding bail bondsman, devises an underhanded plan to steal half a million dollars from the arms dealer while managing to turn him over and make a clean getaway herself. Robert DeNiro also costarred as a burned-out ex-con.

In addition to what some call her "comeback" film, Grier has made strides in her personal life as well. Never married, she hopes to have a child with her boyfriend, record producer Kevin Evans. She maintains a rigorous fitness routine in order to keep her immune system up to fight the cancer, meditates, drinks lots of water, and eats well. She commented in *Time*, "Society says [women in their 40s] are not attractive, have no sex appeal and are thrown away. That's not true.... I feel better than I felt at 19." She also does quite a bit of volunteer work, helping with causes dealing with drug abuse and disadvantaged children.

Grier has likened the character of Jackie Brown to the spitfire character of her youth, Foxy Brown, as well as her own life, telling Keaton in *Interview*, "All I wanted to show when I played Foxy Brown was that here was someone who was independent, who could take care of herself ... and that's a lot about me. It's also a lot about who Jackie Brown is." Grier added, "Jackie [Brown] lives on her wits, and she's a woman that really has to take control of her life, which is something I'm always doing."

Sources

On-line

"Pam Grier," http://www.inetworld.net/garrick/pgbio.htm (February 10, 1998).

Books

Notable Black American Women, Gale Research, 1996.

Periodicals

Ebony, June 1974, p. 33; June 1976, p. 33.
Entertainment Weekly, December 19, 1997, p. 26.
Essence, July 1996, p. 28.
Interview, January 1998, p. 78.
Los Angeles Times, August 19, 1979, calendar section, p. 34; March 12, 1981, section 5, p. 1.
Moviegoer, May 1983.
Ms., August 1975, p. 49.
Time, December 8, 1997, p. 94.

—Geri Speace

Terry Gross

Radio producer and host

Born February 14, 1951, in Brooklyn, NY; daughter of Irving (a businessman) and Anne (Abrams) Gross; married Francis Davis, 1978. *Education:* State University of New York (SUNY) at Buffalo, B.A. in English, 1972, M. Ed. in communications, 1974.

Addresses: *Home*—Philadelphia, PA. *Office*—WHYY, 150 North Sixth St., Philadelphia, PA 19106.

Career

School teacher, Buffalo, NY, c. 1972; WBFO public radio, Buffalo, NY, host and producer, 1973-75; WHYY-FM, Philadelphia, PA, producer and host of *Fresh Air*, 1975—; *Fresh Air* distributed nationally on National Public Radio (NPR), beginning 1985; also guest host for *All Things Considered*, NPR; coanchor of *The Great Comet Crash*, PBS; and guest host for *Nightwatch*, CBS.

Awards: Ohio State Award, 1987, Corporation for Public Broadcasting Award for best live radio program, 1981, Peabody Award, 1994, all for *Fresh Air*; distinguished alumni award, SUNY at Buffalo, 1993.

Sidelights

Terry Gross is the voice and the mind behind the smart and popular *Fresh Air* program heard daily on National Public Radio (NPR). *Fresh Air* focuses mainly on cultural happenings and reviews, and features conversations with a wide array of artists, actors, writers, commentators, politicians, and other movers and shakers. Known for her insightful questions and

choice of hip yet relevant topics and guests, she is considered one of the best interviewers on the air.

Gross grew up in Brooklyn, New York, but never developed the trademark local accent. Her father owned a business in the hat-making industry, and she has a brother who went on to develop qualifying exams in optometry for the Board of Examiners. Gross enrolled in college in 1968 and participated in the social upheavals of the times, more frequently attending protests and watching experimental films than going to class at SUNY Buffalo. After graduating, the petite (5-foot, 1-inch tall) Gross was hired to teach in Buffalo's inner city, where she was "so much more used to challenging than embodying authority," remarked Edmund White in a *Vogue* interview. She was fired after six weeks.

Thanks to a roommate, Gross began volunteering at a local public radio station, WBFO, in Buffalo. She joined the staff in 1973, thanks to her abilities and her voice. White called it "well modulated but not late-night sexy, well informed but not elitist, the voice of someone who is sympathetic but not a pushover." She became the producer and host of several shows on the arts, women's issues, and public affairs, including *This Is Radio,* a daily three-hour magazine that aired live. In 1975, she went aboard WHYY in Philadelphia, Pennsylvania, where she started producing and hosting *Fresh Air,* which at that time was a daily interview and music program with a local flair. Then, in 1985, WHYY began a weekly half-hour edition of *Fresh Air,* which National Public Radio snapped up for national distribution. The show became an hour-long affair each weekday in 1987; by 1998, it was broadcast on over 190 stations to nearly two million listeners.

Since its inception, *Fresh Air* has been hailed by listeners and critics as intelligent, informative discourse. It combines cultural news, book and music reviews, and in-depth interviews with writers, artists, and other thinkers complemented by insights from critics and commentators. Guests have included singer Tony Bennett, playwright David Mamet, authors Toni Morrison and Salman Rushdie, former First Lady Nancy Reagan, and actor Nicholas Cage as well as politicians, journalists, and experts on current affairs. Though Gross gives her interviewees as much time as they want, there are a few who have not let her probe too far. White reported that *Rolling Stone* editor and publisher Jann Wenner left the studio after 2 minutes and 48 seconds, following Gross's inquiries into his subscriber list and advertisers. Lou Reed was unwilling to speak any further when she tried to get him to comment on early Velvet Underground tracks. Other guests have been quite open, such as film director Paul Bartel, who first announced that he was gay on her show.

Gross married *Atlantic Monthly* music critic Francis Davis in 1978; the couple lives in Philadelphia, but Gross admitted that much of their marriage is a phone relationship due to her busy schedule. Her efforts have not gone unnoticed. *Fresh Air* won the Ohio State Award in 1987, a Corporation for Public Broadcasting Award for best live radio program in 1981, and the prestigious Peabody Award in 1994 for its "probing questions, revelatory interviews and unusual insight." In addition to *Fresh Air,* Gross has guest hosted NPR's daily *All Things Considered.* She also co-anchored *The Great Comet Crash,* PBS, and appeared as a guest host on *Nightwatch,* CBS. In 1993, she was honored with a Distinguished Alumni Award from SUNY Buffalo.

Early in 1997, *Fresh Air* got a boost when America's largest bookseller, Barnes & Noble, became the major corporate underwriter for the program. Barnes & Noble saw it as a perfect match for reaching out to the show's literate array of listeners, and WHYY station management was happy to welcome the influx of financial support. Inaugurating the event, Gross made an appearance at Union Square in New York City to discuss how she chooses guests and reveal her best and worst interviews.

Fresh Air generally focuses on the deeper issues and is one of the reasons that Gross is generally regarded as one of the best interviewers in the business. "If you want to understand a political conflict, it helps to understand the culture in which that conflict is taking place," Gross commented on the *Fresh Air* web page at the WHYY web site. She added, "When there is a crisis in a foreign country, we sometimes call up that country's leading novelist or filmmaker to get that cultural perspective." She also tries to get at the connections between a guest's personal life and their work. She noted in the *Utne Reader* that the task is becoming increasingly difficult, since celebrities are so often humiliated in the press. "When I interview celebrities now, I find that their defenses are up the moment the mike is turned on," she commented. Gross, on the other hand, respects her guests and tries to make them comfortable enough to confide things to her. "What puts someone on guard isn't necessarily the fear of being 'found out,'" she expressed on the *Fresh Air* web page. "It sometimes is just the fear of being misunderstood."

Gross, in a role reversal, was the subject of the interview in the *Utne Reader* in 1997. In the article, she revealed the long list of periodicals that she subscribes to in order to keep up on the day's people and events: *New Yorker, Atlantic Monthly, New Republic, Time, Vanity Fair, Columbia Journalism Review, American Journalism Review, Publisher's Weekly,* and *Pulse.* She noted that her favorite singers include Billie Holiday, Maxine Sullivan, Abbey Lincoln, Lee Wiley, Chet Baker, Tony Bennett, Frank Sinatra, and Johnny Adams, and that three of her favorite films are *Taxi Driver, The Umbrellas of Cherbourg,* and *Vertigo.*

Asked how she comes up with ideas, Gross responded in the *Utne Reader,* "I get some of my best ideas when I'm physically occupied, but my mind is free: when I'm driving the car, working on the treadmill, taking a walk." Luckily for her listeners, she seems to keep her mind flowing, despite her hectic pace. She admitted in the *Utne Reader* that her work and personal life are usually one and the same due to her full schedule and her love for her job. As she told the interviewer, "Those of us who are lucky enough to have work that we are passionate about are usually unlucky enough to have more of it than we can handle."

Sources

On-line

"About Terry Gross," WHYY web site (*Fresh Air* page), http://whyy.org/freshair (April 20, 1998).

Periodicals

Business Wire, January 15, 1997.
Utne Reader, March/April 1997, p. 94.
Vogue, May 1997, p. 160.

—*Geri Speace*

Scott Hamilton

Professional figure skater

Full name, Scott Scovell Hamilton; born August 28, 1958, in Toledo, OH; adopted son of Ernest and Dorothy (McIntosh) Hamilton. *Education:* Attended Metro State College, 1979. *Politics:* Republican.

Addresses: *Office*—4242 Van Nuys Boulevard, Sherman Oaks, CA 91403-3710.

Career

Amateur competitive career includes National Figure Skating Championships: junior men's division, first place, 1976, senior men's division, ninth place, 1977, third place, 1978, fourth place, 1979, first place, 1981-84; Mid-Western Figure Skating Championships: senior men's, third place, 1977-79; Norton Skate Championships (now Skate America): men's division, first place, 1979-82; South Atlantic Figure Skating Championships: senior men's division, first place, 1980; Eastern Figure Skating Championships: senior men's, first place, 1980-84; World Figure Skating Championships: men's division, fifth place, 1980, first place, 1981-84; Winter Olympics: men's division, fifth place, Lake Placid, NY, 1980, first place, Sarajevo, Yugoslavia, 1984; National Sports Festival Championships: first place, men's division, 1981; Nippon Hoso Kyaki Figure Skating Championships: men's division, first place, 1982; Golden Spin of Zagreb Championships: men's division, first place, 1983. Professional competitive career includes Nutrasweet/NBC World Professional Figure Skating Championships: men's division, first place, 1984 and 1986, second place 1985 and 1987-89; World Challenge Champions/ABC: men's division, second place, 1985-86. Professional

AP/Wide World Photos

performances include Ice Capades National Arena Tour, 1984-85, 1985-86; Scott Hamilton's Amateur Tour, 1986-87; Discover Card Stars On Ice Tour, 1986—; Concert on Ice, Harrah's Hotel, Lake Tahoe, Nevada, 1987, 1988; Festival on Ice National Theater Tour, 1987; Stars On Ice National Arena Tour, 1987-88, 1988-89, 1989-90; *Ice Capades with Kirk Cameron*, ABC, 1988; *A Very Special Christmas*, ABC, 1988; *An Olympic Calgary Christmas*, ABC, 1988; Scott Hamilton's Celebration of Ice, Sea World of California, 1988; *A Salute to Dorothy Hamill* (television special), 1988; Broadway on Ice National Theater Tour, 1989; *Vail Skating Special*, HBO, 1990, 1992, 1993; *A Disney Christmas On Ice* (television special), 1992; Skates of Gold I and II, 1993, 1994; *Nancy Kerrigan & Friends*, CBS, 1994. CBS commentator for a variety of figure skating competitions, 1981—, including Winter Olympics in Albertville, France, 1992, Lillehamer, Norway, 1994, and Nagano, Japan, 1998.

Awards: Figure Skating Athlete of the Year, 1981-84; Olympic Gold Medal, 1984; March of Dimes Achievement Award, 1984; Professional Skater of the Year Award, *American Skating World* (magazine), 1986; Jacques Favart Award, International Skating Union, 1988; inducted into the U.S. Olympic Hall of Fame and the World Figure Skating Hall of Fame, 1990; Spirit of Giving Award, U.S. Ice Skating Association, 1993;

Friends of Scott Hamilton Foundation named in his honor to produce skate-athons for the benefit of U.S. children's hospitals.

Sidelights

After 30 years on the ice, Olympic gold medal winner Scott Hamilton remains one of the best-loved figure skaters in the sport's history. As an amateur in the early 1980s, he became the best male figure skater in the world and helped increase the sport's emphasis on athleticism. As a professional in the 1990s, Hamilton mounted successful touring shows which contributed to the growing popularity figure skating achieved in the decade. As a television commentator, he displayed a contagious love of the sport, firsthand knowledge of its subtleties and celebrities, and a comfortable, often humorous, broadcasting style.

Hamilton's easy manner belies the hard road he has traveled and the singular determination he has demonstrated with each challenge and setback. As a child, he suffered from a rare disease which paralyzed his intestines, prevented his body from absorbing nutrients, and left him physically stunted.

In 1976 he abruptly quit figure skating, a sport he loved, because of the financial burden it placed upon his parents. Then, when he was a year out of high school, his mother died of breast cancer. Twenty years later, doctors told Hamilton he had testicular cancer. By the time it was diagnosed, the cancer had spread to his abdomen and spawned a tumor twice the size of a grapefruit.

With typical determination and a remarkably positive outlook, Hamilton overcame the cancer and quickly returned to a busy career skating for sold-out crowds in his own touring ice show and serving as a television commentator at skating competitions including the 1992 Winter Olympics in Albertville, France, the 1994 games in Lillehamer, Norway, and the 1998 Olympics in Nagano, Japan.

Scott Scovell Hamilton was born in Toledo, Ohio, on August 28, 1958. Ernest and Dorothy Hamilton adopted him when he was six weeks old and took him home to Bowling Green, Ohio, where both were professors at Bowling Green State University. Ernest was a biologist, and Susan was an expert on marriage and family relations. They had a daughter, Susan, who was five when Scott was adopted, and they later adopted another son, Steven. When Scott was two years old, a mysterious condition caused him to stop growing.

Medical tests showed he was failing to adequately absorb nutrients from food, but doctors did not know how to help him. The child spent much of the next few years traveling to a series of doctors, clinics and children's medical centers. He was prescribed various restrictive diets and treatments—none of which helped.

When he was eight years old, Scott was diagnosed with cystic fibrosis and his parents were told he had six months to live—a diagnosis which later proved to be incorrect. "We grew more and more desperate," Ernest Hamilton told Bob Ottum, a writer for *Sports Illustrated*. The Hamiltons took their frail son to Children's Hospital in Boston, Massachusetts, where a team of specialists identified his ailment. Scott suffered from Schwachmann's syndrome, a disorder that paralyzed two-thirds of his intestinal tract and caused respiratory distress.

Identifying the disease, however, did not help the doctors explain how it had started or ascertain whether it would kill the boy. There was little they could do, besides sending the patient home to Bowling Green with a vitamin-rich, high-protein diet and an exercise regimen. "And then," Ernest Hamilton told Ottum, "one day Susan went skating and Scotty went along to watch."

The ice beckoned that day, and Hamilton began a recovery as mysterious as the disorder which had dogged him. "I'll always remember the sight of him then," his father recalled to Ottum. "He had a feeding tube in place. It went to his stomach. One end of it came out of his nose, and when he wasn't using it, we taped it out of the way behind one ear. This frail little kid with the tube running across his cheek turned and said, 'You know, I think I'd like to try skating.'"

Hamilton began skating relentlessly and within a year he was healthy and growing again. "The consensus of the doctors," Ottum wrote, was "that the intense new activity and the cold atmosphere of the ice rink produced some sort of magical benison. Scott figures he simply skated his way out of it. But whatever it was, Ernie and his son came out of their experience very close, much more so than most fathers and sons."

As his health improved, Hamilton took skating lessons and, despite his diminutive size, joined a hockey team at his elementary school. Soon, he was skating competitively. As a teenager, skating was the center of his world. He left home at age 13 to live and train with Olympic gold medalist Pierre Brunet in Illinois. His training required travel which forced him to change schools regularly; Hamilton's senior year alone was divided between three different schools. Despite his dedication and love of the sport, he quit skating competitively in 1976 because of the financial burden it placed on his parents. He had already enrolled at Bowling Green State University when a wealthy couple, who had been patrons to several world-class figure skaters, stepped forward and offered to sponsor him. Hamilton quickly left college behind and returned to the training rink—first working with legendary skating coach Carlo Fassi in Denver, then with Don Laws in Philadelphia. The couple who financed Hamilton's career have remained anonymous.

> *"I don't want an illness or this episode to stop me from skating.... I love my job. That's been inspiration enough."*

Following his mother's death in 1977, he seemed even more driven to succeed. After finishing ninth in the National Figure Skating Championship in 1977, he climbed to third the following year. He won the Norton Skate Championships, now known as Skate America, four years in a row, from 1979 to 1982, and the Eastern Figure Skating Championship five years running.

At the 1980 Olympic Games in Lake Placid, New York, Hamilton's fellow athletes bestowed upon him the honor of carrying the American flag in the opening ceremonies. "The team had a meeting about who to pick," Hamilton told Ottum, "and someone made this emotional pitch for me, pointing out that I had overcome terrible obstacles, sickness and all, and that my mom had died at a crucial point in my career, and that I was the smallest male Olympian there. And suddenly, there I was, marching along and peering out from under the rim of this cowboy hat a couple sizes too big, leading the parade into the stadium. I was so proud."

Hamilton finished in fifth-place in the men's division at Lake Placid, and over the next four years established himself as the man to beat at the 1984 games. He won both the National Figure Skating Championship and World Figure Skating Championship four years in a row, beginning in 1981. He was the first American male to win the world championship three consecutive years since David Jenkins in the late 1950s.

Although Hamilton never reached normal size (at his competitive prime, the 5-foot, 3-inch skater weighed in at a muscular 115 pounds), he has maintained a self-deprecating humor and quiet self-confidence. "You know me," Hamilton was quoted in *Sports Illustrated* in February 1984. "I go into a department store to buy a new blue blazer; I get the one with the duck on the pocket." At the same time, however, Hamilton perceived his small size as an asset. "I like my size," he told Frank Litsky of the *New York Times*. "I wouldn't change it for anything. Anytime you're different in anything, people will kid you, and I joke about it a lot. But my size is perfect for skating. I have a lower center of balance. I don't have as much body to adjust when I make a mistake, and not as much body to get tired."

As Hamilton climbed to the top of the amateur ranks, he took it upon himself to change the image of male figure skating to a more masculine endeavor. In his performances, he emphasized the athletic over the artistic and substituted costumes with sequins and beads and bangles for utilitarian stretch suits like those worn by speed skaters. And he traded in the sport's ballet-like style for extraordinary speed, and dramatic, athletic leaps and flurries of triple jumps.

"Most sports depend on athletic performance, instead of how you look," Hamilton told Litsky. "I consider myself an athlete and I want people to look at me and my sport that way. Figure skating has been a social event more than a sport.... It's been promoted in this country as a woman's sport. There hasn't been a prominent American male figure skater since 1960."

Building on his performance in the 1980 Winter Olympics, Hamilton changed that. When he arrived in Sarejevo, Yugoslavia, for the 1984 games, he had not lost a competition since September 1980, racking up 15 consecutive first-place finishes. He was the overwhelming favorite to win the gold medal for men's figure skating. It did not come easily, however. Hamilton turned in an uncharacteristically shaky and tentative performance in the short program and finished second, behind Canadian Brian Orser.

But in the end, Hamilton's showing in the competition's school-figures segment and long program earned him the gold. Orser took the silver, and Czechoslovakia's Jozef Sabovtchik claimed the bronze. A month later, Hamilton was victorious at the world championship for the fourth time in a row—then he retired from amateur skating and entered the professional ranks, giving up the thrill of competition but continuing to experience the exhilaration of wowing a crowd.

Since then, Hamilton has skated with several touring ice shows, including the Ice Capades, Festival on Ice, Stars On Ice, Broadway on Ice, and the Discover Card Stars On Ice, a tour Hamilton co-founded in 1986. In addition, he has appeared on numerous television specials and worked as a skating commentator for CBS-TV.

While skating with the Discover Stars on Ice in February 1997, Hamilton began experiencing sharp, shooting pains in his lower back and abdomen. In mid-March, doctors at the St. Francis Medical Center in Peoria, Illinois, found a large tumor in his abdomen. Despite the pain and the devastating news, Hamilton performed in Peoria that night. The next day, doctors at the Cleveland Clinic Foundation concluded that he was suffering from testicular cancer which had spread to his abdomen. The skating world was shaken. "Scott is the symbol of eternal youth in skating," ABC skating commentator Dick Button told *People* magazine. "It comes as a real blow to realize that your symbol is under attack."

In the same article, gold medalist Kristi Yamaguchi said Hamilton "has always been our big brother, someone to turn to. But over the next three months, he'll need our support.... He's the toughest little guy I know." Hamilton's doctors said the condition was curable in 70 to 80 percent of cases. In a prepared statement released to the press and printed in the *Arizona Daily Star*, the skater declared that "the only disability is a bad attitude," and said he was "100 percent confident I can overcome this disease."

Following the diagnosis, Hamilton left the tour and underwent a grueling chemotherapy regimen. By June of 1997, the chemo had shrunk the tumor to the size of a golf ball, and doctors operated to remove it, along with his right testicle. By September, the cancer was gone and Hamilton announced plans to return to the Stars On Ice Tour. Doctors told him there is an 80-percent chance the cancer will not return.

Denver Post sportswriter Terry Frei quoted Hamilton saying that he had drawn strength from memories of his mother's brave fight with cancer as well as his own competitiveness. "I just don't like losing," Hamilton said. "I want to retire on my own terms. I don't want an illness or this episode to stop me from skating.... I love my job. That's been inspiration enough. The cancer, I've tried as hard as I could to make it an inconvenience more than anything else."

Sources

Arizona Daily Star, January 2, 1998, p. F2.
Arizona Republic, January 12, 1998, p. C1.
Buffalo News, December 1, 1997, p. B10.
Cincinnati Enquirer, March 20, 1997, p. C2; October 30, 1997, p. B6.
Denver Post, September 16, 1997, p. D1.
New York Times, March 7, 1983, p. C7.
People, April 7, 1997, pp. 103-104.
St. Louis Post-Dispatch, February 1, 1998, p. C5.
Sports Illustrated, March 16, 1981, pp. 58-59; March 21, 1983, pp. 88-102; February 6, 1984, pp. 68-73.

—*Dave Wilkins*

Dominik Hasek

Hockey player

Born January 29, 1965, in Pardubice, Czechoslovakia (now Czech Republic); married; wife's name, Alena; children: Michael, Dominika. *Education:* Attended University of Hradec Kralove, Czechoslovakia.

Addresses: *Home*—East Amherst, NY. *Office*—Buffalo Sabres, Marine Midland Arena, 1 H. Seymour Knox III Plaza, Buffalo, NY 14203.

Career

Hockey goaltender; drafted 11th pick by Chicago Blackhawks (199th overall), 1983. Named Czechoslovakian First-Team All-Star, 1988, 1989, 1990. Starting goaltender for Team Czechoslovakia during the Canada Cup Tournament, 1991. IHL First All-Star Team, 1991; leader in IHL shutouts and goals against average, 1991. Named to the *Upper Deck*/NHL All Rookie Team following the 1991-92 season. Traded to Buffalo Sabres, 1992; set team records in 1993-94 for goals-against average (GAA) and save percentage; finished regular season with a GAA of 1.95 (joint league leader), becoming first European-trained goaltender to lead NHL in GAA, 1994; league leader for save percentage, 1994; NHL Playoff leader for goals-against average and save percentage, 1994; joint league leader for number of shutouts (no goals allowed in game), 1994, 1995; Official NHL First Team All-Star, 1994; *Sporting News* Second Team All-Star, 1994; Official NHL First Team All-Star and *Sporting News* All Star First Team, 1995; Eastern Conference All-Star Team, 1996; NHL leader in save percentage, 1996, 1997; Eastern Conference All-Star Team, *Hockey News* NHL All Star First Team, and NHL First All-Star Team Goaltender, 1997; became first NHL goalie in 35 years to be named most valuable player, 1997; voted starting goalie for World Team, NHL All Star Game, 1998; goaltender for gold-medal winning Czechoslovakian Olympic team, 1998.

Awards: Czechoslovakian Goaltender of the Year, 1986, 1987, 1988, 1989, 1990; Czechoslovakian Player of the Year, 1987, 1989, 1990; Jennings Trophy (joint winner with Grant Fuhr) for lowest goals-against average, 1994; Vezina Trophy for top goaltender, National Hockey League (NHL), 1994, 1995, 1997; *Sporting News* player of the year, 1994; *Hockey News* goaltender of the year, 1994, 1995; *Upper Deck* goaltender of the year, 1994; Hart Memorial Trophy for most valuable player, NHL, 1997; Lester B. Pearson award for top player as voted by the players, 1997; *Hockey News* most valuable player, player of the year, and goalie of the year, all 1997; Olympic Gold Medal for hockey and Olympic hockey most valuable player, 1998.

Sidelights

Fast and flexible Buffalo Sabres goaltender Dominik Hasek has been called "the human Gumby" by

Michael Farber in *Sports Illustrated*, who also described his style this way: "He tends goal the way Kramer enters Seinfeld's apartment, a package of flailing arms and wild gesticulations that somehow has a perfect logic." The double-jointed, kinetic goalie can do the splits, and boasts some of the quickest reflexes in the league. "They say I am unorthodox, I flop around the ice like some kind of fish," Hasek told Larry Wigge in the *Sporting News*. "I say, who cares as long as I stop the puck." Apparently no one cares *how* he does it. Despite his unusual form, he was named the National Hockey League's top goaltender three times, in 1994, 1995, and 1997, and was the first goalie in 35 years to win the Hart Trophy for most valuable player.

Hasek was born January 29, 1965, in Pardubice, Czechoslovakia (now in the Czech Republic). When he was six, his father took him to hockey tryouts, which would dictate his future. "I didn't even have real skates," Hasek told Wigge. "I had those blades that you screwed onto the soles of your shoes, but I was tall, and the 9-year-olds didn't have a goalie, so they put me in with them." It turned out that he was double-jointed in the knees, which made the doctors worry, but he could make saves that other goalies could not. Hasek watched films of NHL games and decided he would emulate them and someday become an NHL goalie himself.

Hasek moved from his junior team in Pardubice to the Czechoslovakian national team. After a few years, he figured he could show his skills in the NHL. He was an 11th round draft pick in 1983 (199th overall) for the Chicago Blackhawks, but ended up mostly playing for the team's International Hockey League (IHL) affiliate in Indianapolis. He rode a bus back and forth across the heartland, playing only 25 games for the Blackhawks, unable to penetrate the lineup that featured All-Star goaltender Ed Belfour. During those sparse moments when he was able to tend the net, his first NHL win was, ironically, against the Buffalo Sabres on March 8, 1991—the team that would later pick him up in a trade. At that time, though, Hasek was unable to demonstrate his potential. He asked to be sent back to Europe, claiming that he was not good enough for the NHL. Others—including his coach Mike Keenan, now with the St. Louis Blues, who had scouted Hasek in Europe—knew that he was lying, but Chicago could not keep him and Belfour, so they traded him to the Buffalo Sabres in 1992.

In Buffalo, Hasek took turns in goal with Daren Puppa for the first half of the 1992-93 season, until Puppa was traded along with left wing Dave Andreychuk and a first-round draft pick to Toronto for Grant Fuhr and a fifth-round pick. Hasek felt defeated. Five-time Stanley Cup winner Fuhr was sure to knock him out of the running again—until the veteran goalie's knees began acting up. Hasek stepped in and started his reign. "It wasn't fun sitting on the bench," Fuhr remarked to Wigge, "but it was fun watching Dominik stone every opponent he faced." Fuhr later went on to play for Keenan in St. Louis.

The 1993-94 season would further justify the relatively new goalie's position on the team. During that year, Hasek set new Sabres records for shutouts in a season (earning him the nickname "the Blank Czech"), with seven; team shutouts (with Fuhr) for a season; goals-against average (the average number of goals that a goaltender allows through the net in a game), and save percentage (the amount of shots a goaltender prevents from making it through for a scoring goal). He and Fuhr also received the Jennings Trophy for leading the entire NHL in goals-against average, and had the best save percentage, becoming the first European-trained goaltender to lead the league in goals-against average, with 1.95. That achievement made him the first NHL goalie in 20 years with a goals-against average of less than two, and earned him his other nickname, "The Dominator." At the end of the year, his teammates chose him as their most valuable player. In the playoffs that year, he again led the league in goals-against average and save percentage, and at the end of the season, was awarded the Vezina Trophy for being the top goalie in the league. In addition, the *Hockey News* and *Upper Deck* named him their pick for goaltender of the year, and he received the Star of Stars Trophy for most home three-star selections (awarded throughout the year to a game's best players).

Hasek racked up more of the same honors during the 1995-96 season, leading the league in save percentage, winning his teammates' vote as most valuable player, and winning the Star of Stars Trophy. He also made the Eastern Conference All-Star Team. Then after the 1996-97 season, Hasek collected a list of accolades from the *Hockey News:* most valuable player, player of the year, and goalie of the year, as well as being named to the NHL All Start First Team. Also in 1997, Hasek again won the Vezina Trophy.

In addition to all of the other tributes, the 1997 season marked an important pinnacle in Hasek's career as he was honored with the Hart Memorial Trophy for the league's most valuable player, the most prestigious individual award in the NHL. Usually reserved for offensive (high scoring) players, it had been 35 years since a goalie had received the trophy, when

Montreal Canadians' Jacques Plante won it in 1962. Since the top goalie has his own separate award with the Vezina Trophy, many hockey writers who choose the winner feel it is not fair to give both to a netminder, much like the unwritten rule of not nominating a Cy Young Award winner for baseball's most valuable player. However, starting goalies are usually on the ice for almost three-quarters of the time, usually playing an entire game straight through with no rest like other players, who get a line change.

Toward the end of the season, however, before he even had his trophy in hand, Hasek got into trouble for scuffling with *Buffalo News* hockey columnist Jim Kelley. Hasek grabbed Kelley's shirt outside of the locker room, taking offense at Kelley's comments in a column saying that Hasek did not play well under pressure and questioning the extent of the injuries that Hasek said were keeping him out of the game. The NHL fined Hasek $10,000 and suspended him for the first three games of the semifinal conference playoffs against the Philadelphia Flyers. At the start of the following season, sportswriters and booing fans again took him to task, partly because of a poor start as he saw his goals-against average go up to 3.39. They were more displeased, however, at what was seen as his role in the departure of Ted Nolan, the coach of the year much loved by the fans. After fans hurled insults at him after a 3-3 game against the New York Rangers on November 28, "Dom changed.... He realized he couldn't listen to what people said, and he couldn't control the crowd. He could only control the game. He became totally focused," general manager Darcy Regier told Kostya Kennedy in *Sports Illustrated*. In December, Hasek won back friends with a six-game shutout, a tie for the league's single-month record.

In February of 1998, Hasek led his home country, now called the Czech Republic, to a gold medal victory at the Olympics in Nagano, Japan, knocking out a dis-traught Canada in a big upset. Sabres teammate Derek Plante told the CNNSI web site, "When he hits the ice, you're in awe. He makes saves you're not supposed to make and he makes them continually and routinely. He's just awesome He's the Dominator." After the win, Czech President Vaclav Havel called Hasek immediately to tell him that fans in Prague were waving "Hasek for President" banners in the streets. Hasek related to *Washington Post* staff writer William Gildea. "I told him, 'I want to play hockey. You do your job and I play hockey.'"

Sources

On-line

"Awards Won by Dominik Hasek," *Dominik Hasek web site,* http://www.geocities.com/Colosseum/Arena/6265 (April 30, 1998).

"Player Profile #39 Dominik Hasek," *Buffalo Sabres official web site,* http://www.sabres.com (April 30, 1998).

"What Did you Expect? Hasek's Olympic performance no surprise in Buffalo," February 18, 1998, CNNSI web site, http://cnnsi.com (April 30, 1998).

Periodicals

Editor & Publisher, May 24, 1997, p. 17.

Maclean's, July 1, 1997, p. 17.

New York Times, March 2, 1998.

Sporting News, February 14, 1994, p. 51; November 6, 1995, p. 26; May 26, 1997, p. 55; September 15, 1997.

Sports Illustrated, May 2, 1994, p. 52; February 10, 1997, p. 34; April 14, 1997, p. 22; May 5, 1997, p. 42; July 14, 1997, p. 19; November 24, 1997, p. 46; January 12, 1998, p. 68.

Washington Post, March 2, 1998.

—*Geri Speace*

Isaac Hayes

Singer, composer, and actor

Born August 20, 1942, in Covington, TN; son of Isaac and Eula Hayes; married, c. 1960 (divorced); eight children.

Addresses: *Record company*—Columbia Records, 550 Madison Ave., New York, NY 100159- 6119.

Career

Worked in meat packing plant; performed in clubs with Sir Isaac and the Doo-Dads, Memphis, TN; worked as house musician and songwriter, Stax-Volt Records, 1964-67; released debut solo album, *Presenting Isaac Hayes,* 1967; released first ABC/Hot Buttered Soul album, *Chocolate Chip,* 1975; signed to Polydor Records and released *New Horizons,* 1977; film and television actor and radio host, c. 1976—. Television appearances include *The Rockford Files,* 1974; *The A-Team,* 1983; *Hunter,* 1984; *Tales from the Crypt,* 1989; *Sliders,* 1995; and *South Park* (voiceover for animated character Chef), 1997—. Film appearances include *Wattstax,* 1973; *Truck Turner,* 1974; *Escape from New York,* 1981; *I'm Gonna Git You Sucka,* 1988; *Posse,* 1993; *Robin Hood: Men in Tights,* 1993. *Once Upon a Time ... When We Were Colored,* 1995; and *Blues Brothers 2000,* 1998.

Awards: Academy Award for best song from a motion picture, 1971, Grammy Award (with Johnny Allen) for best arranging on an instrumental, 1971, and Grammy Award (with Allen) for best engineered recording (non-classical), 1971, all for "Theme from *Shaft;*" Grammy Award for best album or original instrumental score for a motion picture or for television, 1971 for *Shaft* (soundtrack); Golden Globe Award for best original score, 1972, for "Theme from *Shaft;*" Grammy Award for best instrumental pop performance, 1972, for *Black Moses.*

Sidelights

Starting out as a house player at the Stax-Volt studios in the early 1960s, singer and songwriter Isaac Hayes worked behind the scenes to help shape modern soul music, playing with Otis Redding and writing songs for Sam & Dave. He became a major name with the release of *Hot Buttered Soul* in 1969, an experimental album containing only four songs. In 1971, he was recognized for the funky soundtrack for the film *Shaft,* which won a number of awards and made him a star. He followed up with the acclaimed *Black Moses,* and though he kept busy with music as well as film and television appearances throughout the 1970s and 1980s, Hayes lost his position as a major name until the nostalgia for the 1970s brought him back in the 1990s. Fans enamored with the era facilitated a comeback for Hayes, who personified the outrageous clothes and soul music that defined early 1970s pop culture. Not content to continue rehashing old achievements, Hayes in the mid-1990s began recording again, took a job hosting a radio program, and signed on to provide the voice of Chef, a brash school cafeteria cook on the Comedy Central animated program *South Park.*

Hayes was born August 20, 1942, in Covington, Tennessee, just north of Memphis. His mother, Eula, died before he turned two, and his father, Isaac, left home about the same time. Hayes's grandparents raised him and his sister, Willette Rankin, on a sharecropping farm. When Hayes was about six, the family moved into Memphis in search of better economic opportunities, but were gravely disappointed. At age eight, Hayes was working in cotton fields while trying to attend school, and at age 11, after his grandfather's death, Hayes and his family went on welfare. Hayes continued working odd jobs to supplement the family's meager income by picking cotton, washing dishes, and stocking shelves.

Interested in music from a young age, Hayes would later note that his influences ranged from the Grand Ole Opry to classical, from gospel to jazz greats like Charlie Parker, and even included pop artists like Perry Como and Nat King Cole. He played with a group called the Teen Tones, then sang with gospel act the Morning Stars, and later joined rock and R&B group the Ambassadors. His reputation was building, but Hayes was married while still a teenager and had to quit school and music in order to sustain a steady job. He worked in a meat packing plant but eventually drifted back into playing, forming his own group, Sir Isaac and the Doo-Dads. He struggled as a saxophonist before he got a tip from a friend's sister about a band in need of a keyboard player. "I didn't know how to play—the only things I knew were Chopsticks and Heart and Soul—but I was hungry and had a wife and a new baby, so I had to do something," Hayes recalled to Ira Robbins in *Newsday*. To his relief, none of his bandmates were any good, either, but the drunken New Year's Eve revelers thankfully did not notice. The club later hired the group as its house band.

Hayes eventually learned more chords as he continued to play, and was eventually hired as a sideman to saxophonist Floyd Newman, who was a house player at the legendary Stax-Volt label. This studio was known for a particular sound, exemplified by the smooth, soulful sounds of Booker T and the MGs (who recorded the instrumental "Green Onions"). When Newman in 1963 was offered a chance to cut his own single, Hayes ended up cowriting the song "Frog Stomp" and playing keyboards for him. Soon, the leader of the MGs, Booker T. Jones, left Stax to go to school, and the studio asked Hayes to take his place. Hayes joined the staff, often taking credit as "Ed Lee," as a songwriter,

performer, and producer. His first session was playing on an Otis Redding album.

Hayes would go on to play on almost all of Redding's records, adding behind the scenes an important element in the legendary singer's sound. Later, Hayes teamed up with lyricist David Porter, and the two began composing material for Stax artists. R&B heavyweights Sam & Dave performed a number of their tunes, including "Soul Man," "Hold On! I'm Coming," "I Thank You," and "Wrap It Up." Hayes and Porter's catchy, high-spirited hits would help define sixties soul and make Stax a formidable competitor to Detroit and its Motown sound. The style would also influence generations of music to come, including future R&B, soul, and funk artists, not to mention rock acts like the Rolling Stones. All told, Hayes and Porter wrote over 200 songs for Stax and produced most of them.

Not a classically trained musician, Hayes was unable to read or write music, but managed to get his ideas down by humming into a tape recorder. He also enjoyed the art of improvisation. His first solo album, *Presenting Isaac Hayes*, was born during a Stax office party when the company's vice president made a spur-of-the-moment recording. However, this release, which came out in 1967, did not do well, and it would be three more years before Hayes got another chance. In 1969, the vice president came to him again and asked for an album: any old album would do, he told Hayes; he just needed to make a quota. The result was *Hot Buttered Soul*, an experimental work with only four songs. The album hit number eight on the pop charts and went platinum, propelling Hayes to fame after years as a hidden talent.

Though the typical Stax sound was simple and spare, *Hot Buttered Soul* used strings and backing vocals to make it sound almost symphonic. It also introduced Hayes's deep bass gravelly voice, used to croon as well as to provide a sexy bedroom voice in more of a conversational tone; kind of a mellow precursor to rap. In fact, Hayes called his technique "rapping" even back then. In *Newsday*, he related to Ira Robbins how he got the idea for the extended, improvisational style. As he told it, his introductory rapping was a way to get the audience's attention at a packed Memphis nightclub where he was sitting in with a group called the Bar-Kays, preparing to do a version of the country song "By the Time I Get to Phoenix," made popular by singer Glen Campbell. Hayes noted in *Newsday*, "I started talking, off the top of my head, I had to do something that they could relate to in order to segue into 'Phoenix.' Halfway through my rapping, the conversations began to subside. When I hit the first notes, I had 'em." He later included an 18-minute version of "By the Time I Get to Phoenix" on *Hot Buttered Soul.*

In 1971, Hayes had another big hit with the soundtrack for *Shaft,* which he wrote and coarranged with Johnny Allen. *Shaft* was about a black private detective, John Shaft, a suave and courageous character who is hired to find an underworld boss's kidnapped daughter. The title song featured the wah-wah guitar that would epitomize late 1960s/early 1970s funk music, and included Hayes's trademark "rapping" along with a call-and-response style of singing with female back-ups. The lyrics contained the priceless line, "Who's the black private dick who's a sex machine to all the chicks?" The singers called back, "Shaft!" and Hayes responded, "I'm just talkin' 'bout Shaft."

The film was a hit, and was admired just as much for Hayes's funky theme song as for being one of the rare films to feature an African American hero. "Theme from *Shaft*" hit number one on the pop charts and went platinum, making Hayes a superstar. Hayes in 1971 won an Academy Award for best song, a Grammy Award with Johnny Allen for best arranging on an instrumental, and a Grammy Award with Allen for best engineered recording (non-classical) for "Theme from *Shaft.*" He also won a Grammy Award that year for best album or original instrumental score for a motion picture or for television for the soundtrack, as well as a Golden Globe Award in 1972 for best original score.

In 1972, Hayes followed up with *Black Moses,* honored with a Grammy in 1972 for best pop instrumental performance. He had two gold records in 1973 with *Live at the Sahara Tahoe* and *Joy.* He then provided soundtracks to blaxploitation films *Tough Guys* in 1973 and *Truck Turner* in 1974. He also appeared in these two films, starring as the lead character, Truck Turner, in the latter. As his acting career was gearing up, his music career was chugging along nicely as well, despite legal knots with Stax. He had a disagreement with the record company and then they went bankrupt, after which Hayes founded his own label, Hot Buttered Soul, as an arm of ABC. His first release under his new company was *Chocolate Chip,* which went gold, followed by *Groove-a-Thon,* and then *Juicy Fruit* in 1976. The sound on the last two, however, was mainly a blend of generic disco and ballads.

Perhaps due to manager mishaps as well as his own lavish lifestyle, Hayes went bankrupt in 1976. He

signed with Polydor Records in 1977 and recorded at a quick pace throughout the late 1970s, releasing *A Man and a Woman* with Dionne Warwick in 1977 and *Royal Rappin's* with singer Millie Jackson in 1979, among others. Many of his early Stax albums were reissued around this time as well. Hayes won two Grammy nominations in 1978, and the title track from 1979's *Don't Let Go* went gold. After a hiatus from acting in the late 1970s, he made it back on the big screen in 1981 with a part in *Escape from New York,* and returned to television in *The A-Team.* The early 1980s saw Hayes in occasional television episodes, but he spent most of his time out of the limelight in Atlanta and London. In 1986 he released *U-Turn,* which featured the anti-drug song "Ike's Rap."

Hayes subsequently stayed out of the music business for a while and concentrated on his acting career. As of 1998, he had appeared in almost 30 films since his big-screen debut in *Wattstax* in 1973. He has had roles in *I'm Gonna Git You Sucka,* 1988; *Posse,* 1993; *Robin Hood: Men in Tights,* 1993; *Once Upon a Time ... When We Were Colored,* 1995; *Blues Brothers 2000,* 1998, and many more. In 1995, he reemerged on the music scene with *Raw & Refined,* an instrumental album, and *Branded,* featuring vocals. Around the time he was coming out with new material, cartoon characters Bart and Lisa Simpson were seen on the Fox prime-time animated series *The Simpsons* performing "Theme from *Shaft*" in a karaoke bar. Hayes told Ric Leyva in the *Los Angeles Sentinel,* "That was a riot, man. I thought, 'OK, *Shaft* has arrived. Bart Simpson is doing it.'"

Hayes also in the mid-1990s worked with the British Broadcasting Company (BBC) on a production called *Soul Survivors,* about 1970s soul acts. Around 1996, Hayes took a position at a New York City radio station doing the morning slot from 6 a.m. to 10 a.m. On top of his recording career, the acting, and the radio gig, Hayes was also working as the international spokesman for the World Literacy Crusade, giving speeches to promote the cause of literacy.

Hayes's career, however, got another huge boost when he was asked to provide the voice of Chef, a blunt and rather perverted school cafeteria cook in the Comedy Central series *South Park.* The animated series features a group of third-grade boys who use adult language and get involve in twisted situations, including trying to decide the paternity of one of the children and seeking to discover whether euthanasia is morally right when the grandfather of one of the boys begs to be killed. "I just crack up on the first take," Hayes told Laura Swezey in the *San Francisco Examiner,* later adding, "It's so whacked. I love the character." Unfortunately his success led to an old ghost coming back to haunt him, when a judge ordered Hayes to repay close to $89,000 to a Georgia woman. Hayes had borrowed the money from her during his lean years, 1979 to 1992, and once his career took off again, she wanted it back.

Hayes began shaving his head in the mid-1960s and his smooth pate, along with his penchant for wild clothing and mounds of jewelry, became his trademark look. He has been married at least once and has eight children by three or four partners. In 1993 Hayes converted to the religion Scientology, and has mentioned that it has helped give him the energy and skill to revive his career. A wave of 1970s nostalgia that hit the mainstream and the proliferation of his grooves in contemporary rap music probably did not hurt, either. Tupac Shakur, Ice Cube, Snoop Doggy Dogg, and Dr. Dre have all sampled Hayes's work. In a 1995 *USA Today* article, James T. Jones IV noted, "Rappers sampled (appropriated pieces of) his music on 40 different recordings last year. The godfather of grooves still does the influencing, thank you." Hayes himself in the piece remarked, "When you go to a record company to try and secure a contract, this young A & R (artist and repertoire) person who has no idea about your musical history will say, 'Can I hear something of what you've done lately?' I'm tempted to say, 'Turn on the radio. That's what I've done lately. I'm sampled like hell.'"

Selected discography

On Stax

Presenting Isaac Hayes, 1967.
Hot Buttered Soul, 1969.
Isaac Hayes Movement, 1970.
...To Be Continued, 1970.
Shaft (soundtrack), 1971.
Black Moses, 1971.
Live at the Sahara Tahoe, 1973.
Joy, 1973.
Tough Guys (soundtrack), 1973.
Truck Turner (soundtrack), 1974.
Hotbed, 1978.
Enterprise—His Greatest Hits, 1980.

On ABC/Hot Buttered Soul

Chocolate Chip, 1975.
Groove-a-Thon, 1975.
Juicy Fruit, 1976.

On Polydor

New Horizons, 1977.
(With Dionne Warwick) *A Man and a Woman,* 1977.
For the Sake of Love, 1978.
Don't Let Go, 1979.
(With Millie Jackson) *Royal Rappin's,* 1979.
And Once Again, 1980.
U-Turn, 1986.
The Best of Isaac Hayes—The Polydor Years, 1996.

Other

Love Attack, Sony, 1986.
Branded, Cema/Virgin, 1995.
Raw and Refined, Cema/Virgin, 1995.

Sources

On-line

"Isaac Hayes," Internet Movie Database web site, http://www.imdb.com (July 7, 1998).
"Isaac Hayes," Music Boulevard web site, http://www.musicblvd.com (July 7, 1998).

Books

Contemporary Musicians, Vol. 10, Gale Research, 1994.

Periodicals

Call and Post (Cincinnati, OH), November 7, 1996.
Los Angeles Sentinel, July 5, 1995.
Newsday, May 30, 1995, p. B3.
New York Times, April 23, 1972.
People, July 8, 1996, p. 101.
Reuters, June 29, 1998.
San Francisco Examiner, December 10, 1997, p. 7C.
Star Tribune (Minneapolis, MN), July 7, 1995, p. 15E.
USA Today, June 4, 1995.

—Geri Speace

Caroline Hebard

AP/Wide World Photos

Rescue volunteer

Born Caroline Anne Ruthven Gale, June 20, 1944, in Santiago, Chile; daughter of Malcolm (a British diplomat) and Ilse Gale; married Arthur Hebard (a physicist), 1968; children: Joanne, Andrew, Alastair, Heather. *Education:* American University, B.A. and M.A., and Stanford University, M.A.

Addresses: *Office*—International Rescue Dog Organization, 104 Ballatine Road, Bernardsville, NJ 07924.

Career

Assistant in rescue missions around the world, early 1970s—; co-founder of the U.S. Disaster Response Team (a nonprofit organization that responds to emergencies worldwide), 1988; pioneer in the field of volunteer canine search-and-rescue work.

Member: International Rescue Dog Organization, American Rescue Dog Association, National Association for Search and Rescue.

Sidelights

Pascha is the name of the dog who accompanied Caroline Hebard to the sites of the 1995 bombing of the Alfred P. Murragh Federal Building in Oklahoma City, the earthquake in Kobe, Japan, the same year, and the natural-gas pipeline explosion in Edison, New Jersey, in 1994. Pascha's predecessors include Aly, Ziba, and Jaeger—all German shepherds, all trained to search for lost, trapped, or injured people in response to Hebard's orders. As co-founder and leader of the U.S. Disaster Response Team, a non-profit or-

ganization made up of volunteers who respond to catastrophes both nationally and internationally, Hebard is well-known for her work in the field of volunteer canine search-and-rescue.

Hebard was born in Santiago, Chile, on June 20, 1944, to a British diplomat father and a German mother. Her older brother, Ian, had been born five years earlier. Hebard was only four when her father was transferred to Venezuela, and that is where Hebard first fell in love with dogs. Her parents bought an Airedale named Mike, and he became Hebard's best friend. When they were transferred again, however, her parents were forced to find another home for Mike, and Hebard vowed she would someday have a dog of her own to keep.

When Hebard was 16, her father was transferred to Washington, D.C., where the family stayed for several years and where Hebard earned a bachelor's and a master's degree in applied linguistics from American University. From there, she attended Stanford University in California, where she earned a second master's degree. At Stanford she met her husband-to-be, Arthur Hebard, who was also attending graduate school, studying physics.

Arthur and Caroline Hebard were married in 1968, and shortly thereafter Hebard bought her first purebred German shepherd, Jaeger. She trained Jaeger to respond to commands in German and has trained all her dogs in the same manner since then. But, as Jaeger had disabling dysplasia in both hips, his potential for extensive obedience training was limited, so Hebard acquired a second German shepherd, Zibo, from Germany.

In addition to dogs, the Hebards also wanted to have children, but had been told they could not conceive. So they adopted three-day-old Joanne. A month later, Caroline Hebard found out she was pregnant, and their son Andrew was born when Joanne was 10 months old. Hebard, who is fluent in seven languages (English, German, French, Spanish, Italian, Portuguese, and Turkish), originally intended to teach languages, but instead stayed home to raise her children. Training and raising dogs became her main hobby.

In 1972 Arthur Hebard accepted a position with Bell Laboratories in New Jersey, and the Hebards, their two children, and their two dogs made the cross-country move. Caroline Hebard explained the impact of the move to Hank Whittemore of the *Washington Post*: "I was pushed all of a sudden into suburbia, with two kids in diapers, not knowing anyone, and I wasn't the type to join the Junior League or the bridge club."

Instead, Hebard connected with a group of people who were forming a canine search-and-rescue group close by, and she realized she had found her niche. She told Whittemore, "That's when I realized you can take a well-trained dog and progress even further, so he's actually performing a life-saving mission. It seemed like the perfect use of an intelligent dog, and I was thrilled."

Hebard started to train in earnest for what appeared would be her life's work. She took classes in first aid and compass skills, learned how to climb down the side of steep cliffs and lower a large dog in a harness into tight spaces, worked in two hospital emergency rooms, and volunteered as a local firefighter, eventually becoming a qualified emergency medical technician. She also joined the National Association for Search and Rescue and the American Rescue Dog Association. Working with Zibo, Hebard started going on two or three rescue missions a month in New Jersey and nearby states. Her informal motto was: "Have Dog, Will Travel."

And travel they did; over the next several years, Hebard was called to rescue missions in locations around the world. In 1985 she was part of the first international search-and-rescue unit supported by the United States when she traveled to Mexico City after the earthquake that killed thousands of people and buried thousands more.

By then, Hebard was working with a new dog, Aly, who had arrived from Germany in 1983. Aly also accompanied her to earthquake sites in El Salvador in 1986, where they saved 38 lives; in Armenia in 1988, where he helped find a teen-age girl who had been trapped alive for six days; and in the Philippines in 1990. But earthquakes are certainly not the only disaster Hebard has had close experience with.

In 1990 she and Aly were called to Panama to search for an American solider who had gotten lost in the jungle during survival maneuvers (they found him alive). She has also assisted after such catastrophes as bridge collapses in New York and Tennessee, and Hurricane Hugo's aftermath in South Carolina, as well as floods, fires, plane crashes, and train wrecks.

With Aly's successor, Pascha, also from Germany, Hebard has even participated in homicide investigations. In addition, Hebard and her dogs have helped search for missing people and children. She told Janet Cawley of *Biography*, "A disaster could be one child missing. And if you help a family ease its worry and sorrow and find that child, that alone is rewarding."

Hebard's lifestyle has not been that of the typical suburban homemaker, and she admits that it was sometimes difficult raising a family (she and Arthur had two more children as well, Alastair and Heather). She is on-call 24-hours a day, ready to answer her pager or cellular phone and be on the way to a disaster site within hours. But, as she told Cawley, "Having mom gone was an inconvenience at times, but they understand now that they're older, and they're proud." Her husband, she said, "has always encouraged me in what I've done. He knows I'm not a conventional person."

The family eventually moved to Gainesville, Florida, where her husband received a position as professor of physics at the University of Florida. Meanwhile, Hebard began working with her newest dog, Petro. As a volunteer Hebard is not paid for the rescue work she does.

In addition to going on rescue missions, she leads courses in search management, map and compass skills, and survival skills, and trains canine teams around the world. She has even written a book, *So That Others May Live,* about her most memorable missions. Hebard insists quality control is a priority in search-and-rescue training. As she told Whittemore, "No one is an expert in this field, and you never stop learning."

Sources

On-line

"Search and Rescue," Dog Fancy On-Line, http://www.animalnetwork.com/dogs/library/behavior/general/sar.asp (February 15, 1998).

Books

Whittemore, Hank, and Caroline Hebard, *So That Others May Live: Caroline Hebard & Her Search-and-Rescue Dogs,* Bantam Books (New York), 1995.

Periodicals

Biography, January 1998, p. 45.
Reader's Digest, March 1996, p. 120.
Washington Post, September 12, 1993, p. WSP4.

—Kari Bethel

Jesse Helms

United States Senator

Born October 18, 1921, in Monroe, NC; son of Jesse Alexander and Ethel Mae Helms; married Dorothy Jane Coble, October 31, 1942; children: Jane, Nancy, Charles. *Education:* Attended Wingate (NC) Junior College, Wake Forest College. *Politics:* Republican. *Religion:* Baptist.

Addresses: *Office*—US Senate, 403 Dirsken Senate Building, Washington, DC 20510.

Career

City editor, *Raleigh Times,* 1941-42; news and program director, WRAL, 1948-51; assistant to U.S. senators, 1951-53; executive director, North Carolina Bankers Association, 1953-60; member of Raleigh City Council, 1957-61; executive vice-president, Capital Broadcasting Company, 1960-72; chair of the board, Specialized Agricultural Publications, 1964-72; switched from Democratic to Republican Party, 1970; won U.S. Senate seat, 1972; re-elected to Senate, 1978, 1984, 1990, 1996; chair of the Senate Foreign Relations Committee, 1995—. *Military service:* U.S. Navy, 1942-45.

Awards: Freedom Foundation award, 1962, for best TV editorial; Freedom Foundation award, 1973, for best newspaper article; Southern Baptist national award, 1972, for service to mankind; American Economic Council liberty award, 1978; Public Service Research Council Distinguished Public Service Award, 1978; Women for Constitutional Government, Man of the Year award, 1978; National Rifle Association, Legislator of the Year award, 1978; National Taxpayer's Union, Taxpayer's Best Friend award, 1993.

Member: Rotary Club, Masons, Raleigh Executives, North Carolina Cerebral Palsy Hospital (member of board of directors), United Cerebral Palsy (North Carolina; member of board of directors).

Sidelights

The most powerful conservative in Washington, Senator Jesse Helms has come to symbolize the right wing of the Republican Party. "Far from being a fading figure, he is, at 75, more powerful than ever as the imperious chairman of the Senate's foreign relations committee," noted Andrew Phillips in *Maclean's.* "He has pushed U.S. foreign policy firmly to the right—most recently forcing a shakeup at the United Nations and a major reorganization of the state department."

Helms was so powerful that in 1997, he single-handedly thwarted President Clinton's nomination of Massachusetts Governor William Weld to be ambassador to Mexico. He refused to hold a hearing on the nomination. According to Howard Fineman of *Newsweek,* during a brief meeting with Weld, Helms taunted, "Got your ticket to Mexico yet?" Though Weld is a Republican, he was in the moderate camp of the party and "failed Helms's ideological litmus test on drugs, abortion rights and other issues," noted Phillips. By nominating Weld, Clinton "couldn't have waved a bigger red flag at the old bull," one of Helms's colleagues told Fineman.

> "The paramount thing is whether a man believes in the principles of America and whether he is willing to stand up for them, win or lose."

Since becoming chairman of the Senate Foreign Relations Committee in 1995, Helms had been forced to compromise sometimes, a new position for a stubborn ideologue. Now an insider, Helms cooperated with the Clinton administration on a chemical weapons ban and on paying dues to the United Nations. He has been charmed by Secretary of State Madeleine Albright. Helms says that he now has a cordial relationship with Senator Joe Biden, the ranking Democrat of the Senate Foreign Relations Committee, with Fineman noting that they "have agreed to disagree agreeably." But Helms remained vigilant on most of his right-wing causes, sponsoring the Helms-Burton Act, a boycott of Cuba's government. He led the opposition in Washington to gay rights and was one of the loudest voices calling for an end to The National Endowment for the Arts. In a speech to his colleagues, Helms noted, "It is self-evident that many of the beneficiaries of NEA grants are contemptuous of traditional moral standards." Powerful politicians still regularly traveled to North Carolina "to pay tribute to Helms's power," Phillips noted.

Helms was born in Monroe, North Carolina, in the heart of tobacco country, on October 18, 1921. He studied at Wingate Junior College and Wake Forest College, but never graduated, instead launching a career in journalism. He was city editor at the Raleigh Times in 1941 and 1942, served in the U.S. Navy in World War II, and then turned to broadcast journalism. From 1948 to 1951, he was news and program of WRAL radio in Raleigh.

Helms managed to construct parallel careers in politics, journalism and business. He got his first taste of Washington politics while serving as an aide to senators Willis Smith and Alton Lennon in the early 1950s. He returned to Raleigh and became executive director of the North Carolina Bankers Association from 1953

to 1960. He first won elective office in 1957 and served a four-year term on the Raleigh City Council.

From 1960 to 1972, he was executive vice-president of the Capital Broadcasting Company, operator of WRAL radio and television stations in Raleigh and the Tobacco Radio Network, with stations across the tobacco-growing region. From 1964 to 1972, he was also chairman of the board of Specialized Agricultural Publications Inc. As a leading executive in North Carolina's media, Helms wrote and broadcast daily editorials which challenged what he called the "consistent bias in national television network news," especially concerning the civil rights battles raging across the south.

During his tenure with Capital, Helms filed 500 separate protests with the three major TV networks over "instances of deliberate bias." He termed the Civil Rights Act of 1964 "the single most dangerous piece of legislation ever introduced in the Congress" and called Martin Luther King Jr. a Communist. Helms often editorialized against busing and in favor of military spending. He attacked welfare recipients, judges he felt were too soft on crime, and government interference with the tobacco industry. He also attacked academic freedom, once bringing down a University of North Carolina English teacher for allowing students to recite off-color poems in class.

In 1970, Helms switched from the Democratic Party to the Republican and soon launched his first Senate campaign. When he won in 1972, he became the first Republican to represent North Carolina in the Senate in the twentieth century. During his first term his staunchly conservative voting record earned him a 100 percent rating from the American Security Council and a zero percent rating from the Consumer Federation of America and the League of Women Voters.

Prominent conservative activist Richard Viguerie, the publisher of the *Conservative Digest*, became fundraiser for Helms' 1978 campaign. Viguerie raised an unprecedented $6.2 million in a national direct-mail drive, with two-thirds of the contributions from outside North Carolina. Subsequent Helms campaigns would gather similar nationwide support, from groups such as the National Rifle Association; anti-abortion groups; and oil, tobacco and defense interests, among others. Conservatives saw his re-election as essential to cementing power in Washington, especially as Helms's stature in Congress grew with his seniority. Direct mail organizations sent as many as five million letters a year promoting Helms to conservative Americans. "He was always a step ahead," political scientist Thad Beyle told Phillips, "He built his own personal machine before a lot of people realized we had moved from party politics to personal politics."

In Washington, Helms perfected the politics of refusal. Expert at blocking any measure that met with his disapproval, he earned the nickname "Senator No." His staff once gave him a big red rubber stamp, the traditional metaphor for political acquiescence, emblazoned with the word "No." The tougher the battle, the more Helms would rise to the challenge. "Jesse's got guts," Republican consultant Carter Wrenn told *Maclean's*. "He's got a bit of the barroom brawler in him."

Helms never apologized for his support for American segregation and for South Africa's apartheid government, and he strongly opposed making Martin Luther King's birthday a national holiday. Those stances earned him almost no support from North Carolina's black voters. In 1990 and 1996, Helms won narrow victories over Harvey Gantt, a liberal African American politician. "He doesn't win over his opponents," Wrenn noted. "He polarizes." In 1990, with polls showing the race a dead heat, Helms unleashed a television commercial aimed at white blue-collar voters. It showed two white hands crumpling a rejection letter. The narrator said: "You needed that job, and you were the best qualified. But they had to give it to a minority because of a racial quota." In 1996, the U.S. Justice Department cited his campaign for violating civil rights and voting laws after a mailing of 125,000 postcards to voters in predominantly black precincts warned they could be imprisoned for fraud if they voted. Gantt himself noted Helms's appeal, "He does what every little guy who thinks like him would like to do: stand at the gap and keep out the people they think are trying to change things for the worse. Jesse Helms represents exactly that kind of defiance."

Tobacco giants and foreign governments were among contributors to the Jesse Helms Center, in Wingate, NC, a tax-exempt foundation. The center accumulated $8.3 million in assets. Donors included Kuwait, which gave $140,000 in 1991, and Taiwan, which donated $310,000 in 1993. Tobacco company R.J. Reynolds chipped in $1 million and Philip Morris gave $278,000. The donations became an issue in Helms's 1996 campaign, and he responded: "You can't influence me; nobody can except the truth."

"Next to Ronald Reagan, Jesse Helms is the most important conservative of the last 25 years," wrote Fred Barnes, editor of the *Weekly Standard*, in 1997. "Helms has been a magnetic force on ideology and policy, pulling the entire national debate to the right. Positions he noisily took in Washington two decades ago, almost alone, are now part of mainstream conservatism." Among those were tougher curbs on abortion, a flat tax on income, a balanced-budget amendment to the Constitution, and school prayer.

Helms once said: "The paramount thing is whether a man believes in the principles of America and whether he is willing to stand up for them, win or lose." In 1997, he told the North Carolina general assembly: "Big government cannot and will not solve the multitude of problems confronting our nation ... because big government is the problem."

Selected writings

When Free Men Shall Stand (political philosophy), Zondervan, 1976.

Sources

Knight-Ridder/Tribune Business News, May 28, 1997, p. S28.
Maclean's, September 1, 1997, p. 36.
Nation, October 14, 1996, p. 24.
Nation, April 7, 1997, p. 4.
Newsweek, August 4, 1997, p. 34; September 22, 1997, p. 41.

—*Michael Betzold*

John Lee Hooker

Singer and songwriter

Recorded under numerous pseudonyms, including Delta John, Texas Slim, Birmingham Sam, Johnny Williams, John Lee Cooker, John Lee Booker, John Lee, Johnny Lee, and the Boogie Man; also known as "The Hook," "Doctor Feelgood," and "The Godfather of the Blues"; born August 22, 1917, in Clarksdale, MS; son of William (a sharecropper and minister) and Minnie Hooker; stepson of William Moore (a blues singer and guitarist); married and divorced three times; children: eight, including daughter Zakiya (a blues musician).

Addresses: *Agent*—The Rosebud Agency, P.O. Box 170429, San Francisco, CA 94117-0429; e-mail: rosebudUS@aol.com.

Career

Numerous jukebox hits began in 1948 with "Boogie Chillen" and included "I'm in the Mood" and "Boom Boom"; toured extensively across North America, starting in 1951, and across Europe, starting in 1961; appeared at the Newport Folk Festival (1959, 1960, 1963), the Newport Jazz Festival (1964), the American Folk Blues Festival (1964, 1965, 1968), and at Carnegie Hall (1971, 1983, 1986); recorded more than 100 albums, including *Travelin'* (1961), *Best of John Lee Hooker* (1974), *The Healer* (1988), *Mr. Lucky* (1991), and *Chill Out* (1995). Inspired and collaborated with many famous rock and blues artists, including Rolling Stones, Eric Clapton, Canned Heat, Animals, Richie Havens, Van Morrison, and Bonnie Raitt. Appeared in the film *The Blues Brothers* (1980); television appearances include a Pepsi Cola commercial, *The To-night Show, Late Night with David Letterman,* and the BBC's *Late Show.* Owner of the Boom Boom Room (a blues club), San Francisco, CA, 1997—.

Awards: Folk Heritage Award, Smithsonian Institution, 1983; W.C. Handy Award, top contemporary blues artist, 1990; inducted into Rock and Roll Hall of Fame, 1991; Grammy Awards, for *The Healer,* and 1996, for *Jealous*; Grammy Award, best contemporary blues recording, 1996, for *Chill Out*; Lifetime Achievement Award, Blues Foundation, 1996.

Sidelights

New listeners keep getting hooked on the "deep blues" sound of John Lee Hooker. In March 1997, Hooker, 80, performed with his Coast-to-Coast Blues Band at San Francisco's Fillmore Theatre to celebrate the release of his new CD, *Don't Look Back.* Most of the people who crowded the stage were in their 20s or 30s. "They want to know about the real down blues," Hooker told Dan Oullette of *Down Beat.* "They're beginning to learn that the blues is the root of all music. I looked down at those kids rockin' and smilin', and, that's right, they put energy into me."

For a half-century Hooker has been a driving force in blues music. His adaptation of Mississippi Delta blues to urban audiences was a major factor in the development of modern rock-and-roll and rhythm-and-blues. Hooker has recorded more than 100 albums, several of which have won Grammy Awards. Artists who have credited Hooker as an inspiration include Bonnie Raitt, the Rolling Stones, the Doors, Carlos Santana, Van Morrison, Joe Cocker, Johnny Winter, Gregg Allmann, ZZ Top, and the Who. Hooker has an "inimitable, idiosyncratic style ... a shimmering brand of blues ... with his trademark talkin'-moanin'-stutterin'-mumblin'-chucklin' vocal delivery," Oullette noted. His songs feature sad, one-chord melodies accompanied by his incessant foot-stomping. Hooker often chants the same phrases or words over and over in his deep, earthy voice.

"I don't play a lot of fancy guitar," Hooker told Steve Dougherty of *People.* "I just got this heavy, good rhythm, you know. I play a heck of a funky beat. What I do is soulful, it's the feeling." Hooker wears sunglasses when he plays. He told Jan Obrecht of *Guitar Player* why: "Sometimes I get so emotional, I hear my own voice soundin' good, but it's so sad when I get to singing deep down, the tears run out of my eyes. The dark glasses hide my teardrops."

Hooker grew up poor in Clarksdale, Mississippi, the son of sharecroppers and the fourth of eleven children. His father, William, was a strict Baptist preacher who thought blues was the devil's music. When John was 12, his parents broke up. His mother, Minnie, married William Moore, an amateur blues singer and guitar player. Young Hooker learned the grassroots style of blues playing at country dances with his stepfather.

When Hooker was 14, he ran away from home and moved to Memphis. There he lived in boarding houses and played guitar at house parties. At 15, he migrated to Cincinnati, where he worked as a janitor and movie theater usher, played blues in nightclubs, and sang in gospel groups. Around 1943, he moved to Detroit and got a job as a janitor in a Chrysler plant. Hooker soon became a fixture on Hastings Street, the center of black music and culture in Detroit. He traded his acoustic guitar for an electric guitar to make his music more appealing to urban audiences. Hooker was discovered by Elmer Barber, a record store owner. "Elmer would take me back to his shop each night and record me on blanks," Hooker told Oullette. "He'd give me wine, I'd play and he'd cut the records. That's when I worked up 'Boogie Chillen,'" a song about the Hastings Street scene.

"Boogie Chillen" was released on Sensation Records, a small label. "I was working in a plant as a janitor when 'Boogie Chillen' became a tremendous big hit," Hooker told Melodie McDaniel of *Los Angeles Magazine.* "Everywhere you went, that was all you'd hear. I said, I don't need this broom—I can make it on my own." The song was picked up by a bigger label, Modern Records, and it sold a million copies, climbing to the top spot on the rhythm-and-blues charts in 1949. But the song didn't enrich Hooker. "Modern made money, but they didn't give it to me," Hooker told Oullette. "They made tons. I got peanuts. I knew they were crooks, but I didn't know how to fight 'em." While Hooker's songs—"Hobo Blues," "Boom Boom," "Maudie," "House Rent Boogie"—were becoming jukebox hits, he was forced to go on the road to make money. For nearly half-a-century, he would live much of his life on tour, and among the personal casualties were three marriages that produced eight children.

> *"I don't play a lot of fancy guitar," Hooker told Steve Dougherty of* People. *"I just got this heavy, good rhythm, you know. I play a heck of a funky beat. What I do is soulful, it's the feeling."*

In 1951, Hooker's song "I'm in the Mood" sold another million copies. But with royalty checks from Modern never coming in reliably, Hooker's manager signed him with other labels, using pseudonyms. Between 1949 and 1953, Hooker recorded dozens of albums for at least 24 labels, using many names, including Delta John, Texas Slim, Birmingham Sam, Johnny Williams, John Lee Cooker, John Lee Booker, John Lee, Johnny Lee, and the Boogie Man. "Dimples," a song he released in 1956, became a big hit in England a few years later, paving the way for his enormous popularity in Europe, which was cemented by several appearances at the American Folk Blues Festivals in Europe in the 1960s.

After playing at the Newport Folk Festival in 1963, Hooker became a fixture on American college campuses and the coffeehouse circuit, often using acoustic guitar. "I used to hang out in Central Park with Bob Dylan and Joan Baez and play in coffeehouses with Brownie McGhee, Sonny Terry and Odetta," Hooker recalled. In 1965, he recorded an album with

John Mayall, the first of many collaborations with rock performers.

During the 1960s and 1970s, Hooker continued to release albums, both new material and compilations of older songs, for various labels. His prodigious output was aided by his improvisational studio style. "I don't mess around," he told Oullette. "I do what I do. And I hardly ever make two takes."

In 1980, Hooker made his movie debut in *The Blues Brothers*. In 1986, he recorded a song with Quincy Jones, "Don't Make Me No Never Mind," for *The Color Purple*. He continued touring with his Coast-to-Coast Blues Band, averaging 75 concerts a year. In 1989, Hooker released *The Healer*, which sold more than a million copies. On it, he collaborated with Bonnie Raitt, Carlos Santana, George Thorogood, and others. More collaborations followed. *Don't Look Back* featured several duets with Van Morrison.

Finally, Hooker had achieved both fame and wealth, and he was able to stop touring. But he still did concerts on occasion. In 1996, Hooker joined blues legend Buddy Guy at a star-studded Los Angeles performance. "There's no silencing this man or his deep-souled music," wrote Oullette, noting "the numbing beauty of his guitar's shivery minor chords." Asked by Obrecht why his music brings audiences to their feet, Hooker replied: "That boogie just ride on. It got no end. It just go higher, higher, higher. That get people up. They can't sit down. They can't sit still."

Selected discography

"Boogie Chillen," Sensation Records, c.1949.
I'm John Lee Hooker, Vee Jay, 1959.
House of the Blues, Chess, 1960.
The Folklore of John Lee Hooker, Vee Jay, 1961.
Burnin', Vee Jay, 1962.
The Big Soul of John Lee Hooker, Vee Jay, 1963.
Moanin' and Stompin' the Blues, King, 1970.
Endless Boogie, ABC, 1970.
Hook 'n' Heat, Liberty, 1971.
Mad Man Blues, Chess, 1973.
Free Beer and Chicken, ABC, 1974.
Never Get Out of These Blues Alive, Pickwick, 1978.
The Cream, Tomato, 1978.

The Best of John Lee Hooker, Crescendo, 1987.
Real Folk Blues, MCA, 1987.
Simply the Truth, One Way, 1988.
The Healer, Chameleon, 1989.
Mr. Lucky, Charisma, 1991.
The Country Blues of John Lee Hooker, Riverside, 1991.
John Lee Hooker: The Ultimate Collection 1948-1990, Rhino, 1991.
Boom Boom, Pointblank/Virgin, 1992.
Graveyard Blues, Specialty, 1992.
Chill Out, Pointblank, 1995.
Jealous (originally recorded in 1986), Pointblank/Virgin, 1996.
Alone, Blues Alliance, 1996.
John Lee Hooker and Friends 1984-1992 (video), Rounder, 1996
Live at Cafe Au Go Go (and Soledad Prison), MCA, 1996.
His Best, Chess/MCA, 1997.
Don't Look Back, Virgin, 1997.

Sources

On-line

"John Lee Hooker," The Rosebud Agency, http://www.rosebudus.com/hooker (December 30, 1997).
"John Lee Hooker," Virgin Records, http://www.virginrecords.com/jlhooker (December 30, 1997).

Books

Contemporary Musicians, Volume 1, Gale, 1989.
Hardy, Phil, and Dave Laing, *Encyclopedia of Rock*, Schirmer Books, 1988.
Zalkind, Ronald, *Contemporary Music Almanac*, Macmillan, 1980.

Periodicals

Down Beat, June 1997, p. 20.
Guitar Player, November 1989, p. 50; March 1996, p. 116; June 1996, p. 68.
Los Angeles Magazine, March 1995, p. 62.
People, October 29, 1990, p. 113; May 26, 1997, p. 28.
Playboy, June 1995, p. 30.

—Michael Betzold

Lena Horne

Singer, actress, activist

Born Lena Mary Calhoun Horne, June 30, 1917, in Brooklyn, NY; daughter of Edwin F. ("Teddy"), a civil servant (some sources say hotel operator or numbers banker), and Edna (an actress; maiden name, Calhoun) Horne; married Louis Jones, 1937 (divorced, 1944); married Leonard George ("Lennie") Hayton, December, 1947 (died, early 1970s); children: (first marriage) Gail, Edwin ("Teddy;" died, early 1970s).

Addresses: *Home*—New York, NY. *Office*—5950 Canoga Ave., #200, Woodland Hills, CA 91367.

Career

Began singing at Cotton Club, New York City, 1933; Broadway debut in *Dance with Your Gods,* Mansfield Theatre, 1934; also appeared on stage in *Jamaica,* Imperial Theater, New York City, 1957; *Tony Bennett and Lena Horne Sing,* Minskoff Theatre, New York City, 1974; *Lena Horne: The Lady and Her Music,* Nederlander Theatre, New York City, 1981; and *Pal Joey,* Los Angeles Music Center; featured singer with Noble Sissle's Society Orchestra, 1935-37, and Charlie Barnet Orchestra, 1940-41; appeared in musical *Blackbirds of 1939,* 1939; and at Cafe Society Downtown, 1941; featured performer at Little Troc nightclub, Hollywood, CA, 1942. Appeared in films, including *Duke Is the Tops,* 1938; *Panama Hattie,* 1942; *Cabin in the Sky,* 1943; *I Dood It,* 1943; *Stormy Weather,* 1943; *Swing Fever,* 1943; *Thousands Cheer,* 1943; *Broadway Rhythm,* 1944; *Two Girls and a Sailor,* 1944; *Till the Clouds Roll By,* 1946; *Zeigfield Follies,* 1946; *Words and Music,* 1948; *Duchess of Idaho,* 1950; *Meet Me in Las Vegas,* 1956, *Death of a Gunfighter,* 1969; and *The Wiz,* 1978. Television ap-

pearances include *Music '55,* 1955; *Perry Como Show,* 1959; *Here's to the Ladies,* 1960; *The Milton Berle Special,* 1962; *Bell Telephone Hour,* 1964; *Lena in Concert,* 1969; *Harry and Lena,* 1970; *Keep U.S. Beautiful,* 1973; *Lena Horne: The Lady and Her Music,* 1984; *The Ed Sullivan Show, The Tonight Show, Sanford and Son; The Cosby Show;* and *The Lena Horne Show.*

Awards: Variety New York Drama Critics' Poll Award, best performance by a female lead in a musical, 1958, for *Jamaica;* New York Drama Critics' Circle Award, Special Citation, and Antoinette Perry ("Tony") Special Award, both 1981, for *Lena Horne: The Lady and Her Music;* Grammy Award for best pop vocal performance, female, 1981, for *Lena Horne: The Lady and Her Music Live on Broadway;* Dance Theater of Harlem Emergence Award, 1982; Handel Medallion, 1982; Spingarn Award from the National Association for the Advancement of Colored People (NAACP), 1983; Kennedy Center Honors Award for Lifetime Contribution to the Arts, 1984; Pied Piper Award from the American Association of Composers, Authors, and Publishers, 1987; Lifetime Achievement Award, National Academy of Recording Arts and Sciences, 1989; Frontrunner Award, Sara Lee Corporation, 1990; Essence Award, 1993; Grammy Award for best jazz vocal performance, 1995, for *An Evening with Lena Horne;*

Ella Award for Lifetime Achievement, Society of Singers, 1997; Lifetime Achievement Award, *Ebony* magazine; Paul Robeson Award, Actors' Equity Association.

Sidelights

Silky-voiced singing legend Lena Horne was drawn to the stage early in life, the daughter of a would-be actress who had little success in breaking down the barriers of discrimination. Horne went to work partly out of necessity as a teenager and made herself into a successful entertainer who consciously rejected stereotyping. Enduring all kinds of oppression as an African American performer, she nevertheless managed to establish an image as a glamorous chanteuse and eventually, as a jazz icon in the same league as Billie Holiday, Ella Fitzgerald, and Sarah Vaughan.

Though studios censored her film appearances for audiences in the South in the 1940s, American soldiers both African American and white during World War II admired her sultry beauty. Despite a bump in the road when she was, along with many, blacklisted for being a possible Communist sympathizer, her career buzzed along in the 1950s with a new recording contract and appearances in musicals, films, and television shows. In the 1960s, she became dedicated to civil rights and attended marches and rallies. The early 1970s brought personal tragedies with the death of three loved ones within a short period. By the 1980s, she was as hot as ever, winning a number of awards for her Broadway smash, *Lena Horne: The Lady and Her Music*. The 1990s saw her in the spotlight again, belting out her hits at her eightieth birthday party in New York in 1997 and releasing a new jazz album, *Being Myself*, in 1998.

Horne was born Lena Mary Calhoun Horne in the Bedford-Stuyvesant ("Bed-Stuy") area of Brooklyn in New York City. Six generations prior, one of Horne's ancestors had been a slave who bought her freedom by selling pies. By the time Horne was born, her family was solidly middle-class; her father was a civil servant (though some sources have written that he was a hotel operator or numbers banker) and her mother was an aspiring actress. Horne also spent part of her youth with her grandparents, Frank Edwin and Cora Horne. Her grandfather was a talented poet and cofounder of the lobbying group United Colored Democracy, as well as a member of President Franklin Roosevelt's unofficial council on race relations. Her feminist grandmother was a member of the Urban League and NAACP, enrolling young Lena in the latter when she was only two. Cora Horne once told her granddaughter, "You will look people in the eye and speak distinctly, and you will never let anyone see you cry," according to a *New York Times* profile of Horne.

Edwin "Teddy" and Edna Horne separated when their daughter was just three years old, and Horne's mother took her on the road as she performed in tent shows in the South. Her mother's career never fully took off due to the rampant racism of the era, a grim reality that Horne saw firsthand on their adventures in the southern states. Horne lived with a number of families along the way, and when Horne's mother married Miguel "Mike" Rodriguez, Horne moved in with them, and the family returned to New York. Though her grandmother raised her to be socially conscious and urged her to become a teacher, Horne was smitten by show business. It was also the Depression, and the family needed some extra money, so in 1933, Horne received her first professional booking as a chorus line dancer at the Cotton Club in the Harlem area of New York City, a legendary night spot where numerous African American entertainers got their start.

The Cotton Club was run for whites, by whites in those days; African Americans were only allowed on stage, not in the audience. At 16, Horne fit the bill of the young, attractive, exotic-looking African American with somewhat Caucasian features that the white audiences desired. She quit school to perform three shows a night, seven nights a week for just $25, and recalled in the *New York Times*, "The conditions were really terrible. We couldn't even use the toilet, which was for the customers." However, African Americans were shut out of most other venues at the time, so she persisted, hoping to land a singing gig.

Though she did not headline at the Cotton Club, Horne finally landed a Broadway musical role in *Dance with Your Gods*, 1934, and in 1935, African American bandleader Nobel Sissle hired her to belt out tunes with his Society Orchestra. She still endured racism; many hotels would not rent rooms to African American performers, so the group was forced to sleep in boarding houses in African American neighborhoods, or even on circus grounds. However, Horne enjoyed being in the company of great African American entertainers. She toured with Sissle until 1937 and then at age 19, ran away to get married to Louis Jones, 28. He was a friend of her father's from Pittsburgh who had political aspirations and assumed Horne would become a homemaker. Horne had no interest in being a stay-at-home wife, and she continued working. She appeared in an all-African American film, *The Duke Is Tops*, in 1939, and had a role in the musical *Blackbirds of 1939* that same year, although it ran for only eight nights.

Horne was happy to become a mother, however, and had a daughter, Gail, and a son, Edwin ("Teddy") with Jones. Around the time their son was born in 1940, the couple split up. Horne moved back to New York with her daughter, and Jones kept custody of Teddy. Horne remained an entertainer, joining the Charlie Barnet Orchestra in 1940. But as the only African American member of the group, she was disturbed by the shabby treatment from audiences, hotel owners, and others. She quit in 1941 and began appearing at Café Society Downtown, a hip New York club in Greenwich Village that attracted intellectuals and social activists regardless of race.

At Café Society, Horne was exposed to African American history, politics, and culture; recorded with bandleader Artie Shaw; reportedly had an affair with boxer Joe Louis; and even met legendary performer Paul Robeson. "He taught me about my people," Horne recalled in *People*. She also met Billie Holiday, who was singing at Kelly's Stable, another club in the neighborhood. Holiday was a great influence who taught Horne to sing however she could to get by, and Count Basie was another important mentor who urged Horne to break into Hollywood in order to show that African Americans could be screen idols, not just domestics or other stereotypes.

In the summer of 1941, Horne was offered a job on Sunset Strip and moved to California. She was supposed to work at a new club called the Trocadero, but it fell through and a smaller version of the venue was opened in February of 1942. Horne began singing at the Little Troc and also signed a seven-year deal with MGM studios to make films. The first African American woman to sign with a studio since 1915, she nevertheless refused to take demeaning parts. Her stepfather met with studio boss Louis B. Mayer, and told him, according to *People*, "The only Negroes I ever see are menials or Tarzan extras. I don't see what the movies have to offer my daughter. I can hire a maid for her. Why should she act one?" However, the filmmakers were reluctant to cast her as a romantic lead with a white man, since interracial relationships were still taboo, but they considered her too light to act with other African Americans. Horne thus generally won glamorous roles in which she was cast in elegant, elaborate musical numbers, although she would only make a total of 16 films.

In 1943, Horne starred in the all-African American musical *Stormy Weather*, the title song of which became her trademark, and *Cabin in the Sky*. She was the first African American actor to grace the cover of a major magazine (*Motion Picture*) and was profiled in *Time*, *Life*, and *Newsweek*, and in the 1940s became a "pin-up" for soldiers serving in World War II. She embarked on USO tours around the country and made appearances on Armed Forces Radio. Meanwhile, though, her resistance to be stereotyped brought criticism from other African American actors, who dubbed Horne a puppet of the NAACP. In many of her films with white casts, studios were continuing to cut Horne's singing scenes out of films so that Southern audiences would not have to view an African American woman on the screen, and in other marketing strategies, she was offered as an exotic sex symbol about whom white men could fantasize.

Horne married again in 1947 but did not publicly announce the union until 1950. Her second husband was Lennie Hayton, a white conductor-arranger at MGM, whom she wed in Paris because interracial marriage was still illegal in California at the time. This relationship caused an outpouring of controversy and threats of violence. Hayton built a wall around their home and purchased a shotgun in response. Horne later admitted that she was drawn to Hayton because as a white man, he could boost her career faster, but she later grew to love him. Meanwhile, she grew more and more weary of the racism that she encountered as a black performer, and angry that society still oppressed blacks by segregation and other mistreatment.

Horne was also targeted during the "witch hunts" of the late 1940s and early 1950s instituted by Senator Joseph McCarthy, in which scores were blacklisted (people were fired from jobs, actors were banned from appearing in movies or on television, and so on) for being suspected Communists. Her career was briefly on hiatus, but after being cleared, she was back in the swing. In 1956, Horne signed a contract with RCA Victor and acted again on Broadway in the all-African American musical *Jamaica* in 1957, for which she won the 1958 Variety New York Drama Critics Poll Award for best performance by a female lead in a musical. She also began appearing on a number of television programs, and her album *Lena Horne at the Waldorf-Astoria* became the top-selling recording by a female artist in RCA's history. She was also a sensation in Las Vegas, but was frustrated at the absence of African Americans in the audiences.

In the 1960s, Horne got involved in the civil rights struggle. In a much-publicized incident that seemed to spark her activism, a drunken white man used a racial epithet against her in a restaurant, and she hurled an ashtray, a lamp, and drinking glasses back at him, along with some choice words. "I was this nice, cute young thing who didn't make any trouble, didn't bother anybody, didn't shake things up," Horne commented in *Newsday*. "but I never forgot for a moment who I was or where I came from. It was the acceptance of my people that matters most to me." She subsequently attended marches and rallies, including the 1963 march on Washington, D.C., with Dr. Martin Luther King, Jr., and continued to make appearances on television and to record albums.

Horne separated from her husband in the 1960s and became involved with Billy Strayhorn, Duke Ellington's arranger-composer, whom she called her soulmate. He died in 1967, and then in the early 1970s, within 18 months, she lost three loved ones. Her son Teddy succumbed to kidney disease, leaving three children behind, her father died around the same time, and so did her ex-husband, Hayton, with whom she was still close. Though she was devastated, she told Michiko Kakutani in the *New York Times*, "When I finally woke up and realized there was only me and I was still awake morning after morning, I did what I had to do—I went back to work." Horne appeared with Tony Bennett in 1974 on Broadway in a show called *Tony and Lena*, and made a number of television commercials. In 1978, she was cast as Glinda, the Good Witch, in the all-African American musical *The Wiz*, based on the *Wizard of Oz*.

Though Horne embarked on a farewell tour in the summer 1980, she had a major comeback in 1981 with the one-woman Broadway hit *Lena Horne: The Lady and Her Music*, which opened in May at the Nederlander Theatre. The show ran for two years and won a special Tony Award, a special citation from the New York Drama Critics' Circle, and a Grammy Award for best pop vocal performance for the recorded album of the show. In 1986, her daughter, Gail Lumet Buckley (once married to director Sidney Lumet and later to journalist Kevin Buckley), constructed a family history called *The Hornes: An American Family*, thanks in large part to a load of memorabilia that Horne had saved along the years.

Into the 1990s, a number of Horne's hits were re-released, and she gave a much-admired concert at Lincoln Center in 1993, after which a record producer urged her back into the studio. The albums, *We'll Be Together Again* in 1994 and a live recording, *An Evening with Lena Horne: Live at the Supper Club* in 1995, stirred new interest in the legendary lady's career, leading to a documentary special about her life in 1996. A 1997 birthday bash in New York City brought her into the limelight again to lay out her vocal stylings as she turned 80. She was spotted around 1997 as well in an understated advertisement around the holidays for the clothing store The Gap featuring a few bars from "Win-

ter Wonderland." In 1998, she made news again with the CD release *Being Myself*.

Horne lives alone in a six-room Manhattan apartment on the Upper East Side of New York City. She admits to enjoying the Cartoon Network and late-night movies, especially vampire flicks and old films on the American Movie Classics, and indulges in lamb chops and red wine. Reading is also one of her passions; her favorite authors include Toni Morrison, Alice Walker, and Walter Mosley. She has five grandchildren and a great-grandson. Strangely enough, the woman who has become one of the most-loved voices of the century actually dislikes singing. "I hate to sing!" Horne exclaimed in *Entertainment Weekly*. "I mean, I don't hate it when I'm doing it. But I don't sing in the shower. I don't sing in the kitchen. I don't sing until I have to."

Selected discography

Birth of the Blues, RCA, 1940.
Moanin' Low, RCA, 1940.
Little Girl Blue, RCA, 1942.
A Date with Fletcher Henderson, 1944.
Till the Clouds Roll By, MGM, 1946.
Words and Music, MGM, 1948.
Lena Horne at the Waldorf-Astoria, Victor, 1958.
Sands, Victor, 1961.
Lovely and Alive, Victor, 1962.
On the Blue Side, Victor, 1962.
Lena Horne Sings Your Requests, Charter, 1963.
Like Latin, Charter, 1963.
Lena—A New Album, 1976.
Lena Horne: The Lady and Her Music Live on Broadway, 1982.
(With the Lennie Layton Orchestra) *Lena Goes Latin*, recorded in 1963, DRG, 1987.
(With Sammy Davis and Joe Williams) *The Men in My Life*, Three Cherries, 1989.
Stormy Weather: The Legendary Lena, 1941-1958, Bluebird, 1990.
At Long Last Lena, RCA, 1992.
Greatest Hits, CSI, 1992.
Lena Horne, Royal Collection, 1992.
The Best of Lena Horne, Curb, 1993.
We'll Be Together Again, 1994.
An Evening with Lena Horne: Live at the Supper Club, Blue Note, 1995.
Being Myself, Blue Note, 1998.
Classics in Blue, RCA Victor.
First Lady, Jem.
The Lady is a Tramp, MGM.
Lena, A New Album, RCA.
Lena Horne at the Coconut Grove, RCA Victor.

Lena in Hollywood.
Lena with Lennie Hayton and Marty Gold Orchestras, Jem.
Now, Fox.
The One and Only, Polygram.
Porgy and Bess, RCA.
Standing Room Only, Accord.
Stormy Weather, RCA Victor.

Selected writings

In Person (autobiography), 1950.
(With Richard Schickel) *Lena* (autobiography), 1965.

Sources

Books

Contemporary Black Biography, Volume 11, Gale Research, 1994.

Contemporary Theatre, Film, and Television, Volume 6, Gale Research, 1989.

Periodicals

Atlanta Journal and Constitution, June 30, 1997, p. B6.
Entertainment Weekly, May 13, 1994, p. 26.
Los Angeles Times, May 31, 1990, p. 4.
Newsday, May 15, 1994, p. 15; November 15, 1996, p. A15.
New York Amsterdam News, March 22, 1997, p. 6.
New York Times, May 3, 1981; June 20, 1986; June 5, 1994.
People, July 6, 1998, p. 120.
Time, July 4, 1994, p. 71.
Town & Country Monthly, September 1, 1995, p. 128.
USA Today, May 20, 1994, p. 10.

—*Geri Speace*

Dolores Huerta

Labor activist

Born April 10, 1930, in Dawson, NM; daughter of Juan (a miner and migrant worker, activist, and politician) and Alicia (a hotel and restaurant owner; maiden name, Chavez) Fernandez; married Ralph Head (divorced); married Ventura Huerta (divorced); companion of Richard Chavez; children: (first marriage) Celeste, Lori; (second marriage) Fidel, Emilio, Vincent, Alicia, Angela; (with Chavez) Juanita, Maria Elena, Ricky, Camilla. *Education:* Attended Stockton College.

Address: *Office*—c/o United Farm Workers of America, AFL-CIO, P.O. Box 62, La Paz, Keene, CA 93531.

Career

Worked variously as a manager of a grocery store and teacher; Naval Supply Base, near Stockton, CA, secretary to the commander in charge of public works; worked in records and identifications at the local sheriff's office; associated with Community Service Organization (CSO), Sacramento, CA; associated with Agricultural Workers Association (AWA); Agricultural Workers Organizing Committee (AWOC), secretary-treasurer, c. 1958; National Farm Workers Association (NFWA), cofounder, 1962; United Farm Workers, cofounder, 1962, vice-president, 1962-93, executive board member, administrator, lobbyist, contract negotiator, picket captain, and lecturer.

Awards: Inducted into National Women's Hall of Fame, 1993; Martin Luther King Award, National Association for the Advancement of Colored People (NAACP); Roger Baldwin Award, American Civil Liberties Union (ACLU); Eugene V. Debs Foundation Award; Trumpeters Award, Consumers Union.

Sidelights

Cofounder and first vice president of the United Farm Workers, Dolores Huerta (sometimes referred to as Dolores "Huelga," Spanish for "strike") is the most prominent Chicana labor leader in the United States. For more than 30 years she has dedicated her life to the struggle for justice, dignity, and a decent standard of living for one of the United States's most exploited groups—the men, women, and children who toil in the fields and orchards picking the vegetables and fruits that stock grocery stores. The recipient of countless awards from community service, labor, Hispanic, and women's organizations as well as the subject of *corridos* (ballads) and murals, the vibrant and charismatic Huerta is a much-admired role model for Mexican American women.

Born April 10, 1930, in the small mining town of Dawson in northern New Mexico, Dolores Fernandez Huerta was the second child and only daughter of Juan and Alicia (Chavez) Fernandez. On her mother's side of the family, Huerta is a third-generation New Mexican. Huerta's father was also born in Dawson but to a Mexican immigrant family. The young couple's marriage was a troubled one, and when Huerta was a toddler, her parents divorced. Her mother moved her three children first to Las Vegas, New Mexico, and then to Stockton, California, where Huerta spent the remainder of her childhood.

As a single parent during the Depression, Alicia Chavez Fernandez had a difficult time supporting her young family. To make ends meet, she worked as a waitress during the day and in a cannery at night, relying on her widowed father, Herculano Chavez, to watch her children. Despite the hardships, it was a loving and happy household. The gregarious Huerta was very close to her grandfather, who called her "seven tongues" because she talked so much. (Such verbal skills would serve her well later in life.) As she once recalled in an interview, "My grandfather kind of raised us.... He was really our father.... [His] influence was really the male influence in my family." But Huerta also maintained sporadic contact with her father, a miner and migrant worker whose own political and labor activism later proved inspirational to his daughter.

The family's economic fortunes took a turn for the better during World War II. Alicia Fernandez ran a restaurant and then purchased a hotel in Stockton with her second husband, James Richards, with whom she had another daughter. During summers in particular, Huerta and her brothers helped manage these establishments, which were located on the fringes of skid row and catered to a working-class and farm-worker clientele. She relished the experience and believed it taught her to appreciate all different types of people. "The ethnic community where we lived was all mixed," she explained. "It was Japanese, Chinese. The only Jewish families that lived in Stockton were there in our neighborhood.... There was the Filipino pool hall..., the Mexican drug stores, the Mexican bakeries were there."

In the early 1950s, Alicia Fernandez Richards divorced her husband, whose strained relationship with Huerta had been a source of tension, and married again, this time to a man named Juan Silva. Their union was a happy one that produced another daughter and endured until Alicia's death. Huerta speaks admiringly of her mother's entrepreneurial and personal spirit and her expectations for her children. "My mother was always pushing me to get involved in all these youth activities.... We took violin lessons. I took piano lessons. I took dancing lessons. I belonged to the church choir.... I belonged to the church youth organization.

And I was a very active Girl Scout from the time I was eight to the time I was eighteen." Mother and daughter enjoyed a caring relationship that extended into Huerta's adult years.

Although Huerta counted her mother and grandfather as the primary influences in her life, she also credits her father with inspiring her to be an activist. Like most people in Dawson, Juan Fernandez worked in the coal mines. To supplement his wages, he joined the migrant labor force, traveling to Colorado, Nebraska, and Wyoming for the beet harvests. The inferior working conditions, frequent accidents, and low wages he encountered as a farm worker sparked his interest in labor issues. Leaving Dawson after his divorce from Huerta's mother, Fernandez continued his activism, becoming secretary-treasurer of the Congress of Industrial Organizations (CIO) local at the Terrero Camp of the American Metals Company in Las Vegas, New Mexico. In 1938, using his predominately Hispanic local union as a base, he won election to the New Mexico state legislature. There he worked with other sympathetic members to promote a labor program, including a piece of legislation known as the "Little Wagner Act" and a wages-and-hours bill. Due to his outspoken independence on many issues, Fernandez lasted only one term in the state house.

After her parents' divorce, Huerta saw her father only occasionally. Once she reached adulthood, however, she met up with him more frequently, especially after he settled in Stockton. There he lived in a labor camp for a while, worked in the asparagus fields, held other odd jobs, and returned to school for a college degree. Huerta remained proud of her father's union activism, political achievements, and educational accomplishments, and he in turn supported her labor organizing. But their relationship remained aloof and distant, partly because he disapproved of her personal lifestyle.

After graduating from Stockton High School, Huerta—unlike most Hispanic women of her generation—continued her education at Stockton College. A brief and unsuccessful marriage that produced two daughters prompted her to abandon her studies for a while, but after divorcing her husband, she returned to college and earned her associate's degree with financial and emotional support from her mother.

Huerta held a variety of jobs in Stockton before, during, and after her marriage. Before her marriage, for example, she managed a small neighborhood grocery store that her mother had purchased. (It eventually went bankrupt.) Then she obtained a job at the Naval Supply Base as the secretary to the commander in charge of public works. During and after her divorce, she worked in the sheriff's office in records and identifications. Dissatisfied with these kinds of jobs, Huerta resumed her education and earned a provisional teaching certificate. Once in the classroom, however, she quickly grew frustrated by how little she could really do for those students who didn't have proper clothing or enough to eat.

Huerta's frustration eventually found an outlet in the Community Service Organization (CSO), a Mexican American self-help group that first took shape in Los Angeles in the years after World War II and then spread across California and the Southwest. She joined up during the mid-1950s and became very active in the CSO's many civic and educational programs, including registering voters, setting up citizenship classes, and lobbying local government officials for neighborhood improvements. Huerta showed particular talent for the latter, so much so that the CSO soon hired her to handle similar duties for the group at the state level in Sacramento.

During the course of these activities, Huerta met and married her second husband, Ventura Huerta, who was also involved in community affairs. Their relationship produced five children but gradually deteriorated because of incompatible temperaments and disagreements over Dolores Huerta's juggling of domestic matters, child care, and civic activism. "I knew I wasn't comfortable in a wife's role, but I wasn't clearly facing the issue," she later remarked in the *Progressive*. "I hedged, I made excuses, I didn't come out and tell my husband that I cared more about helping other people than cleaning our house and doing my hair." A series of trial separations eventually led to a bitter divorce, and once again, Huerta turned to her mother for financial and emotional support so that she could continue her work for the CSO.

During the late 1950s, as Huerta was struggling to balance a failing marriage, her family, and a job with her commitment to social activism, she found herself drawn to the plight of Mexican American farm workers. She soon joined a northern California community interest group, the Agricultural Workers Association (AWA), which had been founded by a local priest and his parishioners. It later merged with the American Federation of Labor-Congress of Industrial Organizations (AFL-CIO)-sponsored Agricultural Workers Organizing Committee (AWOC), for which Huerta worked as secretary-treasurer.

It was around this same time that Huerta first met Cesar Chavez, another CSO official who shared her concern for migrant workers. The two worked together to bring rural labor issues to the attention of the more urban-oriented CSO. When they could not interest the CSO in expanding its focus, both Chavez and Huerta left the group to devote their time to organizing this overlooked segment of American society. In 1962, from their base in the town of Delano, they changed the course of agricultural and labor history in California when they founded the National Farm Workers Association (NFWA), the precursor to the United Farm Workers (UFW).

> *"I think we brought to the world, the United States anyway, the whole idea of boycotting as a nonviolent tactic."*

The full extent of the Chavez-Huerta collaboration has only recently been documented as correspondence between the two and others becomes available. For instance, in a 1962 letter to activist Fred Ross, his CSO mentor, Chavez remarked, "Dolores was here [in Delano] for one and a half days. I filled her in on all the plans and asked her to join the parade.... While here we did some work on the list of towns to work in throughout the valley.... Also she, Helen [Chavez's wife], and I decide [sic] on the name of the group. 'Farm Workers Assn.'"

Ever since the founding of the union, Huerta has held decision-making posts and maintained a high public profile. As second in command to Chavez until his death in 1993, she exerted a direct influence on shaping and guiding the fortunes of the UFW. In the famous 1965 Delano strike (the one that first attracted national attention to the union and launched the table grape boycott), she devised strategy and led workers on picket lines. She was also responsible for setting up the UFW's contract negotiation department and served as its director in the early years.

In these and other positions in the union, Huerta had to battle both gender and ethnic stereotypes. Commenting on her uncompromising and forceful personality, for example, one grower declared, "Dolores Huerta is crazy. She is a violent woman, where women, especially Mexican women, are usually peaceful and calm." But she was able to hold her own against hostile Anglo growers who resented the fact that any Mexican American—and a woman, no less—would dare challenge the status quo.

Another major undertaking for Huerta involved running the table grape boycott in New York City in the late 1960s, an effort that eventually expanded to include the entire east coast, the primary distribution point for grapes. The leadership she provided in 1968 and 1969 as the east coast boycott coordinator greatly contributed to the success of the national boycott. Huerta mobilized other unions, political activists, Hispanic associations, community organizations, religious supporters, peace groups, student protestors, and concerned consumers across racial, ethnic, and class lines in a drive to show support for farm workers and keep media attention focused on their cause. Their efforts finally paid off in 1970 when the Delano growers agreed to contracts that ended the five-year-old strike.

It was also while she was living and working in New York that Huerta met feminist Gloria Steinem, who made her aware of the emerging women's movement. Huerta then began to incorporate a feminist critique into her human rights philosophy.

During the early 1970s, Huerta once again found her expertise in demand in New York, where she directed not only the continuing grape boycott but also boycotts against lettuce and Gallo brand wine. As before, the strategy was to maintain nationwide pressure to force changes in California. Victory came in 1975 when the California state legislature passed the Agricultural Labor Relations Act (ALRA), the first law to recognize the collective bargaining rights of farm workers in California.

In the midst of her busy schedule, Huerta began a third relationship, this time with Richard Chavez, Cesar's brother. Their liaison produced four children. Reflecting on the sacrifices all eleven of her children have had to make given her frequent absences from home, Huerta admitted, "I don't feel proud of the suffering that my kids went through. I feel very bad and guilty about it, but by the same token I know that they learned a lot in the process."

During the late 1970s, Huerta assumed the directorship of the UFW's Citizenship Participation Day Department (CPD), the political arm of the union. In this role, she lobbied the California state legislature to protect the new farm labor law. During the 1980s she became involved in another ambitious UFW project, the founding of KUFW-Radio Campesina, the union's radio station. Meanwhile, Huerta also continued to de-

vote a great deal of her time to various other UFW activities, including speaking engagements, fund raising, publicizing the renewed grape boycott, and testifying before state and congressional committees on a wide range of issues, including pesticides, health problems of field workers, Hispanic political issues, and immigration policy.

Huerta's activism has come at great personal cost to her and to her family. Besides the extensive travel that keeps her away from home most of the time, she has been arrested on more than twenty occasions. In 1988, she suffered a life-threatening injury at a peaceful demonstration against the policies of George Bush, who had made a stop in San Francisco during his campaign for the presidency. Rushed to the hospital after a clubbing by baton-swinging police officers, Huerta underwent emergency surgery for removal of her spleen. (She also suffered six broken ribs in the incident.) She later sued the city and settled out of court, receiving a record financial settlement. In addition, as a direct result of the assault on Huerta, the San Francisco police department was forced to change its rules regarding crowd control and police discipline.

After recovering from her injuries, Huerta gradually resumed her work for the farm workers in the 1990s. It was an especially difficult time for the UFW; the political climate had shifted more toward the conservative point of view, the farm workers' cause no longer seemed as pressing, and the union itself was in turmoil as it went through a process of internal reassessment and restructuring. The sudden death of Cesar Chavez in 1993 was also a severe blow, one that some people thought might signal the end of the UFW as well.

Huerta insists, however, that the UFW legacy remains strong in the Hispanic community and beyond. She herself continues to commit her energies to the union as an outspoken leader, executive board member, administrator, lobbyist, contract negotiator, picket captain, and lecturer. And she is very proud of what has been accomplished so far and is still hopeful for the future. "I think we brought to the world, the United States anyway, the whole idea of boycotting as a nonviolent tactic," Huerta once told an interviewer. "I think we showed the world that nonviolence can work to make social change.... I think we have laid a pattern of how farm workers are eventually going to get out of their bondage. It may not happen right now in our foreseeable future, but the pattern is there and farm workers are going to make it."

The current president of the United Farm Workers, Arturo Rodriguez—who happens to be married to

Cesar Chavez's daughter—agrees that the road ahead is challenging. The union has had a tough time holding on to contracts in the grape vineyards and citrus orchards, but it is fighting to reorganize there while also reaching out to new groups such as the rose and mushroom workers. Like his father-in-law before him, Rodriguez depends on Huerta's tireless enthusiasm to help boost membership and hammer away at the growers on issues such as pesticide use. "Early in 1970, Cesar Chavez said [Huerta] is totally fearless, both physically and mentally," Rodriguez recalled in a chat with a reporter for *Hispanic* magazine. "A quarter of a century later she shows no sign of slowing down. [Huerta] is an enduring symbol of the farm worker movement."

Sources

Books

Day, Mark, *Forty Acres: Cesar Chavez and the Farm Workers*, Praeger, 1971.

De Ruiz, Dana Catharine, *La Causa: The Migrant Farmworkers' Story*, Raintree Steck-Vaughn, 1993.

Dunne, John Gregory, *Delano: The Story of the California Grape Strike*, Farrar, 1976.

Levy, Jacques, *Cesar Chavez: Autobiography of La Causa*, Norton, 1975.

Matthiessen, Peter, *Sal Si Puedes: Cesar Chavez and the New American Revolution*, Random House, 1969.

Perez, Frank, *Dolores Huerta*, Raintree Steck-Vaughn, 1996.

Telgen, Diane, and Jim Kamp, editors, *Notable Hispanic American Women*, Gale Research, 1993.

Periodicals

Delano Record, April 28, 1966, p. 1.

Hispanic, August, 1996.

Ms., November, 1976, pp. 11-16.

Nation, February 23, 1974, pp. 232-238.

Progressive, September, 1975, pp. 38-40.

—*Deborah Gillan Straub*

Faisal Husseini

AP/Wide World Photos

Palestinian political leader

Born in 1940 in Baghdad, Iraq; son of Abdel Kader Husseini; married; two sons. *Education:* Attended University of Baghdad and University of Cairo; graduated from military college in Syria, 1967.

Addresses: *Office*—c/o Palestinian National Authority, East Jerusalem, Israel.

Career

Palestine Liberation Army, officer, mid-1960s; Arab Studies Society, East Jerusalem, founder, 1979; Palestinian National Authority, minister of Jerusalem affairs, 1993—.

Sidelights

Palestinian political leader Faisal Husseini started his career in the 1960s with the Palestinian Liberation Organization when it was notorious for its terrorist activities, but managed to shed the image over the years to emerge as an advocate for peace in the region. After spending the turbulent 1980s in and out of jail and under house arrest for being a member of the PLO, Husseini has gained acceptance in the peace process as a moderate negotiator. A senior official in the Palestinian National Authority headed by Yasir Arafat, Husseini champions compromises between Palestine and Israel, foreseeing that one day Palestine can coexist as a state and hold Jerusalem as its capital. Extremists on both sides denounce his work and offer death threats, but he has persisted. He even visualizes that Israel and Palestine can someday join forces with other Middle Eastern nations to form a regional entity that works together for the good of all.

Husseini was born in 1940 in Baghdad, Iraq, and moved to Jerusalem, Israel, as a child. His father, Abdul Kader Husseini, was a war hero who led Arab resistance forces against the creation of Israel. He was killed in 1948 in the Arab-Israeli conflict in the village of Kastel and was subsequently regarded as a martyr among Palestinians. Husseini's grandfather, Musa Kasim Pasha Husseini, was a prominent Palestinian nationalist leader during British rule. Another relative, Haj Amin Husseini, was the top political and Islamic religious leader—known as the Grand Mufti—of Palestine from 1921 until 1948. He vociferously opposed Jewish settlement in Palestine and the British occupation, and was eventually exiled. He settled in Germany and supported the Nazis.

Husseini and others in his family, meanwhile, holed up in Egypt, like many wealthy citizens, while war ravaged their country. About 350 villages were wiped out and about half the population—perhaps 800,000 Palestinians—left the nation in 1948. Husseini attended college at the University of Baghdad and also the University of Cairo, where he became friends with Yasir Arafat, an engineering student who had started Fatah, a liberation group, in the mid-1950s. He would later become leader of the Palestinian Liberation Organization (PLO). Fatah was initiated to lash out using terrorism in order to command attention for the Palestinian cause. Husseini became involved with Fatah and went to a military college in Syria, graduating in 1967 and becoming an officer in the fledgling Palestine Liberation Army. He set up a training camp in Lebanon and assisted with other "military activities," according to an article in the *Christian Science Monitor,* which "included bombings and hijackings most of the world saw as terrorism." Husseini said later that although he did not approve of the tactics, they were effective in publicizing the situation and turning some opinion their way.

On June 5, 1967, Israeli forces began the Six-Day War, an integral point in Arab-Israeli politics. Israel captured the Golan Heights from Syria, the West Bank and East Jerusalem from Jordan, and the Gaza Strip form Egypt. Since then, the ownership of those areas has been in dispute. Husseini moved back to Jerusalem and soon after, Israeli soldiers arrested him for having two submachine guns in his home. He was jailed for a year. Throughout the 1970s, turmoil continued between the two states with another conflict, the October War, breaking out in 1973. Meanwhile, Husseini separated himself from terrorist activities and veered into politics, holding public forums with important Israelis and helping with cooperative protests in conjunction with Israeli groups. Dedicating himself to peaceful solutions, he founded the Arab Studies Society in East Jerusalem in 1979, an institute for researching Palestinian history. In 1974, the Arab Summit named the PLO the official representative body for Palestine and was given observer status at the United Nations. Arafat, heading the PLO, signed the Camp David Agreement peace accords with Israel in 1978.

However, in 1982, Israel invaded Lebanon, where Arafat and other PLO officials held offices. Husseini was arrested and jailed numerous times from 1982 to 1987 for being a PLO member and was not allowed to travel outside of the country. In December of 1987, a Palestinian uprising known as the intifada began on the West Bank and Gaza Strip. This revolt against the Israeli occupation was marked with violence and demonstrations. The Israeli army retaliated by striking back hard at the rioters and locking up Palestinian leaders, including Husseini, who was accused of inciting riots. The military also closed down his Arab Studies Society, though he later reopened it in his home. During Husseini's year-long prison stretch that lasted until January of 1989, he used his time to study Hebrew and English. His release was taken as a sign that Israeli defense minister Yitzhak Rabin was ready to talk in order to help simmer down the intifada. Husseini, however, redirected Rabin to the PLO. That December, Husseini was placed under house arrest, purportedly because his public speeches fueled uprisings.

During the Gulf War in 1991, the PLO set itself back by supporting Saddam Hussein and Iraq during the conflict. After the war, the United States worked to establish peace in the region and arranged a conference in Madrid, Spain, in late October of 1991. Israeli prime minister Yitzhak Shamir, however, refused to negotiate with any known PLO members, so Husseini instead acted as a consultant to the Palestinian delegates. After Rabin took over as prime minister in 1992, he expressed willingness to discuss peace with the PLO, and Husseini was called to the table. However, Husseini and two other negotiators quit the talks in 1993 after having differences with Arafat, who was still living outside the region in Tunisia, but he would not accept their resignations. Subsequently, Israel officially recognized the PLO, and then it was revealed that Rabin, meanwhile, had begun secret discussions with the PLO in Oslo, Norway. In 1993 a peace agreement was signed in Washington, D.C., that allowed Palestinian autonomy in the Gaza Strip and Jericho, a town on the West Bank. It also set up a temporary authority, the Palestinian National Authority. Arafat returned to Gaza and named Husseini the minister of Jerusalem affairs for the Palestinian National Authority.

Rabin was assassinated in 1994 by a right-wing Israeli gunman, shocking both sides, and right-of-center Likud Party member Benjamin Netanyahu was elected prime minister. His rise put new strains on the peace process, and his support of Jewish settlements in the region, including the construction of two Jewish housing projects in East Jerusalem, drove a wedge between the two sides in 1997. This point of contention sparked protests and violence, and Husseini was injured in June of 1998 during an incident when he was hit on the head by a rock. There were also disputes over residency permits and the plans for Israel to extend Jerusalem's boundaries. In addition, relations between Husseini and Arafat seemed to have soured, though Husseini publicly supports the PLO leader. As the fighting raged on well into 1998, Husseini was doubtful that there would be peace with Israel as long as Netanyahu was prime minster. Husseini remained committed to the idea that Palestine should join with other countries such as Israel, Jordan, Lebanon, Syria, and Egypt to form a larger, regional state, much like Europe, which retains individual nations that tend to cooperate as one entity.

Husseini is married and has two sons. He is tall and soft-spoken, and popular in Palestinian intellectual circles. Though some observers feel he is being pushed out of the top ranks of the PLO due to his differences with Arafat, especially on human rights issues, others say he could be in line as a successor, though Husseini denies the talk. He insists that if Jerusalem is not the capital of Palestine, then he will not become its leader.

Sources

On-line

"Jewish Settlers' Move Sparks Palestinian Protest," June 8, 1998, CNN Interactive web site, http://cnn.com (September 1, 1998).

"A Brief History of Palestine," Palestinian National Authority web site, http://www.pna.com (September 1, 1998).

Periodicals

Christian Science Monitor, Feb. 13, 1989; April 30, 1998.
Jerusalem Post, August 18, 1995; July 21, 1995; September 3, 1996, p. 2.
Jewish Telegraphic Agency, April 27, 1993.
Los Angeles Times, May 17, 1998, Opinion, p. 3.
New York Times, October 26, 1991, p. 4.
Northern California Jewish Bulletin, November 25, 1994.
Reuters, June 21, 1998.
Time, August 5, 1991, p. 30.

—Geri Speace

Jesse Jackson, Jr.

AP/Wide World Photos

Politician

Born Jesse Louis Jackson, Jr., March 11, 1965, in Greenville, SC; son of Jesse Louis (a civil rights activist) and Jacqueline (a homemaker; maiden name, Davis) Jackson; married Sandra Stevens (an attorney), June 1, 1991. *Education:* North Carolina Agricultural and Technical University, B.S., 1987; Chicago Theological Seminary, M.A., 1990; University of Illinois College of Law, J.D., 1993.

Addresses: *Home*—Homewood, IL. *Office*—312 Cannon Building, Washington, DC 20515-1302.

Career

Field director for the Rainbow Coalition/Operation PUSH, 1993-95; elected to U.S. House of Representatives, 1995, appointed to the committee on banking and financial services, reelected, 1996.

Sidelights

Jesse Jackson, Jr. carries with him the name of his famous father and much more. The son of the famous civil rights activist was just 30 years old when elected to the U.S. House of Representatives in 1995. Despite his achievements, he continues striving to emerge from his prominent father's shadow. Profiles of Jackson often make the assertion that although Jackson has been heavily influenced by his famous father, he has inherited all of the good qualities—his dedication to social justice, intelligence, religious views—but added a more polished veneer and business skills. Jackson told Laura Blumenfeld in *Newsday* that he is like "Jesse plus," adding a get-it-done approach of

"technology and systematic organizing" to his father's good ideas and intents. Indeed, for all his father's accomplishments, the elder Jackson never was elected to office. To say Jackson, Sr. was nevertheless proud of his son would be an understatement. On the day of Jackson's first swearing in, Jackson's father told Blumenfeld of his feelings, "I wish I had a bigger word. Like, I feel elephant joy, or dinosaur excitement."

Born on March 11, 1965, Jesse Jackson, Jr. is the first son of Jesse, Sr., the charismatic civil rights activist, and Jacqueline Jackson, a homemaker. Jesse, Jr. has an older sister, Santita, and three younger siblings: Jonathan, Yusef, and Jacqueline. The elder Jackson was miles away at the time of his son's birth: he had joined Martin Luther King, Jr. in marching to Selma, Alabama, during the historic demonstration demanding voting rights for African Americans. Later, Jackson learned that his father wanted to name him "Selma" in recognition of this event and to shelter him from the problems of being the namesake of such a famous figure.

The Jackson household, set up in a roomy Tudor on South Constance Avenue in Chicago, Illinois, was quite strict. Friends were not allowed to visit on weekdays, prime-time television was taboo, and the radio volume had to be kept low. Though the family was Baptist, children did not receive Christmas presents; instead, they spent Christmas morning preaching to inmates at Chicago's Cook County Jail. The Jackson children were often in contact with celebrities and the media from a young age, and helped out with their dad's organizations, Operation PUSH (People United to Serve Humanity), an economic empowerment group, and the Rainbow Coalition, a Democratic political action group.

Though the family did not take many vacations except to visit their grandparents in the South, Jackson, Jr. and his siblings were not sheltered by any means. They jetted with their parents to the far reaches of the globe on civil rights missions, seeing Africa, Europe, the Middle East, and Latin America. Jackson and his brother, Jonathan, even accompanied their father to Syria to rescue a U.S. hostage, to Italy to meet the Pope, and to South Africa for a conference with Nelson Mandela. Despite the discipline, rules, and work, Jackson, Jr. was often a handful.

Indeed, tests proved Jackson was hyperactive and aggressive, but also very intelligent. The one thing his father remembered best about Jackson's childhood was the time he stood on a milk crate at age five to deliver a speech at an Operation PUSH workshop, according to Laura Blumenfeld in the *Washington Post*. But Jackson's mother, Jacqueline, felt her sons "needed a more regimented form of discipline," as she noted in *Chicago* magazine, so he and his brother Jonathan were sent to LeMans Academy, a private military school in Indiana.

Jackson fared well at LeMans and subsequently attended St. Albans Episcopal preparatory school in Washington, D.C., known to have high-profile students such as the children of ambassadors. His grades were outstanding, and he excelled as an athlete. Leader of the debate team, he also performed well on the football field, gaining 1,000 yards and 13 touchdowns as a running back during his senior year. His football achievements led to scholarship offers from big-name schools such as Notre Dame, University of Southern California, and the University of Michigan. He declined them all, deciding to follow in his father's footsteps and register at the majority-black North Carolina Agricultural and Technical University.

In just three years at North Carolina A&T, Jackson graduated with a degree in business administration. A quarterback on the football team there, just like his father had been, Jackson left the team during his sophomore year to focus on his studies. He went on to complete his master of arts at Chicago Theological Seminary and a law degree from the University of Illinois, even though he has never practiced law. He told *Chicago* magazine that he paid for tuition with money earned from national speaking engagements (his fees ranged from $2,500 to $7,500). He also spent many of his weekends campaigning for his father or other candidates.

Jackson has declared that his family never pressured him to follow a prescribed path, but allowed him to make his own decisions concerning his future. Not surprisingly, however, he told *Chicago* magazine, "I grew up wanting to be just like Dad." At the podium, he became a powerful presence in his own right. In 1988, he and his siblings introduced their father to the Democratic National Convention, and Jackson, Jr. caused a stir with his charged address.

In 1991, Jackson married his wife Sandra, known as Sandi, whom he had met at a Congressional Black Caucus meeting four years prior. She had worked for Congressman Cleo Fields and for the presidential campaign to elect Michael Dukakis before she married Jackson and moved to Chicago. In Chicago, she obtained her law degree and became a practicing attorney. She commented in *Ebony* magazine, "My husband is a true people person. And he's one of the most sincere people I've ever met. We're great friends, and that has helped us through everything."

Jackson officially joined his father's Rainbow Coalition in 1993, becoming a national field director, serving as a liaison between the Washington, D.C., offices and the local branches. There, he used his computer knowledge and knack for organization to modernize. He brought in computers and trained staff on the equipment, set up an Internet site, instituted a weekly faxed newsletter called "JaxFax," and documented the reorganization in a 200-page manual. He told *Chicago* magazine that his father "doesn't even want to use a typewriter. He's so set in his ways—but he's coming around." He also campaigned for his father's allies, U.S. representatives John Conyers and Maxine Waters, and helped open more local chapters of Operation PUSH. His office became covered in pictures of him next to presidents, world leaders, and other politicians.

In 1994, Jackson moved to Chicago's South Side in the Second Congressional District, prompting rumors that he was planning to challenge the incumbent, Mel Reynolds, for a seat in the House. He skipped running for local office, explaining that he had more important things on his mind. "There's a 28-year-old

Kennedy in Congress," he remarked in 1995 in *Chicago,* adding, "my peers are in Congress, the House of Representatives ... Why shouldn't I function in the national debate?" In addition to receiving help from influential advisors, the time was ripe for Jackson's move. Reynolds resigned his seat in 1995 after being sentenced to jail for having sexual relations with a 16-year-old girl.

Jackson quickly took action, leaving his job with the Rainbow Coalition to begin campaigning. At an emotional meeting at the Salem Baptist Church on September 9, 1995, he declared that he was in the running to fill the national political position. In the Democratic primary, he was up against Illinois state Senate leader Emil Jones, who was heavily backed by Chicago politicians and favored for the win. Jackson crowded his home with several computers set up to track demographics by name, city, ZIP code, hobbies, and religious affiliation. Targeting mainly the 18- to 40-year-old voters, he presented his theme of "Let a New Generation Arise" and vowed to improve the district economically. He took jabs throughout the campaign from those who said he was riding to victory on his dad's name. "I inherit my father's friends, but also his detractors," Jackson later claimed in *Ebony,* "neither of which I have earned."

Rising over four other candidates, three of whom had previous political experience, Jackson won the primary handily with 48 percent of the vote compared to next-closest competitor Jones, who took 39 percent. Jackson faced Republican Thomas J. Somer in a special election on December 12, 1995, to fill the vacancy. During the interim, the *Chicago Tribune* claimed that the Hotel and Restaurant Employees International Union, based in Chicago, had paid Jackson's salary for his final two years with the Rainbow Coalition. The government at the time was investigating the embattled union for alleged links to organized crime. Jackson, however, deflected the accusations. Criticism also came his way for not rejecting the support of a former gang member.

Despite the bumps in the road, Jackson won the general election on December 12th, as expected, with an amazing 76 percent of the vote in a district that is 65 percent black and 35 percent white, with one-third of his constituents living in suburbs. Dirk Johnson in the *New York Times* recognized that his popularity bridges any color barrier, even in racially tense areas like Chicago Heights. Jackson told Johnson, "Ninety percent of the racial debate is really about economics," adding, "If we can frame the discussion in terms of growth, jobs, the economy, we can move beyond the racial

battleground." After his swearing-in ceremony, Jackson addressed other members of the House and received a standing ovation for pledging his intent to be a "freedom fighter in the character and best tradition of Jesus Christ, of Martin Luther King, Jr., of Nelson Mandela, and my dad, Jesse Jackson Sr.," reported *Ebony* magazine. He also vowed to oppose Republican plans to cut Medicare and to work toward saving student loans.

Once in Congress, Jackson had a tough road ahead of him, being a freshman congressman with no experience. But he plugged ahead. He was named to the Banking and Financial Services Committee; not a prestigious position, but one befitting a rookie. Though some of his constituents lived in the well-to-do Flossmoor suburb, most of the 572,000 he served were poor and middle-income. Much of his district was problematic, having suffered economic collapse after the steel industry lost its shine. However, he worked to create jobs and boost the economy. In an effort that crossed party lines, he supported Republican Governor Jim Edgar and teamed up with Republican Congressman Henry J. Hyde to forge a plan for building a new airport in a rural area just south of Chicago. He also launched an effort to register young people to vote, and rapidly became popular with his peers. In his first nine months in office, he received 36 requests from fellow congress people for him to visit their districts.

Jackson easily won reelection to the House seat in 1996, where he continued to prove his diligence. Johnson, in a 1998 *New York Times* article, noted that the young congressman had not missed a vote in over two years, and had only held four press conferences. Jackson made headlines in 1997 for his involvement in the Death Penalty Moratorium Campaign, which calls for independent counsel to review the death penalty process. Jackson, along with many, believed blacks were unfairly targeted and that mistakes could not be tolerated when lives were at stake. He cited nine cases in Illinois alone in which inmates sat on Death Row for years, only to be proven innocent.

Most accounts agree that Jackson has a promising career ahead of him; pundits predicted a breezy reelection in the fall of 1998. His quick rise may be partly as a result of his name, but he has added his own ambition to the equation as well. When a writer for *Chicago* magazine suggested that he acted "like a young man in a hurry," Jackson replied, "Well, let's look at the other side of the coin: If my name had been Jesse Jackson, Jr., and I didn't have certain accomplishments at age 30, the press and so many others would be say-

ing, 'The kid's unqualified; what the hell's he been doing? Look at the opportunities he's had.'"

Sources

Chicago, May 1996, p. 58.
Ebony, January 8, 1996, p. 6; February 1996, p. 154.
Jet, May 31, 1993; December 18, 1995, p. 22; February
    24, 1997, p. 10; May 12, 1997, p. 37.
Knight-Ridder/Tribune News Service, January 4, 1996.
Newsday, January 15, 1996.
New York Times, March 3, 1998.
People Weekly, November 18, 1996, p. 50.
USA Today, December 17, 1995.
USA Weekend, July 27, 1997.
U.S. News & World Report, October 7, 1996, p. 11.

—Geri Speace

Jim Jarmusch

Film director and screenwriter

Born in 1953, in Akron, OH; son of a businessman and reporter. *Education:* Attended Northwestern University's School of Journalism, 1970, and Columbia University, 1971; studied in Paris, 1975; attended New York University, c. 1975-79.

Addresses: *Home*—New York, NY. *Office*—Exoskeleton INC, 208 East 6th St., New York, NY 10003. *Agent*—c/o International Creative Management, 8942 Wilshire Blvd., Beverly Hills, CA 90211.

Career

Film director, screenwriter, and actor. Writer and director, *Permanent Vacation,* 1982; *Stranger than Paradise,* 1984 (initially shot as *The New World*); *Down by Law,* 1986; *Mystery Train,* 1989; *Night on Earth,* 1991; and *Dead Man,* 1995. Director, *Coffee and Cigarettes,* 1986; *Coffee and Cigarettes II,* 1986; *Coffee and Cigarettes III,* 1993; and *Year of the Horse,* 1997. Film appearances include *Fraulein Berlin,* 1982; *American Autobahn,* 1984; *Candy Mountain,* 1987; *Straight to Hell,* 1987; *Running Out of Luck,* 1987; *Helsinki Napoli All Night Long,* 1988; *Leningrad Cowboys Go America,* 1989; *The Golden Boat,* 1990; *In the Soup,* 1992; *Iron Horsemen,* 1994; *Tigrero: A Film that Was Never Made,* 1994; *Blue in the Face,* 1995; *The Typewriter, the Rifle & the Movie Camera,* 1996; *Cannes Man,* 1996; *Sling Blade,* 1996; and *Divine Trash,* 1997. Television appearances include *Fishing with John,* 1991. Has directed music videos for the Talking Heads and Big Audio Dynamite.

Awards: Joseph von Sternberg prize, Mannheim International Critics Prize, and Figueira da Foz (Portugal), all 1981, for *Permanent Vacation;* Rotterdam Film Festival International Critics' Prize, c. 1983, for *The New World;* Cannes Film Festival Camera d'Or, Locarno (Switzerland) Film Festival best film award, and National Society of Film Critics picture of the year, all 1984, for *Stranger than Paradise;* Locarno Film Festival Golden Leopard award, and best foreign film from Norway, Denmark, and Israel, all 1986, for *Down by Law;* Cannes Film Festival highest artistic achievement prize, 1989, for *Mystery Train;* Houston International Film Festival Grand Award for best feature film, 1992, for *Night on Earth;* Cannes Film Festival Palm d'Or, 1993, for short film *Coffee and Cigarettes;* Felix award for best non-European film and New York Critics Circle Award for best cinematography, both 1996, for *Dead Man.*

Sidelights

Jim Jarmusch is not a top name in the Hollywood film industry, and it is that way by design. His arthouse films, though by no means pretentious or inaccessible, have always hung just outside the realm of mainstream audience appeal, because he has refused to make them any other way. They are wry, ironic, and quirky, but with a dry sense of humor and a slower pace than is normally seen on the big screen; they are often "slice of life" stories punctuated with poetic dialogue and illustrated with static shots that resemble artistically executed still photographs. Though not exactly the kind of movie that translates to big bucks at the box office, they rack up awards at international film festivals, like Cannes, and the admiration of many critics and devoted fans. In his own words, the white-haired, black-clad, gravelly-voiced hipster, Jarmusch told Christopher Cook in the *New Statesman* that his films are "not built on the conventional sense of suspense or dramatic tension." He elaborated on his approach to storytelling: "Say a guy breaks up with his girl over the phone and he decides to go to see her and we cut from him leaving his apartment to him entering hers. What I wanted to see was him in between and how he was feeling, what he did and how he got there." Cook appropriately summed him up: "Jarmusch is a reader's director."

Jarmusch was born in the northern Ohio city of Akron, just south of Cleveland, in 1953. His father was a businessman who worked for the city's flagship company, Goodyear Tire and Rubber, and his mother had been a reporter for the *Akron Beacon-Journal* before she married. An aspiring poet and writer, Jarmusch did not see a future in that industrial area of Ohio. He was exposed to culture there, however, as he told Karen Schoemer in the *New York Times:* "I had some friends who had older brothers and sisters. When we were like 14 we started pillaging their stuff—books by [William] Burroughs and [Jack] Kerouac or records by the Mothers of Invention.... That saved me for a while. It kept my mind working."

Jarmusch also recalled that he and his friends would use fake I.D.s to go to the midnight movies to watch Andy Warhol's *Chelsea Girls* and other underground films. He was a part of the "car culture and rock-and-roll," as he told Schoemer. He also took in Japanese horror flicks and James Bond, but two Robert Mitchum movies really opened his eyes: *The Night of the Hunter*, in which Mitchum plays a so-called preacher with "love" tattooed on one set of knuckles and "hate" on the other, and *Thunder Road*, about a band of moonshine producers. Later, during studies in Paris in the mid-1970s, he frequented the Cinémathèque Française, where he was exposed to international films from top Japanese and European directors, as well as some Americans. He devoured works by Yasujiro Ozu, Kenji Mizoguchi, Robert Bresson, Nicholas Ray, and Samuel Fuller.

In 1971, Jarmusch began attending Columbia University in New York City, where he studied literature and planned to become a poet. His teachers included David

Shapiro and Kenneth Koch, mainstays in the city's avant-garde poetry scene of the time. When he returned to New York after his time in Paris, Jarmusch vied for a spot in New York University's prestigious film school. With no technical experience, he submitted an essay and some photographs he had taken, and to his surprise, he was accepted. There, he became a teaching assistant for one of the directors whose films he had often viewed while in Paris: Nicholas Ray, the auteur behind the action-packed *Rebel Without a Cause, Johnny Guitar, In a Lonely Place*, and others. At the time, Ray was working with legendary German director Wim Wenders on *Lightning Over Water*, which dealt with Ray's eventually fatal battle with cancer. Jarmusch got the chance to serve as a production assistant under Wenders, and decided then that he would make filmmaking his life's work.

While Jarmusch was studying at NYU, he also embraced the East Village's thriving post-punk scene, joining a band called the Del-Byzanteens. He sang, played keyboards, and helped write songs such as "Atom Satellite," featuring lyrics pulled from tabloid headlines. His interest in subculture and kitschy Americana would surface again when he began making films, although he would incorporate elements from the Asian and European films he had watched as well. Two weeks after Ray's death, Jarmusch set out to start filming his first project. He had shown his mentor some drafts before his death, and Ray would give him Hollywood-style advice, which Jarmusch ignored. "[Ray] would say, 'There's nothing happening. You need action. The girl should pull a gun out of her purse and shoot the guy,'" the director recalled to Cook in the *New Statesman*. "At which point I'd take the script home and remove even more of the action." Even that early on, while still in the midst of polishing up his first screenplay, Jarmusch was molding the kind of subtle, static-shot filmmaking that would become his trademark style.

Permanent Vacation was Jarmusch's student project for NYU's film school. "It's about two-and- a-half days in the life of a young guy who doesn't really have any ambitions or responsibility. He doesn't live anywhere specifically," Jarmusch noted in the *New York Times*, as quoted in *Contemporary Authors*. Jarmusch also told the *New York Times* that the film was shot in an apartment on East Third Street, and the eccentric painter Jean-Michel Basquiat would often show up to sleep there. This necessitated the director having to drag the artist around in a sleeping bag at times until he was out of the camera's view. "He'd grunt and go back to sleep," Jarmusch remarked to Schoemer in the *New York Times*.

Though the 80-minute release was a bit long for a student film, causing consternation at NYU, it was a hit overseas, winning awards in Portugal and Germany. Unfortunately, it caused no such sensation in his home country. Jarmusch was unaffected. He laid plans to start his second movie, penning the script and hob-nobbing with potential backers, when he came in contact once again with Wenders. Jarmusch had contributed a musical score to Wenders's *The State of Things*, which the director had recently completed, and Wenders offered to give Jarmusch some of the left-over film—about 40 minutes' worth. The normal ratio of film a director needs for shooting is one hour for every ten minutes of finished product, after editing. Jarmusch, however, filmed the entire project in one weekend and culled 38 minutes of final footage from the stock. The sophomore effort, titled *The New World*, was a comedy about dullness. It involves a Hungarian woman, Eve, who is fixated on bluesman Howling Wolf, who comes to America to stay with her cousin, Willie, a cardsharp who immigrated ten years prior. Most of the action takes place in Willie's spartan New York City apartment, where Eve, Willie, and a friend, Eddie, watch television, eat junk food, and sometimes talk to each other.

> "You know, you're lucky for all the people you love in your life that you meet by accident. That's what my films are about: things that we take for granted that may be what life really is."

After finishing the film, Jarmusch thought up some more scenes he wanted to add in which the characters would travel to Cleveland and Miami. He went back to Europe, where *Permanent Vacation* had enjoyed success, hoping to drum up investors. After screening *The New World* around the Continent, Jarmusch won the International Critics' Prize from Rotterdam Film Festival around 1983. A West German producer funded the completion of the two additional episodes: "One Year Later," in which the trio uneventfully treks to Cleveland to stay with Aunt Lottie; and "Paradise," where the team again finds nothing much happening in Miami. After fleshing out the film, Jarmusch retitled it *Stranger than Paradise*. The film won the Camera d'Or at the Cannes Film Festival in 1984. The grand prize that year, the Palm d'Or, was given to Wenders for *Paris, Texas*.

The acclaim continued. In the summer of 1984, *Stranger than Paradise* won first prize at the Locarno Film Festival in Switzerland and was chosen to premier at the New York Film Festival, one of the most important screenings of international films in the United States. Critics raved, finally making Jarmusch a relatively big name in his own country. Vincent Canby of the *New York Times* raved that the film was "one of the most original, wonderfully oddball independent American films ... in years," according to a *Contemporary Authors* sketch. Canby also noted that the film uncovered "the ludicrously sublime in the supremely tacky." *Stranger than Paradise* gained a cult following in New York and other large cities like Chicago and Los Angeles, managing to make a profit and catching the attention of Hollywood. Jarmusch, however, rejected offers to direct from the West Coast studios, preferring to stay true to his style.

Jarmusch did indeed keep it going with his third effort, *Down by Law,* another minimalist comedy featuring two down-and-out jailbirds, a pimp (John Lurie) and an unemployed disc jockey (raspy singer Tom Waits). While in the lockup, a new cellmate is tossed into the pen, an effervescent Italian (played by Italian comedian Roberto Begnini) who has learned what little English he knows from slang and profane put-downs. Nevertheless, he manages to communicate a breakout plan, and the three escapees face further misadventures in the Louisiana bayou country. The odd little black-and-white film was chosen to open the 1986 New York Film Festival, where it was critically revered.

The next gem from Jarmusch was *Mystery Train,* a simultaneous trio of tales, all set in Memphis, Tennessee, that tied together in the end. Shot in color, this film features a photographic appeal and offbeat humor. The first part involves a young Japanese couple making a pilgrimage to Graceland and Sun Studios; the bubbly woman, Mitzuko, is enthralled with Elvis Presley, while the sullen boyfriend, Jun, touts the superiority of Carl Perkins in an accented monotone. Their conversations are held in their native language and subtitled in English. In the second story, Luisa, an Italian widow shipping her husband's remains back to her home country, is forced to make an unexpected stop and is begrudgingly paired at a hotel with a flighty motormouth, DeeDee, who cannot afford her own room. The final leg of the film entails an unhappy Englishman named Johnny, but also called Elvis (played by the Clash's Joe Strummer) who has lost his job and his girlfriend, DeeDee (from the second part). He proceeds to get drunk while driving around with DeeDee's worry-wart brother (Steve Buscemi) and a friend, and ends up shooting a racist liquor store clerk. All three stories are connected by the hotel, where they all stay the night. The role of the dubious desk clerk is filled by Screamin' Jay Hawkins, and his bellhop is played by Spike Lee's brother Cinqué Lee. Some critics faulted the slow pace, but others, like Canby in the *New York Times,* continued their praises; the film won the award for highest artistic achievement at Cannes in 1989. In 1991, Jarmusch came out with a less deadpan—but again segmented—work in *Night on Earth,* a collection of five stories simultaneously taking place in taxicabs around the world. With a higher budget and some bigger stars, such as Winona Ryder, the film is more of a romp than Jarmusch's previous releases, but still possesses the small observances and artistic imagery that originally built his fan base.

In 1996, Jarmusch surprised critics with *Dead Man,* a poetic Western in which he got to direct one of the heroes of his early film days, Robert Mitchum. Boasting Johnny Depp in the lead role as William Blake, an accountant from Cleveland, *Dead Man* was hailed with a New York Critics Circle Award for best cinematography and a Felix award for best non-European film. The story traces Blake's journey to a nonexistent job at a mining company, where he ends up getting wounded while killing the owner's son in a gunfight. The outlaw goes on the run and befriends Nobody (Gary Farmer), a Native American aficionado of English literature. Not to disappoint viewers who have come to relish the odd cameos that Jarmusch tosses in, rocker Iggy Pop turns up as a cross-dressing animal trapper. Jarmusch went back to filming in black-and-white for this release, which David Ansen in *Newsweek* admitted "is not an easy movie to categorize." Ansen liked the film, saying, "Undeniably, it's an original," but acknowledged, "I won't pretend that Jarmusch's austere poetry will speak to everyone."

Guitarist/singer Neil Young, who provided the music for *Dead Man,* was the subject of Jarmusch's next feature, a 1997 documentary called *Year of the Horse,* referring to Young's longtime rock band, Crazy Horse. Young had asked Jarmusch to make a video for a song from the band's *Broken Arrow* album. The director obliged, shooting "Big Time" with a low-budget Super 8 film camera, the grainy kind that people used to use for home movies before videotape. "When Neil saw the finished video," Jarmusch remarked in Detroit's *Metro Times,* "he really loved the way it looked and that was really the genesis of this film." Without a plan, he went on the road, shooting Super 8 concert footage of Crazy Horse's 1996 tour. Between the long

takes of Young's blistering onstage guitar work, Jarmusch added brief clips from backstage interviews with Young's father and band members, as well as some old behind-the-scenes films from 1976 and 1986. The work is more concert film than documentary as well as a big-screen (although often fuzzy) tribute to one of Jarmusch's favorite artists. It was the first time he broke from his traditional narrative form. It did not, however, betray his attachment to static shots. Quick-cuts and other flashy MTV-like bells and whistles had no place in this music movie.

Rolling Stone reported in August of 1997 that Jarmusch was already busy with his next script. Though critics cannot seem to agree on whether Jarmusch's films are good or bad, they all seem to indicate that they are not really *about* anything—much like television's famed *Seinfeld*—but are more about the spaces in between life's action. The director, in one of his adroit statements, seemed to echo this point. "You know, you're lucky for all the people you love in your life that you meet by accident," Jarmusch mused to Schoemer in the *New York Times.* "That's what my films are about: things that we take for granted that may be what life really is."

Sources

Books

Contemporary Authors, Volume 132, Gale Research, 1991.
Contemporary Theatre, Film and Television, Volume 9, Gale Research, 1992.

Periodicals

Entertainment Weekly, January 31, 1997, p. 65.
Film Comment, November-December 1995, p. 80.
Metro Times (Detroit, MI), January 28-February 3, 1998, p. 21.
New Republic, June 3, 1996, p. 30.
New Statesman, July 5, 1996, p. 41.
Newsweek, December 4, 1989, p. 78; June 3, 1996, p. 75.
New York, November 20, 1989, p. 120.
New York Times, April 30, 1992.
Rolling Stone, May 14, 1992, p. 111; August 21, 1997, p. 34.
Video Magazine, January 1993, p. 58; February-March 1997, p. 80.

—Geri Speace

Jenny Jones

Talk show host

Born Janina Stronski, June 7, 1946, in Jerusalem, Palestine (now Israel); daughter of Jan (a Polish army officer) and Zosia (a seamstress) Stronski; first marriage (husband's name not given), 1969 (annulled c. 1969); married Al Gambino (an entertainer), 1970 (divorced 1972); married Buz Wilburn (a businessman), 1973 (divorced 1980). *Education:* GED certificate, 1996.

Addresses: *Office*—P.O. Box 3333, Chicago, IL 60654; and c/o Warner Bros. Television, 645 North Michigan Avenue, Chicago, IL 60611.

Career

Toured small towns in Canada as a drummer in several rock and roll groups, early 1960s; toured bars and clubs in the United States as a musician with several groups, 1965-67; The Swingin' Dolls (an all-girl band), performed in Las Vegas and Lake Tahoe, NV, member of band, 1967-69; The Cover Girls, member of band, 1969-70; *The Wayne Newton Show,* Las Vegas, sang back-up vocals and later arranged vocals and played harmonica, 1971-73; Jenny Jones and Company, Los Angeles, CA, lead singer, 1973-79; Laff Stop, Encino, CA, appeared as comedienne, March 1981; Ed McMahon's *Star Search,* grand prize winner in "Comedy," 1986; worked as the opening act comedienne for Engelbert Humperdinck, Tony Bennett, Sammy Davis, Jr., and others, 1986-88; revised comedy act into a women-only format, Girls' Night Out, 1989; *The Jenny Jones Show,* talk show host, 1991—.

Sidelights

Talk show host Jenny Jones achieved success relatively late in her career as an entertainer. She has performed and struggled as a 17-year-old rock and roll musician, a singer, a caterer, a game show contestant, and a stand-up comedienne. Despite career setbacks, including a scandalous murder trial where a one guest was convicted of killing another, Jones gained national recognition after she candidly disclosed her health problems associated with her breast implants. She has proven to be a survivor whose will to succeed is stronger than the adversity she has faced.

Jones was born Janina Stronski to Polish refugee parents whose World War II experiences left them emotionally scarred, homeless, and without a country. She and her older sister Elizabeth were born in Palestine, which became the state of Israel two years after Jones' birth. The Polish, Roman Catholic family left the country, and lived briefly in Rome before immigrating to Canada in 1948.

Jones was raised in a pleasant, small, eastern Canadian city from the age of two. Her parents opened a bridal shop in London, Ontario. When she was eleven, her parents divorced after her father had an affair with the shop assistant. Their mother took her and her sister to live in Montreal for two years. According to Michael A. Lipton in *People*, Jones' mother was a diet-pill popping, verbally-abusive alcoholic. Jones' sister Elizabeth added, "My mother was a binger. She wasn't a hugger or kisser. She was an old-country mother."

In 1959, their father won custody of the two sisters, and they returned to London. However, according to Jones, things weren't much better there. She constantly sought approval and emotional support from her parents but never really received more than a token of recognition. At the age of 17, the rebellious Jones dropped out of school and left home to become a musician.

Jones had taught herself to play jazz drums. She toured small towns in Canada with various groups in the 1960s, and by the mid-1960s, she was touring across the United States with pick-up groups. Jones was a member of an all-girl rock quartet called The Swingin' Dolls and they had moderate success touring Las Vegas and Lake Tahoe, and later the Far East in the late 1960s. She then joined another band called The Cover Girls and worked the U.S. and Canadian circuit in 1969 and 1970. Jones also married for the first time in 1969, but it was quickly annulled.

Jones' early career as an entertainer had many small successes which brought her into contact with established performers who could advise her and open doors to opportunity. She sang back-up vocals, played harmonica and was later the vocal arranger for *The Wayne Newton Show* in Las Vegas in the early 1970s. Jones also married for the second time in 1970, but was divorced in 1972. She married her third husband in 1973, and also formed her own group, Jenny Jones and Company.

The group played the club circuit around Los Angeles, from 1973 to 1979, with Jones as the lead singer. However, after a severe beating at the hands of a mugger in August of 1979 following a night performance, Jones quit performing and started a catering business out of her California home. She also began to carry a handgun in her purse. Her marriage ended in divorce shortly thereafter, in 1980.

Jones decided to pursue in comedy, and began studying performance techniques of stand-up comedians. By day, Jones was a game show contestant, winning money and prizes on *The Price Is Right, Match Game,* and *Press Your Luck*. At night, Jones paid her dues on the comedy circuit, playing gigs for free and honing her skills. She appeared as comedienne at the Laff Stop in Encino, California, March 1981. It was also during this time that Jones got breast implants as, according to Jane Birnbaum of *Redbook*, "she still believed what she'd heard growing up—that real women have big breasts."

However, Jones didn't get her big break until she was the first woman to win the $100,000 Grand Prize on Ed McMahon's *Star Search* in 1986. Although she literally had everything she wanted, money, fame and more opportunities, within a few years she lost everything. As Jones commented to Lipton of *People*, "I wasn't about being rich or famous. I just wanted to be somebody. I was absolutely driven. I was going to succeed."

In 1989, Jones revised her comedy act into women-only format, Girls' Night Out, and it quickly began breaking attendance records across the country. After an appearance on *20/20*, a prime-time talk show, in 1990, Jones was approached by a Warner Brothers executive who proposed a daytime talk-show. The pilot was filmed in 1990, and *The Jenny Jones Show* was first broadcast September 16, 1991. Although the show was poorly received by critics and initially suffered low ratings, it became one of the top five television talk shows, and was widely syndicated.

In 1992, Jones went public with the health problems associated with her breast implants after she had them removed for good. After six surgeries, "Jones felt compelled to speak out, even at the risk of damaging her career," noted Birnbaum in *Redbook*. Jones received hundreds of letters of support from women with similar health problems. She realized she was lucky she didn't have worse health problems.

According to Marilyn Achiron of *People*, Jones worked at accepting her body and created the "Image Foundation" to "help students realize that beauty is personal." Her longtime companion, TV production executive Denis McCallion, ran the foundation for Jones during its first year.

Jones was also in the public eye in 1995 and 1996 after *The Jenny Jones Show* taped a segment on same-sex, secret crushes. One of the guests was embarrassed by the whole situation, and three days later, he murdered the gay man who had made his feelings public. The press criticized Jones and her talk show.

As noted by Lipton of *People*, the day after the murder, the county prosecutor commented, "*The Jenny*

Jones Show ambushed this defendant with humiliation." Although Jones offered her sympathies to both families, she insisted, "We are definitely not to blame for this murder."

Jones had to appear as a material witness at the murder trial, and the victim's family brought a civil suit against Jones, the show, the distributor, and the parent company, Time Warner. During the trial it was argued whether the perpetrator had gone to the taping aware of its nature, but in the end, he was convicted of second degree murder. The controversial segment has never been broadcast.

Despite the many highs and lows of her career, Jones moves forward. According to Lipton of *People*, "Her show ranks a respectable sixth among the Top 15 daytime talk shows." In 1997, Jones released her autobiography, *Jenny Jones: My Story*, with one hundred percent of the proceeds going to breast cancer research. She commented to Lipton in *People*, "I never thought I had anything to tell. But now that I've written my story, I realize I was a survivor."

Sources

On-Line

http://www.jennyjones.com (March 1, 1998).

Books

Brown, Les, *Encyclopedia of Television,* 4th Edition, Gale, 1992, p. 549.
Jones, Jenny, with Patsi Bale Cox, *Jenny Jones: My Story,* Andrews McMeel Publishing, 1997.
Shattuc, Jane, *The Talking Cure: TV Talk Shows and Women,* Routledge, 1996.

Periodicals

Advocate, December 24, 1996, p. 42.
Detroit News, August 15, 1995; October 24, 1995; February 26, 1996; March 20, 1996; August 21, 1996; October 30, 1996; November 29, 1996.
Entertainment Weekly, November 21, 1997, p. 12.
Newsweek, December 30, 1996, p. 21.
Out Now, November 26, 1996.
People, June 14, 1993; November 18, 1996; November 25, 1996; November 10, 1997.
Redbook, June 1995.

Other

Kravarik, Jason, *The Columbia Chronicle,* Warner Bros. Press Release on Jenny Jones, January 31, 1997, via world wide web.

—*Ralph Westbrook*

Marion Jones

Archive Photos

Track and field athlete

Born in 1975 in Los Angeles, CA; daughter of George Jones and Marion Toler (a legal secretary). *Education:* University of North Carolina at Chapel Hill, degree in communications, 1997.

Addresses: *Home*—Apex, North Carolina.

Career

High school sprinter and basketball player, 1990-93; college basketball player, 1993-96, 1997; professional track and field athlete, 1998—.

Awards: Gatorade Circle of Champions National Girls Track and Field Athlete of the Year award, 1990, 1991, 1992; gold medal as member of South Team in the Olympic Festival, 1994; member of NCAA National Women's Basketball Championship team, 1994; most valuable player, Atlantic Coast Conference, 1997; gold medal, 100-meter run and long jump, USA Track and Field Championships, 1997; gold medal, 100-meter run, World Track and Field Championships, 1997; gold medal, 100-meter run, 200-meter run, and long jump, USA Track and Field Championships, 1998.

Sidelights

In 1993, *Sports Illustrated* writer Merrell Noden wrote, "How good is Marion Jones? Here's an answer straight and simple as the 100 itself: She is the greatest sprint talent ever." Five years later, Tim Layden in *Sports Illustrated* mused, "By the time Jones is finished, it might be fair to ask whether the best athlete in the world wears a jockstrap." As a track star, Jones in 1998

became the first woman in 50 years to win three individual events—the 100-meter and 200-meter run and long jump—and also broke the long jump record and tied Florence Griffith Joyner's time of 10.71 in the 100-meter run. All of these stunning feats came after Jones made a name for herself as one of the best female basketball players in the NCAA. However, her career is by no means complete. She is determined to go to the Olympics in 2000 and bring home five gold medals while surpassing the track records set by Joyner and Jackie Joyner-Kersee.

Jones was born in 1975 to George Jones and Marion Toler, a legal secretary originally from the Central American country of Belize, who also had a son (Albert Kelly) from her first marriage. Jones's mother and father split up after four years of marriage. The family lived in Los Angeles until 1983, when they moved to Palmdale, about 50 miles north, and Jones's mother married Ira Toler. Marion Toler worked while her husband took care of the children; Jones became very close to him. The family was torn when Toler died of a stroke in 1987. However, Jones maintained her tenacity. "Kids on the block called her Hard Nails for her stoicism and spunk," Layden remarked. Jones was a fearless, boisterous girl who did not like dolls, was not scared of the dark, and loved snakes. She would compete in sports against her brother, who is six years older, and his friends.

Jones's mother encouraged her talents, and she moved her children around a number of times so that Jones could attend schools that nurtured her athletic abilities. She attended Pinecrest Junior High in the Los Angeles suburb of Sherman Oaks, then Rio Mesa High School in Camarillo, and finally Thousand Oaks High School, where she played basketball. Jones traveled to Asia during high school for an all-star basketball tournament, and meanwhile, she was ripping up the track. In 1992 her mother recruited Elliot Mason, who had trained with Olympian Evelyn Ashford, to coach Jones. At age 14, only a sophomore, she was the first non-senior to win the Gatorade Circle of Champions National Girls Track and Field Athlete of the Year award after setting the best national time that year—52.91 seconds—in the 400. She repeated the honor as a junior and senior, the only athlete to win that award more than once.

Jones at age 16 became the top junior sprinter in the world, holding the fastest six times for the 100-meter, including her best of 11.14 seconds. She held the nine fastest times for the 200 as well, topped with a time of 22.58 seconds, setting the all-time record for the 200 for a girl younger than 18. She narrowly missed winning a spot on the Olympic team in 1992 by only .07 of a second. Though offered a spot as an alternate, she declined. Also in high school, Jones began long jumping and quickly established herself as a wonder. In her first attempt on the field in March of 1993, she jumped further than any high schooler that year. Later, at a state meet, she came close to breaking a record, jumping 22 feet, 12 inches—the second-longest jump by a high school girl in history. As if all this was not enough, Jones was tearing it up on the basketball court as well, averaging 22.8 points and 14.7 rebounds for Thousand Oaks, earning her the honor of California's Division I Player of the Year. During her two years on the team, their record was 60-4 and they twice made the regional championships.

After high school, Jones's mother encouraged her to take a scholarship from the University of North Carolina at Chapel Hill. Toler was impressed with the school's journalism department as well as the fact that it would work with a two-sport athlete and had a good record for graduating minorities. There, Jones initially concentrated on basketball and helped take the Lady Tar Heels to the 1994 NCAA National Championship as a starting point guard. That year, she also won a gold medal as a member of the South Team in the Olympic Festival in St. Louis, Missouri. In addition, in

1994 she again began giving some time to track and field, competing for two years despite the fact that her body was muscled for the basketball court. While on the team, she won the 100 meter and long jump championships and was second in a photo finish in the 200 during the Atlantic Coast Conference Track and Field Championships, aiding her school to a victory. She planned to redshirt in basketball at the 1996 Olympics in Atlanta, but was left out due to a twice-broken bone in her left foot.

Back on the court in 1997, Jones was named most valuable player in the Atlantic Coast Conference, for which the Lady Tar Heels took the regular season and tournament titles. The team was the number one seed in the East Regional, but was edged out later by George Washington University. She told Peter Brewington in *USA Today* around that time that she would return to track after the basketball season finished. "It (track) was my first love, and it continues to be my love," she noted. Sure enough, after hiring a new coach, Trevor Graham, Jones was flying again with a win in the 100 at the USA Track and Field Championships in Indianapolis, Indiana, with a time of 10.97, and a winning long jump distance of 22 feet, nine inches, beating 1988 Olympic champion Kersee. She also that year won the 100 at the World Track and Field Championships in 1997 with a time of 10.83 seconds.

In 1998, Jones awed spectators and injected a new enthusiasm into track and field when she took the 100-meter, 200-meter, and long jump wins in the USA Track and Field Championships, held in a sweltering heat in New Orleans, Louisiana. She was the first woman to win all three events since Stella Walsh in 1948. Jones's time in the 100 was 10.72 seconds, the seventh-fastest time in the history of women's running. Her time in the 200 was 22.24, and her distance in the long jump was 23 feet, eight inches.

Jones in 1995 met C. J. Hunter, a bronze medal shot-put winner at the 1995 world competition. He was working as throws coach at the university, but stepped down in order to date Jones in early 1996. That spring, they were engaged. The couple lives in a four-bedroom home in Apex, a town about midpoint between Raleigh and Chapel Hill, North Carolina. Jones's mother worries about the relationship (Hunter is divorced, with two children, and declared bankruptcy in 1993), but Jones took steps to rebuild a friendship with her mother so the two would be close again. Happy with Hunter, confident of her abilities, and financially secure with endorsement deals, it does not look like Jones has many, or possibly any, obstacles in the way of her goals, which are nothing to scoff at. "Before my career is over," she told Layden in *Sports Illustrated*, "I will attempt to run faster than any woman has ever run and jump farther than any woman has ever jumped." She also stated in *Newsday*, "I want to be remembered as one of the greatest athletes that ever lived."

Sources

Dallas Morning News, June 21, 1998, p. 19B; June 22, 1998, p. 9B.

Los Angeles Sentinel, May 24, 1995.

Los Angeles Times, June 22, 1998, p. C2.

Newsday, April 3, 1994, p. 7; June 21, 1998, p. C28; June 28, 1998, p. C19.

Sports Illustrated, August 2, 1993, p. 54; February 9, 1995, p. 30; June 23, 1997, p. 58; August 11, 1997, p. 50; June 29, 1998, p. 72.

Star Tribune (Minneapolis, MN), August 4, 1997, p. 8C.

St. Louis Post-Dispatch, August 4, 1997, p. 6D.

USA Today, March 11, 1997, p. 7C.

—Geri Speace

Erica Jong

Author

Born Erica Mann, March 26, 1942, in New York, NY; daughter of Seymour (an importer) and Eda (a painter and designer; maiden name, Mirsky) Mann; married Michael Werthman, 1963 (divorced, 1965); married Allan Jong (a child psychiatrist), 1966 (divorced, September 16, 1975); married Jonathan Fast (a writer), December 1977 (divorced, January 1983); married Kenneth David Burrows (a lawyer), August 5, 1989; children: (third marriage) Molly Miranda. *Education:* Barnard College, B.A., 1963; Columbia University, M.A., 1965; post-graduate study at Columbia School of Fine Arts, 1969-70.

Addresses: *Office*—Erica Jong Productions, c/o Kenneth David Burrows, 425 Park Ave., New York, NY 10022-3506. *Agent*—Ed Victor, 6 Bayley St., Bedford Sq., London WC1, England.

Career

Author and lecturer. Member of English faculty, City College of the City University of New York, 1964-65 and 1969-70; member of faculty, University of Maryland, Overseas Division, Heidelberg, Germany, 1967-69; instructor in English, Manhattan Community College, 1969-70; instructor in poetry, YM/YWCA Poetry Center, New York City, 1971-73; instructor, Bread Loaf Writers Conference, Middlebury, VT, 1982, and Salzburg Seminar, Salzburg, Austria, 1993. Judge in fiction, National Book Award, 1995. Member, New York State Council on the Arts, 1972-74. President of Authors Guild, 1991-93.

Awards: American Academy of Poets Award, 1963; New York State Council on the Arts grant, 1971;

Jerry Bauer

Borestone Mountain Award in poetry and Bess Hokin prize, *Poetry* magazine, both 1971, for *Fruits & Vegetables;* Madeline Sadin award, *New York Quarterly,* and Alice Faye di Castagnolia Award, Poetry Society of America, both 1972, for *Fruits & Vegetables;* Creative Artists Public Service (CAPS) Award, 1973, for *Half-Lives;* National Endowment for the Arts fellowship, 1973-74; Premio International Sigmund Freud (International Sigmund Freud Prize), Italy, 1979; Woman of Achievement, Barnard College, 1987; United Nations Society of Writers Award.

Sidelights

Novelist and poet Erica Jong added some spark to the women's liberation movement during the early 1970s with the satirical novel, *Fear of Flying,* a frank and witty depiction of a woman searching for love while struggling to remain independent. The novel was considered vanguard in feminism and in literature for its innovation of characterizing women as having sexual desires and fantasies, until then usually a masculine domain. A recognized poet before her breakthrough book was published, Jong has continued to produce works of both kinds examining women's issues such as self-definition and sexuality. In 1997, Jong released *Inventing Memory: A Novel of Mothers and Daughters,* which tracks four generations of women, their relationships among themselves, the men in their lives, and their creative pursuits.

Jong was born on March 26, 1942, in New York City, the daughter of Seymour and Eda (Mirsky) Mann. Originally named Samuel Nathaniel Weisman, Jong's father Seymour had been a vaudeville musician who changed his name to separate himself from another man in his union who had the same surname and a bad reputation and because he feared discrimination based on his Polish-Jewish heritage. He later quit his music career for the more practical business of importing antique dolls. Jong's mother, Eda (Mirsky) Mann, born to Russian-Jewish parents hailing from England, was an artist. Jong's maternal grandfather was also a painter, leading Jong to believe she would become an artist as well. The Manns also had two other girls, Suzanna, who was older than Jong, and Claudia, a younger sister. The family lived on Manhattan's Upper West Side and spent summers in the Berkshires and on Fire Island.

Jong attended New York's prestigious High School of Music and Art and then Barnard College of Columbia University, where she decided to abandon her plans of becoming a doctor after an unpleasant dissertation experience with a fetal pig. She decided to pursue English literature, studying all the major authors, including Shakespeare, Chaucer, Alexander Pope, William Blake, and John Keats. Despite the fact that Barnard was for women only, the curriculum did not include women writers, so Jong explored them on her own. At that time, "there were 'no women's studies courses, no anthologies that stressed a female heritage, no public women's movement,'" Jong remarked, as quoted in Feminist Writers. She later gave credit to poets Anne Sexton, Sylvia Plath, Muriel Rukeyser, Carolyn Kizer, and Adrienne Rich for helping her find the way to write from a distinctly female perspective.

In 1963, Jong graduated from Barnard as a member of Phi Beta Kappa and won an Academy of American Poets award and the next year was granted a Woodrow Wilson fellowship. Also in 1963, she married Michael Werthman, but the marriage dissolved after only six months. Jong began teaching in 1964 at the City College of the City University of New York (CUNY) while pursuing her master's degree in eighteenth-century English literature, which she received in 1965 after writing her thesis on Alexander Pope. She told Contemporary Poets that she enjoyed her studies of conventional male poets such as Pope, Auden, Yeats, Keats, and Byron, and from them "cultivated the command of formal verse, and developed an abiding interest in satire," but also later developed an interest in French surrealist poetry and its South American counterparts, such as the work of Pablo Neruda.

After marrying her second husband, Chinese-American Allan Jong, a child psychiatrist, in 1966, Jong left CUNY to accompany him to Heidelberg, Germany, where he was stationed for military service. There, she taught at the University of Maryland Overseas Division for three years and explored her feelings about being Jewish, a topic that she eventually addressed in her writing. The couple returned to New York in 1969 where she was involved in seminars at the Writing Division of the School of Arts at Columbia University, along with poets Stanley Kunitz and Mark Strand. In 1969-70, she resumed teaching at CUNY and joined the English department at Manhattan Community College.

In 1971, Jong published her first book, a collection of poems titled Fruits & Vegetables, thanks to a grant from the New York State Council on the Arts. It was recognized with the Poetry Society of America's Alice Faye di Castagnolia Award, the Bess Hokin prize from Poetry magazine, the Borestone Mountain Award, and New York Quarterly's Madeline Sadin Award. She followed up this success with another book of poetry, Half-Lives, in 1973, which earned the Creative Artists Public Service award. These first two efforts were later combined and released with some other prose and an interview as Here Comes, and Other Poems, in 1975. The next collection, Loveroot, was a Book-of-the-Month club alternate selection. A number of other books of poetry would follow, including The Poetry of Erica Jong, 1976; At the Edge of the Body, 1981, and Becoming Light: Poems, New and Selected, 1991.

After becoming an accomplished poet, in 1973 Jong burst into the public consciousness as a novelist with her debut, Fear of Flying. The book, based heavily on Jong's own life, generated a firestorm of commentary, criticism, and kudos. The protagonist, Isadora Wing, is a poet and writer who seeks an ideal sexual experience. On a trip to Vienna with her Chinese-American psychoanalyst husband, she meets Adrian Goodlove, an English analyst and self-proclaimed free spirit. He persuades her to drop her husband and accompany him on a free-love European vacation, where they can explore their sexual desires without guilt. During the trip, Wing discovers that Goodlove is actually impotent and has promised her a false freedom. Goodlove rejects Wing after two weeks for a pre-planned meeting with his own family, and she returns to her husband, unrepentant though unfulfilled.

Full of wit, energy, and four-letter words, the book addressed the serious concept of what it means for women to be liberated. Many critics, male and female, objected to Jong's use of vulgar language and graphic descriptions of sex. *Contemporary Popular Writers* quoted Anne Z. Mickelson as writing in her book, *Reaching Out: Sensitivity and Order in Recent American Fiction by Women*, "Instead of a woman finding her own self-worth, language and scene crystalize in the kind of male fantasy found in girlie magazines.... By adopting the male language of sexuality, Jong is also fooling herself that she is preempting man's power." Many thought that she encouraged women to have meaningless sex in order to be free. Others, including Jong, disputed that notion. According to *Contemporary Authors*, Jong remarked in *Interview* that *Fear of Flying* is "not an endorsement of promiscuity at all. It [is] about a young woman growing up and finding her own independence and finding the right to think her own thoughts, to fantasize." An *Atlantic* contributor, quoted in *Contemporary Authors*, remarked that the novel includes "a diatribe against marriage—against the dread dullness of habitual, connubial sex, ... against childbearing," and a search for personal creative fulfillment. Translated into 27 languages and selling over 12 million copies, *Fear of Flying* was hailed by author Henry Miller as the female *Tropic of Cancer*.

> "Co-dependency is just a trendy term for being a well-socialized woman.... It's not uniquely feminine, but it's considered normal in women, whereas in men it's considered a disease."

Jong continued the semi-autobiographical tale in *How to Save Your Own Life* (1977), relating Wing's rise to acclaim as a successful author, the divorce from her stifling husband, and her relationship with a young screenwriter, Josh Ace. The love story ends with Wing marrying Ace and having a baby. The trilogy was completed in 1984 with *Parachutes & Kisses*, which details how Ace deserts the family and Wing struggles to be a single, working mother. "It is about having it all in the 1980s," Jong stated in the London *Times*, as quoted in *Contemporary Authors*. "Isadora exemplified the 1970s woman and now, in the 1980s, we are trying to be single parents, breadwinners and feminine at the same time."

Between the second and third installment of the story of Wing, Jong wrote *Fanny: Being the True History of the Adventures of Fanny Hackabout-Jones* (1980), spoofing eighteenth-century epics and delving into the realm of witchcraft. The next year she came out with the collection *Witches*, miscellaneous prose and poetry which continued this theme. In 1987 Jong wrote *Serenissima: A Novel of Venice*, which erases the boundary of time to combine two characters: one is a contemporary actress, the other is a woman from the Middle Ages who knows William Shakespeare. Jong continued to write poetry throughout the 1970s and '80s as well.

Any Woman's Blues was published in 1990, chronicling a wealthy artist who is obsessed by her unfaithful and manipulative young lover. The book outlines the main character's downward spiral into alcoholism, sexual depravity, and drug abuse, although she eventually finds the strength to catch herself and remedy the ills that plague her life. "Co-dependency is just a trendy term for being a well-socialized woman," Jong quipped to Josh Getlin in the *New York Times*, "We're all trained to put other people's needs before our own. We're trained to be validated by what our husbands, children and lovers think of us. It's not uniquely feminine, but it's considered normal in women, whereas in men it's considered a disease."

Jong published *The Devil at Large: Erica Jong on Henry Miller* in 1993, a collection of commentary by Jong, critical essays, a biography of Miller, and letters exchanged between Jong and Miller before his death in 1980. The two had established a friendship after the publication of *Fear of Flying*. In 1994, Jong published *Fear of Fifty*, which she readily subtitled *A Midlife Memoir. Contemporary Authors* quoted Lynn Freed's *Washington Post Book World* review, which called the book "a funny, pungent, and highly entertaining memoir of her growing up, her men, her marriages, her motherhood, her writing, her successes and her failures on all fronts. And she has done so ... with all her customary candor." In 1997, she came out with another novel, *Inventing Memory: A Novel of Mothers and Daughters*, which traced the lives of four generations of women, exploring their relationships and the changes women have gone through during the twentieth century.

Divorced from Allan Jong in 1975, Jong married Jonathan Fast in 1977, with whom she had a daughter, Molly Miranda. After their divorce in 1983, Jong wrote a children's book on coping with divorce titled *Megan's Book of Divorce: A Kid's Book for Adults* (1984), which was revised in 1996 and released as *Megan's Two Houses*. During the 1980s, Jong entered into a couple of romances before meeting attorney Kenneth Burrows on a blind date in 1989. The couple married that same year and made their home an apartment in Manhattan and a Connecticut house in the country. Jong has served as president of the Authors Guild (1991-93) and has won numerous awards for her writing.

Jong told *Contemporary Poets*, "Throughout much of history, women writers have capitulated to male standards, and have paid too much heed to what Virginia Woolf calls 'the angel in the house.' She is that little ghost who sits on one's shoulder while one writes and whispers, 'Be nice, don't say anything that will embarrass the family, don't say anything your man would disapprove of...' The 'angel in the house' castrates one's creativity because it deprives one of essential honesty, and many women writers have yet to win the freedom to be honest with themselves. But once the right to honesty has been established, we can go on to write about anything that interests us."

Selected writings

Novels

Fear of Flying, Holt, 1973.
How to Save Your Own Life: A Novel, Holt, 1977.
Fanny, Being the True History of the Adventures of Fanny Hackabout-Jones, New American Library, 1980.
Parachutes & Kisses, New American Library, 1984.
Serenissima: A Novel of Venice, Houghton, 1987, published as *Shylock's Daughter*, HarperCollins, 1995.
Any Woman's Blues, Harper, 1990.
Inventing Memory: A Novel of Mothers and Daughters, HarperCollins, 1997, published in Britain as *Of Blessed Memory*, Bloomsbury, 1997.

Poetry

Fruits & Vegetables, Holt, 1971.
Half-Lives, Holt, 1973.
Loveroot, Holt, 1975.
Here Comes, and Other Poems, New American Library, 1975.
The Poetry of Erica Jong (three volumes), Holt, 1976.
Selected Poetry, Granada, 1977.
The Poetry Suit, Konglomerati Press, 1978.
At the Edge of the Body, Holt, 1979.
Ordinary Miracles: New Poems, New American Library, 1983.

Becoming Light: New and Selected Poems, HarperCollins, 1991.

Other

Fear of Flying (sound recording; poetry and selections from novel read by author), spoken Arts, 1976.
(Contributor) *Four Visions of America*, Capra Press, 1977.
Witches (miscellany), illustrated by Joseph A. Smith, Abrams, 1981.
Megan's Book of Divorce: A Kid's Book for Adults, illustrated by Freya Tanz, New American Library, 1984; revised edition published as *Megan's Two Houses: A Story of Adjustment* (children's book), illustrated by Freya Tanz, Dove Kids/Penguin USA, 1996.
Serenissima (sound recording from novel, read by author), Brilliance Corp./Houghton, 1987.
Becoming Light (sound recording of book), Dove Audio, 1992.
The Devil at Large: Erica Jong on Henry Miller, Turtle Bay, 1993.
Fear of Fifty: A Midlife Memoir, HarperCollins, 1994.

Sources

Books

Contemporary Authors, New Revision Series, Volume 52, Gale Research, 1996.
Contemporary Novelists, St. James Press, 1996.
Contemporary Poets, St. James Press, 1996.
Feminist Writers, St. James Press, 1996.
Modern Women Writers, Continuum, 1996.

Periodicals

Billboard, June 3, 1995, p. 7.
Economist, November 15, 1997, p. 14.
Library Journal, June 1, 1997, p. 148.
New York Times, August 25, 1973; November 6, 1973; September 7, 1974; June 11, 1975; March 11, 1977; August 4, 1980; August 28, 1980; March 8, 1984, October 10, 1984.
People Weekly, September 12, 1994, p. 77.
Publishers Weekly, July 22, 1996, p. 240; May 5, 1997, p. 193.

—Geri Speace

Ashley Judd

Photograph by Doug Hyun. The Kobal Collection

Actress

Born April 19, 1968, in Los Angeles, CA; daughter of Michael Ciminella (a marketing specialist in the horse-racing industry) and Naomi Judd (a country music singer); sister of Wynonna Judd (a country music singer). *Education:* University of Kentucky, B.A., 1990.

Addresses: *Agent*—William Morris Agency, 151 El Camino Dr., Beverly Hills, CA 90212.

Career

Actress in films, including *Kuffs,* 1992; *Ruby in Paradise,* 1993; *Natural Born Killers* (director's cut), 1994; *Smoke,* 1995; *Heat,* 1995; *The Passion of Darkly Noon,* 1995; *Normal Life,* 1996; *A Time to Kill,* 1996; *Kiss the Girls,* 1997; *The Locusts,* 1997. Television appearances include commercials in the fashion campaign for designer Carmen Marc Valvo; the specials *The Judds: Across the Heartland,* 1989, and *Wynonna: Revelations,* 1996; the series *Star Trek: The Next Generation,* 1991, and *Sisters,* 1991-94; the movies *Till Death Do Us Part,* 1992, and *Norma Jean & Marilyn,* 1996; and a voiceover in the mini-series *Naomi & Wynonna: Love Can Build a Bridge,* 1995. Stage appearances include *Picnic,* New York City, 1994.

Awards: Independent Spirit Award, Sundance Film Festival, 1993, for *Ruby in Paradise.*

Member: Screen Actors Guild, Phi Beta Kappa.

Sidelights

Drawing upon her signature qualities of intelligence and inner strength, Ashley Judd has over-
come difficulties in her personal life to emerge as an actress who is viewed by both critics and the public at large as one of the best in the industry. Although she is the younger sister of country music singing superstar Wynonna and daughter of the glamorous Naomi Judd, who is known as much for her own history of overcoming personal tragedy as she is for her musical and vocal talents, Ashley Judd has not used her family's fame to further her own career. She has managed to carve out a niche for herself among the most sought-after actresses in Hollywood today, and has gained acclaim for her striking, authentic performances in such films as *Ruby in Paradise* (1993), *Smoke* (1995) and *Kiss the Girls,* which was released in 1997. In an interview with *Esquire* contributor Michael Angeli, Judd commented: "I have a responsibility to play my character with the full width and breadth of my own capacity of feeling—that's the only currency I have to invest in my characters. So, if I feel something to here in my real life, I'm looking when I'm playing something to resonate down to that same spot of depth."

Ashley Judd was born in Los Angeles in 1968, the daughter of Naomi Judd and Michael Ciminelli. Judd's parents divorced when she was very young, and she moved with her mother and sister to Kentucky. In Kentucky she attended 12 different schools during the first 13 years of her life and led a truly impoverished existence—often getting by without electricity, running water, or telephone service—as she and her family moved from one run-down house to another. In a brief article by *People* contributor Chuck Arnold detailing Judd's relationship with her sister, Wynonna, Judd recalled: "Mama would say, 'Kids, pour more water in the soup. Better days are coming.'" Looking back on her childhood with *Interview* contributor Ingrid Sischy, Judd remarked: "There's a marvelous synchronicity in my life despite having moved around a lot.... I really believe that I'm designed to be an actor with the immutable facts of this lifestyle—it seems as though what could potentially have been a hardship has actually been sugarcoated for me because of all my experiences."

Judd's mother and sister pursued a career as a country singing duo, but Judd was drawn to reading books, placing herself within the stories and imagining herself as various characters. Asked by Sischy if her family was disappointed that she didn't become a singer, Judd replied, laughing, "I don't think anyone, especially having heard my voice, would be remotely disappointed that I didn't become a singer." Judd was 15 years old when her mother and sister, known as The Judds, became major country music recording stars, but by her own admission, her family's fame did not keep her from leading a steady, fairly typical life as a teenager, as she graduated from high school and went on to graduate with Phi Beta Kappa honors from the University of Kentucky with a bachelor's degree in French in 1990.

Although she spent the majority of her young life with her mother and sister, Judd periodically lived with her father, an arrangement that Judd told Sischy "served me very well because I had a touchstone and a base with him that is the foundation for my relationship with him as a grown-up." Judd also told Sischy that she credits both her maternal and paternal grandparents, with whom she spent summers in Kentucky, with providing unwavering love and care for her as a young girl. Judd declared to Sischy that "the contribution of both sets of grandparents is rock solid," and made it clear that she has tremendous affection for her "Mamaw and Papaw" Ciminella and "Nana and Papaw" Judd. She spent most of her early years living in Kentucky, but Judd also lived in Tennessee beginning in 1979, and spent a few years in Marin County, California. While in Tennessee, Naomi Judd worked as a nurse in a hospital in Franklin, and this is where she believes she contracted the virus Hepatitis C, which is what led to Naomi's ultimate decision to stop performing in 1991.

The shocking public revelation that The Judds were splitting up due to Naomi's illness came about just as Ashley Judd was beginning her career as an actress. Her fledgling acting career was somewhat overshadowed in the public eye by the big news of her family's turmoil, but Judd quietly and with great determination moved to Los Angeles and managed to sign herself with an agent on her first day in Hollywood. The actress prepared for her chosen career by taking classes at the noted Playhouse West and supported herself financially by working as a restaurant hostess. As an indication of her tremendous self-assurance, Judd also landed a role in the very first film she auditioned for, the 1992 film *Kuffs*, which starred popular teen actor Christian Slater. Although she refused to do the topless screen test that was required for the leading role for which she had initially intended to audition, the film's producers were so impressed with the way in which she presented her reasons for refusing that they offered her the role of the wife of the paint store owner, which enabled Judd to secure membership in the Screen Actors Guild.

After *Kuffs*, Judd went on to appear in the recurring role of Ensign Mussler on the television series *Star Trek: The Next Generation*. Watching her play the role of Mussler, Judd's mother was able to witness her daughter's acting abilities onscreen, and, as Judd joked to *People* contributor Cynthia Sanz, it was "perhaps the first time in history someone has wept their way through *Star Trek*." Judd continued to find success in television, receiving high praise from critics for her portrayal of the daughter of Swoosie Kurtz's character on the dramatic series *Sisters* from 1991 to 1994. Kurtz remarked to Sanz that "[Judd] is poised beyond her years. She doesn't want to ride on any coattails or be known for anything except what she herself accomplishes."

Nevertheless, Judd wasn't fulfilled by her work for television, and sought out more film roles. She was rewarded in 1993 with the leading role of Ruby Lee Gissing in the film *Ruby in Paradise*, which won the Grand Jury Prize at the Sundance Film Festival. Judd earned rave reviews from critics and an Independent Spirit Award for her portrayal of Ruby, which *People* contributor Leah Rozen called a "focused, considered performance" in a film that *Playboy*'s Bruce Williamson characterized as "a low-key but stunning showcase for Ashley Judd." Remarking upon her role as Ruby to Ingrid Sischy in *Interview*, Judd enthused: "I felt gripped by the script of *Ruby in Paradise* from the opening paragraph. I thought, This is it. This is for me. This is everything I have been waiting for since the third grade. Here is the story, here is the girl. It could not have been a more perfect piece of material for me to make my debut in."

Judd followed up her starring role in *Ruby in Paradise* with a small role in the 1994 Oliver Stone film *Natural Born Killers*, in which she played the lone survivor of a group of girls massacred during a slumber party by the film's lead characters, serial killers Mickey (played by Woody Harrelson) and Mallory (played by Juliette Lewis). Judd's character sobs hysterically during the film as she recalls—aided by graphic flashbacks—the carnage she witnessed on the night the murders took place. In 1995 Judd appeared in *Smoke,* in which she portrayed the drug-addicted daughter of Stockard Channing's character. The actress received positive reviews for her performance in *Smoke,* which critics praised as realistic and emotionally powerful. In a review in the *Nation,* Stuart Klawans commented: "And then there's Ashley Judd (as Channing's crackhead daughter), whose whitehot performance blows the picture apart from inside. For as long as she's on screen, it feels as if *Smoke* were meant to be more substantial than its title." Judd upheld her reputation as a riveting onscreen presence in her brief but commanding portrayals of the wife of Val Kilmer's character in the 1995 action film *Heat,* and the wife of Matthew McConaughey's character in the 1996 thriller *A Time to Kill,* which was based upon the novel of the same title by John Grisham.

> *"I have a responsibility to play my character with the full width and breadth of my own capacity of feeling—that's the only currency I have to invest in my characters."*

Judd declined to appear in the 1995 miniseries, *Naomi & Wynonna: Love Can Build a Bridge,* which was based on Naomi's autobiography of the same name, but in what she called—according to a *People* article by Shelly Levitt, Kate Klise, and John Griffiths—"a tip of my hat to Mom," she agreed to provide narration for the project. Despite her misgivings over the project and the reported discord in her family, the *People* article reported that Ashley, Wynonna, and Naomi remained close and served as a constant source of support and affection for one another. The article concluded with a quote from Naomi as she described one night spent sitting on the couch with her daughters at her home:

"Wynonna had her head on my right shoulder, and Ashley had her head on my left. I just felt this moment of exquisite completion. They are truly my other halves, the flesh of my flesh, the bone of my bone." In an interview with *People* contributor Cynthia Sanz, Judd spoke of her relationship with her mother and sister, saying "We always think of ourselves, the three of us, as a team. Us against the world. It was that way when I was little, and I think it always will be."

In 1996 Judd starred in *Normal Life* opposite actor Luke Perry, receiving favorable reviews for her performance; in the same year she starred in the Home Box Office (HBO) movie *Norma Jean & Marilyn,* receiving both favorable reviews and an Emmy Award nomination for her portrayal of Norma Jean Dougherty. Although the movie itself, which presents 1950s screen star Marilyn Monroe's life from the perspective of the two halves of her personality, Norma Jean Dougherty and Marilyn Monroe (portrayed by actress Mira Sorvino), was panned by many critics, Judd's performance was often singled out as superior. Indeed, *Time's* Ginia Bellafante, who asserted that Judd's "Norma Jean is a feminist out of a Camille Paglia fever dream—a firecracker of a young woman fully aware of her ravaging sex appeal and ready to use it," went on to declare that "Judd's performance is the high point of this absurd psychoanalytic adventure."

In 1997, Judd played lead roles in two feature films, *Kiss the Girls* and *The Locusts.* The actress appears as a doctor who is hunted and victimized by a psychologically disturbed kidnapper in the thriller *Kiss the Girls,* and although her performance did not merit rave reviews from critics, the film was popular with moviegoers. For her appearance in *The Locusts,* which also fared poorly with critics, Judd was again singled out as exceptional by *People* critic Leah Rozen, who observed that although the entire cast attempts to breathe life into the script "only Judd, playing a refreshingly uncoy sexpot, comes off with her dignity fully intact." Judd expressed enthusiasm for *Locusts* in her *Esquire* interview with Michael Angeli, declaring: "It's such old-fashioned cinema.... It's beautiful composition, gorgeous acting. It's the proudest I've ever been of my work."

Judd's private life continues to be of interest to the public, and she has been linked romantically to actor Robert De Niro, with whom she appeared in *Heat,* and actor Matthew McConaughey, her co-star in *A Time to Kill.* In late 1996 Judd began an on-again, off-again relationship with popular singer Michael Bolton. Although the couple has been seen regularly attending public functions, Judd appears to be more interested in pursuing her acting career and in enriching her personal life. When asked by *Esquire*'s Michael Angeli about her hopes for the future, Judd replied: "What do I want to be? Me—just more so."

Sources

Online

http://www.celebsite.com.

Periodicals

Christian Century, May 15, 1996, p. 546.
Entertainment Weekly, September 15, 1995, p. 10; October 10, 1997, p. 67.
Esquire, February 1997, p. 80.
Interview, August 1993, p. 64; August 1996, p. 85.
Nation, July 10, 1995, p. 68.
Newsweek, December 18, 1995, p. 68; May 20, 1996, p. 64.
People, October 12, 1992, p. 113; November 1, 1993, p. 16; May 22, 1995, p. 64; May 6, 1996, p. 125; May 20, 1996, p. 15; June 23, 1997, p. 45; October 13, 1997, pp. 19, 144; October 20, 1997, p. 21.
Playboy, December 1993, p. 32.
Time, May 20, 1996, p. 71.

—*Lynn M. Spampinato*

Laurent Kabila

Drawing by Bill Bourne. Gale Research

President of the Democratic Republic of Congo

Full name, Laurent Désiré Kabila; born in 1939, in Shaba Province, Belgian Congo. *Education:* Studied political philosophy in France, 1950s. *Religion:* Christian.

Addresses: *Home*—Presidential Palace, Kinshasa, Democratic Republic of Congo. *Office*—c/o Embassy of the Democratic Republic of Congo, 1800 New Hampshire Ave. NW, Washington, DC 20009.

Career

Member of the North Katanga Assembly, Congo (formerly Belgian Congo), beginning 1960; left country after Prime Minister Patrice Lumumba killed, 1961; People's Revolutionary Party, founder, 1963; led assorted engagements against government of Zaire (formerly Congo), early 1960s; established "liberated zone" in Kivu Province, 1970s; forced into exile in Tanzania, 1977; trafficked in diamonds, ivory, and other precious materials, c. 1977-87; leader of opposition to Mobutu regime, beginning October, 1996; president of Zaire (renamed Democratic Republic of Congo), beginning May, 1997.

Sidelights

Few figures emerge on the world stage as suddenly as Laurent Kabila did in the last months of 1996. It is a measure of the speed with which he made his appearance that there were literally hundreds of magazine and newspaper articles about him in the United States and Britain during the first half of 1997—but almost no pieces whatever for the five years preceding that time. In October of 1996, he entered the limelight as the leader of Zairian forces rising up against the corrupted regime of dictator Mobutu Sese Seko. Less than six months later, troops under his command took control of the capital, Kinshasa, and Kabila became the leader of the country, now renamed Democratic Republic of Congo. With its location at the center of Africa, its physical size (as large as Western Europe), and its troubled past, Congo occupies a strategic position in Africa, and suddenly leaders all over the world were asking "Who is Laurent Kabila?" The answer to that question lies beneath layers of mystery, and indeed analysts are far from agreement as to who he is—or what he intends for his country's future.

Kabila was born in 1939, in Shaba Province, part of the region then called Belgian Congo. This was the same land described memorably by Joseph Conrad in his novel *Heart of Darkness* (1902), a vast stretch of jungles, rivers, and mountains nearly one million square miles in area. Belgian rule in the Congo became legendary for its cruelty, but by the time Kabila reached maturity, there were few colonial empires left in Africa. One legacy of the Belgians was the French language; therefore when it came time for Kabila to receive a university education, he went to France and studied political philosophy.

By the time Kabila returned home, the Congo was in a state of turmoil. It had gained its independence from Belgium in 1960, but that was far from the end of the new nation's troubles; in fact, those had only really begun. By now the old struggle of the European colonial empires was an artifact of history, and the new battle over Africa was the Cold War conflict between the Soviet Union and the United States. The Soviets supported Marxist Prime Minister Patrice Lumumba, and so did Kabila, who became a pro-Lumumba member of the North Katanga Assembly, a provincial legislature. The United States, on the other hand, supported Lumumba's chief opposition, an army officer named Joseph Désiré Mobutu.

A bloody civil war ensued, and in 1961, Mobutu allegedly had Lumumba killed. Kabila fled to the Ruzizi lowlands, and tried to wage war against the government from there, but was defeated. In 1963, he formed the People's Revolutionary Party, and set up operations on Lake Tanganyika, at the country's eastern edge. Two years later, he was joined by one of the twentieth century's most prominent revolutionary leaders, a man who in 1959 had helped Fidel Castro take power in Cuba, Ernesto "Che" Guevara. Guevara kept a diary during the six months of 1965 that he spent in Africa, released in English as *Bolivian Diary [of] Ernesto "Che" Guevara* (1968). In the volume, he complained bitterly about Kabila's lack of commitment, and his penchant for spending time away from the front, "in the best hotels, issuing communiques and drinking Scotch in the company of beautiful women." Though admitting that Kabila was young—26 years old—and therefore capable of change, Guevara wrote, "for now, I am willing to express serious doubts, which will only be published many years hence, that he will be able to overcome his defects."

By the end of 1965, it became clear that Mobutu was about to win the war, so Guevara left in disgust. In 1966, Mobutu took power and declared himself head of the nation, which he renamed Zaire in 1971. He also gave himself a new name, the abbreviated form of which was Mobutu Sese Seko, which in full meant something like "the rooster who leaves no hens alone." Zaire came under Mobutu's domination, and he made himself one of the world's richest men while keeping his people in extreme poverty.

Kabila's life during the three decades between the mid-1960s and the mid-1990s are somewhat of a mystery. In the early 1970s, his People's Revolutionary Party

established a "liberated zone" in Kivu Province, and spent the next 20 years in periodic fighting with the government. Kabila himself went into exile in neighboring Tanzania in 1977, and from there he continued to lead guerrilla attacks against the increasingly repressive and corrupt Mobutu regime. While Mobutu stole both from his people and the Western nations who gave him financial aid, Kabila engaged in some questionable dealings himself, not the least of which was the kidnapping of hostages—including some Americans. In addition, Congo expert Gerard Prunier told *ABC News*, "[Kabila] and his supporters killed elephants, quite ecologically, and did mining. Then they smuggled the ivory and diamonds and gold through Burundi."

Burundi was one of three small countries on Zaire's eastern border, and events in the other two nations—Uganda and Rwanda—led to a dramatic change in fortunes for Kabila, who all but disappeared from view by 1988. Tensions began to mount between Rwanda's two main ethnic groups, the Hutus and the Tutsis, in the late 1980s and early 1990s, and because the Hutus were in power, Tutsi refugees were spread throughout Uganda and Zaire. Kabila moved to Uganda in the early 1990s, and became associated with a group of Tutsis who helped a rebel leader named Yoweri Museveni take power in that country. When civil war broke out in Rwanda in 1994 following massacres of Tutsis by Hutus, two things happened: Museveni's Tutsi associate Paul Kagame became the vice president and de facto leader of Rwanda, while fleeing Hutus flooded Zaire.

As the Rwandan civil war spread over into Zaire, Mobutu attempted to conduct a campaign of ethnic cleansing against his country's Tutsi minority. The latter—supported by Kagame in their homeland—began an uprising, and as they took town after town, they were joined by Zairians eager to throw off Mobutu's rule. By October of 1996, Kabila emerged as the leader of the group, which he called the "Alliance of Democratic Forces for the Liberation of Congo-Zaire."

Journalists described Kabila, a large man with a bald head, as jovial in manner, though this was certainly no cause for relief, since Uganda's notorious Idi Amin had been described the same way 25 years before. And it did not help that he refused to speak much about his past: "When he is asked about himself or his family," the *New York Times* reported on April 1, 1997, "Mr. Kabila—a stout man with an easy laugh—invariably changes the subject with a deep chuckle and a wave of the hand." Other journalists, most notably Philip Gourevich of the *New Yorker*, were apt to give Kabila the benefit of a doubt—and so too were representatives of the United Nations, the Clinton Administration, and the continent's most noted political leader, Nelson Mandela of South Africa.

Mobutu was out of power by May of 1997—he died in September of that year, ironically in the same week as Princess Diana and Mother Teresa—and Kabila was the new president. Kabila assumed leadership of the country, which he renamed the Democratic Republic of Congo, on May 29, 1997, and the months that followed did not appear to confirm the high hopes many had expressed for the nation's future. Kabila's troops engaged alternately in lawless robbery, or in strict enforcement of repressive social codes, such as a ban on miniskirts. His foreign minister justified clampdowns on demonstrations, claiming they were unnecessary. Kabila stalled United Nations teams attempting to investigate allegations regarding massacres of Hutus, and he had the chief opposition leader, Etienne Tshisekedi, jailed briefly.

The people of Congo had pinned their hopes on Kabila, who used the same middle name as Mobutu once had: Désiré, which means "the one hoped for" in French. But by September 18, 1997, the *Christian Science Monitor* was reporting that hopes for genuine change were ebbing. People even claimed nostalgia for the Mobutu era, since as one Zairian said, the soldiers under Mobutu could be counted on to spare people who bribed them—unlike the loose cannons of the Kabila regime.

Yet there was still hope to be found in the person of Kabila's backer and mentor, Museveni. The latter has enacted democratic and pro-market reforms in Uganda, exerts enormous sway throughout Africa, and has urged a pro-Western stance on the part of his allies. This may be a pragmatic response to a situation in which there is little choice, as the *New Republic* observed in a June 16, 1997, assessment of the new Kabila regime entitled "The End and the Beginning": with the Cold War over, Africa is no longer a staging ground for superpower conflict, and African leaders cannot count on Western dollars to prop up their regimes. Observers who wish for genuine positive change in the country formerly known as Zaire, a place rich in natural resources and poor in its history of freedom, can only hope that the West will maintain a policy of constructive engagement with Kabila and the other leaders of the Democratic Republic of Congo.

Sources

On-line

"Kabila Was Addicted to Women and Drink," *Sunday Times on the Web,* http://lacnet.org/suntimes (November 26, 1997).
"Laurent Kabila, President of the Democratic Republic of Congo," *ABC News,* http://www.abcnews.com (November 26, 1997).
"President Laurent Kabila of the Democratic Republic of Congo," *MBendi: Information for Africa,* http://mbendi.co.za (November 24, 1997).

Books

Hansen, Carlos P. and Andrew Sinclair, translators, *Bolivian Diary [of] Ernesto "Che" Guevara,* introduced by Fidel Castro, J. Cape (London), 1968.
Waters, Mary-Alice, *The Bolivian Diary of Ernesto Che Guevara,* Pathfinder (New York), 1994.

Periodicals

Christian Science Monitor, November 25, 1996, p. 7; March 31, 1997, p. 6; May 30, 1997, p. 6; September 18, 1997, p. 8.
National Review, June 16, 1997, p. 16.
New Republic, June 16, 1997, pp. 7, 15-18.
Newsweek, December 15, 1997, p. 37-39.
New Yorker, May 19, 1997, pp. 7-8; June 2, 1997, pp. 50-53.
New York Times, April 1, 1997, p. A1; June 28, 1997, p. A3; July 8, 1997, p. A3; July 13, 1997, section 1, p. 9.
Time, May 12, 1997, pp. 52-55.
World Press Review, June 1997, p. 15.

—Judson Knight

Craig Kielburger

Archive Photos

Children's Rights Activist

Born in 1983, in Canada; son of Fred (a school-teacher) and Theresa (a schoolteacher) Kielburger.

Addresses: *Office*—c/o Free the Children, 16 Thornbank Rd., Thornhill, ON L4J 2A2, Canada.

Career

Free the Children (an international children's rights advocacy organization), founder, 1995, leader, 1995—; has testified before two U.S. congressional committees and delivered speeches to a wide variety of groups. Has appeared on the television program *60 Minutes.*

Sidelights

According to United Nations estimates, on any given day, more than 200 million children aged 5 through 14 can be found at work in the fields, factories, and homes of Third World countries in Asia and Africa. Many of these children labor under slave-like conditions for long hours at extremely low pay, often in dangerous or back-breaking occupations such as mining or brick-making. They lack adequate food and medical care, and they rarely (if ever) attend school. Some endure extreme punishments, including torture and occasionally death, for trying to escape their wretched lives. Since 1995, however, these children have had a powerful new voice raised in protest against the exploitation of young workers. Remarkably enough, it belongs to a young Canadian who is himself barely past childhood—Craig Kielburger, an internationally recognized leader in the movement to

focus public attention on child labor and work toward eliminating it.

Craig Kielburger is the youngest of two sons of Fred and Theresa Kielburger, both of whom are school-teachers. He lives with his parents in Thornhill, Canada, a comfortable suburban community just north of Toronto. Until April 17, 1995, Craig lived a life that was fairly typical for a 12-year-old in his neighborhood. When he was not busy with school or homework, he could probably be found hanging out at the mall with friends, playing video games, or shooting basketballs. But on that fateful spring day, the young man read an article in the *Toronto Star* that changed his life forever and perhaps those of countless other children as well.

The article in question told the story of a Pakistani boy named Iqbal Masih who was reportedly sold into slavery by his parents at the age of four to settle a $16 debt. Little Iqbal was then chained to a rug loom and forced to work 12 hours a day, six days a week, for which he was paid about three cents a day. He toiled under those harsh conditions for around six years until he escaped and began a crusade against child labor, particularly in the carpet factories and brick kilns of Pakistan. Iqbal eventually attracted international acclaim for his campaign, traveling to Europe and the United States to discuss his experiences. Just a few months after he began to make headlines, however, the 12-year-old activist was shot and killed while riding his bike in a village just outside the city of Lahore, Pakistan. While no one has ever been convicted of the crime, it is widely believed that angry carpet factory owners wanted very much to get rid of the boy who was causing them so much trouble.

Iqbal's story deeply moved Kielburger for reasons he still does not quite understand; the two had absolutely nothing in common other than their age. And as a family, the Kielburgers had no strong tradition of social or political activism. Yet the young Canadian could not forget what Iqbal's short life had been like and what courage he had shown in taking a stand against adults who were so willing to exploit children for their own gain. So Kielburger began to educate himself on the subject of child labor, contacting organizations around the world that were familiar with the problem and reading everything he could get his hands on.

During the course of his research, Kielburger learned that many popular exports to the United States and Canada—including sneakers, clothes, sporting goods, and toys—are made with child labor. He was also shocked to discover that it is not uncommon for children to be employed in hazardous occupations such as manufacturing fireworks. Others find themselves lured into prostitution, especially in Thailand and the Philippines. "And when I learned that there were 200 million kids being tortured in this way," Kielburger told Elizabeth Shepard of *React*, "I knew I had to do something."

At first, Kielburger appeared before local school groups and service organizations to discuss the problem of child labor. Before the end of 1995, he had recruited about 50 of his friends and classmates to help him launch a new organization, Free the Children (FTC), to publicize the problem of child labor and lobby for its elimination. At its headquarters in Kielburger's home, FTC set up a Web site and soon began receiving letters, e-mail, and donations from around the world.

Thus, what began as a local effort quickly mushroomed into something much bigger—a veritable children's rights movement led by a passionate and charismatic teenager with the poise and oratorical skills of a seasoned politician. In the first months of its existence, FTC managed to gather the signatures of 15,000 people on a petition against child labor and raise $150,000 to build schools in India for former child laborers who had been rescued from their jobs.

During the winter of 1995-96, Kielburger convinced his parents that he needed to see firsthand what he was up against. So, accompanied by an adult chaperon (a social worker with a similar interest in the child labor issue) who doubled as a camera operator, he left Toronto on a nearly eight-week journey through South Asia. Once there, he talked with child workers, took extensive notes, and recorded what he saw on video.

The highlight of Kielburger's trip came in January of 1996, when Canadian Prime Minister Jean Chretien was visiting the same region on a trade mission with several hundred Canadian business leaders. At one press conference after another, the teenager upstaged the prime minister with pointed questions about what actions Chretien planned to take to put a stop to child labor in Asia. The media delighted in the articulate young man's outspokenness and focused even more attention on his cause. Several months later, in April of 1996, Kielburger garnered still more publicity when he made an appearance on the U.S. television program *60 Minutes.*

Within less than a year after establishing FTC, Kielburger had testified before two U.S. congressional committees and delivered speeches to a wide variety of groups, including a number of labor unions, the World Council of Churches, and corporate leaders gathered for a prestigious conference on business ethics at the University of Wisconsin. He also logged more travel time in Canada and the United States as well as in Haiti and South America, alternating speaking engagements with investigations of child labor concerns. In addition, he spoke with numerous carpet manufacturers and urged them to adopt the Rugmark labeling system, a special program that guarantees rugs featuring the distinctive Rugmark logo were not made with child labor. (Manufacturers of other consumer goods, including Reebok, have since agreed to abide by a similar system or are considering doing so.)

While he has concentrated his efforts on Third World nations, Kielburger is keenly aware that exploitation of child labor also flourishes in more affluent Western countries. It is not uncommon, he notes, for young members of ethnic minorities in particular to be employed in agriculture and garment workshops to supplement their families' incomes. And he points out that even in well-to-do suburban areas, it is socially acceptable for children in their early teens to hold after-school and summer jobs. By no means, however, does he equate the magnitude of the problem in the Third World with what goes on in the West.

Despite the uphill battle he and his supporters face, Kielburger remains optimistic that his crusade will eventually put an end to child labor worldwide. He points to increased vigilance by American clothing manufacturers with overseas factories and boycotts of products made with child labor as just two examples of how the public-awareness efforts have already begun to pay off. Besides, as he told Shepard, "I simply do not believe that the adults of this world can put a man on the moon and invent a nuclear bomb and cannot feed or protect the world's children."

As for his own career plans, Kielburger says he would someday like to work as a physician with the international relief agency Doctors Without Borders. Entering politics is also a possibility for the young man many consider a natural for the job. In the meantime, he is intent on turning Free the Children into a true "kid power" movement. "The most important thing I've learned is that kids can make a difference," Kielburger once told a group of high schoolers.

"Knowledge is the key, knowledge is the power. Take that power and bring about change."

Sources

On-line

Free the Children, http://freethechildren.org (November 1997).

Periodicals

Chicago Tribune, December 15, 1996.
Christian Science Monitor, April 26, 1996.
Knight-Ridder/Tribune News Service, April 25, 1996.
Los Angeles Times, December 17, 1996.
Maclean's, May 13, 1996; December 23, 1996.
React, December 9-15, 1996, pp. 10-11.
Saturday Night, November, 1996.
Washington Post, February 23, 1996.

—*Deborah Gillan Straub*

Kim Dae Jung

Reuters/Archive Photos

President of South Korea

Born December 3, 1925, in Hukwang-ri Haewi-myon, Shinangun, Korea; son of Un-shik Kim (a farmer) and Soo-keum Chang; married Yong-ae Cha, 1944 (died, 1959); married Hee-Ho Lee, May 10, 1962; children: (with Yong-ae Cha) Hong-il, Hong-up; (with Hee-ho Lee) Hong-gul. *Education:* Attended University of Korea, Seoul, 1964; Kyunghee University, master's degree in economics, 1970; Diplomatic Academy of Foreign Ministry, Moscow, Russia, Ph.D. in political science, 1992.

Addresses: *Office*—Office of the President, Chong Wa Dae, 1 Sejong-no, Chongnu-ku, Seoul, Republic of Korea.

Career

Mokpo Marine Corps, Chollanam-do, 1947-54; Mokpo Daily News, Mokpo Marine Corps, 1948-52; vice-chief, Navy Police, 1950-51; operated a shipping business, 1950s; spokesman, Democratic Party, 1963-65; member of parliament opposition, Seoul, Korea, 1963-72; spokesman, Masses Party, 1965-67; spokesman, New Democratic Party, 1967-68; presidential candidate, New Democratic Party, 1970-71; presidential candidate, 1987; president, Party for Peace and Democracy, 1987-91; co-leader, Democratic Party, 1991—; president of Republic of Korea, 1997—. Cochair, Council for Promotion of Democracy, Seoul, 1985—; founder, Kim Dae Jung Peace Foundation for Asia-Pacific Region, 1994—. Visiting fellow, Harvard University, 1983-84; advisor, Minnesota Center for Treatment of Victims of Torture, 1983, and Robert F. Kennedy Memorial, Washington, D.C., 1984—; visit-ing fellow, Center for International Studies and Clare Hall College, Cambridge, England, 1993. Author.

Awards: Bruno Kreisky Human Rights Award, 1981; Human Rights Award, North American Coalition for Human Rights in Korea, 1984; George Meany Human Rights Award, AFL-CIO, 1987; Union medal, Union Theological Seminary, 1994.

Sidelights

South Korean President Kim Dae Jung is often called the Nelson Mandela of Asia. Beginning as a representative to the South Korean parliament from a rural province in 1960, Kim's voice championing real democracy and the end of military rule got louder and louder until he challenged the ruling president in 1971. After his defeat in the election, which some observers claim was rigged, he was almost murdered twice and then subjected to house arrest, imprisonment, torture, and a death sentence before the United States finally secured his release in 1982. After returning to Korea in 1985, he was put under house arrest again, but twice more tried to secure the presidency in 1987 and 1992. Kim was finally elected in 1997 and sworn in to office in 1998. But his fight was just beginning, as commentators pointed out the nation's numerous problems that the new president would have to face, not the least of which was an Asian economic crisis that sent international finance into a quandary.

Kim Dae Jung was born the son of a farmer on December 3, 1925, in the most rural province of Korea. The country had at that time been a colony of Japan for 15 years. Not bound to modern-era practices, his parents did not register his birth immediately, which has prompted questions about his exact age. Kim graduated from Mokpo Commercial High School in 1943 and the following year married Yong-ae Cha; the couple had two children, Hong-il and Hong-up. After service with the marine corps from 1947 to 1954, Kim later became president of the marine corps' Mokpo Daily News from 1948 to 1952. He also served as a navy police chief from 1950 to 1951 and operated a shipping business. His first wife died in 1959, and he remarried, to Hee-ho Lee, in 1962. They had one child together, Hong-gul. In 1964, Kim took a management course at the University of Korea in Seoul and in 1967 began courses at Kyunghee University, also in Seoul. He completed his master's degree in economics at Kyunghee in 1970.

The political climate in Korea was rocky throughout the twentieth century. In 1910, Korea became a colony under ruthless Japanese rule until 1945. The northern part of the nation gradually became industrialized, while the south remained agricultural. After Japan was defeated in World War II, the U.S.S.R. occupied the north area, and in 1948 set up the Democratic People's Republic of North Korea. The United States, which had taken hold in the south, worked with the United Nations to ensure elections for South Korea. After the Soviets and Americans pulled out of Korea in 1949, however, the north invaded the south, planning a unification. In 1953, U.N. troops forced the North Koreans and Soviets to retreat north of the thirty-eighth parallel, which established the border between the two nations. Korean military regimes, nevertheless, held tight control over South Korea from 1948 into the 1980s. In 1988, a constitution was drafted which instituted a popularly-elected president and a 299-member parliament, called the National Assembly.

During the 1950s and 1960s, Kim became a gifted orator, speaking out against Korea's authoritarian political and economic system. He was elected to the National Assembly in 1960 and briefly worked as a spokesman for the democratic prime minister, Chang Myon. In 1963, Kim began serving as a spokesman for the Democratic party and also was a member of the party's finance committee. After being reelected in 1965, he held positions as spokesman for the newly created Masses Party and then the New Democratic Party beginning in 1967. As President Park Chung Hee increased his authoritarian hold, Kim became more popular. He continually challenged the ruling conservatives, working fervently to institute true democracy.

In 1971, Kim ran for president against Park, calling for more liberal economic and political policy. Backed by students and the working class, Kim won 46 percent of the vote, but it was not enough to beat Park, who had the backing of big business and the military. World commentators doubted the election results. A month later, Kim was purposely run off the road by a 14-ton truck. Though Kim's driver swerved and saved their lives, the truck killed two people in another vehicle. Kim suffered a broken arm and a limp that has plagued him ever since.

Two years later, still serving in the opposition party, Kim met with a fellow party leader for a secret lunch at Seoul's Grand Palace Hotel on August 8, 1973. Afterward, Kim was abducted in a hallway, beaten, rendered unconscious with a rag soaked in chloroform, bound and gagged, blindfolded, and whisked off in a car. The next night he found himself on a Korean freighter. His captors bound him again, taped his face except for air holes around the nose, and tied him with ropes to a traditional Korean funeral plank for a burial at sea. As weights were hung from his wrists, Kim, a devout Roman Catholic, began to pray. Suddenly, he could hear aircraft above, and the ship made a sharp turn, throwing Kim to the deck. Many years would pass before Kim and the world would learn that Korea's Central Intelligence Agency had masterminded the kidnapping, and that the United States had stepped in to try to rescue him. The details are still sketchy, however, as to where the planes that saved him came from.

The worst was still not over for the outspoken politician. He remained confined to his home, in exile, or in prison for most of the next nine years for his reformist views. In 1976, President Park's power was challenged by a group of religious leaders, professors, and students who signed a letter calling for him to step down. Dissident leaders, including Kim, were arrested and imprisoned, despite riots calling for their release. He was sentenced to eight years in prison for advocating the overthrow of the government, but eventually released, although the government continued to spy on him and harass him.

After President Park was assassinated in 1979, Kim was asked to cooperate with the new military leader,

General Chun Doo Hwan, who had already killed about 200 in Kwangju, where Kim's support was strongest. Kim stood his ground, went on trial for six minutes, and was sentenced to death. An international outcry was heard, and again, the United States stepped in. Newly elected U.S. President Ronald Reagan worked with members of former President Jimmy Carter's administration to effect Kim's release. The Korean government commuted the sentence to life in prison, then finally released him two days before Christmas in 1982. Kim immediately flew to the United States.

In prison Kim endured freezing cells and torture, but he also used the malevolent circumstances to further his education. In fact, as Nicholas D. Kristof related in the *New York Times*, Kim "sometimes complains that the downside of being released from prison was that he lost his best time to read and reflect, although he still works from 6 a.m. to midnight each day and always makes time to read books—in Korean, Japanese and English." Kim learned English and read voraciously during his time in prison and under house arrest, absorbing the works of Mencius, Plato, Bertrand Russell, and Abraham Lincoln. He also became an avid botanist. One of the men hired to spy on him during his house arrest was Lee Yeol, a retired police officer. He was instructed to record foreign journalists' visits to Kim and to root through his garbage, which is how his opinion of Kim began to change. "One day, I was looking through Kim Dae-jung's trash, and I found a piece of his writing entitled 'Resolving Regional Hatreds,'" noted Lee in the *New York Times*. "I was really impressed. I thought he was a genius." Lee added, "I used to look forward to going through his garbage, in hopes of finding some of his writings." Family members must have figured out that Kim was being watched, Lee concluded, because they quit discarding such writings. "I was really disappointed," he remarked.

After arriving in America, Kim took a post as a visiting professor at Harvard University, and served as an advisor to the Minnesota Center for Treatment of Victims of Torture in 1983 and the Robert F. Kennedy Memorial in Washington, D.C., in 1984. In 1985, he returned to Korea, only to be placed immediately under house arrest again. The political climate in the country, however, was changing. After President Park's assassination in 1979, liberal sympathies were on the rise. When President Chun Doo Hwan resigned in 1987, Kim pursued the presidency, but lost in what many believed to be unfair elections. He again lost in 1992, to Roh Tae Woo, who in 1995 was accused of taking over $300 million in bribes. Kim was also im-

plicated in this event, accused of receiving $2.6 million from Roh. The investigation still continues. Meanwhile, a bungling Kim Young Sam took power.

On December 18, 1997, though his party did not have a majority in the National Assembly, Kim finally won his country's highest seat as the first non-military affiliated candidate since 1961. Kim Young Sam's term ended in 1998, and Kim was sworn in. Now in charge of the eleventh-largest economy in the world, Kim was in the midst of an Asian crisis that affected global finance. The nation's financial mess was due mainly to the decades of corrupt officials operating in secrecy and necessitated a bailout by the International Monetary Fund (IMF). Kim ceased being the left-wing dissident and became a more pragmatic world leader, by many accounts. Though prior to the election he promised to try to restructure the terms of the IMF's nearly $60 million bailout, he assured everyone in a speech shortly afterward that he would obey the deal.

In trying to adhere to the plan, Kim also promised to introduce laws that would more readily allow businesses to lay off workers, a frightening prospect for more than half the population who would probably be ineligible for welfare. Unions threatened to strike, but Kim headed it off with a vow to increase government spending for welfare and retraining. However, economic experts predicted that up to two million people—17 percent of the work force—would eventually lose their jobs after needed reforms were implemented, and hundreds of companies were expected to close their doors, including large manufacturers. Interest rates, as decreed by the IMF, were up to between 20 and 25 percent. Also just before taking office, in a move that made for good-guy publicity, Kim pardoned two of his former persecutors, Chun Doo Wan and Roh Tae Woo, who had orchestrated much of the oppression that Kim had suffered. And shortly after taking office, amid a boycott by parliamentary opponents, Kim chose Kim Jong Pil to serve as prime minister: the very man who, as founder of Korea's Central Intelligence Agency, was behind several plots to kill Kim Dae Jung. Kim Jong Pil's appointment was confirmed in March.

Kim Dae Jung was officially sworn in on February 25, 1998, at age 73 and moved into Chong Wa Dae, the Blue House, in Seoul. Among those attending his inauguration were American pop star Michael Jackson and former Philippine president Corazon Aquino. The day before the swearing-in, he told *Time International* that his biggest challenge as president would be the financial crisis and was outspoken in his belief that democracy, human rights, and free markets go hand-in-hand. "I always valued the free-market system," Kim insisted in *Newsweek.* He also commented in *Time International,* "I intend to tear down the dogma pervasive in Asia that democracy is not helpful for economic development," and later added, "I think Asia's economic crisis stems mainly from a lack of democracy."

In addition to the Asian currency crisis, Kim notified communist North Korea, long a mortal foe, that his nation may be amenable to establishing a relationship. North Korea at the time was in the midst of a terrible wave of mass starvation. And although Kim freed two of his former foes before the election, the world continued to watch for the human rights advocate to release other political prisoners; namely, communists. That was slow-going, but Kim did indicate that he might relax the rules on listening to communist radio broadcasts from North Korea and change the National Security Law, which is used against communists sympathizers. Kim also promised that eventually all prisoners of conscience would be liberated. It seemed most of his constituents believed him and felt he would improve their nation. One poll in March of 1998 indicated that he was at a 90 percent approval rating. The world watched to see if it would continue. "All my life I've struggled with all kinds of adversity," commented Kim in *Newsweek.* "Now I've won the presidency, and look what I'm struggling with."

Selected writings

Mass-participatory Economy in Korea, 1971, University Press of America, 1985.

Prison Writings, 1983, University of California Press, 1987.

With the Conscience to Act, 1985.

Building Peace & Democracy: Kim Dae Jung Philosophy & Dialogues, Korean Independent Monitor, 1987.

A New Beginning: A Collection of Essays, translated by Yong Jack Lee and Yong Mok Ki, 1993, Center for Multiethnic and Transnational Studies, 1996.

My Life My Thoughts, 1994.

Korea & Asia: A Collection of Essays, Speeches, and Discussions, Chungdo Publishing Co., 1994.

Sources

Books

Current Leaders of Nations, Gale Research, 1998.

Periodicals

Economist, January 3, 1998, p. 13; January 10, 1998, p. 32; January 31, 1998, p. 41; February 28, 1998.

Knight-Ridder/Tribune News Service, February 24, 1998; February 25, 1998.

Maclean's, December 29, 1997, p. 81.

Newsweek, November 27, 1995, p. 43; March 2, 1998, p. 56.

New York Times, December 21, 1997; February 23, 1998; February 26, 1998; March 10, 1998.

Time, December 29, 1997, p. 111.

Time International, March 2, 1998, pp. 16, 20, 22; March 9, 1998, p. 14; March 16, 1998, p. 15.

—Geri Speace

Mary-Claire King

Scientist, geneticist, and educator

Born February 27, 1946, in Evanston, IL (one source says Wilmette, IL); daughter of Harvey W. (a personnel manager) and Clarice King; married Robert Colwell (a zoologist), 1973 (divorced); children: Emily King Colwell. *Education:* Carleton College, B.A. in mathematics, 1966; University of California at Berkeley, Ph.D. in genetics, 1973.

Addresses: *Office*—University of Washington, Department of Medicine, Division of Medical Genetics, K-160A Health Sciences, Box 357720, Seattle, WA 98195.

Career

Universidad de Chile, Santiago, visiting professor, 1973; University of California at Berkeley, School of Public Health, assistant professor of epidemiology, 1976-80, associate professor, 1980-84, professor, 1984-95; University of Washington, Departments of Medicine and Genetics, professor, c. 1996—. Consultant, United Nations Forensic Anthropology Team. Contributor of articles to professional journals. Member of board of scientific counselors, Division of Cancer Prevention, National Cancer Institute; advisory board, National Institutes of Health Office of Research on Women's Health; Special Commission on Breast Cancer, President's Cancer Panel; consultant, Committee for Investigation of Disappearance of Persons, government of Argentina, 1984—.

Awards: Carleton College Alumni Achievement Award, 1982; Susan G. Komen Foundation Award for Distinguished Achievement in Breast Cancer, 1992; named fellow, American Association for the Advancement of Science, 1993; woman of the year, *Glamour* magazine, 1993; Clowes Award for Basic Research, American Association for Cancer Research, 1994; first recipient of the Walt Disney Research Professorship for Breast Cancer, American Cancer Society, 1994.

Sidelights

In 1990, after 17 years of painstaking work, geneticist Mary-Claire King announced that she was very close to pinpointing the location of a gene that is responsible for a number of cases of inherited breast and ovarian cancer. By locating the chromosome on which the gene was located, she cleared the path for helping to predict who might be at higher risk for the cancer and possibly developing better treatments. Though her research immediately targeted only about five to ten percent of breast cancer cases, those statistics represent a great number of human lives that are tragically affected by the killer disease: about 600,000 women in the United States alone, not to mention families and friends of the victims. The race to find the exact gene ended in 1995 when another scientist made the discovery, but King had opened the floodgates to further research. On the verge of the next millennium, she continues in her quest for further study on breast cancer and actively crusades to keep the effort moving. King is also involved in AIDS studies and is an ardent activist who uses her scientific knowledge to help Argentina's "disappeared" persons by means of genetic testing.

King was born on February 27, 1946, in a suburb of Chicago, Illinois, to Harvey W. and Clarice King. The family also includes King's brother Paul, a mathematician and business consultant, as well as a stepbrother and stepsister. King's father worked at Standard Oil of Indiana managing the personnel department. An avid fan of puzzles, King studied mathematics at Carleton College in Northfield, Minnesota, graduating Phi Beta Kappa in 1966. Eager for a challenge, she enrolled in graduate school studying biostatistics at the University of California at Berkeley, where she planned to use her math background in the field of medicine. After a course with geneticist Curt Stern, King found she enjoyed the concrete applications of genetics and changed her major. She was granted a National Science Foundation fellowship from 1968 to 1972 for her graduate studies.

For a period of time during the turbulent Vietnam War era, King organized a letter-writing campaign and petition drive at the University of California in 1970 protesting the American invasion of Cambodia. After then-Governor Ronald Reagan sent the National Guard to the campus to remove students from the buildings, King became dismayed and dropped out. For a while, she worked with consumer watchdog Ralph Nader investigating the effects of pesticides on farm workers. He offered her a job in Washington, D.C., and she weighed the option heavily. She told her friend Allan Wilson, a professor of biochemistry and molecular biology at Berkeley, that she was disappointed with her academic research. "'I can never get my experiments to work,' I said," recalled King in *Omni*. "'I'm a complete disaster in the lab.' And Allan said, 'If everyone whose experiments failed stopped doing science, there wouldn't be any science.' So I went to work in his lab."

At the time, Wilson was looking into the genetic differences between chimpanzees and humans. King plugged along with him, despite doubts, and finished her dissertation outlining the fact that the DNA of humans and chimps is 99 percent identical. This indicated that the two species possibly had a common ancestor about five million years ago, a time estimate about ten million years sooner than previously thought, based on fossil evidence. The researchers ended up on the cover of *Science* magazine in April of 1975 for their discovery. Meanwhile, King received her doctorate from the University of California in 1973 and married Robert Colwell, a zoologist. (They later had a daughter, Emily, but divorced when she was five.) The couple went to the Universidad de Chile to teach. In September, after the assassination of Socialist government head Salvador Allende Gossens, many left-wing supporters, including some of King's friends and students, were killed, went into hiding, or left Chile.

Returning to the United States, King worked for a year at the University of California in San Francisco in epidemiology from 1974 to 1975, then was hired as an assistant professor in that discipline at the Berkeley campus in 1976. She was promoted to associate professor in 1980 and professor in 1984. She spent her time studying 1,579 women, trying to prove that some breast cancer cases could be traced to a single gene, despite her colleagues' doubts. Aware of the fact that some breast cancer runs in families, she studied chromosomes of related women who had the disease. After tedious work dating from 1974, a new technology breakthrough in the early 1980s made it possible to search for pieces of DNA from blood samples. Finally, in 1990 she presented her findings at the American Society of Human Genetics annual meeting in Cincinnati. She had narrowed down the possibilities to a gene located on chromosome 17.

> "'I can never get my experiments to work,' I said," recalled King in *Omni*. "'I'm a complete disaster in the lab.' And [biochemistry professor] Allan Wilson said, 'If everyone whose experiments failed stopped doing science, there wouldn't be any science.' So I went to work in his lab."

Following this remarkable news, a kind of "holy grail" search ensued in the scientific community, with about a dozen teams of researchers fervently trying to isolate the gene, dubbed BRCA1. In September of 1994, Mark Skolnick of the University of Utah Medical Center and his colleagues finally won the race. King and her group, however, did not fail in their mission. King's original research, coupled with ongoing studies of BRCA1 and another gene that was found a year later, BRCA2, has succeeded in raising awareness of breast cancer and the need for further study. King noted at a conference in Paris in 1996 that immense achievements had been made in figuring out how the gene worked. She and some researchers at Vanderbilt University discovered in February that year that healthy genes may be able to halt or even reverse the effects of the mutant gene. This could lead to the possibility that gene therapy—correcting or replacing the gene—will come into play in the future. Scientists well into the 1990s, however, still had few clues as to why breast cancer rates were increasing in developed nations such as the United States, Canada, and across Europe. "Our grandmothers had far lower risks of getting breast cancer than we do now," King noted in a 1997 lecture at the University of California at Santa Cruz, as reported in *Currents.*

King's breast cancer research also paved the way to figuring out whether other diseases could be inherited. "Before BRCA1, there was a widespread view that diseases like breast cancer were caused by multiple genes that interact with environmental factors. This didn't provide geneticists with a clear road ahead," noted Maynard Olson, a professor with the University of Washington, in *Columns,* the university's alumni magazine. "In the midst of that, Mary-Claire's initial report was a jolt. She told a different story: that in carefully selected families she could find a fairly simple genetic link for breast cancer. It provided us with a powerful path forward. We now know that many important diseases can be attacked in the same way." Several legal and ethical issues arose, however, with the discovery that people can inherit these "mutant" genes: If a person is tested positive, will they be rejected for health insurance or employment? What can be done even if the gene is found? What exactly is a person's risk for developing the disease if they carry the gene? These tests are costly—between $700 and $2,400—and research reported in 1997 suggested that carriers of BRCA1 or BRCA2 have only a 56 percent chance of getting cancer, rather than the 80 to 90 percent originally estimated. King, however, was skeptical of the study. These questions, as with many in a quickly-changing era of science and technology, must be answered on an ongoing basis.

In another project, King combined her activist zeal and her education in genetics to assist grandmothers in Argentina who had lost their grandchildren during the civil war of the 1970s. After a coup in 1975, the military began kidnapping huge numbers of people in order to instill terror. Many of the "disappeared," as they came to be known, were pregnant women or women with children. Older children were killed, and pregnant women were tortured. Their babies were sold or adopted by military members, after which the mothers were killed. The new parents would claim the children as their own, despite no sign of pregnancy by the military wives. Through subversive contacts, such as midwives and obstetricians who were coerced to deliver the babies, as well as janitors, family members tried to keep track of the relatives they had lost. By 1977, families began forming human rights groups to find the missing children.

In 1983, two of the grandmothers, members of Abuelos de Plaza de Mayo, asked the American Association for the Advancement of Science to provide a geneticist who could help determine if certain youngsters were their grandchildren. King went to Argentina in June of 1984 to identify remains as well as perform HLA (human leukocyte antigens) typing on living children, a test that analyzes blood proteins. Thanks to King's help, dozens of children were reunited with their biological families. She also assisted with performing DNA tests on exhumed remains in order to hopefully initiate criminal cases against the murderers. In similar projects, King has helped the U.S. government and the United Nations identify the remains of soldiers who had been missing in action, and she worked to establish the identities of over 500 Salvadoran villagers killed during a bloodbath in 1981. "I've learned not to question the motives of bastards," King asserted in *Omni.* "They just do what they do, and you try to stop it."

In the mid-1990s, King began doing AIDS research, trying to determine whether genetics plays a part in why some people quickly develop full-blown AIDS, while others live for years with the disease. Also around that time, she moved from the University of California at Berkeley to the University of Washington in Seattle, where she teaches in the departments of medicine and genetics. She has also worked with the Human Genome Project, a government-sponsored program to map and analyze all 100,000 human genes. In addition, she has served on the Special Commission on Breast Cancer of the President's Cancer Panel; the advisory board of the National Institutes of Health Office of Research on Women's Health; and on committees of the National Academy of Sciences and the National Institute of Medicine.

King has been published extensively in professional journals and books and has received a number of recognitions for career achievements, including the Susan G. Komen Foundation Award for Distinguished Achievement in Breast Cancer (1992) and the Clowes Award for Basic Research from the American Association for Cancer Research (1994). Also in 1994, she became the first recipient of the Walt Disney Research Professorship for Breast Cancer, the most prestigious award granted by the American Cancer Society. She was named a fellow of the American Association for the Advancement of Science in 1993.

Sources

Periodicals

Columns (University of Washington at Seattle), September 1996.

Currents (University of California at Santa Cruz), September 27-October 5, 1997.

Discover, January 1, 1995, p. 99.

Lancet, June 29, 1996, p. 1823.

Newsday, September 29, 1992, p. 59; May 14, 1996, p. B23; December 8, 1996, p. A6; May 15, 1997, p. A6.

New York Times, April 27, 1993, p. C1.

Omni, July 1993, p. 68.

U.S. News & World Report, September 26, 1994, p. 80.

On-line

"Mary-Claire King: Geneticist and Political Activist," Biographies of Women in Biomedicine web site, http://www.students.haverford.edu (May 19, 1998).

"Mary-Claire King biography," SJSU Virtual Museum web site, http://www.sjsu.edu (May 19, 1998).

—Geri Speace

Stephen King

Horror writer and screenwriter

Full name, Stephen Edwin King; also known as Steve King; author under the pseudonyms Richard Bachman and John Swithen; born September 21, 1947, in Portland, ME; son of Donald (a merchant mariner) and Nellie Ruth (Pillsbury) King; married Tabitha Jane Spruce (a novelist), January 2, 1971; children: Naomi Rachel, Joseph Hill, Owen Phillip. *Education:* University of Maine at Orono, B.Sc., 1970. *Politics:* Democrat.

Addresses: *Office*—P.O. Box 1186, Bangor, ME 04001. *Agent*—Arthur Greene, 101 Park Ave., New York, NY 10178.

Career

Hampden Academy (high school), Hampden, ME, English teacher, 1971-73; University of Maine, Orono, writer-in-residence, 1978-79. Owner, Philtrum Press, a publishing house, and WZON-AM, a rock music radio station, both in Bangor, ME. Director of the film *Maximum Overdrive*, 1986; executive producer of the television series *Stephen King's Golden Years*, 1991, and of the television miniseries *The Stand*, 1994. Has made cameo appearances in films *Knightriders*, 1980, *Creepshow*, 1982, *Maximum Overdrive*, 1986, *Pet Sematary*, 1989, and *Sleepwalkers*, 1992; in television miniseries *The Stand*, 1994, and *The Langoliers*, 1995; and in television documentaries *Fear in the Dark*, 1993, and *Baseball*, 1994; has also appeared in a television commercial for American Express. Served as a judge for the 1977 World Fantasy Awards, 1978. Participated in radio honor panel with George A. Romero, Peter Straub, and Ira Levin, moderated by Dick Cavett on

WNET in New York, October 30-31, 1980. Has worked as a janitor, a laborer in an industrial laundry, and in a knitting mill. Screenplays written by others based on King's novels and stories include *Carrie*, 1976; *The Shining*, 1980; *Cujo*, 1983; *The Dead Zone*, 1983; *Christine*, 1983; *Firestarter*, 1984; *Children of the Corn*, 1984; *Creepshow 2*, 1987; *Stand by Me*, 1986; *The Running Man*, 1987; *Misery*, 1990; *Graveyard Shift*, 1990; *The Dark Half*, 1991; *The Lawnmower Man*, 1992; *Needful Things*, 1993; *Children of the Corn II: The Final Sacrifice*, 1993; *The Shawshank Redemption*, 1994; *The Mangler*, 1995; *Dolores Claiborne*, 1995. Teleplays written by others based on King's novels and stories include *Salem's Lot* (miniseries), 1979; *Stephen King's It* (miniseries), 1990; *The Tommyknockers* (miniseries), 1993; *The Langoliers* (miniseries), 1995; *The Shining* (miniseries), 1997.

Awards: *School Library Journal* Book List citation, 1975, for *Carrie*; Balrog Awards, second place in best novel category for *The Stand*, and second place in best collection category for *Night Shift*, both 1979; American Library Association best books for young adults citation, 1979, for *The Long Walk*, and 1981, for *Firestarter*; World Fantasy Awards, 1980, for contributions to the field, and 1982, for the story "Do the Dead Sing?"; Career Alumni Award, University of Maine at Orono, 1981; special British Fantasy Award for outstanding contribution to the genre, British Fantasy Society, 1982, for *Cujo;* Hugo Award, World Science Fiction Convention, 1982, for *Stephen King's Danse Macabre;* named Best Fiction Writer of the Year, *Us* Magazine, 1982; Locus Award for best collection, Locus Publications, 1986, for *Stephen King's Skeleton Crew;* World Fantasy Award for short story, 1995, for "The Man in the Black Suit." Most of King's books have been Literary Guild or Book-of-the-Month Club selections.

Member: Authors Guild, Authors League of America, Screen Artists Guild, Screen Writers of America, Writers Guild.

Sidelights

Stephen King is among the most successful, popular, productive, and widely-read contemporary authors of horror fiction, and the films and television programs based on his numerous works have made millions. King's ability to produce fantastic, captivating tales combining elements of psychological thrills, mystery, gore, and science fiction, and featuring real-life characters with common worries in everyday settings has endeared him to readers and movie-goers worldwide. Despite his tremendous success, King, whose 1977 novel *The Shining*, which had been adapted and released as a film in 1980 was subsequently adapted for television and broadcast as a miniseries on ABC in 1997, continues to maintain both his popularity and his sense of humor. In a quote which appears on the internet service CelebSite, King joked: "People want to know why I do this, why I write such gross stuff. I like to tell them that I have the heart of a small boy—and I keep it in a jar on my desk."

King was born on September 21, 1947, in Portland, Maine, the second son of Donald Edwin King and Nellie Ruth Pillsbury King. When King was two years old, his father, a merchant mariner, abandoned King, his older brother David Victor, and his mother and left them virtually penniless. Living what King described to *Playboy* contributor Eric Norden as "a pretty shirt-tail existence," King's mother moved frequently with her two young sons during the first half of the 1950s to stay with relatives in a variety of cities in Maine, Massachusetts, Illinois, Wisconsin, Connecticut, and Indiana, and supported them by working at a series of low-paying jobs. King has revealed that by reading to him during his childhood and by encouraging him to submit his manuscripts to publishers, his mother was a tremendous influence on his career as a writer, and in his 1981 nonfiction book *Danse Macabre* he described her as a "talented pianist and a woman with a great and sometimes eccentric sense of humor." King's itin-

erant early years are perhaps the reason he told Norden that as a child, he "had friends and all that, but I often felt unhappy and different, estranged from other kids my age." In 1958 the family settled in Durham, Maine, so that King's mother could care for her elderly parents. King attended elementary school in Durham, and went on to attend high school in Lisbon Falls, where he covered high school sports as a writer for the *Lisbon Enterprise*. He published "I Was a Teenage Grave Robber," his first story, in the fan magazine *Comics Review* in 1965, which was also the year he wrote his first full-length manuscript, called "The Aftermath."

After graduating high school, King went on to attend the University of Maine at Orono on a scholarship; he majored in English and minored in speech. While at the University of Maine, King wrote a column for the campus newspaper and was active in the political and anti-war activities that proliferated on college campuses in the 1960s. In 1967 King first received payment as a writer for "The Glass Floor," which was a story published in *Startling Mystery Stories*. Although he was only an undergraduate student, King taught an English course at the University of Maine called Popular Literature and Culture, which was developed after King took the English department to task for the narrow scope offered in its traditional literature courses. King graduated from college in 1970 and because he was unable to find immediate work as an English teacher, he supported himself by working at a gas station and a laundry until 1971, when he was hired to teach English at Hampden Academy, a private high school in Hampden, Maine. King also married his college sweetheart Tabitha Jane Spruce in 1971; later, in "Why I Was Bachman," his introduction to *The Bachman Books*, King declared: "The only important thing I ever did in my life for a conscious reason was to ask Tabitha Spruce ... if she would marry me."

King wrote the story that became his first novel, *Carrie,* in 1972, but, dissatisfied with it, he quickly threw it away; his wife removed the manuscript from the trash and encouraged him to submit it for publication. Doubleday published *Carrie* in 1974, and although it initially sold only thirteen thousand copies in its first hardcover release, the subsequent paperback editions in 1975 and 1976—the second edition corresponded with the release of the film version of *Carrie*—sold a combined total of 3.5 million copies, and King quickly achieved the status of a best-selling author. The novel depicts Carrie White, a disturbed, lonely teenager who uses her supernatural telekinetic powers to kill the classmates who have tormented her and her own mother, a deranged religious zealot who has taught Carrie to feel self-hatred. In this first novel King displays his affinity for presenting such real-life adolescent problems as peer pressure and his emphasis on the roles and concerns of women. Although the novel was a popular success, critical reception of it was mixed, with some reviewers praising King's realistic, believable portrayal of the terror and outrage that marked Carrie White's life and death, and others faulting King's narrative as excessively violent.

> *"King, more than any other modern master of Dark Fantasy, knows how to activate our primal fears."*
> *—William F. Nolan*

King has, over the course of the ensuing decades, steadily built upon the publishing success he established with the release of *Carrie*, and has sold over one hundred million copies of his works worldwide. "Nothing is as unstoppable as one of King's furies, except perhaps King's word processor," according to *People*'s Gil Schwartz; King was selected by *People* as one of twenty people who defined the 1980s. Critics have offered negative assessments of King's books throughout his career, but the author's commercial success has continued to expand. *American Film* contributors Darrell Ewing and Dennis Meyers called King "the chronicler of contemporary America's dreams, desires, and fears," and in *Kingdom of Fear: The World of Stephen King* Leslie Fiedler noted that "no other writer in the [horror] genre [has] ever before produced so long a series of smash successes ... so that he has indeed finally become—in his own words—a 'brand name.'"

The types of characters and themes King has employed in his many books has greatly varied, and many of his works defy classification; nevertheless, similarities between his works have been noted, specifically concerning King's treatment of his subjects and characters. A defining characteristic of King's style is his emphasis upon the inability of his characters to account for the striking evidence of the presence of evil or the supernatural within their everyday lives. King's characters are all distinctly human, sharing a variety of common human frailties and facing very familiar problems, and it is their humanity in the face of

otherworldly forces that lends credibility to King's stories and thus makes the books more accessible to his readers. The accessibility of King's narratives, the humor and compassion in King's presentation of his stories and characters, and the way in which readers are able to empathize with his characters are also what make the stories frightening and compelling; William F. Nolan declared in *Kingdom of Fear*, "King, more than any other modern master of Dark Fantasy, knows how to activate our primal fears," and asserted that readers "value his unique ability to scare the living daylights out of us." Similarly, Don Herron remarked in *Discovering Stephen King* that readers begin "a new Stephen King book with thrills of expectation, waiting for this guy who's *really* a horror *fan*, see, to jump out of old closet and yell 'Boo!!!'"

Many of King's characters are children and adolescents, and the author has been praised by critics as having a keen insight into the minds of young people, which enables him to create especially realistic, believable young characters, all of whom are in some manner estranged from society. King has expressed his appreciation for the special attraction children have to "ghost stories" and horror in general; in an interview in *High Times* he observed: "We start kids off on things like 'Hansel and Gretel,' which features child abandonment, kidnapping, attempted murder, forcible detention, cannibalism, and finally murder by cremation. And the kids love it." In King's books, the young people are empowered and are able to conquer their antagonists, although sometimes losing their own lives in the process. Some of King's books that feature young people as their main characters include *Carrie*, which relates the terror faced by Carrie White, a shy, awkward teenage girl who suffers abuse both at the hands of her mother and her peers; *Christine*, his 1983 novel in which an isolated teenage boy is placed at the mercy of a demonic automobile; and 1980's *Firestarter*, in which Charlie McGee's telekinetic power to start fires using mental images and emotional impulses is sought after by the U. S. government, which seeks to manipulate Charlie and gain control over the firestarting power. King has asserted that his 1986 novel *It* is the last of his novels to feature children and supernatural monsters; in this narrative, seven children who are members of the "Losers Club" defend themselves and their community against a mysterious demon dwelling in the sewer system. The story begins in 1958 and concludes in 1985, when the now-adult members of the Losers club return to their childhood home and vow to destroy the monster they call "It" using the only weapons to which It appears vulnerable: faith, humor, and childlike fearlessness. *New York Review of Books* contributor Thomas R. Edwards concluded "Only brave and imaginative children, or adults who learn to remember and honor their childish selves can hope to foil It, as the Losers finally do in 1985."

Such traditional horror fiction figures as monsters, ghosts, evil spirits, and demons figure prominently in a number of King's books, including the 1975 novel *Salem's Lot*, which portrays the terror that results from a vampire taking up residence in a small town in Maine. *Cycle of the Werewolf*, King's 1983 novel, features the familiar, conventional werewolf in a contemporary American setting, while 1977's *The Shining* and 1984's *The Talisman*, which King coauthored with Peter Straub, take place in haunted buildings. King's monsters also come in the form of alien life forms and scientific powers, such as in his 1987 novel *The Tommyknockers*, which traces what happens to the residents of a small town after they find a spaceship and in 1978's *The Stand*, which is a fantastical depiction of what results when biological weapons and atomic bombs are unleashed on the world's population.

King has incorporated classic tales of horror and fantasy into his works, such as in *Salem's Lot*, which is in many ways a modern version of Bram Stoker's novel *Dracula*, and in *The Talisman*, in which King's young protagonist creates a fantasy world for himself—where he can find a cure for his mother's cancer—that resembles the dream world in J. R. R. Tolkien's *The Lord of the Rings*. *Pet Sematary*, King's 1983 novel, features a story similar to the classic short story "The Monkey's Paw" by W. W. Jacobs; in King's version of the story, the protagonist discovers ancient Native American burial grounds (now used as a pet cemetery) which house a flesh-eating spirit that will inhabit and resurrect dead bodies, and after his young child is killed in an accident he succumbs to temptation and uses the burial ground's power to resurrect his son, with horrific results. The books in King's "The Dark Tower" series were inspired by the Robert Browning poem "Childe Roland to the Dark Tower Came."

Many of King's works fall under the heading of psychological thrillers, some of which he wrote under the pseudonym Richard Bachman, which he adopted in response to publishers' criticism that he was flooding the market with too many "Stephen King" novels. *Misery*, published in 1987, has as its protagonist a novelist named Paul Sheldon who after an automobile accident finds himself held hostage by a deranged fan who forces him to write a novel resurrecting her favorite character—named Misery Chastaine—who had perished in Sheldon's last novel. Women estranged from society feature prominently in 1992's *Dolores*

Claiborne and *Gerald's Game*, both of which illustrate how seemingly normal families can conceal untold horrors, including child abuse. In 1979's *The Long Walk*, one hundred men enter a race and are tormented by the knowledge that only one of them will win and all the rest of them will die, and in 1994's *Insomnia* the protagonists discover another plane of reality as a result of their inability to sleep.

Because of their far-reaching success and popularity among readers, King's novels and stories have been sought out by producers to serve as the basis for screenplays and teleplays, and the results have been commercially triumphant. Many of King's narratives have been adapted for film, and the vast majority of them have been box office successes, earning millions of dollars. Although many of the films, including *Christine, Cujo*, and *Pet Sematary*, are standard horror films noted more for their ability to captivate and thrill audiences than for their merits as fine cinema, some of the films, including *The Shining* and *Misery*, have been critically acclaimed in spite of their classification as horror films or thrillers. Two of King's short stories have been adapted for films that were decidedly outside of the realm of horror; *Stand by Me*, a film based on King's story "The Body," is a coming-of-age film that was praised for its depiction of the struggle of a group of young boys to come to grip with a variety of life issues, including death, abandonment, and abuse, and *The Shawshank Redemption*, based on King's story "Rita Hayworth and the Shawshank Redemption," was enthusiastically applauded for its portrayal of one innocent man's perseverance and constant faith in the face of years of wrongful imprisonment. One of King's works, his 1977 novel *The Shining*, has been adapted twice, once for the 1980 film that starred prominent actors Jack Nicholson and Shelley Duvall, and again for a 1997 television miniseries that director Mick Garris asserted was much closer in terms of its plot and to King's novel than the earlier film. As Garris told *Entertainment Weekly*'s Kate Meyers, "That was a Kubrick film, this is a King book." According to the Meyers article, King was dissatisfied with the film adaptation of *The Shining*, and served in a supervisory capacity for the television version to ensure that it stayed true to his original work. King's works continue to command extraordinary fees for film rights and the author has continued to write his own screenplays, including one in 1997 for a film based on his novel *Desperation*.

King's commercial success has earned him the position of the richest writer in the world, according to a biography on the internet service CelebSite, which reported that *Forbes* magazine has ranked King among the "forty highest-grossing U.S. entertainers" as a result of King's $25 million in earnings during 1995 and 1996. In 1997 King left his longtime publisher, Viking Penguin, and offered his manuscript entitled *Bag of Bones* to the publisher who would pay more than the $17 million requested for the rights to publish the novel. By all accounts King is enjoying his success, and although he reportedly maintains a grueling writing schedule, taking only 3 days off per year, he relaxes with his family in a sprawling twenty-five room home in Bangor, Maine, and plays poker with his friends, including author Amy Tan and cartoonist Matt Groening (of "The Simpsons" fame).

"People want to know why I do this, why I write such gross stuff. I like to tell them that I have the heart of a small boy— and I keep it in a jar on my desk."

King has been publicly very humble about his own fame, asserting to *Yankee* magazine contributor Mel Allen: "I'm very leery of thinking that I'm somebody. Because nobody really is. Everybody is able to do something well, but in this country there's a premium put on stardom." Despite his modesty concerning his celebrity status, King maintains a pride in his craft, and as he told *Playboy*'s Eric Norden, he aims to elicit fear from his readers by employing a variety of techniques in a hierarchical progression. King explained: "There's terror on top, the finest emotion any writer can induce; then horror; and, on the very lowest level of all, the gag instinct of revulsion. Naturally, I'll try to terrify you first, and if that doesn't work, I'll try to horrify you, and if I can't make it there, I'll try to gross you out. I'm not proud.... I suppose the ultimate triumph would be to have somebody drop dead of a heart attack, literally scared to death. I'd say, 'Gee, that's a shame,' and I'd mean it, but part of me would be thinking, Jesus, that really *worked!*"

Selected writings

Carrie: A Novel of a Girl with a Frightening Power (novel), Doubleday, 1974.
Salem's Lot (novel), Doubleday, 1975.
The Shining (novel), Doubleday, 1977.
(As Richard Bachman) *Rage* (novel), New American Library/Signet, 1977.

The Stand (novel), Doubleday, 1978.
Night Shift (short fiction collection), Doubleday, 1978.
The Dead Zone (novel), Viking, 1979.
(As Bachman) *The Long Walk* (novel), New American Library/Signet, 1979.
Firestarter (novel), Viking, 1980.
Cujo (novel), Viking, 1981.
Stephen King's Danse Macabre (nonfiction), Everest House, 1981.
(As Bachman) *Roadwork: A Novel of the First Energy Crisis* (novel), New American Library/Signet, 1981.
(As Richard Bachman) *The Running Man* (novel), New American Library/Signet, 1982.
Creepshow (screenplay based on King's stories: "Father's Day," "The Lonesome Death of Jordy Verrill," and "They're Creeping Up on You"), Warner Bros., 1982.
Different Seasons (collection; includes the novellas "Rita Hayworth and the Shawshank Redemption: Hope Springs Eternal," "Apt Pupil: Summer of Corruption," "The Body: Fall from Innocence," and "The Breathing Method: A Winter's Tale"), Viking, 1982.
Pet Sematary (novel), Doubleday, 1983.
Christine, Viking, 1983.
(With Peter Straub) *The Talisman* (novel), Viking Press/Putnam, 1984.
Cat's Eye (screenplay based on King's stories: "Quitters, Inc.," "The Ledge," and "The General"), Metro Goldwyn Mayer/United Artists, 1984.
The Eyes of the Dragon (young adult novel), Philtrum Press, 1984.
(As Bachman) *Thinner* (novel), New American Library, 1984.
Cycle of the Werewolf (novella), New American Library, 1985.
Silver Bullet (screenplay based on King's novella, *Cycle of the Werewolf*), Paramount, 1985.
The Bachman Books, New American Library, 1985.
Stephen King's Skeleton Crew (short fiction collection), Viking, 1985.
Maximum Overdrive (screenplay based on King's story, "Trucks"), Dino de Laurentiis' North Carolina Film Corp., 1986.
It (novel), Viking, 1986.
Misery (novel), Viking, 1987.
The Tommyknockers (novel), Putnam, 1987.
The Dark Tower: The Gunslinger (book one of "The Dark Tower" series), New American Library, 1988.
The Drawing of Three (book two of "The Dark Tower" series), New American Library, 1989.
The Dark Half (novel), Viking, 1989.
My Pretty Pony (short fiction), Knopf, 1989.
Pet Sematary (screenplay based on novel of the same name), Laurel Production, 1989.
Four Past Midnight (collection of four novellas), Viking Penguin, 1990.

Needful Things: The Last Castle Rock Story (novel), Viking Penguin, 1991.

Stephen King's Golden Years, CBS-TV, 1991.

The Dark Tower III: The Waste Lands (book three in "The Dark Tower" series), New American Library/Dutton, 1992.

Gerald's Game (novel), Viking Penguin, 1992.

Dolores Claiborne (novel), Viking Penguin, 1992.

Sleepwalkers (also known as *Stephen King's Sleepwalkers*; screenplay), Columbia, 1992.

Nightmares and Dreamscapes (short fiction collection), Viking Penguin, 1993.

The Dark Tower Trilogy: The Gunslinger; The Drawing of Three; The Waste Lands (volume containing the beginning trilogy in "The Dark Tower" series), New American Library/Dutton, 1993.

Insomnia (novel), Viking Penguin, 1994.

The Stand (television miniseries based on King's novel of the same name), ABC-TV, 1994.

The Langoliers (novel; originally published in *Four Past Midnight*), New American Library/Dutton, 1995.

Rose Madder (novel), Viking Penguin, 1995.

The Green Mile (novel), Viking Penguin, 1996.

Desperation (novel), Viking Penguin, 1997.

The Dark Tower IV: Wizard and Glass (fourth book in "The Dark Tower" series), Donald M. Grant, 1997.

Sources

On-line

CelebSite, http://www.celebsite.com/people/stephenking.

Mr. Showbiz, http://www.mrshowbiz.com/news/todays_stories/970418/4_18_97/stephenking.html.

Books

King, Stephen, *The Bachman Books,* New American Library, 1985.

King, Stephen, *Stephen King's Danse Macabre,* Everest House, 1981.

Schweitzer, Darrell, editor, *Discovering Stephen King,* Starmont House, 1985.

Underwood, Tim, and Chuck Miller, editors, *Kingdom of Fear: The World of Stephen King,* Underwood-Miller, 1986.

Periodicals

American Film, June 1986.

Entertainment Weekly, April 11, 1997, p. 44.

High Times, January 1981; June 1981.

New York Review of Books, October 19, 1995, p. 54.

People, March 7, 1977; December 29, 1980; January 5, 1981; May 18, 1981; January 28, 1985; April 1, 1996.

Playboy, June 1983.

Washington Post, August 26, 1979; April 9, 1985; May 8, 1987; October 29, 1990, p. B8; July 16, 1991, p. B1; April 13, 1992, p. C7; May 21, 1993, p. 16; May 27, 1993, p. D9; May 14, 1995, p. G1.

Yankee, March 1979.

—Lynn M. Spampinato

Emeril Lagasse

Chef and television show host

Born in 1959, in Fall River, MA; son of Emeril, Jr. (a textile mill worker) and Hilda (a homemaker) Lagasse; married Elizabeth (a schoolteacher; divorced, c. 1982); married Tari Hohn (a fashion designer), 1989 (divorced, 1996); children: (first marriage) Jillian, Jessica. *Education:* Johnson and Wales University, Providence, RI, culinary arts degree, 1978.

Addresses: *Office*—Emeril's Home Base, 638 Camp St., New Orleans, LA 70130.

Career

Chef, restaurateur, and television show host. Worked in restaurants in Paris and Lyons, France, late 1970s; worked in New York, NY, Boston, MA, and Philadelphia, PA, late 1970s-early 1980s; Commander's Palace, New Orleans, LA, chef, c. 1982-90; Emeril's Restaurant, New Orleans, LA, owner and chef, 1990—; NOLA, New Orleans, LA, owner and chef, 1992—; also owner of Emeril's New Orleans Fish House, South Las Vegas, NV; host of television programs *Essence of Emeril,* Food Network, 1993—, and *Emeril Live,* Food Network. Author of cookbooks.

Awards: Ivy Award, Restaurants & Institutions, 1994.

Sidelights

Viewers probably think the interjections "Whoo!" "Bam!" and "Pow!" are more likely to emanate from a television tuned to the Cartoon Network than the Food Network, but dazzling chef Emeril Lagasse has added zip to the usually sedate world of how-to cooking shows. No longer the domain of snooty gourmets, food programs have been transformed into a world of fast-paced, down-to-earth fun and entertainment thanks to the New Orleans, Louisiana, restaurateur. Although his accent clearly reveals that he hails from the Northeast, Lagasse specializes in Creole and Cajun dishes, which he learned to make in his adopted home of the Big Easy. *Essence of Emeril,* shown three times daily on weekdays, offers culinary instruction as well as theatrical delivery, including exclamations like "Bam!" as spice is pitched into a pan, and "Kick it up a notch!" when the chef is really feeling spunky, which is most of the time. Lagasse has helped spark new interest in the art of food, in a nation where burgers and fries top the list of favorite edibles.

Lagasse was born and raised in the small town of Fall River, Massachusetts, where his French-Canadian father, Emeril, Jr., worked in a textile mill, and his Portuguese mother, Hilda, was a homemaker who loved to cook. The family also included an older sister, Delores, now a computer operator, and younger brother Mark, a sewing machine mechanic. At age seven, after assisting his mother with a pot of vegetable soup, Lagasse realized the joy of cooking. "I was kind of viewed as a weird kid because I liked food," he told *People Weekly.* Active in sports and music, Lagasse played in a Portuguese band with older musicians. He taught himself to play the trombone, trumpet, and flute, but especially favored the drums. However, he always gravitated toward cooking and baking.

Lagasse's first job at age ten was at a Portuguese bakery, where he washed dishes and observed the action. He gradually became skilled at baking bread and cakes, enjoying the fact that customers took pleasure in his products. "I would just see how happy people were when they came into the bakery," he recalled to Molly O'Neill in the *New York Times Magazine.* After graduating from high school, he turned down a scholarship to the New England Conservatory of Music to pursue his dream, trading his drums for pots and pans. He worked his way through the culinary program at Johnson and Wales University, graduating in 1978. After honing his skills in the kitchens of Paris and Lyons, France, Lagasse went home to the United States, displaying his skills in Boston, Massachusetts, New York City, and Philadelphia, Pennsylvania.

Lagasse's expertise caught the eye of Ella Brennan, the noted queen of the New Orleans restaurant scene. Her family owned Commander's Palace and was seeking a new chef to replace Cajun bigwig Paul Prudhomme. In the early 1980s, Brennan became Lagasse's mentor when he took the position at the Washington Avenue eatery. He was thrilled with the city and its epicurean attitude toward food. There, he learned the secrets of the spicy cuisine and how to best interpret the flavors through his Portuguese background. "After coming to New Orleans," Lagasse remarked to Mary Beth Romig-Price in *New Orleans Magazine,* "I instantly fell in love with this place, the heritage, the culture, the food, and the music. The city resembles my own years growing up in Massachusetts, especially in the warmth of the people, and I am very lucky to have enjoyed tremendous acceptance in the community."

After seven-and-a-half years working with Brennan, Lagasse was critically acclaimed as a leading recipe wrangler, and decided he would set off on his own gastronomic venture. Living in the city's warehouse district, he realized the area was becoming dotted with art galleries but only offered one restaurant, open only for breakfast and lunch. Seeing the possibility, in 1990 he obtained an empty space and began drawing evening visitors to the neighborhood. In 1992, he branched out to another location with NOLA, a hip bistro in the French Quarter. Later, he added a third annex with Emeril's New Orleans Fish House in the MGM Grand Hotel in South Las Vegas, Nevada.

Lagasse's menus feature "new New Orleans" cuisine, which is based on traditional Cajun and Creole dishes, but with his own twists inspired by Asian, Italian, and regional American cuisines. Some of his concoctions include stir-fry of crawfish over fried noodles with sesame and ginger sauce, corn cakes with caviar, smoked duck and wild mushroom gumbo, crawfish-stuffed filet mignon, foie gras bread pudding, and pork chops with tamarind-glazed roasted sweet potatoes and green-chile mole sauce. Desserts are equally rich, as exemplified by the goat cheese cheesecake with Creole cream cheese coulis. All of the items are made from scratch. He makes his own cheeses and ice cream, and raises hogs so that he can produce farm-fresh andouille sausage, ham, and bacon. Lagasse believes in using only organically grown produce and the finest of all ingredients, keeping a base of ranchers, farmers, and fishermen on hand to supply him with top-quality goods. Lagasse commented to Rick Marin in *Newsweek,* "America got so wrapped up with healthy, healthy, healthy, they forgot what eating was like." Although he seems to be the archenemy of heart-smart promoters, he asserted to Carolyn Walkup in *Nation's Restaurant News,* "Moderation is everything. I take health into consideration in my cooking."

> *"America got so wrapped up with healthy, healthy, healthy, they forgot what eating was like."*

Meanwhile, Lagasse convinced his parents to move south from Massachusetts and join him in making the business a family operation. His father regularly helps out in just about all of the restaurant operations. Unfortunately, Lagasse's personal life did not enjoy the same success as his career. In the early 1980s, he was divorced from his first wife, Elizabeth, a schoolteacher with whom he had two daughters, Jillian and Jessica. He married fashion designer Tari Hohn in 1989, who helped him design and develop his establishments, but they divorced in 1996. Emeril, nevertheless, focused on his passion and continued building his empire.

In 1993, the cable channel, The Food Network, picked up the charming and exuberant Lagasse to host his own televised cooking show, *Essence of Emeril.* Until then, Lagasse's recipes were a regional treat, accessible only to those who visited him on location. The show propelled the chef into the nation's living rooms and became the highest-rated program on the network. Never using a script, Lagasse bustles around the onstage kitchen with gesticulations and proclamations, slam-dunking ingredients with a "Bam!' or "Hey now!" and encouraging people to "Kick it up a notch," which means to be generous when adding spices. He flies to New York to tape the show, where he always invites a selection of audience members to join him onstage in consuming his creations when they are done. Later, the Food Network added *Emeril Live* to its lineup as well. Also in 1993, Lagasse published *New New Orleans* and made appearances throughout the country promoting the cookbook.

Who knows whether Lagasse will transform a nation of fast-food feeders into *bon vivants*. If his continuing popularity is any indication, perhaps some couch potatoes will indeed be donning aprons and scouting the markets for more than just meatloaf ingredients. He also plans to start reaching the public at a young age, with a children's cookbook reportedly in the works. In any case, it seems Lagasse will certainly continue to provide gastronomes with what they crave because of his unrelenting love of preparing meals and sharing them. Even on his days off, Lagasse says he relaxes by cooking for family and friends, in addition to playing the drums for fun. "I never get up and think that I'm going to work," he insisted to Michelle Green in *People Weekly*. "This is passion! This is art! This is me!"

Selected writings

New New Orleans, William Morrow, 1993.
Louisiana Real and Rustic, William Morrow, 1996.
Emeril's Creole Christmas, William Morrow, 1997.

Sources

On-line

"Chef Emeril Lagasse biography," The Food Network web site, http://www.foodtv.com (April 3, 1998).

Periodicals

Nation's Restaurant News, January 1997, p. 106.
New Orleans Magazine, September 1993, p. 44.
Newsweek, March 31, 1997, p. 67.
New York Times Magazine, February 21, 1993, p. 65.
People Weekly, May 27, 1996, p. 16; December 22, 1997, p. 97.

—*Geri Speace*

Shelly Lazarus

Businesswoman

Born Rochelle Braff, September 1, 1947, in Oceanside, NY; daughter of Lewis L. (an accountant) and Sylvia Ruth (a homemaker) Braff; married George Lazarus (a pediatrician), 1970; children: Teddy, Samantha, Benjamin. *Education:* Smith College, B.A. in psychology, 1968; Columbia University, M.B.A., 1970.

Addresses: *Home*—Manhattan, NY. *Office*—c/o Ogilvy & Mather Worldwide, 309 West 49th St., New York, NY 10019-7316.

Career

General Foods Corporation, intern, 1968; Clairol, assistant product manager, 1970; Ogilvy & Mather Advertising, junior account executive, 1971, account executive, 1973-76, account supervisor, 1976-77, management supervisor, 1977-87; Ogilvy & Mather Direct, general manager of New York office, 1987-89, president, 1989-91; Ogilvy & Mather Advertising, president of New York office, 1991-94, president and chief operating officer (COO) of all North American operations, 1994-96, chief executive officer (CEO), 1996—.

Awards: Woman of the Year, Advertising Women of New York, 1994.

Sidelights

Ogilvy & Mather Worldwide is one of the advertising industry's powerhouses, managing accounts for big-name companies, such as Duracell,

Ford, GTE, Kodak, Mattel, and Shell. Though the clients may come and go, Shelly Lazarus has been at the company since 1971, working her way up from junior account executive to CEO, making her the most important woman in advertising. She is also the mother of three with a reputation as someone who can expertly balance her home life with the hectic pace of leading a multibillion dollar corporation.

Lazarus was born in the suburb of Oceanside, New York, where her father, Lewis, was a certified public accountant, and her mother, Sylvia, was a homemaker. Lazarus also had two younger brothers who grew up to become lawyers. As a straight-A student at Midwood High in Brooklyn, where the family relocated in 1960, Lazarus edited the school newspaper. She went on to attend the prestigious Smith College, obtaining her bachelor of arts in psychology in 1968. As a senior, she went along with a friend to a career conference sponsored by the Advertising Women of New York, which changed her direction. "I was amazed you could do something that fun and make a living," Lazarus commented to Elizabeth Cohen in *People Weekly.*

At that time, Lazarus was engaged to George Lazarus, a pre-med student whom she met at a Yale mixer. She realized that she would need to work in order to support them through the rest of his education, so she went on to get her master's degree in business administration from New York's Columbia University in 1970. They were married the same year, and she was hired in at Clairol as an assistant product manager. After about a year on the job, she took a position as junior account executive at Ogilvy & Mather in 1971, where she was assigned to the Lever Brothers account. "When I started out," she told Cohen, "I was often the only woman at the table." The only female among 100 account managers, she would be called upon for her opinions as to what women would purchase.

By 1973, Lazarus was the only female account supervisor at Ogilvy & Mather—and she was pregnant with her first child, Teddy. The following year, she took a leave to accompany her husband to Dayton, Ohio, where he was required to serve two years' mandatory military service. Though she worked there as a department store buyer, she was not happy, and the family returned to New York after her husband's commitment with the Air Force had been fulfilled. Lazarus would have a daughter, Samantha, about six years later, and another son, Benjamin, about 8 years after that.

Back at Ogilvy & Mather in 1976, Lazarus worked as an account supervisor for Avon, Ralston Purina, Campbell's Soup, Pepsi, and others. She was promoted to management supervisor on the Clairol account in 1977, and started working with one of the company's biggest accounts, American Express, in 1980. Named head of the direct marketing arm of Ogilvy & Mather in 1987, she was unfazed that the area had a reputation as being bland; she was just pleased to be in charge of her own branch. Her career got another boost in 1989, when she became president of the Ogilvy & Mather Direct's main office in New York. In 1991, she went back to her original setting, Ogilvy & Mather Advertising, as president of the New York office, and in 1994 she was appointed president and chief operating officer of all North American operations.

Lazarus especially made her name at Ogilvy & Mather working with American Express. However, the charge-card service in 1991 fired the agency and took its $60 million account to Chiat/Day. The company was shocked, but no one more so than Lazarus, who had spent six years cultivating the client as group account director. She set her sights on wooing them back, contracting new market research and developing creative campaigns. Eleven months later, American Express returned, and when that firm's top guns, Lou Gernster and Abby Kohnstamm, moved over to IBM, they sent that $500 million account (which later grew to about $750 million) to Ogilvy & Mather as well. The IBM account, which had previously been divided among several agencies, was the largest single advertising account at any agency to date.

Lazarus reached the highest point in her career in early September of 1996 when she was named to replace Ogilvy & Mather chief executive officer (CEO) Char-

lotte Beers, who was retiring. With 25 years of respected experience, Lazarus's appointment was expected and hailed by those who knew of her qualifications. Though some pointed to her softer, friendlier, more feminine manner of leadership as a key to her success, others mentioned her business acumen as well as her conservative, low-key image: short, gray hair, and simple outfits accented by a trademark single strand of pearls. Advertising industry executive Michael Baulk called her "one of the best managerial talents in world advertising" in *Campaign*. Lazarus sees success as a direct result of talent, and dismisses the notion of the glass ceiling. "In advertising, success is measured by ideas, creativity is rewarded," she explained to Cohen in *People Weekly*. Though 63 of Ogilvy & Mather's 162 senior partners are women, she does not give preferential treatment, and she will not allow part-time employees to work as department heads, telling Bernice Kanner in *Chief Executive*, "Just because you're a mom doesn't mean we can lower performance standards."

Colleagues describe Lazarus as the ideal working mother, balancing her career with her professional responsibilities. The CEO, however, remarked to Kanner in *Chief Executive*, "Someone once described me as a swan. I look smooth going across the lake but underneath I'm paddling like crazy." Lazarus is known to chat about her family to major clients over lunch, and she told Cohen in *People Weekly* that she will take off work for what she believes are important events or tasks for her kids, like birthdays, doctor visits, and clothes shopping. She keeps long hours at the office, though, and part of her million-dollar salary goes toward the services of a nanny and housekeeper to help her out.

Lazarus lives with her husband and children in an elegant townhouse on the Manhattan's East Side, where he runs a pediatrics office from their home. Their living room, like her office, is decorated with frogs made from ceramic, plastic, crystal, even bean bags. In December of 1994, she was named Woman of the Year by the Advertising Women of New York. She enjoys speed skiing, jogging around Central Park with her husband, and spending time with her children. Lazarus noted in her Ogilvy & Mather biography on the web, "When I'm not working—I'm mothering."

Sources

On-line

"Biography of Shelly Lazarus," Ogilvy & Mather web site, http://www.ogilvy.com (April 21, 1998).

Periodicals

Advertising Age, February 5, 1990, p. 38; May 27, 1991,
    p. 4; September 9, 1996, p. 1.
Adweek, January 16, 1995, p. 20; December 11, 1995, p.
    5.
Campaign, August 16, 1996.
Chief Executive (U.S.), June 1997, p. 23.
Fortune, August 5, 1996, p. 42.
New York Times, February 19, 1997, p. 1.
People Weekly, May 5, 1997, p. 89.
Wall Street Journal, September 9, 1996, p. B9.

—Geri Speace

Martin Lee

AP/Wide World Photos

Hong Kong politician

Born Chu-Ming Lee, June 8, 1938, in Hong Kong; son of Li Yin-wo (a Kuomintang army general and later teacher); married Amelia Yee-ngor Fong, 1969; children: Joseph. *Education:* Attended Wah Yan College; University of Hong Kong, B.A., 1960; received law degree, c. 1966. *Politics:* Democratic Party of Hong Kong. *Religion:* Roman Catholic.

Addresses: *Office*—Admiralty Centre, Room 704A, Tower I, 18 Harcourt Rd., Hong Kong.

Career

Taught high school in Hong Kong, early 1960s; called to the Bar, Lincoln's Inn, 1966; attorney in private practice, Hong Kong, 1966—; served on the Hong Kong Legislative Council, 1985-95; member of the Basic Law Drafting Committee, 1985-90, the Hong Kong Law Reform Commission, 1985-91, the Hong Kong Fight Crime Committee, 1986-92; United Democrats of Hong Kong, founder, 1990, chair, 1990-94; Democratic Party of Hong Kong (formerly United Democrats of Hong Kong), leader, beginning 1994, majority vote-earner, 1995 elections.

Awards: Democracy Award, U.S. National Endowment for Democracy, 1997.

Member: Hong Kong Bar Association (chair, 1980-83).

Sidelights

In 1997, Martin Lee emerged as the voice of Western-style democratic principals during the momentous historical event of the "handover" of the British crown colony of Hong Kong back to the government of China. The successful and prominent attorney, who gave up his caseload as he became increasingly involved in politics in the 1980s, is the son of parents who had fled mainland China when communist forces came to power in 1949. As an outspoken liberal, leader of the Democratic Party of Hong Kong—at the time of the handover the largest political party in Hong Kong—and above all, one of the most popular elected politicians in the colony, Lee received international attention as a vocal thorn in the side of the communist Chinese government.

China planned to retake Hong Kong—the very jewel of capitalist, free-market thinking—with little or no trouble under the terms of an international treaty; Lee gained world renown as the Hong Kong Legislative Council's most vociferous anti-Communist member. Lee's dire, but reasoned warnings about the lives and freedoms of Hong Kong residents under a new master also irritated its business community, who saw nothing but profit ahead in the 1997 deal to become part of the world's most populous nation.

Lee, who has used much of his own wealth to finance his political cause instead of fleeing with his assets to the West—as many of his affluent friends had done in the pre-handover years—has been called a "globe-trotting defender of liberty" by *People* magazine and "the man who's loathed by China" in the *New York Times*. Educated abroad, Lee's impeccable manners, excellent Queen's English, and smooth, unflappable demeanor have helped immensely in his success as a politician. These qualities have also made him a somewhat unlikely figure in his role as a political firebrand; Lee is, wrote *Time* magazine's Sandra Burton and Johanna McGeary, "a man whose mission in life is to fuel resistance to Beijing's attempt to rein in Hong Kong."

For his first eleven years of life, Chu-Ming (Martin) Lee grew up in Canton, China, though he had been born in Hong Kong on June 8, 1938, when his mother was visiting the peninsula for a mah-jongg game. His father had been a general with the Nationalist Army, at the time engaged in a losing struggle to keep China from being overrun by invading Japanese military forces; after Japan's loss in World War II, the Nationalist and Communist forces began battling for control of the country.

When Lee was eleven in 1949, the Communists took power and the Nationalists fled to Taiwan. His father was dismayed, however with the corruption he witnessed inside Nationalist leadership circles, and refused to join the exiled government. Instead, he took his family to Hong Kong. At the time, it was unclear whether Communists forces would be able to gain control of the affluent and thriving British colony; they did not.

In Hong Kong, Lee and his family were nearly destitute. His proud and aristocratic father took a job as a teacher of Chinese at a school run by Roman Catholic missionaries, and through his connections was able to send his son there as well. Lee even converted to Roman Catholicism and, for a time, thought about entering the priesthood, but his love of more frivolous pursuits such as soccer quashed such ideas. He earned a degree in philosophy and English literature from the University of Hong Kong in 1960, then taught high school for three years.

Deciding on a change of career, Lee traveled abroad to London to study law. There he received his law degree as well as met his future wife, Amelia Yee-ngor Fong, whom he married in 1969. Lee soon earned a reputation as an up-and-coming young trial attorney in Hong Kong, known for his eloquence and talents in the high-pressure atmosphere of a courtroom. As he progressed through his thirties and entered middle age, Lee had become a prosperous and prominent Hong Kong barrister and was one of its top-grossing legal professionals. In addition, Lee has served as legal ad-

visor to the Justice and Peace Commission of the Diocese of the Roman Catholic Church of Hong Kong, the Hong Kong Medical Association, Hong Kong Telephone Company Limited Staff Association, Cathay Pacific Airways Flight Attendants Union, and the Hong Kong Journalists' Association, among other bodies.

By the early 1980s, Hong Kong was also thriving. It was an extremely successful commercial center, the eighth largest trading center in the world, and statistically ranked as the most free and competitive economy on the planet. Great Britain's announcement that Hong Kong would revert to China in 1997 after its 99-year lease on the colony expired raised little alarm at the time, and the colonial government, with the approval of British prime minister Margaret Thatcher, moved to introduce some reforms that would allow Hong Kong to have some semblance of a self-governing democracy for a few years prior to the handover. When a Chinese diplomat in Hong Kong criticized this plan, few in Hong Kong even blinked. So Lee's colleagues—he was the onetime chair of the Hong Kong Bar Association—formed a political alliance and asked him to stand for election in the colony's first attempts at free elections.

Prior to 1985, the 60-member Hong Kong Legislative Council was a handpicked group who made little waves in the sea that separated the affluent British colony and its future Communist ruler on the mainland. That year, British officials amended election laws to allow representatives of actual political-interest groups; Lee won a seat representing the Hong Kong legal community. His legal expertise also won him a spot on the Basic Law Committee, which was entrusted with the task of writing a set of legal guidelines to govern what the Sino-British Joint Declaration of 1984 called the "one country, two systems" model. Under this accord, it was stipulated that the daily life, commercial activities, and free port status of Hong Kong citizens would remain "as is" for at least fifty years.

Yet Lee's dissatisfactions with what became the Basic Law, published in 1988, roused the ire of Chinese authorities, and he soon became one of their targets. With a fellow liberal activist, Szeto Wah, Lee coauthored a book published that same year, *The Basic Law: Some Basic Flaws*. This and his other anti-Beijing sentiments caused him to be officially banned from entering China, and he was frequently attacked in its press. In Hong Kong, pro-China legislators in Hong Kong warned that his words and writings would anger the Chinese government and cause future difficulies and possibly economic decline for Hong Kong. During this era, there were others similarly wary of the "one country, two systems" plan, and affluent Hong Kong citizens like Lee were using their connections to obtain visas to the West. Lee and his family—which now included a son, Joseph—opted to stay. "I decided to do my best to help Hong Kong preserve the rule of law," Lee told *People* magazine, "because that to me is the most important thing. That is the one thing we have which they in China do not have."

"But freedom is not divisible between political and economic freedom. The best way to protect political rights is to have democratic elections."

Events that took place in China during June of 1989 injected an element of fear into the minds of remaining Hong Kong residents, however: when massive student protests in Beijing's Tiananmen Square went on for weeks and orders to disperse were ignored, Chinese troops opened fire. The news footage caused international outcry and brought official condemnations from the world community.

In protest, Lee led two immense rallies in Hong Kong, which became an annual event on the anniversary of the Tiananmen debacle. The actions of Chinese leaders served to galvanize the Hong Kong residents into action, and a political movement voicing concern over China's human-rights record arose—a movement centered around Lee.

In 1990, Lee founded Hong Kong's first political party, United Democrats of Hong Kong, which evolved into Democratic Party of Hong Kong four years later. In 1991, the first full legislative elections were held for council seats, and the United Democrats and Lee received the majority of votes. As the *New York Times* noted, not long before Lee had been considered a troublemaker, a political outsider with no real support, but as he told the newspaper's Barbara Basler, "the people here have clearly shown they want democracy, and not only that, they want it knowing they run the risk of offending China."

Over the next few years, Lee continued to lead a pro-democracy movement in Hong Kong, and found he had increasing support among the colony's 6-million-plus, soon-to-be citizens of China. When its governor called 1995 elections, Lee and his Democratic Party of Hong Kong won 19 of 60 seats.

Yet Lee and the party's majority status in the Legislative Council would be a short-lived one. Beijing had named shipping magnate Tung Chee-hwa as the leader of what would become known after the handover as the "Hong Kong Special Administrative Region" (SAR), and Tung's pronouncements about the territory's future were essentially the plans of China's Central Committee. Tung announced the Council would be dissolved upon the official handover at midnight on June 30, 1997, and would be replaced with a "Provisional Legislature" for a year until new elections would be held. The group of "provisional" lawmakers were selected by a committee that had itself been selected by Beijing leaders.

Lee lobbied world leaders and asserted that the Provisional Legislature was illegal, a clear violation of the Joint Declaration; he also pointed out that many of its members had stood for Legislative Council seats in the 1995 elections and lost. As for the future elections, it was likely that changes would be made to existing laws to insure that anti-Beijing elements like Lee's Democratic Party would not gain any real electoral power.

Not all of Hong Kong residents were heeding Lee's warnings that repression and a bleak, totalitarian future were awaiting the new SAR. Many inside Hong Kong's business community looked instead at the bottom line: under the new "one country, two systems" plan, a huge, virtually untapped market of over 1.1 billion people in mainland China meant certain profit.

It was an eager, new-consumer economy that was increasingly moving toward western ideals at the same time as Hong Kong was heading its way politically; China had undergone many economic and political changes since 1989, and had lightened up some of its strictures in an effort to become more of a free-market economy. Even some of Lee's pro-Democratic allies conceded that he may have been somewhat out of step with what China had become in 1997. Still other critics of Lee remarked that under archaic British imperial rule, Hong Kong was hardly a bastion of democracy.

Lee was undeterred. "We have for decades had the benefits of democracy," Lee wrote on the op-ed page of the *Wall Street Journal*, "including clean and accountable government, a free press, an independent judiciary and a civil society." Meanwhile, Lee continued, "the distinguishing characteristic of the Chinese government's rule in China is its intervention in the economic, political and social aspects of life."

He remained an outspoken critic of Tung and his plans, and in the spring of 1997 toured several countries, meeting with U.S. President Bill Clinton and Canadian Prime Minister Jean Chretien in an effort to put international pressure on China to treat Hong Kong well. "The country [my family] left behind," Lee wrote in the *Wall Street Journal* on June 30, "will now have sovereignty over Hong Kong, and we must stand firm against any efforts to erode the freedoms and way of life our people risked so much to reach."

As a fellow Hong Kong politician told *Time* magazine, Lee "convinces people with his reasoning and his principles. As a lawyer, he believes you don't need to shout loud when you are trying to change someone's mind. All you need is the evidence." A few weeks before the handover, Lee spoke with the *Hong Kong Voice of Democracy,* and was asked whether he and the Democratic Party would officially oppose the Provisional Legislature when it became legitimate. Lee replied, "It will never become legitimate, unless it is elected. So says the Joint Declaration, and so says the Basic Law." Lee also asserted that he and the party planned "to continue with our role, we're going to speak up for Hong Kong, and to criticize Chinese policies if they are wrong."

As the handover date neared, Lee was a blunt critic of Tung and the announced reforms set to take place then, especially the new security laws that would restrict the right to assemble in Hong Kong. "Political freedoms are being rolled back and businessman say that is okay because there will still be economic freedom," Lee said in a debate with pro-Beijing politicians reported in the *Canadian Online Explorer* a week before the handover. "But freedom is not divisible between political and economic freedom. The best way

to protect political rights is to have democratic elections."

On the day of the handover—the official ceremonies of which were boycotted by British-elected leaders and U.S. Secretary of State Madeleine Albright in protest of the dismantling of the Legislative Council—Lee spoke from a balcony at the Council Building to a cheering crowd. "We pledge to continue to be the voice of Hong Kong people—in or out of office—and to fight to get democracy back," reported the *Times* of London. "We are prepared to defend the freedoms we cherish.... We declare Hong Kong people want democracy ... the flame of democracy has been ignited and is burning in the hearts of our people. It may not be extinguished."

Selected writings

(With Szeto Wah) *The Basic Law: Some Basic Flaws,* 1988.

Sources

On-line

Canadian Online Explorer, http://cgi.canoe.ca (February 12, 1998).
Hong Kong Voice of Democracy, www.democracy.org.hk (February 12, 1998).

Periodicals

New York Times, October 7, 1991.
People, June 16, 1997, pp. 67-68.
Time, June 2, 1997, pp. 52-57.
Times (London), June 1, 1997.
Wall Street Journal, June 30, 1997, p. A14.

—*Carol Brennan*

Jack Lemmon

Actor, producer, and director

Born John Uhler Lemmon III, February 8, 1925, in Boston, MA; son of John Uhler, Jr. (a company executive) and Mildred LaRue (Noel) Lemmon; married Cynthia Boyd Stone (an actress), May 7, 1950 (divorced, 1956); married Felicia Farr (an actress), August 17, 1962; children: (with Stone) Christopher; (with Farr) Courtney. *Education:* Attended Phillips Andover Academy; Harvard University, B.A. and B.S., 1947.

Addresses: *Office*—Jalem Productions, 141 El Camino Dr., Suite 201, Beverly Hills, CA 90212.

Career

Actor, producer, and director. Appeared in summer stock productions, 1940-48, and on radio, 1948-52; Old Nick Saloon, New York City, waiter, piano player, and master of ceremonies, 1947; actor in radio soap operas, 1948; Jalem Productions, Beverly Hills, CA, founder and president, 1952—. Television debut in "The Times Square Story," *Old Knickerbocker Music Hall*, CBS, 1948; other appearances include series *That Wonderful Guy*, ABC, 1950; and *Road of Life*, CBS, 1954; and numerous episodes and specials. Film debut in *It Should Happen to You*, 1954; has appeared in over 50 films, including *It Should Happen to You*, 1954; *Mister Roberts*, 1955; *Some Like It Hot*, 1959; *Days of Wine and Roses*, 1962; *The Fortune Cookie*, 1966; *The Odd Couple*, 1968; *Save the Tiger*, 1973; *The China Syndrome*, 1979; *Tribute*, 1980; *Buddy Buddy*, 1981; *Dad*, 1989; *Glengarry Glen Ross*, 1992; *Grumpy Old Men*, 1993; *Short Cuts*, 1993; *Grumpier Old Men*, 1995; *My Fellow Americans*, 1996; and *The Odd Couple II*, 1998. Executive producer of *Cool Hand Luke*, 1967; director of *Kotch*, 1971; *Military service:* U.S. Naval Reserve, active duty as communications officer, 1945-46.

Awards: Academy Award for best supporting actor, 1955, for *Mister Roberts*; British Academy of Film and Television Arts Award for best foreign actor, 1959, and Golden Globe award for best motion picture actor in a musical or comedy, 1960, both for *Some Like It Hot*; Golden Apple Award, star of the year, Hollywood women's Press Club, 1960; British Academy of Film and Television Arts Award for best foreign actor, 1960, and Golden Globe award for best motion picture actor in a musical or comedy, 1961, both for *The Apartment*; Emmy Award, outstanding single variety or popular music program, 1972, for *Jack Lemmon in S'Wonderful, S'Marvelous, S'Gershwin*; Academy Award for best actor, 1973, for *Save the Tiger*; Golden Globe Award for best motion picture actor in a musical or comedy, 1973, for *Avanti!*; named Hasty Pudding Man of the Year, Hasty Pudding Theatricals, 1973; British Academy of Film and Television Arts Award for best foreign actor, 1979, and best actor award, Cannes Film Festival, 1979, both for *China Syndrome*; Drama Guild Award, 1979, for the stage version of *Tribute*; Silver Berlin Bear for best actor, Berlin International Film Festival, and Genie Award for best performance by a foreign actor, Academy of Canadian Cinema and Television, both 1981, for the screen version of *Tribute;* best actor award, Cannes Film Festival, 1982, for *Missing;* inducted into Television Academy Hall of Fame, 1987; D. W. Griffith Award, 1987; American Film Institute Life Achievement Award, 1988; Golden Globe Award for best performance by an actor in a miniseries or motion picture made for television, 1988, for *Long Day's Journey into Night;*Annual Achievement Award, Screen Actors Guild, 1989; Lifetime Achievement Award (male), American Comedy Awards, 1991; Cecil B. De Mille Award, Hollywood Foreign Press Association, 1991; Volpi Cup, Venice Film Festival, 1992, for *Glengarry Glen Ross;* Lincoln Center Tribute, 1993; Golden Berlin Bear, Berlin International Film Festival, 1996.

Sidelights

A ward-winning actor Jack Lemmon has made a career being "a clown for the Age of Anxiety," as John Culhane observed in the *New York Times.* Slightly uptight, skittishly nervous but possessing a relatively poised veneer and a tragicomic quality, Lemmon's characters are sympathetic because of his ability to represent the "everyman." Audiences can identify with his realistic portrayals; he is capable of registering a range of emotion with just one look. Even his comedic characters can be full of insecurity and sadness, but manage to keep the laughter flowing, seemingly inadvertently. He is no less successful in forceful dramatic roles. Lemmon started his career mainly in comedies such as *Some Like It Hot* and *The Odd Couple,* but also displayed his range with more serious films, including *Save the Tiger, China Syndrome,* and *Glengarry Glen Ross.* A steady actor since his screen debut in 1954 in *It Could Happen to You,* his popularity reached new heights in the 1990s when he costarred with *Odd Couple* partner Walter Matthau in *Grumpy Old Men* (1993) and *Grumpier Old Men* (1995). The pair teamed up for a sequel to *The Odd Couple* in 1998.

Lemmon was born on February 8, 1925, in Boston, Massachusetts, to John Uhler Lemmon, Jr., a vice president of sales for the Doughnut Corporation of America, and Mildred LaRue (Noel) Lemmon. His mother was engrossed in a bridge game and did not acknowledge the labor pains that brought her son into the world two months early. She did not make it in time and gave birth in the Newton-Wellesley Hospital elevator. Though Lemmon was very close to his parents, they had marital troubles when he was young. When they began sleeping in separate bedrooms, Lemmon's mother told him it was due to his father's snoring. Lemmon then devised a comic routine involving an extensive menu of snoring sounds and would use it to

amuse his parents and guests. "His childish attempt to make snoring seem funny and appealing would not be his last attempt to relieve anxiety with comedy," stated Culhane.

As Lemmon's father took more lengthy business trips, his mother would socialize at the bar of the Ritz-Carlton in Boston. Their escalating difficulties gave birth to Lemmon's cheerful personality. He felt that if he gave them nothing to worry about, then they would be able to devote more time to getting along with each other. His parents never divorced, but they never were happy with each other, either, which caused Lemmon great pain. They finally separated permanently during his senior year in high school. Lemmon attended the exclusive prep school Phillips Academy in Andover, Massachusetts, where he was a champion distance runner and taught himself to play piano. In 1943, he enrolled in Harvard University. Though he lagged in core subjects, he excelled in music and drama and was active in a variety of clubs. He was president of the Hasty Pudding Club and performed in one of its musical reviews; he was vice president of the Dramatic and Delphic clubs; and he was well-known for his acting talent. He also played piano and wrote songs, but seemed to shine more at acting.

Lemmon served in the U.S. Naval Reserve toward the end of World War II in 1945 and 1946 as a communications officer, then graduated from Harvard with his B.A. and B.S. degrees in 1947. He went on to act in summer stock. His father offered him a job at the doughnut company, but Lemmon stubbornly and rather unsuccessfully held out for acting parts, biding his time waiting tables, playing piano, and serving as master of ceremonies at the "Old Knick" show bar in New York City. His father eventually moved to New York and set Lemmon up with an apartment and a steady source of available money. In 1948, he landed his first professional part in a radio soap opera. Although he had only considered acting in the theater, television was developing as a promising new medium, and he ended up finding plenty of work in that arena.

Lemmon's television debut was in "The Times Square Story" for the *Old Knickerbocker Music Hall* program on CBS in 1948. He went on to roles in the *Philco Television Playhouse, Kraft Television Theatre,* and others. These dramatic, live, hour-long shows provided excellent training and helped showcase new talent, including the likes of James Dean, Paul Newman, Grace Kelly, Rod Steiger, Charlton Heston, and others. Lemmon was especially acclaimed for his performance in the 1956 *Ford Star Jubilee* program, "The Day Lincoln Was Shot." It is estimated that he had about 400 parts in those early years. "I had no idea what great experience I was getting," Lemmon recalled in the *St. Louis Post-Dispatch*. "I just accepted it. I realized I was lucky because I was getting a lot of work." Thanks to his prolific appearances on television, Hollywood studios took notice and Columbia Pictures offered Lemmon a contract in 1953.

Lemmon's comic talent won him the lead in his first film, *It Could Happen to You*, costarring with Judy Holliday in 1954. After just his fourth film, *Mister Roberts*, starring Henry Fonda, Lemmon won an Academy Award in 1955 for best supporting actor for his role of Ensign Pulver. In 1959, he had another big hit with Marilyn Monroe in the comedy *Some Like It Hot*, landing his first Oscar nomination for best actor and taking a Golden Globe. He dressed in drag throughout most of the film, masquerading as a woman in order to disguise his identity from the Mafia. Lemmon's next nomination came in 1960 for *The Apartment*; though he did not take the award, the film did get the Academy Award for best picture and Lemmon won another Golden Globe. The tale involved an ambitious clerk who gains favor with corporate bigwigs by loaning them his apartment for their trysts with mistresses.

After lobbying to make a powerful drama about alcoholism, *Days of Wine and Roses*, Lemmon found many of his fans thought that he really was a problem drinker and wrote him letters touting the benefits of Alcoholics Anonymous. Lemmon, though he enjoys a martini or two, claims he never had a drinking problem, despite an arrest for drunk driving in 1976. He later explained that his friends had thrown him a party and did not let him get a bite to eat, and that he only had a small amount of wine and barely flunked the sobriety test. He later, at age 60, gave up drinking, as well as smoking pipes and cigars.

Lemmon followed *Days of Wine and Roses* with another comedy, *Irma La Douce*, costarring Shirley Maclaine, in 1963, and *The Fortune Cookie* in 1966. In the latter, he was first teamed with comic actor Walter Matthau, who won an Oscar for best supporting actor in the picture. In *The Fortune Cookie*, Lemmon plays a television cameraman who is plowed over by a star football player and is talked into faking an injury by his brother-in-law, an unscrupulous attorney (Matthau). The two actors had an undeniable chemistry, working together again in Neil Simon's classic hit *The Odd Couple* in 1968. In one of Lemmon's most memorable parts, he played the neat Felix Ungar to Walter

Matthau's messy Oscar Madison in this hilarious story of two opposites trying to live together.

Lemmon went on to work with Matthau again on a number of projects, including *The Front Page*, 1974; *Buddy Buddy*, 1981; *Grumpy Old Men*, 1993, *Grumpier Old Men*, 1995, *Out to Sea*, 1997, and *The Odd Couple II* in 1998. The *Grumpy Old Men* movies re-established Lemmon and Matthau's presence as an unparalleled comic duo and introduced them to a new generation of viewers. Older audiences continued to enjoy them as longtime favorites, and younger audiences could identify with the feisty older men as they would perhaps their senior relatives. Their rapport, energy, and rapid-fire humor in the films belied the fact that Matthau was 73 and Lemmon 68 when the first *Grumpy* film was released. They delighted fans again in 1998 with Neil Simon's sequel to *The Odd Couple*. In *The Odd Couple II*, Oscar and Felix have led separate lives for decades but are reunited when Oscar's son and Felix's daughter decide to get married.

Lemmon, meanwhile, had a string of other successes. In 1967, he stepped behind the scenes as executive producer of the legendary prison flick, *Cool Hand Luke*, and in 1971 he tried a stint at directing with *Kotch*, starring Matthau. In 1972, he won an Emmy when he returned to his piano-playing roots in the television special *Jack Lemmon in S'Wonderful, S'Marvelous, S'Gershwin*. The following year he picked up an Academy Award for best actor for his performance in *Save the Tiger*, a drama about a day in the life of a pathetic man. In 1979, he was again nominated for an Oscar, but did not win, for *The China Syndrome*, about a reporter who witnesses an accident at a nuclear power plant. Lemmon played the plant manager who decided to speak out even though doing so would likely end his career. The movie was notable, but in addition, a real-life nuclear meltdown at the Three Mile Island reactor in Pennsylvania shortly after the movie's release made it all the more frightening. Lemmon won a best actor award at the Cannes International Film Festival for this role.

In the early 1980s Lemmon was acclaimed for his work in the stage and screen versions of *Tribute*, about a dying publicity agent, earning a Drama Guild Award, Berlin Film Festival Award, Genie Award, and a nomination for another Academy Award. He was again honored with a best actor nod at Cannes in 1982 for his role in *Missing* and was nominated for a Tony in 1986 for the stage version of *A Long Day's Journey into Night*. He also received a Golden Globe in 1988 for the television movie version of that story. Meanwhile, he also kept busy in television, predominantly appearing on awards shows and occasionally in specials such as *Neil Simon: Not Just for Laughs,* 1989.

After playing a dying man, in 1989's *Dad,* Lemmon wanted to move on to new challenges. He got his chance when one of the meatiest parts of his career came in 1992, playing Shelley "The Machine" Levine in the film version of David Mamet's Pulitzer Prize-winning play, *Glengarry Glen Ross.* In this tale of the cutthroat world of real estate, Lemmon portrays a down-and-dirty, desperate, shameless salesperson. He was awarded the Volpi Cup from the Venice Film Festival for his gritty depiction. The next year came the comic hit *Grumpy Old Men,* followed by the sequel, and then the *Odd Couple II.* In the 1990s, he also worked on the Robert Altman films *The Player* and *Short Cuts; 12 Angry Men,* 1997, a cable remake of the classic 1950s jury-room drama; and a television movie in 1998 called *The Long Way Home,* about a retired carpenter on a cross-country road trip with a young woman.

Lemmon in 1950 married Cynthia Boyd Stone, an actress he met in New York. They had a son, Christopher, in 1954, but were divorced in 1956. Lemmon then married actress Felicia Farr on August 17, 1962, in Paris, France, and they have been together since. Their daughter, Courteney, was born on January 7, 1966. Christopher has followed his father into the acting business, and Courteney is a journalist. Lemmon also has a stepdaughter, Farr's daughter, Denise. He enjoys golfing, fishing trips in Alaska, and socializing with friends, including his good pal Matthau. When writer Elizabeth Snead in a 1998 *USA Today* interview asked if the septuagenarian was considering retirement, he responded, "No, not totally. Slowing down, maybe."

Sources

On-line

"Jack Lemmon," Internet Movie Database, http://www.imdb.com (July 7, 1998).

Books

Contemporary Theatre, Film and Television, volume 14, Gale Research, 1996.

Periodicals

Dallas Morning News, April 11, 1998, p. 2C.
Life, October 1, 1992, p. 72.
Los Angeles Times, December 8, 1996; June 29, 1997.
Newsday, September 27, 1992, p. 6.
New York Times, January 16, 1972; July 12, 1981; April 17, 1993.
Parade Magazine, April 5, 1998, p. 26.
St. Louis Post-Dispatch, February 28, 1998, p. 34.
USA Today, April 9, 1998, p. 7D.

—Geri Speace

Elmore Leonard

Author

Born Elmore John Leonard, Jr., October 11, 1925, in New Orleans, LA; son of Elmore John (an automotive executive) and Flora Amerlia (Rive) Leonard; married Beverly Cline, July 30, 1949 (divorced, May 24, 1977); married Joan Shepard, September 15, 1979 (died January 13, 1993); married Christine Kent, August 19, 1993; children: (first marriage) Jane Jones, Peter, Christopher, William, Katherine Dudley. *Education:* University of Detroit, Ph.B., 1950.

Addresses: *Home*—Birmingham, MI. *Agent*—Michael Siegel, Creative Artists Agency, Beverly Hills, CA 90212.

Career

Campbell-Ewald advertising agency, Detroit, MI, copywriter, 1950-61; freelance copywriter and author of educational and industrial films, 1961-63; head of Elmore Leonard Advertising Company, 1963-66; full-time writer, 1967—. *Military service*—U.S. Naval Reserve, 1943-46.

Awards: *Hombre* named one of the 25 best western novels of all time, Western Writers of America, 1977; Edgar Allen Poe Award, Mystery Writers of America, 1984, for *LaBrava;* Michigan Foundation of the Arts Award, 1985; Grand Master Award, Mystery Writers of America, 1992.

Sidelights

Writer Elmore "Dutch" Leonard, the mind behind popular crime novels such as *Get Shorty, Maxi-* *mum Bob, Out of Sight,* and numerous others, was past retirement age when his fun, suspenseful mysteries emerged from their status as above-average genre fiction books into Hollywood hits during the 1990s. He began gaining recognition earlier with 1983's *LaBrava,* and then in 1985, the best-selling *Glitz* enhanced his reputation as one of the best crime writers on the scene. Though he made the cover of *Newsweek* at that time, his name was not truly mainstream until his tale of a starstruck loan shark, *Get Shorty,* made the big screen in 1995 with the newly rediscovered John Travolta in the starring role. Following that, his work was gobbled up by film and television studios, with a series based on his book *Maximum Bob* developed for the 1998 fall lineup. Leonard, often called the "Dickens of Detroit," had been writing fiction full time since 1967 and had seen most of his novels optioned for screenplays, but he did not become a hot item until around age 70. "I am what you call an overnight success," Leonard sarcastically told Frank J. Prial in the *New York Times,* "after writing almost anonymously for 30 years."

Leonard was born on October 11, 1925, in New Orleans, Louisiana, to Elmore John and Flora Amerlia (Rive) Leonard. The family moved around the country as the senior Leonard, an executive at General Motors, was transferred various times. By the time

Leonard was about nine or ten, they had settled in the Detroit area. There, he played football and baseball in high school and earned the nickname "Dutch," after a famous baseball player with the Washington Senators. After graduating, he served in the U.S. Navy during World War II in the Pacific. By the time he went to college at the University of Detroit, he realized he was too small (at five feet, nine inches and only 132 pounds) to play sports. Consequently, his attentions turned toward writing.

After receiving his bachelor of philosophy degree in 1950, Leonard was not sure he could earn a living as a fiction writer, so he went to work at the Detroit advertising agency Campbell-Ewald, where he wrote copy for Chevrolet. However, he would rise early to work on western stories before his day job, and in 1951, he sold his first piece, "Apache Agent," to a men's magazine called *Argosy*. He chose westerns after deciding that they would be most lucrative; he had examined the popular magazines of the day and noticed that many of the short stories published were of that genre. He also enjoyed western movies and wanted to sell his work to the movie industry. Later, he sold a 4,500-word short story, "3:10 to Yuma," to a pulp fiction publisher for $90, but later signed a deal to make $4,000 off of it from Columbia Pictures. However, the publisher ended up taking 25 percent. "I learned then to read the fine print," Leonard told Frank J. Prial in the *New York Times*. In 1953, he sold his first novel, *The Bounty Hunters,* following it up with four more over the next eight years.

In 1961, Leonard had a major breakthrough with *Hombre,* about a white man raised by the Native American Apache tribe. It would later be named one of the 25 best western novels of all time by the Western Writers of America in 1977. Also that year, he came into some money via a company profit-sharing plan and decided to quit the ad firm in order to write full time. However, with five children to raise, he found he needed steadier work. He became a freelance jobber, writing educational and industrial films and continuing to write ad copy on his own. When Twentieth Century-Fox bought the rights to *Hombre* in 1967 for $10,000, Leonard finally had the means to pursue fiction as a career. The story was made into a film starring Paul Newman. However, with westerns becoming passe, Leonard began concentrating on more modern topics. His first attempt was *The Big Bounce,* about a couple of scam artists. Though his Hollywood agent saw great promise, the manuscript was rejected 84 times before finally getting picked up by a paperback publisher. It was later made into a film that Leonard in the *New York Times* called "a terrible, terrible picture."

After briefly going back to westerns, Leonard returned to contemporary crime fiction with 1974's *Fifty-Two Pickup.* An extortion story involving a suburban businessman who comes in contact with the grimy Detroit underworld, critics liked it, but it did not generate much enthusiasm among buyers. Nevertheless, he continued cranking out crime novels such as *Mr. Majestyk,* 1974; *Swag,* 1976; *Unknown Man No. 89,* 1977; and *City Primeval: High Noon in Detroit,* 1980. He also regularly commuted to Los Angeles to write scripts, some based on his work. By 1980, he was keeping busy and doing well as a screenwriter, but his fiction-writing career—his true love—was mired in cult status. Publisher Donald I. Fine of Arbor House in 1980 contacted Leonard and offered him a deal; if the author would agree to less pay than what he was getting from Hollywood, Fine would score the publicity needed to kick-start his novels.

By 1983, Fine's promise panned out, and Leonard finally broke through with *LaBrava,* for which he earned an Edgar Allen Poe Award from the Mystery Writers of America in 1984. After that, his 1985 work, *Glitz,* became a best-seller and Book-of-the-Month selection, thrusting him into the mainstream. That year he also won a Michigan Foundation of the Arts Award. Added to that, Burt Reynolds starred in a film based on his 1983 work *Stick,* and although Leonard was not happy with the film, it brought further recognition. Fans liked the stories that rejected the psychoanalytical aspect of many crime tales and instead focused on the plot, and more importantly, the characters as they move through it. As Ben Yagoda wrote in the *New York Times,* "What's important in these stories is the caper, the scheme, the revenge. Morality rarely if ever comes into question; everyone is implicated to some degree." Later, Leonard introduced more standard good guys, such as law enforcement characters, but they, too, were more subdued and often shopworn, not virtuous one-dimensional crime fighters. Also, the quirky criminals and minor characters often seem to have just as much or more flair than the main players, a Leonard signature that keeps readers coming back and that translates so well to the screen. As of 1998, all but three of his novels had been optioned or made into movies.

Leonard's books continued to be popular throughout the 1980s and into the 1990s, and some—including *52 Pick-Up,* 1986, and *Cat Chaser,* 1989—were made into films during that time but did not fare well. Though many of his books have taken place at least partly in Detroit, he also often expertly uses Florida as a setting, although he has only vacationed there. Leonard's tales involve hoods and hookers, con men and convicts, and often display an intricate knowledge of guns and other implements of the underworld. However, he generally does not prowl the streets and back alleys for his inspiration, besides occasionally hanging around cops to listen to their slang and speech rhythms. He claims to have only been to a shooting range one time, and instead stays cooped up in his safe, suburban home and contracts a researcher to help him out on some of the details, such as how a bail bondsman would talk, or how much it would cost to smuggle horses from Arizona to Cuba in the nineteenth century. As a result, he conveys a sense of realism, and his prose flows naturally.

By the mid-1990s, Hollywood had rediscovered Leonard, and director Barry Sonnenfeld was hired to direct the film adaptation of *Get Shorty*, released in 1995. Though Leonard's books are not known for being especially funny, *Get Shorty*, starring John Travolta, had a vein of humor running through it that surprised Leonard at first. However, as he told Martin Amis in the *Los Angeles Times*, "It was the first contemporary story of mine that I really liked on the screen." Critics and moviegoers alike generally agreed. The story involved a loan shark, played by John Travolta, who goes to California to collect on a debt and gets stars in his eyes, hoping to sell a script. He finds himself involved with a cast of oddballs, including a sleazy producer (Gene Hackman) and a washed-up actress (Rene Russo).

After *Get Shorty*, director Quentin Tarantino, fresh from the success of *Pulp Fiction*, reworked the novel *Rum Punch* into *Jackie Brown*, starring 1970s blaxploitation queen Pam Grier as a flight attendant who is involved with a petty gun runner. Though many critics complained that it did not measure up to *Pulp Fiction*, Leonard was pleased with the product. Subsequently, Leonard saw another big hit in 1998 with the release of *Out of Sight*, which faithfully stuck to the original story. Leonard made $2.5 million off the rights. The film starred George Clooney as an aging bank robber who breaks out of prison, only to find a U.S. marshal (Jennifer Lopez) who unwittingly throws a wrench into his plan. After he abducts her in order to complete his escape, the two become attracted to each other and pursue a romance while he gets mixed up with some seedy gangsters. Leonard claimed his inspiration for the tale was a photograph that he saw in the newspaper of a female marshal with a gun slung on her hip.

In fact, Leonard admitted to Amis in the *Los Angeles Times* that all of his ideas begin with the characters. "By page 100, roughly, I should have my characters assembled," Leonard commented. "I should know my characters because they're sort of auditioned in the opening scenes, and I can find out if they can talk or not. And if they can't talk, they're out. Or they get a minor role." However, he also noted that conversely, minor characters can become major ones if they come alive. Critics more often compare his style to that of Ernest Hemingway than crime writers Raymond Chandler or Dashiell Hammett. Leonard once told an interviewer, according to Yagoda in the *New York Times*, "I never, never do images or metaphors. The second reason is that they slow everything down. The first reason is that I'm no good at them, and I don't do what I don't do well."

By 1998, Quentin Tarantino had purchased the rights to three more Leonard novels, and ABC created a television series based on the 1991 book *Maximum Bob*, about a strict Florida judge and his flaky New Age wife, starring Beau Bridges as the hard-nosed justice. Meanwhile, *Touch* was adapted for film as well, and Leonard pumped out his first non-contemporary novel in years, *Cuba Libre*, a story of horse smugglers set roughly a hundred years ago. Joel and Ethan Coen, who made *Raising Arizona* and *Fargo*, right away began working on bringing it to the screen. Also, Leonard has a sequel to *Get Shorty* in the works, tentatively titled *Be Cool*, in which main character Chili Palmer switches gears from movies to rock and roll. In order to research this one, Leonard even invited members of Aerosmith to his home. In addition, Buck Henry was working on a screenplay for *LaBrava*, which Dustin Hoffman was supposed to bring to life before he backed out of the project a number of years prior.

Leonard has lived in the northern Detroit suburb of Birmingham, Michigan, most of his life, where he has an upscale two-story home with a pool and tennis court. He has been married three times: to Beverly Cline on July 30, 1949 (they divorced on May 24, 1977); to Joan Shepard on September 15, 1979 (she died on January 13, 1993); and to Christine Kent, at the time his gardener and a French instructor at the University of Detroit, on August 19, 1993. He has five children from his first marriage—Jane Jones, Peter, Christopher, William, and Katherine Dudley—and ten grandchildren. *Newsday*'s Patrick Goldstein described Leonard's look, complete with a short gray beard and wire-framed glasses, as "a retired cool-jazz pianist, the kind of crusty old hipster you'd see sitting in at a wee-hours Detroit nightclub," whereas Ben Yagoda in the *New York Times* once compared his casual appearance to that of a college professor. A former alcoholic, Leonard told Yagoda he took his last drink on January 21, 1977. Despite the fact that he is past retirement age, Leonard does not see himself drifting from his 9:30 a.m. to 6 p.m. work schedule. "I still love to tell stories and I still love to create characters and listen to what they say," he explained to Joe Holleman in the *St. Louis Post-Dispatch*. "Why should I retire?"

Selected writings

Western novels

The Bounty Hunters, Houghton, 1953, reprinted, Bantam, 1985.

The Law at Randado, Houghton, 1955, reprinted, Bantam, 1985.

Escape from Five Shadows, Houghton, 1956, reprinted, Bantam, 1985.

Last Stand at Saber River, Dell, 1957, reprinted, Bantam, 1985.

Hombre, Ballantine, 1961, reprinted, 1984.

Valdez Is Coming, Gold Medal, 1970.

Forty Lashes Less One, Bantam, 1972.

Gunsights, Bantam, 1979.

Crime novels

The Big Bounce, Gold Medal, 1969, revised edition, Armchair Detective, 1989.

The Moonshine War, Doubleday, 1969, reprinted, Dell, 1988.

Mr. Majestyk, Dell, 1974.

52 Pick-Up, Delacorte, 1974.

Swag, Delacorte, 1976, published as Ryan's Rules, Dell, 1976.

Unknown Man No. 89, Delacorte, 1977.

The Hunted, Dell, 1977.

The Switch, Bantam, 1978.

City Primeval: High Noon in Detroit, Arbor House, 1980.

Gold Coast, Bantam, 1980, revised edition, 1985.

Split Images, Arbor House, 1981.

Cat Chaser, Arbor House, 1982.

Stick, Arbor House, 1983.

LaBrava, Arbor House, 1983.

Glitz, Arbor House, 1985.

Bandits, Arbor House, 1987.

Touch, Arbor House, 1987.

Freaky Deaky, Morrow, 1988.

Killshot, Morrow, 1989.

Get Shorty, Delacorte, 1990.

Maximum Bob, Delacorte, 1991.

Rum Punch, Delacorte, 1992.

Pronto, Delacorte, 1993.

Riding the Rap, Delacorte, 1995.

Out of Sight, Delacorte, 1996.

Cuba Libre, Delacorte, 1998.

Sources

On-line

"Elmore (John Jr.) Leonard," *Contemporary Authors* database, Gale Literary Databases web site, http://www.galenet.com (July 11, 1998).

Periodicals

Atlanta Journal and Constitution, June 21, 1998, p. L1.

Dallas Morning News, January 19, 1997, p. 2C; January 17, 1998, p. 5C.

Entertainment Weekly, May 31, 1996, p. 66.

Los Angeles Times, June 21, 1998, calendar, p. 21.

Los Angeles Times Book Review, February 1, 1998, p. 8.

Newsday, October 26, 1995, p. B4; September 22, 1996, p. C12.

New York Times, December 30, 1984; February 15, 1996.

St. Louis Post-Dispatch, December 24, 1997, p. E4.

Star Tribune (Minneapolis, MN), October 29, 1995.

USA Today, October 20, 1995.

Other

Fresh Air, National Public Radio, interview with Terry Gross, January 2, 1998.

—Geri Speace

Loida Nicolas Lewis

Businesswoman

Born December 23, 1942, in Sorsogon, Philippines; daughter of a furniture-store chain owner; married Reginald F. Lewis, 1969 (died 1993); children: Leslie, Christina. *Education:* St. Theresa's College, B.A., 1963; University of the Philippines College of Law, LL.B., 1967.

Addresses: *Home*—New York, NY. *Office*—TLC Beatrice International Holdings Inc., 9 West 57th St., 39th Floor, New York, NY 10019.

Career

Immigration attorney for the Immigration and Naturalization Services, New York City, 1979-90; chair and chief executive officer (CEO) of TLC Beatrice International, New York City, 1994—. Author of three books on immigration.

Sidelights

Loida Nicolas Lewis was thrust into the high-stakes world of international business with no real prior experience in 1994. Her husband, Reginald Lewis, had been running the world grocery powerhouse, TLC Beatrice International Holdings since his buyout in 1987, making it the country's largest African American-owned business. He died of brain cancer at age 50 in 1993. Wishing to continue his legacy, Lewis stepped in a year later to keep the company running smoothly. Surrounding herself with savvy leaders and restructuring in order to continue reducing the debt, Lewis raised profits and laid plans to continue expansion.

AP/Wide World Photos

Lewis was born in Sorsogon, the Philippines, where her father founded Nicfur, one of that country's biggest furniture chains. She graduated cum laude from St. Theresa's College and went on to obtain her law degree from the University of the Philippines College of Law. She first saw New York City in 1968 after her father financed a trip for her as a reward for passing the bar exam. While on vacation, she met Reynaldo P. Glover, who set her up on a blind date with Reginald Lewis, an associate at a Wall Street law practice. Married in 1969, the couple had two daughters, Leslie and Christina.

In 1972, when her daughters were young, Lewis started up a monthly magazine for Filipino-Americans. She published it until 1979, when it merged with another publication. She later wrote three books on immigration law. In 1979, she won a case against the Immigration and Naturalization Service (INS) for discrimination on the basis of sex, race, and national origin. Having been the first Asian female to pass the bar exam of New York State without ever studying law in the United States, Lewis was more qualified for the job than the candidates who had been hired. She joined the agency as General Attorney, where she served until 1990.

Lewis' husband, Reginald, bought Beatrice International for close to a billion dollars in December 1987 in a leveraged buyout and renamed it TLC (The Lewis Company) Beatrice International Holdings Inc. Employing 4,500 workers, it became a leader in the grocery and convenience store market in Western Europe, especially Paris, and a manufacturer of ice cream in Spain and potato chips in Ireland. Lewis managed the assets to reduce the company's debt and was leader of the largest African American-owned business in the United States when he fell into a coma and died of brain cancer in January of 1993. He had named Jean S. Fugett, Jr. to the CEO position shortly before his death to keep things on track until his wife could step in.

Lewis mourned her husband for nearly a year before taking over TLC Beatrice. *New York Times* writer Tony Chapelle claimed that Fugett stepped down after shareholders became worried. First, Chapelle reported, the media had announced Fugett's intent to purchase the Baltimore Orioles baseball team, which was out of character for a food corporation. Then, Beatrice opened its books to Wall Street, showing that Reginald Lewis had received $22 million in bonuses for the prior five years amid TLC's large losses and cash-flow problems. Chapelle related, "Quicker than a New York minute, several shareholder groups demanded that the stock be taken public, on the theory that the market would make it liquid enough to pick up some value."

Lewis, however, commented to Chapelle that she just told Fugett that she was ready. The board did not object to her taking the lead, and the largest non-family shareholder (Lewis and her daughter Leslie own about half of the shares), Carlton Investments, no longer declared that the shares be put on the public market. Despite her smooth handling of the potential mutiny, Carlton later filed a lawsuit claiming that the $22 million Lewis' husband earned had violated the stockholders' agreement. TLC Beatrice lawyers fought it, saying that the overworked CEO earned the money.

Lewis continued to demonstrate her business skills despite lack of formal training or experience. She noted to Chapelle in the *New York Times* that her husband taught her a lot about the business. In an audio interview with Ann Devlin on the Ann On-line web site, she noted, "I would not have taken this position if I knew that I [would] not be able to do it." She told Devlin that since she knew her husband's goals, she knew what to strive for, and she surrounded herself with quality management. Her sister, Imelda Nicolas, works as her executive assistant, and the man who was

her matchmaker, Reynaldo P. Glover, is her general counsel.

Lewis took charge, selling under-performing subsidiaries, refinancing a $175 million loan, and laying off employees. She noted to Devlin, however, that the employees were provided with psychologists and given job counseling in order to re-enter the job market. She reduced debt from $321 million to $232 million. Net profits rose 46 percent in 1994 during the first nine months that she was generally making decisions, and 26 percent in her first full quarter as CEO. Critics claimed that her success was due to the healthy European economy at the time, not her business savvy.

However, Lewis boasted to Devlin that the company would branch out into China as well. She said in the interview that her philosophy is that she is in the business to serve. "If you can give them good service, if you are honest, you have integrity, profit will follow," she remarked in the interview. She told Devlin that she believes "all successful businesses have an inner code of conduct, a code of ethics...if a business is constantly cheating its customers, it won't last long." *Working Woman* named her one of the top businesswomen in 1994 and *Business Week* called her a "manager to watch" in 1995, according to her biography on Ann On-line.

Lewis is a cofounder of the Asian-American Legal Defense & Education Fund. She also chairs the Reginald F. Lewis Foundation, founded by her husband in 1987. The private foundation donates millions each year to a variety of institutions, although the emphasis is placed on African American causes. She still considers TLC Beatrice African American-owned due to her daughter's large share and the fact that the board is mostly black. She also has worked to promote her husband's autobiography, *Why Should White Guys Have All the Fun? How Reginald Lewis Created a Billion-Dollar Business Empire*. When asked by Devlin whether she worried about people criticizing her when she took over TLC Beatrice, Lewis replied, "Don't listen to what other people think of you. Believe in your own self.... Don't listen to naysayers."

Selected writings

How the Filipino Veteran of World War II Can Become a U.S. Citizen (According to the Immigration Act of 1990), 1991.
One Hundred One Legal Ways to Stay in the U.S.A., 1992.
How to Get a Green Card: Legal Ways to Stay in the U.S.A., 1993.

Sources

On-line

Biography of Loida Nicolas Lewis, Ann On-line web site, http://www.annonline.com (April 21, 1998).
Interview with Ann Devlin, Ann On-line web site, http://www.annonline.com (April 21, 1998).

Periodicals

Jet, January 24, 1994, p. 38.
New York Times, November 27, 1994.
Star-Ledger (Newark, NJ), June 30, 1996, p. 3.

—*Geri Speace*

Jim Leyland

Baseball manager

Born James Richard Leyland, December 15, 1944, in Toledo, OH; son of James Leyland (a factory worker); married Katie O'Connor, 1987; children: two.

Addresses: *Office*—Florida Marlins, 2267 N.W. 199th Street, Miami, FL 33056.

Career

Detroit Tigers' minor league system, baseball player, 1964-69; coach in the minor leagues, 1970-71; manager in the minor leagues, 1971-81; Chicago White Sox, coach, 1981-85; Pittsburgh Pirates, manager, 1986-96; Florida Marlins, manager, 1997—.

Awards: Named National League Manager of the Year, 1988 and 1990.

Sidelights

Working stiffs applauded when Jim Leyland's team finally won a World Series in 1997. After 34 seasons in professional baseball, 17 of them in the minor leagues, Leyland, who never played in the majors, achieved professional baseball's pinnacle. The irony is that he did it managing the Florida Marlins, a team that epitomized the power of money rather than the nose-to-the-grindstone values Leyland cherishes.

The Marlins were the best team money could buy in 1997. Before the season, owner Wayne Huizenga, the Blockbuster Video multi-millionaire, spent close to $100 million to lure a half dozen top free agents to Miami. Winning was so costly that Huizenga sold the team days after the World Series ended. The new

owners soon held a fire sale, shipping off high-priced stars like Kevin Brown, Moises Alou and Devon White. Fortunately, they held onto Leyland, who proved in his 11 year tenure with the Pittsburgh Pirates that he can make the most of a limited budget.

"Nobody's going to ruin this for me tonight by talking about money," Leyland told S.L. Price of *Sports Illustrated* after his team's victory in the final game of the Series. "We didn't buy this pennant, we won the pennant. We won the World Series. We earned it."

Despite the high payroll, the Marlins were plagued with injuries and lost their best pitcher, Alex Fernandez, in the first round of the playoffs. Leyland made the most of little known players such as Craig Counsell, a longtime minor leaguer who scored the run that won the series, and Livan Hernandez, a Cuban defector who was the unlikely pitching standout.

Prior to the big win, Leyland had certainly paid his dues. Three times, his Pittsburgh Pirates teams had advanced to the National League Championship Series but failed to make it to the World Series. Once, in 1992, the Pirates were two runs ahead with three outs to go to reach the World Series and lost to the Atlanta Braves. Mostly, Leyland earned his reward with the many long, low-paid seasons in towns like Clinton,

Iowa, and Jamestown, New York. In an era where baseball is besotted with millionaires, Leyland is a guy who made the most of his limited talents and clawed his way to the top through courage and respect for the game and his players. "Look, one of the big blessings I have is that I tried to play this game," Leyland told Charles Pierce of *GQ*. "I know how hard it is. When you know how hard it is, you have a greater appreciation for the people who play the game well."

Mike Lupica of *Esquire* wrote of Leyland: "He is as powerful an advertisement for what is still right about baseball, as articulate a spokesman for the game's values and traditions and beauty, as anyone." Leyland is particularly outspoken about a back-to-the-basics approach. He told Michael Knisley of the *Sporting News*: "I personally think baseball makes a mistake by trying to create too many sideshows through marketing, instead of focusing on what the real product is. The real product is your players."

James Richard Leyland grew up in a working class family in Perrysburg, Ohio, a suburb of Toledo. His father worked in an auto glass factory. Jim was one of five sons, all of them athletic except Tom, who became a priest. He also had one sister. As a kid, Jim played baseball constantly, and his father encouraged him to follow his dream.

Eventually, a scout named Herm Cander signed him for the Detroit Tigers. "I knew the first day of minor league training camp that I never was going to play baseball in the major leagues," Leyland told Leigh Montville of *Sports Illustrated*. "I had hopes—everyone who signs a contract has high hopes—but once I saw those other players and how good they were, I knew I didn't have a chance."

Leyland spent seven seasons as a catcher in the Tigers' system, never rising above Double A ball, two steps below the majors. He was a poor hitter who managed only four home runs in six seasons. But Leyland loved the work.

"When I made $400 a month, I thought I was the richest son of a bitch you ever saw," he told Steve Rushin of *Sports Illustrated*. "I always had a buck in my pocket and a pack of cigarettes. My dad always said, 'He's not gonna amount to nothin', because you give him a buck and a pack of cigarettes, and he's the happiest son of a bitch I've ever seen in my life.'"

During the off season, Leyland would return to Perrysburg to work. "I'd come home, I'd be broke again," he told Montville. "I'd have to borrow money....

I worked every winter. I worked in the post office. I worked in the glass company. I worked construction. I drove a truck."

But Leyland refused to give up. "I had the fever," he explained to Montville. "I never considered quitting." At 26, he took a job managing in Bristol, the Tigers' entry in the Appalachian Rookie League, the lowest ring in the minors. "The one thing I decided to do from the beginning was be honest," he told Montville. "That is the most important thing.... Tell a guy what you really think about him. He might not like it, but if he knows you're honest, he has to respect you. You start playing games with people and you're lost."

Leyland spent the 1970s moving from one team to another, trying to move up the mountain he was unable to conquer as a player. "I loved every place I went," he proclaimed to Montville. "People say, 'You managed in Clinton, Iowa?' I loved it. The people would say hello to you on the street, talk about the team. Ladies would bake apple pies and bring them to the ballpark for you. Clinton, Iowa, was wonderful." By 1979, Leyland had worked his way to the top of the minor league system, Triple A, managing the Tigers' Evansville club. But his path to Detroit was blocked by Sparky Anderson, who managed the Tigers from 1979 to 1995.

One of his rival managers in the minors was Tony LaRussa at Des Moines. After LaRussa was promoted to the Chicago White Sox, he hired Leyland as one of his coaches. Leyland coached with Chicago from 1981 to 1985, when he finally got his chance to manage a big league team in Pittsburgh.

"The first game in Pittsburgh, I stood on that field," he told Montville. "I looked into the stands. I saw my father. I was just so proud, and I knew he was proud." A consummate "player's manager," Leyland soon won the respect of the Pirates, their management, and their fans.

Leyland had little use for curfews, dress codes and other off-field rules designed to control behavior. "I don't have a lot of rules, because all they do is get broken," he told Pierce. "Play hard and be on time. That's the baseline for me.... Knowing what a guy throws you, and knowing what he did to you last time—to me, that's discipline, not telling a guy he can't wear saddle shoes."

Leyland's admonitions to his players were simple, as he recounted them to *Esquire*'s Lupica: "I tell them to be decent human beings. I tell them to go out every day and perform to the best of their abilities and sometimes beyond. And I tell 'em to sign an autograph once in a while and make a kid smile."

When Leyland took over the Pirates in 1986, they were rebuilding. In his first season, Leyland's Pirates finished last with a record of 64 wins and 98 losses. Two years later, they were second in their division with 85 wins and 75 losses.

From 1990 to 1992, the Pirates won more games than any team in baseball. "Jim is not a great motivator," shortstop Jay Bell told Knisley. "But the thing he does better than just about anybody else is allow his players to have confidence in themselves, because he shows confidence in them."

> "I tell them to be decent human beings. I tell them to go out every day and perform to the best of their abilities and sometimes beyond. And I tell 'em to sign an autograph once in a while and make a kid smile."

Leyland believes handling players is a manager's biggest job. "Everybody who's managing in the major leagues knows what this game is all about," he told Knisley of the *Sporting News.* "There are no big secrets.... It boils down to players and how you get it out of them."

Mark Starr of *Newsweek* noted: "Leyland has a gritty, blue collar, no b.s. style, which can mask management skills that would be the envy of any white collar organization man. He admits to being a 'dynamic listener,' and seems to understand the modern game as well as the modern player."

When Leyland arrived in Pittsburgh, he had never owned a house or furniture. He asked a woman named Katie O'Connor, who worked in the Pirates promotions department, to accompany him to a furniture store. A year later, Leyland married O'Connor, who is 17 years his junior.

Leyland became a fans' favorite by personally answering their letters to him, often with phone calls. Yet Leyland refused to join in the increasing chorus of baseball fans' criticism of players as overpaid. "It's

common sense that owners would not be paying these kinds of salaries if they could not afford to pay them," Leyland told Rushin of *Sports Illustrated.*

For most of his tenure, Leyland enjoyed managing in Pittsburgh. "It is Leyland's nature to look beleaguered," Rushin noted. "But there are nights, he admits, when he walks through the clubhouse as the players undress, gathers his coaches in his office, shuts the door and leans back in that rocking chair. Then he grins at his staff, as if they're all in on a grand conspiracy, and he says, 'Daaaaamn, what a game!'"

In 1993, superstar Barry Bonds left to sign a lucrative free-agent contract with the San Francisco Giants, and the glory days were over. Management quickly dismantled the team, hoping to save their small market franchise with a rock bottom payroll. In Leyland's last four seasons in Pittsburgh, the Pirates never won more than 75 games.

"He was a good fit for Pittsburgh, an old school manager in a hard knocks town," wrote Knisley . "He stuck with that no hope team for a lot longer than anybody had a right to expect him to, mostly because he thinks in sync with the city's scrappiness." But eventually, even Leyland gave up on the Pirates.

The Marlins' general manager Dave Dombrowski, who knew Leyland from his days with the White Sox, won a fierce competition for Leyland's services. Florida signed Leyland to a five-year contract. Bobby Bonilla, one of the stars on Leyland's pennant winning Pirates clubs, signed with the Marlins to play again for his old boss. Dombrowski told Starr: "It's amazing, once we had Jim here, the number of players who wanted to play for him."

Though the Marlins did not finish in first place in their division, they became the first wild card team to enter a World Series. Leyland's team fulfilled the high expectations set for them. He told Lupica he was flattered by his newfound notoriety, but was trying to keep it in perspective: "There's a saying I've always gone by, and it may sound corny, but here it is: Take the job seriously, but don't take yourself seriously. Because all of this shit can be very fast and fleeting."

And despite managing some of the game's most egotistic superstars, Leyland continued to profess his affection for the players. "I can count on the fingers of one hand the players that I just didn't care for," Leyland told Pierce. "To me, if a guy's a jerk, he's a jerk if he's making $400 a month or $400,000." "I'm a shit ballplayer from a small town." he told Lupica.

"I've already gotten more out of this game than I thought I ever would.... I wake up every morning thinking I'm lucky to have a job like this."

Sources

Esquire, June 1997, p. 36.

GQ, May 1996, p. 61.

Newsweek, March 10, 1997, p. 77.

Sporting News, March 31, 1997, p. S3; November 3, 1997, p. 40.

Sports Illustrated, August 27, 1990, p. 54; October 26, 1992, p. 20; January 25, 1993, p. 42; June 26, 1995, p. 72.

—Michael Betzold

Tara Lipinski

Figure skater

Born Tara Kristen Lipinski, June 10, 1982, in Philadelphia, PA; daughter of Jack (an oil company executive) and Patricia Lipinski.

Addresses: *Home*—Sugarland, TX.

Career

Figure skater. Has competed in regional, world, and Olympic championships; turned professional, 1998. Published *Triumph on Ice: An Autobiography by Tara Lipinski as Told to Emily Costello*, Bantam Books, 1997.

Awards: Blue Swords, first place, Midwestern Novice, first place, Southwestern Novice, first place, National Novice, second place, and U.S. Olympic Festival, first place, all 1994; National Juniors, second place, Nebelhorn Trophy, fourth place, and World Junior Championships, fourth place, all 1995; National Championships, third place, Nations Cup, second place, Skate Canada, second place, Trophee Lalique, third place, South Atlantic Juniors, first place, World Junior selections competition, second place, World Juniors, fifth place, World Championships, fifteenth place, all 1996; Champion Series final, first place, Hershey's Challenge (team), first place, National Championships, first place, Skate America, second place, Trophy Lalique, second place, U. S. Olympic Committee's SportsWoman of the Year, and World Championships, first place, all 1997; Champion Series final, first place, National Championships, second place, Olympic gold medal, all 1998; Skate, Rattle & Roll, first place, 1998.

Sidelights

The tiny Tara Lipinski has accomplished giant feats within her short time in the world. At age 14, the figure skater already had won the U.S. national and world championships, breaking the 70-year record held by the legendary Sonja Henie as skating's youngest world champion. In December of 1997, when she was 15, the United States Olympic Committee named her SportsWoman of the Year, the youngest athlete to ever earn the title. Lipinski continued her reign, grabbing the Olympic gold medal for women's figure skating in Nagano, Japan, in February of 1998, making her the youngest Olympic women's figure skating champion in history.

In early April of 1998, her whirlwind days of competing behind her, Lipinski announced that she was turning pro. The decision made her ineligible for any future Olympic games, but allowed the bubbly teenager to spend more time with her family. Though her success points to a young woman with determination to win, she also comes across as an athlete with a deep love for her sport and a joy of the experiences she has had while competing. During the days leading up to her gold medal at the 1998 Olympics, she spent the majority of her time in the Olympic Village with other athletes, meeting hockey legend Wayne Gretzky, playing games, sending e-mail, and posing for photos as the smallest Olympic athlete (4-foot, 11-inches and 85 pounds) next to the largest, the 516-pound Sumo wrestler Akebono. "I want my Olympic memories. This is my chance to have fun," Lipinski told a friend, according to *Sports Illustrated.* "The Olympics are pretty stressful," claimed Lipinski in *Newsweek,* "and I think I relaxed a little bit and just let myself have fun." The teenager wisely added, "I think it worked."

> "When I go out there [on the ice], I put everything that's on the outside away, and I think about my skating and what I need to do to feel happy."

Lipinski was born in Philadelphia, Pennsylvania, and grew up near Newark, Delaware. She became a regional roller skating champ in New Jersey at age five. Her parents, Jack and Patricia Lipinski, first introduced her to the ice at the University of Delaware Ice Arena at six years old, when they watched her flounder in the rink before going in for hot chocolate. When they returned, Lipinski was already showing that she was a natural. Not quite six years elapsed between her first ice skating lesson and her first national silver medal. In 1991, the family moved just outside of Houston to Sugarland, Texas, which she considers her home town. There she trained diligently, getting up as early as 3 a.m. for lessons and training at the Houston Galleria ice rink before school.

Many young girls aspire to be skaters, but Lipinski showed real talent. When she was barely 12 years old, in 1994, Lipinski's motivation reaped its rewards when she became the youngest athlete ever to win a gold medal at the U.S. Olympic Festival, skating to "Spirit of St. Louis." That year she also placed first in the Midwestern Novice and Southwestern Novice competitions, and made it to second place at the National Novice level. The next year saw her rise to become a silver medalist at the U.S. National Junior championships at age 13, and she captured fourth place at the World Juniors.

The 1996 season saw some awesome achievements by Lipinski-third place at the National Championships, second place at the Nations Cup and Skate Canada, and first place at the South Atlantic Juniors. The prodigy finished a disappointing fifth at World Juniors that year, although she came in fifteenth at the World Championships after moving into the senior division—a remarkable first attempt that she accomplished with seven triple jumps in her long program to boost her up from twenty-third. Getting serious now, Lipinski headed north, to Bloomfield Hills, Michigan, a tiny Detroit suburb, to be coached by the renowned Richard Callaghan. She trained four times daily for 45 minutes at the Detroit Skating Club with Callaghan, whose students included national champions Nicole Bobek and Todd Eldredge. Unfortunately, Lipinski's father remained behind in Sugarland as vice president of the oil firm, Coastal Corporation, flying up for visits on weekends. Lipinski, an "A" student, received four hours of private academic tutoring each day and completed homework in the evenings.

The changes, though stressful, proved fruitful. Coach Callaghan aided with Lipinski's image, giving her a more mature look, yet one befitting a young girl. She also began ballet lessons three times a week to improve her grace. Lipinski had a banner year in 1997, taking the U.S. National Figure Skating Championships by storm at the sold-out Nashville Arena. After a shocking series of falls and stumbles by Michelle Kwan, the 16-year-old favorite, Lipinski wowed the crowd with what was thought to be the first triple loop-triple loop combination ever successfully executed in competition. With her win, the tiny powerhouse broke the record for the youngest U.S. national women's champion, thus beginning a rivalry with Kwan. The young victor also knocked Sonya Klopfer, who was 15 when she won in 1951, off the books. As if that huge accomplishment wasn't enough, Lipinski again out-skated Kwan to capture the World Championship in Switzerland in March of 1997. This time, she unraveled Sonja Henie's record for youngest world champion, which had stood for 70 years.

After upsetting Kwan at World Championship, Lipinski did not stop being her usual charming teenage self, even after appearing on David Letterman's show and being tapped to possibly take home a gold medal in the Olympics. She was in prime position to see it happen, since the ten previous women's world championships winners went on to win gold medals at the following Olympic Games. Lipinski told *Texas Monthly* magazine, "I don't think about being famous or anything like that. I just want to do my best when I'm on the ice." After a brief moment, however, she did say that winning a gold medal at the Olympics would be "pretty neat, you know? Oh, okay, that would be really, really neat." In the meantime,

Lipinski signed a deal to promote Donna Karan's DKNY Kids clothing line, the first of what will most likely be a string of lucrative product endorsements for the photogenic and savvy young skater.

While preparing for the big games, Lipinski broke yet another record with her youth when she was named the United States Olympic Committee's SportsWoman of the Year in December of 1997. Two other athletes were 15 when they received the honor, but Lipinski was younger by a few months. Her skating, however, was not so much to brag about. Her scores were lower throughout the competitions, and she came in second to Kwan's first place at the national championships. Coach Callaghan in *Time* attributed her slight decline to an increase in the judges' scrutiny, since she was the reigning world champ. Lipinski seemed to brush away the pressure, commenting in *Time*, "When I go out there [on the ice], I put everything that's on the outside away, and I think about my skating and what I need to do to feel happy." Lipinski's positive attitude must have worked, because she had plenty to cheer her up at the 1998 Olympics in Nagano, Japan. Her ambition, talent, and drive did not hurt, either. Although by that time Kwan was favored to win the gold, Lipinski took in the Olympic experience with giggles and smiles. It did not seem to matter to coach Callaghan that she wanted to have fun. He remarked in *Sports Illustrated*, "I knew she was organized enough to go to bed on time, get up on time and not miss the bus to practice. Tara has her day structured so she's a giddy teenager between these hours and a really hard worker between these hours." Apparently "balance is best" is the message that could be learned from Lipinski's Olympic experience. Kwan could almost feel the gold medal around her neck with her string of almost-perfect scores. But the judges threw in a few 5.7s for technical merit, and the little Lipinski squeezed into the margin, landing seven triples—the same as Kwan—and layering on top of that her trademark triple loop-triple loop. The lustrous program thrust her into the top spot and sent her into shrieking fits of joy.

Lipinski quickly became a media darling. The skater whose coach initially thought she would be ready for the 2002 Olympics turned out to be a persevering underdog who toppled the favorite at the last minute at the tender age of 15. However, she announced in April of 1998, just two months after her win, that there would be no more Olympic glitter in her future: she was going pro. "I realized after Nagano how important it is to me to be with my mom and dad and be all together and have fun and go out to dinner and really be a family again," she explained in a *New York Times* report. "I owe that to my parents and myself." Shortly thereafter, Lipinski made her professional debut in Skate, Rattle & Roll in North Charleston, South Carolina, taking first place above France's Surya Bonaly and former Olympic gold medalist Oksana Baiul.

In addition, after the gold medal, endorsement deals poured in, including one for Disney World's Animal Kingdom. She also released a chronicle of her 15 years on this planet in 1997, titled *Triumph on Ice: An Autobiography by Tara Lipinski as Told to Emily Costello*, and even has her own domain on the web: www.taralipinski.com, which features graphics of spinning skates as well as photos, diary entries, personal information, appearance schedules, press articles, and an address for fans to send e-mail. How does the diminutive teenager cope with all the fame and possible fortune? "When I'm off the ice, I feel like a normal teen-ager," Lipinski noted in an Associated Press article. "On the ice, I feel like I have something a little special to have and to go for." And what are her plans for the future? As she remarked to ESPN SportsZone interviewer Steve Cyphers, "I'll keep skating and enjoy it. I mean I've won and it's been my dream of my whole life so I can just keep going on from here and trying to improve on everything."

Sources

On-line

"Conversation with Tara Lipinski," ESPN SportsZone, http://espn.sportszone.com (May 4, 1998).

"Lipinski skates away with USOC honor," December 16, 1997, Associated Press sports, http://www.sportserver.com (May 4, 1998).

Tara Lipinski web site, http://www.taralipinski.com (May 4, 1998).

Periodicals

Detroit Free Press, September 25, 1997; April 25, 1998.

Maclean's, March 2, 1998, p. 42.

Newsweek, March 31, 1997, p. 82; March 2, 1998, p. 62.

New York Times, February 6, 1998, p. C3; April 7, 1998.

Sports Illustrated, February 24, 1997, p. 28; March 2, 1998, p. 48.

Texas Monthly, September 1, 1997, p. 134.

Time, February 9, 1998, p. 86; March 2, 1998, p. 66.

—*Geri Speace*

LL Cool J

Corbis-Bettmann

Rap singer and actor

Born James Todd Smith, 1968, in Queens, NY; married, 1995; wife's name, Simone; children: one son, two daughters.

Addresses: *Record company*—Def Jam, 825 Eighth Avenue, New York, NY 10019.

Career

Signed to Def Jam and released first single "I Need a Beat," 1984; albums include *Radio*, 1985; *Bigger & Deffer*, 1987; *Walking with a Panther*, 1989; *Mama Said Knock You Out*, 1990; *14 Shots to the Dome*, 1993; *Mr. Smith*, 1995; *All Change*, 1996; and *Phenomenon*, 1997. Film appearances include *Krush Groove*, 1985; *Hard Way*, 1991; *Toys*, 1992; *Out of Sync*, 1995; *Right to Remain Silent*, 1996; and *Baps*, 1997. Also appeared in the television series *In the House*, 1995-97. Established nonprofit Camp Cool J Foundation, 1992. Released autobiography, *I Make My Own Rules*, 1997.

Awards: Grammy Award, best rap solo performance, 1991, for "Mama Said Knock You Out"; Grammy Award, best rap solo performance, 1996, for "Hey Lover"; Music Television (MTV) Video Vanguard Award, 1997; Image Award, National Association for the Advancement of Colored People (NAACP), for favorite hero; 15 New York Music Awards; ten Soul Train Awards.

Sidelights

Arguably the most popular and influential member of the hip-hop nation, LL Cool J has established himself as a premiere multi-faceted entertainer and entrepreneur. His anti-violence, anti-drugs, and anti-degradation of women approach to rap and hip-hop was often times at odds with the prevailing mood of the genre. Undaunted by this, LL Cool J soldiered on, following his own vision, while the rest of the hip-hop nation tried to keep up the pace.

LL Cool J was never a proponent of the harshly violent urban imagery found in the gangsta rap genre. He explained his stance on violence in the Def Jam website: "I don't like violence. I've seen violence, seen people I love be the victims of violence and there's nothing cool about it. It plainly just doesn't interest me."

While growing up in the St. Alban's area of Queens, New York, LL Cool J was a witness to violence in his own home. He was only four years old when his mother left his father after suffering years of physical and mental abuse. His mother moved in with her parents and tried to make a new life for herself, away from her abusive husband. LL Cool J's father was not so easily deterred, however, and was determined to win back his estranged wife. When she refused to return, LL Cool J's father shot her in the lower back with a 12 gauge shotgun. Rushing to see what had happened, LL Cool J discovered that his grandfather had been shot in the stomach. Commenting on the shooting, LL Cool J related to *Jet* that "I ran to get towels from the bathroom. When I pushed them into my grandfather's stomach, I could see where his flesh had been ripped apart.... The way my family handled that incident—no charges pressed, that forgiveness—showed love in a way I have never seen since. From the way my family dealt with the shooting, I learned forgiveness and gained inner strength. That lesson helped me become who I am today."

Yet, LL Cool J's troubles were not over. As his mother was recovering from the wounds, she met a man who was willing to help and support her during her long period of convalescence. Unfortunately for LL Cool J, his mother's pillar of strength viewed her young son as his personal whipping boy, physically and mentally abusing him.

Seeking some solace and refuge from the abuse, LL Cool J began to immerse himself in rap music. He recalled to *Jet*,"the music and rhymes helped me escape all the pain." He was rapping at nine years old, and soon afterward invented his stage name; LL Cool J was an acronym for ladies love cool James.

A gift from his grandfather was the impetus young LL Cool J needed to start his rap career. The 13-year-old had asked for a dirt bike but his grandfather, fearing for his young grandson's future, declined to honor his request and gave him some musical and recording equipment instead.

Soon the high school student was strutting his stuff and flexing his vocal cords for his enraptured classmates. He began producing his own demo tapes and sending them off to the major labels with rap departments and artists. Yet the only response came from the fledgling New York-based Def Jam label.

LL Cool J signed with Def Jam, and in 1984 released his first single "I Need a Beat." The 16-year-old's song was the first single ever released by Def Jam. LL Cool J's debut album, *Radio*, earned the distinction of being the first album released by Def Jam as well. The year 1985 also marked the beginning of LL Cool J's acting career as he was offered a cameo appearance in the hip-hop film *Krush Groove*. By the following year, he was on tour with some of the biggest and most notorious names in hip-hop and rap at the time, including the Beastie Boys and Run DMC.

His second album, 1987's *Bigger & Deffer*, featured the songs "I'm Bad," which became a top five R&B hit, and "I Need Love," a gentle rap ballad that became the first rap song to reach the top of the Hot Black Singles chart.

Walking with a Panther was released in 1989 and spawned the hit song "Going Back to Cali." The following year saw the phenomenal breakthrough success of *Mama Said Knock You Out*, which tended to overshadow LL Cool J's previous accomplishments. *Mama Said Knock You Out* produced two tremendously popular hit songs. The first was "Around the Way Girl" which topped the rap and R&B charts, and became a *Billboard* top ten single. The album's title track faired even better, earning LL Cool J the 1991 Grammy Award for the best solo rap performance. This recording remained on the *Billboard* Top Pop Albums chart for over a year and lasted nearly 18 months on the Top Black Albums chart. Also in 1991, LL Cool J starred in the film the *Hard Way*.

> *"I don't like violence. I've seen violence, seen people I love be the victims of violence and there's nothing cool about it. It plainly just doesn't interest me."*

In 1992 the rap star established the Camp Cool J Foundation, a non-profit organization that funded free camping, educational, cultural and recreational activities for young people across America. In his website, he explained his motivation behind the founding of Camp Cool J: "it's a place where kids who have achieved good grades in school and performed some community service can go to improve their academic skills and enjoy nature. Kids from around my way never had the chance to get out of the city in the summertime. I wish I had that somebody I looked up to who would scoop me up from the neighborhood and say 'Come on, we're going to put you in camp for free.'" That same year, he appeared in the film *Toys*, and in 1993 released his next album, *14 Shots to the Dome*.

The year 1995 was another watershed for LL Cool J. That autumn, he finally wed Simone, his high school sweetheart and the mother of his three children. They were married in Long Island. LL Cool J also starred in the film *Out of Sync* and began a new career as a television actor. He had the starring role in the television program *In the House*.

On the music front, LL Cool J released his sixth consecutive platinum album, *Mr. Smith*, which was the showcase for a wiser and older performer. The artist claimed that *Mr. Smith* was the most honest and open album that he had created so far.

He also continued to record and release the sensitive and romantic rap ballads that were becoming some of his signature songs. "Hey Lover" was no exception; the platinum single featured backing vocals by the R&B innovators Boyz II Men.

It shot to number three on the *Billboard* Hot 100 chart and earned LL Cool J his second Grammy Award in 1996 for best solo rap performance. He also starred in the film *Right to Remain Silent*. Also in 1996, Def Jam released his greatest hits album *All Change*.

Throughout his career, LL Cool J has received numerous other awards including the 1997 MTV Video Vanguard Award, Rock the Vote's Patrick Lippard Award, ten Soul Train Awards, a *Billboard* Music Award, 15 New York Music Awards, and a NAACP Image Award for favorite hero.

The rapper released his eighth album *Phenomenon,* in 1997. That year, he also starred in the film *Baps* and released his autobiography *I Make My Own Rules.* He commented in the Def Jam website that the release of the book was "a testimony to my growth and development as a human being. It's a way to show people how to go through negativity and come out on top if you just focus, concentrate and believe in spirituality. A lot of the songs on the album [*Phenomenon*] apply to chapters in the book, so there's an inter-relationship to the book and album."

Promoting his book in *Jet,* LL Cool J stated that "I'm a lot more than an entertainer who wears hats and rolls up his pant's leg. I'm a father with three beautiful children. I'm a husband with a wonderful wife. I'm a healing victim of abuse who has made many mistakes along the way. My real name is James Todd Smith, and in real life I am a man."

Selected writings

I Make My Own Rules, St. Martin's Press (New York City), 1997.

Selected discography

"I Need a Beat," Def Jam, 1984.
Radio, Def Jam, 1985.
Bigger & Deffer (includes "I Need Love" and "I'm Bad"), Def Jam, 1987.
Walking with a Panther (includes "Going Back to Cali"), Def Jam, 1989.
Mama Said Knock You Out (includes "Around the Way Girl" and "Mama Said Knock You Out"), Def Jam, 1990.
14 Shots to the Dome, Def Jam, 1993.
Mr. Smith (includes "Hey Lover"), Def Jam, 1995.
All Change, Def Jam, 1996.
Phenomenon, Def Jam, 1997.

Sources

On-line

"LL Cool J," http://www.boomshakamusic.com/mr.smith/ms1.html (February 13, 1998).
"LL Cool J," http://www.defjam.com/artists/llcoolj/coolj03.html (February 13, 1998).

Periodicals

Billboard, January 6, 1996, pp. 12-14.
Entertainment Weekly, December 1, 1995, p. 74; July 11, 1997, p. 61.
Jet, October 9, 1995, p. 40; September 22, 1997, pp. 37-42.
National Review, October 14, 1996, p. 94.

—*Mary Alice Adams*

Kenny Lofton

AP/Wide World Photos

Professional baseball player

Born May 31, 1967, East Chicago, IN; son of Annie; grandson of Rosie Person. *Education:* University of Arizona, B.A., media arts, 1989.

Addresses: *Office*—Cleveland Indians, 2401 Ontario St., Cleveland, OH 44115-4003.

Career

Drafted by Houston Astros, 1988; played in Houston's farm system, 1988-91; promoted to majors, 1991; traded to Cleveland Indians; Cleveland outfielder 1992-96; traded to Atlanta Braves; Atlanta outfielder, 1997; became free agent after 1997 season; re-signed with Cleveland Indians, 1997.

Awards: Gold Glove, outfield, American League, 1993, 1994, 1995, 1996; named East Chicagoan of the Year, 1995.

Sidelights

Speed demon Kenny Lofton has more than just a fine set of wheels. Through hard work, he has developed the tools needed to be a baseball superstar. An excellent, defensive center fielder, Lofton on offense is a catalyst, a fearsome hitter who can get on base and disrupt the defense with his speed. The heir to Rickey Henderson as baseball's best leadoff man, Lofton was slowed in 1997, his first season with the Atlanta Braves, by a pulled groin muscle. During the regular season, the normally unstoppable Lofton was successful in only 27 of his 47 steal attempts. His play in the field also suffered. Yet he batted for a .333 aver-

age (fourth-best in the National League) with a .409 on-base percentage, typically impressive numbers for one of the game's best hitters.

In the first game of the playoffs against the Houston Astros, Lofton led off with a double, audaciously took third on a short fly to right field, and scored on another fly ball, manufacturing a key run in a 2-1 Braves win. However, he didn't do much the rest during the rest of the playoffs. In the National League Championship Series, in the eighth inning of the fifth game, with the Braves down a run, Lofton was caught stealing.

Lofton came to Atlanta and the National League in a controversial trade after five outstanding years with the American League's Cleveland Indians. To get Lofton, the Braves gave up two top players, David Justice and Marquis Grissom. About his disappointing 1997 season, Lofton told Michael Farber of *Sports Illustrated:* "I got recognized for what I didn't do compared to what I did last year. And I didn't get recognized for the transition to this league." Lofton had to learn the moves of new pitchers. In the field, he had to adjust to the tendencies of new hitters. "I couldn't let my guard down, because I had so much to learn, and mentally it started to have an effect," he said.

Lofton grew up in poverty in a rundown neighborhood in East Chicago, Indiana. His mother was 14 when he was born, and although he never knew his father, he kept his father's name. He was raised by his grandmother, Rosie Person. At birth, he weighed only three pounds. His mother, Annie, was afraid to hold him. "She was afraid she would drop him," Person told Michael Silver of *Sports Illustrated*. "So I made a little pillow and we carried him around on that." His grandmother "taught me right and wrong, to respect your elders, keep a level head and don't stray from what you are," Lofton told George Castle of *Sport*. He explained to Silver: "The saddest part about growing up was seeing certain kids with certain things you didn't have and wondering, why can't I have that? If you had a toy, you protected it because if you let someone tear it up, you didn't get another one.... I learned to protect what's mine, and that might be something people don't like about me."

At Washington High School, Lofton played basketball, football and baseball. A 5-foot-10 point guard, Lofton accepted a basketball scholarship to the University of Arizona. In his junior year, the team reached "the Final Four" in the NCAA (National Collegiate Athletic Association) basketball tournament. As a senior, Lofton set a school record for steals. However, he gave up on playing professional basketball. "I wasn't given an opportunity to play my style of basketball," he told Castle. "I felt I should do something else because I wasn't getting the recognition in basketball I should have."

The Houston Astros selected Lofton in the 1988 draft, but not until the 17th round. He played four seasons in the minors, hitting over .300 and stealing 168 bases. But the Astros were unhappy when Lofton twice refused to play in the Florida Instructional league in the fall, choosing instead to return to college to complete his degree in television and radio. When he made the majors in September 1991, he hit only .203 in 20 games. The Astros traded him to Cleveland for Willie Blair and Ed Taubensee. Castle of *Sport* noted that Cleveland had "pulled off the trade of the 90s." For the Astros, it would turn out to be one of the worst trades in baseball.

In 1992, Lofton set an American League record for most stolen bases by a rookie, swiping a league-leading 66. It was a remarkable achievement for a player who had played only five baseball games in college. "I remember how raw he was and I've never seen anybody develop into that type of player that fast," said Milwaukee manager Phil Garner, who saw Lofton play in the

minors. Indians coaches taught him how to hit to the opposite field, read pitchers' moves, and get a jump on fly balls. "He's very coachable, and he was very sincere about improving himself," Cleveland general manager John Hart told Silver of *Sports Illustrated*. After his rookie year, Lofton signed a four-year, $6.3 million contract with the Indians.

> "I'll do anything to get on base," Lofton told Jon Scher of Sports Illustrated for Kids. "And once I get on, a lot of things can happen."

Lofton led the league in steals the next two years and racked 325 in his five years with the Indians. In 1994, he led the league in hits, with 160, batted .349 and reached base in 103 of the Indians' 112 games. He finished fourth in the voting for American League Most Valuable Player. He hit .285 his rookie year, then batted between .310 and .349 the next five seasons. Starting in 1993, he won four consecutive Gold Glove awards for his outstanding fielding. In 1995, he started for the American League in the All-Star game. Later that year, in the American League Championship Series, Lofton stole five bases. In the sixth game, he bunted for a single, stole second, and scored from there on a passed ball.

A left-handed batter and thrower, Lofton is considered a serious student of the game and a quick learner. He keeps a book on pitchers' moves. "Some pitchers are harder than others," he told Castle. "I wrote that in a little book I have. Others who are not as tough, I put that in my mind."

Lofton is adept at working walks, bunting, beating out ground balls, and lining hits to the outfield. "I'll do anything to get on base," Lofton told Jon Scher of *Sports Illustrated for Kids*. "And once I get on, a lot of things can happen." But playing center field is Lofton's favorite part of baseball. "On defense, I can control some people's minds by catching the ball," Lofton told Castle. "The opposing team gets frustrated.... It also helps the pitcher out. You make a catch, he'll feel more confident throwing that pitch."

After the 1997 season, Lofton became a free agent. In early December, Lofton signed a three-year deal worth $24 million with his former team, the Cleveland Indians. Commenting to The *Sporting News*, Lofton said "I'm glad to be back where I belong. Everyone knows I belong here. Hopefully I'll be here for the rest of my career."

Sources

On-line

Cleveland Indians, http://www.indians.com (December 11, 1997).

The Sporting News, December 8, 1997, http://www.sportingnews.com/baseball/teams/indians (December 11, 1997).

Periodicals

Sport, August 1995, p. 12.
Sports Illustrated, May 1, 1995, p. 96; October 13, 1997, p. 50.
Sports Illustrated for Kids, June 1996, p. 36.

—*Michael Betzold*

Jennifer Lopez

Actress

Born July 24, 1970, in the Bronx, New York, NY; daughter of David (a computer specialist) and Guadalupe (a teacher) Lopez; married Ojani Noa, February, 1997 (divorced, 1998).

Addresses: *Agent*—United Talent Agency, 9650 Wilshire Blvd., Suite 500, Beverly Hills, CA 90212.

Career

Actress on television and in films. Television series appearances include series *In Living Color*, 1990; *Second Chances*, 1993; and *Hotel Malibu*, 1994. Television movie appearances include *Nurses on the Line: The Crash of Flight 7*, 1993. Film appearances include *My Little Girl*, 1986; *Mi Familia (My Family)*, 1995; *Money Train*, 1995; *Jack*, 1996; *Blood & Wine*, 1996; *Selena*, 1997; *Anaconda*, 1997; *U Turn*, 1997; and *Out of Sight*, 1998.

Awards: Imagen Foundation Awards, Lasting Image Award, and Lone Star Film & Television Award, both 1998, for *Selena*.

Sidelights

Latina actress Jennifer Lopez's wide range and her motivation to succeed has led to her breakthrough as a leading lady on the big screen. She started her Hollywood career in 1990 as one of the attractive and high-energy "fly girl" dancers on *In Living Color*, then worked her way into acting in some television pilots. Her film debut was in the multigenerational *Mi Familia (My Family)*, with Jimmy Smits, and she went on to work with other giant names including Jack Nicholson and Robin Williams. After a stunning starring role in 1997 in *Selena* as the murdered Tejano singer, Lopez broke through the barrier of being typecast in ethnic roles when she starred in 1998 with George Clooney as a headstrong U.S. marshal in *Out of Sight*. Unabashedly ambitious, Lopez has worked hard and takes credit for her rise. She says that success in Hollywood, rather than being a case of luck, is "about being prepared when your opportunity comes, about being able to perform under pressure," she told Rene Rodriguez for Knight Ridder Newspapers, printed in the *Arizona Republic*. "If you're going in to audition for Oliver Stone or Francis Ford Coppola, are you gonna choke?... If you have a good day that day, then it's not luck. It's because you made it happen."

Lopez was born on July 24, 1970, in the Bronx, New York, the second of three daughters, including her younger sister, Lynda, and older sister, Leslie. Lopez's father, David, is a computer specialist for an insurance firm and her mother, Guadalupe ("Lupe") is a kindergarten teacher at Holy Family School in the Bronx. They are both Puerto Rican. Even as a child, Lopez wanted to be a star, despite the near-absence of Latina role models in Hollywood. David Handelman remarked in *Mirabella*, "She watched *West*

Side Story over and over, dreaming of being the next Rita Moreno." As a teenager, Lopez dressed in a tomboy fashion until seeing Madonna and her ever-changing appearance. "I always admired her, liked her music, her sense of style," Lopez commented to Handelman.

Lopez graduated from Holy Family School, where her mother teaches, and went on to Baruch College in New York City. She dropped out after one semester to pursue her dancing career. While studying jazz and ballet, Lopez aspired to appear on Broadway, and in fact appeared overseas in two productions: *Golden Musicals of Broadway,* which toured Europe, and *Synchronicity,* which toured in Japan. She tried auditioning for commercials, but her heart was not in it. When hip-hop became popular, she found a niche. Lopez competed with over two thousand other hopefuls to win a spot in 1990 as one of the energetic "fly girl" dancers on the Fox comedy *In Living Color.* After staying with that for a while, the husband of one of her fellow dancers cast Lopez in a pilot that he wrote and produced called *South Central.* Though the show never made it, Lopez was getting noticed and won parts in other series pilots as well as a made-for-television movie in 1993 called *Nurses on the Line: The Crash of Flight 7.*

The big-screen breakthrough for Lopez came in 1995 with a supporting part in the film *Mi Familia (My Family),* an epic story covering a number of generations of a Latino family. It also starred Jimmy Smits. Following that, Lopez landed roles in *Money Train* (1995); *Jack* (1996), starring Robin Williams; and the film noir thriller *Blood & Wine* (1997), starring Jack Nicholson. Also in 1997 Lopez made *Anaconda* and Oliver Stone's *U-Turn.* She blossomed, though, with her acclaimed starring performance in the 1997 film *Selena,* about the life of the Tejano singer who was shot to death in 1995. For her portrayal, Lopez reportedly became the first Latina actress to earn $1 million.

Selena was revered throughout the Latino world, and for the picture, Lopez lived with Selena's family for a while to replicate the singer as closely as possible. She lip-synched to Selena's music and wore the reproductions of the singer's colorful original costumes, made from the same patterns and by Selena's own seamstress. Lopez even painted her nails with Selena's favorite color polish, L'Oreal Sangria, thanks to advice from the singer's sister Suzette, and got tips from the family on how to hold the microphone the same way as Selena did. Some Latinos protested Lopez playing the part, since Lopez is from Puerto Rican descent and not Mexican. However, the film and Lopez's portrayal were well-received; Lopez won the Imagen Foundation Lasting Image Award and the Lone Star Film & Television Award for the role, and was nominated for a Golden Globe and MTC Movie Award.

After the filming of *Selena,* Lopez's boyfriend, Ojani Noa, proposed to her at a big party and she accepted. They had met while he was waiting tables in Miami and were married about a year later, in February of 1997, but divorced sometime in 1998. Lopez did not comment on the separation, and Noa has been relatively quiet except to say that Lopez paid for their divorce and gave him some money, and that they are still friends. After their breakup, the press has speculated widely regarding her romantic affairs, linking her with musician and music company executive Sean "Puff Daddy" Combs, Sony music chief Tommy Mottola, and R&B singer Maxwell. She has denied all of the rumors, insisting that she is just friends with all of them.

Also in 1998, Lopez made a splash costarring with George Clooney in the crime story *Out of Sight.* As U.S. marshal Karen Sisco, Lopez is kidnapped by Clooney's character, Jack Foley, a bank robber, just as he is breaking out of prison. Not a violent sort, and in fact rather gentlemanly, Foley only abducts Sisco when she unwittingly messes up the breakout plan. The unlikely pair—cop and crook—develop a romantic attraction to each other, although they know it is doomed. Philip Wuntch of the *Dallas Morning News* noted that "the film retains the wit and tempo of Elmore Leonard's novel.... *Out of Sight* manages to be both wry in tone and energetic in its telling." He added, "Ms. Lopez is terrific."

Despite—or perhaps because of—Lopez's newfound popularity, she went through a backlash after making some comments about fellow actresses in the magazine *Movieline.* Handelman in Mirabella mentioned that she made catty remarks about Gwyneth Paltrow, Winona Ryder, and Cameron Diaz, but Lopez later told Rodriguez that she was misunderstood. She sent apologies to her colleagues, but did not manage to shake her reputation as being "arrogant and temperamental," as Rodriguez put it. Lopez insisted to Handelman, "You know, I am ambitious and I am confident, but who isn't in this business?" She added, "And that [*Movieline*] article depicted me in a diva sort of way, like I'm not a nice person, and that was disturbing to me."

Whether or not she is nice, she is definitely in demand. Oliver Stone told Jeffrey Ressner in *Time,* "She's striking, strong, and has an extremely enthusiastic attitude." Lopez in the summer of 1998 worked on recording an album of pop and R&B songs for Sony and was set to star in a couple more films for 1999. Lopez told Rodriguez that being Latina is still an issue in casting for some directors, and that it is a constant battle to tend with. *Out of Sight* director Steven Soderbergh, however, claimed that he, for one, did not take into account Lopez's background. "I just thought she was the best actress for that part. Jennifer is ebullient, very positive and effervescent," Soderbergh told Rodriguez, adding, "She's really unique, because she can do just about anything, and it's not often you find someone with that kind of range."

Sources

On-line

"Jennifer Lopez," CelebSite web site, http:// www.celebsite.com (July 12, 1998).

"Jennifer Lopez," Internet Movie Database, http:// www.imdb.com (July 7, 1998).

"Jennifer Lopez, Divorcee," June 12, 1998, Mr. Showbiz web site, http://www.mrshowbiz.com (July 12, 1998).

Periodicals

Arizona Republic, June 26, 1998, p. D2.
Dallas Morning News, June 26, 1998, p. 1C.
In Style, May 1, 1997, p. 196.
Mirabella, July/August 1998, p. 82.
Newsday, March 20, 1997, p. A4.
People, March 24, 1997, p. 160.
Time, March 24, 1998, p. 43.
USA Weekend, June 21, 1998, p. 18.
Vanity Fair, July 1998, p. 114.

—Geri Speace

Trent Lott

AP/Wide World Photos

United States Senator

Full name, Chester Trent Lott; born October 9, 1941, in Grenada County, MS; son of Chester (a shipworker) and Iona (a school teacher; maiden name, Waston) Lott; married Patricia Thompson, December 27, 1964; children: Chester, Tyler (daughter). *Education:* University of Mississippi, B.S. (Public Administration), 1963, J.D., 1967. *Politics:* Republican. *Religion:* Baptist.

Addresses: *Office*—487 Russell Senate Office Building, U.S. Senate, Washington, DC 20510. *District Office*—1 Government Plaza, #428 Gulfport, MS 39501.

Career

Attorney and politician. Bryan and Gordon (law firm), attorney, 1967; congressional aide for William M. Colmer, 1968-72; U.S. House of Representatives, congress member for State of Mississippi, 1973-88, member of House Rules Committee, 1975-88; U.S. Senate, senator for State of Mississippi, 1989—, Senate Majority Leader, 1996—.

Awards: Vincent T. Hirsch Maritime Award, 1997.

Member: Sigma Nu Social Fraternity, Phi Alpha Delta Legal Fraternity, Masons.

Sidelights

A U.S. Senator from Mississippi, Trent Lott is a major political figure in the nation's capitol. He first came to Washington as a Democratic congressional aide in the early 1960s. Known for his conser-

vative views, however, Lott served as a Republican in both the House of Representatives and the U.S. Senate. Lott was recognized for his leadership skills in Congress and was able to organize support for important issues among both Republicans and Democrats. Paul Weyrich, a radio news commentator, once described Lott "as a wily Southerner. He likes to make deals, but sometimes, when he feels a great principle is at stake, he can be tough as nails." A skillful politician, the U.S. Senator from Mississippi was elected by fellow senators as Senate Majority Leader on December 3, 1996.

Born on October 9, 1941, in Grenada County, Mississippi, Chester Trent Lott, moved with his family to the costal town of Pascagoula. As an only child, Trent received the full attention and love of his parents. His father, Chester, worked as a shipyard worker who later also tried his hand in the furniture business. In a *U.S. News & World Report* interview with Gloria Borger, Lott described his father as "handsome and outgoing, and I always thought he might actually run for office someday."

Lott's mother, Iona, was a schoolteacher and bookkeeper. Iona Lott recalled to *Time* contributor Dan Goodgame, "People used to say an only child would be spoiled and selfish. And I was determined he wouldn't be that way." She insisted that he share everything, even the pony she and Lott's father gave him before he was ten. Lott was exposed to politics at any early age, as one grandfather was a justice of the peace, the other grandfather a county supervisor, and an uncle who was a tax assessor and a state senator.

> *"Let's see where we can find some commonality, where we can begin to come up with agreements that will help the quality of life for all Americans."*

The family moved to Pascagoula when Lott was in the seventh grade. He adapted to the new location quickly and wasn't afraid to participate in a wide range of school activities. During his school years, he played tuba in the band and was a member of the drama club. He also worked part-time at a local rootbeer stand. Among his classmates, Lott was popular and well-respected. In high school, he was elected president of the drama club, president of the student body, homecoming king, most popular, most likely to succeed, and most polite. Goodgame quoted a high school friend who recalled that Lott found time for everyone "from shy girls to the guys we would describe these days as gang members."

With money earned from summer jobs and support from his parents, Lott entered the University of Mississippi (Ole Miss) in the fall of 1959. While at Ole Miss, Lott had his first real experience at politics. His first year, he pledged the Sigma Nu social fraternity. While he participated in Sigma Nu activities, Lott also made many friends among members of other fraternities and independent student groups. Eventually, he was elected as president of both Sigma Nu and the university's interfraternity council. Cheerleaders at Ole Miss were also elected positions, and running for cheerleader provided Lott another opportunity to gain political skills in forming political blocks, cutting deals and doing door-to-door precinct work.

No African American students attended the University of Mississippi when Lott first entered the school. During Lott's senior year, on September 30, 1962, Air Force veteran James Meredith, protected by armed U.S. marshals, enrolled at Ole Miss. The small group was confronted by rock-throwing students and non-student protestors in violent demonstrations. By the time the violence ended, two people had been killed and many others injured and arrested. Lott worked to keep Sigma Nu fraternity members from taking part. At the same time, he used his campus influence to call for peaceful campus integration. In *National Review*, Rich Lowry quoted Lott as saying, "Yes, you could say that I favored segregation then. The main thing was, I felt the Federal Government had no business sending in troops to tell the state what to do."

Graduating with a bachelor's degree in Public Administration in the spring of 1963, Lott enrolled in the Ole Miss law school. He subsidized his graduate education with a federal student loan and also obtained a job with the university's recruitment office. Later, he was able to work for the alumni association as a fund raiser, a position that enabled him to make valuable political connections throughout his native state.

While he attended law school, the Vietnam War was expanding in scope and troop commitments. Like other college students Lott received a student deferment from the draft. By the time he graduated from law school in 1967 Lott had married Patricia (Tricia) Thompson of Pascagoula, and under Selective Service rules, obtained a hardship exemption due to the birth of their first child, also named Chester.

After graduating from the Ole Miss law school, Lott and his family returned to Pascagoula. For a brief period Lott worked in a private law firm, leaving after less than a year when he was offered a top staff job by Congressman William M. Colmer, a Mississippi Democrat. The Lott family moved to Washington, D.C., in 1968. Tricia Lott explained to Lowry that the family went to Washington "to stay a couple of years and see if we liked it." Political skills learned at Ole Miss in organizing and influencing people earned Lott a reputation as an effective and able congressional aide.

When Congressman Colmer announced his retirement from the House in 1972, Lott announced his candidacy as a Republican to seek the vacant office. Lott was able to win Colmer's endorsement and support. According to Lowry, Lott explained his party switch by vowing to "fight against the ever increasing efforts of the so-called liberals to concentrate more power in the government in Washington." Lott had a well-organized and tireless campaign. With the aid of the landslide re-election of President Richard Nixon he was able to win the House seat with a vote margin of 55 percent.

Arriving in Washington as a freshman Representative, Lott was appointed to membership on the House Judiciary Committee. As the youngest member of this committee Lott became involved in the 1974 hearings to impeach President Nixon. The president had been implicated in the break-in of the Democratic National Committee headquarters at an office complex called Watergate. After the President released tape recordings and transcripts indicating his involvement and a cover-up of the crime, Lott reversed his position as a staunch supporter and joined others in the call for the President's resignation, which occurred less than a week later.

Although Lott had vowed to fight against increased government controls from his seat in the House, he actually supported more federal spending for entitlement programs, farm subsidies, public works projects, and the military. During his 16-year tenure in the U.S. House of Representatives, Lott was never credited with authoring any major legislation. However, he won praise for his work on tax and budget reform. He was an active member of the House, and served on the powerful House Rules Committee from 1975 to 1989. With the support of his fellow Representatives, Lott was elected and served as Minority Whip from 1981-89. As Minority Whip, he was the second ranking Republican in the House of Representatives. He was also named chair of the Republican National Convention's platform committees in 1980 and 1989. Lott, however, did not always support the legislative agenda of his political party. When President Reagan proposed a tax reform bill in 1985, Lott used his political power as Minority Whip to oppose the measure. Two years later, Lott joined with Democrats to override a presidential veto of a highway spending bill which included several highway projects in his home district.

When the Mississippi Democratic Senator, John Stennis, retired in 1988, Lott announced that he would seek the vacant Senate seat. He won the Senate position with a 54 percent majority. As a Senator, Lott continued to focus his political talents on building coalitions and was appointed as a member of the Ethics Committee. He was later appointed as a member of the powerful Senate Budget Committee. Continuing his climb through the ranks of the Senate, Lott was elected as the secretary of the Senate Republican Conference in 1992. In 1994 he won the election for Senate Majority Whip by a one vote margin, making him the first person to be elected Whip in both houses of Congress.

Lott's experiences as House Minority Whip helped him to establish a highly-organized whip system in the Senate. Individual members of Congress were drafted to organize and track colleagues on a regional basis. These regional whips provided daily briefing to Lott on crucial votes. One of the regional whips was also tasked to be on the Senate floor at all times. Lott's ability to work with both parties helped to end what was described in the popular press as budget gridlock. During 1997 budget negotiations, Richard Stevenson, writing in the *New York Times*, described him as "Trent Lott the bad cop" and as "Trent Lott the good cop." Stevenson reported that Lott's message to both parties was, "I'm going to urge that we not waste time talking about what we disagree on. Let's see where we can find some commonality, where we can begin to come up with agreements that will help the quality of life for all Americans." When the Senate Majority Leader, Bob Dole, announced his plans to retire from the Senate in order to run for President, Lott used his well-controlled whip organization to campaign for the vacant Majority Leader position. His organizational and political skills were rewarded, and he was elected Senate Majority Leader on June 13, 1996.

Campaign financing became the focus of national attention after the re-election of President Clinton in 1996. With reports of improper fund-raising activities by the Democrats, many Republicans called for in-depth investigations of campaign practices. While some called for major campaign reforms, Lott had other views. In an interview with *New York Times* contributor Katharine Seelye, Lott described his position on this issue, commenting that "I support people being involved in the political process.... I think for them to have the opportunity to do that is the American way."

The Senator's stance on other major issues facing the nation were widely known. He articulated his views on numerous radio and television interview shows. He also took advantage of the electronic media and maintained an internet home page stating his position on key political and national issues. In regards to a balanced national budget, Lott declared, "I understand the concerns regarding the Balanced Budget Amendment and want to assure you that I do not take amending our Constitution lightly. However, having watched many futile attempts to reduce the deficit through legislation, I am convinced that an amendment to our Constitution is necessary." Lott also described his position concerning prayer in public schools on this site: "I have consistently advocated strong legislative action in support of the rights of students who wish to participate in voluntary prayer in their schools."

Lott's personal beliefs reflect those of his constituency, and his election to both houses of Congress show his successful representation of the people in his home district and home state. In Congress, his ability to mobilize his fellow Representatives and Senators in support of key legislation was recognized with prominent positions in both houses—as Minority Whip in the House of Representatives, and in the Senate as Majority Whip and later Senate Majority Leader. Lott has the distinction of being the first Southerner to be House Minority Whip and the first person to be elected Whip in both houses of Congress.

Sources

On-line

Issue Positions, http://www.senate.gov (November 10, 1997).

Periodicals

National Review, June 30, 1997, pp. 20-23.
New York Times, February 8, 1997; February 21, 1997.
Time, March 10, 1997, pp. 38-39.
U.S. News & World Report, February 24, 1997.

Other

Direct Line with Paul Weyrich (live broadcast on radio station KIUSA), December 3, 1996.

—*Homer Emery*

Patty Loveless

Photograph by Ken Settle

Country singer

Born Patty Ramey, January 4, 1957, in Pikeville, KY; daughter of John (a coal miner) and Naomi Ramey; married Terry Lovelace (a drummer), 1976 (divorced, c. 1987); married Emory Gordy, Jr. (a record producer), February, 1989.

Addresses: *Record company*—Epic, P.O. Box 4450, New York, NY 10101-4450.

Career

Country singer and songwriter, c. 1970—. Singer with brother Roger Ramey's country music band, c. 1970-72; secured a song-publishing contract, c. 1972; worked as the "girl singer" in the Wilburn Brothers road show, c. 1972-76; worked as a singer in night clubs in and near Charlotte, NC, c. 1976-85; moved to Nashville, TN, recorded demo tape with help of Roger Ramey, c. 1985; recording artist with MCA, 1985-92; recording artist with Sony Music, 1992—.

Awards: Inducted into the Grand Ole Opry, 1988; American Music Award, favorite new country artist, 1989; TNN Music City News Country Award, female artist, 1990; Country Music Association Awards, album of the year, 1995, for *When Fallen Angels Fly*, and female vocalist of the year, 1996; Academy of Country Music Awards, both female vocalist of the year, 1996 and 1997.

Sidelights

Dubbed "The Heartbreak Kid" in the headline for an April 1997 article by *TV Guide* contributor Dan DeLuca, country singer Patty Loveless has certainly earned her title. Her ability to belt out the sentimental lyrics of her songs in a way that stirs and inspires her listeners is rooted in the fact that, because of her life experiences, she has become all too familiar with tragedy and misery.

Nevertheless, her hard-luck past has served as her key to a spectacular present and a promising future, as Loveless's songs continue to top the charts, her albums continue to win, and her personal life continues to become richer and fuller. Loveless, named the Academy of Country Music's female vocalist of the year for both 1996 and 1997, told DeLuca: "I think torch songs and heartache songs reach out to people and say, 'Hey, this is life and we've got to live, learn from our mistakes, and continue.' That's what I try to put into the songs. That's what I make music for."

Loveless was born on January 4, 1957, in the Appalachian miningtown of Pikeville, Kentucky. Her father, John Ramey, was a coal miner who ultimately died in 1979 of the black lung disease that plagues many in his occupation, and her mother, Naomi Ramey, was a homemaker who struggled to care for Loveless and her siblings. Loveless began singing at the age of five, primarily to entertain her parents, but by the age of 12 she was singing in her brother Roger's band. Roger introduced his sister to country music stars Dolly Parton and Porter Wagoner in 1971, and Wagoner agreed to give the 14-year-old Loveless a song publishing contract; shortly thereafter the young singer began working with the Wilburn Brothers road show, replacing famous country singer Loretta Lynn, who is Loveless's distant cousin.

It was while working with the road show that Loveless met Wilburn Brothers drummer Terry Lovelace (pronounced "Love-less"). In 1976, despite the disapproval of her family and friends, she married Lovelace and moved to Kings Mountain, North Carolina. In an article by *People* contributor Steve Dougherty, Loveless said that her marriage at the age of 19 was, in part, a rebellion. "So many people had been making decisions for me for so long," she asserted, "I just wanted to feel a sense of freedom."

Unfortunately for the singer, her marriage to Lovelace did not turn out as she had planned. Instead, she began abusing drugs and alcohol and singing cover versions of popular rock songs in Charlotte-area night clubs, in order to support the couple's expensive addictions and to make ends meet. Loveless ultimately overcame her substance abuse, and in 1985, she and Lovelace separated. After changing the spelling of her married name to Loveless, she returned to Nashville to try to rekindle her career as a country singer.

With the help of her brother, Roger, Loveless recorded a demo tape and worked to sell it to record labels; while in the elevator on her way to audition for executives at MCA Records, she met Emory Gordy, Jr.—at the time an MCA producer—who would later become her husband.

In 1985 Loveless signed with MCA and soon began to receive positive reviews from music critics and industry insiders who predicted that she would one day be a country music superstar. She and Terry Lovelace were divorced in 1987, and in 1988 Loveless was honored as an inductee of the Grand Ole Opry.

Loveless's first number one single came in 1989, with "Timber I'm Falling in Love"; that same year she and Gordy were married and she took home an American Music Award for favorite new country artist. Loveless continued to gain notoriety and became increasingly popular among country music fans; in 1990 she was awarded the Tennessee News Network (TNN) Music City News Country Award. The singer's career was most definitely moving her toward stardom.

Between 1990 and 1993 Loveless's luck changed, and she suffered a series of professional and private set-

backs. In 1992, in an attempt to revitalize her career, which was in a slump following the sluggish sales of two of her records, Loveless left MCA Records and fired her brother, Roger Ramey, as her manager, a move which caused a rift in their previously close relationship. Before she was able to begin the work of recording fresh material—with her new label, Epic, and her new producer, Emory Gordy—and getting her career back on track, Loveless encountered another personal obstacle.

In the fall of 1992 she began experiencing hoarseness, and soon learned that she had developed an aneurysm on her vocal cords. The situation was grave; in order to repair the aneurysm, which left untreated could have destroyed her voice, Loveless had to undergo risky laser surgery, which also had the potential to damage her voice permanently. The surgery was performed on October 21, 1992.

After remaining completely silent during November 1992 and recuperating throughout December 1992, Loveless decided to try out her newly-repaired vocal cords and began recording her sixth album in January 1993. The album was an immediate success when it was released in the spring of 1993, and as *People*'s Steve Dougherty noted, "it was clear that Loveless' luck had turned."

Unfortunately, despite the promise with which 1993 had begun, Loveless was to suffer yet another personal challenge. In June 1993 a tabloid article with the headline "Patty Loveless Killed Our Baby!" was published. The story, which quoted as its source Loveless's ex-husband Terry Lovelace, revealed that the singer had had an abortion in 1980. Previously no one had known about the terminated pregnancy, and the singer was devastated to have her private misery made public in such a merciless and tasteless manner.

In the *People* article by Dougherty Loveless discussed the reasons behind her decision to end her pregnancy, indicating that she was frightened that her excessive drug and alcohol consumption during the pregnancy would have produced birth defects or other health traumas for the fetus, and declared that "[t]he abortion was a decision Terry and I both made. We swore we would never tell because of the pain it would cause our families."

Asserting her belief that her ex-husband was attempting to jeopardize her career out of bitterness, Loveless told Dougherty, "I wish [Lovelace] could just get on. I hope that people will understand and that I'll be forgiven." Lovelace has maintained that he was duped into revealing the secret to the press and never intended to subject Loveless to such public embarrassment.

Loveless managed to overcome her personal crises—even reconciling with her brother Roger—and used her familiarity with tragedy to her advantage, producing emotionally powerful songs that touched the hearts of fans and music experts alike. Matraca Berg, a songwriter who penned Loveless's 1990 hit single "That Kind of Girl" and 1996's "You Can Feel Bad," maintained in an article by *TV Guide*'s Dan DeLuca that Loveless has "a lot of class and she's no puppy. She's lived, and she sings like she believes every word of it. And that's a rare gift."

The music industry has continued to bestow upon Loveless some of its highest honors, including making her the first woman ever to win a Country Music Association (CMA) Award for best album, which she won in 1995 for her album, *When Fallen Angels Fly*. In 1996 Loveless was named female vocalist of the year by both the CMA and the Academy of Country Music (ACM), and in 1997, she repeated as the ACM's female vocalist and was nominated for the CMA's award as well.

Loveless's vocal ability, which DeLuca called "a gutbucket emotionalism that places her squarely in the sisterhood of soul," has been applauded by critics since the release of her debut album, *Patty Loveless*, in 1985. The praise continued for her 1988 effort, *If My Heart Had Windows*, and for *Honky Tonk Angel*, released that same year and containing the number-one single "Timber I'm Falling in Love." Although critics lauded her 1990 album *On down the Line*—*People*'s Ralph Novak declared that it represented "just plain quality country singing"—as well as 1991's *Up Against My Heart*, neither of the albums managed to reach the level of commercial success Loveless had attained with her previous albums.

However, with the 1993 release of *Only What I Feel*, Loveless again joined the ranks of the critically acclaimed and popularly successful country music stars. Recorded after her encounter with laser surgery, the album was hailed by critics as irrefutable evidence that Loveless's voice had come through her ordeal intact. *Billboard*'s Peter Cronin declared that on the album Loveless was "singing with more range, more control, more conviction than ever before, effectively combining powerful delivery with fragile emotion." *Entertainment Weekly* contributor Alanna Nash noted the "restored power and character shadings of Loveless'

authentically rural voice," and *People*'s Hal Espen characterized Loveless's vocals as "equal parts Linda Ronstadt and Pasty Cline," referring to her ability to combine elements of traditional country and rock music.

The album quickly produced a number-one hit with "Blame It on Your Heart," an up-tempo tune in which Loveless tells her philandering lover that he is responsible for the breakup of their relationship, urging him to "blame it on your lyin', cheatin', cold-dead beatin', two-timin', double-dealin', mean-mistreatin', lovin' heart."

Only What I Feel also contained the single "How Do I Help You Say Goodbye," a poignant, moving ballad in which Loveless portrays a mother who is attempting to help her child cope first with the loss of a childhood friend, then with the ordeal of a divorce, and finally with the death of the mother herself. That single helped bring *Only What I Feel* out of the sales slump it had entered following the early success of "Blame It on Your Heart," and quickly became a favorite of fans, who expressed to Loveless the many ways in which the song had touched their hearts.

> "I think torch songs and heartache songs reach out to people and say, 'Hey, this is life and we've got to live, learn from our mistakes, and continue.' That's what I try to put into the songs. That's what I make music for."

Loveless told *Entertainment Weekly*'s Alanna Nash: "I hope it makes people think.... And to look at death as a long goodbye, and not necessarily something final." The song, backed by the strength of the album on which it appeared, earned Loveless three 1994 CMA Award nominations for song of the year, album of the year, and female vocalist of the year.

Loveless followed up the success of *Only What I Feel* with her 1994 album, *When Fallen Angels Fly*, which, she told Morris, she wanted "to be one of those that when people listen to it, it gives them some release and hope and encourages them not to give up."

The album garnered both critical and popular success, and the single "You Don't Even Know Who I Am" earned Loveless 1996 Grammy Award nominations for best female country vocal performance and best country song.

In his review of the album, *Entertainment Weekly*'s Bob Cannon called Loveless's performance "emotionally gripping," and *People*'s Craig Tomashoff offered praise for Loveless's "conversational" tone, contending that "listening to [*When Fallen Angels Fly*] is like chatting with a close friend." Loveless's efforts on *When Fallen Angels Fly* were rewarded in 1995 when she became the first woman artist to win the CMA's Award for album of the year.

The Trouble with the Truth, Loveless's 1996 album that *People* contributor Craig Tomashoff asserted "builds a bridge" between country, rock, and pop music, was also a critical and popular success, earning Loveless a 1997 Grammy Award nomination for best country album. The album contains the singles "You Can Feel Bad," in which a woman tells her ex-lover that she has successfully gone on with her life after their breakup, and "A Thousand Times a Day," which critics praised for its powerful vocals. *People*'s Tomashoff called Loveless's singing "warm and inviting" and *Entertainment Weekly*'s Nash asserted that Loveless "uses her backwoods soprano—as rural and unassuming as a mountain brook—to best effect" on this song. The album's title song proclaims that the truth has "ruined the taste of the sweetest lies, / Burned through my best alibis," and as *Time* critic Richard Corliss contended: "The way Loveless sings it, the truth ain't pretty, but it sounds as golden as the Gospel."

According to critics, Loveless's 1997 effort, *Long Stretch of Lonesome,* lived up to the high expectations that followed the singer's 1996 CMA and ACM Awards for best female vocalist as well as her 1997 ACM Award for best female vocalist and her 1997 nomination for the CMA's best female vocalist honors. Jeremy Helligar, writing in *Entertainment Weekly*, observed that "Loveless' Appalachian blues sound torchy with hardly a hint of twang," and *People*'s Tomashoff lauded the singer's "silky voice," concluding that "Loveless' words may tell you how tough life can be, but her voice lets you know that things will work out anyway."

Interviewed by *TV Guide*'s DeLuca while working on her ninth album, Loveless maintained that she was determined not to let her fame weaken her commit-

ment her singing. Loveless told DeLuca: "I like to keep focused on the work. I'm just looking for songs that stir emotions in me. Because if it moves me, then somebody else is going to be stirred in the same way."

Selected discography

Patty Loveless (includes "After All," "Slow Healing Heart," and "You Are Everything"), MCA, 1985, reissued, 1989.

If My Heart Had Windows (includes "A Little Bit on the Lonely Side," "You Saved Me," and "I Can't Get You off My Mind"), MCA, 1988.

Honky Tonk Angel (includes "Timber I'm Falling in Love" and "The Lonely Side of Love"), MCA, 1988.

On down the Line (includes "You Can't Run Away from Your Heart" and "Looking in the Eyes of Love"), MCA, 1990.

Up Against My Heart (includes "I Already Miss You [Like You're Already Gone]" and "If It's the Last Thing I Do"), MCA, 1991.

Greatest Hits, MCA, 1993.

Only What I Feel (includes "Blame It on Your Heart" and "How Can I Help You Say Goodbye"), Epic, 1993.

When Fallen Angels Fly (includes "You Don't Even Know Who I Am"and "I Try to Think about Elvis"), Epic, 1994.

The Trouble with the Truth (includes "You Can Feel Bad" and "A Thousand Times A Day"), Epic, 1996.

Patty Loveless Sings Songs of Love, MCA, 1996.

(With others) *Tin Cup* (soundtrack), Epic, 1996.

Long Stretch of Lonesome (includes "You Don't Seem to Miss Me," a duet with George Jones, and "I Don't Want to Feel Like That"), Epic, 1997.

Sources

Billboard, April 17, 1993, p. 7; April 16, 1994, p. 38; August 13, 1994, p. 1.

Entertainment Weekly, April 23, 1993, p. 56; August 26, 1994, p. 113; September 22, 1995, p. 77; February 2, 1996, p. 56; October 3, 1997, p. 85.

People, June 25, 1990, p. 23; May 3, 1993, p. 25; August 9, 1993, p. 85; September 5, 1994, p. 28; February 12, 1996, p. 27; November 3, 1997, p. 25.

Time, March 11, 1996, p. 71.

TV Guide, April 19, 1997, p. 42.

—*Lynn M. Spampinato*

Adam Cardinal Maida

AP/Wide World Photos

Archbishop of Detroit

Born Adam Joseph Maida, March 18, 1930, in East Vandergrift, PA; son of Adam and Sophie (Cieslak) Maida. *Education:* St. Vincent's College (Latrobe, PA), B.A., 1952; St. Mary's University (Baltimore, MD), S.T.L., 1956; Pontifical Lateran University, Rome, J.C.L., 1960; Duquesne Law School (Pittsburgh, PA), J.D., 1964. *Religion:* Roman Catholic.

Addresses: *Office*—Archdiocese of Detroit, Cardinal's Office, 1234 Washington Blvd., Detroit, MI 48226.

Career

Ordained a Roman Catholic priest, May 26, 1956; served in the Diocese of Pittsburgh, PA, as associate pastor, vice chancellor, and general counsel, La Roche College, assistant professor of theology, Duquesne University Law School, adjunct professor of law, 1956-84; Diocese of Green Bay, WI, bishop, 1984-90; Archbishop of Detroit, 1990—; elevated to College of Cardinals, November 26, 1994.

Member: Congregation for Catholic Education, Congregation for the Clergy, Pontifical Council for the Pastoral Care of Migrants and Itinerant Peoples, Pontifical Council for the Interpretation of Legal Texts, National Conference of Catholic Bishops (NCCB), Bishops' Welfare Emergency Relief Committee, Committee on Migration, Committee on Pro-Life Activities, Committee for the Polish Apostolate (Episcopal Liaison), Catholic Legal Immigration Network, Incorporated (Board of Directors), Catholic University of America (Board of Trustees), Basilica of the National Shrine of the Immaculate Conception (Washington,

DC; Board of Trustees), Pope John XXIII Medical-Moral Research and Education Center (Braintree, MA; Board of Directors), Michigan Catholic Conference (chair, Board of Trustees), Pope John Paul II Cultural Foundation (Rome), Pope John Paul II Cultural Foundation (Washington, DC; President and Advisory Board).

Sidelights

The diplomatic talents of Adam Cardinal Maida has earned him a reputation in cities across the globe. In 1990 he was named head of the Archdiocese of Detroit, Michigan where he brought his spirit and determination to the economically depressed city. Both a priest and a lawyer, Maida is known by his friends and by the members of his archdiocese for his warmth and human compassion.

Adam Joseph Maida, the son of Sophie Cieslak Maida and the late Adam Maida, was born on March 18, 1930, in East Vandergrift, Pennsylvania. Maida's father had immigrated from the Warsaw area of Poland, while his mother was born in the United States. The Maidas were a religious couple, and two of their sons, Adam (the eldest) and Thaddeus, became priests. Their third son, Daniel, married and had a family.

Maida was ordained into the Roman Catholic priesthood on May 26, 1956. The late Archbishop John Dearden of Detroit, who was a bishop at that time, performed the ceremony at St. Paul Cathedral in Pittsburgh, Pennsylvania. Maida served the Diocese of Pittsburgh for over 17 years, in positions of increasing honor and responsibility. Maida ultimately was appointed Vice Chancellor and General Counsel of the Diocese, and became a member of the Diocesan Tribunal.

Maida speaks three languages (Polish, Italian, and Latin) and is considered a highly-educated man. He graduated from St. Mary's High School in Orchard Lake, Michigan in 1948, and then began his formal studies at St. Mary's College (also in Orchard Lake). Two years later he transferred to St. Vincent's College in Latrobe, Pennsylvania. After receiving a Bachelor of Arts degree in philosophy from St. Vincent's, he went on to earn degrees from a number of prominent universities throughout the United States and in Europe.

In 1956 he graduated from St. Mary's University in Baltimore, Maryland, with a Licentiate in Sacred Theology. His studies then took him to Rome, to Pontifical Lateran University where he earned a Licentiate in Canon Law in 1960. In 1964 he graduated as a Doctor of Civil Law (Juris Doctor) from Duquesne University in Pittsburgh. Maida became a member of the Pennsylvania State Bar and was subsequently admitted to practice before the United States Supreme Court.

As a priest and an attorney in Pittsburgh, Maida retained close ties with the academic community. He joined the faculties at La Roche College (as Assistant Professor of Theology), and at Duquesne University Law School (as Adjunct Professor of Law). As a civil lawyer Maida also used his talents to assist the clergy and other religious of the Pittsburgh diocese with legal matters, and to resolve property disputes among Church factions.

In 1970 he edited a case book about marriage annulments in the Catholic Church, and in 1982 he edited a book on the church's perspective on labor relations. Maida wrote his first book, *Ownership, Control, and Sponsorship of Catholic Institutions: a Practical Guide*, in 1975, and in 1984 he collaborated with Nicholas P. Cafardi to publish a handbook on canon law, *Church Property, Church Finances, and Church-related Corporations*.

From 1984 to 1990, Maida lived in Green Bay, Wisconsin. He was installed as the ninth bishop of that diocese on January 25, 1984. In Green Bay, Maida earned a reputation as a resourceful and progressive leader. He addressed the dearth of Catholic priests in the diocese by assigning nuns to administer to parishes. His diocesan chancellor, too, was a nun. Maida's popularity was enhanced when he successfully balanced the diocesan budget through the implementation of drastic cutbacks in spending. Over the years at Green Bay he also managed to pose for photographs with some 80,000 parochial school students, just one of many gestures that endeared him to the diocese.

In May of 1990 Bishop Maida was named Archbishop of Detroit, Michigan by Pope John Paul II. Detroit at the time presented a stark contrast to the quiet, homogeneously populated Green Bay, Wisconsin. Detroit was a city in decay. It had a history of poor race relations and social unrest. Much of the metropolitan area was in virtual ruins, following years of declining economy and dwindling population.

Upon his arrival in Detroit, Maida toured the diocese. He turned his focused on the grim educational facilities in the urban area. Dozens of parish schools had been closed during the years prior to his arrival, and city officials had done little to help offset the loss. The city administration had faltered in other ways too. Major commercial districts were demolished and abandoned from riots and "white flight" (migration to the suburbs). Vacant skyscrapers cluttered the skyline. Not one Catholic hospital remained in Detroit. Indeed the population of Detroit had declined by 50 percent over a 30-year period. "The people are gone but the buildings remain," one observer was quoted by the National Catholic Reporter.

Maida quickly coordinated a contingency of civic leaders, educators, and representatives from the business sector, in an effort to improve education. He employed prudence, in particular when he approached the Economic Club of Detroit, dispensing with critical rhetoric, appealing instead to their sensibilities, he pleaded for a spirit of self-help and regeneration.

The result of his diplomacy was a project called Cornerstone Schools, an effort to bring quality interdenominational education to the predominantly black (70 percent) population of Detroit. Maida successfully enlisted the necessary support to turn the Cornerstone Schools into a viable endeavor. Local companies donated services and furniture, and funding was arranged for tuition assistance. By August of 1991 Cornerstone Schools were operational at two locations, and plans were underway to expand the program to encompass pre-school through eighth grade plus adult education.

Maida won approval easily because of his sensitivity to issues and his warm and caring personality. "Even those who differ with Maida approved of his style.... Reporters in Detroit said they were impressed with Maida's candor and good humor," wrote Jack Kresnak in the National Catholic Reporter. Kresnak went on to quote Monsignor John Schuh, vice-chancellor of the diocese, "He [Maida] senses hurt—he tries to heal."

Maida quickly involved himself in a full spectrum of humanitarian endeavors within the Detroit Archdiocese. He was praised when he initiated a proposal which would require students in Catholic colleges, and eventually in Catholic high schools, to perform community services in the course of their respective curriculums. Maida's vision, that students perform services in soup kitchens, nursing homes, and other charitable outlets, was well received by the interfaith religious community. Tom Fox of National Catholic Reporter commented, "The idea sounds promising. A creative initiative ... ways to bring rich and poor together for the common good. I hope we hear more from Detroit on this.... Projects that open minds, build bonds, and unleash goodness need to find their way into the light."

On November 26, 1994 Archbishop Maida became a member of the College of Cardinals at a Vatican ceremony. Pope John Paul II officiated the consistory (gathering of cardinals). Thousands of Maida well-wishers, members of Maida's family, including his mother, and residents of his archdiocese attended the celebration.

During the course of the Vatican consistory, Pope John Paul II spoke to Maida with private candor. The Pope, whose first language is Polish, indulged Maida with some personal remarks in the mother tongue of their ancestors. Two years later, in 1996, Cardinal Maida, at the request of Pope John Paul II, attended the International Marian Congress in Czestochowa, Poland. Maida was honored to serve as a Papal Legate (a representative) to the conference, in place of the Pope who was unable to attend.

Cardinal Maida continued his mission to the people of the Archdiocese of Detroit. In 1996 he initiated and organized Project Life, a coordinated alliance between social and economic resources in the Detroit area. Project Life was conceived to reinforce the dignity of human life by eliminating casualties from abortion and assisted suicide. The program was well received. The Project Life hotline fielded hundreds of calls in its first few weeks of operation. Most of the callers sought help, while others offered financial assistance, and some offered moral support. Maida's message, "I stand ready to process whatever resources are necessary ... whatever it takes, to respond personally and directly ... [to anyone considering abortion or assisted suicide].

Maida channeled much effort in asserting the position of the Catholic Church with respect to capitol punishment, welfare reform, and other social and moral issues. In 1996 a controversial political group known as Call to Action planned a convention in the Detroit area. Maida discouraged attendance at the conference which fostered beliefs that were contradictory to canon law and church doctrine.

> *Kresnak went on to quote Monsignor John Schuh, vice-chancellor of the diocese, "[Maida] senses hurt—he tries to heal."*

The controversy escalated, because the supporters and members of Call to Action included certain members of the Catholic clergy who were expected to attend the conference in Detroit. Detroit area Catholics expressed concern about the integrity of the event; others protested publicly against those priests and religious who were known to be members of the group. Maida displayed his characteristic diplomacy when he issued a public statement about the Call to Action conference. According to an article in National Catholic Reporter, Maida noted that Catholics had the right to have differing opinions but warned, "What Catholics do not have the right to do ... is to openly dissent from church teaching." He then added, "I do not think it is helpful when individuals or groups ... criticize ... priests ... accusing them of infidelity ... to our church teaching."

Maida was far less tolerant in November of 1997 when Dr. Jack Kevorkian, an assisted suicide activist, claimed that he had helped a woman end her life inside a Detroit area Catholic church. Cardinal Maida reacted critically, condemning Kevorkian's political agenda and calling the doctor a "death broker." Maida took the controversial issue a step further at the National Conference of Catholic (American) Bishops (NCCB) Conference in November of 1997. He put out a call for Catholics to return to "meatless Fridays" as a penance for "attacks against human life and human dignity." According to the website article, Maida added that people wanted to "show their opposition to the culture of death."

Cardinal Maida's dedication to human welfare extends beyond the Archdiocese of Detroit. According to the *Detroit Free Press,* when Pope John Paul II visited Cuba in January of 1998, Cardinal Maida received special permission from the communist administration to travel there as well. On the last day of the visit, Maida joined with the Pope to celebrate the closing mass.

Maida sits on many councils and committees. As the President of the John Paul II Cultural Foundation he spearheads the enormous task of coordinating the construction of an expansive cultural center in Washington D.C. Originally scheduled to be three years in building, ground-breaking ceremonies for the center were held on September 11, 1997. The cultural center was designed to include an expanse of facilities surrounding a central international research center and forum, including a museum, library, auditorium, and seminar facility. Cardinal Maida described the center as follows, "One of the goals of the Cultural Center is to enable people to come to the exhibit in any state of mind and with any orientation toward Catholicism and leave feeling that they have gained something positive from the experience."

Selected Writings

The Tribunal Reporter—Casebook and Commentary on the Grounds for Annulment in the Catholic Church (editor) Vol. 1, Our Sunday Visitor, 1970.

Ownership, Control and Sponsorship of Catholic Institutions: a Practical Guide, Pennsylvania Catholic Conference, 1975.

Issues in the Labor-Management Dialogue: Church Perspectives (Editor), Catholic Health Association, 1982.

(With Nicholas P. Cafardi), *Church Property, Church Finances and Church-Related Corporations, A Canon Law Handbook,* Catholic Health Association of the United States, 1983.

Sources

On-line

"Biography of Cardinal Adam Maida", *Pope John Paul II Cultural Center,* 1997, http://www. jpiicultural center. com/maida.html (March 3, 1998).

"History and Development", *Pope John Paul II Cultural Center,* 1997, http://www.jpiiculturalcenter .com/history.html (March 3, 1998).

"Meatless Fridays," *The American Catholic Bishops - NCCB,* http://www.trosch.org/for/the/abs-main.htm (March 23, 1998).

"Press Release," *Pope John Paul II Cultural Center,* July 22, 1997, http://www.jpiiculturalcenter.com/ press3.html (March 3, 1998).

Periodicals

Associated Press, November 15, 1997; January 25, 1998.

Detroit Free Press, January 20, 1998.

Detroit News, August 15, 1996.

National Catholic Reporter, May 18, 1990, p. 3; August 16, 1991; December 9, 1994, p. 13; December 16, 1994, p. 2; October 25, 1996, p. 12.

—Gloria Cooksey

Norman Mailer

Writer

Born January 31, 1923, in Long Branch, NJ; son of Isaac Barnett (an accountant) and Fanny (owner of a small business; maiden name, Schneider) Mailer; married Beatrice Silverman, 1944 (divorced, 1952); married Adele Morales (an artist), 1954 (divorced, 1962); married Lady Jeanne Campbell, 1962 (divorced, 1963); married Beverly Rentz Bentley (an actress), 1963 (divorced, 1980); married Carol Stevens, 1980 (divorced, 1980); married Norris Church (an artist), 1980; children: (first marriage) Susan; (second marriage) Danielle, Elizabeth Anne; (third marriage) Kate; (fourth marriage) Michael Burks, Stephen McLeod; (fifth marriage) Maggie Alexandra; (sixth marriage) John Buffalo. *Education:* Harvard University, S.B. (cum laude), 1943; graduate studies at Sorbonne, Paris, France, 1947-48. *Politics:* "Left Conservative."

Addresses: *Office*—c/o Rembar, 19 West 44th St., New York, NY 10036. *Agent*—Scott Meredith, Inc., 580 5th Ave., New York, NY 10022.

Career

Writer. Producer, screenwriter, director of and actor in films, including *Wild 90,* 1967, and *Maidstone: A Mystery,* 1968; producer and screenwriter, *Beyond the Law,* 1967; actor, *Ragtime,* 1981; director and screenwriter, *Tough Guys Don't Dance,* 1987; screenwriter for television movie, *The Executioner's Song,* based on his novel, 1982. Lecturer at colleges and universities, 1950-89; University of Pennsylvania Pappas Fellow, 1983. Candidate for democratic nomination in mayoral race, New York City, 1960 and 1969. Cofounding editor of the *Village Voice;* founder, Fifth Es-

tate (merged with Committee for Action Research on the Intelligence Community), 1973. *Military service:* U.S. Army, 1944-46, field artillery observer; became infantry rifleman, served in the Philippines and Japan.

Awards: *Story* magazine college fiction prize, 1941, for "The Greatest Thing in the World"; National Institute and American Academy grant in literature, 1960; elected to National Institute of Arts and Letters, 1967; National Book Award nomination, 1967, for *Why Are We in Vietnam?;* National Book Award for nonfiction, 1968, for *Miami and the Siege of Chicago;* National Book Award for nonfiction, Pulitzer Prize in letters—general nonfiction, and George Polk Award, 1969, all for *Armies of the Night;* Edward MacDowell Medal, MacDowell Colony, 1973, for outstanding service to arts; National Arts Club Gold Medal, 1976; National Book Critics Circle nomination, Notable Book citation from the American Library Association, and Pulitzer Prize in letters, 1979, all for *The Executioner's Song;* Rose Award, Lord & Taylor, 1985, for public accomplishment; Emerson-Thoreau Medal for lifetime literary achievement from American Academy of Arts and Sciences, 1989.

Member: PEN (president of American Center, 1984-86), American Academy and Institute of Arts and Letters.

Sidelights

One of the United States' most prominent and productive contemporary writers, Norman Mailer has resisted literary classification and has continually generated controversy with his works based on such taboo topics as murder, rape, sexuality, suicide, and mental illness. As "the official Bad Boy of contemporary letters," according to *Dictionary of Literary Biography*'s Andrew Gordon, Mailer has aspired to create "a hero fit for our times: a man powerful enough and egotistical enough to resist the drift of history and help to shape the future." Despite his achievements as a two-time Pulitzer Prize and National Book Award winner, the author has not chosen to rest on his laurels and instead has opted to continue to incite animosity within various segments of society by challenging established norms and deeply sacred spiritual beliefs. In his 1997 novel, *The Gospel According to the Son,* Mailer brazenly created a narrative from the perspective of Jesus Christ that is the author's interpretation of the New Testament that blends the Gospels of Matthew, Mark, Luke, and John. According to an article by *New York Times* contributor Dinitia Smith, in a written statement released through his publisher, Random House, Mailer commented on his 1997 novel: "My intent is to be neither pious nor satirical; it is instead to make comprehensible for myself what Fulton Oursler once called 'The Greatest Story Ever Told.'"

Mailer was born January 31, 1923, in Long Branch, New Jersey, the first child of Isaac Barnett and Fanny Schneider Mailer. The Mailers moved to Brooklyn in 1927, and remained there; Isaac worked there as an accountant until his death in 1972. Mailer displayed both his superior intellect and self-assurance at an early age. Always an honor student, the young Mailer enjoyed playing the clarinet, building model airplanes, reading, and writing. He wrote his first story at the age of seven, but he wasn't a published author until high school, when an article he had written on building model planes was printed. When he was only 16, Mailer enrolled at Harvard University, where he planned to study aeronautical engineering. By the time he was 17, he had discovered his affinity for writing and American literature. In 1940 Mailer won his first literary award, *Story* magazine's college fiction prize, for his short story "The Greatest Thing in the World," which was originally published in the *Harvard Advocate* during his sophomore year.

Mailer graduated with honors from Harvard in 1943 with a bachelor's degree in engineering, and in 1944 he married the first of his six successive wives, Beatrice Silverman. During World War II Mailer served in the U.S. Army as a clerk and a rifleman in the Philippines. In September 1947, fifteen months after completing his military service, Mailer finished *The Naked and the Dead,* a hugely successful novel based on his experiences during the war. Following the novel's completion, Mailer moved to Paris, France, where he used the GI bill he had earned during his time in the army to attend the Sorbonne. When he returned to the United States in the mid-1950s, Mailer co-founded the *Village Voice,* a leftist newspaper, with Daniel Wolf and Edwin Fancher. In 1956 Mailer became a columnist for the newspaper. Due to the popularity of his novels and nonfiction writings, Mailer became an American celebrity, and his activities were of tremendous interest to the public.

The media swarmed around Mailer in 1962, reporting on an incident that involved the author stabbing his second wife with a penknife in a drunken rage that followed one of the frequent all-night parties held at the couple's Manhattan apartment. Following the incident, Mailer was held for fifteen days of psychiatric evaluation at Bellevue Hospital in New York City. He and his wife remained together briefly after the stabbing, but they soon divorced. In 1997 Adele Mailer's book, *The Last Party: Scenes from My Life with Norman Mailer,* was published. In her book she provides a detailed account of their 10-year relationship, including the night she was stabbed. The stabbing of his wife was only one of many incidents which propelled Mailer into the media spotlight during the 1960s. During that decade Mailer was arrested in Provincetown, Massachusetts, for inciting and participating in a fight with police, jailed in New York City after a fight with a bartender over his liquor tab, and arrested in Washington, D.C., after crossing a boundary imposed by the U.S. Federal Marshal during an antiwar demonstration. Mailer's exploits earned him an equal share of critics and supporters; some argued that he was simply a publicity monger and a nuisance, while others maintained that the author was simply collecting research for his books.

Indeed, many of Mailer's works, particularly his novels, have main characters who must battle against social or political forces in order to attain their goals. In "The White Negro," an essay included in his 1959 collection *Advertisements for Myself,* Mailer presents his theory that African Americans established the pattern of social rebellion imitated by white American "hipsters," who Mailer described as violent "philosophical psychopath[s]" who have no regard for society's rules or regulations, and who attain their goal of self-knowledge through their involvement with crime, drugs, and other illicit activities. In *The*

Naked and the Dead Mailer presented the experiences of a fictional fourteen-man platoon attempting to seize a Japanese-held island in the Philippines during World War II, and championed the courage of the characters who were able to endure the prevailing threat of death and destruction. In Mailer's narrative, the most courageous soldiers were those who had been forced to live with adversity in their civilian lives and who had survived because of their simple faith and stamina. In Mailer's 1955 novel *The Deer Park*, the hero is a film director whose career is threatened when he is blacklisted by Hollywood producers after refusing to testify before a Congressional committee, and in 1965's *An American Dream* the protagonist murders his wife in order to destroy his socially responsible image as an author and educator and embrace a more self aware, self-serving identity.

While much attention has been given to his novels, Mailer's innovative nonfiction narratives have garnered him numerous awards and accolades throughout his career. Beginning with his 1968 book *The Armies of the Night: History as a Novel, the Novel as History,* in which he relates an actual event—a 1967 antiwar march on the Pentagon—but exaggerates his own role to a ridiculous extent, Mailer wrote several works that examined historical figures and events from a fictionalized insider's perspective. Mailer earned two National Book Awards for nonfiction, one for *The Armies of the Night* (for which he was also awarded the Pulitzer Prize) and the other for *Miami and the Siege of Chicago,* a narrative which examined the events that took place during 1968 political conventions. Following the acclaim for *The Armies of the Night,* Mailer's career entered a slump; although he continued to produce several books based on such events as the 1969 moon landing, boxing matches, political conventions, and fictionalized biographies of famous people, he was considered repetitive, presenting the same ideas—now seen as tired and irrelevant—as he had in his earlier works.

Mailer also continued his pattern of restlessness and rebellion in his private life, divorcing and marrying again and again: ultimately he would marry six times and father eight children. In 1974, following the Watergate political scandal, Mailer organized a group known as the Fifth Estate, which was comprised of private citizens who were dedicated to investigating the Federal Bureau of Investigation (FBI) and Central Intelligence Agency (CIA) to reveal and weed out corrupt people and practices. In 1979 Mailer once again managed to evoke admiration, shock, and controversy with his written work, producing *The Executioner's Song,* a novel based on the life and death of convicted murderer Gary Gilmore, who in 1977 became the first person to be executed under the death penalty in the United States since the late 1960s. The novel was widely discussed, earned Mailer his second Pulitzer Prize, and was eventually adapted by Mailer into an Emmy-nominated television movie in 1982. In 1991 Mailer's novel *Harlot's Ghost* offered a view of the CIA as an "old boys" league that was teeming with corruption and elitism by presenting a fictionalized nonfiction narrative from the perspective of a fictional CIA insider.

> *"My intent is to be neither pious nor satirical; it is instead to make comprehensible for myself what Fulton Oursler once called 'The Greatest Story Ever Told.'" —Mailer describing* The Gospel According to the Son

Mailer has elicited hostility and resentment from feminist leaders as well as from the public at large for his public comments about women and women's issues and for his works which examine issues relating to gender and sexuality. In 1971's *The Prisoner of Sex* he discusses his various sexual relationships and responds to writer Kate Millet's characterization of him as a sexist in her 1970 book *Sexual Politics,* and in his 1976 book *Genius and Lust: A Journey through the Major Writings of Henry Miller* he expressed admiration for author Henry Miller, who is famous for his own erotic literature and who had also been called a sexist by Millet. Mailer also examined the life of one of the most famous American sex symbols, actress Marilyn Monroe, in his 1973 work *Marilyn: A Biography,* which was a fictionalized account of her life, and in *Of Women and Their Elegance,* a 1980 work in which he presents a fictional interview between himself and Monroe.

Although the subjects of Mailer's works have continued to be outrageous and controversial and his books have elicited much debate, critical reception of the author's works in the 1980s and 1990s has been mixed. Although critics continue to acknowledge Mailer's talent as an exceptional writer, many have faulted his later works as superficial and have condemned the author's preoccupation with sordid topics and lurid human behavior. According to some reviewers, because of his reputation as a gifted writer Mailer continues to arouse readers' interest with his new works—even when he covers topics and figures already examined in detail by other authors—and to disappoint those readers who find his writing by turns sloppy, overdone, bombastic, and predictable.

Oswald's Tale: An American Mystery, Mailer's 1995 nonfiction narrative, has as its subject President John F. Kennedy's alleged assassin Lee Harvey Oswald. In a review of the work, *New York Times* critic Michiko Kakutani lamented that although the subject "looks like the perfect magnet for the author's talents and preoccupations," the book is a disappointment, because in Kakutani's estimation, "Mailer declines to use his enormous gifts as a reporter and novelist to create an unvarnished portrait of his subject ... but instead clumsily tries to force his material into an unyielding cookie-cutter shape." Kakutani concluded that "[t]he result is a book that succeeds simultaneously in being boring and presumptuous, derivative and solipsistic. Other assessments of the book were less negative; *Entertainment Weekly*'s reviewer called *Oswald's Tale* "full of interest," but noted that Mailer overstated the assassin's importance as an historical figure. Mailer's *Portrait of Picasso as a Young Man*, a 1995 biography of celebrated artist Pablo Picasso, fared better with critics, who applauded the author's choice of subject and his treatment of artistic themes and philosophies, although some faulted the work as lacking discussion of Picasso's masterpieces and for relying too heavily upon earlier biographies of the artist that failed to capture his true, complete nature. Some critics speculated that the author identified himself with Picasso, and in examining the artist's life Mailer was engaging in self-analysis as well. Mailer told *Entertainment Weekly*'s Rebecca Ascher-Walsh: "There are some ways in which I feel close to Picasso. We had a similar childhood.... I understand something about his competitiveness. But I never for one moment identified with him." The *National Review*'s David Gelernter offered a mixed assessment of the book, but concluded his review by asserting: "I move we vote Mailer a round of thanks and ask him to go home and write a second edition." Eunice Lipton's review for the *Nation* was distinctly negative; the critic found fault with many things in the book, and noted Mailer's particularly harsh treatment of lesbian activist Gertrude Stein, who posed for Picasso. Lipton concluded: "There are many sad things about *Portrait of Picasso as a Young Man*: how luridly nasty it is concerning [Gertrude] Stein's death; how voyeuristic regarding Picasso's lover Fernande Olivier; how vulgar and silly in its sexual references. But saddest of all is its apathetic disingenuousness, its lack of heart and honor."

Mailer's 1997 novel *The Gospel According to the Son* was a popular success, topping bestseller lists for many weeks and generating more than six reprintings. Critical reception of the novel, however, was mixed. Some critics, like *Entertainment Weekly*'s L. S. Klepp, faulted the novel's "failure to shock," given that it was intended as a provocative alternative version of the New Testament audaciously offered from the perspective of Jesus Christ himself. *People*'s Ralph Novak offered a similar assessment, calling Mailer's Christ "a curiously sterile figure," and asserting that the novel would have been more "fascinating ... had Mailer not demurred with such uncharacteristic timidity in the face of his supremely imposing protagonist." The *Nation*'s Mary Gordon disparaged the novel, asking "How can someone who has published so much, some of it admirable, have written such a bad book? A book whose badness leaves the reader first with a sense of reluctance (must I really go on?), then anger (how can he let himself get away with this?), then embarrassment (it is unseemly to cast my eyes on such a spectacle)." The book received some favorable reviews, among them a *Publishers Weekly* assessment that declared that although the novel fails in some regards, it is "also a triumph," and that "[u]ltimately, Mailer convinces, more than any writer before him, that for Jesus the man it could have been just like this; and that is, in itself, some sort of literary miracle." The book also elicited commendatory remarks from the *New Yorker*'s John Updike, and from the *New York Times Book Review*'s Reynolds Price, who, although expressing many of the same reservations as other critics about Mailer's handling of the larger themes and Christ's character, contended that "Mr. Mailer's Jesus impresses in smaller ways. He is able to draw on telling passages from His predecessors among the Hebrew prophets; He possesses an acute eye and a ready gift for the surprising image that crystallizes a moment of intense feeling. And, throughout the swift tale of His brief career, He retains a winning youthful liveliness of vision and response that relieves Him of the dismal and plainly unhistorical solemnity of so many Jesuses of story and film."

In 1996 Mailer, a self-described political "left conservative," interviewed right-wing conservative politician Pat Buchanan (who also asserted himself as a "left conservative") for *Esquire*. The two discussed a variety of topics, including what they both perceived as the sinister power of the American corporate establishment, and Mailer expressed his dissatisfaction with the administration of President Bill Clinton, for whom he had voted in 1992. Mailer was so unhappy with Clinton's performance in office that he considered running for Democratic nomination himself. If he had run for office, it would not have been the first time; in 1960 and 1969 Mailer campaigned as a mayoral candidate in New York City. Mailer asserted in the interview that he felt that not only could he have contributed his unique political wisdom as a presidential candidate, he was certain to avoid scandal based on media scrutiny of his life, due to the extensive media coverage of his past transgressions. As Mailer termed it: "I've been married six times. I committed a felonious assault against my second wife. I've been untrue to every woman I cared about. Gentleman and ladies of the press: Do your worst! I've broken through the media barrier. There's nothing to ransack in the closet." Mailer was also named one of *GQ*'s men of the year in 1996, in recognition of his considerable influence as an author, and by all accounts he has no plans to retire; instead he intends to continue to offer his unique perspective on the past and present, and to accept new challenges, both personal and literary.

Selected writings

The Naked and the Dead (novel), Rinehart, 1948.

Barbary Shore (novel), Rinehart, 1951.

The Deer Park (novel), Putnam, 1955, reprinted with preface and notes by Mailer, Berkley, 1976.

Advertisements for Myself (short stories, verse, articles, and essays, with narrative; includes "The White Negro"), Putnam, 1959.

The Presidential Papers (collected works), Putnam, 1963.

An American Dream (novel; first written in serial form for *Esquire*, January-August, 1964), Dial, 1965.

Cannibals and Christians (collected works), Dial, 1966.

Why Are We in Vietnam? (novel), Putnam, 1967, reprinted with preface by Mailer, 1977.

The Bullfight: A Photographic Narrative with Text by Norman Mailer (nonfiction), CBS Legacy Collection/Macmillan, 1967.

The Short Fiction of Norman Mailer (short fiction collection), Dell, 1967.

The Armies of the Night: History as a Novel, the Novel as History (nonfiction narrative), New American Library, 1968.

Miami and the Siege of Chicago (nonfiction narrative), New American Library, 1968.

King of the Hill: On the Fight of the Century (nonfiction narrative), New American Library, 1971.

The Prisoner of Sex (first published in *Harper's* magazine), Little, Brown, 1971.

St. George and the Godfather (nonfiction narrative), New American Library, 1972.

Marilyn: A Biography (nonfiction), Grosset and Dunlap, 1973, reprinted with new chapter by Mailer, Warner, 1975.

The Faith of Graffiti (nonfiction), photographs by Jon Naar, Praeger, 1974.

The Fight (nonfiction narrative), Little, Brown, 1975.

Some Honorable Men: Political Conventions 1960-1972 (collection of previously unpublished nonfiction narratives), Little, Brown, 1976.

The Executioner's Song (novel; excerpted in *Playboy* in 1979), Little, Brown, 1979.

Of Women and Their Elegance (fictional interview), photographs by Milton H. Greene, Simon & Schuster, 1980.

Ancient Evenings (novel), Little, Brown, 1983.

Tough Guys Don't Dance (novel), Random House, 1984.

Harlot's Ghost (novel), Random House, 1991.

How the Wimp Won the War (nonfiction narrative), Lord John Press, 1991.

Oswald's Tale: An American Mystery (nonfiction narrative), Ballantine, 1995.

Portrait of Picasso as a Young Man: An Interpretive Biography (nonfiction), Atlantic Monthly Press, 1995.

The Gospel According to the Son (novel), Random House, 1997.

Sources

Books

Andrew Gordon, "Norman Mailer," in *Dictionary of Literary Biography*, Volume 28: *Twentieth-Century American-Jewish Fiction Writers*, edited by Daniel Walden, Gale Research, 1984, pp. 154-66.

Periodicals

America, June 21, 1997, p. 2.

Booklist, May 15, 1997, p. 1556.

Entertainment Weekly, November 10, 1995, p. 54; July 19, 1996, p. 71; May 16, 1997, p. 108.

Esquire, August, 1996, p. 54.

GQ, November, 1996, p. 332.

Nation, November 6, 1995, p. 543; June 23, 1997, p. 27.

National Review, February 12, 1996, p. 50; August 12, 1996, p. 62.

New Republic, May 12, 1997, p. 30.

Newsweek, April 28, 1997, p. 74.

New York Times, April 25, 1995; April 14, 1997; February 4, 1997.

New York Times Book Review, May 4, 1997.

People, June 16, 1997, p. 32.

Publishers Weekly, September 11, 1995, p. 69; March 31, 1997, p. 59; May 26, 1997, p. 22.

Time, April 28, 1997, p. 75.

—*Lynn M. Spampinato*

David Mamet

Playwright, screenwriter, and director

Born November 30, 1947, in Chicago, IL; son of Bernard Morris (an attorney) and Lenore June (a teacher; maiden name, Silver) Mamet; married Lindsay Crouse (an actress), December 21, 1977 (divorced); married Rebecca Pidgeon (an actress and singer), 1991; children: (with Crouse) daughters Willa, Zosia; (with Pidgeon) Clara. *Education:* Attended Neighborhood Playhouse School of the Theater, 1968-69; Goddard College, Plainfield, VT, B.A., 1969.

Addresses: Home—Chicago, IL; Vermont. Office—c/o Pantheon Books, 201 East 50th St., New York, NY 10022-7703. *Agent*—Howard Rosenstone, Rosenstone/Wender, 3 East 48th St., New York, NY 10017.

Career

Playwright, screenwriter, director, producer, and actor. St. Nicholas Theater Company, Plainfield, VT, (moved to Chicago, IL, 1973) founder, 1972, artistic director, 1972-76, member of board of directors, beginning 1973; Goodman Theater, Chicago, associate artistic director, 1978-79. Special lecturer in drama, Marlboro College, 1970; artist-in-residence in drama, Goddard College, 1971-73; faculty member, Illinois Arts Council, 1974; visiting lecturer in drama, University of Chicago, 1975-76 and 1979; teaching fellow, School of Drama, Yale University, 1976-77; guest lecturer, New York University, 1981; associate professor of film, Columbia University, 1988. Contributing editor, *Oui*, 1975-76.

Awards: Joseph Jefferson Award, 1975, for *Sexual Perversity in Chicago,* and 1976, for *American Buffalo;* Obie Awards, *Village Voice,* for best new playwright, 1976, for *Sexual Perversity in Chicago* and *American Buffalo,* and for best American play, 1983, for *Edmond;* Children's Theater grant, New York State Council on the Arts, 1976; Rockefeller grant, 1976; New York Drama Critics' Circle Award for best American play, 1977, for *American Buffalo,* and 1984, for *Glengarry Glen Ross;* Outer Critics Circle Award, 1978, for contributions to the American theater; Pulitzer Prize for drama and Joseph Dintenfass Award, both 1984, for *Glengarry Glen Ross;* Hull-Warriner Award, Dramatists Guild, 1984; American Academy and Institute of Arts and Letters Award for Literature, 1986; Venice Film Festival, FIPRESCI Award and Golden Osella Award for best original screenplay, both 1987, for *House of Games.*

Sidelights

American playwright David Mamet (pronounced "*Mam*-it") is the voice of the common man—and lower—in theater. Rather than staging pretentious dramas full of preachy, prancing characters, Mamet shows the audience a gritty reality, often populated by con men, thieves, or morally bereft salesmen whose language is rife with the kind of stuttering, pausing, and obscenities that occur in real-life conversation. Despite the spartan phrasing and lack of eloquence, the staccato rhythm ends up flowing naturally, making Mamet's dialogue unique, though he is sometimes roughly compared to fellow author Harold Pinter. His first big hit was in the mid-1970s with *Sexual Perversity in Chicago*, followed by *American Buffalo*. Mamet was awarded the Pulitzer Prize for drama in 1984 for *Glengarry Glen Ross*, the tale of shady salesmen in a cutthroat real estate sales office.

Later, he became more involved in feature films, writing and producing 1992's fictionalized biopic *Hoffa*, bringing *American Buffalo* to the screen in 1996, and directing a warmly received version of his 1985 work *The Spanish Prisoner* in 1997. He was also responsible for cowriting the screenplay for *Wag the Dog*, the 1997, a sleeper hit about a conspiracy involving a Hollywood director who creates a fake war to detract attention from a presidential sex scandal. The video bounced back into the American consciousness in mid-1998 when it looked as if life might be imitating art.

Mamet was born on November 30, 1947, in a Jewish neighborhood on the south side of Chicago, Illinois. His mother, Lenore June (Silver) Mamet, was a teacher, and his father, Bernard Morris Mamet, was a labor lawyer who instilled in Mamet and his younger sister, Lynn, a keen aptitude for the language. The playwright once recalled that his dad would make them pause during conversation in order to find better words for what they were trying to say. "From the earliest age," Mamet recalled to John Lahr in the *New Yorker*, "one had to think, to be careful about what one was going to say, and also how the other person was going to respond." His parents had high expectations of him in all areas, making for a childhood filled with pressure. However, as he told Lahr, "My childhood, like many people's, was not a bundle of laughs. So what? I always skip that part of the biography."

After his parents went through a difficult divorce when he was about 10 or 11, Mamet and his sister moved with their mother to Olympia Fields on the far reaches of the city. The divorce was especially hard on him because it was still so stigmatized in those days. In 1958, their mother married one of her ex-husband's colleagues and a close family friend, whose name was also Bernie. The children came home from vacationing with their father in Florida to find out the two had tied the knot. Their stepfather was violent, and Mamet became frustrated and clashed with him often. At age 15, he moved in with his father on scenic Lake Shore Drive. This relationship would heavily color the writer's attitudes and later works. Mamet's father died in 1991.

Around the time he moved in with his dad, Mamet got involved doing backstage work and acting in bit parts at Chicago's Hull House Theatre, hoping to someday become an actor. He then went to Vermont to study literature and drama at Goddard College, where he once quipped that he had majored in drugs and sex. After a couple of years, he took a respite from college during his junior year to attend the Neighborhood Playhouse School of the Theater in New York City in 1968-69, where he studied acting under the renowned Sanford Meisner of the Group Theatre. There Mamet studied Meisner's and the Group Theater's interpretation of the Stanislavsky method, which emphasizes constant action and the rhythm of language, and he was also exposed to a Word Repetition Game that was supposed to extract genuine emotion from actors. His later work would reveal the effects of these exercises in his dialogue. After the year in New York, Mamet returned to Chicago to bus tables over the summer break at Chicago's Second City, the influential comedy club, where he became inspired by the improvisational, fast-paced style. He then went back to Goddard and started writing plays, earning his bachelor of arts in 1969.

Mamet's first play, *Camel*, a collection of 34 short scenes, was completed as his senior-year project at Goddard. The work was composed using writings out of his personal journal, a method on which he continues to rely. Mamet charged fifty cents' admission at the staging, which upset fellow students, but as he told Lahr, "I wanted to communicate to the public at large that this was going to be no ordinary theatrical event." In addition, he noted, "I felt like it." After graduation, Mamet worked odd jobs and held small roles in touring productions around New England. Though he was not especially skilled on the stage, he landed a job teaching acting at Marlboro College in Marlboro, Vermont, in 1970, where one of the conditions of his employment required writing a play suitable for production. Later that year his students held the premier of *Lakeboat*, a one-act play about the merchant marine. After a year at Marlboro, Mamet was back in Chicago, adding the items cab driver, short-order cook, factory worker, and telephone salesman to his resume. Many critics have presumed that his immersion in the working class has given him an edge in writing dialogue, but Mamet denies this, insisting he just needed to earn cash.

By 1971, Mamet was back at Goddard as a drama instructor and artist-in-residence. His alma mater was an unconventional college, eschewing grades, tests, and required courses. Mamet was a walking dichotomy in the halls: the conventional iconoclast. He took his art and teaching very seriously and showed no mercy for those who slacked. If students arrived late for class, he would fine them for each minute they were late, then burn their money. One of his pupils and later a cofounder of Mamet's theater group, Steven Schacter, remarked in the *New York Times Magazine*, "We were poor students. We didn't have money to burn. But it was all part of a devotion, a devotion to the art that was not to be taken lightly." During Mamet's time as a teacher, he began penning scenes for his students to act out when he could not find existing material to his liking. This led to his founding an ensemble acting group, the St. Nicholas Company, with a collection of his top students, in Vermont in 1972. They performed modern classics as well as works by Mamet. One such play was *Sexual Perversity in Chicago,* which would become his first big success.

Encouraged by filmmaker friend Mike Nichols, who had just made *Carnal Knowledge,* and by the fact that some small theater groups in Chicago were catching on to his work, Mamet relocated his crew to the Windy City. There, they enlisted actress Patricia Cox and opened their own theater, raising money by holding acting workshops. Mamet also during this time moonlighted waiting tables, cleaning offices, and driving a taxi. His reputation was elevated when he won the Joseph Jefferson Award in 1975 for best new Chicago play for *Sexual Perversity in Chicago*. In December of 1975, the play, along with another called *Duck Variations,* made a double-bill debut Off-Off-Broadway at the St. Clement's Theatre, and after positive response, was staged Off-Broadway at the Cherry Lane Theatre. *Sexual Perversity* is a collection of somewhat raunchy, satirical vignettes focusing on two sets of supposedly "swinging" couples in the 1970s. It examines how sex complicates the communication between men and women. *Duck Variations,* on the other hand, portrayed two old men on a park bench gently spouting observations on an array of topics.

After that round of success, Mamet's *American Buffalo* opened on Broadway in 1977 after spending some time in Chicago. Mamet knew he had a winner on his hands and even ordered his friend, director Gregory Mosher, to produce it, insisting that it would win the Pulitzer Prize. The loosely-written story concerns a trio of small-time crooks who plot to steal a coin collection. In 1975, the *Village Voice* awarded Mamet an Obie Award for best new playwright for this as well as *Sexual Perversity,* and the New York Drama Critics' Circle named *American Buffalo* the best American play in 1977. Though *American Buffalo* did not net him a Pulitzer, this was Mamet's breakthrough work. It es-

tablished him as one of the great language playwrights and fused him with Mosher, who would go on to direct a great many of Mamet's plays. Mamet then left his hometown for New York.

The late 1970s saw Mamet in a flurry of activity, writing sometimes a number of plays within a year, including the children's story, *The Revenge of the Space Pandas, or Binky Rudich and the Two Speed-Clock,* 1977, which earned him a $4,000 grant from the New York State Council on the Arts. The next year he also won the Outer Critics Circle Award for contributions to the American theater, and in 1983 took another Obie Award from the *Village Voice* for best American play for *Edmond*. Mamet's next major work was 1984's *Glengarry Glen Ross,* about a group of huckster real estate agents. This time around, he did win the Pulitzer Prize for drama, as well as the New York Drama Critics' Circle Award for best American play and the Joseph Dintenfass Award, all in 1984. The play was made into an acclaimed film in 1992 starring Jack Lemmon. In 1987, Mamet directed his first film, *House of Games,* and went on to write and produce 1992's *Hoffa,* loosely based on the life of the fiery union boss who disappeared in the 1970s, never to be found. In 1994 Mamet directed the film version of his 1992 play *Oleanna,* about a student who accuses a professor of rape. It was one of his few works to center on a female character. Though it was a Broadway hit, some deemed it misogynist; he has long been criticized for leaving women out of his plays or inserting them only as sex objects or recipients of male violence.

Also in 1994 Mamet staged *The Cryptogram,* considered one of his most personal plays. It draws upon his own emotionally abusive childhood and tells the tale from a young boy's point of view. The same year, Mamet released his first novel, *The Village,* about the inhabitants of a small town in New England, to mixed reviews. In 1997 Mamet wrote and directed the screen version of his 1985 play *The Spanish Prisoner,* about a con artist who develops an updated version of an old trick in order to make millions for his company. Also that year he staged *The Old Neighborhood,* another semi-autobiographical work which Bruce Weber in the *New York Times* noted "may be this most private of writers' most public drama about his own life."

Mamet in 1997 cowrote the screenplay for the political farce *Wag the Dog,* about a secret plot to present a "fake war" to the American public in order to draw attention away from a presidential scandal involving a young girl. Well-received upon its release, the film's pay-per-view subscribers doubled and tripled at many cable companies and video rentals were selling out as well in August of 1998. The popularity boost was due, according to observers, by the fact that just three days after President Bill Clinton testified that he had an "improper" relationship with a White House intern, the United States bombed an alleged terrorist camp and undercover chemical weapons plant in Afghanistan and Sudan. Though the attacks were undoubtedly legit, the situation seemed to mirror the events in *Wag the Dog,* thus generating interest. Insider buzz reported that Mamet and director Barry Levinson were both unhappy that he got second billing on the project after cowriter Hilary Henkin, because the sharp dialogue seems to betray his heavy involvement. Mamet then wrote and directed the films *The Winslow Boy* and *State and Maine* in 1998 and also cowrote the screenplay for *Ronin,* but decided on being credited under the name Richard Weisz for the latter, again owing to a dispute about proper credit. He has also written episodes of the television shows *Hill Street Blues* and *L.A. Law.*

Mamet married actress Lindsay Crouse, the daughter of Russel Crouse (who cowrote *The Sound of Music*) on December 21, 1977; the couple had two daughters, Willa and Zosia. They later divorced and Mamet married Rebecca Pidgeon, an actress and singer whom he met when she was cast in his 1989 production of *Speed-the-Plow* in London. They have a daughter, Clara, and live in a converted farmhouse dating from 1805 in Vermont. Mamet did not practice Judaism until later in life, but when they married, Pidgeon converted to the faith as well. Mamet has taught at a number of institutions throughout his career, including the University of Chicago, Yale University, New York University, and Columbia University. Mamet continues to collect ideas from eavesdropping. "We listen to people talk all the time," Mamet told Peter Howell in the *Toronto Star.* "Everybody says, 'The funniest thing just happened to me' or 'Wow, I saw the weirdest thing!' or 'Wouldn't it be funny if?' or 'I got this strange thought...' We all say that a hundred times a day. The only difference with a writer than the rest of the people is that a writer writes it down. The writer doesn't have any more ideas than other people."

Selected writings

Plays

Lakeboat, produced 1970; Grove, 1981.
Duck Variations, produced 1972; Grove, 1978.
Squirrels, produced 1974.
The Poet and the Rent: A Play for Kids from Seven to 8:15, produced 1974; Grove, 1986.
American Buffalo, produced 1975; Grove, 1977.
Reunion, produced 1976; Grove, 1979.

Dark Pony, produced 1977; Grove, 1979
All Men Are Whores, produced 1977; Dramatist Play Service, 1981.
A Life in the Theatre, produced 1977; Grove, 1978.
The Revenge of the Space Pandas, or Binky Rudich and the Two Speed-Clock, produced 1977; Sergel, 1978.
The Woods, produced 1977; Grove, 1979.
The Water Engine: An American Fable, produced 1977; Grove, 1978.
Mr. Happiness, produced 1978; Grove, 1978.
Lone Canoe, or The Explorer, produced 1979.
The Sanctity of Marriage, produced 1979.
Shoeshine, produced 1981, Dramatist Play Service, 1981.
Short Plays and Monologues, Dramatist Play Service, 1981.
A Sermon, produced 1981.
Donny March, produced 1981.
Litko, produced 1984, Dramatist Play Service, 1981.
Edmond, produced 1982; Grove, 1983.
The Disappearance of the Jews, produced 1983.
The Dog, produced 1983.
Film Crew, produced 1983.
4 A.M., produced 1983.
Glengarry Glen Ross, produced 1983; Grove, 1984.
Yes, But So What, produced 1983; Samuel French, 1985.
Vermont Sketches, produced 1984, Samuel French, 1985.
Five Unrelated Pieces, published 1985.
The Shawl [and] Prairie du Chien, produced 1985, Grove, 1985.
Vint, produced 1985, Grove, 1986.
Speed-the-Plow, produced 1988; Grove, 1988.
Where Were You When It Went Down?, produced 1988.
Goldberg Street, Grove, 1989.
Bobby Gould in Hell, produced 1989.
Oleanna, produced 1992, Pantheon, 1993.
A Life with No Joy In It; and Other Plays and Pieces, Dramatists Play Service, 1994.
The Cryptogram, produced 1995, Dramatists Play Service, 1995.

Screenplays

The Postman Always Rings Twice, 1981.
The Verdict, 1982.
About Last Night..., 1986.
House of Games, 1987.
The Untouchables, 1987.
Things Change, 1988.
We're No Angels, 1989.
Homicide, 1991.
Glengarry Glen Ross, 1992.
The Water Engine (for television), 1992.
Hoffa, 1992.

Rising Sun (uncredited), 1993.
A Life in the Theater (television), 1993.
Vanya on 42nd Street, 1994.
Texan, 1994.
American Buffalo, 1996.
The Spanish Prisoner, 1997.
The Edge, 1997.
(With Hilary Henkin) *Wag the Dog,* 1997.
The Winslow Boy, 1998.
State and Maine, 1998.
Ronin (credited as Richard Weisz), 1998.

Other

Warm and Cold (children's book), Solo Press, 1984.
(With Lindsay Crouse) *The Owl,* Kipling Press, 1987.
Writing in Restaurants (essays, speeches, and articles), Penguin, 1987.
Some Freaks (essays), Viking, 1989.
On Directing Film, Viking, 1992.
The Cabin: Reminiscences and Diversions, Random House, 1992.
The Village (novel), Little, Brown, 1994.
Passover (novel), St. Martin's Press, 1995.
The Duck and the Goat, St. Martin's Press, 1996.
Make-Believe Town: Essays and Remembrances, Little, Brown, 1996.

Sources

On-line

"David Mamet," *Contemporary Authors,* Gale Literary Databases, http://www.galenet.com (July 7, 1998).
"David Mamet," *Dictionary of Literary Biography,* Gale Literary Databases, http://www.galenet.com (July 7, 1998).
"David Mamet," Internet Movie Database, http://us.imdb.com (August 26, 1998).

Books

Contemporary Theatre, Film, and Television, volume 8, Gale Research, 1990.

Periodicals

Economist, January 31, 1998.
Interview, April 1998, p. 66.
Los Angeles Magazine, April 1998, p. 88.
Los Angeles Times, August 5, 1998, calendar, p. 2.
Nation, April 27, 1998, p. 35.
New Republic, February 2, 1998, p. 24.
Newsday, November 20, 1997, p. B11.
New Yorker, November 16, 1992, p. 121; November 17, 1997, p. 70.
New York Times, March 26, 1984, p. C3; October 16, 1987, p. C10; November 8, 1992, sec. 2, p. 1; January 3, 1993, sec. 2, p. 1; November 17, 1994, p. C1; April 14, 1995, p. C3; November 16, 1997, sec. 2, p. 7; November 20, 1997, p. E1.
New York Times Magazine, April 21, 1985, p. 32.
Toronto Star, April 24, 1998.
Vanity Fair, April 1988, p. 32.

—Geri Speace

Dan Mathews

Activist and campaign director

Born in 1965, in Orange County, CA; son of Ray (a restaurateur) and Perry (a secretary) Mathews. *Education:* Attended Pasadena City College; American University, history degree, 1985.

Addresses: *Home*—Alexandria, VA. *Office*—PETA, 501 Front St., Norfolk, VA 23510.

Career

Model and actor, 1983-85; People for the Ethical Treatment of Animals (PETA), receptionist, 1988, campaign director, c. 1989—.

Sidelights

Dan Mathews, campaign director for PETA (People for the Ethical Treatment of Animals) is generally recognized as the mastermind behind the "I'd Rather Go Naked than Wear Fur" crusade to dissuade consumers from purchasing the pelts and bring attention to the group's mission. Mathews's name has become synonymous with PETA, the animal rights group that calls for rejecting all human use of animal products, from eating eggs to wearing leather loafers. Arrested over 20 times on civil disobedience charges, he has helped transform PETA from an obscure nonprofit organization made up of about 60,000 to a household name backed by screen stars and supermodels, with a following of 500,000 and a multimillion dollar budget.

Mathews was born in 1965 in Orange County, California, where he grew up with his two brothers. His father, Ray, a restaurant owner, and mother, Perry, a secretary, divorced when Mathews was seven. Mathews told *Biography* that although his father lent support, his mother raised the family basically as a single parent, and from her he developed his love of animals. She would take strays into their two-bedroom apartment, giving them veterinary care and teaching her sons that animals need human assistance. Mathews's mother also instilled in her sons a strong rejection of homophobia, racism, and sexism, and a love of the *Rocky Horror Picture Show,* which she would show at his slumber parties when he was young.

Mathews, unfortunately, was on the receiving end of prejudice at a young age. Classmates at Davis Middle School picked on him and a friend for crying at the zoo, distraught over seeing the animals in cages. Often beat up in school for being overweight and gay, he found solace being around animals when he returned home. Mathews reached an important conclusion as an adolescent on a fishing trip off the coast of California with his father, when he caught a giant flounder and decided to throw it back. Mathews recalled in *People Weekly* that he "suddenly realized that I had ripped this fish away from his world." The reverse of most vegetarians, who give up fish as the final step in becoming meat-free, Mathews gave up eating seafood at that point, but only became a full vegetarian at age 16. He told *Biography,* "I started realizing just because cats and dogs might be cute, it's unfair to be cruel or insensitive about other animals because they might not be as cute and cuddly."

In high school, Mathews began attending animal rights protests with his friend Connie. Active in the punk rock scene, he initially thought the movement would be too "hippie" for him and figured he would ridicule the effort. Standing outside of a research lab in Orange County that was experimenting on sheep, he was part of a grass-roots coalition of about 10 grandmothers with hand-made signs. His emotions ran high, and he discussed with Connie afterward his feelings of frustration at not being able to help the sheep. He later began reading about fur farms and slaughterhouses and attending protests regularly.

Mathews graduated from Costa Mesa High School at 16 and attended Pasadena City College, then left for Rome in 1983 to study history. There, the handsome, 6-foot-5-inch Mathews worked as a model for two years, getting parts in a Fiat commercial, music videos, and a spaghetti western (*Arapho*), but his heart was with an animal rights group that he had volunteered to help. In 1985, Mathews moved to Washington, D.C., and finished his history degree at American University. Around the time he graduated, he decided to let his family know that he was gay, telling his father and 20 others at a family reunion in Oklahoma. "I think the reason people think gays are unhappy," Mathews remarked in *Out,* "is because we seem unhappy with ourselves when we sit uncomfortably in the closet."

A self-professed "bleeding heart," Mathews attributes his sensitivity to animals in part to his sexual orientation. Because gays are treated unfairly, he believes he has more understanding of what it's like to be the underdog. "I care about everyone's rights, whether they're women, children, minorities, or the environment," he commented in *Out,* adding, "My message to people isn't just to become an animal rights person or a vegetarian, it's to become a more responsible human being."

While in college, Mathews began an animal rights group to stop the school from poisoning pigeons on campus in order to control the population. He was successful in halting the effort, and received much attention. A colleague told him of a position at People for the Ethical Treatment of Animals (PETA), a nonprofit animal-rights group founded in 1980 by Ingrid Newkirk and Alex Pacheco. He started as a receptionist making a $10,400 annual salary. Within a year, he was moved into the campaigns department, where he organized protests and developed campaigns. He flourished in the new area, using his love of pop culture to develop entertainment-oriented messages for the public as opposed to dry, hard news.

> *"My message to people isn't just to become an animal rights person or a vegetarian, it's to become a more responsible human being."*

In one of Mathews's biggest early coups, he chained himself to a million-dollar prototype vehicle at a General Motors (GM) exhibit during an international auto show in San Francisco wearing a sign saying, "GENERAL MURDERERS." He was drawing attention to the company's use of live animals in crash testing. PETA claimed that GM was the last of the Big 3 automakers to use animals in testing; the car company later agreed to stop the tests. As time progressed, he was able to round up big-name celebrities to rally behind the cause, bringing a much-needed element of glamour to the usually low-budget world of nonprofits. PETA's membership increased from 60,000 to 500,000 in the ten-year span between 1985 and 1995, most likely due in large part to Mathews's high-profile protests and advertisements. The budget has grown to $13.4 million.

Though hobnobbing with the rich and famous, Mathews lives on a $30,000 salary in a modest apartment in the Washington, D.C., suburb of Alexandria, Virginia. He admits to never having more than $500 in his checking account at any given time, and owing thousands to credit cards. He keeps giving money to a number of his favorite charities, however, including the National Abortion Rights Action League, the Human Rights Campaign Fund, and local AIDS clinics. When he travels, he stays with friends, although that often does not mean spartan accomodations. Friends who put him up include singer Chrissie Hynde in London and Cassandra "Elvira" Peterson in Los Angeles. Other celebrities who have joined PETA's cause include Sara Gilbert of *Roseanne,* Paul McCartney, Kate Pierson of the B-52's, Mary Tyler Moore, Kirstie Alley, k.d. lang, and Bea Arthur.

Perhaps the most obvious supporters who have helped PETA are the models who have bared almost all in full-page magazine ads and billboards reading, "I'd Rather Go Naked than Wear Fur." Naomi Campbell, Christy Turlington, Tyra Banks, and Cindy Crawford, as well as actress Kim Basinger, have all appeared in the ads. Though the group has seemed to become more mainstream with the involvement of well-known people, their tactics often still run afoul of the law. He was arrested with talk-show host Ricki Lake in November of 1994 for entering designer Karl Lagerfeld's offices in Manhattan and applying "Fur Hurts" stickers to coats. They were, however, legally permitted into the building (someone "buzzed" them in), and Mathews said that the stickers were easily removed. He claimed in *People Weekly*, "PETA doesn't do violence. It's more vaudeville than violence."

Mathews and others also spray-painted anti-fur graffiti on signs—not coats—at the office of Calvin Klein, who agreed to meet with PETA members to view a four-minute video that showed the cruelty endured by animals killed for their fur. The designer then announced he would thereafter only use fake fur, stating that he had reflected "on the humane treatment of animals." Mathews has also disrupted runway fashion shows, such as Karl Lagerfeld's fur show on May 13, 1991, at the Parsons School of Design in New York City. Models wearing flesh-toned undergarments started off the parade carrying "We'd Rather Go Naked than Wear Fur" signs, as puzzled attendees questioned de la Renta's sense of humor, not understanding that a protest was in progress.

Other designers swearing off fur include Giorgio Armani, Bill Blass, Donna Karan, Anne Klein, Ralph Lauren, Isaac Mizrahi, and Todd Oldham, although Anne Klein and Donna Karan claimed that economic, not moral or social, reasons were behind their decisions. PETA's efforts may have caused the decrease in demand by stigmatizing fur fashions for many would-be wearers, but fur trade groups deny it. The *New York Times* reported that fur sales dropped from $1.8 billion in 1987 to $1 billion in 1991, but manufacturers cited mild winters and a recession for the decrease, and noted that fur's popularity was returning. Karen Handel of the Fur Information Council told the *New York Times* in 1994, "The fact sales are up 20 percent in two years says more about what's happening in the fur industry than half a dozen people on the street parading around naked." Mathews disagreed that fur was making a comeback, stating in *People Weekly*, "Fur farms have gone belly-up all over the country."

For all of Mathews's persuasive tactics, he told *USA Today* that PETA feels that people have a right to wear anything they choose. "We simply believe it should be an educated choice," he commented. However, he also noted in the article, "If people won't stop wearing fur because they care about animals, they'll stop wearing fur because they're afraid of spray paint." PETA gained many critics when some anti-fur protestors started getting arrested for spray-painting the coats of private citizens. Despite whether a person thinks wearing fur is right or wrong, most recognize that defacing a person's private property is illegal, and the group was pegged as extremist. Mathews countered in *USA Today* that PETA's tactics were extreme so that the public could be made aware of the animal suffering. Due to PETA's efforts, much of the country became aware of the inhumane ways in which animals were killed for their pelts, such as anal shocks and gruesome traps. The fur industry later claimed that these procedures had been replaced with gentler methods when they introduced a big-budget campaign to increase fur sales in the mid-1990s.

Though his efforts against wearing fur are his most visible, Mathews's campaigns do not end there. He has also been active in trying to persuade consumers not to eat meat and was arrested during a march in Phoenix, Arizona, protesting the National Cattlemen's Association convention. He has confronted carriage operators near Central Park in New York City, accusing them of mistreating the horses. And he organized a protest of Gillette to try to make them stop testing their products on animals. He also takes a firm stand against testing on animals to produce cures for human disease, which has drawn fire from many. Mathews defended himself in *Biography*, insisting that most advances in medicine, especially in regards to AIDS treatment, have stemmed from the study of actual patients. He also noted that despite millions of dollars, numerous animal deaths, and decades of research, there is still no cure for cancer. "[T]he whole idea of trying to infect animals has been really, really pointless and really, really cruel," he opined in *Biography*.

Mathews himself firmly practices what he preaches. In addition to not eating any animal products—including Jell-O, made with horse hooves, and milk, which he believes exploits cows—he does not wear any animal products, either. PETA opposes leather, silk (they say silkworms are boiled during the process), and wool, because of the frequency with which sheep are cut during the shearing, so Mathews sports vinyl Doc Marten boots, canvas suits, and polyester belts. Also, he does not run his campaigns from the home office, preferring to be on the front lines. He has seen the inside of so many jail cells, he even wrote a handy guide for *Details* on how to best cope with getting ar-

344 • Newsmakers • 1998, Cumulative, Issue 4

rested for civil disobedience ("Definitely avoid eating too much before an arrest, unless you enjoy crapping in a cold cell in front of a group of strangers" was one of his many practical tips). Also in *Details,* he related a humorous anecdote about his arrest at a meat-trade conference in Denver, Colorado. The guard who restrained Mathews had him charged with assault with intent to gore him with the papier-mache horns on his cow costume. "I argued that from the inside I could hardly see my outfit, so if I horned him it was unintentional," Mathews wrote in *Details.* The judge dropped the charges.

"Dan's the epitome of the youthful spirit," described PETA cofounder Ingrid Newkirk in *Out* magazine. "He'll do whatever it takes.... Dan has a wonderful zest and a sense of universal justice that applies to all individuals, all species. He'll fight quite vigorously for what he believes in. Practicalities just don't get in his way."

Sources

Arizona Republic, January 28, 1993.
Biography, January 1998.
Details, September 1995.
New Yorker, February 28, 1994.
New York Times, May 14, 1991; May 1, 1994.
Out, August/September 1993.
People Weekly, February 13, 1995.
Philadelphia Inquirer Magazine, August 11, 1994.
USA Today, December 23, 1991.

—*Geri Speace*

John S. McCain

AP/Wide World Photos

U.S. senator

Born John Sidney McCain, August 29, 1936, in the Panama Canal Zone; son of John Sidney, Jr., and Roberta (Wright) McCain; married, 1965; wife's name, Carol (divorced, 1980); married Cindy Hensley, May 17, 1980; children: (adopted; first wife's children) Doug, Andrew; (with first wife) Sidney Ann; (with second wife) Meghan, Jack, Jimmy, Bridget. *Education:* U.S. Naval Academy, graduated, 1958; attended National War College, 1973-74.

Addresses: *Office*—U.S. Senate, 241 Russell Senate Building, Washington, DC 20510.

Career

United States Navy, 1958-81, prisoner of war in Vietnam, 1967-73; became captain, 1977; director of Navy Senate Liaison office, 1977-81; U.S. representative, Arizona's First Congressional District, 1982-86; U.S. senator, Arizona, 1986—; chair of the Senate Commerce, Science, and Transportation Committee; serves on Armed Services and Indian Affairs committee, and subcommittees on readiness, personnel, and seapower; chair of the International Republican Institute, 1993—.

Awards: Silver Star, Bronze Star, Legion of Merit, Purple Heart, Distinguished Flying Cross, Vietnamese Legion of Honor.

Sidelights

Senator John S. McCain spent 22 years in the navy before becoming a Republican congressman, then a senator, from Arizona. He did not, however, have a typical military career. McCain was shot down over Hanoi in the Vietnam War only to endure five-and-a-half years as a prisoner of war (POW), spending most of the time in solitary and enduring incessant torture. When he returned, he put the dismal period behind him and forged on—an awe-inspiring tale of survival that is almost unfathomable. However, as an elected official, he prefers to be known for what he is accomplishing now, rather than living on his reputation as the tough POW. "Nowadays, when somebody introduces me like, 'Here is our great war hero,' I don't like it," McCain remarked to Charles P. Pierce in *Esquire*. "I want to be known as the guy who's trying to reform the telecommunications business, who's trying to see the cable rates deregulated." In 1998, he received his wish when he won credit as the anti-tobacco crusader. McCain's name became synonymous with the drive to sharply decrease smoking in America by raising taxes and yanking tobacco companies' ability to shield themselves from lawsuits. The bill eventually petered out, and the senator redirected his energy into other issues, such as campaign finance reform and telecommunications legislation. A respected Republican with admirers in both parties, McCain's name has been tossed around as a possible presidential candidate for 2000.

John Sidney McCain was born on August 29, 1936, in the Panama Canal Zone to John Sidney McCain, Jr., and Roberta (Wright) McCain. He grew up on naval bases both in the United States and overseas. The elder McCain was an admiral who served as commander of American forces in the Pacific during the Vietnam War. In fact, the family has a long lineage in the military. McCain's paternal grandfather, John S. McCain, Sr., was also an admiral, as well as commander of all aircraft carriers in the Pacific during World War II. He and McCain's father were the first father and son admirals in the history of the navy. Going way back, McCain had a distant ancestor, Captain William Young, who served under General George Washington during the American Revolution. It is not surprising that McCain always set his sights on entering the military. McCain also has a sister and a younger brother.

McCain graduated from Episcopal High School in Alexandria, Virginia, in 1954 and then attended the United States Naval Academy in Annapolis, Maryland, where he took courses in electrical engineering. There he was known as a rowdy and insubordinate student whose demerits for his antics dragged down his otherwise decent grades. He graduated in 1958 toward the bottom of his class (790 out of 795), but was nevertheless accepted to train as a naval aviator. "I enjoyed shooting rockets and dropping bombs and shooting off guns," McCain told Pierce. "Nobody in their right mind wouldn't enjoy that. Here you are you're a single guy, you're in the Mediterranean. You're a young single guy, and you go out and you fly for a couple of weeks, then you come in for a week and carouse like hell. Nobody deserve to get paid for that." It was not all fun and games, though. At one point, McCain was almost killed on the aircraft carrier *Forrestal* when a wayward rocket from a nearby bomber struck his plane's fuel tank as he was getting ready to take off. The explosions and fires killed 130, but McCain managed to emerge unscathed.

A few months later, McCain would not be so lucky. On October 26, 1967, the lieutenant commander lifted off from the carrier Oriskany in an A-4E Skyhawk on a mission over power plants in the Vietnamese capital, Hanoi. Above the city, an anti-aircraft missile sliced off the plane's right wing, forcing McCain to eject. With both arms broken, a shattered knee, and a broken shoulder, he landed in a lake where a Vietnamese man extracted him, then a crowd beat him, stabbed him with a bayonet, and took him into custody. He did not receive care for his wounds for nine days. When officials learned of his father's high rank, they admitted him to the hospital and later placed him with an American cellmate who helped nurse him back to health.

McCain, thanks to his father's status, was offered an early release after just seven months, but he denied it, insisting on following the American prisoner of war code of conduct which states that prisoners should only accept release in the order in which they were captured.

When he refused to leave, the Vietnamese beat McCain severely for about a week straight, almost constantly. After this ordeal, he signed a statement confessing to being a war criminal, an act that he has always regretted. "I failed myself. I failed my fellow prisoners. I failed my family, and I failed my country," McCain related to Pierce. "Is there anybody else?" McCain also endured beatings for trying to communicate with other prisoners by tapping on the walls, and he lost about a third of his weight because of malnutrition. He was not allowed to send or receive mail. The captors hung him up by his broken arms for hours on end, among other tortures. McCain was eventually put in a facility with 50 other prisoners in 1971, but after some men began a riot, he and a number of others were transferred to an even more oppressive jail. One of the worst aspects, however, above the physical pain, was not knowing what would happen next—hearing rumors of impending freedom, only to find they were false, prompted intense emotional trauma.

After five-and-a-half years as a prisoner of war in Vietnam, McCain and the rest of the men in Hanoi were released on March 17, 1973. The years of torture had wracked his small frame. The five-foot, nine-inch pilot had dropped from 160 pounds down to about 100, and his hair had turned a shock of white by the age of 36. He could not bend his knee, raise his right arm all the way, or hold his arms out straight. Arthritis would plague him. After medical treatment in the Philippines and in Florida, McCain was scarred, but remarkably, emerged emotionally stable. "The minute I got off the plane in the Philippines, I put all that behind me," McCain told Pierce. "I really did. I know that's hard to believe, but I did." McCain was given a hero's welcome upon his return to America, meeting President Richard Nixon and California Governor Ronald Reagan and receiving the Silver Star, Bronze Star, Legion of Merit, Purple Heart, and Distinguished Flying Cross. He went to the National War College in Washington, D.C., in 1973 and 1974, but missed flying. After going back into a plane as a training squadron commander, he was promoted to captain in 1977.

That year, the navy named him their liaison to the U.S. Senate, sowing the seeds of his political ambition. He retired from the navy in 1981 and moved to Phoenix to work for his wife's father, a beer distributor. In 1982, despite his newcomer status in the state, he ran for the House of Representatives from Arizona's First Congressional District—a Republican-dominated area taking up much of Phoenix—and won. Unopposed in the 1984 primary, he was re-elected by a large majority over his Democratic contender. His conservative voting record followed the party line rather faithfully during the Reagan years. He gave the nod to prayer in public schools, the Gramm-Rudman deficit reduction bill, the use of lie-detector tests in certain forms of employment, the reintroduction of certain handgun sales, and subsidies for tobacco companies. He voted against the Equal Rights Amendment for women and extra money for the Clean Air Act. Understandably hawkish in his views on the military, he opposed the 1983 nuclear freeze resolution and supported more funding for MX missile development and other programs. However, McCain showed in many ways that he was not afraid to voice his own opinion. He approved of sanctions in the apartheid-era South Africa, voting to override President Reagan's veto, and also spoke out against a maneuver to cut millions from a program providing food to the poverty-stricken in order to gives raises to administrators. He also stood against direct U.S. intervention in Central America.

In 1986, McCain ran unopposed in the primary for the U.S. Senate seat vacated when Arizona's political icon Barry Goldwater retired. He won the general election handily and was appointed to the Armed Services Committee and its subcommittees on readiness, personnel, and seapower; the Indian Affairs Committee; and the Senate Commerce, Science, and Transportation Committee. Of course, he has also lobbied for the rights of veterans and pushed to normalize relations with Vietnam, a goal he realized on July 11, 1995. His early record was punctuated by the passage of the line-item veto, a power given to the president to erase certain elements of a bill, usually inserted by congresspersons trying to add special interest or narrow constituent issues on to a larger, unrelated bill (called "pork barrel" politics). Though the federal courts eventually struck down the law in 1997, McCain became known as the champion fighting against pork, even hiring a staff member to sit in the Senate and spot any instances of such dealings at all hours.

McCain also rankled fellow Republicans when he took up the issue of campaign finance reform. Wanting to make sweeping changes to the way fundraising is handled, he joined forces withDemocrat Russell

Feingold around 1995. They sought to hammer out a bill to limit private donations to public office, as well as to even out the balance between lushly funded incumbents and their opponents. The unpopular measure was not taken seriously at first. "We were like the guys who introduced the metric system," McCain told Michael Lewis in the *New York Times Magazine*. Though Democrats have come out heavily in support of the idea, Lewis observed, "Their enthusiasm derives from their certainty that Republicans will find a way to kill it." The bill's most lofty intention was to close the loophole that allows parties to accept general donations then re-route them to specific candidates; these funds are called "soft money." The House of Representatives passed a version of the bill in August of 1998, but it looked as though the Senate was going to block it.

At perhaps the lowest point in McCain's career, he was embarrassed back in 1989 in a case of campaign financing of his own. One of the notorious "Keating Five," McCain, along with senators John Glenn, Donald Riegle, Dennis DeConcini, and Alan Cranston, were implicated in a scandal to protect Charles Keating, the owner of Lincoln Savings and Loan. Keating gave generously to the senators and in return expected them to shelter him from federal bank regulators after his dealings ruined his financial institution and cost taxpayers more than $3 billion to bail out. The Senate Ethics Committee investigated and found that although McCain exercised "poor judgment," according to Lewis, he was not guilty of any wrongdoing. The affair hurt his reputation in the short term, but not fatally, since he was re-elected in 1992. McCain's later efforts, in addition to campaign reform, included an attention-getting $516 billion proposed bill that made tobacco companies more vulnerable to lawsuits filed by smokers and their families. He further proposed to sharply increase taxes on the substance. It made headlines for much of the first half of 1998, until it was voted down, basically due to its emphasis on raising taxes to those who buy tobacco products. In addition, McCain was also involved in a telecommunications reform measure, pushing to install Internet connections in schools, cut satellite and cable television costs, and introduce local telephone competition.

Though he is often controversial among his colleagues thanks to the campaign reform bill, pork-watching, and more, McCain is widely respected and some have hinted that he might be in the running for a presidential nomination after Clinton's term expires in 2000. In an article by Candy Crowley on the All Politics web site, he noted, "It's flattering, but we also know that I am less than conventional in many respects." However, some are convinced that his high-profile tobacco bill, as well as the campaign contribution bill, were measures to drum up publicity for himself before his bid. House Majority Leader Dick Armey, a Republican, told Todd J. Gilman in the *Dallas Morning News*, "John McCain's whole idea of campaign finance reform was inadequate and unacceptable and not something that I believe John McCain would have been the least interested in if he weren't running for president."

McCain married his first wife, Carol, in 1965 and adopted her two sons, Doug and Andrew. They also had a daughter together, Sidney Ann. After McCain's much-publicized affair with another woman, they divorced in 1980, and he married Cindy Hensley. They have four children, Meghan, Jack, Jimmy, and Bridget. McCain lives about two hours outside of Phoenix, Arizona, where he enjoys socializing with friends and family.

Sources

On-line

"Who Is Sen. John McCain?," May 18, 1998, All Politics web site, http://allpolitics.com (May 27, 1998).

"U.S. Senator John McCain," U.S. Senate web site, http://www.senate.gov (July 12, 1998).

Periodicals

Capitol Hill Press Releases, January 20, 1998.
Dallas Morning News, August 13, 1998, p. 32A.
Esquire, May 1, 1998, p. 94.
New York Times, June 1, 1998; August 9, 1998.
New York Times Magazine, May 25, 1997, p. 32.
Time, November 17, 1986, p. 45.
U.S. News & World Report, March 28, 1983; December 18, 1995.
Wall Street Journal, June 19, 1998, p. A14.

—Geri Speace

Carolyn McCarthy

U.S. Representative

Born Carolyn Cook, January 5, 1944, in Brooklyn, NY; daughter of Thomas (a boilermaker) and Irene (a homemaker and sales clerk) Cook; married Dennis McCarthy (an office manager), 1967 (divorced but re-married; died, 1993); children: Kevin. *Education:* Attended nursing school, received L.P.N.

Addresses: *Home*—Mineola, NY. *Office*—1725 Longworth Bldg., Washington, DC 20515.

Career

Licensed practical nurse and homemaker, c.1967-97; Democratic U.S. Representative, Fourth Congressional District, Long Island, NY, 1997—.

Sidelights

When Carolyn McCarthy returned to her suburban Mineola, New York, home from a Christmas concert in early December of 1993, her brother Tom was waiting outside to tell her that her husband was dead and her son was seriously injured. The former nurse and homemaker would later learn that a gunman had shot 25 people on the Long Island commuter train they were riding, killing six, including her husband, Dennis. Prospects looked extremely bleak for her son Kevin as well, with doctors giving him only a ten percent chance of survival, and even then, they expected him to suffer severe brain damage. The normally mild-mannered McCarthy went into full gear to care for her son with a zeal, who eventually made almost a full recovery and was able to return to work. She then led a vehement campaign for gun con-

trol, and upon learning that her congressman was voting to repeal a ban on assault weapons for which she had helped lobby, she decided to take his place. McCarthy had been a registered Republican for a long time, but found that her party was not willing to support her. She switched tickets and ran as a Democrat, managing to unseat her district's representative, Dan Frisa, 57 percent to 41 percent. She was sworn in on January 1, 1997, just before she turned 53.

McCarthy was born Carolyn Cook in Brooklyn, New York, to Thomas and Irene Cook. Her father was a boilermaker and her mother was a homemaker who also held a job for a while as a salesperson. McCarthy and her family, which included three siblings, grew up in the suburban Long Island town of Mineola, New York, in a house where she would live her whole life and later raise her own son. As a youth, McCarthy enjoyed sports and considered becoming a physical education teacher. However, school was often difficult for her; years later she found out that she was dyslexic. The condition, which affects learning and reading skills, still plagues her.

When McCarthy was in high school, her career plans changed when her boyfriend was in a terrible car accident and his family hired a nurse to take care of him.

The nurse asked McCarthy to assist her, and she was exposed to caring for a person. However, the boy died a few days later, and that very day, McCarthy applied to nursing school. She became a licensed practical nurse and devoted herself to caring for the people "nobody else would touch," as she noted to Jonathan Mandell in *Good Housekeeping*. Chronically ill patients, badly burned patients, all deserved the same high level of care, in her mind. "Even if a person was dying," she told Mandell, "you made that person comfortable, helped them cross over."

After starting her career, McCarthy met Dennis "Whitey" McCarthy at the beach. A tall blond man, McCarthy was from a large Irish-American family, just as his future wife was. She was a little reluctant to date him, since she was suburban and he lived in the city. But he pursued her, and they were married in 1967. Dennis McCarthy was an office manager at Prudential Securities in Manhattan who called his wife "Cookie," after her maiden name, Cook. Their only child, Kevin, was born in 1967, and he grew up to work as a computer analyst in the same firm as his father, riding the commuter train with him each day. Carolyn McCarthy, meanwhile, had left her job in the intensive care unit after a number of years to become an avid gardener and homemaker. Though the McCarthys divorced at one point, reportedly due to Dennis's problems with alcohol, they reunited and remarried. Active in the outdoors, McCarthy and her husband enjoyed fishing, skiing, and golfing, and spent much of their free time at a ski lodge in Killington, Vermont. They had agreed to buy some nearby property as a retirement getaway shortly before McCarthy's pleasant life was shattered.

On December 7, 1993, McCarthy came home at around 11 p.m. from an evening with a friend at a Christmas concert. She found her brother Tom on the front lawn, as well as a bare Christmas tree that she had asked her husband and son to set up in the house. After McCarthy asked why the tree was still in the driveway, McCarthy's brother told her the news. Dennis and Kevin McCarthy were riding the 5:33 Long Island Rail Road out of New York City's Pennsylvania Station to come home when a mentally ill gunman opened fire on 25 passengers in the car, killing six, including Dennis. Kevin was the worst of the injured, as well. About one-seventh of his brain was shot away, and much of the remaining was exposed and riddled with bullet and bone fragments. His hand was blown apart, too. As Kevin lie in a coma, doctors said he had a ten percent chance of pulling through, and even if he did live, he would probably be a vegetable.

McCarthy, however, was determined to help Kevin survive. She had lost her husband and best friend, and decided she was not going to lose her son as well. At the press conference after the shooting, she spoke up and told the doctor, "Excuse me, you're wrong. He will live. And he will move," she recalled in *Good Housekeeping*. McCarthy vigilantly attended to her son at the hospital, and a week later, he was able to speak. As the weeks progressed, he remained paralyzed on the left side and doctors assumed he would never be able to walk. McCarthy enlisted his friends in shifts to provide physical therapy, continuously moving his arms and legs so that they would not become stiff. He was eventually able to move his fingers on his right hand. Though his left hand and foot remained paralyzed, he learned to walk again with the aid of a brace, thanks in large part to his mother's constant push for him to become rehabilitated. Kevin even went back to work, taking the train daily, to the same job he held before the shooting, even working overtime. He told *Good Housekeeping* that his mother "is more outgoing now, more determined."

Once McCarthy learned more about the incident, she put her persistence to work. She found out that the gunman, Colin Ferguson, was carrying his 9-millimeter semiautomatic pistol illegally. He had purchased it in California and did not have a permit for it in New York. However, the 15-round magazine he was using was legal, and so were the destructive Black Talon bullets, designed to spread apart on impact in order to cause greater injury. McCarthy and other victims and victims' families filed lawsuits against the company that produced the gun, the bullets, and the clip, but it was thrown out. In addition, a governor's aide at one point asked her to lend support to a state bill to ban assault weapons. This experience fueled her spirit. As time progressed, McCarthy became a vehement activist.

Trying to garner support for her cause, McCarthy began speaking at rallies and lobbying Congress to ban assault weapons. "I couldn't change those events," McCarthy stated in the *Washington Post*, "but I could try to make sure it never happened again to anyone else." In 1994 the Crime Bill outlawed 19 such weapons, including the 15-round magazine that was used in her husband's shooting. Meanwhile, beginning in February of 1995, McCarthy and the other victims had to endure a horrific trial in which the defendant, Ferguson, acting as his own lawyer, sadistically questioned the very victims that he had wounded. He eventually received 200 years in prison.

After the trial, McCarthy found her battle was starting all over again when a new set of representatives in Congress planned to repeal the bill she worked so hard to get passed. She traveled to Washington, D.C. in order to bend some ears. Her own congressman, Republican Dan Frisa, voted to repeal the bill, despite what had happened on the train. Though he told McCarthy that he wanted to develop a more inclusive bill that would eliminate semiautomatic weapons altogether, McCarthy doubted his sincerity, because the bill seemed destined for failure. According to *Ms.*, McCarthy at the time commented to a friend, "I'm gonna run against this guy and I'm gonna beat this guy." The angry threat gradually became a serious idea. The longtime registered Republican found that her party was unwilling to encourage her, so McCarthy ran as a Democrat. "Carolyn is stronger politically than either the Democrats or Republicans because she's neither," former New York Mayor Mario Cuomo commented in the *Los Angeles Times*. "She is where most Americans are. They'll all call themselves something but they would prefer to tell you what they don't like about either party."

Throughout the race, Frisa and some media commentators criticized McCarthy as being a one-issue candidate. "At least I have an issue!" she retorted in *People*. Also, McCarthy pointed out that her lobbying efforts gave her insight into the workings of Washington, and she further responded by outlining her broader concerns in addition to gun legislation. "It's not about guns alone," she told Dan Barry in the *New York Times*. "It's about Head Start. It's about drug-free schools, it's about job opportunities." She learned the hard way about the flaws in the health care system when Kevin needed emergency treatment after the shooting, and has spoken out about reform in that industry. She has a strong pro-choice stance, and advocates spending for education, environmental protection, and welfare reform. All the other knowledge that she needs, she figured she could get on the job, just like the other freshman congressmen always have. "What did I know about guns three years ago?" McCarthy asked in *People*. "I learned. I had to." She also had an open mind on crime policy, stating that although she personally opposed the death penalty, she would vote for it if her constituents desired it.

On November 5, 1996, McCarthy unseated Frisa after his first term in office with 57 percent of the vote as opposed to Frisa's 41 percent. As the representative from the Fourth CongressionalDistrict of New York, she speaks for a generally suburban area on Long Is-

land composed of a mix of working-class, upper-class, and upper-middle-class people. About a quarter of her constituents are African American and Latino and most commute into New York City for their jobs. Only about two out of three are registered Democrats. As a new representative, McCarthy did not land her preferred committee assignments to the House Commerce, Judiciary, Appropriations, or Ways and Means committees. She was instead placed on the House Education and Workforce Committee, which oversees the entire range of learning in the country from preschool to adult education, and the House Small Business Committee, designed to help and protect small businesses, especially in regards to financial assistance.

After starting her new career, McCarthy was not shy to ask for help. "In nursing, I learned never to be afraid to ask a question, because if you don't ask, someone could die," she told Jeffrey Zaslow in *USA Weekend*. In her first term, she worked with fellow New Yorkers Senator Alfonse D'Amato and Representative Peter T. King to draft a bill helping legal immigrants. Reflecting her pro-choice stand, she voted against a ban on partial birth abortions. She also supported funding for the National Endowment for the Arts and opposed military funding, school choice, and the requirement to notify parents when their children seek family planning. Though she fought for a law requiring child-proof safety locks on all handguns, the measure has not survived. The *New York Times Magazine* reported that she pointed out in an address on the House floor: "It's a simple safety lock. We have bills that make it impossible for children to get in an aspirin bottle. Do my colleagues not think we should do the same thing with a gun?"

In May of 1998, NBC aired a television movie, *The Long Island Incident,* based on McCarthy's life and the events surrounding the shooting and her subsequent political career. Initially, she was against the project, but then learned that since the information was in the public domain, it would be made without her consent if necessary. She cooperated closely with the writers and was allowed quite a bit of control with the script, and she and Kevin were on the set during much of the filming. McCarthy was also on track to write her autobiography, but it was later put on hold. The small-built, blond congresswoman has an apartment in Washington when she is not at home in Mineola. Though she misses her husband, Dennis, McCarthy told Tamara Jones in the *Washington Post*, "You have to keep moving forward."

Sources

On-line

"Carolyn McCarthy Biography," U.S. House of Representatives web site, http://www.house.gov (July 12, 1998).

Periodicals

Good Housekeeping, September 1996, p. 64.
Los Angeles Times, July 5, 1996, p. E1; May 3, 1998, p. 3.
Ms., September/October 1996, p. 19.
Nation, November 1, 1996, p. 15.
Newsday, February 26, 1998, p. B3; May 12, 1998, p. A34.
New York Times, April 12, 1996, p. B6; May 29, 1996, p. B1; October 12, 1996, p. B15; January 8, 1997, p. B6.
New York Times Magazine, June 22, 1997, p. 20.
People, September 9, 1996, p. 75.
USA Weekend, May 1-3, 1998, p. 26.
Washington Post, August 27, 1996, p. B1.

—Geri Speace

Ewan McGregor

Photograph by Liam Longman/ The Kobal Collection

Actor

Born c. 1971, in Crieff, Scotland; married Eve Maurakis (a costume designer and writer), c. 1995; children: Clara. *Education:* Studied acting at Guildhall School of Music and Drama, late 1980s.

Addresses: *Home*—London, England. *Agent*—United Talent Agency, 9560 Wilshire Blvd., Suite 500, Beverly Hills, CA 90212.

Career

Apprenticed at the Perthshire Repertory Theater, mid-1980s; cast in the British television series *Lipstick on Your Collar,* 1992; made film debut with the role of Alvarez in *Being Human;* appeared in first lead role as Alex in *Shallow Grave,* 1994; appeared as Renton in *Trainspotting,* and as Frank Churchill in *Emma,* both 1996; as Robert in *A Life Less Ordinary,* and in *The Pillow Book, Nightwatch, Brassed Off, The Serpent's Kiss,* all 1997; in *Velvet Goldmine,* c. 1998; and as Obi Wan Kenobi in the *Star Wars* prequel.

Sidelights

Scottish actor Ewan McGregor has achieved renown through his performances in several tough, but disparate independent film roles since the mid-1990s. Not yet thirty, McGregor has appeared as a heroin addict, an eighteenth-century seducer, a Seventies-era rock star, and has been cast to play a young Obi Wan Kenobi in the upcoming prequel to the *Star Wars* saga. Moreover, McGregor has become virtually a household name in the United States—not an easy market to crack for an entertainer with both intensity and an accent.

Writing for the *New York Times,* Michael Dwyer compared McGregor to two other successful "Brit Pack" stars, Daniel Day-Lewis and Gary Oldman, and noted that many who have worked with McGregor describe him as "the most interesting actor to come out of Scotland since Sean Connery."

The son of teachers, McGregor grew up in the Scottish town of Crieff and attended Morrison's Academy until he was sixteen. He was an admittedly indifferent student, and was far more interested in following in the footsteps of his uncle, an actor who had appeared in all three *Star Wars* films. McGregor was taken to the theater to see Denis Lawson on the screen when he was just five or six years old, and the experience stuck with him. His uncle continued to be a profound influence in other ways—"he had long hair, beads, and a furry waistcoat," McGregor commented to Richard Corliss of *Time.* "I aspired to be as different as he seemed to me."

By the mid-1980s, still in his teens, McGregor began working behind the scenes at the Perthshire Repertory Theater. He then won entry into London's Guildhall School of Music and Drama, and remained there for three years. His first professional acting job was a plum one—he appeared in the 1992 British television series *Lipstick on Your Collar,* the work of the acclaimed writer Dennis Potter. From there, McGregor was cast in his first film role by Scottish director Bill Forsyth, but spoke only one line in *Being Human,* a movie that bombed at the box office.

McGregor found his metier, however, when director Danny Boyle cast him in a darkly comic 1994 film called *Shallow Grave.* In it, McGregor played a young journalist who is suddenly dealing with the ramifications of a mysterious, freshly deceased roommate and a large sum of cash, both of which he and his two other Edinburgh flatmates have somehow co-inherited. *Shallow Grave* was a surprise hit in the United States as well as in the British Isles, and McGregor's performance led Boyle to cast him in the lead role for his next film.

McGregor played Renton, the central character in *Trainspotting,* a tale of loser Edinburgh junkies waging a futile, halfhearted war against their heroin addiction. Released in both the U.K. and U.S. in 1996, the adaptation of a novel by English writer Irvine Welsh quickly became a cult hit on both sides of the Atlantic. It was a somewhat controversial one as well for the rather objective take on drug abuse at the hands of Welsh, Boyle, and physician-turned-screenwriter John Hodge. For the role, McGregor lost nearly thirty pounds to play a convincingly emaciated junkie, and his comic turn as the cheeky Renton made him almost famous—or at least quite well known among the film's under-30 target audience.

In a rather abrupt departure, McGregor's next role after finishing work on *Trainspotting* called for horseback riding, top hats, and elegant Jane Austen prose—he was cast as Frank Churchill in the screen adaptation of *Emma,* which hit screens in 1996 as well. He admitted the switch from modern-day urban dope fiend to refined literary character was a bit precipitous in the end. "I was terrible in [*Emma*]," McGregor told Dwyer in the *New York Times.* "I didn't believe a word I said."

He was next cast as a deranged kidnapper in another Boyle film, *A Life Less Ordinary,* opposite Cameron Diaz (1997). In a marked departure from *Shallow Grave* and *Trainspotting,* Boyle shot this film in Utah, a state that to McGregor quickly appeared far more "foreign" to him than New York or Los Angeles had been from Scotland.

Another challenging role came when McGregor was cast in acclaimed director Peter Greenaway's 1997 film *The Pillow Book.* In it, the actor played a bisexual man whose skin is the canvas for the calligraphic writings of a Hong Kong woman, played by Vivian Wu. The role called for a great deal of frontal nudity, but McGregor admitted that having to stand for hours while the makeup artists prepared his back was far more excruciating.

Another McGregor film released in the United States came in the form of *Brassed Off,* the saga of an English brass band, a closing coal mine, and a town that will never recover. This script interested McGregor, he later said, more for its pro-labor, anti-Thatcherite political overtones than for the chance it allowed him to use his French horn skills from his youth.

Unique and challenging film scripts seem to find McGregor on their own. Another plum lead—this time as a master gardener—arrived for the actor in the form of *The Serpent's Kiss.* Shown at the Cannes International Film Festival in 1997, the movie was described by Dwyer of the *New York Times* as "a story of landscape gardening, sexual intrigue and deceit set in Gloucestershire, England, in 1699."

From there, McGregor donned glitter makeup and platform shoes for his role in *Velvet Goldmine,* a film in which he plays a London glam-rocker in the early 1970s. Coming full circle to his childhood experience, McGregor was cast by George Lucas as the young Obi Wan Kenobi in the *Star Wars* prequel scheduled to be released later in the decade.

Despite landing the much-coveted role in such a potentially huge movie, McGregor confessed that he has never wished for blockbuster-type stardom. The Hollywood action movie, he noted in an E! Online interview, does not interest him in the least, and mentioned a hit American film laden with aliens and special effects, including an exploding White House. "I would shoot myself in the head before I was in a film like that, I really would," McGregor told E!'s Strauss. "I think it's disgraceful."

Far more challenging tasks than dodging spaceships seem to be in McGregor's future. He lives in London with his wife, a French film production designer, and their toddler daughter Clara—who will be taken to seen her father as Obi Wan Kenobi right about the same age as her father was back in 1977 when he saw his kin in the original *Star Wars.* "I've been very lucky, always having something to go on to when I finish something else," McGregor reflected on his career in the *New York Times* article. "And now I even have the opportunity to choose what I do. It can't get better."

Sources

On-line

"Q & A: Ewan McGregor," *E! Online—The Hot Spot,*
http://www.eonline.com (February 5, 1998).

Periodicals

New York Times, June 1, 1997, section 4, p. 17; October
24, 1997, section E, p. 12.
Time, July 15, 1996, pp. 64-66; November 3, 1997.

—*Carol Brennan*

Sarah McLachlan

Singer, songwriter, and guitarist

Born January 28, 1968, in Halifax, Nova Scotia, Canada; daughter of Jack (a marine biologist) and Dorice McLachlan; married Ashwin Sood (a drummer), February, 1997. *Education:* Attended Nova Scotia College of Art and Design.

Addresses: *Home*—Montreal, Canada. *Office*—c/o Arista Records, 6 West 57th St., New York, NY 10019.

Career

Trained in classical guitar, piano, and voice; worked as a dishwasher and counter person in Halifax, Nova Scotia; performed with new wave band; signed to Nettwerk Records, 1987, and released debut album, *Touch*, 1988; contributed "Hold On" to *No Alternative* compilation, Arista, 1993.

Awards: Grammy Awards, for best female pop vocal performance, for "Building a Mystery," and best pop instrumental performance, for "Last Dance," both 1998; Elizabeth Cady Stanton Visionary Award, 1998, from New York Governor George E. Pataki. Juno Awards, 1998, for album of the year, for *Surfacing*, female vocalist of the year, single of the year, for "Building a Mystery," and songwriter of the year, for "Building a Mystery."

Sidelights

Canadian singer-songwriter Sarah McLachlan helped usher in a new era of women musicians during the 1990s. Along with artists such as Paula Cole, Tori Amos, and Sinead O'Connor, McLachlan permeated the airwaves with a female sound and perspective, one with an ethereal but strong quality and poetic, intelligent lyrics. Her 1994 album, *Fumbling Toward Ecstasy,* firmly established her as one of the preeminent feminist musicians on the charts, a reputation she reinforced when she assembled the popular Lilith Fair music festival in summer of 1997 featuring a strictly female bill. The Lilith Fair was reprised in 1998 to huge crowds, outselling other megatours, H.O.R.D.E. and Lollapalooza. Though Lilith Fair was promoted as being by and about women, McLachlan made it very clear it was not just for women. "I've been clear from the beginning that this isn't about excluding men," she told Chris Dickinson in the *St. Louis Post-Dispatch.* "Men are welcome. It's about celebrating that women finally have a voice after centuries, and people are finally listening."

McLachlan was born on January 28, 1968, in Halifax, Nova Scotia, Canada. She was adopted by Jack and Dorice McLachlan, who also have two adopted sons. Her father was an American marine biologist, and both parents were jazz fans who also exposed their daughter to artists such as Simon and Garfunkel, Joan Baez, and Cat Stevens. "I listened to those records for 10 or 12 years," McLachlan told Nicholas Jennings in *Maclean's.* "That's where my biggest influences lie."

When McLachlan was young, she was a an introvert and outsider who spent much of her time composing songs. Her strict parents limited television watching to half an hour a day, andthey enrolled her in a music conservatory for classical training at age seven. She studied music for years, taking 12 years of guitar lessons, six years of piano, and five years of voice, even though she grew weary of classical and yearned for a change.

While McLachlan was in high school, her parents began to worry when she started befriending punk rockers and dropouts. Before her musical breakthrough, McLachlan toiled away as a dishwasher and counter person at establishments in Halifax. At age 17, the young skate punk was singing for a band called the October Game, a new wave band with a gothic-folk sound that was influenced by Kate Bush and Erasure. One night in 1985, when the band opened for the Vancouver band Moëv at a Dalhousie University club, one of the owners of the Vancouver label Nettwerk, Mark Jowett, caught McLachlan's act and offered to sign her. "Here was this quasi-goofy teenage girl, still wearing braces on her teeth, singing a Blondie cover," Jowett recalled to Jennings in *Maclean's*. "But she had this warmth, and a voice that lured people right in. She really captivated me."

McLachlan's parents, however, were reluctant to let their daughter move clear across the continent (Nova Scotia is on the Atlantic Ocean, while Vancouver is on the west coast) to enter the world of rock and roll. They were concerned that she would fall into drugs. So in 1986 she enrolled at the Nova Scotia College of Art and Design, where she studied jewelry and textiles. While she was there, McLachlan serendipitously found her birth mother, Judy Kaines, an artist who worked with her college roommate. When the roommate noticed a startling resemblance, Kaines and McLachlan realized the connection. Later, McLachlan's parents eventually relented on the record deal, and Nettwerk signed McLachlan in 1987. She released her debut album, *Touch*, in 1988, when she was just 20 years old. From the beginning, McLachlan's voice was compared to singers like Joni Mitchell, Kate Bush, Sinead O'Connor, and Tori Amos, and possessed a remarkable range and clarity. Her debut sold 200,000 copies and dealt with mostly introspective issues.

McLachlan subsequently released *Solace* in 1991, which was widely praised and marked a noticeable step in musical maturity. While *Touch* focused on romance and soul-searching, *Solace* began to fuse self-discovery with subjects like abortion and animal rights, although she continued to explore gender issues and relationships

as well. In 1992 the singer's political perspective was expanded further when she traveled to Cambodia and Thailand for the World Vision charity group. There, she was saddened to view the devastating effects of AIDS, poverty, and prostitution, as well as thousands of photographs of the victims of Cambodian leader Pol Pot's regime during the 1970s. This experience influenced her songwriting immensely, swinging her away from writing about victimization and self-pity. In her next album, *Fumbling Toward Ecstasy*, 1994, critics noted McLachlan's broader, more political scope even while the songs themselves still mainly concerned interpersonal relationships. This album, too, was enthusiastically received, and went platinum She followed it up by releasing a multimedia CD-ROM containing reworked and inherently different-sounding versions of the tunes on *Fumbling*, as well as a cover of Tom Waits's "Ol' 55" (which was used on the soundtrack to the film *Boys on the Side*) and some biographical data.

In 1997, McLachlan came out with her biggest album to date, *Surfacing.* Boasting the hit singles "Sweet Surrender" and "Building a Mystery," this CD also went platinum and won two Grammy Awards in 1998: best female pop vocal performance, for "Building a Mystery," and best pop instrumental performance, for "Last Dance." Her melancholy melodies continued to attract fans and *Surfacing* sold over three million copies. Riding on the wave of this success, McLachlan put together an idea that was brewing for a year or two: an all-women musical tour. She had organized a popular four-date mini-tour in the summer of 1996 and felt that in 1997, she was ready to give it her full effort. Frustrated that the large megatours like H.O.R.D.E. and Lollapalooza were overlooking female talent, McLachlan assembled a list in hopes of showcasing a diverse collection of women artists. She admitted to David E. Thigpen in *Time* that she wanted to see the show come together for selfish reasons: "I was touring a lot and there was an incredible amount of talent out there, musicians that I loved, and I wasn't getting to see anybody play live." In addition, she was angry that promoters felt that having a female-dominated bill would not work. When she would suggest a female opening act for her tours, they would tell her, "You can't put two women on the same bill. There's not a wide enough audience for that," as she recalled to Thigpen. Defiantly, she set out to prove them wrong, and did.

The result of McLachlan's idea was the Lilith Fair, so named after a character in Jewish folklore. Lilith was said to be the first wife of Adam, created out of dust just like him rather than a rib, but her refusal to submit and her insistence on being treated as an equal led to her exile. Later, the headstrong woman's ghost returned to stir trouble in the Garden of Eden. The rotating all-female lineup in 1997 included Tracy Chapman, Joan Osborne, Fiona Apple, Jewel, Paula Cole, and The Cardigans, not to mention McLachlan herself. For every ticket sold, the Lilith Fair donated $1 to a local nonprofit group in each city it played, and in addition donated $700,000 to women's charities. The collection of about 60 singers and songwriters worked in conjunction, rather than competition, thanks in part to a more open attitude toward female artists in mainstream music. After women like Alanis Morissette and Jewel hit the airwaves in the mid-1990s and overtook the charts, the doors were opened for many more. McLachlan told to Christopher John Farley in *Time* that previously, she was pitted against Tori Amos for airplay, noting, "That was very marginalizing because our music is completely different. They were saying, 'Go away—we've added our token female this week." By the end of August, the Lilith Fair had raked in more ticket sales than either H.O.R.D.E. or Lollapalooza, earning over $16 million on its seven-week, 38-date run.

Not surprisingly, the success of Lilith Fair led to a repeat in summer of 1998. This time, McLachlan took pains to get a more representative batch of performers, including those from the country and rap genres. She brought together names such as soul artist Erykah Badu, hip-hop's Missy "Misdemeanor" Elliot, and country singers Emmylou Harris, Bonnie Raitt, and Shawn Colvin, in addition to acts like Luscious Jackson, Lisa Loeb, Natalie Merchant, and the Indigo Girls. The tour expanded to 57 shows, and McLachlan laid plans to take the fair to Europe, Australia, and Japan as well. Roughly 70 percent of the audiences were female, ranging from tattooed teens to middle-aged moms. McLachlan was pleased but not surprised by the overwhelming success. "When we started doing this, they said it wouldn't work because women don't buy tickets and don't buy T-shirts and on and on," she remarked to Robert Hilburn in the *Los Angeles Times*. "And there was all this talk about what a risk we were taking. Well, I guess I am just naive because I didn't see it as that. I knew women liked music ... and guess what? I was right."

In 1998, McLachlan received four Juno Awards (Canada's equivalent of the Grammys), for album of the year, for *Surfacing;* for single of the year, for "Building a Mystery;" for songwriter of the year, for "Building a Mystery;" for female vocalist of the year. Also in 1998, New York Governor George E. Pataki honored her with the Elizabeth Cady Stanton Visionary Award,

named after an important America women's rights activist. When McLachlan is not touring, she lives in Vancouver, British Columbia, Canada, in a neighborhood known as Dunbar. She eloped with her drummer, Ash Sood, in Negril, Jamaica, in February of 1998; the two had worked together since 1991 and been dating since 1995. They had a small reception afterward back in Vancouver. The two enjoy walking their black Labrador retriever, Rex, and socializing with friends. McLachlan also likes to bake cookies and paint, and she sells her artwork through her catalog, Murmur. She has expressed interest in starting a family and is finally comfortable with her position as a role model to many young women. As she told Jennings in *Maclean's*, she used to think, "Don't look up to me— I'm more messed up than anybody I know." Later, as she became more self-confident, she gradually embraced the responsibility. "I'm feeling really strong at the moment," McLachlan stated, "ready for anything the world throws at me."

Selected discography

Touch, Nettwerk, 1988.
Solace, Nettwerk, 1991, BMG/Arista, 1992.
(Contributor) "Hold On," *No Alternative*, BMG/Arista, 1993.
Fumbling Toward Ecstasy, Nettwerk, 1993, BMG/Arista, 1994.
The Freedom Sessions (multimedia CD-ROM), Nettwerk, 1994, BMG/Arista, 1995.
Rarities, B-Sides, and Other Stuff, Nettwerk, 1996.
Surfacing (includes "Building a Mystery" and "Sweet Surrender"), BMG/Arista, 1997.

Sources

On-line

"Sarah McLachlan: Arista Records Official Web Page Biography," Arista Records web site, http://www.aristarec.com/aristaweb/SarahMcLachlan (July 12, 1998).
"Sarah McLachlan," Juno Awards web site, http://www.Juno-Awards.ca (September 24, 1998).
Sarah McLachlan Official web site, http://www.sarahmclachlan.com (August 14, 1998).

Books

Contemporary Musicians, vol. 12, Gale Research, 1994.

Periodicals

Biography, August 1998, p. 106.

Boston Irish Reporter, August 1, 1995.
Business Wire, January 14, 1998.
Entertainment Weekly, June 19, 1998, p. 28.
Los Angeles Times, June 21, 1998, p. 4.
Maclean's, March 28, 1994, p. 59; July 28, 1997, p. 48.
Newsday, March 17, 1995, p. B19; July 20, 1997, p. C12.
People, October 20, 1997, p. 81.
St. Louis Post-Dispatch, July 10, 1997, p.24.
Time, July 21, 1997, pp. 45, 60.

—Geri Speace

Kate Michelman

President of NARAL

Born August 4, 1942; married and divorced; married Frederic Michelman (a professor); children: (from first marriage) Lisa, Natasha, Anya. *Education:* University of Michigan, B.A. in psychology and art history, 1966.

Addresses: *Home*—Washington, D.C. *Office*—National Abortion and Reproductive Rights Action League, 1156 15th St. NW, Suite 700, Washington, D.C. 20005.

Career

Pennsylvania State University, Hershey, PA, clinical assistant professor, 1978-80; Adams County Early Childhood Services, Gettysburg, PA, executive director, 1978; Planned Parenthood of the Capitol Region, Harrisburg, PA, 1980-85; National Abortion and Reproductive Rights Action League, Washington, D.C., president and executive director, 1985—.

Sidelights

Abortion is a topic that raises emotions on both sides of the argument like perhaps no other in contemporary American politics. Coming down firmly on the side of protecting women's right to choose is Kate Michelman, the president and executive director of the National Abortion and Reproductive Rights Action League (NARAL), a lobbying group in Washington, D.C. Taking the reins as the group's leader in 1985, Michelman has fought to keep abortion legal and to prevent the government from attaching restrictions or roadblocks to abortion, such as parental consent. The mother of three and a doting grandmother,

Michelman's zeal for this issue stems from a personal incident which changed her perspective on abortion and the laws that govern it.

Michelman was raised in New Jersey and moved to Ohio as a teenager. Since the time she was young, she had a social conscience. At one point, noticing that the children of Latino farm workers were segregated from the white kids at school, she helped start a club for the groups to get to know each other. As the treasurer of her high school class, she led a drive to sell Christmas trees, with the profits going to buy presents for poor families. Michelman was also suspended once for three days for circulating a petition among students to criticize some of the bad teachers. Growing up in the Catholic faith, she remembered being taught that Catholicism was the only religion to practice. The nuns taught her that "If we ever turned to another religion we'd go to hell, we'd die. At least that's how I took it," Michelman remarked to Jayne Garrison in the *San Francisco Examiner*'s magazine, *Image*. Testing this theory, she once snuck into a Lutheran church to see if God would strike her down. When nothing happened, she realized that perhaps the nuns were incorrect. Nevertheless, she continued to be a practicing Catholic.

Despite her rebellious streak, Michelman married at 20 and settled into the role of being a wife, mother, and homemaker, hoping to eventually have six children. Raised to feel that birth control was against the teachings of God, she had three daughters, Lisa, Natasha, and Anya, in three years. One night, when the girls were still toddlers, ages five, four, and three, Michelman'shusband, a graduate archaeology student at Pennsylvania State University, did not come home. The next day, he reappeared and told her that he was in love with another woman. "Everything I knew about myself and valued, every vision I had, every goal I had, was completely torn asunder," Michelman told Garrison. A couple of weeks later, she learned that she was pregnant again.

Michelman's husband had taken the car and left her with no money and no means to support herself. She signed up for welfare, but felt that she would be unable to get through the rough time and manage her family if she also had to deal with another baby. As a Catholic woman in 1970, a time before abortion was legal, she agonized over her decision alone, without support from family or friends. Finally, she knew that she would never manage to keep her life and her family going if she had to go through the pregnancy. "The all-consuming responsibility for my daughters led me to decide to have an abortion," Michelman wrote in the *Los Angeles Times*. However, the procedure was not easily accessible at that time. Women had to prove that an abortion was necessary for physical or psychological reasons.

Appearing before a panel of four male doctors, Michelman had to explain how she got pregnant, why her husband left her, what kind of a mother she was, and what her finances looked like. After proving that she would not be able to care for her three daughters if she had to go through with the pregnancy, the doctors finally decreed that she could have an abortion. As Michelman waited in the hospital bed for the doctor, the nurse returned and explained that they had forgotten one detail. Married women were required to have their husband's signature in order to get the abortion. Michelman got dressed and searched the campus for her husband, got his agreement, then returned to the hospital. After that, she battled for child support but finally gave up. The local dime store would not even give her credit. She held a part-time job at a campus library and eventually decided that she would not allow herself to become dependent on a man again, reasoning that such reliance leaves women and children in a dangerous position.

Michelman, who earned her bachelor's degree from the University of Michigan in 1966, eventually began working with troubled children as a clinical assistant professor at Pennsylvania State University in 1978 and also served as the executive director of Adams County Early Childhood Services in Gettysburg, Pennsylvania. In 1980 she became executive director of Planned Parenthood of the Capitol Region in Harrisburg, Pennsylvania. In 1985, she became the president and executive director of the National Abortion Rights Action League (NARAL), which promotes the right to a legal and safe abortion. Its group is made up of three areas: a nonprofit group, a lobbying effort, and a charitable arm that donates funds for research and legal work. In 1994 it officially revised its mission to also include reducing the need for abortion through means such as promoting birth control and abstinence and increasing options for contraception, thus changing its name to National Abortion and Reproductive Rights Action League.

Though the federal government legalized abortion in its landmark 1970 decision *Roe v. Wade,* many Americans still vehemently oppose the operation. NARAL, with Michelman at its helm, has been a leading defender of access to abortion, as well as contraception. The group has been cited as one of the most powerful special interest groups in the country. During his time in office, President Bill Clinton issued five executive orders on the issue of abortion and reproductive rights, reversing legislation that banned tests of RU-486, a method of abortion usingpharmaceuticals, and forbid using aborted fetal tissue in medical research, among others. In the late 1990s, NARAL was involved in the hot debate over partial-birth abortion, a procedure used late in pregnancies. A furor arose and many have called for this particular method to be outlawed. The *Dallas Morning News* quoted Michelman as saying, "We're not defending this procedure. That's a medical decision. What I'm defending against is the political intrusion into a medical decision."

Another important issue for the group was getting the word out about the "morning-after" pill, a legal and effective method of preventing pregnancy in which a woman takes a high dosage of birth control pills, which then interrupt the pregnancy, up to 72 hours after having unprotected sex. In addition, individual states have been passing laws that NARAL opposes because they say they restrict free choice. These include waiting periods, by which women seeking abortions must delay the procedure usually for about 24 hours after going into a clinic. Abortion rights proponents argue that this makes it difficult and sometimes impossible for women outside urban areas who must travel long distances to obtain an abortion. Other restrictions include making underage girls have parental consent, which many argue makes sense, since anyone under 18 must have parental consent for other medical operations. However, others say this allows parents to block a girl from going through with the abortion, thus inflicting their choice on the pregnant girl who may not want to complete the pregnancy.

After her first marriage ended, Michelman married Frederic Michelman, now a college professor, whom she met at a campus party when he was a French student. She is reluctant to discuss personal details about her childhood or family, but has agreed to interviews in order to stir publicity for her cause. After her abortion, Michelman opted to leave the Catholic church and became a Quaker. In the *Los Angeles Times,* she called her decision to have an abortion "the right and moral thing to do." Michelman added, "The lessons I learned were that this is a decision we should trust to the women of America. That government and politicians should not interfere in our personal lives. And that ultimately, we must strive to elevate childbear-ing and parenting to a higher moral ground. Our children deserve no less."

Sources

On-line

"About NARAL," NARAL web site, http://www.naral.org (July 12, 1998).

Periodicals

Cosmopolitan, May 1994, p. 206.
Dallas Morning News, June 12, 1997, p. 9A.
Los Angeles Times, August 11, 1996, p. M5; February 27, 1997, p. A18.
Image (San Francisco Examiner), June 21, 1992, p. 6.
Newsday, January 22, 1998, p. A49.
Reuters, January 21, 1997; January 13, 1998.
Rocky Mountain News, January 23, 1997, p. 51A.
San Francisco Chronicle, June 2, 1996.

—Geri Speace

Julianne Moore

Archive Photos

Actress

Born Julie Smith, December 3, 1960, in Fort Bragg, NC; father, an Army colonel and military judge; mother, psychiatric social worker; married John Gould Rubin (actor), 1986 (divorced, 1994); companion of Bart Freundlich (a writer and director); children: (with Freundlich) one son. *Education:* Boston University, School of Fine Arts, B.A.

Address: *Office*—Creative Artists Agency, 9830 Wilshire Blvd., Beverly Hills, CA 90212.

Career

Actress in films, including: *Tales from the Darkside: The Movie,* 1990; *The Hand That Rocks the Cradle,* 1992; *The Gun in Betty Lou's Handbag,* 1992; *Body of Evidence,* 1993; *Benny & Joon,* 1993; *The Fugitive,* 1993; *Short Cuts,* 1993; *Vanya on 42nd Street,* 1994; *Roommates,* 1995; *Safe,* 1995; *Nine Months,* 1995; *Assassins,* 1995; *Surviving Picasso,* 1996; *The Lost World: Jurassic Park,* 1997; *The Myth of Fingerprints,* 1997; *Boogie Nights,* 1997. Television appearances include regular role on *As the World Turns,* 1985-88; role in miniseries, *I'll Take Manhattan,* 1987; and parts in several made-for-TV movies, 1989-91.

Awards: Emmy Award, outstanding ingenue, 1988, for daytime drama *As the World Turns.*

Member: Screen Actors Guild.

Sidelights

Getting attention has always been easy for Julianne Moore. Her long, flaming red hair, and her willingness to play controversial scenes and startling roles in often eccentric films see to that. Portraying a cocaine-addled, maternal porn star in one of the most talked-about films of 1997, *Boogie Nights,* "Moore gives the film its twisted heart," observed Mick LaSalle in the *San Francisco Chronicle.* The *New York Times*'s Janet Maslin called her "wonderful as the vaguely lost soul ... transformed into a porn queen" and said "her studiously bad acting in movie-making scenes is perfect."

Boogie Night's whiz-kid director Paul Thomas Anderson wrote the part of Amber Waves with Moore in mind. The character of Waves, a melancholy, no-talent dropout, is the live-in leading lady for porn director Jack Horner (Burt Reynolds) and a sympathetic den mother to a dysfunctional family of X-rated stars. Moore, who has made a career out of puncturing expectations, plays both sides of the character with disarming directness. When Waves leads rookie Dirk Diggler (Mark Wahlberg) through the paces of his first on-camera sex scene, "Moore plays the scene as though welcoming her son back into the womb," according to LaSalle, who writes that the scene is "many things at once: crude and absurd, a genuine love scene and an initiation, too." LaSalle adds: "On the surface, Amber is a dazed, cocaine-addicted, no-talent, whiny porn star. Yet Moore takes the viewer deep into this woman's pain."

Her ability to show emotional pain in difficult circumstances is one of Moore's most notable talents. She first won widespread notice in 1993 for an unusual scene in Robert Altman's *Short Cuts*. Her character, an emotionally troubled artist, wages a nasty argument with her husband (Matthew Modine), while she is nude from the waist down. Doing the scene was easy, she told Carol Lawson of *Cosmopolitan*, because Altman "makes you feel protected and not exploited.... It's everyday nudity—like when you have no clothes on around your husband." Still, the scene was startling, not only for the unconventional nudity but for Moore's ability to overcome embarrassment and concentrate on her angry lines.

Yet perhaps Moore's most daring role was her first lead performance, in Todd Haynes' 1995 art film *Safe*. She portrayed an upscale but emotionally troubled Los Angeles housewife who develops an overwhelming allergic reaction to almost every aspect of 20th-century life. Recalling her first brush with the film, Moore told James Ryan of *GQ:* "I got to page 10 of that script and I was shaking." She lost ten pounds for the part because, as she put it, "I wanted to look sick." Moore so thoroughly immersed herself in the role that she actually did get sick. "It took me close to a year to recover," she told Ryan.

Her unconventional roles appear to be Moore's way of defining herself with more complexity than her screaming auburn hair does. In interviews, Moore often expresses ambivalence about her striking appearance and a desire to escape its confining definition. "If I wear a hat, people walk right by me," she complained to Ryan. "That's one of the things I don't like. Redheadedness defines me." Still, filmmakers and their audiences continue to be fixated with what's atop Moore's head. "I don't know what's going on with her hair," the late Louis Malle, who directed her in *Vanya on 42nd Street,* once told *People* magazine, (which christened Moore one of the 50 most beautiful people in the world in 1995), "but even in the shadow it shines."

Like many successful entertainers, Moore was a military brat who was a globetrotting child. Born at Fort Bragg, North Carolina, she was one of three children. Her mother was a psychiatric social worker. Her father was an Army colonel and a helicopter pilot who went to law school and became a judge on the U.S. Military Court of Appeals. Family dinner, Moore told Ryan of *GQ*, was "therapy on trial." Moore was raised in 23 different locations, mostly on military bases. The constant relocation, she told Ryan, "makes you adaptable and needy. It makes you open to different societies and mores, but it makes you crave attention."

Moore, a self-described "drama dweeb" as an adolescent, began acting while in high school in Frankfurt, Germany, where her drama coach encouraged her to make a career of it. Her parents, however, wanted her to become a doctor or a lawyer, and so Moore went to Boston University, rather than a drama school, as a compromise. After graduating with a degree in performing arts, Moore moved to Manhattan, where she launched a career in theater and television and married actor John Gould Rubin.

Moore's first notable television role was a short-lived part on the soap opera *Edge of Night*. In 1985, she debuted on *As the World Turns*. For the next three years she played a dual role on the long-running soap as Frannie Hughes and her evil half-sister Sabrina. Moore won an Emmy for her work in 1988. The previous year, she played Valerie Bertinelli's friend in the Judith Krantz miniseries, *I'll Take Manhattan.* Several less notable TV movies followed. During this period, Moore also appeared in a number of off-Broadway plays, including the American premieres of Carol Churchill's *Serious Money* and *Ice Cream with Hot Fudge* at the Public Theatre in New York. She also played Ophelia in a Guthrie Theater production of *Hamlet* in Minneapolis in 1988.

In 1990, Moore made her feature film debut. In *Tales from the Darkside: The Movie,* she played the victim of a deadly mummy. It wasn't much of a part or a movie, but it was a start. Moore got much more notice two years later in the hit movie *The Hand That Rocks the Cradle.* She played an outspoken, glamorous real estate agent who was the best friend of the character played by Annabella Sciorra. Again, Moore's character met a grisly demise, this time in a greenhouse.

The hard-working Moore broke through with multiple roles in 1993. On stage, she played opposite Al Pacino in a theatrical workshop production of Strindberg's *The Father*. On the big screen, in *Body of Evidence,* she played the thankless role of Willem Dafoe's cuckolded wife. In *Benny & Joon,* she was Ruthie, a sexy waitress who is wooed by auto mechanic Aidan Quinn. In *The Fugitive,* she gave a pivotal three-minute performance as Harrison Ford's doctor colleague. She was also part of the large ensemble in *Short Cuts.* Stealing scenes in all four films, Moore became known as someone with a compelling screen presence.

Her success was a little overwhelming for the shy Moore, who once admitted she had trouble breathing in a room full of famous people. Altman's film was full of famous people. "*Short Cuts* really threw me into the fray," she told interviewer Ryan. "It was like a cavalcade of stars. Things got a little easier after that."

Besieged with scripts, Moore showed a strong preference for independent, offbeat films. In 1994, in *Vanya on 42nd Street,* a movie based on Chekhov's novel *Uncle Vanya,* she played the beguiling Yelena, a role she had been performing in theater workshops. The next year, her performance in *Safe* enthralled critics, but failed to excite mass audiences. Also in 1995, in the family drama *Roommates,* Moore played D.B. Sweeney's social worker wife. However, she also played lighter roles in more conventional fare. Now well-known enough to secure parts opposite top male stars, Moore cracked the million-dollar salary mark in the action movie *The Assassins,* where she portrayed a tough, electronics security expert who was also Sylvester Stallone's love interest. She also teamed up with Hugh Grant in the light romantic comedy *Nine Months,* playing Grant's pregnant girlfriend. To prepare for the part, she went to Lamaze classes, and during filming she wore a prosthetic stomach. "It not only looked terrible but it also smelled like a big ol' rotten egg," she told Kim Cunningham of *People* magazine. Ironically, during the making of the film, she was in the process of divorcing her husband, but playing the part heightened her interest in having children.

In 1996, Moore continued to chart her own waters, portraying painter Dora Maar, the long-suffering partner of Pablo Picasso (Anthony Hopkins) in *Surviving Picasso.* Moore's short performance in *The Fugitive* had convinced Stephen Spielberg to cast her, without an audition, in the lead female role of a paleontologist in *The Lost World,* his sequel to *Jurassic Park.* Opening in the summer of 1997, it became a record-breaking, box-office smash, but filming the blockbuster posed special challenges. In one scene, Moore had to hang out of a motor home that had been pushed off a cliff by a *Tyrannosaurus rex.* "I was in a harness that was hoisted 20 feet off the ground," she told Chuck Arnold of *People.* "And the scene went on and on. It was a little scary."

Moore was serving as a judge at the 1995 Sundance Film Festival when someone handed her a script. Its

writer (and future director) was Bart Freundlich, and his story, about an upscale New England family confronting their emotional demons over Thanksgiving dinner, was called *The Myth of Fingerprints.* Moore signed on to play Mia, the oldest, most sophisticated and angriest sibling, and co-starred with Noah Wyle and Blythe Danner. During filming, she connected to Freundlich's understanding of Mia's vulnerability and sense of loss. Despite Moore's feelings that getting involved with a director during a film was off limits, the pair fell in love. When the film opened in late 1997, the couple was living together in Los Angeles, and expecting a baby around Thanksgiving. It was announced in mid-December that Moore had given birth to a boy on December 4.

Moore's prolific but offbeat career continued with a role in Joel and Ethan Coen's *The Big Lebowski,* scheduled for release in 1998. In the film, Moore appears in the brothers' first choreographed production number, wearing a Styrofoam outfit. In *Chicago Cab* (working title *Hellcab*), also scheduled for release in 1998, Moore teamed up with Gillian Anderson and John Cusack. The film is a comedy about a day in the life of a Chicago cabbie during the Christmas season.

Sources

On-line

"Julianne Moore," *Tony Tang Productions,* www.tonytang.com/moore (November 21, 1997).

Periodicals

Cosmopolitan, November 1993, p. 168.
Entertainment Weekly, April 21, 1995, p. 271.
GQ, May 1995, p. 154.
Maclean's, December 1, 1997, p. 76.
People, May 8, 1995, p. 170; August 7, 1995, p. 110; June 9, 1997, p. 124.
Premiere, September 1993, p. 31.
Rolling Stone, October 14, 1993, p. 103.
San Francisco Chronicle, October 17, 1997, p. C1.

—*Michael Betzold*

Toni Morrison

Author

Born Chloe Anthony Wofford, February 18, 1931, in Lorain, OH; daughter of George (a shipyard welder) and Ramah (Willis) Wofford; married Harold Morrison (an architect), 1958 (divorced, 1964); children: Harold Ford, Slade Kevin. *Education:* Howard University, B.A., 1953; Cornell University, M.A., 1955.

Addresses: *Office*—Random House, 201 East 50th St., New York, NY 10022. *Agent*—Lynn Nesbit, International Creative Management, 40 West 57th St., New York, NY 10019.

Career

Texas Southern University, Houston, instructor in English, 1955-57; Howard University, Washington, DC, instructor in English, 1957-64; State University of New York at Purchase, associate professor of English, 1971-72; State University of New York at Albany, Schweitzer Professor of the Humanities, 1984-89; Princeton University, Princeton, NJ, Robert F. Goheen Professor of the Humanities, 1989—. Visiting lecturer, Yale University, 1976-77, and Bard College, 1986-88. Random House, New York City, senior editor, 1965—.

Awards: National Book Award nomination and Ohioana Book Award, both 1975, both for *Sula*; National Book Critics Circle Award and American Academy and Institute of Arts and Letters Award, both 1977, both for *Song of Solomon*; Matrix Award from New York Women in Communications, 1995; New York State Governor's Art Award, 1986; National Book Award nomination and National Book Critics Circle

Award nomination, both 1987, and Pulitzer Prize for fiction and Robert F. Kennedy Award, both 1988, all for *Beloved*; Washington College Literary Award, 1987; Elizabeth Cady Stanton Award from the National Organization of Women; Nobel Prize in literature, 1993; National Book Foundation Medal for Distinguished Contribution to American Letters, 1996.

Member: American Academy and Institute of Arts and Letters, National Council on the Arts, Authors Guild (council), Authors League of America.

Sidelights

Prior to October 1996, Nobel laureate and Pulitzer Prize-winning author Toni Morrison was no stranger to notoriety. She had received media attention for her highly regarded written works, and events in her personal life had gained public attention. Three of her six novels had been bestsellers, and the others had been steady sellers throughout their years in print. Nevertheless, Morrison's fame increased considerably when television talk show host Oprah Winfrey announced on her October 18, 1996, broadcast of *The Oprah Winfrey Show* that Morrison's 1977 novel *Song of Solomon* was the latest selection for Oprah's Book Club. Soon after Winfrey's announcement, Morrison's novel, of which 360,000 paperback copies had been printed between 1987 and October 1996, became a runaway commercial success, selling over 500,000 copies in paperback, hardcover, and on audio cassette and appearing in the top five on the *New York Times* bestseller list.

Song of Solomon, which depicts a black man's quest for identity and discovery of his heritage, is "not an easy read," according to Morrison in an interview with *People*'s Lan N. Nguyen; the narrative style is dense and poetic, and the characters and events are multifaceted and complex. Remarkably, Winfrey's popularity and status as a public role model for many Americans has enabled her to persuade people to read *Song of Solomon* despite the novel's intimidating qualities, and Toni Morrison's works are now being read by an entirely new audience. In a November 19, 1996, online chat led by the *Oprah* show's online host, Morrison was asked by one reader if she had planned "to reach a particular group of readers" with her novels. Morrison replied: "My aim is to reach all readers who are not fearful of being challenged and are willing to take this human journey with me."

Morrison's own "human journey" began on February 18, 1931, in Lorain, Ohio, when she was born Chloe Anthony Wofford, daughter of George and Ramah Wofford. Although her novels are not explicitly autobiographical, they are grounded in her experiences as a child growing up in Ohio, where as an adolescent she read the works of English author Jane Austen, French writer Gustave Flaubert, and classic Russian novelists. In an essay in *Black Women Writers at Work,* Morrison explained the influence of her early years in Ohio on her writing: "I am from the Midwest so I have a special affection for it. My beginnings are always there.... No matter what I write, I begin there.... It's the matrix for me.... Ohio also offers an escape from stereotyped black settings. It is neither plantation nor ghetto."

Morrison's parents were hardworking and very proud of their African American heritage, instilling in their children self-esteem and a desire to distinguish themselves by leading honorable, principled lives. Morrison's father often worked several jobs to support his family, and her mother took a series of low-paying, menial jobs in order to send Morrison money while she was attending college. After graduating with honors from Lorain High School, Morrison attended Howard University in Washington, D.C., where she studied English and earned a bachelor's degree in 1953. It was while she was a student at Howard University that Morrison changed her first name to Toni, because

she had encountered difficulty with people who could not pronounce Chloe. She went on to receive a master's degree in English from Columbia University in 1955.

From 1955 to 1957 Morrison taught English at Texas Southern University in Houston; in 1957 she returned to Howard University as an English instructor. While working at the university, she met a Jamaican architect named Harold Morrison, whom she married in 1958. Ultimately the Morrisons divorced, and in 1964 Toni Morrison took the couple's two young sons, Harold Ford and Slade Kevin, to stay with her at her parent's home in Ohio. After living with her parents for over a year, Morrison found a job as an editor with a textbook subsidiary of Random House in Syracuse, New York. Although she was a single working mother, Morrison managed to compose her first novel, *The Bluest Eye,* by working late into the evenings after her children were asleep.

In 1969 *The Bluest Eye,* which relates the experiences of three pre-teenaged black girls in Lorain, Ohio, was published. The title of the novel comes from the character of Pecola Breedlove, who considers herself ugly and wishes she had blue eyes, which she believes would make her beautiful. After a series of tragedies in her life, Pecola sinks into madness and believes that she possesses the bluest eyes of anyone. *Black American Literature Forum* contributor Phyllis R. Klotman commented: "*The Bluest Eye* is an extraordinarily passionate yet gentle work, the language lyrical yet precise—it is a novel for all seasons."

Morrison's first novel was well received by critics, and in 1973 she followed it with *Sula,* which earned her a 1974 National Book Award nomination. *Sula* focuses on a peculiar relationship between two women, Nel and Sula. Sula, who is regarded within her community as an evil woman, commits murder, stands by as her own mother dies in a fire, and has an affair with her best friend's husband. Nevertheless, she achieves some measure of respect for the personal freedom she demonstrates by her actions. In *Reaching Out: Sensitivity and Order in Recent American Fiction by Women,* Anne Z. Mickelson remarked: "The novel bears the same incompleteness as Sula's search for freedom.... Sula makes of life a defiant gesture which liberates her to an extent, and keeps her from self-pity. She is sustained by her pride in the fact that she walks through life with no blinders on. Yet, there is no happy ending. Sula collapses in the loneliness of the search for freedom, and proves what? That love is necessary? That the human heart cannot entertain equal proportions of good and evil? That everything is not relative? These and other unanswered questions are given more scope in ... *Song of Solomon.*"

Published in 1977, *Song of Solomon* was awarded the National Book Critics Circle Award that same year. The main character of the novel is Milkman Dead, an African American man who acquired his first name when his mother was discovered breast-feeding him when he was four years old. His last name was the result of an error made by a drunken Yankee soldier working for the Freedmen's Bureau, who mistakenly recorded Milkman's grandfather's name as Macon Dead after the man told the soldier that he was born in Macon, Georgia, and his father was dead. Milkman's search for his own identity as well as for his ancestors is the dominant idea in the novel, in which Mickelson declared Morrison "deals ... with the black man who yearns to fly—to break out of the confining life into the realm of possibility—and who embarks on a series of dramatic adventures." Although Milkman figures prominently in the novel, his aunt, named Pilate, according to Mickelson, "emerges as the most powerful figure in the book with her calm acceptance of this world, as well as of another reality other than the fixed one of the world. She is thoroughly at home with herself, and has the kind of sensibility which is not disturbed by anything she experiences or witnesses."

In the *Oprah Winfrey Show*-sponsored online chat with readers, Morrison commented that her favorite underlying theme in *Song of Solomon* is "[t]he place that love plays in the process of becoming an adult." At the beginning of the novel Milkman is torn between Pilate's charitable and generous philosophy and his father's value of material things, and after he searches his roots for an answer to his dilemma, he discovers the importance of community and the nature of love and faith. Critics applauded Morrison's ability to portray Milkman's journey toward understanding, her blending of elements of fantasy and reality, and her use of myths and folklore in the novel. *Song of Solomon* was Morrison's first best-selling novel and established her as a major American writer.

Tar Baby, Morrison's 1981 novel, is set on an isolated West Indian island and focuses on the relationship between Jadine, a black model who was educated in Paris, and Son, a rebellious drifter from Florida. Jadine is attracted to Son but is torn between the young black man and a wealthy white man who has asked her to marry him. Critics interpreted the novel as an examination of what results when one attempts to deny one's heritage and praised Morrison's capacity for presenting such a cultural dilemma in an accessible manner

without resolving the question for the reader. Some commentators faulted the novel as obscure and described the characters as lacking motivation; however, many applauded *Tar Baby*'s intricate symbolism and its insightful treatment of the themes of race, identity, love, and power.

> "*My aim is to reach all readers who are not fearful of being challenged and are willing to take this human journey with me.*"

Morrison's fifth novel, 1987's *Beloved*, is set in a small Ohio town shortly after the end of the Civil War and portrays the trials and tribulations of Sethe, a former slave woman. Sethe, who mistakenly believes that she is going to be returned to slavery, murders her baby daughter, Beloved, so that she will not have to endure the misery of life as a slave. The story of Sethe is based on an actual nineteenth-century magazine article Morrison read while conducting research for *The Black Book*, a history book she was editing. In *Beloved*, twenty years after her death, Sethe's daughter returns from the grave to revenge her murder, and Morrison uses flashbacks, fragmented dialogue, and myths to illustrate the events leading up to Beloved's murder, and why Sethe refused to atone for her crime in the black community.

Critics hailed *Beloved* as a masterpiece, lauding it as one of the finest representations of the hardships of slavery and its psychological consequences ever written. Nevertheless, despite the critical acclaim with which the novel was greeted, it failed to win either the 1987 National Book Award or the National Book Critics Circle Award. In response to what they believed was an outrageous failure to recognize Morrison's talent, forty-eight prominent black American writers and critics, including Maya Angelou, Angela Davis, Alice Walker, John Wideman, and Houston A. Baker, Jr., signed a letter to the editor that appeared in the January 24, 1988, edition of the *New York Times Book Review*. The letter expressed the authors' desire to have Morrison's achievements acknowledged with the "keystone honors," either a National Book Award or a Pulitzer Prize, expressed dismay at what they called the "oversight and harmful whimsy" that had resulted in Morrison's failure to win an award for *Beloved*, and asserted their opinion that "[t]he legitimate need for our own critical voice in relation to our own literature can no longer be denied." The letter concluded with a tribute, in which the authors expressed to Morrison: "For all of America, for all of American letters, you have advanced the moral and artistic standards by which we must measure the daring and the love of our national imagination and our collective intelligence as a people."

The letter generated fierce debate within the New York literary community, with some critics accusing the authors of the letter of racist manipulation. *Beloved* was awarded the Pulitzer Prize for fiction in 1988. In a *New York Times* article by Herbert Mitgang, Morrison, who had no knowledge of the 1987 letter to the editor before it was published, responded to the news that she had won the Pulitzer by remarking, "I think I know what I feel. It's true that I had no doubt about the value of the book and that it was really worth serious recognition. But I had some dark thoughts about whether the book's merits would be allowed to be the only consideration of the Pulitzer committee. The book had begun to take on a responsibility, an extra-literary responsibility that it was never designed for." Most commentators observed that Morrison's winning of the Pulitzer Prize ended the debate sparked by the letter to the editor.

Morrison followed *Beloved* with *Jazz,* a 1992 novel that focuses on the turbulent relationship between its two main characters, Joe and Violet Trace, a black couple from Virginia who move to Harlem in 1906. The novel is set in 1926, but flashes back to events in the past, including Joe's murder of a young girl with whom he had had an affair. *Jazz* explores the themes of jealousy and forgiveness and portrays Harlem in the 1920s as symbolic of freedom and excitement for many African Americans. In a review of *Jazz* in the *Chicago Tribune,* Michael Dorris asserted that the novel is "about change and continuity, about immigration: the belongingness you leave behind and the tied-together suitcase you carry under your arm. It's about coping with arrival in a destination that doesn't let you stay the same person." The novel was generally well received by critics, with only a few objecting to the narrative structure as confusing.

In 1993 Morrison became the first black woman to receive the Nobel Prize in literature. In awarding her the honor, the Swedish Academy called Morrison "a literary artist of the first rank," and commended her ability to give "life to an essential aspect of American reality" in novels "characterized by visionary force and poetic import." The Academy also asserted that Morrison "delves into the language itself, a language

she wants to liberate from the fetters of race. And she addresses us with the luster of poetry." In an article in the *New York Times* William Grimes quoted Morrison as saying: "This is a palpable tremor of delight for me. It was wholly unexpected and so satisfying. Regardless of what we all say and truly believe about the irrelevance of prizes and their relationship to real work, nevertheless this is a signal honor for me." Only two weeks after she had traveled to Stockholm to receive the Nobel Prize, Morrison's Hudson River home was ravaged by fire. The house was almost entirely gutted, but a portion of Morrison's papers kept in a basement study, including some of her original manuscripts, were spared. The fire was started when an ember from the fireplace burst onto a nearby sofa.

Before the auspicious occasion of receiving her Nobel Prize, Morrison had already begun her seventh novel, *Paradise,* which was published in early 1998. The author noted in a *Time* article that she was relieved she had already begun to research the book's historical setting, given the expectations of a Nobel Prize-winning author. "I was so happy that I had a real book idea in progress," Morrison recalled. "If I hadn't, I would have thought, `Uh-oh, can I ever write a novel again?'"

Paradise was generally warmly received by critics who found that the novel lived up to Morrison's previous works. The backdrop of the story is the settling of former slaves in the western United States in the nineteenth century. A group of African American men bring their wives and children to Oklahoma and found the town of Haven, where the inhabitants are haunted throughout the twentieth century by a past of bondage and the rejection they suffer by light-skinned members of their own race. The novel also tackles the issues of female rebellion against a patriarchal society and the search for paradise—some sort of happiness and security—in a less than perfect world. "One of the many pleasures of *Paradise,* for longtime Morrison readers," commented Paul Gray in *Time,* "is watching the way it picks up and elaborates on subjects and themes from the author's earlier works." "With Paradise," declared Brooke Allen in the *New York Times Book Review,* Morrison has brought it all together: the poetry, the emotion, the broad symbolic plan.... It is an ambitious, troubling, and complicated piece of work, proof that Toni Morrison continues to change and mature in surprising new directions."

In addition to her award-winning fiction, Morrison also published *Playing in the Dark: Whiteness and the*

Literary Imagination, her first work of literary criticism. In the 1992 book, which began as a series of lectures she presented at Harvard University, Morrison argues that the importance of black characters in American literature has been downplayed by literary critics. *Playing in the Dark,* which critics praised as an attentive and innovative study of the history of the treatment of race in American literary criticism, is Morrison's attempt to increase the scope of American literary criticism through a type of study she calls American Africanism. In the preface to the book, Morrison explained: "[Until] very recently, and regardless of the race of the author, the readers of virtually all of American fiction have been positioned as white. I am interested to know what that assumption has meant to the literary imagination. When does racial 'unconsciousness' or awareness of race enrich interpretive language, and when does it impoverish it? What does positing one's writerly self, in the wholly racialized society that is the United States, as unraced and all others as raced entail? What happens to the writerly imagination of a black author who is at some level *always* conscious of representing one's own race to, or in spite of, a race of reader that understands itself to be 'universal' or race-free? In other words, how is 'literary whiteness' and 'literary blackness' made, and what is the consequence of that construction?"

With the help of Oprah Winfrey, Morrison's singular writing talents are becoming known to readers who, if they had not been introduced to her works through *The Oprah Winfrey Show,* may never have heard of her. Winfrey's method of getting her audience to identify personally with the authors whose works she has selected for her Book Club has proven effective for Morrison and for other authors. And with Morrison, Winfrey went one step further, buying the rights to adapt *Beloved* for film. The Jonathan Demme-directed motion picture was scheduled for release in the fall of 1998.

An article by the *New York Times*'s Caryn James quoted a comment made by Winfrey on her program as she recalled a telephone conversation she had had with Morrison. Regarding the complex nature of her narrative style, Oprah asked Morrison, "Do people tell you they have to keep going over the words sometimes?" Morrison responded simply: "That, my dear, is called reading." During her appearance on Winfrey's talk show, Morrison commented on the staggering growth of interest in her novel *Song of Solomon* that had been generated by the talk show host's promotion of it, asserting, "To give it a new life that is larger than its original life is a revolution."

Selected writings

The Bluest Eye (novel), Holt, 1969.
Sula (novel), Knopf, 1973.
(Editor) *The Black Book* (anthology), Random House, 1974.
Song of Solomon (novel), Knopf, 1977.
Tar Baby (novel), Knopf, 1981.
Beloved (novel), Knopf, 1987.
Jazz (novel), Knopf, 1992.
Playing in the Dark: Whiteness and the Literary Imagination (nonfiction) Harvard University Press, 1992.
(With Taylor Guthrie and Danille Kathleen) *Conversations with Toni Morrison,* University Press of Mississippi, 1994.
(Editor) *To Die for the People: The Writings of Huey P. Newton,* Writers and Readers, 1995.
Paradise (novel), Knopf, 1998.

Sources

On-line

Swedish Academy Press Release, *The Permanent Secretary,* October 7, 1993, Nobel Prize Internet Archive, http://www.almaz.com.
Transcript of online chat session with Toni Morrison, November 19, 1996, *The Oprah Winfrey Show* website on America Online.

Books

Mickelson, Anne Z., *Reaching Out: Sensitivity and Order in Recent American Fiction by Women,* Scarecrow Press, 1979, pp. 112-74.
Morrison, Toni, *Playing in the Dark: Whiteness and the Literary Imagination,* Harvard University Press, 1992.
Tate, Claudia, editor, *Black Women Writers at Work,* Continuum, 1986, pp. 117-31.

Periodicals

Black American Literature Forum, Winter, 1979, pp. 123-25.
Chicago Tribune—Books, April 19, 1992, pp. 1, 5.
New York Times, January 24, 1988, section 7, p. 36; April 1, 1988, p. B5; October 8, 1993; December 28, 1993; November 21, 1996.
New York Times Book Review, January 11, 1998.
People, December 2, 1996, p. 36.
Time, December 2, 1996, p. 84; January 19, 1998.

—*Lynn M. Spampinato*

Olivia Newton-John

Singer and actress

Born September 26, 1948, in Cambridge, England; daughter of Bryn (a university professor and dean) and Irene (Born) Newton-John; married Matt Lattanzi (a dancer and actor), c. 1984 (divorced, 1995); children: Chloe Rose.

Addresses: *Home*—Malibu, CA. *Office*—c/o MCA, 70 Universal City Plaza, Universal City, CA 91608-1011. *Agent*—c/o Bill Sammeth Organization, P.O. Box 960, Beverly Hills, CA 90213- 0960.

Career

Singer and actress. Recorded over 25 top 40 singles, including five number one hits. Film appearances include *Funny Things Happen Down Under*, 1966; *Toomorrow*, 1970; *Grease*, 1978; *Xanadu*, 1980; *Two of a Kind*, 1983; and *It's My Party*, 1995. Television appearances include movies *The Case*, 1972; *A Mom for Christmas*, 1990; *A Christmas Romance*, 1994; and *Snowden on Ice* (voice over), 1997; and episodes of *Saturday Night Live*, 1982; *Snowy River: The McGregor Saga*, 1994; and *Murphy Brown*, 1997.

Awards: Created Officer of the British Empire (O.B.E.); Best British Girl Singer Award, 1971; Academy of Country Music Award for most promising female vocalist, 1973; Grammy Award for best female country vocal performance, 1973, for "Let Me Be There;" Country Music Association Award, 1974, for female vocalist of the year; Country Music Association (U.K.), female vocalist of the year, 1974 and 1975; American Guild of Variety Artists Award, 1974; *Billboard* magazine awards, 1974, 1975, and 1982; *Cashbox* Award, 1974 and 1975, for number one new female vocalist

(singles), and 1975, for number one new female vocalist (albums); Grammy Award for record of the year, 1974, for "I Honestly Love You;" Grammy Award for best female pop vocal performance, 1974, for "I Honestly Love You;" Record World awards, 1974, 1975, 1976, and 1978; TNN *Music City News* Country Award for Star of Tomorrow, 1974; American Music Awards, 1975 and 1976, for country favorite female vocalist; American Music Award, 1975, for country favorite album, for *Let Me Be There*; American Music Awards, 1975, 1976, 1977, and 1983, for pop/rock favorite female vocalist; American Music Award, 1975, for pop/ rock favorite single, for "I Honestly Love You;" American Music Award, 1976, for pop/rock favorite album, for *Have You Never Been Mellow*; American Society of Composers, Authors and Publishers (ASCAP) Country Music Award, 1975, for "Please Mr. Please;" People's Choice Award, 1975, 1977, and 1979, for female musical performer; People's Choice Award, 1979, for motion picture actress; National Juke Box Award, 1980; Grammy Award for video of the year, 1982, for "Let's Get Physical."

Sidelights

Many fans remember singer Olivia Newton-John as the bubbly blonde cheerleader Sandy in the 1978 film *Grease*, with John Travolta. What they may not remember is that she was also one of the biggest names in music in the 1970s, scoring hit after hit and winning a truckload of awardsfor her country and pop favorites like "Let Me Be There," "I Honestly Love You," "Have You Never Been Mellow," and "Please Mr. Please." With a clean-cut image and gentle, clear voice, Newton-John had a "girl next door" persona, although she did, in fact, hail all the way from Australia. In 1981, she modified her style to come out with the throbbing album *Physical,* helping define that decade as well, with a spunky new hairdo, exercise togs, and a hint of sexual innuendo.

"I appreciate the basic things—spending time at the beach, watching the sun come up. I've learned to value the day.... I try to keep in touch with the fact that life is a gift—that every day is a gift."

Though she continued making records in the 1980s and 1990s, Newton-John backed off of her career for a time to devote herself to raising her daughter and starting a line of fashion stores. Though her business went bankrupt, Newton-John soon had more on her mind when she was diagnosed with cancer in 1992. She pulled through, and by 1998, was back in the spotlight as a re-release of *Grease* on its twenty-year anniversary found fans wondering about the stars. Meanwhile, the singer also healed herself by releasing *Gaia: One Woman's Journey,* a collection of songs about her bout with cancer, in Australia in 1994, and in 1998 offered up *Back with a Heart,* a country-themed release that includes a remake of "I Honestly Love You" with a backing vocal by Kenneth "Babyface" Edmonds.

Newton-John was born on September 26, 1948, in Cambridge, England, to Bryn and Irene (Born) Newton-John. Her mother is the daughter of German scientist Max Born, who won a Nobel Prize for physics in 1954. Newton-John's father was from Wales and taught German literature at King's College of Cambridge University. The family also included an older sister and brother. When she was just five, the family moved from England to Melbourne, Australia, where her father was named dean of a college. Newton-John was greatly influenced by her father's love of music and his extensive collection of classical records, although she also

appreciated contemporary artists such as Tennessee Ernie Ford, Ray Charles, and Joan Baez. When Newton-John was about ten or eleven, her parents divorced, and her mother was given custody.

Newton-John began singing at her brother-in-law's coffeehouse in Melbourne when she was in her teens and eventually won a talent contest, earning her a free trip to London. Though she was not happy to leave her boyfriend behind, the singer's mother thought the trip would be a good experience, and they went to England in 1965. Once there, she and her mother stayed for an extended period of time, with Newton-John singing in "some pretty divey clubs," as she recalled to Gregory Tasker in *Parade.* She released her first single, "Till You Say You'll Be Mine," with the B-side "For Ever," on Decca Records in May of 1966. The rare recording was re-released in 1994 on the British compilation *Pop Inside the '60s.* Also in 1966, Newton-John acted in the Australian film *Funny Things Happen Down Under.*

The young singer began appearing with a variety of groups, eventually joining forces with another Australian female singer, Pat Carroll. They performed as Pat and Olivia at clubs and on television shows as they dreamed of stardom. Newton-John's mother's visa eventually ran out in 1969, but she had obtained an English passport for her daughter so that she could remain in the country and continue working. "I was very upset," Newton-John noted in *Parade.* "I wanted to go back to Australia, to my boyfriend." Instead, she became part of a canned futuristic combo dubbed Toomorrow, which British sponsors hoped would become the next big thing. They filmed an embarrassing self-titled space-age musical in 1970, but the concept never managed to blast off.

After Carroll went back to Australia, Newton-John found producer John Farrar, who produced her first hit single, a rendition of the Bob Dylan song "If Not for You." Released in 1971, the record was popular in Great Britain and led to a tour. She followed this up with a couple more hits, including a cover of John Denver's "Take Me Home Country Roads," which tuned her in to an appreciation of country music. Before then, she had concentrated on folk songs. By 1972, Newton-John was regularly appearing on a top-rated English television show hosted by singer Cliff Richard, and performing in area clubs. She began releasing albums, including *Olivia Newton- John* and *Music Makes My Day* in 1971, and *Olivia* in 1972.

In 1973, Newton-John hit the American charts in 1973 with the song "Let Me Be There," which won a

Grammy Award in 1973 for best country female vocal performance. Soon, the singer was at the peak of her game, invading the top 40 charts at a stunning pace and charting five number one hits, including "Have You Never Been Mellow" and "I Honestly Love You." She also won an astounding number of awards throughout the 1970s. She earned two more Grammys in 1974, for best female pop vocalist and record of the year, for "I Honestly Love You." In 1974 the Country Music Association in America and in Britain named her female vocalist of the year, and the British association tapped her for the title again in 1975. Meanwhile, she was burning up the American Music Awards, with honors for country favorite female vocalist in 1975 and 1976; for country favorite album in 1975 for *Let Me Be There;* for pop/rock favorite female vocalist in 1975, 1976, 1977, and 1983; for pop/rock favorite single in 1975 for "I Honestly Love You;" and for pop/rock favorite album in 1976 for *Have You Never Been Mellow. Billboard* honored her with four awards in 1975, *Cashbox* doled out one in 1974 and two in 1975, and the American Society of Composers, Authors and Publishers (ASCAP) gave her its Country Music Award in 1975 for "Please Mr. Please." Newton-John also took the People's Choice Awards for top female musical performer in 1975, 1977, and 1979, and also for top motion picture actress in 1979. Newton-John's lengthy list of awards also includes the prestigious Order of the British Empire (O.B.E.).

After her huge success in both country and pop, Newton-John was already a superstar when she was asked to appear opposite heartthrob John Travolta in the film version of *Grease,* which had been a Broadway musical. A love story set at a high school in the 1950s, *Grease,* released in 1978, was a smash success. It unwound the tale of a bad boy greaser, Danny (Travolta), who falls in love with a lily-pure cheerleader, Sandy (Newton-John). The two try to make it work despite the differences in their cliques, enduring taunts from their friends along the way. *Grease,* featuring a catchy soundtrack and vibrant choreography, became one of the top-grossing musicals of all time. When it was re-released on its 20-year anniversary in 1998, the event caused a resurgence in popularity for the movie, and won over a whole new generation of fans, who flocked to the box office and then the music stores.

Following *Grease,* Newton-John decided to stick with cinema and starred in the roller disco extravaganza *Xanadu,* which did not fare nearly as well. The soundtrack, however, was popular, with the song "Magic" topping the charts. The next year, she shed her wholesome image to put out *Physical,* which paved the way for people to freely wear their gym clothes in

public. It was accompanied by a full-length video featuring a new, more athletic and slightly devilish Newton-John. Sporting close-cropped hair, a headband, and aerobic workout gear, Newton-John shattered her doe-like image with the title song *Let's Get Physical,* which was considered too risque for some radio stations due to its naughty double entendres. The trend-setting album sold over two million copies and spent 10 weeks on the *Billboard* Hot 100, a record for a female vocalist, starting on November 21, 1981.

Newton-John during the 1970s had an ongoing relationship with American businessman Lee Kramer, who was also her manager. In 1979, she met Matt Lattanzi, a dancer and aspiring actor eleven years her junior (she was 31, he was 20), on the set of *Xanadu.* They married in the mid-1980s and had a daughter, Chloe Rose, in 1986. Though Newton-John continued recording, her albums did not stir up as much attention, as she was perhaps more concerned with raising her daughter and starting up a new business, Koala Blue. She founded the enterprise, a chain of sportswear stores, in 1983. "It sounds kind of boring to say I've been at home," Newton-John remarked in a 1990 *People* article. "But that's the truth." Unfortunately, her peaceful life would suffer a series of shake-ups. First, Koala Blue filed for bankruptcy in February of 1991. Then on July 2, 1992, she was diagnosed with breast cancer, the same day her father died of cancer. After a year of chemotherapy and a partial mastectomy, doctors decreed that Newton-John was clean. Then on April 24, 1995, she and her husband announced they were separating.

Despite these setbacks, Newton-John managed to keep her spirits up, releasing a 1994 album containing non-self-pitying songs about her struggle with cancer. *Gaia,* which is Greek for "Mother Earth," went gold in Australia, although no American company released it. "Once you face your fear," Newton-John told Tasker in *Parade,* "nothing is ever as hard as you think." Later, the singer was back in action for the twenty-year anniversary of *Grease* in 1998, gracing the covers of magazines and appearing with Travolta in the media for the revival. Also that year, she released her first U.S. album since 1992. *Back with a Heart* featured a country sound and boasted a new version of her early 1970s hit "I Honestly Love You," which included a backing vocal by R&B star Kenneth "Babyface" Edmonds.

Newton-John lives in an environmentally-friendly adobe-style home on a ranch in the mountains in Malibu, California, sharing the property with a variety of dogs, cats, birds, and horses. She also has a 15-acre farm near Byron Bay, Australia, complete with rolling green hills and citrus trees. After her recovery, Newton-John hosted a documentary about environmental factors that may cause cancer, and cowrote an environmentally-themed children's book called *A Pig Tale*. She also helped found the Children's Health Environmental Coalition (CHEC), after a good friend's young daughter died of a rare cancer, and is lobbying for legislation to cut down toxins in the environment. "The levels of toxicity that the government considers safe in the environment are judged by a fully grown male," Newton-John explained to Elizabeth Snead in *USA Today*. "Children are ingesting levels that are much too high…. As a result, childhood cancers are on the rise." Newton-John does not smoke or drink caffeine, practices good nutrition, and meditates. She told Tasker in *Parade*, "I appreciate the basic things—spending time at the beach, watching the sun come up. I've learned to value the day…. I try to keep in touch with the fact that life is a gift—that every day is a gift."

Selected discography

Toomorrow, 1970.
Olivia Newton-John, 1971.
Music Makes My Day, 1971.
Olivia, 1972.
Long Live Love, 1974.
Have You Never Been Mellow, 1975.
Clearly Love, 1975.
Come On Over, 1976.
Don't Stop Believin', 1976.
Making a Good Thing Better, 1977.
Greatest Hits, 1978.
Totally Hot, 1978.
(With John Travolta and others) *Grease*, 1978.
Xanadu, 1980.
Love Performance (live), 1981.
Physical, 1981.
Greatest Hits 2, 1982.
(With Travolta) *Two of a Kind*, 1983.
Soul Kiss, 1985.
The Rumour, 1989.
Warm and Tender, 1990.
Back to Basics, 1992.
Gaia: One Woman's Journey, 1994.
(With Cliff Richard) *Heathcliff*, 1995.
Back with a Heart, 1998.

Sources

On-line

International Only Olivia Fan Club web site, http://www.onlyolivia.com (August 20, 1998).
"Olivia Newton-John," Internet Movie Database web site, http://us.imdb.com (July 7, 1998).

Books

Contemporary Theatre, Film, and Television, volume 5, Gale Research, 1988.

Periodicals

Columbian, June 14, 1998.
Good Housekeeping, May 1, 1998, p. 30.
Los Angeles Times, May 9, 1998, calendar, p. 6.
New York Times, June 11, 1978.
Parade, Sunday, July 5, 1998, p. 4.
People, December 24, 1990; August 19, 1991; August 3, 1992; May 15, 1995; April 13, 1998.
USA Today, May 7, 1998, p. 1D.

—Geri Speace

Christiane Nuesslein-Volhard

Genetic researcher

Born October 20, 1942, in Magdeburg, Germany; daughter of Rolf (an architect) and Brigitte (Haas) Volhard. *Education:* Received doctorate from the University of Tuebingen, early 1970s.

Addresses: *Office*—Max-Planck-Institut fuer Entwicklungsbiologie, Spemannstrasse 35/III, 7400 Tuebingen, Germany.

Career

Max-Planck-Institut fuer Virusforschung, Tuebingen, Germany, research fellow, 1972-74; Biozentrum Basel, Basel, Switzerland, postdoctoral fellow, 1975-76; affiliated with the laboratory of Dr. K. Sander, University of Freiburg, Freiburg, Germany, 1977; European Molecular Biology Laboratory, Heidelberg, Germany, member of head group, 1978-80; Friedrich-Miescher-Laboratorium, Max-Planck-Gesellschaft, Tuebingen, 1981-85, scientific member, 1985-90; Max-Planck-Institut fuer Entwicklungsbiologie, Tuebingen, director, 1985-90, director of department of genetics, 1990—.

Awards: Nobel Prize for Medicine (with Edward B. Lewis and Eric F. Wieschaus), 1995, for discoveries concerning the genetic control of early embryonic development; Leibnizpreis der Deutschen Forschungsgemeinschaft; Franz-Vogt-Preis, University of Giessen; Rosenstiel Medal, Brandeis University.

Sidelights

In 1995 Christiane Nuesslein-Volhard became only the tenth woman in history to win a Nobel Prize

for medicine. The German biologist shared this award with fellow scientists Eric Wieschaus and Edward Lewis for their discoveries into the process by which genetic coding determines the development of an organism. American embryologist Donald Brown told the *New York Times Magazine* that "Nuesslein-Volhard is the most important developmental biologist of the second half of this century. Perhaps of all time."

Nuesslein-Volhard was born in 1942 in Magdeburg, Germany, but grew up in Frankfurt. She was the second of architect Rolf Volhard and his wife Brigitte's five children, and was raised in an art-appreciative environment. Even as adults, all the Volhard siblings paint. This emphasis on the visual helped Nuesslein-Volhard develop excellent observatory powers which she later put to use in her scientific research, but it also had drawbacks. From an early age she exhibited a passion for science, but "intelligence didn't matter in my family," she told Jennifer Ackerman in the *New York Times Magazine*. "What counted was artistic accomplishment, wittiness, beauty. There was a certain feeling of loneliness in this."

As a young adult, Nuesslein-Volhard studied biochemistry at the University of Tuebingen, a famed, centuries-old center of learning near Stuttgart, and in 1975 moved to Basel, Switzerland for her postdoctoral work. At the time, she didn't fully grasp the fruit-fly research that was so integral to developmental biology, she recalled in the *New York Times Magazine*. "I had no idea what I was looking at. I would just sit and watch, not able to make heads or tails of anything." In time, however, she began to catch on, and was even able to improve some of the research techniques used at the Biozentrum Basel.

In 1978 Nuesslein-Volhard became affiliated with the European Molecular Biology Laboratory (EMBL) in Heidelberg, Germany, and for the next two years was a member of its head group. It was here she began her collaboration with another developmental biologist, Eric Wieschaus. They were curious as to how a single-cell egg—the immediate union of a sperm cell and egg—develops into a complex organism; it was known that the cell began dividing itself over and over until there were trillions of separate cells that made up all the different parts of the organism, whether it was a fruit fly, housecat, or human being. Nuesslein-Volhard and Wieschaus wanted to answer the question of how the cells "knew" to become legs, skin, or brain matter.

To accomplish this, Nuesslein-Volhard and her colleague, who would later head the Department of Molecular Biology at Princeton University, mutated all the genes in an adult male fruit fly with a tainted sugar-water compound, then tracked his descendants. By scrutinizing the defective dead embryos that resulted, the scientists were able to identify the genes that were markers for body shape and organ arrangement. In several professional papers published over the next few years, Nuesslein-Volhard and Wieschaus demonstrated this and further discoveries. One of their findings was that a mother's genes pass on genetic codes to a developing embryo that are known as morphogens, which release chemicals that activate developmental genes. In essence, the morphogens tell the other genes where to go and what to do.

Much of Nuesslein-Volhard's work with Wieschaus built upon genetic research pioneered by Edward Lewis in the 1940s, but the findings of the two EMBL colleagues opened up new territory for research into human birth defects. Because of their work, an international project to map out a genetic blueprint for all life forms beyond the fruit fly was launched. This would prove immeasurable to researchers working toward the eradication of congenital birth defects and miscarriages. For this Nuesslein-Volhard was awarded the Nobel Prize for Medicine in 1995 along with Wieschaus and Lewis. "They let the genie out of the bottle," declared Nobel committee member Bjorn Vennstrom, according to the *Boston Globe*. "Their re-

search has stimulated other research in many other fields."

A decade earlier, in 1985, Nuesslein-Volhard had returned to Tuebingen to serve as director of the Max-Planck-Institut for Developmental Biology. After carrying out additional research into fruit-fly genetics, the iconoclast scientist then decided to force her research further up the developmental ladder; she launched a project to track genetic development in the common zebra fish. This announcement was greeted in some scientific quarters with bafflement and murmurs of heresy, but Nuesslein-Volhard felt the fish was an excellent candidate for large-scale research because it develops from a transparent embryo, which would allow her to observe organ growth. Furthermore, it possesses a notochord, or rudimentary spinal cord, which classifies it as a vertebrate, unlike the fruit fly.

Since 1993, Nuesslein-Volhard's ultramodern, 7,000-tank Fischhaus in Tuebingen and her team of sixteen researchers have made new inroads into genetic inquiry. "This vast piscine library supports a city-size population of fish with a dazzling array of mutations," wrote Ackerman, and Nuesslein-Volhard's new methodology has since gained acceptance in the scientific community. In 1996 she and fellow researchers working overseas at Boston's Massachusetts General Hospital published a 481-page guide to the genetic structure of a zebra fish. The scientific treatise has been described as groundbreaking, and other researchers are using it as a guide to identify similar genetic mutations in humans. Its findings also show Nuesslein-Volhard's sense of humor—she gave telltale names many of the individual genes. One that causes a zebra fish to develop an enlarged heart she called *santa*, for instance; the *mercedes* gene yields a split tail fin not unlike the luxury car's distinctive tripartite hood ornament.

Nuesslein-Volhard continues her research into genetic development and zebra fish in Tuebingen. She lives in the millhouse of a monastery dating from the fourteenth century not far from the university town. She keeps her own zebra fish at home as pets, and for a hobby makes her own jigsaw puzzles by cutting apart art reproductions. Seemingly undeterred by the most daunting of challenges, Nuesslein-Volhard actually cuts the pieces apart along color and shape lines. Her scientific colleagues describe her as both meek and strong-willed. "When she wants to do something, she does it and does it right," Wieschaus told the *New York Times Magazine*. "If she lived in the Stone Age, she would have figured out how to make fire."

Sources

Boston Globe, October 10, 1995, p. 3.
Lancet, October 14, 1995, p. 1028.
New York Times Magazine, October 12, 1997.
Science News, October 14, 1995, p. 246.

—*Carol Brennan*

Gary Oldman

Actor

Born March 21, 1958, in New Cross, London, England; son of Kay Oldman; father, an itinerant seaman, welder, and pipe fitter; married Lesley Manville (an actress), late 1980s (divorced, 1990); married Uma Thurman (an actress), 1990 (divorced, 1992); married Donya Fiorentino (a photographer), mid-1990s; children: (with Manville) Alfie, (with Fiorentino) Gulliver Flyn. *Education:* Rose Bruford College of Speech and Drama, London, B.A., 1979; also studied with Greenwich Young People's Theatre.

Career

Began acting career in repertory theater in Theater Royal, York, England, and later Glasgow Citizens Theatre, Scotland; appeared with the Royal Court Theater, London, productions include *The Pope's Wedding* and *Serious Money* and the Royal Shakespeare Company, 1984-87; British television credits include the films *Remembrance, Honest, Decent and True,* and *Fallen Angels;* motion picture debut in the Alex Cox film *Sid and Nancy,* 1986; screenwriting and directorial debut, *Nil by Mouth,* 1997.

Awards: Best Actor citation, British Theatre Association *Drama* Magazine, 1985, and *TimeOut* magazine Fringe Awards, best newcomer of 1985-86, both for *The Pope's Wedding; Evening Standard* Film Award, best newcomer, 1986; Director's Award of the Edinburgh Film Festival, Channel Four Television, 1997, for *Nil by Mouth.*

Member: Fellow, Rose Bruford College of Speech and Drama, 1997.

Sidelights

British stage and screen veteran Gary Oldman has been called one of the most outstanding actors of the modern era. Since he first appeared before American filmgoers in the 1986 punk-rock love story *Sid and Nancy,* Oldman has consistently frightened audiences with his often murderously-inclined characters, but is also known as an actor who is willing to test his own limits; his roles have ranged from Ludwig van Beethoven to Lee Harvey Oswald. Oldman's personal life has been rich in drama as well, but the actor maintains he considers himself fortunate to have found a professional outlet for his proclivity toward the amoral. "My mum would say I fell in with the wrong crowd," Oldman once said about his youth in a *Rolling Stone* interview. "I could have a career, I suppose, in crime."

Oldman was born in 1958, in London, England. His father was a laborer who drank before permanently abandoning Oldman and his two sisters in the early 1960s. Their neighborhood, New Cross, was a notoriously impoverished and dangerous part of London, and with his mother working and his sisters far older, Oldman led a solitary existence. "I spent a lot of time alone when I was growing up," Oldman told *New York*

Times Magazine writer Susan Dworkin. "It doesn't come as a surprise to me that acting is what I ended up doing." As a teenager Oldman drifted into delinquency when he joined a gang—following the career path of both his sisters' husbands—but he also found his inspiration to escape New Cross on television. Two early films that featured iconoclastic young British actor Malcolm McDowell—*Long Ago Tomorrow* and *If*—made a dramatic impression on him.

Oldman auditioned for the Royal Academy of Dramatic Art, but was informed that he should probably pursue other career options. Undaunted, he won a scholarship to London's Rose Bruford College of Speech and Drama, and earned a degree in 1979; from there he began doing repertory theater. At the Theater Royal in York, and later with the Glasgow Citizens Theatre, Oldman learned to channel his energies into the forceful characters he portrayed onstage, and within a few years had moved on to London. With the Royal Court Theater he appeared in *Serious Money* and *Women Beware,* and at the Royal Shakespeare Company Oldman performed in *The Desert Air* and *War Play,* among other works. He also found challenging work in numerous British television films. One memorable role came as a skinhead in the 1984 Mike Leigh telefilm *Meantime.* "Coxy was an extraordinary creation," wrote Graham Fuller of this character in *American Film.* "Rolling around in a dustbin, trampling a sofa in a neighbor's flat, he was as deeply touching an inarticulate, glue-sniffing lout as British television has seen."

> "If you can make audiences gasp, that's the best you get," Oldman told Rolling Stone's Fred Schruers. "Somewhere way down inside, I must think I'm a good actor, 'cause if I thought I was terrible, I couldn't get up there and do it."

Oldman told Fuller that finding the inspiration to portray society's more marginal members was not a stretch; he only thought back to his own formative years and what might have been had he not found shelter in the thespian world—his schooling, for instance, was far from adequate. "[It] isn't even a school anymore," Oldman said of his alma mater in the *American Film* interview. "They closed it down because it was so bloody terrible. I was constantly told, 'Oldman, you're stupid, you're thick, you'll never amount to anything.' What do you do if you're seventeen years old in Thatcherite Britain and you can't get a job? You become a football [soccer] hooligan."

It was his reputation as an intense stage presence that brought Oldman to feature films. In 1985, Oldman appeared at the Royal Court as Scopey in *The Pope's Wedding,* and for this he tied with Anthony Hopkins for the Best Actor award from *Drama* magazine. Around the same time, filmmakers Eric Fellner and Alex Cox were planning their cinematic re-telling of the debauched end of Sid Vicious. The sorry guitarist of the Sex Pistols had died of a drug overdose while free on bail after the unsolved stabbing death of his American girlfriend, Nancy Spungen. Fellner and Cox went to see Oldman onstage in London. "We had never heard of Gary," Fellner told Dworkin in the *New York Times Magazine.* "We went to see him in a play which was unbelievably long and artistic and weird. He was completely mind-bogglingly amazing." They offered him the *Sid and Nancy* lead and, in what would become standard practice for Oldman, he began preparing intensely. He met with Vicious's mother, who gave him some things her son used to wear. He lost so much weight for role that at one point he had to be hospitalized.

Oldman became a cult icon when *Sid and Nancy* was released, but he has admitted dissatisfaction with the final cut. On-set artistic disagreements between Oldman and Cox, the director, were commonplace; in some cases their disputes about the on-screen interpretation of events were indeed valid, since many of the police-file details about Spungen's death were murky to begin with. Despite these conflicts, Oldman's performance garnered positive reviews. In the 1988 *American Film* article, Fuller declared that within the first few frames of *Sid and Nancy* is "the exact moment Gary Oldman became a star." Chloe Webb, as Spungen, is lying near him in the seedy Chelsea Hotel, and "Oldman holds the camera transfixed as the cops mill around him in one of the longest reveries in movies," Fuller wrote.

Oldman next appeared as doomed English playwright Joe Orton in the 1987 film *Prick Up Your Ears.* Orton was a notorious Oscar Wilde-like personality who was murdered by his lover; for this role, Oldman put on enough weight to give him a nice paunch. "Although the movie had no great commercial success, it established Oldman as an actor other actors admire," Dworkin wrote. Over the next several years, Oldman took on a variety of personae in quirky or decidedly uncommercial movies. He played a rough-around-the-edges sailor from London in the 1988 film *We Think the World of You*—"it wasn't a very enormous stretch," Oldman said in an interview with *Rolling Stone*'s Fred Schruers—and appeared in Nic Roeg's bizarre *Track 29* that same year. In 1989, he tried out his first American accent in portraying a Boston attorney in *Criminal Law* who has just won a case for his client, a criminal defendant portrayed by Kevin Bacon; Oldman's character then discovers the other really is a serial killer.

In 1990, Oldman had a small role in *Henry & June*, appearing under the pseudonym "Maurice Escargot," and that same year appeared as a damaged Irish-American gangster in *State of Grace* opposite Sean Penn. Schruers termed Oldman "the scene stealer" of the movie—"his Jackie is a shambling, mercurial baby-faced killer." In an interview with Robert Seidenberg in *American Film*, Oldman explained that to create such a repugnant personality on-screen, it was first necessary for him to come up with "something I can like about a character," and he termed the alcoholic murderer Jackie "an innocent.... rather a tortured spirit." He admitted that in *State of Grace*'s church scene, where Jackie weeps, "that's me crying.... You bring a lot of you to a performance. I'm using my feelings and bringing my baggage to it."

Scripts calling for damaged criminals often came Oldman's way—for a time, he seemed to be typecast in deviant roles, but they were also meaty parts in which he excelled and earned critical approval. Perhaps Oldman's apotheosis as an aberrant actor came with his portrayal of the Texan thought to have assassinated an American president in the 1991 Oliver Stone film *JFK*; the following year, he played the lead in Francis Ford Coppola's 1992 remake, *Bram Stoker's Dracula*. Oldman then made appearances in a pair of sinister crime films, *True Romance* and *Romeo Is Bleeding*, both in 1993, before abruptly changing gears to take on the part of Ludwig van Beethoven in the 1995 period film *Immortal Beloved*. Its plot traced the origins of a love letter the composer had written, and by retracing his romantic life gave a more intimate view into Beethoven's creative powers. Reviewing it for *New York*, David Denby termed *Immortal Beloved* "repeatedly embarrassing," but granted that Oldman furnished "a fiery, sullen Beethoven."

An excellent mimic, accents are Oldman's forte, and he is comfortable with dialogue that calls for him to abandon his New Cross inflections for a Transylvanian lilt or a Texan drawl. Archaic seventeenth-century language was necessary for *The Scarlet Letter*, another love story in which he appeared opposite Demi Moore as the Puritan minister with whom she commits adultery; the movie received a thrashing from critics. Next, Oldman vaulted back to the twentieth century with his role in *Basquiat*, one of the most talked-about films of 1996. Oldman played blustery New York artist Albert Milo, really the celluloid alter-ego of real-life painter Julian Schnabel; Schnabel wrote, directed, and financed the biopic about the stellar of rise and tragic end of Jean-Michel Basquiat, a young, streetwise artist who rose to fame in the New York art world of the 1980s. Other cast members included David Bowie as Andy Warhol and Dennis Hopper.

For his next role, Oldman modeled his accent on yet another Texan, H. Ross Perot, when he appeared in the 1997 sci-fi thriller *The Fifth Element*. He played Zorg, "the film's mega-hammy villain," as the *New York Times* film critic Janet Maslin described him; she also remarked that "Oldman preens evilly enough to leave tooth marks on the scenery." He also appeared as a Russian terrorist in another summer blockbuster of the same year, *Air Force One*, as the hijacker of the American president's plane. "Oldman's deft underplaying (no *Fifth Element* hamming here) adds unexpected humanity to a role that could have slipped into caricature," wrote Peter Travers in *Rolling Stone*.

Yet Oldman's years of admittedly unrestrained drinking began to catch up with him, and he found he had inherited the same tendency toward alcoholism that eventually killed his father. He stopped altogether, and took a year off from acting in order to write his first screenplay. *Nil by Mouth* premiered at the Cannes Film Festival in 1997, and Oldman, who also directed it, credits his newfound sobriety for allowing him to focus clearly on the tale of substance abuse and its damaging effects on human relationships. An intense, bleak tale, *Nil by Mouth* chronicled the neighborhood thug, his abused wife, and a tragic drug addict—characters taken from Oldman's youth in New Cross. *Film Comment* writer Harlan Kennedy found some technical fault with Oldman as a director, but granted he "has a rhythmic intuition about when to draw breath between dementias."

Oldman's personal life also settled down somewhat as he neared forty. Before a well-publicized romance with actress Isabella Rossellini that began during the filming of *Immortal Beloved* in Eastern Europe, he had been married to Uma Thurman, for whom he had left his first wife, actress Lesley Manville. He is now married a photographer, Donya Fiorentino, also the mother of his second child, and the actor admits to taking on fewer roles now in order to spend time with his sons. Though he is still the consummate on-screen villain, Oldman's 1998 work perhaps reflects his newly kid-friendly lifestyle: he will give voice to one of the characters in the 1998 animation feature *The Quest for Camelot,* and will then revive the nefarious Dr. Smith character in the celluloid version of 1960s cult television series *Lost In Space.* "If you can make audiences gasp, that's the best you get," Oldman told *Rolling Stone*'s Schruers. "Somewhere way down inside, I must think I'm a good actor, 'cause if I thought I was terrible, I couldn't get up there and do it."

Selected filmography

Sid and Nancy, 1986.
Prick Up Your Ears, 1987.
We Think the World of You, 1988.
Track 29, 1988.
Criminal Law, 1989.
State of Grace, 1990.
Henry & June (under name "Maurice Escargot"), 1990.
Rosencrantz and Guildenstern Are Dead, 1990.
Chattahoochee, 1990.
JFK, 1991.
Bram Stoker's Dracula, 1992.
True Romance, 1993.
Romeo Is Bleeding, 1993.
Immortal Beloved, 1995.
The Scarlet Letter, 1995.
Basquiat, 1996.
The Fifth Element, 1997.
Air Force One, 1997.
The Quest for Camelot (voice only), 1998.
Lost In Space, 1998.

Sources

American Film, April 1988, pp. 24-30; October 1990, pp. 54-55.
Film Comment, July/August 1997, pp. 5-7.
New York, January 9, 1995.
New Yorker, July 24, 1995, p. 41.
New York Times, October 13, 1995; May 9, 1997.
New York Times Magazine, November 8, 1992, pp. 50-54.
Premiere, January 1995, pp. 68-69.
Rolling Stone, October 18, 1990, pp. 63-64; August 7, 1997, pp. 67-68.

—*Carol Brennan*

Trey Parker and Matt Stone

Co-creators of *South Park*

Trey Parker born in 1969, in Conifer, CO; son of Randy (a geologist) and Sharon (an insurance representative) Parker. *Education:* Attended University of Colorado at Boulder.

Matt Stone born in 1971, in Houston, TX; son of Bud (an economics professor) and Sheila (a homemaker) Stone. *Education:* University of Colorado at Boulder, B.S. in mathematics.

Addresses: *Office*—c/o Comedy Central, 1775 Broadway, 10th Floor, New York, NY 10019. *Internet*—www.comedycentral.com.

Career

Wrote, produced, and directed *The Spirit of Christmas* (animated short film), 1995; wrote produced, and directed *South Park* (animated television series), 1997—. Parker: wrote, produced, directed, and appeared in *Cannibal! the Musical*, 1996; wrote, produced, and directed short film, *Your Studio and You*, 1996; wrote, produced, directed and appeared in *Orgasmo*, 1997. Stone: appeared in *Cannibal! the Musical*, 1996, and *Orgasmo*, 1997.

Sidelights

Alien abductions, anal probes, a singing stool specimen, abundant flatulence, genetic aberrations, and some of the most foul-mouthed eight year olds ever imagined inhabit the bizarre, yet oddly down to earth, Colorado hamlet known as South Park. For *South Park's* creators, Trey Parker and Matt Stone, the show is a brutal and vicious, but honest depiction of young children and their world. According to Rick Marin in *Newsweek,* the show depicts kids "who abuse each other, delight in dissing authority figures and yet possess a dumb innocence that makes their bad behavior forgivable." The caustic cruelty exhibited by the children of *South Park* has struck a responsive chord in many of the program's viewers and rabid fans.

Parker discussed the "children's lost innocence" theme with David Wild of *Rolling Stone* when he said "there's this whole thing out there [in the media and society] about how kids are so innocent and pure. That's bull.... Kids are malicious.... They totally jump on any bandwagon and rip on the weak guy at any chance. They say whatever bad word they can think of. They are total bastards, but for some reason, everyone has kids and forgets about what they were like when they have kids. It's [*South Park's* vicious cruelty] a total projection of what I remember. I remember making the poor kid eat the worm. I remember thinking 'What's the meanest thing I could possible do here?'"

According to James Collins of *Time,* Parker's childhood refusal to flush the toilet and his father's reaction, led to the creation of South Park's infamous singing stool specimen, Mr. Hankey, the Christmas Poo. Collins added that this was "very revealing," and shows that *South Park's* "creators are not simply out to offend people but are exploring the surreal terrors of childhood."

Parker was raised in Jefferson County, Colorado, which was adjacent to the real South Park. He remarked to Wild of *Rolling Stone* that he "was extremely introverted except with good friends. It was all about math and science and tae kwan do." When he was 13, Parker's father purchased a video camera for him and almost immediately, his young life and world began to change as he spent his weekends shooting movies.

Stone, less than two years younger than Parker, was born in Houston, Texas, although he grew up in the Denver, Colorado suburb of Littleton. He was an honor student who was able to take trigonometry classes in the local high school when he was in the sixth grade. Despite this, Stone's excellence in academics did not save him from getting into trouble. Commenting on his academic record to Wild, Stone's mother asserted that "I wouldn't say he was a troublemaker. I'd say he was always a good kid. He did have one teacher in elementary school who said he wasn't reading the novels she had picked out during reading time. I asked what he was doing. She said he was reading the encyclopedia."

In *Newsweek,* Marin noted that Parker and Stone did not have a publicist, as "the story of how this goofball duo made it writes itself." Parker and Stone met in the early 1990s when they were both attending the University of Colorado at Boulder. At the time, Parker was working on a film project entitled *The Giant Beaver of Sri Lanka.* According to Parker, the film focused on a young girl who wore a beaver costume and then would go out and terrorize the town. He noted that it was quite similar to the premise of the Godzilla movies.

Parker was eventually kicked out of the University of Colorado at Boulder for failing to attend a good deal of his classes. Stone, however, stayed on at the University of Colorado at Boulder and pursued studies in both mathematics and film. He earned his bachelor's degree in mathematics and hooked up with his friend Parker.

Undeterred by his less than perfect academic track record, Parker began work on his first feature film, which was eventually completed a few years later. The film was called *Cannibal! the Musical* and was envisioned by Parker as a mutant hybrid melding the musical stylings of *Oklahoma!* with the slasher film chic of *Friday the 13th.* The budget for the film was $125,000, which was a relatively small amount for a feature film. Parker managed to raise the money from donations and contributions from his family and friends. He not only wrote, produced, and directed the musical send up, but he starred in it as well. Stone also had a role in *Cannibal! the Musical.*

By 1995, the two roommates were struggling to survive. Parker was completing *Cannibal! the Musical* and

as Stone related to Wild "we were seriously starving. Down to one meal a day." Parker and Stone's fortunes were about to change when they were commissioned by an ardent supporter, former Fox executive Brian Graden, to create a video Christmas card for him. Graden paid the pair $1,200 for the five minute animated short film *The Spirit of Christmas.* The result was an obscene, rude, crude, and slightly blasphemous story about the battle for the hearts and the minds of the children of South Park. The dueling combatants were Jesus and Santa Claus. As Santa and Jesus duked it out, four of South Park Elementary School's third grade students watched in horrified excitement, anxious to learn of the outcome of the fight. The foul-mouthed little scamps who provided the blow by blow commentaries were: Stan Marsh, the so-called leader of the bunch; Kyle Broslofski, who was a member of one of South Park's only Jewish families; Eric Cartman, the chubby bully who was spoiled rotten and claimed to be big-boned; and Kenny Mc Cormick, the one who came from a poor family, mumbles, and gets killed.

According to Comedy Central's Debbie Liebling, South Park *serves as a release valve "in an age of political correctness. It's like a release of these restrictions. There's a vicarious thrill to going to a world that's seemingly forbidden. These children make it less threatening."*

The impact of *The Spirit of Christmas* was phenomenal. According to Marin in *Newsweek,* "the video became an underground bootleg obsession. Actor George Clooney alone duped dozens of copies." (Clooney later recorded the "Grrrs" of Sparky, Stan's gay dog.) The video immediately gained a cult status among those who saw it and the two creators of *The Spirit of Christmas* were soon inundated with offers for their services. The offers of the major film studios ranged from asking Parker to direct *Barney: the Movie* to creating a television series based on the characters from *The Spirit of Christmas.* Most of the offers, according to Parker, missed the point. Parker and Stone believed that the appeal of *The Spirit of Christmas* was due to a combination of the behaviors, situations, and encounters the children's characters found themselves in, as opposed to the prevailing view, of the vast majority of the studios, who felt, that the rampant profanity drove the short and without it there would be nothing.

Parker and Stone eventually managed to find an understanding and kindred soul in Comedy Central's Debbie Liebling who was willing to let them do what they wanted to do with their show within reason. Liebling recalled her reaction to first viewing *The Spirit of Christmas*, to Mike Duffy of the *Detroit Free Press*, "I just jumped through the roof. I though this is what we have to have."

In 1996, Parker signed up with Celluloid Studios to function as his production house. At about the same time, Universal Studios commissioned him to create a promotional video for them. The resulting product was *Your Studio and You*, a 15 minute campy send up of the instructional films from the 1950s. The mini documentary featured performances by such luminaries as directors Steven Spielberg and James Cameron, as well as Sylvester Stallone and Demi Moore.

With Liebling and Comedy Central's blessings, Parker and Stone began to develop *South Park*. According to Marin in *Newsweek*, Parker, who does the voices of Stan and Cartman "is the one people call the 'genius' of the pair, the self-directed hustler." Stone, who does the voices of Kyle and Kenny, "is more practical and business-savvy." Anne Garefino, a co-executive producer of the show commented to *Newsweek*, "Trey and Matt both have a sweetness that balances out the grossness." Marin concluded, "Both still come off like dorks."

Fleshed out the world of *The Spirit of Christmas*, Jesus was a resident of the town and had a cable access show called *Jesus and Pals*. Stan's gun crazy Uncle Jimbo and his buddy Ned, the Vietnam veteran with a voice box, ran the gun shop. The children's teacher, Mr. Garrison, spread misinformation and untruths via his alter ego, hand puppet Mr. Hat. Chef was the school's cook and the children's adult confidant who believed that sweet love solved all problems. In *South Park*, the children were cruel and the adults were inept and ineffectual. One critic noted that *South Park* was a crude cross between the immature hijinks *Beavis and Butthead* and the sometimes skewed morality of *The Simpsons*. In *Time*, Collins noted that "It [*South Park*] is the only regular series to carry a Mature or MA rating, the harshest." Marin of *Newsweek* added that even though parents and educators complain about the show, "it's worth remembering that the show's core viewers are

of voting age. Almost 60 percent of them are 18-34." No one or thing was safe from *South Park*'s scathing pop cultural analysis as Parker explained to Duffy in the *Detroit Free Press*, "the challenge is to go as far out as you can but then keep it totally grounded in reality." Furthering this train of thought, Liebling told Duffy that *South Park* served as a release valve "in an age of political correctness. It's like a release of these restrictions. There's a vicarious thrill to going to a world that's seemingly forbidden. These children make it less threatening." Parker later joked to Duffy, "*South Park* is our therapy. We don't need any (shrinks)."

Not content to rest on his laurels, Parker started to work on his next feature length film, *Orgsamo*. It was a live action send up of the pornography industry. Parker, the writer, director, and producer starred as a Mormon who was transformed into a porn star shortly before he was about to be married. Stone also had a role in *Orgasmo*, as a pornography photographer. *Orgasmo* made its American debut at the Sundance Film Festival in January of 1998. About the same time, Parker's first film, *Cannibal! the Musical* was premiering at the anti-Sundance alternative movie celebration the Slamdance Festival.

The over the top success of *South Park* went well beyond Parker, Stone and Comedy Central's wildest expectations. The show has earned for the network its highest ratings ever. However, there was some friction between the co-creators and the network. Parker and Stone complained that they were receiving a fraction of their show's profits. Parker commented to Marin in *Newsweek*, "I have a friend who writes for *Just Shoot Me*, who makes more a week than I do. Thirty million in T-shirt sales, and I got a check for $7,000." After publicly airing their financial complaints, Marin noted that "William Morris is renegotiating their deal, and Comedy Central wants to keep its star attractions happy." In April of 1998, a new contract was announced that will pay Parker and Stone a minimum of $15 million for new episodes of *South Park* into the year 2000, plus a feature-length film. Parker and Stone's work has been recognized in other ways, as they were honored with a nomination for a Cable Ace Award in early 1998.

Sources

On-Line

"Filmography for Trey Parker," *South Park HQ*, http://eccentrica.org/cheesegod/soxmas/trey.html (February 13, 1998).

"South Park," *Comedy Central Online,* http://www.comedycentral.com (February 13, 1998).

"Trey Parker Interview," *Surf Park,* http://www.zdnet.com/yil/content/mag/9802/parker.html (February 13, 1998).

Periodicals

Detroit Free Press, December 16, 1997; February 4, 1998.
Entertainment Weekly, January 30, 1998, p. 69.
Newsweek, March 23, 1998, pp. 56-62.
People, August 11, 1997, p. 17.
Rolling Stone, February 19, 1998, pp. 32-41.
Shoot, October 18, 1996, pp. 7-9.
Spin, March 1998, pp. 66-75.
Time, August 18, 1997, p. 74; March 23, 1998, pp.74-76.

Other

ABC World News Tonight, March 21, 1998.

—Mary Alice Adams

Steve Perlman

President of WebTV Networks Inc.

Born c. 1961. *Education:* Attended Columbia University, c. 1979-82.

Addresses: *Office*—WebTV Networks Inc., Headquarters, 305 Lytton Avenue, Palo Alto, CA 94301.

Career

Computer and multi-media innovator. Atari, computer product development, c. 1982; Coleco, computer product development, c. 1982-84; associated with Apple Computer, 1984-90; General Magic, managing director for advanced products, 1990-94; Catapult Entertainment, founder, 1994, chief technology officer, 1994-95; WebTV Networks Inc., Palo Alto, CA, co-founder, 1996, president and chief executive officer, 1996—.

Sidelights

Steve Perlman, a computer visionary, is credited with developing much of the technology enabling television users to connect to the internet and world wide web. With early career work at computer giants Atari, Coleco, and Apple Computer, he gained a reputation for simple and ingenious solutions to complicated technical problems. Not content to work only for other computer companies, Perlman started his own business and developed a video game modem that allowed local players to compete with one another over phone lines. His innovative ideas combining computer technology and television gave birth to a new industry. "Fifty years ago, television brought the world into our homes.... WebTV will connect our homes to the world," Perlman declared in a press release on the WebTV Networks website. Perlman's technological skills have earned him 11 patents for innovations involving computer graphics, video, animation, and modems.

Born around 1961, Perlman showed an early aptitude and a genuine interest in computers and telecommunications. He was creating sophisticated computer graphic systems by the age of 17. While attending Columbia University in New York, Perlman was under contract with Atari to develop modems, graphic systems, and programs for speech and music. During this time, he also created programs for Dun and Bradstreet. For Perlman, necessity was truly the mother of invention. When assigned to write a research paper at Columbia, he used his knowledge of computers to connect to the school's mainframe system. Soon afterwards, other students were seeking help to bring their word processing systems into the information age.

After attending Columbia University as a liberal arts major, Perlman worked for a short time for Atari in computer product development. He later moved to Coleco, again developing computer products. In 1984, Perlman joined the staff at Apple Computers, remaining there for six years. During this period, his reputation as a technology genius grew. One of his major challenges at Apple was solving a problem with monitor flicker and resolution in low-cost units. Perlman's simple and inexpensive fix—using noise-cancellation techniques developed by the space industry for satellite imagery and a software filter program—kept the Apple system affordable for the average computer user.

Leaving Apple Computer in 1990, Perlman became managing director for advanced products at General Magic. Developing the company's second-generation computer system, he produced an inexpensive but high-performance unit. Perlman was also responsible for creating a low-cost microprocessor with modem capabilities and Magic TV. In 1994 he left General Magic to form his own company, Catapult Entertainment, where he was the chief technology officer (CTO) responsible for product concept, research, and development. As CTO Perlman produced a new type of modem, the innovative XBAND, for video games that allowed competition among players through the phone lines. Using games for the Super Nintendo Entertainment System and the Sega Genesis that the players owned, entire video games could be played with another person without leaving home or even seeing the other person.

With the growing popularity of the internet, Perlman became convinced that it was possible for the home television set to be connected to the world wide web at a low cost. Using his experience and expertise in computers, multimedia, video, and telecommunications technology, Perlman began to make his vision a reality. By April of 1995 he had assembled an inexpensive array of electronic components inside a simple black box that made it possible to surf the internet using a regular television. With the help of friends and fellow computer enthusiasts Bruce Leak and Phil Goldman, Perlman assembled a high tech team working in secrecy under the name of Artemis Research to transform his black box into a marketable product. On July 10, 1996, WebTV was announced to the world, with on-line service beginning on September 18, 1996.

In less than a year WebTV grew to more than 150,000 subscribers. Robert Hof, writing in *Business Week*, described Perlman's creation as "very easy to use, letting users send E-mail and click on favorite web sites with a TV remote." During the early months of 1997 major hotels in the San Francisco Bay area tested the use of WebTV, providing guests with a high-speed internet connection for accessing their e-mail or simply surfing the internet from the comfort of their own hotel room. The experiment was a success, and Robert

Kavner, president of On Command Corp., the world's leading provider of entertainment services to the hotel industry, noted in a press release, "After evaluation of other systems in the marketplace, we are convinced that WebTV provides the most reliable, user-friendly Internet access solution. Our goal is to greatly expand the in-room information and entertainment options available to hotel guests by building on WebTV's technology, services and brand." On August 29, 1997, Fujitsu Ltd., a major Japanese electronic corporation, announced the introduction of WebTV in Japan. The joint venture linked Japanese homes to the internet using a Japanese-language version of WebTV.

Perlman also sees success for WebTV in the children's market. In an interview with *Digital Kids Report*, Perlman noted that "kids think of it as a video game." Parents, on the other hand, see WebTV as a learning tool that they can share with their children. The technology is also a lower cost alternative to on-line access than a computer, priced under $400 in 1997 with future estimates even less. Perlman told *Digital Kids Report*, "It's our view that in five years you won't be able to buy a set without this capability. It will be viewed as a natural extension of the television-viewing experience."

During 1997 Perlman and his partners sold WebTV to the Microsoft Corporation for $425 million. *Wall Street Journal* contributor Lee Gome described the deal with Microsoft as "vindication [for Perlman] after his exile at Apple." Perlman reassured product users in an April 1997 column in *Club WebTV* that despite the sale, "we will continue to operate as an independent company." He continued to fine tune his creation with new enhancements that make surfing the web easier for the television audience. In an interview with Margaret Kane for *PC Week Online*, Perlman explained a new method for sending WebTV data that "solves a problem no one thought could be solved. You're going to see WebTV associated less and less with the Internet and more as an extension to television." The new technique developed by Perlman allowed nearly instantaneous transmission of data, enhancing the use of game devices with WebTV. Perlman told Kane, "It's not just a matter of putting the Internet on television, it's doing it in a simple way."

Sources

On-line

Club WebTV, April 1997, http://www.webtv.net/corp (November 15, 1997); May 1997 (November 15, 1997); October 1997 (November 20, 1997).

"Interview with Steve Perlman," *PC World Online*, http://www.pcworld.com/news (November 20, 1997).

"Press Release," WebTV, http://www.webtv.net/corp (November 15, 1997).

Periodicals

Business Week, March 24, 1997.
Computer Retail Week, January 6, 1997.
Digital Kids Report, April 1, 1997.
Television Digest, February 3, 1997.
Wall Street Journal, April 9, 1997.

Other

Communication with Carol Sacks, Director of Corporate Communications for WebTV Networks Inc., November 25, 1997.

—Homer Emery

Tom Peters

Tom Peters Group

Writer and motivational speaker

Full name, Thomas J. Peters; born November 7, 1942, in Baltimore, MD; son of Frank J. E. and Evelyn C. (Snow) Peters; married Anne C. Hartman, November 22, 1975 (marriage ended); married Kate Abbe. *Education:* Cornell University, B.C.E., 1965, M.C.E., 1966; Stanford University, M.B.A., 1972, Ph.D., 1977.

Addresses: *Office*—The Tom Peters Group, 555 Hamilton Avenue, Palo Alto, CA 94301-2015.

Career

Peate, Marwick, Mitchell & Co., Washington, DC, business management consultant, 1970; Office of Management and Budget, Washington, DC, began as director of cabinet committee on international narcotics control, became assistant to director for federal drug-abuse policy, 1973-74; McKinsey & Co. (a management consulting firm), San Francisco, CA, began as an associate, became principal practice leader in organizational effectiveness, 1974-81; Tom Peters Group, Palo Alto, CA, founder, 1982, chief of The Skunkworks, Inc., TPG Communications, and TPG/Learning Systems, 1982—; writer and speaker, 1982—. *Military service:* U.S. Navy, 1966-70; served in Vietnam.

Awards: Ford Foundation grant, c. 1975.

Sidelights

Tom Peters stormed onto the business scene in 1982 with one of the best-selling business books of all-time, *In Search of Excellence: Lessons from America's Best-run Companies,* which he co-wrote with Robert H.

Waterman, Jr. The volume spent 130 weeks on the *New York Times* bestseller list and is still widely recommended today as a must read for any executive wanting to learn the essential ingredients to success. *New York Times Book Review* contributor Fran R. Schumer praised "this highly readable and sensible book" that "finds the secret of business success ... [in] good old-fashioned values—respect for the individual, devotion to service and attention to the customer." In the text, Peters and Waterman profile what they judge to be the best run organizations in America—including McDonald's, I.B.M., and Hewlett-Packard—and outline eight basic principles these companies follow. Ironically, fourteen of the forty-three companies they praised were either bankrupt or in severe financial trouble only three years later. Still, *In Search of Excellence* made many trenchant points and Peters became one of the most sought after speakers in the corporate world.

Peters was born in Baltimore, Maryland, in November of 1942. He earned civil engineering degrees from Cornell University, continuing his education at Stanford University, where he graduated with an M.B.A. in 1972 and earned a doctorate in business five years later. Before entering Stanford, Peters served in the U.S. Navy for four years, including active duty in

Vietnam. While earning his doctorate, he was employed by McKinsey & Co. as a practice leader in organizational effectiveness. He left this post in 1981 and formed his own company, the Tom Peters Group, the following year. Peters created the company to handle his consulting and management business, as well as organize and publish his print, audio, and video projects.

In 1985, Peters co-wrote his second book *A Passion for Excellence: The Leadership Difference*. This time, his co-author was Nancy Austin. Written in the same pattern as *In Search of Excellence,* this volume looks into five key areas of competence that create organizational excellence, focusing mainly on company leadership. It gives hundreds of examples, often in anecdotal form, of how corporations—again using real-life examples such as an Edison, New Jersey, Ford Motor Company plant, Campbell Soup Company, Texas Instruments, and the city of Baltimore—should look at customers, innovation, employees, leadership, and common sense. Peters called these insights a blinding flash of the obvious because it was really about taking a simple and rational approach to business. Webster Schott, writing in the *Washington Post Book World,* declared: "While there is not much that is new in *A Passion for Excellence*—other than that great organizations start at the top, which both Harry Truman and Emerson told us—there is much that is instructive here." *New York Times Book Review* contributor Malcolm S. Forbes, Jr. also noted the educational quality of *A Passion for Excellence,* noting that "a good number of executives should find the authors' themes instructive and parts of the book inspirational." Forbes concluded that the volume serves as a "useful reminder that ... good management remains an art, not a science." *A Passion for Excellence* spent forty weeks on the *New York Times* bestseller list.

Then, in 1987, a few days before the stock market took its big 508 point drop on an October morning known as Black Monday, Peters came out with his third book and first solo effort, *Thriving on Chaos: Handbook for a Management Revolution.* The volume couldn't have been more appropriately titled or come at a more appropriate time. Readers scooped up the book based on the title alone and Peters enjoyed a sixty-week coast on the *New York Times* bestseller list. The text took another look at the same five areas described in *A Passion for Excellence* but this time the section on common sense was changed to systems and examined how bureaucracy (which Peters calls the antithesis of common sense) prevents all these ideas from getting implemented. In fact, Peters, speaking on a live seminar audio cassette that came out shortly after *Thriving on Chaos,* declared: "Getting rid of bureaucracy is more important than getting customer oriented because it is easy for people to be customer oriented if there is nobody on top of them telling them what to do."

Those words were a departure from Peters' first two books where he seemed to continually focus on customer service. With his third work, Peters' stance shifted to say that customer service was only a symptom and the real source of the problem was that people were handcuffed by overly cumbersome, bureaucratic structures. Peters quoted Peter Drucker on the live seminar audio cassette as saying, "90 percent of what we call management consists of making it difficult for employees to do their job." Peters also advocated constant change and market responsiveness within the company structure. Robert Krulwich of the *New York Times Book Review* judged Peters as a speaker who "knows he can thrill, frighten and motivate with the skill of an old-time preacher, and *Thriving on Chaos* is just as effective."

If customer service was the theme of the first two books, dismantling organizational systems and focusing on team work seemed to be the theme of the next two. Peters' fourth book, *Liberation Management: Necessary Disorganization for Nanosecond Nineties,* discusses the organizational model of the future. It explores the transition from a vertical to a horizontal structure, with employees taking on more responsibility under less management, and is described as flat and flexible. Peters stresses that employees work in small groups or teams, rather than as individuals. In his new concept of business, managers become project creators or consultants. The model is built for speed, as Peters commented in the seminar cassette, "There is no such thing as a slow, effective decision maker ... [and] if you do something fast, you can screw it up and fix it while the other guy is still thinking about it." Although the text is approximately 834 pages in length, *Liberation Management* is written in "a chatty and engaging style," according to John A. Byrne of *Business Week.* Byrne further commented: "Peters is very good at making management advice lively, even interesting, for busy executives."

Symbolic of his message of the faster and smaller company, Peters changed his book style as well. Although his first four books were large, hardcover tomes ranging from 360 to 834 pages of academic jargon, his later books became shorter and easier for the general reader to understand. *The Tom Peters Seminar: Crazy Times Call for Crazy Organizations,* released in 1994, is a paperback and the concepts are broken up into smaller pieces. The volume also contains many humorous pictures, quotes, and metaphors. It was conceived after many attendees came up to him during his seminars requesting copies of his pictures and quotes. So, Peters decided to put his whole seminar in a book. Although those familiar with Peters previous work may see some repetition, *Library Journal* contributor Steven Silkunas praised *The Tom Peters Seminar*, noting "[T]he presentation is fresh, mixing opinions with measures of puck, pluck, and petulance."

A follow-up to *The Tom Peters Seminar*, called *The Pursuit of Wow: Every Person's Guide to Topsy-Turvy Times*, was released as a paperback in 1994. Focusing on actual people at work rather than companies, Peters suggests ways to improve both employee and customer relations. Even the cover of the book makes a statement, with the back cover showing Peters in a suit with his sleeves rolled up, wearing a baseball cap, and under the suit he is wearing a T-shirt with a cartoon face. In the text, Peters laments over stupid dress codes and voices his preference to work in shorts and a T-shirt. These and other thoughts are organized into 210 concepts that range in length from a quote to three or four pages. The book consists of a collection of lists, questions and answers, quotes, transcripts of interviews, tips, and other bullet points of lessons Peters learned along the way to excellence. He also includes an informative roundtable discussion by Federal Express employees talking about diversity in the workplace. Andrew E. Serwer, writing in *Fortune*, noted that many of Peters' points were superficial, and that *The Pursuit of Wow* "is really just a sort of *Reader's Digest* for the new management order." Serwer lamented the lack of in-depth answers from Peters, an author who "possesses a first-rate mind and can certainly be stimulating."

In Peters' 1997 book, *Circle of Innovation: You Can't Shrink Your Way to Greatness*, Peters revisits the concept of speed covered in earlier works. In support of his theory, he quoted Klaus Schwab, head of the prestigious World Economic Forum in Zurich as saying, "We are moving from a world where the big eat the small to a world in which the fast eat the slow." He also discusses the issue of total quality management. "The problem with quality," Peters noted in his seminar titled after his book, *Circle of Innovation*, "is that everyone is doing it.... Quality is no longer enough because your competitors have quality too. You have to go beyond that and get the customer to say wow!" But Peters takes aim at customer service, too. He declared in his *Circle of Innovation* seminar, "If you want to improve customer service, the first thing to do is eliminate your customer service department. This will prevent your employees from pawning off customers to somebody else.... When you have a customer service department your employees in other departments will think customer service is not their responsibility."

On the other hand, if your company does have a customer service department, Peters suggests jazzing it up. He gave an assignment to one customer service representative to review their existing document and rewrite it to reflect her true personality. She came back with a document that read, "Please complain! Thanks for your order! We want everything to go perfectly! If the order was late. Or wrong. Or if any of the goods are damaged in the slightest. Or if you're just having a lousy day and want to unload on someone ... call our customer care hotline." Peters loved it. And so did his seminar audience. Peters calls this the Beautiful Systems Initiative in his book *Circle of Innovation*, and suggests that it can be applied to any department and any document.

> "90 percent of what we call management consists of making it difficult for employees to do their job."

Care and treatment of employees is an important subject for Peters. In his earlier books though, Peters wrote to bosses about maximizing employees' potential. In later works, Peters writes directly to employees about taking responsibility for their own career. Stuart Crainer of *Management Today* noted this trend: "Peters' ideas have been refined and, in many cases, entirely changed. While academics shift directions slowly and quietly in the obscurity of academic journals, Peters does so in front of audiences of hundreds, if not thousands." Crainer concluded, "While making things happen is a consistent refrain in Peters' books, the shift in emphasis has been dramatic. Over 15 years, he has moved from a corporate world view to one centered on individuals."

In an article by Peters for *Fast Company*, titled "The Brand Called You," Peters describes branding as the identity and reputation an employee creates for himself or herself. He sights Nike, Starbucks, and Nordstrom as examples of brands that sell their products mostly because of the reputation they have with their customers. Peters noted in *Fast Company*, "The brand is a promise of the value you'll receive." Just as there are brands of companies, Peters says people can become a brand, too. He uses Martha Stewart as an example, noting in the article, "[Stewart represents] the ultimate in 'how to' information to raise the quality of life at home." People buy her products because they want to be like her. This gives job security because a competitor can come up with a similar product, but the competitor can't duplicate the reputation which prompted people to buy that specific product in the first place. This reputation makes a person stand out.

Peters often uses controversial quotes in his texts, using the shock value of flying in the face of conventional wisdom to get his points across. In *The Pursuit of Wow*, Peters quoted Brian Quinn: "A good deal of corporate planning ... is like a ritual rain dance. It has no effect on the weather that follows, but those who engage in it think it does." Peters used Quinn's comment to stress his own concept of strategic planning. And Peters encourages people to get fired. He told the graduating business class at the University of California at Berkeley in his commencement speech, "If you don't get fired then you're not trying new things and are probably one of those people who just agrees with everything the boss says.... Make it impossible for them not to fire you. Screw up so much they have to fire you."

Standing out and being different are important to Peters. When he encourages people to get fired, he can point to his personal experience of being fired from McKinsey & Co. when he was partner and making over $1 million per year. By encouraging others to take risks, he echoes his own lifestyle, pointing to his books and identifying how they are different from all the other business management volumes out there. And when he encourages managers and business owners to treat employees and customers in a certain manner, he can point to his own multi-million dollar company and the way he treats his customers and employees. His personal success has made his books, seminars, and audio cassettes popular management tools.

Selected writings

(As Thomas J. Peters; with Robert H. Waterman, Jr.) *In Search of Excellence: Lessons from America's Best-run Companies*, Harper, 1982.

(With Nancy Austin) *A Passion for Excellence: The Leadership Difference*, Random House, 1985.

Thriving on Chaos: Handbook for a Management Revolution, Knopf, 1987.

Liberation Management: Necessary Disorganization for Nanosecond Nineties, Ballantine, 1992.

The Tom Peters Seminar: Crazy Times Call for Crazy Organizations, Vintage Books, 1994.

The Pursuit of Wow!: Every Person's Guide to Topsy-Turvy Times, Vintage Books, 1994.

Circle of Innovation: You Can't Shrink Your Way to Greatness, Knopf, 1997.

Tom Peter's Career Survival Guide (CD-Rom), Houghton Mifflin Interactive, 1997.

Sources

On-line

"Bio," *Tom Peters*, http://www.tompetersgroup.com/ tomsbio.html (December 2, 1997).

Novak, Carol, "Interview with Tom Peters," *Technos Quarterly: For Education and Technology* (fall 1994), http://www.ait.net/journal/volume3/ 3peters.htm (December 2, 1997).

Books

Peters, Thomas J., and Waterman, Robert H. Jr., *In Search of Excellence: Lessons from America's Best-run Companies*, Harper, 1982.

Peters, Tom, and Austin, Nancy, *A Passion for Excellence: The Leadership Difference*, Random House, 1985.

Peters, *Thriving on Chaos: Handbook for a Management Revolution*, Knopf, 1987.

Peters, *Liberation Management: Necessary Disorganization for Nanosecond Nineties*, Ballantine Books, 1992.

Peters, *The Pursuit of Wow!: Every Person's Guide to Topsy-Turvy Times*, Vintage Books, 1994.

Peters, *Circle of Innovation: You Can't Shrink Your Way to Greatness*, Knopf, 1997.

Periodicals

Business Week, November 16, 1992, pp. 14, 18.
Business Wire, May 5, 1997.
Fast Company, August/September 1997, pp. 83-94.
Fortune, December 26, 1994, p. 221.
Library Journal, June 1, 1994, p. 126.
Los Angeles Times Book Review, October 11, 1987.
Management Today, May 1997, p. 74.
Nation, May 24, 1993, pp. 712-13.
New York Times Book Review, March 6, 1983, p. 16; May 26, 1985, p. 9; October 25, 1987, p. 30.
Washington Post Book World, January 9, 1983, p. 5; May 26, 1985, pp. 1, 8.

Other

Tom Peters Live (audio cassette), CareerTrack, 1991.
Circle of Innovation (live seminar), Lessons in Leadership, 1997.

Additional material supplied by the Tom Peters Group Headquarters, 1997.

—*Colin Maiorano*

Eckhard Pfeiffer

CEO of Compaq Computer Corp.

Born August 20, 1941, in Lauban, Germany (now in Poland). *Education:* Kaufmaennissche Berufsschule, Nuremberg, Germany, B.A. in business, 1963; Southern Methodist University, M.B.A., 1983.

Addresses: *Office*—Compaq Computer Corp., P.O. Box 692000, 20555 State Hwy., Houston, TX 77269-2000.

Career

Texas Instruments, Munich, Germany, office manager, became head of subsidiary, 1964-74, head of European consumer products group, 1974-79, vice-president of strategic marketing, 1979-83; Compaq Computer Corp., head of overseas expansion, 1983, chief operating officer, 1991, president and chief executive officer, 1991—.

Awards: MSNBC, CEO of the year, 1994; Prime Minister's Trade Award, Japan, 1996.

Sidelights

German businessman Eckhard Pfeiffer gave up a successful, longstanding career with Texas Instruments to get involved in the early 1980s with a small startup computer firm. As head of the European division of Compaq Computer Corporation, Pfeiffer plumped up sales year after year, finally seeing Compaq overtake IBM as the number one computer seller in Europe by 1992. Meanwhile, other corporate bigwigs saw that his talents were needed at home base to breathe life into their sagging U.S. sales. He shipped out to Houston in 1991 to take over as chief operating

officer, and by year's end was boosted into the top spot of president and chief executive officer, replacing Compaq's founder after the board became unsatisfied with the company's strategy. Pfeiffer then set out in late 1993 to make Compaq the largest provider of personal computers in the world by 1996, but reached the goal by 1994.

In addition to taking over the market with IBM "clones," or machines that carry generally the same kind of hardware and run the same kind of software as higher-cost IBM personal computers (PCs), Pfeiffer moved Compaq up a notch by snatching business away from bigger mainframe producers as well. With an eye on selling to businesses as well as individuals, Pfeiffer expanded Compaq into marketing "servers," or high-end, powerful computers that serve as central processors for an entire department, or for an Internet provider. Personal computers were still its bread and butter, though, accounting for about 10 million units and two-thirds of its sales in 1997. The remarkable fact about its PC sales was that it managed to make them profitable: While other firms were still seeing losses from PCs or managing to squeak by with minimal gains, Compaq was showing a healthy 8.4 percent profit margin on the machines.

In 1998 Compaq purchased Digital Equipment Corporation, a firm known for its mini-computers, smaller alternates to mainframes that became outdated when servers startedgaining momentum. One of its better-known products was the Unix operating system. Though Digital's sales were gradually falling, Pfeiffer saw the opportunity to combine forces in order to beef up large corporate accounts, thus competing with IBM and Hewlett-Packard. Though it had been trying its hand at selling servers, Compaq had mainly specialized in low-cost PCs sold through dealers, who handled service needs. Bigger clients, however, were looking for a more intensive support structure, such as installation, programming, and sometimes even operation of systems that Digital could help provide. The merger was the largest in the history of the computer industry. Stockholders sealed the deal by June of 1998, making Compaq the second largest overall computer firm in the world. Though Pfeiffer's willingness to venture in new directions characterizes him as somewhat of a risk-taker in the business world, he is also known to be very focused and calculating. Unwilling to talk about himself too much, he simply told David Kirkpatrick in *Fortune,* "I am a very thorough person."

Pfeiffer was born in a small town just east of Dresden, Germany, called Lauban (which is now part of Poland), on August 20, 1941. His father, a German soldier, was taken prisoner of war during World War II, and as Russian troops steadily forged on in Europe, his mother piled the family's belongings in a hand cart and ran. Pfeiffer was only four years old at the time. She settled with her children in Nuremberg, then part of West Germany. His father was held prisoner until 1948. Pfeiffer ended up attending the Kaufmaennissche Berufsschule in Nuremberg, graduating with a bachelor of arts degree in business in 1963. The following year, he began working for Texas Instruments, an American company, in Munich, Germany, as a financial controller and office manager. At one point while working in Germany, Pfeiffer went along with an associate to act as a translator at a sales meeting and later decided to leave accounting and join the sales crew. He was eventually promoted to head of the Munich subsidiary and in 1974 began leading the European consumer products group, the marketing arm of Texas Instruments in Europe. In 1979, he was named vice-president of corporate marketing and began working out of the Dallas offices.

After almost two decades with Texas Instruments, Pfeiffer was approached by a former Texas Instruments employee who had ventured out on his own. Joseph R. "Rod" Canion, an American engineer, started up Compaq Computer Corporation in 1982. His goal was to copy the technology from IBM personal computers, improve upon it, and sell the enhanced machines for about the same price. The next year, 1983, Canion recruited Pfeiffer to head the new computer firm's European division. Pfeiffer started his new job on September 1, 1983, arriving in Germany a week later with $20,000 to get things going. He set up headquarters in Munich, since Compaq decided the largest markets for PCs would probably be in Germany. In April of 1984, Compaq began a British subsidiary, and French operations started about five months after that. By 1991, Compaq Europe was selling about $2 billion in products a year. "Our timing was just right," Pfeiffer commented to Steve Lohr in the *New York Times* about Compaq's growth in the European market. "When the demand exploded, we were in place. Had we started much later, we would have missed that window of opportunity."

Meanwhile, however, Pfeiffer noticed that due to a strong U.S. currency, Compaq's machines were more expensive than their competitors' products. In addition, corporations in Europe were wary of dealing with an unproven firm. Pfeiffer thus argued that for Compaq to grow its business, it should establish manufacturing plants in Europe. This would not only lower its cost,but also raise its profile and affirm its commitment to operations in Europe. Compaq gave the green light to set up shop overseas in 1985. After narrowing down a list of potential sites, Compaq chose Erskine, Scotland, and announced in 1986 that it would begin building a plant. With its abundance of universities and technical schools, that area of Scotland, home also to Glasgow and Edinburgh, is sometimes known as "Silicon Glen." Compaq thus knew that there, they could amass the skilled labor essential for their operations, and as an added bonus, wages were lower than in most areas on the Continent and unemployment was running high.

Pfeiffer made Compaq's European division a rousing success thanks to his strategy of dealer-only distribution. Sales increased from less than $20 million in 1984 to $733 million in 1988. That figure represented about 36 percent of the firm's total sales. By 1990, sales had jumped about 50 percent to roughly $1.8 billion, capturing the number two spot in European computer sales, behind IBM, making up about half of the company's sales. By 1992, they had sprinted past IBM to take the lead. The company was also going global, acquiring subsidiaries in Australia, Latin America, and Asia. However, Compaq was falling behind in the United States. The average growth rate in America for computer firms was about seven percent in 1990, but Compaq was dragging its feet at about four percent. Its LTE 386 laptop was a disappointment, and the competition was selling machines for up to 35 percent cheaper than Compaq.

In January of 1991, Pfeiffer moved to Compaq headquarters in Houston to take over as COO, at Canion's request. Later that year, after Compaq announced its first-ever round of layoffs and a $70 million loss, the board in an October meeting ousted Canion, the firm's founder, and instituted Pfeiffer as president and CEO. Canion reportedly did not want to make drastic enough changes in the company's strategy, and Pfeiffer was an established performer. He trimmed the work force—letting go of 2,700 employees—and cut computer prices in the marketplace. The boom in PC sales, in addition to contracting out production of their components, allowed Compaq to slash prices by about 50 percent, making them the first computer firm to offer a PC for under $1000. He also introduced a number of new models, increased the number of retail outlets carrying Compaq products, and toned down the technical jargon in ads in order to make them easier to understand. The winning combination of offering a Windows operating system with an Intel processor in the machine was also part of Compaq's success. By 1994, Compaq had surpassed IBM as the number one vendor of PCs. As Marshall Loeb noted in a 1995 *Fortune* article, "Nobody complained when the board recently raised his salary, bonus, and other annual compensation from $2.5 million to $5.05 million."

Perhaps one of Pfeiffer's most important decisions, however, was to branch out from just offering low-cost PCs to individuals into marketing high-end megasystems known as servers, which function as a hub in a network of PCs. These smaller, powerful computers began replacing mainframes in businesses, and Pfeiffer wanted to get in on the action. However, to do so, the company would have to offer more support directly to its customers, rather than relying on service from retailers, as was its previous method. Compaq thus bought mainframe manufacturer Tandem Computers in 1996, doubling its field sales force and expanding its crew of people knowledgeable about larger data-centered systems. *Forbes* magazine was sufficiently impressed with his success in this area, in addition to the firm's strong growth, high returns, and large buildup of assets—$6 billion in cash and no debt—to name Compaq its Company of the Year in 1997. At the time, Eric Nee wrote in the *Forbes* article, "Even with the Tandem acquisition, Compaq has only 8,000 sales and support people in the field, one twentieth the number that IBM has. Don't be surprised if

Compaq spends some of that cash hoard buying some or all of Digital or Unisys."

Sure enough, in January of 1998, Compaq announced it was buying Digital Equipment Corporation for roughly $9 billion. The sale became final in June when stockholders approved the union. Compaq, with Digital, had a combined revenue of $37 billion in 1997 compared to IBM's sales of $78.5 billion, making it the second largest overall computer firm in the world. Digital had previously risen to become the number two computer manufacturer, providing mammoth machines to universities and big businesses, but their profits had been falling due to a turnaround in demand for the large systems. With the buyout, Compaq added Digital's skill at serving large corporations to its mix, thereby opening up the road to getting a greater slice of the pie from business and other major accounts. "Frequently we weren't invited to the party," Pfeiffer noted in the *New York Times*. "Now Compaq can provide service and support capability that is a prerequisite for most of our major customers." Along with the news of the merger came word that up to 17,000 workers could be laid off during restructuring. Compaq, however, has generally been known as a benevolent corporation, giving generously to nonprofit groups.

Pfeiffer in 1994 was named CEO of the year by online news service MSNBC, and in 1996 received the Prime Minister's Trade Award from Japan's Ryutaro Hashimoto. The soft-spoken, conservative businessman has a reputation as a calm, meticulous, leader, sometimes to the point of being a bit boring. He does, however, have his wild side. A fan of James Dean, Pfeiffer is known to favor leather jackets and classic sports cars, driving a 1988 black convertible Porsche Turbo at speeds up to 100 miles per hour on his way to work. Though he works about 65 to 70 hours a week, he does go out socially, sometimes with a female companion. He has also been seen around town with Houston Rockets' basketball player Hakeem Olajuwon. An avid dancer, he cuts loose at company parties and has been seen sporting a four-foot-wide cowboy hat at company meetings. He lives in the upscale Tanglewood section of Houston in a luxury high-rise.

Sources

On-line

Compaq Computer Corporation web site, http://www.compaq.com (August 24, 1998).

Periodicals

Business Week, June 26, 1989, p. 150; February 4, 1991,
p. 86; November 11, 1991, p. 41; February 9, 1998,
p. 90.
Computer Reseller News, November 18, 1996, p. 151.
Electronic Engineering Times, June 15, 1998, p. 8.
Forbes, January 12, 1998, p. 90.
Fortune, December 14, 1992, p. 80; February 21, 1994,
p. 90; April 17, 1995, p. 217; April 1, 1996, p. 120.
New York Times, July 9, 1989, sec. 3, p. 4; October 25,
1992, sec. 3, p. 9; January 28, 1998, p. A1.
Popular Science, July 1, 1997, p. 75.

—Geri Speace

Mike Piazza

Baseball player

Born Michael Joseph Piazza, September 4, 1968, in Norristown, PA; son of Vincent, Sr. (a businessman) and Veronica Piazza. *Education:* Attended University of Miami, 1986, and Miami- Dade (North) Community College, 1987.

Addresses: *Office*—c/o New York Mets, 12301 Roosevelt Ave., Flushing, NY 11368.

Career

Professional baseball player; catcher and designated hitter. Los Angeles Dodgers, 1988-98; traded to Florida Marlins, 1998; New York Mets, 1998—.

Awards: Baseball Writer's Association of America and *The Sporting News* both named him National League Rookie of the Year, 1993; most valuable player award, 67th Annual All-Star Game, 1996.

Sidelights

Baseball player Mike Piazza stated to Bob Nightengale of the *Sporting News,* "I'll never take this game for granted, never. I've worked too hard to get here. It's something that I've always been taught, and lived by. I know this can be gone as easily as it came." Piazza's spectacular professional baseball career might never have gotten started if it were not for family friend Tommy Lasorda, manager of the Los Angeles Dodgers, who talked the team into using a draft pick on the relatively unpromising hopeful. Since the initial push, however, Piazza's record has stood on its own. Though Lasorda pulled strings to get Pi-

azza drafted—barely—in 1988, it was up to the tenacious player to prove his worth. After a record-breaking season in 1993, Piazza was unanimously named Rookie of the Year. As a catcher he is not outstanding, but his power-packed batting skills have put him in the top rank as one of the best players in the league. In 1998, Number 31 was traded to the Florida Marlins in a multi-player deal considered the biggest trade in baseball history, and only a week later he was shuttled again, this time to the New York Mets, who nabbed him in exchange for three prospects.

Piazza was born on September 4, 1968, in Norristown, Pennsylvania, one of five sons of Vincent and Veronica Piazza. He was raised in Phoenixville, near Philadelphia. His father, a first-generation Sicilian, left high school in order to go to work, and eventually became a self-made millionaire. He ran a used-car dealership and went on to manage a number of business operations, including new car sales, real estate, and computers, working his up to become worth about $70 million. When he reached success, he moved his family to Valley Forge, Pennsylvania, in an expensive home overlooking Valley Forge National Park. Piazza's father is also the fourth cousin of Los Angeles Dodgers manager Tommy Lasorda, and the two have been close friends throughout their lives. The elder Piazza even named his youngest son, Tommy, after Lasorda, who asked to become the child's godfather. Lasorda, however, is not the godfather of Mike Piazza, as many sources have erroneously reported. "In the Italian culture, once you're godfather to one child, in a sense you're godfather to them all," Mike Piazza explained to Lisa Winston in *Baseball Weekly*. "But it got blown out of proportion."

Piazza grew up loving baseball. He used to bounce balls off a mattress that leaned against a wall in his basement and swing at them. Later, he used a batting tee, or his father would pitch to him. When Piazza was still in elementary school, he and his father put together a batting cage and pitching machine so that the youngster could practice all the time. Piazza even warmed up baseballs on the stove and went out in the dead of winter, prompting his father to build a roof on top, add side paneling, and set up a heater inside. Each year Piazza improved, until his father and Lasorda began joking that someday he would join the Dodgers. At one point, Ted Williams, through a mutual friend, stopped by the Piazza household to see the young player. Piazza recalled to Winston, "The first thing he said after watching me hit was, 'He hits the ball better than I did when I was 16.'" In 1986, Piazza, a senior at Phoenixville High School, broke his school's record for career home runs (previously held by major league player Andre Thornton).

However, the major league scouts just did not seem enthused about Piazza. "I have talked to a lot of scouts since then who said they didn't like anything about me," Piazza told Kelly Whiteside in *Sports Illustrated.* "They said that I couldn't run or hit." Lasorda intervened and landed Piazza a spot as a college freshman on the University of Miami Hurricanes. After one disappointing season in which he had one hit in nine at bats, Piazza transferred to Miami-Dade Community College and hit .364, but was out much of the year because of a hand injury. In order to stir interest among four-year universities and hopefully snag a scholarship, Lasorda managed to have the Dodgers draft Piazza in June of 1988. He was their last pick in the 62nd round.

In August, a scout called up to see where Piazza would be attending school, and Piazza requested a tryout, optimistic about a real future with the team. As Dodgers scouting director Ben Wade watched Piazza hit balls into the blue seats, Lasorda suggested that he could be a catcher, despite the fact that the player had never held that position. They asked Piazza to throw, and he gave it his all. "I think my arm is still hurting from that day," he told Whiteside. The director offered him

a $15,000 signing bonus and Piazza accepted before even hearing the whole offer. "If he would have said, 'You have to pay me $15,000,'" Piazza remarked to Whiteside, "I would have said, 'Well, let's see. I have 10 grand in the bank and ...' I said 'yes' before he said thousand.' He could have said $15, and it wouldn't have mattered."

After his 1989 rookie season in Arizona on the Dodgers' instructional league team, Piazza asked to be sent to Campo Las Palmas, the Dodgers' academy for Latino recruits in the Dominican Republic, to hone his talents. There he endured tarantulas and a spartan meal plan, but did improve his skill. By 1991 he was catching full-time at Class A Bakersfield, leading the team with 29 home runs. He shined in 1992, hitting .350 with 23 home runs and 89 runs batted in (RBIs) between playing in Double-A San Antonio and Triple-A Albuquerque. After a 25-game hitting streak, he was called to play for the Dodgers against the Chicago Cubs on September 1, 1992, going 3-for-3 and blasting his first major-league hit. In 1993, he won the Dodgers' "triple crown," hitting .318, landing 112 RBIs, and nailing 35 home runs—the most ever by a rookie catcher. He was also named National League Rookie of the Year in 1993, providing the losing Dodgers with a hero to flaunt. After that fantastic season, the Dodgers offered him three-year, $4.2 million contract, the highest guaranteed amount ever for a second-year player.

Piazza did not succumb to the dreaded "sophomore slump" in 1994, his second year in the major league. He led the team in batting, home runs, and RBIs, becoming only the second player in Dodgers history to hit 20 homers in his first two seasons. In 1995 after a knee injury, he was on the disabled list for almost a month, but returned to fly through a 16-game hitting streak from July 29 to August 16, setting a career high. He also became the first Dodger in team history to hit 20 or more homers in his first three seasons, a record he extended in 1996. Also in 1996 he topped his previous best with a 19-game hitting streak from August 22 to September 12. He was only the second person in the history of Dodgers Stadium to hit a home run over the left-field roof in 1997, and his record continued to show that he was the best-hitting catcher in the league. Piazza played in the 1994, 1995, and 1996 All-Star games and was the most valuable player of the game in 1996, an honor that both he and his father cherished.

In 1998, the baseball world was abuzz with news that the Dodgers had traded Piazza to the Florida Marlins on May 15 after contract negotiations sputtered out when he declined a six-year, $80 million offer, asking instead for a seven-year, $105 million deal. The trade was perhaps the biggest in baseball history, involving seven players: the Dodgers gave up Piazza and Todd Zeile in exchange for Gary Sheffield, Charles Johnson, Bobby Bonilla, Jim Eisenreich, and Manuel Barrios. However, the Marlins did not want to take on Piazza's salary either, and instead used him as a bargaining chip one week later in another trade involving three New York Mets players—Preston Wilson, Ed Yarnall, and Geoff Goetz. Thus Piazza ended up with the Mets, who welcomed him warmly and did not seem to shy away from a probable triple-digit contract request. "I've gone from a player who thought he would spend his whole career with one organization to a player who's been with three organizations in a week," Piazza commented to Ross Newhan in the *Los Angeles Times.* "I'm in shock, but I'm also very excited to be going to New York." Though attendance rose wildly at first at Shea Stadium to see the slugger, he was then plagued by "boos" for the first few weeks—perhaps due to his immodest salary request and his reluctance to fully commit to New York right away—but gradually gained fans' acceptance.

In addition to playing baseball, Piazza is an avid drummer who began at age 18 and is self-taught. He is a spokesperson for Hooked on Drums, a group that promotes drum-playing to youngsters, and loves the heavy metal music of Anthrax, Slayer, Motorhead, AC/DC, and others. He is also a big hockey fan and names Wayne Gretzky as one of his favorite athletes, in addition to football's Randall Cunningham. The six-foot, three-inch catcher weighs in at 215 pounds and has dark hair and a handsome face. His good looks and charm have led to guest appearances on the television shows *Married ... with Children* and *Baywatch,* a spot on MTV, and a cameo in the film *Spy Hard.* Known to have a hot temper on the field, Piazza is otherwise a laid-back guy except for his intensity for practicing his hitting.

Sources

On-line

"Mike Piazza Profile & Scouting Report," ESPN web site, http://espn.sportszoe.com (August 25, 1998).

"31 Career Notes," Mighty Mike Piazza web site, http://www.geocities.com/Colosseum/2331/careernotes.html (August 25, 1998).

"Mike Piazza," *Sporting News* web site, http://www.sportingnews.com (August 25, 1998).

Periodicals

Baseball Weekly, January 12, 1994, p. 6; May 27, 1998, p. 6.

Los Angeles Times, May 29, 1996, Sports, p. 1; July 8, 1996, Sports, p. 1; July 10, 1996, Sports, p. 1; July 14, 1996, Sports, p. 1, May 23, 1998, Sports, p. 1.

Newsday, May 23, 1998, p. A50; May 24, 1998, p. C2.

New York Times, August 24, 1998.

Sport, May 1994, p. 26.

Sporting News, February 28, 1994, p. 8; April 24, 1995, p. 38; May 23, 1998.

Sports Illustrated, July 5, 1993, p. 12; May 13, 1996, p. 74; April 28, 1998, p. 82; May 25, 1998, p. 32; June 1, 1998, p. 89.

Sports Illustrated for Kids, June 1, 1995, pp. 32, 35.

Star Tribune (Minneapolis, MN), May 24, 1998, p. 15C.

—Geri Speace

Jada Pinkett Smith

Actress

Born September 18, 1971; daughter of Robsol Pinkett, Jr. (a contractor) and Adrienne Banfield (a nurse); married Will Smith (an actor), December 31, 1997; children: Jaden (son). *Education:* Graduated from Baltimore School for the Arts high school; attended North Carolina School for the Arts.

Addresses: *Publicist*—Bragman, Nyman, Caffarelli, 9171 Wilshire Blvd., Penthouse Suite, Beverly Hills, CA 90210.

Career

Actress. Television series appearances include *A Different World,* NBC, 1991-93. Film appearances include *Menace II Society,* 1993; *The Inkwell,* 1994; *Jason's Lyric,* 1994; *A Low Down Dirty Shame,* 1994; *Tales from the Crypt: Demon Knight,* 1995; *The Nutty Professor,* 1996; *If These Walls Could Talk,* 1996; *Set It Off,* 1996; *Scream 2,* 1997; *Woo,* 1998; and *Return to Paradise,* 1998. Directed videos for Y?N—Vee and Shug & Dap, 1994; designed clothes for own Maja line, 1994-95; performed poetry readings around the U.S.; appeared at schools and shelters as motivational speaker.

Sidelights

Barely out of her teens and just finished with her freshman year at college, Jada Pinkett Smith made her way to Los Angeles and forged an illustrious acting career thanks to her self-confidence, talent, and beauty. Beginning with a role on the hot television comedy, *A Different World,* she played a smart-mouthed, street-smart Baltimore college student—not far from her real-life persona. She caught the attention of a couple of rookie filmmakers who gave her her first film role in the gritty *Menace II Society,* and the rest has been Hollywood history. Only five feet tall and weighing 100 pounds, the petite dazzler is known for portraying strong, even abrasive women on the silver screen, even though in real life she is known to relish slinky gowns and exudes a glamorous aura. Though Pinkett Smith's successful acting career is enough to guarantee her prominence in the press for a long time to come, she really swept the media off of its feet with her fairy-tale romance with handsome television and film star Will Smith, whom she married in 1997. Her gushing husband told *Ebony,* "Jada is an intellectual goddess. She just understands life ... the parameters of living."

Pinkett Smith was born in Baltimore, Maryland, the daughter of Robsol Pinkett, Jr., a contractor, and Adrienne Banfield, a nurse. Her parents divorced after only a few months of marriage around the time she was born. Pinkett Smith was raised by her mother and grandmother, Marion Banfield, in a rough neighborhood of northwest Baltimore called Pimlico. Pinkett Smith later recalled that her grandmother, a social worker, sowed the seeds of ambition in her as a child and started nurturing her talents. "She taught me that I can achieve whatever I want to achieve," Pinkett Smith remarked to Shelley Levitt in *People*. "Grandma wanted her grandchildren to have every possible experience—ballet, tap dancing, piano lessons, gymnastics. She didn't ever want us to ever think we were deprived."

At age 14, Pinkett Smith was accepted to the prestigious Baltimore School for the Arts, where she befriended fellow classmate Tupac Shakur, who later became a famous rapper and actor. The two were close until his death in 1996; she even contributed $100,000 in 1995 to help post his $3 million bail when he was appealing a sexual abuse conviction. Slightly rebellious, she was known to dye her hair bright colors, and confessed to Karen Brailsford in *Interview* that she "barely graduated," but says she never really got into too much trouble as a teen. After high school, Pinkett Smith's mother shipped her off to college at the North Carolina School for the Arts. After her freshman year, she went out to Los Angeles for the summer and met Keenen Ivory Wayans, the creator and star of the television show *In Living Color*, at a party. She boldly asked him for a job as a choreographer for his show, though she freely acknowledged having no professional experience except for chipping in with some dance numbers at a school play. He did not hire her, but saw some promise and told her to get an agent. Pinkett Smith related to Heather Keets in *Entertainment Weekly*, "He encouraged me to get off my lazy tail, get an agent, and do something."

Pinkett Smith did just that, and after fifteen auditions for the part, in 1991 landed a role on the smash television sitcom, *A Different World*. Playing college student Lena James, a Baltimore ruffian with a soft spot, she drew upon her own experiences growing up to give Lena the edge and sassiness required. She also blossomed as an actress during this two-year stint, which led to a movie offer. Teenage brothers Allen and Albert Hughes, who had directed some music videos, scraped together a $2 million budget to produce *Menace II Society*, casting her as a single mother. Turned off at first because of the violence, Pinkett Smith reconsidered after discussing the project with the creators. As she noted in *Interview*, "When I started to look at my character, Ronnie, I realized that for the first time you're seeing a young, responsible single mother.... Most of the time black women within that element are drug addicts, hookers, loudmouths, what have you. I had to give the [Hughes] brothers props."

After her acclaimed performance in *Menace*, Pinkett Smith took a part that she described in *Interview* as "a snooty don't-know nothing" in the 1994 comedy-

drama *The Inkwell*. Another romantic role followed in the violent, gang-inhabited *Jason's Lyric*, also in 1994. That same year, Pinkett Smith got her chance to team up with her old friend Wayans in his action-comedy *A Low Down Dirty Shame*, playing Peaches, the helping hand to Shame, a private eye played by Wayans. She told Keets in *Entertainment Weekly* that Wayans "busted my ass. I had to read twice, no three times, for him!" Though the film was plagued by lukewarm critical reception, it did not do badly at the box office, and Pinkett Smith was a standout. Owen Glieberman in *Entertainment Weekly* called Pinkett Smith "a hyperkinetic comic sprite," while *People Weekly* quoted two other publications' raves: Stephen Holden of the *New York Times* commented that her performance "is as sassy and sizzling as a Salt-n-Pepa recording" and Kevin Thomas in the *Los Angeles Times* cheered that she "lights up the screen."

Pinkett Smith transformed her appearance for her next role, dying her hair platinum blonde to do battle with evil forces in 1995's *Tales from the Crypt: Demon Knight*. She told Brailsford in *Interview*, "It was something I thought would really work for my character." That character, Jeryline, was the first female African American action hero on the big screen in almost 20 years, when Pam Grier took her revenge in blaxploitation films of the 1970s (with whom she would later work in the 1997 romantic comedy *Woo*). Pinkett Smith made three films in 1996: *The Nutty Professor, If These Walls Could Talk,* and *Set It Off.*

Although Pinkett Smith had been generating attention for a few years, *Cosmopolitan* asserted in 1996, "*The Nutty Professor* propelled her film career into high gear." The Eddie Murphy remake had audiences rolling in the aisles, and brought Pinkett Smith fully into the limelight. After that, she switched gears for the female fugitive foursome film, *Set It Off*, about a team of women bank robbers. Also in 1996 she appeared in *If These Walls Could Talk*, a made-for-cable trilogy on HBO about abortion set in three different eras: 1952, 1974, and 1996. The next year, she and her movie boyfriend (Omar Epps) were the killer's very first victims in the horror film *Scream 2*. In 1998, she starred in *Woo*, a romantic comedy in which she plays a heartbreaker who goes out on a blind date with an attorney, and she appeared in *Force Majeure*, a drama about three friends who are torn when one is arrested for drug possession in Malaysia.

In addition to detailing her performances, magazine articles abounded on Pinkett Smith's offscreen love life. Back in 1994, Pinkett Smith was living single with just her two cats in a two-bedroom rental house in

Studio City, California, telling Levitt in *People,* "I don't have time to be serious about anyone, and that's been a real sacrifice for me." That all changed when she and actor Will Smith (of *Fresh Prince of Bel-Air* television series and *Men in Black* film fame, among others) began seeing each other after his divorce in 1995 and fell in love. They moved into a suburban Los Angeles home on three acres in 1996 and announced in December of 1997 that they were expecting a child. On New Year's Eve that year, they secretly wed in a ceremony at Cloister's Mansion just outside of Baltimore. In addition to family and friends, the high-profile guest list included Jasmine Guy, Tisha Campbell of television's *Martin* and her husband, Duane Martin, and *Fresh Prince of Bel-Air* costars James Avery, Karyn Parsons, and Alfonso Ribeiro. In July of 1998, Pinkett Smith gave birth to a son, whom she named Jaden.

Though Will Smith had already been divorced and had a child, Will III (known as Trey), reports characterized the couple as being true soul mates. Lynn Norment wrote in *Ebony,* "They are seen together at movie premieres, club openings, celebrity charity bashes, weddings, awards shows, restaurants, and sometimes just hanging out at the mall. Inseparable, they always appear to be happy." Will Smith told Dream Hampton in *Essence,* "Jada Pinkett is my best friend. Not my best female friend. She's my best friend, period. And that's the only way a relationship can work." And Pinkett Smith had remarked in 1996 in *Jet,* "When I decide to get married, that is going to be the man I spend the rest of my life with."

Pinkett Smith began designing her own fashion line, Maja, which featured the slogan "Sister Power" on dresses and T-shirts, in 1994. Though the project went on hiatus after her business partner died in 1995, Pinkett Smith indicated that she would like to restart the endeavor, specializing in a line for very petite women such as herself. Dabbling behind the camera as well, she has directed music videos for rap artists Y?N—Vee and hip-hoppers Shug & Dap and collaborated with Will Smith in 1997 on a script. She also has been spotted at New York sites like Mama's Kitchen giving poetry readings. Her plans for the future will include more scriptwriting, as she mentioned to Alore D. Collier in *Ebony:* "I want to write about things that empower women in all different ways, whether comedy or drama." She also told Collier, however, that she plans to be a full-time mom when the day comes. Even before she got pregnant, she was adamant about her personal position on mothering, saying that she will not have a live-in nanny to take over her duties. "It's going to be 24 hours a day, seven days a week. That's my child, and I'm raising the child," she insisted to Collier, although she noted that her husband urged her to make at least one movie a year.

Pinkett Smith bought a horse ranch near her hometown of Baltimore in 1996, where she goes back to relax on a regular basis. She has maintained her tiny size-one physique by avoiding red meat and working out regularly, although she mentioned to Collier in *Ebony* that her husband has a tendency to whip up high-calorie specialties like fried chicken, sweet potato pie, and apple and banana pancakes. Though her life seems to be at the peak of perfection, with a "Prince" for a husband and a glamorous career well underway, Pinkett Smith often shows up in urban schools and shelters to give motivational speeches. As she noted in *People Weekly,* she tells kids that "from struggle comes strength. And if everything's easy, then how do you know how to survive when, inevitably, there comes a time when things aren't so happy-go-lucky?"

Sources

Cosmopolitan, December 1996, p. 114.
Ebony, December 1996, p. 144; September 1997, p. 134.
Entertainment Weekly, October 7, 1994, p. 54; December 9, 1994, p. 48; December 23, 1994, p. 48; February 24, 1995, p. 132; May 19, 1995, p. 72; November 8, 1996, pp. 48, 77; May 2, 1997, p. 68.
Essence, January 1995, p. 80; July 1997, p. 60.
Interview, September 1994, p. 136.
Jet, February 13, 1995, p. 30; October 21, 1996, p. 36; December 15, 1997, p. 32; January 19, 1998, p. 64.
New Republic, July 5, 1993, p. 26.
People Weekly, December 5, 1994, p. 18; December 19, 1994, p. 55; January 30, 1995, p. 17; July 29, 1996, p. 96; November 18, 1996, p. 21; January 19, 1998, p. 52.
Time, April 21, 1997, p. 125.
Variety, December 8, 1997, p. 111.

—Geri Speace

Jeanine Pirro

Attorney

Born in 1951, in Elmira, NY; daughter of Esther Ferris; married Albert Pirro (a real estate development attorney), early 1970s; children: Cristi, Alexander. *Education:* Earned degree from University of Buffalo; earned law degree from Albany Law School. *Politics:* Republican. *Religion:* Roman Catholic.

Addresses: *Home*—Harrison, NY. *Office*—Westchester County District Attorney's Office, 111 Dr. Martin Luther King Jr. Blvd., White Plains, NY 10601.

Career

Became assistant district attorney for Westchester County, New York, c. 1975; headed one of the first domestic-violence crimes prosecution units in the United States, 1977; elected Westchester County Court judge, 1990; elected Westchester County district attorney, 1993 and 1997.

Awards: Inducted into the Westchester County Women's Hall of Fame, 1993; Kate Stoneman Award, Albany Law School, 1995, for career achievements.

Sidelights

As her official biography from the Westchester County District Attorney's office points out, Jeanine Pirro's career has been one of numerous firsts. She was Westchester's first female D.A. to argue a murder case; she was the first woman elected as a judge in the county, an enclave that includes Yonkers, White Plains, and some of New York City's poshest suburbs; and in 1993 she became Westchester County's first woman district attorney. She was re-elected to the post in 1997 by an overwhelming majority. She also may have been the first female district attorney ever to land on *People* magazine's "50 Most Beautiful People" list. *New Yorker* writer John Heilemann described her as "telegenic, articulate, and a politically ambitious firebrand."

Pirro was born Jeanine Ferris in 1951 and grew up in Elmira, New York, a city not far from the state's border with Pennsylvania. Her mother was once a model, and as Pirro admitted in her *People* profile, Esther Ferris "taught me that being the best you can be in your personal appearance as well as your intellect was primary." Pirro, however, did not let herself be deterred by the usual constraints of growing up female and Roman Catholic in the 1960s—she has said that she knew from the age of six that she wanted to be a lawyer. While still in high school, Pirro began working as a volunteer in the local district attorney's office, and from that experience realized that the prosecutorial side of the law was her forte. She received her undergraduate degree from the University of Buffalo, and then went on to Albany Law School, where she made law review.

It was at Albany that she began dating Albert Pirro, who returned to his home turf of Westchester County to begin a career as one of the state's most successful real estate development lawyers. The two were married, and the new Mrs. Pirro began working as an assistant district attorney in the county prosecutor's office. Pirro began to take a particular interest in crimes against women and children—sexual abuse and domestic violence breaches of law that at the time were usually handled in family court. In the mid-1970s, it was still legally permissible for a husband to sexually assault his wife, for instance, and in cases of physical violence against children, many law-enforcement authorities as well as the general public saw that as simply a parents' prerogative. Furthermore, in regard to the matter of the sexual abuse of children, it was an issue so shocking that it was rarely discussed openly.

Pirro helped change many of those attitudes. She learned that President Jimmy Carter was about to make funds available to set up four domestic-crimes units on a test basis in 1977. She asked her boss, the Westchester County district attorney, to apply for the funds, which he did, and then let her run the unit, which he also did to the surprise of some. She met resistance at every level for trying to bring cases that many judges felt should be handled in "family" court into the criminal arena. Even "juries didn't think that parents should be prosecuted for abusing a child," Pirro told Heilemann in the New Yorker. "I would go into court with a battered woman, and there were judges who would call me out of court, and they'd tell me, `Get that case out of here.'"

Pirro headed the Westchester County domestic-crimes unit for several years, and achieved an excellent conviction rate for the cases she brought to trial. She ran for a seat on the county bench herself in 1990, and held it until her former boss at the D.A.'s office decided to retire. She ran for his job as Westchester County D.A., and despite a rather ugly campaign—her opponent's political advisor was none other than Dick Morris, the Clinton insider who resigned after a sordid scandal—Pirro won by a solid majority. Her first day in office was a tough one: an heiress from Westchester's affluent Bronxville suburb had disappeared; Pirro launched a nationwide search for her missing husband. Later that year, she began appearing on news programs when the O.J. Simpson case broke; her specialty in domestic-violence issues, combined with her ease and eloquence before the camera, made her a frequent guest on Nightline, Court TV, and the Geraldo Rivera show.

Pirro's first term as D.A. was marked by several successes. Crime in Westchester County fell nearly ten percent, while the rate of prosecutions rose 15 percent; the largest seizure of drugs in county history landed Pirro in the spotlight when she successfully prosecuted those responsible. Her office also launched special units for crimes against the elderly, hate crimes, and misdeeds by public officials. Ironically, Pirro's own husband came under fire when a Federal Bureau of Investigation inquiry into a possible bribery scandal was derailed shortly after she took office. These and other charges do not appear to bother Pirro, who issued a standard reply to the charges volleyed by her detractors: "I stand on my own record," reported the New York Times.

Another controversial issue in Pirro's first term as D.A. again brought her national media attention. Long a champion of children's rights, Pirro felt that the growing access of the Internet—and pedophiles' access to minors on it—was a serious matter. After some well-publicized incidents in which adults were actively soliciting underage pen pals on the Internet and then attempting to meet them in person—with one occurrence in Westchester County a bit too close to home for Pirro, the mother of two—she submitted a legal remedy to the New York State legislature that was one of the first of its kind. Signed into law in late 1996, her "cybersex" statute amended the state penal code to allow felony prosecution of anyone who engaged in "indecent communications" with a minor over a computer network. Many objected to what they saw as a violation of free-speech rights and outright censorship, but as Pirro told Heilemann, "my mission is alerting people that our children are being handed to pedophiles on a pedestal because the courts are claiming everything is protected by the First Amendment."

A Republican, Pirro is a member of her New York State's highest political echelons. She and her husband count Senator Alfonse D'Amato and Governor George Pataki and his wife as friends, and real-estate tycoon Donald Trump is one of Albert Pirro's clients. The couple lives in Harrison, New York, in an Italianate villa built with marble they personally shopped for in Italy; their two children are Cristi and Alexander. Pirro is known as a workaholic who rises at 6 a.m. to exercise, but who gets through her twelve-hour days by snacking on candy. Despite her no-nonsense demeanor Pirro is an unabashed animal lover; her villa's grounds are home to four dogs and two pot-bellied pigs, among other creatures.

Pirro was re-elected in a landslide in 1997 for her second term, but both her supporters and detractors consider her to possess far greater political ambitions. There is talk she may appear on the next gubernatorial ticket as lieutenant governor, a stepping stone to the governor's office itself should her friend Pataki decide to make a bid for the White House in the year 2000. "She's brilliant, she's tough, she's extremely articulate, and she has all the skills needed for higher office," Pataki told the *New Yorker*. "I don't know if she'll want to do that, but if she does I wouldn't want to be in her way."

Sources

On-line

"Jeanine Pirro," *Westchester County—DA's Office,* http://www.da.westchester.ny.us (February 5, 1998).

Periodicals

New Yorker, February 24, 1997, pp. 122-126.
New York Times, May 21, 1997, p. B5; October 12, 1997, Section WC, pp. 1, 12; November 1, 1997.
People, May 12, 1997.
Village Voice, November 12, 1996, p. 15.

—*Carol Brennan*

Charley Pride

Country singer, guitarist, and producer

Born Charley Frank Pride, March 18, 1938 (some sources say 1939), in Sledge, MS; son of Mack Pride, Sr. (a sharecropper); married, December 28, 1956; wife's name, Rozene (a former cosmetologist, currently coordinator of Pride's business affairs); children: Kraig, Dion, Angela. *Religion:* Baptist. *Avocational interests:* Baseball and golf.

Addresses: *Home*—Dallas, TX, and Branson, MO. *Manager*—Jack D. Johnson, Nashville, TN. *Contact*—c/o PLA Media-Nashville, 1303 16th Avenue South, Nashville, TN 37212; fax: 615-320-1061.

Career

Played semi-professional and professional baseball in the Negro American League, including the Birmingham Black Browns, and later the Memphis Red Sox; joined Pioneer League, playing for the Timberjacks, Great Falls, MT, 1960-63; Anaconda Mining Company, Great Falls, tin smelter, 1960-64; played for Montana Amvets, 1961; sang at local Montana clubs and at baseball games, beginning c. 1962; signed with RCA records, 1964; performer in professional music tours across the globe, including Japan, New Zealand, Norway, Canada, Australia, Europe, and Fiji, 1966—; debuted at the Grand Ole Opry, 1967; moved to 16th Avenue Records, 1986; moved to Intersound Records, c. 1990; performed at the White House, c. 1995. First Texas Bank, Dallas, TX, majority stock holder; Cecca Productions, co-owner; Charley Pride Theatre, Branson, MO, owner, 1994—. Television appearances include *Hee Haw; Tom Jones Show; Lawrence Welk Show; Joey Bishop Show; Encore; Flip Wilson Show; Vibrations; Johnny Cash Show; Eddy Arnold Christmas Show,* 1970; *American All, Merv Griffin Show, Feeling Good, Christmas with Oral Roberts,* and *Midnight Special,* 1974; *Merv Griffin Show, Pop! Goes the Country, Como Country ... Perry and his Nashville Friends, American Music Awards, Mike Douglas Show, Tonight Show, Dinah!, Phil Donahue Show, Today, Grand Ole Opry at 50 (A Nashville Celebration),* and *Country Music Association Awards,* 1975; *Saturday Night Live with Howard Cosell* and *Donny and Marie,* 1976; *General Electric All-Star Anniversary,* 1978; *Sha Na Na* and *Games People Play,* 1980; *Solid Gold, Down Home Country Music,* and *Nashville Palace,* 1982; *NAACP Image Awards Show, Austin City Limits,* and *Music City News Country Awards,* 1983; *Colorsounds, Break Away,* and *Today,* 1984; *Nashville Now* and *Essence,* 1986; *Hollywood Squares,* 1987. Theater appearances include Felt Forum, 1975, and at Madison Square Garden, 1981. *Military service:* U.S. Army, 1956-58; performs in United Service Organizations (USO) tours.

Awards: Named Country Song Roundup's Most Promising Male Artist, 1967; Billboard's Trendsetter Award, 1970; Grammy Awards, best sacred performance, 1971, for *Did You Think to Pray,* and best gospel performance, 1971, for "Let Me Live"; named

Entertainer of the Year, Country Music Association, 1971; named Entertainer of the Year, Music Operators of America, 1971; named Male Vocalist of the Year, Country Music Association, 1971 and 1972; named Cashbox's top male vocalist; named Billboard's top male vocalist and top country artist; Grammy Award, best country performance, 1972, for *Charley Pride Sings Heart Songs;* inducted into Mississippi Hall of Fame, 1976; member of Grand Ole Opry, 1993; Pioneer Award, Academy of Country Music, 1994; Trumpet Award, outstanding African-American achievement, Turner Broadcasting, 1996; has had thirty-one gold and four platinum albums, and thirty-six singles reach number one on Billboard's chart.

Member: American Federation of Music.

Sidelights

One of a sharecropper's eleven children who helped his father chop and pick cotton from the age of five, Charley Pride wanted to be in another field when he grew up: a baseball field. Little did he know, all the Grand Ole Opry broadcasts to which he listened on Saturday nights and all the lyrics of Hank Williams he memorized would be what made Pride a recognized figure in both African-American and Caucasian circles. The first African-American to command country music charts with his warm baritone, Pride has recorded 36 number-one hit singles and has sold more than 35 million copies. One of the top 20 best-selling country artists of all time, Pride's RCA Records album sales are second only to Elvis Presley.

Charley Frank Pride was born in rural Sledge, Mississippi, a town imbued with the blues influence of Memphis's Beale Street 60 miles to the north. Pride dreamt of playing baseball and becoming the next Jackie Robinson, who played for the Brooklyn Dodgers and made history as one of the first African-American ball players in the nation. Pride began running around the diamond at 14 years old, the same age at which he bought his first guitar—a ten dollar Silverstone from Sears, Roebuck and Company. He taught himself how to play the guitar by listening carefully to Grand Ole Opry broadcasts and mimicking the picking styles he heard, but still hoped for a professional baseball career. He left Sledge after finishing junior high school, arriving in Memphis in 1955 where he joined the now-defunct Negro American League.

Pride played for Detroit and then for the Birmingham Black Browns before returning to Memphis, where he played for the Memphis Red Sox. It was in Memphis where Pride unofficially began his music career, en-tertaining his teammates with his guitar on the road between playing fields. As the Red Sox traveled throughout the country, Pride would often hop on stage and perform with various bands. It was also in Memphis where Pride met the woman he would marry, a former cosmetologist named Rozene. Soon after their relationship began in 1956, Pride was drafted and his baseball career was put on hold while he served two years in the army. "I got to thinking I didn't want nobody else being with her. I went back home for Christmas and married her," Pride told *Jet* in an interview conducted after their 40-year anniversary. They were married in a civil ceremony in Hernando, Mississippi. When his service was over, he returned to the Red Sox in 1958, where he pitched and played outfield for a year before he quit. After his Red Sox managers refused to give him a pay raise, Pride signed on with the Pioneer League's semiprofessional Montana Timberjacks in Great Falls.

Finding it necessary to supplement his salary from the Timberjacks, Pride took a job with the Anaconda Mining Company working in a tin smelter. African-Americans at the Anaconda mines were rare, and he was one of the only African-Americans working there. Still hoping to make it big as a baseball player, Pride traveled to the training camp of the Los Angeles Angels in February of 1961. Coach Marv Grissom told him his pitching arm wasn't strong or fast enough for the major leagues, but Pride persisted. He next appealed to the team's manager, Bill Rigney, and the Angels' owner, Gene Autry, to let him stay on. They all refused and after only two and a half weeks, Pride returned to Montana.

Working the swing shift back at the smelting factory and playing semiprofessional ball with the Helena (Montana) Amvets wasn't turning out to be the kind of existence Pride had expected to be living. Focusing on his work became difficult as well when his sleep was continuously interrupted by neighbors practicing their country music. He introduced himself to the group and in no time he was appearing with them as a singer and guitar player in local clubs. The Amvets also let Pride sing at games over the public address system, where the crowds begged for more. After one game where Pride had sung and played baseball particularly well, he was approached by the local press. After being featured as "the singing baseball player," Pride's serious music career began almost immediately. A phone call from the secretary of the local musicians' union came in one day to make sure Pride was a member. Pride remarked, as told to Bruce Cook in the *National Observer*, "[S]ure, I paid my dues at the smeltery," completely unaware that music stars got some union backing, too, if they wanted. "[I]t looked like I was going to get into this a little deeper. And so I joined up," he commented to Cook.

Pride continued to work at the mining company, but on weekends he began to perform regularly in various nightclubs. One evening in 1963, Grand Ole Opry greats Red Sovine and Red Foley happened to stop in at the club in Great Falls where Pride was performing. They were so impressed with his talent that Sovine and Foley promised that if he came to Nashville, they would get him an audition. Pride was not ready to give up the prospects of getting famous by belting out home-runs instead of hits and tried to reach the major leagues one more time. A new team in the league, the Mets, had not had many successes in their 1962 and 1963 seasons and Pride thought he could be a benefit to the team's roster. He showed up at the Mets' Tampa, Florida, training camp in 1964. Unfortunately, Pride was viewed as another mediocre talent bucking for a try-out and he was refused because Tampa was for training, he overheard the coach say, not for try-outs.

Disheartened and disappointed, Pride headed home to Montana, but soothed himself with a side trip to Nashville. Recalling Sovine's offer for an audition, Pride arranged to sing for music manager Jack D. Johnson. By the time Pride had returned home, a contract was in the works. On March 5, 1964—less than a week after singing for Johnson—Pride had a management contract. By 1965, Pride was ready to record a demonstration tape. He decided to personally deliver the finished product, a seven-track recording, to Nashville himself. Johnson had been having a difficult time promoting Pride, an African-American man in the South who sang country music in an era fraught with racial unrest and civil rights battles. Once Chet Atkins, the country guitarist who was head of RCA Victor in Nashville, heard two of Pride's test recordings, he signed him to a long-term contract with the company. Pride cut his first record and the single "Snakes Crawl at Night" quickly rose to the top of the country music charts.

RCA was still somewhat hesitant about the reception of an African-American by listeners who were predominately white so they promoted Pride by shipping records with no liner notes on or photographs of him. The intention was to let Pride's singing win fans over before letting them know about his race. Pride's first three recordings were all well-received; his second, "Just Between You and Me," won him a Grammy Award nomination for best country and western male vocal performance in 1966. Pride was quickly attract-

ing a large following but none of his fans knew he was African-American until his first major concert performance in Detroit in 1966. Upon the introduction of Pride, the crowd broke out in resounding applause which quickly died down when Pride walked out on stage. This sort of reception was typical early in his career. According to an interview in *Jet*, he told audiences his first year of touring: "'Now ladies and gentlemen, we realize it's a little unique me coming out here on a country music show wearing this permanent tan.'" Apparently this comment about his appearance was a hit. "Automatically, it's another big applause because I'm saying exactly what they're thinking," Pride explained in *Jet*.

> "I tried to be myself.... All I'm trying to do is just be a total individual who can fit into what society has become over the years. It goes beyond music."

As the first African-American country singer, Pride met with racism as well as the confusion and misunderstanding of fellow African-Americans. Even members of his family, he recalled to *Jet*, would say, "Why are you singing White folks' music?" Some African-Americans thought his career was "a gimmick" and that he was trying to prove something to the world. Pride always maintained that race was not an issue and that he was merely an American singing what he termed "American music." Once the initial shock of his color wore off, audiences quickly recovered their adoration for his rich and versatile voice. Pride said he always knew it would be his music that would make his audiences colorblind. "I didn't have any doubts," he reflected in Jerry Parker's 1971 *Newsday* article. "I always have felt people were just people. I guess society had to adjust to me, but I came along at a time when society was ready to accept me for what I am: plain old Charley Pride." He was right. Before the end of 1966, he was getting standing ovations, requests for encores at performances, and several country music awards. Pride knew he had gained the acceptance of his fans and peers alike when he appeared for the first time at the Grand Ole Opry and was the first African-American to grace their stage.

Concurrent with his Grand Ole Opry performance was the release of *Country Charlie Pride* (1967), his first-recorded album which eventually sold over a million copies. Throughout the 1960s, Pride continued to record best-selling albums and singles and receive high-rotation air play on country radio all over the country. He made numerous television appearances and continued touring. In 1970, he won his first Gold Single award for "Kiss An Angel Good Morning." In that year, Pride grossed approximately $2 million and was selected as the winner of *Billboard*'s 1970 Trendsetter Award. Pride's fame and recognition endured with myriad awards, including three Grammy Awards and several nominations. Pride was starting to be seen not only as a talent, but also as a popular performer able to break racial barriers. Pride insists that his intention was never to become a role model or transcend any boundaries. He only wanted to sing the music to which he grew up listening and which he loved. "I tried to be myself," he told *Jet*. "All I'm trying to do is just be a total individual who can fit into what society has become over the years. It goes beyond music," Pride once commented in the New York *Sunday News*.

Not only has Pride crossed the racial barriers in music, he has also taken great strides beyond music itself. He still performs and, in fact, owns the Charley Pride Theatre in Branson, Missouri, as well as the office building which is the home of his production company (Cecca Productions) and a recording studio. Completely outside of the realm of music, Pride bought the 124-acre farm of his childhood and rents it to a farmer in Sledge. He also owns a 248-acre cattle ranch in Texas and is a major stock holder of the First Texas Bank in Dallas, which reported assets of $134 million in 1997 and was number seven on *Black Enterprise*'s list of top financial companies. His wife serves on the bank's board of directors. She also helps behind the scenes of Pride's career to coordinate his performances, fan club, tour activities, and other business interests.

Pride told *Jet* that the reason his 40-year marriage has withstood the trials and tribulations that sometimes accompany fame and fortune is because they've always shared his successes and reveled in them together. They work together as a couple, yet still maintain their individuality. Most importantly, they told *Jet*, they understand the necessity of communication and working at differences without trying to change one another. What has worked for Pride in marriage to his wife has also worked for keeping up his relationship with his audiences. He performs in 70 or more concerts a year, and with 30 million albums in the hands of admirers, there is little doubt that Pride can easily charm those he loves and who love him back. And Pride has hardly forgotten his first love: baseball. He reportedly keeps in shape by working out with the Texas Rangers during their Spring Training.

Selected discography

"Snakes Crawl at Night," RCA 1964.
"Just between You and Me," RCA, 1966.
Country Charlie Pride, RCA, 1967.
Pride of Country Music, RCA, 1967.
Make Mine Country, RCA, 1968.
Songs of Pride ... Charley, That Is, RCA, 1968.
Charley Pride in Person at Panther Hall, RCA, 1968.
The Sensational Charley Pride, RCA, 1969.
The Best of Charley Pride, RCA, 1969.
Did You Think to Pray (includes "Let Me Live"), RCA, 1970.
Just Plain Charley, RCA, 1970.
Kiss an Angel Good Morning, RCA, c. 1970.
Christmas in My Home Town, RCA, 1970.
From Me to You, RCA, 1971.
I'm Just Me, RCA, 1971.
Charley Pride Sings Heart Songs, RCA, 1971.
The Best of Charley Pride, Volume 2, RCA, 1972.
A Sunshiny Day with Charley Pride, RCA, 1972.
Songs of Love by Charley Pride, RCA, 1973.
Sweet Country, RCA, 1973.
Amazing Love, RCA, 1973.
Country Feelin', RCA, 1974.
Pride of America, RCA, 1974.
Charley, RCA, 1975.
The Happiness of Having You, RCA, 1975.
Sunday Morning with Charley Pride, RCA, 1976.
She's Just an Old Love Turned Memory, RCA, 1977.
The Best of Charley Pride, Volume 3, RCA, 1977.
Someone Loves You, Honey, RCA, 1978.
When I Stop Leavin' I'll Be Gone (also known as *Burgers and Fries*), RCA, 1979.
You're My Jamaica, RCA, 1979.
There's a Little Bit of Hank in Me, RCA, 1980.
Roll on Mississippi, RCA, 1981.
Charley Pride Live, RCA, 1982.
Charley Pride Sings Everybody's Choice, RCA, 1982.
Night Games, RCA, 1983.
The Power of Love, RCA, 1984.
Greatest Hits, Volume 2, RCA, 1985.
Back to the Country, RCA, 1986.
After All This Time, Capitol, 1987.
I'm Gonna Love Her on the Radio, Capitol, 1988.
Moody Woman, Capitol, 1989.
Platinum Pride, Volumes 1 and 2, Honest Entertainment, 1994.
My Six Latest and Six Greatest, Honest Entertainment, 1994.
Super Hits, RCA, 1996.

Classics with Pride, Honest Entertainment, 1996.
The Essential Charley Pride, RCA, 1997.

Selected writings

(With Jim Henderson) *Pride: The Charley Pride Story* (autobiography), William Morrow (New York), 1994.

Sources

On-line

"Charley Pride," *Music City News,* http://www.hsv.tis.net/mcn (December 22, 1997).
"Charley Pride," PLA Media, http://www.plamedia.com/pride.html (December 22, 1997).

Books

African-American Reference Library, Gale Research, 1994.
Contemporary Musicians, Volume 4, Gale, 1990.
Estell, Kenneth, editor, *African-American Almanac,* Gale Research, 1994.
Mapp, Edward, *Directory of Blacks in the Performing Arts,* The Scarecrow Press, 1990.

Periodicals

Jet, August 5, 1996, p. 63; February 10, 1997, p. 32.
National Observer, April 1, 1972, p. 1.
Newsday, November 15, 1971, p. 3.
Sunday News (New York), December 2, 1973.

—Audrey Gebber

Stanley Prusiner

Neurologist and biochemist

Born Stanley Ben Prusiner, May 28, 1942, in Des Moines, IA; son of Lawrence (an architect) and Miriam (Spigel) Prusiner; married Sandra Lee Turk, 1970; children: Helen Chloe, Leah Anne. *Education*: University of Pennsylvania, A.B., 1964, M.D., 1968. *Religion*: Jewish.

Addresses: *Office*—Department of Neurology, HSE-781, University of California, San Francisco, San Francisco, CA 94143-0518. *Home*—400 Pacheco St., San Francisco, CA 94116-1419.

Career

University of California, San Francisco (UCSF), neurology resident, 1972-74, assistant professor, 1974-80, associate professor, 1980-84, professor of neurology, 1984—, simultaneously lectured in biochemistry and biophysics, 1976; associated with Howard Hughes Medical Institute, 1976-81; Alfred P. Sloan research fellow, 1976-78; University of California, Berkeley, professor of virology, 1984—; Senator Jacob Javits Center for Excellence in Neuroscience, National Institutes of Health, principal investigator and director, 1985-90.

Awards: Roy G. Williams Basic Sciences Research Award, 1968; George Cotzias Award, American Academy of Neurology, 1987; PotamKin Prize for Alzheimer's Disease Research, 1991; Christopher Columbus Quincentennial Discovery Award in Biomedical Research, National Institutes of Health, 1992; Richard Lounsbery Award, National Academy of Sciences, 1993; Albert and Mary Lasker Basic Medical

Research Award, 1994; Wolf Prize, 1996; Louisa Gross Horwitz Prize; Nobel Prize for Medicine, 1997.

Member: National Academy of Sciences, Institute of Medical-Natural Academic Sciences, American Society of Biological Chemists, American Society for Clinical Investigation, American Association of Immunologists, American Chemistry Society, American Academy of Neurologists, Sigma Xi.

Sidelights

Described in the *Wall Street Journal* by his friend Allen D. Roses as "a towering figure in American neurology," Stanley Prusiner has become an international presence for his discovery and research on prions (pronounced "PREE-ons"). Prions, according to Brendan I. Koerner of *U.S. News & World Report* are "infections proteins believed responsible for a range of brain-wasting ailments, including Creutzfeldt-Jakob disease, mad cow disease, and possibly Alzheimer's." The radical theories Prusiner has forced the medical community to acknowledge have garnered much controversy, even more so after he was awarded the Nobel Prize for Medicine in October of 1997. According to an article in *Time*, many critics still doubt the "maverick neurologist," and "not even the Nobel Prize will convince them otherwise."

Stanley Ben Prusiner was born on May 28, 1942 in Des Moines, Iowa, and grew up in Cleveland, Ohio. He earned his bachelor's degree at the University of Pennsylvania in 1964 and then remained another four years, earning his M.D. in 1968. The next four years were spent in biochemical research before Prusiner became a resident in neurology at the University of California, San Francisco, School of Medicine in 1972. When a 60 year-old female patient died of Creutzfeldt-Jakob disease (CJD), a fatal brain disease with symptoms of dementia, muscle spasms, brain deterioration, Prusiner resolved to find out the exact cause of neurodegenerative diseases.

While reviewing data on CJD and other such afflictions, Prusiner learned that all spongiform encephalopathies (diseases which cause the brain to become riddled with sponge-like holes) were thought to be infections caused by a type of "slow-acting virus," he wrote in his article for *Scientific American*, despite the fact that no one had actually managed to secure tangible proof. He was also inspired by the research of Tikvah Alper and her colleagues at the Hammersmith Hospital in London, and rushed to set up a lab at UCSF, which he did in 1974. By 1982, Prusiner and scientists at his laboratory were able to hypothesize a single infectious agent. Prusiner decided that since this agent was not a virus, it must be a protein-based agent. With this revelation, Prusiner coined the phrase "prion," short for "proteinaceous infectious particle."

Instead of being overwhelmed with praise for his findings, Prusiner was instead flooded with skepticism and severe criticism, as according to Gina Kolata in her *New York Times* article, "proteins had not been known to cause infectious diseases because, unlike viruses or bacteria, they did not have genetic material and so could not multiply." These claims practically made him an outcast in the scientific world. "He was challenging the conventional wisdom and he was aggressive about it," commented Dr. Zaven Khatchaturian, a former director of neurology at the U.S. government's National Institute of Aging, to the *Wall Street Journal*. "People didn't like that." Soon after, according to Robert Matthews in an article in *Focus*, Prusiner and his colleagues determined that "prions consist of a very resilient protein they call 'protease resistant protein or PrP.'" Matthews added that "PrP comes in two forms. In its natural form it plays some unknown role in the brain. But if the instructions for making it go wrong, brain cells make a different, and lethal, form of PrP—the prion protein."

In what Kolata described as a "slow-motion chain reaction," in the *New York Times*, more and more normal prions were reformed into the shape of the abnormal ones. As the process continued, the infectious proteins ate away at the brain, leading to inevitable death. In sum, what made the proteins disease-causing agents, Prusiner theorized, was their shape. Altman of the *New York Times* shared the analogy "that the prion could fold into two distinct formations ... a normal, friendly Dr. Jekyll and a dangerous, disease-causing Mr. Hyde."

> *"Awards do not vindicate a piece of science, only data does that."*

Considered brash and controversial, Prusiner's work initially did not gain him any respect or many supporters. In 1986, an outbreak in southeastern England of mad cow disease had the British in a frenzy. According to an article by Mark Caldwell in *Discover*, up to 300 cows a week were coming down with apprehensive, twitchy, and aggressive behavior that lead to their deaths. Matthews in *Focus* commented that scientists noted the similarities of the this epidemic with those of sheep who first contracted scrapies (so called because it drove sheep to scrape their heads against fences) in 1967. Caldwell added in his *Discover* article, that when veterinary researchers realized that British cattle were fed protein-laden feed made from sheep carcasses, manufacturers were forced to reconsider their processes for production. When another severe outbreak descended upon England in 1996, this time affecting humans who had eaten the meat of infected cattle, Prusiner was thrust into the scientific spotlight. Even some of his harshest critics began to reconsider their disbelief. He became more widely recognized and acknowledged for the value of his discoveries.

Early in the morning on October 6, 1997, Stanley Prusiner received a phone call in his hotel room in Bethesda, Maryland, where he was attending a U.S. Food and Drug Administration committee meeting on prion disease. He learned he had been awarded the $1 million Nobel Prize for Medicine. Many scientists praised Prusiner's work after the announcement of his award was publicized, but Dr. Laura Maneulidis, head of neuropathology at Yale Medical School, remained a leading critic of Prusiner's claims. She told the *New York Times* that she feared that the endorsement of the prion theory by the Nobel committee might block or discourage other researchers testing other possibilities. Maneulidis told Jonathan Knight and Nell Boyce in *New Scientist* that while she congratulates Prusiner on winning the Nobel Prize, "the real prize is scientific truth." Along with Robert Rohwer of Baltimore's Veteran Administration Medical Center, Maneulidis remarked that Prusiner sometimes would pass over data that did not fit his theory.

Prusiner himself, although unyielding in his beliefs about prions, understands controversy and thinks it is necessary for people to question findings until they are convinced. "Awards do not vindicate a piece of science," *New Scientist* reported Prusiner as saying, "only data does that." Prusiner would also like to see the creation of a drug that would stop the progression of CJD once it is detected. Usually, CJD is diagnosed posthumously with a brain biopsy, but scientists are working on a test to diagnose CJD earlier. Genetic engineering also remains a possibility.

Since a 1986 article in *Discover* profiled Prusiner, he has refused to speak to the press. He let down his guard, however, once he was honored with a Nobel Prize. When reporters tracked him down at his meeting with the FDA after his accolade hit the media, Prusiner acquiesced and agreed to respond to questions. According to a Reuters on-line source, when asked what he was going to do with the $1 million in prize money, the man who never joked about his research joked with reporters: "I am going to use it to pay my taxes."

Sources

On-line

Knight, Jonathan and Nell Boyce, "Nobel Splits Top Brains," *NewScientist,* http://www.newscientist .com/ns/971011/nnobel.html (November 2, 1997).

"Prusiner Wins Horwitz and Nobel Prizes," *Columbia University Record,* http://www.columbia.edu/cu/ record/23/07/18.html (November 2, 1997).

Books

Gale Encyclopedia of Science, Volume 5, Gale, 1996.

Periodicals

Discover, April 1991, p. 68.

Economist, January 18, 1997, p. 76.

Focus, January 1996, p. 36.

Newsweek, October 20, 1997, p. 51.

New York Times, October 4, 1994, p. C1; October 7, 1997, p. A1, pA12.

Science, March 1, 1991, p. 1022; June 14, 1991, p. 1515; July 12, 1996, p. 184; December 20, 1996, p. 2079.

Scientific American, January 1995, p. 48.

Time, October 20, 1997, p. 29.

U.S. News & World Report, October 20, 1997, p. 18.

Wall Street Journal, March 25, 1996.

—*Audrey Gebber*

Muammar Qaddhafi

Corbis

President of Libya

Born Mu'ammar Abu Minyar al-Qaddhafi (sources cite various spellings of name), in 1942, in Sirte, Libya; son of Abu Minyar (a shepherd) and Aisha Al-Qaddhafi; married Fathia Nouri Khaled, December, 1969 (divorced); married Safiya, 1970; children: (with Khaled) one son; (with Safiya) six children. *Education:* Military Academy of Benghazi, Libya, graduated, 1965; attended Beaconsfield Military Academy, Great Britain, 1966, and University of Benghazi, 1960s, studied history.

Addresses: *Office*—Office of the Secretary of Information & Culture, Tripoli, Libya.

Career

Leader of Libya, 1969—. Overthrew monarchy in nonviolent coup d'etat and was declared president of the Revolutionary Command Council (RCC), 1969; changed country's name to Socialist People's Libyan Arab Jamahiriya and became president, 1977. Author.

Sidelights

Muammar Qaddhafi, the longtime leader of the oil-rich country of Libya, is one of the United States' major foes. Considered a zealot and terrorist, he is driven by the idea of a united Islamic "Arab nation" linking the region from the Persian Gulf to the north Coast of Africa on the Atlantic Ocean. He began making headlines in 1969, when he and a group of supporters nonviolently seized power from the Libyan monarchy. Since then, Qaddhafi has remained in the forefront of world politics, first for his dramatic changes in Libya, then for his plan to fuse all Middle Eastern countries, and later for various political moves, the most notorious of which was his refusal to extradite two suspects in the bombing of a civilian aircraft over Lockerbie, Scotland, in 1988, which killed 270. He has also been in the spotlight for offering in 1996 to donate money to African American civil rights activist Louis Farrakhan, and for his writings, including 1998's *Escape to Hell and Other Stories*.

Mu'ammar Abu Minyar al-Qaddhafi's name has been transliterated into the English language in at least 30 different ways, including Muammar Qaddafi, Mu'ammar al-Qadafi, Moammar Ghadhafi, and other variants. The youngest child of four and the only son in his family, he was born in 1942 in a tent in the desert 20 miles south of Sirte, Libya, on the Mediterranean Sea. Sources cannot pinpoint the exact date. His father was a camel and goat herder, the main occupation for centuries for those in the Bedouin tribe of the Qadhdhafa. He and one of Qaddhafi's uncles had spent time in prison for resisting Italian colonial forces until Libya's independence in 1951. Qaddhafi was taught the Koran, the sacred book of Islam, as a child, and attended elementary school in Sirte from 1953 to 1955, where classmates teased him for being a poor nomad. When his family moved to Fezzan, an area south of Tripolitania, he continued his education in Sidra at the Sebha preparatory school from 1956 to 1961. During this time, he became fascinated with the ideas and political actions of Egypt's independence leader Gamal Abdel Nasser, whose impassioned pleas for Arab unity, condemnation of Western influences, and overthrow of King Farouk inspired many youths of the day.

Qaddhafi, a bright student, memorized Nasser's speeches and developed his political awareness. He formed a secret revolutionary society in which students discussed current events, led demonstrations supporting Nasser, and recruited others to the cause. His militant views and activities resulted in his expulsion in 1961. He and his family relocated to Misuratu in Tripolitania, where Qaddhafi finished his secondary education in 1963. He then enrolled in the Military Academy of Benghazi, where he and two of his best friends formed the core of the Free Unionist Officers Movement, an organization that intended to overthrow King Idris al Sanusi. After graduating from the military academy, Qaddhafi was sent to Britain to attend a signals course at Beaconsfield Military Academy. Also around this time, he took history classes at the University of Benghazi, but sources do not indicate that he graduated. Instead, Qaddhafi was commissioned in 1966 to the signal corps of the Libyan army, where he served just outside of Benghazi.

After three years in the army, Qaddhafi and his fellow Free Unionist Officers on the night of September 1, 1969, staged a bloodless coup overthrowing the Libyan monarchy. King Idris al Sanusi had been out of the country for several months due to health problems, so after a number of delays, Qaddhafi and his cronies found the right moment. After a relatively easy coup d'etat lasting only a few days, the Libyan Arab Republic was declared. Roughly two weeks later, it was announced that the 27-year-old Colonel Qaddhafi was the president of the Revolutionary Command Council (RCC), the power structure of the new regime. A slight power struggle ensued between Qaddhafi and his young officers on one hand and older officers and civilian supporters on the other, but the new leader crushed his opposition and by January of 1970 was totally in control.

Qaddhafi quickly instituted a plethora of reforms under what he deemed "Islamic socialism." He erased perks enjoyed by those in the former system, and he worked to smooth over tribal differences. American and British military bases were removed by June of 1970, and Italians were harassed and eventually all banished by October of the same year. Qaddhafi also nationalized finance, business, and industry, including big oil interests, and did away with wages. Vehemently Islamic, he abolished alcohol and nightclubs, declared the Koran the law of the land, and ceased the teaching of English in schools. In April of 1973, he declared a cultural revolution for changing society and politics, and the next month announced his "Third International Theory," which further distributed wealth among citizens and outlined new social programs. Using the wealth from oil companies, now partnered with the government, he funded housing, agriculture, and health care. By December of 1971, he had even nationalized British Petroleum, which operated in Libya. Other foreign companies met with the same fate.

For the first few years in power, Qaddhafi also tried desperately to link all Arab states into one nation. General Nasser, who died in 1970, had also espoused this idea of Pan-Arabism. Qaddhafi managed to get the cooperation of Egypt and Syria and proclaimed the Federation of Arab Republics in 1972, but the arrangement soon collapsed when the three countries could not agree on terms for the merger. Early in his reign Qaddhafi had tried to overthrow Sudan and fought with other nations that he considered too pro-Israel or pro-Western. He also established strong ties with the U.S.S.R., and, as a fervent opponent of Israel, supported the Palestine Liberation Organization (PLO). After some splits developed in the RCC in early 1974, Qaddhafi temporarily stepped down, but later that year emerged with more changes in mind. He set up the people's congresses, meant to handle local and regional issues, and the General People's Congress, to take over legislative power from the RCC. Qaddhafi remained in control, however, as secretary-general of this body. He claimed that his intent was for the state to eventually fade out so that the people would govern themselves at all levels.

Qaddhafi began outlining his political philosophy in the *Green Book*, published in three parts. The first part, released in 1976, dealt with politics; the second, in 1977, focused on economics, and the third, in 1979, concentrated on social aspects. This manifesto declared that the idea of a representative democracy was a hoax and encouraged the direct participation in government by all citizens. It also trumpeted true socialism, dismissing capitalism as well as Marxist Communism. Qaddhafi urged workers to begin managing all businesses as partners, rather than employees, and he decided that everyone was suddenly a homeowner: renters were given the titles to the houses they lived in, and began paying their rent to the state as a mortgage payment. On March 2, 1977, the country's name was changed to the Socialist People's Libyan Arab Jamahiriya, with Qaddhafi in position as president and leader of the "people's revolution."

Also throughout the 1970s, Libya stirred up trouble with its neighbors. In 1973, Libya invaded Chad, annexing the Aozou Strip, which is rich in minerals. The troubles between the two countries dragged on until 1988. In 1977, Libya briefly went to war with Egypt, and in January of 1980, after Libya-backed forces purportedly invaded a Tunisian mining town, France sent forces to support Tunisia. Libya was also implicated in the 1988 overthrow of Jafar Mohammed Nimeiri in the Sudan. Qaddhafi's sympathies, however, were erratic: in 1986 Libya entered a political union treaty with Morocco, in 1987 forged a political agreement with Algeria, and in April of 1988 signed a cooperation pact with Tunisia.

In 1978, Qaddhafi began to encourage people to form vaguely defined "revolutionary committees" in order to defend the people's revolution. In 1980, these groups began traveling abroad to kill any Libyan expatriate dissidents. In 1984, for example, Libyan representatives fired at Libyan dissidents during a demonstration in London, killing a British policewoman. Libya has also been accused of numerous terrorist plots, supposedly financing and providing military assistance to terrorist and revolutionary groups worldwide. Qaddhafi's support of Palestinian terrorist groups, the Irish Republican Army, and the Japanese Red Army have created hostile relations between Libya and Western powers, especially the United States. Though some opposition has simmered within the country and a number of reported attempts were made to overthrow Qaddhafi—many sponsored by other countries—he has maintained control.

When U.S. President Ronald Reagan took office in 1980, he stepped up efforts to impose political and economic sanctions on Libya and depose Qaddhafi. The decade saw heightened tension between the nations. In 1981, during American naval maneuvers in the Gulf of Sidra, two American planes shot down two approaching Libyan fighters. The United States accused Libya of manufacturing chemical weapons and seeking to obtain nuclear weapons. Libya-based Abu Nidal terrorists bombed airports in Rome and Vienna. In March of 1986, Libya fired ground-to-air missiles at American aircraft in the Gulf of Sidra, claiming they were violating Libyan air space. American forces then bombed missile and radar centers in Sirte, on the coast. The next month, the United States asserted that Libya had sponsored a terrorist attack on a disco in Berlin, Germany, which killed a U.S. soldier.

In retaliation for the disco incident, the Reagan administration ordered attacks on military bases, suspected terrorist camps, and government buildings. The raids killed 37, including Qaddhafi's adopted daughter. Later, in 1989, amid accusation that Libya was producing biological and chemical weapons, two Libyan planes inexplicably flew directly at American forces over international waters. The Americans then shot them down, and the pilots parachuted to safety. An Italian official, quoted in *Time,* considered it a way for Qaddhafi to make Americans appear bloodthirsty. "[Qaddhafi] must be pleased over the incident," the official noted. "It gives him a chance to play the victim."

> *Richard Z. Chesnoff in* U.S. News & World Report *wrote, "[D]aily life for most of Libya's 4.9 million people has vastly improved since September 1969 [when Qaddhafi came to power].... [D]espite current sanctions, foreign businessmen have replaced most of the global terrorists and revolutionaries who used to jam Libyan hotels."*

In yet another notorious international incident, two Libyan nationals were accused of blowing up a civilian commercial jet, Pan Am Flight 103, over Lockerbie, Scotland, in 1988. The United Nations demanded extradition of the suspects, but Qaddhafi steadfastly refused, provoking stiff economic sanctions. Despite a downturn in the country's economy, Richard Z. Chesnoff in *U.S. News & World Report* wrote, "[D]aily life for most of Libya's 4.9 million people has vastly improved since September 1969.... [D]espite current sanctions, foreign businessmen have replaced most of the global terrorists and revolutionaries who used to jam Libyan hotels." Indeed, it seemed the times were changing for what Americans had come to regard as an evil empire. Qaddhafi himself in *U.S. News & World Report* called President Bill Clinton "a nice man," and in 1994, the opponent of all things Western invited American activist Stokely Carmichael to a party for the twenty-fifth anniversary of his revolution. Following that, Qaddhafi caused a stir when he offered African American civil rights activist Louis Farrakhan, architect of the "Million Man March" in October of 1995, a $250,000 award as part of his Qaddhafi Human Rights Award and $1 billion for lobbying efforts. Despite Farrakhan's vocal protests, the Clinton Administration forbade him to accept the money, citing continuing sanctions against Libya.

Qaddhafi continued making headlines throughout the late 1990s for various, sometimes surprising, reasons. In 1995, he began expelling Palestinians from Libya, many of whom were families who had been in the country for decades. "It was his way, he said, of protesting the Palestine Liberation Organization's peace treaty with Israel," reported Alan Sipress for the Knight-Ridder/Tribune News Service. Then in October of 1996, South African President Nelson Mandela, a living symbol for human rights activists, called Qaddhafi "my dear brother leader" and presented him with South Africa's highest award for foreigners, the Order of Good Hope. Libya had supported Mandela's outlawed African National Congress, which sought to end apartheid in South Africa, landing Mandela in prison for 27 years. Then, in early January of 1997, President Clinton extended sanctions on Libya for executing eight spies allegedly linked to the United States because they used CIA-provided equipment. Also that month, Qaddhafi caused troubled for American millionaire Steve Fossett, who was attempting to fly a hot-air balloon around the world. When Libyan officials denied him permission to cross over the country, Fossett made plans to circumvent the region. A year later, during Fossett's journey, Qaddhafi personally reversed the decision, but the balloon pilot was already on a new course.

In 1997, Qaddhafi maintained his reputation as a thorn in the side of the United States when he demanded that America extradite the persons responsible for the previous decades' air raids on Libya before he would consider extraditing the suspects in the Lockerbie plane bombing. In March of 1998, the World Court in the Hague, Netherlands, decided that it will be the ruling body in the case of the bombing suspects, instead of ordering them to be extradited to the United States or Britain. Enforcement of their ruling, however, will be dependent on the U.N. Security Council. Also in 1997, Qaddhafi accused French and British secret service personnel, as well as members of the British royal family, for being responsible for a conspiracy which killed Princess Diana and her companion, Dodi al-Fayed, in a car crash in France on August 31, 1997. Meanwhile, Qaddhafi's name surprisingly popped up as the author of two collections of stories and essays, *The Village, the Village, the Earth, the Earth, and the Suicide of the Astronaut* in 1995 and *Escape to Hell and Other Stories* in 1998, which included a lengthy preface by President John F. Kennedy's former press secretary Pierre Salinger. Nurith C. Aizenman in the *New Republic* argued, "Notwithstanding the book's title, none of the works in *Escape to Hell and Other Stories* can really be called stories; they are more like stream-of-consciousness rants." Aizenman indicated that the book was redundant, and added, "Alas, the downside of being an absolute ruler seems to be that it's hard to find an aggressive editor."

On a personal level, Qaddhafi married a former schoolteacher named Fathia Nouri Khaled in December of 1969, and although they had a son together, they soon divorced. In July of 1970 he married a woman named Safiya, with whom he has six children. His family stays in a large two-story home, but Qaddhafi prefers to keep to himself, living outside on the property in a tent set up on a pile of sand brought in from the desert. Ruggedly handsome and extremely wealthy, some have declared Qaddhafi's charisma to be almost mystical. Many in the Middle East consider him somewhat of a folk hero for his dedication to Islam and his unrelenting opposition to Western ways. However, much of the world scorns him as a madman, one of the most feared and most powerful terrorists of the modern age.

Selected writings

Green Book, three parts, 1976, 1977, 1979.
The Village, the Village, the Earth, the Earth, and the Suicide of the Astronaut (stories and essays), 1995.
Escape to Hell and Other Stories (stories and essays), Stanke International Publishing, 1998.

Sources

On-line

"Gadhafi calls for extraditions over Dodi's death, U.S. air raids," September 29, 1997, Nando Times web site, http://wedge.nando.net/newsroom/ntn/world (May 22, 1998).
"Mandela Honors Libya's Gadhafi," October 29, 1997, Black News Today web site, http://www.blackvoices.com (May 22, 1998).
"Mandela presents Gadhafi with South Africa's highest award," October 30, 1997, from Associated Press report on Athenaeum web site, http://www.athensnewspapers.com (May 22, 1998).
"Mu'ammar al-Qaddafi," *DISCovering World History*, GaleNet web site, http://galenet.gale.com (May 22, 1998).

"Muammar Qaddhafi Role Profile," Arab-Israeli Politics Profiles Archive 1996, http://link.lanic.utexas.edu/meclass/aipol/mail/profiles96 (May 22, 1998).

Books

Current Leaders of Nations, Gale Research, 1998.
Encyclopedia of World Biography, second edition, Gale Research, 1997.

Periodicals

Economist, October 25, 1997, p. 48.
Independent, September 4, 1996, p. 2; January 18, 1997, p. 2; January 5, 1998, p. 3.

Knight-Ridder/Tribune News Service, September 20, 1995; January 30, 1996; August 28, 1996.
Los Angeles Times, August 31, 1996, p. A5.
New Republic, May 31, 1993, p. 19; November 17, 1997, p. 7; May 4, 1998.
Newsday, January 30, 1996, p. A30; October 8, 1996.
Reuters News Service, February 11, 1996; January 2, 1997; May 8, 1997.
Time, April 21, 1986, p.18; April 6, 1987, p. 42; January 16, 1989, p. 18; November 17, 1997, p. 26.
U.S. News & World Report, February 21, 1994, p. 55.
World Press Review, June 1995, p. 45.

—*Geri Speace*

Chris Rock

Comedian and actor

Born c. 1967, in Bedford-Stuyvesant, Brooklyn, NY; son of Julius (a truck driver) and Rose (a teacher) Rock; married Malaak Compton (a public relations coordinator), November, 1996. *Politics:* "[R]egistered Democrat with a Republican wallet."

Addresses: *Agent*—Michael Rotenberg, 3 Arts Entertainment, 9460 Wilshire Blvd., 7th Floor, Beverly Hills, CA 90212.

Career

Stand-up comedian, 1984—; *Saturday Night Live,* cast member, 1990-93; *In Living Color,* Fox, series regular, 1993-94; *The Chris Rock Show,* host, 1996—. Actor in films, including *Beverly Hills Cop II,* 1987; *I'm Gonna Git You Sucka,* 1988; *New Jack City,* 1991; *Boomerang,* 1992; *CB4,* 1993; *Panther,* 1995; *Sgt. Bilko,* 1996; *Beverly Hills Ninja,* 1997; *Lethal Weapon 4,* 1998. Released comedy albums, including *Born Suspect,* 1991; and *Roll with the New,* 1997. Host of numerous TV specials, including *Big Ass Jokes; Saturday Night Live,* 1996; *1997 MTV Music Video Awards*; and covered the 1996 presidential elections for *Politically Incorrect.*

Awards: CableAce Award, best stand-up comedy special, 1995, for *Chris Rock: Big Ass Jokes;* Emmy Award, outstanding variety, music, or comedy special and outstanding writing for variety or music program 1997, both for *Bring the Pain.*

Sidelights

Chris Rock's last name invites all sorts of puns to describe his popularity. *Us* magazine had the idea as early as 1993, when it ran a story called "Rock's Roll." In 1997, *Entertainment Weekly* called him "The Hot Rock," and *Ebony* combined motifs with the title of its 1997 profile: "Hot Comic Is on the Roll of His Life." Such wordplay is fitting, considering the fact that Rock has built his career around making people laugh. With a successful show on HBO, an enormously popular appearance as host of the *MTV Video Music Awards,* a new comedy album, and numerous upcoming film appearances, Rock was unquestionably on a roll in 1997. But Rock refused to succumb to vanity, or to believe in the illusion that the roll would last forever: "I know I'm going to fall," he told *Ebony.* "All this hoopla that's going on now is going to stop. But as long as I put in the proper amount of work, the fall won't be that steep." This modesty is characteristic of Rock, who speaks almost with reverence of comic influences such as Dick Gregory and Eddie Murphy, and who nearly gave up comedy forever just before the "roll" began.

As for the name, he was born with it. "It was the worst name as a kid to have," he said in a Prodigy on-line chat. "They called me Piece of the Rock, Plymouth Rock...." Unfortunately, those were not the worst names he heard as a boy growing up in Brooklyn's Bedford-Stuyvesant district. It was the era of busing in the 1970s, when children were required to attend schools outside of their home areas in an attempt to create racial balance. As a result, Rock had to go to school in an equally tough—but predominantly white—neighborhood, Bensonhurst. Years later, his memories remained vivid: "It was horrible," he told *Ebony*. "It was like Vietnam. They spit on me, called me n——r, not once in a while, every single day."

Fortunately, as Rock has pointed out, he came from a loving home, and it was there that he had his self-confidence restored after every day of such verbal—and sometimes physical—abuse. The oldest of six children, Rock was close to all of his family, but especially his father. "My father led by example," Rock said in an interview with *Ebony*. "[H]e made no excuses about anything. What I got from my father is his work ethic and a sense of what's right and wrong. He was always training me to be a man. If I would do something wrong, he would say 'A man doesn't do that.'"

Closely tied with his family, who became his first audience, was the other sustaining factor in his life: comedy. After quitting school at age 17—he later obtained a general equivalency diploma—Rock began building a career as a stand-up comic while working variously as a busboy, a mental hospital orderly, and a laborer unloading trucks for the *New York Daily News*, where his father was employed. In 1984, he started doing shows, and one night at Manhattan's Comic Strip Club in 1986, superstar comedian Eddie Murphy caught Rock's act.

Murphy, who was one of Rock's idols, liked what he saw, and gave the young comedian a minor role in his film *Beverly Hills Cop II*. Soon afterward, Rock played "the rib joint customer" in the 1988 comedy *I'm Gonna Git You Sucka*, and his performance attracted the attention of late-night talk-show host Arsenio Hall. The spot on *The Arsenio Hall Show*, in turn, led to an audition for *Saturday Night Live* in 1990. Soon afterward, Rock became a featured player on the popular show, which had launched the careers of numerous comic successes, including Murphy himself. It seemed that Rock's career was unfolding with the precision of a falling string of dominoes, and the next year saw his memorable appearance in Mario Van Peebles's critically acclaimed *New Jack City*. To prepare for the role of the crack addict Pookie, Rock spent time with a real crack addict, and his performance proved that he could play drama as well as comedy.

But even when he seemed perched on the edge of unbridled success, Rock faced challenges in his personal and professional life. The first had come in 1988, when his father died of complications resulting from an ul-

cer. In an interview with *Ebony*, Rock called this "the most traumatic experience of my life," and it may have contributed to what he has described as his "lackadaisical" attitude on *Saturday Night Live*. Though he gained a wide fan base with roles such as the militant talk-show host Nat X, critics complained that he wasn't giving his all, and Rock has been quick to admit this in the years since. "Back then," he said in an interview with *Ebony*, "I had a Jheri curl. I was missing a tooth. I was like straight off everybody. There were some awkward years there."

> *"I'm trying to do good work.... So the attention I get is really based on my work, and not some fad. I'm not the flavor of the month."*

Dissatisfied with *Saturday Night Live*—"SNL was great," he said in a 1996 *Up Close* internet chat, "but I felt like the adopted [black] kid with the great white parents"—he left the show in 1993 and signed on with its chief competition, the primarily black *In Living Color* on Fox. "Then I went to the black family," he recalled, "and it was like I really fit in. But then they canceled the show." He followed his one season on *In Living Color* with a starring role in the rap parody *CB4*, which he co-produced and wrote. In spite of the acclaim the latter received, Rock's career seemed to stall in the mid-1990s. He had done some shows on cable network HBO, but he had no upcoming TV series, and there were no movie offers to consider either. Hoping to drum up some interest with a different agent, he left the William Morris Agency, and "after I left," he later told *Entertainment Weekly*, "no one wanted me. Literally every agent in town turned me down."

At the beginning of 1996, Rock made two decisions. The first was a renewed commitment to improving his work by studying the greats who had gone before him. The other was an ultimatum to himself: if nothing significant happened for him by the end of the year, it was a sign that his career had peaked, and he needed to find something else to do with his life. In line with the first objective, the high school dropout studied like he never had, educating himself on the work of heroes such as Bill Cosby, Eddie Murphy, Richard Pryor, Woody Allen, and Don Rickles. Meanwhile he went to the Takoma Theatre in Washington, D.C., to tape his HBO special, *Bring the Pain*.

But a funny thing happened for Chris Rock. As a result of his intensive study and his hard work, his show was good—very good. Comedy Central's *Politically Incorrect* invited him to cover the 1996 presidential elections, and HBO signed him to host his own half-hour show. By the end of 1996, when Rock married public-relations executive Malaak Compton, he was gaining momentum. With prominent spots in 1-800-Collect and Nike commercials—the latter as the voice of the puppet Li'l Penny—it seemed that one saw or heard Rock everywhere. In 1997, he continued his string of successes with the release of a book, *Rock This!*, two Emmy awards for *Bring the Pain*, and an appearance as host of the *MTV Music Video Awards*.

The latter, which aired on September 4, had the third-highest ratings in the video awards show's history, and for months afterward, people were quoting Rock's quips, such as "You know how it is in music: fickle. Here today, gone today!" No doubt Rock was talking to himself as well. Regarding his four brothers and one sister, he said in an *Ebony Man* article, "I don't want my relatives working for me.... I want my brothers to go to college and get good jobs. Show business is shaky. So if that doesn't work out, I want to be able to work for them." His humility is not a put-on: Rock lives in an ordinary house in Brooklyn, with a plumber for a next-door neighbor. He goes to the local barbershop to get his hair cut, and aside from a few celebrity friends, his closest relationships are with family members.

Rock's humor is laced with a profound wisdom: "Any show on television," he told *Ebony Man*, "especially with kids, the smart kid is always made out to be the kid you would least want to be like. So it's kind of like an anti-education thing that we promote.... To me, [that's] worse than violence and profanity." He has often engendered controversy, not just for his sometimes obscene humor, but for his criticism of prominent black figures such as Washington, D.C., Mayor Marion Barry, who was re-elected in spite of his record as a crack user, and O. J. Simpson. But none of his qualities—fearless honesty, wisdom, or modesty—mean much to Rock if he's not able to make audiences laugh. "I'm trying to do good work," he said in an *Ebony Man* interview. "So the attention I get is really based on my work, and not some fad. I'm not the flavor of the month."

Selected discography

Born Suspect (includes "Crack Mayor"), Atlantic, 1991.
Bring the Pain, Dreamworks SKG, 1996.
Roll with the New (includes "Marion Barry/Million Man March"), Dreamworks SKG, 1997.

Selected writings

CB4 (screenplay), Universal, 1993.
"What's Up, Shaq? Shaq Diseal by Shaquille O'Neal," *Village Voice*, January 11, 1994, pp. 71-72.
Rock This!, Hyperion, 1997.

Sources

On-line

"Chris Rock," *Internet Movie Databank*, http://us.imdb.com (November 25, 1997).
"HBO-The Chris Rock Show," http://www.hbo.com/chrisrock (December 4, 1997).
"Meet Mr. Rock," *Up Close* (June 6, 1996), http://www.chatsoup.com (November 25, 1997).

Periodicals

Billboard, September 28, 1996, p. 100.
Ebony, May 1997, pp. 132-136.
Ebony Man, April 1997, p. 64.
Elle, September 1997, p. 274.
Entertainment Weekly, May 31, 1996, p. 49; September 19, 1997, p. 6; November 28, 1997, p. 61.
Esquire, March 1997, p. 50.
Jet, May 9, 1994, pp. 58-61; February 6, 1995, p. 40; December 30, 1996-January 6, 1997; April 14, 1997, p. 37; September 29, 1997, p. 63; October 20, 1997.
TV Guide, April 6, 1996, pp. 38-41.
Us, April 1993, pp. 68-73.
U.S. News & World Report, May 12, 1997, p. 82.
Village Voice, July 2, 1996, p. 55.

—*Judson Knight*

Tim Roth

AP/Wide World Photos

Actor and director

Born May 14, 1961, in London, England; son of Ernie (a journalist) and Anne (a teacher and painter) Roth; married Nicki Butler, 1993; children: (with Lori Baker) Jack; (with Butler) Timothy Hunter, Cormac. *Education:* Attended Camberwell School of Art.

Addresses: *Office*—Fine Line Features, 888 7th Ave., Floor 19, New York, NY 10106-2599.

Career

Actor in films, including *The Hit*, 1984; *Return to Waterloo*, 1986; *A World Apart*, 1988; *To Kill a Priest*, 1988; *The Cook, The Thief, His Wife and Her Lover*, 1989; *Vincent and Theo*, 1990; *Rosencratz and Guildenstern Are Dead*, 1990; *Jumpin' at the Boneyard*, 1991; *Backsliding*, 1991; *Reservoir Dogs*, 1992; *The Perfect Husband*, 1992; *Bodies, Rest, and Motion*, 1993; *Pulp Fiction*, 1994; *Little Odessa*, 1994; *Captives*, 1994; *Rob Roy*, 1995; *Four Rooms*, 1995; *Everyone Says I Love You*, 1996; *Gridlock'd*, 1997; *Hoodlum*, 1997; *No Way Home*, 1997; *Deceiver*, 1997; *Prophecy II: Ashtown*, 1997; *Legend of a Pianist on the Ocean*, 1998. Actor in television movies, including *Made in Britain*, 1982; *Meantime*, 1982; *The Metamorphosis*, 1987; *Yellowbacks*, 1990; *Murder in the Heartland*, 1993; and *Heart of Darkness*, 1993. Director of film *The War Zone*, 1998.

Sidelights

If the character is psychotic, criminal, or simply strange, and the film is cutting-edge and low budget, Tim Roth is likely to be the first choice for the job.

Roth is a British-born actor who excels at making decidedly unglamourous individuals intense and believable. And he has gained a massive cult following among fans of the "indies."

"He sniffs out roles that take his fancy and plays them with feral intensity: hooligans, hoods, lost souls, degenerates, and all manner of edgy lowlifes," noted Theresa Sturley in *Interview* magazine. "He can be an atavistic killer, and he has a knack for being clownish in films that show the comic side of pain." Unlike some of his contemporaries, Roth breathes heart and soul into his roles, keeping them authentic even when they are outrageous. Hillary Johnson in *Harper's Bazaar* noted: "It is his ability to play the ridiculous without resorting to camp that makes him independent cinema's favorite everyman."

In the 1980s and 1990s, Roth appeared in more than two dozen feature films, only two of which were Hollywood studio productions. The rest were mostly offbeat independent movies, often with inexperienced young directors. "Studio films are really not what I'd be good at, in the end," Roth told Steve Pond of *US* magazine. "Because it's got a lot to do with what you look like, as opposed to what's going on in your head."

Although Roth does not possess the looks of a traditional leading man, he enjoys being a character actor. "With a schnozz like a shark fin and a bod that defines non-definition, Roth is hardly Hollywood's idea of a movie star," wrote Steve Wulf in *Entertainment Weekly.* That's just fine with Roth. "There is less pressure as a character actor," he said in an interview on America On Line (AOL). "It generally means that you will be acting for all of your life, which is my intention. It is not my intention to just be a rich and famous person. That would be pretty boring." Working at a prolific pace, Roth has had little chance to get bored since coming to America in 1990. After completing a shoot, "usually there is a comedown period of two weeks, and then I'm desperate to get back to work again," he told his AOL audience. "I'm a workaholic."

> *"There is less pressure as a character actor. It generally means that you will be acting for all of your life, which is my intention. It is not my intention to just be a rich and famous person. That would be pretty boring."*

Roth is well known to the new breed of young filmmakers that have carved out a larger audience for independently produced movies than at any time in history. "Edgy, perverse, provocative ... he represents the spirit of the new Hollywood," wrote Jessica Berens in British *GQ.* "His lips, around a Camel, are usually seen with blood frothing out between them. His nose says he could do comedy. His manner is as uncuddly as you could get without a firearms license.... His voice is slightly nasal."

Interview's Sturley noted that Roth's physical attributes fit perfectly with the demands of his off-the-wall characters: "he's a quick-change artist who can contort his face into a myriad of expressions: his eyes pop, his eyebrows soar, his mouth twists. But it's the way his personality twists that has made him the favorite British vagabond in American movies."

Roth's father was an eccentric, left wing British journalist whose ambition, Roth told Berens of *GQ,* was to invent "a machine that dropped Margaret Thatcher's knickers in public." His mother, Anne, was a teacher

and painter. His parents separated when Roth was young but his father lived nearby and remained close to him. Roth's lower-middle-class upbringing gave him a feel for the streetwise characters he would later play. At a rough public school in South London, Roth picked up a Cockney accent for sheer survival. He showed no interest in sports or right wing politics. "Small, bright and bullied, he was forced into social exile, and these experiences, in some respects, have affected everything he has done since," Berens observed. Roth told her: "Nobody liked me when I was a teenager. I wanted to be liked but I didn't have any friends."

His first acting part came at age 16 when he appeared in a school musical production of the Dracula legend. At a British art college, Roth started off studying sculpture but soon switched to acting. He began on stage "because it was the only work I could get," Roth told AOL. Working with the Glasgow Citizens' Theatre and at the Royal Court, he "specialized in working-class outsiders and punkish rude boys," according to Pond. But once Roth broke into film, he never went back to theater.

Landing the lead role of a young Nazi skinhead in Alan Clarke's *Made in Britain* was a dream come true for Roth. "I'd always harbored the notion of doing film acting, more so than stage acting," he told Sturley. "I had the lead role, first time out. I'd never been in front of a camera before, and I loved it." The part has remained his favorite role.

After *Made in Britain,* controversial directors started to seek him out. Mike Leigh cast him in his made-for-TV movie *Meantime,* Stephen Frears used him in *The Hit,* and Roth appeared in Peter Greenaway's controversial 1989 film *The Cook, The Thief, His Wife and Her Lover.* His work in the 1980s also including a remarkable performance, playing a man turned into a beetle in *The Metamorphosis,* a 1987 TV movie based on Franz Kafka's short story.

While living in Britain in the 1980s, Roth had a relationship with Lori Baker and together they had a son, Jack. After moving to the United States, he was at the Sundance Film Festival when he met Nikki Butler, a fashion designer. They married in 1993 in Belize and had two sons, Timothy Hunter, named after Hunter S. Thompson, and Cormac.

Two acclaimed performances in films that were released in 1990 catapulted Roth onto the radar screen of international critics. He played Guildenstern opposite Gary Oldman in the film version of *Rosencratz and Guildenstern Are Dead.* Next he portrayed painter

Vincent Van Gogh in Robert Altman's *Vincent and Theo*. Wulf commented that "from the first shot, of him chomping on his pipe, to the penultimate shot, of him bleeding in the street, Roth paints a much truer and more poignant self-portrait of Van Gogh than [Kirk] Douglas did in *Lust for Life*."

Though Roth won praise for both portrayals, he still had trouble finding work. He settled for a role in the Australian bomb *Backsliding*, which was so bad that audiences at the Cannes Film Festival walked out in droves.

Roth's first American film was the little-known *Jumpin' at the Boneyard*, where he played a Bronx crackhead's brother. When he arrived in Hollywood in 1990, "he had no friends and no car," Berens wrote. Roth told Pond: "It was like a private club that was impossible to break into." But soon he connected, first to actor Sean Penn and then to the not-yet-famous director Quentin Tarantino. Tarantino asked Roth to play Mr. Blond or Mr. Pink in his film *Reservoir Dogs*, but Roth insisted on playing Mr. Orange, because he found that character more fascinating than the others. The portrayal immediately placed Roth into cult stardom. That status was cemented by his performance in Tarantino's much noticed *Pulp Fiction*, where Roth played a petty criminal who, in scenes that begin and end the film, terrorizes a coffee shop by brandishing a pistol.

Despite increasing notoriety, Roth continued to gravitate to low-budget productions by little-known directors. "There's no shortage of interesting scripts in the independent world," Roth explained to Sturley. "And even if the film doesn't work, the experiences are often amazing." Roth signed on to newcomer James Gray's *Little Odessa* to play hit man Joshua Shapiro, a part in which "he conveyed the cold, complicated criminality that marks his best work," according to Berens. Roth told Hillary Johnson of *Harper's Bazaar* that the film is "sad and relentless. I like it because the only sentimentality comes from a complete asshole." Gray was grateful for Roth's help, as was Buddy Giovinazzo, the novice director of *No Way Home*. "He put his name to it without asking for money up front," Giovinazzo told Berens."That is practically unheard of, and I will always love him for it." Brother directing team Jonas and Josh Pate enlisted him for *Deceiver*, a psychological thriller in which Roth played a brilliant but manipulative Southern aristocrat accused of murder. In *Captives,* he played a convict who falls for Julia Ormond, a prison dentist.

A departure for Roth was his appearance in the 18th Century swordplay-and-costume epic, *Rob Roy*, a big budget studio film based on the Walter Scott novel and released in 1995. He signed on, he told Sturley, because "it was made by a bunch of people I knew and the part was juicy." His role was that of a cold-blooded, foppish, sadistic villain, Archibald Cunningham. Although Roth admits that his acting in the film was a bit over the top, he claimed that director Michael Jones encouraged him to make his performance even more outrageous. "And he was right," he told Sturley. "It really worked. I think it's hysterical. And horrible." John Simon of *National Review* said Roth played the part with "wonderful loathsomeness." About a scene where he rapes Jessica Lange's character on a table, Roth told Berens: "I wanted to be as foul as possible." Johnson of *Harper's Bazaar* wrote: "It's an over-the-top, enchanting—nay, festive performance that nonetheless manages to glance at the soul of evil with tender and devastating pity. And it's all done in a wig that would embarrass Dolly Parton." For his portrayal, Roth was nominated for both a Golden Globe and an Academy Award for best supporting actor, although he failed to win either prize.

"I don't always play bastards," Roth told Berens. "It's just that people remember them. I'm always amused and I always find it good fun.... Actually, the more depressing they are, the more fun you have." Fun was what Roth and four hot young directors, including Tarantino, had in mind with the ensemble piece *Four Rooms*, released late in 1995. Roth's comic role as the rubber-faced Ted the Bellhop reminded some critics of Charlie Chaplin, while others found it very unappealing. Ralph Novak of *People* termed Roth's character "a bellhop all jitters and head tilting in what seems a pathetic imitation of Stan Laurel." The film was a critical and box office failure.

Roth's next film continued to stretch his persona. In Woody Allen's *Everyone Says I Love You*, he played an ex-con who croons a love song for society girl Drew Barrymore. His edgy performance "gave Woody Allen's parlor comedy a jolt of adrenaline," wrote Pond in *US*. The prolific Roth had parts in five films released in 1997. His co star in *Gridlock'd* was rapper Tupac Shakur, who was murdered between the end of shooting and the film's release. They played heroin-addict musicians who are trying to kick the habit but are constantly thwarted by bureaucracy. Also that year, Roth played the ruthless mobster Dutch Schulz in *Hoodlum*. Unfortunately, neither film was successful.

Late in 1997, Roth went to the Ukraine to play the hero in *The Legend of the Pianist on the Ocean*, by *Cinema Paradiso* director Guiseppe Tornatore. In 1998, Roth set his sights on a new goal. On many movie sets, other actors noted that Roth was thinking all the time, sometimes giving suggestions to his young directors. After having worked with virtually every maverick director of note, Roth decided to try working *behind* the camera. He directed the film *The War Zone*, based on Alexander Stewart's dark novel about a boy who discovers his father and sister have an incestuous relationship. Of his new job, Roth confessed to Pond: "I'm terrified. I mean, as an actor, you show up and do your stuff and after about six weeks you're done. But this is a year ... and you get about 700 questions a day. And you have to have the answers, even if they're the wrong ones."

Sources

On-line

http://www.geocities.com/Hollywood/Lot/8133/ (March 23, 1998).

http://www.geocities.com/Hollywood/Lot/9968/ (March 23, 1998).

http://www.celebsite.com/people/timroth/ (March 23, 1998).

http://members.aol.com.blknpkins/TimRoth.html/ (March 23, 1998).

Periodicals

Entertainment Weekly, June 30, 1995, p. 34; November-December 1997, p. 44.
GQ (British edition), May 1997, p. 126.
Harper's Bazaar, April 1995, p. 212.
Interview, February 1997, p. 97.
National Review, May 15, 1995, p. 70.
People, January 15, 1996, p. 19.
US, December 1997.

—*Michael Betzold*

Mary Schiavo

Political activist and author

Born America Mary Fackler, September 4, 1955, in Pioneer, OH; daughter of Harland "Barney" (an Air Force veteran) and Nina Fackler; married Ed Sterling, 1982 (divorced 1990); married Alexander Schiavo, 1992; children: (second marriage) Larissa, Alexander. *Education:* Harvard University, B.A., 1976; Ohio State University, Master of Public Administration; New York University, Juris Doctor. *Politics:* Republican.

Addresses: *Office*—Ohio State University, School of Public Policy and Management, Haggerty Hall, 202-C, 1775 College Road, Columbus, OH 43210.

Career

U.S. Department of Justice, assistant U.S. attorney, western district of Missouri, 1982-85, federal prosecutor, racketeering strike force, 1985-86; U.S. Department of Labor, assistant secretary for labor management standards, 1989-90; U.S. Department of Transportation, Inspector General, 1990-96; Ohio State University School of Public Policy and Management, professor of government ethics and government management, 1997—.

Awards: Enarson Executive-in-Residence, Ohio State University School of Public Policy and Management, 1997.

Sidelights

Mary Schiavo made a powerful political statement in 1996 by her surprising resignation from a high-ranking position as the Inspector General of the United States Department of Transportation. Schiavo cited the Federal Aeronautics Agency (FAA) and its lack of concern for the safety of the flying public as the motive behind her decision. In justification of her own action Schiavo was quoted by *Time* (in an excerpt from her first book), "If I expected change, I knew I had to devise yet another strategy to circumvent the FAA.... I had to resign.... I couldn't continue working in a place where all we did was sit around waiting for people to die."

Schiavo, during her tenure as inspector general, attempted to expose and to rectify previously ignored deficiencies in airline safety. She was increasingly appalled that only in the wake of a major crash, "With people dead and sobbing survivors filling television screens, does the FAA step up to the plate and make changes."

Schiavo, born America Mary Fackler on September 4, 1955 (Labor Day), was raised in rural Ohio. When she was nine years old she took her first airplane ride in a small propeller plane. She was thrilled by the experience, and she determined herself to learn to fly. An intelligent and enterprising young woman, she earned money as a ventriloquist to finance her own flying lessons. By age 18 she was a licensed private pilot, although she could not qualify for a commercial pilot's license because she was too nearsighted.

She went to Harvard, earned a bachelor's degree in 1976, and then returned to Ohio State University where she earned a Masters Degree in Public Administration. Schiavo went on to earn a law degree at New York University. She married Ed Sterling in 1982; they divorced in 1990. She married Alexander Schiavo in 1992. They had two children, a daughter, Larissa, born in 1994, and a son, Alex, born in 1996.

Schiavo worked in the Midwest before moving to Washington D.C. From 1982-85 she was an assistant U.S. attorney in the Federal prosecutor's office in Kansas City, Missouri where she developed a reputation as a tough and effective prosecutor. Then from 1985-1986 she worked as a federal prosecutor on the racketeering strike force. Her colleagues in Kansas City dubbed her "Maximum Mary," because she believed in imposition of maximum penalties.

In 1987 Schiavo received a White House fellowship appointment from President Ronald Reagan. In 1988 she headed the Bush/Quayle presidential campaign in Missouri. She also served as the assistant secretary for labor management standards at the U.S. Department of Labor, then worked with the Secretary of Labor, investigating election tampering in the labor unions.

Schiavo's rising career reached a new height in 1990 when President George Bush appointed her to the position of Inspector General of the Department of Transportation (DOT). Schiavo was unusually well suited to her new post which combined the challenges of investigation, aviation, public service, and law. Schiavo, with her characteristic dynamism, redefined the job. She turned the focus to safety issues, where her predecessors were concerned with finance and administration. She set out to combat what she perceived as a lack of humanitarian concern that permeated both DOT and the Federal Aviation Administration (FAA).

Six years later, on July 8, 1996, she submitted her resignation to President Bill Clinton. This dramatic move came just weeks after the tragic crash of a commercial airliner (ValuJet flight 592) over Florida on May 11. No one aboard the plane survived the crash. The wreckage, strewn across the Everglades, was a particularly gruesome site.

During the years of Schiavo's incumbency at DOT, airport security took the forefront. Schiavo sent undercover inspectors to international airports. Her agents reported back that they successfully entered "secure" areas without appropriate authorization in well over one-half of their attempts. Schiavo further uncovered a frightening pattern of irregularities in the sale of aircraft replacement parts. This "bogus parts" issue grew into an exhaustive investigation revealing that parts brokers were dealing in uncertified parts over 90 percent of the time. The investigation of counterfeit parts led to scores of convictions.

When the ValuJet crash occurred Schiavo appeared the following evening on Ted Koppel's news show, *Nightline*. During the course of the interview she announced, "I wouldn't fly ValuJet." She was quick to question the safety records of other commercial airlines as well, including a number of commuter airlines. Less than two months later, Schiavo bluntly submitted her resignation to President Clinton. She took harsh criticism for her abrupt decision and for her dissident response to the ValuJet crash. Many insiders insisted that she lacked experience in issues of airline security and therefore had no right to her "whistle blowing" tactics. According to Annie Groer of *Biography*, "critics called her an irresponsible alarmist ... who ... inspires baseless fear among the flying public."

Among Schiavo's supporters a sense of bewilderment prevailed. Representative Frank R. Wolf (R-VA) expressed this sentiment to the Washington Post, "I was with her just [last] Monday, and she didn't mention anything.... I'm very surprised. But Mary is a bold person, a very tough person. I'm sure she had her reasons. I just hope we get someone to replace her who's equally as tough." Another supporter, according to Groer, called her "the Ralph Nader of the skies."

Schiavo explained later that she believed she could more effectively stimulate change in some other capacity, "It was not time to hang up my spurs but to change horses." After her headline-grabbing resignation, she spoke out publicly against the FAA many times on mainstream television shows and magazines, and in May of 1997 she published the expose, *Flying High, Flying Safe*.

In her book Schiavo stepped forward to stigmatize airport security once again. This time she assigned a fourth-rate (D) rating to the national airline security establishment. She blamed the FAA for poorly monitored operations. Security breaches could be simulated with ease, Schiavo maintained. Unauthorized "shills" reported successfully entering so-called secure areas at international airports as often as 75 percent of the time.

In 1997 Schiavo was appointed the Enarson Professor-in-Residence at Ohio State University School of Public Policy. She continues to teach government ethics and government management at the university as well.

Selected writings

Flying Blind, Flying Safe, Avon Books, 1997.

Sources

Biography, November 1997, pp. 50-53.
Business Week, June 24, 1996; April 14, 1997.
Newsweek, May 20, 1996, p. 32.
People, June 2, 1997, p. 117.
Time, March 31, 1997.
Washington Post, July 9, 1996, p. A13.

—Gloria Cooksey

Charles M. Schulz

Cartoonist

Born Charles Monroe Schulz, November 26, 1922, in Minneapolis, MN; son of Carl (a barber) and Dena Schulz; married Joyce Halverson, April 18, 1949 (divorced, 1972); married Jean Clyde, 1973; children: (first marriage) Meredith, Charles, Craig, Amy, Jill.

Addresses: *Office*—Number One Snoopy Place, Santa Rosa, CA 95401; also, United Features Syndicate, 200 Park Avenue, New York, NY 10016-0005.

Career

Cartoonist for *St. Paul Pioneer Press* and *Saturday Evening Post*, 1948-49; created *Peanuts* comic strip, 1950, currently syndicated worldwide; author of dozens of collections of *Peanuts* strips and cartoons and other books; wrote television plays and feature films based on the *Peanuts* strip. *Military service:* U.S. Army, 1943-45.

Awards: Outstanding Cartoonist award, National Cartoonist Society, 1955, 1964; Yale Humor award, 1956; School Bell award, National Education Association, 1960; Emmy and Peabody Awards, 1966, for TV special *A Charlie Brown Christmas*; inducted into Cartoonists Hall of Fame; honorary degrees: Anderson College (1963), St. Mary's College of California (1969).

Sidelights

The creator of *Peanuts*, one of the most successful comic strips in history, Charles M. Schulz has built an entire industry on insecurity. His comic alter ego, Charlie Brown, has been analyzed as an Everyman for the modern age of anxiety. Schulz himself said in his book *Peanuts Jubilee:* "Charlie Brown has to be the one who suffers because he is a caricature of the average person. Most of us are much more acquainted with losing than we are with winning. Winning is great, but it isn't funny."

Schulz's lovable loser is the center of the comic strip. He is constantly being frustrated, but he never gives up. Lucy, the tyrannical and inventive girl who loves to torture and ridicule Charlie Brown, holds a football for him to kick. Though for decades she has jerked it away when he runs up, and he falls on his face, Charlie Brown always keeps trying to kick it. The beleaguered pitcher and manager of a sandlot baseball game, Charlie Brown can't ever pull his team of losers together. He can't ever win the attention, much less the affection, of the little red-haired girl he loves. His dog, Snoopy, frequently disobeys him. Trees devour every kite he tries to fly. His friends ridicule his appearance and disparage his intelligence, but he never loses faith and hope.

Though Schulz dismisses the idea that Charlie Brown is an extension of his own personality, he has not convinced many interviewers. "This whole business about my being like Charlie Brown, that's just talk," Schulz once said. Yet the parallels between the artist and his protagonist are striking. Schulz is fearful of travel and is a habitual worrier. Despite his position as the most famous cartoonist ever, and despite millions annually in revenue from his ideas, Schulz does not seem all that sure of himself. Dianna Waggoner and Roger Wolmuth in *People* described him as "a connoisseur of dread." Schulz told them, "I sometimes feel people only like me because I draw those silly little pictures. If I didn't, they wouldn't care if I were ever born."

> *"Perhaps the most important contribution a comic strip can make is to bring humor into people's everyday language, and to help them slip right into the language of a different world."*

Charles Monroe Schulz was born in a working-class family in Minneapolis. His father had only a third-grade education and worked as a barber six days a week. They lived frugally. His father read newspaper comics daily and nicknamed his son "Sparky" after the cartoon racehorse, Spark Plug, in the comic strip *Barney Google and Snuffy Smith*. His friends still called him by that name 70 years later. Young Schulz grew to love comics, too, especially admiring the work of Al Capp, Milt Caniff, Roy Crane and George Gerriman. At 15, he had his first cartoon published, in *Ripley's Believe It or Not!*, but it was years before he had any other commercial success as an artist.

When Schulz was 17, he enrolled in an art correspondence course. He did well, but his worst grade, a C+, came in a lesson on drawing children. Drafted into the Army during World War II, he went to Europe as an infantry machine gunner. After the war, he landed a job as an instructor at the same art correspondence school. There, he fell in love with a red-haired young woman named Donna Johnson. She would become his inspiration for Charlie Brown's unrequited love, the nameless little red-haired girl. Johnson's mother didn't like Schulz, so he backed off.

Schulz became a cartoonist for the *St. Paul Pioneer Press* and sold a few cartoons to the *Saturday Evening Post* in 1948 and 1949. He created a comic strip he called *L'il Ones,* borrowing the name for his luckless protagonist from an art school colleague. In 1949, Schulz married

Joyce Halverson. The next year, he sold his strip to United Features Syndicate, which changed the name to *Peanuts* over his objections. In 1994, Schulz told a National Cartoonists Society meeting that he never liked the name, because it suggested a character who didn't exist in the strip.

Drawing from his own childhood and eventually from his experiences in raising five children, Schulz created a gallery of memorable characters: Lucy, the spoiled brat and tyrant; Linus, the little boy with his security blanket; Schroeder, the kid genius who plays Beethoven; Snoopy, the dog with an elaborate fantasy life of great adventure and heroics; Snoopy's friend, Woodstock the bird; and Peppermint Patty, who always falls asleep in class. Snoopy was inspired by a beloved childhood pet, Spike. Schulz got the idea for Snoopy's skirmishes with the Red Baron when his son was playing with a plane. He got the idea for the blanket because his oldest daughter and two sons carried around blue blankets when they were toddlers.

His children became some of his biggest fans. "They always liked the strip, and this was very important to me and very gratifying," Schulz once commented. "I would have been quite disappointed if they had felt that it wasn't really worthwhile or it wasn't funny, or it was just silly or trite; but they always read all the books, and I guess the most flattering thing of all is that they would frequently ask for some of the originals themselves."

Over time, the strip evolved, with minor characters coming and going. In the early years, the characters' identities became firmly shaped. Charlie Brown originally dragged around the blanket, but gave it to Linus. The major characters and their personalities never changed, and they did not age. Stock situations, like the kick-the-football trick, developed and remained constant over many years. Critics said Schulz became a master at recycling the same material over and over, but he always added a slightly different twist. One thing remained constant: No adult characters ever appeared, at least until a 1991 TV movie. "I've never drawn for children, although kids read the strip and we get lots of mail from them," Schulz told Roxanne Farmanfarmaian of *Publishers Weekly*. "I never felt good enough to draw for children.... I draw for myself." In 1955, the National Cartoonists Society awarded Schulz its top honor, the Reuben. Schulz later said it was his most thrilling honor because it meant he was accepted in his chosen profession by his peers. He won the award again in 1964; Schulz is the only cartoonist to win it twice.

In 1965, Charlie Brown and his friends were introduced to television when Schulz wrote a teleplay for CBS. *A Charlie Brown Christmas* won an Emmy award and a Peabody award. In the years to come it became one of the most repeated animated features in TV history. An annual string of TV specials followed for many years. *You're a Good Man, Charlie Brown,* a hit musical adapted from the comic strip by Clark Gesner, debuted off-Broadway in 1967 and in years to follow played all over the world; it spawned a book and a record album. Another musical, *Snoopy!!!* opened in 1975 in San Francisco. Snoopy's skirmishes with the Red Baron became immortalized in song by a rock group named the Royal Guardsmen.

Peanuts merchandise—everything from clothing to lunch boxes to cosmetics and furniture—provided Schulz a gold mine. Subsidiaries licensed by Schulz's Creative Associates, Inc., manufactured millions of items. *Peanuts* books, mostly compilations of material from the strip, rolled out at least once a year for decades, and sales of the collected works reached over 100 million copies worldwide. The National Aeronautics and Space Administration (NASA) adopted Snoopy as a promotional mascot. In 1969, on the Apollo 10 moon mission, American astronauts used a Lunar Excursion Module named Snoopy. Snoopy and other characters from the strip became frequent product endorsers, appearing in countless commercials. Schulz's characters became familiar all over the globe. Schulz himself owns and operates Snoopy's Gallery & Gift Shop near his California home.

By 1969, Schulz, a hockey and golf fanatic, was so wealthy that he built a $2 million ice rink near his home. That year, the first *Peanuts* feature film, written by Schulz, opened. In 1972, Schulz and his wife divorced. The next year, he met a woman named Jeanne Clyde at the ice rink and married her.

His prodigious output of work continued as Schulz grew older. Besides writing a daily strip and overseeing the merchandising of his work, he was responsible for annual compilations of his material, numerous television screenplays, and several feature-length films. "Everything we've ever done beyond the strip is because someone came to us," Schulz told Farmanfarmaian in 1996. Despite his numerous projects, Schulz did almost all the work of drawing the strip himself. Continuing to play golf, hockey and tennis, he made his home in a secluded hilltop retreat in Santa Rosa, California, working in a modest office nearby with the address One Snoopy Place.

A heart attack and quadruple bypass operation in 1981 didn't slow Schulz down. Since then, he sometimes has had to steady his right hand atop his left to draw the strip. In his 70s, Schulz still was creating every pen-and-ink drawing by himself, using only his own ideas. *Peanuts* remained the most widely syndicated comic strip in the world. "I work harder now," he told the National Cartoonists Society meeting in 1994. "I'm more particular about everything I draw than I have ever been."

By 1989, *People* magazine reported, retail sales of *Peanuts* products totaled a billion dollars a year, with Schulz reportedly getting about five percent of that in royalties. By 1990, *Peanuts* was being run in 26 languages, including Chinese and Serbo-Croatian. In 1993, Schulz finally let Charlie Brown hit his first home run, after 43 years of trying. He explained why to reporters: "I think it's a mistake to be unfaithful to your readers, always to be letting them down."

For his part, Schulz feels the magic of his creations lies mainly in their universal appeal and straightforward, familiar human predicaments tinged with humor. "Perhaps the most important contribution a comic strip can make is to bring humor into people's everyday language, and to help them slip right into the language of a different world," he told Farmanfarmaian. "There's a market still for 'nice' cartoons. But really funny cartoons are harder to do than repeating underground vulgarities over and over." As his career continued with the same characters and same situations repeated over and over, some critics said it was time for Schulz to hang up his pen. *Chicago Tribune* columnist Eric Zorn in 1993 wrote that "*Peanuts*" was "a once-mighty force that is hanging on too long past its prime" and that the strip "simply isn't amusing or relevant anymore." Yet it remained the most widely syndicated strip in the world, even as Schulz resisted the temptation to stir interest by changing things too much.

In late 1997, Schulz decided to take a five-week leave of absence to celebrate his 75th birthday. He had never taken a break in the 47 years he has been drawing the strip. He was quoted in *Time* as saying, "I've been thinking of taking some time off for a long time." He has said the strip will not continue after he retires or dies. As John Tebbel wrote in a 1969 article in *Saturday Review:* "*Peanuts* is so much a projection of the Schulz personality that it is inconceivable that anyone else could do it.... Perhaps it is because the strip is so personal that it elicits an unprecedented identification and affection from its vast readership."

Selected writings

Peanuts, Rinehart, 1952.
More Peanuts, Rinehart, 1954.
Good Grief, More Peanuts, Rinehart, 1954.
Good Ol' Charlie Brown, Rinehart, 1957.
Snoopy, Rinehart, 1958.
But We Love You, Charlie Brown, Rinehart, 1959.
Happiness Is a Warm Puppy, Determined Productions, 1962.
Security Is a Thumb and a Blanket, Determined Productions, 1963.
I Need All the Friends I Can Get, Determined Productions, 1964.
Love Is Walking Hand in Hand, Determined Productions, 1965.
(With Kenneth F. Hall) *Two-by-Fours: A Sort of Serious Book about Small Children*, Warner Press, 1965.
A Charlie Brown Christmas (teleplay), CBS, 1965.
Home Is on Top of a Doghouse, Determined Productions, 1966.
Charlie Brown's All-Stars (teleplay), CBS, 1966.
It's the Great Pumpkin, Charlie Brown (teleplay), CBS, 1966.
Happiness Is a Sad Song, Determined Productions, 1967.
You're in Love, Charlie Brown (teleplay), CBS, 1967.
Charlie Brown's Yearbook, World Publishing, 1969.
A Boy Named Charlie Brown (screenplay), 1969.
It Was a Short Summer, Charlie Brown (teleplay), CBS, 1969.
It Really Doesn't Take Much to Make a Dad Happy, Determined Productions, 1970.
The World According to Lucy, Hallmark, 1970.
Peanuts Classics, Holt, 1970.
It's the Easter Beagle, Charlie Brown (teleplay), CBS, 1972.
Snoopy, Come Home (screenplay), 1972.
The Peanuts Philosophers, Hallmark, 1972.
A Charlie Brown Thanksgiving, Random House, 1974.
Peanuts Jubilee: My Life and Art with Charlie Brown and Others (autobiography), Holt, 1975.
You're a Good Sport, Charlie Brown, Random House, 1976.
Don't Hassle Me with Your Sighs, Chuck, Holt, 1976.
The Loves of Snoopy, Hodder & Stoughton, 1978.
It's Your First Kiss, Charlie Brown (teleplay), 1978.
They're Playing Your Song, Charlie Brown, Fawcett, 1978.
(With R. Smith Kiliper) *Charlie Brown, Snoopy and Me: And All the Other Peanuts Characters* (autobiography), Doubleday, 1980.
Bon Voyage, Charlie Brown, and Don't Come Back (screenplay), 1980.
Here Comes the April Fool!, Holt, 1980.
Things I Learned After It Was Too Late (and Other Minor Truths), Holt, 1981.
She's a Good Skate, Charlie Brown (teleplay), CBS, 1981.
Sweet Dreams, Charlie Brown, Fawcett Crest, 1983.
A Boy Named Charlie Brown (video), CBS/Fox Video, 1984.
Snoopy's Getting Married, Charlie Brown, Random House, 1986.
You're Supposed to Lead, Charlie Brown, Fawcett Crest, 1988.
School's Out, Charlie Brown, Fawcett Crest, 1990.
There Goes the Shutout, Holt, 1990.
What Makes You Think You're Happy?, Holt, 1990.
You're Not Alone, Charlie Brown, Ballantine, 1992.
I'll Be Home Soon, Snoopy, Harper Festival, 1996.
Kick the Ball, Marcie!, Harper Festival, 1996.

Sources

On-line

Press Democrat on-line, http://www.pressdemo.com/news/schulz/ (December 11, 1997).
Snoopy's Gallery & Gift Shop, http://www.snoopygift.com (December 11, 1997).

Books

Reitberger, Reinhold, and Fuchs, Wolfgang, *Comics: Anatomy of a Mass Medium* (translated by Nadia Fowler), Studio Vista, 1972.
Short, Robert L., *The Gospel According to Peanuts*, John Knox, 1965.
Short, *The Parables of Peanuts*, Harper, 1968.

Periodicals

Art in America, March-April 1976.
Editor & Publisher, May 28, 1994, p. 30.
Ladies Home Journal, October 1990, p. 96.
New York Times Magazine, April 16, 1967.
People, October 30, 1989, p. 81.
Publishers Weekly, July 7, 1975; November 4, 1996, p. 21.
Saturday Review, April 12, 1969.
Sports Illustrated, April 12, 1993, p. 18.
Time, December 8, 1997, p. 21.

—*Michael Betzold*

Gary Sheffield

AP/Wide World Photos

Professional baseball player

Born Gary Antonian Sheffield, November 18, 1968, in Tampa, FL; children: Ebony, Carissa, Gary Jr.

Addresses: *Office*—Florida Marlins, 2267 N.W. 199th Street, Miami, FL 33056.

Career

Drafted by Milwaukee Brewers, 1986; played in Brewers minor league system, 1986-89; played for Milwaukee in American League, 1988-91; traded to San Diego Padres; played for San Diego, 1992-93; traded to Florida Marlins; played for Florida, 1993—; member of Marlins' World Championship team, 1997.

Awards: *Sporting News* Major League Player of the Year, 1992.

Sidelights

Once notorious for his temper, Gary Sheffield has learned to be patient. One of baseball's most-feared sluggers, Sheffield crowds the plate and dares pitchers to throw inside. He has stopped swinging at bad pitches and added a new dimension to his game. His ability to get on base and drive in runs helped lead the Florida Marlins to their first world championship in 1997.

Sheffield's post-season success followed a disappointing regular season. Playing right field and batting third, Sheffield didn't find his batting stroke until September. By that time, Florida had fallen hopelessly behind the Atlanta Braves in the National League's

Eastern Division. But with the help of Sheffield, the Marlins became the first wild-card team in baseball history to compete in the World Series.

Prior to 1997, Sheffield's career had mixed high expectations and bursts of remarkable achievement with frequent injuries, suspensions and off-field trouble. The nephew of major league pitcher Dwight Gooden, Sheffield grew up in Belmont Heights, a tough neighborhood in Tampa. His mother was 17 when he was born, and he never knew his father. When he was two, his stepfather, Harold Jones, moved in. By the time Gary was six, his 10-year-old Uncle Dwight was pulling him out of bed to make him go outside and catch his already terrifying fastball. He also dared him to hit it, and this early training helped Sheffield developed his quick hands. The scrappy kid became a terror on the field and off it, getting into frequent fights. One time, after being benched for missing a practice, he chased his Little League coach around the field with a bat. As punishment, he had to sit out the league championship game. He later appeared in the Little League World Series. By the time he was a senior at Hillsborough High, Sheffield had fathered two children by different mothers and had been selected the nation's top high school player by *USA Today*.

The Milwaukee Brewers picked him as the sixth selection in the first round of the 1986 draft. Sheffield wasn't happy with his midwestern destination, and he was angry when the Brewers shifted him from shortstop to third base after his rookie season in 1988. "Everything you asked for in Milwaukee, you didn't get," Sheffield complained to Tim Kurkjian of *Sports Illustrated*. "Ask for good weather, you don't get it. Ask for a good playing surface, you don't get it. Ask for a first-class organization, you don't get it." During his Milwaukee years, Sheffield was frequently injured. Management accused him of faking, while Sheffield accused management of asking him to play hurt. Fans frequently booed him, and he often criticized teammates. During the 1990 season, he left the team without permission. He ended up in a hospital with a mysterious illness. The following spring, he was fined after refusing to run sprints.

Before the 1992 season, Sheffield was traded to the San Diego Padres. To him, it was like being let out of prison. "After four years of scowling and snarling in Milwaukee, Sheffield, 23, finally seems comfortable and relaxed," observed Kurkjian. San Diego management took a hands-off attitude, and Sheffield responded with an injury-free year that demonstrated his potential was real. Hitting .330 with 33 home runs and 100 runs batted in, he was named Major League Player of the Year by the *Sporting News.*

The Padres cleaned house in a cost-cutting frenzy and shipped Sheffield to Florida in the middle of the 1993 season. The Marlins moved him from third base to right field. Not known for his defense, Sheffield worked hard to learn his new position. Only 25, Sheffield already was a millionaire. Back in his home state playing for the Marlins, Sheffield again seemed poised for superstardom. "He has the greatest bat speed of any player," wrote Bob Nightengale in the *Sporting News*. "Sheffield also has a brilliant baseball mind. He could out-manage half the men in this game on strategy alone."

But when Sheffield moved back to the Tampa area, trouble followed. His bayfront home in St. Petersburg was broken into. He had an aggravated battery complaint filed against him. He allegedly threatened his son's mother. There was a murder plot against his mother. A female fan stalked him, and anonymous callers harassed him. He was convicted of drunk driving. A former girlfriend sued him. He fathered another child out of wedlock. Sitting at a traffic light in Tampa, he was shot at, but luckily the slug merely grazed his shoulder. He was pulled off a team flight and searched for drugs by sheriff's deputies. With his uncle's [Gooden] career derailed by cocaine addiction,

Sheffield was tested frequently for drugs, but was always clean. Among all his off-field troubles, he also battled injuries and his playing time suffered in 1994 and 1995.

In 1996, Sheffield hired a public relations agent and embarked on an image makeover. He took public speaking lessons, started his own charity, did a magazine fashion shoot, and moved to a more secure Miami high-rise, fading into the elegance of the South Beach neighborhood. Recovered from his injuries, and finally at peace, Sheffield had his second great season, batting .314 with 42 home runs and 120 RBIs.

As the 1997 season opened, Sheffield signed a six-year, $61 million contract extension, at the time the richest in baseball history. Sheffield then went into a slump which lasted most of the season. Pitchers refused to throw him strikes. He hit only .250 with 21 homers and 71 RBIs, but walked 121 times. But he came alive in the last month of the season and in the post-season playoffs he was an on-base machine. In the first round, against the San Francisco Giants, Sheffield reached base 10 times in 14 appearances. In the second round, the Marlins beat the heavily favored Atlanta Braves in six games to advance to the World Series, and then went on to beat another heavily favored team, the Cleveland Indians, to become world champions. Even though the Marlins won the World Series, owner Wayne Huizenga made plans to sell the team, claiming he had lost $40 million. According to Tom Verducci of *Sports Illustrated*, Huizenga ordered his general manager to cut payroll from $53 million to $25 million. The GM began to get rid of the team's high-priced players, and it was rumored that he was trying to deal Sheffield and his $61 million salary to the New York Mets.

Sources

Books

Shatzkin, Mike, *The Ballplayers*, William Morrow, 1990.

Periodicals

Sporting News, May 6, 1991, p. 35; November 2, 1992, p. 18; April 15, 1996, p. 18; July 1, 1996, p. 7; April 14, 1997, p. 37; October 13, 1997, p. 8.
Sports Illustrated, April 27, 1992, p. 54; September 14, 1992, p. 54; May 24, 1993, p. 60; May 27, 1996, p. 68; October 13, 1997, p. 57; November 24, 1997.

—Michael Betzold

Jenny Shipley

Reuters/Ho/Archive Photos

Prime Minister of New Zealand

Born Jennifer Robson, February 4, 1952, in Gore, New Zealand; daughter of a Presbyterian minister and a homemaker; married Burton Shipley (a farmer), c. 1972; children: Ben and Anna. *Education:* Attended Marlborough Girls' College, Christchurch Teachers' College and Lincoln College.

Addresses: *Office*—Office of the Prime Minister, Parliament House, Wellington, New Zealand.

Career

Primary school teacher, 1972-76; Joined National Party, 1975, held executive positions; child safety officer, Plunket, 1979-81; Malvern Plunket executive, 1979-84; playcentre president, 1980-82; Malvern County councillor, beginning 1983; Aged Peoples Welfare Committee, beginning 1983; Malvern Community Arts Council, beginning 1983; Lincoln College Conference Committee, beginning 1985; Divisional Councillor, beginning 1985; member of parliament for Ashburton, beginning 1987; Minister of Social Affairs and Minister of Women's Affairs, beginning 1990; Health Minister, 1993-96; Transport Minister and Minister of State-Owned Enterprises, 1996-97; Prime Minister of New Zealand, 1997—.

Sidelights

Jenny Shipley in just a decade and a half transformed herself from a homemaker raising two children on her husband's farm to one of the most powerful women in New Zealand's government. Seven years later, she took over as prime minster of the country. A former schoolteacher, Shipley got started in politics at the grass-roots level in the National Party in 1975 and by 1990 was the Minister of Social Welfare. In that post, she earned a reputation as a hard-line right-wing hatchet woman, cutting benefits to the poor while some outraged citizens burned her in effigy. Often called "the toughest man in the cabinet," she garnered comparisons to conservative Prime Minister Margaret Thatcher of England. In 1997, she craftily orchestrated a takeover from Prime Minister Jim Bolger, making her New Zealand's first female prime minister. After Bolger stepped down, David Barber in the *Independent* wrote, "Mr. Bolger is seen by many in the National Party to have been too soft with his big-spending coalition partners in New Zealand First at the cost of National's traditional right-wing policies and fiscal restraint. Mrs. Shipley has never been accused of being too soft on anyone."

Shipley was born in Gore, New Zealand, on February 4, 1952, the second of four girls. Her father was a Presbyterian minister, and her mother was a homemaker. She was raised in Marlborough on New Zealand's South Island and attended Marlborough Girls' College in Blenheim. After failing her university entrance exam, she enrolled at Christchurch Teachers' College. From 1972 to 1976, she taught primary school, and at age 20 married Burton Shipley, a farmer. The couple lived in Ashburton on South Island. After they had two children, Ben and Anna, Shipley quit her teaching job to raise them while her husband tended the 480-hectare farm.

Meanwhile, Shipley became active in politics, joining the National Party in 1975. She would eventually hold a number of executive positions. She was also involved with grass-roots groups and community service, especially in the area of child care, serving as a child safety officer from 1979 to 1981 and the playcentre president from 1980 to 1982. In 1983, Shipley ran for county council and was elected, serving on the Aged Peoples Welfare Committee and the Malvern Community Arts Council, among others. In 1987, she was elected to the national parliament from Ashburton. Upon this momentous occasion, her husband sold the farm to take care of the family while his wife pursued her political career.

The National Party did not hold a majority in 1987, which helped facilitate Shipley's rapid rise. By the time the party regained prominence in 1990, she was in place for a high-level cabinet appointment. Jim Bolger, leader of the National Party, was elected prime minister and named Shipley his minister of social affairs. Along with Minister of Finance Ruth Richardson, Shipley effected quick change in the welfare system, making deep cuts to benefits, imposing a six-month hold on all unemployment assistance, and hacking away at fraud. She intended to lessen public dependence on government assistance, but the moves were unpopular. "Protesters burned her in effigy and likened her to a tank commander for her singleminded determination to achieve her goals," wrote Simon Robinson in TIME International.

Bolger made Shipley the minister of health in 1993, where she continued to trim government spending, implementing a reform that asked hospitals and clinics to turn a profit. During that stint, however, she also decreed that the government would distribute free birth control pills to all women. Her plan called for spending $13.7 million (in U.S. funds) over three years to reduce the country's abortion rate. In 1994-95, New Zealand had 221 abortions for every 1,000 births, an increase from 202. Comparatively, the United States at that time had almost twice the rate—401 abortions for every 1,000 live births—but Germany only had 108, and the Netherlands had 96. Shipley announced at the time, "This won't change overnight, but I think that a modern society like ours should be up-front, realistic and ambitious about having a positive attitude toward our sexual reproductive health and set ourselves spe-cific goals," according to Brendan Boyle in the Reuters news service. As part of the effort, Shipley authorized a survey of sex education, which was not mandatory in schools.

After her role as health minister, Shipley asked for a less controversial appointment and was made transport minister in 1996, while also serving as minister for women's affairs and minister of state-owned enterprises. In this capacity, Shipley set out to unseat Prime Minister Jim Bolger, who had formed a coalition government in 1996 with the minority New Zealand First party, led by Winston Peters. Toward the end of 1997, opinion polls rated only a ten percent approval of the power structure. Shipley wanted to wrest control from Bolger and continue her right-wing reforms, which were often compared to those of England's Prime Minister Margaret Thatcher. Indeed, many National Party members of parliament (MPs) felt their party had lost direction and were unhappy with scandals that took place in the New Zealand First party after Bolger formed the coalition government. Late in October, with Bolger out of the country, Shipley circulated a letter to all National party MPs, in effect staging a peaceful coup. Robinson in TIME International reported that the letter read, "I understand that it is your intention to challenge for the leadership of the National Party on November 4, 1997. I give you my undertaking that I will vote for you in the ballot." The numbers of those signing the letter escalated to 30 out of the 44 National Party MPs.

On November 3, 1997, shortly after Bolger returned to New Zealand, Shipley presented her evidence that the government did not support his leadership. She warned him that he would have to go through an embarrassing vote of confidence, so the next day, Bolger announced that he would step down at the end of the month. New Zealand First leader Winston Peters initially balked at supporting Shipley, who was much too right-wing for his tastes, but Shipley remained committed to coalition government. On December 8, 1997, she was sworn in as the first female prime minister in the history of New Zealand. Her first meeting with the new cabinet dealt with a proposal for funding the country's roadways, including possibly a toll for drivers. Other actions soon after her assumption of power included proposals for a one-stop job agency, abolition of car tariffs, and simplification of the tax system. She also indicated that she wanted to require welfare recipients to earn a "community wage," meaning that they would have to do community service or other work for their benefits, and hoped to trim the number of people on disability by changing the definition of "invalid."

In 1998, Shipley noted at a factory opening that the nation's business climate was good, despite troubles in Asia. (New Zealand depends closely on Asian tourists for a large segment of their economy.) In February of that year, Shipley celebrated the opening of her country's biggest cultural project to date, the Museum of New Zealand. This national museum cost $185 million (in U.S. funds) to build, and contained works from the indigenous Maori people as well as later-arriving Europeans, known as "pakeha." Shipley hoped that the museum would help ease tension between the two groups. On an international level, U.S. President Bill Clinton called Shipley in February to ask for support in a possible military action against Iraq. Forces were being assembled to ensure that Iraq would comply with a United Nations mandate that they not produce biological weapons, and Shipley agreed to send a small number of troops for potential search and rescue operations. In April, former Prime Minister Bolger became an ambassador to the United States.

Meanwhile, Shipley saw her popularity rise above that of opposition Labour Party leader Helen Clark, despite her reputation among critics as "an armoured personnel carrier," as an *Economist* article noted. "Jenny can tell you in wonderful warm tones how she's going to garrotte you and then disembowel you and throw your intestines over her left shoulder," remarked Michael Laws, a New Zealand First member of parliament, in the *Independent*. "She never raises her voice and never uses bad language, but the assault is deadly."

Sources

Books

Current Leaders of Nations, Gale Research, 1998.

Periodicals

Daily Telegraph, November 4, 1997, p. 27.
Economist, November 8, 1997, p. 43.
Independent, November 4, 1997; November 5, 1997.
Reuters news service, May 2, 1996; February 13, 1998; February 15, 1998; February 16, 1998; February 16, 1998.
Rocky Mountain News, November 4, 1997, p. 33A.
TIME International, November 17, 1997, p. 50.
Xinhua News Agency, November 4, 1997; November 22, 1997; December 5, 1997; December 7, 1997; January 23, 1998; February 13, 1998.

—Geri Speace

Thomas Sowell

AP/Wide World Photos

Economist, author, and educator

Born June 30, 1930, in Gastonia, NC; married Alma Jean Parr (divorced); remarried; children: (first marriage) two. *Education:* Harvard University, B.A., 1958; Columbia University, M.A., 1959; University of Chicago, Ph.D., 1968.

Addresses: *Office*—Stanford University, Hoover Institution, Stanford, CA 94305.

Career

U.S. Department of Labor, Washington, DC, economist, 1961-62; Rutgers University, Douglass College, New Brunswick, NJ, instructor in economics, 1962-63; Howard University, Washington, DC, lecturer in economics, 1963-64; American Telephone & Telegraph (AT&T) Co., New York City, economic analyst, 1964-65; Cornell University, Ithaca, NY, assistant professor of economics, 1965-69, director of Summer Intensive Training Program in Economic Theory, 1968; Brandeis University, Waltham, MA, associate professor of economics, 1969-70; University of California, Los Angeles, associate professor, 1970-74, professor of economics, 1974-80; Urban Institute, Washington, DC, project director, 1972-74; Center for Advanced Study in the Behavioral Sciences, Stanford, CA, fellow, 1976-77; Hoover Institution, Stanford, fellow, 1977, senior fellow, 1980—. Visiting professor, Amherst College, 1977. Columnist, Scripps-Howard News Service, 1984-90, Creators Syndicate, 1991—, *Forbes* magazine, 1991—. Contributor to various publications. *Military service:* U.S. Marine Corps, 1951-53.

Awards: Francis Boyer Award, American Enterprise Institute, 1990.

Sidelights

Author and economist Thomas Sowell is noted for his right-wing opinions on racial issues surrounding economic and social policy. An African American who opposes such programs as affirmative action, busing, quotas, minimum wage, and welfare, he has drawn fire from liberals and a number of African American leaders, while generating applause from fellow conservatives. Sowell is an advocate of the "pull yourself up by the bootstraps" philosophy, which encourages people to improve their positions not by government intervention, but by personal ambition and hard work. He believes that government's initiatives to ensure a fair playing field for African Americans have actually hurt their chances for equality. Regardless of whether one agrees with his politics or not, Sowell is also known as a top economic expert, having published extensively in economics journals and general periodicals. He also spent the better part of three decades teaching in respected academic institutions. Into the 1990s, his name was commonly seen as a weekly byline in *Forbes* magazine and on his syndicated column appearing in newspapers nationwide. Sowell is the author of over 20 books and has edited or contributed to others. "The word 'genius' is thrown around so much that it's becoming meaningless," remarked renowned economist Milton Friedman in

Forbes, "but nevertheless I think Tom Sowell is close to being one."

Sowell was born June 30, 1930, in Gastonia, North Carolina, and spent much of his youth in Charlotte, North Carolina. Secretive about his personal life, not much is known about his family or early years, except that he moved to Harlem in New York City with his parents at around age eight or nine, and his father worked in construction. Sowell attended classes for gifted students and was ranked at the top of his class at the prestigious Stuyvesant High School, but dropped out in tenth grade to go to work for four years. He took jobs in a factory, as a delivery person, and as a Western Union messenger making 65 cents an hour. These lean early years would heavily influence his politics later in life and provide him with arguments during debates with liberal leaders.

> *"I wish that I may never think the smiles of the great and powerful a sufficient inducement to turn aside from the straight path of honesty and the convictions of my own mind."*

Sowell finally finished high school by going to night classes, then was drafted to serve in the U.S. Marine Corps in 1951. He spent two years at Camp Lejeune, North Carolina, where he worked as a photographer in the Korean War. Thanks to the G.I. Bill, he enrolled at Howard University in Washington, D.C., a majority-African American institution, while working part-time as a photographer and as a civil service clerk for the General Accounting Office. After three semesters, he transferred to Harvard. There, Sowell wrote his senior thesis on left-wing German political philosopher Karl Marx and graduated magna cum laude with a bachelor's degree in economics in 1958. A Marxist sympathizer as an undergraduate, Sowell gradually became more conservative as he pursued his master's degree at Columbia University and later during his doctoral studies at University of Chicago, where he studied under economist and Nobel laureate Milton Friedman and Professor George Stigler. Sowell obtained his M.A. from Columbia in 1959 and his Ph.D. from the University of Chicago in 1968.

Sowell spent much of the 1960s in academics after beginning his career first as a summer intern in 1960, then as an employee of the U.S. Department of Labor in 1960-61 as an economist. From there, he taught at Rutgers (1962-63) and Howard (1963-64) universities, later taking a post as an economic analyst with AT&T from 1964-65. Sowell taught from 1965-69 as an assistant professor of economics at Cornell and spent the summer of 1968 there as the director of the Summer Intensive Training Program in Economic Theory. After teaching from 1969-70 at Brandeis, Sowell went to the University of California, Los Angeles (UCLA) as an associate professor of economics, where he was promoted to full professor in 1974. He also served as project director of the Urban Institute from 1972-74. Sowell stayed at UCLA until 1980 and also taught there from 1984-89. In 1980, he was named a senior fellow at Stanford University's Hoover Institution.

Also in 1980, Republican President Ronald Reagan took office and ushered in a wave of conservativism in politics that would last most of the decade. It seemed that Sowell's time had come. He organized a Black Alternatives Conference in San Francisco to publicize the conservative voice of African Americans. About 100 Republican business professionals and educators attended, advocating right-wing policies such as lowering the minimum wage, doing away with rent control, and reorganizing federal programs. After that event, Edwin Meese III, then the director of Reagan's transition team, announced that the new president would appoint African Americans to his cabinet and other high-level positions. Sowell was offered a cabinet post, but did not even entertain the notion. According to a *Newsweek* piece from the time, "Such active participation in politics ... would only damage his scholarly reputation." In February of 1981, however, Sowell did accept a post on the White House Economic Advisory Board, but resigned after one meeting. The commute to Washington, D.C., from his home in Palo Alto, California, was "too much of a strain," as *People Weekly* reported.

Instead, Sowell continued working at the Hoover Institute, teaching at UCLA for part of the decade, and penning his controversial ideas. A prolific writer for much of his career, Sowell has churned out books nearly every year since 1971 and has contributed regularly to scholarly economics journals as well as periodicals, such as the *New York Times Magazine* and *Spectator.* His topics range from law to education in addition to economics and race issues. In 1984, Sowell began writing a newspaper column, figuring that if George Will could make a point in 750 words, so could he. He was a regular columnist for the Scripps-Howard news service from 1984-90, then began writing a column for the weekly *Forbes* magazine as well as newspaper columns for the Creators Syndicate in 1991. He has been criticized by fellow economists who think his academic papers are not "formal" enough, but *Forbes* defended him by saying that his work was readable and not bogged down in algebraic formulas. A biography of Sowell on the web jabbed back at the academics, explaining his desire to publish in the mass media: "Writing for the general public enables him to address the heart of issues without the smoke and mirrors that so often accompany academic writing."

Readers, however, have also been taken aback by Sowell's authorship, but in a different way—his conservative opinions, not his writing style, have been the cause of dissent. One of Sowell's often-targeted beliefs is that poverty among minority groups is less a result of racial and social discrimination than of a group's values, ethics, and attitudes. He contends that if discrimination is to blame for a group's lack of progress, then many of the Japanese, Chinese, and Jewish groups in America would never have reached the level of prosperity that they enjoy. As an example, he says that Chinese immigrants from a certain province have had more success in America than those from other areas. Those older immigrants from the Toishan district of the Kwantung Province are affluent, whereas newer immigrants from various other areas work in sweatshops and live in poverty. As he asserted in *U.S. News & World Report,* "The two have different cultures, and that accounts for the contrast in their situations.... The enormous difference between the groups cannot in any way be attributed to how the larger society treats Chinese people, because the average American employer cannot tell the two apart." He also cited statistics on West Indian blacks, who have higher incomes than whites in the United States, yet cannot be distinguished from other African Americans.

Sowell believes that government programs such as busing black children to white schools, welfare, affirmative action programs, and other social programs have hurt, not helped, blacks by causing them to rely too heavily on government safety nets instead of using their own motivation to succeed. He also has said that government programs will harm African Americans by fueling racist sentiments of whites upset by busing, quotas, and other laws that Sowell feels discriminate against the majority. He claimed in *U.S. News and World Report* that the status of African Americans was rising prior to the Civil Rights Act of 1964 and that they were making strides in housing integration and career advancement, thus the act did not really have the impact that people think it did.

Sowell's 1990 book, *Preferential Policies: An International Perspective,* deals specifically with the issue of affirmative action. In it, he vehemently opposes quotas in college admissions and jobs, using examples not just from American society, but from around the world. He argues that preferential treatment leads to relaxed standards, which cause people to fail to reach their true potential. Quotas can cause underprepared minorities to suffer frustration and a higher drop-out rate, or may be a reason they are steered to "softer" fields of concentration instead of more practical pursuits at schools that fit their pace. Sowell also believes that quotas can lead to more interracial tension on campuses. Andrew Hacker in the *New York Times Book Review* related Sowell's claims that policies such as affirmative action make the "trendy middle classes" feel virtuous, as if they are somehow making up for slavery or for overrunning a native culture. Sowell disagrees with those who call for reparations to be paid by the government to African Americans for the slavery they endured, arguing that African Americans today should progress to thinking about the present, not the past.

Not surprisingly, many liberal African American leaders, including Jesse Jackson and Benjamin Hooks, as well as left-wing whites have taken offense with Sowell's arguments, saying, ironically, that he is the one promoting racism, and that his arguments are too simplistic. Economist Bernard Anderson of University of Pennsylvania's Wharton School asserted in *Newsweek,* "We cannot separate the incredible gains that have been made [by blacks] from the strong role that the government has played." He added that the U.S. government is the largest single employer of middle-class African Americans in the nation. *People Weekly* reported that Carl T. Rowan charged that Sowell gives "aid and comfort to America's racists," but that "Sowell has dismissed Rowan as an 'idiot' whose 'dumb remarks' intimidate blacks holding differing views."

Sowell also had strong opinions in 1995 after publication of the controversial study, *The Bell Curve.* Emotions were highly charged when the book was released asserting that intelligence quotient (IQ) is genetic and that blacks score lower on IQ tests than whites. Though it was derided by many as having a cultural bias, Sowell defended much of the study, detailing his arguments in a lengthy article in *American Spectator.* He did point out aspects that troubled him, but overall, he stated, "Contrary to much hysteria in the media, this is not a book about race, nor is it trying to prove that blacks are capable only of being hewers of wood and drawers of water."

With the repealing of affirmative action laws and the ensuing debates in the late 1990s, Sowell's works are more salient than ever. He continues to write a weekly column for *Forbes,* publish books, and make numerous appearances on the lecture circuit. Divorced from his first wife, Alma Jean Parr, he married again in the early 1980s, but he remains secretive about his personal life; his name is not even posted on his office door at the Hoover Institute. He is reputed to be blunt and impatient, but humorous and outgoing among friends. Indeed, his wit often shows through in his writing. Known for his satirical jabs as well as his serious messages, *Forbes* once reprinted Sowell's "glossary of common political terms" as published in *National Review,* which included gems such as "Equal opportunity: Preferential treatment," "Stereotypes: Behavior patterns you don't want to think about," "Demonstration: A riot by people you agree with," "Mob violence: A riot by people you disagree with," "A proud people: Chauvinists you like," and "Bigots: Chauvinists you don't like."

Sowell's intent not to be swayed by voices of dissent among other African American leaders may be illustrated by one of his favorite quotations, as listed on his own home page and attributed to David Ricardo: "I wish that I may never think the smiles of the great and powerful a sufficient inducement to turn aside from the straight path of honesty and the convictions of my own mind."

Selected writings

Economics: Analysis and Issues, Scott, Foresman, 1971.
Black Education: Myths and Tragedies, McKay, 1972.
Say's Law: An Historical Analysis, Princeton University Press, 1972.
Classical Economics Reconsidered, Princeton University Press, 1974.
Affirmative Action: Was It Necessary in Academia?, American Enterprise Institute for Public Policy Research, 1975.
Race and Economics, McKay, 1975.
Patterns of Black Excellence, Ethics and Public Policy Center, Georgetown University, 1977.
(Editor) *American Ethnic Groups,* Urban Institute, 1978.
(Editor) *Essays and Data on American Ethnic Groups,* Urban Institute, 1978.
Knowledge and Decision, Basic Books, 1980.
Ethnic America: A History, Basic Books, 1981.
Markets and Minorities, Basic Books, 1981.
(Editor, with others) *The Fairmont Papers: Black Alternatives Conference, December, 1980,* ICS Press, 1981.

Pink and Brown People, and Other Controversial Essays, Hoover Institution, 1981.
The Economics and Politics of Race: An International Perspective, Morrow, 1983.
Civil Rights: Rhetoric or Reality?, Morrow, 1984.
Marxism: Philosophy and Economics, Morrow, 1985.
Education: Assumption Versus History, Hoover Institution, 1986.
Compassion Versus Guilt, and Other Essays, Morrow, 1987.
A Conflict of Visions, Morrow, 1987.
Choosing a College: A Guide for Parents and Students, Harper & Row, 1989.
Judicial Activism Reconsidered, Hoover Institution, 1989.
Preferential Policies: An International Perspective, Morrow, 1990.
Inside American Education: The Decline, the Deception, the Dogmas, Macmillan, 1993.
Is Reality Optional?: And Other Essays, Hoover Institution, 1993.
Race and Culture: A World View, Basic Books, 1994.
The Vision of the Anointed: Self-Congratulation as a Basis for Social Policy, Basic Books, 1995.
Migrations and Cultures: A World View, Basic Books, 1996.
Late-Talking Children, Basic Books, 1997.
Conquests and Cultures, Basic Books, 1997.

Sources

On-line

"Biography of Thomas Sowell," Conservative Current web site, http://www.townhall.com (April 28, 1998).
"Favorite Quotations," Thomas Sowell home page, http://www.tsowell.com (April 28, 1998).
"Online NewsHour: A Gergen Dialogue with Thomas Sowell—July 11, 1996," PBS web site, http://www.pbs.org (April 28, 1998).

Periodicals

American Spectator, February 1, 1995, p. 32.
Forbes, August 24, 1987, p. 40; August 26, 1996.
Newsweek, March 9, 1981, p. 29.
New York Times Book Review, July 1, 1990.
People Weekly, December 28, 1981, p. 66.
U.S. News & World Report, October 12, 1981, p. 74.
Washington Times, September 18, 1995.

—*Geri Space*

Art Spiegelman

Author, cartoonist

Born February 15, 1948, in Stockholm, Sweden; immigrated to U.S., 1951; naturalized citizen; son of Vladek (a salesperson and businessman) and Anja (Zylberberg) Spiegelman; married Françoise Mouly (a publisher), July 12, 1977; children: Nadja Rachel, Dashiell Alan. *Education:* Attended Harpur College (now State University of New York at Binghamton), 1965-68.

Addresses: *Home*—New York, NY. *Office*—Raw Books & Graphics, 27 Greene St., New York, NY 10013-2537. *Agent*—Deborah Karl, 52 West Clinton Ave., Irvington, NY 10533.

Career

Freelance artist and writer, 1965—; Topps Chewing Gum, Inc., Brooklyn, NY, creative consultant, artist, designer, editor, and writer for novelty packaging and bubble gum cards and stickers, including "Wacky Packages" and "Garbage Pail Kids," 1966-88; editor, *Douglas Comix*, 1972; editor (with Bill Griffith) and contributor, *Arcade, the Comics Revue*, 1975-76; founding editor, *Raw*, 1980—; artist and contributing editor to the *New Yorker*, 1992—. Instructor in studio class on comics, San Francisco Academy of Art, 1974-75; instructor in history and aesthetics of comics at New York School of Visual Arts, 1979-87. Contributor to numerous underground comics.

Awards: *Playboy* Editorial Award for best comic strip, 1982; Yellow Kid Award for best comic strip author, 1982; Regional Design Award, *Print* magazine, 1983, 1984, 1985; Joel M. Cavior Award for Jewish Writing,

1986, for *Maus: A Survivors Tale, My Father Bleeds History*; Inkpot Award, San Diego Comics Convention, 1987; Stripschappening Award for best foreign comics album, 1987; Before Columbus Foundation Award, *Los Angeles Times* book prize, National Book Critics Circle Award, and Pulitzer Prize special citation, all 1992, for *Maus: A Survivors Tale II, and Here My Troubles Begin*; Alpha Art Award, Angoulerne, France, 1993; Guggenheim fellowship.

Sidelights

Underground comics guru Art Spiegelman surfaced into the mainstream in the 1980s with his acclaimed two-part graphic novel *Maus*, an account of his parents' experiences as Jews in the concentration camps during the Holocaust. Formerly known as a mainstay in the quirky world of self-published and offbeat comics, Spiegelman was also responsible for many of the kooky ideas and artwork for Topps Chewing Gum's Wacky Packages and Garbage Pail Kids— trading cards and stickers that, not surprisingly, featured irreverent pokes at popular culture. Spiegelman was awarded a Pulitzer Prize special citation for *Maus* and went on to put the whole collection on CD-ROM in 1994 for the information age. He is also known for the avant-garde graphic magazine *Raw*, which he and his wife began publishing in 1980. Since 1991, he has served as a contributing editor for the *New Yorker*, producing sometimes controversial covers, and in 1996 he published a children's book titled *Open Me, I'm a Dog.*

Spiegelman was born on February 15, 1948, in Stockholm, Sweden, to Vladek, a businessman, and Anja (Zylberberg) Spiegelman. Before World War II, Vladek earned a great deal of money as a salesman, but during the rise of Nazism in Europe, he and his wife and first son were imprisoned at Auschwitz, Poland, one of the most notorious concentration camps where Jews were killed. Their son, Richieu, did not make it through the ordeal, but the couple survived the horror, although Spiegelman later shared the fact that they woke up screaming during the night on a regular basis. They moved to Sweden, where they had their second child, Art. The Spiegelmans immigrated to the United States in 1951, when Art was three, and settled in the Rego Park area of Queens in New York City, where his father was involved in the garment industry and with the diamond business.

Spiegelman's father wanted him to become a dentist, explaining that he could always draw after work, but he could not draw all day and moonlight as a dentist. Spiegelman also noted to *Washington Post* writer Judith Weinraub that his parents were concerned about his future based on their experiences during the Holocaust: "If you were a dentist, in the camps you became a doctor if you were lucky. And if you were a doctor, you had a better chance for survival because you were needed." Spiegelman, following his own wishes, began copying drawings from his favorite comics and *Mad* magazine at an early age, and quickly became obsessed. By age 13, he was supplying art for the school newspaper at Russell Sage Junior High, and at 14, he sold his first piece for $15, a cover for the *Long Island Post.*

Spiegelman attended the High School of Art and Design in New York, which Weinraub described as "the blue-collar version of New York's better-known High School of Music and Art." The school focused on commercial, rather than fine, art, and Spiegelman thrived, getting his work published in alternative and local publications. While still a high school student, Spiegelman was approached by a United Features Syndicate representative, who had noticed some of the young artist's designs such as the Ink Blot, the Mad Hatter, and the Termite. Offered a chance at a daily strip, Spiegelman decided he would get bored. Besides, he knew his quirky style would be inappropriate for a general audience, and he did not want to modify it.

Instead, Spiegelman continued writing for underground comics, which are often self-published or printed in small publications or by minor companies. Unlike traditional comics, which usually feature superhero action-adventure or silly humor, underground comics often deal with social issues or taboos, feature black humor or no humor at all, and have been known to offend. Spiegelman enrolled at Harpur College, which later became the State University of New York at Binghamton, and studied art and philosophy. His works were often published in his college newspaper and the *East Village Other*, an unconventional New York publication.

After his freshman year in college Spiegelman went to work for Topps Chewing Gum Inc. When he was younger, he had sent a copy of his self-published magazine, *Blase*, to Topps, hoping they would send him some baseball cards drawn by Jack Davis, whose art he admired. Topps responded with an invitation to lunch at their production studios and gave him a number of Davis' originals. Remembering the bright young artist years later, Topps called Spiegelman in 1966 to offer him a summer job at their offices, where he developed novelty toys and streamlined their procedures. At the end of the summer, the firm asked him to stay on. Spiegelman would continue his relationship with Topps for over 20 years.

At Topps, Spiegelman was responsible for creating the "Wacky Packages" and "Garbage Pail Kids" series of trading cards and stickers. Wacky Packages was born after an executive had visualized a set of cards showing reproductions of typical supermarket items. Spiegelman twisted the idea into a parody, creating stickers and cards for goofy products like "Fright Guard" deodorant, "Bustedfingers" candy bars, and even mocking itself, "Wormy Packages" bubble gum cards. Later, in a spoof of the popular Cabbage Patch Kids craze, Spiegelman came out with "Garbage Pail Kids" cards, featuring unkempt little ones with names like Acne Annie and Wrinkled Rita.

Despite his success, Spiegelman suffered a breakdown in 1968 and spent some time recovering in a mental hospital. Shortly thereafter, his mother, depressed on and off her whole life since the Holocaust, committed suicide after her brother died. Spiegelman then moved to San Francisco, where underground comics were flourishing, thanks to artists like R. Crumb. Under the pseudonyms Joe Cutrate and Skeeter Grant, Spiegelman's cartoons were published in periodicals such as *Real Pulp*. Around this time, in the early 1970s, he produced the books *The Complete Mr. Infinity*, 1970; *The Viper Vicar of Vice, Villainy, and*

Vickedness, 1972; *Zip-a-Tune and More Melodies,* 1972; and *Ace Hole, Midget Detective,* 1974. He also drew a strip for *Short Order Comix* in 1972 dealing with his mother's suicide, and that same year developed the idea for his later masterpiece, *Maus,* when he produced a short cartoon for *Funny Aminals* (sic) using the idea of Jews in the Holocaust as mice. Originally, he intended to draw a depiction of oppression of African Americans, until he realized that he, as a white Jewish man, would probably not be the best candidate to speak for African Americans.

Spiegelman taught for a short time at the San Francisco Academy of Art in 1974-75, and also around this time collaborated with Bill Griffith, creator of *Zippy the Pinhead,* to form the comic anthology *Arcade* in order to showcase new material. Later in the 1970s, Spiegelman returned to New York, where he met Françoise Mouly, an editor and graphic designer. The two married on July 12, 1977, and joined creative forces, publishing *Raw,* an underground comics anthology magazine, beginning in 1980.

In 1978, Spiegelman turned 30 and took inventory. "If I was going to stay alive past 30," he told the *Washington Post*'s Weinraub, "I thought I'd better do something to justify it." He started the research he would use to flesh out *Maus* by interviewing his father. The tape-recorded conversations eased the tension that had existed between father and son for most of Spiegelman's life. "It gave us a reason to be together, and it gave me a weapon to keep him at bay, and it gave him someone who would listen to him, someone who would respect his memories," Spiegelman explained to Esther B. Fein in the *New York Times.* Traveling to Auschwitz in 1978 and 1986, Spiegelman saw drawings that the inmates made to record their surroundings, which also profoundly affected him.

The first book of the oral history was published in 1986 as *Maus: A Survivor's Tale, My Father Bleeds History.* (Unfortunately, Spiegelman's father had died in 1982 and would never see the acclaim that was to come.) The story begins with the author, as a mouse, asking his father, Vladek, to recall the Holocaust. Vladek obliges, telling him that he is living in Poland with his wife, Anja, and their son, Richieu, as World War II begins. The Nazis, drawn as cats, occupy most of Eastern Europe. Though they oppress everyone, they specifically target the Jews (mice). After serving with the Polish army, Vladek is locked up in a German war prison. When he returns to his family, the Nazis are implementing their "Final Solution" to kill the entire Jewish race. People are aware that Jews are being shipped off to concentration camps, where they are forced to do hard labor, and most are killed or die of disease. Vladek and Anja try to escape, but are rounded up and sent to Auschwitz (Mauschwitz), Poland, to one of the most infamous camps of the Holocaust.

> *"The language I speak is comics. I'm a rotten ballet dancer. So it would never be possible for me to make* Maus *as a ballet."*

Initially, people were stunned that someone would dare make a cartoon out of such a serious issue as the Holocaust, perhaps not realizing that *Maus* was a graphic novel, not a funny comic book. In fact, he had a difficult time finding a publisher. "Many of the rejections were quite loving," he remarked to Fein in the *New York Times,* "But the bottom line was they all said, 'How on earth! It's just not publishable.'" Finally, Pantheon reconsidered, and the book became a sensation. "I've gotten responses from Holocaust survivors, and they've been uniformly positive, except when they haven't read the book," Spiegelman noted in *ARTNews.* "Then they're appalled by the concept." In fact, Spiegelman's cousin, Lolek, another survivor, praised him for his accurate depictions. "I count that as the best review I could have gotten," Spiegelman remarked in *ARTNews,* "because he was there."

Spiegelman followed this volume with *Maus: A Survivors Tale II, and Here My Troubles Began,* which continues with Vladek's tale, starting at the gates of Auschwitz. Vladek recalls being separated from his wife—he is put in Auschwitz, while she goes to nearby Birkenau. The gruesome and inhumane details of life in the camps are drawn with graphic precision: the crowding of four men on one bunk, the constant scavenging for food, the agonizing physical labor, the extreme abuse from Nazi guards, and the looming fear that he or his wife will be sent to the gas chamber. Somehow, Vladek retains hope due to his clandestine meetings with Anja and the camaraderie of other prisoners. He is also told by a former priest that the sum of his tattooed serial numbers is 18, meaning life. Despite a bout with typhus and other threats, Vladek pulls through and manages to flee the camp at the end of the war. In the rush, he loses contact with Anja and is not sure if she is alive. They are reunited and move to Sweden, where Anja gives birth to Art. The family moves to America, but Anja, scarred from her ordeal, never recovers, committing suicide in 1968. The saga ends with Art visiting his father prior to his death in 1982.

Maus was overwhelmingly praised, especially for its ability to make the reader deal with the events through the use of animals instead of humans (not unlike George Orwell's *Animal Farm*). "By relating a story of hideous inhumanity in non-human terms," commented James Colbert in the *Los Angeles Times Book Review,* "*Maus* and *Maus II* allow us as readers to go outside ourselves and to look objectively at ourselves and at otherwise unspeakable events." Though some criticized his use of metaphors—Poles as pigs, Jews as mice, Germans as cats, Americans as dogs—Spiegelman pointed out that that was how Hitler saw the races, not how he saw them. Spiegelman also noted that Hitler even used the word "extermination," typically used only in the context of ridding one's home vermin and pests, to refer to his plan of genocide. Interestingly, due to the book's use of animal characterizations, the best-seller lists could not agree on a category; the *New York Times* listed it as fiction due to its anthropomorphism, while *Publisher's Weekly* tagged it nonfiction.

In 1992, Spiegelman was awarded a special citation Pulitzer Prize for his *Maus* graphic novels. The books were eventually translated into 18 languages. *The Complete Maus* came out on CD-ROM in 1994, augmented by video segments in which Spiegelman talks about his work, rough drafts and photographs, essays by the artist, and transcripts of the interviews he did with his father. After *Maus,* Spiegelman became a contributing editor and artist in 1992 for the *New Yorker,* where his wife works as an art director. He stirred controversy in 1993 with two of his covers for that magazine that were seen by some as politically incorrect, one of which depicted a kiss between a Hasidic Jew and an African American woman, the other, a drawing of a child wearing Arabic headgear destroying sand castles. Another cover drawn for the Christmas issue, featuring Santa Claus urinating in the snow, was deemed unpublishable and never seen by the public.

Spiegelman took off in a slightly different direction in 1994 when he illustrated *The Wild Party: A Lost Classic,* a hard-boiled poem about drinking, fighting, and a party that ends in murder, banned when it was first released in 1928. He really changed course, however, in 1996 with *Open Me, I'm a Dog,* a children's book that claims it is not a book at all, but a real dog in the form of a book, due to a curse. Made with soft orange fur to pet while it is read, the book even comes with a cloth leash for a bookmark.

In addition to the Pulitzer, Spiegelman has received numerous awards for his work, including the National Book Critics Circle Award in 1992 and a Guggenheim fellowship. In 1997, he was busy organizing an international retrospective exhibition of his work, some parts of which made appearances in U.S. cities during that year. He and Mouly have a daughter, Nadja Rachel, and a son, Dashiell Alan; the family resides in the SoHo area of Manhattan in New York City. When asked whether he felt comic books were the appropriate medium for exploring the Holocaust, the wry Spiegelman replied in *Time,* "The language I speak is comics. I'm a rotten ballet dancer. So it would never be possible for me to make *Maus* as a ballet."

Selected writings

The Complete Mr. Infinity, S. F. Book Co., 1970.

The Viper Vicar of Vice, Villainy, and Vickedness, privately printed, 1972.

Zip-a-Tune and More Melodies, S. F. Book Co., 1972.

(Compiling editor with Bob Schneider) *Whole Grains: A Book of Quotations,* D. Links, 1972.

Ace Hole, Midget Detective, Apex Novelties, 1974.

Language of Comics, State University of New York at Binghamton, 1974.

(Contributor) Don Donahue and Susan Goodrich, editors, *The Apex Treasury of Underground Comics,* D. Links, 1974.

Breakdowns: From Maus to Now, an Anthology of Strips, Belier Press, 1977.

Work and Turn, Raw Books, 1979.

Every Day Has Its Dog, Raw Books, 1979.

Two-Fisted Painters Action Adventure, Raw Books, 1980.

(Contributor) Nicole Hollander, Skip Morrow, and Ron Wolin, editors, *Drawn Together: Relationships Lampooned, Harpooned, and Cartooned,* Crown, 1983.

Maus: A Survivors Tale, My Father Bleeds History, Pantheon, 1986.

(Editor with wife, Françoise Mouly, and contributor) *Read Yourself Raw: Comix Anthology for Damned Intellectuals,* Pantheon, 1987.

(With Mouly) *Jimbo: Adventures in Paradise,* Pantheon, 1988.

(Contributor) *The Complete Color Polly and Her Pals, Vol. 1: The Surrealist Period, 1926-1927,* Remco Worldservice Books, 1990.

Raw, Penguin, 1990.

(Editor with Mouly and R. Sikoryak) *Warts and All/ Drew Friedman and John Alan Friedman,* Penguin, 1990.

Maus: A Survivors Tale II, and Here My Troubles Began, Pantheon, 1991.

Raw 3: High Culture for Lowbrows, Viking, 1991.

(Editor with R. Sikoryak) Charles Burns, *Skin Deep: Tales of Doomed Romance*, Penguin, 1992.

The Complete Maus (CD-ROM), Voyager, 1994.

(Illustrator) Joseph Moncura March, *The Wild Party: The Lost Classic*, Pantheon, 1994.

Open Me, I'm a Dog (for children), HarperCollins, 1996.

Sources

On-line

"Art Spiegelman Biography," http://galenet.com (March, 1998).

Books

Artists & Authors for Young Adults, Volume 10, Gale Research, 1993.

Contemporary Authors, New Revision Series, Volume 55, Gale Research, 1997.

Periodicals

ARTNews, May 1993, p. 63.

Entertainment Weekly, December 13, 1991; November 18, 1994, p. 98.

Los Angeles Times Book Review, November 8, 1992, p. 2.

MacUser, August 1994, p. 64.

Nation, January 17, 1994, p. 45.

Newsday, November 27, 1994.

New York Times, December 10, 1991, p. C15.

Publishers Weekly, October 10, 1994, p. 61.

Rocky Mountain News, December 22, 1997.

Time, November 1, 1993.

Washington Post, December 24, 1991, p. C1.

—*Geri Speace*

Jerry Springer

Talk show host

Born February 13, 1944, in London, England; married but separated; children: Katie. *Education:* Tulane University, B.A. in political science, 1965; Northwestern University, J.D., 1968.

Addresses: *Office*—Jerry Springer Show, 454 N. Columbus Dr., 2nd Floor, Chicago, IL 60611.

Career

Senator Robert F. Kennedy campaign aide, 1968; lawyer, Cincinnati, OH, 1968-71; Cincinnati City Council member, 1971-75; 1976-77; mayor of Cincinnati, 1977-81; WLWT-TV, political reporter and commentator, 1982-84; news anchor and managing editor, 1984-93; *Jerry Springer Show,* host, 1991—.

Awards: Seven Emmy Awards for news commentaries.

Sidelights

Talk show host Jerry Springer, the "King of Trash TV," has carved out a niche for himself in popular culture by becoming the impetus for the array of shocking, usually fascinating, characters who parade across the television screen on a daily basis, often engaging in down-and-dirty onstage brawls. Proving again that truth is often stranger than fiction, Springer's guests are real people from around the country who have jumped at the chance to air their dirty laundry—the dirtier, the better—for television viewers in exchange for little more than a few minutes of fame (or notoriety). Many loathe this barrage of incestuous lesbian sisters, bisexual love triangles, secret transvestites, mothers who want to marry their stepsons, and numerous other outrageous participants, calling the show disgusting and perverse. However, many others tune in, boosting his ratings to a solid 8 million watchers per day. "Why is the show so popular?" asks Marvin Kitman in *Newsday.* He answers, "What Jerry is doing is an old-fashioned kind of freak show. It's like going to the circus and seeing the bearded lady, the man who bites off chicken heads, sword swallowers, and so on." The *Jerry Springer Show* has stirred controversy, amassing a cadre of critics. However, as is often noted, if fans did not watch, the show would not be on the air.

Springer was born in London, England, on February 13, 1944, during World War II. At age five, he and his parents, who were Jewish, fled the horrors of the Holocaust, which was responsible for the deaths of a number of their relatives, and arrived in New York City. They settled in the Kew Gardens area of Queens, with his mother working as a bank clerk while his father sold stuffed animals. Springer, who loved the Yankees, recalled that he was a well-mannered boy who never caused his parents any trouble. He enrolled at Tulane University in New Orleans, where he served as his fraternity president and appeared in a couple of plays. After graduating in 1965 with his bachelor's degree in political science, he moved north to Chicago and attended law school at Northwestern University. Upon graduation, he was hired as a campaign aide for Senator Robert F. (Bobby) Kennedy's 1968 presidential bid, and he also ran for a seat in Congress from Ohio, losing by a small margin.

After Bobby Kennedy was assassinated, Springer worked at a Cincinnati law firm and ran for the city council. In 1971, he won a place on the council-at-large and immediately drafted a motion making it illegal for city residents to be drafted into the Vietnam War. He soon worked his way up to the position of vice-mayor. During his tenure, in 1974, Springer ran afoul of the law. When local police across the state line in Kentucky raided a house of prostitution, they confiscated a receipt bearing Springer's name. He stepped down from his office, but a year later, reconsidered his initial reaction and figured there were worse things he could have done. The voters apparently agreed. He ran again for the council and was elected.

Despite his legal snafu, Springer established himself as a popular politician. He ran for mayor of Cincinnati in 1977 and won by the largest percentage in that city's history. At age 33, he was dubbed the "Boy Mayor" and served two terms. He aspired to bigger things, though, and campaigned to become governor of Ohio. His opponent ran negative ads focusing on Springer's seedy incident, but the mayor countered in his commercial by airing a confession and then pointing out his honesty as a virtue. According to Erik Hedegaard in *Rolling Stone*, Springer at the time remarked, "You have to remember, I'm not running for God. What's wrong with the public knowing I'm a human being with warts?" Citizens did not support him this time, however, and he lost the race.

In 1982, Springer started a new career, embarking on a job at Cincinnati's WLWT-TV News 5 as a political reporter and commentator, covering conventions, primaries, and elections. He rose to anchor and managing editor in 1984, holding the number one anchor spot until January of 1993. For his efforts, he won five Emmy awards for newscasting and was voted best television anchor five years running in readers' polls taken by *Cincinnati Magazine*. One of his proudest moments during these years came when he went to Ethiopia and Sudan to report "Cincinnati Reaches Out," about local help for famine relief there. In 1993, Springer stepped down to devote his time to his own show.

In 1991, Multimedia Entertainment, which owned WLWT-TV as well as the *Phil Donahue Show,* ap-proached Springer to host a new talk show. As with the Donahue show, Springer's employers pictured him as a caring host and also told him that he could produce it. Early on, he welcomed top-name guests including Jesse Jackson and Oliver North, but had his doubts about the program's longevity in an already saturated genre. It seemed a new celebrity talk show was popping up every week: Vicki Lawrence, Tempestt Bledsoe, George Hamilton, Danny Bonaduce, and more. "I remember when we announced the show in (June) 1991," Springer recalled to John Kiesewetter in the *Cincinnati Enquirer,* "and I was thinking: `Who are we kidding? We'll be lucky to last 13 weeks!" The *Jerry Springer Show* began basically as a replica of Donahue, with topics like "Grandparents Raising Grandkids," but Springer was not comfortable mimicking the formula.

Instead, Springer took note of his more raunchy competition, such as the topics involving call girls and transvestites that Jenny Jones, Ricki Lake, and Rolanda Watts were covering. He grew his hair a little longer and began courting guests like topless maids and male exotic dancers, and the ratings started to climb. In 1994, producer Richard Dominick took the reins, and the show became infamous. "We made it wild in '94," Dominick related in the *Atlanta Journal and Constitution.* "That's when I told Jerry, 'Put away the issues. Let Ted Koppel do the issues at night. Let's not save the world. We are television.'" Meanwhile, in March of 1995, a *Jenny Jones* show guest, outraged and embarrassed when it was revealed during the taping that a male friend had a crush on him, killed the gay friend. The public was appalled, the show was never aired, and Jones was even called to the witness stand during the trial. Soon, many of the other programs dropped off, and Oprah, the undisputed queen of daytime talk, vowed to rise above the sleaze.

However, once the backlash died down, Springer continued to fill audiences' desire to peek into the sordid lives of others. His ratings rose 40 percent from 1994 to 1995, and 70 percent from late 1996 to late 1997. *The Jerry Springer Show* jumped from being the fifth-ranked talk show in 1995 to becoming runner-up to number one, *The Oprah Winfrey Show,* in 1997. In some markets, including Cleveland, Atlanta, and New Orleans, he regularly beat Oprah, and in late 1998, he began surpassing her numbers. In many markets, his program is on twice a day, in the afternoon and late-night. That is not to say he has not continued to endure the wrath of critics. Opponents chastise him for exploiting people. Tom Teepen in the Minneapolis *Star Tribune* opined, "Springer's show is one of the too many that daily assembles a human sinkhole of life's losers and then turns a rabid audience loose on their depravity." He cited as an example the topic, "Pregnant Women Who Work in the Sex Industry." ABC media commentator Jeff Greenfield noted in an *Entertainment Weekly* article, "I don't think Jerry Springer goes home and pulls the wings off flies. But that's exactly what he does on the show."

Nevertheless, people actively seek to become guests; the show receives over 15,000 calls each week from hopefuls. Many are pranksters, but there is also a constant flow of true stories for the producers to choose from. When chosen to appear, guests receive airfare to Chicago, free meals and hotel, and a limousine ride to the studio. Springer is dedicated to weeding out people trying to pull a hoax, making them sign a form stating that they will pay production costs if their stories turn out to be false. A Canadian comedy troupe tried to pull a fast one in 1995 and faced a possible $80,000 lawsuit. Perhaps just as amazing as some of the stories is the fact that people willingly subject themselves, knowing that nary an episode ends without a fistfight. Those seeking happiness and healing need not appear on Springer, although he does provide a personal commentary, called "Final Thought," at the end of each show to recap the traumas exposed.

In addition to the off-color topics, the extensive fighting on Springer caught attention and flak. The violence, including face slapping, hair-pulling, and chair-throwing, is augmented by shots of women's underwear as they tumble onto the stage, while Springer, in his Armani suits, cooly steps aside. Off-duty Chicago cops are hired to provide security, and they work hard for their money. The incessant use of profanity, and resultant censoring with "bleeps," often makes it nearly impossible to discern more than one word out of every few. Kitman in *Newsday* railed against these aspects of the show, noting that it airs usually during the afternoon when children are likely to be viewing. He also noted, "According to research, it is watched by the lowest-income, least-educated segment of the audience." Other articles point out that it is highly popular with college students, many of whom congregate in restaurants and bars to watch as a group. By 1997, Springer was so vilified that when he took a job moonlighting as a bona fide commentator of Chicago's NBC affiliate, WMAQ-TV, anchor Carol Marin quit in a huff. "She acted as if the prospect were as unsanitary as being asked to go halves on a toothbrush," remarked Teepen in the *Star Tribune*. A week later, Springer backed away from the job in order to douse the fire. He argued afterward that the fan's enemies were being elitist: "I was a liberal populist politician, and my show is populist," he insisted to

Jefferson Graham in *USA Today*. "It's something the hoity-toity don't like. I'm speaking to the same crowd on a power, cultural, educational, and style level." Fans got an extra treat when Universal Television, the show's distributor, sold outtakes to the Real Television company, which in early 1998 released *Jerry Springer: Too Hot for TV*. It is full of uncensored clips, mostly of women who felt the need to bare their breasts in from of the studio audience, and also contains some nasty brawls.

Meanwhile, in 1998 a *Rolling Stone* article suggested that many of the fights were egged on by staffers, with guests receiving coaching before the shoots. Springer professed no knowledge of the staging. The arguments about the moral responsibility of letting the show continue its antics came to a head about the same time, and the syndicate, concerned about its image, ordered Springer to chop out all of the gratuitous violence. Springer initially refuted the news, saying that his show would proceed as usual, but the next day went along with it. The following day, however, according to Kitman in *Newsday,* Springer stated, "If people start to fight, they fight. How am I supposed to know?" The fights slowed down at first, but later picked up the pace again to be a usual occurrence.

Springer is separated from his wife and has a grown daughter, Katie. Intensely private, he refuses to discuss many details about himself, but his official web site offers a quick look at the multifaceted man: "Consider that this one-time mayor has impersonated Elvis, opened for Billy Ray Cyrus, sung rock-and-roll at Johnny Depp's Viper Room, sat astride a Harley Davidson in a leather jacket and suited up to play goalie for the International Hockey League's Milwaukee Admirals." He has also done a few stints as cohost of Jerry Lewis's "Stars Across America" Muscular Dystrophy Telethon and for many years has served on the board of the Audrey Hepburn Hollywood for Children Fund, a charity for needy kids. In addition, he set up a scholarship fund at the urban Kellman School in Chicago.

Another side of him likes to loosen up with music; he recorded a country CD called *Dr. Talk* and even opened a show for Billy Ray Cyrus. "It struck me that the subjects of country songs and the subjects of talk shows are very similar," Springer quipped on his official web site. The loved and hated host generally answers his critics with sage words about the nature of entertainment. "We're just a wild, silly show," Springer stated to Kiesewetter in the *Cincinnati Enquirer*. "As I've said many times before, it's not going to save humanity or destroy it."

Sources

On-line

"Meet Jerry," The Jerry Springer Show web site, http://www.universalstudios.com/tv/jerryspringer (July 12, 1998).

Periodicals

Atlanta Journal and Constitution, December 17, 1997, p. B1.
Columbus Times (OH), February 15, 1994.
Entertainment Weekly, May 12, 1995, p. 34.
Gannett News Service, May 9, 1997, December 11, 1997; January 29, 1998.
Newsday, February 18, 1998, p. B31; June 17, 1998, p. B39.
Rolling Stone, May 14, 1998, p. 41.
Star Tribune (Minneapolis, MN), May 13, 1997, p. 15A.
USA Today, January 22, 1998, p. 3D.

—Geri Speace

Kenneth Starr

Attorney

Born July 21, 1946, in Vernon, TX; son of W. D. (a minister) and Vannie Maude (Trimble) Starr; married Alice Jean Mendell (a public relations executive), August 23, 1970; children: Randall Postley, Carolyn Marie, Cynthia Anne. *Education:* George Washington University, B.A., 1968; Brown University, M.A., 1969; Duke University, J.D., 1973.

Addresses: *Home*—McLean, VA. *Office*—Kirkland & Ellis, 655 Fifteenth St. NW, Suite 1200, Washington, DC 20005.

Career

Law clerk to Judge David Dyer, U.S. Court of Appeals (fifth circuit), Miami, FL, 1973-74; law clerk to U.S. Supreme Court Chief Justice Warren E. Burger, 1975-77; Gibson, Dunn, & Crutcher law firm, associate and partner, 1977-81; counselor to attorney general of the U.S. Department of Justice, Washington, D.C., 1981-83; U.S. Court of Appeals judge, Washington, D.C. circuit, 1983-89; Department of Justice, solicitor general, 1989-93; Kirkland & Ellis law firm, partner, 1993—; independent counsel for Whitewater, beginning 1994. Contributor to legal journals. Legal advisor, CAB transition team of president-elect, 1980-81; legal advisor, SEC transition team, 1980-81; board of advisors, Duke Law Journal. Fellow, American Bar Foundation (judicial fellows committee, judicial conference committee on bicentennial of U.S. constitution). Member, American Bar Association, American Law Institute, American Judicature Society, Institute of Judicial Administration (president), Supreme Court Historical Society, California Bar Association, D.C. Bar Association, Virginia Bar Association, Phi Delta Phi (Hughes chapter Man of the Year, 1973).

Awards: Distinguished alumni awards, George Washington University, Duke University; Attorney General's Award for Distinguished Service, 1993; American Values Award.

Sidelights

Attorney Kenneth Starr could have remained a legal bigwig in private practice, raking in an enormous salary yet staying relatively anonymous. The pull of politics, however, has always been in his blood. He served as a law clerk to U.S. Supreme Court Justice Warren E. Burger right out of law school, and after a few years with a private firm, President Ronald Reagan appointed him to the U.S. Court of Appeals in Washington, D.C. In an unusual move, he stepped down in 1989 when Republican President George Bush asked him to become the solicitor general. Perhaps hoping to work his way on to the Supreme Court, his name was circulated for a seat on that bench, but opponents—both liberal and conservative—threatened a fight. When Bush lost his reelection bid, and Democrat Bill Clinton entered the White House, Starr returned to private practice with a major Chicago-based firm, Kirkland & Ellis. But the government called upon Starr again, first in 1993 to help out with the Senator Bob Packwood sexual misconduct case, then the next year when they asked him to become an independent counsel. Soon Starr would hold center stage with Clinton in an ongoing investigation of the president's ethics, morals, and actions, from supposed shifty land deals to a rumored sexual encounter with a 21-year-old intern. The case spawned comparisons to Watergate, which resulted in President Richard Nixon's resignation, and twice the word "impeachment" arose. Though commentators seemed divided as to whether Starr was a conservative right-winger with a vendetta or just a morally sound man doing his duty to preserve the standards of the United States' highest office, Americans made it clear that they supported Clinton through the storm. Amid a booming economy, the president's approval ratings kept climbing—as high as 80 percent, in some polls—despite Starr's continuing investigation, which had raged on since August of 1994.

> *Kenneth Starr was recruited to replace Robert Fiske as an independent counsel. In this position, an attorney is chosen to investigate high-profile cases in the government. They are meant to be nonpartisan and neutral and do not have to answer to any governmental body.*

Starr was born the youngest of three children on July 21, 1946, in Vernon, Texas, to W. D. and Vannie Maude (Trimble) Starr. His father was a Church of Christ minister in the town of Thalia and moonlighted as a barber for extra money. He raised Starr to shun smoking and drinking. The family, which included Starr's older sister Billie and his big brother Jerry, moved to San Antonio, Texas when Starr was still in grade school. Starr was an immaculate youngster who as an adolescent polished his and his father's shoes each night. By the time he entered Sam Houston High School, he was already interested in politics. He once remarked in an interview, according to Richard Lacayo and Adam Cohen in *Time,* that he greatly admired Richard Nixon when he was vying for the presidency in 1960 against John F. Kennedy. "I really identified with Nixon because of his rather humble roots and the way he worked his way up," Starr was quoted as saying in *Time.*

Starr briefly attended Harding College, a Christian campus in Searcy, Arkansas, selling Bibles door-to-door during the summer to raise tuition money. He transferred to George Washington University after a year and a half, where he was an editor at the college newspaper. When most students were letting their hair grow, adopting a casual dress, and protesting the Vietnam War, Starr suited up in a jacket and tie daily and supported American troops in Vietnam, although his psoriasis prevented him from entering military service. Though he disagreed with anti-war activists, he did support their right to demonstrate, as he outlined in the campus paper, and actively campaigned for Lyndon B. Johnson as a member of the Young Democrats. Starr graduated from George Washington in 1968 and got his master's degree from Brown University the following year. He went on to excel in law school at Duke University, obtaining his juris doctorate in 1973. Meanwhile, on August 23, 1970, he married Alice Jean Mendell, who is now a public relations executive. Right out of law school, Starr began clerking for the U.S. Court of Appeals Judge David Dyer in Miami's fifth circuit from 1973 to 1974, then nabbed a coveted position as a clerk for Warren E. Burger, chief justice of the U.S. Supreme Court, from 1975 to 1977.

After that important role, Starr joined the law firm of Gibson, Dunn & Crutcher in Washington, D.C., as an associate in 1977 and worked his way up to partner. There he met William French Smith, a friend of Ronald Reagan. Smith was named Reagan's first attorney general in 1981, and asked Starr to be his chief of staff. Though it was a financial step down from his six-figure salary in the private sector, Starr took the position. He figured it could be a stepping stone to the U.S. Court of Appeals in Washington, D.C., where many Supreme Court justices got their start, and he was right. Reagan appointed him to the court in 1983. In this role, Starr developed a reputation as a moderate conservative. He was against affirmative action, but protective of the First Amendment, most memorably in a decision for the *Washington Post* protecting it from a libel suit brought by William P. Tavoulareas, chair of the Mobil Corporation.

In a move rare among justices, Starr stepped down from the bench in 1989 to become the solicitor general under President George Bush. The solicitor general bridges the executive and judicial branches of the government, arguing the position of the president's administration in front of the Supreme Court. Starr did not jump on this offer right away, taking several days to contemplate it. "I really loved being a judge on that court," he told Neil A. Lewis in the *New York Times*. Though liberals were initially relieved that the office was no longer held by Charles Fried, a Reagan conservative who many believed used the office to further right-wing causes, Starr proved to hold many of the same positions. Regarding a case in Minnesota, he supported anti-abortion forces, who wanted a law stating that both parents must be notified when a minor seeks an abortion. He also argued that burning the U.S. flag should be illegal. Liberals disliked his harsh stance against abortion rights, yet his own party felt he was too moderate to warrant an appointment to the Supreme Court when a seat became vacant on the bench in 1990. Bush named David Souter instead, and when Democrat Bill Clinton was elected president in 1992, Starr returned to private practice with the Washington, D.C., office of the Chicago-based firm, Kirkland & Ellis, with a salary reported to be in excess of a million dollars.

After leaving the solicitor general job, Starr considered running in Virginia's Republican senate primary before taking the position with Kirkland & Ellis. The government, however, soon beckoned again. In November of 1993, the Senate Ethics Committee called upon Starr, asking him to peruse Senator Bob Packwood's diaries when he was embroiled in sexual misconduct accusations. Then, Starr was recruited to replace Robert Fiske as an independent counsel. In this position, an attorney is chosen to investigate high-profile cases in the government. They are meant to be nonpartisan and neutral and do not have to answer to any governmental body. A number of vocal Democrats, and even some Republicans, felt that Starr was too involved in Republican politics to satisfy the terms of the job, but Starr vowed objectivity. The law creating the role, forged in the late 1970s, was about to expire in 1994 when Clinton renewed it, against the warning of former President George Bush. Five weeks later, a panel of three federal judges put Starr to work investigating The Whitewater Scandal.

The Whitewater case involved a defunct corporation called Whitewater Development that dealt with real estate, and Madison Guaranty, a bankrupt savings and loan. Allegedly, President Clinton and First Lady Hillary Rodham Clinton were enmeshed in some illegal dealings with these firms. Starr, following his nose, began turning up more and more activities of persons related to the case that he thought should be pursued. He began investigating Webster Hubbell, the former deputy attorney general and a partner in Hillary Clinton's law firm, for fraud and tax evasion. He also accused Arkansas Governor Jim Guy Tucker and James and Susan McDougal, longstanding business partners of President Clinton, of fraud. All were even-

tually convicted of wrongdoing or entered pleas, which led to the unseating and imprisonment of Governor Tucker and jail time for others as well. Quite a few others were also brought down in the process—13 in all. In 1996, *Insight on the News* reported that "senior Democratic leaders had been meeting regularly to make contingency plans to deal with the possible impeachment of President Clinton, as cumulative investigations of growing scandals continue to build."

Starr also sought testimony from Susan McDougal in front of an Arkansas grand jury regarding the Clinton's involvement in Whitewater, but she refused. She went to jail for contempt of court. Starr later pursued Hubbell, his wife, their accountant, and their tax attorney in 1998 for tax evasion in what some thought was a hardball move to get Hubbell to confess wrongdoing on the part of the Clintons. "I want you to know that the office of independent counsel can indict my dog," Hubbell remarked on National Public Radio in May of 1998. "They can indict my cat. But I'm not going to lie about the president. I'm not going to lie about the first lady or anyone else."

Meanwhile, Bill Clinton was caught up in yet another case. Paula Corbin Jones had filed a sexual harassment suit against the president claiming that he asked her for sexual favors in a hotel room. Though the case was eventually dropped, a number of women were called to the stand to testify whether or not they had sexual encounters with the president. One of the witnesses was Monica Lewinsky, a young White House intern. When asked under oath if this was true, both she and Clinton denied it. In a move that riled up the American public, Starr in January of 1998 revealed that Clinton may have lied under oath and pressured Lewinsky to lie in court to protect himself. If this was proven to be true, the president would be guilty of perjury. Immediately, more cries of impeachment were heard, but Republicans backed off when the president's approval ratings soared up to 80 percent in some polls.

After that allegation, Starr focused his energies on trying to prove whether or not the president lied about his relationship with Lewinsky. Clinton again publicly declared that he never had sexual relations with her, but Starr produced a set of tapes indicating that he had. Linda Tripp, a colleague of Lewinsky's, had made numerous recordings of conversations when the two of them had been friends working together at the Pentagon. The tapes also implied that Clinton urged Lewinsky to lie about their affair. A flurry of stories emerged in the media questioning motives and probing into the characters of both women.

Starr plugged away, calling Lewinsky's mother to testify against her daughter in a move that was heavily criticized and did nothing to increase sympathy for the prosecution. Sordid details were revealed in the press, from the particular sex act that Clinton and Lewinsky supposedly engaged in, to rumors that she owned a dress that was stained with presidential semen. Starr even obtained bookstore receipts revealing the young woman's choice of reading materials. People who knew Starr personally were surprised to see him wrapped up in such a steamy situation. A *People Weekly* article quoted family friend Ellen Field claiming, "Kenny is the last person I could imagine in the middle of all this. He would just die if you told a dirty joke in front of him." Starr probed further into the case, calling on White House aides and Secret Service personnel to testify against the president and requiring Lewinsky to submit fingerprints and handwriting samples.

Critics sniped at Starr continuously throughout the investigation. Early on, his detractors accused him of partisanship; this peaked in early 1998 when First Lady Hilary Rodham Clinton publicly charged him with being part of a right-wing conspiracy against her husband. Then, some took him to task for continuing his private work while pursuing Whitewater. Even though it was not illegal, many believed it was improper and unusual and came very close to being a conflict of interest. Starr, it was noted, had been representing big-business clients, such as General Motors, Brown & Williamson tobacco company, Southwestern Bell Telephone, and the NFL Players Association. Others complained that well over $30 million and close to four years had been spent on investigating a popular president, without proving any wrongdoing on his part. As the Whitewater case dragged on for years, the complaints grew louder. However, Starr's supporters, including Senator Orrin G. Hatch, have insisted that he is an effective and noble lawyer that is being thwarted by Democratic efforts to impede his progress. Even some Democrats have come out in his support. Some media commentators have accused the Clintons and their supporters for effectively putting a negative "spin" on Starr's actions in order to make him look like "an out-of-control federal cop who preys on innocent victims," as worded by Timothy W. Maier in *Insight on the News.*

The investigation reached a critical point in the summer of 1998 when Starr submitted a lengthy report to Congress, which was made available to the public over the Internet and in book form. Tapes of the president's grand jury testimony regarding his relationship with Lewinsky were soon made public as well. Though Clinton did not admit, technically, to having sexual relations with Lewinsky, he revealed that he had an "improper relationship" with the intern, who was 21 years old when the incidents began. He apologized to his wife and family, but did not bow to pressure from some to resign. In September, Judiciary Committee Chairman Henry Hyde (R-Illinois) announced that the committee would begin looking into possible impeachment procedures in an open session in early October of 1998. If the measure passed, the House would vote on proceedings shortly thereafter. The country was embroiled in the scandal and potential loss of a president, the first time since Richard Nixon resigned in 1974 after impeachment proceedings began as a result of his involvement in the Watergate affair. However, polls consistently indicated a majority of the country approved of the president and did not support impeachment.

Starr has indicated that after the high-profile case is over, he will no longer serve as independent counsel. In 1996, Starr commented in *Newsweek* that he was not enjoying spending so much time in Little Rock, Arkansas for his work. "I have not coached Little League in two years," he remarked. "I don't teach Sunday School now. There are things I used to do and find personal satisfaction and fulfillment in doing that I do not do now." His wife, Alice Jean (Mendell) Starr, works in public relations for a commercial development firm in McLean, and they have three children: Randall Postley, Carolyn Marie, and Cynthia Anne. Starr tried walking away from the affair in February of 1997 to accept two deanships at Pepperdine University in Malibu, California, but quickly reversed his decision amid criticism that he was a quitter. The posts are being held open for him, and hopefully his new career will not be as time-consuming and controversial.

Sources

On-line

"More Starr Documents on the Way," September 25, 1998, CNN Interactive web site, http://www.cnn.com.

Periodicals

Insight on the News, November 13, 1995, p. 8; November 4, 1996, p. 8; March 30, 1998, p. 10.
New Republic, March 23, 1998, p. 10.
Newsday, December 14, 1994, p. A5; October 6, 1995, p. A6; May 15, 1998, p. A19.
Newsweek, December 2, 1996, p. 31.

New York Times, June 1, 1990; February 16, 1998.

People Weekly, February 16, 1998, p. 182.

Time, February 2, 1998, p. 49; February 9, 1998, p. 42.

USA Today, February 23, 1998, p. 14A.

U.S. News & World Report, February 9, 1998, p. 30; February 23, 1998, p. 32; May 25, 1998, p. 41.

Washington Times, March 22, 1998, p. 33.

Other

Additional information for this profile was obtained from transcripts of National Public Radio's *Morning Edition,* May 6, 1998, and *All Things Considered,* May 8, 1998.

—*Geri Speace*

George Strait

Singer

Born May 18, 1952, in Poteet, TX; son of a high school math teacher; married Norma Voss, 1971; children: Jenifer (died, 1986), George, Jr. *Education:* Southwest Texas State University, B.S. in agriculture and education, 1978.

Addresses: *Home*—San Marcos, TX. *Record company*—MCA Records, 70 Universal City Plaza, Universal City, CA 91608. *Fan club*—George Strait Fanclub, P.O. Box 2119, Hendersonville, TN 37077.

Career

Country singer, 1973—; began singing with U.S. Army band in Hawaii; signed with MCA Records, 1981; first top ten country hit, "Unwound," 1981. *Military service:* U.S. Army, 1971-75.

Awards: Academy of Country Music male vocalist of the year, 1984, 1985, 1988, 1997, album of the year, 1985, for *Does Fort Worth Ever Cross Your Mind?*, and 1997, for *Carrying Your Love with Me*, entertainer of the year, 1989, top male country vocalist of the year, 1991, Tex Ritter Award, 1993, "Pure Country" single of the year, 1996, for "Check Yes or No," male entertainer of the year, 1997, and album of the year, 1997, for *Blue Clear Sky;* American Music Awards top male country vocalist, 1991, and favorite country album, 1996, for *Blue Clear Sky;* ASCAP Voice of Music award, 1995; *Billboard* magazine male album artist of the year, 1981, male single artist of the year, 1983, male vocalist of the year, 1984, top male artist and overall top artist, 1986, number one top country artist of the year, 1987, hot country singles and tracks artist, 1995, 1996, and

top male country artist and overall top artist, 1996; Country Music Association male vocalist of the year and album of the year, 1985, for *Does Fort Worth Ever Cross Your Mind?*, male vocalist of the year, 1986, entertainer of the year, 1989, 1990; album of the year, 1996, for *Blue Clear Sky*, single of the year, 1996, for "Check Yes or No," and male vocalist of the year, 1996; *Country Weekly* favorite video entertainer, favorite video for "Check Yes or No," and favorite album, for *Blue Clear Sky; Music City News,* male vocalist of the year, 1986, and song of the year, video of the year, and album of the year, all 1996; *Music Wire* readers' poll, best country artist, 1996; R&R country performer of the year, 1990, and top country artist, 1996; SRO touring artist of the year, 1990.

Sidelights

George Strait, one of the biggest names in country music, has not lost his stronghold on the charts since he first signed with MCA Records in 1981. He is a hit on the airwaves and a collector of awards, including a number of top male vocalist and top entertainer honors from the likes of *Billboard* magazine, the Country Music Association, the American Music Awards, and others. In addition to talent, he has the charm and good looks to woo female fans. His concerts draw throngs to see the man voted "Sexiest Country Singer" by *People* in 1997. Country singer Patty Loveless in *People* remarked, "George is the gentleman cowboy we all used to dream about."

Strait was born the second of three children on May 18, 1952, in Poteet, Texas and raised in nearby Pearsall. His father taught math at a high school, but Strait was a real-life cowboy on his grandparents' ranch. There he roped, rode, and branded cattle on their 2,000 acres of land. After graduation, he eloped with longtime love interest Norma Voss and briefly enrolled at Southwest Texas State University. Deciding against college for the time, Strait joined the army in 1971 and was shipped off to Hawaii. There, he auditioned for a country band at the Schofield Barracks to entertain soldiers on the base and got the job of lead singer. During his formative years, Strait enjoyed 1960s rock and roll, but his tastes began to change when he heard Merle Haggard, Hank Williams, and George Jones, who became big influences on his own music.

After his discharge in 1975, Strait went back to Southwest Texas State University to get his degree in agriculture and education. Meanwhile, he was traveling in a pickup in the evenings to perform, sometimes up to 200 miles away. Though he tried time and again to prove himself worthy of a recording contract, he was shot down repeatedly. "I was 27 or 28 years old," Strait recalled in *People*. "I didn't think I was ever going to really get anywhere in the music business." He was all set to take a job with a ranch equipment manufacturer in Uvalde, Texas, and give up his dream of a career in music when his wife urged him to reconsider. "George was moping around the house so much I couldn't stand it," Norma Strait told *People*, adding, "[W]e talked about his hopes in music. I wanted him to give it one more try."

The timing seemed right. It was the early 1980s, and the nation was in the midst of a country craze with the popularity of the John Travolta-Debra Winger film, *Urban Cowboy*. Around eight months after turning down the job offer, MCA promotions person Erv Woolsey snagged some studio time and helped Strait record a few tunes. One of the songs, "Unwound," shot to number four on the country charts, a major accomplishment for an unknown singer with obscure material. Despite MCA's initial concern that real-life cowboy Strait was not slick enough, they signed him, and Strait hired Woolsey as his manager.

Since his 1981 debut, Strait has managed to maintain a presence on the top 100 charts almost continuously. His lack of glitz and glamour, once a concern for record executives who wanted to see more crossover hits, has only enhanced his popularity. Fans love his "good ol' boy" persona, someone who is just "ordinary people." Though Strait's clear voice and smooth good looks have the makings of a less roots-oriented country star, his catalog of honky-tonk songs deal with lost love and all the usual staples. An article by Ryan Craig on the University Wire claimed that into 1998, Strait did not stray from the formula, explaining that his album *One Step at a Time* contained the usual kind of country song that "reaches in and rips out your heart, kicking it around on the ground. You know, the good stuff." Craig added, "It's like that old joke: what would you get if you play a country song backwards? You'd get your trailer, truck, and wife back and your mamma wouldn't be in prison." Strait is not, however, a scruffy rough-rider: David Gates in *Newsweek* called the singer "clean-cut, almost preppy" and compared the atmosphere at his concerts—with their legions of swooning women waving undergarments—to those of the late crooner, Frank Sinatra.

Strait's albums are almost always guaranteed to be a hit. Though he generally does not write his own material, he is a whiz at choosing which songs to perform off of demo tapes. His 1995 release *Strait Out of the Box* is country's best-selling boxed set of all time and is tied with rock dinosaurs Led Zeppelin for second place in boxed set sales across all genres (Bruce Springsteen holds top honors). All of Strait's more than 20 albums as of 1998 have gone gold, platinum, or multi-platinum in sales, and over 30 singles have hit number one on the *Billboard* country charts. In April of 1998, *One Step at a Time* debuted at number one on the country album charts (his fourteenth number one album) and in May, he got his fifty-fifth top ten single when "I Just Want to Dance With You" moved to number seven. In addition, he has racked up a laundry list of top album and top performer awards from the likes of the Academy of Country Music, the American Music Awards, *Billboard* magazine, the Country Music Association, *Country Weekly*, *Music City News*, and *Music Wire*.

Strait is vehement about keeping his offstage life private, living on a secluded ranch in San Marcos, Texas, with his wife, Norma, and son, George, Jr, who is nicknamed "Bubba." Their daughter, Jenifer, died in a car crash in 1986. A dedicated husband and father, Strait has been known to fly his family from their home to meet his tour bus at various locations around the country. And in April of 1998, he announced that he would introduce a new approach to touring in order to be able to spend more time at home. Though his 1996 concert attendance broke records set by Hank

Williams, Sr., Elvis Presley, and himself, he began a national tour in 1998 that saw him only performing on weekends. He also planned to be done by summer so that he could get back to the ranch full-time. The arrangement increased touring costs and cut down on ticket receipts, but Strait was willing to make the sacrifice. He continued to do well regardless: the first four spring dates sold out, drawing between 44,000 and 63,000 fans. Other dates were near sell-outs, even in cities like Detroit, where promoters were not aware that country was so popular. Though his large stadium shows boasted five video screens, Strait remained true to his style. "You're not going to see George spit fire or blood; you're not going to see him on strings flying across the stage," commented tour promoter Louis Messina in the *Los Angeles Times*. "It's all about the music and what he represents. If you're a George Strait fan, it's pure country."

Selected discography, all on MCA Records

Strait Country, 1981.
Strait from the Heart, 1982.
Right or Wrong, 1983.
Does Fort Worth Ever Cross Your Mind?, 1984.
George Strait's Greatest Hits, 1985.
Something Special, 1985.
Number 7, 1986.
Merry Christmas Strait to You, 1986.
Ocean Front Property, 1987.
George Strait's Greatest Hits, volume 2, 1987.
If You Ain't Lovin' (You Ain't Livin'), 1988.
Beyond the Blue Neon, 1989.
Livin' It Up, 1990.
Chill of an Early Fall, 1991.
Ten Strait Hits, 1991.
Holding My Own, 1992.
Pure Country (soundtrack), 1992.
Easy Come, Easy Go, 1993.
Lead On, 1994.
Strait Out of the Box, 1995.
Blue Clear Sky, 1996.
Carrying Your Love with Me, 1997.
One Step at a Time, 1998.

Sources

On-line

"George Strait Fan Club," http://www.georgestraitfans.com (May 15, 1998).

Periodicals

Los Angeles Times, April 22, 1998, p. F2.
Music Wire, February 1997.
Newsweek, January 9, 1984, p. 93.
People, June 3, 1985, p. 106; November 17, 1997, p. 111.
St. Louis Post-Dispatch, November 2, 1995, p. 8; February 13, 1997, p. 13; May 1, 1997, p. 8; April 21, 1998.
University Wire, May 6, 1998.

—Geri Speace

Arthur O. Sulzberger, Jr.

Newspaper publisher

Born Arthur Ochs Sulzberger, Jr., September 22, 1951, in Mt. Kisco, NY; son of Arthur Ochs (a newspaper publisher) and Barbara Winslow Grant Sulzberger; married Gail Gregg (a journalist and artist), 1975; children: Arthur Gregg, Ann Alden. *Education:* Tufts University, B.A., 1974; attended Harvard University Business School, 1985

Addresses: *Home*—New York, NY. *Office*—*The New York Times,* 229 West 43rd St., New York, NY 10036-3913.

Career

Worked at the *Boston Globe,* Boston, MA, and *Vineyard Gazette,* Martha's Vineyard, MA, early 1970s; *Raleigh Times,* Raleigh, NC, reporter, 1974-76; Associated Press, London, correspondent, 1976-78; *New York Times,* Washington, D.C. correspondent, 1978-81, city hall reporter, 1981, assistant metro editor, 1981-82, group manager, advertising department, 1983-84; senior analyst, corporate planning, 1985, production coordinator, 1985-87, assistant publisher, 1987-88, deputy publisher, 1988-92, publisher, 1992—. New York Times Co., chairman, 1997—. Board of directors, Times Square Business Improvement District and New York City Outward Bound (chairman, 1992).

Sidelights

Family control of the *New York Times* has been in effect for over 100 years, since Adolph Ochs purchased the newspaper in 1896. In 1992, his great-grandson, Arthur Ochs Sulzberger, Jr., became the fifth

relative to act as its publisher and has since established himself as a strong yet personable manager and something of a pioneer at the old "Gray Lady." The newspaper got its nickname due to its longtime colorless look, with black-and-white columns running on and on and headlines bumping into each other, leaving little room for pleasing graphic layouts. Despite the stodgy appearance, its reputation as arguably the best newspaper in the world kept readers hooked. In fact, many of them relished the paper's unwillingness to deviate from its traditional design. Approaching the new millennium, however, Sulzberger knew that he needed to reel in some new, younger readers. He gradually phased in the use of full color, first in some Sunday sections, then gradually on the inside front pages of daily editions, and eventually on page one. Perhaps an even larger contribution, although not as immediately apparent, was Sulzberger's commitment to making the company a more diverse workplace. By encouraging the hiring of women and minorities and displaying tolerance toward gays, he has hoped to vary the voice of all facets of the paper, thus maintaining its relevance in a country where more and more people are not white men.

The lineage of *Times* leadership includes Adolph S. Ochs (Sulzberger's great-grandfather); his son, Arthur

Hayes Sulzberger (Sulzberger's grandfather); Orvil E. Dryfoos (Sulzberger's uncle, the husband of his father's sister Marian); Arthur Ochs "Punch" Sulzberger (Sulzberger's father); and Sulzberger, Jr. He was born into the newspaper dynasty to Arthur Ochs and Barbara Winslow Grant Sulzberger in Mount Kisco, New York, on September 22, 1951. His parents divorced in 1956, but Sulzberger and his sister, Karen, still spent time with their father, often at their grandparents' estate near Stamford, Connecticut. The 262-acre property included a private lake taking up five acres, an Olympic-size swimming pool, and an indoor tennis court. As an adolescent, Sulzberger decided to go to Manhattan to live with his father and stepmother, Carol Fox Fuhrman, in their apartment on Fifth Avenue. There he enrolled in a college preparatory academy, the Browning School, where he was on the debating club, played junior varsity football, and spent three years on the school newspaper. Though he went through a typical anti-authoritarian spurt that would last into his college years, growing his hair long, donning his father's old Marine Corps jacket, and getting arrested at peace rallies, he remained close to his supportive father.

> "I don't think leadership demands yes or no answers; I think leadership is providing the forum for making the right decision, which doesn't demand unanimity."

Sulzberger graduated from high school in 1970 and went to college at Tufts University in Medford, Massachusetts, obtaining a bachelor of arts in political science in 1974. On breaks, he worked at the *Boston Globe* and *Vineyard Gazette* newspapers in Massachusetts, knowing that his future was in publishing. He told Alex S. Jones in the *New York Times*, "I was not pushed to do it either by myself or some strange sense of responsibility. It was something I wanted to do as long as I can recall." Sulzberger officially started his professional career at the *Raleigh Times* in North Carolina as reporter in 1974.

While visiting his mother in Topeka, Kansas during a Thanksgiving holiday while still in college, Sulzberger met the girl next door, literally. She was Gail Gregg, also a journalist, and they married in 1975. The following year, they relocated to London, where they held wire service jobs. Although Gregg was adept as a journalist, often beating her husband to stories, she opted for a change when the couple moved back to America in 1978 and became an artist. Sulzberger knew when he returned to the United States that he was preparing for a permanent career at the *New York Times*. He stuck close with family and did not fraternize with staff members, causing a rift between him and some who used to be pals. "When I moved back to New York, I decided for my own mental health that my closest friends should be outside the *Times*," Sulzberger told Margaret Carlson in *Time*. "They can afford to be honest with me."

Sulzberger served at all levels of the newspaper on his way to the top. He held positions as the *New York Times*' Washington, D.C., correspondent from 1978 to 1981, the city hall reporter in 1981, assistant metro editor from 1981 to 1982, group manager of the advertising department from 1983 to 1984; senior analyst in corporate planning in 1985, production coordinator from 1985 to 1987, assistant publisher from 1987 to 1988, and deputy publisher from 1988 to 1992. This was all before reaching the apex of his career when his father named him to take over as publisher in 1992. Although he basically knew a path would be cleared for him, Sulzberger did not take it for granted, establishing a reputation as a down-to-earth, hard-working guy. *New York Times* columnist Anna Quindlen told Carlson, "From the moment he walked in the door, there were people desperately trying to dislike him. It proved to be impossible."

After working in the Washington, D.C., bureau from 1978 to 1981, Sulzberger returned to Manhattan as a general reporter on the metropolitan beat, where he covered the second term of Mayor Edward Koch, among other stories. He was promoted to assignment editor in 1982, which he called "the single most exhausting job I ever had," according to Carlson. As a rookie manager, he endeared himself to the reporters, operating a democratic newsroom and being available to his workers. He also learned that motivation was the key duty of a solid manager. After getting a dose of the editorial operations of the newspaper, Sulzberger transferred over to the business side. In 1983, he began selling advertising and overseeing a team of sales people. Around this time, he seriously began considering his future role in the paper's management and assessing his own style of supervision. As he told Alex S. Jones in the *New York Times*, "I don't think leadership demands yes or no answers; I think leadership is providing the forum for making the right decision, which doesn't demand unanimity."

In 1985, Sulzberger spent some time as a senior analyst in corporate planning before taking the job of production coordinator. In that capacity, he spent two nights a week supervising the printing of the paper. He was named assistant publisher in 1987, dealing with budget issues, and his father promoted him to deputy publisher just over a year later. In that capacity, he was in charge of both the news and business sides. He had a hand in redesigning the metro and sports sections and also worked to infuse color into the "Gray Lady." Sulzberger also was eager to bring more women and minorities on board. Female employees had filed a discrimination lawsuit against the *New York Times* in 1978, and into the 1990s, the demographics of the top positions were still mainly white males. However, one of Sulzberger's trademarks has been his commitment to diversity, which he continued to pursue his appointment to publisher.

On January 16, 1992, Sulzberger's career reached its pinnacle when he was chosen to fill his father's shoes as publisher of the *New York Times*. He immediately pledged to continue the paper's outstanding quality, but soon gave notice to the bottom line, announcing in early 1993 that the paper wanted to trim ten percent of its workforce. Also in 1993, the *New York Times* bought the *Boston Globe* for well over one billion dollars. In late 1995, executives reported that another 190 jobs would be cut. Despite the job losses, Ken Auletta in the *New Yorker* remarked that Sulzberger eagerly worked to democratize the office climate, hoping to wage a war "against an authoritarian decision-making process that exists on both the news and the business sides of the *Times*—a process that he believes breeds insularity and saps initiative." Auletta also noted that Sulzberger and his executive editor, Max Frankel "have improved the writing in the *Times,* have provided readers with more analytical stories, have sharpened the Sunday magazine and the sports and metropolitan sections, have hired more women and minorities for the newsroom, and have given individual writers greater freedom in how they write." Auletta added, however, that employees thought Sulzberger still appeared to concentrate too much on how far the paper still had to go, rather than how far it had come.

Although in 1993, the *New York Times* only boasted about ten percent women executives on the news side of its masthead, some workers pointed out that Sulzberger's pace was not to blame. Auletta quoted Rebecca Sinkler, editor of the *New York Times Book Review,* as saying, "The *Times* is so big and powerful that changing it is like teaching a hippopotamus how to tango. Moving the hippopotamus around is frustrat-

ingly slow," confounding even the publisher, Auletta commented. To help effect change more quickly, Sulzberger has held numerous retreats in order to spawn communication. "He believes that self-discovery and candor flow from conflict and adversity and that improved teamwork will follow," Auletta explained, noting that Sulzberger's theories seemed to stem from his experiences with the group Outward Bound, of which he was chairman for the New York City center. Sulzberger also actively recruited minorities by holding dinners at National Association of Black Journalists conventions, and noticeably stepped up coverage of gay issues.

Perhaps Sulzberger's most shocking decision as publisher, however, was to introduce color into the newspaper's main sections late in 1997. Other newspapers had been adding color to their pages for over 30 years, but the *Times* never followed suit. Worried that some traditionalists would protest, Sulzberger nevertheless saw the need to give the "Gray Lady" a makeover in order to keep the readers' interest and attract newer, younger subscribers. "We admit we're taking a risk," he told Lee Berton in the *Columbia Journalism Review.* "But we feel that not changing would be even riskier with our readers and advertisers." Sulzberger also assured shareholders, Berton reported, that "color design will reflect the taste and moderation that have always distinguished the *Times*'s news judgment."

When Sulzberger's father turned 70 in 1996, many were anxious to see who would become the company's chairman and chief executive officer. Though he had certainly earned the title with the sweat he had poured into the paper, Sulzberger also had four male cousins and a female cousin in executive positions at the *New York Times.* The *New Yorker* reported at the time that although "Punch" Sulzberger would probably like to move his son up into the position, he shared with his three sisters 85 percent of the controlling stock, and they may have other ideas. The senior Sulzberger remained tight-lipped about it before finally stepping down on October 16, 1997 and announcing that his son would assume duties as chairman while company president Russell T. Lewis would become chief executive officer.

Despite Sulzberger's privileged background as heir apparent to the *New York Times,* Margaret Carlson in *Time* characterized him as making a conscious effort to be an "average Joe." Carlson noted that Sulzberger uses public transportation, toured Europe on a used motorcycle, pitches in at homeless shelters, and prefers inexpensive eateries. However, his veneer is not quite so humble. Known as a dapper dresser, a friend of Sulzberger's in the *New Yorker* mentioned that he looks like "an English gentleman." Sulzberger on his off time enjoys rock climbing and *Star Trek: The Next Generation.* He and his wife have two children, Arthur Gregg and Ann Alden, and the family has lived on Central Park on the Upper West Side of Manhattan in New York City since the early 1980s.

Sources

Columbia Journalism Review, September-October 1997.
Editor & Publisher, January 22, 1994; January 11, 1997.
Fortune, November 24, 1997, p. 46.
HR Focus, May 1994, p. 22.
Mediaweek, January 13, 1997, p. 6; October 20, 1997, p. 8.
Newsweek, September 15, 1997, p. 76.
New Yorker, June 28, 1993, p. 55; June 10, 1996, p. 44.
New York Times, January 17, 1992, p. A1; December 6, 1995, p. C4.
Time, August 17, 1992, p. 46.
Wall Street Journal, October 17, 1997, p. B5.

—*Geri Speace*

Sheryl Swoopes

AP/Wide World Photos

Professional basketball player

Born Sheryl Denise Swoopes, March 25, 1971, in Brownfield, TX; daughter of Louise Swoopes; married Eric Jackson, June 17, 1995; children: Jordan Eric Jackson. *Education:* Attended South Plains Junior College, 1989-91; Texas Tech University, B.A., 1994.

Addresses: *Office*—c/o Nike, Inc., One Bowerman Drive, Beaverton, OR 97005.

Career

Played college basketball at South Plains Junior College, Levelland, TX, 1989-91, and Texas Tech University, 1991-93; briefly played professional basketball in Italy, 1993; member of U.S. women's national basketball team, 1995; member of U.S. women's team in the Summer Olympics, 1996; member of Houston Comets, Women's National Basketball Association, 1997.

Awards: Southwest Conference Newcomer of the Year and Player of the Year, 1992; National Collegiate Athletic Association (NCAA) national title as a member of the Texas Tech University Lady Red Raiders, 1993; Most Valuable Player, NCAA Final Four, 1993; Collegiate Player of the Year, 1993; Naismith and Sullivan Awards for amateur athletics, 1993; Sportswoman of the Year, Women's Sports Foundation, 1993; bronze medal as member of the U.S. team competing at the world championships, 1994; gold medal as member of U.S. team at Goodwill Games, 1994; gold medal as member of the U.S. women's team at the Summer Olympics, 1996.

Sidelights

Sheryl Swoopes led the Texas Tech University women's basketball team to a national title in 1993, earned a Gold Medal at the 1996 Olympic Games in Atlanta, and helped the Houston Comets win the league championship in the inaugural season of the Women's National Basketball Association (WNBA) in 1997. "Sheryl Swoopes is a once-in-a-lifetime superstar," sports columnist Corky Simpson wrote in the *Tucson Citizen*, "an athlete so gifted as to lift up an entire sport and inspire a generation of kids to go for the same brass ring." Like her male contemporary Michael Jordan, Nike has even named a shoe after her. More impressive, however, is the way the 6-foot shooting guard took the concept of "working mom" to a whole new level. Just six weeks after delivering her first child, 7-pound 9-ounce Jordan Eric Jackson, Swoopes was back on the job, playing her physically grueling sport in the heat of a title race. "What Sheryl has done is nothing short of remarkable, trust me," Phoenix guard Nancy Lieberman-Cline, who has a son, told the *Sacramento Bee*. "I think of myself as one of the athletes that's always in great shape, and I could not have come back in six weeks. I think she's done a great job."

Swoopes was born in Brownfield, a small town about 40 miles from Lubbock in west Texas. After her parents divorced, she and her brothers were raised by their mother, Louise. She grew up playing basketball with her three brothers in neighborhood pickup games. As a result of playing with boys, she learned an aggressive, physical style of play and to deftly control the ball. She was the star of her high school girl's basketball team, an All-State and All-American athlete, and Texas Player of the Year as a junior. Heavily recruited by colleges, Swoopes accepted a full scholarship to play at the University of Texas, which had long been a major power in women's basketball.

When she arrived at the school in the fall of 1989, however, she was overwhelmed by the huge campus and became acutely homesick. After four days, she gave up her scholarship and returned home to Brownfield. "Texas was the only school I really considered out of high school," Swoopes told the Los Angeles Times. "It was a big national basketball power, and I thought they could take my game to another level. But once I got there, well, I just didn't realize how far it was from home." Critics concluded that Swoopes let a bout of freshman jitters ruin her career.

Undeterred, she enrolled at South Plains Junior College in Levelland, Texas, commuting from home. Playing at South Plains, Swoopes set nearly 30 records and became a junior college All-American and Player of the Year. In her second and final season at South Plains, Swoopes averaged 21.5 points per game, 11.9 rebounds, 4.6 assists, and 4.7 steals. In the fall of 1991, she transferred to nearby Texas Tech University in Lubbock, where the women's basketball program was, at best, a modest regional power. That changed quickly, however, after Swoopes' arrival.

In her two years at Texas Tech, the team compiled a record of 58-8, twice captured the Southwest Conference title, and won its first-ever national championship. Swoopes recorded astonishing numbers: 14 games scoring 30 points or more, an average of 28.1 points and nearly ten rebounds per game in her senior year, a record-setting 53 points against the University of Texas in the 1993 Southwest Conference final.

In 1993 Swoopes led the Lady Red Raiders to the Final Four round of the National Collegiate Athletic Association (NCAA) championship tournament. In a semifinal contest with Vanderbilt, Swoopes scored 31 points to seal Tech's easy 60-46 victory. The next day, she dominated the national title game, pouring in 47 points—and breaking Bill Walton's 20-year-old record for most points in an NCAA championship game. The Red Raiders beat the Ohio State Buckeyes, 84-82. In the course of the tournament, Swoopes set ten records and earned the Final Four's Most Valuable Player Award. "You don't really appreciate Sheryl Swoopes until you try and stop her," noted Ohio State coach Nancy Darsch in the Washington Post. "She's an absolutely tremendous player. She showed why she's national player of the year."

Swoopes, in fact, was named player of the year by at least nine organizations, including the Associated Press, the Converse company, and USA Today. She also won the prestigious Naismith Award, the Sullivan Award, and the Women's Sports Foundation's Sportswoman of the Year award. In February 1994, Texas Tech retired Swoopes' jersey number, 22.

A man with that talent and those accomplishments, of course, would be the NBA's top draft pick and recipient of a multi-million dollar contract. Swoopes did not have that option. "American women basketball players have no place to play after college," Michael Knisley wrote in Sporting News. "Women's pro leagues have never sustained themselves in the United States, so most women either sign contracts to play overseas or give up the notion of making a living on the court. The system is frustrating and unjust and abominable."

In August 1993, Swoopes left Texas for Bari, Italy, where she played for the Basket Bari team in the Italian women's league. But after only ten games she returned home, claiming the team had not met its contractual obligations. Back in Texas, Swoopes completed her degree in sports science, worked occasionally as a radio commentator, played pickup basketball at the Lubbock recreation center, volunteered as a coach—and felt her skills deteriorate.

In 1994 Swoopes played on the American teams that won the bronze medal at the world championships in Sydney, Australia, and the gold medal at the Goodwill Games in St. Petersburg. In early 1995, she made the U.S. team that was to play in the Pan American Games in South America, but the tournament was canceled because too few teams committed to play. So, in the two years following her golden moment, the 1993 NCAA championship, Swoopes played 22 organized games—ten in Italy, eight in Australia, and four in Russia.

Fortunately, Swoopes' luck began to change later that year, when she was chosen to join the U.S. women's national basketball team—which gave her an opportunity to play competitive ball and hone her skills in preparation for her next goal, the 1996 Summer Olympics in Atlanta, Georgia. Team USA spent the 1995-96 season playing NCAA teams and touring Europe, Asia and Australia. The players were paid approximately $50,000 for their year on the team. Swoopes, meanwhile, landed endorsement contracts with Kellogg Co. and Nike, which introduced the "Air Swoopes" athletic shoe for women. She promoted the shoe in personal appearances and a TV commercial directed by noted filmmaker Spike Lee. In June 1995, Swoopes married Eric Jackson, whom she had met at Texas Tech. At the Olympic Games in Atlanta in 1996, the U.S. women's team played teams from Australia, Cuba, Zaire, Ukraine and South Korea in the preliminary rounds, then competed with Canada, China, Brazil, Japan and Russia in the quarterfinals. On August 4, Swoopes and her teammates beat Brazil by a score of 111-87 to capture the gold medal.

> "You don't really appreciate Sheryl Swoopes until you try and stop her," noted Ohio State coach Nancy Darsch in the Washington Post. "She's an absolutely tremendous player. She showed why she's national player of the year."

Swoopes' good fortune continued when women's professional basketball got another chance in the United States with the formation of two leagues—the NBA-sponsored Women's National Basketball Association and the American Basketball League (ABL). Swoopes signed with the WNBA's Houston Comets, where she became one of three league stars to receive personal service contracts which push their earnings well above the league maximum salary of $50,000.

Under the agreement, Swoopes and fellow Olympians Rebecca Lobo and Lisa Leslie earn six-figure salaries, over and above their playing wages, to serve as central figures in the WNBA's promotional campaigns. The ABL, which started playing ball in the fall of 1996, pays its players more than the WNBA, arguably has attracted a greater pool of talent, and plays a more substantial 44-game schedule, compared with the WNBA's 28 games. Even so, the ABL has generated far less attention and significantly smaller crowds. This is primarily due to the financial, managerial, and

marketing support the WNBA receives from its corporate big brother, the NBA. "Ever-present promos during the NBA playoffs lured a TV audience of 50 million to WNBA games on NBC, ESPN and Lifetime, while attendance averaged 9,669—more than double the league's preseason projection," Barbara Huebner wrote in the Boston Globe.

In its inaugural season in the summer of 1997, the WNBA also attracted more TV viewers, corporate sponsors and fan enthusiasm than anticipated, USA Today reported. The league's affiliation with the NBA means that "for the first time women get some of the same support and resources as men," the newspaper editorialized. "That's a leveling that's long overdue."

Yet Swoopes was sidelined before the WNBA's 1997 season began when she became pregnant. Jordan Eric Jackson, who was named after Swoopes' friend, Chicago Bulls superstar Michael Jordan, arrived on June 25, 1997. His Mom, astonishingly, stepped onto the hardwood ready to play a mere six weeks later. Swoopes' husband, Eric Jackson, quit school and shelved plans to play on Houston's team in the Arena Football League, the Texas Terror, in order to be a house-husband. "He has been extremely helpful to me and to my career," Swoopes told Tucson Citizen sports columnist Corky Simpson. "He said, 'Sheryl, you do what you do and I'll take care of the baby.' I can't think of another man who, in Eric's shoes, would do the same. I'm playing in this pro league while he sits at home and takes care of the baby."

Swoopes was able to return to the game so quickly because she worked hard to stay in excellent condition. She continued playing in pickup games into the sixth month of her pregnancy, and kept riding a stationary bike and shooting free throws even after that. She was back lifting weights, running, and shooting two weeks after giving birth. "Swoopes wanted to play in the WNBA's first season, help her team win a championship, and prove that basketball and motherhood can go hand in hand," John Schumacher wrote in the Sacramento Bee.

Her decision to return to the game so quickly drew criticism from Reggie Miller, who plays for the Indiana Pacers and is an analyst for WNBA games on the Lifetime TV network. "I know it's the inaugural WNBA season, but why come back?" Miller said on the air. "Take time and be with your newborn and play next year." Swoopes responded that she would not have returned if she were not ready. "He was trying to make it seem like I was just abandoning my baby," Swoopes was quoted by Simpson. "My baby is with me everywhere I go. He's on the road with me, at practice with me, at the games with me, and when I'm not at the gym, I'm at home with him."

When Swoopes joined the Comets at mid-season her play was inconsistent, but her contribution was undeniable. As Swoopes settled into a supporting role on the team behind guard Cynthia Cooper (who would later be named the league's MVP), the Comets won six of their next eight games, increasing their record to 18-9 and moving past the New York Liberty in the race for a division title. The Comets finished the season with an 18-ten record and entered the playoffs as the top-seed. They beat Charlotte in the semi-finals, then triumphed over New York, 65-51, to become the first-ever champions of the Women's National Basketball Association. "My biggest concern was once I did come back, I didn't want to mess up the chemistry with the team or disrupt anything they had going on," Swoopes was quoted in the *St. Louis Dispatch*. "The most important thing to me was to be able to come back and show my teammates that I was here because I wanted to be here."

Sources

Arizona Republic, November 26, 1997, p. D7; December 24, 1997, p. D5.

Boston Globe, October 11, 1997, p. E7.

Contemporary Black Biography, volume 12, Gale Research, 1996.

Ebony, December 1997, pp. 102-106.

Fort Lauderdale Sun-Sentinel, August 28, 1997, p, C8.

Minneapolis Star-Tribune, December 20, 1997, p. B4.

Pittsburgh Post-Gazette, September 1, 1997, p. D7.

Sacramento Bee, August 23, 1997, p. C1.

St. Louis Post-Dispatch, August 22, 1997, p. D8.

Sporting News, May 22, 1995, p. 53.

Sports Illustrated, September 8, 1997, pp. 56-58; December, 29, 1997, pp. 94-95.

Time, August 18, 1997, p. 79.

Tucson Citizen, August 21, 1997.

USA Today, August 28, 1997, p. A14; September 17, 1997, p. C10.

—Dave Wilkins

Amy Tan

Archive Photos

Author

Born Amy (Chinese name, En-Mai) Ruth Tan, February 19, 1952, in Oakland, CA; daughter of John Yuehhan (an electrical engineer and minister) and Daisy (a vocational nurse; maiden name, Tu Ching) Tan; married Louis DeMattei (a tax attorney), April 6, 1974. *Education:* San Jose (CA) State University, B.A. in linguistics and English, 1973, M.A. in linguistics, 1974; post-graduate studies at University of California at Berkeley, 1974-76.

Addresses: *Home*—San Francisco, CA, and New York, NY. *Office*—c/o Random House, Publicity, 201 East 50th St., 22nd Floor, New York, NY 10022.

Career

Author. Alameda County Association for the Mentally Retarded, Oakland, CA, specialist in language development, 1976-81; M.O.R.E. Project, San Francisco, CA, project director, 1980-81; reporter, managing editor, and associate publisher, *Emergency Room Reports*, 1981-83; technical writer, 1983-87. Author of *The Joy Luck Club*, 1989; screenplay by Tan and Ronald Bass, 1993. Also author of short stories, including "The Rules of the Game," and contributor to periodicals, including *Atlantic Monthly, McCall's Threepenny Review, Grand Street,* and *Seventeen.*

Awards: Gold Award for fiction, Commonwealth Club Bay Area Book Reviewers Award for best fiction, 1989, 1990 and American Library Association's best book for young adults award, 1989, all for *The Joy Luck Club*; Best American Essays award, 1991.

Sidelights

Amy Tan first gained acclaim in 1989 for *The Joy Luck Club*, a beautifully spun tale of generational and cultural differences in Asian American families focusing on mother-daughter relationships. Though her novels eloquently convey elements of the rich Chinese culture, they have universal appeal due to their insightful treatment, human emotions, and themes common to everyone: loss and hope, family ties and reconciliation, failure and success. The tales in her books are told from the points of view of a number of the characters, lending a more personal, storytelling appeal. Her novels have made the bestsellers lists, and she has continued to remain a popular writer with works such as *The Kitchen God's Wife* (1991) and *The Hundred Secret Senses* (1995).

Tan was born February 19, 1952, in Oakland, California, and grew up in the San Francisco Bay area. Her parents gave her the Chinese name En-mai, meaning Blessing of America. Tan's father, John Yuehhan Tan, immigrated to the United States in 1947 and got a job in electrical engineering before becoming a Baptist minister. Tan's mother, Daisy, was also a Chinese immigrant from Shanghai who had been abused by her husband in China. When she came to America, however, Chinese law would not grant custody of children to a divorced woman, so she kept her three children a secret from her new husband and offspring. While Tan was a teenager, her father and 16-year-old brother Peter died of brain tumors within six months of each other in 1967 and 1968. Only after this loss did her mother reveal that she had two living daughters back in China. Tan would later incorporate her mother's tale into her novels.

> *Though Amy Tan's novels eloquently convey elements of the rich Chinese culture, they have universal appeal due to their insightful treatment, human emotions, and themes common to everyone: loss and hope, family ties and reconciliation, failure and success.*

After the deaths, Tan's mother consulted a Chinese geomancer and decided to relocate in order to rid their home in Santa Clara of evil influences. At age 15, Tan and her younger brother went to Europe for three years with their mother. They settled first in the Netherlands, then found an affordable century-old chalet nestled among fourteenth-century houses in Montreux, Switzerland. Tan graduated from high school at the College Monte Rosa Internationale in Montreux, where she was in the company of the children of ambassadors, wealthy businesspeople, and princes. Nevertheless, her anger at the deaths of her father and brother turned her to rebellion, and she made friends with drug-dealing hippie types. After being arrested at age 16, she later fell in love with a mental patient who claimed he was a German army deserter and almost eloped with him to Australia.

After Tan's graduation, the family returned to the United States. She attended Linfield College in McMinnville, Oregon, where she planned to fulfill her mother's wishes that she become a neurosurgeon, but changed her mind when she became interested in English literature. She transferred to San Jose City College, then San Jose State University, where she received her bachelor of arts degree with a double major in English and linguistics in 1973. She worked her way through school on a scholarship and by working in a pizza parlor.

Tan reportedly transferred to attend college in San Jose after meeting Lou DeMattei, a law student at San Jose State, on a blind date. After getting her undergraduate degree, Tan went on to obtain a master of arts in linguistics in 1974. That year, she married DeMattei. After some study at the University of California at Santa Cruz and the University of California at Berkeley, Tan decided to forego academic life when her best friend's murder in 1976 renewed her feelings of anger and loss. In 1976, Tan began working as a specialist in language development with disabled children at the Alameda County Association for the Mentally Retarded in Oakland, California. Her work led to a deeper understanding of people. "I was meeting with families every day who'd just found out that their child had been diagnosed with a disability," Tan told George Gurley for the Knight-Ridder/Tribune News Service. "That experience was a crash course about humanity, what hope means and the things that matter most. It was rewarding and sad and it helped me identify with many different kinds of people." After holding that position until 1980, she served as a reporter, managing editor, and associate publisher for *Emergency Room Reports* from 1981 to 1983. She then became a freelance technical writer specializing in corporate business tax proposals.

In 1987, Tan finally met her half-sisters from China and about that time, began pursuing fiction writing after gaining inspiration from Louise Erdrich's novel *Love Medicine,* which deals with Native American family life, and *The Bean Trees* by Barbara Kingsolver. She also wrote as a form of therapy. A workaholic logging about 90 hours a week as a technical writer, Tan began seeing a counselor to break her habit, but the therapist kept falling asleep during sessions. Tan decided to enroll in jazz piano lessons and try her hand at fiction writing in order to diversify her pursuits. Her stories soon earned her a place with a fiction writers' workshop, Squaw Valley Community of Writers, and the publisher G.P. Putnam bought her short story "Rules of the Game" and the outline for a novel.

Tan's first novel, *The Joy Luck Club,* published in 1989, was an immediate success. It revolves around a young Chinese-American woman, June, and three of her mother's friends, and describes generational and cultural differences as well as ties among family and friends, especially mother-daughter relationships. The Joy Luck Club in the book is a weekly social get-together to play mah jong, formed in 1949 by June's mother and the three "aunties." After her mother's death, June takes her mother's place at the table, where the older women weave stories of their pasts, trying to instill in June their strength and hope. Tan also intersperses chapters about June's and her mother's life and the lives of the auntie's American-born daughters. When the friends decide that June should travel to China to meet her stepsisters and tell them of their mother's death, June is reluctant, and the women are disappointed, but she finally agrees.

The Joy Luck Club was hailed by many critics and spent nine months on the New York Times best-seller list. The Toronto Globe and Mail's Nancy Wigston remarked that the novel "is that rare find, a first novel that you keep thinking about, keep telling your friends about long after you've finished reading it," according to a Contemporary Authors sketch. Some reviewers complained that it contained too many stories for one book, a criticism that arose again when the film was released in 1993 (Tan cowrote the screenplay with Ronald Bass). However, Tan received the Gold award for fiction from Commonwealth Club and Bay Area Book Reviewers Award for best fiction for the work, as well as nominations for the National Book Critics Circle award and the Los Angeles Times Book award.

Much like Waverly Jong in The Joy Luck Club, Tan often felt pressure from her mother to excel. Tan's mother, Daisy, had hoped for her daughter to have a career as a brain surgeon while performing as a concert pianist as a hobby. She was disappointed with her daughter's decision to study English literature. When the novel was fourth on the best-seller list, Tan's mother told her that she should have been in first place, claiming that since Amy was so talented, she deserved to be the best. Tan, in fact, wrote the novel mainly to fulfill a promise to her mother, who almost died of a heart attack in 1986. She dedicated her first novel to her mother and grandmother, promising that their stories would not be forgotten.

Tan's next novel, The Kitchen God's Wife, again explores the connection of mothers and daughters. Kathryn Hughes in New Statesman and Society, excerpted in Modern Women Writers, summarizes the book as "a big, bold story set in pre-revolutionary Shanghai and framed by a contemporary family drama whose near-misses of communication, secret trade-offs, and emotional culs-de-sac brilliantly describe its own culture while refusing its limitations." The novel concentrates on one mother and daughter sharing their secrets and bridging the generation gap that has confounded

them. Generally autobiographical about Tan and her mother, The Kitchen God's Wife was spawned from videotapes Tan made of her mother relating stories about her past life in China and the terrible oppression that she suffered in a patriarchal society.

Tan's next novel, The Hundred Secret Senses, relates details of a relationship between half-sisters Olivia and Kwan. Olivia is the daughter of an American mother and a Chinese father who died before she turned four years old. On his deathbed, the father reveals he has a daughter in a small village back in China by a previous wife whom he left behind, and asks his American wife to get her and bring her to America. Six-year-old Olivia, dreading the attention the exotic sister may receive from her mother, is shocked when the 18-year-old Kwan arrives. Clumsy, bubbly, and completely unfamiliar with American language or customs, Kwan is taunted and Olivia is embarrassed by her presence. Nevertheless, Kwan unconditionally loves Olivia and remains devoted to her, leaving Olivia with a sense of bewilderment and guilt. Olivia gradually realizes that Kwan is convinced that she communicates with the spirit world and believes that she and Olivia were close friends in a previous life. Through Kwan's stories, Olivia learns volumes about her Chinese heritage as well as truths about her personal life and suffering marriage.

Tan affirmed that ghosts ("yin people," as they are called in the book) actually assisted her when she was writing The Hundred Secret Senses. "So many things happened during the writing of the book," she told Gurley, "it knocked away any doubts I had. Literally, the ghosts came and helped me." She explained to him, for example, that she would ask the ghosts to get her an archaeologist specializing in prehistoric China, and the next day she would receive a call inviting her to a reception for esteemed Chinese archaeologists. Tan also remarked to Erica K. Cardozo in Entertainment Weekly that the ghosts actually told her to write about them: "They are telling me this is important. To not write the story would be ... rude." Though some reviewers disliked the book, calling it unconvincing, many praised it, and it spent three months on the New York Times best-seller list.

Tan has also written two children's books, The Moon Lady (1992) and The Chinese Siamese Cat (1994). She and her husband have residences on both coasts, in San Francisco and New York City. During her time away from the keyboard, Tan has been known to sing with the Rock and Roll Remainders, a group of writers who perform at publishing conventions. She is also reported to be quite a pool shooter, and says her specialty game is nine ball. She told *Life* magazine that the game improves her motor skills and well as her mental ability. "The concentration is almost identical to what I need to write. In both, you have to be so focused on what's going on in front of you."

Selected writings

Novels

The Joy Luck Club, Putnam, 1989 (screenplay adaptation by Tan and Ronald Bass for Hollywood Pictures, 1993).
The Kitchen God's Wife, Putnam, 1991 (sound recording read by Tan, Dove Audio, 1991).
The Hundred Secret Senses, Putnam, 1995.
The Year of No Flood, Putnam, 1995.

Children's books; illustrated by Gretchen Shields

The Moon Lady, Macmillan, 1992.
The Chinese Siamese Cat, Macmillan, 1994.

Sources

Books

Contemporary Authors, New Revision Series, Volume 54, Gale Research, 1997.
Contemporary Novelists, St. James Press, 1996.
Contemporary Popular Writers, St. James Press, 1997.
Dictionary of Literary Biography, Volume 173: *American Novelists Since World War II, Fifth Series,* Gale Research, 1997.
Encyclopedia of World Biography, second edition, Gale Research, 1998.
Feminist Writers, St. James Press, 1996.
Modern Women Writers, Continuum, 1996.

Periodicals

America, May 4, 1996, p. 27.
Economist, April 6, 1996, p. 39.
Entertainment Weekly, October 27, 1995, p. 84.
Knight-Ridder/Tribune News Service, June 14, 1995; April 22, 1998.
Life, April 1994, p. 108.

—Geri Speace

Susan L. Taylor

Editor, *Essence* magazine

Born January 23, 1946, in New York, NY; daughter of Lawrency and Violet (Weekes) Taylor; married William Bowles, c. 1966 (divorced, c. 1967); married Khephra Burns (a television writer), 1989; children: Shana-Nequai. *Education:* Fordham University, B.A., 1991.

Addresses: *Office*—Essence, 1500 Broadway, New York, NY 10036-4015.

Career

Negro Ensemble Company, actor, mid-1960s; co-founder of Nequai Cosmetics, late 1960s; *Essence* magazine, New York City, began as freelance beauty editor, 1971, became fashion and beauty editor, promoted to current position as editor-in-chief, 1981; named vice-president of Essence Communications, 1986.

Sidelights

Under the guidance of editor in chief Susan L. Taylor, *Essence* magazine has set itself apart from other publications by emphasizing that beauty is a decidedly inner as well as outer quality. Taylor has been involved with magazine almost from its launch date in 1970, and put much of her own personal stamp on this positive-minded, spiritually-focused style publication for African-American women in the years since. Though not as well-known outside the African-American community, Taylor is a tireless crusader for her ideals, and her *Essence* editorials, motivational books, and popular lectures have earned her the respect and

admiration of women of color around the world. "Susan has truly believed in something that has always been intrinsic to the Essence message: *you can*," her predecessor, *Ms.* editor Marcia Gillespie told *New York Times Magazine* writer Veronica Chambers. "She was interested in more than what people were wearing. She was interested in black women in their entirety."

Born in 1946, Taylor was the daughter of two Harlem entrepreneurs and grew up both there and in the borough of Queens. Her parents both hailed from Caribbean islands, and she came from a long line of savvy women—many in her family had run businesses, including a great-grandmother who had a hot-pepper-sauce business in Trinidad. "My parents always made me feel I could do anything I wanted to," Taylor told Michele Willens of *Cosmopolitan*. Independent-minded, she was eager to strike out on her own, and took a job as a receptionist in New York City's Garment District in order to have her own apartment. Practical-minded, she then took a typing course and more than doubled her salary.

Taylor's life as a single, career-minded woman came to an end when she married at the age of twenty. She had always dreamed of acting on the stage, and won a spot with the Negro Ensemble Company. After a time, though, she left the theater group. "The roles that were available to me as a black woman in the 1970s were not interesting enough to keep me acting," Taylor told Chambers of the *New York Times Magazine*. "I also knew I wasn't the best actress in the world." With an increasing confidence in other abilities, Taylor decided to explore the possibilities of fulfilling another dream—to start her own cosmetics line for black women. She went to cosmetology school while pregnant, and worked at a department-store makeup counter to learn first-hand what was missing from the market. With her husband, she founded Nequai Cosmetics, which they named after their daughter, Shana-Nequai.

Taylor suffered a serious setback when her marriage didn't work out and Nequai Cosmetics went under. She found herself a single mother, living in Harlem, still in her early twenties, and at a loss for a job to support them both. Her cosmetics experience, however, earned her an assignment with *Essence* magazine in 1971 shortly after its debut. Aimed at young African-American women, the journal was practically a revolutionary act in and of itself, challenging both Caucasian standards of beauty as well as those of the established, but conservative black publishing realm. She began with freelance beauty assignments, and then was made its official beauty editor.

Yet Taylor's hiring at *Essence* brought new personal and spiritual challenges. It was sometimes difficult for her—the other staffers were not single mothers living in Harlem, and moreover, had earned degrees from prestigious black colleges. Taylor had never gone to college, a missing element on her resume that would haunt her for many years. In time, she took over the fashion pages of *Essence* as well, and is credited with bringing a more realistic vision to its editorial layouts: it was one of the first mainstream, non-niche magazines to use full-figured models.

Taylor had far more in mind for *Essence* than clothes updates and skincare issues, however. In 1981, when *Essence*'s editor's slot was vacant, Taylor gave Ed Lewis, its founding publisher, a thorough plan with a new vision for the eighties, one that would take the magazine into a positive-minded, yet still stylish, new direction. Lewis told Chambers in the *New York Times Magazine* interview that he received anonymous phone calls chastising him for thinking about hiring someone for the job who didn't have a college degree. Some staff members even quit after his decision to promote Taylor was announced, but as Lewis told Chambers, it was "the best decision I ever made."

Since that era, Taylor's plan and her ability to carry out that vision have helped make *Essence* phenomenally successful. "Like all good magazines, Essence is the vision of its editor," a journalism consultant explained to Chambers in the *New York Times Magazine* profile. During her tenure, circulation has risen from 600,000 to one million; audits estimate it reaches about 5.2 million readers a month. *Essence* earns praise for keeping current on rising African Americans from all walks of life, and has usually profiled them before the mainstream media does. It is sometimes faulted, however, for taking too soft an approach and avoiding more salacious topics, which might well reflect Taylor's firm belief in the power of positive thinking. In her monthly editorial called "In the Spirit" (her predecessor's column was entitled "Getting Down") Taylor discusses "her fears, her mistakes and her triumphs, assuring readers that they, too, could overcome," noted Chambers in the *New York Times Magazine*. Chambers also likened Taylor to Oprah Winfrey, for her ability to use an entity of the mass media to project forth her own spirituality, inner strength, and charismatic personal warmth.

True to form, Taylor decided to rectify her past and began taking night classes at Fordham University in the 1980s, and earned her B.A. in 1991. Again, plunging into the unknown presented her with new challenges: she was already a household name among many African Americans by that time, in part because of her hosting of a weekly television show also called *Essence*. Sometimes her fellow students would stop her on campus and ask her what class she was teaching, and she would then be chagrined to admit she was an undergraduate just like them. The degree opened up more possibilities for Taylor, however: she began a career as an author. Still editor-in-chief at *Essence*, Taylor penned her first book, *In the Spirit: The Inspirational Writings of Susan L. Taylor*, which was published in 1993. Two years later she followed it up with *Lessons in Living*.

Taylor's third book was a co-editor's project undertaken with her husband since 1989, PBS documentary writer Khephra Burns. Published in 1997, *Confirmation: The Spiritual Wisdom That Has Shaped Our Lives*, is a collection of inspirational writings and speeches Taylor and Burns culled from their own favorite books. Both admitted that undertaking the project, with its chapters organized around such topics as forgiveness, compromise, and relationships, was sometimes difficult. "The process of working on the book helped us to practice every tenet in the book," Taylor told *Detroit Free Press* writer Cassandra Spratling.

An author, editor of a top magazine, popular guest lecturer, and also senior vice-president at Essence Communications, Taylor plans to add the challenges of being a graduate student to her list by studying world religions at Columbia University beginning in late 1997. When asked by Willens of *Cosmopolitan* if she thought of herself as a role model, Taylor replied, "I used to resist it, but now I accept that I am. And it gives me some of the discipline I wouldn't have otherwise." She also dreams of earning an M.B.A., and envisions someday launching projects that would create investment opportunities for African Americans. "We are about to have the first generation of black people who are going to have the money to retire and I think it would be wonderful if we could retire in ways that bring us together and keep our culture alive," she told the *New York Times Magazine*. Her own retirement, however, is likely to be far from near.

Selected writings

In the Spirit: The Inspirational Writings of Susan L. Taylor, Amistad, 1993.
Lessons in Living, Anchor Books, 1995.
(Editor, with Khephra Burns) *Confirmation: The Spiritual Wisdom That Has Shaped Our Lives,* Anchor Books, 1997.

Sources

Cosmopolitan, July 1988, pp. 100-104.
Detroit Free Press, April 28, 1997, p. 1E.
Essence, December 1994, p. 61.
New York Times Magazine, June 18, 1995, pp. 24-27.

—*Carol Brennan*

Fred Thompson

United States Senator

Born Fred Dalton Thompson, August 19, 1942, in Sheffield, AL; children: Fred Jr., Elizabeth Thompson Hollins, Daniel. *Education:* Memphis State University, B.S., 1964; Vanderbilt University, Nashville, J.D., 1967. *Politics:* Republican.

Addresses: *Office*—523 Dirksen Senate Office Building, Washington, DC 20510; 3322 West End Ave., Ste. 120, Nashville, TN 37203.

Career

Assistant U.S. attorney, 1969-72; Senate Select Committee on Presidential Campaign Activities, minority counsel, 1973-74; attorney in private practice, 1975-94; special counsel to Governor Lamar Alexander, 1980; Senate Foreign Relations Committee, special counsel, 1980-81; Senate Intelligence Committee, special counsel, 1982; member of Appellate Court Nominating Commission for the State of Tennessee, 1985-87; elected member of U.S. Senate, 1994—, served as chair of Governmental Affairs Committee and on the Judiciary Committee. Actor in motion pictures, including *Marie* (1985), *No Way Out* (1987), *Feds* (1988), *Fat Man and Little Boy* (1989), *Flight of the Intruder* (1990), *The Hunt for Red October* (1990), *Die Hard 2* (1990), *Days of Thunder* (1990), *Necessary Roughness* (1991), *Cape Fear* (1991), *Class Action* (1991), *Curly Sue* (1991), *Aces: Iron Eagle III* (1992), *White Sands* (1992), *Thunderheart* (1992), *Born Yesterday* (1993), *In the Line of Fire* (1993), and *Baby's Day Out* (1994); television appearances include episodes of *China Beach, Matlock, Wiseguy* (1987), *Roseanne* (1988), and the movies *Unholy Matrimony* (1988), *Bed of Lies* (1992), *Stay the Night* (1992), *Day-O* (1992), *Keep the Change* (1992), *Barbarians at the Gate* (1993).

Member: Nashville Bar Association, American Bar Association.

Sidelights

On October 31, 1997, the Senate Governmental Affairs Committee concluded its hearings regarding alleged campaign finance abuses during the 1996 elections. Before the hearings, which had begun in July of that year, committee chair Fred Thompson had earned accolades from observers across the ideological spectrum of mainstream politics. Republicans praised him because he was investigating apparent misconduct by the Clinton Administration in accepting large donations from Chinese and other overseas interests. Democrats were pleased that Thompson, a Republican, had vowed to pursue wrongdoing by his own party with as much vigor as he did actions by Clinton and other Democrats. The media noted his courage in standing up to powerful interests within the Senate. In the words of Kent Jenkins Jr. in *US News & World Report*, "this 6-foot-6, glamorous, baritone-voiced movie-star Tennessean is in many ways a political version of The Natural, so overloaded with talent that even the presidency seems within his reach."

Thompson, who had assumed his Senate seat in a special 1994 election to fill the position vacated by Al Gore when he resigned to become Vice President, has appeared to be a likely 2000 presidential candidate. Many observers have judged Thompson as possessing a magnetism akin to that of an earlier Republican actor who took the White House, Ronald Reagan. But with the cessation of the Senate hearings on an inconclusive note at the end of October, 1997, criticisms of Thompson were rampant. Journalist Brit Hume, in the *Fox News Sunday* program of November 2, said Thompson had "failed to give any focus" to the hearings; the *Detroit Free Press* called the hearings "little short of a disaster" (November 2); and the Baltimore *Sun* on November 3 editorialized that "Thompson will not ride his committee's hearings on campaign fund-raising abuses to the White House."

"I wanted to try out whether I could walk into the middle of grass-roots Republicans from the Midwest ... and look them in the eye and say we need campaign finance reform. And I did."

Despite all the criticisms, Thompson clearly had enjoyed a varied and successful career in two of the notable arenas of American life: politics and film. A popular misconception about Thompson is that, as in the case of Reagan, his film career predated his political role. On the contrary; it was politics that paved the way for the secondary on-screen vocation Thompson has pursued in 18 feature films and numerous television appearances.

Fred Dalton Thompson grew up in Lawrenceburg, Tennessee, and earned his undergraduate degree at Memphis State University (now the University of Memphis) in 1964. Working his way through school, he obtained his law degree from Vanderbilt University in 1967. In 1969 he became an Assistant United States Attorney; four years later, the 30-year-old Thompson received an appointment as Minority Counsel to the Senate Watergate Committee.

When he arrived in Washington in 1973 to work with his mentor, Senator Howard Baker of Tennessee, Thompson did not create a sophisticated image: according to Jenkins's profile in *US News and World Report,* a

Baker aide recalled Thompson "arriving on Capitol Hill in a white suit and white patent leather shoes." But Thompson would also prove his shrewdness when he "flushed out" a senator whom he suspected was leaking key information to reporters. According to Jenkins, Thompson shared a piece of information only with that senator. Thompson first came to nationwide attention with his role in the Watergate hearings. Particularly noteworthy was an incident in 1974 when, during nationally televised hearings, he asked former Nixon aide Alexander Butterfield a question regarding White House tapes. Butterfield's answer revealed for the first time the fact that the Nixon Administration had maintained an extensive taping system.

By pursuing questionable acts on the part of a Republican administration, Thompson had defied partisan loyalty in favor of adherence to the law. The next significant chapter of his career would find him in a somewhat similar situation. Having returned to Tennessee, he engaged in private practice as an attorney while maintaining an advisory role within the state government. In 1977, Marie Ragghianti, a former state parole board worker, came to Thompson with a claim that she had been fired when she uncovered a scheme whereby Governor Ray Blanton was selling pardons to prisoners. Thompson's successful defense of Ragghianti, which led to the governor's resignation, attracted notice well beyond Tennessee.

In fact, he gained the attention of Hollywood, which produced the 1985 film *Marie* with actress Sissy Spacek in the title role, and Thompson as himself. The attorney proved to be an exceptional actor, garnering several film roles over the next nine years. Melissa Burdick Harmon of *Biography* magazine noted that "in 14 movies he smiled a total of four times." This, she suggested, was because Thompson tended to play authority figures, including an admiral in *The Hunt for Red October* (1990), a chief air traffic controller in *Die Hard 2* (1990), a senator in *Born Yesterday* (1993), a White House chief of staff in *In the Line of Fire* (1993), and an FBI agent in *Baby's Day Out* (1994). Thompson also played a military officer in *Flight of the Intruder* (1990) and a Wall Street broker in *Barbarians at the Gate* (1993).

In November of 1994, however, Thompson placed himself in the running for a real-life authority role, as U.S. Senator from Tennessee. Initially, he lagged 30 points behind the Democratic candidate, Congressman Jim Cooper; then Thompson devised a piece of symbolism that Jenkins in *US News and World Report* called "inspired." Wearing a designer business suit and cowboy boots, as Harmon reported in *Biography,* Thompson toured the state in a red pickup truck and "shrewdly advised voters that 'Ol' Fred' would bring common sense to Washington." He managed to maintain this folksy persona, Harmon observed, in spite of the fact that he himself was a Washington insider and experienced lobbyist.

Journalists praised his ability as a speaker, as well as his promise as a reformer. By his own account, Thompson sponsored the first Senate legislation in 50 years to establish term limits. According to Thompson's plan, both senators and representatives would be limited to 12 years on Capitol Hill, and though the bill failed to win a majority, Thompson vowed to continue sponsoring the plan as long as he remained in the Senate. He also co-sponsored a balanced budget amendment to the constitution, and successfully called for legislation to abolish automatic cost-of-living pay raises for members of Congress. He also supported a September 1997 Governmental Affairs Committee plan to put members of Congress under the same rules, with regard to pensions, as all other federal employees. He also joined with fellow Republican John McCain of Arizona, and Democrat Russ Feingold of Wisconsin, in groundbreaking bipartisan legislation to place limits on what his Web page called "the overwhelming influence of money in politics."

On July 8, 1997, Thompson, as chairman of the Governmental Affairs Committee, opened hearings on campaign finance abuses in the preceding election year. The aim of these hearings, as Thompson announced at the outset, was to determine whether the laws regarding campaign finance should be changed; and to uncover instances of wrongdoing. Chief among the persons against whom allegations had been made was President Clinton, who had been accused of accepting large donations from a number of questionable sources, including figures with close ties to the Chinese government.

As William Schneider of the *National Journal* reported, Thompson told the Senate at the outset, "Our work will include any improper activities by Republicans, Democrats, or other political partisans." Thus he placed himself in a position that, while it may have been laudable, did not guarantee him strong support from his own party. Furthermore, as Jenkins noted, for all his gregarious and charismatic qualities, Thompson did not have a large number of close friendships in the "notoriously clubby Senate." According to Gloria Borger of *US News and World Report,* Thompson then found "himself undercut by both Democrats and his own Republicans." Fellow senators, she noted,

had criticized the cost of Thompson's investigation, and his "fair-weather GOP friends [are] fretting that his big budget means he will investigate them, too."

Thompson concluded the first round of the hearings, to examine the need for a change in the laws, in the latter part of the summer. By the time he had taken the committee to the second phase—an investigation of wrongdoing by specific persons—John B. Judis in the September 22, 1997 *New Republic* was already predicting failure. Thompson, Judis wrote, had promised too much and offered too little. At the outset he had stated that the committee had evidence of involvement by the Chinese government in a plan "designed to pour illegal money into American political campaigns." But, as Judis wrote, "the ploy would prove a disastrous blunder: it set up expectations about the hearings that Thompson and his committee would never meet."

By taking on corruption in parties, Thompson had found himself in what Jenkins called a "lonely" position. And though his investigation did not prove a success according to most accounts, the senator stood by his stated principles: at an Indianapolis rally for Republican presidential hopefuls, Thompson told Ken Foskett of the *Atlanta Journal and Constitution,* "I wanted to try out whether I could walk into the middle of grass-roots Republicans from the Midwest ... and look them in the eye and say we need campaign finance reform. And I did."

Selected writings

At That Point in Time: The Inside Story of the Senate Watergate Committee, Quadrangle/New York Times Book Co. (New York City), 1975.

Sources

On-line

"Biography," *Fred Thompson, U.S. Senator, Tennessee,* http://www.senate.gov/(February 23, 1998).

Periodicals

Atlanta Journal and Constitution, November 6, 1997.
Biography, February 1998, p. 26.
Insight on the News, December 1, 1997, pp. 28-29.
National Journal, February 8, 1997; November 8, 1997.
New Republic, September 22, 1997, pp. 18-23.
US News & World Report, March 3, 1997; July 14, 1997.

—*Judson Knight*

Kenny A. Troutt

Founder of Excel Communications

Born Kenneth A. Troutt, January 8, 1948, in Mt. Vernon, IL; son of Nadine (a bartender); married, 1993; wife's name, Lisa; children: Preston, Grant. *Education:* Southern Illinois University at Carbondale, B.S., 1970.

Addresses: *Office*—Excel Communications, Inc., P.O. Box 650582, Dallas, TX 75265-0582.

Career

Sold life insurance to pay his way through college, c. 1966-70; owner and operator of a real estate and construction company, Omaha, NE, 1970s; founder of an oil and gas exploration company, Dallas, TX, 1980s; Excel Communications, Dallas, founder, 1988, chief executive officer and president, 1988—.

Awards: Ernst and Young Entrepreneur of the Year, emerging company category, 1996; Southwest Area Entrepreneur of the Year, service category, 1996; University of Houston's Center for Entrepreneurship and Innovation, Future 500 Upside Down Award, 1996.

Sidelights

In the business of telecommunications services, Excel Communications is considered one of the fastest growing providers in the United States. In June 1997, the company announced a $1.2 billion merger with Telco Communications Group, Inc. According to the on-line source *Newsbytes News Network,* when Kenny A. Troutt, chair and chief executive officer (CEO) of Excel announced this merger, he noted that

the company would continue towards its goal of entering "the $100 billion local telephone market and ultimately provide a bundled package of local, long distance and wireless services." The proposed merger would also solidify the company's position as the fifth largest long distance company in the United States.

Troutt, the ambitious architect of this merger, was born in 1948 and the son of a single mother who worked as a bartender. Troutt spent his formative years in a Mt. Vernon, Illinois housing project. Determined to succeed, he earned a partial football scholarship to Southern Illinois University at Carbondale (SIUC) and paid for the rest of his education by selling life insurance. In an interview with the SIUC campus newspaper, *Daily Egyptian,* Troutt talked of his college experience and noted, "I think what SIUC did for me was allow me, for the first time, to know that if I really worked hard, my life could be better."

After graduating from college in 1970, Troutt moved to Omaha, Nebraska where he started a real estate construction company. In the 1980s, he moved to Dallas, Texas and founded an oil and gas exploration company. As he noted in his *Forbes 400 Richest People in America* profile, "I was good at sales." He also developed his vision of a perfect company: "find product everybody uses; periodic payments after initial sale (like insurance); nonvolatile product (unlike oil)." Troutt was ready to make an impact.

With the break up of AT&T, and the rise of such additional major long distance carriers as MCI and Sprint, Troutt recognized an opportunity to profit from the reorganization and still be of service to the consumer. Armed with an innovative idea and the skills of a first-rate salesman, Troutt launched Excel Communications in 1988 as a regional reseller of long distance telephone services. In 1989, the company began national operations.

Troutt realized that he could purchase blocks of long-distance time, especially those that were owned by businesses and not in use in the prime residential calling times (evenings and weekends) on existing transmission lines, and resell them as a profit to residential customers. He contacted such companies as WorldCom, AllNet and MCI Business, not as a potential rival but as a customer, asking to purchase their off-peak blocks for deep discounts. Troutt then was able to couple this business concept with a commission-based sales force or multi-level marketing (MLM) structure. With Stephen R. Smith, an experienced network marketing executive, he designed a program where Independent Representatives (the sales force) stream down sales and build a long-term customer base.

There have been other successful MLM's, such as Amway and Avon, where the representatives earn a percentage of what they sell and sign up more representatives for the company. Excel representatives sell their product and earn bonuses for the performance of their recruits. However, according to Susan Caminiti of *Fortune*, "Multilevel marketing companies are sometimes regarded with suspicion because of the potential for pyramid abuses." It seemed though, that Excel was an exception to the MLM scam rule. Simply, the concept worked. According to Caminiti of *Fortune*, in 1995, "Excel had sales of $507 million, up from $31 million in 1993, while earnings jumped from $2.3 million to $44.5 million." The head of Kagan Telecom Associates, Jeffrey Kagan, added to the *Fortune* article, "The company's selling something everyone needs, it isn't selling vitamins."

Troutt's belief in a commission-based sales force reflected of his own drive, ambition and hunger. He holds rallies for his independent representatives, and some consider his motivational style almost evangelical. According to Caminiti of *Fortune*, Troutt boomed, "The real money is coming," at a 1995 rally, yet he remembers where he came from. "We change lives," he told *Money*, "Because of the way I grew up, because I was poor, I know what $200 a month can mean to people. It is the difference between a vacation and no vacation, a house instead of an apartment.... I know why the lottery is so popular. You buy hope for a dollar.... That's the one thing Wall Street will never under-stand—the difference $100 or $200 makes in a person's life."

For the most part, Troutt's MLM concepts have been successful, but in 1996 complaints and a few lawsuits were filed against the company, citing that some of the representatives claims were false. The Dallas Better Business Bureau temporarily revoked Excel's membership, but reinstated it when it found that it had safeguards in place to reduce violations of company policy and unauthorized switching of long distance services. And when Troutt received his 1996 Southwest Area Entrepreneur of the Year award, he gratefully accepted the honor, commenting, "all this growth has been possible with the support of our employees and the commitment of our independent representatives who believe in the entrepreneurial dream and all the personal and professional awards it offers."

In 1997, SIUC made plans to present him with an honorary doctoral degree and featured him in the Fall 1997 issue of *Southern Alumni* magazine. As Troutt noted to *Daily Egyptian*, "I've always been an entrepreneur because I've always had companies. I got bit by the entrepreneur bug, and it never left me." Poised to take his company into the new century, Troutt and his communications empire have consolidated their position as a leader in the communications field by offering a full range of services to consumers—long distance, Internet, local and international—as well as nurturing and developing a first rate sales force that reflected the philosophy of its founder. The innovative combination of business and marketing strategies catapulted Excel to the forefront of telecommunications. As Troutt's company biography states, "His entrepreneurial spirit is not only the spark that created the company, it is also the fundamental principle that continues to fuel its spectacular growth."

Sources

On-line

Daily Egyptian (July 31, 1997), http://www.dailyegyptian.com (December 22, 1997).

Excel Communications Website, http://www.exceltel.com (December 22, 1997).

"Forbes 400 Richest People in America-Kenneth Troutt," *Forbes*, http://www.forbes.com/Richlist/9768.htm (December 22, 1997).

"Merger to Make $2 Billion Long Distance Company," *Newsbytes News Network* (June 6, 1997), http://www.newsbytes.com (December 22, 1997).

Books

Robinson, James W., *The Excel Phenomenon*, Prima Publishing, 1997.

Periodicals

Discount Long Distance Digest News, July 5, 1996, p.79.
Forbes, March 24, 1997, p. 63.
Fortune, May 27, 1996, pp. 24.
Money, October 1, 1997, pp. 168.
Wall Street Journal, June 9, 1997, p. B8.

—Paula M. Kalamaras and Paul T. Kraly

Atal Behari Vajpayee

AP/Wide World Photos

Prime Minister of India

Born December 25, 1926, in Gwalior, Madahya Pradesh, India; son of Shri Krishna Behari (a teacher). *Education:* Victoria (now Laximbai) College, Gwalior, graduated; Dayanand Anglo-Vedic College, Kanpur. M.A. in political science.

Addresses: *Office*—6 Raisina Rd., New Delhi, India 110011.

Career

Worked as a journalist and social worker; arrested during freedom movement, 1942; founder member of Jana Sangh, 1951-77; leader of Jana Sangh Parliamentary Party, 1957-77; president, Bharatiya Jana Sangh, 1968-73; founder member, Janata Party, 1977-80; External Affairs Minister in Janata government, 1977-80; founding member, Bharatiya Janata Party (BJP), 1980— (president and leader of BJP party, 1980-86). Member of Lok Sabha (House of the People), 1957-62 and 1967-84; member of Rajya Sabha (Council of States, or parliament), 1962-67 and 1986-91. Served on Indian Delegation to Commonwealth Parliamentary Association meetings held in Canada, 1966, Zambia, 1980, and Isle of Man, 1984; Committee on Government Assurances, 1966-67; Public Accounts, 1969-70; Parliamentary Goodwill Mission to East Africa, 1965; Parliamentary Delegation to Australia, 1967; Indian Delegation to Inter-Parliamentary Union Conference held in Japan, 1974, Sri Lanka, 1975, and Switzerland, 1984; Parliamentary Delegation to European Parliament, 1983; and Delegation to UN General Assembly, 1988, 1989, 1990, 1991. Served on National Integration Council, 1958-62, 1967-73, 1986, and 1991—

Awards: India's second highest civilian honor, the Padma Vibhushan, 1992; named Best Parliamentarian, 1994.

Sidelights

Prime Minister of India Atal Behari Vajpayee made global news in May of 1998 when his country detonated three nuclear devices, catching American security watchers off guard. In the post-Cold War era, nuclear capability became an even more volatile subject, with a number of players on the world stage developing weapons besides just the major superpowers. The United States denounced the tests and vowed to institute sanctions as punishment for what many considered a reckless deed. However, in India, citizens cheered their leader's decision to flaunt their might. What kind of person was behind the orders to set off these bombs? By all accounts, a charming leader and published poet, a popular man who spent his entire career in service to his country, from early years in the 1950s in India's parliament to a 13-day stint as prime minister in 1996 until his right-wing Bharatiya Janata Party (BJP; translated as Indian People's Party) failed to round up a majority in parliament. In March of 1998 he came back to firmly take the seat as prime minister representing the BJP, thanks to his favored standing as a moderate in a party long considered hostile to Muslims. As Tim McGirk wrote in the *Independent*, "Vajpayee has a reputation as a bright, decent man, a liberal who keeps his distance from the Hindu extremistswithin the BJP who wave tridents and saffron-coloured flags and shout anti-Muslim slogans."

Vajpayee was born December 25, 1926, in the Central Indian city of Gwalior, Madahya Pradesh, one of seven children of Shri Krishna Behari, a secondary school teacher and Hindu scholar. They belonged to the Brahmin caste, one of the high social levels that separates the classes in India. (These castes are grouped hierarchically according to the occupation of a family, passed down through generations, and serve as a notion of purity; based on Hindu religious concepts, the castes are binding at birth, and many feel they are unfair.) As a teenager, Vajpayee joined Rashtriya Swayamsevak Sangh (RSS), a secretive right-wing Hindu youth organization whose name means National Voluntary Service, and participated in the movement to liberate India from British colonial rule. As a result, he was imprisoned in 1942 during the freedom movement and jailed for 24 days. Vajpayee graduated from Victoria College (now called Laximbai College) in Gwalior and went on to earn a master's degree in political science from Dayanand Anglo-Vedic (D.A.V.) College in Kanpur.

Vajpayee started taking courses for a law degree in Lucknow, the capital of Uttar Pradesh, but left school to take a job as the editor of a magazine published by the RSS. The RSS, according to John F. Burns in the *New York Times*, "is considered the fountainhead of Hindu nationalism." On its own party's web site, the group reveals that the "RSS has always been dubbed 'communal,' 'reactionary,' and what not by its detractors." It was founded in 1925 and was nurtured in the 1940s by M.S. Golwalkar, who opposed Mahatma Gandhi's position of "Muslim appeasement." Although the RSS had "the greatest respect for the Mahatma," according to the BJP web site, 17,000 members of the group, including the leader, were accused of conspiracy in his murder. One Hindu nationalist, Naturam Vinayak Godse, was found guilty of the 1948 assassination, just a few months after Gandhi helped free India from British control.

In 1951 Vajpayee, who always wanted to become a journalist, "came into politics by mistake," as he told Hari Ramachandran in the Reuters news service. He joined

an early conservative political party, Jana Sangh, which was heavily influenced by Hindu nationalism, and somehow ended up serving as private secretary to its founder and president, Shyama Prasad Mukherjee. When Mukherjee died in 1953, Vajpayee stood out as a top name in the party, especially since he had also kept busy editing and writing for party publications, in addition to spending some time as a social worker. He became leader of the Jana Sangh party, which was the predecessor to the BJP, in 1957 and was elected to the lower house of parliament, Lok Sabha (House of the People) that same year, serving until 1962. During this time, the country's leader was Jawaharlal Nehru, who led India from its independence in 1947 to his death in 1964.

In 1962 Vajpayee was elected to the other house of parliament, Rajya Sabha, or Council of States, where he served until 1967, and again from 1986 to 1991. The legislator served as president of his party, Jana Sangh, until 1977, the whole time spent as the opposition in parliament. On June 26, 1975, he was arrested during Prime Minister Indira Gandhi's "emergency," a point at which she outlawed the RSS and arrested thousands. After that, in 1977 Vajpayee became minister of external affairs, or foreign minister, at a time during a backlash against the Congress party. He held the post until 1980, when he helped found the BJP, serving as its president from 1980 to 1986. He was elected to Rajya Sabha again in 1986, serving until 1991. In 1992 Vajpayee's party suffered a serious blow when Hindu extremists destroyed asixteenth-century mosque in the northen town of Ayodhya, spurring nationwide riots that ended in more than 3,000 deaths.

Vajpayee, however, had cultivated the position of moderation within the staunchly pro-Hindu BJP and built an impressive resume of government activity. He served on the Indian Delegation to Commonwealth Parliamentary Association meetings held in Canada in 1966, Zambia in 1980, and Isle of Man in 1984. He held positions on the Committee on Government Assurances from 1966 to 1967 and the Committee on Public Accounts from 1969 to 1970. An avid traveler, he attended a Parliamentary Goodwill Mission to East Africa in 1965, a Parliamentary Delegation to Australia in 1967, and an Indian Delegation to an Inter-Parliamentary Union Conference held in Japan in 1974, Sri Lanka in 1975, and Switzerland in 1984. In addition, he was part of a Parliamentary Delegation to European Parliament in 1983 and went along on a Delegation to the United Nations General Assembly in 1988, 1989, 1990, and 1991. He also served on the National Integration Council in 1958-62, 1967-73, 1986, and again beginning in 1991. Vajpayee briefly held the seat of prime minister in 1996, when the BJP took the most number of seats in parliament. Since no party held a majority, BJP was given the first shot at establishing a new government. In order to gain control, the BJP would have to swing support from other parties. However, there was a rift with the two other mainstream parties, the Congress Party and United Front, who feared that the BJP would be too divisive, given its strong pro-Hindu stance. Though Vajpayee had cultivated a reputation as a moderate who put great distance between himself and more of the nationalistic aspects of his party, the BJP could not drum up enough partners. After just 13 days in office, Vajpayee stepped down. Afterward, the United Front, a loose coalition of left-wing and regional parties, was sworn in, but in November of 1997, the Congress party withdrew support and Prime Minister I.K. Gujral's government fell. The president subsequently dissolved the Lok Sabha.

Early in 1998 India held elections again, and no party emerged with a clear majority. However, the BJP roused enough support to lead a coalition government, and once again, Vajpayee was named prime minister. This time, after taking oath, he won a vote of confidence from parliament and maintained his position. Then, in May, the world was stunned to discover that India had detonated three nuclear devices underground as a series of tests in order to demonstrate the strength of their national security. Shortly thereafter, neighboring Pakistan, one of India's fierce rivals, responded with tests of their own. Many nations around the globe condemned the tests, and the United States was embarrassed that they failed to be able to predict the impending detonations, citing a massive failure on the part of American intelligence.

In the face of economic sanctions from America and other nations, Vajpayee defended the action, stating in *India Today*, "The decision to carry out these tests was guided by the paramount importance we attach to national security." He later added in the interview, "I would like to assure the people of the world, especially in our part of the world, that there is no cause for worry at all, much less any alarm, on account of India's action." (India had fought three wars with Pakistan since 1947 and went to war with China in 1962.) He insisted that hundreds of nuclear tests have been performed by various countries, with no violent repercussions, and admitted that no further tests were scheduled. Vajpayee remarked, "Millions of Indians have viewed this occasion as the beginning of the rise of a strong and self-confident India," and brushed off threats of political and economic effects, saying, "Yes, our action has entailed a price. But we should not worry about it. India has an immense reservoir of resources and inner strength.... Sanctions cannot and will not hurt us."

Vajpayee has never married and instead has lived since the late 1950s with the daughter of a close friend, Namita Bhattachariya; her husband, Ranjan; and their daughter, Neharika; first on the campus of Delhi University and later in a white colonial in central Delhi. He has adopted her family as his own and is secretive about his private life. Vajpayee is a noted poet in his country who has published several volumes of verse. He is also revered as a colorful orator who never prepares a speech, preferring to speak off the cuff. Collections of some of his addresses have been published. The statesman and poet's favorite activities are reading and writing, and he also enjoys travel, the arts, film, gardening, and fine cuisine. He is opposed to the caste system and promotes women's liberation efforts.

Sources

On-line

"Atal Behari Vajpayee: A Profile," Bharatiya Janata Party web site, http://www.bjp.org (July 12, 1998).
"BJP History: Its Birth, Growth & Onward March," Bharatiya Janata Party web site, http://www.bjp.org (July 12, 1998).
"Vajpayee to Become India's Prime Minister," May 15, 1996, CNN web site, http://www.cnn.com (July 12, 1998).

Books

Current Leaders of Nations, Gale Research, 1998.

Periodicals

Arizona Republic, May 13, 1998, p. A6.
Dallas Morning News, March 16, 1998; March 20, 1998.
Independent, May 2, 1996, p. 11.
India Today, May 25, 1998.
Los Angeles Times, May 19, 1996; May 29, 1996.
Maclean's, May 27, 1996, p. 28.
New York Times, March 28, 1977; May 16, 1996.
Reuters, May 15, 1996; May 28, 1996; February 16, 1998; June 8, 1998.

—Geri Speace

Mary Verdi-Fletcher

Photograph by Al Fuchs

Dancer, dance teacher, and dance company director

Born Mary Regina Verdi, June 4, 1955, in Bratenahl, OH; daughter of Sylvio (a quality control technician) and Nancy (Baruzzi) Verdi; married Robert A. Fletcher (a financial consultant), August 11, 1984. *Education:* Studied marketing and public relations at Lakeland Community College, 1980.

Addresses: *Office*—Cleveland Ballet Dancing Wheels and Professional Flair, 1501 Euclid Ave., Ste. 412, Cleveland, OH 44115. *Agent*—G.G. Greg Agency, 1288 East 168 St., Cleveland, OH 44110.

Career

Cleveland Ballet Dancing Wheels (a dance company for people with disabilities), founder, 1980, and principal dancer, beginning 1980; Professional Flair (a non-profit arts/disability organization), founder, 1989, and president, beginning 1989; conductor of dance workshops for children and adults with and without disabilities, 1990s—.

Awards: Outstanding Young Clevelanders Awards, 1990 and 1992; Oracle Merit Award for Outstanding Educational and Outreach Programming, 1991; Invacare Award of Excellence in the Arts, 1994; Ohio Theater Alliance Award for Accessibility in Theater, 1996.

Member: Ohio Dance, Very Special Arts Ohio, Ohio Alliance for Arts Education.

Sidelights

As a dancer, Mary Verdi-Fletcher performs more than 150 times a year in such diverse settings as universities, performing arts festivals, and concert halls, often to rave reviews. But there is one big difference between Verdi-Fletcher and most other dancers: she is physically disabled and performs in a wheelchair. She is co-founder and president of the Cleveland Ballet Dancing Wheels, the first professional troupe of its kind in the United States. Members of Dancing Wheels are comprised of both able-bodied and disabled dancers.

Mary Verdi-Fletcher was born Mary Regina Verdi on June 4, 1955, to Sylvio Verdi and Nancy (Baruzzi) Verdi in Bratenahl, a suburb of Cleveland, Ohio. She had one older brother and lived with extended family in a 28-room house. Verdi-Fletcher was born with spina bifida, a disabling disease that results from a weakness in the spinal column. She had her first operation—one of many—when she was five weeks old. At the age of four, she began wearing braces and was able to walk with crutches. Yet before then, Verdi-Fletcher knew what she wanted to do with her life. "Right from the time I was 3 years old, I wanted to dance," she told Anjuman Ali of the *Standard Times.* "As a child you don't have any preconceived ideas of what is possible. So I just kept saying that I wanted to be a dancer, and everybody would say, 'Oh, that's cute. You can't walk, how can you be a dancer?'"

But Verdi-Fletcher did dance, sometimes with her brother, and sometimes by herself. She was guided by her mother, who had been a professional dancer. She danced so vigorously that her braces broke repeatedly, and after being fitted with stronger braces, the activity took its toll on her legs. After breaking one of her legs for the third time, when she was 12, Verdi-Fletcher became confined to a wheelchair.

Verdi-Fletcher's parents insisted that their daughter receive a good education, despite her disability. She attended a Catholic girls high school at a time when integration was virtually unheard of. Her mother carried her up flights of stairs every day so that she could attend school with able-bodied children. Her parents were very supportive, but also very protective, as Verdi-Fletcher recalled in *Chronicles of Courage*: "Once I graduated from high school, both my parents became very protective, very much afraid of letting me pursue my own personal goals.... It was a very hard struggle to become truly independent because of my family situation—yet their caring was out of love, not out of any kind of possessiveness."

After graduation from high school, Verdi-Fletcher took a course in keypunch operation and obtained a position as a keypunch operator, which she hated. She quit that job and the next year, at age 23, moved with her parents to the rural community of Perry, Ohio. Shortly thereafter, Verdi-Fletcher learned to drive a car and moved back to Cleveland where she shared an apartment with a friend. She also started a job as the director of Services for Independent Living for the Independent Living Center, an organization that creates specially equipped housing for disabled people. She later became its director of development.

During this time, Verdi-Fletcher continued dancing; she and friends would go to dance clubs together. One night she met David Brewster, whose wife was Verdi-Fletcher's best friend from high school. Brewster was not disabled, but he was a dance enthusiast, and he and Verdi-Fletcher became dancing partners. Friends encouraged them to enter the *Dance Fever* competition that was coming to Cleveland. Verdi-Fletcher described the experience in *Chronicles of Courage*: "When I got onstage, there was a major hush. You could tell people were thinking, 'What is a person in a wheelchair do-

ing in a dance competition?'" But the audience gave the couple a standing ovation after their performance, and they were named first runners-up.

After the *Dance Fever* performance, Verdi-Fletcher and Brewster began receiving requests to do performances. In 1980 they made their partnership formal and started performing as Dancing Wheels. They were sponsored by Invacare, a wheelchair manufacturer. Verdi-Fletcher danced part-time for several years while also working at the Independent Living Center. On August 11, 1984, she married Robert Fletcher, whom she met in a bar. In 1989, when his career as a financial consultant had become established, Verdi-Fletcher resigned from her job and became a full-time dancer. She also founded Professional Flair, a nonprofit organization with three divisions: Dancing Wheels; Theatrical Expressions, which works with actors; and Career Insight, which assists people in developing personal skills.

Verdi-Fletcher worked as a tour director for the Cleveland Ballet for six months, beginning in September 1989. In 1990 she proposed that the Cleveland Ballet, along with Dancing Wheels, offer performances together to give audiences the chance to see the possibilities for disabled dancers. The proposal was accepted, and the Cleveland Ballet Dancing Wheels was created in September 1990, with Verdi-Fletcher as the director. The members of Dancing Wheels—three men and five women, some of whom are disabled—began performing around the country, appearing 108 times in the first 15 months of existence. Since then, they have performed around the world for as many as 125,000 people a year.

In addition to dancing, Verdi-Fletcher teaches dance classes to both disabled and able-bodied children and adults. She and Sabatino Verlezza, the co-artistic director and choreographer for the company, teach the May O'Donnell dance technique, which is especially suited for sit-down dancers because of the emphasis on upper torso movements.

Verdi-Fletcher told Michele San Filippo of *Exceptional Parent* that her mission is twofold: "First, Dancing Wheels opens the eyes of able-bodied children to see the possibilities and similarities—rather than the differences—in all of us. And, second, the dance itself inspires children and adults with disabilities to feel a change within themselves." Verdi-Fletcher believes that disabled people need to realize their ability to participate in activities that were once thought possible only for able-bodied people. After all, as Verdi-

Fletcher says in her Dancing Wheels motto, "Whoever made up the rule that you can only dance on your two feet?" As she stated in *Chronicles of Courage,* "Dance is an expression, an emotion; it comes from within and can be demonstrated in many different ways."

Sources

On-line

Ali, Anjuman, "Breaking New Ground in Dance," *Standard Times,* http://www/s-t.com/daily/11-96/11-03-96/e08ae134.htm (February 14, 1998).

Carlson, Joe, "On Wheels, on Foot, Ballet Company Dazzles U's Eyes," *Minnesota Daily,* http://www.daily.umn.edu/daily/1996/11/14/news/wheels/ (February 14, 1998).

Cleveland Ballet Dancing Wheels, http://www.oac.ohio.gov/artstour/dance/dawheels.htm (February 14, 1998).

Dancers Collective archives, http://www.dancerscollective.org/cleveland-ballet/ (February 14, 1998).

Books

Plimpton, George, and Jean Kennedy Smith, *Chronicles of Courage: Very Special Artists,* Random House (New York), 1993.

Periodicals

Chicago Tribune, September 18, 1995, p. 2MC8.

Exceptional Parent, June 1995, p. 68.

—*Kari Bethel*

Kurt Vonnegut

Archive Photos / Saga 1991 Frank Capri

Author

Born November 11, 1922, in Indianapolis, IN; son of Kurt (an architect) and Edith (Lieber) Vonnegut; married Jane Marie Cox, September 1, 1945 (divorced, 1979); married Jill Krementz (a photographer), November, 1979; children: (from first marriage) Mark, Edith, Nanette; (adopted deceased sister's children) James, Steven, and Kurt Adams; (second marriage) Lily (adopted). *Education:* Attended Cornell University, 1940-42; attended Carnegie Institute of Technology (now Carnegie-Mellon University) and the University of Tennessee, 1943; attended University of Chicago, 1945-47, M.A. in anthropology, 1971.

Addresses: *Home*—New York, NY. *Agent*—Donald C. Farber, Tanner, Propp & Farber, 32nd Floor, 1370 Avenue of the Americas, New York, NY 10019-4602.

Career

Cornell Daily Sun, editor, 1941-42; Chicago City News Bureau, Chicago, IL, police reporter, 1947; General Electric Co., Schenectady, NY, public relations writer, 1947-50; writer, 1950—; Hopefield School, Sandwich, MA, teacher, 1965—; City College of the City University of New York, NY, Distinguished Professor of English Prose, 1973-74. Lecturer at University of Iowa Writers' Workshop, 1965-67, and at Harvard University, 1970-71. Actor in several films, including *Between Time and Timbuktu,* 1972, *Back to School,* 1986, and *That Day in November,* 1988. Contributor of fiction to numerous periodicals, including *Cosmopolitan, Collier's, Esquire, Galaxy Science Fiction, Ladies' Home Journal, Magazine of Fantasy and Science Fiction, McCall's, Playboy,* and *Saturday Evening Post.*

Speaker, National Coalition Against Censorship briefing for the Attorney General's Commission on Pornography hearing, 1986. One-man exhibition of drawings, New York City, 1980. Member, Authors League of America, PEN, National Institute of Arts and Letters (American Center; vice president, 1972), Delta Upsilon, Barnstable Yacht Club, Barnstable Comedy Club. *Military service*—U.S. Army, Infantry, 1942- 45; was POW; received Purple Heart.

Awards: Guggenheim Fellow, Germany, 1967; National Institute of Arts and Letters grant, 1970; Literary Lion award, New York Public Library, 1981; Eugene V. Debs Award, Eugene V. Debs Foundation, 1981, for public service; Freedom to Read Award from Playboy Enterprises and the Friends of the Chicago Public Library, 1982; Emmy Award for outstanding children's program, 1985, for *Displaced Person;* Bronze Medallion, Guild Hall, 1986.

Sidelights

Author Kurt Vonnegut has become a cultural icon known for his humorous, biting social commentaries that probe the effects of science, technology, and human behavior on the world. Though he has been labeled a science fiction author, his works are more postmodern pastiches owing to a number of influences, from the wit of Mark Twain and Laurel and Hardy to the satire of Voltaire and Jonathan Swift. His short, informal style of writing has roots in his background as a journalist, and his themes of economic inequality, environmental exploitation, military might, and social injustice perhaps stem from his upbringing during the Great Depression and his experience as a POW during World War II. Though his first novel, *Player Piano*, was published in 1952, Vonnegut's career did not reach its zenith until the release of *Slaughterhouse Five* in 1969. Based heavily on his wartime ordeal, the novel struck a chord with a nation embroiled in the Vietnam War, and the account became required reading in many classrooms (although it was banned in some schools and libraries for its use of obscenity). Its popularity stirred new interest in the author's older works and led to overwhelming sales for his subsequent book, *Breakfast of Champions*, in 1973, although it did not achieve as great a critical reception. Since then, Vonnegut has written a number of other works, all respectable efforts but none as enthusiastically praised as *Slaughterhouse Five*. In 1997 he declared that his latest novel, *Timequake*, would be his last.

Vonnegut was born on November 11, 1922, in Indianapolis, Indiana, to Kurt and Edith (Lieber) Vonnegut. His father was an architect who designed and built the family home on North Illinois Street in 1922, and his mother was the daughter of one of the wealthiest men in town, a brewer. Vonnegut was the youngest of three children. His sister, Alice, grew up to become a sculptor, and his brother, Bernard, became a physicist. Until he was about ten years old, Vonnegut was virtually raised by the housekeeper and cook, an African American woman named Ida Young. As a fourth-generation German-American, he was not taught the German language because of the heavy anti-German sentiment in the United States after World War I. He became proficient at telling jokes around his family and started to read humor books. He was also a fan of the many radio comedians during the 1930s. Vonnegut was sent to an elite private school, but after the Great Depression of 1929, his parents' fortunes fell, and he began attending public high school. Meanwhile, his mother, an aspiring writer who never had much luck prior, began to make some money selling short stories. But to her dismay, the family never regained their status.

After graduating from Shortridge High School, where he worked on the daily newspaper, Vonnegut went on to Cornell University in 1940 and majored in chemistry, upon the urging of his father. "Chemistry was everything then," he remarked to Richard Todd in the *New York Times*. "It was a magic word in the thirties." Vonnegut, however, wished to become a journalist and eventually served as editor of the *Cornell Daily Sun*. Working at newspapers taught him the short, concise journalistic writing style that he would continue to use when writing fiction. After obtaining helpful instruction in writing but nearly failing his science courses, Vonnegut volunteered to join the army in 1942 during World War II. The army sent him to the Carnegie Institute of Technology (now Carnegie-Mellon University) and the University of Tennessee in 1943 to study mechanical engineering, but he did poorly there as well. Although he was a decent soldier, he held the rank of private for the three years he served.

In May of 1944, Vonnegut went home on Mother's Day on a special pass to see his mom, but found that she died the night before of an overdose of sleeping pills. Three months later he was shipped overseas and on December 2, 1944, was captured by Germans at the Battle of the Bulge. Vonnegut was a prisoner of war in Dresden until his discharge in October of 1945. Most of the time he was held in a slaughterhouse—albeit a modern, relatively clean facility—and worked during the day in a factory producing vitamin-enriched syrup for pregnant women. The city was bombed on February 13, 1945, and the prisoners huddled two stories underground while the whole area was destroyed in the ensuing firestorm, which combusted or asphyxiated about 135,000 residents, even in their shelters. Later, he helped the Germans retrieve the dead bodies so that disease would not spread. After Vonnegut returned home, he was granted the Purple Heart and decided that he would write about his wartime experiences, although he would not tackle the project for almost another 25 years.

Instead, Vonnegut went back to school at the University of Chicago from 1945 to 1947 to study anthropology, a subject that intrigued him greatly. He ventured into social anthropology, but upon completing his course work, the school rejected all of his ideas for a master's thesis, so he never wrote one. (Later, in 1971, as his career was reaching its peak, the school granted the anthropology degree on the basis that his novel *Cat's Cradle* was relatively anthropological.) Vonnegut worked in Chicago in 1947 at the Chicago City News Bureau as a police reporter, then later that year headed to Schenectady, New York, to take a $90-a-week job as a public relations writer with General Electric, where his brother was employed. In the meantime, he began submitting short stories to magazines such as *Collier's*, who paid him $750 for his first piece. Earning more as a fiction writer than at his day job, he left GE in 1950 and moved to Cape Cod, Massachusetts, to concentrate on writing full time. He later denounced public relations and would include references in his novels indicating that public relations work was demeaning to writers.

In 1952 Vonnegut published his first novel, *Player Piano,* a social satire about a futuristic town—based on Schenectady—run by computers. Though his short stories were quite lucrative, Vonnegut's first novel was ignored by critics and initially sold a meager 3,500 copies. Slightly derivative of the dystopian work of Aldous Huxley (*Brave New World*), the novel was pegged as science fiction, much to the author's dismay. He rejected the tag because he felt it was too simplistic in describing the totality of the ideas in his novels. Vonnegut continued to submit work to the popular magazines of the day, including *Cosmopolitan, Esquire, Ladies' Home Journal,* and *Saturday Evening Post,* but would later claim he just used that work to pay the bills while writing his novels. While these shorter pieces should not be critically dismissed, he often had to hold other jobs as well to make ends meet. Some of his positions included teaching at Hopefield High School on Cape Cod, working for an advertising agency, and even opening one of the first Saab dealerships in the United States. He did not publish his second novel, *Sirens of Titan,* until 1959. That, too, was pegged as science fiction and was indeed more in the vein, given that it was a parody of the genre. It was also overlooked except for a small college following.

Vonnegut finally reached the public consciousness with his fourth novel, 1963's *Cat's Cradle,* about a man investigating the actions of people on the day the atomic bomb was dropped on Hiroshima. During his journey, he reaches a Caribbean island where he converts to a nonsensical religion. The title is based on the string game that Eskimos used in vain to trap sunlight, symbolizing the uselessness of many human endeavors. This book is considered one of Vonnegut's best and introduced him to a large base of fans, including many fellow writers. Nevertheless, he was yet to witness his big breakthrough. His next work was *God Bless You, Mr. Rosewater,* in 1965, which deals with economic forces on the psychology of people. Vonnegut spent two years in residence at the University of Iowa Writers' Workshop from 1965 to 1967. While in residence, he traveled back to Dresden to cull material for his next novel, based on the time he spent there during the war.

Vonnegut's *Slaughterhouse Five* was published to great admiration, especially among college students who were enmeshed in the politics of the time. The United States was back at war, this time with Vietnam, and the author's intent on making the Dresden affair a universal statement was well understood. The fact that opposition to the war was growing perhaps boosted the novel's sales and led to a film version by 1972. After two decades as an aspiring writer, Vonnegut was thrust into fame and fortune as a cultural leader of the Sixties generation. From there, he was taken seriously by readers who recognized his acerbic social observations, leading to its use in classrooms as required reading, at the same time that other schools and libraries were banning it because of its obscene language. After this enormous success, Vonnegut claimed that he would never write another novel and instead concentrated on lecturing and writing plays.

Later, Vonnegut completed a half-finished novel he had started earlier and discarded. *Breakfast of Champions* was not as critically acclaimed as his prior work, but sold a quarter of a million copies in less than a year. His next work, *Slapstick,* published in 1976, was a rumination about his sister's death and a rather bleak treatment of the loneliness of contemporary American society that also did not win much applause. Then Vonnegut composed *Jailbird,* one of his most blatantly political novels, fusing the McCarthy witch hunts of the 1950s, the Watergate affair, and the Sacco and Vanzetti trials with the Sermon on the Mount. His tenth novel, *Deadeye Dick,* is one of his funniest and recycles aspects from his earlier works, such as *Breakfast of Champions,* to create the effect of a fiction within a fiction. In 1985, *Galapagos* was born out of the author's trip to the islands off of the Pacific coast of South America. Paying careful attention to the science involved, Vonnegut centered the novel on Charles Darwin's theory of natural selection. He was rewarded when famous biologist Stephen Jay Gould affirmed that the facts were accurate. Vonnegut's 1990 work *Hocus Pocus* again culls elements from previous books and features a protagonist named Eugene Debs Hartke, after the socialist labor leader. It predicts a grim social deterioration yet manages to avoid a despondent tone.

Vonnegut penned what he again said was his final novel in 1997, claiming during a National Public Radio interview that writing books is "too hard," adding, "And also, television and movies are doing a much better job of holding people's attention than books." *Timequake* is based on the idea that due to a time-space error, the universe must replay the 1990s. As a diversion from writing, Vonnegut enjoys painting and has exhibited in New York and Denver; a silk screener makes prints of his works. Also during the

1990s, he designed a beer label—complete with a short story—for Kurt's Mile High Malt, a microbrewery beer named after him and using his grandfather's recipe.

Vonnegut lectured at Harvard University from 1970 to 1971 and was named Distinguished Professor of English Prose at the City College of the City University of New York for the 1973-74 year. He also served as the vice president of the National Institute of Arts and Letters in 1975. In 1967 he was named a Guggenheim Fellow, and in 1970 he received a National Institute of Arts and Letters grant. The New York Public Library gave him their Literary Lion award in 1981. He has also received the Eugene V. Debs Award for public service in 1981, the Freedom to Read Award from Playboy Enterprises and the Friends of the Chicago Public Library in 1982, an Emmy Award for outstanding children's program in 1985 for *Displaced Person,* and a Bronze Medallion from the Guild Hall in 1986.

Vonnegut married his high school sweetheart, Jane Marie Cox, on September 1, 1945. They had three children—Mark, Edith, Nanette—and in 1957 adopted three of his sister's children as well when she died of cancer a couple of days after her husband perished in a train crash. Vonnegut and his wife separated in 1970 and were divorced in 1979; later that year, he married Jill Krementz, a photographer he met when she was on assignment to take pictures of him. Vonnegut is a rumpled-looking man with glasses and a brown mop of hair. His conversation is punctuated by wheezes, thanks to years of smoking Pall Mall cigarettes. He told Alan Dumas of the *Rocky Mountain News* that he feels he has finished his life's work: "Many writers died young with a sense of being incomplete. Thank God I lived long enough to finish." Vonnegut added, "How many people have lives worth living? I'd say 17% seems about right. Thank God mine was one of them."

Selected writings

Novels

Player Piano, Scribner, 1952.
The Sirens of Titan, Dell, 1959.
Mother Night, Gold Medal Books, 1961.
Cat's Cradle, Holt, 1963.
God Bless You, Mr. Rosewater; or, Pearls before Swine, Holt, 1965.
Slaughterhouse Five; or, the Children's Crusade: A Duty-Dance with Death, by Kurt Vonnegut, Jr., a Fourth-Generation German-American Now Living in Easy Circumstances on Cape Cod (and Smoking Too Much) Who, as an American Infantry Scout Hors de Combat, as a Prisoner of War, Witnessed the Fire-Bombing of Dresden, Germany, the Florence of the Elbe, a Long Time Ago, and Survived to Tell the Tale: This Is a Novel Somewhat in the Telegraphic Schizophrenic Manner of Tales of the Planet Tralfamadore, Where the Flying Saucers Come From, Seymour Lawrence/Delacorte, 1969.
Breakfast of Champions; or, Goodbye, Monday, Seymour Lawrence/Delacorte, 1973.
Slapstick; or, Lonesome No More!, Seymour Lawrence/Delacorte, 1976.
Jailbird, Seymour Lawrence/Delacorte, 1979.
Deadeye Dick, Seymour Lawrence/Delacorte, 1982.
Galapagos: A Novel, Seymour Lawrence/Delacorte, 1985.
Bluebeard, Delacorte, 1987.
Hocus Pocus, Putnam, 1990.
Timequake, Putnam, 1997.

Short fiction

Canary in a Cathouse, Fawcett, 1961.
Welcome to the Monkey House: A Collection of Short Works, Seymour Lawrence/Delacorte, 1968.
Who Am I This Time? For Romeos and Juliets (illustrated by Michael McCurdy), Redpath Press.

Plays

Penelope, first produced in Cape Cod, MA, 1960; Seymour Lawrence/Delacorte, 1971.
Happy Birthday, Wanda June, produced in New York, 1970.
Between Time and Timbuktu; or, Prometheus Five: A Space Fantasy, (television play) produced on National Educational Television Network, Seymour Lawrence/Delacorte, 1972.
Miss Temptation, Dramatic Publishing Company, 1993.

Other

Wampeters, Foma, and Granfalloons: (Opinions) (essays), Seymour Lawrence/Delacorte, 1974.
(With Ivan Chermayeff) *Sun, Moon, Star* (juvenile), Harper, 1980.
Palm Sunday: An Autobiographical Collage, Seymour Lawrence/Delacorte, 1981.
(Contributor) *Bob and Ray: A Retrospective,* June 15-July 10, 1982, Museum of Broadcasting, 1982.
(Contributor) W. E. Block and M. A. Walker, editors, *Discrimination, Affirmative Action, and Equal Opportunity: An Economic and Social Perspective,* Fraser Institute, 1982.
Nothing Is Lost Save Honor: Two Essays (includes "The Worst Addiction of Them All" and "Fates Worse Than Death: Lecture at St. John the Divine, New York City, May 23, 1982") Toothpaste Press, 1984.

Sources

On-line

"Kurt Vonnegut," *Contemporary Authors*, Gale Literary Databases, http://www.galenet.com (July 7, 1998).

"Kurt Vonnegut," *Dictionary of Literary Biography*, Gale Literary Databases, http://www.galenet.com (July 7, 1998).

Books

Authors & Artists for Young Adults, volume 6, Gale Research, 1991.

Periodicals

Daily Telegraph, October 11, 1997, p. 50.
Dallas Morning News, October 12, 1997, p. 8J.
Los Angeles Times, October 2, 1997, Life & Style, p. 2.
Newsday, October 8, 1997, p. B6.
New York Times, January 24, 1971.
Rocky Mountain News, October 7, 1997, p. 6D.
Star Tribune (Minneapolis, MN), October 26, 1996.

Other

All Things Considered (radio transcript), National Public Radio, September 22, 1997.

—*Geri Speace*

Barbara Walters

Television journalist, anchor, and host

Born September 25, 1931, in Boston, MA; daughter of Louis Edward (a nightclub operator and theatrical producer) and Dena (a homemaker; maiden name, Selett) Walters; married Robert Henry Katz (a businessman; annulled, May 21, 1958); married Lee Guber (a theatrical producer), December 8, 1963 (divorced, 1976); married Merv Adelson (a television production executive), May 10, 1986 (divorced, 1992); children: (adopted in 1968) Jacqueline Dena. *Education:* Sarah Lawrence College, B.A. in English, 1953.

Addresses: *Office—20/20,* 147 Columbus Ave., Floor 10, New York, NY 10023-5900; Barwall Productions, The Barbara Walters Specials, 825 7th Ave., Floor 3, New York, NY 10019-6014.

Career

Television journalist, writer, anchor, host, and producer. Writer-producer, WNBT-TV, WNBC-TV, WPIX, CBS-TV, 1952-58; Tex McCrary Inc., publicist, c. 1958-61; *Today* show, writer and reporter, 1961, regular panel member, 1964-74, co-host, 1974-76; *Not For Women Only* syndicated television show, moderator, 1974-76; *ABC Evening News* (now *ABC World News Tonight*), newscaster, 1976-78; *Barbara Walters Specials,* host, 1976—, host and executive producer, 1992—; *20/20* news show, ABC, correspondent, c. 1979-84; co-host, 1984—; and *The View,* ABC, co-creator and co-host, 1997—. Contributor to *Issues and Answers,* ABC. Author of *How to Talk with Practically Anybody about Practically Anything,* Doubleday, 1970; contributor to *Reader's Digest, Good Housekeeping, and Family Weekly.*

Archive Photos

Awards: Named among One Hundred Women of Accomplishment, *Harper's Bazaar,* 1967, 1971; named one of America's Seventy-Five Most Important Women, *Ladies' Home Journal,* 1970; Woman of the Year in Communications, 1974; named one of Two Hundred Leaders of the Future, *Time,* 1974; Award of the Year, National Association of Television Program Executives, 1975; Emmy Award, best host or hostess of a talk, service, or variety series, 1975, for the *Today Show;* Mass Media Award, American Jewish Committee's Institute for Human Relations, 1975; Woman of the Year, Theta Sigma Phi, and Broadcaster of the Year, International Radio and Television Society, 1975; Gold Medal, National Institute of Social Sciences, 1976; Matrix Award, New York Women in Communications, 1977; Lowell Thomas Award, International Platform Association, 1977; Hubert H. Humphrey Freedom Prize, B'nai B'rith's Anti-Defamation League, 1978; named one of the Ten Women of the Decade, *Ladies' Home Journal,* 1979; named one of the Most Important Women of 1979, Roper Report, 1979; Emmy Award, best news program segment, and shared Emmy Award, best news and documentary programs and program segments, both 1980, for *Nightline;* named one of the Women Most Admired by the American People, Gallup Poll, 1982, 1984; named one of America's One Hundred Most Important Women,

Ladies' Home Journal, 1983; Emmy Award, best interviewer, 1983, and best interview segment, 1988, for 20/20; two Emmy Awards for best interviewer, for *The Barbara Walters Special;* President's Award, Overseas Press Club of America, 1988; Lowell Thomas Award, Marist College, 1990; elected to Hall of Fame, Academy of Television Arts and Sciences, 1990; Lifetime Achievement award, International Women's Media Foundation, 1992; Distinguished Service Award, National Association of Broadcasters, 1997; numerous honorary degrees and Emmy Award nominations.

Sidelights

One of the most influential women on television, Barbara Walters became the highest-paid television news anchor in history when she signed a $1 million annual contract in 1976 to co-host the *ABC Evening News* with Harry Reasoner. Before that accomplishment, she had established herself on the *Today* show as a competent all-around journalist, with a knack for lining up important guests. Around the same time that she started hosting the *ABC News,* she began airing her own brand of personal interview program, *The Barbara Walters Specials,* which have made her a household name. Her probing yet nonaggressive manner, insightful questions, and obvious delight with her guests made those shows some of the highest-rated on television and have featured some of the biggest names in the news. She arranged the first joint interview with Egyptian President Anwar Sadat and Israeli Prime Minister Menachem Begin in 1977, and since then has covered a catalog of leaders and celebrities, from the late Princess Diana (after her split from Prince Charles) to Colin Powell to George Clooney. After leaving *ABC News,* Walters joined the staff at *20/20,* a prime time news magazine program designed to compete with *60 Minutes.* She became a co-anchor with Hugh Downs in 1984 and has remained there since. In 1997 she began appearing in a much earlier time slot on *The View,* which she and producer Bill Geddie created for the daytime talk show market.

Although Walters is a respected television professional with numerous awards and honors, she has endured her share of bumps in the road. From her humble beginnings behind the scenes on the *Today* show, she was eventually offered a spot as a *"Today* girl" in the early 1960s, a job previously held by attractive females functioning mainly as scenery. Walters was the show's first shot at putting an intelligent woman in the position, and she became popular with audiences, while facing daily tension with host Frank McGee. When McGee died, she was given his job. After her pricey appointment at *ABC News,* Reasoner bristled at having to share

the camera and acted hostile toward her. Critics were dubious of her credentials: despite her *Today* background, many felt her celebrity connections tainted her reputation. And she was reportedly hurt by the ribbing she got for her imperfect speech patterns, as exemplified in a recurring *Saturday Night Live* skit featuring late comedian Gilda Radner as "Baba Wawa." Walters rose above the obstacles and criticism, becoming more and more successful as her career continued. A *Working Woman* article quoted television critic Tom Shales of the *Washington Post* summing up Walters's success: "She became very splashy about her career. And she overcame a lot of male chauvinism in television." He added, "She simply got more intimate than anyone else had before her. She pioneered the style of getting the guest to cry. And she's genuinely nosy, which is a good thing for a journalist to be."

Walters was born on September 25, 1931, in Boston, Massachusetts, to Louis Edward and Dena (Selett) Walters. The Walters also had a son, Burton, who died of pneumonia at only a year old, and a daughter, Jacqueline, who was developmentally disabled. "She was a great influence on my life," Walters recalled to Allison Adato in *Life.* "I think she made me more understanding and compassionate because people were not as tolerant as they maybe are today." Walters' father, Louis, was a busy and well-known theatrical producer who booked vaudeville acts. Though he became quite wealthy, he also spent a lot, and then lost everything during the Great Depression. In 1937, he opened the Latin Quarter nightclub in Boston, and later expanded to New York City and Miami. Walters' father bounced his family from city to city as his business grew; she went to Miami at age 11 and New York two years later, then returned to Miami at age 15 and New York at 16. Her father's fortunes reversed again, however, and he lost his Boston Latin Quarter club in a card game. Walters decided that she would always be self-supporting in order to avoid this type of predicament later in life.

Walters went to Sarah Lawrence College and received a bachelor of arts degree in English. With help from her father's entertainment-world connections, she began working as a writer and producer for WNBT-TV in New York. In 1955, she began booking guests for the *Morning Show* with Dick Van Dyke on CBS, and after the show was canceled in 1956, she continued on its replacement, *Good Morning with Will Rogers, Jr.* It eventually went off the air, and Walters found work at the public relations firm Tex McCrary Inc. as a publicist, trying to book clients on television shows and generate positive press. In 1961, she started writing for the *Today* show.

After managing to get on camera a few times to appear in the stories she wrote, Walters was given the chance to report a full story. Previously, the "*Today* girl" was an attractive young woman relegated to reporting on lightweight topics geared for female audience members. Walters started to change that. She was sent to India to accompany First Lady Jacqueline Kennedy and was the only reporter there to be granted an interview, albeit short. She continued writing and reporting, and although she was passed up twice to be a *Today* girl, the producer eventually realized he needed a woman with credentials, and hired Walters on a trial basis in 1963.

Walters fine-tuned her talents, especially for interviewing, on *Today,* and in 1974 took a position hosting a daytime talk show, *Not for Women Only* (Walters insisted on adding the "not" to the show's proposed title). Around the same time, she was promoted to co-host of the *Today* show when Frank McGee died of bone cancer, making her the first ever female co-host on a TV network news or public affairs show. However, she would soon break another barrier. In 1976, she was the center of attention when ABC extended an offer to co-anchor the *ABC Evening News* and produce four specials—for a salary of $1 million. No newscaster had ever made that much; most were making less than half that. NBC told Walters they would match the salary, but wanted her to stay on *Today.* Walters moved to ABC and began anchoring the news with Harry Reasoner.

Walters came under fire for the salary as well as for her style. She was known for being more entertainment-oriented, and many questioned her hard news credentials. However, she was extremely popular with audiences, which was how she justified demanding such a hefty amount. Reasoner was reportedly unreasonable about her appointment to his desk. Though Walters made attempts to calm the waters, the duo's dynamics clashed. They never got along, and eventually would not even speak to each other. In addition, Walters did not help boost the third-place ratings (before cable, when there were only three competing networks), and ABC eventually abolished the anchor positions. Walters remained a correspondent, and began devoting more time to her specials.

Since her first *Barbara Walters Special* on December 14, 1976, with President and First Lady Jimmy and Rosalyn Carter and entertainer, Barbra Streisand, Walter's shows have been ratings successes. Throughout the years, her slant has changed to focus mainly on celebrities and less on politicians, but she has interviewed every American president since Richard Nixon, as well as other world leaders, including Cuban leader Fidel Castro (he even made her and the crew grilled cheese sandwiches after the shoot). She is known for her incisive and intimate interviews with a bevy of stars, from Jim Carrey to Bette Davis. Usually informal and often held in the person's home, the interviews encourage public figures to reveal sensitive details about their personal lives. Her interview with actor Christopher Reeve after he became paralyzed in a horse-riding accident was seen by 29 million viewers and received the George Foster Peabody Award. Walters told Melina Gerosa in *Ladies' Home Journal,* "I think this interview had a greater effect than anything that I have done in all the years at ABC, because there are not that many times when you come across that extraordinary true, shining love that Chris [Reeve] and his wife have for each other."

> *Katie Couric, anchor on the* Today *show, noted:* "What a lot of women in the business admire is that she is still hungry and so competitive. She will never rest on her laurels. She's in her 60s and still on the air. It gives all women a real boost."

Around the late 1970s or early 1980s, Walters began contributing to the news magazine program *20/20.* Though the anchor, Hugh Downs, had originally suggested Walters for the spot on the *Today* show in the early 1960s that got her career moving, he was reluctant to have her on board as a *20/20* co-host. She was given the position in 1984 and remains a major presence. Her specials continue to earn high ratings, and the Lifetime cable channel in 1994 announced they would recycle Walters's past interviews for a new hour long series, *Barbara Walters: Interviews of a Lifetime.* Throughout the 1980s and 1990s, thanks in large part to Walters opening the door, more and more women entered television. However, Walters noted in a 1996 *TV Guide* article that there were no women on the nightly network news.

After spending her career since the 1970s in evening time slots, Walters returned to morning television in 1997 with the premiere of *The View,* which she put together with her longtime producer, Bill Geddie. Jane Hall in the *Los Angeles Times* described the effort as "the ABC daytime talk show that aims to combine *Live with Regis & Kathie Lee* with *This Week with David Brinkley,*" and noted that critics have applauded it "for being a positive, smart alternative to some dysfunctional daytime talkers." The show's panel features five women co-hosts who represent different stages of a woman's life: Walters, in her 60s, who appears twice a week, alternating days with Joy Behar; Behar, a comedian and radio show host in her 50s who is seen three days a week; Meredith Vieira, the moderator, a former *60 Minutes* correspondent who is in her 40s; Star Jones, a former prosecutor in her 30s; and Debbie Matenopolous, a former MTV crew member in her 20s. *The View* was nominated for eight Emmy awards in spring of 1998 after its first season. Despite the below-average ratings, ABC executives renewed the show for the 1998 season because it performed better that the show it replaced (*Caryl & Marilyn*) and it had increased 38 percent in popularity with the coveted market of 18- to 49-year-old women. Walters is involved in all aspects of the production. "I love doing this show, and I'm committed to it," she told Hall in the *Los Angeles Times.*

Although Walters no longer commands the highest salary in television, she does not do poorly, with estimates ranging from $5 to $10 million per year. And, as Stephanie Mansfield noted in *Working Woman,* "She may be the best value," with her highly-rated specials and the ongoing popularity of *20/20.* Colleagues praise her skills and motivation, and she is a role model for many. In an industry where other female newscasters have been fired due to their age, Walters keeps working harder. Katie Couric, anchor on the *Today* show, told Mansfield in *Working Woman,* "What a lot of women in the business admire is that she is still hungry and so competitive. She will never rest on her laurels. She's in her 60s and still on the air. It gives all women a real boost." Steve Wulf in *Time* quoted ABC News president Roone Arledge commenting on Walters: "She just keeps getting better and better. She has a way that has matured over the years of getting people to say things on the air that they never thought they were going to say."

Walters married and divorced three times. Her first husband, Robert Henry Katz, was a businessman; they divorced shortly before their three-year anniversary. Her second marriage, to theatrical producer Lee Guber, lasted from 1963 to 1976. They adopted a daughter, Jacqueline, in 1968 after Walters had a series of miscarriages. She married a third time, to Merv Adelson, chairman of Lorimar Production Company, but it ended in 1992. She told Melina Gerosa in *Ladies' Home Journal* that she does not think her career caused her marriages to break up. "Maybe they broke up because if I wasn't really happy in them, " Walters mused. "I could walk away knowing that I could earn enough money. I could go places alone." Walters has remained single since her third divorce from television executive Merv Adelson and now lives with two other women who provide friendship and help her at home. Revealing some of her regrets to Gerosa, Walters said that she wishes she had more children, and would have liked to have been more patient with her sister, Jacqueline, who died in 1988. However, Walters remarked, no one can have everything in life. "Along with living, there are always some regrets," Walters observed. "At a certain point, you say, 'It may not be the best, but it's what I chose, and you know what? It's pretty darn good.'"

Sources

On-line

"Barbara Walters biography," *The View* web site, http://www.abc.com/theview (May 13, 1998).

Books

Baldwin, Louis, *Women of Strength: Biographies of 106 Who Have Excelled in Traditionally Male Fields, A.D. 61 to the Present,* McFarland & Co., 1996.

Contemporary Theatre, Film, and Television, Volume 13, Gale Research, 1995.

Encyclopedia of World Biography, second edition, Gale Research, 1997.

Signorielli, Nancy, editor, *Women in Communication: A Biographical Sourcebook,* Greenwood Press, 1996.

Periodicals

Broadcasting & Cable, April 9, 1997, p. 11.

Cosmopolitan, May 1994, p. 208.

Entertainment Weekly, December 16, 1994, p. 88.

Ladies' Home Journal, April 1996, p. 128.

Life, November 1997, p. 36.

Los Angeles Times, April 27, 1998, p. F11.

Maclean's, May 26, 1997, p. 36.

Mediaweek, July 21, 1997, p. 8.

Time, November 6, 1995, p. 68.

TV Guide, April 27, 1996, p. 24.

Vanity Fair, August 1994, p. 88.

Variety, August 25, 1997, p. 33.

Working Woman, November/December 1996.

—*Geri Speace*

Vera Wang

Courtesy of Vera Wang

Designer

Born June 27, 1949, in New York, NY; daughter of Cheng Ching (a businessman) and Florence Wu (a translator) Wang; married Arthur Becker (a businessman), June, 1989; children: Cecilia and Josephine (both adopted). *Education:* Sarah Lawrence College, B.A. in art history, 1971.

Addresses: *Home*—New York, NY. *Office*—Vera Wang Bridal House, 991 Madison Ave., New York, NY 10021-1825.

Career

*V*ogue magazine, New York City, 1971-87, became senior fashion editor; Ralph Lauren, design director, 1987-89; opened first wedding dress boutique, Vera Wang Bridal House, Ltd., New York City, 1990, began designing bridal dresses, 1992, and evening wear, 1993; owner of Vera Wang, Ltd., Bridal House, Ltd., Bridal Collections; Made to Order; and Ready to Wear Collection of Evening.

Sidelights

Energetic and creative fashion guru Vera Wang became known as the designer to the stars in the 1990s with her trademark up-to-date wedding dresses, in addition to sleek evening gowns and elegant figure skating costumes. Using sheer materials and emphasizing minimalist styles, she has amassed a legion of famous fans from actresses Sharon Stone and Holly Hunter to skater Nancy Kerrigan, whose 1994 Olympic outfits made Wang a household name. Wang's creations are not just for the elite, however; she has a ready-to-wear line of bridal and evening dresses that can be found at over stores across the nation. A former almost-Olympic figure skater herself, Wang used her extensive experience as a fashion editor at *Vogue* and her stint designing for Ralph Lauren to launch her own lines. Her incentive for starting with bridal wear stemmed from her own frustration at not being able to find a suitable dress for her own 1989 wedding. "They were over-the-top and ornate and looked like wedding cakes," Wang told Jane Sharp in *Biography*. "I wanted something more elegant and subdued, but there wasn't anything. I realized the desire to fill that niche."

Wang was born on June 27, 1949, in New York City, to Cheng Ching Wang and Florence Wang. The couple fled China during World War II and were separated for a few years, but reunited in the United States. Wang's father studied chemical engineering at the Massachusetts Institute of Technology, but acknowledged that he could make more money as a businessman. As the chairman of the U.S. Summit Company, a multimillion dollar oil and pharmaceuticals firm, he later also became the primary investor in Wang's fashion designing business. Florence Wang was formerly a translator at the United Nations, and Wang's younger brother, Kenneth, would grow up to become president of the family business.

Wang was an achiever from a young age. She attended prestigious schools such as Chapin school in Manhattan and the School of American Ballet. When she was seven, she received figure skates for Christmas and embraced the sport fervently. As a teenager, Wang and her partner, James Stuart, placed fifth in the junior pairs competition at the U.S. national championships in 1968 and 1969. Stuart, however, subsequently opted to skate solo, and Wang enrolled in Sarah Lawrence College in Bronxville, New York, thus dashing her dream of competing in the Olympics. There was not enough time to study and train, and this led to the greatest disappointment of her life. As a sophomore, she dropped out and moved to Paris, where she lived with Olympic skater Patrick Pera and studied at the Sorbonne. After a year there, Wang went back to Sarah Lawrence and finished her bachelor's degree in art history.

After graduating, Wang in the early 1970s landed a job at *Vogue* magazine, doing "everything from Xeroxing messenger slips to packing and unpacking for photo shoots," as she recalled in *People*. Fast making an impression on her superiors, Wang was a senior fashion editor by her mid-20s. In that position, she oversaw all of the photographs in the magazine, an extremely important position. She stayed there about 16 years, living a fast life of hanging out at places like the legendary Studio 54 disco, sometimes hailing a cab directly to work after a night on the town. In 1987, she left *Vogue* to take a job with Ralph Lauren as a design director for 13 lines of accessories.

Meanwhile, Wang met real estate entrepreneur and golf equipment manufacturer Arthur Becker at a country club in 1980, but did not want to become too deeply involved. "At that point I was like, 'No way! I have a career, I have places to go, people to see," Wang remarked in *People*. Seven years down the line, though, she ran into him again and they got serious. When it was time to choose the dress, Wang was disappointed that the styles were very fussy or too young-looking for a bride who was edging 40. She eventually settled on a custom-made satin beaded number that ran $10,000. The wedding took place in June of 1989 at the Pierre Hotel in Manhattan; 400 guests from the realm of fashion, film, and media attended.

After her wedding, Wang began taking fertility drugs in order to start a family and found that her work was being compromised. "I was getting shots every day, having blood tests and sonograms," she explained to Alex Witchel in the *New York Times*. "And I couldn't do that and work for Ralph [Lauren] at the same time." Six months after the wedding, Wang reluctantly left her job. Though she never became pregnant, Wang later adopted daughters Cecilia and Josephine. Her father, meanwhile, suggested that she open her own business in order to assist other brides-to-be with a better selection of dresses. He loaned her $4 million and she opened Vera Wang Bridal House, Ltd., in Manhattan's Carlyle Hotel in 1990. Though she began carrying only other designers' gowns, she was busy sketching out her own ideas anytime she could—at home watching television, or in a taxi or plane. She told Witchel, "I have to really squeeze it in because I run the business full time, too." The shop immediately attracted an upscale clientele.

Wang's own bridal dresses soon became highly sought-after for their minimalist lines and modern designs. More fashionable and less frou-frou, they flatter women from the very petite to larger figures. Interjecting sexiness into weddings, some of Wang's creations feature low-cut backs, velvet trim, and sheer fabrics. "My fitting model has a big behind, big shoulders," Wang told Witchel. "If garments look beautiful on her then that's the thing to do. If it looks beautiful on a model, so what?" Wang's ready-to-wear dresses run from about $2,200 to $4,800 and are sold at numerous stores across the country, but she will also create custom works starting at $10,000. Some famous brides who have worn her designs include Mariah Carey, Holly Hunter, Elizabeth Shue, Mary Matalin, and Karenna Gore, the vice president's daughter.

After her successful bridal line, Wang introduced evening wear in 1993, and Hollywood was impressed. Stars such as Halle Berry, Goldie Hawn, Sharon Stone, and Meg Ryan went to her for Oscar night finery. In 1994, Wang won a boost of publicity when she designed elegant costumes for Olympic silver medal figure skater Nancy Kerrigan. In addition to her bridal and evening wear, Wang has worked with Mattel to create one of a trio of collectible Barbie dolls, has laid plans to write a wedding guide, and intends to offer a line of housewares such as dishes and linens. She also aims to expand into women's sportswear and active wear, as well as offer an accessory line of shoes and handbags and possibly a fragrance.

Wang looks many years younger than her age and exudes an air of confidence and perennial energy. She and her husband, Becker, own a 12-room, 6-bedroom apartment on Park Avenue, and her brother and sister-in-law live in the building next door. Her parents are close by as well. Wang and Becker also have homes in Pound Ridge, New York, and Palm Beach, Florida, in addition to a nine-bedroom beach home in Southampton, New York. They also enjoy golfing.

Wang herself is an admitted clothes horse, her closets bulging with outfits by other designers, including Jil Sander, Prada, and Gaultier. Though she seems to keep everything running smoothly, she admits that the glamour has a gritty side as well. "It's tremendous pressure," Wang told Witchel in the *New York Times*. "I see myself as a madwoman scrambling to keep 100 marbles on the tables before they fall off." So far, she is coping just fine.

Sources

On-line

"Designer to the Stars Vera Wang," Women's Wire web site, http://www.womenswire.com (July 7, 1998).

Periodicals

AsianWeek, January 21, 1994.
Biography, June 1998, p. 60.
In Style, May 1, 1997, p. 220.
New York Times, June 19, 1994.
People, July 8, 1991, p. 65; February 13, 1995, p. 78; July 20, 1998, p. 129.
USA Weekend, May 10, 1998, p. 19.
Working Woman, May 1995, p. 62.

—*Geri Speace*

Maxine Waters

U.S. Representative

Born Maxine Carr, August 15, 1938, in St. Louis, MO; daughter of Remus and Velma (Moore) Carr; married Edward Waters (divorced, 1972); married Sidney Williams, July 23, 1977; children: (from first marriage) Edward Keith, Karen. *Education:* California State University, Los Angeles, B.A. in sociology, 1972.

Addresses: *Office*—2344 Rayburn House Office Building, Washington, DC 20515; 10124 S. Broadway, Suite 1, Los Angeles, CA 90003.

Career

Head Start program, teacher; California State Assembly, member, district 48, 1976-90; member of Rules Committee, 1984; U.S. House of Representatives, Washington, DC, congresswoman from California's district 29, 1991-92, and district 35, 1992—; chair of Congressional Black Caucus, 1996—; member of Banking, Finance, and Urban Affairs committee; Small Business Committee; Veterans' Affairs Committee; House subcommittee on banking; capitol subcommittee on banking; and employment and training subcommittee on veterans. Delegate to Democratic National Convention, 1972, 1976, 1980, 1984, and 1988; member of National Advisory Committee of Women, 1978—; Democratic Caucus chair, 1984; member of Democratic National Committee, 1980—, and Democratic Congressional Campaign Committee. Board of directors, TransAfrica Foundation, Center for National Policy, National Women's Political Caucus, Clara Elizabeth Jackson Carter Foundation, Spellman College, National Minority AIDS Project, Women for a Meaningful Summit, National Council of Negro Women, Black Women's Agenda; *Ms.* Foundation for Women; *Essence* magazine. Cofounder, National Political Congress of Black Women, 1984; Black Women's Forum.

Sidelights

United States representative Maxine Waters has long been known as one of the champions of minorities, women, children, and the poor, first in state politics and then in Congress. A tough legislator not known to back down from issues about which she feels strongly, she was instrumental in passing bills in California that protected citizens' rights, supported affirmative action, and prevented the state from investing in South Africa during the reign of apartheid. The first African American and first female majority whip of the state assembly, Waters was also the first woman chair of the Democratic Caucus. Her zeal for politics began early, when she was coordinating volunteers in a Head Start program in Los Angeles and managed to get involved with the city council. Since then, her career has been on the move, a blur of high-energy lobbying and leadership. As a congresswoman, she holds her own in the mostly white male legislature, continuing to try to improve society, especially in the inner cities. "I feel it is my responsibility to do these things," Waters stated to Ron Harris in *Essence*, "and I think that is a feeling born out of a belief that I can cause change."

Waters was born Maxine Carr on August 15, 1938, in St. Louis, Missouri, the fifth of 13 children of Remus and Velma (Moore) Carr. Her parents divorced when she was two, and her mother later remarried a number of times. Though Waters's mother diligently tried to make a good life for her family, working low-paying jobs and supplementing her income with welfare, the family lived in a housing project and remained poor. In order to help out, Waters got a job at 13 as a busgirl in a segregated restaurant and later worked as a floor girl in a factory. She was also a good student and active in school activities such as swimming, track, and theater. One of her classmates even predicted that someday she would be speaker of the U.S. House of Representatives. Waters credits her upbringing with instilling her determined and outspoken nature. "Some people say I'm feisty," she remarked to Beverly Beyette in *Ms.* "Some say I'm tough. Combative.... In the community where I come from, the community of survival, those were considered good qualities."

Just out of high school, at age 18, Waters married Edward Waters. He immediately went into military service, and when he came back, there were not many opportunities for him in St. Louis. He took a factory job, but money remained tight, so they set their sights on heading West. In the early 1960s, with their two young children, Edward Keith and Karen, the couple moved to Los Angeles, California, and lived in the Watts section. However, jobs were scarce there also, so Waters went to work earning $1.75 a hour in the sweatshops of the garment district while her husband toiled in a silk screen printing plant. Later, she became an operator for Pacific Telephone, but had to quit in the mid-1960s after suffering complications from a miscarriage. When Waters was ready to go back to work in 1966, she was pleased to get involved with a new federally funded program called Head Start, which helps preschool children from low-income families. There, she was hired as an assistant teacher and "got really motivated, turned on," she recalled to Beyette. She was eventually promoted to supervisor in charge of coordinating volunteers.

Waters earned her sociology degree from California State University at Los Angeles in 1972. It took her just three-and-a-half years. However, she was divorced the same year, due in great part to her passionate devotion to college and her growing political involvement which tore her away from home. "I had this drive, this need to fulfill certain things," Waters commented to

Ron Harris in *Essence*, "and I just plugged away at it." With Head Start, Waters came into contact with a number of politicians and had become a paid political volunteer. This led to a position as deputy to a city councilman, and later, as chief deputy to city councilman David Cunningham. In this role, Waters managed Cunningham's campaigns and became involved with campaigns for Senator Alan Cranston and Los Angeles Mayor Tom Bradley, among others. She would also serve as a delegate at the Democratic National Convention in 1972, 1976, 1980, 1984, and 1988, and as an alternate delegate at numerous others.

In 1976, Waters decided to run for the California State Assembly and ended up serving in the legislature for 14 years. Though she initially met with resistance from other assembly members, she found a friend in Willie Brown, the speaker of the assembly who later became mayor of San Francisco. Though Waters was elected to serve the 48th district, she traveled throughout the state promoting women's issues and became known as a powerful presence in the assembly. A tireless fighter for a bevy of issues, she helped enact legislation on tenants' rights and limits on strip-searches. After six attempts, she managed to push through a bill in 1986 preventing the state of California from investing in South African businesses during the apartheid era. Other issues she sponsored included the nation's first Child Abuse Prevention Training Program, an environmental protection bill, a bill to ensure that workers would be notified of plant closings, and measures assisting victims of sexual assault. Waters rose to become the first African American and first female majority whip of the state assembly. She was also the first woman in the state to be elected chair of the Democratic Caucus, in 1984.

Waters gave special attention to women's rights during her tenure in the state assembly. She has served as a member of the National Advisory Committee of Women since 1978, and she cofounded the Black Women's Forum in order to get more women involved in political activity that effects them. In 1984, Waters worked with a collection of prominent people, including Coretta Scott King, Barbara Rose Collins, and others to form the National Political Congress of Black Women in order to empower African American women and involve them in working to improve their quality of life. In addition, Waters has served on the board of directors of a variety of groups involved in women's causes as well as other issues, including the National Women's Political Caucus, Women for a Meaningful Summit, the National Council of Negro Women, the Black Women's Agenda, the Clara Elizabeth Jackson Carter Foundation, TransAfrica Foundation, the Center for National Policy, the National Minority AIDS Project, *Ms.* Foundation for Women, *Essence* magazine, and Spellman College.

Waters was also known to institute programs to assist her urban constituents with training and jobs. For the residents of a half dozen Los Angeles housing projects, she established Project Build, which provides job training as well as information on child care, day care, and health concerns. Also, Waters lobbied for an affirmative action bill that required the state, when contracting companies for jobs, to hire at least 15 percent minority-owned firms and five percent female-owned. This landmark bill was the first of its kind. Expanding on the Watts Skills Center, founded in 1966, she started up the Maxine Waters Employment Preparation Center in the late 1980s to supply vocational training to young adults. Waters was also instrumental in Jesse Jackson's presidential bids in 1984 and 1988, acting as his campaign manager in the latter race.

In 1990 Waters ran for the U.S. congressional seat from the 29th district, left open when Augustus Hawkins retired. He had served for over three decades, and observers had predicted for some time that she would be his successor. The area encompassed the south part of Los Angeles, familiar territory for Waters. Although the Democrats supported her opponent in the primary, Waters handily took 88 percent of the vote and won the general election with 80 percent of the support. In 1992 she ran from the larger 35th district and won 83 percent of the votes. One of the more liberal members of Congress, Waters has served on the Banking, Finance, and Urban Affairs Committee; the Small Business Committee; and the Veterans' Affairs Committee, as well as the House subcommittee on banking; capitol subcommittee on banking; and employment and training subcommittee on veterans.

While in Congress, Waters continued her mission of helping urban areas, women, and minorities. In 1992 her Emergency Development Loan Guarantee Program was enacted, offering $2 billion to the nation's cities for economic development, housing, and small businesses, and later, another $360 million was authorized for the Community Development Bank Bill for lending to areas not well served by nearby banks. She also worked to give women and minorities preference in acquiring failed financial institutions in underserved areas. In addition, in July of 1993 President Bill Clinton signed a $50 million bill for job and life skills training for unemployed people from 17 to 30 years old.

In 1992 Waters, like most of the nation, was shocked when riots devastated a great deal of Los Angeles after four white police officers were found innocent of using unnecessary force in the beating of African American motorist Rodney King, an incident that had been caught on videotape by a witness. The case demonstrated that racial and class tensions had reached a boiling point, the very thing that Waters had tried conscientiously to prevent by her work with social programs. After a second trial, this time in federal court, two of the officers were sentenced to 30 months in prison. Waters used this controversial situation to shed light on the need for more opportunity in inner cities. Also in 1992, Waters seconded Bill Clinton's presidential nomination at the Democratic convention and later served as national co-chair of the Clinton campaign.

Waters has gained a reputation in Washington for stirring controversy. From her first day on the Veterans' Affairs Committee in January of 1991, she ruffled feathers when she clashed with committee chair G. V. "Sonny" Montgomery. Other members of Congress, too, have remarked about her aggressive nature. She dismisses the criticism, explaining that men do things the same way and asserting that she is targeted because she is female. Despite the accusations that she is audacious, she is also highly respected for her tenacity and was named to the prestigious seat of chair of the Congressional Black Caucus in November of 1996. However, she heavily irked the Democratic party in 1996, when she was outspoken about as yet unproven allegations that the CIA supplied crack cocaine to inner cities. A hotly disputed series on the topic ran in the *San Jose Mercury News,* but other major newspapers such as the *New York Times* and *Washington Post* investigated and could not back up the claims, and the *San Jose Mercury News* later ran a retraction. Waters, however, remained dedicated to the issue, calling for a Congressional investigation in early 1998. She also continued to fight to keep federal affirmative action programs.

Waters met Sidney Williams, a Mercedes-Benz dealer and former Cleveland Browns linebacker, in 1972, and they married in 1977. He would later be named the United States Ambassador to the Commonwealth of the Bahamas. In her spare time, Waters enjoys tennis, swimming, antique shopping, and collecting African American dolls. What drives this powerhouse to keep such a hectic schedule and keep advocating for the so-called little guy? "I just want to make life better for some people," Waters commented to Julianne Malveaux in *Essence.* "Everybody deserves a good quality of life. There is too great a divide between the haves and have-nots, and I believe I can do something to change that."

Sources

On-line

"Congresswoman Maxine Waters Biography," U.S. House of Representatives web site, http://www.house.gov (July 12, 1998).

Books

Contemporary Black Biography, volume 3, Gale Research, 1993.

Notable Black American Women, Book II, Gale Research, 1996.

Periodicals

Black Enterprise, February 1998, p. 30.
Ebony, August 1984, p. 56; January 1991, p. 105.
Essence, March 1984, p. 79; November 1990, p. 55.
Gannett News Service, March 23, 1998.2, 1998, p. 33.
Jet, December 9, 1991, p. 38; October 28, 1996, p. 46; January 20, 1997, p. 47; February 2, 1998, p. 33.
Knight-Ridder/Tribune News Service, December 19, 1997.
Los Angeles Times, November 22, 1996; March 4, 1997.
Ms., January 1984, p. 42.
New Republic, June 30, 1997, p. 11.

—*Geri Speace*

Damon Wayans

Actor

Born September 4, 1960, in New York, NY: son of Howell and Elvira Wayans; married; wife's name, Lisa; children: Damon, Jr.; Michael; Cara Mia; Kyla.

Addresses: *Agent*—Jeff Krask, Triad, 10100 Santa Monica Blvd., 16th Floor, Los Angeles, CA 90067. *Office*—Wife & Kid Productions, 102202 West Washington Blvd., Culver City, CA 90232.

Career

Actor and stand-up comedian; performer in various nightclubs, 1982—, including Good Times nightclub, New York City; host of Miller Lite Comedy Search Finals, 1989. Television appearances include series *Saturday Night Live,* NBC, 1985-86; *In Living Color* (also cowriter), Fox, 1990-92; and *Damon,* Fox, 1998; and television specials *Take No Prisoners: Robert Townsend and His Partners in Crime,* HBO, 1988 *The Mutiny Has Just Begun: Robert Townsend and His Partners in Crime,* HBO, 1989; *One Night Stand,* HBO, 1989; and "Damon Wayans: The Last Stand?," *HBO Comedy Hour,* 1991. Also creator and executive producer of television series *413 Hope St.,* Fox, 1997, and *Damon,* Fox, 1998. Film appearances include *Beverly Hills Cop,* 1984; *Hollywood Shuffle,* 1987; *Roxanne,* 1987; *Colors,* 1988; *I'm Gonna Git You Sucka,* 1988; *Punchline,* 1988; *Earth Girls Are Easy,* 1989; *Look Who's Talking Too* (voiceover), 1990; *The Last Boy Scout,* 1991; *Mo' Money* (also executive producer and screenplay writer) 1992; *Blankman* (also executive producer and cowriter), 1994; *Major Payne* (also cowriter) 1995; *Celtic Pride,* 1996; *The Great White Hype,* 1996; and *Bulletproof,* 1996.

The Kobal Collection

Sidelights

After making a name on the stand-up comedy circuit in the 1980s, Damon Wayans really caught the public eye in the early 1990s with his HBO comedy shows and his contributions to the Fox television series *In Living Color.* As Homey the Clown and one of the outrageous Men on Film, Wayans's performances and writing made an integral addition to the talented cast, which also boasted brother Keenen Ivory Wayans (the show's creator), sister Kim Wayans, as well as actor Jim Carrey, the show's only white cast member. By, for, and about African Americans, *In Living Color* was raucously funny and was just one stop in Wayans's career in the entertainment industry, which also had included a number of feature film roles in the late 1980s. In 1992, Wayans got his chance to run the show as writer, executive producer, and star of *Mo' Money.* He went on to make more films and in 1998, burst back onto television sets with the controversial comedy series *Damon.*

Wayans was born September 4, 1960, in New York City, the fourth of ten children of Howell and Elvira Wayans, and raised in the Chelsea district. Until age 15, Wayans had to wear orthopedic shoes and leg braces for a foot deformity, provoking taunts from other children. That experience, he told James Ryan in *Newsday*, inspired his "affinity for misfits and underdogs" that would later shine through in his comedy routines. Though he and his siblings joked around with each otherquite a bit, his youth really was not much of a laughing matter. His family was poor, and he often went to school hungry. Lacking the ability to concentrate, he failed most of his classes, but managed to get his general equivalency degree. Wayans admitted to Ryan that at age 14 and 15, he used to mug people, and he was also arrested for car theft. Though he went straight for a while, he ran afoul of the law again in his early 20s and was arrested for credit card fraud. He revealed that his parents raised him to be honest and work for a living, but he fell in with the wrong crowd.

Meanwhile, Wayans's brother, Keenen Ivory Wayans, was making a name for himself on the comedy circuit. In 1982, Damon followed his lead and took the stage at Good Times, a club in New York City and soon became a headlining act at numerous venues around the country. In 1984 he landed a small part in the blockbuster movie *Beverly Hills Cop*, starring Eddie Murphy, and the next year, joined the cast of the long-running NBC comedy skit show, *Saturday Night Live.* He only stayed one year, however, giving it up to return to stand-up. Soon, he won more minor parts in major films with top comic stars, including Robert Townsend's hilarious spoof of the acting business, *Hollywood Shuffle*, 1987; the Cyrano de Bergerac-inspired love story *Roxanne*, 1987, with Steve Martin and Daryl Hannah; *Punchline*, 1988, about aspiring comedians; and Townsend's blaxploitation satire *I'm Gonna Git You Sucka*, 1988, directed by his brother Keenen. He also had a part in the 1988 gangs-vs.-cops thriller *Colors*. Working with Townsend led to appearances on the television specials *Take No Prisoners: Robert Townsend and His Partners in Crime*, HBO, 1988, and *The Mutiny Has Just Begun: Robert Townsend and His Partners in Crime*, HBO, 1989.

Wayans landed his first big part in 1989's *Earth Girls Are Easy*, starring Geena Davis and Jeff Goldblum, and was one of the voices in *Look Who's Talking Too*, 1990. Also in 1990, he began working on his brother Keenen's comedy skit show, *In Living Color*, which also featured some other Wayans siblings, including Kim, Marlon, and Shawn. As one of the show's writers, Wayans was nominated twice for Emmy awards, and as a performer, he brought to life two favorite characters, Homey the Clown and one of the flamboyant movie film critics in the skit "Men on Film," which popularized "two snaps up" as votes of appreciation. He stayed for three seasons on *In Living Color*, and meanwhile, in 1989, appeared on the HBO comedy show, *One Night Stand.* In 1991 he taped his first solo comedy show for HBO, "Damon Wayans: The Last Stand?" at the legendary Apollo Theater in Harlem, New York, for the *HBO Comedy Hour.*

Finding that television and stand-up were not as substantive as he would like, Wayans left *In Living Color* in 1992 and decided to pursue film work, including behind the scenes activities. Inspired by his earlier legal woes with the credit card scam, Wayans used the traumatic experience to write and star in a romantic comedy called *Mo' Money*. Released in 1992, the story concerns a con man who gets hired in at a credit card company, falls in love with a coworker, and attempts to give up crime. Though reviews were mixed, Wayans felt that he finally achieved the same element of control in his film work as he had performing stand-up, and it was a hit at the box office.

Wayans went on to co-write and appear in *Major Payne,* 1994, about a tough Marine officer who is forced to retire, and the same year co-wrote and produced *Blankman,* about a bumbling but good-intentioned urban crime fighter who is motivated to be a hero despite his meager budget. Wayans told Ryan in *Newsday* that some of his inspiration for the story came from his love of the Batman series and old Bruce Lee martial arts films. "Some of it is so campy, but it's smart humor—silly but very tongue-in-cheek," Wayans noted. He cast his son, Damon, Jr., as the young version of Blankman. Following those creative attempts, Wayans acted in a couple more films, including *Bulletproof*, 1996, and *The Great White Hype,* 1996. In 1997 he broke from creating comedy with the television series *413 Hope St.*, a gritty drama set in a teen crisis center in New York City. Though the series impressed the president of Fox, it was doomed when the network ran it in a time slot against the wildly popular *Seinfeld.*

Moving on after losing *413 Hope St.*, Wayans developed another comedy series, *Damon,* to air mid-season in 1998. In it, Wayans plays a sharp-witted undercover officer with the Chicago police department. Fellow *In Living Color* alumnus David Alan Grier (Wayans's sidekick in the skit "Men on Film") plays his bungling younger brother. Wayans's disguises are the nucleus of the program, and the humor is decidedly not politically correct. Initial reaction focused on the bawdy comedy surrounding body parts, sex, and bodily functions, as well as questionable jokes about sexual harassment. However, as Bark pointed out, Comedy Central had a hit the same season with animated series *South Park*, "in which 8-year-old cartoon characters discuss the intricacies of anal probes."

Meanwhile, Greg Braxton in the *Los Angeles Times* focused on Wayans's repartee with Grier, commenting that the two actors "display their kinetic chemistry that explodes into impromptu riffs of punch lines and movements. Their interaction is not unlike veteran jazz musicians who take pride in their solos but get the most pleasure out of their harmony."

Wayans and his wife, Lisa, have four children: Damon, Jr., Michael, Cara Mia, and Kyla. They live in a mostly African American, middle-class area called Baldwin Hills on the border of South Central Los Angeles. He curbs their television watching and sends them to private school. In case his show *Damon* does not work out, Wayans will undoubtedly forge ahead again. "*Hope St.* was not the cure to cancer, and if [*Damon*] doesn't work, I'll come up with something else that does work," Wayans told Ed Bark in the *Dallas Morning News*. "One show doesn't stop my creative flow." Also, though he has begun to spend more time as a writer and producer, fans should not worry about Wayans disappearing from the screen anytime soon. He loves acting too much, telling Barry Koltnow in the *Orange County Register*, "I love the moments between 'action' and 'cut.' I can't get enough of those moments. I live for those moments."

Sources

On-line

"Damon Wayans," Internet Movie Database, http://us.imdb.com (August 12, 1998).

Books

Contemporary Black Biography, volume 8, Gale Research, 1995.
Contemporary Theatre, Film, and Television, volume 10, Gale Research, 1993.

Periodicals

Atlanta Journal and Constitution, March 22, 1998, p. L1.
Dallas Morning News, September 6, 1996, p. 5C; January 11, 1998, p. 37A; March 22, 1998, p. 1C.
Los Angeles Times, September 10, 1997; March 29, 1998.
Newsday, August 13, 1994, p. B5; March 22, 1998, p. 3.
People, April 10, 1995, p. 130.
St. Louis Post-Dispatch, March 30, 1998, p. E1.
Washington Post, July 25, 1992.

—*Geri Speace*

Wei Jingsheng

Human rights activist

Born May 20, 1950, in the People's Republic of China; son of Wei Zilin (a deputy director, State Capital Construction Commission) and Du Peijun (a Communist party official).

Addresses: *Office*—School of International and Public Affairs, Columbia University, New York, NY 10027.

Career

Participated in the Great Proletarian Cultural Revolution, 1966-68; exiled in Anhui Province, 1968-69; member of People's Liberation Army, 1969-73; electrician, 1973-78; "Democracy Wall" activist, 1978; imprisoned for "Democracy Wall" protests, 1979-93; released and rearrested after six months; sentenced to 14 years in prison, 1995; released and exiled to United States, 1997; Columbia University, School of International and Public Affairs, visiting scholar, 1997—.

Awards: Olaf Palme Award; Sakharov Prize for Freedom of Thought, European Parliament; Democracy Award, National Endowment for Democracy, 1998.

Sidelights

On November 16, 1997, Chinese dissident Wei Jingsheng was released from prison in his country and allowed to fly to the United States. Imprisoned for all but six months since 1979, Wei's crime had not been a physical act but an intellectual one: questioning the policies of his country's Communist government. For his participation in the "Democracy Wall" movement in 1978, Wei had spent 14 years in

AP/Wide World Photos

prison. When, upon his release in 1993, he had proven himself unwilling to keep quiet about the abridgement of freedoms under China's totalitarian system, he was sentenced to another 14 years. But following talks between President Bill Clinton and China's President Jiang Zemin, Wei had been released and flown to Detroit, Michigan, where he received special treatment for medical conditions exacerbated by his long imprisonment. In the next few months, the Nobel Peace Prize nominee would embark on a new career as a free man, an outspoken proponent of human rights. Though he now resided in a country where he was free to speak his mind, it was clear that Wei desired something more: to enjoy that freedom in his homeland, the country for which he had endured nearly 18 years of imprisonment.

In his early days, Wei would hardly have seemed like a future opponent of Communism. His parents were high-ranking officials in the regime established by Mao Zedong, who took power in 1949. The oldest of four, Wei grew up in Beijing, where he was well-acquainted with Mao and his wife, Jiang Qing. Young Wei was steeped in Communist doctrine, learning the precepts not only of his country's leader, but of Mao's intellectual forebears, including Marx, Engels, Lenin, and Stalin. In 1966 Wei was a student at one of China's top-ranking high schools, attached to the People's University in Beijing. That was the year when his country entered a tumultuous series of events called the Great Proletarian Cultural Revolution, which would sweep up Wei and the rest of China.

> "I suddenly realized that my determination to help others was the great cause which had been helping me to withstand physical and mental suffering and helped me maintain my optimism and strength."

At the beginning of the Cultural Revolution in August, 1966, Mao called for a reinvigoration of Chinese Communism, and urged young people in the "Red Guards" to direct their energies to the task of rooting out all forces opposed to revolution. In practice this meant enormous bloodshed, with millions of teenagers allowed to wreak violence on the country. One of those teens was Wei, and by the end of 1966 he had graduated from the Red Guards to the elite United Action Committee, a group composed of children of high-ranking party officials. By then, however, the Cultural Revolution had gotten so completely out of hand that even Mao was committed to suppressing the revolutionary fervor he had unleashed. As a result, Wei spent the first months of 1967 in prison, and upon his release became involved in a propaganda movement that included publication of a revolutionary periodical called *Preparation*. The following year saw an increased backlash against the perpetrators of the Cultural Revolution, and Wei fled to Chao County, Anhui Province, in the hinterlands of China.

As he recalled in a 1998 interview with *China News Daily*, Wei's year in the country had a large impact on his political views. Up until that time, Wei had been a fervent believer in Communism, and throughout the upheavals of the Cultural Revolution had remained assured that Mao's system would produce peace and prosperity for the people of China. Now, for the first time removed from the relative luxury of the big city, he glimpsed firsthand the poverty wrought by Mao's forced modernization of agriculture. A subsequent stint in the army (1969-73) further broadened Wei's awareness of conditions in his country, as he realized that most of his fellow soldiers were peasants.

Wei then began to seriously reevaluate the precepts he had accepted without question since childhood. Particularly troublesome was the claim that China under Mao represented a "people's democratic dictatorship." He came to recognize the contradiction in terms inherent in this phrase, as he told the *China News Daily*: "If you want democracy, folks will get together to discuss diverse opinions. If you have dictatorship, nobody can discuss with you.... [I]f you still had to listen to [the leader], then what was the point of democracy?"

Events in his personal life contributed further to Wei's questioning of political conditions in China. His mother died in 1976, discredited by the party leadership, and his father suffered in a labor camp. Because his family lost their high position, Wei did not have a variety of career options available to him when he completed his army service in 1973. He became an electrician, and obtained employment at the Beijing Zoo. During this time he met and became engaged to Ping Ni, a Tibetan who had suffered greatly as a result of the Maoist takeover of her country in the 1950s. Her father, formerly a leader in the Communist Party of Tibet, had been in prison since 1961; and her mother committed suicide in 1968. Many years later, while in prison, Wei would write a long letter to Deng Xiaoping (who assumed leadership of China after a power struggle that followed Mao's death) criticizing the Chinese Communist Party for poisoning its people's minds against the Tibetans.

Mao died in 1976, and by 1978, the youth of China had begun to agitate for greater freedom. A focal point for this opposition became the "Democracy Wall," an area near Tienanmen Square in Beijing where students displayed manifestoes called "big-character posters." Particularly noteworthy was a poster by Wei in response to Deng's call for "Four Modernizations": in addition to modernization of areas such as defense and technology, as Deng had outlined, Wei demanded a "Fifth Modernization"—democracy.

He had posted the message, Wei told the *China News Daily* 20 years later, to prove "that not all Chinese were spineless." His poster, written in one night and posted the next day, became particularly popular, and aroused repeated readings and discussions. Wei then wrote his name and address on the poster in the middle of the night, and soon a group of the fiercest agitators for freedom gathered around him. The risks and consequences of such activities, Wei remembered, were quite clear, and he and the others faced them willingly. "In fact," he told Fang Wu in an interview for *China News Digest*, "which country has acquired democracy, freedom, and human rights without hard struggle, and shedding blood and sweat? You could not possibly wait for someone to present you with a democracy. There might have been exceptions with very small countries, but for a major people in the world to achieve democracy, methodical efforts with donations of life, blood, sweat, and pain would be required. Could the Chinese achieve democracy without such donations? Impossible!"

With limited time to act before the inevitable government crackdown, Wei and the small group who joined him proceeded to print and distribute a publication called *Exploration*. As funds were limited, the group took what was considered a highly unusual step: instead of giving away copies of their journal, they sold copies to pay for future issues. Word of the monthly grew, and Wei became so involved in his activities that he had to take an extended leave from his job. A doctor friend wrote him fake medical passes, and when that physician came under scrutiny for it, an elderly doctor stepped in and promised to provide Wei with leave permits.

But Wei knew the end of his freedom was near, and as he told the *China News Daily*, the Chinese withdrawal from the war with Vietnam in March, 1979 signaled the end: "Once the troops were pulled out, I knew it was time to deal with us." He conducted a quick rearguard action, destroying his records. He also met with Ping Ni one last time, and told her that once he was arrested, she would announce that she and Wei had broken off their relationship—thus protecting herself and her family from harm. He was arrested at the end of March, and tried on October 16. Held in various institutions in Beijing, he was routinely denied medical and dental care, and lost a number of his teeth. After five years of imprisonment, he was moved to a labor camp of whose location he was never certain, though it seems to have been in the northwest part of the country. Five more years passed before he was placed in the Nangpu New Life Salt Works in 1989.

Then in 1993, while China was involved in its ultimately unsuccessful bid to host the 2000 Olympics in Beijing, the government announced that Wei would be released a year early. But Wei, physically depleted as he was, refused to accept freedom until the authorities returned to him the large volume of letters he had written over the preceding years but had not been allowed to send. These letters would form the basis for Wei's 1997 publication in the United States, *The Courage to Stand Alone*.

Once he was released from prison on September 14, 1993, Wei returned to his political activities with vigor. Wei's friend and assistant Tong Yi, in her *New York Times* editorial, wrote that Wei met with an American official and told him that "The U.S. should be at least as firm in its position on human rights in China as the Chinese government is." Five days later, both Wei and Tong were arrested. Tong Yi wrote an editorial urging President Clinton in an upcoming meeting with President Jiang, to call for Wei's release. The article was published on September 29, 1997, and six weeks later, on November 16, Wei was released. According to Simon Beck of the *South China Morning Post*, "His release was hailed as a sign of bilateral progress made during the recent Sino-U.S. summit."

On December 5, Columbia University announced that Wei had accepted a position as a visiting scholar in its School of International and Public Affairs, where he would work with Tong Yi.

In a speech at Amnesty International, published in *Index online*, Wei recalled a discussion with a prison guard in which he discovered his purpose in life: "I suddenly realized that my determination to help others was the great cause which had been helping me to withstand physical and mental suffering and helped me maintain my optimism and strength. Once I realized this point, I became aware that I could not shake off my life-long responsibility to other people."

Selected writings

The Courage to Stand Alone: Letters from Prison and Other Writings, edited and translated by Kristina M. Torgeson, Viking Penguin (New York City), 1997.

Sources

On-line

"China Rights Forum," *Human Rights in China*, http://www.igc.apc.org/hric (February 22, 1998).
"Further Information on Wei Jingsheng's Release," *Writers in Prison Committee*, http://www.democracy.org (February 22, 1998).
"A Handful of Pennies" (Amnesty International Address), *Index online*, http://www.oneworld.org (February 22, 1998).
"Interview with Wei Jingsheng," *World News Tonight*, http://www.abcnews.com (February 22, 1998).
"Newsmaker: Wei Jingsheng," *Online Newshour*, http://www.pbs.org (February 22, 1998).

Books

Wei Jingsheng, *The Courage to Stand Alone: Letters from Prison and Other Writings*, edited and translated by Kristina M. Torgeson, Viking Penguin, 1997.

Periodicals

China News Digest, January 15, 1998.
Columbia University Record, December 5, 1997.
New York Times, September 29, 1997.
San Francisco Chronicle, December 23, 1997.
South China Morning Post, November 17, 1997.

—*Judson Knight*

Vivienne Westwood

Archive Photos/Propperfoto

Fashion designer

Born Vivienne Isabel Swire, April 8, 1941, in Glossop, Derbyshire county, England; daughter of Gordon and Dora Swire; married Derek Westwood (a dance hall manager; divorced); married Andreas Kronthaller (a designer and model), 1993; children: (with Westwood) Ben; (with Malcolm McLaren) Joseph Corre. *Education:* Attended Harrow Art School; trained as a teacher.

Addresses: *Home*—Clapham, South London, England. *Office*—Unit 3, Old School House, The Lanterns, Bridge Lane, Battersea, London SW11 3AD, England.

Career

Fashion designer. Schoolteacher, c. 1971. With partner Malcolm McLaren, proprietor of boutique, beginning in 1970 (shop has operated under various names: Let It Rock, 1971, Too Fast to Live, Too Young to Die, 1972, Sex, 1974, Seditionaries, 1977, and World's End, 1980); opened second shop, Nostalgia of Mud, 1982; Mayfair shop opened, 1990; Tokyo shop opened, 1996. First fashion show under own name, 1982. Created Pirate Collection, c. 1980; Savages Collection, 1982; Witches Collection, 1983; mini-crini, 1985; Harris Tweed Collection, 1987; Anglomania Collection, 1992; Cafe Society Collection, 1993; On Liberty, 1994; Erotic Zones, 1994; Vive la Cocotte, 1995; Les Femmes S/S, 1996; MAN Collection, 1996; Storm in a Tea Cup, 1996-97; Red Label Collection, 1997. Professor of fashion, Academy of Applied Arts, Vienna, Austria, 1989-91; professor, Hochschule der Künste-Berlin, 1993—. *Exhibitions:* Retrospective, Galerie Buchholz & Schipper, Cologne, Germany, 1991; retrospective, Bordeaux, France, 1992.

Awards: British Designer of the Year, 1990, 1991; Order of the British Empire (O.B.E.), 1992.

Sidelights

From punk rocker to couture designer, Vivienne Westwood has been an influential force in shaping how people look since the early 1970s. Westwood became famous as the woman who helped dress 1970s punk legends The Sex Pistols, and as co-owner of Sex, the London boutique that catered to the wild-looking, mohawk-and-safety pin crowd. When that fad began to burn out, Westwood swept the fashion world with the New Romantics movement of the early 1980s, with pirate shirts and petticoats. Since her first show under her own name in 1982, she has kept the runways alive with bizarre displays, including "hobo" inspired looks, graffiti-covered sweatshirts, models teetering on (and sometimes falling off of) towering platform shoes, fake fur G-strings, and tweed corsets. Known as an inspiration for many other designers, some credit Westwood solely with the craze of producing undergarments to wear as actual clothing. In the mid-1990s she introduced a number of new collections, including an exclusive Gold Line and less expensive Red Line, the mass-market Anglomania, and a full menswear line, MAN, as well as announcing that she would produce couture, or custom-ordered, pieces.

Westwood was born Vivienne Isabel Swire to Gordon and Dora Swire in Glossop, Derbyshire county, England, on April 8, 1941. Creative at a young age, she experimented with new ways to form letters of the alphabet. Though her mother dressed her conservatively, Westwood's fashion flair reared its head on her first trip to buy her own clothes: she picked out a tight skirt and high heels. Though not vain about her physical looks, she prided herself on the way she clothed herself.

Westwood attended Harrow Art School for one semester then tried a teacher's training college. She married dance hall manager Derek Westwood and had a son, Ben, but she eventually split from Westwood in the early 1970s to pursue a relationship with Malcolm McLaren. With him, she had another son, Joseph Corre, and the couple maintained a professional relationship as well. Westwood and McLaren, who managed the 1970s punk band, The Sex Pistols, designed outrageous gear for the group to wear, creating its then-unique image. The couple decided to open a boutique on King's Road in London in 1970 to feature their work. Initially it was called Let It Rock when it opened in 1971. The shop assumed new identities every couple of years or so, using and discarding the names Too Fast to Live, Too Young to Die, 1972, Sex, 1974, and Seditionaries, 1977. In 1980, it became World's End and has remained so. The store is remembered primarily for the name Sex, its moniker during punk rock's heyday in the mid-1970s, which appeared above the door in pink puffy letters.

Westwood and McLaren's shop catered to the burgeoning London punk scene, later immortalized on postcards featuring the colorfully coiffed youth of the city wearing Westwood's designs, or facsimiles thereof. Clothes were reminiscent of 1950s "teddy boys" and "teddy girls," the rebellious rock-and-roll youth of that era, and also drawn from biker culture and sadomasochistic sex imagery. Mainly offered in black, often in leather, rubber, or pre-ripped fabric, the designs were adorned with decorative zippers, chains, metal studs, and safety pins. "Bondage" shirts and pants were the rage for a while; the shirts were adorned with sleeves that wrapped around like a straitjacket, and the pants were made with straps that could be used to attach the legs together. Westwood was also noted for her fetish-inspired shoes, such as leopard print stiletto heels, monstrous platforms, and multi-buckle and multi-strap boots.

Westwood's T-shirts proved popular as well, with shocking, and at times, profane messages printed on them, some referring to rape and child molestation or instructing people, "F— your mother." Anti-monarchy sentiments were used as well. One classic design was a picture of Queen Elizabeth II with a safety pin piercing her lip; another featured the word "Destroy" superimposed over a swastika and the Queen's face. Westwood was once convicted for selling a pornographic shirt that displayed cowboys with their genitals exposed. The original T-shirts, despite their lewd and offensive nature, have since fetched prices in the hundreds at various auction houses. Though McLaren would later claim to be the brains of the operation, coming up with the slogans for the shirts, Westwood insists that the designs were her own, although she has admitted that McLaren introduced her to the how-to's of putting together a collection.

In 1982, Westwood had her first show under her own name and opened another shop, Nostalgia of Mud. Her designs, meanwhile, were evolving. After the punk look had been exhausted, Westwood in the early 1980s had created a line based on the pirate look, ushering in a new fashion era—the New Romantics movement. Billowy shirts, large buckles, loose-fitting boots, petticoats, and ruffles became the hot ticket. Post-punk singer Adam Ant made the style his trademark, and Westwood also made contributions to the image of British pop stars Boy George (of the Culture Club) and Bananarama. After that, the Witches Collection came out in 1983. Westwood and McLaren dissolved their partnership in 1984, and by the next year, Westwood had abandoned the punk look entirely. She partnered with Carlo D'Amario and continued to be a major name on the runways.

Though Westwood relied heavily on fashions from past decades and even centuries, she was also known to be ahead of her time. In 1985, Westwood showed her "mini-crini," a puffed-out super-short crinoline (a netted slip dating from the Victorian age meant to wear under long skirts to fill them out), paired with a tailored jacket and platform shoes. The ensemble was not warmly received. She was chided for being impractical, a charge that seemed to vindicate critics when supermodel Naomi Campbell fell off of her Westwood platform shoes on the catwalk in 1993. Later, designer Christian Lacroix appropriated the general feel of the mini-crini and popularized the pouf skirt. In addition, some writers have attributed the mid-1990s platform shoe revival to Westwood. Then in 1987, when she showed a lightweight Harris tweed corset on the outside of an outfit, the idea launched an underwear-as-outerwear craze that lasted well into the 1990s. Some of her other groundbreaking work has included a see-through bodysuit with strategically placed fig leaves, a fake fur thong and matching coat, and a barely-there miniskirt, modeled on a topless Kate Moss.

Westwood has always been known for her predilection towards showing off the rounded female form, rather than designing only for youthful, thin women. She took that approach to a hilarious extreme in 1994 when she introduced the padded bottom, a bubbly backside addition to skirts, sweater dresses, and panties. "All in all, it was a very cheeky affair," an article in *Women's Wear Daily* proclaimed. Westwood, meanwhile, was producing with business partner Carlo D'Amario a couple of less outrageous lines. The Gold Line, produced in London, was a higher-priced select group, whereas the Red Line, made in Italy at lower cost, was more affordable and accessible. Also, in 1994 they reorganized Vivienne Westwood Ltd. to offer accessories such as shoes and purses.

Westwood's popularity blossomed in the mid-1990s. A *Women's Wear Daily* article from October of 1994 commented that "the Westwood collection looks better than it ever has," and added that the designs were becoming more commercial. She had not stopped creating her more peculiar pieces, however. One 1994 show featured a tight black velvet corset as well as a skirt whose fabric was pushed up in the front. In 1996, the designer opened up her first shop outside of England in Tokyo, Japan. Also that year she showed her first full line of menswear, MAN, and announced that she was beginning a couture (made-to-order) line. In early 1997, she signed a fragrance license deal with German beauty firm Lancaster.

Westwood drew fire in 1997 with her first show in London in over six years, but not for her designs. The British media were flustered by the models: private school girls as young as age 13. Later that year, Westwood decided, however, to target that market rather than hire them. In a decidedly more commercial move than ever before, she revealed a new line, Anglomania. For it, she drew upon some of her favorite work dating from 1970 to her current fashions, reworking them for a lower-priced mass market line. The clothes were made out of mainstream fabrics, with 35 percent of the line consisting of denim, but also using jersey, cotton, Lycra spandex blends, and knits. Anglomania was made up of 60 percent women's wear, included shoes, hats, bags, belts, and jewelry, and was manufactured and distributed by the Italian firm GTR. Jeans were expected to start at $48, with tops ranging from $27 to $96. "We want **Vivienne**

Westwood to become a label and not just a designer," remarked Vivienne Westwood, Ltd. sales and marketing director Christopher di Pietro in *Women's Wear Daily*. "The awareness of the brand will become much, much bigger, because of this and the launch of our perfume next year. So we expect a boom in sales of all our lines."

Westwood continued to woo the runway set, however. Robert Lohrer in the *Daily News Record* described her 1998 men's collection as "the personification of pheasant under glass." He noted that models resembled peacocks, with eye-masks reminiscent of the Lone Ranger, billowy structures, and brightly colored faux leopard print. He deemed the show entertaining, saying, "Westwood's production, as they have been in the past, was equal part fashion and equal part show. It was unabashed pomp, pageantry, and costume." Westwood herself explained to Lohrer, "What I think my clothes have to offer is that they're dynamic. They give empowerment to the people who wear them. People can express themselves through the clothes."

Divorced from her first husband, Derek Westwood, during her early career, Westwood had a son, Ben, with him. She and McLaren also had a son, Joseph Corre. Westwood taught classes at the Academy of Applied Arts in Vienna, Austria, from 1989 to 1991, and has been a professor at the Hochschule der Künste-Berlin since 1993. Also in 1993, she married one of her students, Andreas Kronthaller, who is younger than Westwood by 25 years. He helps her with designs and struts the catwalk in her menswear lines. Westwood has lived in Clapham, South London, for over twenty years.

Sources

Books

Contemporary Fashion, St. James Press, 1995.

Periodicals

Daily News Record, August 22, 1996, p. 8; July 2, 1997, p. 2; January 16, 1998, p. 12.
Sunday Times (London), August 18, 1996, p. S3.
Vogue, September 1994, p. 187.
Women's Wear Daily, March 7, 1994, p. 5; September 13, 1994, p. 20; September 16, 1994, p. 12; October 13, 1994, p. 5; July 21, 1995, p. 5; August 20, 1996, p. 2; September 17, 1996, p. 1; January 24, 1997, p. 1; February 24, 1997, p. 8; July 18, 1997, p. 2; August 28, 1997, p. 1.

—*Geri Speace*

Elie Wiesel

Archive Photos

Author

Full name, Eliezer Wiesel; born September 30, 1928, in Sighet, Romania; came to the United States, 1956, naturalized U.S. citizen, 1963; son of Shlomo (a grocer) and Sarah (Feig) Wiesel; married Marion Erster Rose, 1969; children: Shlomo Elisha. *Education:* Attended Sorbonne, University of Paris, 1948-51. *Religion:* Jewish.

Addresses: *Office*—University Professors, Boston University, 745 Commonwealth Ave., Boston, MA 02215. *Agent*—Georges Borchardt, 136 East 57th St., New York, NY 10022.

Career

Arche, Paris, France, journalist, c. 1949-52; *Yediot Ahronot*, Tel Aviv, Israel, journalist, 1952-56; *Jewish Daily Forward*, New York City, journalist, then later foreign correspondent, 1957—; City College of the City University of New York, New York City, distinguished professor, 1972-76; Boston University, Boston, MA, Andrew Mellon professor in the humanities, 1976—; Whitney Humanities Center, Yale University, New Haven, CT, Henry Luce visiting scholar in Humanities and Social Thought, 1982-83; Florida International University, Miami, distinguished visiting professor of literature and philosophy, 1982. Chairman, United States President's Commission on the Holocaust.

Awards: Prix Rivarol, 1963; Remembrance Award, 1965, for *The Town beyond the Wall* and all other writings; William and Janice Epstein Fiction Award, Jewish Book Council, 1965, for *The Town beyond the Wall*; Jewish Heritage Award, 1966, for excellence in litera-

ture; Prix Medicis, 1969, for *Le Mendiant de Jerusalem*; Prix Bordin, French Academy, 1972; Eleanor Roosevelt Memorial Award, 1972; American Liberties Medallion, American Jewish Committee, 1972; Frank and Ethel S. Cohen Award, Jewish Book Council, 1973, for *Souls on Fire*; Martin Luther King, Jr., Award, City College of the City University of New York, 1973; Faculty Distinguished Scholar Award, Hofstra University, 1973-74; Joseph Prize for Human Rights, Anti-Defamation League of B'nai B'rith, 1978; Zalman Shazar Award, State of Israel, 1979; Jabotinsky Medal, State of Israel, 1980; Prix Livre-International, 1980, and Prix des Bibliothecaires, 1981, both for *Le Testament d'un poete juif assassine*; Anatoly Scharansky Humanitarian Award, 1983; Congressional Gold Medal, 1984; humanitarian award, International League for Human Rights, 1985; Freedom Cup award, Women's League of Israel, 1986; Nobel Peace Prize, 1986; Special Christopher Book Award, 1987; achievement award, Artists and Writers for Peace in the Middle East, 1987; Profiles of Courage Award, B'nai B'rith, 1987; Human Rights Law Award, International Human Rights Law Group, 1988; S. Y. Agnon Gold Medal.

Member: Amnesty International, PEN, Authors League, Foreign Press Association (honorary lifetime member), Writers and Artists for Peace in the Middle

East, Royal Norwegian Society of Sciences and Letters, Phi Beta Kappa.

Sidelights

Holocaust survivor Elie Wiesel, whose 1960 memoir *Night* relates the torture and atrocities he endured and witnessed as a prisoner in Nazi concentration camps and is widely considered one of the finest and most powerful works of Holocaust literature, has continued his pledge to speak out on behalf of all persecuted peoples and take action to end oppression worldwide. Wiesel, who was awarded the Nobel Peace Prize in 1986 for his "commitment, which originated in the suffering of the Jewish people, [and] has been widened to embrace all oppressed people and races," has also authored *All Rivers Run to the Sea*, the first half of a promised two-part memoir. The 1995 work examines some of the same material in *Night*, but provides a broader view of the author's life, including a depiction of what life was like for him in his orthodox Jewish community prior to his imprisonment and what life was like for him following his release. The inclusion of this material, according to the *New York Times*'s Michiko Kakutani, leaves readers "with a profound sense of how an entire community was brutally erased by the Nazis without warning, how abruptly the mundane business of work and study and play gave way to unimaginable horror." *Memoir in Two Voices*, a 1996 volume on which Wiesel collaborated with former French President Francois Mitterrand, offered a glimpse into the life of the French leader, with Wiesel asking sometimes provocative questions of Mitterrand, including his knowledge of the treatment of Jews during World War II. In May 1997 Wiesel was appointed as a member of a board in charge of overseeing a fund to supply financial aid to Holocaust victims.

Eliezer Wiesel was born on September 30, 1928, in Sighet, Romania, a well-known center of Jewish culture near Transylvania. His parents, Shlomo and Sarah Feig Wiesel, were dedicated to their religious life and encouraged Elie to learn all he could about the teachings of the Hasidic masters, the traditions of the Torah, Talmud, and Kabbala, and to master Hebrew and Yiddish. Wiesel's childhood and early adolescence were spent in the warm, supportive, traditional environment of his orthodox Jewish family and community. When Nazi forces arrived in 1944, the ideal life Wiesel had been living was cut horrifically short as all of the approximately 15,000 Jews living in Sighet were forced into cattle cars and taken by train to the concentration camp known as Auschwitz, in Poland. Wiesel, then 15 years old, was able to stay with his father at the camp, but the two men were separated from the women in their family, Wiesel's mother and three sisters, upon their arrival at Auschwitz. When Nazi officials learned that Soviet troops were nearing Auschwitz in early 1945, Wiesel and his father were forced to march to the camp known as Buchenwald. It was at Buchenwald that Wiesel witnessed his father's death from starvation and dysentery; later, after the camp was liberated in April 1945, Wiesel learned that his mother and one sister, Tzipora, had been murdered in Auschwitz's gas chambers, while his other sisters, Hilda and Batya, had managed to survive. Wiesel would not be reunited with his sisters until years later.

Following the liberation of Buchenwald, Wiesel wanted to travel to Palestine, but because of immigration restrictions he was placed on a train bound for Belgium, a train which was subsequently rerouted to France, at the insistence of General Charles de Gaulle, who wanted to provide shelter for the homeless in France. Wiesel first lived in Normandy, but then moved to Paris and studied literature at the Sorbonne. Later he became a reporter for the French-Jewish periodical *Arche* and was sent to Israel on assignment. In 1952 Wiesel began working as a reporter for *Yediot Ahronot*, a newspaper in Tel Aviv, and in 1954 he conducted an interview with Roman Catholic novelist and Nobel laureate Francois Mauriac, who convinced Wiesel to relate his wartime experiences so that the world would find out first-hand about the atrocities that had been committed by the Nazis. In 1956 Wiesel completed an 800-page memoir entitled *Un di Velt Hot Geshvign*, which eventually was condensed into the slimmer volume, 1956's *La Nuit*, which was then translated into English and published as *Night* in 1958.

Wiesel traveled to New York City in 1956 as a United Nations correspondent for *Yediot Ahronot*, and was injured after being hit by a taxicab. Because of his injuries, which kept him confined to a wheelchair for almost a year, Wiesel was unable to return overseas, and when his French travel papers expired he applied for and received U.S. citizenship. After recovering from his accident, Wiesel went to work for the *Jewish Daily Forward* in 1957. Beginning with *Night*, Wiesel wrote numerous books, some fiction, others nonfiction, based on his memories of the Holocaust; the books were initially published in French, but were quickly translated and published in English. For Wiesel, telling his stories was a way to honor those who had survived, honor those who had perished, and ensure that such a tragedy would never be repeated. In 1969 Wiesel married Marion Erster Rose, a fellow Holocaust survivor who became the primary

English translator of his works. He became a respected educator as well, serving on the faculties of the City College of the City University of New York and Boston University, where he was named the Andrew Mellon professor in the humanities in 1976. Later Wiesel received the honor of being named the chairman of the United States President's Commission on the Holocaust.

Night, Wiesel's most famous work, was published in English in 1960, and has since been hailed as one of the defining works of Holocaust literature. In the volume, Wiesel relates the horrors he witnessed while imprisoned at Auschwitz and Buchenwald, and expresses his feelings of guilt because he had survived and anger at God, who he blamed for allowing the destruction of His devoted followers. The emotional tone of *Night* was carried over into Wiesel's next novels, *Dawn* and *The Accident,* both of which concern Holocaust survivors whose faith in God has been shaken and who must try to find meaning in their suffering before they can feel hopeful about their future and feel positive about God and humanity.

"No one is as capable of gratitude as one who has emerged from the kingdom of night. We know that every moment is a moment of grace, every hour an offering; not to share them would mean to betray them. Our lives no longer belong to us alone; they belong to all those who need us desperately."

In his later novels, Wiesel continued to offer narratives dealing with the experiences of Holocaust survivors, but focused more upon issues of morality rather than questions of faith in God and humanity. In novels such as *The Town Beyond the Wall, The Gates of the Forest,* and *The Fifth Son,* Wiesel's survivors choose between life and death, apathy and action, and suffering and mercy. Beginning in the mid-1960s, Wiesel expanded his literary scope and wrote nonfiction books that raised awareness of contemporary oppression of Jews in such places as the former Soviet Union. *The Jews of Silence, Legends of Our Time,* and *One Generation After* are all works of nonfiction which

examine the effects of persecution on various peoples worldwide. In his 1976 collection *A Jew Today* Wiesel presented autobiographical sketches, essays, and dialogues that communicated a sense of shame about the past and careful optimism for the future of the Jewish people. In this volume he asserted that contemporary Jews have a responsibility to remain aware of their history and to keep it alive in the public consciousness by "singing ... louder and louder." Wiesel has also written books—*Souls on Fire, Four Hasidic Masters and Their Struggle against Melancholy, Five Biblical Figures,* and *Somewhere a Master*—on biblical and religious issues, specifically examining Jewish biblical figures and legends and the relevance of Judaism in modern times.

In an essay in *Contemporary Authors Autobiography Series,* Wiesel commented: "What have I learned since I began to write? I have learned that the literature of the Holocaust has this in common with the Holocaust: they do not change people, they only intensify them: the good become better and the bad worse. But there are exceptions, happily. There are surprises, and then words become prayers. I am still waiting." Some critics have argued that Wiesel's works should be considered discussions on historical, moral, and religious topics rather than as literature, but most commentators have praised the author for providing powerfully affecting literature. Reviewers have applauded Wiesel's ability to produce sensitive, insightful works which illuminate human behavior, his straightforward, self-revealing approach, and his objectivity in examining the effects of the Holocaust and modern Jewish thought. Aside from questions of literary merit, Wiesel's works are almost unanimously acknowledged as among the most heartfelt and poignant of works by Holocaust survivors.

In addition to his writings and speeches regarding the persecution of Jews both past and present, Wiesel has made an effort to speak out on behalf of all persecuted people, regardless of their race, religion, or national origin. He has taken up the cause of victims of apartheid in South Africa, of political prisoners such as Nelson Mandela and Andrei Sakharov, and of victims of "ethnic cleansing" in the war in Bosnia. At the dedication of the United States Holocaust Memorial Museum in 1993 Wiesel stirred up some controversy with his admonishment of President Bill Clinton over what he perceived to be the leader's indifference to the war in Bosnia. In an interview with Cable News Network (CNN) correspondent Joel Hochmuth, Wiesel commented on his drive to speak out about oppression regardless of the consequences: "I tell you," Wiesel asserted, "I have a luxury which I've always had. I can speak my mind. What do I have to lose, really?

What can people do to me?" Following the incident at the Holocaust Museum Wiesel and Clinton arrived at a level of mutual respect and understanding. Wiesel told Hochmuth, "That is really how I began my relationship with the president. And we became close and I like him."

Wiesel was awarded the Nobel Peace Prize in 1986, because as Nobel Committee chair Egel Aarvik asserted, Wiesel "has emerged as one of the most spiritual leaders and guides in an age when violence, repression and racism continue to characterize the world.... Wiesel is a messenger to Mankind. His message is one of peace, atonement, and human dignity. His belief that the forces fighting evil in the world can be victorious is a hard-won belief." In his Nobel Peace Prize acceptance speech delivered on December 10, 1986, Wiesel expressed his feelings about receiving the award, revealing that he felt frightened to accept the award on behalf of the Jews murdered during World War II because he knew that "no one may really speak for the dead, no one may interpret their mutilated dreams and visions." He also added that he was pleased to accept the award because he knew that "this honor belongs to all the survivors and their children, and through us, to the Jewish people with whose destiny I have always identified." Wiesel concluded his speech by expressing his "deepest gratitude," and declaring that "[n]o one is as capable of gratitude as one who has emerged from the kingdom of night. We know that every moment is a moment of grace, every hour an offering; not to share them would mean to betray them. Our lives no longer belong to us alone; they belong to all those who need us desperately."

In 1995, *All Rivers Run to the Sea*, the first part of what was projected to be Wiesel's two-part memoir, was published. The volume was greeted with enthusiasm by critics who asserted that although Wiesel's earlier autobiography, *Night*, was powerful and moving, *All Rivers* was perhaps even more profound because of the maturity, the lifetime of experience, and the years of perspective with which the author was able to enhance the narrative. The *New York Times*'s Michiko Kakutani noted a "new richness of emotional detail" in *All Rivers*, and a highly favorable review in *Publishers Weekly* concluded: "This haunting, impassioned book will make you cry yet, somehow, leave you renewed with a cautious hope for humanity's future." Although most critics offered similarly positive assessments of *All Rivers Run to the Sea*, some critics objected to what they characterized as Wiesel promoting himself and disparaging others, using his memoir as an opportunity to get revenge on celebrities and other notable people who had maligned him in the past. The *New Leader*'s

James E. Young, who acknowledged the complaints over Wiesel's treatment of himself and others in *All Rivers*, concluded his review by defending Wiesel, arguing: "Rather than taking Wiesel to task for his part in nourishing our culture's voracious appetite for celebrity victims, we need to ask whether it is possible today to speak out effectively on behalf of the world's oppressed without having a gift for public relations. After all, had every witness obeyed our society's squeamish laws of decorum and taste, the Holocaust might have remained an untold story altogether."

In 1996 *Memoir in Two Voices*, which Wiesel coauthored with his friend, former French President Francois Mitterrand, was published. The volume offers a glimpse into the life of the former leader, who served as France's president from 1981 to 1995; the topics covered are driven by Wiesel's questions, which are intended to elicit explanations from Mitterrand. The book was characterized by a *Publishers Weekly* reviewer as containing insights into Mitterrand's personal life that were "as fascinating for their revelations as they [were] for their silences," indicating that the book did not probe as deeply into the mind of the French leader as the critic would have liked. Bonnie Smothers, reviewing *Memoir in Two Voices* for *Booklist*, assessed the section of the book in which Wiesel questions Mitterrand about the leader's knowledge of the Nazis' treatment of Jews during World War II as providing "a very enlightening exchange" between the two authors, and called the volume as a whole "a very special book, powerful at times, always provoking the reader's inner thoughts."

Wiesel's 1997 appointment as a member of the board that oversees a Swiss fund designed to aid Holocaust survivors was not only a reflection of his reputation as a spokesperson for survivors but also an indication of his continuing efforts to act in their behalf. The author has also kept himself at the forefront of the battle to return riches stolen from Jews by the Nazis during World War II to the survivors of the Holocaust. In a February 1997 *U.S. News & World Report* article on the subject of revealing truths about apartheid in South Africa, Jerelyn Eddings quoted Wiesel, who had addressed an audience at the U.S. Holocaust Museum with the following words: "There is no compensation for what happened. But at least a certain balance can be established that opposing fear there is hope, hope that when we remember the fear ... our memory becomes a shield for the future." That Wiesel firmly believes that his efforts and the efforts of others like him to educate the public about the Holocaust and to keep the memory of its devastation alive in the public consciousness will prevent such a tragedy from recurring was evident when he told CNN's Joel Hochmuth: "There I am an optimist. I think it cannot happen again. I think the Holocaust was a unique event, therefore it will remain unique."

Selected writings

Un Di Velt Hot Geshvign (title means "And the World Has Remained Silent"), [Buenos Aires], 1956, abridged French translation published as *La Nuit*, foreword by Francois Mauriac, Editions de Minuit, 1958, English translation by Stella Rodway published as *Night*, Hill & Wang, 1960.

L'Aube, Editions du Seuil, 1961, translation by Frances Frenaye published as *Dawn*, Hill & Wang, 1961.

Le Jour, Editions du Seuil, 1961, translation by Anne Borchardt published as *The Accident*, Hill & Wang, 1962.

La Ville de la Chance, Editions du Seuil, 1962, translation by Stephen Becker published as *The Town beyond the Wall*, Atheneum, 1964, new edition, Holt, 1967.

Les Portes de la foret, Editions du Seuil, 1964, translation published as *The Gates of the Forest*, Holt, 1966.

Le Chant des morts, Editions du Seuil, 1966, translation published as *Legends of Our Time*, Holt, 1968.

The Jews of Silence: A Personal Report on Soviet Jewry (nonfiction; originally published in Hebrew as a series of articles for the newspaper *Yedioth Ahronoth*), translation and afterword by Neal Kozodoy, Holt, 1966, 2nd edition, Vallentine, Mitchell, 1973.

Zalmen; ou, la Folie de Dieu (play), 1966, translation by Lily and Nathan Edelman published as *Zalmen; or, The Madness of God*, Holt, 1968.

Le Mendiant de Jerusalem, 1968, translation by the author and L. Edelman published as *A Beggar in Jerusalem*, Random House, 1970.

La Nuit, Le Jour, Editions du Seuil, 1969, translation published as *The Accident: Three Tales*, Hill & Wang, 1972, reprinted as *The Night Trilogy: Night, Dawn, The Accident*, Farrar, Straus, 1987, translation by Rodway published as *Night, Dawn, Day*, Aronson, 1985.

Entre deux soleils, Editions du Seuil, 1970, translation by the author and L. Edelman published as *One Generation After*, Random House, 1970.

Celebration Hassidique: Portraits et legendes, Editions du Seuil, 1972, translation by wife, Marion Wiesel, published as *Souls on Fire: Portraits and Legends of Hasidic Masters*, Random House, 1972.

Le Serment de Kolvillag, Editions du Seuil, 1973, translation by M. Wiesel published as *The Oath*, Random House, 1973.

Ani maamin: A Song Lost and Found Again (cantata), music composed by Darius Milhaud, Random House, 1974.

Celebration Biblique: Portraits et legendes, Editions du Seuil, 1975, translation by M. Wiesel published as *Messengers of God: Biblical Portraits and Legends*, Random House, 1976.

Un Juif aujourd'hui: Recits, essais, dialogues, Editions du Seuil, 1977, translation by M. Wiesel published as *A Jew Today*, Random House, 1978.

(With others) *Dimensions of the Holocaust*, Indiana University Press, 1977.

Four Hasidic Masters and Their Struggle against Melancholy, University of Notre Dame Press, 1978.

Le Proces de Shamgorod tel qu'il se deroula le 25 fevrier 1649: Piece en trois actes, Editions du Seuil, 1979, translation by M. Wiesel published as *The Trial of God (as It Was Held on February 25, 1649, in Shamgorod): A Play in Three Acts*, Random House, 1979.

Images from the Bible, illustrated and with paintings by Shalom of Safed, Overlook Press, 1980.

Le Testament d'un poete Juif assassine, Editions du Seuil, 1980, translation by M. Wiesel published as *The Testament*, Simon & Schuster, 1981.

Five Biblical Portraits, University of Notre Dame Press, 1981.

Somewhere a Master, Simon & Schuster, 1982, reprinted as *Somewhere a Master: Further Tales of the Hasidic Masters*, Summit Books, 1984.

Paroles d'etranger, Editions du Seuil, 1982.

The Golem: The Story of a Legend as Told by Elie Wiesel (fiction), illustrated by Mark Podwal, Summit Books, 1983.

Le Cinquieme Fils, Grasset (Paris), 1983, translation by M. Wiesel published as *The Fifth Son*, Summit Books, 1985.

Against Silence: The Voice and Vision of Elie Wiesel, three volumes, edited by Irving Abrahamson, Holocaust Library, 1985.

Signes d'exode, Grasset & Fasquelle (Paris), 1985.

Job ou Dieu dans la tempete, Grasset & Fasquelle, 1986.

Le Crepuscule au loin, Grasset & Fasquelle, 1987, translation by M. Wiesel published as *Twilight*, Summit Books, 1988.

(With Albert H. Friedlander) *The Six Days of Destruction*, Paulist Press, 1989.

L'Oublie: Roman, Seuil, 1989.

(With Philippe-Michael de Saint-Cheron) *Evil and Exile*, translated by Jon Rothschild, University of Notre Dame Press, 1990.

The Forgotten (novel), translated by Stephen Becker, Summit, 1992.

All Rivers Run to the Sea: Memoirs, Knopf, 1995.

(With Francois Mitterrand) *Memoir in Two Voices*, translated by Richard Seaver and Timothy Bent, Arcade, 1996.

Sources

On-line

Cable News Network (CNN) Interactive, http://www.cnn.com (November 1997).

Nobel Prize Internet Archive, http://www.almaz.com (November 1997).

U.S. News & World Report Online, February 10, 1997, http://www.usnewscom/usnews/issue/10week.hm (November 1997).

Books

Contemporary Authors Autobiography Series, Volume 4, Gale Research, 1986.

Wiesel, Elie, *A Jew Today,* translated by Marion Wiesel, Random House, 1978.

Periodicals

Booklist, July 1996, p. 1798.

New Leader, December 18, 1995, p. 17.

New York Times, December 5, 1995.

Publishers Weekly, October 16, 1995, p. 49; May 20, 1996.

—*Lynn M. Spampinato*

Venus Williams

Professional tennis player

Born Venus Ebone Starr Williams, June 17, 1980, in Los Angeles, CA; daughter of Richard (a security-business owner and daughters' coach) and Oracene (a nurse) Williams. *Religion:* Jehovah's Witness.

Addresses: *Home*—Palm Beach Gardens, FL.

Career

Played junior tennis until 1991; became professional tennis player, October, 1994.

Sidelights

When Venus Williams made her debut in professional women's tennis in 1994, the *New York Times*'s Robin Finn called her "the most unorthodox tennis prodigy her sport has ever seen." Three years later, the seventeen-year-old, six-foot-two-inch athlete was an international celebrity: photographs of Williams with the beads in her cornrowed hair clicking through the air, her face a study in determination as her racket smacked the ball to her opponent, were some of the most memorable of the 1997 tennis season. Though she enjoyed success at Wimbledon and the U.S. Open, her opponents were often younger and had been playing competitive tennis longer; moreover, the blunt remarks of Williams's outspoken father sometimes overshadowed her rising star.

Williams was born in the Watts area of Los Angeles in June of 1980, the fourth of Richard and Oracene Williams's five daughters. Richard Williams was part-owner of a security business, and her mother was a

nurse. A few years later the family moved from Watts to nearby Compton. All five Williams daughters played tennis as youngsters, but the two youngest, Venus and Serena, were outstanding players from an early age. Compton was a city somewhat infamous for its troubles with gang-related activity, and the girls practiced the game at a court in a park that gang members frequented. Nevertheless, Venus Williams began entering competitions, went unbeaten in 63 games, and by the age of ten had won the Southern California girls' title in the under-12 division.

Both *Sports Illustrated* and *Tennis* magazine noticed Williams's talent, and ran stories on her in the summer of 1991 calling her "tennis's newest pixie" and "a prodigy." Her father contacted Rick Macci, a tennis coach in Florida, and asked him to come to Compton to meet his daughter and judge her potential. "I hear it all the time: `I've got the next Jennifer [Capriati],'" Macci told *Tennis* magazine's David Higdon. "Richard said he'd like to meet me but the only thing he could promise me was that I wouldn't get shot. All I could think of was: `Who is this guy?'" he recalled. Early one morning Richard drove the visiting Macci to the park. "There must have been 30 guys there already playing basketball and another 20 lying on the grass passed out," Macci recollected in *Tennis* magazine. He played a few games with Venus, and was unimpressed. Then, he remembered, she "asks to go to the bathroom and as she walks out the gate, she walks at least 10 yards on her hands. Then she went into these backward cartwheels for another 10 yards. I'm watching this and the first thing I thought was: 'I've got a female Michael Jordan on my hands.'"

> *"I never thought anyone was better than me.... Once you do that, you lose."*

The Williams family moved to Florida when Venus enrolled in Macci's tennis academy there. She also withdrew from junior tennis that year at the age of 11. Instead of mixing practice with the competition circuit, Williams stayed put, was schooled at home, and practiced six hours a day, six times a week. She did this for four years—a decision, Macci said, that Williams and her family had made based on her unique temperament. "Putting her in a traditional development system would be like putting her in prison," the coach told Finn in the *New York Times*. When she was thirteen, companies were already contacting Williams and her family to offer endorsement contracts if she did turn pro.

Tennis-watchers wondered when Williams would succumb to the lure—some young women in tennis entered professional competition at the age of fourteen, dropping out of school and playing the tournament circuit, and earning large sums of money either by winning prize purses or by signing lucrative product endorsement contracts. It was a potentially disastrous situation for many young players. Richard Williams appeared on the ABC news program *Nightline* in the summer of 1994, after former preteen tennis prodigy Jennifer Capriati was arrested and faced drug charges, declaring he'd never allow Venus to turn pro at such a young age. He was criticized, however for wearing a hat and vest with both bearing the logo of a sports-energy food product during the television interview.

Surprisingly, Williams turned pro just a few months later. Her debut came in October of 1994 at the Bank of the West Classic in Oakland, California. There, the fourteen-year-old beat the woman ranked Number 59 in the world, Shaun Stafford, then went on to give Arantxa Sanchez Vicario—women tennis's Number 2 player—a good game before losing. "She's going to be great for women's tennis," Stafford told the *New York*

Times's Finn. Some wondered, however, why Williams had suddenly entered the professional circuit, but new rules adopted by the Women's Tennis Council of the World Tennis Association at the time may have provided just cause. After the close of 1994, fourteen-year-olds were barred from turning pro, and young women under 18 who entered the competition level from 1995 onward were limited in the number of tournaments in which they could participate.

Though she had skated into the professional level exempt from these rules, Williams restricted her schedule anyway. She stayed in school and did not appear again on the pro circuit until an August 1995 event, the Acura Classic in Manhattan Beach, California; she lost in the first round. Some tennis analysts noted that because she lacked the junior-tournament experience, Williams had not learned to inject a competitive edge to her game. Her father has tried to rectify this, sometimes by rooting against her in public matches. Conversely, he told *New York Times Magazine* writer Pat Jordan, "Every time she loses, I pay her $50."

As the *New York Times Magazine* profile pointed out, however, the dedicated fathers of women's tennis are sometimes problematic: Steffi Graf's father was charged with tax evasion, and she herself was nearly arrested for complicity; and an American teenage player, Mary Pierce, had to obtain a court restraining order against her parent. Richard Williams was well aware of the dangers of the sport on young women, though, and controlled his daughter's career in order to avoid problems. He saw the lesson in Capriati, who turned pro at 14. "At 15, she lost her smile," he told Jordan in the *New York Times Magazine*. "At 16, there were problems. What happened? I want to make sure that doesn't happen to my kids," he added.

Williams's younger sister, Serena, also showed great promise as a player. Richard Williams predicted that some day the pair would have to play against one another for the women's world title; in January of 1998 Venus defeated Serena in their first professional pairing at the Australian Open. However, Richard Williams often received more press than either of his daughters. "Richard Williams has been called a 'liar' and 'genius' and everything in between," wrote Higdon in *Tennis* magazine. The senior Williams asserted that his family did not receive any endorsement money from wearing the logo-emblazoned clothing of one sportswear maker at public appearances, but a spokesperson for the company said they had indeed paid him a consultant's fee. Yet Williams has also been lauded for shepherding his daughter's career down a non-traditional path that kept the focus on her education and allowed her to mature outside of the competitive pressures of the pro circuit. Newspaper reportage about Venus Williams often remarks on her self-assuredness and impressive vocabulary. Her father and coach Macci, declared Finn in the *New York Times*, "have produced a player who appears to possess wit and wisdom beyond her years—with a serve, volley, and vocabulary to match."

Again, Williams stayed out of the limelight for much of 1996, and in the spring of 1997 made her debut at the French Open. A month later, as she turned seventeen, she traveled to England for Wimbledon, perhaps the sport's most famous tournament. Serena and Oracene Williams came with her to lend support, but her father stayed home. She received a great deal of attention, but had a poor showing and lost to Magdalena Grzybowska. "By the time it was over ... Williams stood revealed as a huge talent with little idea of how to adjust to an opponent or adversity," wrote S. L. Price in *Sports Illustrated*. She remained imperturbable, though. "It's my first Wimbledon," she told reporters. "There will be many more," she added, according to *Sports Illustrated*.

Her father asserted in the *New York Times Magazine* that his daughter's "only weakness is she's overconfident." Williams's U.S. Open performance in the late summer of 1997 went somewhat better: she advanced from 66th to 25th in the rankings in one day. "Williams's progress as a player was undeniable; almost overnight she had become a force every player but one fears," wrote Price in *Sports Illustrated*, referring to Martina Hingis, who would take home the title. Both young women were the same age, but Hingis had far more professional competition experience. Still, insiders predicted future greatness for Williams. Pam Shriver, a former U.S. Open titleholder, once played in a training match against Serena and Venus, and she told Higdon in *Tennis* magazine that Venus "didn't know tactically how to play points yet, but she had weapons and has this natural way of intimidating."

Unfortunately, Williams's U.S. Open showing was clouded by charges of racism. Her father, in a telephone interview, told journalists that some of the other players had directed racial epithets toward his daughter. Gracefully, the teenager tried to deflect attention from the potential furor at a press conference, but her father's comments caused some watchers of the sport to note this may limit her chances of obtaining endorsement contracts. Other African American players have hinted that subtle discrimination does indeed occur in what has been called a "country-club" sport, and some of Williams's white competitors on the divarife circuit have accused her of not smiling, or of not being friendly enough. "Why don't you guys tell me what they want me to do?" she queried reporters at one press conference, according to *Sports Illustrated*. "They should come up to me and say, 'Venus, I want you to smile so I can feel better,'" she continued.

Despite the excitement of being a tennis prodigy, Williams remains a rather ordinary—though somewhat extraordinarily intelligent and athletically gifted—teenager. She lives with her family in Palm Beach Gardens, is close to sister Serena, and along with the rest of her family is a practicing Jehovah's Witness. She plans to become a paleontologist, listens to Rage Against the Machine, and has a shed-full of toys that include a drum kit and a full-sized surfboard. Regarding the game of tennis, however, she does concede some recognition of her own ability. "I never thought anyone was better than me," she told Finn in the *New York Times* when she was still ranked No. 211. "Once you do that, you lose," she added.

Sources

New York Times, November 1, 1994, p. B10; November 2, 1994, p. B9; March 10, 1997, p. C2; September 7, 1997; September 9, 1997.

New York Times Magazine, March 16, 1997.

Sport, February 1995, p. 14.

Sports Illustrated, June 13, 1994, p. 10; November 14, 1994, pp. 30-32; July 7, 1997, p. 26; September 15, 1997, pp. 32.

Tennis, July 1997, pp. 46-55.

USA Weekend, April 10-12, 1998, pp. 4-5.

—Carol Brennan

B. D. Wong

Actor, playwright, and Asian-American activist

Born Bradley Darryl Wong, October 4, 1962, in San Francisco, CA; son of William D. and Roberta Christine (Leong) Wong. *Education:* Attended college briefly.

Addresses: *Office*—Agency for the Performing Arts, 888 Seventh Ave., New York, NY 10019.

Career

Stage credits include *Anything Goes; Androcles and the Lion*, 1982; *M. Butterfly*, 1988; *The Tempest*, 1989; *A Chorus Line;* and *La Cage Aux Folles.* Film appearances include *The Karate Kid II*, 1986; *Family Business*, 1989; *The Freshman*, 1990; *Mystery Date*, and *Father of the Bride*, both 1991; *And The Band Played On* and *Jurassic Park*, both 1993; *The Ref*, 1994; *Father of the Bride, Part II* and *Men of War*, both 1995; *Executive Decision*, 1996; *Seven Years in Tibet*, 1997; and *Slappy and the Stinkers* and *Substitute II*, both 1998. Has appeared in television movies, including *Crash Course, Goodnight Sweet Wife: A Murder in Boston*, and *Judith Krantz's 'Dazzle';* appeared on an episode of *The X-Files*; as Stuart, *All-American Girl* (series), ABC, 1994; and as Father Ray Mukada, *Oz* (series), HBO, 1997—. Also speaks on Asian-American identity issues.

Awards: Antoinette Perry Award, Drama Desk Award, Clarence Derwent Award, Outer Critics Circle Award, and *Theatre World* Award, all c. 1988, all for *M. Butterfly;* Asian Pacific Council recognition, entertainment category, Mainstream America, 1992.

Member: Actors Equity Association, Screen Actors Guild, American Federation of Television and Radio Artists, Asian Pacific Alliance for Greater Equality (founder), Alliance of Resident Theatres (member of board of directors).

Sidelights

Besides acting, B. D. Wong spends much time campaigning for equality and emphasizing the importance of identity for Asian Americans. Still, as he told Gerard Raymond in his article on the internet, he would love the chance to wear a stereotypical Chinese outfit and talk with a funny accent one day. "I can't wait for the time when I can make fun of my culture and my heritage, ... but that can't be done until there is a ground-level awareness that we are all equal. Only then can we have a good time fooling around," Wong declared to Raymond. Often having to remind directors to avoid certain stereotypical presentations and prejudicial attitudes, Wong has earned a reputation as a talented actor who can transcend even the worst roles in poorly-reviewed films. While making a name for himself as an actor, probably the most important role Wong has taken on is his one as an activist for Asian-American artists.

Bradley Darryl Wong was born and raised in San Francisco, California, in 1962, and acknowledges dealing with issues of self-image at an early age. He speaks to audiences about his personal struggles with his Asian-American identity and notes that growing up during the time of John F. Kennedy's assassination, the war in Vietnam, and raging civil rights battles contributed to his fear of never being perceived as equal. Wong diagnosed his afflictions as "racial anorexia" in terms of the similarity in how people perceive themselves . "Just as someone with anorexia looks into the mirror and sees themselves as fat, I looked into the mirror and thought to myself that I wanted to be white," Stephen Armour quoted Wong as saying in a speech excerpted in *The University Daily*. "All my life Americans were idealized as blond and Caucasians. It was difficult to find out where I fit in."

Wong also noted that the lack of Asians on television in positive roles added to the questioning of an Asian's worth. Asian-American children grew up with role models, but he noted that none of them were Asian-American paradigms. Instead, Asian stereotypes were the only portrayals he saw in the media. With the outbreak of the Vietnam War, the images of Asians splashed across magazines, newspapers, and television were those of murdered Vietnamese. "I identified with 'those people,'" Wong commented, as noted by Armour. "I wasn't sure if people thought of me in the same way they thought of the people in Vietnam. 'Was I the enemy?' I thought. I couldn't find the reassurance to believe that I wasn't the typical American boy." Wong said it wasn't until he reached adulthood that he realized how difficult it was for him to establish his own self-image.

Wong turned to acting following a brief college experience. After honing his talent in dinner theater productions and showcases, he blazed into the public eye when he got the role of Song Liling, the transvestite opera star who becomes the mistress to a French diplomat in David Henry Hwang's *M. Butterfly*. The diplomat finds out twenty years later that not only is his lover a spy, but she is also a he. Wong had already landed his first Broadway role in an unsuccessful musical, *Mail,* and his decision to withdraw from that performance and perfect instead his part as Song Liling paid off: he was honored with five awards—one of which was an Antoinette Perry Award—all for *M. Butterfly*.

Wong had a bit part on the movie screen before he became known through his *M. Butterfly* performance, appearing in *Karate Kid II* in 1986. After his role as Song Liling, Wong landed the part of the assistant to Martin Short's "wedding coordinator from hell," as Raymond described the character, in *Father of the Bride* in 1991. The film was a breakthrough for Wong for two reasons: one, he was all over the big screen with well-known (and popular) actors Steve Martin, Diane Keaton, and Martin Short; second, filmmakers chose Wong not because of his race, but because they needed someone comical. Short, Raymond reported, was amazed at Wong's improvisational abilities.

Wong had minor roles early in his career, including a tiny part in Sidney Lumet's 1989 film *Family Business.* If the audience stepped out for popcorn at the wrong time, Raymond wrote, they missed Wong in a small role alongside Marlon Brando in 1990's *The Freshman.* In the same year that *Father of the Bride* premiered, Wong also appeared in *Mystery Date* with Ethan Hawke. Despite disappointing reviews, critics praised Wong's performance, such as a *Library Journal* contributor who commended Wong's "amusingly skewed portrayal of the crooked art dealer Mr. Lew." Lew was Wong's first co-starring role, associating Asians with the underworld and crime, and was potentially stereotypical. Wong worked to make his character less of an "other" and tried to emphasize the comic aspects of his role, which garnered some of the only positive comments the movie received.

Although more well-known for his theater work, including roles in *Androcles and the Lion* (1982), *The Tempest* (1989), *A Chorus Line* and *La Cage Aux Folles,* Wong has several films on his resume. He is steadily gaining recognition (and a build up of admirers) for his silver screen work. Wong acted in 1993's *And The Band Played On* and the smash hit *Jurassic Park.* Busy in 1995, he appeared in *Judith Krantz's 'Dazzle,' Men of War,* and returned for an encore performance in *Father of the Bride, Part II.* He was seen in the 1996 release *Executive Decision* and with Brad Pitt in the 1997 film *Seven Years in Tibet* as Ngawang Jigme. Cable viewers familiarized themselves with Wong in HBO's series *Oz.*

Wong suspects that Asian stereotypes, particularly those of being frail and delicate, are part of the reason why Asian actors are more frequently typecast in roles emphasizing their ethnicity rather than in roles where true character and personality are developed. "A rugged image is what commands respect in this society," Wong told Donald Suggs in his 1989 *Village Voice* article. "So Asian men aren't taken seriously as men.... I think that white Americans are afraid to allow any other kind of man to represent success and power." When Wong was cast as the spirit Ariel in

The Tempest, he was the only minority actor in the production. Wong commented to Suggs: "I understand that even though they don't realize it, the fact that I'm not white makes it easier for many people to accept the premise that I'm not human." Wong also mentioned the difficulty of trying to get casting agents and directors to consider that artists of color are indeed human and have the ability to play any role involving everyday activities.

It is tough enough for an Asian actor to find lead roles that have nothing to do with his or her race, but Wong told Suggs that the fact that he became famous for playing a transvestite in *M. Butterfly* hasn't done much to help his case, either. Wong recalled an instance where he was asked to audition for a role in person rather than send a tape, because his performance in *M. Butterfly* had caused those casting the role to question his ability to appear masculine.

Because of the obstacles Asian Americans constantly confront, Wong has used his acting status and personal experiences to try to encourage others to cure themselves of "racial anorexia." Wong believes that the "Asian sensibility" and traditional cultural values stifle any urges Asian minorities might have to stand up and fight for equality. At the same time, he feels that it's wrong for those demanding the same respect as the majority to deny their heritage. Now in a position to be a role model himself for others who may never have had someone to look up to, Wong acknowledges that being Asian allows him to be a messenger for Asian Americans who so desperately need one. Wong's talent will undoubtedly bring him fame as an actor, but his concern for identity and equality will make him known as one who campaigned for, and furthered, the positive attention paid to Asian artists in a world that has too often overlooked them.

Sources

On-line

Armour, Stephen, "Asian Actor Recovering From 'Racial Anorexia,'" *The University Daily,* http://www.arches.uga.edu/~acaasy97/anorexia (November 10, 1997).

"E! Online=Fact Sheet=B. D. Wong," http://el.eonline.com/Facts/People/0.12.22510.00 (November 10, 1997).

"Hollywood Online=The Press Room," http://www.hollywood.com/pressroom/premieres/sevenyears (November 10, 1997).

"Movie Guide: B. D. Wong Film Credits," http://www.mrshowbiz.com/reviews/moviereviews/stars/bdwong (November 10, 1997).

Raymond, Gerard, "Premier, Actor B. D. Wong," http://www.arches.uga.edu/~acaasu97/premiere (November 10, 1997).

Suggs, Donald, "Butterflies Are Free? B. D. Wong on Acting Identity," *Village Voice* (November, 1989), http://www.arches.uga.edu/~acaasu97/butterflies (November 10, 1997).

Periodicals

Back Stage West, December 1, 1994, p. 4.
Library Journal, March 1, 1992, p. 133.

—Audrey Gebber

Chuck Yeager

Pilot

Born Charles Elwood Yeager, February 13, 1923, in Myra, WV; son of Albert (a gas driller) and Susie May (Sizemore) Yeager; married Glennis Faye Dickhouse, February 26, 1945; children: Sharon, Susan, Donald, Michael. *Education:* Air Command and Staff School, graduated 1952; Air War College, graduated 1961. *Politics:* Republican. *Religion:* Methodist.

Addresses: *Home*—Box 128, Cedar Ridge, CA 95924-0128.

Career

Served in the U.S. Air Force, 1941-75; flew missions in World War II in Europe; became an experimental flight test pilot and the first man to break the sound barrier in 1947; continued test flights until 1954; various command assignments in Europe and the United States, 1954-62; became brigadier general and vice-commander of 17th Air Force, 1969; flew missions in Vietnam War; U.S. defense representative to Pakistan, 1971-73; director of aerospace safety, 1973-75; president of Yeager Consulting, 1975—; numerous appearances on television, film, and commercials; wrote autobiographies in 1985 and 1988.

Awards: Distinguished Service Medal, Silver Star, Legion of Merit, Distinguished Flying Cross, Bronze Star, Air Medal, Air Force Commendation Medal, Purple Heart, all for military service; Mackay Trophy and Robert J. Collier Trophy, National Aeronautic Association, 1947, for first supersonic flight; Gold Medal, International Aeronautical Foundation, 1948; inducted into International Space Hall of Fame, 1981; Theodore Roosevelt Distinguished Service Medal, Theodore Roosevelt Association, 1985; Presidential Medal of Freedom, 1985; Bradford Washburn Award, Boston Museum of Science, 1985; honorary degrees from West Virginia University (1948), Marshall University (1969), Salem College (1975).

Sidelights

The first man to break the sound barrier, Chuck Yeager celebrated the 50th anniversary of his historic test flight by taking an F-15 Eagle high above the California desert at the age of 74 in 1997. After punching into Mach speed, he radioed: "I'm smoking along." However, he promised that it would be his last supersonic flight. "I just decided to go out on top rather than wait for some doctor to ground me," he told reporters. The next day, a British pilot broke the speed of sound in a land vehicle.

Fifty years earlier, flying a tiny, bullet-shaped Bell X-1, Yeager became the first human being to fly faster than the speed of sound. As Yeager's speed reached 700 m.p.h., observers on the ground heard the first sonic boom in history, and a new era of aviation had begun. Yeager performed the feat on October 14, 1947, but the world did not know about it until an article appeared in *Aviation Week* in December, and the U.S. Air Force did not officially confirm the achievement until June 1948.

For Yeager, it was the high point of a long Air Force career that included decorated combat missions in World War II and in the Vietnam War, numerous command assignments, and retirement as a brigadier general. Eventually, his feats were immortalized in the 1979 Tom Wolfe novel *The Right Stuff* and its popular 1983 movie adaptation. The film was nominated for several Academy Awards, including a Best Supporting Actor nomination for Sam Shepard, the actor who portrayed Yeager. Belinda Luscombe of *Time* called him [Yeager] "the enduring symbol of flyboy coolheadedness under pressure."

> *"In an emergency situation, a pilot thinks only about one thing—survival. You battle to survive right down to the ground; you think about nothing else."*

Yeager was born into a large family in 1923 in West Virginia's hills, the second of five children. In his autobiography, Yeager described his mother, Susie May, as "a big-boned no-nonsense churchgoer who lowered the boom on any of us if we got out of hand," and his father, Albert, as "a great prankster, and a real marksman with a slingshot." His father worked in the coal fields, made moonshine, and then got a job as a natural gas driller. "Some evenings we'd have only corn bread and buttermilk," Yeager recalled. "Mom and Dad taught us by example. Mom worked as hard as any of the pioneer women, from dawn to dark, cooking and mending and cleaning. Dad got home late Friday and left on Sunday; in between he worked like a dog. They never complained."

Yeager grew fond of hunting and fishing. "I was a competitive kid," he wrote in his memoirs. "Whether it was swinging from vines over the swimming hole or skiing down hills on barrel staves during the first snowfall, I always tried to do my best. We made and raced our own bobsleds too, so I knew what a skid was when I first learned to fly." Yeager also inherited his father's mechanical ability. When he joined the Army Air Corps as a mechanic in 1941, Yeager had never even seen the inside of an airplane. "Unlike others in the squadron, I

had never dreamed of being an aviator," Yeager said. During his first few training flights, he became violently ill. But by the end of the war he had shot down 13 German fighters, including five in one day. On one mission, however, he was shot down. He was picked up by French resistance fighters who helped him escape to Spain, but there he was captured and imprisoned. He escaped by cutting the bars of his cell with a small saw he had hidden in his uniform. For his wartime feats, he earned a Purple Heart and several other medals.

After the war, Yeager became an Air Force flight instructor and then an experimental test pilot, flying high-speed rocket planes. No one knew for sure what might happen when the sound barrier was broken. When the planes of that era approached supersonic speeds, their cockpit controls would lock up and they would shake uncontrollably. Several men died trying to surpass the speed of sound. The X-1 was designed specifically to break the sound barrier. Yeager, small in stature, was chosen for the project partly because he could fit into the X-1's tiny cockpit. The tiny plane was ejected from the belly of a B-29 at 25,000 feet. "Anyone with brain cells would have to wonder what in hell he was doing in such a situation—strapped inside a live bomb that's about to be dropped out of a bomb bay." Yeager wrote in his autobiography. "But risks are the spice of life, and this is the kind of moment that a test pilot lives for. The butterflies are fluttering, but you feed off fear as if it's a high-energy candy bar." The flight went surprisingly well. "The faster I got, the smoother the ride was," Yeager wrote in his autobiography. "It was so smooth that Grandma would be sitting up there sipping lemonade."

In subsequent years, Yeager continued to break flight records. In all, he spent 15 years as a test pilot, flying mostly secret missions over the Mojave Desert. Once, he climbed into the X-1 without telling superiors he had broken ribs. He always nicknamed his planes "Glamorous Glennis," after his wife. "I flew, flew, flew," Yeager recalled in his 1985 book. "I was probably logging more flying time than the entire air force of some damned banana republic, but all of us were." On one of his test flights, in 1953, Yeager set a new record of 1,650 miles per hour, but his plane went out of control at 70,000 feet. He dropped 50,000 feet until he was able to regain control and land the plane. Yeager attributed his survival not only to luck but to extensive preparation and knowledge of his equipment. He wrote: "You know when you're in sync with the machine, so plugged into its instruments and controls that your mind and your hand become the heart of its operating system.... You know what you can get away with. And you can be wrong only once.... In an emergency situation, a pilot thinks only about one thing—survival. You battle to survive right down to the ground; you think about nothing else."

On another occasion he describes in his book, Yeager flew a Lockheed Starfighter at twice the speed of sound in 1963. "I went over the top at 104,000 feet, and as the airplane completed its long arc, it fell over," Yeager recalled in his book. "My nose was stuck high, and the damned airplane finally fell off flat and went into a spin. I was spinning down like a record on a turntable.... I had no hydraulic pressure because that operated off the engine, which had wound down to the point where it stopped and locked at about 40,000 feet. I was feeling kind of hopeless about this ride. The data recorder would later indicate that the airplane made fourteen flat spins from 104,000 until impact on the desert floor. I stayed with it through thirteen of those spins before I punched out [parachuted away]. I hated to lose an expensive airplane, but I couldn't think of anything else to do."

Between 1954 and 1962, Yeager's promotions earned him various command assignments in Germany, Spain, France, and the United States. In Europe in this period, Yeager was on the front lines of the Cold War. "A week seldom passed in the 1950s when East German or Czech pilots didn't invade our air space and cause us to scramble to intercept," Yeager recalled in his first book. "Often they staged their sweeps to coincide with our end-of-the-day beer calls, but there was more to it than just harassment. They were testing our reaction time." He later became commander of a squadron that possessed tactical nuclear weapons.

In the early 1960s, Yeager studied at the Air War College and then headed the new Air Force Aerospace Research Pilots School at Edwards Air Force Base in California, training military astronauts. The school was one of the first to study the effects of long-term weightlessness in space travel. Yeager ran the school for six years but then President Lyndon Johnson scrubbed the plans for a military space program.

During the Vietnam War, he flew several missions. In 1968 and 1969, he was commander of the 405th Fighter Wing, based at the Seymour Johnson Air Force Base in North Carolina. He reached the rank of brigadier general in 1969 and became vice-commander of the 17th Air Force at Ramstein Air Base in Germany. Between 1971 and 1973, he served as the U.S. Defense

Department's representative to Pakistan, during a time of open conflict between Pakistan and India. "I didn't get involved in the actual combat because that would have been too touchy," Yeager wrote. "but I did fly around and pick up shot-down Indian pilots and take them back to prisoner-of-war camps for questioning."

In 1973, he became director of aerospace safety for the Air Force. Two years later, at age 52, Yeager retired from the military. Before his retirement, he was enshrined in the Aviation Hall of Fame in Dayton, Ohio, as the hall's youngest member. At his retirement, Yeager was annoyed that no planes flew over, telling his friend Bud Anderson: "I spent my life flying and there wasn't even a pigeon in the air when I said goodbye."

Yeager started his own consulting firm after he retired, advising aircraft manufacturers. In 1979, Tom Wolfe's book, *The Right Stuff*, which focused on the achievements of Yeager and his colleagues, was published. After a hit movie was made from the book in 1983, Yeager became more famous than ever. His public speaking engagements skyrocketed and he started doing numerous television commercials, including ones for Delco Batteries. Following the success of *The Right Stuff*, Yeager's autobiography, published in 1985, was a best seller. He followed up with a second volume of reminiscences in 1988 that focused mainly on his wilderness expeditions and his newfound fame. Writing about *Yeager: An Autobiography*, critic Christopher Lehmann-Haupt of the *New York Times* said readers "glimpse the features of an authentic American hero—a good old country boy who wanted nothing out of life but to fish and hunt and fly, yet who was cool in the face of death."

In *Yeager: An Autobiography*, the man with "the right stuff" admitted: "I was always afraid of dying. Always. It was my fear that made me learn everything I could about my airplane and my emergency equipment, and kept me flying respectful of my machine and always alert in a cockpit. Death is the great enemy and robber in my profession, taking away so many friends over the years, all of them young." About winning the Congressional Medal of Honor, Yeager wrote: "the nicest part about winning that medal was that I'd receive it standing up."

Selected writings

Yeager: An Autobiography (with Leo Janos), Bantam, 1985.
Press On! Further Adventures in the Good Life (autobiography, with Charles Leerhsen), Bantam, 1988.

Sources

Books

Ayres, Carter M., *Chuck Yeager: Fighter Pilot,* Lerner, 1988.

Cox, Donald W., *America's Explorers of Space,* Hammond, 1967.

Levinson, Nancy S., *Chuck Yeager: The Man Who Broke the Sound Barrier: A Science Biography,* Walker & Co., 1988.

Lundgren, William R., *Across the High Frontier: The Story of a Test Pilot, Major Charles E. Yeager, USAF,* Morrow, 1955.

Wolfe, Tom, *The Right Stuff,* Farrar, Straus, 1979.

Periodicals

American Heritage, October 1997, p. 114.

Aviation Week & Space Technology, October 13, 1997, p. 58.

Forbes, October 23, 1995, p. S74.

New York Times, June 26, 1985; July 1, 1985; December 2, 1985.

Time, July 29, 1985, p. 69; October 27, 1997, p. 131.

U.S. News & World Report, January 13, 1986, p. 65; October 27, 1997, p. 12.

Vogue, June 1986, p. 248.

—Michael Betzold

Alex Zanardi

Race car driver

Born Alessandro Zanardi, October 23, 1966, in Bologna, Italy; married Daniela Manni, 1996.

Addresses: *Home*—Bologna, Italy; and Monte Carlo, Monaco. *Office*—Target/Chip Ganassi Racing, 3821 Industrial Blvd., Indianapolis, IN 46254.

Career

Driver of go-carts, Italy, 1980-87; Team Coperchini e Guareschi (Formula Three), driver, 1988; Team Racing for Italy (Formula Three), 1989; RC Motorsport (Formula Three), driver, 1990; Il Barone Rampante (Formula Three), 1991; Team Jordan (Formula One), driver, 1991; Minardi (Formula One), driver, 1992; Team Benetton (Formula One), official test and development driver, 1992; Team Lotus (Formula One), driver, 1993-94; Lotus Esprit (GT2), British Racing Production championship, England, driver, 1995; Target/Chip Ganassi Racing (Indy car/CART), United States, driver, 1996—.

Awards: Second place, Italian Formula Three Championship, 1990; second place, European Formula 3000 Championship, 1991; Casco d'Oro Tricolore award, Italian motorsports journalists, 1991; Jim Truman Rookie of the Year award, 1996; first place, PPG CART Championship, 1997; named Man of the Year, *Automobile* magazine, 1998.

Sidelights

When Alex Zanardi wins a race, he detours on his way to the victory lane by spinning the rear end of his car 360-degrees to leave rubberized doughnuts on the pavements. Why does he do this? "When I drive, I have to keep the emotions in. It's very hard. So when the race is over, I let everything out," he told *USA Today.* Since his impressive debut in the PPG Championship Auto Racing Teams (CART) series in 1996, he has had many opportunities to practice his victory spin. In his first season in the series he won three races. He captured the 1997 PPG CART Championship in his second season, winning five races and over $2 million in prize money.

Alessandro Zanardi was born in Bologna, Italy, on October 23, 1966. His driving career began at the tender age of 14 when he started racing go-karts in his native Italy. For seven years, he honed these fundamental driving skills, until in 1988 he began driving Formula Three cars for a number of Italian teams. By 1995, Zanardi had switched to Formula One racing and was associated with Team Lotus. Unfortunately, the team could not support another racing season, and Zanardi was unable to find a new team for the year. Instead, he sold pizzas and watched races on Eurosport TV. "When Team Lotus folded, I felt my career was not going in the right direction," Zanardi told the *Los Angeles Times.* "I decided I needed a change. The options were Formula 3000, the Japanese championship, European touring cars or Indy cars." He decided on Indy cars and came to the United States.

Unlike other European drivers, Zanardi had no financial backing that would enable him to buy his way onto a team. Instead, he was highly recommend by Reynard, the company that built his race car chassis, and given an introduction to Chip Ganassi of Team Target. Luckily Ganassi was looking for a second driver. When Zanardi passed the test, he was hired and advised to prepare for his first race. It was at that point his first name became Alex after a suggestion by Chip Ganassi, who claimed that Alessandro was too hard for Americans to remember.

The first season of driving for PPG CART found Zanardi setting a course record with six consecutive poles. "Whatever it is you do in life, you always want to be the best. I don't know why I keep winning the poles, but it is very satisfying. I am enjoying it.... Truthfully though, I don't really know why I'm suddenly so good.... I like to drive fast. Maybe that is my secret, " he told Shav Glick of the *Los Angeles Times*. It was in this impressive season that Zanardi was awarded the Jim Truman Rookie of the Year award, a $50,000 prize that honored his remarkable accomplishments in driving. In addition to his six pole starts, he topped CART drivers in laps led with 610 (doubling Michael Andretti's old record of 329) and won three races. He finished third in points for the season, behind his teammate Jimmy Vassar and Michael Andretti. Zanardi actually tied Andretti in points, but Andretti was given precedence over Zanardi because Andretti won four races to Zanardi's three.

Zanardi's second season on the Indy car circuit was even more successful than his first. His innate sense of the dramatic injected a sense of flair and personality into the CART series, while it also increased his popularity with fans of Indy car racing. Overall, Zanardi won five races and had four pole positions that season. He was consistently the fastest driver on the circuit. At the end of the season, he was awarded the 1997 PPG CART Championship. In his honor, the Italian pasta company Barilla donated 195 cases of pasta to the United States hunger organization Second Harvest, the number reflecting the total points Zanardi earned in the season.

Although Zanardi did work his way though the European ranks, he attributed his success in the U.S. as much to luck as the diligent effort he had put into his sport. A talented driver, he acknowledged to T. E. Hale of *SpeedCenter Internet Publishing*, "Motor racing is a question of preparation, dedication." Zanardi also noted to Hale that a driver must maintain his or her concentration, even on an oval course such as the Michigan International Speedway, "Because if you lose your concentration—and I can guarantee that it is very easy to do—sometimes you [make] maybe a little mistake and the time of recovering is less than a thou-

sandth of a second." That time spent correcting a mistake can lose the race. On the other hand, Zanardi also feels luck played a role in his success. He explained to Hale, "Well, I believe that in ... sport, like in life, you do have good periods of your life where things go right and you do have bad periods where things go wrong. And, it certainly ... changes your effort a little bit. In other words, it is easier to do everything right when you get a little bit of help from luck.... So, you actually give that maybe 5 extra percent that ... may be crucial."

Zanardi is considered by many to be one of the finest drivers to come along in years. He is the quintessential racer always striving to push himself and his machine to the limits. But he doesn't try to push the machine beyond those limits. Perhaps this comes from his early training as a test driver and one of the developers of new systems for Team Lotus. He not only understands how to drive a vehicle, but also what makes that vehicle operate at peak performance. He is able to communicate with his crew about what makes his car work and how to improve its performance. Zanardi told Hale that his relationship with his race engineer, Morris Nunn, "is very good. Morris ... helps me a lot because we now have a perfect understanding and we always find the little tricks that finally make the car work very well." Zanardi is a student of the mechanics of racing as well as of driving and that makes the difference between a good driver and a great one.

In 1996, after the season ended, Zanardi married his long-time companion Daniela. He has no problem putting aside his personal life to engage in discussion that enhances his sport. "I am a student of the sport but I really enjoy the study.... I don't mind staying long hours and having my wife get mad at me. [Morris] Nunn and me, we have many big discussions about little things," Zanardi told *USA Today*. "My philosophy is to be happy and enjoy what you have in life each day, but never be happy enough not to try for more."

Zanardi's combination of skill, determination, and intelligence make him a formidable opponent on the racing circuit. While he may be relatively new to the American racing scene, he has put in long hours of training and development in such places as Europe and the Middle East to become one of the best drivers in the world. His cool objectivity and understanding of the limits of his machine give him the ability to take the kind of risks that put him in the winner's circle time and again. The emotions come later.

Sources

On-line

"Alex Zanardi: Get the 120 Percent out of It Every Lap," *SpeedCenter Internet Publishing*, http://www.speedcenter.com (December 30, 1997).
"CART Circuit, Driver: Alex Zanardi," *STP Website*, http://www.stp.co/zanardi.html (March 11, 1998).
"CART Drivers—Alex Zanardi," *CART PPG*, http://www.cart.com (December 30, 1997).
"Firestone Drivers—Alex Zanardi," *Firestone*, http//www.firestonetire.com (December 30, 1997).

Periodicals

Autoweek, February 19, 1997, p. 79.
Detroit News, March 12, 1998.
Los Angeles Times, April 9, 1997, Sports section, p. 1.
PR Newswire, September 29, 1997.
USA Today, August 28, 1997, p. C11.

—Paula M. Kalamaras and Paul T. Kraly

Obituaries

Sani Abacha

Born September 20, 1943, in Kano, Nigeria (some sources say in Minna, Nigeria, or near Maiduguri, Nigeria); died of a heart attack, June 8, 1998. Sani Abacha was the seventh military officer to take power by force in Nigeria since the country gained independence from Britain in 1960. A brutal and oppressive ruler, he pilfered riches from the oil-laden land and cracked down hard on all opposition. His human rights record was horrendous, but became especially well-known after author and human rights activist Ken Saro-Wiwa was hanged along with eight others in 1995. Despite global sanctions, it seemed Abacha was not willing to let go of his control, rigging the "democratic" elections held in April of 1998 and the presidential ballot scheduled for August that year. Abacha was married to Mariam Jidah and had six sons, one of whom died in a plane crash caused by Nigerian liberation terrorists in 1996, and three daughters.

Abacha was born in northern Nigeria, but various sources list his exact birthplace as Maiduguri, Minna, or Kano. Official sources list Kano, the political hub of northern Nigeria and thus a more prestigious pedigree, but scholars and diplomats place his origin either in the smaller town of Minna, or near the city of Maiduguri, to the west. His early life is a mystery, and not much is known except that he attended the City Senior Primary School in Kano as a youth, then went on to Provincial Secondary School (now Government College) in Kano from 1957 to 1962. After that, he enrolled at the Nigerian Military Training College at Kaduna.

Although the army rule stated that soldiers had to be five feet, six inches tall, Abacha—only five feet, four inches at full growth—was accepted anyway. Abacha was commissioned second lieutenant in the Nigerian Army in 1963 and then quickly worked his way up the military ranks. He was promoted to lieutenant in 1966, captain in 1967, major in 1969, lieutenant colonel in 1972, commanding officer in 1975, and briga-

dier in 1980. He also attended military training schools in Great Britain in 1963, 1966, and 1971, and took the Senior International Defense Course in Monterey, California, in 1982.

On December 31, 1983, Abacha first made headlines when he announced on television that General Muhammad Buhari was staging a military coup of the civilian government. President Alhaji Shehu Shagari, elected in 1979, was toppled after falling oil prices in the early 1980s created a crisis in the oil-rich country. Buhari, however, did not help to improve the economy and cracked down on human rights and freedom of speech, causing more troubles. Two years later, on August 27, 1985, Abacha announced that General Ibrahim Babangida would be assuming control. Babangida made Abacha his defense minister and put him in charge of quelling any further takeovers. Abacha joined the Armed Forces Ruling Council (AFRC) that year, and later, in 1989, he was named chairman of the Joint Chiefs of Staff. The following year, he became minister of defense.

Abacha was part of the military government's plan to restructure the political system, a development that would allow multiparty elections and eventually, institute a civilian government. Babangida made the elections a central goal, but soon decided to create just two parties to vie for seats instead of the 13 that were previously running candidates. The new factions were generally in line with the politics of the ruling government, one slightly left-leaning, the other a little to the right. After the elections took place, the military government had them annulled anyway. Chief Mashood Abiola, a wealthy businessman and publisher from the southwest area of Nigeria, took the lead for president, and the northern-controlled military was against him. Citizens protested the disregard for their votes, and more than 150 were killed as the army tried to quash the demonstrations. Many human rights and pro-democracy advocates were arrested, opposition newspapers were silenced, and opposition politicians went into exile. Babangida stepped down.

After the confusion, a civilian named Chief Ernest Shonekan was placed as the head of government, and he named Abacha his defense minister. Shonekan was unable to get a handle on the country's unrest, and plans for another coup began brewing among junior military officers. Abacha saw this, and on November 17, 1993, took over himself, forcing Shonekan to resign after just 82 days in office. He immediately outlawed the two parties created during elections and banned all other political actions as well. On June 22, 1994, Abiola tried to declare himself the rightful president, and Abacha had him jailed for treason. He remained in prison at the time of Abacha's death.

Abacha's record of human rights offenses became notorious, with former chairman of the U.S. Joint Chiefs of Staff Colin Powell stating that Abacha "has the worst CIA bio I've ever read, and I've read lots of them," according to the *Chicago Tribune*. Abacha shut down newspapers and jailed numerous journalists. Nobel Prize-winning Nigerian author Wole Soyinka went into exile to avoid Abacha's wrath, and for good reason. In one of his most infamous acts, Abacha—in the face of an international outcry—executed playwright and human rights activist Ken Saro-Wiwa, who spoke out for Nigeria to share their oil wealth with the ethnic Ogoni people. Eight of his associates were also killed. This led to Western nations imposing sanctions on the country, as well as its expulsion from the British Commonwealth. In March of 1995, reports surfaced that Abacha's government killed between 60 and 300 military officers and about 40 civilians in a suppression of a coup attempt, an explanation many found suspicious. Moreover, various watchdog groups around the globe declared Nigeria, a notorious "kleptocracy," the world's most corrupt country under Abacha's rule.

Meanwhile, Abacha instituted a cult of personality in Nigeria. His face—usually masked with dark glasses—loomed at citizens from billboards claiming "Abacha is the Answer," and he named housing projects, rice, soap, and television sets after himself. However, he was extremely secretive and rarely ventured out in person, preferring to hole up in a mansion called Aso Rock with a few trusted advisors and numerous security personnel. His Special Bodyguard forces consisted of about 2,000 members. As worldwide condemnation swelled against Nigeria, Abacha ironically sent troops into the nation of Sierra Leone on the eastern coast in order to dismantle a junta and allow for the return of democratic elections. However, he still was not keen on freedoms in his own land. Though he had promised democratic reform, parliamentary elections in April of 1998 were worthless. Fear of violence at the polls—staffed heavily by soldiers and police—kept most voters away, and even if people did cast ballots, it was reported that Abacha had propped up most candidates anyway.

Abacha was supposedly preparing to run for president in August of 1998, but again, critics noted that his opposition were mainly token candidates that Abacha had selected. He would not live to see election by "popular" vote, however. Abacha died of a heart attack on June 8, 1998, and was buried in Kano. The ruling junta immediately named General Abdulsalam Abubakar, previously the defense minister, to the office of president, dampening hopes that Nigeria would enter a new realm of democracy. Though Abubakar did call for the release of political prisoners, Abiola died in prison in July of 1998 before he saw freedom. His death sparked days of rioting in Nigeria. **Sources:** *Chicago Tribune,* June 9, 1998; "Nigeria's Military Ruler Abacha Dead at 54," June 8, 1998, CNNin web site, http://cnn.com (June 9, 1998); *Newsmakers,* 1996 Cumulation, Gale Research, 1996; *New York Times,* June 9, 1998; *Times* (London), June 9, 1998; *USA Today,* June 9, 1998; *Washington Post,* June 9, 1998.

—*Geri Speace*

Joseph L. Alioto

Born Joseph Lawrence Alioto, February 12, 1916, in San Francisco, CA; died of pneumonia, January 29, 1998, at his home in San Francisco, CA. Mayor, lawyer, politician. Former San Francisco Mayor Joseph L. Alioto was known for keeping peace in the city during the turbulent Vietnam War era and for standing up for minorities' rights. Mayor for two terms, Alioto was already well-known in the legal field when he was elected in 1968. Though many projected a bright political future, a spell of negative media attention fizzled the rising star, and he returned to private practice as an antitrust lawyer in the mid-1970s.

Joseph Lawrence Alioto was the only son of the four children born to Sicilian immigrant Giuseppe Alioto, a fisherman, and Domenica (Lazio) Alioto, a second-generation Sicilian living in San Francisco. The couple met out on the San Francisco Bay, on a fishing boat seeking refuge from the devastating 1906 earthquake and fire that destroyed much of the city. Alioto, at a young age, began assisting his father with his business, the International Fish Company, on the famous Fisherman's Wharf in San Francisco. He attended St.

Peter and St. Paul Elementary School and then Sacred Heart High School, where he showed his colors as a leader, editing the school paper, serving as student body president, and joining the basketball and debate teams. After graduating in 1933, Alioto majored in philosophy and English at St. Mary's College in Moraga, California. There, too, he stood out, editing the yearbook, becoming student body president, and graduating valedictorian of his class in 1937. He received a scholarship and went on to study law at the Catholic University of America in Washington, D.C., graduating in 1940. In 1941, he married Angelina Genaro.

Soon after graduation, Alioto began his law career with the Antitrust Division of the Justice Department in Washington, D.C. Two years later, in 1942, he moved to the Board of Economic Warfare, where, among other assignments, he studied overseas enemy factories in order for the military to choose Allied bomb targets. After World War II, Alioto returned to his home town to open a private practice. He specialized in suing businesses engaged in antitrust practices, such as price-fixing and trade restraint. His high-profile client list included Walt Disney, Samuel Goldwyn, and Walter Wanger. In one of his larger cases, Alioto in 1951 sued Twentieth Century-Fox (on behalf of Goldwyn) alleging that they stymied competition. Fifteen years later, the courts issued a $1,900,000 judgment in favor of Goldwyn, which helped open up the arena of film distribution for all producers. Between 1964 and 1966, Alioto's court winnings were estimated at $61 million.

The charismatic Alioto served on the San Francisco Board of Education from 1948 to 1954 and was its president from 1953 to 1954. He also became involved with the Rice Growers Association of California, serving as the group's executive vice-president beginning in 1959 and becoming president in 1964. During a stint as chair of the San Francisco Redevelopment Agency, he urged new building while trying to protect homes from razing. During this time, he gained a reputation as an innovative and competent leader. Almost as an accident, Alioto entered the San Francisco mayoral race when the incumbent bowed out, and his successor died with less than two months to go toward election day. The incumbent, John L. Shelly, threw his support to Alioto, who won in a landslide over 17 other hopefuls.

Alioto was a popular mayor, representing the interests of minorities, striving to improve social and economic conditions, developing cultural institutions, and subduing the rampant Vietnam-era protests. Amid criticism, he lobbied for two new skyscrapers,

the Transamerica Building and Embarcadero Center, which thereafter changed the look of the cityscape; he also urged for many more new structures. The *Washington Post* reported that the mayor of San Francisco at the time of Alioto's death, Willie Brown, remarked that Alioto was "a champion of racial diversity long before it was fashionable," and that "[h]is imprint on San Francisco is indelible—from the city's downtown landscape to its cultural institutions to its public parks." Alioto's political future seemed secure when he was asked to make the nominating speech for Democratic presidential candidate Hubert H. Humphrey, then vice president under Lyndon B. Johnson. Rumors abounded that Alioto was in the running for vice president, and many suspected he would throw his hat in the ring to become the next governor of California.

Alioto's reputation was dealt a blow when a story in *Look* magazine on July 23, 1969, tied him to the Mafia. He sued for libel for $12.5 million and eventually received $450,000 after four trials and 11 years had passed. However, around the same time, the state of Washington filed suit against him, charging that he illegally took $2.3 million of a $16 million antitrust case. That case was dismissed before it got to a jury, but the government later indicted him on bribery charges. Those, too, were dropped. Alioto claimed that the bad press ruined his chances at a seat in the state house of representatives and contributed to his defeat to Jerry Brown for the job of governor. Despite the controversy and the other failures, the energetic and optimistic Alioto was reelected as mayor for the 1972-76 term.

After his run as mayor, Alioto went back to practicing antitrust law in 1976. In 1977, he divorced his wife, Angelina, with whom he had had five sons and one daughter. The next year he married Kathleen Sullivan; they had one son and one daughter. Alioto had suffered from prostate cancer since 1991. **Sources:** "Former San Francisco Mayor Alioto dies at 81," CNN Interactive web site, http://cnn.com (January 30, 1998); *Los Angeles Times,* January 30, 1998; *Washington Post,* January 31, 1998.

—*Geri Speace*

Sonny Bono

Born Salvatore Philip Bono, February 16, 1935, in Detroit, MI; died of massive head injuries after crashing into a tree while skiing, January 5, 1998, in South Lake Tahoe, CA. The son of Sicilian immigrants, Bono became a popular singer, songwriter, and television star in the 1960s and 1970s and a successful businessman and Republican politician in the 1980s and 1990s. With his former wife and singing partner, Cher, Bono crafted enduring pop classics such as "I Got You, Babe" and "The Beat Goes On" as well as the endearing *The Sonny and Cher Comedy Hour* on CBS-TV in the early 1970s. Following their 1974 divorce, Bono traded in the entertainment business to become a restaurateur in Palm Springs, California. In 1988, he was elected mayor of Palm Springs—after acknowledging that he had never voted until he ran for office at age 53. Six years later, voters from Southern California's 44th Congressional District sent Bono to the U.S. House of Representatives, where he served until his death.

When Bono was seven years old, his family moved to Los Angeles, California, from his native Detroit. A poor student, he dropped out of high school and supported himself working a series of jobs—including waiter, construction worker, butcher's assistant, truck driver—while struggling to become a songwriter. Legend has it that while working as a truck driver with a meat delivery route, Bono would stop at record companies he passed to submit songs. His first break came in 1957, when singer Larry Williams recorded his song "High School Dance" for the b-side of a single. The record reached number 90 on the music charts. Bono then landed a job at Specialty Records, where he worked his way up to staff producer and worked with music legends such as Sam Cooke and Little Richard.

In the late 1950s and early 1960s he was famed producer Phil Spector's assistant at Phillies Records, where he gained experience arranging, engineering, producing, songwriting, and singing backup for groups including the Ronettes, the Crystals, and the Righteous Brothers. His composition, "Needles and Pins," became a hit for both Jackie DeShannon and later the British group the Searchers; the Righteous Brothers scored big with Bono's song "Koko Joe." On the home front, Bono married Donna Rankin in 1954; they had a daughter named Christy. The couple divorced in 1962.

In the early 1960s, Bono met Cherilyn Sarkisian (known professionally as Cher), an exotic-looking 16-year-old who longed to be an entertainer. Bono, who was 27, taught Cher to sing backup and persuaded Spector to hire her. In 1964, the couple married and began performing as Sonny and Cher. They had a modest hit with the Bono composition "Baby Don't Go" and landed a contract with the major label Atco-Atlantic Records. The duo had a string of hits over the next two years, most penned by Bono, including "I Got You, Babe," which reached number 1 in America and Europe. Sonny and Cher shared 10 Top-40 hits by the end of the decade. They also portrayed themselves in the film *Good Times*, released in 1967. Two years later, Bono wrote and produced the film *Chastity*, starring Cher, which told the story of a teenage runaway who hitchhikes through the Southwest and Mexico. Unfortunately, neither film was a critical or financial success. It was around this time that the couple's daughter was born and they named her Chastity.

In 1971, CBS aired *The Sonny and Cher Comedy Hour* as a five-week summer replacement series. The variety show became a surprise hit. The format was based on their popular night club act—a mix of song and comedy. Cher played the glamorous, sharp-tongued wife to Sonny's hapless, overmatched husband as the couple engaged in entertaining verbal sparring in which Cher inevitably skewered Sonny. Regardless of how many barbs and off-color remarks the duo exchanged, the act always ended on a happy note as they sang their signature song, "I've Got You Babe." After their divorce in 1974, Cher flourished in films and won an Academy Award for her performance in 1987's *Moonstruck*. Bono's show business career stalled, however.

Eventually, Bono became a successful restaurateur in the desert resort Palm Springs where, angered by bureaucratic red tape he confronted at City Hall, he ran for mayor in 1988 and won. Bono's portrayal of a buffoonish second banana on *The Sonny and Cher Comedy Hour* helped make the program a success in the early 1970s, but the image followed him into politics, where he was derided as a "vacuous lightweight," as noted in the *Detroit Free Press*. "People underestimate me, but I've always been a stretch runner," he once told the *Washington Post*, as quoted in the *New York Times*. "If people would take a look—and I don't mean this arrogantly—if they would take a look at what I've done in my life, you can't be a dummy and have the achievements I've had in my lifetime."

As mayor of Palm Springs, Bono helped erase the city's $2.5 million deficit and promoted tourism. He lost the Republican primary in the 1992 U.S. Senate race, but rebounded two years later to win a seat in Congress. Bono was part of a conservative Republican tide which in 1994 seized control of the House of Representatives for the first time in 40 years. Bono was denigrated for his lack of experience, but "[h]e quickly proved engaging and shrewd, a fairly dutiful legislator and an engaging speaker," the *Chicago Tribune* reported. In fact, Bono's speaking style and self-deprecating wit made him one of the most popular speakers at his Republican colleagues' fund-raising events. "Bono almost took pride in his lack of qualifications for Congress," Bernard Weinraub wrote in the *New York Times*. "What is qualified?" Bono told the *Los Angeles Times* in 1992, as quoted by Weinraub. "What have I been qualified for in my life? I haven't been qualified to be a mayor. I'm not qualified to be a songwriter. I'm not qualified to be a TV producer. I'm not qualified to be a successful businessman. And so, I don't know what qualified means." Bono was re-elected to Congress in 1996.

Bono married model Susie Coelho in 1982; they divorced in 1984. He met his fourth wife, Mary Whitaker, in 1985. They married the following year and had two children, Chesare and Chianna. **Sources:** *Chicago Tribune,* January 7, 1998; *CNN Interactive,* January 6, 1998; *Detroit Free Press,* January 6, 1998, and January 7, 1998; *Los Angeles Times,* January 6, 1998; *New York Times,* January 7, 1998; *Times* (London), January 7, 1998; *USA Today,* January 6, 1998.

—Dave Wilkins

Lloyd Bridges

Born Lloyd Vernet Bridges II, January 15, 1913, in San Leandro, CA; died March 10, 1998, of natural causes in Los Angeles, CA. Actor. Rugged, versatile, and prolific actor Lloyd Bridges got his start in Hollywood in 1941 when he signed with Columbia Pictures. His lengthy list of credits includes *Sahara*, with Humphrey Bogart, 1943; *A Walk in the Sun*, 1945; *Home of the Brave*, 1949; *High Noon*, 1952; *Around the World Under the Sea*, 1966; *Running Wild*, 1973; *Airplane!*, 1980; *Hot Shots!*, 1991; and *The War at Home*, 1996. He also appeared on television, making a name for himself in the series *Sea Hunt* (1957-61) and acting in numerous other series, miniseries, and made-for-television movies. He is the father of actors Beau and Jeff Bridges.

Bridges was born in San Leandro, California, near San Francisco, to Lloyd Vernet Bridges, Sr. and Harriet (Brown) Bridges, but grew up in an assortment of towns in northern California. His father owned a theater, among other businesses, so Bridges early on became a film buff. At Petaluma High School, he took drama classes. He went on to play basketball, baseball, and football at the University of California, Los Angeles, where he majored in political science and took legal courses. Though his father wanted him to

become a lawyer, he became a member and eventually president of the University Drama Society and was convinced to pursue acting by fellow student Dorothy Simpson, whom he later married in 1939. Trained as a classical actor, he performed the plays of Shakespeare and had a part in Sophocles's *Oedipus Rex*.

Producer Rollo Peters caught Bridges performing in Sidney Howard's *Yellowjack* at the university and offered him the part of Lucentio in a modern-dress production of Shakespeare's *The Taming of the Shrew*. Initially just a regional show debuting in Berkeley, California, the production went on to dates in Los Angeles and New York. While in New York, Bridges landed a small walk-on role in *Othello*, which starred Walter Huston and Brian Aherne, and made his first Broadway appearance on January 6, 1937. The same year, Bridges cofounded The Playroom Club in order to stage modern off-Broadway plays. He also taught drama at the private Cherry Lawn School in Darien, Connecticut, with his wife, and appeared in stock theater. In 1941, a Columbia Pictures producer saw him and signed him to a contract for $75 a week.

Bridges followed his first picture, *Lone Wolf Takes a Chance* (1941), with a string of other small roles in forgettable B-flicks. He even appeared in a Three Stooges short, *They Stooge to Conga*, in 1943. That same year, he gained some attention playing British soldier Fred Clarkson in the Humphrey Bogart World War II thriller *Sahara*. In 1944, the actor branched out into radio, costarring with Irene Rich in the CBS serial *The Woman from Nowhere*, and the following year, he received critical praise for his role as Sergeant Ward in Lewis Milestone's *Walk in the Sun*, another World War II story.

After working for some of the major studios and independent houses, Bridges signed on to Universal Pictures in the mid-1940s. There he was cast as the lead in a serial called *Secret Agent X-9*, based on a comic strip by Alex Raymond. Around this time, he was also a member of the radical theater group, the Actors' Lab. Finally, in 1949, he won his first starring role in a major film, *Home of the Brave*, directed by Stanley Kramer, and received much critical praise. *Home of the Brave* was one of the first Hollywood movies to focus on the state of race relations in the United States.

Bridges appeared in no less than 20 movies during the years 1946 to 1949, playing a fisherman and former navy diver in *16 Fathoms* (1948); a criminal cooperating to shut down counterfeiters in *Trapped* (1949); a mountain climber in *The White Tower* (1950); a pilot chosen to fly to the moon in *Rocketship X-M* (1950);

and one of General Custer's officers in *Little Big Horn* (1951). He also starred in westerns. Then in 1952, Bridges got his big break in one of the most memorable roles of his career: he played a crafty, revenge-seeking deputy sheriff in the classic *High Noon*, starring Gary Cooper. The film won six Academy Awards and almost ensured stardom for Bridges. Politics would unfortunately intervene, however.

During the early 1950s, U.S. Senator Joseph McCarthy launched his infamous campaign against Communists that caused numerous people throughout the country to lose their jobs and be shunned in their communities. Bridges was a target of these "witch hunts" due to his earlier involvement with the Actors' Lab, a politically-oriented group that staged plays around Hollywood. The FBI later cleared him, and he was allowed to return to work, although his career suffered due to the accusations. For two years, he mainly acted in low-budget independent productions and also returned to Broadway after a 13-year hiatus. He got back into the mainstream of Hollywood with 1956's *The Rainmaker*, starring Katharine Hepburn and Burt Lancaster.

Around this time Bridges also regularly appeared in television dramas and eventually agreed to star in the series *Sea Hunt* as daring undersea investigator Mike Nelson. The popular show aired from 1957 to 1961. Throughout the 1960s and 1970s, Bridges made numerous appearances on television, including *The Lloyd Bridges Show*, 1962-63, and the miniseries *Roots*, 1977. He also continued to act, sporadically, in films. In 1980, his film career was revived with his comedic role as a gruff, drunken controller trying in vain to safely land planes in the hilarious spoof *Airplane!*, a role he played again in 1982's *Airplane II*. He worked steadily throughout the 1980s in film and television, with roles in the miniseries *How the West Was Won*, *East of Eden*, and *North and South, Book II*, as well as the comedy films *Hot Shots!*, 1991, and *Hot Shots! Part Deux*, 1993.

Bridges had two sons, Beau and Jeff, who went on to forge successful careers of their own in Hollywood. He acted with Jeff in 1988's *Tucker: The Man and His Dream* and with Beau in *Meeting Daddy*, which was completed shortly his death. Bridges also had a daughter, Lucinda (Cindy). He was active in social causes such as ending world hunger, CARE, and the liberal lobbying group People for the American Way. In 1994, Bridges and his wife of over 50 years, Dorothy, were awarded the Ralph Bunche Peace Award commemorating the United Nations Year of the Family. **Sources:** *Chicago Tribune*, March 11, 1998; "Actor Lloyd Bridges dead at age 85," CNN Interactive, http://cnn.com, March 10, 1998; *Contemporary Theatre, Film, and Televi-*

sion, Volume 11, Gale Research, 1994; *Los Angeles Times*, March 11, 1998; *New York Times*, March 11, 1998; *Times* (London), March 12, 1998; *USA Today*, March 10, 1998.

—Geri Speace

Leo Buscaglia

Born March 31, 1924, in Los Angeles, CA; died of a heart attack in Lake Tahoe, NV, June 12, 1998. Author. Leo Buscaglia was a self-help guru who wrote over 15 books and gave hundreds of lectures on the power of love. His trademark was giving everyone in the audience at his speeches a hug, no matter how many lined up. This earned him the nickname "Dr. Hug." Five of his books were on the *New York Times* bestseller lists at one time, and he had a long-running syndicated column called "Living and Loving." Though he advocated a simple message and one that was not in the least a new or radical concept—loving one's own self and others—he was passionate in his speeches and writings and urged people to lead more caring and responsible lives.

Felice Leonardo Buscaglia was born in East Los Angeles, California, to Italian immigrants Tulio Bartolomeo, a restaurant owner, and Rosa (Cagna) Buscaglia. The family included ten children and was very tight-knit. Buscaglia later recounted stereotypical but heartwarming stories of an Italian mother singing as she prepared heaping bowls of spaghetti and of a family drawn together by telling each other tales of their day at the dinner table. Shortly after he was born, Buscaglia's parents took him to Italy, where he lived until he was five years old. During his European upbringing, he learned to speak Italian as well as a little French and Spanish. When he returned to Los Angeles and began school, however, he could not speak English. Thus, school officials put him a special education class. There, Buscaglia was pleased with the warm manner in which the teacher interacted with the children, and he would later note that the rest of his public education experience in regular classrooms was extremely boring.

Buscaglia served in the Navy during World War II from 1941 to 1944 and earned a bachelor's degree in education in 1950 from the University of Southern California. He followed this up with a master's degree in 1954, and later, a Ph.D. in speech pathology in 1963. In 1951, he began working as a speech therapist and teacher in the Pasadena (California) City School System. In 1960, he was promoted to special education supervisor, but he ached to work again in the classroom. He took some time off to travel and went to Asia, where he studied Zen Buddhism and Hinduism and came to the realization that all religions share the belief that love is at the basic core of humanity. Upon his return, Buscaglia took a cut in pay and joined the faculty at the University of Southern California school of education, working his way up to full professor.

Buscaglia was deeply affected when one of his star students committed suicide and began seriously considering his earlier thoughts on the subject of love. He started teaching courses on love, which rattled the other faculty members, especially when 600 students signed up. Subsequently, it became one of the school's most popular courses, causing Buscaglia to venture out of the university to give lectures as well. Around this time, his first book, *Love*, consisting of his classroom lectures, was published in 1972, and steadily attracted fans. Buscaglia would go on to write various other self-help books, including *Living, Loving and Learning* (1982), *Loving Each Other* (1984), *Bus 9 to Paradise* (1986), and *Sounds of Love* (1989); some children's fiction; and even a cookbook—his last endeavor—titled *The Love Cookbook* (1994). The cookbook combined the author's passions: people and food. Cooking, eating, and good wines were three of his hobbies, in addition to traveling, meeting people, and opera. Buscaglia's lectures were frequently taped for broadcast on the Public Broadcasting System (PBS), and he began writing a column for the New York Times Syndicate in 1984 called "Living and Loving." One of his children's books, *The Fall of Freddy the Leaf* (subtitled *A Story of Life for All Ages*), was adapted for audiocassette, educational film, and an hour long ballet. It used a leaf and the seasons to symbolize the changes during human life and the natural cycle of birth and death.

Though his critics chastised him for not marrying and producing children, Buscaglia responded by saying that he loved everyone, not just a select few people in his own life. He was also sometimes attacked for his sentimentality and a lack of more thorough substance. However, Buscaglia had a great deal of fans; his books sold over 11 million copies in 20 languages. In 1991, he was honored with the establishment of the Leo F. Buscaglia Scholarship for Inner City Teachers Education at the University of Southern California. Buscaglia died at age 74 of a heart attack at his home on the shores of Lake Tahoe in Nevada. According to a *USA Today* obituary, he once noted at a lecture in Denver that death "is only morbid if you never lived."

Sources: *Chicago Tribune,* June 13, 1998, p. 25; "Self-Help Author Buscaglia Dead at 74," June 12, 1998, CNNin web site, http://cnn.com (June 15, 1998); "Contemporary Authors," Gale Literary Database web site, 1998, http://www.galenet.com (July 9, 1998); *Los Angeles Times,* June 13, 1998; *New York Times,* June 13, 1998, p. A10; *USA Today,* June 12, 1998; *Washington Post,* June 13, 1998.

—Geri Speace

Harry Caray

Born Harry Christopher Carabina, March 1, 1914 (some sources cite as 1917 or 1920), in St. Louis, MO; died of cardiac arrest and subsequent brain damage, February 18, 1998, at the Eisenhower Medical Center in Rancho Mirage, CA. Sports broadcaster. Harry Caray, with his trademark oversized Coke-bottle spectacles and distinctive voice, was a colorful and controversial play-by-play announcer in Chicago baseball since 1971. Throughout his 53-year career, Caray stirred emotions. Not only did he add an element of zest to the game thanks to his passion for the sport, he also was widely known for having an oversized ego and making blunt, often offensive, comments about players, management, and fellow broadcasters. Fans, however, never seemed to tire of the outspoken icon and did not mind that he was at times derided as a cheerleader for the teams he covered. He often exclaimed his signature line, "Holy Cow!," immediately after a home run by the home team.

Caray was born to Christopher and Daisy (Argint) Carabina in St. Louis, Missouri. He was coy throughout his life about his year of birth; most sources place it around 1919, but a *Los Angeles Times* obituary noted that the *St. Louis Post-Dispatch* had uncovered birth records showing the date as 1914. He was orphaned at age ten and brought up in foster homes and by his strict aunt. After playing baseball for Webster Groves High School in St. Louis, Caray declined an athletic scholarship with the University of Alabama in order to vie for a position with the St. Louis Cardinals professional baseball team. When that did not materialize, he held various odd jobs, including a gig selling basketball backboards, and then decided to try announcing.

Caray wrote a letter to the manager at KMOX in St. Louis criticizing the station's baseball announcers and touting himself as a better choice. The manager, impressed by Caray's confidence, helped him land a job at WCLS in Joliet, Illinois, in 1941. From there, he went to WKZO in Kalamazoo, Michigan, where he worked with Paul Harvey (now known for his home-spun radio show *The Rest of the Story*), who was then the news director there. In the mid-1940s Caray made it back to his home town to work for KXOK announcing hockey and then WIL-AM, where he debuted as a baseball announcer. He then was hired in at KMOX, where he became the station's number one announcer and the voice of the St. Louis Cardinals for 25 years. A *Chicago Tribune* obituary quoted Caray as saying, "I always thought I'd die at the microphone doing a Cardinals game." That was not the case. The team fired Caray after the 1969 season amid rumors that he was having an affair with an executive's wife. He did not deny the charges and went on to broadcast for California's Oakland A's in 1970.

The next year, 1971, Caray landed a job with the Chicago White Sox, where he would stay for 11 years. In Chicago, he developed a reputation as a heavy drinker, earning the nickname "Mayor of Rush Street," after the town's nightlife district. It was with the White Sox that he debuted his raspy, off-key rendition of "Take Me Out to the Ballgame" and the interjection, "Holy Cow!" Despite the down-to-earth qualities that endeared him to fans, he was known to have shouting matches with players as well as team manager Chuck Tanner. In 1975, the team's owner, John Allyn, fired Caray. The radio station that carried the games, however, threatened to drop the contract unless Caray came back. In 1976, Bill Veeck bought the team, and Caray was re-hired.

In 1981, Jerry Reinsdorf and Eddie Einhorn bought the Cubs and decided to begin a pay-television business. The next season, 1982, Caray left for the cross-town Chicago Cubs. Fans of both were shocked and upset, but many followed Caray to the other ballpark. There, he gained a national audience on superstation WGN, a Chicago channel carried by cable companies across the country. He continued his showmanship and personal brand of commentary, boosting the team's popularity with his candid criticism of players and musings about the backward spelling of various names as well as his everlasting enthusiasm for the team and the game. "He could be critical, contentious and bombastic," the *Chicago Tribune* quoted Dodgers' Hall of Fame announcer Vin Scully as saying. "Or he could be lovable and full of praise.... He said what he honestly felt should be said, like a fan, and sometimes at the expense of his own team." He sometimes gave his broadcast from a seat in the bleachers, surrounded by fans.

Caray's fellow WGN broadcaster, Steve Stone, remarked in the *Chicago Tribune*, "He is the single greatest salesman of the game who ever lived."

In 1987, Caray suffered a near-fatal stroke which benched him for the first six weeks of the season. When he returned to work on May 19, Illinois Governor James Thompson deemed it "Harry Caray Day" and attended the ball game. Even President Ronald Reagan, a former Cubs announcer, called him with a greeting that was broadcast on the air. Into the 1990s, though, Caray was often criticized for mangling players' names and getting plays wrong. Some said his age was a factor in the mixups and that he should retire. A *USA Today* obituary recalled, however, that Caray often boasted, "I'll keep going until I die on the job someday." After a fall resulting from a bout with the extreme heat in Miami, Florida, in July of 1994, Caray did concede to only announcing home games.

Caray was elected to the National Sportscasters and Sportswriters Hall of Fame in 1988. In 1989, he entered the Baseball Hall of Fame when he was awarded the Ford C. Frick award, which honors a broadcaster for meritorious service. Also in 1989, he wrote his autobiography, aptly titled *Holy Cow!* Three generations of Carays would eventually be involved in baseball play-by-play. In 1991, Caray teamed up during a Cubs-Braves game with his son, Skip, the announcer for the Atlanta Braves, and his grandson, Chip, who was also a Braves announcer at the time. Caray was looking forward to working regularly with Chip on WGN, who had been a studio host for Fox Sports and had moved to the Chicago station shortly before Caray's death.

Caray collapsed at a restaurant in Palm Springs, California, on February 14, 1988, during a Valentine's Day dinner with his third wife, Dolores, also known as "Dutchie." Survivors include his wife; two sons, Harry ("Skip"), Jr. and Christopher; three daughters, Patricia, Elizabeth, and Michelle; five stepchildren, Mark, Roger, Donald, Gloria, and Elizabeth; 14 grandchildren; and one great-grandchild. **Sources:** *Chicago Tribune*, February 19, 1998; "Baseball loses a legend," CNNSI web site, http://cnnsi.com (February 18, 1998); *Los Angeles Times*, February 19, 1998; "Baseball legend Harry Caray dies at age 83," MSNBC News Service online, http://www.msnbc.com (February 18, 1998); *New York Times*, February 19, 1998; *USA Today*, February 19, 1998.

—Geri Speace

Carlos Castaneda

Born December 25, 1931 (some sources say 1925), in Sao Paolo, Brazil (some sources say Cajmarca, Peru); died of liver cancer, April 27, 1998, in Los Angeles, CA. Anthropologist, author. Carlos Castaneda was best known for his first publication, *The Teachings of Don Juan: A Yaqui Way of Knowledge* (1968), which recorded his experiences with a mysterious man who was supposedly a sorcerer who taught the author to reach new levels of consciousness. These realms were initially coaxed along, according to Castaneda, by the use of hallucinogenic drugs such as peyote. The book was generally regarded as an imaginative work of fiction, but Castaneda insisted it was factual. He went on to pen a total of ten books which sold millions of copies in 17 different languages, all expounding on Castaneda's journey into new realities and fueling a rise in New Age mysticism and reviving interest in the culture of Native Americans and the Southwest.

Castaneda's life, like his writing, remains somewhat of a mystery. He listed his birth date and place as December 25, 1931, in Sao Paulo, Brazil, and said that Castaneda was not his true last name. According to his own story, he was raised by his grandparents on a chicken farm because his mother and father were not ready for parenthood. He noted that he went to a boarding school in Buenos Aires, Argentina, then moved to Los Angeles at age 16 to live with a foster family and attend high school. However, immigration records have shown that he was born Carlos Cesar Aranha Castaneda on December 25, 1925, in Cajmarca, Peru, and was educated at the Colegio Nacional de Nuestra Senora and the National School of Fine Arts in Lima. The official account says he emigrated to the United States in 1951 and later attended the University of California at Los Angeles. He graduated from college in 1962, received a master's degree from UCLA in 1964, and was granted a doctoral degree in 1970, after he wrote his tale of Don Juan as his thesis.

Castaneda began focusing on ethnomethodolgy at UCLA, a way of studying linguistics in a holistic manner, while pursuing his anthropology degree. He claimed that he met a Yaqui Indian sorcerer named Don Juan Matus in Arizona in the early 1960s while conducting research on medicinal plants. According to his own description, the shaman took Castaneda under his wing in order to mentor him in the ways of knowledge, and the two later moved to the Sonoran Desert just south of the Arizona border in Mexico. During this apprenticeship, the two frequently took peyote and other drugs to induce hallucinations to transport them through time and space. Castaneda claimed that he did eventually reach a higher state of reality and became a "man of knowledge" like his tutor.

Castaneda published his thesis in 1968, and surprisingly, though it read like a work of fiction, it was accepted by the academic powers at UCLA. *The Teachings of Don Juan: A Yaqui Way of Knowledge* also hit a note with the psychedelic 1960s society, as the book was chock full of drug trips and tales of expanded consciousness. It became a bestseller and established Castaneda as a folk icon. The book also inspired a resurgence of interest in the culture of the Southwest and Native Americans, and many commentators later placed Castaneda as the impetus for the New Age movement that swelled in subsequent decades. Many readers were also inspired themselves to indulge in drug use to reach new heights of knowing, but Castaneda saw them as misguided. He was apparently disappointed that recreational drug use was being substituted for what he saw as a difficult path to enlightenment.

The author followed his smash success with *A Separate Reality: Further Conversations with Don Juan,* and *Journey to Ixtlan: The Lessons of Don Juan.* Castaneda penned a total of ten works, not all of which were as enthusiastically received. In addition, doubts surfaced about the existence of Don Juan, despite Castaneda's continuing insistence that he was real. Numerous would-be followers searched in vain for such a person, and a general assessment developed that Castaneda's writings were a hoax. Though the consensus eliminated the works' anthropological value, they did not diminish the power and importance of the works as genius-level fiction.

Castaneda shunned the spotlight, and he refused to be recorded or photographed, thus lending even more mystery to his persona. Though journalists hounded him, he eluded them. American Express once offered him a million dollars to appear in a commercial for ten seconds, which he turned down. He rarely appeared in public, although in his later years he became less of a recluse, holding some seminars and giving an occasional interview. He died of liver cancer on April 27, 1998, at his home in the Westwood area of Los Angeles, California.

Castaneda's death was not reported until almost two months after the fact, and even then, his friends and associates refused to discuss him with the media, which discovered that Castaneda's death certificate contained a bevy of misinformation. It listed him as never having been married, which was blatantly untrue: from 1960 to 1963, he was married to Margaret Runyan Castaneda, who wrote a humorous 1997 memoir called *A Magical Journey with Carlos Castaneda.* Throughout his life and on his death certificate, Castaneda denied having a child, C. J. Castaneda, insisting that the boy was his wife's by another man. Castaneda was estranged from his ex-wife and son, who maintained that Castaneda was indeed his real father and was listed as such on his birth certificate. **Sources:** "Author Carlos Castaneda, Guru of New Age Movement, Dies," June 19, 1998, CNNin web site, http://cnn.com (June 23, 1998); "Contemporary Authors," Gale Literary Databases web site, http://www.galenet.com (July 9, 1998); *Chicago Tribune,* June 20, 1998, section 1, p. 19; *Encyclopedia of Occultism and Parapsychology,* second edition, Gale Research, 1984-85; *Los Angeles Times,* June 19, 1998; *New York Times,* June 19, 1998; *Times* (London), June 20, 1998; *Washington Post,* June 20, 1998, p. C1.

—*Geri Space*

Eldridge Cleaver

Born August 31, 1935 (some sources say June 5, 1935), in Wabbaseka, AR; died May 1, 1998, in Pomona, CA. Activist and author. Eldridge Cleaver was a hardened criminal, serving time for assault with intent to kill after raping a number of women, when he became involved with the Black Muslims and the preaching of Malcolm X. Eschewing the life of crime, he won parole and fought diligently to improve the lot of African Americans, becoming a noted author and helping to found a black cultural center. His 1968 book *Soul on Ice,* consisting of essays written in prison, shockingly related the condition of life for African Americans and outlined how incarceration fueled his own violence and anger. *Soul on Ice* established Cleaver as a prominent social critic. One of the original Black Panthers, Cleaver was caught up in a shootout in 1968 and subsequently fled the country. While in exile, he soured on socialism and communism and adhered to Christian principles. After his return in 1975, his life took a series of odd turns; he became a sought-after speaker, designer of unusual fashions, founder of a new religion, recycling business proprietor, ceramic pottery artisan, and would-be politician in the Republican party.

Leroy Eldridge Cleaver was born in the small town of Wabbaseka, near Little Rock, Arkansas. His father,

Leroy, played piano and waited tables in a nightclub in Little Rock, and his mother, Thelma, was an elementary school teacher. Cleaver's father later worked as a waiter in a dining car on the Super Chief train from Chicago to Los Angeles, and because of that job, the family moved to Phoenix, Arizona, one of the stops on the route, when Cleaver was young. Two years after moving to Phoenix, the family moved to the Watts section of Los Angeles, and Cleaver's life took a downturn. After moving to California, Cleaver's parents separated. Then, soon after entering Abraham Lincoln Junior High School, where his mother took work as a janitor, Cleaver dropped out and turned to crime.

Cleaver's criminal record began at age 12, when he was arrested for stealing a bicycle. A trip to the Fred C. Nelles School for Boys in Whittier, California, put him in the company of older boys who inspired him to commit more serious crimes. After his release from Nelles in 1953, he quickly found himself in another reform school for selling marijuana. Subsequently, Cleaver faced arrest again for possession of marijuana, and in June of 1954 he received a two and a half-year sentence to the California State Prison at Soledad. In prison, Cleaver studied heartily and obtained his high school diploma. However, soon after his release, he returned to selling marijuana, and this time, began raping women regularly. After "practicing" on African American girls in the ghetto, he moved to raping white women as "an insurrectionary act" to get revenge on white men, as he noted in his book *Soul on Ice,* quoted in the *New York Times.*

Cleaver was eventually arrested for the assaults and received two to fourteen years at San Quentin Prison, but was later transferred to Folsom Prison. While incarcerated, he embraced the teachings of Elijah Muhammad and the Black Muslims, and when Malcolm X broke with the Nation of Islam, Cleaver turned to his leadership for inspiration. Furthermore, Cleaver studied the Bible, vowing to give up crime. He also began writing essays on black nationalism and racial pride, some of which were published in 1962 in the *Negro History Bulletin,* and others in *Ramparts* magazine.

Eight years into his prison sentence, Cleaver contacted Beverly Axelrod, a prominent white attorney in San Francisco known for civil liberties cases. She was the person who took his writing to *Ramparts,* and she worked successfully to gain his parole. By the time he was eligible for release, Cleaver had a job waiting for him at *Ramparts,* thanks to left-wing editor Edward M. Keating. In late 1966, Cleaver left prison and started his new career in San Francisco. Transformed from a maximum-security felon to a well-known writer, he hobnobbed with other community leaders and intellectuals. He also helped to start up Black House, a cultural center in San Francisco for African Americans, where he met Huey Newton and Bobby Seale, the founders of the newly-formed Black Panther Party.

Cleaver joined the Black Panthers and was named minister of information. As a top official, he was outspoken and high-profile, which led his parole officer to ask him to step down from the position. However, Cleaver wanted to make a difference in the quality of life for African Americans and continued his efforts, especially working to end police violence and harassment. He also helped bring the Panthers together with a white group, the Peace and Freedom Party, to organize a political campaign and put candidates on the ballot. Cleaver's wife, Kathleen Neal (whom he married in 1967), ran for the California State Assembly, in addition to Newton and Seale. Around this time, Cleaver also taught an experimental course at the University of California at Berkeley in the fall of 1968.

Cleaver would again run afoul of the law on April 6, 1968, when he was involved in a shootout between members of the Black Panthers and the Oakland, California, police. *New York Times Magazine* writer T. D. Allman painted the scene as such: "Cleaver and a companion, Black Panther Treasurer Bobby Hutton, were holed up in a house with a rifle and a few pistols. The police poured thousands of rounds of ammunition into the house. Though some fire was returned, no policemen were wounded. Hutton, however, was shot dead, apparently while trying to surrender." The *New York Times* obituary on Cleaver, however, noted that two police officers were wounded at the scene. In addition, Cleaver was wounded and his parole revoked, and he was potentially facing more jail time. After this incident, Cleaver ran for president on the Peace and Freedom ticket and received 30,000 votes. Also in 1968, he published his best-selling essay collection, *Soul on Ice*.

Finally, a local judge ruled that the charges were politically motivated and enabled Cleaver to go free. However, in late 1968, a higher court disagreed, stating that he should return to prison for violating parole and slapping him with new charges for the shootout. At 33 years old, Cleaver did not want to be locked up again, after spending so much time incarcerated already. Thus, he fled to Cuba with his wife Kathleen, son Maceo, and daughter Joju, and also spent time in Algeria, France, and the Soviet Union.

While abroad, he quit the Black Panthers, dismissed communism and socialism, and took up Christianity. After eight years, he returned to the United States and received a sentence of community service.

Though Cleaver was initially much in demand as a speaker, his years after his return were marked by strange endeavors. He opened a store in Hollywood, selling men's pants with a special codpiece to accentuate the genitals. Then he founded a religious group in 1979 in Nevada, the Cleaver Crusade for Christ, only to establish a new religion altogether—Christlam—the following year. Accompanying this idea was a group called Guardians of the Sperm. He then took up Mormonism. He tried his hand at a recycling business, but other companies accused him of taking their trash. At some point, he made ceramic flowerpots, and he tried in vain to start up a political career with the Republican party. He and his wife, a law professor, divorced in the mid-1980s. Also in the 1980s, he was reportedly arrested for burglary and possession of cocaine, and in 1990 he was treated for an addiction to crack cocaine. In 1994 he underwent brain surgery after receiving a head injury during a drug buy.

After this low period, Cleaver attended Harvard Law School for some time, then returned to Berkeley and became a preacher. He spent much of his later years speaking in schools, prisons, and churches about drug recovery and nonviolence, and served as a consultant to the Coalition for Diversity at the University of La Verne in southern California. Once branded the "nation's greatest threat" by FBI director J. Edgar Hoover, according to the *Los Angeles Times*, Cleaver continued to craft ceramics and also spent many evenings giving poetry readings at local coffeehouses in the Pomona area. He died at Pomona Valley Hospital Medical Center in California at age 62. Hospital spokespersons did not reveal the cause of death, but a neighbor told the press that Cleaver had suffered from prostate cancer and that his illness may have been caused by an interaction of medications. **Sources:** "'He Was a Symbol': Eldridge Cleaver Dies at 62," CNNin web site, May 1, 1998, http://cnn.com (May 4, 1998); *Contemporary Authors, New Revision Series*, volume 16, Gale Research, 1986; *Contemporary Black Biography*, volume 5, Gale Research, 1994; *Encyclopedia of World Biography*, second edition, Gale Research, 1997; *Los Angeles Times*, May 2, 1998; *New York Times*, May 2, 1998, p. A11; *New York Times Magazine*, January 16, 1977, p. 10; *Times* (London), May 4, 1998; *USA Today*, May 1, 1998; *Washington Post*, May 2, 1998.

—Geri Speace

Henry Steele Commager

Born October 25, 1902, in Pittsburgh, PA; died March 2, 1998, at his home in Amherst, MA. Historian. History scholar Henry Steele Commager was best known for cowriting *The Growth of the American Republic,* which remained a staple textbook in college classrooms for over 40 years. An educator for almost seven decades, he was also known as a scholar of the U.S. Constitution. He made news in the 1950s for his opposition to Senator Joseph McCarthy and in the 1960s for his opposition to the U.S. involvement in the Vietnam War.

Commager was born in Pittsburgh, Pennsylvania, to James Williams and Anna Elizabeth Commager. Orphaned as a child, he was raised by his grandfather, who was one of the founders of American Lutheranism. After growing up in Toledo, Ohio, and Chicago, Illinois, he graduated from high school in Chicago, Illinois, and enrolled at the University of Chicago. He went on to earn his bachelor's degree in philosophy and a master's degree and doctorate in history from the University of Chicago, in addition to a master's degree in politics from Oxford University in England. He also attended the University of Copenhagen, where he studied Danish naval history.

In 1926, Commager joined the faculty of New York University and rose through the ranks to become a professor in 1931. He moved to Columbia University in 1939, where he taught American history until 1956, when he accepted a post at Amherst University. He taught there until 1972, when he was named Simpson lecturer, the school's most prestigious faculty appointment, which he held until the age of 92. Robert Frost and Archibald MacLeish were two who previously held the title. During his many years of academia, Commager also lectured and held visiting professorships at numerous other institutions, including Boston University, Oxford University, Northwestern University, and many others.

Commager was a lively presence on campus. CNN Interactive cited a *New York Times* article which claimed that the professor was known for his "No. 1 Rule," which was "I'm right." Not especially intent on remembering students' names, Commager often referred to people as Miss or Mr. McGillicuddy. His scholarly and teaching career was briefly interrupted during the 1940s when he worked for the Office of War Information in Europe during World War II and served as an official war historian.

Commager's reputation was cemented upon the release in 1931 of *The Growth of the American Republic,* which he wrote with Samuel Eliot Morison of Harvard University. This work became a leading text in college history classrooms throughout the country. In a *Washington Post* obituary, noted historian Allan Nevins was quoted as calling the book "the most entertaining, stimulating and instructive single-volume history of the United States as yet written." In the work, readers could discern Commager's view that the U.S. Constitution was "the greatest monument to political science in literature," as the CNN Interactive web site quoted. As successful as this project was, Commager himself deemed his most significant contribution to be his editorship of *Documents of American History,* a collection of primary sources relevant to the establishment of the United States. The two-volume work was first published in 1934.

Commager was the author, coauthor, or editor of numerous works of history throughout his lengthy and distinguished career. In 1941, he published what would serve as a standard reading for high school students of U.S. history, and the following year cowrote with Nevins the general interest book, *America: The Story of a Free People,* which covered the country's history from the first settlers to the attack on Pearl Harbor in December of 1941. It became a best seller. He first applied constitutional history to contemporary events in *Majority Rule and Minority Rights* (1943). In 1950, he published his magisterial work, *The American Mind: An Interpretation of American Thought and Character Since the 1880s.* In this, he recounted the tremendous progress of the first century of the country, with the exception of slavery and the Civil War.

About the time he was working on *The American Mind,* Commager began to take note of political events that he believed seriously threatened the principles of the Constitution. Senator Joseph McCarthy, in his crusade to seek out Communists, was forcing citizens to sign loyalty oaths or else risk losing their jobs. Commager saw this as a more sinister threat to democracy that communism itself. He outspokenly opposed McCarthy and persevered toward upholding free speech.

During the 1960s, despite his staunch pride in the United States, Commager decried America's involvement in the Vietnam War, publishing articles on the subject, giving speeches, and even appealing to Congress not to send U.S. troops. The following decades saw many more works by the scholar, including the 1977 book, *The Empire of Reason: How Europe Imagined and America Realized the Enlightenment*, which was called "his most brilliant work" by the *New York Times*, as reported by CNN Interactive. His final book, *Commager on Tocqueville*, published when he was 91, was praised by a *New York Times Book Review* critic.

Commager received the Herbert B. Adams Award of the American Historical Association in 1929; a special award from the Hillman Foundation in 1954 for the work *Freedom, Loyalty, Dissent*; a Guggenheim Fellowship in 1960-61; a Gold Medal Award for history from the American Academy and Institute of Arts and Letters, 1972; the Sarah Josepha Hale Award, 1973; and numerous honorary degrees and tributes. Commager married Evan Carroll on July 3, 1928; she died in 1968. He married Mary E. Powlesland in 1979. He is survived by his wife; two daughters from his first marriage, Nell Lasch and Lisa Demlinger; five grandchildren; and five great-grandchildren. His son, Henry Steele Commager, Jr., a Columbia professor, died in 1985. **Sources:** "Commager left his mark on American history," CNN Interactive web site, http://www.cnn.com (March 3, 1998); *Contemporary Authors*, Volumes 21-24, 1st revision, Gale Research, 1977; *New York Times*, March 3, 1998; *Times* (London), March 9, 1998; *Washington Post*, March 3, 1998.

—Geri Speace

Jacques-Yves Cousteau

Born June 11, 1910, in St.-Andre-de-Cubzac, France; died of a heart attack on June 25, 1997, at his home in Paris. Cousteau spent most of his life exploring the Earth's oceans and capturing their wonders, secrets and frailties on film for a worldwide television audience. He co-invented the first underwater breathing device, developed a one-person, jet-propelled submarine, established the first manned undersea colonies, and pioneered the craft of undersea film making. "For 50 years, his films conveyed a wonderful excitement about nature," wrote Christopher Dickey in *Newsweek*. "The spectacle beneath the seas was wildly alien, but through Cousteau it became ... accessible.... He changed the way we see the world and the way we live in it." In the process, Cousteau attracted a worldwide following. "He was one of the most familiar faces on the planet, one of the most enduring and one of the most comforting," Dickey wrote. Late in life, according to *Maclean's*, Cousteau embraced environmentalism and advocated protection of the marine ecosystem's delicate balance.

Cousteau was born in a prosperous small town near Bordeaux, France. His father, a lawyer, traveled constantly and kept his family on the move. Cousteau, a sickly, anemic child, was entranced by the sea at an early age; he began swimming at age 4. As he grew up and grew stronger, Cousteau decided on a career as a naval officer. Following World War I, his father's work took the family to the United States for two years, where young Jacques played stickball on Manhattan's Upper West Side and made his first dive in Vermont's Lake Harvey. An indifferent student, Cousteau once was expelled for breaking 17 windows at his high school. Ultimately, his parents sent him to a rigorous boarding school and, in 1930, he entered the French naval academy.

Six years later, while stationed in Toulon as an artillery instructor, he swam in the Mediterranean and, with help from two friends, experimented with water-tight goggles. "The naked human eye is almost blind underwater," Gerald Jonas wrote in the *New York Times*, "so the submarine vistas that Mr. Cousteau beheld when he first put on the goggles in 1936 were a revelation.... Determined to dive deeper, stay down longer and see more, (he) and his friends began tinkering with homemade snorkel hoses, insulated body suits, and portable breathing devices based on the recent invention of compressed air." Before long, Cousteau and French engineer Emile Gagnan patented the "Aqua-lung," the first underwater breathing apparatus.

In 1937, Cousteau married Simone Melchior. They had two sons, Jean-Michel, born in 1938, and Philippe, born in 1940. He served in the Navy through World War II, spying for the French Resistance and establishing a military unit which taught sailors scuba diving and underwater photography techniques and cleared German mines from French ports. After the war he received the French Legion of Honor, his country's highest honor.

"In the 1950s," Jonas wrote, "Mr. Cousteau came into his own as an innovator and entrepreneur of undersea exploration. On permanent leave from the navy, he formed the first in a series of corporations and nonprofit organizations through which he financed expeditions, advanced environmental causes dear to him, and projected his image as the leading explorer of the day." In 1953, Cousteau gained celebrity with the publication of *The Silent World*, an account of the development and promise of scuba diving. The book sold millions of copies worldwide. A documentary film version of the story won Cousteau the first of his three

Academy Awards as well as the top prize at the 1956 Cannes Film Festival.

In the 1960s, Cousteau experimented with underwater habitats—known as Conshelf I, II, and III—which allowed "oceanauts" to live and work beneath the sea. A documentary exploring the Conshelf expeditions, *World Without Sun*, won an Oscar in 1964. Following an acclaimed National Geographic television special on the project, Cousteau began a nine-year relationship in which he delivered four one-hour specials a year to ABC-TV. The series was titled *The Undersea World of Jacques Cousteau*. He later produced television documentaries under the title *The Cousteau Odyssey* for the Public Broadcasting System; the series *Cousteau's Amazon* premiered in 1984 on the Turner Broadcasting System. The TV series, which earned more than 40 Emmy nominations, brought the wonders of the Earth's oceans into people's homes, along with the pollution that was degrading them. "I think Captain Cousteau might be the father of the environmental movement," said TBS founder Ted Turner. Cousteau's environmental activism, in fact, grew stronger as he got older. "In the '60s he talked about the sea as an exploitable resource," Jonas wrote. "By 1970 he was warning that life in the oceans had diminished 40 percent in just 20 years."

Cousteau's youngest son, Philippe, died in a seaplane crash in 1979. His wife, Simone, died in 1990, by which time he had two children with Francine Triplett, who became his second wife in 1991. Cousteau once commented, "Curiosity and passion is what keeps us alive." He is survived by his second wife and his three children, Jean-Michel, Diane, and Pierre-Yves. **Sources:** *CNN Interactive*, June 25, 1997; *Maclean's*, July 7, 1997, p. 15; *Notable 20th Century Scientists*, Gale Research, 1995, pp. 413-417; *New York Times*, June 26, 1997, p. A1; *Newsweek*, July 7, 1997, p. 56; *People*, July 7, 1997, p. 113; *Time*, July 7, 1997, p. 25.

—Dave Wilkins

John Denver

Born Henry John Deutschendorf, Jr., December 31, 1943, in Roswell, NM; died October 12, 1997, in Pacific Grove, CA, in a plane crash while flying solo off the California coast. Denver broke onto the pop, country, and folk music scene as a songwriter when his 1969 hit, "Leaving On a Jet Plane," was covered by Peter, Paul and Mary and sold one million copies. Soon af-

ter, Denver began his solo career and won popularity with uplifting songs celebrating the appreciation of one's surroundings, such as "Rocky Mountain High," and "Sunshine On My Shoulders." Despite criticism that his music was "as bland as Wonder Bread" and "as cloying as toffee," as noted by Mary Curtius and Louis Sahagun in the *Los Angeles Times*, Denver maintained a cadre of followers. As his concern for environmental issues increased during the 1980s, the number of Denver's recordings and hit songs began to decrease. He started the nonprofit educational and research group, Windstar Foundation, that ran symposiums. He also made documentaries about hunger, campaigned for the preservation of wildlife, sat on the board of the Cousteau Society, and helped found the reforestation project called Plant-It 2000, and the Hunger Project, aiming to end world hunger.

The son of an Air Force pilot who later became a Lear Jet flying instructor, it was the senior Henry John Deutschendorf who taught Denver how to fly. Bounced around from state to state due to his father's transfers with the Air Force, Denver grew up in Oklahoma, Arizona, Alabama, Japan, Ohio, and Texas. His grandmother gave him his first guitar, a 1910 Gibson, when he was in seventh grade. At that time, he was fairly disinterested in learning to play. Influenced by Elvis Presley's revolutionary effect on the music world, Denver eventually began to take lessons and to practice diligently, becoming good enough to perform with local groups, play at parties, and entertain audiences with folk songs while still in high school. He headed for Texas Tech University in Lubbock in 1961 where he planned to major in architecture. To defray the costs of college, Denver played guitar in a rhythm and blues band and performed at coffeehouses. After two and a half years, Denver dropped out of college in 1964. He found himself spending more time on his music than on his studies, so he packed up his three guitars and the $125 he had to his name and headed to Los Angeles. Working as a draftsman by day, Denver sang at lounges and clubs at night. His first musical break was as a regular performer at Leadbetters nightclub. He met a Capital Records producer who helped move along Denver's career and suggested he find a new surname. "I guess he thought [Deutschendorf] wouldn't fit on a record label," Denver once joked as quoted in the *Los Angeles Times*. Denver chose his stage name in homage to the clean air and mountains he so loved and that the city's name evoked.

In Los Angeles, Denver became a member of the musical group Back Porch Majority. His big break came in 1965, however, when he beat out 250 hopefuls to replace Chad Mitchell as the lead singer in the Chad Mitchell Trio, a pop-folk group that toured college folk circuits. In 1967, Denver had written "Leaving On a Jet Plane." But it wasn't until a Peter, Paul and Mary recording sold a million copies in 1969 that Denver's talents as a lyricist, as well as a guitar player, were recognized. With the popularity of the Chad Mitchell Trio fading, Denver set out on his own to establish a solo career. Enlisting the help of Milt Okun, who was the producer for both the Chad Mitchell Trio and Peter, Paul and Mary, Denver produced his first solo album, *Rhymes and Reasons,* in 1969 on the RCA label.

In 1971, "Take Me Home, Country Roads" became Denver's first million-selling single and served as the catalyst for a string of hits that brought him fame and fortune throughout the decade. Following "Take Me Home, Country Roads," which was co-written by Denver and Bill and Taffy Danoff and became the unofficial state song for West Virginia, Denver's successive hits included "Rocky Mountain High," "Annie's Song" (written in ten minutes for his first wife while riding up a ski-lift after the couple had an argument), and "Thank God I'm a Country Boy" (still a favorite at Baltimore Orioles games). He earned the honor of being named the Country Music Association's entertainer of the year in 1975.

In the 1980s, Denver's musical career began to falter; after recording 1981's *Perhaps Love* with tenor Placido Domingo, the title song was his last hit. Denver was frustrated and hurt when his music's popularity decreased. "It was very disturbing to him," said former Chad Mitchell Trio member Joe Frazier in the *Los Angeles Times.* "I don't think he ever got over not being up there." Denver, still wanting to inspire and be "a role model for young people," as he once told Alice Steinbach in the *Saturday Review,* threw himself into numerous causes. He founded the Windstar Foundation, an environmental education center, and donated song royalties to the United Nations International Children's Emergency Fund (UNICEF). His patronage also went to The Wilderness Society, Friends of the Earth, and the World Wildlife Fund. He served on a presidential commission on hunger and toured the Soviet Union, China, and Vietnam long before such altruism and concern became popular. When Denver traveled to Africa as part of a fact-finding trip on behalf of the Hunger Project, President Reagan presented him with the Presidential World Without Hunger Award. Plant-It 2000 was a group Denver created in hopes of planting a million indigenous tress around the world by the turn of the millennium. Also interested in astronomy, Denver tried repeatedly to convince the National Aeronautics and Space Administration (NASA) to allow him on a space mission. When they rejected him, he asked the Soviet Union to let him aboard the Mir space station.

Denver also dabbled in television and movies. He had his own show in Britain and specials with the Muppets. He appeared on the TV drama *McCloud* and hosted the Grammy Awards six times. 1977 saw his movie debut when he appeared with George Burns in *Oh, God.* He later filmed his own documentaries dealing with environmental concerns and had been seen in the film *Walking Thunder.* In 1994, Denver published his autobiography, *Take Me Home.*

In his 53 years, Denver wrote more than 200 songs, and had just penned "Yellowstone," for a documentary that had yet to be released at the time of his death. He had signed a contract with Sony records and had recorded *Best of John Denver Live* in 1997. Fourteen of his albums went gold and eight were platinum. Denver is survived by his two former wives, two daughters and a son, a brother, and his mother. **Sources:** Associated Press on-line, http://wire.ap.org (October 14, 1997); *Atlanta Journal and Constitution* on-line, http://www.accessatlanta.com (October 14, 1997); *Chicago Tribune* on-line, http://www.chicago .tribune.com (October 4, 1997); CNN Interactive on-line, http://cnn.com (October 13, 1997); *Contemporary Musicians,* Volume 1, Gale Research, 1989; *Detroit Free Press,* October 14, 1997, p. D1; *Detroit News* on-line, http://www.detnews.com (October 14, 1997); *Los Angeles Times,* October 14, 1997, p. A1; *New York Times,* October 14, 1997, p. B11; *Saturday Review,* September/ October, 1985; *Times* (London) on-line, http:// www.the-times.co.uk (October 14, 1997); *USA Today* on-line, http://www.usatoday.com (October 14, 1997); *Washington Post* on-line, http://search.washingtonpost .com (October 14, 1997).

—*Audrey Gebber*

Nancy H. Dickerson

Born January 27, 1927, Wauwatosa, WI; died October 18, 1997, in New York, NY, after a long illness. Nancy Hanschman Dickerson fought her way into the male-dominated ranks of broadcast journalism to become the first woman reporter at a national American political convention in 1960. She enjoyed a long career as a network correspondent, producer of news specials, and Washington insider.

The daughter of an architect, Dickerson grew up in the midwest through the Great Depression and World War II. She studied English, Spanish and Portuguese at the University of Wisconsin and graduated in 1948 with degree in education. For the next few years, Dickerson taught school in Milwaukee, but grew dissatisfied in the profession and sought greater challenges. In 1951 she moved New York City, but had little luck finding a job; she then moved to Washington, D.C., where she secured an administrative position with Georgetown University. In a short time, however, Dickerson was hired as a staff researcher for the United States Senate Foreign Relations Committee, a plum assignment.

From that moment forward, Dickerson consistently avoided the so-called "women's ghetto" in her career choices. A leading Washington newspaper once offered her its women's-page editor post, but she declined, saying "it seemed outlandish to try to change the world," according to her *Washington Post* obituary, in feature stories devoted to fashion and domestic concerns, which were the staples of such sections in that day.

In 1954 she bluffed her way into a new career as an assistant producer at CBS Radio for a show called *The Leading Question.* She excelled, despite her inexperience, and was given the same job with the just-launched *Face the Nation* program in 1956. Four years later, she became the network's first female correspondent; CBS was the last of the three American networks to hire a woman as an on-air reporter. She covered the 1960 presidential campaign for her first major assignment and did so well that management offered her a weekday radio show of her own. *One Woman's Washington* made Dickerson the first woman to host her own daily news show on a network. On it, she broke new ground in news aimed at female audiences by exploring political, legislative, and judicial happenings in the nation's capital that affected American women.

Dickerson left CBS for rival network NBC in 1963, and remained there as an on-air corespondent for the next seven years. During that time, she covered a series of memorable events on the American political landscape—the funeral of assassinated President John F. Kennedy, the civil rights marches, and the national political conventions of the decade. In 1970 she left NBC, and the following year founded her own company and began appearing as an analyst on the nationally syndicated show *Inside Washington.* Dickerson's firm produced and syndicated news programs, and she continued to work as a journalist in this capacity. In 1980, she launched another company, the Television Corporation of America, which produced similar programming. Her 1982 special on the Nixon Administration, *784 Days That Changed America—From Watergate to Resignation,* won her the prestigious George Foster Peabody Award for excellence in broadcasting. The judge who had presided over the court cases that forced Nixon out of office, John Sirica, declared that because of the historical value of Dickerson's documentary, "it would be a great thing if this program could be shown in every high school and college in the country," reported the *Chicago Tribune.*

Dickerson was known as a legendary party-giver in the nation's capital, and over the years became friends with a host of well-known personalities, including the Reagan family and several cabinet members of various administrations. By the time of her 1962 marriage to real-estate developer C. Wyatt Dickerson, she was such an affirmed Washington social and political insider that a party co-hosted by a Supreme Court Justice, a senator, and Vice-President Lyndon Johnson feted the couple. They began a family that would eventually number five children, and acquired the McLean, Virginia, estate known as Merrywood that had been the childhood home of Jacqueline Kennedy Onassis. Dickerson had once dated Jack Kennedy when both were singles in Washington, she admitted in her 1976 biography *Among Those Present: A Reporter's View of Twenty-Five Years in Washington.*

During the 1980s, Dickerson focused much of her interests on the turmoil in the Middle East and brought back interviews with leaders such as Egyptian President Anwar Sadat, Prince Saud of Saudi Arabia, and Israeli Prime Minister Menachem Begin. She produced a special on women in Arab society, *Islam: The Veil and the Future,* that aired on PBS, and had served as a commentator for Fox News since the mid-1980s. She was divorced from C. Wyatt Dickerson in 1983; six years later she wed the former Deputy Secretary of State in the Reagan Administration, John C. Whitehead. They lived at Merrywood, and she was active in a number of charitable causes. She was working on a follow-up memoir when she suffered a stroke in early 1996. She died at New York Hospital on October 18, 1997. She is survived by her husband, five children, four step-children, eleven grandchildren, and one sister. **Sources:** *Chicago Tribune,* October 19, 1997, p. C8; *Los Angeles Times,* October 19, 1997, p. B5; *New York Times,* October 19, 1997, sec. 1, p. 45; *Washington Post,* October 19, 1997.

—Carol Brennan

James Dickey

Born February 2, 1923, in Buckhead, GA (a suburb of Atlanta); died January 19, 1997, in Columbia, SC, of complications from lung disease. James Dickey published more than 20 volumes of poetry, earning him a National Book Award and a seat in the American Academy of Arts and Letters. Hailed by critics for his "impeccable ear," "joyous imagination" and "intense clarity," Dickey was appointed a consultant in poetry to the Library of Congress in 1966, which was, at that time, the American equivalent of the British poet laureate. Despite his acclaim as a poet and a critic, Dickey is perhaps best known for his novel-turned-movie, *Deliverance*. Dickey helped write the screenplay for the Academy Award-nominated film and even appeared in it as the hefty Georgia sheriff.

Considering himself a novelist only when he needed to pay the rent, Dickey was always fiercely loyal to the poetic genre. "The strength of my life always has been and always will be poetry," he once said. "Poetry is the center of the creative wheel."

The son of Eugene and Maibelle (Swift) Dickey, James Lafayette Dickey grew up listening to his lawyer father dramatically reading the speeches of Robert Ingersoll, a 19th-century agnostic orator who enjoyed confrontations with the fundamentalist preachers of the time. Raised primarily by his grandmother because his mother was an invalid, Dickey spent a good deal of time with his father, traveling frequently to the Appalachian Mountain-area of Eugene's family. Dickey admitted that his family had "no interest in the arts, and none had as little interest as I." An avid outdoorsman, Dickey entered Clemson College where he was a varsity wingback on the football team his freshman year. He also took up archery, canoeing, weight lifting, hunting, and other sports he continued to pursue during his lifetime. He also became an excellent guitarist, and could pluck out a decent tune on a banjo. He loved life and was known for his boisterous behavior, enthusiastic drinking, and attraction to women.

After his first year at Clemson, Dickey quit school and enlisted in the Army Air Corps in 1942 and volunteered for the 418th Night Fighter Squadron. Dickey flew more than 100 missions during his service in the Pacific, and his war experiences often appeared in his writing. It was during the boring gaps between air missions that Dickey became interested in literature, devouring the books in the base library in Okinawa.

After tearing through the prose selections, Dickey became captivated with a poetry anthology he came across. He began "tinkering" with language himself, saying his initial attempts were "erotic love letters to girls back in Atlanta and Montgomery. I guess I started being a writer the day I found myself thinking, 'Gosh, that's pretty good,' instead of 'That ought to knock her dead.'"

Dickey returned to college after World War II, this time to Vanderbilt University where he majored in English. While there, he was a track star, winning the Tennessee state championship in the 120-yard high hurdles. He graduated *magna cum laude* in 1949 and received his masters degree, also from Vanderbilt, the following year. In 1951, Dickey sold his first poem, "Shark at the Window" to the *Sewanee Review*. He earned $28.50.

The years 1952-54 were spent teaching English at Rice University and the University of Florida. In 1954, the *Sewanee Review* awarded Dickey with a $3,500 fellowship, allowing him to spend a year writing in Europe. Dickey also returned to the skies when he served in the Air Force during the Korean War. In 1956, with a wife, Maxine, and two sons, Christopher and Kevin, Dickey had to leave poetry behind to support his family. He joined the McCann-Erickson advertising agency, where he wrote jingles for Coca-Cola, Lay's potato chips, Delta Airlines, and Armour fertilizer.

By 1960, Dickey felt he had saved enough money writing advertising copy to be able to quit and focus his attentions on being a full-time poet. His first collection, *Into the Stone and Other Poems*, was published by Charles Scribner's Sons that year. Although it was favorably received, Dickey only earned $114 in royalties. In 1961, Dickey went on welfare for a short time, but then obtained a $5,000 Guggenheim grant. He sold his home in Atlanta and spent a year in Italy. When he returned to the States, he served as a poet-in-residence at Reed College, San Fernando Valley State College, and the University of Wisconsin.

Between 1962 and 1964, Dickey published three more volumes of poetry and a selection of his critical essays. Known for his brashness, his criticisms were not of the standard scholarly, academic set. In one essay, he described John Milton as among "the great stuffed goats of English literature." In 1966, Dickey succeeded Stephen Spender as the Library of Congress's poetry consultant and won the National Book Award for poetry for his collection entitled *Buckdancer's Choice*.

Dickey became the poet-in-residence and an English instructor at the University of South Carolina in 1968, a position he held up to his death, even wheeling his oxygen tank into the classroom only days before he died. *Deliverance* was published in 1970, a work on which he toiled for seven years. A thriller about four friends encountering disaster on a canoe trip down a North Georgia river, the book won him the French Prix Medicis in 1971. In 1972, the movie version won an Academy Award nomination. Much to Dickey's dismay, the book overshadowed his talent as a poet for most of the general public. Dickey once told an interviewer, "There are times when I wish I could be rid of that book." President Jimmy Carter did not overlook the poet, however, and he asked Dickey to compose a poem for his inauguration. The country heard Dickey's smooth, Southern drawl read "The Strength of Fields," reminding Carter of the "profound, unstoppable craving of nations" he would be forced to address.

Maxine, Dickey's first wife, died in 1976; and two months later, he married Deborah Dodson, a former student, with whom he had a daughter, Bronwen Elaine. Married to Maxine for nearly 30 years, his second marriage was a struggle, with several separations. The couple was separated at the time of Dickey's death.

Dickey's health began its decline in 1986, when he underwent surgery to remove a blood clot in his brain. He still managed to put out a second novel, *Alnilam*, in 1987, about a men's group seeking world dominance, another book in *Deliverance*'s epic form, pitting men against each other as well as nature. He published one more novel, *To the White Sea*, in 1993, about a B-29 tailgunner shot down over Tokyo in the last days of World War II. In late 1994, he was admitted to the hospital twice for jaundice and related problems. On January 15, 1997, Dickey entered Providence Hospital for the last time, dying four days later.

Of her father, Bronwen Dickey described his memory in a guest column for *Newsweek* as, "Not the greatness of the writer but the greatness of the father and the teacher. One time in the class he taught, my father was reading his poem, 'Good-bye to Big Daddy,' about the death of football player Big Daddy Lipscomb, and this big ox-headed football player in the class started bawling in the middle of the reading. The class was dismissed and my dad just went over to this guy and held him while he wept like a child, saying, 'It's all right, Big Boy; it's gonna be OK.' That is the kind of teacher James Dickey was. There are no words for the kind of father he was."

Among the many awards Dickey won were the Longview, Vachel Lindsay and Melville Cane Awards for poetry. Dickey once said that as "a creature of the military" his main value was always survival. The legacy of work he has left the world is testimony to his instinct. **Sources:** CNN interactive online, http://www.cnn.com; *Los Angeles Times*, January 21, 1997, p. B8; *Newsweek*, August 30, 1993, p. 54, February 3, 1997, p. 53, March 24, 1997, p. 19; *New York Times*, January 21, 1997, p. D22; *New York Times Book Review*, March 23, 1997, p. 31; *Time*, February 3, 1997; *Washington Post*, January 21, 1997, p. B5.

—*Audrey Gebber*

Walter E. Diemer

Born c. 1904; died January 8, 1998, in Lancaster, PA, from congestive heart failure. An accountant by profession, Walter E. Diemer was the unlikely inventor of one of the world's most popular confections. One day in 1928, Diemer was testing some of his ideas in the laboratory of his employer, the Fleer Chewing Gum Company, and concocted, quite by accident, what turned out to be the perfect recipe for bubble gum.

Then in his mid-twenties, Diemer had worked for the Philadelphia-based Fleer since finishing high school. The company's president encouraged all employees to play around in the Fleer laboratories, and Diemer had been working on coming up with a formula for a better chewing gum—not for a bubble-producing product. Finding a pliant gum base, and one that held flavor longer, had been a leading research goal for Fleer and its competitors since the first American chewing gum hit the market in 1870. "It was an accident," Diemer later said of his successful experiment in an interview with the *Lancaster Intelligencer Journal* in 1996. "I was doing something else and ended up with something with bubbles." His batch yielded a much softer type of gum and could stretch much farther. It enabled the chewer to blow bubbles—yet did not stick to the face when popped—something that Fleer and other American chewing-gum makers had been trying to achieve for over two decades. When he and his colleagues sampled the batch that night, Diemer said, they became quite excited and began "blowing bubbles all over the office. Everyone said, 'What a great product!' and it really went to our heads," he reminisced in *The Great American Chewing Gum Book*. Another accident related to the invention of bubble gum was its appetizing bright pink hue—which only occurred because pink food coloring was the only shade Diemer had close at hand in the lab that day.

The success of the product that Fleer executives trade-marked as Dubble Bubble would not, however, go to Diemer's pockets; he never received any royalties from the invention. He was, however, the official company "expert" on Dubble Bubble, having been sent out to a local grocery store with one of the first batches as a test; it sold out immediately and the company moved quickly to mass-produce and market it. Fleer put Diemer's confection in yellow wrappers and sold it for a penny apiece, and he trained the salespeople hired to market the bubble gum nationally in the art of bubble blowing. Eventually he rose to the post of a senior vice-president at Fleer, and he felt that his promotion was ample compensation for his contribution to the company fortunes.

For two decades Dubble Bubble was the only bubble gum on the market; only after World War II, when the Brooklyn, New York-based Topps Co. came up with their own recipe and began selling it wrapped inside miniature comics—the Bazooka brand—did another competitor encroach upon Fleer's healthy market share. Nor surprisingly, parents, teachers, and dentists were vociferous critics of Dubble Bubble and the later brands, but by the 1990s it was estimated that around 150,000 pounds of the product—much of it still the requisite pink color—were being chewed around the world daily.

Before he retired from Fleer in 1970, Diemer supervised construction of manufacturing plants and oversaw marketing efforts for the product in numerous countries. He remained on company's board of directors until 1980. After his first wife died in 1991, Diemer moved from the New Jersey resort town of Ocean City, to which he had retired, to Lancaster, Pennsylvania. There he was a familiar sight to townspeople as he rode about on a giant tricycle. According to his second wife, Florence Freeman Kohler Diemer, he also enjoyed entertaining neighborhood children by giving a brief history lesson of his invention and then staging a bubble-blowing contest. Diemer had two children from his first marriage, who both died in 1986; he is survived by five grandchildren and nine great-grandchildren. Over the years, the accountant had received hundreds of letters from children around the world thanking him for his invention. "He would say to me: 'I've done something with my life,'" Diemer's widow told the *New York Times*. "'I've made kids happy around the world.'" **Sources:** *Los Angeles Times*, January 13, 1998; *New York Times*, January 12, 1998; *Times* (London), January 13, 1998.

—*Carol Brennan*

Lillian Disney

Born Lillian Bounds, in 1899, in Spalding, ID; died after a stroke on December 16, 1997, at her home in Holmby Hills, CA. Businesswoman, philanthropist. Lillian Disney was the wife of businessman and animator Walt Disney, who built an entertainment empire of film studios, amusement parks, and merchandising. Lillian Disney was her husband's business partner and an integral part of his success. The *Los Angeles Times* reported that in the 1920s, Walt Disney had suggested a new animated character that he wished to name "Mortimer Mouse." Lillian Disney, according to the *Times*, replied, "It's too formal. How about Mickey?" Mickey Mouse went on to become the most famous rodent in history. At a White House ceremony in 1969, President Richard Nixon presented Lillian Disney with a gold Commemorative Medal honoring her late husband; it had Walt Disney's profile on one side and Mickey Mouse's on the other.

Lillian Disney was born into a family that admired music in Spalding, Idaho, the youngest of ten children of Willard and Jeanette (Short) Bounds. Her father was a government employee who worked as a blacksmith and federal marshal on the Nez Pierce Indian Reservation in Lapwai, Idaho, where Disney was raised. In 1923, she moved to Los Angeles, California, where her sister, Hazel, was living. Through a friend, she was hired at the Walt Disney Studio for $15 a week to ink film frames. She and Walt Disney were married on July 13, 1925, in Lewiston, Idaho. Their daughter, Diane Disney Miller, revealed in the *Los Angeles Times*, "I think my dad fell in love with her almost immediately.... She was a very independent little lady." The Disneys had one adopted daughter, Sharon Disney Lund, who died of cancer in 1993.

Lillian Disney stayed in the background as her husband's sounding board for ideas and helpmate for 41 years. She provided advice on ideas from *Snow White* to Disneyland, often denouncing some of his revolutionary ideas until he had given them more thought. Her *Los Angeles Times* obituary reported a statement from company chairman Michael D. Eisner: "Mrs. Disney was a full-time partner to Walt, and we are all grateful for her contributions in the creation of Mickey Mouse and the Disney Co. and for the example she set for family life and community service."

After her husband's death in 1966, Lillian Disney, with other family members, founded the California Institute of the Arts, a multidisciplinary school that brought up many of the finest animators in the film business. She assisted with many charities for young people and the arts and also headed a giving foundation. Three years after Walt Disney's death, Lillian Disney married John Truyens, who died in 1981.

Among her numerous philanthropic deeds, on May 13, 1987, Lillian Disney donated $50 million to the Music Center of Los Angeles to build the world-class Walt Disney Concert Hall in downtown Los Angeles across from the Dorothy Chandler Pavilion. She hoped for it to possess perfect acoustics for the Los Angeles Philharmonic, as well as a garden, and to be a place for the masses to enjoy music—not just the elite. At that time, she announced, "I have always had a deep love and admiration for my husband, and I wanted to find a way to honor him, as well as give something to Los Angeles which would have lasting qualities," the *Los Angeles Times* recalled in her obituary.

Renowned Santa Monica architect Frank Gehry was chosen to design the building. Unfortunately, the project experienced numerous delays, and the original groundbreaking date of 1990 was pushed back to 1992, although it was mainly symbolic. In 1994, revised cost estimates doubled the initial price, and the following year, the county threatened to leave the project and the work was halted. Late in 1996, some new funds were donated from outside sources, and on December 1, 1997, the Walt Disney Company gave $25 million, practically sealing the completion of the new hall. Though the planned opening date at the beginning of the project was 1997, it looked like the grand opening of the 2,350 seat structure would be seen in 2001, with construction ensuing in 1998.

Disney received the Governor's Award for the Arts recognizing her contributions to the arts in California, and in 1988 was given a cultural award from the Los Angeles Headquarters City Association for her funds to build the Walt Disney Concert Hall. In 1996, she donated $100,000 to the Nez Pierce Indians to purchase ancient tribal artifacts. In one of her infrequent public comments, as quoted in the *Los Angeles Times*, she reacted to a negative biography of her husband—*Walt Disney: Hollywood's Dark Prince,* by Marc Eliot—by stating, "We shared a wonderful, exciting life, and we loved every minute of it. He was a wonderful husband to me and wonderful and joyful father and grandfather." Lillian Disney suffered a stroke exactly 31 years after the death of her husband on December 15, 1966. She is survived by her daughter, Diane Disney Miller, 10 grandchildren, and 13 great-grandchildren. **Sources:** *Chicago Tribune,* December 18, 1997; "Lillian Disney, widow of Walt Disney, dies at 98," CNN Interactive web site, http://cnn.com (December 17, 1998); *Los Angeles Times,* December 18, 1997; *USA Today,* December 17, 1997; December 18, 1997.

—*Geri Speace*

Marjory Stoneman Douglas

Born April 7, 1890, in Minneapolis, MN; died of natural causes, May 14, 1998, in Miami, FL. Author, activist. Marjory Stoneman Douglas was a fervent activist dedicated to saving the Florida Everglades. Her 1947 book, *The Everglades: A River of Grass,* opposed the general outlook on the area as being a region of untamed, worthless swamp that needed to be drained and converted to farmland and commercial property. Her sparkling prose stirred preservation efforts, the area was declared a national park in 1947, and successive generations have continued to work to save the wetlands. Douglas also continued to write novels and short stories for magazines throughout her lengthy career, many of which concerned the Everglades, or at least included them as a setting.

Douglas was the daughter of Frank Bryant Stoneman, a judge and newspaper editor, and Lillian (Trefethen) Stoneman, a concert violinist, in Minneapolis, Minnesota. Her mother and father separated when Douglas was young, and she grew up in Taunton, Massachusetts, with her mother, who suffered from a number of nervous breakdowns. Douglas graduated from Wellesley College in 1912 and soon after, married a newspaper editor, Kenneth Douglas. He passed bad checks and tried to scam money from her relatives, so she quickly divorced him and never remarried. In 1915, Douglas moved to Miami, Florida, where her father, whom she had not seen in 20 years, was the editor of a newspaper that later became the *Miami Herald*. He gave her a job as a reporter and society page editor.

During World War I, Douglas served with the American Red Cross in France, Belgium, Italy, and in the Balkans. When she returned in 1920, she worked as an assistant editor and began writing columns on a variety of issues, including the plight of migrant workers and labor camp convicts. She also raised the ire of local politicians and developers when she began a crusade to save the Florida Everglades, proposing that it should become a national park. She was asked to serve on the committee, and 1.6 million acres of the area was later designated Everglades National Park in 1947.

After a few years, Douglas in 1923 decided to leave her job in order to freelance and began selling stories to magazines. The *Saturday Evening Post* bought her first piece, and in 1928, she took second place in the O. Henry Memorial Prize for short stories. In 1937, the *Saturday Evening Post* chose her contribution "Story of a Homely Woman" as one of the best of the year. Many of the her stories during this time used the Everglades as a backdrop or subject. In 1941, Douglas' father died, which slowed down her career temporarily as she was trying to complete a novel. However, *Road to the Sun,* for young readers, was finally published in 1951, and in the meantime, an editor called to ask if she wanted to write a book for a series on the nation's rivers.

Douglas, however, was not interested in taking the assignment to write about the Miami River, which she considered rather minor. She countered with the suggestion to write a book on the Everglades, which in effect, according to an expert she consulted, was a "river of grass." The work, *The Everglades: A River of Grass,* was published in 1947, the same year that the area became protected as a national park. Until this call to arms, the public was generally under the impression that the precious wetlands were useless swamps that should be drained and filled in order to serve a practical purpose for commercial building or farming. Douglas blended colorful local history and folk tales with sharply written scientific fact to create the captivating and informative book. The lively volume sold out just one month after its release.

Douglas continued to write, and around 1969, she took charge of the Everglades battle again when a proposed airport threatened part of the preserve. At age 78, she founded Friends of the Everglades, a group that fought successfully to oppose the airport. It has grown to about 7,000 members. Soon after that, she began researching the life of naturalist W. H. Hudson, traveling to remote areas of South America for her work even though her eyesight was failing. She also spoke out to save the endangered Florida panther and Key Largo's coral reefs, in addition to continuing her protection of the Everglades.

In 1990, Douglas was honored on her one hundredth birthday with book signings, interviews, and banquets, and in 1992, she was back in action. That year, Douglas spoke out against President George Bush's proposal to modify the definition of "wetlands," a move that critics pointed out could open the door to future development. President Bill Clinton in 1993 called to wish her a happy birthday as she turned 103, and a few months later, awarded her the Presidential Medal of Freedom. In 1994, Florida state lawmakers passed the Everglades Forever Act, and also in the 1990s the federal government committed hundreds of millions of dollars to restore and protect the area. In 1996, Florida voters passed an amendment to their state's constitution that makes Everglades polluters, particularly sugar farmers, pay for clean-up costs, and more plans to save the wetlands were expected. However, voters did not pass a law to tax sugar at a penny a pound to assist with the effort; sugar producers had successfully argued that the ruling would cost many jobs.

Douglas received a bevy of honors in her lifetime, including Floridian of the Year in 1983 and a number of buildings, schools, and parks named after her. The building in Florida's capitol of Tallahassee that is home to the state Department of Natural Resources also bears her name, as does a special conservation award. Douglas wrote a number of works in addition to *The Everglades,* including *Freedom River,* 1953; *Alligator Crossing,* 1959; and *The Key to Paris,* 1960, all for young readers. She also taught at the University of Miami from 1925 to 1927 and served as editor of the University of Miami Press from 1960 to 1963. Douglas had lived in the Miami, Florida, neighborhood of Coconut Grove since 1926; she died in her sleep at home on May 14, 1998. **Sources:** *Chicago Tribune,* May 15, 1998; "'Mother of the Everglades' Dead at 108," May 14, 1998, CNN web site, http://cnn.com (May 15, 1998); *Contemporary Authors, New Revision Series,* Volume 2, Gale Research, 1981; *Los Angeles Times,* May 15, 1998; *Newsmakers,* 1993, issue 1, Gale Research, 1993; *New York Times,* May 15, 1998; *USA Today,* May 14, 1998; *Washington Post,* May 15, 1998, p. B6.

—Geri Speace

Todd Duncan

Born February 12, 1903, in Danville, KY; died of a heart ailment, February 28, 1998, at his home in Washington, DC. Opera singer, actor. Baritone Todd Duncan became famous for his portrayal of Porgy in George Gershwin's *Porgy and Bess.* He is also noted for breaking the color barrier in American opera, becoming the first African American in the New York City Opera when he performed as Tonio in Leoncavallo's *I Pagliacci* in 1945. Noted for his eloquence and persuasive dramatic stylings, his stage credits also included Vernon Duke's *Cabin in the Sky* and Kurt Weill's *Lost in the Stars.*

Duncan was born in Danville, Kentucky, to John and Lettie Cooper Duncan. He earned his bachelor's degree from Butler University in Indianapolis, Indiana, in 1925 and went on to receive his master's degree from Columbia University Teachers College in 1930. The following year, he became a professor of voice at Howard University in Washington, D.C., where he obtained a doctorate. He decided to stay in the capital city and made it his permanent home. Anne Brown, who starred opposite Duncan in *Porgy and Bess*, remarked in a *Washington Post* obituary, "He always lived in Washington. It was his city." Duncan would stay on the faculty at Howard throughout three runs of *Porgy and Bess*.

Duncan started out with the Aeolian Opera, an African American company in New York. His first appearance was in 1934 in Mascagni's *Cavalleria Rusticana*. When Duncan auditioned for George Gershwin, he had reservations about the famous composer's music, claiming that he thought of Gershwin's music as more of a Tin Pan Alley style. A *New York Times* obituary recalled a statement by Duncan made in the paper in 1978 in which he commented, "I didn't have sense enough to know that here was the most successful man on Broadway who had never had a failure."

Gershwin, on the other hand, was more enthusiastic about Duncan. The composer had sat through 100 baritones and was not thrilled by any of them when Olin Downes, the *New York Times* music critic, suggested that he contact Duncan. Downes had recently been impressed by Duncan's performance with the Aeolian Opera. Gershwin heard less than one minute of Duncan's recital of a Giuseppe Sarti aria from the eighteenth century before interrupting him to offer him the part of Porgy. Duncan went on to play in 124 original productions of *Porgy and Bess* at the Alvin Theater on Broadway, beginning in 1935, and also starred in the 1937 and 1942 revivals. Though many critics would attack the play for being racist and perpetuating stereotypes, the production was an important step for African American performers.

Duncan later forged a successful career as a concert singer, appearing in 56 countries and giving over 2,000 performances. He claimed to enjoy these recitals even more than opera and theater productions. His film roles included *Syncopation* in 1942 and *Unchained* in 1955, and he also made an appearance in a 1990 PBS documentary on singer Marian Anderson. Although his busy recital schedule led to his retirement from Howard University in 1945, he taught privately in his basement studio until he was into his 90s. He also spent some time at Curtis Institute of Music in Philadelphia,

Pennsylvania. In 1998 at age 95, invited to a symposium at the University of Michigan, he could not attend but sent a tape recorded greeting and sang, "Bess, You Is My Woman Now."

Throughout his teaching career, Duncan mentored hundreds of students. Soprano Carolyn Grant was one who studied under him and went on to become the principal voice teacher for Jessye Norman. Another student, Elizabeth Daniels, claimed in a *Washington Post* obituary that the Duncan technique was easily recognizable in the singing world. "More than once during auditions, someone has said to me, 'You have studied with Todd Duncan, haven't you?'" She added, "There is a certain elegance in the way his students do things, a naturalness." Another former pupil recounted in the *Washington Post* that Duncan sat in to watch hundreds of vocal surgeries so that he could completely understand the physical workings of the voice, and he passed this knowledge along in classes.

Gershwin's sound recordings were few. They include *Gershwin: A Self-Portrait in Sound*, which contains the original 1935 studio rehearsal of *Porgy and Bess*; *George Gershwin Memorial Concert*, recorded in 1937; *Porgy and Bess*, 1937, with the Hall Johnson Choir, and Weill's *Lost in the Stars*. In 1984, Duncan won the George Peabody Medal from the Peabody Conservatory of Music of the Johns Hopkins University, and he was also awarded a medal of honor from Haiti, an NAACP award, the Donaldson Award, the New York Drama Critics' Award for *Lost in the Stars*, and honorary doctorates from Valparaiso and Butler universities. He is survived by his wife of 63 years, Gladys Jackson Duncan, who had been a public school teacher in Washington, D.C.; his son, Charles C. Duncan; a grandson; and two great-grandchildren. **Sources:** Smith, Eric Ledell, *Blacks in Opera*, McFarland, 1995, p. 65; *Los Angeles Times*, March 1, 1998; *New York Times*, March 2, 1998; *Washington Post*, March 1, 1998, p. B8.

—*Geri Speace*

Chris Farley

Born February 15, 1964; died of an accidental drug overdose, December 18, 1997, at home in Chicago, IL. Former *Saturday Night Live* (*SNL*) ensemble member and film actor Chris Farley idolized his predecessors in the brethren of oversized, slightly out-of-control comics like Jackie Gleason and John Belushi. Weighing in at almost three hundred pounds at the time of his death, Farley was a talented and well-liked comedian who based much of his screen demeanor on what he once described as the "fatty falls down" routine. Yet many saw Farley headed toward a future not unlike that of Belushi and John Candy, both of whom met untimely ends as a result of excess living; Farley was admittedly plagued by a host of inner torments. "I used to think that you could get to a level of success where the laws of the universe didn't apply," Farley said in a *Playboy* magazine interview a few months before his death, quoted in his *New York Times* obituary. "Once I thought that if I just had enough in the bank, if I had enough fame, that it would be all right. but I'm a human being like everyone else. I'm not exempt."

Farley grew up in Madison, Wisconsin, one of five children. He once recalled a story in which his Catholic-school teachers told his mother—in front of him—that his classmates were laughing *at* him, not with him; as an adult, Farley would point out that making people laugh was the key to not becoming the butt of jokes yourself. Part of his motivation for this came from the way people treated his father, who weighed close to 650 pounds. His strategy went so far as to turn it into a career plan: he went from being the class clown in Madison to the campus cut-up at Marquette University, from which he graduated in 1986 with a degree in theater and communication. He then headed to Chicago, to follow in the footsteps of Belushi and Candy, both of whom had gotten their break with the famed Second City improvisational comedy theater.

Farley joined the touring company of Second City in 1987 and went on to main stage productions a year later. He was invited to audition for *SNL* and became a cast member with the 1990 season. It was the pinnacle of success for most young American comedians—Farley had been a fan of the show since childhood, though his parents forbade him to watch it for many years. The memorable sketch-comedy characters he created included Cindy the Gap Girl; the excitable, often apoplectic motivational speaker Matt Foley; and a "Superfan," one of a trio of blue-collar, bratwurst-snacking Chicago Bears devotees.

The *SNL* show was considered a preliminary to Hollywood film roles, and Farley's first big-screen appearance came in the spin-off of a popular *SNL* skit, the 1992 hit *Wayne's World*. He appeared in a few more secondary parts, but was then teamed with *SNL* castmate David Spade, who often played "straight man" to Farley's out-of-control persona. The two co-starred in *Tommy Boy* (1995) and *Black Sheep* (1996); by 1995 Farley had left *SNL* to officially to pursue his film career. He was the lead in the 1997 film *Beverly Hills Ninja* and was set to take on several other good parts in upcoming films. His film appearances were usually characters described by the *Los Angeles Times* as "the same kind of lovable, bumbling slob," but Farley battled to keep his public and private personas separate. "Sometimes I feel trapped by always having to be the most outrageous guy in the room," the *Detroit Free Press* reported Farley as telling another newspaper a year before his death. "In particular, I'm working not to be that guy in my private life."

Even as his success as a comic actor was increasingly praised—he made a special appearance before Congress in 1995 impersonating Newt Gingrich, with Gingrich amicably laughing alongside—reportedly Farley's control over his addictions was slipping. He was known for gargantuan appetites—for food, for alcohol, for cigarettes, and other controlled substances. He had made several attempts to stick with Alcoholics Anonymous programs and was already taking high blood pressure medication. By 1997, a magazine ran a story entitled "Chris Farley: On the Edge of Disaster," and Spade appeared on a tabloid television show in the fall to ask Farley publicly to pull himself together. In October, Farley hosted *SNL* in what some saw as a disastrous move; at times he appeared inebriated and much of the humor was directed at him and his battles to keep himself together.

A week before Christmas, Farley was found by his brother in the entrance hallway to his apartment on the 60th floor of Chicago's John Hancock Tower; by the time paramedics arrived, Farley was dead. Reportedly he had been on a days-long drinking and drug binge. He was 33—ironically, the same age as John Belushi when he died in 1982. "There are a lot of people shedding tears because they were unable to stop this from happening," former *SNL* co-star Tim Kazurinsky told the *Chicago Tribune*. "I hate to think that people will think his friends and loved ones didn't care. They did." His last film, *Almost Heroes*, was scheduled to be released in 1998. **Sources:** *Chicago Tribune*, December 19, 1997; *Detroit Free Press*, December 19, 1997; *Detroit News*, December 19, 1997; http://cnn.com/SHOWBIZ (January 2, 1998); *Los Angeles Times*, December 19, 1997; *New York Times*, December 19, 1997; *USA Today*, December 19, 1997.

—Carol Brennan

Viktor E. Frankl

Born March 26, 1905, in Vienna, Austria-Hungary (present-day Austria); died September 2, 1997, in Vienna, Austria, of heart failure. Viktor E. Frankl, a Jewish psychiatrist and author, drew on his experiences as a survivor of the Holocaust (Nazi Germany's campaign to exterminate the Jewish population of Europe during World War II) to develop the discipline of logotherapy, a form of psychotherapy that, by stressing the need to find meaning even in the most tragic circumstances, offered solace to millions of readers of his classic work, *Man's Search for Meaning: An Introduction to Logotherapy.*

Frankl grew up in Vienna, the birthplace of modern psychiatry and home of the renowned psychiatrists Sigmund Freud and Alfred Adler. A brilliant student, Frankl became interested in psychiatry in his teens. At age 16 he began writing to Freud, and on one occasion sent him a short paper, which Freud regarded so highly that he passed it on to the *International Journal of Psychoanalysis,* where it was published three years later. Frankl earned a medical degree from the University of Vienna in 1930 and was put in charge of a Vienna hospital ward for the treatment of females who had attempted suicide. When Germany seized control of Austria eight years later, the Nazis made Frankl head of the Rothschild Hospital, the only Jewish hospital that was allowed to remain open in Vienna.

After taking power in Austria, the Nazis began removing the Jews of Vienna to the death camps that had been set up in Eastern Europe. Frankl was deported to the Theresienstadt camp near Prague in January 1942, one month after marrying Mathilde Grosser. He was later sent to the Auschwitz camp in Poland, where the camp doctor, Josef Mengele, was supervising the division of the incoming prisoners into two lines. Those in the line moving left were to go to the gas chambers, while those in the line moving right were to be spared. Frankl was directed to join the line moving left, but managed to save his life by slipping into the other line without being noticed. Other members of his family were not so fortunate, however, and by war's end Frankl had lost his pregnant wife, his parents, and a brother.

Before the war Frankl had begun to develop a theory that psychological health depends on finding meaning in one's life. The death camps, he wrote, confirmed his initial insights in a fashion he could never have anticipated. In the camps one lost everything, he once commented as quoted by Holcomb B. Noble in the *New York Times,* except "the last of the human freedoms, to choose one's attitude in any given set of circumstances, to choose one's own way." Prisoners who allowed themselves to be overwhelmed by despair, who gave up their freedom to choose, often descended into paralytic apathy and depression. The key to helping such people was to show them how they could find meaning even in the face of unimaginable horror. Meaning might consist of holding onto pleasant memories, or helping other prisoners turn away from suicide. Every prisoner had a moral choice to make: to surrender one's inner self to the Nazis, or to find the meaning in one's life that would give one the strength to go on.

On returning to Vienna after Germany's defeat in 1945, Frankl, who had secretly been keeping a record of his observations in the camps on scraps of paper taken from the Nazis, published a book in German setting out his ideas on logotherapy (a term derived from the Greek word for "meaning"). This was translated into English in 1959, and in a revised and enlarged edition appeared as *Man's Search for Meaning: An Introduction to Logotherapy* in 1963. By the time of his death, Frankl's book had been translated into 24 languages and reprinted 73 times, and had long been used as a standard text in high school and university courses in psychology, philosophy, and theology. According to the *Los Angeles Times,* Frankl's theory of a psychotherapy that emphasized "the will to meaning" was described as "the Third Vienna School of Psychotherapy," the first being Freud's, which emphasized "the will to pleasure," and the second being Adler's, which emphasized "the will to power." It exerted an important influence on psychiatrists of varying theoretical perspectives, who often recommended Frankl's book to despairing patients who could find no value in their lives.

In 1947, after confirming that his first wife had died in the camps, Frankl married Eleonore Schwindt, who survived him, as did a daughter, Dr. Gabrielle Frankl-Vesely. Frankl's postwar career was spent as a professor of neurology and psychiatry in Vienna, where he taught until he was 85. He was also chief of neurology at the Vienna Polyclinic Hospital for 25 years. Frankl received numerous honorary doctorates, wrote over 30 books, became the first non-American to be awarded the American Psychiatric Association's prestigious Oskar Pfister Prize, and was a visiting professor at Harvard, Stanford, and other universities. His hobbies included mountain climbing, and at 67 he obtained his pilot's license.

Frankl's message that "man is capable of defying and braving even the worst conditions conceivable," as quoted in the *Chicago Tribune,* resonated with people around the world. In a 1991 survey of general-interest readers conducted by the Library of Congress and the Book of the Month Club, *Man's Search for Meaning* was ranked among the ten books that had most influenced the respondents. For them, and for millions of others, Frankl's writings were an inspiration and a reminder that it is "essential to keep practicing the art of living," as quoted by Noble, even when life seems most hopeless. **Sources:** *Chicago Tribune,* http://www.chicago.tribune.com (September 4, 1997); CNN Interactive, http://cnn.com (September 4, 1997); "Viktor E(mil) Frankl," *Contemporary Authors,* http://galenet.gale.com (November 10, 1997); *Los Angeles Times,* http://www.latimes.com (September 4, 1997); *New York Times,* http://www.nytimes.com (September 4, 1997); *Times* (London), http://www.the-times.co.uk (September 30, 1997); *Washington Post,* September 4, 1997, p. B06.

—*Howard Baker*

Roberto Goizueta

Born November 18, 1931, in Havana, Cuba; died October 18, 1997, in Atlanta, GA, of lung cancer. On the day of his funeral, offices around the world of the soft-drink giant Coca-Cola closed in memory of Roberto Goizueta, the Cuban immigrant who had headed the company for its previous sixteen years. The *New York Times* eulogized him as "one of the legends of American business development" for his clever management of what is arguably the world's best-known consumer product. Goizueta was born in Cuba during that island country's heyday as a sugar grower and gambling playground. His mother was heiress to a sugar fortune, and his father was an architect who hoped his son would one day join the family construction business. The teenage Goizueta was sent to New England for schooling, and graduated from Yale University in 1953 with a degree in chemical engineering. He returned to Havana that same year, and answering a newspaper ad for a bilingual engineer launched his career with Coca-Cola.

But political turmoil during the decade forced Goizueta and his young family to flee to Florida in 1960 after the rise of Communist leader Fidel Castro. For a time, the Goizuetas lived in a Miami motel room, but his job with the company remained secure, and

he continued his work as an engineer for Coke's Latin American operations. He was promoted to its Atlanta world headquarters in 1964, where he became well known among management ranks for his tidy desk at the end of every business day and well-tailored suits. In 1979, he was promoted to vice-president, and became responsible for several different areas of the company, including its laboratories and legal department.

The vice-presidency was a stepping stone to the eventual chairmanship, and the naming of Goizueta to that top post in 1981 surprised many in the business world. He became the first non-Georgian head of Coca-Cola, but corporate analysts also questioned his ascendancy since much of the leadership duties involved marketing, an area in which Goizueta had virtually no experience. Yet because of time spent heading the Coca-Cola labs, Goizueta did possess one advantage over his fellow contenders among the vice-presidents—he was familiar with what is called "the knowledge" in company lore—Coca-Cola's highly secretive formula. Reportedly he was one of only two people in the company who knew it.

In the end, Goizueta did prove to be a savvy marketing executive; at the time, Coca-Cola was losing market share to its major competitor, Pepsi, and its stock was not performing well. Though it was a strong international presence, Coke's brand image was perceived as old-fashioned and conservative. Goizueta reversed all of these deficiencies. One of his first decisions was to allow a new diet drink to trade on the success of the Coke trademark by taking the name "Diet Coke" in 1982. Goizueta broke corporate rules in other areas. He launched what became known as the "cola wars," the intense competition with archrival Pepsi. Goizueta's strategy revolved around a much more aggressive marketing campaign that would effectively halt and reverse Pepsi's gains in market share and triple Coke sales during his tenure.

As an executive, Goizueta knew the value of having a rival—"if you don't have an enemy, the best thing is you create one," he once told the *New York Times.* Goizueta retired the wimpy "Have a Coke and a Smile!" slogan in favor of the more aggressive "Coke Is It!" He focused on increasing international sales, and also targeted company resources at revamping its complex network of bottlers and distributors, which increased shelf space and profits. In one case, Goizueta directed the buyout of Pepsi's Venezuelan bottler, effectively ending Pepsi sales in the only Latin American country where it led Coke in sales. Goizueta told the *New York Times* that "people ask me if I sleep well at night with all of the competition. I tell them I sleep like a baby—I wake up every two hours and cry."

This sense of humor carried Goizueta through what was perhaps his only misstep during his years as Coca-Cola chair—the infamous "New Coke" launch in 1985. In what was initially a huge marketing effort that instead became a famous marketing blunder, Coke introduced a sweeter reformulation with less bite—more similar to Pepsi—and Coke's loyal, extremely addicted consumers revolted clamorously. The company quickly backtracked, reintroducing the old version, and cynics later questioned whether the whole debacle was simply an attention-getting corporate plot, to which Goizueta responded, "we're not that smart, and we're not that dumb," reported the *Washington Post*.

It was Goizueta's savvy management of the Coca-Cola bottom line that eventually earned him a place in corporate annals. His era at the company ushered in a new focus on stock performance and keeping shareholders happy with a healthy annual return on their investment. From 1981 to 1997 its stock value increased over 7000 percent—purchasing $1,000 in shares when Goizueta took over would net an investor $71,000 if sold sixteen years later. He owned 16 million shares himself, and was the first American executive to become a billionaire through owning stock in a company he had not founded or taken public on Wall Street.

Goizueta used some of his wealth to establish the Goizueta Foundation, which donated money to various social and educational causes. He also sat on the boards of several other major companies. One such stockholder, Atlanta's Emory University, named its business school after him in 1994 after the Coke shares held in the college's endowment fund greatly enriched it. In the summer of 1997, however, Goizueta, a lifelong smoker, was diagnosed with lung cancer. He had a fax machine and stock terminal installed in his hospital room, but missed his first board meeting during his executive career the week before his death. Goizueta is survived by his wife Olga, three children, and eight grandchildren. "Perhaps no other corporate leader in modern times has so beautifully exemplified the American dream," former U.S. President Jimmy Carter told the Associated Press. "He believed that in America, all things are possible." **Sources:** *Detroit Free Press*, October 19, 1997; *Los Angeles Times*, October 18, 1997, p. A1, A18; *New York Times*, October 19, 1997, sec. 1, p. 45; *Times* (London), October 20, 1997; *Washington Post*, October 19, 1997, p. B8.

—*Carol Brennan*

Barry Goldwater

Born January 1, 1909, in Phoenix, AZ; died of natural causes, May 29, 1998, in Paradise Valley, AZ. Politician. Barry Goldwater was one of the most famous right-wing American politicians in the twentieth century. An outspoken critic of big government, social spending, communism, and unions, he also touted personal freedoms and was highly ethical and well-respected, both personally and professionally. The five-term Republican senator from Arizona earned the nickname "Mr. Conservative" for his views. He ran for president in 1964 but lost by a huge margin to Lyndon B. Johnson, who had entered office when President John F. Kennedy was assassinated. Later in his career, Goldwater began breaking with party line stances, which were becoming more involved with moral issues. He retired from the Senate in 1986.

Barry Morris Goldwater was born in Phoenix, Arizona, the oldest child of Baron and Josephine Williams Goldwater. His Jewish father was the son of a Polish immigrant tailor, Michael Goldwater, who had set up a chain of department stores in Arizona—back then just a United States territory—and became quite wealthy. The first store was established in the 1860s, and by the turn of the century, the stores were the premier shopping centers around the state. Goldwater's mother was a nurse from Nebraska who raised her son as an Episcopalian.

Goldwater was not an exceptional student at Phoenix's Union High School, although he was elected president of his freshman class. After failing half of his courses that first year, his parents sent him to Staunton Military Academy in Virginia, where he flourished, winning a medal for best all-around cadet and graduating in 1928. Goldwater liked the military and expressed interest in attending college at West Point, but his father demanded that he return west and enroll at the University of Arizona at Tucson. He only completed one year before leaving school to work in the family business in Phoenix in 1929, around the time his father died.

Goldwater displayed a natural talent for running the family stores. By 1937, at age 29, he was president of the company. As a manager, he instituted a five-day work week, became the first in the mercantile industry in Arizona to offer health benefits, and was the first businessman to hire African Americans. However, the stress took its toll, and his heart was elsewhere. Although he had poor vision, he took flying lessons beginning in 1930 and would later become a major general in the Air Force Reserve while serving in the U.S. Senate. In 1934, Goldwater married Margaret (Peggy) Johnson; the couple had four children: Joanne, Barry, Jr., Michael, and Peggy.

Despite his eyesight problems and his age, Goldwater joined the Army Air Force in 1941 during World War II and lobbied, in vain, for a combat assignment. For most of his service, he flew supplies to troops in the India-Burma theater and across the Atlantic. When he returned to Arizona in 1945, he founded the Arizona Air National Guard—an integrated unit—and became involved in local politics. In 1949, he was named Phoenix's "Man of the Year," and also that year won a seat on the city council. In 1950, he helped Republican Howard Pyle's successful campaign for governor in a state that had traditionally been Democratic.

In 1952, Goldwater challenged incumbent Democrat Ernest W. McFarland, Senate majority leader, for his seat and won. Goldwater was elected senator four more times until 1980, taking a respite in 1964 to unsuccessfully run for president against Lyndon B. Johnson, who had succeeded to president after the assassination of John F. Kennedy. The defeat was one of the worst in American history. Not only was he running against the memory of the popular Kennedy, but he also fueled concern among voters when he stated in his nomination acceptance speech, "Extremism in defense of liberty is no vice and ... moderation in the pursuit of justice is no virtue." Although Goldwater's uncle Morris was one of the founders of the Arizona Democratic party, Goldwater himself became known as one of the most staunch conservatives in twentieth-century American politics. He supported Senator Joseph McCarthy's anti-Communist crusade during the 1950s, and he argued to downsize the federal government. He also opposed the graduated income tax, foreign aid, and a bevy of social programs. Though he personally favored civil rights, he spoke out against the 1957 *Brown v. Board of Education* case that established integration in public schools. In 1960, he wrote the *Conscience of a Conservative*, which eventually sold three-and-a-half million copies and firmly established his place in right-wing politics.

After Goldwater's presidential bid in 1964, he stayed out of office until 1968, winning a Senate seat the same year Richard Nixon was elected president. On August 7, 1974, to his dismay, he and other Republican leaders met with Nixon to urge him to resign after the Watergate scandal. In 1980, Goldwater was elected to his final term in the Senate, just squeaking by this time, possibly due to his age (71) and his increasing health problems. During this last term, as chairman of the Armed Services Committee, he was instrumental in getting an important bill passed in 1986 to decrease rivalry among the branches of the armed services. Goldwater was also influential in pushing through the nomination of Sandra Day O'Connor, the first woman on the Supreme Court and a fellow Arizonian.

However, during much of his later time in office, Goldwater disagreed with other conservatives during the "Reagan Era," in which Republican President Ronald Reagan held office from 1980 to 1988. He became known for blunt, sometimes humorous comments while serving as a respected Senate leader. He spoke out against the Moral Majority and stirred controversy when he supported abortion rights and gays in the military. According to the *New York Times,* he wrote a letter to the *Washington Post* stating, "You don't need to be 'straight' to fight and die for your country. You just need to shoot straight." Goldwater insisted that his politics were not leaning more liberal, but that the Republicans were veering off into new and unnecessary territory, with the "New Right" interfering in moral issues and personal lives. He noted in 1989, according to the *Arizona Republic,* that the Republican party had been overrun by "a bunch of kooks."

In 1985, Goldwater's wife of 51 years, Peggy, died. He married Susan Schaffer Wechsler, a hospice director, in 1992 at the age of 83. After his retirement from the Senate in 1987, Goldwater remained an outspoken public commentator, offering his views on personal freedoms. In 1996, Goldwater suffered a stroke that impaired his memory. He died of natural causes at his home in Paradise Valley, an upscale suburb of Phoenix, Arizona, at age 89. **Sources:** "Barry Goldwater Dead at 89," May 29, 1998, AllPolitics web site, http://allpolitics.com (June 1, 1998); "GOP Icon Barry Goldwater Dead at 89," May 29, 1998, Associated Press web site, http://wire.ap.com (May 29, 1998); *Arizona Republic,* May 31, 1998; "Contemporary Authors," Gale Literary Databases web site, http://www.galenet.com (June 19, 1998); *Detroit Free Press,* May 30, 1998, p. 1A; *Encyclopedia of World Biography,* second edition, Gale Research, 1997; *Los Angeles Times,* May 30, 1998; *New York Times,* May 30, 1998, p. A1; *Newsweek,* June 8, 1998, p. 35; *USA Today,* May 31, 1998; *Washington Post,* May 30, 1998, p. A1.

—*Geri Speace*

Stephane Grappelli

Born September 26 (some sources say January 25 or January 26), 1908, in Paris, France; died December 1, 1997, in Paris, from complications following hernia surgery. Violinist Stephane Grappelli was a legendary figure in European music circles and was often termed the continent's first significant non-American jazz musician. He influenced subsequent generations of jazz artists, and collaborated with nearly all the legendary names in the genre, from Duke Ellington to Miles Davis. Grappelli's *Los Angeles Times* obituary quoted music scholar Leonard Feather—if jazz had been of French origins, Feather opined of Grappelli, "this is how it might all have sounded—suave and sophisticated, its rhythms infinitely gentle yet quintessentially swinging."

Grappelli, the son of philosophy professor, was born in France in the years before World War I. His mother died when he was just three, and his father placed him in an orphanage, but later retrieved him after the war ended. Grappelli's musical education began informally when his father took him along to free musical performances, and was formally underway when he began violin lessons at the age of twelve; he also displayed a talent for the piano. The Grappellis' precarious financial situation forced him to support himself from an early age, however, and to do this the teen worked as a piano player for six hours a day at a movie theater, accompanying the silent films shown there. He won a scholarship to the renowned Isadora Duncan School and studied the violin and piano, and in 1924 was admitted for further study at the Paris Conservatory.

Yet as the heady music of the "Jazz Age" migrated from American shores to the European capitals, Grappelli, like many others, grew passionate about it. He first heard the records of trumpet great Louis Armstrong when he was nineteen, and dropped out of the Conservatory shortly after. Jazz had not yet gained wide acceptance abroad, however, and French listeners exhibited suspicion toward those of their own heritage who attempted to play it, believing that only the American-born had the true soul to play it. Sometimes Grappelli played on the streets of Paris to earn coins, especially in the destitute years following the Great Depression of 1929.

Legend has it that it was as a busker that Grappelli first met guitarist Django Reinhardt, but other tales recount a meeting at a Montparnasse nightclub known as the Le Croix du Sud. Reinhardt was of Gypsy descent and was gaining a reputation for his wild interpretive style; the pair played well together. By 1933, Grappelli and Reinhardt were part of Paris's Hotel Claridges house orchestra and were gaining a reputation as crowd-dazzling virtuosos. When the "Hot Club," France's organization of jazz fans, was formed, they became its official combo. With two other guitarists playing alongside Reinhardt, a bassist, and Grappelli on violin, the Quintet "created a new form of subtle but fiery jazz," wrote the *Times* of London. With the Quintet, Grappelli recorded several works during the 1930s, such as *Minor Swing,* which came to showcase "one of the first successful meldings of black American jazz with European idioms," wrote Peter Watrous of the *New York Times*. These releases, Watrous further noted, "are ranked among jazz's greatest." Even American musicians journeyed to Paris to cut records with them.

The onset of World War II effectively disbanded the Quintet, and Grappelli took asylum in England from Nazi-occupied France. There he played with pianist George Shearing, and returned to the Continent after the war's end. He and Reinhardt reunited and did a swing version of the French national anthem, which was met with some rightist rancor, but the serious reunion of the Quintet never materialized; it was lost forever when Reinhardt died in 1953. By then, Grappelli's forte, swing music, had been eclipsed by the newer form called bebop. Over the next several years, Grappelli languished in obscurity, but his career picked up again in 1960s. He reformed the Quintet with new members, and played at the Newport Jazz Festival in 1969 in his American stage debut. He appeared at Carnegie Hall in 1974.

By this era, Grappelli had become fluent in a range of musical styles; he could interpret classical favorites, traditional French ballads, and even contemporary pop tunes. Beginning in the early 1970s, he collaborated with classical violinist Yehudi Menuhin; the duo recorded and performed together. Grappelli had also become a great influence on a new generation of jazz violinists, most notably his fellow French string virtuoso Jean-Luc Ponty. The 1973 LP *Jean-Luc Ponty/ Stephane Grappelli* showcased the jazz great and the avant-garde younger musician.

Grappelli continued to perform even in his eighties. One of his last releases was *Live at the Blue Note* (1995). He lived in one of his homes in Paris or in the Mediterranean resort of Cannes when not on the road, but was increasingly impeded by health problems; he received a pacemaker in 1991, suffered a stroke in 1993, and was plagued by artery problems the following year. His last public appearance came in September of 1997 when he received France's highest civilian honor, the Commander of the Legion of Honor, from President Jacques Chirac. He died at the age of 89 less than three months later. Grappelli is survived by his daughter Evelyne and grandson Gilles, but his remarkable talent also lives on though his hundred-plus recorded works. "I know of no other violinist with that extraordinary command of improvising in the jazz medium," classical violinist Yehudi Menuhin told the *New York Times*. "It is like the juggler who throws his pots and plates to the wind and yet retrieves them every time." **Sources:** *Los Angeles Times,* December 2, 1997; *New York Times,* December 2, 1997; *Times* (London), December 2, 1997.

—Carol Brennan

Phil Hartman

Born Phil Edward Hartmann, September 24, 1948 in Brantford, Ontario, Canada; died of gunshot wounds, May 28, 1998, in Encino, CA. Actor. Phil Hartman rose to fame in the 1980s as a regular on the cast of the late-night NBC skit show, *Saturday Night Live.* After eight seasons on the show, in which he performed rollicking impressions of Bill Clinton, Frank Sinatra, Ed McMahon, and numerous others, he landed the role of conceited anchorman Bill McNeal on *NewsRadio.* He also provided several voices on the hit nighttime cartoon series *The Simpsons,* and enjoyed a flourishing film career playing supporting characters.

Hartman was born in Canada, the fourth of eight children (three boys, five girls), to Doris and Rupert Hartmann, a building and roofing supplies salesperson. The family moved to the United States in the late 1950s or early 1960s and lived in Connecticut and then southern California. Hartman later became a United States citizen in 1990. At Westchester High, he entertained friends with impersonations of John Wayne, Jack Benny, John F. Kennedy, and others. Known as the class clown, he never thought he could make a career in comedy. He later studied art at Santa Monica College and California State University at Northridge and ended up in graphic design. He created the logo for the group Crosby, Stills and Nash, and also designed rock album covers.

In 1975 Hartman went to see The Groundlings, an improvisational troupe in Los Angeles, and was hooked. He joined the group, which also spawned

entertainers Laraine Newman, a 1970s *Saturday Night Live* cast member; Julia Sweeny, another *SNL* comedian; and Paul Reubens, better known as Pee-Wee Herman. Hartman helped Reubens create the Pee-Wee character after the two met in 1978, and he co-wrote the 1985 film *Pee-Wee's Big Adventure.* Hartman struggled through go-nowhere television pilots and subpar movies until 1986, when he joined *Saturday Night Live* and became an integral and popular addition to the show.

Hartman, with his everyman looks and his talent for mimicry, provided characterizations of a wide range of people, including President Bill Clinton, singer Frank Sinatra, talk show sidekick Ed McMahon, televangelist Jimmy Swaggart, and former First Lady Barbara Bush. He was also an expert at hosting many of the show's faux game shows, and played the fire-fearing Frankenstein in a recurring skit involving Tarzan and Tonto, two other linguistically challenged characters. Although he served as a mainstay during one of the more humorous periods in the show's history (fellow actors on the show called him "The Glue" because he held them together), Hartman never achieved big-time stardom as did fellow cast members Mike Meyers and Dana Carvey (*Wayne's World*). However, he set a record for appearances on the program, acting for eight seasons and in 153 episodes.

Meanwhile, Hartman began providing voices for the Fox animated comedy series *The Simpsons,* a stint he continued until his death. He left *Saturday Night Live* after the 1993-1994 season, partly because he felt the show's material was pandering to a younger and less sophisticated audience. He then received the opportunity to invent a less slapstick, more wry character in 1995 when he was cast as Bill McNeal, the snarky and egotistical news anchor on the NBC sitcom *NewsRadio.* Though the show's ratings were not always impressive, it was a critical favorite and its troubles were often blamed on its fickle time slot. The show faced possible cancellation, but was finally scheduled to return in fall of 1998.

Hartman also enjoyed a successful film career as a supporting actor. He appeared in *Blind Date,* 1986; *Three Amigos,* 1986; *Fletch Lives,* 1989; *So I Married an Axe Murderer,* 1992; and *Jingle All the Way,* 1996, among others. He was highly in demand in the movie industry, despite the fact that he was not a leading man, and was reportedly very pleased with his career. Friends described him as a happy and humorous man who remained down-to-earth. Married and divorced twice, he married Brynn (original given name, Vicky Joe) Omdahl, a model and aspiring actress, in 1987, and the two had a son, Sean, and daughter, Birgen. He was reportedly a doting father and lived with his family in the Los Angeles suburb of Encino in a three-bedroom ranch home. Some called the Hartmans a very happy couple. According to the *Los Angeles Times*, Hartman shortly before his death told director Joe Dante, "I have a plane. I have a boat. I have a great house. I have a great family. In fact I have everything I ever wanted. It feels great."

However, troubles brewed with the pair. Actress Cassandra Peterson, known for her character Elvira, Mistress of the Dark, told CNN, "They fought a lot. I don't know what the problems were. I have suspicions. But for the moment, they seemed to be doing fine." Early in the morning on May 28, 1998, a gunshot was reported to the 911 emergency service. When police arrived, they heard another shot, and found Brynn Hartman dead of a self-inflicted gunshot wound, with Phil Hartman dead as well. There were no signs of struggle. Later reports indicated that Hartman was involved with another woman and seeking separation, and Brynn Hartman, who had a history of troubles, had become enraged. The murder-suicide shook the entertainment world because Hartman was known as one of the more stable Hollywood players. The children were unharmed and were apparently going to be taken care of by family members. **Sources:** "Phil Hartman Reportedly Shot Dead," May 28, 1998, Associated Press web site, http://wire.ap.org (May 28, 1998); *Chicago Tribune*, May 29, 1998; "Actor Phil Hartman Found Dead of Gunshot Wound," May 28, 1998, CNNin web site, http://cnn.com (May 28, 1998); "Phil Hartman, Wife Die in Apparent Murder-Suicide," May 28, 1998, CNNin web site, http://cnn.com (May 29, 1998); "Police: 'Domestic Discord' behind Hartman Slayings," May 28, 1998, CNNin web site, http://cnn.com (May 29, 1998); *Los Angeles Times*, May 29, 1998; *Newsmakers*, 1996 Cumulation, Gale Research, 1997; *New York Times*, May 29, 1998; *USA Today*, May 29, 1998; *Washington Post*, May 29, 1998, p. B1.

—Geri Speace

Michael Hutchence

Born January 22, 1960, in Sydney, Australia; died November 22, 1997, in Double Bay, Sydney, Australia, of an apparent suicide. The death of this lead singer for the wildly successful Australian rock band INXS left fans in disbelief. Just 37 years old, Michael Hutchence seemed to possess it all: movie-star looks, phenomenal wealth, and the affections of equally famous women. Fronting INXS and writing many of its hit songs as well, Hutchence helped INXS sell over 20 million records during a twenty-year career. His *Times* (London) obituary mentioned "his sultry good looks and bad boy charisma" and called him "the closest Australia has come to having an equivalent of rock rebels such as Mick Jagger and Jim Morrison."

Hutchence was born in Sydney to relatively affluent parents whose marriage later dissolved. Because of this, he lived in various Pacific Rim cities, including Hong Kong and Los Angeles, as a youth, and admitted to suffering some loneliness as a teenager because of this lack of stability. He worked the turmoil out creatively, however, and wrote prodigious amounts of prose and poetry. When he returned to Australia in his late teens, he joined up with three brothers and two other friends, some of whom he knew from a Sydney high school, and they formed a band—reportedly on the same day Elvis Presley died.

Hutchence sang with "The Farris Brothers" under sometimes squalid conditions in rural bars around Australia. The manager of other popular Australian alternative rock band, Midnight Oil, discovered them, and suggested a name change. They became INXS by the time their first record came out in Australia in 1980. Over the next few years, they enjoyed chart success around the country and in 1982 signed the Australian division of the giant WEA label. Early in 1983, they landed a contract for North America through the "A" in WEA, Atlantic Records.

Major success came quickly for Hutchence and INXS from that moment forward. Their single "The One Thing" and the album it appeared on, *Shabooh Shoobah*, did phenomenally well in 1983, as did subsequent LPs over the next few years. Part of their success came through a savvy understanding of the new medium of music videos; Hutchence's telegenic looks seemed tailor-made for the new MTV cable channel and, over the course of their career, INXS would make over three dozen videos. During the mid-1980s, the band enjoyed worldwide success with albums like *Listen Like Thieves*, released in 1985, which featured songs such as "This Time" and "What You Need" that helped land them a gold record; their 1987 follow-up, *Kick*, went both gold and platinum the same week. Three of its songs—"Devil Inside," "New Sensation," and "Never Tear Us Apart," made the Billboard Top 10.

By the late 1980s, INXS was a major rock band on par with U2 in commercial success. Tours were massive stadium events, especially in their native Australia, where they remained hugely popular. In the early 1990s they became the first international rock act to play Mexico since the Doors. Hutchence became a well-known name in the gossip columns, and squired around female companions such as pop star Kylie Minogue and model Helena Christensen. Though he and INXS produced several other albums for Atlantic, each were less successful than the previous. Critics declared that the trademark INXS sound, which blended funk and rock and had been heavily copied by many alternative acts, had begun to sound dated. The band signed with Mercury/Polygram in 1993 and made their debut with the label in 1997 with *Elegantly Wasted.*

Hutchence was not simply the lead singer of INXS but also a celebrity on the international level, and a post-rock film career seemed certain. He had appeared in two movies, the 1986 Australian feature *Dogs in Space,* in which he portrayed a punk rocker on drugs, and a few years later played the Romantic poet Percy Bysshe Shelley in a Roger Corman film, *Frankenstein Unbound.* Actor/director/producer Michael Douglas was reportedly interested in casting Hutchence in some upcoming projects. Yet Hutchence's personal life was spiraling out of control; he had become involved with Paula Yates, a British television personality married to rock star Bob Geldof, and during 1996 and 1997 the trio became embroiled in a contentious divorce and custody battle that sometimes turned vicious. Hutchence and Yates had a daughter in 1996, and were planning to wed in Tahiti in early 1998.

At the time of Hutchence's mysterious death, INXS was about to begin a tour marking their twentieth anniversary. They were scheduled to appear on Australian television together, but Hutchence failed to arrive for the taping. A maid at the Ritz-Carlton Hotel in the Sydney suburb of Double Bay discovered his body, and sadly, his bandmates learned of the death from reporters. An autopsy ruled it death by asphyxiation, but rumors of foul play abounded. Both Hutchence and Yates had grown distressed over a custody battle with Geldof that kept them on opposite sides of the globe, and police were questioning some who had visited Hutchence in the several hours before his death; friends and associates asserted he had not been despondent and only a month before his death had said he was "the luckiest man alive," according to the *Times.* Sales of the INXS back catalogue soared in the days following Hutchence's death. **Sources:** *Chicago Tribune,* November 22, 1997; *Detroit Free Press,* November 22, 1997; *Los Angeles Times,* November 22, 1997; *New York Times,* November 23, 1997; *Times* (London), November 24, 1997.

—Carol Brennan

Juzo Itami

Born in 1933, in Kyoto, Japan; died December 20, 1997, in Tokyo, after leaping from the roof of an eight-story building. Juzo Itami was an internationally acclaimed film director and screenwriter whose movies offered a biting, satirical view of Japanese society and culture. "His macabre death stood in vivid contrast to his films, which were often droll, witty, subtle, surprising and incisive," Sheryl WuDunn wrote in the *New York Times.* "In a society known for its gravity, Itami's films brought smiles and laughter to his audiences."

The director committed suicide, leaping from the condominium where he lived and worked, just two days before *Flash,* a weekly magazine, intended to publish an article and photographs intimating he had an affair with a 26-year-old woman. Itami was married to Nobuko Miyamoto, a popular actress who had starred in most of his films, and the couple had two sons. In one of the suicide notes left on the desk of his office, Itami wrote, "Please take care of Ms. Miyamoto. She is the best wife, mother and actress in Japan."

In another one of the notes he penned before taking his life, he vehemently denied having an affair and suggested that he killed himself to prove his innocence. "I cannot find any other means to prove that there was nothing," he wrote. Following Itami's death, *Flash* editor Kenji Kaneto issued a statement standing behind the article on Itami's purported infidelity, and the article was published as scheduled.

Itami was the son of noted pre-war film director Mansaku Itami, but he traveled a circuitous route to the director's chair. Early on, he was an amateur boxer and a commercial designer; he became an actor in 1960. He built a successful career performing in the theater, on television, and in numerous films, sometimes appearing under the name Ichizo Itami. He also was a TV talk show host, author, translator, and editor of a magazine on psychoanalysis. Itami was 50 years old before he moved to the other side of the camera and began directing films based on his own screenplays.

His first film, a black comedy called *Ososhiki* (The Funeral), was a hit in 1984. The offbeat movie "is a satirical view of ritualized society performances and their emptiness, exposing the manifold hypocrisies they generate," Robin Wood wrote in *The International Dictionary of Films and Filmmakers.* "*The Funeral* analyzes the traditional elaborate rites in documentary detail and precision, while undercutting the reverence they are supposed to express with a pervasive sense of absurdity." Wood, like other reviewers, has praised Itami's ability to portray strong female characters, an uncommon trait in Japanese cinema.

With his second film, *Tampopo* (Dandelion), released in 1986, Itami gained an international reputation. Ostensibly about the quest of a restaurant-owner (played by Miyamoto) to concoct the perfect bowl of noodles, *Tampopo* "is a lyrically funny look at Japanese noodle-eating habits," WuDunn wrote. The *London Times* suggested the film "artfully demonstrated the link between eating and sex, with constant close-ups of erotically mouthwatering dishes to provoke unrest in audience taste buds." The article went on to call Itami the mostly widely renowned Japanese director after the legendary Akira Kurosawa. "His acerbic attacks on Japanese capitalism, organized crime, bureaucrats, the law, and his skill at combining satirical comedy with examinations of serious social issues, brought him huge popularity with domestic audiences and respect abroad," the newspaper concluded.

In the 1992 film *Minbo—or the Gentle Art of Japanese Extortion,* Itami satirized Japanese gangster culture—and the movie triggered a violent attack by five knife-wielding yakuza mobsters. Itami suffered serious lacerations on his face, neck and arms. He was hospitalized for several weeks, spent time in a witness protection program, and emerged with a deep, craggy scar on his face. "They cut very slowly. They took their time," the director said afterward. "They could have killed me if they wanted.... I won't be giving up. I hope we can all continue to struggle together." His attackers were later convicted and imprisoned.

Itami directed ten films. At the time of his death, he was planning his eleventh film, a movie based on the 1995 nerve-gas attack which killed 12 people on a Tokyo subway. "He was in some ways," WuDunn wrote in the *New York Times*, "fighting a losing war ... trying to explore penetrating themes about Japanese society when Japanese audiences were flocking to Western or animated films instead." **Sources:** *Associated Press,* 1997; *Chicago Tribune,* December 22, 1997; *International Dictionary of Films and Filmmakers,* Volume 2, St. James Press, 1991; *Los Angeles Times,* December, 21, 1997; *New York Times*, December 22, 1997; *Times* (London), December 22, 1997.

—Dave Wilkins

William R. Kelly

Born November 21, 1905, in Koksilah, Victoria, British Columbia, Canada; died January 3, 1998, at his home in Fort Lauderdale, FL, of cancer. William Russell Kelly founded what may arguably be North America's best known temporary staffing agency. In the half-century since its founding, his Troy, Michigan-based Kelly Services has become virtually synonymous with the very industry it launched—especially its onetime army of temporary clerical staffers who were once referred to as "Kelly Girls." Yet the company's success owes much to Kelly's original vision and its own ability to expand with changing business practices and new workforce demands, and has since branched out far beyond the typing pool. This helped earn Kelly, a onetime car salesperson, a fortune estimated at over $540 million.

Kelly was born in a small town in British Columbia, one of seven children of a very successful oil prospector. He was sent to Gulfcoast Military Academy in Gulfport, Mississippi, from which he graduated in 1922, then attended Tennessee's Vanderbilt University and later the University of Pittsburgh; his summers were spent at the family's chateau in France. That elegant lifestyle changed, however, in 1926 when his father suffered a stroke; Kelly had to leave college in order to support the family. In Pittsburgh he sold cars for a time, then became an auditor for the tea and grocery chain Great Atlantic & Pacific Tea Co. for a decade. When World War II began, he tried to join the armed forces, but failed the physical because of his defective feet. Instead he was offered a job as a civilian fiscal management analyst for the Quartermaster Corps of the U.S. Army, which he accepted.

Kelly came to Detroit in 1946. During the war, the city and its environs had grown into a huge manufacturing center, and a good percentage of the war-related factory jobs had been occupied by women. They lost those jobs, however, when returning servicemen resumed their civilian lives; at the same time, the American business and manufacturing sectors were about to enjoy an unprecedented period of growth. Many companies found themselves short of staff, and thus Kelly began the "Russell Kelly Office

Service" to provide outsourcing help for companies with backed-up paperwork. It took in $848 in revenues its first year in operation, with three employees and twelve clients. The jobs he contracted to do for automotive suppliers and other firms—mainly typing and duplicating—were at first done at the Kelly offices, but he also began purchasing office equipment and renting it out to companies. In many cases, Kelly would send an employee along to operate it on site. When companies began purchasing their own machines, as his *New York Times* obituary quoted Kelly as saying, "it just seemed to be a natural development from that point to send the girls and forget about the machines."

Kelly Services soon grew into a thriving business fulfilling companies' needs on a temporary basis, whether for the occasional seasonal rush or as a way to replace vacationing or sick workers with well-trained, available personnel on short notice. Kelly's pool of female temporaries—many of them housewives who had held jobs during the war, but then married and did not want to work full-time—became known as "Kelly Girls." "I remember we had our employees view a film strip to help them explain to their husbands or fathers why it was all right for a woman to be working," Kelly said of this era in a speech at the company's 50th anniversary celebration. Many women often began as temporary staffers with Kelly Services, and were then offered permanent, full-time positions at the client companies when such openings arose; at a time when not many females were part of the workforce, the Kelly innovation inadvertently helped better the economic lives of many single or struggling women who needed it most.

Kelly himself was known as "Ol' Dad" around the company offices, and he recruited his brothers to hold executive posts. He retired from the day-to-day operations in 1967, but the company would continue to thrive: by the 1990s, Kelly had expanded into meeting temporary staffing needs in nearly all sectors of the workforce, from engineering and manufacturing to computer programming and health care. At the time of its founder's death, the Fortune 500 company had 1,500 offices around the world and placed over 700,000 people in jobs in 1997, according to his *New York Times* obituary. Revenues for that same year exceeded $3 billion. Though it had gone public in a Wall Street stock offering in 1962, it was still a family-controlled business, with Kelly's adopted son Terence Adderley as its chief executive officer and president. Adderley and other family members still held majority voting stock.

Kelly, who lived in both Bloomfield Hills, Michigan, and Fort Lauderdale, had earned a spot as one of the 400 wealthiest Americans on the annual *Forbes* magazine list since 1985. He would be respected as one of the most influential business entrepreneurs of the century, but was also feared for his dry wit. "If you weren't paying attention, you'd find out he was having a good time at your expense," one Kelly executive recalled of his boss in the *Detroit Free Press*. In his retirement Kelly was involved in thoroughbred breeding and racing, and also liked to play bridge and enjoy time with his family. That family included his son Terence, a wife of forty-six years, Margaret, six grandchildren, and three great-grandchildren. **Sources:** *Detroit Free Press*, January 5, 1998; *Los Angeles Times*, January 5, 1998; *New York Times*, January 8, 1998.

—Carol Brennan

Charles Kuralt

Born Charles Bishop Kuralt, September 10, 1934, in Wilmington, NC; died of heart failure, July 4, 1997, at New York Hospital, New York, NY. Television journalist. Charles Kuralt started his career as a newsman for CBS covering political events and wars, but made his name seeking out offbeat human interest stories for his show *On the Road*. His poetic narrations and enthusiasm for his subjects made him an admired reporter among his fellow journalists as well as the general public.

Kuralt was born the son of social worker Wallace Hamilton Kuralt and teacher Ina (Bishop) Kuralt in Wilmington, North Carolina. He spent much of his youth on his grandparents' tobacco farm and engrossed in reading *National Geographic* magazines. When he was 14, he began broadcasting minor-league baseball games and later hosted a music program. In high school, he won the national "Voice of Democracy" essay contest sponsored by the American Legion. Legendary broadcaster Edward R. Murrow read the paper over CBS radio, and Kuralt also traveled to Washington, D.C., to meet President Harry S. Truman.

Kuralt was the editor of the campus newspaper, the *Daily Tar Heel,* at the University of North Carolina. He graduated in 1955 and went to work as a reporter and columnist for the *Charlotte News*. In 1956, he received the Ernie Pyle Memorial Award for his quirky human-interest stories. In 1957, when he was just 23, he got a job writing news for CBS's radio division in New York City and the following year began writing for the 15-minute CBS television news program. He was promoted to correspondent in 1959. In 1960, Kuralt covered the presidential election, and became the first host of the prime-time program, *Eyewitness*. After that, he was moved to CBS's new Latin American bureau, where he was based in Rio de Janeiro for three years. He then returned to the United States to manage the Los Angeles office, continuing to travel around the world to cover stories. During the 1960s, he went to Vietnam four times to report on the war, even going to the front lines with a camera on one occasion in 1965.

Weary of the bleakness of war and the mixed emotions boiling about it in the United States, Kuralt wondered about his future in the field of hard news and doubted his abilities. In 1967 he came up with the plan to seek out unusual stories from everyday folks in America's small towns and boon docks. He took the idea for *On the Road* to CBS, which allowed him to roam free in a used motor home with one camera operator and one technician. The *New York Times* quoted him as saying about the decision, "Wishing to escape hawks, doves, gurus and acid rock, I took to the road."

Kuralt's resonant voice, natural curiosity, adventurousness, literary writing style, and eye for unrecognized yet interesting qualities made him the perfect guide to a previously unseen America. He transcended the everyday by his lush narrations and keen observations. A *USA Today* obituary recalled two lines from his first broadcast on fall colors in Vermont: "It is death that causes this blinding show of color, but it is a fierce and flaming death. To drive along a Vermont country road in this season is to be dazzled by the shower of lemon and scarlet and gold that washes across your windshield." His camera operator for 15 years, Isadore Bleckman, commented in the *New York Times*, "He gave a depth to my pictures that I could not have got otherwise, with color or anything else."

At some points during the show's span, Kuralt spent 50,000 miles a year on the road, and he deeply enjoyed covering the human interest stories. Some of his programs highlighted unicyclists, horse traders, professional wrestlers, lumberjacks, whittlers, and a swimming pig. He even found a butcher who could hold 30 eggs in one hand, a gas station that doubled as a poetry factory, and an entertainer who visited nursing homes—at the age of 104. "The chronicle of the country and the nation that he brought was among the most beautiful and vivid journalism that I've ever heard in broadcast," remarked CNN Washington Bureau Chief Frank Sesno in an obituary on the CNN Interactive web site. "He created an art form, really, in television broadcast."

Throughout his years at CBS, Kuralt held numerous other positions as well as host of *On The Road*. In 1979, he became the anchor for *CBS News Sunday Morning,* and in 1980-81 anchored the weekday show *Morning with Charles Kuralt*. In 1989, he reported on the push for democracy in China. He was made anchor of *America Tonight* in 1992, a news magazine show created to compete with ABC's *Nightline*. He retired from CBS in 1994 after 37 years of service, claiming, "I aim to do some traveling and reading and writing," as *USA Today* reported in an obituary. However, in 1997 he went back to work hosting the syndicated show *An American Moment,* consisting of 90-second segments of American life broadcast three times a week. He also that year headed up *I Remember,* a weekly hour-long program examining major news events of the past three decades. However, his health was declining due to the onset of the inflammatory disease lupus, although the *New York Times* reported that a family spokeswoman said that it did not contribute to his sudden death from heart failure.

Kuralt wrote several books, including *On the Road with Charles Kuralt,* 1985, and contributed articles to various periodicals. He was the recipient of three George Foster Peabody Broadcasting awards, in 1969, 1976, and 1979; ten Emmy awards; and the George Polk Memorial Award for national television reporting in 1980. He was named Broadcaster of the Year in 1985 by the International Radio-Television Society. He was married to Sory Guthery in 1957 and had two daughters. They divorced, and he married Suzanna Folson Baird on June 1, 1962. He is survived by his wife; his brother, Wallace; his sister, Catherine Harris; two daughters, Susan Guthery Bowers and Lisa Catherine White; and three grandsons. **Sources:** "Charles Kuralt, CBS' poet of small-town America, dies at 62," CNN Interactive web site, http://cnn.com (July 4, 1997); *Contemporary Authors, New Revision Series*, Volume 43, Gale Research, 1994; *New York Times*, July 5, 1997; *USA Today*, July 4, 1997.

—*Geri Speace*

Roy Lichtenstein

Born October 27, 1923, in New York, NY; died September 29, 1997, in New York, NY, of pneumonia. Roy Lichtenstein, a leading figure in the American pop art movement of the 1960s, was famous for paintings that mimicked yet slyly and subtly altered the conventions of the comic strip. "I take a cliché and try to organize its forms to make it monumental," he once said, as quoted by David Zimmerman in *USA Today*. "The difference is often not great, but it is crucial." Like fellow American pop artist Andy Warhol, Lichtenstein profoundly influenced modern life by changing forever how people experience their relationship to the artifacts of consumer culture.

Lichtenstein grew up in New York City and became interested in art during his teens. In the 1940s he studied art at Ohio State University and served in the U.S. Army. After graduating from Ohio State with a master's degree in fine arts in 1949, he financed his artistic career for more than a decade by teaching at various universities and working as a commercial artist. During this period American art was dominated by abstract expressionism, an art form, pioneered by Jackson Pollock in the later 1940s, that relied on splashing or spraying paint over a large canvas to unleash the artistic potential of the unconscious mind. Throughout the 1950s Lichtenstein experimented with abstract expressionism—a style from which he ultimately became estranged—and other approaches, but his efforts were largely within the artistic mainstream and attracted limited critical and public attention.

Lichtenstein's development of a distinctly personal artistic style came relatively late in life. In the mid-1950s British artists had pioneered a movement known as pop, which appropriated images from popular or mass culture (news photographs, billboard advertisements, supermarket packaging, and the like) as a basis for artistic expression. Within a few years pop style was beginning to influence artists in the United States. It was at this juncture that Lichtenstein, by then in his late thirties, hit on the idea of transforming the comic strip form into high art. His initial effort in this direction was the celebrated *Look Mickey* (1961), a full-size painting inspired by a Mickey Mouse and Donald Duck cartoon on a bubblegum wrapper. Although at first glance *Look Mickey* and the many other comic strip paintings that Lichtenstein produced during the first half of the 1960s seemed to be no more than unimaginative copies of consumerist ephemera, "each image," art critic Robert Hughes remarked in *Time*, "underwent fastidious tweaking, reshaping and restyling." The result was art that offered an ironic commentary on modern—particularly American—life, struck a blow against abstract expressionism by rejoicing in the power of the representational image and, in Hughes's words, "approached real monumentality on the foundation of images that *bien pensant* taste regarded as trash."

The first exhibition of Lichtenstein's comic strip paintings was mounted at the Leo Castelli Gallery in New York City in 1962. The show was a tremendous hit with the public and sold out even before it opened. Other triumphs followed, including an exhibition at the Tate Gallery in London in 1968, the first time that institution featured the work of a living American artist. Some critics, however, reacted to Lichtenstein's paintings with loathing. Zimmerman, writing in *USA Today*, noted that as early as 1963 journalist Brian O'Doherty of the *New York Times* called Lichtenstein "one of the worst artists in America." And when the Tate purchased Lichtenstein's *Whaam!* (1963), a comic strip rendition of a scene from an aerial dogfight, considerable outrage ensued. But *Whaam!* became one of the Tate's most popular works, and in time the bulk of critical opinion on both sides of the Atlantic joined public opinion in recognizing Lichtenstein as a witty, original, and perceptive anatomist of contemporary life. Nor did his popularity wane over the years. In 1993, a Lichtenstein retrospective, presented by the Guggenheim Museum in New York City, attracted more than three thousand visitors a day and later toured widely in North America and Europe. And unlike the works of many of his pop contemporaries, Lichtenstein's paintings commanded huge prices even during the art market slump of the 1990s. In 1997, for instance, *Blang* sold at auction for $2.9 million.

Lichtenstein was survived by his second wife, Dorothy Herzka, whom he married in 1968, and by two sons from his first marriage in 1949 to Isabel Wilson, which ended in divorce in 1965. After 1965, Lichtenstein largely abandoned the comic strip form but remained a prolific artist for the rest of his life, producing paintings, sculptures, and other works in a variety of media. In the 1990s, his creations included paintings inspired by Chinese scrolls and a series of "interiors" that explored how works by Lichtenstein and other artists had fared in the hands of private collectors. One of his interiors, which took as its subject the White House's Oval Office, was transformed into a campaign poster and button for U.S. presidential candidate Bill Clinton. Nothing could have better illustrated how deeply embedded Lichtenstein's work had become in modern consciousness. As Clare Bell, a curator of the 1993 Guggenheim show, observed to Zimmerman, "He began by quoting the comics, and now advertising quotes him." After Lichtenstein, no bubblegum wrapper ever seemed quite the same again. **Sources:** *Chicago Tribune*, http://www.chicago.tribune.com (October 3, 1997); *Detroit Free Press*, September 30, 1997, p. 2B; *Los Angeles Times*, http://www.latimes.com (September 30, 1997);

MSNBC, http://www.msnbc.com (October 1, 1997); *New York Times*, http://www.nytimes.com (September 30, 1997); *Time*, October 13, 1997, p. 101; *Times* (London), http://www.the-times.co.uk (September 30 and October 1, 1997); *USA Today*, http://www.usatoday.com (September 30, 1997); *Washington Post*, http://search.washingtonpost.com (October 1, 1997).

—*Howard Baker*

Jack Lord

Born John Joseph Patrick Ryan on December 30, 1920, in Brooklyn, NY; died of heart failure on January 21, 1998, at his beachfront home in Honolulu, HI. The actor was best known for his portrayal of no-nonsense Detective Steve McGarrett on *Hawaii Five-O*, the longest running crime show in television history. Lord also produced the show, which aired on CBS from 1968-1980.

According to the London *Times*, Lord had a "comfortable and cultured upbringing" and learned horsemanship as a boy while riding on his mother's fruit farm along the banks of the Hudson River. His father, William Lawrence Ryan, was a steamship company executive. As a teenager, Lord traveled the world on freighters owned by his father's company and pursued his first love: painting. From the freighters' decks he painted scenes of the Mediterranean, the Caribbean, Africa, and China. He later studied art at New York University, which he attended on a football scholarship. Lord's paintings have been exhibited in more than 40 museums, including the Bibliotheque in Paris, the Library of Congress in Washington, D.C., and New York's Whitney Museum, Metropolitan Museum of Art and Museum of Modern Art.

At NYU, Lord took an interest in theater, and after graduating, he studied acting at the Neighborhood Playhouse while supporting himself as a car salesman at a Manhattan Cadillac dealership. He worked with Marlon Brando, Paul Newman and Marilyn Monroe at the Actors Studio. Under the name Jack Ryan, he played small parts in two 1949 films *The Red Menace* and *Project X*. In the early 1950s, after taking the stage name Jack Lord, he performed in numerous live television dramas and toured in the play *Flame Out*. In 1954, he made his New York stage debut in *The Illegitimist*. A year later, he portrayed Brick in Elia Kazan's Broadway production of *Cat on a Hot Tin Roof*, the role which propelled him to Hollywood.

Lord's early movie roles included *The Court-Martial of Billy Mitchell*, *Tip on a Dead Jockey*, *God's Little Acre*, and *The True Story of Lynn Stuart*. He also landed guest roles on television shows such as *The Untouchables* and *Have Gun, Will Travel*. In 1962, Lord played CIA agent Felix Leighter in *Dr. No*, the first James Bond movie, and launched the TV series *Stoney Burke*, in which he portrayed a rodeo cowboy. The show folded after a single season. Lord continued making television guest appearances in the 1960s, but he turned down leading roles in the popular dramas *Ben Casey* and *Wagon Train*.

According to the *New York Times*, when *Hawaii Five-O* came along, Lord was ready to play "strait-laced" Steve McGarrett, the head of a police force called "Five-0" which worked for the governor of Hawaii. Shot entirely on location, the show blended standard crime fare with an exotic tropical setting. "It's costing us 25 percent to 30 percent more to film here than in Hollywood," Lord told the *Los Angeles Times* during the show's debut season. "But we feel it's worth it, because we're getting a fresh kind of hot look from this new environment." The series spanned 284 episodes over 12 years, spawned the catch phrase "Book 'em, Danno," attracted a weekly audience of more than 300 million people in 80 countries, and served as a precursor to other Hawaii-based shows, such as *Magnum, P.I.* As the show's producer and occasional director, Lord had control over dramatic decisions on every episode of "Five-0," and he reigned with an iron hand. "He was always a strict taskmaster, a perfectionist," noted Kam Fong, who portrayed Detective Chin Ho Kelly on the show for 10 years, in the *New York Times*. "When we were on the set, it was strictly business; he wouldn't stand for any horseplay. And he was not the social type. After work, he had nothing to do with us socially. But I learned quite a lot from him and so did others. We always had a lot of local actors on the show who were inexperienced and ... he would yell at them, but always to help them learn."

Hawaii Five-0 pumped millions of dollars into the state's economy and was credited with a significant increase in tourism. "It was considered the ultimate travelogue for Hawaii," CBS executive David Poltrack told the *New York Times*. "The ascent of Hawaii as a major tourist location coincided with the strong years of that program. It really hit a chord." Ironically, Hawaiian officials initially had opposed the show, fearing it would portray the islands as crime-ridden.

After declining ratings triggered the show's cancellation, Lord retired from acting, stayed in Hawaii, painted, and invested heavily in real estate. For years, the vanity plate on his Cadillac bore the phrase "Five-0." Marie Lord, his wife of more than 50 years, was at his side when he died at their Honolulu home. The couple was reclusive—especially in their later years, when Lord's health deteriorated and he suffered from Alzheimer's disease. **Sources:** *Associated Press*, January 22, 1998; *Chicago Tribune*, January 22, 1998; *Les Brown's Encyclopedia of Television*, 3rd edition, Gale Research, 1992; *Los Angeles Times*, January 23, 1998; *New York Times*, January 23, 1998; *Times* (London), January 23, 1998.

—Dave Wilkins

Jorge Mas Canosa

Born on September 21, 1939, in Santiago, Cuba; died November 23, 1997, in Miami, FL, from respiratory and cardiac failure caused by lung cancer. He had also suffered from Paget's disease, a degenerative bone disorder. Jorge Mas Canosa was exiled from his homeland in 1960, arrived in Miami penniless, built a business empire worth a half-billion dollars, and led a tenacious, and ultimately unsuccessful, campaign to overthrow Cuban dictator Fidel Castro. Mas established one of the most effective lobbying groups in Washington, pushed relentlessly for political and economic sanctions against Cuba, generously supported anti-Castro lawmakers and heads of state, and advised three U.S. presidents on Cuban affairs. President Bill Clinton called Mas a "born leader and organizer whose tenacity, strength of conviction and passion I greatly admired." U.S. Rep. Ileana Ros-Lehtinen, a Florida Republican, concurred, commenting to the *Washington Post*, "Jorge has been a very important part of shaping U.S.-Cuba policy for a number of years, formulating and passing important legislation."

Mas' father was a member of Cuban dictator Fulgenico Batista's army. At age 14, the boy was arrested and detained briefly for broadcasting anti-Batista slogans on the radio. To keep his son out of further trouble, Ramon Mas sent him to study at Presbyterian Junior College in North Carolina. Mas returned home to Cuba in 1959, shortly after Castro and his guerrilla force had seized control of the country. It wasn't long before Mas' support for Castro disintegrated; he soon was jailed for publicly criticizing the new dictator. After serving a short sentence, Mas, who was then 21, left the country for Miami.

Once in the United States, he joined a team of exiled Cubans who were being trained by the CIA for the Bay of Pigs invasion. The ship he was assigned to, however, remained offshore during the mission. After a short stint in the U.S. Army, Mas returned to Miami and landed various blue collar jobs—washing dishes, selling shoes, loading ships, delivering milk—while plotting Castro's overthrow. "According to his associates of that time," Larry Rohter wrote in the *New York Times*, "he helped raise money, obtain weapons and scout possible sites in the Caribbean and Central America from which Cuba could be attacked or invaded." Mas also brought his high school sweetheart, Irma Santos, to Miami. They married and had three children, Jorge Jr., Juan Carlos, and Jose Ramon.

In the early 1970s, Mas borrowed $50,000 to buy a small company, called Iglesias y Torres, that worked for the phone company in Puerto Rico. He changed the company's name to Church & Tower and landed contracts to install cable and telephone poles for Southern Bell. "Over the years, Church & Tower became the foundation of a telecommunications empire that transformed Mas into one of the wealthiest Hispanic businessmen in the United States," Rohter wrote. "The family business, now called Mastec, today has interests in the United States and in telephone companies and other ventures throughout Latin America and in Spain." At the time of his death, the value of Mastec was estimated at $475 million. Building a fortune, however, did not distract him from continuing to focus on his homeland—although he did change tactics. He gave up the idea of a military assault and instead began waging a political war.

Following Ronald Reagan's election in 1980, Mas, by then an American citizen, founded the Cuban-American National Foundation. The CANF grew to 50,000 members and lobbied intensely for a stream of legislation to tighten sanctions against Cuba and isolate the country politically and economically. Mas' influence grew significantly during the Reagan years, when he deftly delivered Cuban votes to the Republicans. He also developed relationships with George Bush and Bill Clinton, who called on Mas when he was searching for ways to stop the flood of Cuban refugees arriving in Florida on rafts. "Had it not been for Jorge Mas Canosa, we probably would have had normal relations with Cuba. He almost singlehandedly blocked all that," Wayne Smith, head of the U.S. Interest Section in Havana during the Carter administration, commented to the *Chicago Tribune*. Mas also traveled extensively seeking allies in his fight. He met with Russian leader Boris Yeltsin, Czech President Vaclav Havel, and Carlos Menem of Argentina, among others.

Mas had his share of critics as well. The *Los Angeles Times* noted he had been called "irascible and combative," while *CNN* noted he had been called "an arrogant megalomaniac prone to tirades." Another critic noted that he was covetous of the Cuban presidency. "His many detractors ... saw in Mas the same dictatorial streak, relish for power and intolerance of opposing views that characterized Castro's rule," Rohter wrote. "Over the airwaves of Spanish-language radio stations in Miami and in letters to the editor and public debates, Mas repeatedly questioned the patriotism of those who disagreed with him, and threatened in some cases to ruin their lives or careers."

According to the *Los Angeles Times*, he had a legendary string of conflicts. He once challenged a Miami politician to a duel. He lost a $1 million libel judgment in a suit brought by his brother. He engineered a boycott of the *Miami Herald* over its coverage of Cuba and "hate, disinformation and reckless disregard" of Miami's Cuban community. He lashed out at the television show *60 Minutes*, after it broadcast an unflattering profile of him and sued the *New Republic* after it labeled him a "mobster." Mas won a settlement and an apology.

"He was able to create ... the only Cuban-American organization to insert itself into the structure of American political power," University of Miami sociologist and critic of Mas Max Castro told Mireya Navarrothe of the *New York Times*. He added, "The problem was how that power was exercised, and in my view the policies he pursued were not effective in bringing democracy to Cuba, and aggravated the suffering of the Cuban people."

At a press conference following his death, his son, Jorge Jr., said of his father: "Unfortunately, he will never set foot in a free Cuba.... But his spirit and the legacy that he has left us will." Mas is survived by his wife and three sons. **Sources:** *Chicago Tribune,* November 24, 1997; *CNN Interactive,* November 23, 1997; *Los Angeles Times,* November 24, 1997; *New York Times,* November 24, 1997; *Washington Post,* November 24, 1997.

—*Dave Wilkins*

Linda McCartney

Born September 24, 1942, in New York, NY; died of cancer, April 19, 1998, near Tucson, AZ. Photographer, musician. Linda McCartney started her career photographing rock stars and eventually married one of the most famous and successful of them all. She married Beatles singer Paul McCartney in 1969, and the couple enjoyed one of the closest relationships in show business. Linda McCartney joined her husband's band, Wings, and collaborated with him on various projects. She was also a talented photographer who shot nature pictures and other subjects in addition to stars, and her work ended up on a number of Wings album covers and in galleries around the globe. A devoted vegetarian and animal-rights activist, Linda McCartney started her own line of meatless frozen foods and published a few cookbooks. Avoiding the limelight, the McCartneys spent most of their time raising their children on a farm in England. McCartney was diagnosed with breast cancer in 1995.

McCartney was born Linda Louise Eastman in New York City and grew up in Scarsdale, New York. Her father, Lee, was a wealthy lawyer specializing in copyrights and as such, was often retained by entertainment personalities and other well-known figures, including songwriter Hoagy Carmichael, artist Willem de Kooning, and musician Tommy Dorsey. Celebrities were relatively common at the Eastman household. When McCartney was 18 or 19, her mother was killed in a plane crash. McCartney attended Sarah Lawrence College before transferring to the University of Arizona, majoring in art history. During her college years, she married and had a daughter, but the marriage soon ended in 1963.

McCartney later started a photography course in Tucson, Arizona, displaying a real ability. In 1965 she returned to New York, where she worked as a receptionist at *Town and Country* magazine. Stealing an invitation out of the mail to a press reception on a yacht for the rock group the Rolling Stones, she managed to get the lucky break of being the only photographer allowed on board. These exclusive pictures established her as a new talent and would set the course for her life. Over the next few years, the young shutterbug became friendly with numerous major acts of the 1960s, including Jimi Hendrix, Janis Joplin, the Doors, Bob Dylan, Frank Zappa, the Grateful Dead, and others. *Rolling Stone* and other music magazines bought her gritty pictures, and she became an acclaimed photographer. Her proximity to celebrities led her to date Warren Beatty and Chris Stamp, the manager of British rock group The Who.

McCartney's reputation for photography took her to London in May of 1967 to shoot the Beatles, the enormously popular British foursome, on the launch of their groundbreaking album, *Sgt. Pepper's Lonely Hearts Club Band*. It was there she met her future husband, singer Paul McCartney, one of the most desired men of the era. They began a relationship, and were married two years later. Linda broke many young girls' hearts by winning the "cute" Beatle. Together they had three children, Mary, Stella, and James; Paul also adopted McCartney's daughter Heather from her first marriage.

The couple were inseparable and reportedly never spent a night apart from each other throughout their entire marriage, except for a ten-day spell in which Paul McCartney was jailed in Tokyo for possession of marijuana. They formed one of the closest families in the entertainment world. Shortly after the Beatles broke up in 1970, Paul started a new group, Wings, and insisted that his wife join the band, despite her lack of musical training, and according to most, ability. However, Paul could not bear to spend time away from Linda, and thus set her up on keyboards and backing vocals. Her off-key singing and missed notes were scorned by critics, but the band itself was a success throughout the 1970s. She also worked with Paul on other projects and with unnamed groups in the 1980s and 1990s.

Meanwhile, the McCartney family generally shied away from publicity when not touring, with Paul and Linda raising their children on a secluded farm in West Sussex, England, and a getaway in Scotland. Linda did not hire servants, such as cooks or nannies, and she sent their children to state schools rather than private. The family enjoyed a number of pets, including horses, and Linda grew her own organic produce. Though Paul and Linda McCartney were fined for possessing marijuana in 1972 and again apprehended for carrying it through an airport in 1984, they otherwise led healthful lives. Linda was a vegetarian for many years before it caught on in the mainstream, and she created a line of meat-free frozen foods and wrote a few cookbooks. She also was active with environmentalism and animal rights, strongly supporting the work of People for the Ethical Treatment of Animals (PETA).

Linda McCartney's photographs graced many of the album covers for the band Wings. She won a prize in 1980 at the Cannes Film Festival for the music in the animated *Seaside Woman*, and also contributed music to the animated film *Oriental Nightfish*. In 1992, she published a collection of several hundred old photographs, including many of the Beatles, in *Linda McCartney's Sixties: Portrait of an Era*. Some of her other

photography books include *Linda's Pictures, Sun Prints, Photographs,* and *Road Works*. She turned the lens on plants, animals, rock formations, and local people as well as celebrities, and her work has been exhibited in numerous galleries worldwide, including the Victoria and Albert Museum in London. Her husband Paul was knighted in 1997 by Queen Elizabeth II, and the same year, their daughter Stella had her first big show as a designer for the house of Chloe.

But the family faced hardship in 1995 when McCartney was diagnosed with breast cancer. A lumpectomy was performed, but in 1996 the disease returned. She flew to California for chemotherapy treatments, and it was thought that she was in the clear. However, by March of 1998 the cancer had spread to McCartney's liver. On April 19, 1998, the McCartney's publicist reported that she died at age 56 outside Santa Barbara, California, but reports in the ensuing days indicated that no death certificate was ever filed there. Later, the McCartney spokesman verified that Linda had actually spent her last hours at the family's ranch outside Tucson, Arizona, where Linda had often spent time riding horses; in fact, she had been out riding just two days before her death. Paul McCartney admitted to throwing off the press so that he could have a few days to grieve without distraction. At Linda's memorial service in Manhattan, Paul and other mourners sang the Beatles tune "Let It Be," which he had written for his mother, who had died of breast cancer when he was just 14 years old. **Sources:** *Arizona Republic,* April 24, 1998; Browne, Turner, and Elaine Partnow, *Macmillan Biographical Encyclopedia of Photographic Artists & Innovators,* Macmillan, 1983; *Chicago Tribune,* April 20, 1998; "Linda McCartney Loses Battle with Cancer," CNNin web site, April 19, 1998, http://cnn.com (April 20, 1998); *Los Angeles Times,* April 20, 1998; *Newsday,* April 23, 1998, p. A7; *New York Times,* April 20, 1998; *Times* (London), April 20, 1998, April 21, 1998; *USA Today,* April 19, 1998.

—Geri Speace

Burgess Meredith

Born November 16, 1909, in Cleveland, OH; died September 9, 1997, in Malibu, CA, from Alzheimer's disease and melanoma. Among those who grew up in the 1960s and 1970s, Burgess Meredith was most recognizable as the Penguin, a maniacal villain in the 1960s camp television show *Batman*, and as Sylvester Stallone's gruff boxing trainer in the *Rocky* movies, the first of which appeared in 1976. In the mid-1990s, movie audiences came to know him as Jack Lemmon's randy and foul-mouthed father in *Grumpy Old Men* (1993) and *Grumpier Old Men* (1995). But these were only a few of the dozens of memorable or noteworthy roles that Meredith played during his more than 65 years as a stage, screen, radio, and television actor and as a writer, producer, and director.

In his 1994 autobiography, *So Far, So Good,* Meredith recalled a father who was a violent alcoholic. Meredith's parents separated when he was four, and a few years later he and his mother went to live in New York City, where he soon demonstrated talent as an actor and singer. After leaving school he worked at various jobs, including reporter and merchant sailor, and spent some time at Amherst College in Massachusetts. His adult career on the stage began in 1929 when he joined the Civic Repertory Company in New York City. The young actor's early appearances were so successful that Maxwell Anderson, a leading playwright of the era, wrote a blank verse drama, *Winterset,* for him. This work, inspired by the controversial murder trial and execution of the Italian-American anarchists Nicola Sacco and Bartolomeo Vanzetti in the 1920s, was staged on Broadway in 1935. In the play, Meredith played Mio, a young man in search of the truth behind his father's wrongful execution for murder.

Winterset was a hit on Broadway and gave Meredith his entrée into the movies when he was invited to repeat the role of Mio in the 1936 screen version. Other movie appearances followed, one of the most affecting being his 1939 performance as George, the friend of the slow-witted Lenny in John Steinbeck's *Of Mice and Men.* During World War II Meredith joined the U.S. Army Air Corps, serving as a captain and producing and acting in movies for the Office of War Information. He was also cast as famous war correspondent Ernie Pyle in *The Story of G.I. Joe* (1945), a movie whose popularity led to the creation of the G.I. Joe action figures for children. After the war Meredith continued to work regularly in the movies as an actor, writer, producer, and director, but as an actor was confined to supporting roles. He received two Academy Award nominations, for *Day of the Locust* (1975) and *Rocky* (1976). Michael Wilmington of the *Chicago Tribune,* who called Meredith "one of the finest American movie actors never to win an Oscar," explained that his "diminutive, 5-foot-7-inch stature, pleasantly gnarly features and obvious sophistication doomed him to supporting roles, usually as a humorous or frightening eccentric. Yet he always filled those roles with wit, warmth, imagination, high intensity and flashing intelligence."

Although Meredith gained most public attention as a movie and television actor, the theater was, as a writer for the London *Times* remarked, "his true love, and he was happiest when either acting or directing for the stage." Meredith's stage career after *Winterset* included leading roles in works by Eugene O'Neill and Samuel Beckett; an appearance as William Shakespeare's Prince Hal opposite Orson Welles in *The Five Kings* (1939); and an Antoinette Perry Award nomination for directing the James Joyce adaptation *Ulysses in Nighttown* (1958). He also worked as an actor and narrator on radio for many years. On television he appeared not only as the Penguin but also in commercials and in several unforgettable episodes of *The Twilight Zone,* Rod Serling's science-fiction series of 1959-64.

Meredith was known as an intellectual and as an ardent supporter of social and political causes. During the 1950s, the decade of U.S. Senator Joseph McCarthy's crusade to root out supposed Communist subversion in American institutions, Meredith was blacklisted by the movie industry for his left-wing views, but was able to return to screen acting when director Otto Preminger offered him roles in *Advise and Consent* (1962) and other productions. In 1977 Meredith won an Emmy Award for his supporting performance as lawyer and McCarthy opponent Joseph Welch in *Tail Gunner Joe,* a television docudrama about the McCarthy era. Meredith once said, as quoted by Mel Gussow in the *New York Times,* that *Tail Gunner Joe* was a favorite of his, for it had given him a chance to wreak "'a splendid revenge' on 'the McCarthy gang.'"

Meredith's first three marriages (including one to well-known actress Paulette Goddard) ended in divorce. Between marriages, according to his autobiography, he was romantically involved with stage and screen goddesses Tallulah Bankhead, Ingrid Bergman, and Marlene Dietrich. In 1950 he married ballet dancer Kaja Sundsten, who survived him, as did a son and a daughter.

The most remarkable feature of Meredith's career was, perhaps, its versatility. In his eighties, for instance, he made a foray into a new medium, co-starring with Christopher Walken in *Ripper* (1994), an interactive computer game based on the crimes of nineteenth-century murderer Jack the Ripper. Although after 1945 he was denied the leading-man movie roles that he had proved so capable of filling during his early years as an actor, he appeared to take any disappointment he may have felt in his stride. When asked by an interviewer in 1967 why he often

accepted parts that were less than challenging for an actor of his abilities, Meredith replied as quoted by Gussow, "If I spent all my time in Shakespearean companies and only did art movies like [Laurence] Olivier, my position would be more dignified and more serious. I might even be a better actor.... But this is America, and I'm a man moved by the rhythms of his time, so I'll just take amusement at being a paradox."
Sources: *Chicago Tribune*, September 11, 1997, section 1, p. 10; CNN Interactive, http://cnn.com (September 16, 1997); "Burgess Meredith," *Contemporary Authors*, http://galenet.gale.com (November 10, 1997); *Los Angeles Times*, September 11, 1997, p. A1; *New York Times*, September 11, 1997, p. B7; *Times* (London), http://www.the-times.co.uk (September 24, 1997); *USA Today*, September 11, 1997, p. 5D.

—*Howard Baker*

James A. Michener

Born c. February 3, 1907, probably in New York, NY; died October 16, 1997, in Austin, TX, of kidney failure after choosing to discontinue his dialysis treatments. The author or coauthor of more than 50 fiction and nonfiction books, James A. Michener was best known for producing immensely popular novels that explored the history of a country or region over hundreds or thousands of years by chronicling the experiences of several fictional families through the generations. Reviewers praised Michener for his skill in conveying a sense of place, for his exhaustive research and attention to detail, and for the moral seriousness that characterized his work. Less charitable critics, however, pointed to Michener's shortcomings as a literary stylist and the lack of psychological depth in his characters, and slighted his historical novels—which often exceeded the 1,000-page mark—as "doorstoppers" and "beach books."

Michener never knew his parents or the circumstances of his birth. At a very early age he was sent to live with Mabel Haddock Michener, a young, impoverished widow in Doylestown, Pennsylvania, who earned a living doing laundry and caring for orphans. Mabel Michener raised the future author as a Quaker and read to him from Dickens and other nineteenth-century novelists. Commenting on the love of books and music that his foster mother inspired in him, Michener once commented, as quoted by Paul Galloway in the *Chicago Tribune*, "I learned from my mother that there is a world into which even the most abjectly poor can pass freely. It saved me." At age 14 Michener left home to travel around the United States, and by age 20 had visited 45 states. He won a scholarship to Swarthmore College, where he studied English and history and earned a bachelor's degree summa cum laude in 1929. Following graduation he worked as a schoolteacher, travelled and studied in Europe for two years on a scholarship, taught at Harvard, and edited textbooks for a New York City publisher.

After Japan attacked Pearl Harbor in 1941, prompting the United States to enter World War II, Michener enlisted in the U.S. Navy and was posted to the South Pacific, where he served as an officer. His duties, which were clerical and administrative, left him with lots of free time, and he began to write short stories based on his military experiences and on the unusual characters he encountered in his travels throughout the region. In 1947 these stories were published in book form as *Tales of the South Pacific,* which won a Pulitzer Prize and inspired *South Pacific,* a hit Broadway musical by Richard Rodgers and Oscar Hammerstein that opened in 1949. The musical's great success propelled Michener's book onto the best-seller lists, and it eventually sold more than two million copies.

In *Hawaii,* published in 1959, Michener established the formula on which his popularity as a novelist would rest for nearly four decades. Michener was living in Hawaii at the time, and drew on personal experiences and meticulous historical research to craft a 1,140-page fictional account of Hawaii's history from prehistoric to modern times. The author later recalled, as quoted by Stephanie Simon in the *Los Angeles Times,* that with *Hawaii* he had "stumbled on the device of the long novel, and the crazy things sold unbelievably." More historical blockbusters followed: *The Source* (on Israel) in 1965, *Centennial* (on Colorado) in 1974, *Chesapeake* (on the Chesapeake Bay area of the eastern United States) in 1978, *The Covenant* (on South Africa) in 1980, *Space* (on the exploration of outer space) in 1982, *Poland* in 1983, *Texas* in 1985, *Alaska* in 1988, *Caribbean* in 1989, and *Mexico* in 1992.

By the time of his death Michener had sold perhaps 100 million books and was one of only a handful of authors to have had six or more titles on the *New York Times* best-seller list. Several of his novels were made into movies or television miniseries. In his 50-year career as an author, Michener earned tens of millions of dollars in royalties, much of which he gave away to educational, cultural, and other charitable causes, including $37 million to the University of Texas. In 1996 *Fortune* listed him as one of the top 25 American philanthropists. Michener's other nonliterary activities included an unsuccessful campaign for a seat in the U.S. House of Representatives in 1962 and service on several government advisory councils. He received, among other awards, the Medal of Freedom, the highest U.S. civilian honor.

Michener's first two marriages, to Patti Koon in 1935 and Vange Nord in 1948, ended in divorce. His third wife, Mari Yoriko Sabusawa, whom he married in 1955, died in 1994. None of these marriages produced children. Michener remained a prolific author into his seventies and eighties, despite deteriorating health. By October of 1997 he was receiving kidney dialysis treatments three times a week. An advocate of doctor-assisted suicide for the terminally ill (a subject he explored in *Recessional,* a novel published in 1994), Michener ended his life by refusing further medical intervention.

Michener himself was the first to admit that his books were popular works of fiction rather than great works of literature such as those of his childhood. But unlike many of the multimillionaire bestselling novelists who were his contemporaries, he sought to enlighten and uplift as well as entertain, and eschewed vulgarity and sensationalism. As Jonathan Yardley commented in the *New York Times Book Review,* Michener "earned his enormous popularity honorably." **Sources:** Associated Press, http://wire.ap.org (October 17, 1997); *Chicago Tribune,* http://www.chicago.tribune.com (October 17, 1997); CNN Interactive, http://cnn.com (October 17, 1997); "James A(lbert) Michener," *Contemporary Authors,* http://galenet.gale.com (November 10, 1997); *Los Angeles Times,* http://www.latimes.com (October 17, 1997); *New York Times,* http://www.nytimes.com (October 17, 1997); *USA Today,* http://www.usatoday .com (October 17, 1997), and October 17, 1997, p. 4A; *Washington Post,* http://www.washingtonpost.com (October 17, 1997).

—*Howard Baker*

Rodney Milburn Jr.

Born May 18, 1950, in Opelousas, LA; died November 11, 1997, as a result of burns suffered in an industrial accident at a paper mill in Baton Rouge, Louisiana. Rodney Milburn Jr., who took home a gold medal in the 1972 Munich Olympics in a track and field event, was inexplicably living in a homeless shelter and sold his plasma at a Baton Rouge clinic on the morning of what would be his last day. He needed the quick money

from it to pay for a cab to get to his job at a paper mill, where he was later found in a tank of bleach solution by co-workers. Those who knew him at various times of his life, especially in his heyday as a record-breaking hurdler, were puzzled by Milburn's tragic decline. "The assurance and purpose that ushered him safely through sport's most difficult challenges ultimately failed to guide Milburn through life's obstacles," remarked his *Los Angeles Times* obituary.

Milburn grew up in the Louisiana town of Opelousas and had a difficult, impoverished childhood after the death of his father. The town was extremely segregated at the time, and he attended the all-African American Clark High School, which had a third-rate grass and dirt track. He would sneak into the town's white high school at night to run their smooth, regulation surface and practice on their hurdles. Jumping quickly became Milburn's forte, and his coaches gave him much encouragement. He was a standout high school athlete, and enrolled in Southern University. There his prowess in track and field events continued to flourish, and Milburn was receiving national attention even during his 1970 freshman year. As a sophomore, he went virtually undefeated, and won all three national college titles; he also earned a gold medal in the Pan-American Games in 1971. That same year, he set his first world record in 120-yard hurdles, clearing them in 13 seconds; it was a record he would hold for eight years.

By 1972, Milburn had won the American Athletic Union championship and was pegged as a serious Olympic contender. Yet in the Olympic tryouts, he did not do very well and almost failed to win a spot; the aberration was corrected at the Munich Summer Games when he outshone his American teammates and won the gold medal for the 110-meter hurdle. The African-American section of Opelousas renamed a street in his honor. In 1974, Milburn decided to try his hand at the professional track and field circuit, but the sport never succeeded. He failed to earn a living, and when the entire enterprise failed, it set him back several years. Because he had turned "pro," Milburn was then barred from competing in the 1976 Olympics, but by 1980 he had had his amateur status reinstated. He was slated to compete in the 1980 Games, but that year's Summer Olympics in Moscow were boycotted by the United States, and American athletes had to remain at home.

Still, even in the early 1980s Milburn was still doing well in track and field events, though he was then in his early thirties. For a time, he taught track at Southern University, but was fired along with several other members of the athletic department in some administrative maneuvering within the college. He then took a well-paying job at a Georgia-Pacific paper mill in Port Hudson, Louisiana. For his duties at the bleaching facility, Milburn earned $37,000 a year, which made it difficult for many to understand why he was living in a homeless shelter. Yet Milburn was going through a bitter divorce, and had lived with relatives for a time but then felt he was perhaps taking advantage of them. He had six children, and was still paying child support on two minors. Moreover, his soon-to-be ex-wife had put all of his medals and trophies in a storage locker, and when the rent was not paid its contents were auctioned off in the summer of 1997.

Tragically, Milburn—who had set track records through his swift and decisive agility—probably died because he lost his balance while opening a hatch to check the drainage of a railroad car filled with crystallized sodium chlorate. His body was found in the tank, and accident investigators assumed he fell into the car from a catwalk after the intense steam from the hatch knocked him off guard. He had third-degree burns on 100 percent of his body, and had inhaled the poisonous substance as well. Former Olympians Willie Davenport and Thomas Hill attended his Opelousas funeral. Davenport, his 1972 Olympic teammate, told a reporter that he had received numerous phone calls from other former Olympians, saddened by the circumstances of Milburn's death. Even Milburn's former classmate and president of his class at Clark High flew in from New York City. "I can't tell you that I knew him well," James Thomas told the *Los Angeles Times*. "But this man carried himself with such dignity, all the while growing up in this ... place." **Sources:** *Los Angeles Times*, November 17, 1997; *New York Times*, November 13, 1997.

—*Carol Brennan*

Mobutu Sese Seko

Born Joseph Desire-Mobutu, October 14, 1930, in Lisala, Belgian Congo (now Congo); died September 7, 1997, in Rabat, Morocco, of complications due to prostate cancer. Calling himself the "Great Helmsman," Mobutu Sese Seko ruled the immense Central African nation of Zaire (now the Democratic Republic of the Congo) for over three decades. His *Chicago Tribune* obituary called him "the last of Africa's Cold War relics, an autocrat in a leopard-skin hat who lived like a king while leading his potentially magnificent country down a ruinous path."

Born in 1930, Joseph Desire-Mobutu was the illegitimate son of a tribal chief and a hotel maid; the man who later married his mother then adopted him. Mobutu was of Ngbandi heritage, a Sudanese tribal group, just one of the many ethnic groups of what was then called the Belgian Congo. Reflecting the country's European colonial flavor, Mobutu was raised in the Roman Catholic faith and attended missionary schools. He was expelled from one in 1948 for throwing ink at a teacher and was then drafted into the Force Publique, the Belgian Congo's colonial army. Over the next few years Mobutu rose to the highest rank attainable for an African, and held a desk job as an accountant.

After his decommissioning, he became a journalist in Leopoldville, the colonial capital, and excelled in this profession. From 1956 to 1959 he edited the weekly *Actualites Africaines,* and his prominence led to a cordial association with leftist Patrice Lumumba, who was then leading the fight for self-rule in the Belgian Congo. Lumumba was elected president in 1960 in the first elections and appointed Mobutu secretary of state, but then made him commander in chief after some internal strife. Lumumba turned to the Soviet bloc for assistance, but a few months later, in September of 1960, Mobutu gained control with the help of the United States Central Intelligence Agency.

Remaining head of the army, Mobutu appointed a cadre of university graduates to rule, and turned Lumumba over to his enemies; his body was never found. More internal chaos occurred over the next few years and, in November of 1965, Mobutu engineered a military coup and declared himself head of state. He nationalized the copper- and diamond-rich country's major industry by seizing the assets of the Union Miniere, and declared a one-party system under the Popular Revolutionary Movement (MPR). The MPR was the only binding element in a country with hundreds of clashing ethnic groups and lack of infrastructure.

Over the next few years Mobutu consolidated power by expelling potential political threats and even publicly executing rebel leaders. In 1971 he renamed the country Zaire, after its main river, and instated an "authenticity" program. His decrees banned Western music and dress, the straightening of hair, and instructed Zairians to lead a traditionally African way of life. He changed all European-language place names to those of Bantu, and changed his own name to

Mobutu Sese Seko Ngbendu Wazabanga, translated as "the warrior who knows no defeat because of his endurance and inflexible will and is all powerful, leaving fire in his wake as he goes from conquest to conquest."

Mobutu also retained tight control of Zaire through a cult of personality—his image was everywhere in the country, often depicting him in signature style with a leopard hat—and he was the only person allowed to speak on behalf of Zaire. Pressured by Western superpowers to rescind some of the more demagogic aspects of his regime, he eventually allowed elections—in which voters could either vote to retain Mobutu with the green ballot, whose color symbolized "progress," or against him with a red ballot that signified "chaos." He maintained further control by a secret police system and heavy military presence; a patronage system kept his cadre of government appointees loyal through their access to a highly corrupt bureaucracy; it is estimated that insiders pilfered as much as 60 percent of national Zaire revenues over the years.

Political analysts coined the term "kleptocracy" to describe Mobutu's pillage of Zaire's natural resources and treasury. His salary was seventeen percent of the national budget, and the government also footed the bill for the tuition for several of his children at private European schools which ran to half a million dollars annually. Mobutu had homes in France and Switzerland, a vineyard in Portugal, a Spanish castle, an opulent yacht anchored in the Zaire River, and palace a thousand miles north of Kinshasa, the capital, that was called the "Versailles of the Jungle." Before his death, it is believed that Mobutu had built up a personal fortune between $5 and $8 billion.

Zaire suffered increasing internal strife in the 1990s. Mobutu's elite presidential guard massacred students after a revolt in 1990, alienating the dictatorship further from its dwindling Western allies, and at times the country could not meet its civil-service and military payroll. In 1993, when Mobutu issued new currency to pay the army, stores refused to accept it and mutiny resulted; in the strife the French ambassador to Zaire was killed. Civil war in neighboring Rwanda the following year brought a flood of refugees into the eastern provinces of Zaire, and out of the abysmal refugee camps a rebel army of Hutu, Tutsi, Ugandan, and Angolan elements arose who harbored longstanding grudges against Mobutu's regime. In October of 1996, when it was by then known that Mobutu was ill with prostate cancer, the Alliance of Democratic Forces for the Liberation of the Congo-Zaire, led by Laurent Kabila, began a serious offensive that gained them control of the eastern provinces. In May of 1997 Kabila's forces overtook Kinshasa, and Mobutu requested asylum from France, his longtime ally, who refused. Eventually Morocco granted him sanctuary, but in late June, Mobutu entered a hospital in Rabat when his health worsened. He died on September 7.

Only Mobutu's immediate family—headed by Boby Ladawa, his second wife—attended the funeral. There was virtually no diplomatic representation at his funeral, save for one official from the rechristened Congo—prophetically, Mobutu had once asserted that his country would not survive without him, and Kabila had restored the name in his first official presidential act. **Sources:** *Chicago Tribune*, September 7, 1997, sec. 1, p. 4; *Detroit Free Press*, September 8, 1997, p. 5A, September 14, 1997, p. 12A; *Los Angeles Times*, September 8, 1997, p. A1, A12; *New York Times,* September 8, 1997, p. A1, p. B8; *Times* (London), September 9, 1997; *USA Today*, September 8, 1997, p. 10A.

—Carol Brennan

Mother Teresa

Born Agnes Gonxha Bojaxhiu, August 26, 1910, in Skopje, Yugoslavia (now in Macedonia); died September 5, 1997, in Calcutta, India, of cardiac arrest. Mother Teresa, often referred to as "the saint of the gutters," spent the majority of her life serving others, beginning at age 18 when she first entered the Order of the Sisters of Our Lady of Loretto. Barely five feet tall and under 100 pounds, her diminutive stature was in stark contrast to the magnitude of her deeds.

Mother Teresa knew, even as a young child, she would devote her life to God. At 12, she told her mother she wanted to become a nun. In 1928, she joined the Sisters of Loretto, an Irish order with missions in India like those she had heard about as a young girl. Her first teaching job was in Darjeeling, India, in the foothills of the Himalayan mountains. In 1929, she was assigned a position at St. Mary's High School near Calcutta. She took her first vows as a nun on May 24, 1931. Exactly six years later, she took her final vows. She continued to teach at St. Mary's and later became principal.

In 1946, she said she received "a call within a call," from God, the *Washington Post* reported. "The message," she said, "was quite clear: I was to leave the convent and help the poor while living among them," she was quoted as saying in the *Los Angeles Times*. Two years later, with the Pope's consent to live as an independent nun, she chose her trademark habit—a plain white sari with a blue border and a cross pinned to the left shoulder, which has remained the official dress of her Missionaries of Charity—and began her duty to the poor.

Now an Indian citizen, Mother Teresa began to see the need not only for education for the poor, but for a place for the street people of Calcutta to die with dignity. "They lived like animals," Mother Teresa said of those she cared for. "At least they die like human beings." She founded her order the Missionaries of Charity in 1950 and in 1952, she opened *Nirml Hriday* ("Pure Heart") Home for Dying and Destitute.

In the mid-1950s, Mother Teresa expanded her care-taking to abandoned children, lepers, and the elderly. She went on to establish welfare institutions, including family clinics, mobile leprosy and tuberculosis clinics, schools, malnutrition centers, night shelters, and nurseries. When she won the 1979 Nobel Peace Prize, accepting her award in the same $1 white sari she donned when she began her order, she convinced the committee to forego the traditional ceremonial dinner and to add the money to her prize winnings, a total near $192,000. She used the money to build more homes for victims of leprosy.

Although widely hailed as a saint on earth, Mother Teresa was not without her critics. A 1994 British television documentary *Hell's Angel: Mother Teresa of Calcutta,* accused her of taking donations without questioning the sources, such as from Haitian dictator Jean-Claude "Baby Doc" Duvalier and Charles Keating, who played a large part in the U.S. savings and loan scandal. She insisted that she had no political interests, saying "I reject politics completely. The poor are poor no matter if they live under a democracy or a dictatorship. In both cases they need love and care," the *Chicago Tribune* reported. Still, the United States was chagrined when she traveled to Iraq after the Persian Gulf war to meet with Saddam Hussein, who allowed her to open centers for orphans and the disabled in his country. While addressing the National Prayer Breakfast in Washington, she shocked the attendees, including President Clinton and Vice President Gore and their wives, with a furious and emphatic denunciation of the administration's stance on abortion rights.

Despite frequent health problems in the last 14 years of her life, Mother Teresa continued to travel, spread her message of generosity, and care for those who needed it most. In 1983, during a visit to Rome to see Pope John Paul II, she suffered her first heart attack. Her second heart attack in 1989 was almost fatal and doctors found it necessary to implant a pacemaker. In 1993, Mother Teresa fell and broke three ribs while in Rome. Mother Teresa's physical condition took a particularly rapid decline in 1996. She fell and broke her collar bone, suffered malarial fever and the failure of her left heart ventricle, was treated for a chest infection and recurring heart problems, and was readmitted to the hospital yet again with chest pains and breathing problems. Realizing she could not carry out her leadership of the Missionaries of Charity (she first tried to resign in 1990, but was voted back into her supervisory position), her successor, Sister Nirmala, was chosen as head of the order on March 13, 1997.

The woman who brought in millions of dollars to support her causes lived on a rupee (about four cents) of food per day and little more than four hours of sleep per night. She owned only three saris and packed two when she traveled. The *Detroit News/Free Press* quoted Mother Teresa as she relayed a dream about continuing her work to Prince Michael of Greece in 1996: "The other day I dreamed that I was at the gates of heaven. And St. Peter said: 'Go back to Earth, there are no slums up here.'"

Mother Teresa had intended on leading prayer services in honor of Princess Diana who died only a week earlier. In her convent the night before Diana's funeral, Mother Teresa was standing by her bed when she said to those around her, "I cannot breathe." She fell to her bed and died. **Sources:** CNN Interactive On-line, http://cnn.com (September 5, 1997); *Detroit News and Free Press,* September 6, 1997, p. 1A; *Los Angeles Times,* September 6, 1997, p. A1; *New York Times* On-line, http://search.nytimes.com (September 6, 1997); *Times* (London) On-line, http://www.the-times.co.uk (September 6, 1997); *Washington Post,* September 6, 1997, p. A17.

—*Audrey Gebber*

Maureen O'Sullivan

Born May 17, 1911, in Boyle, Roscommon County, Ireland; died June 22, 1998, in Scottsdale, AZ. Actress. Maureen O'Sullivan made her name on the silver screen starring as the beautiful Jane opposite Tarzan, played by Johnny Weissmuller, in a series of popular jungle adventure films during the 1930s and 1940s.

The accomplished actress had roles in more than 60 films, including *Pride and Prejudice, The Thin Man, Anna Karenina,* and *David Copperfield.* She even starred opposite the Marx Brothers and future U.S. President Ronald Reagan. In 1942, she left show business for the most part to raise a family with director John Farrow; their seven children included actress Mia Farrow. Later she returned to the stage, and in the 1980s had a few appearances on television and in films. In 1986, she was cast in Woody Allen's *Hannah and Her Sisters,* in which she costarred with her daughter, playing Farrow's onscreen mother.

O'Sullivan was born in Boyle, Roscommon County, Ireland, to Major Charles Joseph and Mary Lovatt (Fraser) O'Sullivan. She went to school at the convent of the Sacred Heart in Dublin and London, and a finishing school in Paris. While attending a horse show in Dublin, American director Frank Borzage took note of O'Sullivan's attractive looks and signed her to work for Fox studios. Her first acting job was in the director's second sound film, *Song O' My Heart,* starring John McCormack, in 1930. After appearing in a number of Fox movies, she moved to Metro-Goldwyn-Mayer (MGM).

At MGM, O'Sullivan made her name acting with Johnny Weissmuller in Tarzan films, based on the story by Edgar Rice Burroughs. Her first such role was in *Tarzan, the Ape Man,* in 1932, in which she played Jane Parker, a woman who is rescued by Tarzan and decides to stay with him in the jungle and be his companion. In a skimpy sarong-style outfit, she appeared with Weismuller in a total of six Tarzan movies until 1942. O'Sullivan would later complain that their chimpanzee costar, Cheetah, often bit her out of jealousy. However, she would later make other films with chimp actors, including *Bedtime for Bonzo,* which also starred future President Ronald Reagan, and *Bonzo Goes to College,* without Reagan but with the chimp. O'Sullivan also took on more refined roles, including Henrietta in *The Barretts of Wimpole Street* (1934), Dora in *David Copperfield* (1935), and Kitty in *Anna Karenina* (1935). She also portrayed Norah Charles in *The Thin Man* (1934) and a romantic interest in the Marx Brothers' *A Day at the Races* (1937). In 1940 she acted in *Pride and Prejudice,* and in 1948 she made *The Big Clock,* directed by her husband, John Farrow.

O'Sullivan married Farrow in 1936 and would take frequent breaks from her career to raise a family of seven children—three boys, four girls—although her oldest son, Michael, died in an airplane crash in 1958. Her most famous offspring was daughter Mia Farrow, who launched a successful acting career of her own.

In the 1960s, O'Sullivan began a stage career, first appearing as Nancy Fallon in *A Roomful of Roses* at Drury Lane Theatre in Chicago. Her Broadway debut was as Edith Lambert, a middle-aged woman who finds herself pregnant, in *Never Too Late* at the Playhouse Theatre in 1962. O'Sullivan acted on the stage in Britain, Florida, and Los Angeles, as well as New York throughout the 1960s and 1970s. Her husband died in 1963, and she married James E. Cushing, a construction company executive, in 1983.

In 1984, O'Sullivan took a role on the television soap opera *The Guiding Light,* and in 1985, appeared on *The Search for Tomorrow.* Also in 1985, at age 75, she costarred with her daughter, Mia Farrow, as her screen-character mother in the Woody Allen film *Hannah and Her Sisters.* O'Sullivan also acted in the 1986 movie *Peggy Sue Gets Married.* Her last role was in 1987's *Stranded.*

O'Sullivan won an award from the Roman Catholic Interracial Council in 1980 for her work to combat racial and religious discrimination. She died at age 87 on June 22, 1998, at Scottsdale Memorial Hospital in Scottsdale, Arizona. She owned a home in the Phoenix area in addition to a residence in Grantham, New Hampshire. Her daughter Stephanie Farrow told the media that she thought her mother had died of old age. **Sources:** *Chicago Tribune,* June 24, 1998; "Maureen O'Sullivan, Who Played Tarzan's Jane, Dead at 87," June 23, 1998, CNNin web site, http://cnn.com (June 24, 1998); *Contemporary Theatre, Film, and Television,* volume 3, Gale Research, 1986; *Los Angeles Times,* June 24, 1998; *New York Times,* June 24, 1998; *People,* July 6, 1998, p. 66; *Times* (London), June 25, 1998; *USA Today,* June 23, 1998; *Washington Post,* June 24, 1998, p. B6.

—*Geri Speace*

Carl Perkins

Born April 9, 1932, in Tiptonville, TN; died January 19, 1998, in Nashville, TN, following a series of strokes. Carl Perkins was a sharecropper's son who in the 1950s, helped plant the seeds of rock 'n' roll. Perkins was a pioneer of "rockabilly," which melded country, gospel, and rhythm 'n' blues into a swaggering, freewheeling sound exemplified by his 1955 composition "Blue Suede Shoes." Rockabilly and Perkins' guitar playing had a profound influence on some of rock 'n' roll's most important artists—the

Beatles, Rolling Stones, Bob Dylan, Eric Clapton, and Paul Simon among them. However, misfortune would keep from Perkins from achieving the popular acclaim his innovative talent foretold.

At age four, Perkins began picking cotton for a penny a pound alongside his father and brother in the fields of Tiptonville, Tennessee, where the music of the rural south blended. By day, young Carl soaked up the gospel songs sung by the African American field hands his family worked with; by night, he absorbed the country music his father tuned in on the radio. When he was seven, the boy began strumming a guitar his father made from a cigar box, a broomstick and baling wire. Later, an old field hand taught him to play the blues on a cheap, second-hand guitar.

Perkins dropped out of school after the eighth grade to help support his family. At various times he worked in a dairy, a bakery and a radio station—all the while performing at night in local saloons with his brothers, Jay and Clayton. It was during those early years playing for rowdy honkytonk crowds that Perkins developed a drinking problem which would plague him. At age 20, he married Valda Crider and began working full-time as a musician. Success did not come quickly, however. The Perkins Brothers demo tapes were routinely rejected by record company executives who weren't sure what to make of their unusual sound.

Perkins' fortunes improved in 1954, when he heard Elvis Presley's rockabilly version of the bluegrass classic "Blue Moon of Kentucky," a song he and his brothers performed. Presley's record was a revelation. "Elvis sounded identical to what our band was doing," Perkins once said, "and I just knew we could make it in the record business after that." Perkins traveled to Presley's record label, Sun Records in Memphis, and landed an audition with producer Sam Phillips. Soon, Perkins was recording for Sun, releasing the regional hits "Turn Around" and "Gone Gone Gone," and opening shows for Presley. Another Sun artist, Johnny Cash, suggested Perkins write a song about a current teen fad—blue suede shoes. The idea was reinforced when Perkins overheard a couple arguing at a dance. "Don't step on my suedes," the boy snapped at his date. Later that night, Perkins wrote the lyrics to "Blue Suede Shoes" on a potato sack. Recorded on December 19, 1955, the song was played on country, pop and rhythm 'n' blues radio stations, sold a million copies in few months, and reached Number 2 on the Billboard chart—behind the Presley hit "Heartbreak Hotel."

In March 1956, the Perkins Brothers were driving to New York City to play "Blue Suede Shoes" on *The Perry Como Show,* a performance that promised to help legitimize rockabilly and boost the trio's popularity. En route, however, they crashed into a truck, and Carl and Jay were seriously hurt. There would be no national TV exposure. Presley went on to release a version of "Blue Suede Shoes" which would ultimately be best remembered. According to Myrna Oliver of the *Los Angeles Times,* the crash prevented Perkins from enjoying fame that might have rivaled Presley's career. In 1986, Perkins commented, "I was bucking a good-looking cat called Elvis who had beautiful hair, wasn't married and had all kinds of great moves."

Despite that, and his ongoing battle with alcohol, Perkins persevered, returned to the road, and penned a string of rockabilly standards including "Boppin' the Blues," "Matchbox," "Everybody's Trying to Be My Baby" and "Dixie Fried." He never again achieved the success of "Blue Suede Shoes," never released a hit album, never attained the popularity of his peers—Presley, Cash, Lewis, and Roy Orbison. In 1958, Perkins signed with Columbia Records and began "decades of false career starts and rediscoveries," Jon Pareles wrote in the *New York Times.*

While touring England with Chuck Berry in 1964, Perkins was invited to Abbey Road Studios to jam with the Beatles, who would later release their versions of the Perkins compositions "Matchbox," "Honey Don't," and "Everybody's Trying to Be My Baby." In the mid-1960s, Perkins began a decade touring as Cash's opening act. During that period, he wrote "Daddy Sang Bass," which became a Number 1 hit for Cash, co-wrote Cash's classic "A Boy Named Sue," and collaborated with Bob Dylan on a song called "Champaign, Illinois." Perkins embraced Christianity in 1966 and quit drinking in 1967.

Over the years, Perkins worked with many of the artists he influenced. He performed on Paul McCartney's 1981 album *Tug of War,* recorded with the progressive rock band NRBQ, and appeared with George Harrison, Ringo Starr and Eric Clapton on the Cinemax television special *A Rockabilly Session: Carl Perkins and Friends.* He received a Career Achievement Award from the Academy of Country Music in 1986 and was inducted into the Rock and Roll Hall of Fame in 1987. Perkins' songs, meanwhile, became hits for country artists such as Dolly Parton, George Strait, and The Judds. In 1996, he released his last album, "Go, Cat, Go!," which included collaborations with McCartney, Harrison, Cash, Paul Simon, John Fogerty and Tom Petty.

After Perkins made a rare public appearance in 1997, *Los Angeles Times* reviewer Richard Cromelin commented that Perkins had "the dignity and poise of a modest man who's supremely comfortable with himself." Cromelin added, "Perkins survival is a testament to the value of solid craftsmanship and honest expression." He is survived by his wife, Valda, three sons, a daughter, and several grandchildren. **Sources:** *Associated Press,* January 19, 1998; *Chicago Tribune,* January 20, 1998; *Contemporary Musicians,* Volume 9, Gale Research, 1993; *CNN Interactive,* January 19, 1998; *Detroit Free Press,* January 20, 1998; *Los Angeles Times,* January 20, 1998; *New York Times,* January 20, 1998; *Times* (London), January 21, 1998.

—*Dave Wilkins*

Robert Pilatus

Born c. 1966, in New York, NY; died of a heart attack, April 4, 1998, in Frankfurt, Germany. Model, entertainer. The name Robert Pilatus may not ring a bell for most pop music fans, but Pilatus's so-called singing duo Milli Vanilli may always be remembered as one of the most infamous hoaxes in the entertainment world. Pilatus, along with partner Fabrice Morvan, won a Grammy Award in 1989 for best new artist, but they were forced to return the award in 1990 after it was revealed that they did not actually sing on their own album.

Born in New York City in the mid-1960s, Pilatus's father was a U.S. soldier and his mother was a German exotic dancer. Shortly after his birth, he was adopted by a German couple and raised in Munich. In the early 1980s, he was a member of a break dancing troupe that performed in international competitions, and he also worked as a model. He met Morvan, a gymnast from Paris who had become interested in dance, at a club in Los Angeles, California. The two joined forces and moved to Munich. The two adopted eye-catching long, thin braids in their hair, because, as Pilatus remarked in a 1989 *Rolling Stone* article, all the big stars had unique hairstyles. *Contemporary Musicians* quoted him as saying in the article, "I looked at all the superstars. What is their different thing? Their *hair.* Beatles, Elvis, James Dean, James Brown, Marilyn Monroe. I wanted to be a star. I said, 'I have to fix my hair.'"

Unable to get a foothold in the business, the duo approached producer Frankie Farian to help with their careers. Spotting potential, Farian found that their ap-

pearance and dancing may have had star quality, but their singing was lacking. Farian assembled an anonymous group of studio musicians to record some generic, catchy dance-pop tracks and released the album *Girl, You Know It's True* under the name Milli Vanilli. The duo lip-synched to the music during appearances. Later, Morvan stated in an interview on the cable music network VH-1 that he and Pilatus were misled into attaching themselves to the fraud. VH-1 in the late 1990s made a documentary on the group's rise and fall, and Morvan was planning to transform the project into a full-length film.

Before the public knew the truth, Milli Vanilli's album was a hit, producing three number-one singles and selling around ten million copies. Some of the popular tracks included "Blame It on the Rain," "Baby, Don't Forget My Number," "Girl, I'm Gonna Miss You," "It's Your Thing," and "All or Nothing." The instant "success" led Milli Vanilli to brag to the press that they were more talented than legendary songwriters Bob Dylan and Paul McCartney. In 1990, they were given a Grammy Award for best new artist. When an Army veteran came forward to reveal that he was the actual voice on the recordings, however, the stunt was over. Milli Vanilli had to give back the award in a humiliating public appearance, both Pilatus and Morvan started therapy sessions. Later, Pilatus slashed his wrists, tried to jump from a ninth-story hotel room in Los Angeles, and was known to have drug problems.

Pilatus teamed up once again with Morvan in 1993 to try to re-enter the music business. They released an album as Rob and Fab, but it was a failure and the label, Taj, went bankrupt. In 1996, Pilatus pleaded no contest to assaulting two people—one with a metal lamp base—and breaking into a car. A judge sentenced him to 90 days in jail and 180 days in a drug rehabilitation center. It apparently did not work, because at the time of his death, Pilatus had been in Germany since the fall of 1997 for drug withdrawal treatments. However, he was still not clean. Pilatus died alone in his Frankfurt hotel room after drinking alcohol and taking pills. The German newspaper *Bild am Sonntag* had reported that producer Farian knew that Pilatus had been drinking, but did not know he was mixing pills with the alcohol. Farian mentioned that Pilatus, in fact, had planned to go to India to finish his drug treatments, as he was anxious for a new beginning. Frankfurt police later said the cause of death was a heart attack. **Sources:** *Chicago Tribune,* April 6, 1998; *Contemporary Musicians,* Volume 4, Gale Research, 1991; "Milli Vanilli star Pilatus found dead," MSNBC web site, http://www.msnbc.com (April 5,

1998); *New York Times,* April 6, 1998; April 7, 1998; *USA Today,* April 5, 1998; *Washington Post,* April 6, 1998.

—*Geri Speace*

Pol Pot

Born May 19, 1928 (various sources cite other birth days and years); died of a heart attack or natural causes, April 15, 1998, in Cambodia. Dictator. Cambodian leader Pol Pot, one of the most brutal rulers of the modern world, was a genocidal despot often compared to Adolf Hitler. Under his rule, roughly two million of his nation's people were killed, according to most estimates. With his political group, the Khmer Rouge, Pol Pot took over the country in 1975 and renamed Cambodia "Kampuchea." He aimed to develop a nation of Communist worker-peasants, eradicating personal freedoms and instituting a reign of terror that resulted in deaths from murder, starvation, and disease. Because so many died or were killed on the farming communes, they came to be known as the "killing fields." In January of 1979, Pol Pot was forced out of the capital city of Phnom Penh and later stepped down as prime minister. He went into hiding and was captured on June 18, 1997, and sentenced to life in prison. While under house arrest, he died on April 15, 1998, in a hut in the jungles of northern Cambodia.

Pol Pot was born Saloth Sar in Prek Sabu, a small Cambodian village in the province of Kompong Thom, about 70 miles north of the capital city of Phnom Penh. Various sources cite the year of his birth anywhere from 1920 to 1928, and his birthdate has been placed at May 19 or sometime in January. Later in his life he changed his name to Pol Pot, which has no special meaning. He was the eighth of nine children born to Pen Saloth, a farmer, and his wife, Nok Sem. His father, a small land owner, knew people in Cambodia's royal court, and officials would often visit their home. At the age of six, Pol Pot went to live in Phnom Penh with an uncle, a clerk at the royal palace, and his wife, a ballet dancer. He was schooled at a Buddhist monastery, which was the norm for Cambodian education, and then attended a private Catholic school.

After failing the exams needed to enter high school, Pol Pot enrolled at a trade school and studied carpentry. Fellow classmates remembered that he loved sports and was a friendly person, but lacked ambition. In fact, throughout Pol Pot's life, people had commented that his gentle, warm, and almost shy personality was in sharp contrast with his ruthless public policy. In 1949, Pol Pot went to France on a scholarship to study radio technology in France, which controlled Cambodia as a colony. In Paris, he embraced the ideas of Soviet Communist leader Joseph Stalin and soon began neglecting his studies for his radical activities, although he continued to read poetry. He longed to free Cambodia from French colonists, the urban elite, and the royal court, headed by Prince Norodom Sihanouk.

Also in Paris, Pol Pot met Khieu Ponnary, a fellow Communist and schoolteacher several years his senior, whom he later married in 1956. Back in Cambodia in 1953, Pol Pot taught French, geography, history, and civics at a private high school. His students recalled him as a gentle and soft-spoken man who loved the French classics, but they did not realize that he was already devising a plan to overthrow the government as he climbed the ranks of the Cambodian Communist party. In 1954, Cambodia won independence from France, and many Cambodian communists fled to Vietnam. Pol Pot stayed and became involved with an official Communist party.

On September 28, 1960, Pol Pot met secretly in a railway yard in the capital city with Ieng Sary, Tou Samouth, and other Communists to discuss plans for a new political group. Later, in about 1963 or 1964, Sihanouk cracked down on the Khmer Rouge, and Pol Pot and his colleagues went into hiding. In September of 1966, Pol Pot returned to Cambodia and changed his party's name to the Communist Party of Kampuchea (CPK), which began brewing the plot to overthrow Sihanouk. However, the National Assembly on March 18, 1970, ousted Sihanouk instead, and Lon Nol was named president. Sihanouk then joined the Khmer Rouge, and Cambodia was drawn into the Vietnam War. From the underground, Pol Pot—supported by Sihanouk, China, and to an extent, Vietnam—organized a citizen uprising. The United States, hoping to quell the communist forces, in 1973 began bombing suspected Khmer Rouge posts. Angry and homeless, thousands of Cambodians joined Pol Pot's army.

On April 17, 1975, Pol Pot and the Khmer Rouge army took over the Cambodian capital, Phnom Penh. The Revolutionary Army evacuated the city and ordered everyone to flee to the villages. Even the very young, very old, blind, sick, and otherwise at risk were forced out, and perhaps 20,000 patients were wheeled out of hospitals still in their beds. Within two weeks, tens of thousands died of starvation and disease, and numerous others were executed. Pol Pot renamed the state

Democratic Kampuchea and began his tyrannical era of gruesome murder and oppression. Up to two million citizens lost their lives. Children and the elderly were put to work on the farms, schools and churches were closed, and religion was outlawed. Money was no longer used, and food was scarce.

Thousands died from overwork and malnutrition. Many were shot and dumped in mass graves, and rebellious children were buried alive. The Khmer Rouge even took photographs and kept track of those they jailed and tortured, which later became valuable evidence against them during trials. Many on these communes were killed by blows from farming tools. For those who were spared, the communists split up families and banned holidays, music, and entertainment. Because millions died in the farming communes, the term "killing fields" was coined to describe the bloody regime's camps. Today, exhibits at the Toul Sleng Genocidal Museum in Phnom Penh grimly recall this sad history.

With the nation in turmoil, Pol Pot did not back off. Instead, he closed the country to the outside world. However, in 1978 he invaded Vietnam to force them to recognize the Cambodian-Vietnamese border, which brought to light the extent of the tragedy within the nation. In 1979, he was forced out of the capital city of Phnom Penh and fled to the jungle, subsequently remaining in seclusion for the rest of his life. Reports occasionally surfaced about his whereabouts throughout the 1980s and 1990s, hinting that he might try to seize power again. He even remarried in 1987, after his first wife, who was mentally troubled, gave him permission to do so. He reportedly had at least one daughter with his second wife.

On June 18, 1997, a rival faction of the Khmer Rouge located Pol Pot and captured him, placing him under house arrest and sentencing him to life in prison. In a modest jungle in northern Cambodia, Pol Pot died shortly before midnight on April 15, 1998. It was reported that he either had a heart attack or died of natural causes in his sleep. The timing of his death seemed strangely convenient, however, since he had just been captured. Some theorized that his captors may have killed him, but no obvious foul play was discovered. It was widely known that he had been suffering from poor health, and his body was viewed and photographed. By all accounts, Pol Pot was indeed dead. He remained unrepentant to the end, telling a journalist in October of 1997, according to *Time*, "My conscience is clear." **Sources:** *Arizona Republic*, April 19, 1998, p. A26; "Reviled Pol Pot Cremated by Khmer Rouge Comrades," April 18, 1998, CNNin web site,

http://cnn.com (April 20, 1998); *Encyclopedia of World Biography*, second edition, Gale Research, 1997; *Los Angeles Times*, April 17, 1998; *New York Times*, April 17, 1998, p. A1; April 18, 1998, p. A5; *Times* (London), April 17, 1998; *Washington Post*, April 17, 1998, p. A1.

—*Geri Speace*

Ferdinand Porsche

Born September 19, 1909, in Wiener Neustadt, Austria; died March 27, 1998, in Zell am See, Austria. Car designer. Austrian Ferdinand Porsche and his father, an early designer for Daimler-Benz, collaborated on designing the Volkswagen Beetle, the most popular car in the world, as well as lightweight race cars. After World War II, Porsche gained control of the business and concentrated on building sports cars for races, as well as automobiles for normal driving situations. The Porsche coupe became a status symbol, aligned with royalty and movie stars. By the 1980s, the fast, expensive cars reached their peak of popularity. Though a 1987 American recession hit hard, by 1996, Porsche's profits were up and new models were coming out of production. The company went public in 1972, but it continued to be plagued by strife, no thanks to family feuds brought on by Porsche's son and nephew. Porsche remained involved in the business until his retirement in 1993.

Ferdinand Anton Ernst "Ferry" Porsche was born in Wiener Neustadt, Austria, near Vienna, to Ferdinand and Aloysia Johanna (Kaes) Porsche. His Czech-born father was a technical director at the Austro-Daimler automobile company, which became Daimler-Benz, manufacturer of the Mercedes-Benz. The elder Porsche had designed the Lohner-Porsche Chaise in 1900, powered by four electric motors. The year after his son was born, the senior Porsche designed a car that traveled 85 miles per hour. In 1923, the family moved to Stuttgart, Germany, where he took a job with Daimler-Benz as a board member and technical director. The senior Porsche began tinkering in his own workshop as well, and by 1930 opened his own automobile shop building race cars.

"Ferry" Porsche thus grew up with an innate love of cars. In 1920, his father gave him for Christmas a small two-seater that he designed and built. It ran on a 3.5 horsepower, two-cylinder engine. Porsche began helping out in his father's business as soon as it opened; they developed the Auto Union grand prix car, which had a lightweight design and 16-cylinder engine. Porsche liked to test drive this machine, but his father soon nixed his runs, fearing for his safety. At the age of 12, Porsche had witnessed a fatal car crash during a race, and while everyone else shielded their eyes from the carnage, he was engrossed in the wreck—not out of a macabre sense, but to analyze the cause of the tragic accident. Later investigation showed that his original assessment was correct; a tire wheel had collapsed. This scientific curiosity would translate to a successful future in building automobiles.

One of Porsche's greatest claims to fame was his involvement on the prototype Volkswagen ("VW"), meaning "people's car" in German. The first model had its debut run in 1936, and two years later, the first VW plant was built. Porsche's father had been recruited to build the car by German Chancellor Adolf Hitler, who wanted an affordable auto for the working class. In a savvy business move, the younger Porsche made certain that he and his father would receive a portion of the profits for every car sold. Eventually the VW "Beetle," so called for its small size and rounded body style, would become the world's most popular car. Under the Nazi regime, the Porsches' firm flourished as they manufactured military vehicles, airplane engines, and tanks. Porsche later, like most businesspeople who had dealings with the Third Reich, stated that he had no way to refuse Hitler's wishes. The factory during this time operated with what Porsche would later recall as 15,000 to 20,000 Russian employees, although he did not point out that these were prisoners of war who provided slave labor.

After World War II, the French threw Porsche's father and his son-in-law in prison until 1947, but he and his son did not stand trial for war crimes. Instead, as the *New York Times* reported, "The real reason for their arrest seems to have been an attempt to force them to collaborate with the French auto industry." In any case, the Porsche factory moved from the rubble of Stuttgart to Gmund, Austria, in 1944, where Porsche decided to create a new sports car. Because the new German government had canceled their contract to produce cars, Porsche pursued plans for the vehicle that he had initiated back in 1939. It was based on the light, compact model of the VW, with an aluminum body and a four-cylinder, 1131cc engine.

Porsche completed his first car, the 356, by hand in the spring of 1948. He moved production back to Stuttgart in March of 1950 and began working on creating a unique Porsche engine, the Carrera. By March of 1951 Porsche had sold 500 of his new sports cars, and throughout its production life until 1965, the Porsche Carrera sold 78,000 models. Porsche's father died in 1951, but Porsche was already generally in control of the business. The company continued to churn out high-performance, race-winning cars that could also be driven on regular roadways. In 1964, the company introduced its classic 911 series, thanks to the idea of Porsche's son, Ferdinand (nicknamed "Butzi"). The Carrera RS was introduced in 1973, followed by the 930 later that year.

The Porsche sports coupe quickly became a status symbol. Prince Bertil of Sweden and Prince Abd el Moneim of Egypt bought the new coupe, and Hollywood stars were avid fans. Legendary actor James Dean was killed in a Porsche Spyder 550, and despite the tragedy, it added to the aura of the German automobile. Porsche and his sister, Louise, became multimillionaires, but they shunned the spotlight. The Porsche company went public in 1972, but voting stock remained family-owned and generally divided equally. This apparently did little to smooth over family infighting, however. Porsche's son Butzi and his nephew, Ferdinand Piech, were often at odds throughout the company's history. The company was listed on the German stock exchange in 1984.

In the 1970s, critics berated the lower-cost, fuel-conscious Porsche 924 developed for the oil-deprived decade, but the firm rebounded and had its peak year in 1986, selling close to 50,000 cars. After the American stock exchange crash in 1987, sales fell, but a decade later, sales were up and the product line featured a cheaper, retro-style Porsche similar to the originals called the Boxster. Much of this success was credited to engineer Wendelin Wiedeking, who took over as Porsche chairman after decades of family feuding and scandals, in addition to the financial crises that were weathered.

Short and stocky, colleagues often painted Porsche as a soft-spoken and modest man. He married Dorothea Reitz in 1935; she died in 1985. Porsche retired from his company in 1993. He is survived by his four sons, Ferdinand, Gerhard, Peter, and Wolfgang. **Sources:** *Contemporary Authors,* volumes 89-92, Gale Research, 1980; *Chicago Tribune,* March 29, 1998, section 4, p. 9; *Los Angeles Times,* March 28, 1998, section 1, p. 21; *New York Times,* March 28, 1998, p. A11; *Times* (London), March 31, 1998; *Washington Post,* March 28, 1998, p. B6.

—*Geri Speace*

Eddie Rabbitt

Born Edward Thomas, November 27, 1941, in Brooklyn, NY; died May 7, 1998, in Nashville, TN. Eddie Rabbitt was a country-pop crossover hit known for his infectious tunes and his clean act. He wrote almost all of his own songs and churned out 26 number one country singles. However, he did not even perform his first big hit, "Kentucky Rain," which was bought and recorded by Elvis Presley in 1970. Rabbitt was best known for the songs "I Love a Rainy Night," "Drivin' My Life Away," "Step by Step," "Every Which Way but Loose," and a duet with Crystal Gayle, "You and I."

Rabbitt was born Edward Thomas, the son of an oil refinery worker, and raised in East Orange, New Jersey. His parents were Irish immigrants, and his father spent many evenings playing fiddle and accordion in the traditional Irish style in Manhattan dance halls. From a young age, Rabbitt was influenced by country music. At age 16, he dropped out of high school to play clubs around the area in New Jersey and New York under the name Eddie Rabbitt. One day, considering that his stage name sounded more like a magician or clown than a singer, he changed it to Eddie Martin. After a subsequent lack of success with that name, he changed it back.

Rabbitt left on a bus bound for Nashville in 1968 carrying only $1,000 and no prospects for a recording contract. He knew no one in the business, but tried to sell his songs as he paid the bills with odd jobs, including driving a truck, picking fruit, and working at a soda counter. He managed to sell his first song, "Working My Way Up to the Bottom," in 1968, and it was recorded by Roy Drusky. In 1970, he got his big break when Elvis Presley bought "Kentucky Rain," which became a million seller. The country-pop hit hinted at a bright future for the young songwriter.

By 1975, Rabbitt had signed on with Elektra Records and began cranking out about two albums each year. Some of his most popular tunes were "Drivin' My Life Away," based on his earlier job as a truck driver; the cheery love song "Step by Step;" and the catchy "I Love a Rainy Night." He also penned and performed the title song for the Clint Eastwood film *Every Which Way but Loose.* By the end of the 1970s, Rabbitt was a top-name performer and was the first to receive a plaque on the Country Music Walk of Fame in Hollywood. He was named top new male artist by the Academy of Country Music in 1978.

Rabbitt's songs and shows were clean, and in his private life, he was an old-fashioned family man. In 1983, his son Timmy was born with a fatal liver disease that required constant care. The singer sharply cut back his schedule of touring and recording so that he could be with his son every day. A liver transplant in 1985 failed, and Timmy died. Rabbitt withdrew to spend time with his wife, Janine, and daughter, Dimelza. He went back to entertaining after about a year, and in 1986, his wife gave birth to another son, Tommy. However, instead of retreating into melancholy tunes, Rabbitt kept his music positive and uplifting, telling the *Wichita Eagle-Beacon,* "There are enough heavy downers in the world; you can turn on the news for them. I think music should sooth the wild beast in us. It should take people away from the hard stuff in life—the hard jobs, the bad times."

Rabbitt switched to Capitol Records and continued to record and tour. He had had another big hit in 1982 with "You and I," a duet with Crystal Gayle, and his upbeat music was a favorite of American troops during the Gulf War. It was even played during campaign rallies in 1996 for presidential hopeful Bob Dole. After his son's death, Rabbitt became involved with various health care organizations; he was an honorary chairman of the American Council on Transplantation and a spokesman for the Muscular Dystrophy Association and for United Cerebral Palsy.

In the early 1990s, Rabbitt spoke out against the tawdry aspects of music videos, including scantily clad women and sexually explicit lyrics. According to *USA Today,* he once commented that MTV "distorted our youth mentally so that science and math are so far away from a child's mind that anyone thinking about it is a nerd." Rabbitt was diagnosed with lung cancer in March of 1997 and underwent radiation treatment. In May of 1998, he had part of his left lung removed, and he died on May 7, 1998, at Baptist Hospital in Nashville. **Sources:** *Chicago Tribune,* May 9, 1998, p. 17; "Singer-songwriter Eddie Rabbitt dead at 53," May 8, 1998, CNN web site, http://cnn.com (May 12, 1998); *Contemporary Musicians,* Volume 5, Gale Research, 1991; *Los Angeles Times,* May 9, 1998; *New York Times,* May 9, 1998; *USA Today,* May 10, 1998.

—*Geri Speace*

James Earl Ray

Born March 10, 1928, in Alton, IL; died of liver failure, April 23, 1998, in Nashville, TN. Convicted assassin. James Earl Ray was a drifter and escaped convict when he was arrested in 1968 for the murder of legendary civil rights leader Dr. Martin Luther King, Jr. Evidence suggested that Ray shot King, dumped the gun, and fled the scene before leaving the country. He was finally apprehended in London at Heathrow Airport and returned to the United States to face the courts. After pleading guilty and waiving his right to a jury trial in order to elude the death penalty, Ray three days later protested that he was framed. He insisted throughout his time in prison that a larger conspiracy was to blame for King's death, but that he was not aware of all the facts in order to accurately outline his case. Although investigations concluded that Ray acted alone, King's family shortly before Ray's death called for a new trial, convinced that he was an unwitting patsy and that the FBI was behind the assassination. Although he attempted several escapes and even made it out once for a few days, Ray died in prison at the age of 70.

Ray was born the oldest child in a large family in Alton, Illinois. His father, James, would often leave the family for stretches of time, and his mother, Lucie, was an alcoholic. The Ray family and their friends maintained a history of criminal activity. They lived in a shady area of St. Louis before moving to a run-down farm in Ewing, Missouri, a backwoods town with no water or sewage system and no paved roads. Ray dropped out of school in the eighth grade and left home at age 16 to work in a tannery in Hartford, Connecticut, and two years later joined the army. He served as a military police officer in Germany, but was discharged in December of 1948 due to "ineptness and lack of adaptability to military service," according to *The Civil Rights Struggle: Leaders in Profile* by John D'Emilio. Consequently, Ray began a life of crime, holding up stores and committing break-ins.

Ray's criminal escapades were often unsuccessful. He was arrested several times for vagrancy, burglary, and robbery. In 1949, Ray was arrested for holding up a cabdriver, a plan that ended in defeat when he was chased down and caught. In 1950, he was sentenced to 90 days in jail for stealing a typewriter. On one occasion, thinking he was grabbing a taxicab to flee the scene of a crime, he actually jumped into a patrol car. After breaking into a dry cleaners, he cut himself badly on broken glass and accidentally left his wallet on the ground. In 1955, he was sentenced to three years in Leavenworth federal prison for cashing forged Post Office money orders, and in 1959 he landed 20 years in the Missouri State Penitentiary for holding up a supermarket in St. Louis.

During his numerous incarcerations, Ray was known to devise and occasionally attempt escapes. He finally succeeded in breaking out of the Missouri prison in April of 1967 by hiding in a large breadbox being shipped out of the jail's bakery. While he was free, he reportedly spent time in Chicago; Birmingham, Alabama; and Los Angeles. He also traveled to Louisiana; Atlanta, Georgia; and Canada. Ray later claimed that in Canada, he had been involved in a smuggling ring led by a blond man named Raoul.

In March of 1968, Ray bought two guns at a marine supply store in Birmingham, and on April 4, he had checked into a seedy rooming house across from the Lorraine Motel. That evening, about six o'clock, as prominent civil rights leader Martin Luther King, Jr., stood on a second-floor balcony at the Lorraine Motel, he was shot in the neck by a sniper and pronounced dead at 7:05 p.m. He had been in Memphis to support a sanitation workers' strike. Police found a .30-06 Remington hunting rifle on the sidewalk near the motel, in front of the flophouse where Ray had rented a room under a false name. Police later determined that the gun was likely the murder weapon, and that the shot came from the bathroom of the room that Ray had rented. The gun bore Ray's fingerprints, and witnesses said they saw Ray flee the area in a white Mustang after the shooting.

After King's death, riots broke out and a manhunt ensued. Ray went to Canada on April 8, and on April 24, he obtained a Canadian passport. He flew from Toronto to London, then to Lisbon, Portugal, then returned to London again on May 17. The next month, Scotland Yard detectives nabbed him at London's Heathrow Airport and he was returned to Memphis. Back in the United States, police charged Ray with King's murder. On March 10, 1969, Ray pleaded guilty and waived his right to a trial in order to avoid the death penalty. He was sentenced to 99 years in prison with eligibility for parole after half of the time was served.

Three days later, Ray recanted his confession, claiming that he never shot King. He stated that the shadowy gun smuggler named Raoul had set him up to take the blame for the killing, and that evidence was planted to frame him. Ray insisted throughout the years that a larger conspiracy was responsible for King's death, and he fought to clear his name in the ensuing years. He also attempted to win his freedom in other ways. He tried slipping out of incarceration in 1971 and 1972 through a steam tunnel and a hole in the ceiling, but did not succeed. In 1977, he and six other inmates managed to escape from the Brushy Mountain Penitentiary in Petros, Tennessee, a break that prison officials said Ray masterminded. He was rounded up within a few days, but tried again to sneak out in 1979.

Ray was the target of a number of violent episodes in prison, and in 1981, four other prisoners stabbed Ray 22 times. Though he would not identify his attackers, three African Americans were convicted, and authorities added time to their sentences. In 1987, Ray wrote a book called *Tennessee Waltz: The Making of a Political Prisoner*, in which he tried to state his side of the case. However, he later tried to detach himself from the effort, insisting that the publisher planted errors into the text. Meanwhile, a variety of people and groups began to question Ray's role, if any, in the murder. Many, including journalists, civil rights leaders, and congressional investigators, were unlikely advocates who did not personally like Ray, but doubted how a bungling petty criminal could have plotted King's killing as well as the elusive getaway. In 1978, the U.S. House Committee on Assassinations found that Ray was the killer, but that he could have been part of a larger conspiracy, or looking to collect a $50,000 bounty that had been placed on King. They did not agree with those who suggested that the FBI was behind the assassination and noted that they had located Raoul, but that he had nothing to do with the murder. The complete files used in the House investigation were sealed until 2029. Ray's jailhouse pals, incidentally, recalled that he was a racist who always hated King and had spoken of killing him if he was ever freed.

The most surprising supporters of Ray, perhaps, were King's family themselves. In 1995, activist William Pepper wrote a book called *Orders to Kill*, which again argued that King had been killed by a government conspiracy. Furthermore, Pepper noted that "Raoul" was living in New York and still connected with the Mafia and the CIA. Members of the King family were convinced that Pepper's theories had merit. King's son, Dexter, in 1997 met with Ray and asked him, as they were being televised, whether he killed his father. Ray denied it, and King told him that he believed him. King's widow, Coretta Scott King, shortly before Ray's death was pushing for a trial, and many of the King family friends and associates became convinced that the FBI was the source of a conspiracy. Reverend Joseph Lawson, who had invited King to Memphis on that fateful trip, even performed Ray's marriage ceremony in prison in 1978 (his wife, courtroom artist Anna Sandhu Ray, divorced him in 1993). Nevertheless, the Memphis district attorney's office finished up

a four-year investigation a month before Ray's death, only to conclude once again that he acted alone.

In 1992, Ray authored another book about the case, *Who Killed Martin Luther King, Jr.?: The True Story by the Alleged Assassin*. However, around the time of Ray's death, Gerald Posner released a study of the case called *Killing the Dream*, which refuted all of Ray's claims to conspiracies and cover-ups. Also, the Memphis prosecutor, William Gibbons, was quoted as saying in *USA Today*, "About the only thing I can say is I believe the history books will accurately record that James Earl Ray was the killer of Dr. King." In 1996, Ray experienced liver and kidney failure after a battle with cirrhosis of the liver caused by hepatitis, probably contracted from a blood transfusion he received after the 1981 prison stabbing. He died at Columbia Nashville Memorial Hospital on April 23, 1998. **Sources:** *Chicago Tribune*, April 24, 1998; "James Earl Ray, Convicted King Assassin, Dies," CNNin web site, http://cnn.com (April 24, 1998); D'Emilio, John, *The Civil Rights Struggle: Leaders in Profile*, Facts on File, 1979; *Los Angeles Times*, April 24, 1998; *New York Times*, April 24, 1998; *Times* (London), April 24, 1998; *USA Today*, April 23, 1998; *Washington Post*, April 24, 1998.

—*Geri Speace*

Abraham Ribicoff

Born Abraham Alexander Ribicoff, April 9, 1910, in New Britain, CT; died of heart failure, February 22, 1998, at the Hebrew Home for the Aged at Riverdale in the Bronx, New York, NY. Politician. Democrat Abraham Ribicoff was the son of poor immigrants who worked his way through law school and steadily rose up the ranks to become an integral voice in American politics over many decades. He was perhaps best remembered for his participation in the violent 1968 Democratic National Convention, in which he nominated South Dakota Senator George McGovern for president and derided Chicago Mayor Richard J. Daley for his handling of the rioters. He also served two terms as governor of Connecticut, three terms in the U.S. Senate, and was named Secretary of Health, Education and Welfare in President John F. Kennedy's cabinet.

Ribicoff was born to Samuel (a factory worker) and Rose (Sable) Ribicoff, Polish-Jewish immigrants. Growing up in a tenement on Star Street in New Britain, Connecticut, Ribicoff attended Smalley Elementary School. He was a tackle for the New Britain High School football team and worked road construction during his summers. After graduating from high school, he went to work for the G. E. Prentice Company in a factory making buckles and zippers in order to make money for tuition. After a year at New York University, the company offered Ribicoff a job as the Midwest representative in a Chicago office.

Ribicoff took the position and in 1929 moved to Chicago. He began attending afternoon courses at the University of Chicago Law School (some law schools at the time allowed entrance without an undergraduate degree). His academic career was outstanding, and he was named editor of the University's Law Review. He was married to Ruth M. Siegel in 1931; they had two children, Peter and Jane. In 1933, he moved back East, passed the Connecticut bar exam, and went to work for a law office in Hartford. Though the Tennessee Valley Authority offered him a job, he preferred working in a small town, and held an office in Kensington for a while.

The call of politics intrigued Ribicoff, and he began his steady rise in 1938 with two terms in the Connecticut General Assembly, where he was recognized by reporters as the state's most promising new legislator. After that, in 1941, he served as a Hartford Police Court judge and was also elected chairman of the Connecticut Assembly of Municipal Court Judges. From there, he was involved with numerous committees and commissions, including one investigating alcoholism and crime. Finally, in November of 1948, he defeated a Republican incumbent to win the election to the U.S. Congress from his state's First District. He won by an even bigger margin of votes during the next election two years later. While a representative, he was a strong supporter of President Harry S. Truman's policies and supported the Marshall Plan to protect American investments in Europe. He lost a bid for the Senate in 1952 to Prescott S. Bush, father of President George Bush.

In 1954, Ribicoff was elected governor of Connecticut, serving two terms before stepping down in 1961 to join President John F. Kennedy's cabinet. Ribicoff and Kennedy had been friends since 1949, when they were both greenhorns from New England in the U.S. Congress. In fact, Ribicoff nominated Kennedy as vice president under Adlai E. Stevenson in 1956, and was the convention floor manager for his successful bid for the presidential nomination in 1960. Initially offered the post of attorney general, Ribicoff insisted that

Kennedy name his brother, Robert, to the post instead. Ribicoff took the job of Secretary of Health, Education, and Welfare, but later regretted the move. The CNN Interactive web site quoted Ribicoff as saying, "It was the only job I really didn't like because all my life I had been the No. 1 man and suddenly I found that in the Cabinet I was advocating positions I didn't believe in and was against positions that I did believe in." He resigned in 1962.

Ribicoff successfully entered the Senate race again in 1962, and was re-elected in 1968 and 1974. One of the most often recalled moments of his career came in 1968, when he nominated George McGovern for the presidency at the Democratic National Convention. The assembly was marred by protests and riots, and Ribicoff accused the angered Chicago Mayor Richard Daley of using "Gestapo tactics" to quell the crowds. Police had sprayed the demonstrators with tear gas and beaten them with billy clubs. Ribicoff pointed to the need for a candidate who opposed the Vietnam War in order to stop such violence within the country's own borders, and his statements were hailed by many.

Ribicoff , a staunch liberal Democrat, supported integration of urban and suburban school districts, Medicare, environmental regulations, highway safety, and civil service reform. At one point, he sought federal subsidies for a group of his constituents, Connecticut tobacco farmers, but later battled to stop the legislation. Ribicoff decided not to seek re-election to a fourth term in 1981. The 71-year-old retired from the Senate, but kept active by serving as special counsel to the New York law firm of Kaye, Scholer, Fierman, Hays & Handler. Ribicoff was stricken with Alzheimer's disease in his later years. His wife, Lois Mell Mathes, known as Casey, received support throughout her husband's illness from former First Lady Nancy Reagan. It was revealed in 1994 that former President Ronald Reagan was suffering from Alzheimer's.

After retirement, Ribicoff had residences in Manhattan and on a 92-acre estate in Cornwall Bridge, Connecticut. The building that housed his early offices when he was a lawyer and while he was a senator was renamed the Abraham A. Ribicoff Federal Building U.S. Courthouse when he left politics. Ribicoff's first wife, Ruth, died after 40 years of marriage, and he had married Mathes in 1972. He is survived by his wife; his children, Peter and Jane Bishop; a stepson, Peter Mathes; and six grandchildren. **Sources:** *Chicago Tribune*, February 23, 1998; "Ribicoff, former U.S. senator and HEW secretary, dead at 87," CNN Interactive web site, http://cnn.com (February 22, 1998); *Contemporary*

Authors, Volume 108, Gale Research, 1983; *Los Angeles Times*, February 23, 1998; *New York Times*, February 23, 1998.

—*Geri Speace*

Harold Robbins

Born May 21, 1916, in New York, NY; died October 14, 1997, in Palm Springs, CA, of heart failure. Harold Robbins, who began life as an orphan, delinquent, and high school dropout, went on to become one of the top-selling novelists of all time. In books such as *The Carpetbaggers* (1961), he offered his readers an escape into a jet set world populated by extravagantly wealthy and sexually voracious movie moguls, crime bosses, and captains of industry. Although most critics dismissed his books (except for some early works that showed literary promise) as badly written and one-dimensional, Robbins earned a place in literary history by pioneering the genre of what the London *Times* called the "airport novel," the escapist saga that caters to readers' fantasies by chronicling the power struggles and sexual escapades of the rich and beautiful.

Robbins's first years were spent in a Catholic orphanage in New York City, where he was given the name Francis Kane. He became Harold Rubin after being sent to live with a Jewish foster family. Some years later, Rubin was transformed into Robbins on the advice of his publisher. In his early teens Robbins worked as an errand-boy for bookies, prostitutes, and a drug dealer. At age 15 he dropped out of high school and, lying about his age, enlisted in the U.S. Navy, where he spent two years stationed in Florida. Afterwards he returned to New York City and took a job as a grocery store clerk. It was at this point that his talent for making money became evident. Perceiving that the existing system for getting food from the country to the city was grossly inefficient, he borrowed $800 and went into the food brokerage business for himself. His business acumen was such that by age 20 he was a millionaire. In 1939, however, he gambled his entire fortune on sugar futures, reasoning that the coming world war would drive up the cost of sugar. But he failed to anticipate that the United States government would soon freeze sugar prices, and when it did, he was forced into bankruptcy.

In 1940 the then-penniless Robbins joined Universal Pictures in New York City as a shipping clerk making $27 a week. When he discovered that the company was losing thousands of dollars to overcharges, he was rewarded with a promotion and sent to Los Angeles, where he eventually became executive director of film budgets and planning. He remained with Universal until turning to writing full time in 1957. By his own account, his literary career was launched in 1947 when, after grousing to a fellow executive about the poor quality of a novel the studio intended to film, he accepted a $100 bet to produce a better story. The result was *Never Love a Stranger* (1948), a tale, based on Robbins's own experiences, of a tough New York City orphan growing up during the Depression. It was published to good reviews. His next novel, *The Dream Merchants* (1949), was the first of several books on the Hollywood movie industry. It was followed by *A Stone for Danny Fisher* (1952), about a young Jewish boxer striving to make his way in the corrupt world of New York City prizefighting. Like *Never Love a Stranger,* it was a coming-of-age tale inspired by events in Robbins's youth, and was well received by the critics.

With the appearance of *A Stone for Danny Fisher*, Robbins seemed destined for a career as a literary novelist, but any expectations the critics had in that direction were laid to rest by the publication of *The Carpetbaggers,* the book that established his reputation as a popular novelist. *The Carpetbaggers* told the story of Hollywood movie mogul Jonas Cord, a character based loosely on real-life billionaire Howard Hughes. Condemned by the critics, *The Carpetbaggers* became Robbins's most popular book, selling more than eight million copies and making him a wealthy man for the second time in his life. Many more best-sellers followed over the next three-and-a-half decades, each relying on the formula of sex, money, and power to capture a wide readership. Despite the acid comments of most reviewers, Robbins's success rested not merely on exploiting the public's taste for the lurid and the scandalous, but on a genuine talent for creating sharp-edged, fast-paced narratives that opened a window on the undeniably fascinating world of international high society.

Robbins's earnings from his books, and from the many movies and television miniseries they inspired, enabled him to live the life of a character from one of his novels, with houses in Beverly Hills, Acapulco, and the south of France; an 85-foot yacht; and lots of expensive cars. His drug taking was notorious, as were his Hollywood parties. In 1982, however, he suffered a stroke that resulted in aphasia, a neurological condition that impaired—although it did not rob him of—his writing ability. Three years later he fractured both hips in a fall, which put him in a wheelchair for the rest of his life. In the 1980s and 1990s his medical bills, alimony payments (he married approximately five times), and lavish spending probably dissipated much of his fortune. But with the help of his last wife, Jann Stapp, whom he married in 1992, he staged a career comeback in the mid-1990s, publishing three new novels. Despite his poor health and financial troubles, Robbins remarked to Bettijane Levine of the *Los Angeles Times* that he was "very happy.... I may have lost a lot, in terms of money, but I don't miss it. In fact, I have more now than I ever had. Without Jann, I'd be nothing.... Our home, our relationship, the things we share and look forward to together. It's more meaningful than anything.... Maybe I'm finally growing up." **Sources:** Associated Press, http://wire.ap.org (October 15, 1997); CNN Interactive, http://cnn.com (October 15, 1997); *Contemporary Authors New Revision Series*, Volume 54, Gale, 1997; *Los Angeles Times*, May 31, 1991, p. E1, March 15, 1995, pp. E1, E4, http://www.latimes.com (October 15, 1997); *New York Times*, http://www.nytimes.com (October 15, 1997); *Times* (London), http://www.the-times.co.uk (October 16, 1997); *Washington Post*, http://www.washingtonpost.com (October 15, 1997).

—*Howard Baker*

Roy Rogers

Born Leonard Franklin Slye, November 5, 1911, in Cincinnati, OH; died of heart failure, July 6, 1998, in Apple Valley, CA. Singer, actor. Roy Rogers was known as the "King of the Cowboys," the good-guy hero of a past era of television and film, and the voice of the legendary tune "Happy Trails." With his white hat and good looks, Rogers was one of the best-known of the singing cowboys that graced the silver screen from the 1930s to 1950s. Riding into the sunset on his horse, Trigger, he helped define the western genre. After making about 90 films, he sustained a successful television career and continued to record songs and albums. As late as 1991, he was still making music, releasing a CD called *Tribute*, featuring younger performers in duets with him.

Though studio biographers painted Rogers as a real-life cowboy, born in Cody, Wyoming, spending his early years ranching cattle, the truth stands elsewhere. He was born Leonard Franklin Slye, the son of Andrew, a shoe factory worker, and Hattie (Womack) Slye, a homemaker, in Cincinnati, Ohio. His family lived in a brick tenement, then a houseboat in Portsmouth, Ohio. They eventually settled on a farm in Duck Run, Ohio, where Rogers attended a one-room schoolhouse. His parents and three sisters were all musically talented, and Rogers himself played clarinet, guitar, and mandolin, sang in the church choir, and called square dances. An average student, Rogers spent much of his time working on the farm. When he was 17, the family, down on its luck, returned to Cincinnati so that Rogers' father could resume work at the shoe factory. Rogers dropped out of school to join him.

After a year in the factory, Rogers and his family, like many others during the Great Depression, packed up and headed west for the promise of a better future. Rogers later compared the experience to the grim John Steinbeck novel, *The Grapes of Wrath*. During this time of picking fruit and driving trucks, Rogers passed the evenings with other migrant workers singing songs and playing the guitar. He and his cousin, Stanley Slye, formed a duo called the Slye Brothers and supplemented their income playing parties and square dances. Soon, Rogers entered a talent contest sponsored by a local radio station in Inglewood, California. Though he did not win, a promoter took notice and asked Rogers to join a country and western band called the Rocky Mountaineers. Although they did not hit it big, Rogers met two songwriters, Bob Nolan and Tim Spencer, with whom he later formed the Sons of the Pioneers.

Before teaming with Nolan and Spencer, Rogers tried working with a couple of other groups, including the O-Bar-O Cowboys and the Texas Outlaws. Around this time he met Arlene Wilkins, whom he married in 1936. Later, Rogers convinced Nolan and Spencer to form the Pioneer Trio, a name which was eventually changed to the Sons of the Pioneers. The group later welcomed Texas brothers Hugh and Karl Farr, and the band would develop the sound that would set the standard for western music for many years, with sharp instrumental ability, smoothly harmonized vocals, and complementary yodeling. By 1935, the group had snagged jobs in Hollywood, appearing with Bing Crosby in *Rhythm on the Range* and in Gene Autry's debut film, *Tumbling Tumbleweeds*.

Autry became the leading cowboy at Republic Studios, a company known for its westerns, but soon began demanding more money. Rogers, while getting his Stetson hat cleaned, overheard that Republic was going to audition for a new star, so he slipped into the building as workers were going back in from lunch. The studio cast Rogers in *Under Western Stars* and gave him his new name, which he officially changed in 1942.

Autry was drafted soon into World War II, but Rogers' lottery number was not picked. He thus took over as the "King of the Cowboys" and developed his persona as the white-hat-wearing, good-looking, gentlemanly good-guy cowboy. He never even harmed the ne'er-do-wells; instead, he carefully shot their pistol out of their hand, leaving them unscathed but captured. He did not ever kiss his leading lady, either, in any of his films, preferring a chaste image.

Rogers' popularity soared, but his happiness was cut short in 1946 after his wife died six days after giving birth to Roy Rogers, Jr. Eventually, Rogers returned to work and looked up an old co-star, Dale Evans, whom he had met in 1944 during the making of *The Cowboy and the Senorita*. The two starred in numerous films together and married on December 31, 1947. In 1951 Evans wrote "Happy Trails" as the theme song of their new television program, *The Roy Rogers Show*; the song became Rogers' trademark and the show ran from 1951 until 1957. The couple also hosted a variety show beginning in 1962 called *The Roy Rogers and Dale Evans Show*. In movies and television, the couple was accompanied by Rogers' famous palomino, Trigger, as well as his dog, Bullet. Their sidekick in films was Gabby Hayes, and on television, Pat Brady. From 1943 to 1954, Rogers was the top box-office draw in westerns, according to theater owner polls. During the 1960s, Rogers and Evans were featured on television western series and specials, and he continued recording on the Capitol label.

Unfortunately, amid the couple's success and rewarding relationship, they had tragic moments when they lost three of their children. Rogers had two biological children and one adopted child with his first wife; Evans had one by a previous marriage; and together they had one biological child, four by adoption, and one by foster parenthood. Rogers' and Evans' biological child, Robin Elizabeth, was born with Down's syndrome and died shortly before her second birthday after coming down with the mumps. An adopted Korean girl, Debbie, was killed in a church bus accident in 1964 with seven others, and their adopted son John choked to death while he was in the army in Germany. Rogers and Evans held a deep Christian faith to help them through their troubles. They supported televangelist Billy Graham and were also active in other Christian groups.

In 1967, Rogers and Evans opened an 18,000-square-foot museum near their Apple Valley, California, home, about 90 miles east of Los Angeles, featuring memorabilia and showcasing Trigger, who died in 1965 and was mounted for display. In 1991 Rogers recorded *Trib-ute*, a CD of old and new songs in duets with younger performers, including Clint Black, Randy Travis, Kathy Mattea, Alan Jackson, and Tanya Tucker. Rogers died in his sleep of congestive heart failure at age 86. He was survived by his wife, Dale Evans; two children from his first marriage, Roy Rogers, Jr., and Linda Lou Johnson; an adopted daughter from his first marriage, Cheryl Barnett; a daughter adopted with Evans, Dodie Sailors; 15 grandchildren; and 33 great-grandchildren. **Sources:** *Chicago Tribune*, July 7, 1998; "Cowboy 'King' Roy Rogers Dead at 86," July 6, 1998, CNN in web site, http://cnn.com (July 6, 1998); *Contemporary Musicians*, volume 9, Gale Research, 1993; *Los Angeles Times*, July 7, 1998; *Times* (London), July 6, 1998; *New York Times*, July 7, 1998; *USA Today*, July 6, 1998; *Washington Post*, July 7, 1998.

—Geri Speace

Frank Sinatra

Born December 12, 1915, in Hoboken, NJ; died of a heart attack, May 14, 1998, in Los Angeles, CA. Singer, actor. Frank Sinatra was one of the top American icons of the twentieth century, known to his fans as "The Voice," "The Sultan of Swoon," "Ol' Blue Eyes," and "The Chairman of the Board." He started out in the early 1940s as an unlikely teen singing idol, skinny with a crooked smile, but with an intriguing sex appeal and sparkling blue eyes. He complemented his soaring music career in 1946 with a contract to make films for MGM. Though his popularity soon fell, by 1953 he was back in business with more acting roles and a new record contract. His style may have seemed corny as the 1960s progressed, but he retained his charisma and continued to make movies, a total of 60 in all. His later career was mainly entrenched in the lounge lifestyle of Las Vegas, where he, Dean Martin, and Sammy Davis, Jr., were known as the "Rat Pack." Though his career suffered through stops and starts, he established himself as one of the premier voices of romantic ballads and maintained a following while paying little heed to what others thought about him. He was known as a brash, outspoken man who drank, smoked, and chased women while retaining a soft side. Some of his most famous tunes include "My Way," "Strangers in the Night," "Love and Marriage," and "High Hopes."

Francis Albert Sinatra was born in the gritty waterfront working-class town of Hoboken, New Jersey, across the Hudson River from Manhattan. He was the son of Anthony Martin ("Marty"), an Italian immigrant who was a firefighter and boxer, and Natalie Della ("Dolly;" maiden name, Garaventi), a bartender and political activist with the Democratic party. Some reports also indicate that Dolly was a nurse, others say she ran an abortion service. Sinatra's existence was rough from the beginning; during his birth, his left earlobe was severed and the forceps caught him on the throat, and the doctor did not even think Sinatra was alive. After his grandmother rinsed him under cold water, he showed signs of life. An only child, Sinatra would grow up spoiled by his mother and maternal grandmother, showered with gifts and nice clothes. He led a small street gang as a youth until his family moved to a better neighborhood.

Sinatra dropped out of high school at about age 15 or 16. His first job was as a copy boy at a local newspaper, the *Jersey Observer,* but his heart was drawn to entertainment as soon as he saw Bing Crosby in concert in the 1930s. He sang at various Democratic functions, thanks to his mother's involvement in the party, and assembled a singing group, the Hoboken Four. In 1935, Sinatra's quartet won a radio contest, the Major Bowes Amateur Hour, after which they would make regular appearances on the program. Sinatra later took off on his own, and thanks to his mother's influence, landed a gig at the Rustic Cabin nightclub in 1939. There he performed with bandleader Harry James and his group, the Music Makers, and recorded his first album with that band, titled *From the Bottom of My Heart,* in July of 1939. Shortly thereafter, he left the band to work with trombonist Tommy Dorsey, who taught him a great deal about showmanship and breath control. Sinatra around this time practiced underwater exercises in order to boost the power of his lungs, and he also studied the style of jazz singer Billie Holiday.

After working with Dorsey for a few years, Sinatra forged his solo career beginning in 1942. By then, the United States was enmeshed in World War II, and many men were off to war. Sinatra, however, was not drafted because of a punctured eardrum. The timing was right for his laid-back crooning that was similar in style to Bing Crosby's, but more relaxed and sexually suggestive. Sinatra became a huge hit, especially with teenage girls (called bobby-soxers). A *Newsweek* article in 1998 reprinted a quote from their own magazine dating from 1943: "As a visible male object of adulation Sinatra is ... baffling. He is undersized and looks underfed—but the slightest suggestion of his twisted smile brings squeals of agonized rapture from his adolescent adorers." Later, he would display more

of his tough-guy swagger and often coarse language, winning him a strong cadre of male followers as well.

Columbia Records billed Sinatra during the 1940s as simply "The Voice," and in 1946, he signed with MGM to embark on an acting career. However, by the end of the decade, the quality of Sinatra's singing was hit or miss, and his popularity was starting to lag. Part of his downturn was also the result of the public's disapproval of his personal life. The singer had married Nancy Barbato in 1939, and drew fire for leaving her in 1951. They had three children together: Nancy Sandra, Franklin Wayne, and Christina. Sinatra in 1951 married actress Ava Gardner, and they divorced in 1957. At the age of 50, he tied the knot with 21-year-old Mia Farrow in 1966 (they divorced in 1968), and finally settled down with dancer Barbara Jane Blakeley Marx (the widow of comedian Zeppo Marx) in 1976, with whom he stayed until his death. Sinatra also in the 1950s became plagued with rumors that he was connected to the Mafia; these allegations would haunt him throughout his lifetime.

In 1952, Sinatra lobbied fiercely for the role of Maggio, a soldier in the war epic film *From Here to Eternity.* His performance earned him an Academy Award for best supporting actor and revived his screen and singing careers. He had also signed a contract with Capitol Records in 1953 and began churning out discs featuring a deeper voice and a swinging jazz influence, thus revitalizing the genre of vocal music. He began recording long-playing discs (LPs) instead of just singles, including *Songs for Young Lovers,* 1954; *Swing Easy,* 1954; *In the Wee Small Hours,* 1955; and *Songs for Swingin' Lovers,* 1956.

Though Sinatra's albums steadily made the charts, he had trouble cracking the top ten singles list in the 1960s, probably because of a new shift in musical tastes. Rock groups such as the Beatles were taking over the youth consciousness, and Sinatra became a symbol of an older generation, what with his dapper fedora tilted rakishly. Nevertheless, he founded his own record company, Reprise, and continued recording. After he hit the charts in 1969 with "My Way," a tune that developed into his trademark, he attempted a comeback by singing some light rock, but the effort failed. He went into retirement from 1971 to 1973, but made his way back into entertainment in 1974.

During this respite from the limelight, Sinatra's politics shifted from liberal to conservative. Although he was a staunch Democrat and an outspoken supporter of liberal causes including civil rights in his younger years, he joined the Republican party in the 1970s and would become a close friend of Ronald Reagan. His later career was generally limited to his presence in the glittering casino lounges of Las Vegas, where he was one of the famous "Rat Pack" that included Sammy Davis, Jr., and Dean Martin. Despite his heavier build and signs of age, the romantic crooner continued to draw in audiences. In 1988, Sinatra, Davis, and Martin tried touring, but the plan ended after just one week. A 1992 tour with Shirley MacLaine fared much better, but by 1994, Sinatra's health was failing.

Sinatra, with his endearing use of dated slang and his Vegas persona, epitomized the lounge culture, which made a comeback in the 1990s amid a craze of cigar bars and martini shakers. He teamed up with an assortment of other singers, including Barbara Streisand, Julio Iglesias, and Bono of U2, on his popular 1990s albums *Duets* and *Duets II*, the latter of which won a Grammy. Considered one of the consummate professionals in the industry, Sinatra was known for saying, "An audience is like a broad. If you're indifferent, Endsville," cited in a *USA Today* obituary. Sinatra won a bevy of awards throughout his distinguished career, including Grammy Awards for best album and best male vocalist in 1959, 1965, and 1966; a Grammy for record of the year in 1966; an Emmy Award and a George Foster Peabody Award in 1965; the Presidential Medal of Freedom in 1985; and a Lifetime Achievement Award from the NAACP in 1987, among many others. He is survived by his wife and three children. **Sources:** *Arizona Republic*, May 16, 1998; "Legendary Singer Frank Sinatra Dies," CNNin web site, http://cnn.com (May 15, 1998); Detroit News and Free Press, May 16, 1998, p. 1A; *Contemporary Musicians*, volume 1, Gale Research, 1989; *Encyclopedia of World Biography*, second edition, Gale Research, 1997; *Newsweek*, May 25, 1998, p. 54; *New York Times*, May 15, 1998; *Time*, May 25, 1998, p. 67; *Times* (London), May 16, 1998; *USA Today*, May 15, 1998.

—*Geri Speace*

Red Skelton

Born Richard Bernard Skelton, July 18, 1913, in Vincennes, IN; died September 17, 1997, at Eisenhower Medical Center in Rancho Mirage, CA. Red Skelton just wanted to make people laugh. His routines revolutionized comedy, and his programs became the prototype for television's musical-comedy variety shows, inspiring the likes of Jackie Gleason and Carol Burnett.

He was one of America's best-known and best-loved clowns for almost seven decades.

Skelton's father died two months before Red was born. His mother was left with four boys to raise. She worked various jobs, but didn't make enough on her own to sustain the family. Red went to work at the age of seven, singing in the street for pennies, racking balls in a local pool hall, and delivering newspapers. Despite the family's poverty, Red's mother was able to instill an appreciation for art in her youngest child (which would lead to a profitable side career as a painter). She also gave him tickets to vaudeville shows, which likely inspired his career.

At the age of ten, Skelton auditioned for a job as a "mammy singer," with a traveling medicine show. An accidental fall during the audition got him the job. "When I got up, the audience laughed," Skelton once explained. "I decided to fall again to see if I could get another laugh. But that time I jumped up real quick to let them know I wasn't hurt, and the laugh was louder." His pratfalls got him ten dollars a week.

Skelton eventually dropped out of school and tried his hand at drama. He worked in a stock company, in a minstrel show and on a showboat, but moved on to burlesque shows, doing a vaudeville routine at the Gaiety Theater in Kansas City in 1930 where he met his first wife, usher Edna Stilwell. She began writing scripts for him and served as his manager, writer, and partner even after their divorce in the early 1940s.

In 1932, Skelton failed a screen test and moved to Canada where he developed a pantomime sketch for a show at Montreal's Loew's Theater. He also appeared on Rudy Vallee's radio show. Child star Mickey Rooney caught his act and suggested Skelton try another screen test. Skelton auditioned for MGM's Louis B. Mayer, who cast him in his first film, *Having a Wonderful Time* in 1941. Skelton appeared in 43 movies during his career, including *Watch the Birdie, Whistling in Brooklyn, I Dood It, Ziegfield Follies,* and *The Fuller Brush Man*.

In 1941, Skelton had his own radio show, and with the help of his wife, and the musical talents of Ozzie and Harriet Nelson, it became a national hit. It was through this show that Americans came to know characters such as Skelton's Clem Kadiddlehopper, Freddie the Freeloader, the Mean Widdle Kid, and Cauliflower McPugg.

Skelton moved these characters to television when NBC put him on the air in 1951. He moved to CBS in

1953, and although he placed among the Top 10 shows eight times and never fell below the Top 20, CBS canceled the show in 1970. NBC briefly aired a half-hour version of his show, but canceled it in less than a year. Each show ended with Skelton's signature farewell, "Good night, and God bless."

After his television shows were canceled, Skelton turned to painting, a hobby that ended up netting him almost $2.5 million a year. A clown at heart, Skelton's oil paintings were all of clown faces and fetched him $80,000 or more a piece. He continued to tour, doing about 75 shows a year, but focused more and more on painting, running a mail-order business offering his original paintings, reproductions on canvas, and lithographs.

For a man who worked hard at making other people laugh, Skelton had a difficult time finding joy for himself. Although he could often be seen cracking up on stage in the middle of routine, he nevertheless was burdened with personal despair. Arthur Marx, who wrote a 1979 biography of Skelton, told the *Detroit Free Press* that when he wrote his book, he expected to tell "a nice little tale about a comedian who said `God bless' at the end of his show." Instead, he uncovered stories of a lonely, vulnerable man. Besides growing up fatherless, Skelton's first two marriages ended in divorce. Skelton and his second wife, Georgia, had two children—Valentina and Richard, but in 1958, his son died of leukemia, during the peak of Skelton's television career.

After his son's death, Skelton endured several bouts of depression. Marital problems ensued. Skelton and his second wife divorced in the early 1970s, and she committed suicide on the 18th anniversary of her son's death. Skelton also never got over the cancellation of his show, not understanding why it happened if people were still laughing at him. Still, Skelton persevered, continuing to tour, to paint and to support children's charities, including the Red Skelton Foundation in his hometown of Vincennes, which cares for needy children.

Skelton earned several awards and honors during his career, namely three Emmys and one Golden Globe, as well as awards from Amvets, Freedom Foundation, and the American Legion. He was inducted to the Academy of Television Arts and Sciences Hall of Fame in 1986. Skelton was honored, as well, with honorary degrees from Vincennes University, Emerson College, and Indiana University. "Not bad for a guy who had trouble getting through grade school," he once commented to the *Los Angeles Times*.

His last years were spent writing short stories, watching old movies on TV, and painting clown portraits. "The world lost a gem, an icon, an original," said comedian and friend Milton Berle. He is survived by his third wife, Lothian, his daughter, Valentina, and a granddaughter. **Sources:** CNN On-line, http://cnn.com (September 17, 1997); *Contemporary Authors, New Revisions Series,* Volume 28, Gale, 1990; *Detroit Free Press,* September 18, 1997, p. 1A; *Los Angeles Times,* September 18, 1997, p. B11; *USA Today,* September 18, 1997, p. D1.

—*Audrey Gebber*

Sir Georg Solti

Born Gyorgy Solti, October 21, 1912 in Budapest, Hungary; died September 5, 1997, in Antibes, France, after suffering a heart attack on September 2. A world-renowned conductor, Solti's distinctive style refined the reputations and performances of numerous groups, including London's Royal Opera House at Covent Garden, the London Philharmonic, and most notably, the Chicago Symphony Orchestra. Solti was considered "the undisputed Grand Old Man of music" at the time of his death.

Solti was born into a Jewish-Hungarian family and showed his affinity for the piano at an early age. When he was 13, he enrolled in the Franz Liszt Academy of Music, and graduated in 1930 at the age of 18. He went to work for the Budapest Opera as a *repetiteur,* one who assisted backstage, coached singers, and acted as a rehearsal pianist. In 1936, Solti assisted two famous conductors of that era, Bruno Walter and Arturo Toscanini, at the Salzburg Festival. One year later, at age 25, Solti made his conducting debut with a performance of Mozart's *Marriage of Figaro* in Budapest. He was the first Jewish conductor at the Budapest Opera since Gustav Mahler in the 19th century.

Solti's first conducting experience was also his last for more than eight years, as it was on the day that Hitler invaded Austria. The *New York Times* noted Solti as saying, "All my friends left at intermission.... This was a damp ending to my debut." Later, right before the start of World War II, Solti was in Switzerland when his mother wired him not to return to Hungary. His family was later wiped out in the Holocaust.

Unable to get a visa to the United States, he survived the war years as a pianist. Always keeping his eyes open for opportunities, Solti learned that a friend from Budapest was involved with reconstructing musical life in Munich after the war. Solti was eventually offered the post of music director of the Bavarian State Opera. During his tenure in Munich, Solti had become friendly with composer Richard Strauss and conducted Strauss's *Der Rosenkavalier* with Strauss in the audience. Solti also conducted at Strauss's funeral in 1949 and began his 50-year connection with Decca records.

In 1952, Solti moved to Frankfurt, West Germany, where he accepted the post of *generalmusikdirector*. He made his first American appearance in 1953 when he conducted the San Francisco Opera. With his prestige growing and a recording contract in his hands, Decca approached him to record Richard Wagner's *Der Ring des Nibelungen*, a cycle which consists of the four operas *Das Rheingold*, *Die Walkure*, *Siegfried*, and *Gotterdammerung*. Solti knew that recordings were essential for promoting a conductor and his group, and he worked for seven years to complete the project.

The pivotal point in Solti's career came when he was named music director of London's Royal Opera, Covent Garden. The *Chicago Tribune* noted that Solti announced his intention to make Covent Garden "quite simply, the best opera house in the world." Although critics and musicians were not prepared for him, it was perceived that he achieved his goal. For his contributions to music in England, Queen Elizabeth made him a Commander of the Order of the British Empire and later knighted him.

In 1969, Solti became the music director of the Chicago Symphony Orchestra. The 22 years he spent with the CSO marked the acme of his career and brought the orchestra to new levels of "artistic achievement and international celebrity." He tried to hold on to his Covent Garden position while working with the Chicago Symphony, but relinquished the London post in 1971. When Herbert Von Karajan, the conductor of the Orchestre de Paris stepped down, Solti jumped at the opportunity and split his time between Paris and Chicago for five years. However, he felt he could do little with the French musicians, and became conductor and artistic director of the London Philharmonic in 1979. He held these positions until 1983, when he was named conductor emeritus.

When Solti accepted the position in Chicago, he was confronted with a group of technically superior musicians who were lacking "the spark of inspiration," the *Chicago Tribune* reported. Solti immediately set out to reshape the orchestra. Establishing the "Solti Sound," he brought about unprecedented improvement and the CSO became known for its "enormous power, precision and intensity, with a lean, hard brilliance." By the mid-1970s, the orchestra's seasons were regularly sold out.

Solti remained active throughout his career, but was frustrated by the public's declining interest in and appreciation of classical music. He told the *Los Angeles Times*, "Bloody TV and movies ruin everything. People don't want to hear music." Solti turned over his CSO baton to Daniel Barenboim in 1991 and became music director laureate. He continued to make guest conducting appearances, and also took over as artistic director of the Salzburg Easter Festival beginning in 1992. In June of 1994, he began the Solti Orchestra Project at Carnegie Hall, designed to give younger players a chance to perform with and to learn from experienced orchestral instrumentalists.

Solti had won 32 Grammy awards, more than any other artist in the world. He had earned several honorary degrees and international awards. His first marriage ended in divorce in 1966 after 20 years of marriage. In 1967, Solti married BBC journalist Valerie Pitts, with whom he had two children, Gabrielle and Claudia. The *New York Times* reported that Solti suffered a heart attack on September 2, 1997, while vacationing in the south of France. Three days later, it was reported that Sir Georg Solti had died peacefully in his sleep.

He is survived by his second wife and their children.
Sources: *Chicago Tribune*, September 6, 1997, p. 1; CNN Interactive On-line, http://cnn.com (September 6, 1997); *Contemporary Musicians*, Volume 13, Gale Research, 1995; *Los Angeles Times*, September 6, 1997, p. A 24; *New York Times*, September 6, 1997, section 1, p. 1; *Washington Post*, September 7, 1997, p. B8.

—Audrey Gebber

Benjamin Spock

Born Benjamin McLane Spock, May 2, 1903, in New Haven, CT; died of natural causes, March 15, 1998, at his home in La Jolla, CA. Pediatrician, author, activist. Dr. Benjamin Spock became a household name during the "baby boom" of the 1950s with his book, *Baby and Child Care*. The guide has sold more than 40 million copies in 39 languages, making it the second top-seller of all time after the Bible. Spock advocated a more permissive and affectionate atmosphere for child-rearing and told parents to trust their own common sense. He was also a dedicated peace activist, opposing the Vietnam War and nuclear weapons.

Spock was born the oldest of six children—four girls, two boys—to the conservative Benjamin Ives (a lawyer for New Haven Railroad) and Mildred Louise (maiden name, Stoughton) Spock, both of Dutch descent. Growing up in a middle-class home in New Haven, Connecticut, Spock recalled his upbringing as stern and strict. The children ate meals separately from their parents, were required to be in bed by 6:45 p.m., and not allowed to eat certain foods, such as bananas. "There must be easier and pleasanter ways to raise children than the severity we had," Spock remarked in *Time*.

After attending Hamden Hall Country Day School in Manden, Connecticut, Spock transferred in his junior year to Phillips Academy, a college preparatory school in Andover, Massachusetts. He went on to attend Yale University, where he was on the rowing team that won the 1924 Olympic Gold Medal in Paris, France. He initially wanted to study architecture, but after working at a camp run by the Newington Crippled Children's Home in Connecticut, he switched to medicine. After graduating with his bachelor's degree in 1925, he attended Yale Medical School for two years, then transferred to Columbia University's College of Physicians of Surgeons, where he graduated at the head of his class in 1929.

After serving residencies at three hospitals in New York, Spock opened a private practice in New York City in 1933. Being the Great Depression, people were not having a lot of children, and his business was slow, so from 1933 to 1938, Spock continued his training at the New York Psychoanalytic Institute. He was concerned about the way child behaviors were handled, and curious about the underlying reasons why they were committed. Developing some theories, Spock began to test his ideas on his patients and their parents. He was known to have a gentle face and relaxed manner—he wore business suits rather than a white doctor's coat—and to genuinely enjoy being around little ones. Meanwhile, he taught pediatrics at the Cornell University Medical College and was the assistant attending physician at New York Hospital. He also served as a consultant in pediatric psychiatry to the New York City Department of Health.

In 1944, he joined the war effort, serving in the Medical Corps of the U.S. Naval Reserve as a psychiatrist. In 1946, he was discharged as a lieutenant commander. During these years, he took time to write *Baby and Child*

Care, the first edition of which was published in 1945. An immediate sensation, more than 750,000 copies were sold each year for many years. Spock's advice was considered to revolutionize child rearing, which had traditionally espoused a "spare the rod, spoil the child" mentality, as well as the thought that "children should be seen, not heard."

Spock broke with old-school behaviorists, such as Dr. John B. Watson, who, in the earlier part of the twentieth century, advised parents not to show affection toward children, limit their physical closeness, and adhere to regularly timed schedules for toilet training and feeding. Spock, on the other hand, wrote in *Baby and Child Care*, "Don't be afraid to kiss your baby when you feel like it," and asked parents to follow their common sense. He wrote with a down-to-earth manner and began each edition with the maxim, "Trust yourself. You know more than you think you do." He dismissed stern rules and regulations, and urged parents to talk to and play with their babies more.

Many criticized Spock's approach, claiming that his views were too permissive and promoted the loosening of parental responsibility and the development of rebellious behaviors in their children. Some, including Reverend Norman Vincent Peale and Vice President Spiro Agnew, pointed fingers at him for the irresponsibility and lack of discipline of American youth during the 1960s. Spock deflected these accusations, however, as political blather, claiming that he never encouraged parents to teach children instant gratification. A *Los Angeles Times* obituary quoted him as saying, "A lot of Americans still think that my advice is to let children do anything, that it's all right to let them act uncooperatively or impolitely." He insisted, however, "Right from the start, the book said, give your children firm, clear leadership, ask them for politeness and cooperation. Respect your children, but ask them for respect also."

Baby and Child Care went through four revisions in order to address new questions, such as television watching, divorce and single parenting, teenage pregnancy, and the role of fathers during pregnancy. Also, after charges of sexism, he stopped using the pronoun "she" for the parent and "he" for the baby, recognized that the father has just as great a role in the child's life as the mother, and admitted it was all right for mothers to work outside the home.

In 1962, Spock's name became associated with peace activism when he joined the National Committee for a Sane Nuclear Policy and bought a full-page ad in the *New York Times* warning of radioactive contamination from nuclear tests. He became the first prominent personality to openly oppose the Vietnam War—even getting arrested for protest actions—and he ran for president in 1972 with the People's Party. Found guilty in 1968 of conspiring to aid draft dodgers and sentenced to two years in prison, Spock was cleared when the decision was overturned in appeals court on the grounds that he had an unfair trial. Spock gave frequent anti-nuclear lectures and was active in left-wing political groups. "What is the use of physicians like myself trying to bring up children, healthy and happy, to have them killed in such numbers for a cause that is ignoble?," a *Contemporary Authors* sketch quoted him as saying about his peace activism.

Despite his professional success in the area of child rearing, Spock's own family had shortcomings. Married to Jane Davenport Cheney in 1927, he divorced her in 1976 and married feminist Mary Morgan, who was about 40 years younger than Spock. His two sons from his first marriage, Michael and John, matured to have successful careers, though Spock revealed that he did not use his own methods on them and, in fact, never even kissed them. He was reputed to be a distant, rather unaffectionate figure with them. His second wife had an 11-year-old daughter, Ginger, with whom Spock had a stormy first few years as stepfather, but the two later became friends.

Spock wrote or cowrote 12 other books besides *Baby and Child Care*, including *Caring for Your Disabled Child*, 1965; *Decent and Indecent: Our Personal and Political Behavior*, 1970; *Spock on Spock: A Memoir of Growing Up with the Century*; and *A Better World for Our Children: Rebuilding American Family Values*, 1994. He received the E. Mead Johnson Award for Research in Pediatrics in 1948, the Thomas Paine Award from the National Emergency Civil Liberties Committee in 1968, and the SANE Education Fund/Consider the Alternative Peace Award in 1963 and 1988. Spock well into his later years enjoyed his hobbies, boating and rowing, and spent time in Arkansas, Maine, and the Caribbean. Though he had enjoyed excellent health into his 90s, he had suffered a heart attack, stroke, and several bouts with pneumonia in the months before his death. **Sources:** *Chicago Tribune*, March 17, 1998; "Famed pediatrician Dr. Spock dies at age 94," CNN Interactive web site, http://cnn.com (March 16, 1998); *Contemporary Authors, New Revision Series*, Volume 35, Gale Research, 1992; *Los Angeles Times*, March 17, 1998; *New York Times*, March 17, 1998; *Time*, April 8, 1985; *Times* (London), March 17, 1998; *USA Today*, March 16, 1998; *Washington Post*, March 17, 1998.

—*Geri Speace*

Dawn Steel

Born August 19, 1946, in New York, NY; died of brain cancer, December 20, 1997, in Los Angeles, CA. Dawn Steel was the first woman to head a major Hollywood studio, and was responsible for some of the most successful box-office hits of the eighties. Yet Steel was also remembered as a savvy, vivacious, and sometimes feared mover and shaker in the film industry who, it is said, cleared a path for other women behind her to enter the executive suites in the male-dominated entertainment business.

Steel was born in 1946 into a family that would be plagued by money troubles during her youth. Her father sold zippers, but suffered a nervous breakdown that ended his breadwinning days; Steel's mother supported them by working as a bookkeeper. The family lived first in Manhattan and later on Long Island, in a poor section of the posh suburb of Great Neck. Unlike her affluent classmates, Steel had to work in a shoe store to earn spending money. She spent just a year at Boston University, ran out of money, and moved back to New York; by 1967 she had also dropped out of New York University's School of Commerce.

Though less than thrilled with academic challenges, Steel was ambitious and determined, and found work as a receptionist for a sports-magazine publishing company; she eventually rose to become a sportswriter herself for it. In 1969 she took a job with the fledgling *Penthouse* magazine. First published abroad because of American censorship laws, the early *Penthouse* quickly became one of the most outrageous adult magazines of its day. Steel told her parents she was working at *Mademoiselle* instead. For the next several years, Steel would hold a number of jobs at the magazine, including staff writer, but made a name for herself as its merchandising director. This particular post entailed devising mail-order products that fit in with its free-wheeling, sexual revolution-era spirit, and she had several notable successes.

Steel left the magazine in 1975 to begin her own company that manufactured and sold "designer" toilet paper. She called the enterprise "Oh Dawn!," which mimicked the reactions of friends and family when she explained to them her concept. She soon expanded into an array of products—toilet paper with famous quotations, for instance—but Oh Dawn! gained its founder glaring New York media attention for its Gucci-logo toilet paper; the actual Gucci family sued, and the newspapers had a field day with the story. Her attorney then helped her land a job as director of merchandising for Paramount Pictures.

Arriving in Los Angeles in 1978, Steel initially made a name for herself with her savvy promotional efforts for the first *Star Trek* movie, which used tie-ins with McDonald's and Coca-Cola—quite an innovative plan at the time. Executives realized she had an especially keen sense for what the American public liked, and in 1980 she was made a senior vice-president for production. This sometimes difficult job entailed getting screenplays off the ground by working with various studio departments. One idea that many of her male colleagues were lukewarm on was a tale of a beautiful steel welder who dreams of becoming a professional ballet dancer. Steel fought for and shepherded into production what became the 1983 film *Flashdance,* a massive hit for Paramount. Several other successes occurred during her tenure—she was promoted to president of production in 1985—including *Top Gun* and *Fatal Attraction.*

Steel remarried in 1985, and her husband, Charles Roven, broke the news to her in early 1987 not long after she had given birth to their first child that Paramount executives had fired her while she was in labor. By this time, however, Steel was known as a dynamic and revenue-producing studio executive—though she was also considered rather intense and driven—and she was offered the presidency of Columbia Pictures. She spent three years there, but inherited too many problems from previous management to guide the studio into any real financial success. After 1990, Steel worked as an independent producer (she formed a production company, Atlas Productions, with her husband), and took the occasional producer jobs for Disney Studios, such as the 1992 movie *Cool Runnings.*

Steel wrote an autobiography of sorts, *They Can Kill You But They Can't Eat You,* published in 1993. Its title reflected its author's motivational maxims, presented in trademark frank style, to help women readers channel their ambitions. It was not out of line with her own actions; many remembered Steel as someone who succeeded in breaking down barriers for women in management positions in Hollywood by the sheer force of her personality and confidence in her abilities, and who then held the door open for others behind her. "She was one of the first women who wanted to make sure she wasn't the only powerful woman at the table," writer/director Nora Ephron told the *Los Angeles Times.* Many women now in positions of influence at Hollywood lots had been given a job somewhere along the way by Steel; Ephron herself was talked into her first directing job by Steel.

Film mogul Jeffrey Katzenberg told the *Los Angeles Times* that Steel "just was an exhilarating personality to be around," and that personality and her reputation for being somewhat contentious even managed to intimidate a president. Steel was born on same day as Bill Clinton and became one of his biggest supporters in Hollywood; upon their first meeting, Clinton reportedly told her, "You're not as bad as I thought you'd be," according to the *New York Times.* She continued to work as an independent producer, even after she was diagnosed with brain cancer in 1995. One her last films was the spiritual-themed thriller *Fallen,* an early 1998 release that starred Denzel Washington. Steel's doctors told her husband that most patients afflicted with the same kind of tumor die within six months; she endured for twenty months. "It goes to show what spirit she had," Roven told the *Los Angeles Times.* She died on December 2, 1997, at Cedars-Sinai Hospital in Los Angeles. She is survived by her husband, daughter, and brother. **Sources:** *Chicago Tribune,* December 22, 1997; *Detroit News,* December 22, 1997; *Los Angeles Times,* December 22, 1997; *New York Times,* December 22, 1997.

—Carol Brennan

Shin'ichi Suzuki

Born October 17, 1898, in Nagoya, Aichi, Japan; died of heart failure, January 26, 1998, at his home in Matsumoto, Japan. Educator, music instructor. Violinist Shin'ichi Suzuki was a pioneer in teaching children to play music. He believed that since children learn complex languages when they are small, starting children in a nurturing environment at a very young age playing music by ear—without reading music until later—would best foster their capabilities. He built an international following of teachers who used his methods to introduce youngsters to music.

Suzuki was born in 1898 to Masakichi and Ryoh (Fujie) Suzuki during the Meiji era, in which Japan became less isolated and began to reach out to Western forms of music. His father created traditional Japanese instruments and violins in a workshop, exposing Suzuki to music at a young age. When he was 17, he began to teach himself the violin after hearing a recording of Mischa Elman performing a composition by Haydn. In 1921, he began studying the violin in Berlin with the leader of the Klinger Quartet, Karl Klinger. There, Suzuki met and became friends with scientist Albert Einstein, who became his guardian for most of Suzuki's eight years in Germany. Also in Berlin, Suzuki met soprano Waltraud Prange, and they married in 1928. Prange was an essential force in Suzuki's work in addition to accompanying him as a lifetime partner. Her family introduced him to many prominent musicians, such as Fritz Kreisler and Bruno Walter.

Suzuki returned to Japan in 1928 and formed the Suzuki Quartet with three of his brothers, becoming Japan's first professional concert violinist. In 1935, he was appointed to the Imperial School of Music in addition to teaching at the Kunitachi College of Music. During World War II, he moved to Kiso Fukushima to help his father build pontoons for aircraft. Afterward, in 1946, he formed a music school which became the Talent Education Research Institute in the old castle town of Matsumoto, central Japan. At this institute, he applied what would become internationally known as the "Suzuki method" of music instruction, although the teacher himself deemed it the "mother-tongue" approach.

Suzuki's unique approach to learning how to play music was based on his idea that since children learn to speak their native language through listening and imitation, the same theory should apply to music. He insisted that since young children are able to speak complex languages, such as Japanese, without formal instruction, they can pick up a musical instrument the same way, provided they begin early—as young as three years old—and are offered a supportive, nurturing environment. He even advocated playing classical music for babies in their cribs, although he did not condone asking young children to read sheet music, preferring to let them play by ear, with lots of practice. "Talent is not something given naturally. It is something you foster," a New York Times obituary quoted Suzuki as often having claimed. "Every child can foster his talent."

In the 1950s, Suzuki started to hold annual concerts to display his young proteges' talents, and in 1964 gathered a group of ten violinists to appear before the Music Educators' national conference and the American String Teachers' Association. He came under fire from some who thought that the children might be under too much pressure. Suzuki was not interested in creating prodigies for the professional world, however. In a London Times obituary, Yehudi Menuhin remembered Suzuki telling him that "his ambition was to create amateurs so that they might bring themselves the joy of music-making and might contribute to the har-

mony of society." Widely known for having a gift with children, Suzuki was a gentle man who often gave chocolate treats to students. He also required a great deal of commitment from parents. In Suzuki classes, children are encouraged and praised before their mistakes are corrected, and parents are asked to be present during courses to take notes when the instructor makes remarks to the students.

Suzuki's methods were considered revolutionary. Though his critics claim that students trained to play by ear cannot sight read as well as those trained traditionally, Suzuki did not agree. Indeed, numerous orchestra musicians throughout the world were trained by his schools, including Toshiya Eto and Koji Toyoda, two of his first students. Today, an estimated 300,000 in 34 countries are learning music the Suzuki way. Though Suzuki initially started with just the violin, his methods have been applied to other instruments as well. The European Suzuki Association was formed in the late 1970s to help train instructors, and regular conferences on the method are now held. To keep the teachers in contact with their mentor, the International Suzuki Association was formed in 1983. There is also a Suzuki Association of the Americas. Today there are about 8,000 instructors in the Suzuki method around the globe.

Suzuki penned his most famous book, *Nurtured by Love,* in 1966. His honors are numerous, including the Chunchi Culture Award, Japan, 1951; Shinmai Culture Award, Japan, 1961; Ysayi Award, Belgium, 1969; Mobil Music Award, Japan, 1976; Palmes Academiques, French Government, 1982; Kohl International Achievement Award, U.S., 1994; and various honorary citizenships and degrees. He was also decorated with the Order of the Sacred Treasure, Third Class, by the Emperor of Japan. Suzuki is survived by his wife and his sister, Namiko Fujie; he had no children. **Sources:** *Los Angeles Times*, January 27, 1998; *New York Times*, January 27, 1998; *Times* (London), January 28, 1998; *USA Today*, January 26, 1998.

—*Geri Speace*

Brandon Tartikoff

Born January 13, 1949, in Freeport, Long Island, NY; died August 27, 1997, in Los Angeles, CA, of Hodgkin's disease. Brandon Tartikoff's career as a wunderkind television executive made him responsible for some of the most-watched shows of the Eighties, programs that literally attracted cult followings. During his years at NBC, Tartikoff was credited with almost single-handedly turning the company from a veritable joke into the top-rated television network in the United States. Yet his untimely death at the age of 48 from cancer brought forth remembrances of another kind, as his fellow entertainment-industry movers and shakers eulogized him as one of their field's most popular, well-liked executives.

Tartikoff grew up in a Long Island suburb and, as he often pointed out, was the part of that first American generation to come of age in the television era. In fact, Tartikoff loved the medium to such an extent that he often faked illness in order to stay home from school and tune in all day long. On one occasion, he informed his parents that the child actor cast to play title role in the 1950s series *Dennis the Menace* was all wrong for the part. Accepted into Yale University, Tartikoff studied with the American poet Robert Penn Warren, to whom he once expressed the opinion that a short story by nineteenth-century British novelist D. H. Lawrence suffered from too weak a plot. Warren somewhat cuttingly replied that Tartikoff probably had a career in television ahead of him.

Indeed, after a brief stint at an advertising agency after graduating from Yale in 1970, Tartikoff landed a job as promotional director for an ABC affiliate in Connecticut. In 1973, he jumped to a much larger market when he was hired by Chicago's ABC station, WLS. There he gained a reputation as a savvy advertising and promotion director, but these stellar early years were nearly cut short when Tartikoff was diagnosed with Hodgkin's disease. He underwent chemotherapy and through the harsh course of treatment never missed a day of work. The brash young executive would later remark that the experience changed his life by helping him to focus far better, and also taught him a lesson in personal humility.

After vacationing in Los Angeles for several years in order to land a network job, Tartikoff spent a year at ABC as director of dramatic programming in the era of *Starsky & Hutch* and *Charlie's Angels*. A year later, he was hired away by Fred Silverman, the president of NBC at the time. The network had been at the bottom of the ratings heap for a number of years. Silverman put him in charge of comedy, perhaps the only area in which NBC had a quirky lead with *Saturday Night Live*. (Once, Tartikoff had tried to get a job as an *SNL* writer; he later hosted the show and became the only network executive ever to do so.) In 1978 he was promoted to vice-president of program-

ming. When NBC made him president of programming, he became the youngest such executive in television history at the age of 31.

Tartikoff took NBC from the last-place ratings slot to Number One over the next decade. The hit shows he helped create made up a roster of legendary Eighties television: *Cheers, The Cosby Show, Miami Vice, St. Elsewhere, Hill Street Blues, L.A. Law,* and *Family Ties* were perhaps the biggest successes. In many cases, these shows were Tartikoff's own ideas passed on to development staffers, or were his personal favorites despite their initial poor showing in the ratings. At creative meetings, Tartikoff became famous for coming up with brief phrases to conceptualize programming ideas: "four old ladies in Florida" became *Golden Girls,* while "MTV cops" scribbled on a piece of paper became *Miami Vice.* Yet Tartikoff's early years at NBC were marred by a recurrence of the Hodgkin's disease. Once, he donned a wig and fake eyebrows (chemotherapy had eradicated both for a time) and still presented the fall schedule at the all-important affiliates meeting.

Under Tartikoff's guidance, the network that had not beat the other two competitors for three decades managed to pull off an unrivaled ratings lead of 68 weeks in a row at Number One, which had never been equaled in television history. "At the last great moment when network television was a communal experience for America, Brandon was the one in charge of delivering the programs that created that experience," former NBC colleague Dick Ebersol told the *New York Times.* During his last years at the network, Tartikoff signed a relatively unknown comedian named Jerry Seinfeld. In 1990 he was named chairman, but left television for good in 1991 to head Paramount Studios, where his biggest success came with the 1991 film *Wayne's World,* based on a *Saturday Night Live* skit.

Tartikoff left Paramount late in 1992 after a Nevada car accident left both him and his daughter injured; she suffered the brunt of the collision and spent the next five years in rehabilitation at Tulane Medical Center. Tartikoff and his wife Lilly Samuels, a former professional ballet dancer whom he married in 1982, moved to New Orleans to be near her, and he began a third career as an independent producer. He named his company H. Beale, after the television programming executive character in the 1976 film *Network* who comes famously undone. The company was eventually sold to New World Cinema, and Tartikoff was made an executive with the company.

In early 1997 Tartikoff was hired away by Internet provider America Online to develop its entertainment-based content, but shortly thereafter suffered his third bout with cancer. Reportedly he was still working a week before his death in late August, and his death shocked many in the industry. "His combination of passion and love for [television] was so infectious, I think he's irreplaceable," onetime ABC president Ted Harbert told the *Los Angeles Times*. "He raised the bar for all the executives that competed against him." Tartikoff is survived by his wife, and daughters Calla and Elisabeth. He chronicled his years at NBC in the 1992 autobiography, *The Last Great Ride*. **Sources:** *Los Angeles Times*, August 28, 1997; *New York Times*, August 28, 1997, p. B8; *Times* (London), August 30, 1997; *USA Today*, August 28, 1997; *Washington Post*, August 28, 1997, p. B6.

—*Carol Brennan*

Gianni Versace

Born December 2, 1946, in Reggio Calabria, Italy; died July 15, 1997, in Miami, FL, after being shot to death. One of the world's best known and most successful fashion designers, Versace built a $1 billion empire by injecting the world of fashion with glamour and glitz. He gained fame in the 1980s for sexy, flamboyant, brilliantly colorful clothing collections which combined classicism and kitsch. His fashion shows featured a pounding rock beat, floodlights, giant video screens, supermodels, and celebrity-filled audiences. "He understood that fashion was about more than clothes," the *Washington Post* reported, "that it was connected to the art world, film, music and architecture." Versace adorned and befriended celebrities including Elton John, Princess Diana, Madonna, Sting, Prince, Jon Bon Jovi, Demi Moore, Elizabeth Hurley, and Sylvester Stallone.

Some critics considered the designer a visionary; others viewed him as vulgar and garish. Most agreed, however, that he was bigger than life and had an enormous influence on fashion and pop culture. "He was the first to bring stars to the shows, the first to mix the worlds of rock 'n' roll and Hollywood with fashion," *Harper's Bazaar* editor Liz Tilberis told *USA Today*. "He was a driving force who loved fashion as much as he loved life."

Versace was shot twice in the head at point-blank range by serial killer Andrew Cunanan as he returned to his $6.2 million Miami Beach mansion, Casa Casuarina, after an early morning walk to a nearby newsstand. Cunanan, a 27-year-old gigolo, traveled in elite social circles and sought out wealthy gay men to support him. He is believed to have committed five brutal murders during a cross-country killing spree that culminated with Versace's death. He eluded an intense manhunt for eight days after the fashion designer's murder—then killed himself on a houseboat 2 1/2 miles from Versace's home.

Born in Reggio Calabria, an industrial town in southern Italy, Versace was the son of an appliance salesman and a dressmaker. His mother employed 45 seamstresses in her boutique, and at age 18, Versace went to work for her. As a buyer, he went to fashion shows in Paris, London, Rome and Florence. Within a few years, he was creating his own designs, and in 1972, he moved to Milan and designed women's clothing for several prestigious labels, including Complice, Callaghan and Genny.

Three years later, Versace opened a boutique and unveiled a women's ready-to-wear line under his own name. He soon added a men's collection. Versace continually pushed fashion in new and provocative directions as he absorbed and melded disparate influences. He merged high culture with low culture. He borrowed from the classic Greco-Roman imagery which surrounded him as a boy as well as the punk rock movement and sadomasochistic underground. He coupled materials in unusual ways: rubber with leather, fur with silk, metal with cotton, denim with plastic.

"There were no apologies for Versace's fashion," designer Marc Jacobs told *Time* magazine. "No apologies for something being too gold or too sexy or too overt. 'Too' was not a problem." Versace was equally adept creating outrageous designs for Madonna or Elton John and sublime costumes for operas and ballets. He paired T-shirts with linen jackets, a look popularized by the 1980s police drama *Miami Vice*, and he saw his work displayed in numerous museum exhibitions around the world. "You look at his work as a whole, and there is a through line of the Versace energy and spirit. It's all him," Ingrid Sischy, the editor of *Interview* magazine, told the *New York Times*. "But then on top of it is a diary of the things that have been going on in the world, in the pop culture."

With the help of his sister, Donatella, and brother, Santo, Versace turned his vision into a $1 billion fashion empire and "became, along with Giorgio Armani, Italy's leading ready-to-wear designer," according to the *Washington Post.* The Versace name graces clothing that ranges from blue jeans to $30,000 dresses, along with fragrances, china, lingerie, bath products, wallpaper, sunglasses, leather goods, home furnishings, and more. "It is difficult to imagine," Amy Spindler wrote in the *New York Times,* "another designer whose death would drain more life from the (fashion) industry, an industry now driven by contemporary culture because Mr. Versace made it that way." He is survived by his longtime companion, Antonio D'Amico, his brother and sister, as well as nieces and nephews. **Sources:** *Business Week,* July 28, 1977; *Detroit Free Press,* July 16, 1997; *Los Angeles Times,* July 16, 1997; *Maclean's,* July 28, 1997; *New York Times,* July 16, 1997, July 17, 1997; *People,* October 6, 1997; *Time,* July 28, 1997; *Times* (London), July 16, 1997; *USA Today,* July 15, 1997, July 16, 1997; *Washington Post,* July 16, 1997.

—Dave Wilkins

Carl Wilson

Born December 21, 1946, in Los Angeles, CA; died February 6, 1998, in Los Angeles, CA, of complications from lung cancer. Of the three brothers that comprised the core of venerable sixties surf-rock group the Beach Boys, Carl Wilson was perhaps its least infamous. Described by many as the soul that held the group together through their troubled, post-hit years, the guitarist and youngest of the Wilsons led a relatively quiet life—unlike one of his brothers who once recorded tracks with Charles Manson. His *Los Angeles Times* obituary described Wilson as "a stabilizing presence over the years, as the group was torn by family feuds, drug abuse, fame and the death of" one brother and a legal battle against another. "Carl was like a rock for the group. He was the steady one. He was the tiller," the band's publicist for seventeen years, Sandy Freedman, told the *Los Angeles Times.*

Carl Dean Wilson had just turned fifteen when the Beach Boys—the Wilsons plus cousin Mike Love and friend Alan Jardine—gave their first public performance at the Long Beach Municipal Auditorium on New Year's Eve of 1961. Wilson played guitar, studying the instrument by copying Chuck Berry songs, while brother Brian wrote the songs; Brian also taught his brothers to sing the harmonies that would make the group famous. It was drummer Dennis Wilson's idea to capitalize on the surf-rock music that was extremely popular at the time in their hometown of

Hawthorne, a Los Angeles suburb, and throughout Southern California. Over the next five years, the band would become huge in the United States, even as British invaders the Beatles and Rolling Stones were emerging as stiff competition. The Beach Boys enjoyed a string of hits, including the No. 1 singles "I Get Around" and "Help Me, Rhonda," and a total of twelve Top 20 successes. Most were innocent, chiming paeans to the elements of the Southern California myth: girls, cars, sun, and surf.

Carl Wilson first took the microphone with his lead vocal for the 1965 track "Girl Don't Tell Me." He went on to perform on the ballad "God Only Knows" as well as "Good Vibrations"—the latter becoming, over the years, perhaps the signature Beach Boys tune. Bandmates admired his perfect pitch—the ability to hit a note on key. "Wilson's guileless voice and his gleaming surf-rock guitar lines were an essential part of the Beach Boys' music," declared the *New York Times* Jon Pareles in Wilson's obituary. But like the "golden years" of rock music itself—when happy, optimistic songs were the norm and a scrubbed, all-American look set the standard—the Beach Boys' career took a turn down a far different road as the sixties progressed. In 1965, Brian Wilson suffered a nervous breakdown from which he never fully recovered; he also spoke harshly about their father and the senior Wilson's management of the band during its early years; drug problems would plague him for decades from then on. His ability to tour and craft hit songs came to an end, and he later became involved with a psychologist whom some—brother Carl among them—thought was exercising far too much financial control over his [Brian Wilson's] affairs. A divisive, media-chronicled court battle eventually transpired.

The Beach Boys did manage to recover, but never enjoyed the string of hits that Brian had written in the early sixties. Instead, they turned to resurrecting their former image, over the years coming to serve as ageless harbingers from another, more innocent era. There were successful tours each summer, but in 1981 Wilson dropped out, frustrated by the lack of musical growth. He publicly disparaged the group's reliance on their timeworn hits, their penchant for playing lucrative Las Vegas dates, and their indifference about rehearsing. He embarked upon a solo career in 1981, releasing the album *Carl Wilson,* which he had recorded with Myrna Smith of the Sweet Inspirations. He released *Young Blood* in 1983.

Wilson soon found that solo waters were far rougher than the placid Beach Boy shore. He rejoined the band in 1982, but the following year brought yet another tragedy in the Wilson family—the death of brother Dennis in a swimming accident. It was also during this time that Wilson launched the well-publicized legal battles with his brother Brian and his psychologist. Yet in 1988, in a Lazarus-like triumph, the Beach Boys enjoyed their first No. 1 hit in over twenty years with "Kokomo." That year, they were inducted into the Rock and Roll Hall of Fame. They continued to tour every summer, and Wilson seemed to have made his peace with the nostalgia aspect of it. "We have a way, somehow, of bringing it new again," Wilson said a 1988 interview with the Cable News Network. "What we found is that when you really put yourself into it, it makes it newer, it makes it more present. It doesn't get older."

In the spring of 1997, the 51-year-old Wilson was diagnosed with lung and brain cancer; he refused to let the illness keep him from the annual summer dates. He played over 130 shows that year, though he often had to bow out of other dates for treatment or rest. The Beach Boys' current publicist, Alyson Dutch, told *USA Today* that the rest of the band "looked to Carl as a steady force. He was also a peaceful force. Despite everything negative ... when they got on stage or in the studio—the magic, the love, the brotherhood that existed between them never failed." Wilson died with his family—with the exception of brother Brian—at his bedside on February 6, 1998. He is survived by his wife Gina and two adult sons, Jonah and Justyn. "He was one of the kindest and nicest people that I'd met that had become a star," a former high school friend, Rich Henn, told the *Los Angeles Times*. "He was a genuinely sweet, caring and loving guy." **Sources:** *Los Angeles Tims*, February 8, 1998; *New York Times*, February 9, 1998; *Times* (London), February 9, 1998; *USA Today*, February 9, 1998.

—Carol Brennan

Tammy Wynette

Born Virginia Wynette Pugh, May 5, 1942, in Itawamba County, MS; died of a blood clot, April 6, 1998, in Nashville, TN. Singer. Tammy Wynette was known as the "first lady of country music," producing over 50 albums, 39 top ten songs, and 20 number one hits between 1967 and 1988. She sold over 30 million records featuring her twangy, melancholy soprano. Her voice gave the impression that she was often on the verge of tears although it was simultaneously enriched with the qualities of determination and nurturing. The country chart-toppers she belted out were often about romance, both devoted and failed, as well as the kind of hard life that she herself endured. Her 1968 trademark hit *Stand By Your Man* made headlines again in 1992 when Hillary Rodham Clinton, wife of presidential candidate Bill Clinton, derogatorily referred to it and its unfeminist message during a televised interview.

Wynette was born in 1942 near Tupelo, Mississippi, but her father died when she was a baby and her mother went to work in Birmingham, Alabama, for the war effort. Wynette was raised on her grandparents' farm, where she helped pick cotton and taught herself guitar and piano with some instruments that her father had left. She was able to take voice lessons also and hoped to someday sing in the Grand Ole Opry. Her career had to wait, however. She married Euple Byrd, a construction worker, one month before her high school graduation. They were divorced in 1965 just before the birth of their third child, who developed spinal meningitis. Wynette moved to Birmingham, where her father's family lived, and worked as a beautician to help pay her baby's medical bills as well as support her family in the housing project where they lived. She also got her start as a singer on a local television program, getting up a 4 a.m. to be at the station for her appearance before going to work at the salon.

The next year, Wynette and her children moved to Nashville, Tennessee, so she could pursue her dreams. She got the attention of producer Billy Sherill, who changed her name to Tammy and let her record "Apartment No. 9," a Johnny Paycheck song, in 1966. James Hunter in a *Rolling Stone* obituary called the release "brilliant" and commented, "Wynette summoned the courage to lace her self-styled vocal rhythms with sweetness and personal drama instead of trying to impersonate the big voice and dulcet phrasing with which Patsy Cline had triumphed." Soon she reached number three on the country charts with "Your Good Girl's Gonna Go Bad," then had more hits with "I Don't Wanna Play House," about a small boy affected by his parents' marital troubles, the hopeful "Take Me To Your World," and "D-I-V-O-R-C-E," another tale of how breakups are difficult for children.

In 1968, Wynette and Sherill co-wrote the number one hit "Stand By Your Man," which would become her trademark song. This, as well as numerous other tunes, portrayed the ideal woman as a wife and homemaker who should endure the failings of her husband. Feminists were none too pleased with this depiction, but soon-to-be First Lady Hillary Rodham Clinton in 1992 openly condemned the song's values with an off-handed remark in an appearance on the CBS television program *60 Minutes.* Clinton stressed that she was heavily involved in helping her husband, Bill Clinton, run for president, and told the interviewer, "I'm not sitting here like some little woman standing by my man like Tammy Wynette," according to the *Chicago Tribune.* The angry singer publicly defended herself, homemakers across the nation were outraged, and Clinton apologized and announced that she never meant to offend anyone; she only wanted to emphasize her strong support for her husband. Later, Wynette was invited to perform at a fund-raiser for Bill Clinton.

Ironically, Wynette's personal life was not always the picture of devotion so often conveyed in her material. She was married five times. After her divorce from Byrd, she married Don Chapel, a small-time singer/songwriter, in 1967. They divorced the next year, and Wynette fell for the legendary country star, George Jones. They sustained a stormy marriage despite his drinking problems, and had a daughter, Georgette. The couple recorded an array of successful duets, including the number one hits, "Golden Ring" and "Near You." After their divorce, they continued to make music together. In 1976, Wynette married Nashville real estate executive, Michael Tomlin, but they were divorced within a month and a half. Wynette entered matrimony for the final time in 1978 with George Richey, a producer, arranger, and songwriter, who also served as her manager. Unfortunately that year also brought trauma when Wynette was abducted from a Nashville shopping center by a man in a mask who drove her 80 miles in her luxury car, beat her, and robbed her. No arrest was made.

Wynette published her autobiography, *Stand By Your Man,* in 1979, and continued recording into the next decade. She churned out top ten songs such as "Another Chance" in 1982 and "Sometimes When We Touch" in 1985 with Mark Gray, and tried her hand at acting, appearing in the soap opera *Capitol* in 1986. The 1980s also saw her admission to the Betty Ford Clinic to battle an addiction to painkillers, and in 1988 an investment in two Florida shopping centers left her bankrupt. She made the charts again in 1992, however, when she ventured into new musical territory, singing on "Justified and Ancient" for the British group the KLF. The catchy electronic dance song was an international club sensation. The next year, she teamed with fellow country celebrities Dolly Parton and Loretta Lynn (a lifelong close friend) to produce *Honkytonk Angels.* Although her health went into decline after a number of stomach surgeries and ailments from 1992 to 1994, she recorded another album with Jones, *One,* in 1996, and had been planning to perform live on May 8, 1998, on The Nashville Network (TNN) with Melissa Etheridge and Trisha Yearwood.

Wynette won Grammy Awards for best female country vocal performance in 1967 for "I Don't Wannna Play House" and in 1969 for "Stand By Your Man." She was a three-time Country Music Association female vocalist of the year, winning in 1968, 1969, and 1970. She also was named the Academy of Country Music top female vocalist in 1969. Wynette died after a blood clot reached her lungs while she was sleeping at her home in Nashville. She is survived by her husband, Richey; five daughters, Jackie Daly, Gwen Ignaczak, Tina Jones, Georgette Smith, and Deirdre Richardson; a son, Kelly Richardson; and seven grandchildren. **Sources:** *Chicago Tribune,* April 7, 1998; "Tammy Wynette, country music's first lady, dies at 55," CNN Interactive web site, April 7, 1998, http://cnn.com (April 8, 1998); *Los Angeles Times,* April 7, 1998; *New York Times,* April 7, 1998; *Rolling Stone,* May 14, 1998; *Times* (London), April 8, 1998; *USA Today,* April 7, 1998; *Washington Post,* April 7, 1998.

—*Geri Speace*

Coleman A. Young

Born May 24, 1918, in Tuscaloosa, AL; died November 29, 1997, in Detroit, MI, of respiratory failure. One of the first African Americans ever elected to lead a major American city, Coleman A. Young roused both admiration and disdain during his five-term, two-decade service as mayor of Detroit. Beloved by his majority black constituency, often criticized by the local media with whom he seemed to enjoy sparring, and wrongly blamed for Detroit's downfall by the white suburbanites who had fled it, "Hizzoner," as Young was known, left an imprint upon his city that is nearly unrivaled in American urban political legacies.

Like many of the black Detroiters who would later elect him, Coleman Alexander Young was born in the South and came to the Midwest with his family in the years following World War I. The son of a tailor and the oldest of five children, he grew up in what was then known as Black Bottom, the segregated Detroit neighborhood later razed by freeway construction. Though Young excelled in school, he faced racism when he sought scholarships, and such discrimination, both official and of the more subtle stripe, would fuel Young's political ambitions. He worked on the assembly line for Ford Motor Company after winning entry into a pilot training program that normally did not accept minorities, and later worked at the post office. During World War II, he served with the prestigious Tuskegee Airmen, the first all-black Army Air Corps unit, and successfully integrated an officers' club after he and several other African American servicemen were barred. Young then returned to the post office after the war's end, but was fired for labor-organizing activities.

At this point Young began to channel his energies into politics and the labor movement as a full-time vocation. He became involved in Progressive Party politics, and helped found the National Negro Labor Council in 1951. The following year, Young was called before the United States House of Representatives Un-American Activities Committee for questioning about his labor activities and suspected "Communist sympathies." With a typically cantankerous attitude, he refused to answer the panel's questions. Yet Young's demeanor also alienated him from the more mainstream labor movement, and he could not find a job as an organizer since he was considered too much of a radical. At various times during the 1950s, he earned a living as a bartender, salesperson, and even a cab driver.

Young's political career was launched when he won his second bid for a seat in the Michigan Senate in 1963. In Lansing, he fought for open-housing laws (at the time, real-estate companies worked together to racially segregate neighborhoods), and paid attention to the reactions of both black and white Detroiters in the summer of 1967 when the city burned in some of the worst racially-motivated rioting of the century. The event galvanized the city—whites fled to the suburbs in even greater numbers, while its minorities searched for a political voice. By the mayoral election of 1973, police brutality was a divisive issue in the city, with a largely white police force and an undercover squad thought responsible for several suspicious African American deaths. Young ran against the city's white police commissioner and won by small margin.

When Young took office in early 1974, he immediately alienated whites inside and outside the city in his first public speeches. His actions, however, earned him approval from his black supporters. That first year, he abolished the controversial undercover unit within the police department, and implemented minority-hiring program on the force. Yet Young's first years in office

were also witness to a massive bleeding of Detroit's most valuable elements—middle-class taxpayers continued to move out, and the businesses that served them followed; worse, the auto industry hit a disastrous slump and sunk into economic disarray for several years.

By 1981 the city was near bankruptcy, but Young, re-elected for his third term that same year, asked his loyal city employees—many of them new minority hires—to agree to take wage freezes and even pay cuts. Yet Young knew the real key to Detroit's revival would be the showpiece projects—and not the massive concrete and glass hotel and office structure known as the Renaissance Center (launched before his mayorship by private financing and opened in 1977), whose mammoth presence and empty floors seemed to symbolize Detroit's perpetual can't-win situation. Instead Young launched more accessible projects—a riverfront plaza, a monorail system, luxury apartment buildings, and a revitalization of the theater district—that launched the city into a new, more optimistic era.

Young was re-elected by huge majorities again in 1985 and 1989, but his public and private life were plagued by more than one scandal. A paternity suit by a former city employee became public in his fourth term, and in his fifth term, his police chief came under federal investigation and eventually went to prison. In 1992, after an African American man died after being beaten by two white police officers, Young appeared on television before the trial and labeled the two as "murderers." His health was also on the decline. However, he waited until the last possible moment to announce his decision not to seek re-election in 1993. He retired to one of the luxury riverfront condominium complexes he helped launch, and wrote his autobiography, *Hard Stuff*.

Midway through 1997, Young began experiencing more serious emphysema-related setbacks, but kept surprising his doctors by pulling through. After a heart attack on November 12, his heart stopped for over a half-hour but was revived, and a more benign local media reported to its viewers that as always, "Hizzoner" seemed to enjoy a good fight. His death on November 29 was less of surprise than the groundswell of tribute surrounding his funeral. His body lay in state for several days at the city's dazzling Museum of African American History, which he had pushed for, and thousands stood in line even in the middle of the night cold to pay their respects. "The people of this city have lost a great warrior," his successor, Mayor Dennis W. Archer, told the *Los*

Angeles Times, and even those who represented the adversaries of Young came around: former U.S. Senator Donald Riegle told the *Detroit News* that "Young was the Joe Louis of urban electoral politics.... He was a trailblazer his entire public life and he leaves legendary accomplishments." Perhaps fittingly, it rained heavily the day of his passing. "That was the city crying for the mayor," one citizen told the *Detroit News.* "He kept our city alive. He kept us alive." Young is survived by his son, Coleman A. Young, Jr., and two sisters. **Sources:** *Detroit News/Free Press,* November 30, 1997; *Detroit News* (special commemorative section), November 30, 1997; *Los Angeles Times,* November 30, 1997; *New York Times,* December 1, 1997.

—*Carol Brennan*

Henny Youngman

Born Henry Youngman, March 16, 1906 (some sources say 1905 or 1902), in England; died February 24, 1998, in Mt. Sinai Hospital, New York after a bout of pneumonia. Comedian. Universally known as the "King of the One-Liners," Henny Youngman was a legendary comedian whose quick cracks and groan-provoking gags were infused into the mass consciousness for much of the twentieth century. His trademark line, "Take my wife, please," was first used by accident on an usher prior to an appearance on a Kate Smith radio program in the 1930s.

Youngman, who would come to represent an integral part of American humor, was actually born in England (some sources say Liverpool; others, London). His early life is a bit of a mystery. Some articles say he grew up in London's East End, while others say he came to the United States when he was six months old. A *New York Times* obituary reported that Youngman's father, Yonkel Yungman, a hatmaker originally from Friedrichstadt, Russia, had married Olga Chetkin in New York and the two went to London, where Yungman's parents lived, for their honeymoon. Their son was subsequently born, and they returned to New York after a year and a half, when they had saved enough money.

Youngman grew up in a tenement that his uncle owned in the Bay Ridge section of Brooklyn, New York. As a student at P.S. 2 there, he was perennially in trouble and often expelled from classes. His family bought him a violin and his father, a music aficionado, paid for lessons, hoping that Youngman would make

it to the Metropolitan Orchestra. Youngman attended trade school for a couple of years and worked at a Manhattan print shop near the theater district. He was friends with neighbor and fellow performer-to-be Jackie Gleason, and now-legendary comedian Milton Berle would sometimes drop by his shop after gigs at area clubs. A *USA Today* obituary quoted Youngman as saying, "I was a groupie for Berle. I picked up a lot of stuff from him. Learned a lot."

During this time, in the 1920s, Youngman headed a band called Henny Youngman and the Swanee Syncopators. A *New York Times* obituary reported that though Youngman had been called "Hen" (short for his real name, Henry) until age 18, he didn't like the way it looked when he saw the headline "Hen Youngman and the Syncopators Play Coney Island Boardwalk" because, as he noted, "hens lay eggs." He thus became Henny. Around this same time, he was working in downtown Brooklyn serving summonses and printing business cards at a Kresge's store, where he met a red-haired saleswoman in the sheet music department. He was married to the quiet Sadie Cohen for 58 years until her death in 1987. She apparently was not affected by his barrage of onstage insults about her. The *New York Times* quoted him as explaining, "She knew I was just joking. She always stuck by me, and that's what counts."

Youngman's rapid-fire, often offending humor soon became his livelihood. An anecdote in a *USA Today* obituary claimed that the frugal owner of the Swan Lake Inn, where the band was performing, enjoyed Youngman's between-song banter so much that he fired the band and hired Youngman to be a one-person comic act. The *New York Times,* however, recounted that Youngman got his big break at the Nut Club in Mountainside, New Jersey, when he was called upon to fill in for a comedy team that did not show up for their performance. *USA Today* recited a 1991 Associated Press interview in which Youngman insisted, "My whole life's an accident. I've never planned anything. It's just all happened."

Youngman traveled around the East Coast for several years and found a fan in the prominent gossip columnist of the day, Walter Winchell. Winchell often included Youngman's humor in his columns and was the one who dubbed him the "King of the One-Liners." Finally, Youngman hit the big time in 1937 when he was booked for a six-minute spot on Kate Smith's radio program on CBS. The audience laughed so much, they stretched his debut to ten minutes; and thereafter, he was a regular and was signed for two years.

In 1938 Youngman left the Kate Smith show, aspiring to a film career. When it did not work out, he returned to comedy clubs, averaging over 200 dates a year for over four decades. Though his violin never made it to the Metropolitan Orchestra, he often used it in gags onstage during his routine. His trademark style, though, was a machine-gun pace of one-liners. He prided himself on being able to tell eight jokes a minute, and the E! online web site reported that he had a personal memory bank of about 1,600 jokes. The *Los Angeles Times* recounted some of them, including: "I miss my wife's cooking—as often as I can;" "I just got back from a pleasure trip—I took my mother-in-law to the airport," and "A man goes to a psychiatrist who tells him, `You're crazy.' The man says, `I want a second opinion.' The psychiatrist says, `OK, you're ugly, too.'" Much of his humor was from an era past, where women and minorities bore the brunt of the joke. Though it was not politically correct by current standards, he often boasted that he never told "dirty" jokes.

Youngman's career slowed down in the 1960s, when his lines were considered corny and outdated. Thanks to the popular television show, *Rowan and Martin's Laugh-In,* he returned to the spotlight and became known to never refuse a booking. A *New York Times* obituary remembered a 1977 article in that paper in which writer Tony Hiss dubbed him "the world's hardest-working comedian." He would do gigs on college campuses, at fraternal roasts, for trade shows and sales meetings, and bar mitzvahs. He even performed in San Francisco, California, in December of 1997, just a couple of months before his death.

Youngman starred in the television series *Henny and Rocky* in 1955 and *Joey and Dad,* 1975, and appeared in the films *A Wave, A Wac, and A Marine; Nashville Rebel; Won Ton Ton; The Dog Who Saved Hollywood; Silent Movie, History of the World, Part I; The Comeback Trail; Death Wish II;* and *Goodfellas.* Many of Youngman's appearances were in cameo roles portraying himself. He also worked late in his life with director Steven Spielberg on his animated series, *Tiny Toons.* Youngman's 1973 autobiography was appropriately titled after his signature line, *Take My Wife ... Please! My Life and Laughs* (Putnam), and he also penned a number of joke books, including *Four Hundred Traveling Salesmen's Jokes,* Citadel, 1966; *Don't Put My Name on This Book,* Woodhill, 1978; *Insults for Everyone,* Woodhill, 1979; and *Henny Youngman's Giant Book of Jokes,* Citadel, 1983. He was also the first comedian on the Dial-A-Joke call-in service, which drew three million calls in its first month of operation in 1974.

Before he died, Youngman assembled the media to a restaurant in Manhattan to read his "Last Will and Testament." *USA Today* reported that there, he proclaimed, "To my nephew Irving, who still keeps asking me to mention him in my will: `Hello, Irving!'" Youngman is survived by his son, Gary; his daughter, Marilyn Kelly; and two grandchildren. **Sources:** *Contemporary Authors,* Volume 134, Gale Research, 1992; "Henny Youngman, king of the one-liners, dead at 91," CNN Interactive web site, http://cnn.com (February 24, 1998); "King of One-Liners Henny Youngman Dies," E! online web site, http://eonline .com (February 25, 1998); *Los Angeles Times,* February 25, 1998, p. A14; *New York Times,* February 25, 1998, p. B8; *Times* (London), February 26, 1998; *USA Today,* February 25, 1998.

—Geri Speace

1998 Nationality Index

This index lists all newsmakers alphabetically under their respective nationalities. Indexes in softbound issues allow access to the current year's entries; indexes in annual hardbound volumes are cumulative, covering the entire *Newsmakers* series.

Listee names are followed by a year and issue number; thus **1996**:3 indicates that an entry on that individual appears in both 1996, Issue 3 and the 1996 cumulation. For access to newsmakers appearing earlier than the current softbound issue, see the previous year's cumulation.

ALGERIAN
    Zeroual, Liamine **1996**:2

AMERICAN
    Abbey, Edward
      Obituary **1989**:3
    Abbott, George
      Obituary **1995**:3
    Abbott, Jim **1988**:3
    Abdul, Paula **1990**:3
    Abercrombie, Josephine **1987**:2
    Abernathy, Ralph
      Obituary **1990**:3
    Abraham, Spencer **1991**:4
    Abrams, Elliott **1987**:1
    Abramson, Lyn **1986**:3
    Abzug, Bella **1998**:2
    Achtenberg, Roberta **1993**:4
    Ackerman, Will **1987**:4
    Acuff, Roy
      Obituary **1993**:2
    Adair, Red **1987**:3
    Adams, Scott **1996**:4
    Addams, Charles
      Obituary **1989**:1
    Agassi, Andre **1990**:2
    Agnew, Spiro Theodore
      Obituary **1997**:1
    Aiello, Danny **1990**:4
    Aikman, Troy **1994**:2
    Ailes, Roger **1989**:3
    Ailey, Alvin **1989**:2
      Obituary **1990**:2
    Ainge, Danny **1987**:1
    Akers, John F. **1988**:3
    Akers, Michelle **1996**:1
    Akin, Phil
      Brief Entry **1987**:3
    Albee, Edward **1997**:1
    Albert, Marv **1994**:3
    Albert, Stephen **1986**:1
    Albright, Madeleine **1994**:3
    Alda, Robert
      Obituary **1986**:3
    Alexander, Jane **1994**:2
    Alexander, Jason **1993**:3
    Alexander, Lamar **1991**:2
    Alexie, Sherman **1998**:4
    Ali, Muhammad **1997**:2
    Alioto, Joseph L.
      Obituary **1998**:3
    Allaire, Paul **1995**:1

    Allen, Bob **1992**:4
    Allen, Debbie **1998**:2
    Allen, Joan **1998**:1
    Allen, John **1992**:1
    Allen, Mel
      Obituary **1996**:4
    Allen, Tim **1993**:1
    Allen, Woody **1994**:1
    Alley, Kirstie **1990**:3
    Allred, Gloria **1985**:2
    Alter, Hobie
      Brief Entry **1985**:1
    Altman, Robert **1993**:2
    Altman, Sidney **1997**:2
    Ameche, Don
      Obituary **1994**:2
    Amos, Tori **1995**:1
    Amsterdam, Morey
      Obituary **1997**:1
    Anastas, Robert
      Brief Entry **1985**:2
    Ancier, Garth **1989**:1
    Anderson, Gillian **1997**:1
    Anderson, Harry **1988**:2
    Anderson, Marion
      Obituary **1993**:4
    Andreessen, Marc **1996**:2
    Andrews, Maxene
      Obituary **1996**:2
    Angelos, Peter **1995**:4
    Angelou, Maya **1993**:4
    Annenberg, Walter **1992**:3
    Antonini, Joseph **1991**:2
    Applewhite, Marshall Herff
      Obituary **1997**:3
    Archer, Dennis **1994**:4
    Arden, Eve
      Obituary **1991**:2
    Aretsky, Ken **1988**:1
    Arison, Ted **1990**:3
    Arledge, Roone **1992**:2
    Arlen, Harold
      Obituary **1986**:3
    Arman **1993**:1
    Armstrong, Henry
      Obituary **1989**:1
    Arnaz, Desi
      Obituary **1987**:1
    Arnold, Tom **1993**:2
    Arquette, Rosanna **1985**:2
    Arrau, Claudio
      Obituary **1992**:1
    Arrested Development **1994**:2

    Arthur, Jean
      Obituary **1992**:1
    Ash, Mary Kay **1996**:1
    Ashe, Arthur
      Obituary **1993**:3
    Aspin, Les
      Obituary **1996**:1
    Astaire, Fred
      Obituary **1987**:4
    Astor, Mary
      Obituary **1988**:1
    Atwater, Lee **1989**:4
      Obituary **1991**:4
    Aurre, Laura
      Brief Entry **1986**:3
    Avedon, Richard **1993**:4
    Axthelm, Pete
      Obituary **1991**:3
    Aykroyd, Dan **1989**:3 **1997**:3
    Azinger, Paul **1995**:2
    Babbitt, Bruce **1994**:1
    Babilonia, Tai **1997**:2
    Bacall, Lauren **1997**:3
    Backus, Jim
      Obituary **1990**:1
    Bacon, Kevin **1995**:3
    Baez, Joan **1998**:3
    Bailey, F. Lee **1995**:4
    Bailey, Pearl
      Obituary **1991**:1
    Baird, Bill
      Brief Entry **1987**:2
    Baiul, Oksana **1995**:3
    Baker, Anita **1987**:4
    Baker, James A. III **1991**:2
    Baker, Kathy
      Brief Entry **1986**:1
    Bakker, Robert T. **1991**:3
    Baldessari, John **1991**:4
    Baldrige, Malcolm
      Obituary **1988**:1
    Baldwin, James
      Obituary **1988**:2
    Ball, Lucille
      Obituary **1989**:3
    Ballard, Robert D. **1998**:4
    Ballmer, Steven **1997**:2
    Banks, Dennis J. **1986**:4
    Banks, Jeffrey **1998**:2
    Banks, Tyra **1996**:3
    Barad, Jill **1994**:2
    Barber, Red
      Obituary **1993**:2

Caliguiri, Richard S.
  Obituary **1988:3**
Calloway, Cab
  Obituary **1995:2**
Calloway, D. Wayne **1987:3**
Cameron, David
  Brief Entry **1988:1**
Cammermeyer, Margarethe **1995:2**
Campanella, Roy
  Obituary **1994:1**
Campbell, Bebe Moore **1996:2**
Campbell, Ben Nighthorse **1998:1**
Campbell, Bill **1997:1**
Canfield, Alan B.
  Brief Entry **1986:3**
Cantrell, Ed
  Brief Entry **1985:3**
Capriati, Jennifer **1991:1**
Caray, Harry **1988:3**
Caray, Harry
  Obituary **1998:3**
Carcaterra, Lorenzo **1996:1**
Carey, Drew **1997:4**
Carey, Mariah **1991:3**
Carey, Ron **1993:3**
Carlin, George **1996:3**
Carlisle, Belinda **1989:3**
Carpenter, Mary-Chapin **1994:1**
Carradine, John
  Obituary **1989:2**
Carson, Ben **1998:2**
Carter, Amy **1987:4**
Carter, Billy
  Obituary **1989:1**
Carter, Gary **1987:1**
Carter, Jimmy **1995:1**
Carter, Joe **1994:2**
Carter, Ron **1987:3**
Caruso, David **1994:3**
Carver, Raymond
  Obituary **1989:1**
Carvey, Dana **1994:1**
Case, Steve **1995:4**
Case, Steve **1996:4**
Casey, William
  Obituary **1987:3**
Cash, Johnny **1995:3**
Cassavetes, John
  Obituary **1989:2**
Caulfield, Joan
  Obituary **1992:1**
Cavazos, Lauro F. **1989:2**
Chancellor, John
  Obituary **1997:1**
Chaney, John **1989:1**
Channing, Stockard **1991:3**
Chapman, Tracy **1989:2**
Chase, Chevy **1990:1**
Chast, Roz **1992:4**
Chatham, Russell **1990:1**
Chaudhari, Praveen **1989:4**
Chavez, Cesar
  Obituary **1993:4**
Chavis, Benjamin **1993:4**
Cheatham, Adolphus "Doc"
  Obituary **1997:4**
Cheek, James Edward
  Brief Entry **1987:1**
Cheney, Dick **1991:3**
Cheney, Lynne V. **1990:4**
Cher **1993:1**
Chia, Sandro **1987:2**
Chihuly, Dale **1995:2**
Cho, Margaret **1995:2**
Christopher, Warren **1996:3**
Chu, Paul C.W. **1988:2**

Chung, Connie **1988:4**
Cisneros, Henry **1987:2**
Claiborne, Liz **1986:3**
Clancy, Tom **1998:4**
Clark, J. E.
  Brief Entry **1986:1**
Clark, Jim **1997:1**
Clark, Marcia **1995:1**
Clarke, Stanley **1985:4**
Clavell, James
  Obituary **1995:1**
Clay, Andrew Dice **1991:1**
Cleaver, Eldridge
  Obituary **1998:4**
Clemens, Roger **1991:4**
Clements, George **1985:1**
Cleveland, James
  Obituary **1991:3**
Cliburn, Van **1995:1**
Clinton, Bill **1992:1**
Clinton, Hillary Rodham **1993:2**
Clooney, George **1996:4**
Close, Glenn **1988:3**
Cobain, Kurt
  Obituary **1994:3**
Cochran, Johnnie **1996:1**
Coco, James
  Obituary **1987:2**
Codrescu, André **1997:3**
Coen, Joel and Ethan **1992:1**
Coffin, William Sloane, Jr. **1990:3**
Cohen, William S. **1998:1**
Colasanto, Nicholas
  Obituary **1985:2**
Colby, William E.
  Obituary **1996:4**
Cole, Johnetta B. **1994:3**
Cole, Natalie **1992:4**
Coleman, Dabney **1988:3**
Coleman, Sheldon, Jr. **1990:2**
Coles, Robert **1995:1**
Collins, Albert
  Obituary **1994:2**
Collins, Cardiss **1995:3**
Collins, Eileen **1995:3**
Combs, Sean "Puffy" **1998:4**
Commager, Henry Steele
  Obituary **1998:3**
Condon, Richard
  Obituary **1996:4**
Conigliaro, Tony
  Obituary **1990:3**
Connally, John
  Obituary **1994:1**
Conner, Dennis **1987:2**
Connick, Harry, Jr. **1991:1**
Convy, Bert
  Obituary **1992:1**
Cook, Robin **1996:3**
Coolio **1996:4**
Cooper, Alexander **1988:4**
Coors, William K.
  Brief Entry **1985:1**
Copeland, Al **1988:3**
Copland, Aaron
  Obituary **1991:2**
Copperfield, David **1986:3**
Coppola, Carmine
  Obituary **1991:4**
Coppola, Francis Ford **1989:4**
Corea, Chick **1986:3**
Cosell, Howard
  Obituary **1995:4**
Costas, Bob **1986:4**
Costner, Kevin **1989:4**
Couples, Fred **1994:4**

Couric, Katherine **1991:4**
Courier, Jim **1993:2**
Cousteau, Jean-Michel **1988:2**
Covey, Stephen R. **1994:4**
Cowley, Malcolm
  Obituary **1989:3**
Cox, Courteney **1996:2**
Cox, Richard Joseph
  Brief Entry **1985:1**
Crandall, Robert L. **1992:1**
Craven, Wes **1997:3**
Crawford, Broderick
  Obituary **1986:3**
Crawford, Cheryl
  Obituary **1987:1**
Crawford, Cindy **1993:3**
Cray, Robert **1988:2**
Cray, Seymour R.
  Brief Entry **1986:3**
  Obituary **1997:2**
Crichton, Michael **1995:3**
Cronkite, Walter Leland **1997:3**
Crothers, Scatman
  Obituary **1987:1**
Crow, Sheryl **1995:2**
Cruise, Tom **1985:4**
Crumb, R. **1995:4**
Cruzan, Nancy
  Obituary **1991:3**
Crystal, Billy **1985:3**
Cugat, Xavier
  Obituary **1991:2**
Culkin, Macaulay **1991:3**
Cunningham, Merce **1998:1**
Cunningham, Randall **1990:1**
Cunningham, Reverend William
  Obituary **1997:4**
Cuomo, Mario **1992:2**
Curran, Charles E. **1989:2**
Curren, Tommy
  Brief Entry **1987:4**
Curtis, Jamie Lee **1995:1**
Cyrus, Billy Ray **1993:1**
Dafoe, Willem **1988:1**
Dahmer, Jeffrey
  Obituary **1995:2**
Daily, Bishop Thomas V. **1990:4**
D'Alessio, Kitty
  Brief Entry **1987:3**
D'Amato, Al **1996:1**
Daniels, Faith **1993:3**
Daniels, Jeff **1989:4**
Danza, Tony **1989:1**
D'Arby, Terence Trent **1988:4**
Darden, Christopher **1996:4**
Davis, Angela **1998:3**
Davis, Bette
  Obituary **1990:1**
Davis, Eric **1987:4**
Davis, Geena **1992:1**
Davis, Miles
  Obituary **1992:2**
Davis, Noel **1990:3**
Davis, Patti **1995:1**
Davis, Sammy, Jr.
  Obituary **1990:4**
Davis, Terrell **1998:2**
Day, Dennis
  Obituary **1988:4**
Day, Pat **1995:2**
Dean, Laura **1989:4**
Dearden, John Cardinal
  Obituary **1988:4**
DeBartolo, Edward J., Jr. **1989:3**
DeCarava, Roy **1996:3**
De Cordova, Frederick **1985:2**

Fosse, Bob
  Obituary **1988:1**
Fossey, Dian
  Obituary **1986:1**
Foster, David **1988:2**
Foster, Jodie **1989:2**
Foster, Phil
  Obituary **1985:3**
Foster, Tabatha
  Obituary **1988:3**
Foster, Vincent
  Obituary **1994:1**
Fox, Matthew **1992:2**
Foxworthy, Jeff **1996:1**
Foxx, Redd
  Obituary **1992:2**
France, Johnny
  Brief Entry **1987:1**
Franciscus, James
  Obituary **1992:1**
Frank, Barney **1989:2**
Frank, Robert **1995:2**
Franken, Al **1996:3**
Frankenthaler, Helen **1990:1**
Franklin, Aretha **1998:3**
Franklin, Melvin
  Obituary **1995:3**
Franz, Dennis **1995:2**
Freeh, Louis J. **1994:2**
Freeman, Cliff **1996:1**
Freeman, Morgan **1990:4**
Freleng, Friz
  Obituary **1995:4**
Friedan, Betty **1994:2**
Fulbright, J. William
  Obituary **1995:3**
Fulghum, Robert **1996:1**
Furman, Rosemary
  Brief Entry **1986:4**
Futrell, Mary Hatwood **1986:1**
Futter, Ellen V. **1995:1**
Gabor, Eva
  Obituary **1996:1**
Gacy, John Wayne
  Obituary **1994:4**
Gaines, William M.
  Obituary **1993:1**
Gale, Robert Peter **1986:4**
Gallo, Robert **1991:1**
Galvin, John R. **1990:1**
Galvin, Martin
  Brief Entry **1985:3**
Garbo, Greta
  Obituary **1990:3**
Garcia, Cristina **1997:4**
Garcia, Jerry **1988:3**
  Obituary **1996:1**
Garcia, Joe
  Brief Entry **1986:4**
Gardner, Ava Lavinia
  Obituary **1990:2**
Gardner, Randy **1997:2**
Garofalo, Janeane **1996:4**
Garr, Teri **1988:4**
Garrison, Jim
  Obituary **1993:2**
Garson, Greer
  Obituary **1996:4**
Garzarelli, Elaine M. **1992:3**
Gates, Bill **1993:3** **1987:4**
Gates, Robert M. **1992:2**
Gathers, Hank
  Obituary **1990:3**
Gault, Willie **1991:2**
Gebbie, Kristine **1994:2**
Geffen, David **1985:3** **1997:3**
Gehry, Frank O. **1987:1**

Geisel, Theodor
  Obituary **1992:2**
Geller, Margaret Joan **1998:2**
Gephardt, Richard **1987:3**
Gere, Richard **1994:3**
Gergen, David **1994:1**
Gerstner, Lou **1993:4**
Gertz, Alison
  Obituary **1993:2**
Gerulaitis, Vitas
  Obituary **1995:1**
Getz, Stan
  Obituary **1991:4**
Giamatti, A. Bartlett **1988:4**
  Obituary **1990:1**
Gibson, Kirk **1985:2**
Gibson, William Ford, III
  1997:2
Gifford, Kathie Lee **1992:2**
Gilbert, Walter **1988:3**
Gilford, Jack
  Obituary **1990:4**
Gill, Vince **1995:2**
Gillespie, Dizzy
  Obituary **1993:2**
Gillett, George **1988:1**
Gingrich, Newt **1991:1** **1997:3**
Ginsberg, Allen
  Obituary **1997:3**
Ginsburg, Ruth Bader **1993:4**
Gish, Lillian
  Obituary **1993:4**
Giuliani, Rudolph **1994:2**
Glaser, Elizabeth
  Obituary **1995:2**
Glass, David **1996:1**
Glass, Philip **1991:4**
Glasser, Ira **1989:1**
Gleason, Jackie
  Obituary **1987:4**
Glenn, John **1998:3**
Gless, Sharon **1989:3**
Glover, Danny **1998:4**
Glover, Savion **1997:1**
Gobel, George
  Obituary **1991:4**
Gober, Robert **1996:3**
Goetz, Bernhard Hugo **1985:3**
Goizueta, Roberto **1996:1**
  Obituary **1998:1**
Goldberg, Gary David **1989:4**
Goldberg, Leonard **1988:4**
Goldberg, Whoopi **1993:3**
Goldblum, Jeff **1988:1** **1997:3**
Goldhaber, Fred
  Brief Entry **1986:3**
Goldwater, Barry
  Obituary **1998:4**
Gomez, "Lefty"
  Obituary **1989:3**
Gooden, Dwight **1985:2**
Gooding, Cuba, Jr. **1997:3**
Goodman, Benny
  Obituary **1986:3**
Goodman, John **1990:3**
Goody, Joan **1990:2**
Goody, Sam
  Obituary **1992:1**
Gordon, Dexter **1987:1**
  Obituary **1990:4**
Gordon, Gale
  Obituary **1996:1**
Gordon, Jeff **1996:1**
Gore, Albert Jr. **1993:2**
Gore, Tipper **1985:4**
Goren, Charles H.
  Obituary **1991:4**

Gorman, Leon
  Brief Entry **1987:1**
Gossett, Louis, Jr. **1989:3**
Gould, Chester
  Obituary **1985:2**
Gould, Gordon **1987:1**
Grace, J. Peter **1990:2**
Graham, Bill **1986:4**
  Obituary **1992:2**
Graham, Billy **1992:1**
Graham, Donald **1985:4**
Graham, Katharine Meyer **1997:3**
Graham, Martha
  Obituary **1991:4**
Gramm, Phil **1995:2**
Grammer, Kelsey **1995:1**
Grange, Red
  Obituary **1991:3**
Grant, Amy **1985:4**
Grant, Cary
  Obituary **1987:1**
Grant, Charity
  Brief Entry **1985:2**
Grant, Rodney A. **1992:1**
Graves, Nancy **1989:3**
Gray, Hanna **1992:4**
Gray, John **1995:3**
Graziano, Rocky
  Obituary **1990:4**
Green, Richard R. **1988:3**
Greenberg, Hank
  Obituary **1986:4**
Green Day **1995:4**
Greenspan, Alan **1992:2**
Gregorian, Vartan **1990:3**
Gregory, Cynthia **1990:2**
Gregory, Dick **1990:3**
Grier, Pam **1998:3**
Griffey, Ken Jr. **1994:1**
Griffith, Melanie **1989:2**
Griffith Joyner, Florence **1989:2**
Grisham, John **1994:4**
Grodin, Charles **1997:3**
Groening, Matt **1990:4**
Gross, Terry **1998:3**
Grove, Andrew S. **1995:3**
Grucci, Felix **1987:1**
Grusin, Dave
  Brief Entry **1987:2**
Guccione, Bob **1986:1**
Guccione, Bob, Jr. **1991:4**
Gumbel, Bryant **1990:2**
Gumbel, Greg **1996:4**
Gund, Agnes **1993:2**
Gunn, Hartford N., Jr.
  Obituary **1986:2**
Guyer, David
  Brief Entry **1988:1**
Gwynn, Tony **1995:1**
Haas, Robert D. **1986:4**
Hackman, Gene **1989:3**
Hackney, Sheldon **1995:1**
Hagelstein, Peter
  Brief Entry **1986:3**
Hagler, Marvelous Marvin **1985:2**
Hahn, Jessica **1989:4**
Hair, Jay D. **1994:3**
Hakuta, Ken
  Brief Entry **1986:1**
Haldeman, H. R.
  Obituary **1994:2**
Hale, Alan **1997:3**
Hale, Clara
  Obituary **1993:3**
Haley, Alex
  Obituary **1992:3**
Hall, Anthony Michael **1986:3**

Schwab, Charles **1989:3**
Schwartz, David **1988:3**
Schwarzenegger, Arnold **1991:1**
Schwarzkopf, Norman **1991:3**
Schwimmer, David **1996:2**
Schwinn, Edward R., Jr.
    Brief Entry **1985:4**
Scorsese, Martin **1989:1**
Scott, Gene
    Brief Entry **1986:1**
Scott, Randolph
    Obituary **1987:2**
Sculley, John **1989:4**
Secretariat
    Obituary **1990:1**
Sedelmaier, Joe **1985:3**
Seger, Bob **1987:1**
Seidelman, Susan **1985:4**
Seinfeld, Jerry **1992:4**
Selena
    Obituary **1995:4**
Selig, Bud **1995:2**
Sevareid, Eric
    Obituary **1993:1**
Shabazz, Betty
    Obituary **1997:4**
Shakur, Tupac
    Obituary **1997:1**
Shalala, Donna **1992:3**
Shalikashvili, John **1994:2**
Shandling, Garry **1995:1**
Sharkey, Ray
    Obituary **1994:1**
Sharpe, Sterling **1994:3**
Sharpton, Al **1991:2**
Shawn, Dick
    Obituary **1987:3**
Shawn, William
    Obituary **1993:3**
Sheedy, Ally **1989:1**
Sheehan, Daniel P. **1989:1**
Sheffield, Gary **1998:1**
Shepard, Sam **1996:4**
Shepherd, Cybill **1996:3**
Sherman, Cindy **1992:3**
Sherman, Russell **1987:4**
Shields, Brooke **1996:3**
Shilts, Randy **1993:4**
    Obituary **1994:3**
Shimomura, Tsutomu **1996:1**
Shocked, Michelle **1989:4**
Shore, Dinah
    Obituary **1994:3**
Shriver, Maria
    Brief Entry **1986:2**
Shue, Andrew **1994:4**
Shula, Don **1992:2**
Sidney, Ivan
    Brief Entry **1987:2**
Siebert, Muriel **1987:2**
Sigmund, Barbara Boggs
    Obituary **1991:1**
Silber, John **1990:1**
Silverman, Jonathan **1997:2**
Silvers, Phil
    Obituary **1985:4**
Silverstone, Alicia **1997:4**
Simmons, Adele Smith **1988:4**
Simmons, Ruth **1995:2**
Simon, Paul **1992:2**
Simpson, Wallis
    Obituary **1986:3**
Sinatra, Frank
    Obituary **1998:4**
Sinclair, Mary **1985:2**
Singer, Isaac Bashevis
    Obituary **1992:1**

Singleton, John **1994:3**
Sinise, Gary **1996:1**
Sirica, John
    Obituary **1993:2**
Skelton, Red
    Obituary **1998:1**
Skinner, B.F.
    Obituary **1991:1**
Skinner, Sam **1992:3**
Slater, Christian **1994:1**
Slater, Rodney E. **1997:4**
Slotnick, Barry
    Brief Entry **1987:4**
Smale, John G. **1987:3**
Smiley, Jane **1995:4**
Smirnoff, Yakov **1987:2**
Smith, Emmitt **1994:1**
Smith, Frederick W. **1985:4**
Smith, Jack **1994:3**
Smith, Jeff **1991:4**
Smith, Jerry
    Obituary **1987:1**
Smith, Kate
    Obituary **1986:3**
Smith, Roger **1990:3**
Smith, Samantha
    Obituary **1985:3**
Smith, Will **1997:2**
Smith, Willi
    Obituary **1987:3**
Smits, Jimmy **1990:1**
Smoot, George F. **1993:3**
Snider, Dee **1986:1**
Snipes, Wesley **1993:1**
Snoop Doggy Dogg **1995:2**
Snowe, Olympia **1995:3**
Snyder, Jimmy
    Obituary **1996:4**
Snyder, Mitch
    Obituary **1991:1**
Sondheim, Stephen **1994:4**
Soren, David
    Brief Entry **1986:3**
Sorvino, Mira **1996:3**
Souter, David **1991:3**
Southern, Terry
    Obituary **1996:2**
Sowell, Thomas **1998:3**
Spacey, Kevin **1996:4**
Spader, James **1991:2**
Spector, Phil **1989:1**
Spheeris, Penelope **1989:2**
Spiegelman, Art **1998:3**
Spielberg, Steven **1993:4** **1997:4**
Spock, Benjamin **1995:2**
    Obituary **1998:3**
Spong, John **1991:3**
Stahl, Lesley **1997:1**
Stallings, George A., Jr. **1990:1**
Stallone, Sylvester **1994:2**
Starr, Kenneth **1998:3**
Steel, Dawn **1990:1**
    Obituary **1998:2**
Steele, Shelby **1991:2**
Steger, Will **1990:4**
Steinberg, Leigh **1987:3**
Steinbrenner, George **1991:1**
Steinem, Gloria **1996:2**
Stella, Frank **1996:2**
Stempel, Robert **1991:3**
Stephanopoulos, George **1994:3**
Sterling, Bruce **1995:4**
Stern, David **1991:4**
Stern, Howard **1988:2** **1993:3**
Stevens, Eileen **1987:3**
Stevenson, McLean
    Obituary **1996:3**

Stewart, Dave **1991:1**
Stewart, Jimmy
    Obituary **1997:4**
Stewart, Martha **1992:1**
Stewart, Potter
    Obituary **1986:1**
Stockton, John Houston **1997:3**
Stofflet, Ty
    Brief Entry **1987:1**
Stokes, Carl
    Obituary **1996:4**
Stone, I.F.
    Obituary **1990:1**
Stone, Irving
    Obituary **1990:2**
Stone, Oliver **1990:4**
Stone, Sharon **1993:4**
Stonesifer, Patty **1997:1**
Strait, George **1998:3**
Strange, Curtis **1988:4**
Strauss, Robert **1991:4**
Streep, Meryl **1990:2**
Streisand, Barbra **1992:2**
Stroh, Peter W. **1985:2**
Strug, Kerri **1997:3**
Studi, Wes **1994:3**
Styne, Jule
    Obituary **1995:1**
Suarez, Xavier
    Brief Entry **1986:2**
Sui, Anna **1995:1**
Sullivan, Louis **1990:4**
Sulzberger, Arthur O., Jr. **1998:3**
Sun Ra
    Obituary **1994:1**
Sununu, John **1989:2**
Susskind, David
    Obituary **1987:2**
Swaggart, Jimmy **1987:3**
Swayze, John Cameron
    Obituary **1996:1**
Swoopes, Sheryl **1998:2**
Szent-Gyoergyi, Albert
    Obituary **1987:2**
Tagliabue, Paul **1990:2**
Tan, Amy **1998:3**
Tandy, Jessica **1990:4**
    Obituary **1995:1**
Tannen, Deborah **1995:1**
Tanny, Vic
    Obituary **1985:3**
Tarantino, Quentin **1995:1**
Tarkenian, Jerry **1990:4**
Tartikoff, Brandon **1985:2**
    Obituary **1998:1**
Taylor, Lawrence **1987:3**
Taylor, Maxwell
    Obituary **1987:3**
Taylor, Paul **1992:3**
Taylor, Susan L. **1998:2**
Terry, Randall **1991:4**
Tesh, John **1996:3**
Testaverde, Vinny **1987:2**
Thalheimer, Richard
    Brief Entry **1988:3**
Tharp, Twyla **1992:4**
Thiebaud, Wayne **1991:1**
Thomas, Clarence **1992:2**
Thomas, Danny
    Obituary **1991:3**
Thomas, Dave **1986:2** **1993:2**
Thomas, Debi **1987:2**
Thomas, Frank **1994:3**
Thomas, Helen **1988:4**
Thomas, Isiah **1989:2**
Thomas, Michael Tilson **1990:3**
Thomas, Michel **1987:4**

York, Dick
  Obituary **1992:4**
Young, Coleman A.
  Obituary **1998:1**
Young, Steve **1995:2**
Youngblood, Johnny Ray **1994:1**
Youngman, Henny
  Obituary **1998:3**
Zahn, Paula **1992:3**
Zamboni, Frank J.
  Brief Entry **1986:4**
Zamora, Pedro
  Obituary **1995:2**
Zanker, Bill
  Brief Entry **1987:3**
Zanuck, Lili Fini **1994:2**
Zappa, Frank
  Obituary **1994:2**
Zech, Lando W.
  Brief Entry **1987:4**
Ziff, William B., Jr. **1986:4**
Zigler, Edward **1994:1**
Zinnemann, Fred
  Obituary **1997:3**
Zucker, Jeff **1993:3**
Zuckerman, Mortimer **1986:3**
Zwilich, Ellen **1990:1**

ANGOLAN
Savimbi, Jonas **1986:2** **1994:2**

ARGENTINE
Bocca, Julio **1995:3**
Herrera, Paloma **1996:2**
Maradona, Diego **1991:3**
Pelli, Cesar **1991:4**
Sabatini, Gabriela
  Brief Entry **1985:4**

AUSTRALIAN
Allen, Peter
  Obituary **1993:1**
Anderson, Judith
  Obituary **1992:3**
Bee Gees, The **1997:4**
Bond, Alan **1989:2**
Clavell, James
  Obituary **1995:1**
Gibb, Andy
  Obituary **1988:3**
Gibson, Mel **1990:1**
Helfgott, David **1997:2**
Hughes, Robert **1996:4**
Humphries, Barry **1993:1**
Hutchence, Michael
  Obituary **1998:1**
Kidman, Nicole **1992:4**
Murdoch, Rupert **1988:4**
Norman, Greg **1988:3**
Powter, Susan **1994:3**
Summers, Anne **1990:2**
Travers, P.L.
  Obituary **1996:4**
Tyler, Richard **1995:3**

AUSTRIAN
Brandauer, Klaus Maria **1987:3**
Drucker, Peter F. **1992:3**
Falco
  Brief Entry **1987:2**
Frankl, Viktor E.
  Obituary **1998:1**
Hrabal, Bohumil
  Obituary **1997:3**
Lorenz, Konrad
  Obituary **1989:3**

Porsche, Ferdinand
  Obituary **1998:4**
Puck, Wolfgang **1990:1**
von Karajan, Herbert
  Obituary **1989:4**
von Trapp, Maria
  Obituary **1987:3**

BANGLADESHI
Nasrin, Taslima **1995:1**

BELGIAN
Hepburn, Audrey
  Obituary **1993:2**
von Furstenberg, Diane **1994:2**

BOSNIAN
Izetbegovic, Alija **1996:4**

BRAZILIAN
Cardoso, Fernando Henrique **1996:4**
Castaneda, Carlos
  Obituary **1998:4**
Collor de Mello, Fernando **1992:4**
Fittipaldi, Emerson **1994:2**
Salgado, Sebastiao **1994:2**
Senna, Ayrton **1991:4**
  Obituary **1994:4**
Xuxa **1994:2**

BRITISH
Adamson, George
  Obituary **1990:2**
Altea, Rosemary **1996:3**
Amanpour, Christiane **1997:2**
Amis, Kingsley
  Obituary **1996:2**
Andrews, Julie **1996:1**
Ashcroft, Peggy
  Obituary **1992:1**
Baddeley, Hermione
  Obituary **1986:4**
Beckett, Wendy (Sister) **1998:3**
Bee Gees, The **1997:4**
Berners-Lee, Tim **1997:4**
Blair, Tony **1996:3**
Blair, Tony **1997:4**
Bonham Carter, Helena **1998:4**
Bowie, David **1998:2**
Branson, Richard **1987:1**
Brown, Tina **1992:1**
Burgess, Anthony
  Obituary **1994:2**
Bush, Kate **1994:3**
Carey, George **1992:3**
Charles, Prince of Wales **1995:3**
Chatwin, Bruce
  Obituary **1989:2**
Clapton, Eric **1993:3**
Cleese, John **1989:2**
Cook, Peter
  Obituary **1995:2**
Costello, Elvis **1994:4**
Crawford, Michael **1994:2**
Cummings, Sam **1986:3**
Cushing, Peter
  Obituary **1995:1**
Dalton, Timothy **1988:4**
Davison, Ian Hay **1986:1**
Day-Lewis, Daniel **1989:4** **1994:4**
Diana, Princess of Wales **1993:1**
  Obituary **1997:4**
Egan, John **1987:2**
Elliott, Denholm
  Obituary **1993:2**
Eno, Brian **1986:2**

Everything But The Girl **1996:4**
Faldo, Nick **1993:3**
Ferguson, Sarah **1990:3**
Fiennes, Ralph **1996:2**
Fiennes, Ranulph **1990:3**
Fonteyn, Margot
  Obituary **1991:3**
Gift, Roland **1990:2**
Goodall, Jane **1991:1**
Grant, Hugh **1995:3**
Greene, Graham
  Obituary **1991:4**
Hamilton, Hamish
  Obituary **1988:4**
Harrison, Rex
  Obituary **1990:4**
Harvey, Polly Jean **1995:4**
Hawking, Stephen W. **1990:1**
Headroom, Max **1986:4**
Hebard, Caroline **1998:2**
Hill, Benny
  Obituary **1992:3**
Hockney, David **1988:3**
Hoskins, Bob **1989:1**
Hounsfield, Godfrey **1989:2**
Howard, Trevor
  Obituary **1988:2**
Humphry, Derek **1992:2**
Ireland, Jill
  Obituary **1990:4**
Irons, Jeremy **1991:4**
John, Elton **1995:4**
Knopfler, Mark **1986:2**
Laing, R.D.
  Obituary **1990:1**
Lane, Ronnie
  Obituary **1997:4**
Lawrence, Ruth
  Brief Entry **1986:3**
Leach, Penelope **1992:4**
Leach, Robin
  Brief Entry **1985:4**
Leakey, Mary Douglas
  Obituary **1997:2**
Lennox, Annie **1985:4** **1996:4**
LeVay, Simon **1992:2**
Livingstone, Ken **1988:3**
Lloyd Webber, Andrew **1989:1**
Lupino, Ida
  Obituary **1996:1**
Lyne, Adrian **1997:2**
Macmillan, Harold
  Obituary **1987:2**
MacMillan, Kenneth
  Obituary **1993:2**
Major, John **1991:2**
Maxwell, Robert **1990:1**
McKellen, Ian **1994:1**
Mercury, Freddie
  Obituary **1992:2**
Michael, George **1989:2**
Milne, Christopher Robin
  Obituary **1996:4**
Moore, Henry
  Obituary **1986:4**
Moss, Kate **1995:3**
Newkirk, Ingrid **1992:3**
Newton-John, Olivia **1998:4**
Norrington, Roger **1989:4**
Oasis **1996:3**
Oldman, Gary **1998:1**
Olivier, Laurence
  Obituary **1989:4**
Osborne, John
  Obituary **1995:2**
Park, Nick **1997:3**

Singer, Isaac Bashevis
  Obituary **1992:1**
Walesa, Lech **1991:2**

PUERTO RICAN
Ferrer, Jose
  Obituary **1992:3**
Julia, Raul
  Obituary **1995:1**
Novello, Antonia **1991:2**

ROMANIAN
Ceausescu, Nicolae
  Obituary **1990:2**
Codrescu, André **1997:3**

RUSSIAN
Brodsky, Joseph
  Obituary **1996:3**
Gordeeva, Ekaterina **1996:4**
Grinkov, Sergei
  Obituary **1996:2**
Kasparov, Garry **1997:4**
Konstantinov, Vladimir **1997:4**
Lebed, Alexander **1997:1**
Schneerson, Menachem Mendel
1992:4
  Obituary **1994:4**

SALVADORAN
Duarte, Jose Napoleon
  Obituary **1990:3**

SCOTTISH
Blair, Tony **1997:4**
Connery, Sean **1990:4**
McGregor, Ewan **1998:2**

SERBIAN
Karadzic, Radovan **1995:3**
Milosevic, Slobodan **1993:2**

SOUTH AFRICAN
Blackburn, Molly
  Obituary **1985:4**
Buthelezi, Mangosuthu Gatsha
1989:3
de Klerk, F.W. **1990:1**
Duncan, Sheena
  Brief Entry **1987:1**
Fugard, Athol **1992:3**
Hani, Chris
  Obituary **1993:4**
Makeba, Miriam **1989:2**
Mandela, Nelson **1990:3**
Mandela, Winnie **1989:3**
Paton, Alan
  Obituary **1988:3**
Ramaphosa, Cyril **1988:2**
Slovo, Joe **1989:2**

Suzman, Helen **1989:3**
Tambo, Oliver **1991:3**
Treurnicht, Andries **1992:2**

SOVIET
Asimov, Isaac
  Obituary **1992:3**
Chernenko, Konstantin
  Obituary **1985:1**
Dubinin, Yuri **1987:4**
Dzhanibekov, Vladimir **1988:1**
Erte
  Obituary **1990:4**
Federov, Sergei **1995:1**
Godunov, Alexander
  Obituary **1995:4**
Gorbachev, Mikhail **1985:2**
Grebenshikov, Boris **1990:1**
Gromyko, Andrei
  Obituary **1990:2**
Molotov, Vyacheslav Mikhailovich
  Obituary **1987:1**
Nureyev, Rudolf
  Obituary **1993:2**
Sakharov, Andrei Dmitrievich
  Obituary **1990:2**
Smirnoff, Yakov **1987:2**
Vidov, Oleg **1987:4**
Yeltsin, Boris **1991:1**
Zhirinovsky, Vladimir **1994:2**

SPANISH
Banderas, Antonio **1996:2**
Carreras, Jose **1995:2**
Dali, Salvador
  Obituary **1989:2**
de Pinies, Jamie
  Brief Entry **1986:3**
Domingo, Placido **1993:2**
Juan Carlos I **1993:1**
Lopez de Arriortua, Jose Ignacio **1993:4**
Miro, Joan
  Obituary **1985:1**
Moneo, Jose Rafael **1996:4**
Montoya, Carlos
  Obituary **1993:4**
Samaranch, Juan Antonio **1986:2**
Segovia, Andrés
  Obituary **1987:3**

SRI LANKAN
Ondaatje, Philip Michael **1997:3**

SUDANESE
Turabi, Hassan **1995:4**

SWEDISH
Cardigans, The **1997:4**
Garbo, Greta
  Obituary **1990:3**

Lindbergh, Pelle
  Obituary **1985:4**
Olin, Lena **1991:2**
Palme, Olof
  Obituary **1986:2**
Renvall, Johan
  Brief Entry **1987:4**

SWISS
Frank, Robert **1995:2**
Vollenweider, Andreas **1985:2**

SYRIAN
Assad, Hafez al- **1992:1**
Assad, Rifaat **1986:3**

TAHITIAN
Brando, Cheyenne
  Obituary **1995:4**

TAIWANESE
Ho, David **1997:2**

TIBETAN
Dalai Lama **1989:1**

UKRAINE
Baiul, Oksana **1995:3**

VENEZUELAN
Herrera, Carolina **1997:1**
Perez, Carlos Andre **1990:2**

VIETNAMESE
Le Duan
  Obituary **1986:4**
Le Duc Tho
  Obituary **1991:1**

WELSH
Dahl, Roald
  Obituary **1991:2**
Hopkins, Anthony **1992:4**
Jones, Tom **1993:4**

YUGOSLAV
Filipovic, Zlata **1994:4**
Pogorelich, Ivo **1986:4**
Seles, Monica **1991:3**

ZAIREAN
Mobutu Sese Seko **1993:4**
  Obituary **1998:1**

ZAMBIAN
Chiluba, Frederick **1992:3**

ZIMBABWEAN
Mugabe, Robert **1988:4**

1998 Occupation Index

This index lists all newsmakers alphabetically by their occupations or fields of primary activity. Indexes in softbound issues allow access to the current year's entries; indexes in annual hardbound volumes are cumulative, covering the entire *Newsmakers* series.

Listee names are followed by a year and issue number; thus **1996**:3 indicates that an entry on that individual appears in both 1996, Issue 3 and the 1996 cumulation. For access to newsmakers appearing earlier than the current softbound issue, see the previous year's cumulation.

Smith, Roger **1990:3**
Spector, Phil **1989:1**
Steel, Dawn **1990:1**
  Obituary **1998:2**
Steinberg, Leigh **1987:3**
Steinbrenner, George **1991:1**
Stempel, Robert **1991:3**
Stern, David **1991:4**
Stewart, Martha **1992:1**
Stonesifer, Patty **1997:1**
Stroh, Peter W. **1985:2**
Strong, Maurice **1993:1**
Sullivan, Andrew **1996:1**
Summers, Anne **1990:2**
Tagliabue, Paul **1990:2**
Tanny, Vic
  Obituary **1985:3**
Tartikoff, Brandon **1985:2**
  Obituary **1998:1**
Thalheimer, Richard
  Brief Entry **1988:3**
Thomas, Dave **1986:2** **1993:2**
Thomas, Michel **1987:4**
Tilberis, Elizabeth **1994:3**
Tisch, Laurence A. **1988:2**
Tompkins, Susie
  Brief Entry **1987:2**
Toyoda, Eiji **1985:2**
Traub, Marvin
  Brief Entry **1987:3**
Treybig, James G. **1988:3**
Trotman, Alex **1995:4**
Troutt, Kenny A. **1998:1**
Trump, Donald **1989:2**
Trump, Ivana **1995:2**
Turner, Ted **1989:1**
Tyler, Richard **1995:3**
Tyson, Don **1995:3**
Upshaw, Gene **1988:1**
Vagelos, P. Roy **1989:4**
Veeck, Bill
  Obituary **1986:1**
Versace, Gianni
  Brief Entry **1988:1**
  Obituary **1998:2**
Vinton, Will
  Brief Entry **1988:1**
von Furstenberg, Diane **1994:2**
Wachner, Linda **1988:3** **1997:2**
Waitt, Ted **1997:4**
Waldron, Hicks B. **1987:3**
Walgreen, Charles III
  Brief Entry **1987:4**
Walton, Sam **1986:2**
  Obituary **1993:1**
Wang, An **1986:1**
  Obituary **1990:3**
Weill, Sandy **1990:4**
Weintraub, Jerry **1986:1**
Welch, Jack **1993:3**
Westwood, Vivienne **1998:3**
Whittle, Christopher **1989:3**
Williams, Edward Bennett
  Obituary **1988:4**
Williams, Lynn **1986:4**
Wilson, Jerry
  Brief Entry **1986:2**
Wilson, Peter C.
  Obituary **1985:2**
Wintour, Anna **1990:4**
Wolf, Stephen M. **1989:3**
Woodruff, Robert Winship
  Obituary **1985:1**
Wynn, Stephen A. **1994:3**
Yamamoto, Kenichi **1989:1**
Yetnikoff, Walter **1988:1**

Zamboni, Frank J.
  Brief Entry **1986:4**
Zanker, Bill
  Brief Entry **1987:3**
Ziff, William B., Jr. **1986:4**
Zuckerman, Mortimer **1986:3**

DANCE

Abdul, Paula **1990:3**
Acosta, Carlos **1997:4**
Ailey, Alvin **1989:2**
  Obituary **1990:2**
Allen, Debbie **1998:2**
Astaire, Fred
  Obituary **1987:4**
Baryshnikov, Mikhail Nikolaevich
  1997:3
Bennett, Michael
  Obituary **1988:1**
Bissell, Patrick
  Obituary **1988:2**
Bocca, Julio **1995:3**
Campbell, Neve **1998:2**
Cunningham, Merce **1998:1**
Davis, Sammy, Jr.
  Obituary **1990:4**
Dean, Laura **1989:4**
de Mille, Agnes
  Obituary **1994:2**
Englund, Richard
  Obituary **1991:3**
Farrell, Suzanne **1996:3**
Feld, Eliot **1996:1**
Fenley, Molissa **1988:3**
Ferri, Alessandra **1987:2**
Flatley, Michael **1997:3**
Fonteyn, Margot
  Obituary **1991:3**
Forsythe, William **1993:2**
Fosse, Bob
  Obituary **1988:1**
Garr, Teri **1988:4**
Glover, Savion **1997:1**
Godunov, Alexander
  Obituary **1995:4**
Graham, Martha
  Obituary **1991:4**
Gregory, Cynthia **1990:2**
Guillem, Sylvie **1988:2**
Herrera, Paloma **1996:2**
Hines, Gregory **1992:4**
Jackson, Janet **1990:4**
Jamison, Judith **1990:3**
Joffrey, Robert
  Obituary **1988:3**
Jones, Bill T. **1991:4**
Kaye, Nora
  Obituary **1987:4**
Keeler, Ruby
  Obituary **1993:4**
Kelly, Gene
  Obituary **1996:3**
Kistler, Darci **1993:1**
Lander, Toni
  Obituary **1985:4**
MacMillan, Kenneth
  Obituary **1993:2**
Madonna **1985:2**
Mitchell, Arthur **1995:1**
Morris, Mark **1991:1**
Murray, Arthur
  Obituary **1991:3**
North, Alex **1986:3**
Nureyev, Rudolf
  Obituary **1993:2**
Parsons, David **1993:4**

Perez, Rosie **1994:2**
Prowse, Juliet
  Obituary **1997:1**
Rauschenberg, Robert **1991:2**
Renvall, Johan
  Brief Entry **1987:4**
Rogers, Ginger
  Obituary **1995:4**
Takei, Kei **1990:2**
Taylor, Paul **1992:3**
Tharp, Twyla **1992:4**
Tudor, Antony
  Obituary **1987:4**
Tune, Tommy **1994:2**
Verdi-Fletcher, Mary **1998:2**

EDUCATION

Abramson, Lyn **1986:3**
Alexander, Lamar **1991:2**
Bakker, Robert T. **1991:3**
Bayley, Corrine
  Brief Entry **1986:4**
Billington, James **1990:3**
Botstein, Leon **1985:3**
Bush, Millie **1992:1**
Campbell, Bebe Moore **1996:2**
Casper, Gerhard **1993:1**
Cavazos, Lauro F. **1989:2**
Cheek, James Edward
  Brief Entry **1987:1**
Cheney, Lynne V. **1990:4**
Clements, George **1985:1**
Cole, Johnetta B. **1994:3**
Coles, Robert **1995:1**
Commager, Henry Steele
  Obituary **1998:3**
Curran, Charles E. **1989:2**
Davis, Angela **1998:3**
Deming, W. Edwards **1992:2**
  Obituary **1994:2**
Dershowitz, Alan **1992:1**
Dove, Rita **1994:3**
Drucker, Peter F. **1992:3**
Edelman, Marian Wright **1990:4**
Edwards, Harry **1989:4**
Etzioni, Amitai **1994:3**
Feldman, Sandra **1987:3**
Fernandez, Joseph **1991:3**
Fox, Matthew **1992:2**
Fulbright, J. William
  Obituary **1995:3**
Futrell, Mary Hatwood **1986:1**
Futter, Ellen V. **1995:1**
Ghali, Boutros Boutros **1992:3**
Giamatti, A. Bartlett **1988:4**
  Obituary **1990:1**
Goldhaber, Fred
  Brief Entry **1986:3**
Gray, Hanna **1992:4**
Green, Richard R. **1988:3**
Gregorian, Vartan **1990:3**
Gund, Agnes **1993:2**
Hackney, Sheldon **1995:1**
Hair, Jay D. **1994:3**
Hayakawa, Samuel Ichiye
  Obituary **1992:3**
Healy, Bernadine **1993:1**
Healy, Timothy S. **1990:2**
Heaney, Seamus **1996:2**
Heller, Walter
  Obituary **1987:4**
Hill, Anita **1994:1**
Hillegass, Clifton Keith **1989:4**
Hunter, Madeline **1991:2**
Janzen, Daniel H. **1988:4**
Jordan, King **1990:1**

Sharkey, Ray
  Obituary 1994:1
Shawn, Dick
  Obituary 1987:3
Sheedy, Ally 1989:1
Shepard, Sam 1996:4
Shields, Brooke 1996:3
Shore, Dinah
  Obituary 1994:3
Short, Martin 1986:1
Shue, Andrew 1994:4
Silverman, Jonathan 1997:2
Silvers, Phil
  Obituary 1985:4
Silverstone, Alicia 1997:4
Sinatra, Frank
  Obituary 1998:4
Singleton, John 1994:3
Sinise, Gary 1996:1
Slater, Christian 1994:1
Smirnoff, Yakov 1987:2
Smith, Will 1997:2
Smits, Jimmy 1990:1
Snipes, Wesley 1993:1
Sondheim, Stephen 1994:4
Sorvino, Mira 1996:3
Southern, Terry
  Obituary 1996:2
Spacey, Kevin 1996:4
Spader, James 1991:2
Spheeris, Penelope 1989:2
Spielberg, Steven 1993:4 1997:4
Staller, Ilona 1988:3
Stallone, Sylvester 1994:2
Steel, Dawn 1990:1
  Obituary 1998:2
Stevenson, McLean
  Obituary 1996:3
Stewart, Jimmy
  Obituary 1997:4
Stewart, Patrick 1996:1
Sting 1991:4
Stone, Oliver 1990:4
Stone, Sharon 1993:4
Stoppard, Tom 1995:4
Streep, Meryl 1990:2
Streisand, Barbra 1992:2
Studi, Wes 1994:3
Styne, Jule
  Obituary 1995:1
Susskind, David
  Obituary 1987:2
Tanaka, Tomoyuki
  Obituary 1997:3
Tandy, Jessica 1990:4
  Obituary 1995:1
Tarantino, Quentin 1995:1
Taylor, Elizabeth 1993:3
Thiebaud, Wayne 1991:1
Thompson, Emma 1993:2
Thompson, Fred 1998:2
Thornton, Billy Bob 1997:4
Thurman, Uma 1994:2
Tilly, Jennifer 1997:2
Tomei, Marisa 1995:2
Travolta, John 1995:2
Tucker, Forrest
  Obituary 1987:1
Turner, Janine 1993:2
Turner, Kathleen 1985:3
Turner, Lana
  Obituary 1996:1
Tyler, Liv 1997:2
Ullman, Tracey 1988:3
Urich, Robert 1988:1
Vanilla Ice 1991:3
Van Sant, Gus 1992:2

Vidal, Gore 1996:2
Vidov, Oleg 1987:4
Villechaize, Herve
  Obituary 1994:1
Vincent, Fay 1990:2
Walker, Nancy
  Obituary 1992:3
Wallis, Hal
  Obituary 1987:1
Warhol, Andy
  Obituary 1987:2
Washington, Denzel 1993:2
Waters, John 1988:3
Wayans, Damon 1998:4
Wayans, Keenen Ivory 1991:1
Wayne, David
  Obituary 1995:3
Weaver, Sigourney 1988:3
Wegman, William 1991:1
Weintraub, Jerry 1986:1
Whitaker, Forest 1996:2
Wiest, Dianne 1995:2
Williams, Robin 1988:4
Willis, Bruce 1986:4
Winfrey, Oprah 1986:4 1997:3
Winger, Debra 1994:3
Wolfman Jack
  Obituary 1996:1
Wong, B.D. 1998:1
Woo, John 1994:2
Woods, James 1988:3
Wyle, Noah 1997:3
Wynn, Keenan
  Obituary 1987:1
Zanuck, Lili Fini 1994:2
Zeffirelli, Franco 1991:3

LAW

Abzug, Bella 1998:2
Achtenberg, Roberta 1993:4
Allred, Gloria 1985:2
Angelos, Peter 1995:4
Archer, Dennis 1994:4
Astorga, Nora 1988:2
Babbitt, Bruce 1994:1
Bailey, F. Lee 1995:4
Baker, James A. III 1991:2
Bikoff, James L.
  Brief Entry 1986:2
Brennan, William
  Obituary 1997:4
Breyer, Stephen Gerald 1994:4
  1997:2
Brown, Willie 1996:4
Brown, Willie L. 1985:2
Burger, Warren E.
  Obituary 1995:4
Burnison, Chantal Simone 1988:3
Campbell, Kim 1993:4
Cantrell, Ed
  Brief Entry 1985:3
Casey, William
  Obituary 1987:3
Casper, Gerhard 1993:1
Clark, Marcia 1995:1
Clinton, Bill 1992:1
Clinton, Hillary Rodham 1993:2
Cochran, Johnnie 1996:1
Colby, William E.
  Obituary 1996:4
Cuomo, Mario 1992:2
Darden, Christopher 1996:4
Dees, Morris 1992:1
Dershowitz, Alan 1992:1
Deutch, John 1996:4
Dole, Elizabeth Hanford 1990:1
Dukakis, Michael 1988:3

Eagleson, Alan 1987:4
Ervin, Sam
  Obituary 1985:2
Estrich, Susan 1989:1
Fairstein, Linda 1991:1
Fehr, Donald 1987:2
Florio, James J. 1991:2
Foster, Vincent
  Obituary 1994:1
France, Johnny
  Brief Entry 1987:1
Freeh, Louis J. 1994:2
Fulbright, J. William
  Obituary 1995:3
Furman, Rosemary
  Brief Entry 1986:4
Garrison, Jim
  Obituary 1993:2
Ginsburg, Ruth Bader 1993:4
Giuliani, Rudolph 1994:2
Glasser, Ira 1989:1
Grisham, John 1994:4
Harvard, Beverly 1995:2
Hayes, Robert M. 1986:3
Hill, Anita 1994:1
Hills, Carla 1990:3
Hirschhorn, Joel
  Brief Entry 1986:1
Hyatt, Joel 1985:3
Ireland, Patricia 1992:2
Ito, Lance 1995:3
Janklow, Morton 1989:3
Kennedy, John F., Jr. 1990:1
Kennedy, Weldon 1997:3
Kunstler, William 1992:3
Kunstler, William
  Obituary 1996:1
Kurzban, Ira 1987:2
Lee, Henry C. 1997:1
Lee, Martin 1998:2
Lewis, Loida Nicolas 1998:3
Lewis, Reginald F. 1988:4
  Obituary 1993:3
Lightner, Candy 1985:1
Liman, Arthur 1989:4
Lipsig, Harry H. 1985:1
Lipton, Martin 1987:3
MacKinnon, Catharine 1993:2
Marshall, Thurgood
  Obituary 1993:3
McCloskey, James 1993:1
Mitchell, George J. 1989:3
Mitchell, John
  Obituary 1989:2
Mitchelson, Marvin 1989:2
Morrison, Trudi
  Brief Entry 1986:2
Nader, Ralph 1989:4
Napolitano, Janet 1997:1
Neal, James Foster 1986:2
O'Connor, Sandra Day 1991:1
O'Leary, Hazel 1993:4
O'Steen, Van
  Brief Entry 1986:3
Panetta, Leon 1995:1
Pirro, Jeanine 1998:2
Puccio, Thomas P. 1986:4
Quayle, Dan 1989:2
Raines, Franklin 1997:4
Ramaphosa, Cyril 1988:2
Ramo, Roberta Cooper 1996:1
Reno, Janet 1993:3
Rothwax, Harold 1996:3
Scalia, Antonin 1988:2
Schily, Otto
  Brief Entry 1987:4
Sheehan, Daniel P. 1989:1

Sirica, John
  Obituary   **1993:2**
Skinner, Sam   **1992:3**
Slater, Rodney E.   **1997:4**
Slotnick, Barry
  Brief Entry   **1987:4**
Souter, David   **1991:3**
Starr, Kenneth   **1998:3**
Steinberg, Leigh   **1987:3**
Stern, David   **1991:4**
Stewart, Potter
  Obituary   **1986:1**
Strauss, Robert   **1991:4**
Tagliabue, Paul   **1990:2**
Thomas, Clarence   **1992:2**
Thompson, Fred   **1998:2**
Tribe, Laurence H.   **1988:1**
Vincent, Fay   **1990:2**
Violet, Arlene   **1985:3**
Wapner, Joseph A.   **1987:1**
Watson, Elizabeth   **1991:2**
Williams, Edward Bennett
  Obituary   **1988:4**
Williams, Willie L.   **1993:1**
Wilson, Bertha
  Brief Entry   **1986:1**

MUSIC
  Abdul, Paula   **1990:3**
  Ackerman, Will   **1987:4**
  Acuff, Roy
    Obituary   **1993:2**
  Albert, Stephen   **1986:1**
  Allen, Peter
    Obituary   **1993:1**
  Amos, Tori   **1995:1**
  Anderson, Marion
    Obituary   **1993:4**
  Andrews, Julie   **1996:1**
  Andrews, Maxene
    Obituary   **1996:2**
  Arlen, Harold
    Obituary   **1986:3**
  Arnaz, Desi
    Obituary   **1987:1**
  Arrau, Claudio
    Obituary   **1992:1**
  Arrested Development   **1994:2**
  Astaire, Fred
    Obituary   **1987:4**
  Baez, Joan   **1998:3**
  Bailey, Pearl
    Obituary   **1991:1**
  Baker, Anita   **1987:4**
  Bartoli, Cecilia   **1994:1**
  Basie, Count
    Obituary   **1985:1**
  Battle, Kathleen   **1998:1**
  Bee Gees, The   **1997:4**
  Benatar, Pat   **1986:1**
  Bennett, Tony   **1994:4**
  Berlin, Irving
    Obituary   **1990:1**
  Bernhard, Sandra   **1989:4**
  Bernstein, Leonard
    Obituary   **1991:1**
  Bjork   **1996:1**
  Blades, Ruben   **1998:2**
  Blakey, Art
    Obituary   **1991:1**
  Blige, Mary J.   **1995:3**
  Bolton, Michael   **1993:2**
  Bon Jovi, Jon   **1987:4**
  Bono   **1988:4**
  Bono, Sonny   **1992:2**
    Obituary   **1998:2**
  Botstein, Leon   **1985:3**

Bowie, David   **1998:2**
Boyz II Men   **1995:1**
Brandy   **1996:4**
Branson, Richard   **1987:1**
Braxton, Toni   **1994:3**
Brooks, Garth   **1992:1**
Brown, James   **1991:4**
Buckley, Jeff
  Obituary   **1997:4**
Bush, Kate   **1994:3**
Butterfield, Paul
  Obituary   **1987:3**
Cage, John
  Obituary   **1993:1**
Calloway, Cab
  Obituary   **1995:2**
Cardigans, The   **1997:4**
Carey, Mariah   **1991:3**
Carlisle, Belinda   **1989:3**
Carpenter, Mary-Chapin   **1994:1**
Carreras, Jose   **1995:2**
Carter, Ron   **1987:3**
Cash, Johnny   **1995:3**
Cerovsek, Corey
  Brief Entry   **1987:4**
Chapman, Tracy   **1989:2**
Cheatham, Adolphus "Doc"
  Obituary   **1997:4**
Cher   **1993:1**
Clapton, Eric   **1993:3**
Clarke, Stanley   **1985:4**
Cleveland, James
  Obituary   **1991:3**
Cliburn, Van   **1995:1**
Cobain, Kurt
  Obituary   **1994:3**
Cole, Natalie   **1992:4**
Collins, Albert
  Obituary   **1994:2**
Combs, Sean "Puffy"   **1998:4**
Connick, Harry, Jr.   **1991:1**
Coolio   **1996:4**
Copland, Aaron
  Obituary   **1991:2**
Coppola, Carmine
  Obituary   **1991:4**
Corea, Chick   **1986:3**
Costello, Elvis   **1994:4**
Crawford, Michael   **1994:2**
Cray, Robert   **1988:2**
Crothers, Scatman
  Obituary   **1987:1**
Crow, Sheryl   **1995:2**
Cugat, Xavier
  Obituary   **1991:2**
Cyrus, Billy Ray   **1993:1**
D'Arby, Terence Trent   **1988:4**
Davis, Miles
  Obituary   **1992:2**
Davis, Sammy, Jr.
  Obituary   **1990:4**
Day, Dennis
  Obituary   **1988:4**
Dean, Laura   **1989:4**
Denver, John
  Obituary   **1998:1**
de Passe, Suzanne   **1990:4**
DiFranco, Ani   **1997:1**
Di Meola, Al   **1986:4**
Dimitrova, Ghena   **1987:1**
Dion, Celine   **1995:3**
Dr. Demento   **1986:1**
Dr. Dre   **1994:3**
Dolenz, Micky   **1986:4**
Domingo, Placido   **1993:2**
Dorati, Antal
  Obituary   **1989:2**

Dorsey, Thomas A.
  Obituary   **1993:3**
Duncan, Todd
  Obituary   **1998:3**
Dylan, Bob   **1998:1**
Eazy-E
  Obituary   **1995:3**
Eckstine, Billy
  Obituary   **1993:4**
Edmonds, Kenneth "Babyface"
  1995:3
Eldridge, Roy
  Obituary   **1989:3**
Eno, Brian   **1986:2**
En Vogue   **1994:1**
Enya   **1992:3**
Ertegun, Ahmet   **1986:3**
Esquivel, Juan   **1996:2**
Estefan, Gloria   **1991:4**
Etheridge, Melissa   **1995:4**
Everything But The Girl   **1996:4**
Falco
  Brief Entry   **1987:2**
Farrell, Perry   **1992:2**
Fender, Leo
  Obituary   **1992:1**
Fitzgerald, Ella
  Obituary   **1996:4**
Ford, Tennessee Ernie
  Obituary   **1992:2**
Foster, David   **1988:2**
Franklin, Aretha   **1998:3**
Franklin, Melvin
  Obituary   **1995:3**
Garcia, Jerry   **1988:3**
  Obituary   **1996:1**
Geffen, David   **1985:3**   **1997:3**
Geldof, Bob   **1985:3**
Getz, Stan
  Obituary   **1991:4**
Gibb, Andy
  Obituary   **1988:3**
Gifford, Kathie Lee   **1992:2**
Gift, Roland   **1990:2**
Gill, Vince   **1995:2**
Gillespie, Dizzy
  Obituary   **1993:2**
Glass, Philip   **1991:4**
Goodman, Benny
  Obituary   **1986:3**
Goody, Sam
  Obituary   **1992:1**
Gordon, Dexter   **1987:1**
  Obituary   **1990:4**
Gore, Tipper   **1985:4**
Graham, Bill   **1986:4**
  Obituary   **1992:2**
Grant, Amy   **1985:4**
Grappelli, Stephane
  Obituary   **1998:1**
Grebenshikov, Boris   **1990:1**
Green Day   **1995:4**
Grusin, Dave
  Brief Entry   **1987:2**
Guccione, Bob, Jr.   **1991:4**
Hammer, Jan   **1987:3**
Hammer, M. C.   **1991:2**
Hammond, John
  Obituary   **1988:2**
Hancock, Herbie   **1985:1**
Harris, Emmylou   **1991:3**
Harry, Deborah   **1990:1**
Hart, Mary
  Brief Entry   **1988:1**
Hart, Mickey   **1991:2**
Harvey, Polly Jean   **1995:4**
Hayes, Isaac   **1998:4**

Strait, George **1998:3**
Streisand, Barbra **1992:2**
Styne, Jule
    Obituary **1995:1**
Sun Ra
    Obituary **1994:1**
Suzuki, Sin'ichi
    Obituary **1998:3**
Tesh, John **1996:3**
Thomas, Michael Tilson **1990:3**
Tiffany **1989:1**
TLC **1996:1**
Tone-Loc **1990:3**
Tosh, Peter
    Obituary **1988:2**
Travis, Randy **1988:4**
Tritt, Travis **1995:1**
Tune, Tommy **1994:2**
Twain, Shania **1996:3**
Twitty, Conway
    Obituary **1994:1**
Tyner, Rob
    Obituary **1992:2**
Uchida, Mitsuko **1989:3**
Ullman, Tracey **1988:3**
Upshaw, Dawn **1991:2**
Valente, Benita **1985:3**
Van Halen, Edward **1985:2**
Vanilla Ice **1991:3**
Vaughan, Sarah
    Obituary **1990:3**
Vaughan, Stevie Ray
    Obituary **1991:1**
Vega, Suzanne **1988:1**
Vollenweider, Andreas **1985:2**
von Karajan, Herbert
    Obituary **1989:4**
von Trapp, Maria
    Obituary **1987:3**
Walker, Junior
    Obituary **1996:2**
Washington, Grover, Jr. **1989:1**
Weintraub, Jerry **1986:1**
Wells, Mary
    Obituary **1993:1**
West, Dottie
    Obituary **1992:2**
Willis, Bruce **1986:4**
Wilson, Brian **1996:1**
Wilson, Carl
    Obituary **1998:2**
Wilson, Cassandra **1996:3**
Winston, George **1987:1**
Winter, Paul **1990:2**
Wynette, Tammy
    Obituary **1998:3**
Wynonna **1993:3**
Yankovic, "Weird Al" **1985:4**
Yoakam, Dwight **1992:4**
Young, Neil **1991:2**
Zappa, Frank
    Obituary **1994:2**
Zinnemann, Fred
    Obituary **1997:3**
Zwilich, Ellen **1990:1**

POLITICS AND GOVERNMENT—FOREIGN

Abacha, Sani **1996:3**
Adams, Gerald **1994:1**
Akihito, Emperor of Japan **1990:1**
Albright, Madeleine **1994:3**
Aquino, Corazon **1986:2**
Arafat, Yasser **1989:3** **1997:3**
Arens, Moshe **1985:1**
Arias Sanchez, Oscar **1989:3**
Aristide, Jean-Bertrand **1991:3**

Assad, Hafez al- **1992:1**
Assad, Rifaat **1986:3**
Astorga, Nora **1988:2**
Babangida, Ibrahim Badamosi **1992:4**
Banda, Hastings **1994:3**
Barbie, Klaus
    Obituary **1992:2**
Begin, Menachem
    Obituary **1992:3**
Berlusconi, Silvio **1994:4**
Berri, Nabih **1985:2**
Bhutto, Benazir **1989:4**
Blair, Tony **1996:3**
Blair, Tony **1997:4**
Bolkiah, Sultan Muda Hassanal **1985:4**
Bourassa, Robert
    Obituary **1997:1**
Brandt, Willy
    Obituary **1993:2**
Buthelezi, Mangosuthu Gatsha **1989:3**
Campbell, Kim **1993:4**
Cardoso, Fernando Henrique **1996:4**
Castro, Fidel **1991:4**
Ceausescu, Nicolae
    Obituary **1990:2**
Cedras, Raoul **1994:4**
Chernenko, Konstantin
    Obituary **1985:1**
Chiluba, Frederick **1992:3**
Chirac, Jacques **1995:4**
Chissano, Joaquim **1987:4**
Chretien, Jean **1990:4** **1997:2**
Collor de Mello, Fernando **1992:4**
Colosio, Luis Donaldo **1994:3**
Copps, Sheila **1986:4**
Cresson, Edith **1992:1**
Cruz, Arturo **1985:1**
Dalai Lama **1989:1**
de Klerk, F.W. **1990:1**
Delors, Jacques **1990:2**
Deng Xiaoping **1995:1**
    Obituary **1997:3**
de Pinies, Jamie
    Brief Entry **1986:3**
Dhlakama, Afonso **1993:3**
Doe, Samuel
    Obituary **1991:1**
Doi, Takako
    Brief Entry **1987:4**
Duarte, Jose Napoleon
    Obituary **1990:3**
Dubinin, Yuri **1987:4**
Ferguson, Sarah **1990:3**
Finnbogadóttir, Vigdís
    Brief Entry **1986:2**
Freij, Elias **1986:4**
Fujimori, Alberto **1992:4**
Galvin, Martin
    Brief Entry **1985:3**
Gandhi, Indira
    Obituary **1985:1**
Gandhi, Rajiv
    Obituary **1991:4**
Garneau, Marc **1985:1**
Ghali, Boutros Boutros **1992:3**
Gorbachev, Mikhail **1985:2**
Gowda, H. D. Deve **1997:1**
Gromyko, Andrei
    Obituary **1990:2**
Habash, George **1986:1**
Hani, Chris
    Obituary **1993:4**
Harriman, Pamela **1994:4**
Harris, Michael Deane **1997:2**

Havel, Vaclav **1990:3**
Herzog, Chaim
    Obituary **1997:3**
Hess, Rudolph
    Obituary **1988:1**
Hirohito, Emperor of Japan
    Obituary **1989:2**
Honecker, Erich
    Obituary **1994:4**
Hosokawa, Morihiro **1994:1**
Hume, John **1987:1**
Hussein, Saddam **1991:1**
Husseini, Faisal **1998:4**
Hussein I, King **1997:3**
Hu Yaobang
    Obituary **1989:4**
Izetbegovic, Alija **1996:4**
Jiang Quing
    Obituary **1992:1**
Jiang Zemin **1996:1**
Johnson, Pierre Marc **1985:4**
Juan Carlos I **1993:1**
Jumblatt, Walid **1987:4**
Juneau, Pierre **1988:3**
Kabila, Laurent **1998:1**
Kamel, Hussein **1996:1**
Karadzic, Radovan **1995:3**
Kekkonen, Urho
    Obituary **1986:4**
Khatami, Mohammed **1997:4**
Khomeini, Ayatollah Ruhollah
    Obituary **1989:4**
Kim Dae Jung **1998:3**
Kim Il Sung
    Obituary **1994:4**
Kim Jong Il **1995:2**
Kohl, Helmut **1994:1**
Lalonde, Marc **1985:1**
Landsbergis, Vytautas **1991:3**
Lebed, Alexander **1997:1**
Le Duan
    Obituary **1986:4**
Le Duc Tho
    Obituary **1991:1**
Lee, Martin **1998:2**
Lévesque, René
    Obituary **1988:1**
Levy, David **1987:2**
Lewis, Stephen **1987:2**
Livingstone, Ken **1988:3**
Lon Nol
    Obituary **1986:1**
Machel, Samora
    Obituary **1987:1**
Macmillan, Harold
    Obituary **1987:2**
Major, John **1991:2**
Mandela, Nelson **1990:3**
Mandela, Winnie **1989:3**
Marcos, Ferdinand
    Obituary **1990:1**
Masako, Crown Princess **1993:4**
Mas Canosa, Jorge
    Obituary **1998:2**
McGuinness, Martin **1985:4**
McLaughlin, Audrey **1990:3**
Milosevic, Slobodan **1993:2**
Mitterrand, Francois
    Obituary **1996:2**
Miyazawa, Kiichi **1992:2**
Mobutu Sese Seko **1993:4**
    Obituary **1998:1**
Mobutu Sese Seko
    Obituary **1998:4**
Moi, Daniel arap **1993:2**
Molotov, Vyacheslav Mikhailovich
    Obituary **1987:1**

Novello, Antonia   1991:2
Nuesslein-Volhard, Christiane
  1998:1
Nye, Bill   1997:2
Owens, Delia and Mark   1993:3
Pauling, Linus
  Obituary   1995:1
Penrose, Roger   1991:4
Peterson, Roger Tory
  Obituary   1997:1
Plotkin, Mark   1994:3
Pough, Richard Hooper   1989:1
Profet, Margie   1994:4
Prusiner, Stanley   1998:2
Quill, Timothy E.   1997:3
Radecki, Thomas
  Brief Entry   1986:2
Redenbacher, Orville
  Obituary   1996:1
Redig, Patrick   1985:3
Richter, Charles Francis
  Obituary   1985:4
Rifkin, Jeremy   1990:3
Rock, John
  Obituary   1985:1
Rosenberg, Steven   1989:1
Rosendahl, Bruce R.
  Brief Entry   1986:4
Sabin, Albert
  Obituary   1993:4
Sacks, Oliver   1995:4
Sagan, Carl
  Obituary   1997:2
Sakharov, Andrei Dmitrievich
  Obituary   1990:2
Salk, Jonas   1994:4
Salk, Jonas
  Obituary   1995:4
Schank, Roger   1989:2
Schroeder, William J.
  Obituary   1986:4
Shimomura, Tsutomu   1996:1
Skinner, B.F.
  Obituary   1991:1
Smoot, George F.   1993:3
Soren, David
  Brief Entry   1986:3
Spock, Benjamin   1995:2
  Obituary   1998:3
Steger, Will   1990:4
Steptoe, Patrick
  Obituary   1988:3
Sullivan, Louis   1990:4
Szent-Gyoergyi, Albert
  Obituary   1987:2
Thompson, Starley
  Brief Entry   1987:3
Toone, Bill
  Brief Entry   1987:2
Vagelos, P. Roy   1989:4
Vickrey, William S.
  Obituary   1997:2
Waddell, Thomas F.
  Obituary   1988:2
Weil, Andrew   1997:4
Wexler, Nancy S.   1992:3
Wigler, Michael
  Brief Entry   1985:1
Wiles, Andrew   1994:1
Wilmut, Ian   1997:3
Wilson, Edward O.   1994:4
Woodwell, George S.   1987:2
Yeager, Chuck   1998:1
Yen, Samuel   1996:4
Zech, Lando W.
  Brief Entry   1987:4

SOCIAL ISSUES

Abbey, Edward
  Obituary   1989:3
Abernathy, Ralph
  Obituary   1990:3
Ali, Muhammad   1997:2
Allred, Gloria   1985:2
Anastas, Robert
  Brief Entry   1985:2
Aristide, Jean-Bertrand   1991:3
Baez, Joan   1998:3
Baird, Bill
  Brief Entry   1987:2
Baldwin, James
  Obituary   1988:2
Banks, Dennis J.   1986:4
Bayley, Corrine
  Brief Entry   1986:4
Ben & Jerry   1991:3
Bergalis, Kimberly
  Obituary   1992:3
Berresford, Susan V.   1998:4
Biehl, Amy
  Obituary   1994:1
Blackburn, Molly
  Obituary   1985:4
Bly, Robert   1992:4
Bradshaw, John   1992:1
Brady, Sarah and James S.   1991:4
Bravo, Ellen   1998:2
Bristow, Lonnie   1996:1
Brooks, Gwendolyn   1998:1
Brower, David   1990:4
Brown, Jim   1993:2
Brown, Judie   1986:2
Bush, Barbara   1989:3
Cammermeyer, Margarethe   1995:2
Carter, Amy   1987:4
Chavez, Cesar
  Obituary   1993:4
Chavis, Benjamin   1993:4
Cleaver, Eldridge
  Obituary   1998:4
Clements, George   1985:1
Clinton, Hillary Rodham   1993:2
Coffin, William Sloane, Jr.   1990:3
Cole, Johnetta B.   1994:3
Coles, Robert   1995:1
Coors, William K.
  Brief Entry   1985:1
Cruzan, Nancy
  Obituary   1991:3
Davis, Angela   1998:3
Dees, Morris   1992:1
Devi, Phoolan   1986:1
Dickinson, Brian   1998:2
Dorris, Michael
  Obituary   1997:3
Douglas, Marjory Stoneman   1993:1
  Obituary   1998:4
Downey, Morton, Jr.   1988:4
Duncan, Sheena
  Brief Entry   1987:1
Edelman, Marian Wright   1990:4
Edwards, Harry   1989:4
Elders, Joycelyn   1994:1
Ellison, Ralph
  Obituary   1994:4
Etzioni, Amitai   1994:3
Evers-Williams, Myrlie   1995:4
Falkenberg, Nanette   1985:2
Faludi, Susan   1992:4
Farrakhan, Louis   1990:4
Faubus, Orval
  Obituary   1995:2
Faulkner, Shannon   1994:4

Ferrell, Trevor
  Brief Entry   1985:2
Filipovic, Zlata   1994:4
Finley, Karen   1992:4
Fisher, Mary   1994:3
Fonyo, Steve
  Brief Entry   1985:4
Foreman, Dave   1990:3
Friedan, Betty   1994:2
Galvin, Martin
  Brief Entry   1985:3
Garcia, Jerry   1988:3
  Obituary   1996:1
Gebbie, Kristine   1994:2
Geldof, Bob   1985:3
Gertz, Alison
  Obituary   1993:2
Glaser, Elizabeth
  Obituary   1995:2
Glasser, Ira   1989:1
Goetz, Bernhard Hugo   1985:3
Goldhaber, Fred
  Brief Entry   1986:3
Goodall, Jane   1991:1
Gore, Tipper   1985:4
Grant, Charity
  Brief Entry   1985:2
Greenberg, Hank
  Obituary   1986:4
Guyer, David
  Brief Entry   1988:1
Hackney, Sheldon   1995:1
Hahn, Jessica   1989:4
Hale, Clara
  Obituary   1993:3
Hayes, Robert M.   1986:3
Healey, Jack   1990:1
Hebard, Caroline   1998:2
Hefner, Christie   1985:1
Hepburn, Audrey
  Obituary   1993:2
Hoffman, Abbie
  Obituary   1989:3
Hudson, Rock
  Obituary   1985:4
Huerta, Dolores   1998:1
Huffington, Arianna   1996:2
Hullinger, Charlotte
  Brief Entry   1985:1
Hume, John   1987:1
Humphry, Derek   1992:2
Ireland, Jill
  Obituary   1990:4
Ireland, Patricia   1992:2
Jackson, Jesse   1996:1
Jacobs, Joe   1994:1
Jordan, King   1990:1
Jorgensen, Christine
  Obituary   1989:4
Judkins, Reba
  Brief Entry   1987:3
Kennedy, Rose
  Obituary   1995:3
Kevorkian, Jack   1991:3
Kielburger, Craig   1998:1
Kissling, Frances   1989:2
Klarsfeld, Beate   1989:1
Kozol, Jonathan   1992:1
Kramer, Larry   1991:2
Krim, Mathilde   1989:2
Kunstler, William
  Obituary   1996:1
Kurzban, Ira   1987:2
LaDuke, Winona   1995:2
Lang, Eugene M.   1990:3

Reasoner, Harry
  Obituary **1992:1**
Redgrave, Vanessa **1989:2**
Reed, Donna
  Obituary **1986:1**
Reed, Robert
  Obituary **1992:4**
Reeve, Christopher **1997:2**
Reiner, Rob **1991:2**
Reiser, Paul **1995:2**
Remick, Lee
  Obituary **1992:1**
Reubens, Paul **1987:2**
Richards, Michael **1993:4**
Riddle, Nelson
  Obituary **1985:4**
Rivera, Geraldo **1989:1**
Robbins, Tim **1993:1**
Roberts, Cokie **1993:4**
Roberts, Julia **1991:3**
Robertson, Pat **1988:2**
Robinson, Max
  Obituary **1989:2**
Rock, Chris **1998:1**
Roddenberry, Gene
  Obituary **1992:2**
Rogers, Roy
  Obituary **1998:4**
Roker, Roxie
  Obituary **1996:2**
Rollins, Howard E., Jr. **1986:1**
Rose, Charlie **1994:2**
Rourke, Mickey **1988:4**
Rowan, Dan
  Obituary **1988:1**
Rudner, Rita **1993:2**
Ryan, Meg **1994:1**
Sagansky, Jeff **1993:2**
Sajak, Pat
  Brief Entry **1985:4**
Sarandon, Susan **1995:3**
Savage, Fred **1990:1**
Savalas, Telly
  Obituary **1994:3**
Sawyer, Diane **1994:4**
Schneider, Rob **1997:4**
Schwimmer, David **1996:2**
Scott, Gene
  Brief Entry **1986:1**
Sedelmaier, Joe **1985:3**
Seinfeld, Jerry **1992:4**
Sevareid, Eric
  Obituary **1993:1**
Seymour, Jane **1994:4**
Shaffer, Paul **1987:1**
Shandling, Garry **1995:1**
Sharkey, Ray
  Obituary **1994:1**
Shawn, Dick
  Obituary **1987:3**
Sheedy, Ally **1989:1**
Shepherd, Cybill **1996:3**
Shields, Brooke **1996:3**
Shore, Dinah
  Obituary **1994:3**
Short, Martin **1986:1**
Shriver, Maria
  Brief Entry **1986:2**
Shue, Andrew **1994:4**
Silverman, Jonathan **1997:2**
Silvers, Phil
  Obituary **1985:4**
Silverstone, Alicia **1997:4**
Sinise, Gary **1996:1**
Skelton, Red
  Obituary **1998:1**

Slater, Christian **1994:1**
Smirnoff, Yakov **1987:2**
Smith, Jeff **1991:4**
Smith, Kate
  Obituary **1986:3**
Smits, Jimmy **1990:1**
Snipes, Wesley **1993:1**
Sondheim, Stephen **1994:4**
Southern, Terry
  Obituary **1996:2**
Spheeris, Penelope **1989:2**
Spielberg, Steven **1993:4 1997:4**
Springer, Jerry **1998:4**
Stern, Howard **1988:2 1993:3**
Stevenson, McLean
  Obituary **1996:3**
Stewart, Martha **1992:1**
Stewart, Patrick **1996:1**
Stone, Sharon **1993:4**
Stoppard, Tom **1995:4**
Streisand, Barbra **1992:2**
Studi, Wes **1994:3**
Susskind, David
  Obituary **1987:2**
Swaggart, Jimmy **1987:3**
Swayze, John Cameron
  Obituary **1996:1**
Tandy, Jessica **1990:4**
  Obituary **1995:1**
Tartikoff, Brandon **1985:2**
  Obituary **1998:1**
Taylor, Elizabeth **1993:3**
Tesh, John **1996:3**
Thomas, Danny
  Obituary **1991:3**
Thompson, Emma **1993:2**
Thornton, Billy Bob **1997:4**
Tillstrom, Burr
  Obituary **1986:1**
Tilly, Jennifer **1997:2**
Tisch, Laurence A. **1988:2**
Tomei, Marisa **1995:2**
Totenberg, Nina **1992:2**
Travolta, John **1995:2**
Trudeau, Garry **1991:2**
Tucker, Forrest
  Obituary **1987:1**
Turner, Janine **1993:2**
Turner, Lana
  Obituary **1996:1**
Turner, Ted **1989:1**
Ullman, Tracey **1988:3**
Urich, Robert **1988:1**
Vanilla Ice **1991:3**
Varney, Jim
  Brief Entry **1985:4**
Vidal, Gore **1996:2**
Villechaize, Herve
  Obituary **1994:1**
Vitale, Dick **1988:4 1994:4**
Walker, Nancy
  Obituary **1992:3**
Walters, Barbara **1998:3**
Wapner, Joseph A. **1987:1**
Washington, Denzel **1993:2**
Wayans, Damon **1998:4**
Wayans, Keenen Ivory **1991:1**
Wayne, David
  Obituary **1995:3**
Weitz, Bruce **1985:4**
Whitaker, Forest **1996:2**
White, Jaleel **1992:3**
Whittle, Christopher **1989:3**
Williams, Robin **1988:4**
Willis, Bruce **1986:4**
Winfrey, Oprah **1986:4 1997:3**

Winger, Debra **1994:3**
Wolfman Jack
  Obituary **1996:1**
Wong, B.D. **1998:1**
Woods, James **1988:3**
Wright, Steven **1986:3**
Wyle, Noah **1997:3**
Wynn, Keenan
  Obituary **1987:1**
Xuxa **1994:2**
Yetnikoff, Walter **1988:1**
York, Dick
  Obituary **1992:4**
Youngman, Henny
  Obituary **1998:3**
Zahn, Paula **1992:3**
Zamora, Pedro
  Obituary **1995:2**
Zucker, Jeff **1993:3**

THEATER
Abbott, George
  Obituary **1995:3**
Adjani, Isabelle **1991:1**
Albee, Edward **1997:1**
Alda, Robert
  Obituary **1986:3**
Alexander, Jane **1994:2**
Alexander, Jason **1993:3**
Allen, Joan **1998:1**
Allen, Peter
  Obituary **1993:1**
Ameche, Don
  Obituary **1994:2**
Andrews, Julie **1996:1**
Angelou, Maya **1993:4**
Arden, Eve
  Obituary **1991:2**
Ashcroft, Peggy
  Obituary **1992:1**
Aykroyd, Dan **1989:3 1997:3**
Bacall, Lauren **1997:3**
Bacon, Kevin **1995:3**
Baddeley, Hermione
  Obituary **1986:4**
Bailey, Pearl
  Obituary **1991:1**
Barkin, Ellen **1987:3**
Barry, Lynda **1992:1**
Bassett, Angela **1994:4**
Bates, Kathy **1991:4**
Beckett, Samuel Barclay
  Obituary **1990:2**
Belushi, Jim **1986:2**
Bening, Annette **1992:1**
Bennett, Joan
  Obituary **1991:2**
Bennett, Michael
  Obituary **1988:1**
Bernardi, Herschel
  Obituary **1986:4**
Bernhard, Sandra **1989:4**
Bernstein, Leonard
  Obituary **1991:1**
Blackstone, Harry Jr.
  Obituary **1997:4**
Bloch, Ivan **1986:3**
Bogosian, Eric **1990:4**
Bolger, Ray
  Obituary **1987:2**
Bonham Carter, Helena **1998:4**
Booth, Shirley
  Obituary **1993:2**
Bowie, David **1998:2**
Branagh, Kenneth **1992:2**
Brandauer, Klaus Maria **1987:3**

1998 Subject Index

This index lists all newsmakers subjects, company names, products, organizations, issues, awards, and professional specialties. Indexes in softbound issues allow access to the current year's entries; indexes in annual hardbound volumes are cumulative, covering the entire *Newsmakers* series.

Listee names are followed by a year and issue number; thus **1996**:3 indicates that an entry on that individual appears in both 1996, Issue 3 and the 1996 cumulation. For access to newsmakers appearing earlier than the current softbound issue, see the previous year's cumulation.

California Angels baseball team
Abbott, Jim **1988**:3
Conigliaro, Tony
Obituary **1990**:3
Ryan, Nolan **1989**:4

California state government
Brown, Edmund G., Sr.
Obituary **1996**:3
Brown, Jerry **1992**:4
Brown, Willie L. **1985**:2
Wilson, Pete **1992**:3

Camping equipment
Bauer, Eddie
Obituary **1986**:3
Coleman, Sheldon, Jr. **1990**:2

Canadian Broadcasting Corp. [CBC]
Juneau, Pierre **1988**:3

Cancer research
DeVita, Vincent T., Jr. **1987**:3
Fonyo, Steve
Brief Entry **1985**:4
Gale, Robert Peter **1986**:4
Hammond, E. Cuyler
Obituary **1987**:1
King, Mary-Claire **1998**:3
Krim, Mathilde **1989**:2
Love, Susan **1995**:2
Rosenberg, Steven **1989**:1
Szent-Gyoergyi, Albert
Obituary **1987**:2
Wigler, Michael
Brief Entry **1985**:1

Carnival Cruise Lines
Arison, Ted **1990**:3

Car repair
Magliozzi, Tom and Ray **1991**:4

Cartoons
Addams, Charles
Obituary **1989**:1
Barbera, Joseph **1988**:2
Barry, Lynda **1992**:1
Blanc, Mel
Obituary **1989**:4
Chast, Roz **1992**:4
Disney, Roy E. **1986**:3
Freleng, Friz
Obituary **1995**:4
Gaines, William M.
Obituary **1993**:1
Gould, Chester
Obituary **1985**:2
Groening, Matt **1990**:4
Judge, Mike **1994**:2
Parker, Trey and Matt Stone **1998**:2
Schulz, Charles M. **1998**:1
Spiegelman, Art **1998**:3
Trudeau, Garry **1991**:2
Watterson, Bill **1990**:3

Catholic Church
Beckett, Wendy (Sister) **1998**:3
Bernardin, Cardinal Joseph **1997**:2
Burns, Charles R.
Brief Entry **1988**:1
Clements, George **1985**:1
Cunningham, Reverend William
Obituary **1997**:4
Curran, Charles E. **1989**:2
Daily, Bishop Thomas V. **1990**:4

Dearden, John Cardinal
Obituary **1988**:4
Fox, Matthew **1992**:2
Healy, Timothy S. **1990**:2
John Paul II, Pope **1995**:3
Kissling, Frances **1989**:2
Krol, John
Obituary **1996**:3
Lefebvre, Marcel **1988**:4
Mahony, Roger M. **1988**:2
Maida, Adam Cardinal **1998**:2
Obando, Miguel **1986**:4
O'Connor, Cardinal John **1990**:3
Peter, Valentine J. **1988**:2
Rock, John
Obituary **1985**:1
Stallings, George A., Jr. **1990**:1

CAT Scanner
Hounsfield, Godfrey **1989**:2

Cattle rustling
Cantrell, Ed
Brief Entry **1985**:3

Caviar
Petrossian, Christian
Brief Entry **1985**:3

CBC
See: Canadian Broadcasting Corp.

CBS, Inc.
Cox, Richard Joseph
Brief Entry **1985**:1
Cronkite, Walter Leland **1997**:3
Paley, William S.
Obituary **1991**:2
Reasoner, Harry
Obituary **1992**:1
Sagansky, Jeff **1993**:2
Tisch, Laurence A. **1988**:2
Yetnikoff, Walter **1988**:1

CDF
See: Children's Defense Fund

Centers for Living
Williamson, Marianne **1991**:4

Central America
Astorga, Nora **1988**:2
Cruz, Arturo **1985**:1
Obando, Miguel **1986**:4
Robelo, Alfonso **1988**:1

Central Intelligence Agency [CIA]
Carter, Amy **1987**:4
Casey, William
Obituary **1987**:3
Colby, William E.
Obituary **1996**:4
Deutch, John **1996**:4
Gates, Robert M. **1992**:2
Inman, Bobby Ray **1985**:1

Centurion Ministries
McCloskey, James **1993**:1

Cesar Awards
Adjani, Isabelle **1991**:1
Depardieu, Gerard **1991**:2

Chanel, Inc.
D'Alessio, Kitty
Brief Entry **1987**:3

Chantal Pharmacentical Corp.
Burnison, Chantal Simone **1988**:3

Charlotte Hornets basketball team
Bryant, Kobe **1998**:3
Johnson, Larry **1993**:3
Mourning, Alonzo **1994**:2

Chef Boy-ar-dee
Boiardi, Hector
Obituary **1985**:3

Chess
Kasparov, Garry **1997**:4
Polgar, Judit **1993**:3

Chicago Bears football team
McMahon, Jim **1985**:4

Chicago Bulls basketball team
Jackson, Phil **1996**:3
Jordan, Michael **1987**:2
Kukoc, Toni **1995**:4
Pippen, Scottie **1992**:2
Rodman, Dennis **1996**:4

Chicago Blackhawks
Hasek, Dominik **1998**:3

Chicago Cubs baseball team
Caray, Harry **1988**:3

Chicago, Ill., city government
Washington, Harold
Obituary **1988**:1

Chicago White Sox baseball team
Caray, Harry **1988**:3
Leyland, Jim **1998**:2
Thomas, Frank **1994**:3
Veeck, Bill
Obituary **1986**:1

Child care
Hale, Clara
Obituary **1993**:3
Leach, Penelope **1992**:4
Spock, Benjamin **1995**:2
Obituary **1998**:3

Children's Defense Fund [CDF]
Clinton, Hillary Rodham **1993**:2
Edelman, Marian Wright **1990**:4

Chimpanzees
Goodall, Jane **1991**:1

Choreography
Abdul, Paula **1990**:3
Ailey, Alvin **1989**:2
Obituary **1990**:2
Astaire, Fred
Obituary **1987**:4
Bennett, Michael
Obituary **1988**:1
Cunningham, Merce **1998**:1
Dean, Laura **1989**:4
de Mille, Agnes
Obituary **1994**:2
Feld, Eliot **1996**:1
Fenley, Molissa **1988**:3
Forsythe, William **1993**:2
Fosse, Bob
Obituary **1988**:1
Glover, Savion **1997**:1
Graham, Martha
Obituary **1991**:4

Entrepreneurs
Akin, Phil
  Brief Entry   1987:3
Allen, John   1992:1
Alter, Hobie
  Brief Entry   1985:1
Aoki, Rocky   1990:2
Arison, Ted   1990:3
Aurre, Laura
  Brief Entry   1986:3
Bauer, Eddie
  Obituary   1986:3
Ben & Jerry   1991:3
Berlusconi, Silvio   1994:4
Black, Conrad   1986:2
Bloomberg, Michael   1997:1
Boiardi, Hector
  Obituary   1985:3
Bose, Amar
  Brief Entry   1986:4
Branson, Richard   1987:1
Buffett, Warren   1995:2
Burr, Donald Calvin   1985:3
Bushnell, Nolan   1985:1
Campeau, Robert   1990:1
Clark, Jim   1997:1
Covey, Stephen R.   1994:4
Craig, Sid and Jenny   1993:4
Cray, Seymour R.
  Brief Entry   1986:3
  Obituary   1997:2
Cummings, Sam   1986:3
Dell, Michael   1996:2
DiFranco, Ani   1997:1
Ertegun, Ahmet   1986:3
Garcia, Joe
  Brief Entry   1986:4
Gates, Bill   1993:3   1987:4
Gatien, Peter
  Brief Entry   1986:1
Gillett, George   1988:1
Graham, Bill   1986:4
  Obituary   1992:2
Guccione, Bob   1986:1
Haney, Chris
  Brief Entry   1985:1
Herrera, Carolina   1997:1
Hilbert, Stephen C.   1997:4
Honda, Soichiro   1986:1
Hughes, Mark   1985:3
Hyatt, Joel   1985:3
Ilitch, Mike   1993:4
Inatome, Rick   1985:4
Isaacson, Portia
  Brief Entry   1986:1
Jacuzzi, Candido
  Obituary   1987:1
Jones, Arthur A.   1985:3
Katz, Lillian   1987:4
Kerkorian, Kirk   1996:2
Kingsborough, Donald
  Brief Entry   1986:2
Knight, Philip H.   1994:1
Koplovitz, Kay   1986:3
Kurzweil, Raymond   1986:3
Mahesh Yogi, Maharishi   1991:3
Markle, C. Wilson   1988:1
Marriott, J. Willard
  Obituary   1985:4
McGowan, William   1985:2
McIntyre, Richard
  Brief Entry   1986:2
Melman, Richard
  Brief Entry   1986:1
Monaghan, Tom   1985:1
Moody, John   1985:3
Morgan, Dodge   1987:1

Murdoch, Rupert   1988:4
Murray, Arthur
  Obituary   1991:3
Olsen, Kenneth H.   1986:4
Paulucci, Jeno
  Brief Entry   1986:3
Penske, Roger   1988:3
Pocklington, Peter H.   1985:2
Radocy, Robert
  Brief Entry   1986:3
Roberts, Xavier   1985:3
Roddick, Anita   1989:4
Sasakawa, Ryoichi
  Brief Entry   1988:1
Schlessinger, David
  Brief Entry   1985:1
Smith, Frederick W.   1985:4
Tanny, Vic
  Obituary   1985:3
Thalheimer, Richard
  Brief Entry   1988:3
Thomas, Michel   1987:4
Tompkins, Susie
  Brief Entry   1987:2
Trump, Donald   1989:2
Trump, Ivana   1995:2
Turner, Ted   1989:1
Waitt, Ted   1997:4
Wilson, Jerry
  Brief Entry   1986:2
Wilson, Peter C.
  Obituary   1985:2
Wynn, Stephen A.   1994:3
Zanker, Bill
  Brief Entry   1987:3

Environmentalism
Ben & Jerry   1991:3
Brower, David   1990:4
Denver, John
  Obituary   1998:1
Douglas, Marjory Stoneman   1993:1
  Obituary   1998:4
Foreman, Dave   1990:3
Gore, Albert Jr.   1993:2
Hair, Jay D.   1994:3
Ngau, Harrison   1991:3
Plotkin, Mark   1994:3
Strong, Maurice   1993:1

Environmental Protection Agency [EPA]
Browner, Carol M.   1994:1

EPA
  See: Environmental Protection Agency

Episcopal Church
Browning, Edmond
  Brief Entry   1986:2
Harris, Barbara   1989:3
Harris, Barbara   1996:3
Spong, John   1991:3

Espionage
Philby, Kim
  Obituary   1988:3

Esprit clothing
Tompkins, Susie
  Brief Entry   1987:2

Essence magazine
Taylor, Susan L.   1998:2

Estee Lauder
Burns, Robin   1991:2
Lauder, Estee   1992:2

Ethnobotany
Plotkin, Mark   1994:3

European Commission
Delors, Jacques   1990:2

Euthanasia
Cruzan, Nancy
  Obituary   1991:3
Humphry, Derek   1992:2
Kevorkian, Jack   1991:3

Excel Communications
Troutt, Kenny A.   1998:1

Exploration
Ballard, Robert D.   1998:4
Fiennes, Ranulph   1990:3
Steger, Will   1990:4

Fabbrica Italiana Automobili Torino SpA [Fiat]
Agnelli, Giovanni   1989:4

Faith Center Church
Scott, Gene
  Brief Entry   1986:1

Fallon McElligott
McElligott, Thomas J.   1987:4

Fashion
Armani, Giorgio   1991:2
Avedon, Richard   1993:4
Bacall, Lauren   1997:3
Banks, Jeffrey   1998:2
Benetton, Luciano   1988:1
Cameron, David
  Brief Entry   1988:1
Claiborne, Liz   1986:3
Crawford, Cindy   1993:3
D'Alessio, Kitty
  Brief Entry   1987:3
Ellis, Perry
  Obituary   1986:3
Erte
  Obituary   1990:4
Gaultier, Jean-Paul   1998:1
Gucci, Maurizio
  Brief Entry   1985:4
Haas, Robert D.   1986:4
Halston
  Obituary   1990:3
Herrera, Carolina   1997:1
Hilfiger, Tommy   1993:3
Johnson, Betsey   1996:2
Kamali, Norma   1989:1
Karan, Donna   1988:1
Kelly, Patrick
  Obituary   1990:2
Klein, Calvin   1996:2
Lauren, Ralph   1990:1
Mellinger, Frederick
  Obituary   1990:4
Mello, Dawn   1992:2
Miller, Nicole   1995:4
Miyake, Issey   1985:2
Mizrahi, Isaac   1991:1
Natori, Josie   1994:3
Nipon, Albert
  Brief Entry   1986:4
Oldham, Todd   1995:4
Picasso, Paloma   1991:1
Porizkova, Paulina
  Brief Entry   1986:4
Potok, Anna Maximilian
  Brief Entry   1985:2

Cumulative Newsmakers Index

This index lists all newsmakers included in the entire *Newsmakers* series.

Listee names are followed by a year and issue number; thus **1996**:3 indicates that an entry on that individual appears in both 1996, Issue 3 and the 1996 cumulation.